TORTS

G. H. L. FRIDMAN, Q.C., M.A., B.C.L., LL.M. studied law at St John's College, Oxford and was called to the Bar by the Middle Temple in 1950. After practice in London he went to Australia and taught law at the University of Adelaide. Returning to England, he taught first at University College, London and then at the University of Sheffield before moving to Canada in 1969. There he was Dean of the Faculty at the University of Alberta before taking up his present post of Professor of Law at the University of Western Ontario.

He is the author of several books including *The Law of Agency, The Modern Law of Employment, Sale of Goods, Bankruptcy Law and Practice, Sale of Goods in Canada, The Law of Contract in Canada* and *The Law of Torts in Canada*, as well as co-author of a book on the law of restitution in Canada. He has also published many articles in leading law journals in England, Australia, Canada and the U.S.A.

Professor Fridman was called to the South Australia Bar in 1955, the Bar of Alberta in 1972 and the Ontario Bar in 1977. He was made a Queen's Counsel for Ontario in 1985.

TORTS

G. H. L. FRIDMAN, QC, MA, BCL, LLM
Of the Ontario Bar
and of the Middle Temple, Barrister,
Professor of Law,
University of Western Ontario

WATERLOW PUBLISHERS

First edition 1990

Waterlow Publishers
50 Fetter Lane
London EC4 1AA
A division of Pergamon Professional & Financial Services PLC

ISBN 0 08 033080 0

British Library Cataloguing in Publication Data

Fridman, G. H. L. (Gerald Henry Louis)
Torts.
1. Torts. Law
I. Title
342.63

Origination by BPCC Whitefriars Ltd, Tunbridge Wells, and printed and bound in Great Britain by BPCC Wheatons Ltd, Exeter.

In memory of NATASHA and CHARBONNEL

"Who can believe that there is no soul behind those luminous eyes?"

Théophile Gauthier

Acknowledgements

I wish to record my thanks to a number of people: Dr Gavin McFarlane for having suggested that I write this book; Mr James Lamb for having undertaken to publish it; Mr George Orsini, a student at the Faculty of Law, University of Western Ontario, for having done some useful research on recent English cases; and Mrs Teresa Bourne for having taken my typescript and made it presentable on a word processor. My thanks must also go to the Ontario Law Foundation for providing the funds for Mr Orsini during a summer vacation. Whatever flaws or blemishes are present in this work are, of course, my responsibility. The book is presented in the hope that it will serve a useful purpose and will provide information and insight.

The law is stated at April 1st 1990.

G. H. L. F.
London, Ontario, Canada
Anzac Day 1990

Contents

Para.		*Page*
	Table of cases	xvi
	Table of statutes	lxxv
Chapter 1—THE NATURE OF TORT LIABILITY		1
1.01	Introduction	1
1.02	The meaning and scope of torts	1
	The idea of wrong	1
1.03	Legal and non-legal wrong	2
1.07	Torts and other forms of legal wrong	4
1.08	Tort and crime	4
1.10	Torts and breaches of contract	5
1.13	Torts and restitution	7
1.14	Torts and breaches of trust	8
1.15	The function of tort liability	8
1.20	Fundamental principles of liability	12
1.21	Intention	12
1.27	Negligence	15
1.31	Strict liability	16
1.32	Fault	17
1.35	The future of tort liability	18
Chapter 2—THE SCOPE OF TORT LIABILITY		20
2.02	The Crown	20
	At common law	20
2.04	Statutory change	22
2.08	Act of state	24
2.13	Foreign sovereigns	25
2.16	Corporations	27
2.20	Unincorporated bodies	29
2.24	Persons under disability	32
	Minors	32
	Actions by minors	32
2.28	Actions against minors	36
2.31	Mental incompetents	37
2.34	Bankrupts	39
2.36	Personal representatives	40
Chapter 3—VICARIOUS LIABILITY		44
3.01	Rationale	44
3.03	Application	46
3.08	Authority	50
	Meaning	50
3.09	Prohibitions	51
3.11	Actual authority	52
3.14	Ostensible authority	54
3.17	The course of employment	56
	Meaning	56
3.19	Acts within the course of employment	57
3.25	Prohibited acts	61
3.27	Acts not in the interest of the master	62
3.30	Acts outside the course of employment	64

3.34 Independent contractors 66
3.40 The personal liability of employers 70

Chapter 4—JOINT AND SEVERAL TORTFEASORS 72

4.01 Nature of the distinction 72
4.04 Importance of the distinction 73
4.07 Contribution between tortfeasors 76
4.12 Contracts of indemnity 79

Chapter 5—TRESPASS TO LAND 81

5.01 Elements of liability 81
General characteristics 81
5.04 Interference 82
Acts of trespass 82
5.08 Continuing trespass 85
5.09 Trespass ab initio 86
5.10 The mental element 87
5.13 Possession 89
The basis of the action 89
5.16 Claims not based on possession: (1) Trespass by relation 91
5.17 (2) Injuries to reversionary interest 92
5.18 (3) The right to possess: ejectment 92
5.20 Land 93
Below the surface 93
5.22 Above the ground 94
5.28 Defences 98
Inevitable accident and mistake 98
5.30 Necessity 98
5.33 Recaption of chattels 100
5.37 Liberum tenementum 101
5.39 Leave and licence 102
5.44 Lawful entry 105
5.48 Remedies 107
Self-help 107
5.49 Judicial remedies 108

Chapter 6—TRESPASS TO THE PERSON 111

6.01 General characteristics 111
6.10 Varieties of trespass 118
Battery 118
6.14 Assault 119
6.18 False imprisonment 122
6.23 Defences 125
Accident 125
6.26 Self-defence 127
6.29 Parental or other authority 128
6.34 Necessity 130
6.36 Consent 131
6.43 Lawful arrest 135

Chapter 7—WRONGFUL INTERFERENCE WITH GOODS 142

7.01 The legislation of 1977 142
7.03 Varieties of wrongful interference 143
Trespass to goods 143
7.04 Interference 144
7.06 Possession 145
7.12 Wrongfulness 147

7.16	Conversion	150
	Definition	150
7.19	Acts of conversion	152
	Taking possession of goods	152
7.22	Abusing possession of goods	155
7.26	Destruction of the goods	158
7.28	The mental element	159
7.31	The plaintiff's title	162
7.37	Defences	165
7.41	Replevin, rescous and pound-breach	168
7.44	Other wrongs	169
7.46	Remedies	170
	Where goods are detailed	170
7.47	Damages	171
7.48	Trespass	171
7.49	Conversion	172
7.52	Improvement of the goods	174
7.54	Extinction of title	175

Chapter 8—NUISANCE 176

8.01	The forms of nuisance	176
	The meaning of nuisance	176
8.03	Varities of nuisance	176
8.05	Private nuisance	178
	Definition	178
8.08	Elements of liability	180
	A continuing state of affairs	180
8.11	Personal comfort or enjoyment of property	181
8.13	Locality	183
8.15	Standards	184
8.18	Utility	186
8.19	Malice	186
8.24	Negligence	188
8.30	Damage	192
8.32	Entitlement to sue	193
8.36	Incidence of liability	195
	Creator of nuisance	195
8.37	Occupier	195
8.42	Landlord out of possession	198
8.47	Defences	201
	Coming to the nuisance	201
8.49	Jus tertii	202
8.50	Prescription	203
8.54	Statutory authority	204
8.60	Remedies	207
	Abatement	207
8.65	Damages	209
8.69	Injunction	211
8.72	Injuries to servitudes	212
8.75	Public nuisance	213
8.79	Nuisance to the highway	216
	Obstruction causing loss to adjoining owners	216
8.80	Disrepair	216
8.82	Obstruction to users	218
8.84	Projections over the highway	219

Chapter 9—THE RULE IN *RYLANDS V. FLETCHER* 221

9.01	The rule stated	221
9.02	Sources of the rule	222

9.07 Character of the rule 225
9.12 Analysis of the rule 227
Parties 227
9.16 Escape 229
9.19 Dangerous things 231
9.23 Non-natural user 234
9.31 Damage 237
9.35 Qualifications to the rule 239
Act of plaintiff 239
9.38 Consent of plaintiff 240
9.41 Statutory authority 242
9.43 Act of a stranger 243
9.46 Act of God 244
9.50 Necessity 246

Chapter 10—FIRE 247

10.01 Sources of liability 247
10.02 Early strict liability 247
10.05 The introduction of negligence 249
10.07 The impact of *Rylands v. Fletcher* 250
10.12 The modern situation 253

Chapter 11—LIABILITY FOR ANIMALS 255

11.01 The common law before 1971 255
11.07 The legislation of 1971 258
General effect 258
11.10 Dangerous animals 259
Definition 259
11.13 Liability 260
11.20 Incidence of liability 261
11.22 Exceptions from liability 262
11.25 Dogs which attack livestock 265
11.28 Trespassing livestock 266
Liability 266
11.32 Detention 267
11.34 Animals on the highway 268

Chapter 12—NEGLIGENCE 270

12.01 The tort of negligence 270
12.05 The duty of care 273
Relevant factors 273
12.11 Foreseeability 277
12.15 Risk 279
12.21 Foreseeable plaintiffs and foreseeable harm 282
12.24 Nervous shock 283
12.29 Rescuers 287
12.35 Negligent mis-statements 289
12.40 Economic loss 295
12.53 Extensions of duty 303
Limitations 303
12.55 Developments 304
Animals 304
12.56 Defective buildings 304
12.58 Omissions 306
12.61 Acts of third parties 307
12.62 Statutory powers 308
12.64 Exclusion of duty 309
12.70 Duty of care and contract 313

12.73 Breach of duty of care 314
Standard of care 314
12.77 Objectivity 316
12.80 Customary or general practices 319
12.83 Proof of breach 320
12.86 *Res ipsa loguitur* 322
12.87 Application 322
12.88 Control 323
12.90 An ordinary occurrence 324
12.92 Effect of the maxim 325
12.94 Damage 327
Causation and remoteness 327
12.97 Proof of causation 329
12.98 Several defendants 329
12.99 Successive accidents 330
12.103 The McGhee case and its aftermath 332
12.110 Remoteness of damage 336
Introduction 336
12.111 Direct consequences 337
12.116 The rise of foreseeability 340
12.121 Directness versus foreseeability 343

Chapter 13—DEFENCES TO NEGLIGENCE 346

13.01 Introduction 346
13.02 Inevitable accident 346
13.05 Consent 348
Volenti non fit injuria 348
13.10 Express consent 350
13.11 Implied consent 351
13.13 Knowledge 351
13.18 Consent 354
13.22 The decline of consent 356
13.23 Contributory negligence 356
Historical survey 356
13.26 The common law doctrine 357
Not dependent on duty 357
13.27 Neglience which causes or contributes to the damage 358
13.29 Negligence not considered contributory 359
Defendant obliged to protect plaintiff 359
13.30 Where the plaintiff was a child 360
13.31 Where the plaintiff acted in the agony of the moment 361
13.32 The doctrine of "last opportunity" or "last clear chance" 361
13.37 The effect of the statute 364
In general 364
13.38 Last opportunity 365
13.39 Apportionment 366
13.44 The plaintiff's illegality 369

Chapter 14—SOME VARIETIES OF NEGLIGENCE 372

14.01 Liability for chattels 372
The immediate transferee 372
Under contract 372
14.03 Where there is no contract 373
14.04 Ultimate transferees and others 374
Before *Donoghue v. Stevenson* 374
14.06 The decision in *Donoghue v. Stevenson* 375
14.07 Extension of the decision 376
14.12 The demise of chattels dangerous *per se* 380

14.15 Occupiers' liability 382
The common law 382
14.17 The statutory law 383
Scope of the Acts 383
Premises 383
14.19 Occupiers 385
14.20 Visitors 386
14.24 Damage 388
14.28 The occupier's duty 390
The common duty of care 390
Contents of the duty 390
14.31 Children 392
14.33 Knowledgeable visitors 393
14.34 Discharge of the duty 393
Warnings 393
14.36 Independent contractors 394
14.37 Exclusion of the duty 395
14.39 Defences to liability 397
14.42 Duty to those entering under contract with third parties 398
14.43 Duty to trespassers 399
14.46 Employer's liability 401
14.47 The common law duty 402
14.48 Nature of the duty 403
14.49 Content of the duty 403
14.50 Competent staff 404
14.51 Plant, equipment and premises 404
14.53 Safe system of work 405
14.54 Defences 406
Lack of causation 406
14.55 *Volenti* 406
14.56 Contributory negligence 407

Chapter 15—DAMAGES FOR NEGLIGENCE 408

15.01 Introduction 408
The only remedy 408
15.03 Kinds of damages 409
15.08 Compensation 411
15.10 Mitigation of loss 412
15.12 Property 413
Loss 413
15.15 Damage 414
15.18 Date of assessment 415
15.19 Limitations of actions 416
15.22 Non-fatal personal injuries 418
Pecuniary and non-pecuniary loss 418
15.24 Pecuniary loss 419
Lost earnings 419
15.26 Future earnings 420
15.30 Expenses 422
15.35 Deductions 424
15.38 Interest 425
15.39 Non-pecuniary loss 426
Pain and suffering 426
15.41 Loss of amenities 427
15.44 The injury 428
15.45 Assessment of the award 428
15.47 Limitation of actions 429
15.51 Death 432
Survival of actions 432

15.52 Dependents' claims 433
The Fatal Accidents Act 433
15.53 The right to sue 433
15.56 Beneficiaries of the action 435
15.57 Recoverable damages 435
Bereavement 435
15.58 Loss of support 436

Chapter 16—BREACH OF STATUTORY DUTY 439

16.01 Introduction 439
16.03 Construction of statutes 440
The role of the courts 440
16.06 Rules of construction 441
16.11 Elements of liability 444
A duty owed to the plaintiff 444
16.12 Breach of the duty 445
16.15 Causation of damage 447
16.17 Injury within the scope of the statute 448
16.19 Defences 449
Volenti 449
16.20 Contributory negligence 449
16.21 Delegation 450

Chapter 17—DECEIT 451

17.01 Fraud 451
17.04 Elements of liability 452
A false statement of fact 452
17.09 Knowledge of falsity 454
17.11 The defendant's intent 455
17.15 Reliance by the plaintiff 457
17.16 Damage 458

Chapter 18—DEFAMATION 461

18.01 Definition and rationale 461
18.03 Requirements of liability 462
Capacity to be defamed 462
18.04 Falsity 462
18.07 A defamatory allegation 464
The meaning of "defamatory" 464
18.13 Innuendo 467
18.19 Functions of judge and jury 470
18.21 Reference to the plaintiff 471
18.26 Defamation of a class 474
18.29 Publication 475
18.37 Libel and slander 479
Nature of the distinction 479
18.41 Its effect 481
Criminal law 481
18.42 Law of torts 482
Proof of damage 482
18.45 Exceptions 484
18.54 Defences 487
Unintentional defamation 487
18.56 Consent 489
18.58 Justification 489
18.61 Fair comment 491
Nature of the plea 491
18.64 Essential elements 493

	Public interest	493
18.65	Opinion not fact	494
18.67	Fairness	494
18.71	Privilege	497
	Nature of privilege	497
18.74	Cases of absolute privilege	498
	Statements made in Parliament	498
18.75	Parliamentary papers	499
18.76	Judicial proceedings	499
18.83	Communications between solicitor and client	502
18.84	Official communications by officers of state	502
18.86	Fair and accurate reports of judicial proceedings	503
18.89	Cases of qualified privilege	505
	Privileged reports	505
18.95	Statements made under a duty	508
18.99	Loss of qualified privilege	511
18.103	Remedies	513
	Damages	513
	Assessment	513
18.111	Mitigation	516
18.115	Apology	518
18.118	Injunction	519

Chapter 19—PRIVACY 521

19.01	A questionable concept	521
19.03	The scope of privacy	522
19.07	Different types of wrongdoing	525

Chapter 20—BREACH OF CONFIDENCE 527

20.01	A new tort?	528
20.04	The meaning of confidence	529
20.07	The scope of protection	530
20.10	Defences	532
20.13	Remedies	533

Chapter 21—WRONGFUL INTERFERENCE WITH TRADE, BUSINESS OR EMPLOYMENT 536

21.01	Introduction	536
21.03	Conspiracy	538
	Definition and scope	538
21.06	Elements of liability	539
	Agreement and combination	539
21.09	Unlawful means	540
21.11	Unlawful purpose	541
21.16	Intimidation	545
	Emergence of the tort	545
21.20	Unlawful means	547
21.25	Varieties of intimidation	550
21.28	Justification	552
21.30	Inducing breach of contract	553
	Origins	554
21.31	Elements of liability	554
	A contract	554
21.33	Knowledge of its terms	555
21.35	Intention	556
21.38	Inducement	557
21.39	Direct	557
21.41	Indirect	558

21.45 Damage 561
21.47 Justification 562
21.52 The importance of breach 564
21.54 Injurious falsehood 566
Nature of the liability 566
21.58 Instances of liability 568
21.60 Elements of liability 569
A false statement 569
21.61 Malice 569
21.63 Damage 570
21.65 Passing-off 571
Nature and development of the action 571
21.70 Classical passing-off 574
21.73 Modern extension 576

Chapter 22—ABUSE OF PROCESS 579

22.01 Malicious prosecution 579
The nature of the action 579
22.04 Elements of liability 580
Favourable end to prosecution 580
22.06 Lack of reasonable and probable cause 581
22.11 Malice 583
22.13 Damage 584
22.18 Other improperly instituted proceedings 587
22.22 Non-liability for abuse of process 588

Index 592

Table of Cases

A

A.M.F. International Ltd v. Magnet Bowling Ltd [1968] 2 All E.R. 789 3.36, 14.25, 14.36
Abbassy v. Commissioner of Police of the Metropolis [1990] 1 All E.R. 193 6.44, 6.48
Abbott v. Refuge Assurance Co. Ltd [1962] 1 Q.B. 432 22.03, 22.08
Abbott v. Sullivan [1952] 1 K.B. 189 8.19
Abidin Daver, The [1984] A.C. 398 1.17
Abingdon R.D.C. v. O'Gorman [1968] 2 Q.B. 811 7.43
Abington v. Lipscomb (1841) 1 Q.B. 776 7.20
Abraham v. Bullock (1902) 86 L.T. 796 3.32
Abrahams v. Deakin [1891] 1 Q.B. 516 3.29
Abrath v. North Eastern Railway Co. (1883) 11 Q.B.D. 440; (1886) 11 App.Cas.247 22.03, 22.07
Acrecrest Ltd v. W.S. Haskell & Partners [1983] 1 All E.R. 17 12.63
Acrow (Automation) Ltd v. Rex Chainbelts Inc. [1971] 3 All E.R. 1175 21.44, 21.52
Ad Lib Club Ltd v. Granville [1972] R.P.C. 673 21.72
Adam v. Ward [1917] A.C. 309 18.71, 18.73, 18.95, 18.99, 18.100, 18.101
Adams v. Lancashire & Yorkshire Railway (1869) L.R. 4 C.P. 739 12.114
Adams v. Naylor [1946] A.C. 543 2.02, 2.04
Adams v. Ursell [1913] 1 Ch. 269 8.11
Adamson v. Jarvis (1827) 4 Bing. 66 4.14
Addie & Sons (Collieries) Ltd v. Dumbreck [1929] A.C. 358 14.15, 14.43
Addis v. Crocker [1960] 2 All E.R. 629 18.80
Admiralty Commissioners v. S.S. Amerika [1917] A.C. 38 2.36
Adsett v. West [1983] 2 All E.R. 985 2.38
Aga Khan v. Times Publishing Co. [1924] 1 K.B. 675 18.62
Agincourt, The (1824) 1 Hagg.Ecc. 271 6.32
Aikman v. George Mills Co. Ltd [1934] O.R. 597 9.20
Aitchison v. Page Motors Ltd (1936) 154 L.T. 128 3.19
Akerhielm v. De Mar [1959] A.C. 789 17.09
Akerib v. Booth Ltd [1960] 1 W.L.R. 454 H.C.; [1961] 1 W.L.R. 367 A.C. 9.39
Albert v. Lavin [1981] 3 All E.R. 878 6.24, 6.45
Albert (Prince) v. Strange (1849) 1 Mac. & Gr. 25 20.04
Alberta Geophysical Products Ltd v. Geo. E. Failing Supply Co. Ltd (1964) D.L.R. (2d) 681 21.59
Alcott v. Millar's Karri & Jarah Forests Ltd (1904) 21 T.L.R. 30 21.54
Alder v. Dickson [1954] 1 W.L.R. 1482 14.06
Alderson v. Booth [1969] 2 Q.B. 216 6.20, 6.43
Aldham v. United Dairies [1940] 1 K.B. 507 12.114
Aldred's Case (1610) 9 Co. 57b 11.04
Aldridge v. Van Patter [1952] 4 D.L.R. 93 9.33
Aldworth v. Stewart (1866) 4 F. & F. 957 6.32
Alexander v. Jenkins [1892] 1 Q.B. 797 18.37, 18.51
Alexander v. North Eastern Railway Co. (1865) 6 B. & S. 340 18.58
Alexander v. Southey (1821) 5 B. & Ald. 247 7.20
Alford v. Magee [1952] A.L.R. 101 13.32, 13.33, 13.38
Albionby v. Cohen [1955] 1 Q.B. 558 5.48
Alicia Hosiery Co. Ltd v. Brown Shipley & Co. Ltd [1970] 1 Q.B. 195 5.16, 7.46

Al-Kandari v. J.R. Brown & Co. [1988] 1 All E.R. 833 12.68
Allan v. Liverpool Overseers (1874) L.R. 9 Q.B. 180 5.15
Allbutt v. General Council of Medical Education (1889) 23 Q.B.D. 400 18.89, 18.90
Allen v. Flood [1898] A.C. 1 1.22, 8.19, 21.04, 21.14
Allen v. Gulf Oil Refining Ltd [1981] 1 All E.R. 353 8.55–6
Allen v. Roughley (1955) 94 C.L.R. 95 5.19
Allied Arab Bank Ltd v. Heffer (No. 2) [1988] 3 All E.R. 103 21.04
Allsop v. Allsop (1860) 4 H. & N. 534 18.43, 18.44
Allsopp v. Church of England Newspaper Ltd [1972] 2 All E.R. 26 18.13, 18.60
Almaroth v. Chivers [1948] 1 All E.R. 53 13.29
Al Saudi Banque v. Clark Pixley [1989] 3 All E.R. 361 12.36, 12.37
Aluminium Industrie Vaasen B.V. v. Romalpa Aluminium Ltd [1976] 2 All E.R. 582 7.26
American Cyanamid Co. v. Ethicon Ltd [1975] A.C. 296 8.69, 18.118, 21.01
American Express Co. v. British Airways Board [1983] 1 All E.R. 557 1.10, 2.07, 7.37, 16.01
Ancona v. Rogers (1876) 1 Ex.D. 285 7.09
Anchor Brewhouse Developments v. Berkley House (Docklands) Developments (1987) 38 Build.L.R. 82 5.05, 5.25
Anderson v. Gorrie [1894] 1 Q.B. 618 18.88
Anderson (W.B.) & Sons Ltd v. Rhodes (Liverpool) Ltd [1967] 2 All E.R. 850 12.37, 17.08
Andrabell Ltd, re [1984] 3 All E.R. 407 7.26
André et Cie S.A. v. Ets. Michel Blanc & Fils [1979] 2 Lloyd's Rep. 427 17.05
Andrews v. Chapman (1853) 3 C. & K. 286 18.65, 18.90
Andrews v. Freeborough [1967] 1 Q.B. 1 15.41
Andrews v. Grand & Toy Alberta Ltd (1978) 83 D.L.R. (3d) 492 15.31, 15.46
Andrews v. Hopkinson [1957] 1 Q.B. 224 14.01, 14.07
Andrews v. Mockford [1896] 1 Q.B. 372 17.12
Andrews v. Nott-Bower [1895] 1 Q.B. 888 18.97
Angel v. H.H. Bushell & Co. Ltd [1968] 1 Q.B. 813 18.08, 18.95
Anglo-Celtic Shipping Co. Ltd v. Elliott (1926) 42 T.L.R. 297 14.04
Anglo-Newfoundland Development Co. v. Pacific Steam Navigation Co. [1924] A.C. 406 13.32
Anglo-Scottish Beet Sugar Corporation Ltd v. Spalding U.D.C. [1937] K.B. 607 17.14
Angus v. Clifford [1891] 2 Ch. 449 17.04, 17.09
Anheuser Bush Inc. v. Budweiser Budvor Brewery [1984] F.S.R. 413 21.76
Annabel's (Berkeley Square) Ltd v. G. Schock [1972] F.S.R. 261 21.70
Anns v. Merton London Borough Council [1978] A.C. 728 12.06, 12.44, 12.45, **12.56–7**, 12.59, 12.62, 12.63, 14.07, 14.11
Anon, re (1582) Cro. Eliz.10 10.02
Anon, re (1704) 6 Mod. 25 16.02
Anthony v. Haney (1832) 8 Bing. 186 5.33, 5.35
Apley Estates Co. Ltd v. de Bernales [1947] Ch. 217 4.06
Appleby v. Percy (1874) L.R. 9 Q.B. 647 11.03
Arbon v. Anderson [1943] K.B. 252 6.20
Archer v. Brown [1984] 2 All E.R. 267; [1985] Q.B. 401 1.08, 12.113, 17.17, **17.18**, 17.19
Arenson v. Casson, Beckman, Rutley & Co. [1977] A.C. 405 12.37, 12.66, 22.23
Argentino, The (1889) 14 App.Cas. 519 15.16
Argy Trading Development Co. v. Lapid Development Ltd [1977] 1 W.L.R. 444 12.36
Argyll (Duchess of) v. Argyll (Duke of) [1967] Ch. 302 20.02, 20.08, 20.14

Argyll (Duchess of) v. Beuselinck [1972] 2 Lloyd's Rep. 172 12.78
Arkwright v. Newbould (1881) 17 Ch.D. 301 17.07
Armagas Ltd v. Mundogas SA [1985] 3 All E.R. 795 C.A.; [1986] 2 All E.R. 385 H.L. 3.02, 3.10, 3.14, 3.15, 17.13
Armand v. Carr [1926] S.C.R. 575 12.76
Armory v. Delamirie (1721) 1 Stra. 505 7.06, 7.07, 7.35, 7.39, 7.50
Armstrong v. Sheppard & Short Ltd [1959] 2 Q.B. 384 5.39
Armstrong v. Strain [1951] 1 T.L.R. 866 H.C.; [1952] 1 K.B. 232 C.A. 17.14
Arneil v. Paterson [1931] A.C. 560 4.01
Arnold v. Teno (1978) 83 D.L.R. (3d) 609 15.31
Arpad, The [1934] P. 189 7.50, 12.111
Ashby v. Tolhurst [1937] 2 K.B. 242 7.18
Ashby v. White (1703) 2 Ld. Raym. 938 5.01, 16.02
Ashcroft v. Mersey Regional Health Authority [1983] 2 All E.R. 245 12.78
Ashdown v. Samuel Williams & Sons Ltd [1957] 1 Q.B. 409 14.37
Asher v.Whitlock (1865) L.R. 1 Q.B. 1 5.19
Ashton v. Jennings (1672) 2 Lev. 133 6.11
Ashton v. Turner [1981] Q.B. 137 13.16, 13.44, 13.45
Associated British Ports v. T.&G.W.U. [1989] 3 All E.R. 796, *reversed* [1989] 3 All E.R. 822 16.01, 16.08, 21.30, 21.53
Associated Newspapers v. Dingle — *see* Dingle
Astaire v. Campling [1965] 3 All E.R. 666 18.12
Astley Industrial Trust Ltd v. Grimley [1963] 2 All E.R. 33 14.07
Athans v. Canadian Adventure Camps Ltd (1978) 80 D.L.R. (3d) 583 19.01
Atkinson v. Fitzwalter [1987] 1 All E.R. 483 18.58
Atkinson v. Newcastle & Gateshead Waterworks Co. (1877) 2 Ex. D. 441 16.02, 16.07, 16.09
Atland Containers Ltd v. Macs Corporation Ltd (1975) 7 O.R. (2d) 107 22.20
Atlantic Aviation v. Nova Scotia Light & Power Co. (1965) D.L.R. (2d) 554 5.26
Atlas Tiles v. Briars (1978) 21 A.L.R. 129 15.35
Attersoll v. Stevens (1808) 1 Taunt. 183 5.13
Attia v. British Gas plc [1987] 3 All E.R. 455 12.25, 12.26, **12.28**
Attorney-General v. B.B.C. [1980] 3 All E.R. 161 20.02
Attorney-General v. Clough [1963] 1 All E.R. 420 19.05
Attorney-General v. Corke [1933] Ch. 89 9.20
Attorney-General v. Cory Bros. [1921] 1 A.C. 521 9.09, 9.20, 9.38
Attorney-General v. De Keyser's Royal Hotel [1920] A.C. 508 2.08
Attorney-General v. Great Western Railway [1924] 2 K.B.1 10.07
Attorney-General v. Guardian Newspapers Ltd [1987] 3 All E.R. 316 20.02
Attorney-General v. Guardian Newspapers Ltd (No. 2) [1988] 3 All E.R. 545 20.02
Attorney-General v. Jonathan Cape Ltd [1976] Q.B. 752 20.02, 20.09
Attorney-General v. Manchester Corporation [1893] 2 Ch. 87 8.69
Attorney-General v. Mulholland [1963] 2 Q.B. 477 19.05
Attorney-General v. Nissan [1969] 1 All E.R. 629 2.02, 2.09, 2.10
Attorney-General v. P.Y.A. Quarries [1957] 2 Q.B. 169 8.01, 8.75
Attorney-General v. Sheffield Gas Co. (1853) 3 De G.M. & G. 304 8.67
Attorney-General v. Stone (1895) 12 T.L.R. 76 8.37
Attorney-General v. Valle-Jones [1935] 2 K.B. 209 2.02
Attorney-General for New South Wales v. Perpetual Trustee Co. [1955] A.C. 457 2.02
Attorney-General of Canada v. Jackson [1946] S.C.R. 489 2.02
Attorney-General of Canada v. Nykorak [1962] S.C.R. 333 2.02
Attorney-General of Duchy of Lancaster v. G.E. Overton (Farms) Ltd [1982] 1 All E.R. 524 7.35
Attorney-General of Nova Scotia v. Beaver (1985) 32 C.C.L.T. 170 8.78

Attorney-General of St. Christopher, Nevis & Anguilla v. Reynolds [1980] A.C. 637 15.05
Attorney-General's Reference (No. 6 of 1980) [1981] 2 All E.R. 1057 6.12, 6.36, **6.39–41**
Austin v. Culpepper (1683) 2 Show. K.B. 313 18.38
Austin v. Mirror Newspapers Ltd [1986] 2 W.L.R. 57 18.95
Austin v. Dowling (1870) L.R. 5 C.P. 534 5.33, 6.22, 22.04
Australian Blue Metals Ltd v. Hughes [1962] 3 All E.R. 335 5.40
Austria (Emperor of) v. Day & Kossuth (1861) 3 De G.F. & J. 217 16.08
Auty v. National Coal Board [1985] 1 All E.R. 930 15.26
Avery v. London & North-Eastern Railway [1938] A.C. 606 15.53
Aynsley v. Toronto General Hospital (1969) 7 D.L.R. (3d) 193; *Affirmed* [1972] S.C.R. 435 3.41

B

B. (a minor), re [1981] 1 W.L.R. 1421 6.38
Bacon v. Cooper (Metals) Ltd [1982] 1 All E.R. 397 15.12
Bainbridge v. Postmaster-General [1906] 1 K.B. 178 2.02
Baird v. Williamson (1863) 15 C.B. (N.S.) 376 9.24
Baker v. Barclays Bank Ltd [1955] 1 W.L.R. 822 7.27
Baker v. Berkeley (1827) 3 C. & P. 32 5.12
Baker v. Bolton (1808) 1 Camp. 493 2.36
Baker v. Hopkins (T.E.) & Sons Ltd [1959] 3 All E.R. 225 12.33
Baker v. Longhurst [1933] 2 K.B. 461 13.33
Baker v. Market Harbourough Industrial Co-operative Society Ltd [1953] 1 W.L.R. 1472 12.85, 12.98
Baker v. Snell [1908] 2 K.B. 825 11.03
Baker v. Willoughby [1969] 3 All E.R. 1528; [1970] A.C. 467 H.L. 4.02, 4.11, **12.100**, 12.101
Balden v. Shorter [1933] Ch. 427 21.61, 21.62
Baldwin v. Casella (1872) L.R. 7 Ex. 325 11.03
Balfour v. Barty-King; Hyder & Sons (Builders), Third Parties [1957] 1 Q.B. 496 3.37, 9.45, 10.02, 10.03, 10.06, 10.08
Ball v. London County Council [1949] 2 K.B. 159 12.53, 14.13
Ballard v. North British Co. 1923 S.C. 43 12.86
Ballett v. Mingay [1943] K.B. 281 2.29
Balme v. Hulton (1837) 9 Bing. 471 7.19
Bamford v. Turnley (1862) 3 B. & S. 66 8.01, 8.17, 8.23, 8.41
Bank of Montreal v. Dominion Guarantee Co. Ltd [1930] A.C. 659 12.80
Bank of Nova Scotia v. Gaudreau (1985) 27 B.L.R. 101 21.48
Bank of Nova Scotia v. Hellenic Mutual War Risks Association (Bermuda) Ltd [1989] 3 All E.R. 628 12.70
Banque Financière de la Cité S.A. v. Westgate Insurance Co. Ltd [1989] 2 All E.R. 952 12.36, 12.70, 12.118
Banque Keyser SA v. Skandia (U.K.) Insurance Co. Ltd [1989] 2 All E.R. 952; *reversing* [1987] 2 W.L.R. 1300 12.10, 12.59, 12.72
Barker v. Furlong [1891] 2 Ch. 172 7.23, 7.28, 7.29
Barker v. Herbert [1911] 2 K.B. 633 8.85, 9.23
Barkway v. South Wales Transport Co. [1950] 1 All E.R. 392 12.86, 12.91
Barnes v. Irwell Valley Water Board [1938] 2 All E.R. 650; [1939] 1 K.B. 21 14.01, 14.08
Barnes v. Lucille Ltd (1907) 23 T.L.R. 393 11.22
Barnes v. Ward (1850) 9 C.B. 392 8.80
Barnett v. Chelsea & Kensington Hospital Management Committee [1969] 1 Q.B. 428 12.96
Barnett v. Guildford (Earl of) (1855) 11 Ex.19 5.16
Barnett v. Parker [1940] 3 All E.R. 575 14.08

Barrett v. Associated Newspapers Ltd (1907) 23 T.L.R. 666 21.54
Barrette v. Franki Compressed Pile Co. of Canada [1955] 2 D.L.R. 665 9.20
Barritt v. Attorney-General [1971] 1 W.L.R. 1713 19.05
Barrow v. Arnaud (1946) 8 Q.B. 595 7.49
Bartlett v. Tottenham [1932] 1 Ch. 114 9.21, 9.23
Barton v. Sadock (1611) 1 Bulst. 103 3.01
Bartonshill Coal Co. v. Reid (1858) 3 Macq. 266 14.46
Barty-King v. Ministry of Defence [1979] 2 All E.R. 80 12.122
Barrick v. Brighton Corporation [1949] 1 K.B. 339 16.16, 16.21
Barwick v. English Joint Stock Bank (1867) L.R. 2 Ex. 259 3.09
Basely v. Clarkson (1681) 3 Lev. 37 5.10, 5.29
Baston's Case (1610) 9 Co. Rep. 53b 8.61
Batcheller v. Tunbridge Wells Gas Co. (1901) 84 L.T. 765 9.20
Bates v. Batey [1913] 3 K.B. 351 14.04
Bates v. Parker [1953] 2 Q.B. 231 14.33, 14.52
Batty v. Metropolitan Property Realisations Ltd [1978] Q.B. 554 12.44, 14.11
Baty v. Parkdale Farms Ltd (1986) 37 C.C.L.T. 9 11.05
Bauer v. Richardson Construction Ltd [1938] 2 D.L.R. 309 9.20
Baugh v. Delta Water Fittings [1971] 3 All E.R. 258 6.42
Baxhaven Holdings Ltd v. Attorney-General [1974] 2 N.Z.L.R. 195 8.36
Baxter v. Gordon Ironside & Fares Ltd (1907) 13 O.L.R. 598 22.05
Baxter v. Taylor (1832) 4 B. & Ad. 72 5.17
Bayley v. Manchester, Sheffield & Lincolnshire Railway Co. (1873) L.R. 8 C.P. 148 3.19, 3.26
B.D.C. Ltd v. Hofstrand Farms Ltd (1986) 26 D.L.R. (4d) 1 12.43
Beals v. Hayward [1960] N.Z.L.R. 131 6.08
Beaman v. A.R.T.S. [1948] 2 All E.R. 89 H.C.; [1949] 1 K.B. 150 A.C. 7.40
Beard v. London General Omnibus Co. [1900] 2 Q.B. 530 3.31
Beattie v. Lord Ebury (1872) L.R. 7 Ch.App. 777 17.05
Beaudesert Shire Council v. Smith (1969) 120 C.L.R. 145 1.06, 16.11
Beaulieu v. Finglam (1401) Y.B. 2 Hen. IV f.18 10.02, 10.04
Bebee v. Sales (1916) 32 T.L.R. 413 2.30, 4.02
Beckett v. Newalls Insulation Co. [1953] 1 All E.R. 250 12.78
Beckett Ltd v. Lyons [1967] Ch. 449 5.07
Beckham v. Drake (1849) 2 H.L.C. 576 2.34
Beckwith v. Philbey (1827) 6 B. & C. 635 6.46
Beckwith v. Shordike & Hatch (1767) 4 Burr. 2093 5.10, 5.12
Becquet v. MacCarty (1831) 2 B. & Ad. 951 10.05
Beesly v. Hallwood Estates Ltd [1960] 2 All E.R. 314 17.05
Behrens v. Bertram Mills Circus [1957] 2 Q.B. 1 11.03
Beim v. Goyer [1965] S.C.R. 638 12.65
Bell v. Lever Bros [1932] A.C. 161 17.06
Bell v. London County Council [1949] 2 K.B. 159 14.04
Bellador Silk Ltd, Re [1965] 1 All E.R. 667 22.20
Belmont Finance Corporation v. Williams Furniture Ltd [1979] 1 All E.R. 118 21.08
Belmont Finance Corporation v. Williams Furniture Ltd (No. 2) [1980] 1 All E.R. 393 21.04
Beloff v. Pressdram Ltd [1973] 1 All E.R. 241 3.04
Bemax v. Austin Motor Co. Ltd [1955] A.C. 370 12.84
Bendall v. McWhirter [1952] 2 Q.B. 466 5.42
Benham v. Gambling [1941] A.C. 157 15.40
Benjamin v. Storr (1874) L.R. 9 C.P. 400 8.76, 8.77, 8.79, 16.06
Bennett v. Tugwell [1971] 2 Q.B. 267 13.10, 13.19
Benning v. Wong (1969) 43 A.L.J.R. 467 8.07, 9.19, 9.33, 9.43
Benson v. Biggs Wall & Co. Ltd [1982] 3 All E.R. 300 2.38, 15.60
Benson v. Lee [1972] V.R. 879 12.25

Bernstein of Leigh (Lord) v. Skyviews & General Ltd [1978] Q.B. 479; [1977] 2 All E.R. 902 5.20, 5.23, **5.26–27**, 7.05, 19.03
Berry v. British Transport Commission [1960] 3 All E.R. 322 H.C.; [1962] 1 Q.B. 306; [1961] 3 All E.R. 65 C.A. 1.27, 22.13, 22.14, **22.15–17**
Berry v. Humm [1915] 1 K.B. 627 15.60
Besozzi v. Harris (1858) 1 F. & F. 92 11.03
Bettel v. Yim (1978) 20 O.R. (2d) 617 6.10, 6.14
Bettenson v. Johnson (1980) 18 A.R. 343 11.05
Bhoomidas v. Singapore Harbour Authority [1978] 1 All E.R. 956 3.05
Biba Group Ltd v. Biba Boutique [1980] R.P.C. 413 21.66, 21.71
Biddle v. Bond (1865) 6 B. & S. 225 7.24, 7.39
Bielirski v. Obadiski (1922) 65 D.L.R. 627 21.59
Big Point Club v. Logan [1943] 4 D.L.R. 136 5.24
Billings (A.C.) & Sons Ltd v. Riden [1958] A.C. 240 1.32, 3.37, 13.13, 13.21
Birch v. Thomas [1972] 1 All E.R. 905 13.10
Bird v. Fort Francis [1949] 2 D.L.R. 791 7.06, 7.35
Bird v. Jones (1845) 7 Q.B. 742 6.18
Bird v. King Line Ltd [1970] 1 Lloyd's Rep. 349 14.33, 14.40
Bird v. O'Neil [1960] A.C. 907 3.05
Birkett v. Hayes [1982] 2 All E.R. 710 15.38
Bishop v. Cunard White Star Ltd; Appleby v. same [1950] P. 240 15.39
Biss v. Lambeth, Southwark, & Lewisham Area Health Authority [1978] 2 All E.R. 125 15.49
Bisset v. Wilkinson [1927] A.C. 177 17.04
Black v. Christchurch Finance Co. [1894] A.C. 48 3.37, 10.11
Blacker v. Lake & Elliott (1912) 106 L.T. 533 14.04
Blackshaw v. Lord [1983] 2 All E.R. 311 18.71, 18.73, **18.89**, 18.90, 18.94, 18.95, **18.97**
Blades v. Higgs (1861) 10 C.B.N.S. 713 5.33, 5.34, 7.11, 7.48
Blake v. Barnard (1840) 9 C. & P. 626 6.15
Blakemore v. Bristol & Exeter Railway Co. (1858) 8 E. & B. 1035 14.02
Blankley v. Godley [1952] 1 All E.R. 436n 5.27
Blee v. London & North Eastern Railway Co. [1938] A.C. 126 3.21
Bliss v. Hall (1838) 4 Bing. N.C. 183 8.47
Bloodworth v. Gray (1844) 7 Man. & Gr. 334 18.49
Bloxham v. Sanders (1825) 9 B. & C. 941 7.33
Blundell v. Catterall (1821) 5 B. & Ald. 268 5.07
Blyth v. Birmingham Waterworks (1856) 11 Ex. 781 9.02, 12.73
Boardman v. Sanderson [1964] 1 W.L.R. 1317 12.25
Boden v. Roscoe [1894] 1 Q.B. 608 11.02
Bodlewell, The [1907] P. 286 15.16
Bognor Regis U.D.C. v. Campion [1972] 2 All E.R. 61 2.17, 18.03, 18.47
Bolam v. Friern Hospital Management Committee [1957] 2 All E.R. 118 12.73, 12.78, 12.80
Bolduc v. R. [1967] S.C.R. 677 6.38
Bollinger v. Costa Brava Wine Co. Ltd [1960] Ch. 262 21.73–75
Bolton v. Stone [1951] A.C. 850 8.06, 8.09, 8.18, **8.27**, **12.15**, 12.19, 12.61, 12.74
Bonarenko v. Sommers (1967) 69 S.R. (N.S.W.) 269 13.45
Bond v. Loutit [1979] 2 W.W.R. 154 13.45
Bond Worth Ltd, re [1979] 3 All E.R. 919 7.26
Bone v. Seale [1975] 1 All E.R. 787 8.11
Bonita, The (1861) 1 Lush. 252 3.08
Bonnard v. Perryman [1891] 2 Ch. 269 18.118
Bonnington Castings Ltd v. Wardlaw [1956] A.C. 613 12.94, **12.103**, 12.108, 16.15
Bonomi v. Backhouse (1867) L.R. 2 Q.B. 223 8.41
Boomer v. Penn [1966] 1 O.R. 119 12.78

Borden (U.K.) Ltd v. Scottish Timber Products Ltd [1979] 3 All E.R. 961 7.26
Borroughes v. Bayne (1860) 5 H. & N. 296 7.20
Borrowdail v. Hunter (1843) 5 Man. & Gr. 639 6.06
Bosada v. Pines (1984) 5 D.L.R. (4th) 334 22.24, 22.26
Boston v. Tatam (1621) Cro. Jac. 623 18.48
Boston v. W.S. Bagshaw & Sons Ltd [1966] 2 All E.R. 906 18.90
Bottomley v. Bannister [1932] 1 K.B. 458 12.53, 14.04, 14.13
Bottomley v. F.W. Woolworth (1932) 48 T.L.R. 521 18.36
Boulcott Golf Club Inc. v. Engelbrecht [1945] N.Z.L.R. 556 10.03
Boulton v. Arlesden (1697) 3 Salk. 324 3.02
Bourgoin S.A. v. Ministry of Agriculture [1986] Q.B. 716 1.22
Bourhill v. Young [1943] A.C. 92 9.32, **12.12**, 12.20, 12.21, 12.25, 12.26, 12.113
Bourke v. Warren (1826) 2 C. & P. 307 18.21, 18.23
Bowater v. Rowley Regis Corporation [1944] K.B. 476 13.13
Bowen v. Hall (1881) 6 Q.B.D. 333 21.30
Bower v. Peate (1876) 1 Q.B.D. 34 3.37, 8.37, 9.09
Bowyer v. Cooke (1847) 4 C.B. 236 5.08
Box v. Jubb (1879) 4 Ex.D. 76 9.22, 9.44
Box v. Midland Bank Ltd [1979] 2 Lloyd's Rep. 391 12.36
Boxsius v. Goblet Freres [1894] 1 Q.B. 842 18.32, 18.95, 18.99
Boy Andrew, The [1948] P. 140 13.27, 13.34, 13.37, 13.38
Boyce v. Paddington Borough Council [1903] 1 Ch. 109 16.06
Boychuk v. Northwest Territories Housing Corporation (1985) 33 C.C.L.T. 28 21.33, 21.53
Boyle v. Kodak Ltd [1969] 2 All E.R. 439 13.47, 14.53, 16.06, 16.16
Brackenborough v. Spalding U.D.C. [1942] A.C. 310 11.04, 11.34, 12.53
Bradburn v. Great Western Railway (1874) L.R. 10 Ex. 1 15.37
Bradburn v. Lindsay [1983] 2 All E.R. 408 8.28, 8.33
Braddock v. Bevins [1948] 1 K.B. 380 18.11, 18.98
Bradford v. Robinson Rentals Ltd [1967] 1 All E.R. 267 12.74, 12.118
Bradford Building Society v. Borders [1941] 2 All E.R. 205 17.07, 17.09
Bradford Corporation v. Pickles [1895] A.C. 587 1.22, 8.20, 8.23
Bradlaugh v. Gossett (1884) 12 Q.B.D. 271 18.74
Bradley v. Copley (1845) 1 Q.B. 685 7.33
Bradley v. Reynolds (1846) 8 Q.B. 729 7.50
Bradshaw v. Waterlow & Sons Ltd [1913] 3 K.B. 527 22.08
Brandeis Goldschmidt & Co. Ltd v. Western Transport Ltd [1982] 1 All E.R. 28 **7.49**
Brandon v. Osborne Garrett & Co. [1924] 1 K.B. 548 12.30
Bravery v. Bravery [1954] 3 All E.R. 59 13.18
Brearley v. London & North Western Railway (1899) 15 T.L.R. 237 18.20
Brekkes v. Cattel [1971] 1 All E.R. 1031 21.44
Brelitski v. Obadiah (1922) 65 D.L.R. 627 6.17
Bresden v. Johnson [1945] 1 W.W.R. 273 21.59
Brew Bros. Ltd v. Snax (Ross) Ltd [1970] 1 All E.R. 587 8.44, **8.45**
Brezinski v. Schultz [1975] 3 W.W.R. 467 3.22
Bridges v. Hawkesworth (1851) 21 L.J.Q.B. 75 7.07, 7.35
Bridges Bros. Ltd v. Forest Products Ltd (1977) 72 D.L.R. (3d) 335 9.15, 9.18
Bridgman v. Stockdale [1953] 1 All E.R. 1166 18.53
Bridlington Relay Ltd v. Yorkshire Electricity Board [1965] Ch. 436 8.11
Brierly v. Kendall (1852) 17 Q.B. 937 7.48
Briess v. Woolley [1954] A.C. 333 3.08, 17.07
Brimelow v. Casson [1924] 1 Ch. 302 21.12, **21.49**
Brinsmead v. Harrison (1871) L.R. 6 C.P. 584; (1872) L.R. 7 C.P. 547 4.05, 7.54
British Airports Authority v. Ashton [1983] 3 All E.R. 6 6.18

British Airways Board v. Laker Airways [1985] A.C. 58 1.06
British Airways Board v. Taylor [1976] 1 All E.R. 65 17.04
British Aviator, The [1965] 1 Lloyd's Rep. 271 13.41
British Celanese Ltd v. A.H. Hunt (Capacitors) Ltd [1969] 2 All E.R. 1252 9.14, 12.46
British Columbia Electric Railway Co. v. Gentile [1914] A.C. 1034 15.54
British Columbia Electric Railway Co. Ltd v. Loach [1916] 1 A.C. 719 13.27, 13.35
British Columbia Electric Railway Co. Ltd (Owners), re [1953] A.C. 291 13.39
British Economical Lamp Co. v. Empire, Mile End (1913) 29 T.L.R. 386 5.35
British Motor Trade Association v. Salvadori [1949] Ch. 556 21.12, 21.46
British Railway Traffic & Electricity Co. v. C.R.C. Co. [1922] 2 K.B. 260 21.54, 21.61
British Railways Board v. Herrington [1972] A.C. 877 H.L. 12.14, 14.15, 14.28, **14.44**, 14.45
British Road Services v. Slater [1964] 1 W.L.R. 498 8.85
British South Africa Co. v. Companhia de Mocambique [1893] A.C. 602 2.09, 5.18
British Steel Corporation v. Granada Television [1981] 1 All E.R. 417 18.62, 19.05
British Transport Commission v. Gourley [1956] A.C. 185 15.08, 15.09, 15.24, 15.35, 15.59
Broad v. Ham (1839) 5 Bing. N.C. 722 22.07, 22.12
Broadbent v. Ramsbotham (1856) 11 Ex. 602 8.20
Broadway Approvals Ltd v. Odhams Press Ltd [1964] 2 Q.B. 683 H.C.; [1965] 2 All E.R. 523 C.A. 18.63, 18.69, 18.106, 18.110
Brock v. Coupland (1794) 1 Esp. 203 11.23
Brock v. Richards [1951] 1 K.B. 529 11.05, 12.53
Bromage v. Prosser (1825) 4 B. & C. 247 1.22, 18.05
Brooke v. Bool [1928] 2 K.B. 578 3.37, 4.01
Broom v. Morgan [1953] 1 Q.B. 597 3.02, 3.40
Broome v. Agar (1928) 44 T.L.R. 339 18.20
Brown v. Boorman (1842) 3 Q.B. 511; (1844) 11 Cl. & Fin. 1 12.70
Brown v. Chapman (1848) 6 C.B. 368 6.22
Brown v. Cooke (1846) 16 L.J. Ch. 140 18.115
Brown v. Cotterill (1934) 51 T.L.R. 21 12.02, 14.07, 14.08
Brown v. Doe & Astor Hotel Ltd (1980) 23 B.C.L.R. 30 3.22
Brown v. Giles (1823) 1 C. & P. 118 11.02
Brown v. Harrison (1947) 177 L.T. 281 8.85
Brown v. Hawkes [1891] 2 Q.B. 718 22.11, 22.12
Brown v. Lewis (1896) 12 T.L.R. 455 2.21
Brown v. National Coal Board [1962] A.C. 574 16.12
Brown v. Raphael [1958] Ch. 636 17.04
Brown v. Rolls Royce Ltd [1960] 1 All E.R. 577 12.80, 12.83
Brown v. Spamberger (1960) 21 D.L.R. (2d) 630 21.32
Brown v. Thompson [1968] 2 All E.R. 708 4.11, 13.41
Brown v. Wootton (1605) Cro. Jac. 73 4.05
Brown Jenkinson & Co. Ltd v. Percy Dalton (London) Ltd [1957] 2 Q.B. 621 17.16
Browne v. D.C. Thomson 1912 S.C. 359 18.27
Brownlie v. Campbell (1880) 5 App.Cas. 925 17.07
Bruce v. Odhams Press Ltd [1936] 1 All E.R. 287 18.21
Brunsden v. Humphrey (1884) 14 Q.B.D. 141 15.02
Bryanston Finance Ltd v. de Vries [1975] Q.B. 703; [1975] 2 All E.R. 609 4.05, 4.06, 18.32, 18.99

Bryanston Leasings Ltd v. Principality Finance Ltd [1977] R.T.R. 45 7.18, 7.25
Bryce v. Swan Hunter Group plc [1988] 1 All E.R. 659 12.103
Bryden v. Stewart (1855) 2 Macq. 30 14.46
Buchan v. Ortho Pharmaceuticals (Canada) Ltd (1986) 25 D.L.R. (4th) 658 13.17, 14.07
Buck v. Conway (1973) 9 N.B.R. (2d) 124 12.79
Buck v. English electric Co. Ltd [1978] 1 All E.R. 271 15.48, 15.49
Buckland v. Guildford Gas Light & Coke Co. [1949] 1 K.B. 410 12.14, 14.16
Buckle v. Bayswater Road Board (1936) 57 C.L.R. 259 8.80
Buckle v. Holmes [1926] 2 K.B. 125 11.02, 11.03, 11.06
Buckley v. Smith Transport Ltd [1946] 4 D.L.R. 721 2.33
Buckpitt v. Oates [1968] 1 All E.R. 1145 2.24, 13.06, 13.10, 13.19
Building & Civil Engineering Holidays Scheme Management Ltd v. Post Office [1966] 1 Q.B. 247 2.07, 7.19
Bull v. Vazquez [1947] 1 All E.R. 334 18.52
Bulli Coal Mining Co. v. Osborne [1899] A.C. 351 5.21
Bulmer (H.P.) Ltd and Showerings Ltd v. J. Bollinger SA and Champagne Lanson Père et Fils [1978] R.P.C. 79 21.73
Bundy, Clark & Co. v. London & North Eastern Railway [1931] 2 K.B. 334 8.76
Bunker v. Charles Brand & Son Ltd [1969] 2 Q.B. 480 14.17, 14.35, 14.40
Bunyan v. Jordan (1936) 57 C.L.R. 1 6.17
Burfitt v. Kille [1939] 2 K.B. 743 14.04, 14.07, 14.14
Burgess v. Florence Nightingale Hospital for Gentlewomen [1955] 1 Q.B. 349 15.60
Burmah Oil Co. v. Lord Advocate [1965] A.C. 75 2.08
Burnard v. Haggis (1863) 14 C.B.N.S. 45 2.29
Burnett & Hallamshire Fuel Ltd v. Sheffield Telegraph & Star Ltd [1960] 2 All E.R. 157 18.86
Burns v. Edman [1970] 2 Q.B. 451 15.59
Buron v. Denman (1848) 2 Ex. 167 2.08, 3.08
Burrows v. Rhodes [1899] 1 Q.B. 816 17.16
Burton v. Hughes (1824) 2 Bing N.C. 173 7.33
Bush v. Steinman (1799) 1 Box. & Paul 404 3.01
Bushel v. Miller (1718) 1 Stra. 128 7.19
Business Computers International Ltd v. Registrar of Companies [1987] 3 All E.R. 465 12.06, 12.10
Bute (Marquess of) v. Barclays Bank Ltd [1955] 1 Q.B. 202 7.33
Butler v. Manchester Sheffield & Lincolnshire Railway (1888) 21 Q.B.D. 207 5.42
Butterfield v. Forrester (1809) 11 East 60 13.23
Buttes Gas and Oil Co. v. Hammer (Nos. 2 & 3) [1982] A.C. 888; [1981] 3 All E.R. 616 2.09, 21.04
Bux v. Slough Metals Ltd [1973] 1 W.L.R. 1358 14.47
Byrne v. Boadle (1863) 2 H. & C. 722 12.86, 12.90
Byrne v. Deane [1937] 1 K.B. 818 18.09, 18.34
Bywell Castle (1879) 4 P.D. 219 12.114, 13.31

C

C.B.S. Songs Ltd v. Amstrad Consumer Electronics plc [1987] 3 All E.R. 151 16.08
C.P.R. v. Frechette [1915] A.C. 871 13.23
C.P.R. v. Gaud [1949] 2 K.B. 239 5.01
C.P.R. v. Lockhart [1942] A.C. 591 3.10, 3.21, 3.25
C.P.R. v. R. [1931] A.C. 414 5.40
C.P. Hotels Ltd v. Bank of Montreal (1988) 40 D.L.R. (4th) 385 1.11

Cadbury Schweppes Pty Ltd v. Pub Squash Co. Pty Ltd [1981] 1 All E.R. 213 21.69, 21.70
Cahoon v. Franks (1967) 63 D.L.R. (2d) 274 15.02
Cakebread v. Hopping Bros. (Whetstone) Ltd [1947] K.B. 641 13.46
Calliope, The [1952] A.C. 242 12.114, 12.119
Caltex Oil (Australia) Pty Ltd v. Dredge Willemstad (1976) 136 C.L.R. 529 12.46
Calveley v. Chief Constable of Merseyside [1989] 1 All E.R. 1025 1.22, **12.65**
Calvert v. Gosling (1887) 5 T.L.R. 185 5.12
Calvert v. Pick [1954] 1 W.L.R. 456 4.07
Camden Nominees v. Forcey [1940] Ch. 352 21.49
Caminer v. Northern and London Investment Trust [1951] A.C. 88 8.40, 8.85
Camkin v. Bishop [1941] 2 All E.R. 713 12.78
Campbell v. Paddington Corporation [1911] 1 K.B. 869 2.19
Campbell v. Spottiswode (1863) 3 B. & S. 769 18.61, 18.68, 18.114
Campbell v. Thompson [1953] 1 Q.B. 445 2.21
Campbell & Cousans v. U.K. (1982) 4 E.H.R.R. 293 6.30
Campbell Davys v. Lloyd [1901] 2 Ch. 518 8.63
Canada Cement La Farge Ltd v. B.C. Lightwight Aggregate Ltd (1983) 145 D.L.R. (3d) 385 21.04, 21.15
Canada Safeway v. Manitoba Food & Commercial Workers Union Local 832 (1981) 25 C.C.L.T. 1 1.06
Canadian National Railway Co. v. Norsk Pacific Steamship Co. Ltd. (1990) 65 D.L.R. (4th) 321 12.43
Canadian Pacific Hotels Ltd v. Bank of Montreal (1988) 40 D.L.R. (4th) 385 12.71
Canadian Pacific Railway Co. v. Building Material Construction & Fuel Drivers Union Local 213 [1971] 5 W.W.R. 1 21.28
Canadian Pacific Railway Co. v. Kelvin Shipping Co. Ltd (1927) 138 L.T. 369 12.33
Canadian Pacific Steamships Ltd v. Bryers [1958] A.C. 485 16.11
Canadian Pacific Wine Co. v. Tuley [1921] 2 A.C. 417 5.09
Canadian Southern Railway Co. v. Philps (1884) 14 S.C.R. 132 10.11
Canadian Training & Development Group Inc. v. Air Canada (1987) 39 C.C.L.T. 72 21.15
Candler v. Crane, Christmas & Co. [1951] 2 K.B. 164 12.02, 12.35
Candlewood Navigation Corporation Ltd v. Mitsui OSK Lines Ltd [1985] 2 All E.R. 935 12.46, 12.47, 12.48
Cann v. Wilson (1888) 39 Ch.D. 39 12.35
Cant v. Cant (1985) 49 O.R. (2d) 25 6.17
Canterbury (Viscount of) v. Attorney-General (1843) 1 Ph. 306 2.02, 10.05
Caparo Industries PLC v. Dickman [1990] 1 All E.R. 568 H.L.; *reversing* [1989] 1 All E.R. 798 12.10, **12.37,** 12.38, 12.39
Capital & Counties Bank v. Henty (1882) 7 App.Cas. 741 18.13, 18.14, 18.17, 18.20
Capital Finance Co. Ltd v. Bray [Bray] 1 W.L.R. 323 5.35
Capps v. Miller [1989] 2 All E.R. 333 13.26, 13.37, 13.39, **13.42**
Car & General Insurance Corporation Ltd v. Seymour & Maloney [1956] S.C.R. 322 13.16
Carberry v. Davies [1968] 2 All E.R. 817 3.13
Carlgrath, The [1927] P. 93 5.07, 10.04
Carmarthenshire C.C. v. Lewis [1955] A.C. 549 2.30, 3.41, 11.05, 12.13
Carpenters Co. v. British Mutual Banking Co. [1937] 3 All E.R. 811 12.80
Carrington v. Taylor (1809) 11 East 571 21.16
Carroll v. A. Barclay & Sons Ltd [1948] A.C. 477 1.31, 16.12
Carslake v. Mapledoram (1788) 2 T.R. 473 18.48
Carstairs v. Taylor (1871) L.R. 6 Ex. 257 9.39, 9.48

Carter (John) (Fine Worsteds) Ltd v. Hanson Haulage (Leeds) Ltd [1965] 2 Q.B. 495 — 3.27, 3.32
Cartledge v. E. Jopling & Sons Ltd [1963] A.C. 758 — 15.19
Case of Thorns (1466) Y.B. 6 Ed. IV 7 — 5.06, 5.35
Casey v. Arnott (1876) 2 C.P.D. 24 — 21.59
Casey v. Automobiles Renault Canada Ltd [1965] S.C.R. 607 — 22.04, 22.05
Cassell & Co. Ltd v. Broome [1971] 2 All E.R. 187 C.A.; [1972] 1 All E.R. 801; [1972] A.C. 1027 H.L. — 4.04, 6.18, 15.05, 17.19, **18.104**, 18.106, **18.108–10**, 21.46
Cassidy v. Daily Mirror Newspapers Ltd [1929] 2 K.B. 331 — 18.05, 18.06, 18.14, 18.23, 18.54(a)
Cassidy v. Ministry of Health [1951] 2 K.B. 343 — 3.04, 3.05, 3.34, 3.41, 12.85, 12.87
Castle v. St. Augustine Links (1922) 38 T.L.R. 615 — 8.09
Castrique v. Behrens (1861) 3 E. & E. 709 — 22.05
Caswell v. Powell Duffryn Associated Collieries Ltd [1940] A.C. 152 — 13.27, 16.13, 16.20
Castle v. Stockton Waterworks Co. (1875) L.R. 10 Q.B. 453 — 9.32, 12.46
Cavalier v. Pope [1906] A.C. 428 — 12.53, 14.19
Cavanagh v. Ulster Weaving Co. Ltd [1960] A.C. 145 — 12.80, 12.81
Cawdor v. Lewis (1835) 1 Y. & C. 427 — 5.50
Caxton Publishing Co. Ltd v. Sutherland Publishing Co. [1939] A.C. 178 — 7.16, 7.50, 7.52
Central Asbestos Co. Ltd v. Dodd [1973] A.C. 518 — 15.48
Central Canada Potash Co. Ltd v. Government of Saskatchewan (1976) 57 D.L.R. (3d) 7; (1977) 79 D.L.R. (3d) 297; (1979) 88 D.L.R. (3d) 609 — 21.18, 21.23, 21.24
Central Newbury Car Auctions Ltd v. Unity Finance Ltd [1957] 1 Q.B. 371 — 7.30
Central Railway Co. of Venezuela v Kisch (1867) L.R. 2 H.L. 99 — 17.15
Central Trust Co. v. Rafuse (1986) 31 D.L.R. (4th) 481; [1986] 2 S.C.R. 147 — 1.11, 12.68
Century Insurance Co. Ltd v. Northern Ireland Road Transport Board [1942] A.C. 509 — 3.22
Chabbra Corporation — *see* Jag Shakti
Chadwick v. British Transport Commission [1967] 2 All E.R. 945 — 12.25, 12.31
Chadwick v. Herapath (1847) 3 C.B. 885 — 18.116
Chamberlain v. Boyd (1883) 11 Q.B.D. 407 — 18.43, 18.44
Chambers v. Donaldson (1809) 11 East 65 — 5.13
Chan Wai Jong v. Li Ping [1985] 2 W.L.R. 396 — 15.27
Chandler v. Broughton (1832) 1 Cr. & M. 29 — 6.02
Chapman v. Hearse (1961) 106 C.L.R. 112 — 12.31
Chapman v. Ellesmere (Lord) [1932] 2 K.B. 431; [1932] All E.R. Rep. 221 — 13.05, 18.29, 18.56, 18.88, 18.90, 18.99
Chapman v. Honig [1963] 2 Q.B. 502 — 1.22
Chapman v. Oakleigh Animal Products Ltd (1970) 8 K.I.R. 1063 — 3.20
Chaproniere v. Mason (1905) 21 T.L.R. 633 — 12.90
Charing Cross Electricity Supply Co. v. Hydraulic Power Co. [1914] 3 K.B. 772 — 8.54, 9.09, **9.13**, 9.20, 9.41
Chasemore v. Richards (1859) 7 H.L.C. 349 — 8.20
Chatterton v. Gerson [1981] 1 All E.R. 257 — 6.08, 6.36, 13.17
Chatterton v. Secretary of State for India in Council [1895] 2 Q.B. 189 — 18.84, 18.85
Chaudhry v. Prabhaker [1988] 3 All E.R. 718 — 12.36, 12.42
Cheater v. Cater [1918] 1 K.B. 247 — 9.16
Chenard & Co. v. Joachim Arisol [1949] A.C. 127 — 18.74
Cheney Bros. v. Doris Silk Corporation (1929) 35 F. (2d) 279 — 21.69

Chernesky v. Armadale Publications Ltd [1979] 1 S.C.R. 1967 18.35, 18.67
Cheshire v. Bailey [1905] 1 K.B. 237 3.32
Chester v. Waverley Municipal Council (1939) 62 C.L.R. 1 12.25
Cherry Ltd v. Allied Insurance Brokers Ltd [1978] 1 Lloyd's Rep. 274 12.37
Chic Fashions (West Wales) Ltd v. Jones [1968] 2 Q.B. 299 5.09, 5.46, 7.14
China-Pacific S.A. v. Food Coop. of India; The Winson [1981] 3 All E.R. 688 7.13, 7.37
Chipcase v. British Titan Products Co. [1956] 1 Q.B. 545 16.13
Christie v. Davey [1893] 1 Ch. 316 8.21, 8.23
Christie v. Griggs (1809) 2 Camp. 791 12.86
Christie v. Leachinsky [1947] A.C. 573 6.44
Christina, The [1938] A.C. 485 2.13
Christmas v. General Cleaning Contractors Ltd [1953] A.C. 180 14.33
Christos Industry Ltd v. S. Bedford D.C. [1986] 1 Q.B. 1034 12.62
Chubb Cash Ltd v. John Colley & Son [1983] 2 All E.R. 294 7.50
Church of Scientology of California v. Johnson-Smith [1972] 1 All E.R. 378 18.74
Churchill v. Walton [1967] 2 A.C. 227 21.09
Cilia v. H.M. James & Sons [1954] 2 All E.R. 9 14.92
Cinnamond v. British Airports Authority [1980] 1 W.L.R. 582 5.09
Citizens' Life Assurance Co. v. Brown [1904] A.C. 423 2.19
City of Lincoln, The [1899] P. 15 12.114
Claridge v. Mackenzie (1842) 4 Man. & Gr. 142 5.19
Clarke v. Bruce Lane & Co. [1988] 1 All E.R. 364 12.43
Clarke v. Chambers (1878) 3 Q.B.D. 327 12.114
Clarke v. J. Lyons & Co. Ltd [1912] 3 K.B. 198 14.24
Clarke v. Rotax Aircraft Equipment Ltd [1975] 3 All E.R. 794 15.28
Clarke and Wife v. Brims [1947] K.B. 497 16.04
Clay v. Crump Co. Ltd [1964] 1 Q.B. 533 14.06, 14.09
Clay v. Pooler [1982] 3 All E.R. 570 2.38, 15.33
Clayton v. LeRoy [1911] 2 K.B. 1031 7.20
Clayton v. Woodman & Son (Builders) Ltd [1962] 2 Q.B. 533 12.35, 14.36
Claywards v. Dethick (1848) 12 Q.B. 439 13.13, 13.21, 13.31
Clearlite Holdings Ltd v. Auckland City Council [1976] 2 N.Z.L.R. 729 8.05, 8.36
Clearbrook Property Holdings Ltd v. Verrier [1973] 3 All E.R. 614 21.62
Cleery v. Booth [1893] 1 Q.B. 465 6.29
Clegg v. Dearden (1849) 12 Q.B. 576 5.08
Cleghorn v. Sadler [1945] K.B. 325 18.51
Clifton v. Bury (Viscount) (1887) 4 T.L.R. 8 5.24
Clifton Securities v. Huntley [1948] 2 All E.R. 283 5.48
Clinton v. Lyons [1912] 3 K.B. 198 11.03
Clippers Oil Co. v. Edinburgh & District Water Trustees [1907] A.C. 291 12.113
Close v. Steel Co. of Wales Ltd [1962] A.C. 367 16.18
Clough Mill Ltd v. Martin [1984] 1 All E.R. 721 7.26
Clough v. Bussan [1990] 1 All E.R. 431 12.06, 12.08, 12.10, 12.62, 12.64
Clydesdale Bank Ltd v. Paton [1896] A.C. 381 17.08
Cobb v. Great Western Railway [1894] A.C. 419 12.114
Cochrane v. Rymill (1879) 40 L.T. 44 7.23, 7.29
Cocke v. Jenner (1614) Hob. 66 4.06
Cockroft v. Smith (1705) 11 Mod. 43 6.26
Cocks v. Thanet District Council [1982] 3 All E.R. 1135 16.06
Coco v. A. N. Clark (Engineering) Ltd [1969] R.P.C. 41 20.04
Coddington v. International Harvester Co. of Gt. Britain (1969) 6 K.I.R. 146 3.20, 14.50
Coderre v. Ethier (1978) 85 D.L.R. (3d) 621 15.32
Coggs v. Barnard (1704) 2 Ld. Raym. 909 12.77

Cohen, re [1953] 1 Ch. 88 7.07, 7.35
Cole v. Turner (1704) 6 Mod. 149 6.03
Collett v. Gray (1850) 4 Ex. 729 6.19
Collingwood v. Home & Colonial Stores Ltd [1936] 2 All E.R. 200 9.26, 10.08, 10.11, 10.13
Collings v. Hertfordshire C.C. [1947] K.B. 598 3.04
Collins v. Wilcock [1984] 3 All E.R. 374 6.01, 6.04, 6.10, 6.14, 6.23
Colls v. Home & Colonial Stores [1904] A.C. 179 8.15, 8.74
Colvilles Ltd v. Devine [1969] 2 All E.R. 53 12.90, 12.93
Colwell v. St. Pancras B.C. [1904] Ch. 707 8.33
Commercial & Estates Co. of Egypt v. Board of Trade [1925] 1 K.B. 271 2.08
Commissioner for Railways v. McDermott [1967] 1 A.C. 169 14.16
Commissioner for Railways v. Quinlan [1964] A.C. 1054 14.15, 14.16
Commissioner for Railways v. Valuer-General [1974] A.C. 328 5.20, 5.25
Commonwealth v. Quince (1944) 68 C.L.R. 227 2.02
Compania Financiera Soleada S.A. & ors. v. Hamoor Tanker Corp. Inc.; The Borag [1981] 1 All E.R. 856 12.113
Condon v. Basi [1985] 2 All E.R. 453 13.07
Congresso de Partido, I — *see* Playa Larga (Cargo Owners)
Connolly v. Camden & Islington Area Health Authority [1981] 3 All E.R. 250 15.29
Connor v. Port of Liverpool Stevedoring Co. [1953] 2 Lloyd's Rep. 606 13.41
Conry v. Simpson [1983] 3 All E.R. 369 15.49
Consolidated Co. v. Curtis & Son [1892] 2 Q.B. 495 7.23, 7.24, 7.29
Control Risks Ltd v. New English Library Ltd [1989] 3 All E.R. 577 18.60, 18.65
Conway v. George Wimpey Ltd [1951] 2 K.B. 325 3.25, 5.11
Cook v. Alexander [1974] Q.B. 279 8.89
Cook v. Beal (1697) 1 Ld. Raym. 176 6.27
Cook v. Cook (1986) 68 A.L.R. 353 12.77, 12.78, **13.14**, 13.16
Cook v. Lewis [1951] S.C.R. 830 6.07, 12.85, **12.98**, 12.99, 12.104, 12.109
Cookson v. Harewood [1932] 2 K.B. 478n 18.57
Cookson v. Knowles [1979] A.C. 556 15.23, 15.24, 15.26, 15.45, 15.59
Cooper v. Crabtree (1882) 20 Ch.D. 589 5.17, 8.33
Cooper v. Firth Brown Ltd [1963] 2 All E.R. 31 15.24
Cooper v. Southern Portland Cement Ltd [1974] A.C. 623 14.16
Cooper v. Williams [1963] 2 Q.B. 567 15.53
Cope v. Sharpe (No. 2) [1912] 1 K.B. 496 5.30, 5.32, 6.35
Corbet v. Hill (1870) L.R. 9 Eq. 671 5.20
Corbett v. Burger Warren & Ridgley Ltd (1932) 48 T.L.R. 626 22.17
Corelli v. Ward (1906) 22 T.L.R. 532 19.06
Cork v. Kirkby Maclean Ltd [1952] 2 All E.R. 402 12.96
Cormier v. McCarthy (1969) 1 N.B.R. (2d) 866 11.05
Cornfoot v. Fowke (1840) 6 M. & W. 358 17.14
Cornish v. Stubbs (1870) L.R. 5 C.P. 234 5.40
Cornwall v. Myskow [1987] 2 All E.R. 504 18.67, 18.68, 18.105
Corothers v. Slobodian (1975) 51 D.L.R. (3d) 1 12.31
Cory (W.) & Sons Ltd v. Lambton & Hetton Collieries Ltd (1916) 86 L.J.K.B. 401 4.13
Cory Lighterage Ltd v. T. & G.W.U. [1973] 14 K.I.R. 463 21.28
Cosgrove v. Horsfall (1945) 62 T.L.R. 140 14.37
Cotic v. Gray (1981) 33 O.R. (2d) 356 12.119
Couch v. Steel (1854) 3 E. & B. 402 16.02
Coughlin v. Gillison [1899] 1 Q.B. 145 14.03
Coughlin v. Kuntz (1987) 42 C.C.L.T. 142 15.05
Courchene v. Marlborough Hotels Ltd (1971) 20 D.L.R. (3d) 109; (1971) 22 D.L.R. (3d) 157 18.26

Covell v. Laming (1808) 1 Camp. 497 6.02, 7.04
Coventry City Council v. Doyle [1981] 2 All E.R. 184 8.03, 8.75
Coward v. Braddeley (1859) 4 H. & N. 478 6.11
Cowell v. Rosehill Racecourse Co. Ltd (1936) 56 C.L.R. 605 5.42
Cowley v. Newmarket Local Board [1892] A.C. 345 8.80
Cox v. Burbridge (1863) 13 C.B.N.S. 431 11.02, 11.03
Cox v. Coulson [1916] 2 K.B. 177 14.16
Cox v. Glue (1848) 5 C.B. 533 5.21
Cresswell v. Sirl [1948] 1 K.B. 241 7.04, 7.13, 11.27
Crits v. Sylvester (1956) 1 D.L.R. (2d) 502 12.80
Crocker v. Sundance Northwest Resorts Ltd (1989) 51 D.L.R. (4th) 321 13.19
Croft v. Day (1984) 7 Beav. 84 21.65
Crofter Hand Woven Harris Tweed Co. Ltd v. Veitch [1942] A.C. 435 12.94, 21.03, 21.04, 21.06, **21.11–12**, 21.13–14
Croke v. Wiseman [1981] 3 All E.R. 852 15.29, 15.33, **15.39**, 15.42
Crook v. Derbyshire Stone Co. Ltd [1956] 1 W.L.R. 432 3.30
Crowhurst v. Amersham Burial Board (1878) 4 Ex.D 5 9.16, 9.20
Cudney v. Clement's Motor Sales Ltd (1969) 5 D.L.R. (3d) 3 12.93
Cullen v. Trappel (1980) 29 A.L.R. 1 15.35
Cummings v. Granger [1975] 2 All E.R. 1129 H.C.; [1977] 1 All E.R. 104 C.A. **11.15**, **11.17**, **11.22**, 11.23, **11.24**
Cunard v. Antifyre Ltd [1933] 1 K.B. 441 8.08, 8.11, 8.32, 8.34
Cunliffe v. Bankes [1945] 1 All E.R. 459 8.39, 8.85
Cunningham v. Harrison [1950] 2 K.B. 43 15.30
Cunningham Howie v. Dimbleby & Sons Ltd [1950] 2 K.B. 882 18.62
Curran v. Northern Ireland Co-ownership Housing Association Ltd [1987] 2 All E.R. 13 12.06, 12.44, 12.59
Cushing v. Walker & Son [1941] 2 All E.R. 700 8.40
Cutler v. McPhail [1962] 2 Q.B. 292; [1962] 2 All E.R. 474 4.06, 18.35, 18.103
Cutler v. United Dairies [1932] 2 K.B. 297 12.30
Cutler v. Vauxhall Motors Ltd [1971] 1 Q.B. 418 15.25, 15.39
Cutler v. Wandsworth Stadium [1949] A.C. 398 H.L.; *Affirming* [1948] 1 K.B. 291 C.A. 16.03, 16.07, 21.69
Cynat Ltd v. Landbuild Ltd [1984] 3 All E.R. 513 3.39
Czarnikow (C.) Ltd v. Koufos; Heron II [1969] 1 A.C. 350 1.10, 12.118
Czarnikow (C.) Ltd v. Rolimpex [1979] A.C. 351 2.13

D

D v. N.S.P.C.C. [1978] A.C. 171 19.05, 20.02
D. & C. Builders Ltd v. Rees [1966] 2 Q.B. 617 21.23
D. & F. Estates Ltd v. Church Commissioners [1988] 2 All E.R. 992 12.10, **12.44**
D. & L. Caterers Ltd v. D'Ajou [1945] K.B. 210 H.C.; [1945] K.B. 364 C.A. 2.17, 18.03, 18.47
DDSA Pharmaceuticals Ltd v. Times Newspapers Ltd [1973] Q.B. 21 18.13, 18.60
D.P.P. v. Hawkins [1988] 3 All E.R. 673 6.44
D.P.P. v. Humphrys [1977] A.C. 1 22.18
Daborn v. Bath Tramways Motor Co. [1946] 2 All E.R. 333 12.16
Dahlberg v. Naydiuk (1970) 10 D.L.R. (2d) 319 6.08
Dahler v. Bruvold [1981] 5 W.W.R. 706 10.11
Daily Mirror Newspapers Ltd v. Gardner [1968] 2 Q.B. 762 21.32, 21.33, 21.36, 21.43, 21.44
Dallison v. Caffey [1965] 1 Q.B. 348 6.46
Dalton v. Angus (1881) 6 App.Cas 740 3.34, 3.37, 8.11, 8.37
Daly v. General Steam Navigation Ltd [1980] 3 All E.R. 696 15.32

Danford v. McAnulty (1883) 8 App.Cas. 456 5.19
Daniel v. Rickett, Cockerell Ltd [1938] 2 K.B. 322 3.39
Daniels v. Whetstone Entertainments Ltd [1962] 2 Lloyd's Rep. 1 3.22
Danluk v. Birkner [1946] 3 D.L.R. 172 13.46
Danku v. Fort Francis (Town of) (1977) 73 D.L.R. (3d) 377 9.40
Dann v. Hamilton [1939] 1 K.B. 509 13.16, 13.18
Darbyshire v. Warran [1963] 3 All E.R. 310 15.15
Darling v. Attorney-General [1950] 2 All E.R. 793 3.36, 5.04
Darrell v. Mengen Institute (1983) 72 C.P.R. (2d) 238 19.01
Davey v. Harrow Corporation [1958] 1 Q.B. 60 5.01, 8.11
David v. Britannic Merthyr Coal Co. [1909] 2 K.B. 146 16.10, 16.13
David v. Toronto Transit Commission (1976) 16 O.R. (2d) 248 12.119
Davidson v. Handley Page [1945] 1 All E.R. 235 14.52
Davie v. New Merton Board Mills [1959] A.C. 609 1.17, 3.36, 14.47, 14.51
Davies v. Bennion (1927) 22 Tas.L.R. 52 5.24
Davies v. Davies [1974] 3 All E.R. 817; [1975] Q.B. 172 11.35, 12.55
Davies v. Mann (1842) 10 M. & W. 546 13.24, **13.32**
Davies v. Powell Duffryn Associated Collieries Ltd (No. 2) [1942] A.C. 601 2.38, 15.59
Davies v. Snead (1870) L.R. 5 Q.B. 608 18.95
Davies v. Solomon (1871) L.R. 7 Q.B. 112 18.43
Davies v. Swan Motor Co. (Swansea) Ltd [1949] 2 K.B. 291 13.26, **13.32**, 13.33, 13.37, 13.38, 13.41, 13.43
Davies v. Taylor [1974] A.C. 207 15.60
Davis v. Danks (1849) 5 Ex. 435 7.08
Davis v. Foots [1940] 1 K.B. 116 12.53
Davis v. New England College of Arundel [1977] I.C.R. 6 3.05
Davis v. Williams (1851) 16 Q.B. 546 8.64
Davison v. Gent (1857) 1 H. & N. 744 5.19
Davy v. Spelthorne Borough Council [1983] 3 All E.R. 298 12.63
Dawkins v. Lord Paulet (1869) L.R. 5 Q.B. 94 18.84
Dawkins v. Lord Rokeby (1873 L.R. 8 Q.B. 255; (1875) L.R. 7 H.L. 744 18.80
Dawrant v. Nutt [1960] 3 All E.R. 681 13.16
Day v. Edwards (1794) 5 T.R. 648 6.02
Dean v. Hogg (1834) 10 Bing. 245 5.48
Dean v. McCarty (1884) 5. O.R. 531 10.11
Deaton's Pty Ltd v. Flew (1949) 79 C.L.R. 370 3.22
Dedy & Co. Ltd v. Weldon (No. 3) [1989] 3 All E.R. 118 21.04
Dee Conservancy Board v. McConnell [1928] 2 K.B. 159 12.114
Deen v. Davies [1935] 2 K.B. 282 11.05, 12.53
Deerness v. John R. Keele & Son (Brantham) [1983] 2 Lloyd's Rep. 260 15.49
De Lambert v. Ongley [1924] N.Z.L.R. 430 5.34
De Libellis Famosis (1605) 5 Co. Rep. 125a 18.38
De L'Isle (Viscount) v. Times Newspapers Ltd [1987] 3 All E.R. 499 18.19, 18.60
Delaney v. T.P. Smith Ltd [1946] K.B. 393 5.13, 5.37
Demarco v. Ungaro (1979) 95 D.L.R. (3d) 385 12.68
De Medina v. Grove (1847) 10 Q.B. 172 22.19
Denham v. Midland Employers Mutual Assurance Ltd [1955] 2 Q.B. 437 3.05
Dennis v. London Passenger Transport Board [1948] 1 All E.R. 779 15.37
Dennis v. Charnwood Borough Council [1982] 3 All E.R. 486 12.63
Denny v. Supplies and Transport Co. Ltd [1950] 2 K.B. 374 12.02, 12.11, 14.09
Denyer v. Charles Skipper & East Ltd [1970] 2 All E.R. 382 16.13

Department of Environment v. Thomas Baker & Sons Ltd [1989] 1 All E.R. 1075 12.44
Department of Transport v. North West Water Authority [1983] 3 All E.R. 273 8.57, 8.59
Derry v. Peek (1889) 14 App.Cas. 337 12.35, **17.02**, **17.09**, 17.14
Despina R, The [1977] 1 Lloyd's Rep. 618 H.C.; [1979] A.C. 685 A.C. 12.118, 16.01
Dessaint v. Carriere [1958] O.W.N. 481 12.78
Devon Lumbar Co. Ltd. v. MacNeill (1988) 45 D.L.R. (4th) 200 8.35
Devoe v. Long [1951] 1 D.L.R. 203 5.34
Dewall v. Sanders (1618) Cro.Jac. 490 8.50
Dews v. National Coal Board [1986] 2 All E.R. 769 15.24, 15.33
Deyong v. Kingston Speedway Ltd [1954] O.R. 227 9.33
Deyong v. Shenburn [1946] K.B. 227 14.27, 14.49
Dhalia v. Jodrey (1985) 16 D.L.R. (4th) 732 15.46
Diamond v. Bank of London & Montreal Ltd [1979] Q.B. 337 17.03, 17.08, 17.16
Diamond v. Minter [1941] 1 K.B. 656 647
Dickinson v. Del Solar [1930] 1 K.B. 376 2.14
Didow v. Alberta Power Ltd (1986) 37 C.C.L.T. 90; [1988] 5 W.W.R. 606 5.20, 5.26
Digby v. Financial News Ltd [1907] 1 K.B. 502 18.62
Dimbleby & Sons Ltd v. National Union of Journalists [1984] 1 All E.R. 751 2.23, 21.01, 21.53
Dimes v. Petley (1850) 15 Q.B. 276 8.64
Dingle v. Associated Newspapers Ltd [1960] 2 Q.B. 405 H.C.; [1961] 2 All E.R. 897 C.A.; [1962] 2 All E.R. 737 H.L. 18.74, 18.111
Dirassar & Jones v. Kelly Douglas & Co. Ltd (1967) 59 D.L.R. (2d) 452 21.34, 21.48
Distillers Co. (Biochemicals) Ltd. v. Thompson [1971] A.C. 458 2.25, 14.07
Dixon v. Bell (1816) 5 M. & S. 198 2.30
Dixon v. Calcraft [1892] 1 Q.B. 458 7.42
Dodd Properties (Kent) Ltd v. Canterbury City Council [1951] 1 All E.R. 928 8.66
Dixon v. Cementation Co. Ltd [1960] 3 All E.R. 417 14.54
Dockwell v. Dougall (1899) 80 L.T. 556 19.06
Dodd Properties (Kent) Ltd v. Canterbury City Council [1980] 1 All E.R. 928 12.113, 15.17, 15.18, 17.18
Dodds v. Dodds [1978] Q.B. 543 15.54
Doe d. Bishop of Rochester v. Bridges (1831) 1 B. & Ald. 847 16.06
Doe d. Carter v. Barnard (1849) 13 Q.B. 954 5.19
Doe d. Johnson v. Baytup (1835) 3 Ad. & E. 188 5.19
Dokuchia v. Domansch [1945] O.R. 141 9.15
Domsalla v. Barr [1969] 1 W.L.R. 630 15.09, 15.27
Dominion Natural Gas Co. v. Collins [1909] A.C. 640 14.05, 14.14
Donaghey v. Boulton & Paul Ltd [1968] A.C. 1 3.36, 16.16, 16.18, 16.21
Donaghy v. Brennan (1901) 19 N.Z.L.R. 289 6.06
Donald v. Baldwyn [1953] N.Z.L.R. 313 5.41, 5.42
Donald v. Suckling (1866) L.R. 1 Q.B. 585 7.36
Donaldson v. McNiven [1952] 2 All E.R. 692 2.30
Donnelly v. Jackman [1970] 1 W.L.R. 562 6.45
Donnelly v. Joyce [1974] Q.B. 454 15.32
Donoghue v. Stevenson [1932] A.C. 562 1.04, 1.29, **12.02–04**, 12.05, 12.12, 12.15, 12.21, 12.22, 12.35, 12.52, **12.53**, 12.64, 12.65, 12.68, 12.70, 12.111, 12.116, 12.122, **14.05–14**, 14.15–16, 14.46
Donovan v. Laing Syndicate Ltd [1893] 1 Q.B. 629 3.05
Donovan v. Union Cartage Co. [1933] 2 K.B. 71 12.114, 13.30
Dooley v. Cammell Laird & Co. [1951] 1 Lloyd's Rep. 271 12.25, 14.24

Dorling v. Honnor Marine Ltd [1965] Ch. 1 C.A.; reversing in part [1964] Ch. 560 5.40
Dorset Yacht Club v. Home Office [1970] A.C. 1004 1.03, 12.05
Doughty v. Turner Manufacturing Co. Ltd [1964] 1 Q.B. 518 12.74, 12.118
Douglas Valley Finance Co. Ltd v. S. Hughes (Hires) Ltd [1969] 1 Q.B. 738 7.25
Dovaston v. Payne (1975) 2 H.Bl 527 5.07, 11.02
Dove v. Banham Patent Locks Ltd [1983] 2 All E.R. 833 15.20
Dowson & Mason Ltd v. Potter [1986] 2 All E.R. 418 20.15, 20.16
Doyle v. Olby (Ironmongers) Ltd [1969] 2 Q.B. 158 17.17
Doyley v. Roberts (1837) 3 Bing. N.C. 835 18.52
Drane v. Evangelou [1978] 2 All E.R. 437 5.01, 5.51, 15.05
Dranfield v. Bristol Insulated Cables (1937) 54 T.L.R. 11 12.02
Draper v. Hodder [1972] 2 Q.B. 556 11.04, 12.74
Drummond-Jackson v. British Medical Association [1970] 1 All E.R. 1094 18.07, 18.08, **18.09–10**, 18.20
Dube v. Latour (1986) 27 D.L.R. (4d) 653 13.16
Duck v. Mayeu [1892] 2 Q.B. 511 4.06
Dulieu v. White [1901] 2 K.B. 664 12.25, 12.26, 12.113
Dumbell v. Roberts [1944] 1 All E.R. 320 6.46
Duncan v. Cammell Laird (1944) 171 L.T. 186 14.19
Dunlop v. Macedo (1891) 8 T.L.R. 43 5.16
Dunlop v. Woollahra Municipal Council [1981] 1 All E.R. 12.02; [1982] A.C. 158 1.06, 16.11
Dunlop Pneumatic Tyre Co. v. Maison Talbot (1904) 20 T.L.R. 579 21.54
Dunlop Rubber Co. Ltd v. Dunlop [1921] A.C. 367 19.06
Dunn v. Birmingham Canal Co. (1872) L.R. 7 Q.B. 244 9.35
Dunn v. Legge (1783) 3 Doug. 335 5.50
Dunne v. North West Gas Board [1964] 2 Q.B. 806 9.41
Dunster v. Abbott [1953] 2 All E.R. 1572 14.22
Dunwich (Bailiffs of) v. Sterry (1831) 1 B. & Ald. 831 7.06
Duport Steels Ltd v. Sirs [1980] 1 All E.R. 529 21.01
Durant v. Childe (1611) 1 Brownl. 221 7.04
Dutton v. Bognor Regis United Building Co. Ltd [1972] 1 Q.B. 373 12.56
Duval v. Seguin (1972) 26 D.L.R. (3d) 418 2.25
Dwyer v. Mansfield [1946] K.D. 437 8.16, 8.76, 8.79
Dwyer v. Staunton [1947] 4 D.L.R. 293 5.30
Dyck v. Manitoba Snowmobile Association [1985] 4 W.W.R. 319 13.10
Dyer v. Munday [1895] 1 Q.B. 742 6.13
Dymond v. Pearce [1972] 1 Q.B. 496 8.48, **8.82**

E

Eaglesfield v. Marquis of Londonderry (1876) 4 Ch.D. 693 17.05
Eales v. Jones (1979) 17 N. & P.E.I.R. 242 11.05
Earl v. Lubbock [1905] 1 K.B. 263 14.04
Easson v. London & North Eastern Railway [1944] 2 K.B. 421 12.88
East Suffolk Rivers Catchment Board v. Kent [1941] A.C. 74 8.58, 8.59, 12.02, **12.54**, 12.62
Eastern & S. African Telegraph Co. Ltd v. Cape Town Tramways [1902] A.C. 381 9.13, 9.20, 9.35
Eastern Construction Co. Ltd v. National Trust Ltd [1914] A.C. 197 3.08, 7.39
Eastman Photographic Materials Co. Ltd v. John Griffiths Cycle Corporation Ltd (1898) 15 R.P.C. 105 21.70
Eastwood v. Holmes (1858) 1 F. & F. 347 18.26
Eddis v. Chichester Constable [1969] 2 Ch. 345 7.40
Edgington v. Fitzmaurice (1885) 29 Ch.D. 459 17.04, 17.09

Edmondson v. Birch & Co. Ltd [1907] 1 K.B. 371 18.32, 18.99
Edwards v. Thames Board Mills Ltd [1969] 2 Q.B. 67 6.42
Edwards v. Railway Executive [1952] A.C. 737 14.22
Edwards v. National Coal Board [1949] 1 K.B. 704 12.16
Edwards v. W. Herts. Group Hospital Management Committee [1957] 1 All E.R. 541 14.27, 14.49
Egger v. Chelmsford (Viscount) [1965] 1 Q.B. 248; [1964] 3 All E.R. 406 3.23, 4.03, **18.102**
Eid v. Dumas [1969] S.C.R. 668 13.16
Einhorn v. Westmount Industries Ltd (1969) 5 D.L.R. (3d) 71; (1970) 11 D.L.R. (3d) 509 21.53
Eisener v. Maxwell [1951] 3 D.L.R. 345 6.08
Electrical, Electronic, Telecommunication and Plumbing Union v. Times Newspapers [1980] 1 All E.R. 1097 2.22, 18.03
Electrochrome Ltd v. Welsh Plastics Ltd [1968] 2 All E.R. 205 12.43
Elias v. Pasmore [1934] 2 K.B. 164 5.09
Elliott v. Boynton [1924] 1 Ch. 236 5.16, 5.50
Elliott Steam Tug Co. Ltd v. Shipping Controller [1922] 1 K.B. 127 12.46
Ellis v. Burton [1975] 1 All E.R. 395 6.13
Ellis v. Johnstone [1963] 2 Q.B. 8 11.05, 12.53
Ellis v. Loftus Iron Co. (1874) L.R. 10 C.P. 10 1.32, 5.24, 7.12, 11.02
Ellis v. Stenning [1952] 2 Ch. 81 7.54
Elvin & Powell Ltd v. Plummer Roddis Ltd (1934) 50 T.L.R. 158 **7.21**, 7.30
Elwes v. Brigg Gas Co. (1886) 33 Ch.D. 563 5.21, 7.07, 7.35
Embery v. Owen (1851) 6 Ex 353 8.74
Emanuel (H. & N.) Ltd v. Greater London Council [1971] 2 All E.R. 835 10.03, 10.04, 10.06, 10.12
Emerald Construction Co. Ltd v. Lowthian [1966] 1 All E.R. 1013 21.32, 21.33, 21.34, 21.36, 21.45
Emmens v. Pottle (1885) 16 Q.B.D. 354 18.06, 18.36
Emmerson v. Maddison [1906] A.C. 569 5.19
Empire Jamaica, The [1957] A.C. 386 12.96
Engelke v. Mussman [1938] A.C. 433 2.14
England v. Cowley (1872) L.R. 8 Ex. 126 7.25
English & Scottish Co-operative Properties Mortgage and Investment Co. Ltd v. Odhams Press Ltd [1940] 1 K.B. 440 18.58
Entick v. Carrington (1765) 19 St.Tr. 1029 2.02, 5.01
Erikson v. Clifton [1963] N.Z.L.R. 705 10.04
Errington v. Errington [1952] 1 All E.R. 149 5.42
Erven Warnink BV v. J. Townsend & Son (Hull) Ltd [1979] 2 All E.R. 927 21.65, 21.67–68, 21.73, **21.75–76**
Esso Petroleum Co. Ltd v. Kingswood Motors Ltd [1973] 3 All E.R. 1057 21.53
Esso Petroleum Co. Ltd v. Mardon [1976] 1 Q.B. 801 12.36, 12.70
Esso Petroleum Co. v. Southport Corporation — *see under* Southport Corporation
Euro Diam. v. Bathurst [1988] 2 All E.R. 23 13.46
Eurymedon, The [1938] P. 41 13.32, **13.33–4**
Evans v. London Hospital Medical College [1981] 1 All E.R. 714 22.04, **22.02**
Evans v. Triplex Safety Glass Co. Ltd [1936] 1 All E.R. 283 14.09
Evans (C.) & Sons Ltd v. Spritebrand Ltd [1985] 2 All E.R. 416 3.06
Evaskow v. International Brotherhood of Boilermakers (1969) 9 D.L.R. (3d) 715 21.09
Everitt v. Martin [1953] N.Z.L.R. 298 7.04, **8.33**
Everett v. Ribbands [1952] 2 Q.B. 198 22.05
Excelsior Wire Rope Co. v. Callan [1930] A.C. 404 14.19
Exchange Telegraph Co. Ltd v. Gregory & Co. [1896] 1 Q.B. 147 21.46
Express Newspapers Ltd v. MacShane [1980] 1 All E.R. 65 21.01

F

F, re [1977] Fam 58, 98 19.05
Fagan v. Metropolitan Police Commissioner [1969] 1 Q.B. 439 6.10, 6.12
Fairley v. John Thompson (Design & Contracting Division) Ltd [1973] 2 Lloyd's Rep. 40 15.28
Fairline Shipping Corporation v. Adamson [1975] Q.B. 181 3.06, 3.41, 7.18
Fairman v. Perpetual Investment Building Society [1923] A.C. 74 14.19
Fardon & Harcourt-Rivington (1932) 46 L.T. 391 12.15
Farmer v. Hunt (1610) 1 Brownl. 220 7.04
Farmer v. Hyde [1937] 1 K.B. 728 18.86, 18.87
Farndon v. Harcourt-Rivington (1932) 146 L.T. 391 11.20
Farnworth v. Manchester Corporation [1929] 1 K.B. 533 8.59
Farquharson Bros. v. King [1902] A.C. 325 3.02
Farr v. Butters Bros. [1932] 2 K.B. 605 12.02, 14.09
Farrant v. Barnes (1862) 11 C.B.N.S. 553 14.03
Farwell v. Boston & Worcester Railroad Corporation (1842) 4 Metcalf 49 14.46
Faulkner v. Willetts [1982] R.T.R. 159 5.46, 6.45
Fawcett v. Tyrrell (1893) 9 T.L.R. 257 18.39
Fay v. Prentice (1845) 1 C.B. 828 5.23, 8.30, 8.65
Fayed v. Al-Tajir [1987] 2 All E.R. 396 18.84, **18.85**
Fazlic v. Milingimbi Community Inc. (1981) 38 A.L.R. 424 15.11
Feather v. The Queen (1865) 6 B.& S. 257 2.02
Fellowes v. Rother District Council [1983] 1 All E.R. 513 12.54, **12.62**
Fenwick v. Schwartz (1868) L.R. 3 C.P. 313 9.47
Ferguson v. John Dawson & Partners (Contractors) Ltd [1976] 1 W.L.R. 1213 3.04
Ferguson v. Welsh [1987] 3 All E.R. 777 14.19, 14.21, 14.45, 14.48, 14.52
Ferris v. Stubbs (1978) 89 D.L.R. (3d) 364 13.06
Ferris v. Weaven [1952] 2 All E.R. 283 5.42
Field v. Davis [1955] C.L.Y. 1543 18.07
Fielding v. Variety Incorporated [1967] 2 Q.B. 841; [1967] 2 All E.R. 497 18.110, 21.59, 21.62, 21.63, 21.64
Filburn v. People's Palace (1890) 25 Q.B.D. 250 11.03
Filipowich v. Nahachewsky (1969) 3 D.L.R. (3d) 544 6.10, 6.14
Filliter v. Phippard (1847) 11 Q.B. 347 10.05, 10.10
Firman v. Ellis [1978] Q.B. 886 15.49, 15.50
Fishenden v. Higgs & Hill (1935) 153 L.T. 128 8.48
Fisher v. C.H.T. Ltd [1966] 2 Q.B. 475 C.A. 14.19
Fisher v. Oldham Corporation [1930] 2 K.B. 364 2.05
Fisher v. Ruislip-Northwood U.D.C. [1945] K.B. 584 8.58
Fitter v. Beale (1701) 1 Ld.Raym. 339, 692 15.02
Fitzgerald v. E.D. & A.D. Cook Bourne (Farms) Ltd [1964] 1 Q.B. 249 11.34
Fitzgerald v. Firbank [1897] 4 Ch. 96 8.33, 8.49
Fitzgerald v. Lane [1988] 2 All E.R. 961 13.43
Fitzjohn v. Mackinder (1861) 9 C.B.N.S. 505 22.04
Flame Bar-B-Q Ltd v. Hoar (1980) 106 D.L.R. (3d) 438 22.20
Fleming v. Atkinson [1959] S.C.R. 513 11.05
Fletcher v. Autocar and Transporters Ltd [1968] 2 Q.B. 322 15.02, 15.08, 15.23, 15.39
Fletcher v. Bealy (1885) 28 Ch.D. 688 8.69
Flint v. Lovell [1935] 1 K.B. 354 15.40
Flowers v. George Wimpey & Co. Ltd [1956] 1 Q.B. 73 14.47
Foley v. Enso-Gutzeit [1962] 1 Lloyd's Rep. 247 14.40
Fogg v. Kenora [1941] 1 D.L.R. 100 12.113
Fookes v. Slaytor [1979] 1 All E.R. 137 13.37
Forde v. Skinner (1830) 4 C. & P. 239 6.11

Fortin v. Daw (1920) 19 O.W.N. 14 10.11
Fortunity, The [1961] 1 W.L.R. 351 15.13
Fosbrooke-Hobbes v. Airwook Ltd [1937] 1 All E.R. 108 12.90, 14.17, 14.42
Foster v. Outred & Co. [1982] 2 All E.R. 753 15.19
Foster v. Tyne & Wear County Council [1986] 1 All E.R. 567 15.28
Fouldes v. Willoughby (1841) 8 M. & W. 538 7.04, **7.16**, 7.19, 7.26
Foulkes v. Metropolitan District Railway Co. (1880) 5 C.P.D. 157 14.17
Four Point Garage Ltd. v. Carter [1985] 3 All E.R. 12 7.26
Fowler v. Dowdney (1838) 2 Moo. & Rob. 119 18.48
Fowler v. Lanning [1959] 1 Q.B. 426 1.27, 6.08
Fowler Marine (Emsworth) Ltd v. Gafford [1968] 2 Q.B. 618; *reversing* [1967] 2 Q.B. 808 5.07, 5.13, 5.19
Fox v. Chief Constable of Gwent [1985] 1 All E.R. 230 5.46, 6.45
Fox v. Macreth (1788) 2 Cox Eq.Cas. 320 17.06
Fox v. Wood (1981) 35 A.L.R. 607 12.113
Foxcroft v. Lacey (1613) Hob. 89 18.27
Foxley v. Olton [1965] 2 Q.B. 306 15.35
France v. Parkinson [1954] 1 All E.R. 739 13.30
Francis v. Cockerell (1870) L.R. 5 Q.B. 501 14.17
Francome v. Mirror Group Newspapers Ltd [1984] 2 All E.R. 408 19.03
Franklin v. Attorney-General [1974] Q.B. 185 2.03
Franklin v. South Eastern Railway (1858) 3 H. & N. 211 15.58, 15.60
Franks v. Sanderson (1986) 35 C.C.L.T. 307 10.01
Fraser v. Board of Trustees of Central United Church (1983) 38 O.R. (2d) 97 21.08, 21.35
Fraser v. Evans [1969] 1 All E.R. 8 18.118, 19.06
Fraser v. Thames Television Ltd [1983] 2 All E.R. 101 20.07
Freeman v. Home Office [1983] 3 All E.R. 589 H.C.; [1984] 1 All E.R. 1036; [1984] 1 Q.B. 524 C.A. 6.33, 6.36, **6.42**, 13.17
Freeman v. Rosher (1849) 13 Q.B. 780 3.08
Fritz v. Hobson (1880) 14 Ch.D. 542 8.76
Frogley v. Lovelace (1859) Johns. 333 5.40
Froom v. Butcher [1976] Q.B. 286 13.26, 13.42
Fryer v. Salford Corporation [1937] 1 All E.R. 617 12.78
Fulham v. Newcastle Chronicle & Journal Ltd [1977] 3 All E.R. 32 18.14, 18.16, 18.18
Funk v. Clapp (1984) 12 D.L.R. (4th) 62 12.119, 13.45

G

G.W.K. Ltd v. Dunlop Rubber Co. Ltd (1962) 42 T.L.R. 376 7.04, 21.40
Gaffrey v. Aviation & Shipping Co. Ltd [1966] 1 Lloyd's Rep. 249 14.36
Gainsford v. Tuke (1619) Cro.Jac. 536 18.48
Galashiels Gas Co. Ltd v. O'Donnell (or Miller) [1949] A.C. 275 1.31, 3.36, 16.12
Gallagher v. McDowell Ltd [1961] N.I. 26 12.56
Gallant v. Fulkov (1989) 69 O.R. 2d 297 12.105
Gambell v. Caparelli (1974) 54 D.L.R. (3d) 661 6.14
Gammell v. Wilson [1982] A.C. 27; [1981] 1 All E.R. 578 H.L. 2.36, 2.37, 2.38, 15.29
Garden Cottage Foods Ltd v. Milk Marketing Board [1983] 2 All E.R. 770; [1984] A.C. 130 H.L. 1.07, 1035, 16.03, 16.05
Gardiner v. Miller 1967 S.L.T. 29 11.05
Gardiner v. Moore (No. 2) [1966] 1 All E.R. 365 4.03, 4.06
Gardner v. Moore [1984] 1 All E.R. 1100 4.13
Garrard v. Southey & Co. [1952] 2 Q.B. 174 3.05
Garrett v. Taylor (1620) Cro.Jac. 567 21.16

Garry v. Sherritt Gordon Mines Ltd (1988) 42 C.C.L.T. 241 21.53
Garston Warehousing Co. Ltd v. O.F. Smart (Liverpool) Ltd [1973] R.T.R. 377 12.85
Gartside v. Outram (1856) 26 L.J. Ch. 113 20.11
Gaskell v. Preston [1981] 3 All E.R. 427 15.24
Gautret v. Egerton (1867) L.R. 2 C.P. 371 1.03, **14.03**, 14.15
Gavely v. Codd [1967] 1 W.L.R. 19 6.15
Gayler & Pope v. Davies & Son [1942] 2 K.B. 75 6.38, 7.15, 11.31, 12.75
Geddis v. Proprietors of Ban Reservoir (1878) 3 App. Cas. 430 8.54, 8.55
Gee v. Metropolitan Railway (1873) L.R. 8 Q.B. 161 12.88, 13.29
General & Finance Facilities Ltd v. Cooke Cars (Romford) Ltd [1963] 2 All E.R. 314 7.46
General Cleaning Contractors v. Christmas [1953] A.C. 180 12.80, 14.52, 14.53
General Engineering Services Ltd v. Kingston & St. Andrew Corporation [1988] 3 All E.R. 867 3.19
General Tire and Rubber Co. Ltd v. Firestone Tyre & Rubber Co. Ltd [1975] 2 All E.R. 173 15.08, 20.15
Genys v. Matthews [1965] 3 All E.R. 24 14.37
George v. Skivington (1869) L.R. 5 Ex. 1 14.04
Gertsen v. Metro Toronto (1973) 41 D.L.R. (3d) 646 9.18
Ghani v. Jones [1970] 1 Q.B. 693 7.14, 7.37
George & Richard, The (1871) L.R. 3 Ad. & E. 466 2.24, 15.56
Gershman v. Manitoba Vegetable Producers' Marketing Board (1975) 65 D.L.R. (3d) 181; [1976] 4 W.W.R. 406 21.23, 21.53
Gibbons v. Duffield (1923) 47 C.L.R. 520 18.84
Gibbons v. MacDonald (1985) 70 N.S.R. (2d) 441 11.05
Giblan v. National Amalgamated Labourers' Union [1903] 2 K.B. 600 21.12
Gibson v. Skibs A/S, Marina and Orkla Grobe A/B and Smith Coggins [1966] 2 All E.R. 476 14.36
Gifford v. Dent [1962] W.N. 336 5.25
Gibert v. Stone (1647) Aleyn 35 6.34
Gilbertson v. Harland & Wolff Ltd [1966] 2 Lloyd's Rep. 190 15.59
Giles v. Walker (1890) 24 Q.B.D. 656 9.20, 9.21
Gill & Duffus (Liverpool) Ltd v. Scruttons Ltd [1953] 1 W.L.R. 1407 7.26
Gillick v. West Norfolk & Wisbech Area Health Authority [1986] A.C. 112 6.38
Gilpin v. Fowler (1854) 9 Ex. 615 18.73
Gilson v. Kerrier D.C. [1976] 1 W.L.R. 904 8.48
Ginty v. Belmont Building Supplies Lt [1959] 1 All E.R. 414 16.16
Glamorgan Coal Co. Ltd v. S. Wales Miners' Federation — *see* South Wales
Glanville v. Sutton [1928] 1 K.B. 571 11.03
Glasgow Corporation v. Muir [1943] A.C. 448 1.32, 12.11, 12.19, 12.77, 14.14, 14.16, 14.17
Gleaves v. Deakin [1979] 2 All E.R. 497 18.41
Gledhill v. Liverpool Abattoir Utility Co. [1957] 3 All E.R. 117 14.51
Glegg v. Dearden (1848) 12 C.B. 576 5.21
Glendenning & Board of Police Commissioners for City of Belleville, Re (1976) 75 D.L.R. (3d) 33 22.26
Glinski v. McIver [1962] 1 All E.R. 969 22.06, 22.07, 22.08, 22.09–10, 22.11
Global Paint Ltd v. Secretary of State for Social Services [1972] 1 Q.B. 139 3.04
Glo-Klen Distributors Ltd v. B.C. Chemicals Ltd (1959) 14 D.L.R. (2d) 635 21.64
Goddard v. Smith (1795) 6 Mod. 252 22.05
Godley v. Perry [1960] 1 All E.R. 36 14.01

Gogo v. Eureka Sawmills Ltd [1944] 3 W.W.R. 268; [1945] 3 W.W.R. 446 10.11
Gold v. Essex C.C. [1942] 2 K.B. 293 3.04
Gold v. Haringey Health Authority [1987] 2 All E.R. 888 12.78, 12.80
Goldman v. Hargrave [1967] 1 A.C. 645 8.29, 8.41, 10.13, 12.13, 12.16, 12.59, 12.78
Goldsmith v. Pressdram Ltd [1987] 3 All E.R. 485 18.19, 18.41
Goldsmith v. Sperrings Ltd [1977] 2 All E.R. 566 18.36, 18.41, 22.18, 22.21
Gollins v. Gollins [1964] A.C. 644 1.26
Gomberg v. Smith [1963] 1 Q.B. 25 11.05, 12.53
Gootson v. The King [1948] 4 D.L.R. 33 12.78
Gordon v. Harper (1796) 7 T.R. 9 7.33, 7.36
Gordon v. Trottier [1974] S.C.R. 156 12.85, 12.89
Gordon v. Walker (1973) 42 D.L.R. (3d) 342 2.33
Gore v. Van der Lamm [1967] 2 Q.B. 31 14.37
Gorely v. Codd [1967] 1 W.L.R. 19 2.28
Gorringe v. Transport Commission (1950) 80 C.L.R. 357 8.80
Gorris v. Scott (1874) L.R. 9 Ex. 125 12.118, 16.02, **16.17**
Gott v. Measures [1948] 1 K.B. 234 7.04, 7.13
Gough v. Thorne [1966] 3 All E.R. 398 2.24, 2.28, 12.79, 13.30
Gough v. Wood & Co. [1894] 1 Q.B. 713 7.26
Gouriet v. Union of Post Office Workers [1978] A.C. 435 1.07, 8.78, 16.02
Government Insurance Officer of New South Wales v. Frederickberg (1968) 118 C.L.R. 430 12.93
Graham v. Dodds [1983] 2 All E.R. 953 15.59
Graham v. Hodgkinson (1983) 40 O.R. (2d) 697 13.04
Graham v. Peat (1801) 1 East 244 5.13, 7.06
Granada Group Ltd v. Ford Motor Co. Ltd [1972] F.S.R. 103 21.66, 21.71
Grand Trunk Railway v. McAlpine [1913] A.C. 808 13.33
Granger v. Hill (1838) 4 Bing. N.C. 212 22.19
Grant v. Australian Knitting Mills [1936] A.C. 85 12.02, 12.74, 12.85, 12.90, 14.01, 14.08, 14.09
Grant v. National Coal Board [1958] A.C. 549 16.18
Grant v. Sun Shipping Co. Ltd [1948] A.C. 549 13.29, 13.38
Grappelli v. Derek Block (Holdings) Ltd [1981] 2 All E.R. 272 18.14, 18.15, 18.18, **18.22**
Gravesham B.C. v. British Railways Board [1972] 3 All E.R. 853 8.03, **8.76**, 8.79
Gray v. Barr [1971] 2 Q.B. 554 6.23
Gray v. Jones [1939] 1 All E.R. 798 18.47
Grayson v. Ellerman Lines Ltd [1920] A.C. 468 13.23, 13.33
Great Central Railway v. Bates [1921] 3 K.B. 578 5.46
Great Orme Tramways Co., re (1934) 50 T.L.R. 450 2.35
Greater Nottingham Co-operative Soceity Ltd v. Cementation Piling & Foundations Ltd [1989] Q.B. 71 12.39, 12.44, 12.47, **12.51**, 12.72
Greech v. Odhams Press Ltd [1958] 2 All E.R. 462 18.62
Green v. Chelsea Waterworks (1894) 70 L.T. 547 9.18, 9.32, 9.41
Green v. Fibreglass Ltd [1958] 2 Q.B. 245 14.36
Green v. Goddard (1702) 2 Salk. 641 5.48, 6.26
Greenaway v. C.P.R. [1925] 1 W.W.R. 667 15.32
Greenhalgh v. British Railways Board [1969] 2 Q.B. 286 14.15, 14.20
Greenhalgh v. Mallard [1947] 2 All E.R. 255 21.05
Greenland v. Chaplin (1805) 5 Ex. 243 12.116
Greenock Corporation v. Caledonia Railway and Glasgow & S.W. Railway [1917] A.C. 556 9.46, **9.48–9**
Greenwood v. Bennett [1973] 1 Q.B. 195 7.52
Greenwood v. Central Service Co. [1940] 2 K.B. 447 16.12
Gregory v. Kelly [1978] R.T.R. 426 13.16, 13.39

Gregory v. Piper (1829) 2 B. & C. 591 5.01, 5.05, 6.02
Grieg v. Insole [1978] 3 All E.R. 449 21.30, 21.32, 21.33, 21.36, 21.37, 21.38, 21.39, 21.41, 21.43, 21.44, 21.45, 21.47, **21.50**
Griffiths v. Arch Engineering Co. Ltd [1968] 3 All E.R. 217 14.09
Griffiths v. Liverpool Corporation [1967] 1 Q.B. 374 8.81, 12.58, 12.75
Grill v. General Iron Screw Colliery Co. (1866) L.R. 1 C.P. 600 12.01
Grinham v. Willey (1859) 4 H. & N. 496 6.22
Groom v. Great Western Railway (1892) 8 T.L.R. 253 10.07
Gross v. Lewis Hillman Ltd [1970] 1 Ch. 445 17.09
Grove v. Eastern Gas Board [1952] 1 K.B. 77 5.44
Groves v. Lord Wimborne [1898] 2 Q.B. 402 16.02, 16.06, 16.07
Grubb v. Bristol United Press Ltd [1962] 2 All E.R. 380 18.14, 18.16, 18.21
Guay v. Sun Publishing Co. Ltd [1953] 2 S.C.R. 216 12.25, 12.35
Guildford, The [1956] P. 364 12.114
Guildford Industries Ltd v. Hankinson Management Services Ltd (1974) 40 D.L.R. (3d) 398 22.20
Gunter v. James (1908) 24 T.L.R. 868 10.07
Gutek v. Sunshine Village Corporation (1990) 65 D.L.R. (4th) 406 16.11
Gwilliam v. Twist [1895] 2 Q.B. 84 3.25, 3.31
Gwinnell v. Eamer (1875) L.R. 10 C.P. 658 8.44

H

Habib Bank Ltd v. Habib Bank A.G. Zurich [1981] 2 All E.R. 650 21.71, 21.72
Hackney London Borough v. Ezedinna [1981] 3 All E.R. 438 11.19
Hadley v. Baxendale (1854) 9 Ex. 341 1.12
Hadmor Productions Ltd v. Hamilton [1981] 2 All E.R. 724 C.A.; *reversed by* [1982] 1 All E.R. 1042 H.L. 21.01, 21.04, 21.52
Haig v. Bamford (1977) 72 D.L.R. (3d) 68 12.37
Hailes v. Marks (1861) 7 H. & N. 56 22.06
Hale v. Jennings Bros. [1938] 1 All E.R. 579 9.28, 9.32, **9.45**
Haley v. London Electricity Board [1965] A.C. 778 12.20, 12.74
Hall v. Barclay [1937] 3 All E.R. 620 7.50
Hall v. Brooklands Auto Racing Club [1933] 1 K.B. 205 1.32, 13.05, 13.07
Hall v. Cotton [1986] 3 All E.R. 322 7.06
Hall v. Pickard (1812) 3 Camp. 186 7.09
Hall & Co. Ltd v. Pearlberg [1956] 1 W.L.R. 244 5.50
Hall (Edwin) & Partners v. First National Finance Corporation [1988] 3 All E.R. 801 21.51
Halleck v. Doroshuk (1985) 35 C.C.L.T. 81 10.01
Halliday v. Holgate (1868) L.R. 3 Ex. 299 7.36
Halsey v. Brotherhood (1851) 19 Ch.D. 386 21.54
Halsey v. Esso Petroleum Co. Ltd [1961] 2 All E.R. 145 8.11, 8.12, 8.15, **9.14**, 9.20
Hambrook v. Stokes Bros. [1925] 1 K.B. 141 12.25, 12.26, 12.111
Hammersmith (London Borough) v. Magnus Automated Forecourts Ltd [1978] 1 All E.R. 401 8.03, 8.75
Hammersmith & City Railway Co. v. Brand (1867) L.R. 1 Q.B. 130; L; R. 2 Q.B. 223; (1869) L.R. 4 H.L. 171 8.12, 8.55
Hammond v. St. Pancras Vestry (1874) L.R. 4 C.P. 3126 8.54
Hamps v. Darby [1948] 2 K.B. 311 7.04, 7.13
Handcock v. Baker (1800) 2 Bos. & P. 260 5.47
Handraft Co. v. Commissioner for Railways (1959) 77 W.N. (N.S.W.) 84 10.11
Hannah v. Peel [1945] K.B. 509 7.07, 7.35
Hannam v. Mockett (1824) 2 B. & C. 943 11.04
Hanson v. Michelin Tyre Co. Ltd [1985] 1 All E.R. 918 3.20

Hanson v. Wearmouth Coal Co. Ltd [1939] 3 All E.R. 47 4.11
Harakas v. Baltic Mercantile & Shipping Exchange Ltd [1982] 2 All E.R. 710 18.05, 18.118
Harbutt's Plasticine Ltd v. Wayne Tank & Pump Co. Ltd [1970] 1 Q.B. 447 15.14, 15.17
Hardaker v. Idle D.C. [1896] 1 Q.B. 335 8.81
Hardy v. Motor Insurers' Bureau [1964] 2 Q.B. 745 4.13
Hargreaves v. Brotherton [1959] 1 Q.B. 45 1.05, 18.79
Harman v. Secretary of State for the Home Department [1982] 2 W.L.R. 338 19.05
Harnett v. Bond [1924] 2 K.B. 517; [1925] A.C. 669 12.60, 12.114
Harold v. Watney [1898] 2 Q.B. 320 13.30
Harper v. Charlesworth (1825) 4 B. & C. 574 5.13
Harper v. Haden & Sons [1933] 1 Ch. 298 8.01, 8.76, 8.79, 8.82
Harris v. Birkenhead Corporation [1976] 1 All E.R. 341 14.19
Harris v. Bright's Asphalt Contractors Ltd [1953] 1 Q.B. 617 15.24
Harris v. Empress Motors Ltd [1983] 3 All E.R. 561 C.A.; *reversing* [1982] 3 All E.R. 306 2.38, 15.29, 15.59
Harris v. James (1876) 45 L.J.Q.B. 545 8.42
Harrison v. Rutland (Duke of) [1893] 1 Q.B. 142 5.07, 5.11, 5.48
Harrison v. Southwark Water Co. [1891] 2 Ch. 409 8.18
Harrods Ltd v. R. Harrod Ltd (1923) 41 R.P.C. 74 21.66
Harrold v. Watney [1898] 2 Q.B. 320 8.80
Hart v. Basset (1681) T. Jones 156 8.76
Hart v. Chief Constable of Kent [1983] R.T.R. 484 6.20, 6.45
Hart v. Griffiths-Jones [1948] 2 All E.R. 729 15.58
Hart v. Hart & Pickles Ltd [1969] 1 Q.B. 405 4.08
Hartley v. Mayoh & Co. [1954] 1 Q.B. 383 13.20, 16.11
Hartley v. Sandholme Iron Co. [1975] Q.B. 602 15.35
Hartwell v. Grayson Rollo & Clover Docks Ltd [1947] K.B. 901 14.19
Harvey v. R.G. O'Dell Ltd [1958] 2 Q.B. 78 3.21, 3.40, 4.09, 4.10, 4.14
Harvey v. Pocock (1843) 11 M. & W. 740 5.09
Harvey v. Road Haulage Executive [1952] 1 K.B. 120 13.38
Harvey v. Walkers (1873) L.R. 8 C.P. 162 8.53
Haseldine v. Daw [1941] 2 K.B. 343 12.02, 14.07, 14.08, 14.19, 14.36
Haseldine v. Hosken [1933] 1 K.B. 822 4.13
Hasselblad (GB) Ltd v. Orbinson [1985] 1 All E.R. 173 **18.81**, 18.84
Haste v. Sandell Perkins Ltd; Denman v. Essex Area Health Authority [1984] Q.B. 735 1.16, 15.24
Hatton v. Henderson (1981) 126 D.L.R. (3d) 50 15.46
Haverkate v. Toronto Harbour Commissioner (1986) 30 D.L.R. (4th) 125 12.89
Hawkins v. Coulsdon & Purley U.D.C. [1954] 1 Q.B. 319 1.32
Hay v. Hughes [1975] Q.B. 790 15.60
Haydon v. Kent C.C. [1978] 2 W.L.R. 485 8.81, 12.58
Haynes v. Harwood [1935] 1 K.B. 146 12.13, **12.30**
Haynes v. Qualcast — *see* Qualcast
Hayward v. Thompson [1981] 3 All E.R. 450 18.01, 18.21, **18.22**
Hazelwood v. Webber (1934) 52 C.L.R. 268 10.11
Healey v. Healey [1915] 1 K.B. 938 7.34
Heap v. Ind Coope & Allsop Ltd [1940] 2 K.B. 476 8.44
Heaps v. Perrite Ltd [1937] 2 All E.R. 60 15.39, 15.41
Heath v. Weist & Barron School of Television (Canada) Ltd (1981) 18 C.C.L.T. 129 19.01
Heatons Transport (St. Helens) Ltd v. Transport & General Workers' Union [1973] A.C. 15 2.23, 3.07
Heaven v. Pender (1883) 11 Q.B.D. 503 12.01, 14.17
Hebditch v. MacIlwaine [1894] 2 Q.B. 54 18.39

Heddick v. Haslop (1844) 12 Q.B. 267 22.06
Hedley Byrne & Co. v. Heller & Partners [1964] A.C. 465 1.04, 12.05, 12.35, **12.36**, 12.37, 12.40, 12.41, 12.42, 12.45, 12.46, 12.51, 12.52, 17.02
Hegarty v. Shine (1878) 14 Cox C.C. 145; 4 L.R. Ir. 288 6.38, 13.18
Heisler v. Moke (1972) 25 D.L.R. (3d) 670 2.28, 12.79
Hellenius v. Lees (1971) 15 D.L.R. (3d) 147; (1971) 20 D.L.R. (3d) 369 12.91
Hellwig v. Mitchell [1910] 1 K.B. 609 18.46
Heming v. Power (1842) 10 M. & W. 564 18.48
Hemmings v. Stoke Poges Golf Club [1920] 1 K.B. 720 5.48, 6.27
Henderson v. Henry E. Jenkins & Sons [1970] A.C. 282 H.L.; *reversing* [1969] 1 All E.R. 401 C.A. 9.20, 12.93, 14.51
Hendy Lennox (Industrial Engines) Ltd v. Grahame Puttick Ltd [1984] 2 All E.R. 152 7.26
Henley v. Burstall (1657) T. Raym. 180 22.14
Henley v. Cameron (1948) 65 T.L.R. 17 13.33, 13.38
Henwood v. Harrison (1872) L.R. 7 C.P. 606 18.70
Henwood v. Municipal Tramways Trust (1938) 60 C.L.R. 438 13.47
Hepburn v. A. Tomlinson (Hauliers) Ltd [1966] A.C. 451 7.39
Herbage v. Pressdram Ltd [1984] 2 All E.R. 769 18.58, 18.118, **18.119**
Herbert v. Harold Shaw Ltd [1959] 2 Q.B. 138 16.11
Herd v. Weardale Steel Coal & Coke Co. [1913] 3 K.B. 771; [1915] A.C. 67 H.L. 6.20
Herdman v. Walker (Tooting) Ltd [1956] 1 W.L.R. 209 3.05
Hern v. Nichols (1701) 1 Salk. 289 3.02
Hernager v. S.S. Diamond [1939] A.C. 94 13.37
Herniman v. Smith [1938] A.C. 305 22.05, 22.07
Heron II — *see* Czarnikow v. Koufos
Herring v. Boyle (1834) 6 C. & P. 496 6.20
Herrington v. British Railways Board — *see* British Railways
Herschel v. Stewart & Arden [1940] 1 K.B. 155 14.07, 14.08
Hesperides Hotels v. Aegean Turkish Holdings Ltd [1977] 3 W.L.R. 656 1.01
Hesperides Hotels Ltd v. Muftizade [1978] 2 All E.R. 1168; [1979] A.C. 508 2.09, 5.18, 7.06, 7.32
Hewitt v. Bonvin [1940] 1 K.B. 108 3.13
Hewlett v. Crutchley (1813) 5 Taunt. 277 22.08
Hey v. Moorhouse (1839) 6 Bing. N.C. 52 5.01
Heyn v. Ocean Steamship Ltd (1927) L.T. 158 3.27
Hibberd's Foundry v. Hardy [1953] N.Z.L.R. 14 12.14
Hibbert v. McKiernan [1948] 2 K.B. 142 7.06, 7.35
Hickman v. Maisey [1900] 1 Q.B. 752 5.07, 5.11
Hickey v. Electric Reduction Co. of Canada Ltd (1970) 21 D.L.R. (3d) 368 8.77
Hicks v. Faulkner (1878) 8 P.B.D. 167 22.07
Higgins v. Andrews (1619) 2 Roll. Rep. 55 5.35
Hilbery v. Hatton (1864) 2 H. & C. 822 3.08, **7.19**
Hilder v. Associated Portland Cement Manufacturers Ltd [1961] 3 All E.R. 709 12.15
Hill v. Baxter [1958] 1 Q.B. 227 2.33
Hill v. Chief Constable of W. Yorkshire [1987] 1 All E.R. 1173 12.08, **12.61**, 12.64, 12.65
Hill v. Tupper (1863) 2 H. & C. 121 5.15
Hill (Gordon) Trust Ltd v. Segall [1941] 2 All E.R. 379 17.14
Hillen v. I.C.I. (Alkali) Ltd [1936] A.C. 65 3.29, 5.01, 13.46, 14.22
Hillesden Securities Ltd v. Ryjak Ltd [1983] 2 All E.R. 184 7.46, 7.49, 7.50
Hills v. Potter [1983] 1 All E.R. 716 6.08, 12.78, 13.17
Hillyer v. St. Bartholomew's Hospital [1909] 2 K.B. 820 3.04
Hilton v. Sutton Steam Laundry [1946] K.B. 65 2.37

Hilton v. Thomas Burton (Rhodes) LTd [1961] 1 W.L.R. 705 3.33
Hinton v. Heather (1845) 14 M. & W. 131 22.06
Hinz v. Berry [1970] 2 Q.B. 40 12.24, **12.25**, 15.39
Hiort v. Bott (1864) L.R. 9 Ex. 86 7.16, **7.21**, 7.30
Hoare & Co. v. McAlpine [1923] 1 Ch. 167 8.11, 9.20, 9.35
Hobbs v. Peoples Newspaper Publishing Co. (1926) unreported 18.62
Hobbs v. Tinling [1929] 2 K.B. 1 18.111
Hodge v. Anglo-American Oil Co. (1922) 12 Ll.L.R. 183 14.13
Hodgson v. Trapp [1988] 3 All E.R. 870 15.26, 15.30, 15.35
Hoffman v. Sofner [1982] 1 W.L.R. 1250 15.01
Hoffman La-Roche (F.) & Co. AG v. DDSA Pharmaceuticals Ltd [1972] R.P.C. 1 21.66, **21.70**, 21.71
Hogan v. Bentinck West Hartley Collieries [1949] 1 All E.R. 588 12.113
Holden v. Chief Constable of Lancashire [1986] 3 All E.R. 836 15.05
Holden v. White [1982] 2 All E.R. 328 14.15, 14.21
Hole v. Sittingbourne Railway (1861) 6 H. & N. 488 9.09
Holgate-Mohammed v. Duke [1984] 1 All E.R. 1054 6.43, 6.44, 6.48
Hollebone v. Barnard [1954] O.R. 236 6.08
Holliday v. National Telephone Co. [1899] 2 Q.B. 392 3.38, 9.09
Hollington v. F. Hewthorn & Co. Ltd [1943] K.B. 587 12.83
Hollins v. Fowler (1875) L.R. 7 H.L. 757 7.20, **7.22**, 7.23, 7.24, 7.28, 7.29
Hollins v. J. Davy Ltd [1963] 1 Q.B. 844 7.18
Hollywood Silver Fox Farm v. Emmett [1936] 2 K.B. 468 8.22, 8.23
Holmes v. Ashford [1950] 2 All E.R. 76 14.07, 14.08
Holmes v. Bagge (1853) 1 E. & B. 782 5.48
Holmes v. Board of Hospital Trustees of City of London (1977) 5 C.C.L.T. 1 12.80, 12.93
Holmes v. Mather (1875) L.R. 10 Ex. 261 6.38, 12.75, 13.20
Holmes v. Wilson (1839) 10 M. & W. 503 5.08
Holt v. Astrigg (1608) Cro.Jac. 184 18.45
Holt v. Nesbitt [1951] O.R. 601; [1953] S.C.R. 143 12.87
Home Brewery plc v. Davis & Co. [1987] 1 All E.R. 637 8.02, 8.20, 8.23, 8.28
Home Office v. Dorset Yacht Co. Ltd [1970] A.C. 1004 12.13, **12.61**, 12.118, 12.119
Honeywell & Stein Ltd v. Larkin Bros. [1934] 1 K.B. 191 3.04, 3.37
Hook v. Cunard Steamship Co. Ltd [1953] 1 All E.R. 1021 6.32, 6.34
Hope v. W.C. Leng & Co. Ltd (1907) 2 T.L.R. 243 18.88
Hopkins v. Crowe (1836) 4 Ad. & El. 774 6.22
Hopp v. Lepp [1980] 2 S.C.R. 192 13.17
Hopper v. Reeve (1817) 7 Taunt. 698 6.11
Hopper v. Rogers [1975] Ch.43 8.69
Hopwood v. Muirson [1945] K.B. 313 18.52, 18.53
Hornal v. Neuberger Products Ltd [1957] 1 Q.B. 247 17.10
Hornsby Building Information Pty Ltd v. Sydney Building Information Centre (1978) 52 A.L.J. L.R. 312 21.70
Horrocks v. Lowe [1975] A.C. 135 18.72, 18.101
Horsfall v. Brown [1932] 1 K.B. 358 6.47
Horsfall v. Thomas (1862) 1 H. & C. 90 17.15
Horsley v. MacLaren (or McLaren); The Ogopogo (1971) 22 D.L.R. (3d) 545; [1972] S.C.R. 441 1.03, 12.31, 12.32, 12.34, 12.53
Hoskins v. Robins (1671) 2 Saund. 319 11.35
Hotson v. East Berkshire Area Health Authority; Hotson v. Fitzgerald [1987] 2 All E.R. 909 H.L. 12.107
Hough v. London Express Newspapers Ltd [1940] 2 K.B. 507 18.06, 18.18
Houghland v. R.R. Low (Luxury Coaches) Ltd [1962] 1 Q.B. 694 12.77
Houldsworth v. City of Glasgow Bank (1880) 5 App.Cas 317 2.18, 17.01
Hounslow London Borough v. Twickenham Garden Developments [1971] Ch. 233 5.15

Hourani v. Harrison (1927) 96 L.J. K.B. 1025 3.27
Howard v. Harris (1884) Cab. & Ell. 253 7.21
Howard v. Houlder Liness Howard v. Furness Houlder Ltd [1936] 2 All E.R. 781 9.16, 14.04, 14.07
Howard Marine & Dredging Co. Ltd v. A. Ogden & Sons [1978] Q.B. 534 12.36
Howell v. London General Omnibus Co. (1877) 2 Ex.D. 365 4.04
Hubbard v. Pitt [1976] Q.B. 142 5.07, 8.69
Hudson v. Nicholson (1839) 5 M. & W. 437 5.08
Hudson v. Ridge Manufacturing Co. Ltd [1957] 2 Q.B. 348 3.20, 14.50
Hudson v. Roberts (1851) 6 Ex. 697 11.03
Hughes v. Lord Advocate [1963] A.C. 837 12.74, **12.118**, 13.28
Hughes v. Percival (1883) 8 App.Cas 443 3.37
Hull v. Canterbury Municipal Council [1974] 1 N.S.W.L.R. 300 16.11
Hulley v. Silversprings Bleaching Co. [1922] 2 Ch. 268 8.53
Hulton & Co. v. Jones [1909] 2 K.B. 444; [1910] A.C. 20 C.A. 18.06, 18.21, 18.54(a)
Hultquist v. Universal Pattern & Engineering Co. Ltd [1960] 2 Q.B. 467 14.47
Hummerstone v. Leary [1921] 2 K.B. 664 12.98
Humphrey v. Bowers (1929) 45 T.L.R. 297 12.35
Hunt v. Star Newspaper Co. Ltd [1908–10] All E.R. Rep. 513 18.65
Hunt v. T.W. Johnstone Ltd (1976) 12 O.R. (2d) 623 12.43
Hunter v. Chief Constable of W. Midlands [1981] 3 All E.R. 727 12.83, 22.18
Huntley v. Thornton [1957] 1 All E.R. 234 21.12
Hurley v. Sanders & Co. Ltd [1955] 1 All E.R. 833 14.52, 14.55
Hurst v. Picture Theatres Ltd [1915] 1 K.B. 1 5.15, 5.42
Hussien v. Chong Fook Kam [1970] A.C. 942 6.43, 6.46
Huth v. Huth [1915] 3 K.B. 32 18.30
Hutton v. Eyre (1815) 6 Taunt. 289 4.06
Hyett v. Great Western Railway [1948] 1 K.B. 345 12.31

I

I.C.I. v. Shatwell [1956] A.C. 656 3.02, 13.05, 13.19, 13.46, **16.19**
I.R.C. v. Hoogstraten [1985] Q.B. 1007 12.78
I.R.C. v. Muller & Co's Margarine Ltd [1910] A.C. 217 21.66
I.R.C. v. Rossminster Ltd [1980] 1 All E.R. 80; [1980] A.C. 952 5.96, 7.14, 7.37
Ichard v. Frangoulis [1977] 2 All E.R. 461 15.39
Ilkiw v. Samuels [1963] 2 All E.R. 879 3.10, 3.25
Illott v. Wilkes (1820) 2 B. & Ald. 304 11.22
Incledon v. Watson (1862) 2 F. & F. 841 17.07
Indemaur v. Dames (1866) L.R. 1 C.P. 274 9.02, 14.23
Infabrics Ltd v. Laytex Ltd [1981] 1 All E.R. 1057 7.16
Ingall v. Moran [1944] K.B. 160 2.37
Ingram v. Little [1961] 1 Q.B. 31 7.19
Initial Services Ltd v. Putterill [1967] 3 All E.R. 145 20.11
Innis v. Wylie (1844) 1 C. & K. 257 6.15
Insurance Commissioner v. Joyce (1948) 7 C.L.R. 39 13.06, 13.16
International Brotherhood of Teamsters v. Therien [1960] S.C.R. 265 21.42
International Factors Ltd v. Rodrigues [1979] Q.B. 351 7.23, **7.34**
International News Service v. Associated Press (1918) 248 U.S. 215 21.69
Investors in Industry Commercial Properties Ltd v. South Bedfordshire District Council [1986] 1 All E.R. 787 15.20
Isaac v. Hotel de Paris Ltd [1960] 1 W.L.R. 239 5.40
Isaac (M.) & Sons Ltd v. Cook [1925] 2 K.B. 391 18.84, 18.99

Island Records, ex p. [1978] Ch. 122 16.02, 16.08
Islington Metal & Plating Works Ltd, re [1983] 3 All E.R. 218 2.35
Ital-Canadian Investments Ltd v. North Shore Plumbing & Heating Co. Ltd [1978] 4 W.W.R. 289 14.10
Iveson v. Moore (1699) 1 Ld.Ray 486 8.75

J

Jackman v. Corbett [1987] 2 All E.R. 699 **15.24**, 15.28, 15.35
Jackson v. Harrison (1978) 19 A.L.R. 129 13.45, 13.46
Jackson v. Hopperton (1864) 16 C.B.N.S. 829 18.97
Jackson v. McGrath (1947) 75 C.L.R. 293 18.34
Jackson v. Miller (1976) 59 D.L.R. (3d) 246 12.93
Jackson v. Smithson (1846) 15 M. &W. 563 11.03
Jacobs v. London County Council [1950] A.C. 361 14.19
Jag Shakti, The, Chabbra Corporation Pte Ltd v. Owners of Jag Shakti [1986] 1 All E.R. 480 **7.51**,17.17
James v. River East School Division No. 9 [1976] 2 W.W.R. 557 12.80
James v. Rutlech (1599) 4 Co.Rep. 17a, 17b 18.23, 18.49
James v. Woodall Duckham Construction Ltd [1969] 2 All E.R. 794 15.39
Janiak v. Ippolito (1985) 16 D.L.R. (4th) 1, [1985] 1 S.C.R. 146 6.42, 12.119, 15.11
Janvier v. Sweeney [1919] 2 K.B. 316 6.17, 12.24
Jarvis v. Williams [1955] 1 All E.R. 108 7.34
Jays Ltd v. Jacobi [1933] Ch. 411 21.66, 21.70
JEB Fasteners v. Marks Bloom & Co. [1983] 1 All E.R. 583 12.37
Jefferson v. Derbyshire Farmers [1921] 2 K.B. 281 3.22
Jefford v. Gee [1970] 2 Q.B. 130 15.23, 15.38
Jenkins v. Allied Ironfounders Ltd [1969] 3 All E.R. 1609 16.12
Jennings v. Hannon (1969) 89 W.N. (Pt. 2) N.S.W. 232 3.13
Jennings v. Rundall (1799) 8 T.R. 335 2.29
Job Edwards v. Birmingham Canal Navigation Co. [1924] 1 K.B. 341 8.38
Jobling v. Associated Dairies Ltd [1981] 2 All E.R. 752 12.101
Joel v. Morrison (1834) 6 C. & P. 501 3.30
Johnson v. F.E. Callow Ltd [1971] A.C. 335 16.18
Johnson v. Jackson (1889) 40 Ch.D. 71 8.42
Johnson v. Pye (1665) 1 Sid. 258 2.29
Johnson v. Rea Ltd [1962] 1 Q.B. 373 12.60
Johnson v. Tennant Bros. Ltd (1954) (unreported) 13.42
Johnstone v. Pedlar [1921] 2 A.C. 262 2.02, 2.08, 2.11
Johnstone v. Sutton (1786) 1 T.R. 493 22.10, 22.12
Jones v. Boyce (1816) 1 Starke 493 12.114, 13.31
Jones v. Chapman (1849) 2 Ex. 803 5.13
Jones v. Chappell (1875) L.R. 20 Eq. 539 8.08, 8.33
Jones v. Dennison [1971] R.T.R. 174 2.33
Jones v. Department of Employment [1988] 1 All E.R. 725 12.06, 12.10, 12.39, 12.66
Jones v. Fabbi (1973) 37 D.L.R. (3d) 27 21.46
Jones v. Festiniog Railway (1868) L.R. 3 Q.B. 733 9.13, 10.07
Jones v. Foley [1891] 1 Q.B. 730 5.48
Jones v. Gooday (1841) 8 M. & W. 146 15.17
Jones v. Great Western Railway (1931) 142 L.T. 194 12.84
Jones v. Jones (1862) 1 H. & C. 1 8.64
Jones v. Jones [1916] 2 A.C. 481 18.50, 18.51, **18.52**, 18.53
Jones v. Jones [1985] Q.B. 704 C.A.; *reversing* [1983] 1 All E.R. 1037 15.33
Jones v. Lawrence [1969] 3 All E.R. 267 2.24
Jones v. Livox Quarries [1952] 1 T.L.R. 1337 13.27–8, 13.38
Jones v. Llanwrast U.D.C. [1911] 1 Ch. 393 8.33

Jones v. Manchester Corporation [1952] 2 Q.B. 852 4.11
Jones v. Price [1965] 2 Q.B. 618 11.02
Jones v. Pritchard [1908] 1 Ch. 630 8.53
Jones v. Sherwood [1942] 1 K.B. 127 6.17
Jones v. Stroud District Council [1988] 1 All E.R. 5 15.16
Jones v. Swansea City Council [1989] 3 All E.R. 162 1.22
Jones v. Williams (1943) 11 M. & W. 176 8.61
Jones & Sons Ltd v. Tankerville [1909] 2 Ch. 440 5.40
Jones Bros. (Hunstanton) Ltd v. Stevens [1955] 1 Q.B. 275 21.35–36
Jordan House v. Menow (1973) 38 D.L.R. (3d) 105 12.53
Joyce v. Yeomans [1981] 2 All E.R. 21 15.27
Judd v. Board of Governors of Hammersmith, West London and St. Mark's Hospitals [1960] 1 All E.R. 607 15.33
Junior Books Ltd v. Veitchi Co. Ltd [1983] A.C. 520; [1983] 2 All E.R. 201 12.10–11, 12.36, 12.44, **12.45–47**, 12.48

K

Kahler v. Midland Bank [1950] A.C. 24 7.24
Kamloops (City of) v. Nielsen (1984) 10 D.L.R. (4d) 641 12.45, 14.11
Kandalla v. British Airways Board (British European Airways) [1980] 1 All E.R. 341 2.37, 2.38, 15.60
Kark (Norman) Publications Ltd v. Odhams Press Ltd [1962] 1 All E.R. 636 21.72
Kasapis v. Laimos Bros. [1959] 2 Lloyd's Rep. 378 12.53, 14.49
Kassam v. Kampala Aerated Water Co. Ltd [1965] 1 W.L.R. 668 15.59
Kay v. Ayrshire and Arran Health Board [1987] 2 All E.R. 417 12.106
Kay v. I.T.W. Ltd [1968] 1 Q.B. 140 3.10, 3.19
Kealey v. Heard [1983] 1 All E.R. 973 12.90, 12.93
Kearney v. British Railways Board [1968] 2 All E.R. 532 13.41
Kearney v. Eric Waller Ltd [1967] 1 Q.B. 29 14.18
Kearry v. Pattinson [1939] 1 K.B. 471 7.37
Keeble v. Hickersgill (1796) 11 East 547n 21.16
Keegan v. Young [1963] N.Z.L.R. 770 8.74
Keighley Maxsted & Co. v. Durant [1901] A.C. 240 3.08
Kelly v. W.R.N. Contracting Ltd [1968] 1 All E.R. 369 16.13
Kelsen v. Imperial Tobacco Co. Ltd [1957] 2 Q.B. 334 5.25
Kemlin v. Gardiner [1967] 2 Q.B. 510 6.45
Kemsley v. Foot [1952] 345 18.62, 18.63
Kennaway v. Thompson [1980] 3 All E.R. 329 8.17, 8.69
Kenyon v. Hart (1865) 6 B. & S. 249 5.24
Keppel Bus Co. Ltd v. Ahmad [1974] 1 W.L.R. 1082 3.33
Kerr v. Kennedy [1942] 1 K.B. 409 18.50
Kerry v. Carter [1969] 3 All E.R. 723 13.39
Ketteman v. Hansel Properties Ltd [1988] 1 All E.R. 38 15.19
Kettlewell v. Watson (1882) 21 Ch.D. 685 12.01
Keyworth v. Hill (1820) 3 B. & Ald. 685 7.26
Kiddle v. City Business Properties Ltd [1942] 1 K.B. 268 8.47, 9.39
Kimber v. Press Association [1893] 1 Q.B. 65 18.90
King v. Hoare (1844) 13 M. & W. 494 4.05
King v. Lake (1668) Hardr. 470 18.38, 18.45
King v. Liverpool City Council [1986] 3 All E.R. 344 12.53, 12.61
King v. Phillips [1953] 1 Q.B. 429 12.25
Kirk v. Gregory (1876) 1 Ex.D. 55 7.04, **7.13**
Kirk v. McLaughlin Coal & Supplies Ltd [1968] 1 O.R. 311 12.88
Kirkham v. Anderton (1990) The Times, 4 January 12.64, 12.119, 13.11
Kitano v. Commonwealth (1973) 129 C.L.R. 151 16.11
Klein v. Calouri [1971] 2 All E.R. 701 3.13

Klein v. Jenoves [1932] O.R. 504 21.48
Knight & Searle v. Dove [1964] 2 Q.B. 631 2.22
Knightley v. Johns [1982] 1 All E.R. 851 12.29, 12.33, 12.94, **12.120**
Knott v. London County Council [1934] 1 K.B. 126 11.03
Knuppfer v. London Express Newspapers Ltd [1944] A.C. 116 18.27–28
Konsiker v. Goodman [1928] 1 K.B. 421 5.08, 15.02
Kooragang Ltd v. Richardson & Wrench Ltd [1981] 3 All E.R. 65 3.02, 3.09, 3.14, 3.28, 3.31
Koursk, The [1924] P. 140 4.01, 4.02
Kralj v. McGrath [1986] 1 All E.R. 54 15.06
Krouse v. Chrysler Canada Ltd (1974) 40 D.L.R. (3d) 15; (1972) 25 D.L.R. (3d) 49 19.01
Kruber v. Grzesiak [1963] V.L.R. 621 6.08
Kuchenmeister v. Home Office [1958] 1 Q.B. 496 6.18
Kulbach v. Hollands [1939] 3 All E.R. 907 14.09

L

LAC Minerals Ltd v. International Corona Resources Ltd (1989) 61 D.L.R (4d) 14 20.16
Lacroix v. R. [1954] 4 D.L.R. 470 5.26
Lady Gwendolen [1965] P. 294 2.19, 12.78
Lagan Navigation Co. v. Lambey Bleaching Co. [1927] A.C. 226 8.58, 8.59, **8.61**
Lamb v. Camden London Borough Council [1981] Q.B. 625; [1981] 2 All E.R. 408 1.17, 12.14, 12.61, 12.119, 12.123
Lambair Ltd v. Aero Trades (Western) Ltd (No. 2) [1977] 6 W.W.R. 212 21.53
Lambert v. Lastoplex Chemicals Co. [1972] S.C.R. 569 14.07
Lambert v. Lewis [1982] A.C. 225 12.44, 14.04
Lambart v. Roberts [1981] R.T.R. 113 5.39
Lamber (A.) Flat Management Ltd v. Lomas [1981] 2 All E.R. 280 8.03, 8.75
Lambton v. Mellish & Cox [1894] 3 Ch. 163 8.14
Lancashire & Yorkshire Railway Co. v. MacNicoll (1919) 88 L.J.K.B. 601 7.16, **7.22**
Lancashire Waggon Co. v. Fitzhugh (1861) 6 H. & N. 502 7.24
Lane v. Bied (1971) 17 D.L.R. (3d) 632 11.05
Lane v. Dixon (1847) 2 C.B. 776 5.15
Lane v. Holloway [1968] 1 Q.B. 379 6.27, 6.28, 6.39
Lang v. London Transport Executive [1989] 3 All E.R. 609 13.29
Langdon's Coach Lines Ltd v. Toronto Transit Commission [1956] O.R. 45 21.62
Langlands (Swanley) Ltd v. British Transport Commission [1956] 1 W.L.R. 890 10.07
Langridge v. Levy (1837) 2 M. & W. 519 12.35, 14.03, 14.04
Larlee v. Cyr (1970) 2 N.B.R. (2d) 50 12.79
Latimer v. A.E.C. Ltd [1953] A.C. 643 12.16, 12.75, 14.52
Laugher v. Pointer (1826) 5 B. & C. 547 9.04
Laurie v. Raglan Building Co. Ltd [1943] 1 K.B. 152 12.90
Lavell & Co. v. O'Leary [1933] 2 K.B. 200 7.43
Lavender v. Diamints [1948] 2 All E.R. 249 13.41
Law v. Railway Executive (1949) 65 T.L.R. 288 8.58
Lawrence v. Obee (1815) 1 Stra. 22 5.05
Lawrysysn v. Town of Kipling (1965) 50 W.W.R. 430 9.40
Laws v. Florinplace Ltd [1981] 1 All E.R. 659 8.11
Le Fanu v. Malcolmson (1848) 1 H.L.C. 637 18.21, 18.26
Lea v. Charrington (1889) 23 Q.B.D. 45 6.22

Leach v. Standard Telephones & Cables Ltd [1966] 2 All E.R. 523 16.16, 16.21
League Against Cruel Sports v. Scott [1985] 2 All E.R. 489 5.01, **5.04**, 5.12, 7.04, 11.04
Leake v. Loveday (1842) 4 Man. & G. 972 7.39
Leakey v. National Trust [1980] 1 All E.R. 17 **8.28–9**, 8.40, 8.41, 9.01, 9.09, 9.21, 9.24, 10.13
Leame v. Bray (1803) 3 East 593 1.31, 6.02, 7.04
Leanse v. Egerton [1943] K.B. 323 8.40
Leather Cloth Co. v. American Leather Cloth Co. (1865) 11 H.L.C. 523 21.65
Lee v. Riley (1865) 18 C.B.N.S. 722 11.02
Lee v. Sheard [1956] 1 Q.B. 192 15.24
Lee v. Walters (1940) 162 L.T. 89 11.03
Lee v. Wilson & Mackinnon (1934) 51 C.L.R. 276 18.28
Lee (Joe) Ltd v. Lord Dalmeny [1927] 1 Ch. 300 21.32
Lee Kar Choo v. Lee Lian Choon [1967] 1 A.C. 602 21.66, 21.72
Leeds City Council v. W. Yorkshire Police [1983] A.C. 29 2.30
Leeds Industrial Co-operative Society v. Slack [1924] A.C. 851 8.68
Leeman v. Montagu [1936] 2 All E.R. 1677 11.04
Leesh River Tea Co. Ltd v. British India Steam Navigation Co. Ltd [1966] 3 All E.R. 593 3.27
LeFanu v. Malcholmson (1848) 1 H.L.C. 639 8.14
Lefroy v. Burnside (1879) 4 L.R. Ir. 566 18.65
Legh v. Legh (1936) 143 L.T. 151 17.06
Lehndorff Canadian Pension Properties Ltd v. Davis & Co. (1987) 10 B.C.L.R. (2d) 342 21.08, 21.15
Lehnert v. Stein [1963] S.C.R. 35 13.16
Leibo v. Buckman Ltd [1952] 2 All E.R. 1057 22.06, 22.07
Leigh v. Gladstone (1909) 26 T.L.R. 139 6.33, 6.35
Leigh v. Jack (1879) 5 Ex.D. 264 5.15
Leigh & Sillivan Ltd v. Aliakmon Shipping Co. [1986] 2 All E.R. 145 7.32, 12.06, 12.10, 12.47, **12.48**
Leitch & Co. v. Leydon [1931] A.C. 90 7.04
Le Lievre v. Gould [1893] 1 Q.B. 491 12.35, 17.02
Lemmon v. Webb [1894] 3 Ch. 1; [1895] A.C. 1 5.23, 8.61, 8.63
Lepine v. University Hospital Board (1965) 50 W.W.R. 709; [1966] S.C.R. 565 12.80
Leslie (R.) Ltd v. Sheill [1914] 3 K.B. 607 2.29
Letang v. Cooper [1965] 1 Q.B. 232 1.01, 1.27, 6.08, 7.04, 7.15
Letang v. Ottawa Electric Railway Co. [1926] A.C. 725 13.13
Lethbridge v. Phillips (1819) 2 Stark. 544 7.21
Letnik v. Municipality of Metropolitan Toronto (1988) 44 C.C.L.T. 69 12.104
Levesque v. Pickard (1986) 34 C.C.L.T. 276 22.26
Levesque v. St. Laurant (1981) 35 N.B.R. (2d) 315 12.79
Levi v. Colgate-Palmolive (1941) 41 S.R. (N.S.W.) 48 12.18
Levy v. Langridge (1837) 4 M. & W. 337 17.11, 17.16
Leward v. Bosely (1699) 1 Ld. Raym. 62 6.27
Lewis v. Daily Telegraph Ltd [1963] 2 All E.R. 151 18.16, **18.17**, 18.20, 18.60, 18.113
Lewis v. Denys [1940] A.C. 921 13.27, 16.13, 16.20
Lewis v. Read (1845) 13 M. & W. 834 3.08
Lewis (John) & Co. v. Tims [1952] A.C. 676 6.46
Lewis's Declaration of Trust, Re [1953] Ch. 423 21.62, 21.63
Lewvest Ltd v. Scotia Towers Ltd (1981) 126 D.L.R. (3d) 239 5.25
Lickbarrow v. Mason (1787) 2 T.R. 63 3.02
Liddle v. Yorkshire (North Riding) C.C. [1934] 2 K.B. 101 5.07
Liesbosch Dredger v. Edison [1933] A.C. 449 8.66, **12.113**, 12.122, 15.08, 15.12, 15.13, 15.18, 17.18

Liffen v. Watson [1940] 1 K.B. 556 15.33
Lilley v. Ray (1892) 61 L.J.Q.B. 727 18.81
Lim v. Camden Area Health Authority [1980] A.C. 174 15.26, 15.31, 15.39, 15.41, 15.42
Limpus v. London General Omnibus Co. (1862) 1 H.C. 526 3.02, 3.25, 3.31
Lincoln v. Daniels [1961] 3 All E.R. 740 18.81, **18.82**
Lincoln v. Hayman [1982] 2 All E.R. 819 15.35
Lindsey County Council v. Marshall [1937] A.C. 97 14.24
Lion Laboratories Ltd v. Evans [1984] 2 All E.R. 417 20.09, **20.11**
Lister v. Perryman (1878) L.R. 4 H.L. 521 22.06
Lister v. Romford Ice & Cold Storage Co. Ltd [1957] A.C. 555 1.17, 3.40, 4.14
Littler v. Liverpool Corporation [1968] 2 All E.R. 343 8.81, 12.58
Liverpool Corporation v. H. Coghill & Son Ltd [1918] 1 Ch. 307 8.50
Lloyd v. Grace, Smith & Co. [1912] A.C. 716 3.01, 3.04, 3.09, 3.15, **3.27**, 3.32
Lloyd v. West Midland Gas Board [1971] 2 All E.R. 1240 12.88, 12.93
Lloyds Bank Ltd v. Chartered Bank of India, Australia and China [1929] 1 K.B. 40 7.19
Lloyds Bank v. Savory & Co. [1933] A.C. 201 12.80
Lochgelly Iron & Coal Co. Ltd v. M'Mullen [1934] A.C. 1 12.03, 16.10, 16.13, 16.21
Lock v. Ashton (1848) 12 Q.B. 871 6.21
Lockhart v. Harrison (1928) 44 T.L.R. 714 18.20
Lockwood v. Brentwood Park Investments Ltd (1970) 10 D.L.R. (3d) 143 8.11
Lodge Holes Colliery v. Wednesbury Corporation [1908] A.C. 323 5.51
Lezgenkamp v. Bennett (1950) 80 C.L.R. 292 13.16
Lomax v. Arsenault [1986] 1 W.W.R. 68 12.94
London (HMS) [1914] P.72 12.111
London & Brighton Railway v. Truman (1885) 11 App.Cas 45 8.58
London Armoury Co. Ltd v. Ever Ready Co. (Gt. Britain) Ltd [1941] 1 K.B. 742 21.69
London Artists Ltd & ors. v. Littler [1968] 1 All E.R. 1075 H.C.; [1969] 2 All E.R. 193; [1969] 2 Q.B. 375 C.A. 18.62, **18.64**, 18.65, 18.91
London Association for Trade Protection v. Greenlands [1916] 2 A.C. 15 18.73
London City Corporation v. Appleyard [1963] 2 All E.R. 834 7.07, 7.35
London Congregational Union Inc. v. Harriss [1985] 1 All E.R. 335 H.C.; [1988] 1 All E.R. 15 C.A. 12.47, 15.18, 15.19
London Corporation, The [1935] P. 70 15.15
London County Council v. Cattermoles (Garages) Ltd 3.25
London County Freehold Properties Ltd v. Berkeley Properties & Investment Co. Ltd [1936] 2 All E.R. 1039 17.14
London Graving Dock Co. v. Horton [1915] A.C. 737 14.17, 14.23, 14.34
London Jewellers Ltd v. Sutton (1934) 50 T.L.R. 193 7.20
London Passenger Transport Board v. Upson [1949] A.C. 155 1.32, 12.13, 13.29, 13.37, 16.09, 16.13
Long v. Hepworth [1968] 1 W.L.R. 1299 6.01
Longdon-Griffiths v. Smith [1951] 1 K.B. 295 2.22, 18.102
Longhurst v. Guildford Water Board [1963] A.C. 265 16.13
Longmead v. Holliday (1851) 20 L.J. Ex. 430 14.04
Longhurst v. Metropolitan Water Board [1948] 2 All E.R. 834 8.58
Lonrho plc v. Fayed [1989] 2 All E.R. 65 19.10, 21.04, 21.53
Lonrho Ltd v. Shell Petroleum Ltd [1981] 2 All E.R. 456 16.02, **16.06**, 16.08, 16.11, 16.14, 21.03, 21.04, 21.09, **21.13**
Lonrho Ltd v. Shell Petroleum Ltd (No. 2) [1982] A.C. 173 1.06
Lonsdale (Earl of) v. Nelson (1823) 2 B. & C. 302 8.63
Loosemore v. Radford (1842) 9 M. & W. 657 7.19

Lord v. Price (1874) L.R. 9 Ex. 54 7.33
Lord v. Sunday Telegraph Ltd [1970] 3 All E.R. 504 18.62
Lord Citrine, The v. The Hebridean Coast [1961] A.C. 545 15.09, 15.16
Lotan v. Cross (1810) 2 Camp. 464 5.15, 7.09
Loughans v. Odhams Press Ltd [1962] 1 All E.R. 404 18.16
Lovejoy v. Murray (1866) 3 Wall 1 4.05
Lovelidge v. Anselm Olding & Sons Ltd [1967] 2 Q.B. 351 14.51
Lovell v. Blundells & Crompton & Co. [1944] 1 K.B. 502 14.51
Low v. Berdmore (1665) T. Raym. 135 22.14
Lowery v. Walker [1911] A.C. 10 14.22
Lucas-Box v. News Group Newspapers Ltd [1986] 1 All E.R. 177 18.60
Ludgate v. Lovett [1969] 2 All E.R. 1235 12.92
Ludgater v. Love (1881) 44 L.T. 695 17.13
Lumley v. Gye (1853) 2 E. & B. 216 21.30, 21.39, 21.44, 21.46, 21.52, 21.54
Lumsden v. London Trustee Savings Bank [1971] 1 Lloyd's Rep. 114 7.30
Lynch v. Knight (1861) 9 H.L.C. 577 18.43, 18.44
Lynch v. Nurdin (1841) 1 Q.B. 29 12.114, 13.30
Lyon v. Daily Telegraph Ltd [1943] K.B. 746 18.35, 18.61, 18.67, **18.68**

M

Maberley v. Peabody & Co. [1946] 2 All E.R. 192 8.67
McArdle v. Andmac Roofing Co. [1967] 1 All E.R. 583 3.34
McArdle v. Egan (1934) 150 L.T. 412 6.46
McC v. Mullan [1984] 3 All E.R. 908 22.25, 22.26
McCafferty v. Metropolitan Police Receiver [1977] 2 All E.R. 756 **14.49**, 14.51, 15.48, 15.49
McCall v. Abelesz [1976] Q.B. 585 5.05
McCarey v. Associated Newspapers Ltd [1964] 2 All E.R. 335 H.C.; [1965] 3 All E.R. 947 C.A. 18.87, 18.88, 18.90, 18.103, 18.107, 18.110
McCarthy v. Young (1861) 6 H. & N. 329 14.02
McCone v. Oxford [1982] 3 W.L.R. 423 6.45
McCullie v. Butler (1959) The Times 19 March; [1959] C.L.Y. 2207 14.32
McDermid v. Nash Dredging & Reclamation Co. Ltd [1987] 3 W.L.R. 212 3.34, 14.96, 14.47
McDonald v. Associated Fuels [1954] 3 D.L.R. 775 5.06
McEllistrum v. Etches [1956] S.C.R. 787 2.28, 12.79
McGhee v. National Coal Board [1972] 3 All E.R. 1008 12.94, 12.98, **12.103–109**, 16.15
M'Glone v. British Railways Board 1966 S.C. 1 14.41
Macgregor [1943] A.C. 197 4.11
McHale v. Watson (1966) 155 C.L.R. 199; (1966) 38 A.L.J.R. 267 2.28, 6.06, 12.79
Machray v. Stewarts & Lloyds Ltd [1964] 3 All E.R. 716 14.56
McInerney v. Lloyds Bank Ltd [1974] 1 Lloyd's Rep. 246 12.36, 12.37
Macintosh v. Dun [1908] A.C. 390 18.73
Mackay v. Attorney-General of Trinidad and Tobago (No. 2) [1979] A.C. 385 22.24
McKay v. Essex Area Health Authority [1982] 2 All E.R. 771 2.26, 2.27
McKee v. Chief Constable for N. Ireland [1985] 1 All E.R. 1 6.45
MacKeigan v. Hickman (1989) 61 D.L.R. (4th) 688 22.26
Mackenzie v. Sloss [1959] N.Z.L.R. 533 10.11
McKernan v. Foster (1931) 46 C.L.R. 343 21.12
McKew v. Holland & Hannen & Cubitts (Scotland) Ltd [1969] 3 All E.R. 1621 12.119
McKinnon Industries Ltd v. Walker [1951] 3 D.L.R. 577 8.16, 8.66
M'Kone v. Wood (1831) 5 C. & P.I. 11.03

McLaren v. British Columbia Institute of Technology (1978) 94 D.L.R. (3d) 411 21.35
MacLaughlan & Mitchell Homes Ltd v. Frank's Rentals & Sons Ltd (1980) 106 D.L.R. (3d) 245 12.88, 12.93, 14.09
McLeod v. McGhue (1841) 2 Man. & G. 771 7.26
Maclean v. Bell (1932) 112 L.T. 262 13.33
McLoughlin v. O'Brian [1982] 2 All E.R. 298; [1983] 1 A.C. 410 12.06, **12.24–25**, 12.26, 12.27, 12.28
McLone v. Oxford [1982] 2 W.L.R. 423 5.46
McPhail v. Persons Unknown; Bristol Corporation v. Ross [1973] Ch. 447 5.01, 5.48
McQuaker, v. Goddard [1940] 1 K.B. 687 11.03
McQuire v. Western Morning News Co. [1900–03] All E.R. Rep. 673 18.67, 18.70
McVittie v. Bolton Corporation [1945] K.B. 281 8.73
McWilliams v. Sir William Arrol & Co. [1962] 1 All E.R. 623 12.94, 16.15
Madalena v. Kuhn (1987) 35 D.L.R. (4d) 222 12.96
Mafo v. Adams [1970] 1 Q.B. 548 15.05, 17.16, 17.18, 17.19
Maguire v. Calgary [1983] 4 W.W.R. 342 21.08
Mahon v. Osborne [1939] 2 K.B. 14 12.87, 12.91
Maitland v. Raisbeck [1944] K.B. 689 8.82
Makin (J. & J.) Ltd v. London & North-Eastern Railway [1943] K.B. 467 9.49, 13.02
Malcolm v. Broadhurst [1970] 3 All E.R. 508 12.118
Malfroot v. Noxal (1934) 51 T.L.R. 551 12.02, 14.07
Mallett v. McMonagle [1970] A.C. 166 15.26
Malone v. Commissioner of Police of the Metropolis (No. 2) [1979] 2 All E.R. 620 19.03
Malone v. Laskey [1907] 2 K.B. 141 8.32, 8.34, 8.35
Malone v. Metropolitan Police Commissioner [1979] Ch. 344 7.05
Malyon v. Plummer [1964] 1 Q.B. 330 15.60
Malz v. Rosen [1966] 1 W.L.R. 1008 22.07
Manawatu County v. Rowe [1956] N.Z.L.R. 78 3.13
Manchester Corporation v. Farnworth [1930] A.C. 171 8.11, 8.54, 9.42
Manchester Corporation v. Williams [1891] 1 Q.B. 94 2.17, 18.03, 18.47
Manders v. Williams (1849) 3 Ex. 339 7.33
Mangena v. Wright [1909] 2 K.B. 958 18.66
Manitoba Free Press Co. v. Nagy (1908) 39 S.C.R. 340 21.55, 21.62
Mansell v. Griffin [1908] 1 K.B. 160, 947 6.29
Mansell v. Webb (1918) 88 L.J.K.B. 323 10.07
Manson v. Associated Newspapers Ltd [1965] 2 All E.R. 954 18.110
Manton v. Brocklebank [1923] 2 K.B. 212 7.04, 7.12, 11.02, 11.03, 11.04
Marfani Co. Ltd v. Midland Bank Ltd [1968] 1 W.L.R. 956 7.38
Margarine Union GmbH v. Cambay Prince Steamship Co. Ltd [1967] 3 All E.R. 775 12.48
Marina Shipping Ltd v. Laughton [1982] 1 All E.R. 481 21.01
Marjory, Re [1955] Ch.600 22.20, 22.21
Mark Fishing Co. Ltd v. United Fishermen's & Allied Workers Union (1972) 24 D.L.R. (3d) 585 21.39, 21.42
Market Investigations Ltd v. Minister of Social Security [1969] 2 Q.B. 173 3.04
Marks v. Samuel [1904] 2 K.B. 287 18.46
Marlor v. Ball (1906) 16 T.L.R. 239 11.03
Marpesia, The (1872) L.R. 4 P.C. 212 6.07, 13.02
Marriage v. East Norfolk Rivers Catchment Board [1950] 1 K.B. 284 8.54, 8.57
Marrinan v. Vibart [1962] 1 All E.R. 869 H.C.; [1962] 3 All E.R. 380 C.A. 18.79, 22.22

Marsh v. Moores [1949] 2 K.B. 208 3.25
Marshall v. Gotham Co. Ltd [1954] A.C. 360 12.16
Marshall v. Lionel Enterprises (1971) 25 D.L.R. (3d) 141 12.25
Marshall v. Osmond [1982] 2 All E.R. 610 12.65, 12.78, 13.45
Marston v. British Railways Board [1976] I.C.R. 124 15.48
Martin v. Denn [1971] 2 Q.B. 208 16.10
Martin v. Tregonwell & Strachan (1742) 5 T.R. 107n 5.19
Mason v. Clarke [1955] A.C. 778 8.72
Mason v. Hill (1833) 5 B. & Ad. 1 8.20
Mason v. Keeling (1699) 12 Mod. 232 11.03
Mason v. Levy Auto Parts of England Ltd [1967] 2 All E.R. 62 10.02, 10.06, 10.08, 10.09, 10.12
Mason v. Williams & Williams Ltd [1955] 1 All E.R. 808 14.09
Maspro v. Brown (1876) 1 C.P.D. 97 6.13
Massey v. Crown Life Insurance Co. [1978] 1 W.L.R. 676 3.05
Masters v. Brent L.B.C. [1978] Q.B. 841; [1978] 2 All E.R. 664 5.08, **8.33**
Matania v. National Provincial Bank (1936) 155 L.T. 74 3.37, 8.37, 9.09
Matheson v. Northcote College [1975] 2 N.Z.L.R. 106 9.20
Matheson v. Smiley [1932] 2 D.L.R. 787 6.35
Matthews v. Kuwait Bechtel Corporation [1959] 2 Q.B. 57 1.07, 14.48
Maughan v. International Harvester Co. of Canada Ltd (1981) 112 D.L.R. (3d) 243 14.10
Maxfield v. Llewellyn [1961] 3 All E.R. 95 4.11
Maxim's Ltd v. Dye [1977] 1 W.L.R. 1155 21.72
May v. Burdett (1845) 9 Q.B. 101 11.03
Maynard v. West Midlands Regional Health Authority [1985] 1 All E.R. 635 12.80
Maynegrain Pty Ltd v. Campofine Bank [1984] 1 N.S.W.L.R. 258 7.37
Meade v. Haringey L.B.C. [1929] 2 All E.R. 1016 16.01
Meade's & Belt's Case (1823) 1 Lewin 184 6.15
Meah v. McCreamer [1985] 1 All E.R. 36 12.96, 13.16, 13.44, 13.46
Meah v. McCreamer (No. 2) [1986] 1 All E.R. 943 6.13, 12.118, 12.119, 12.123, **15.34**
Mears v. London & S.W. Railway (1862) 11 C.B.N.S. 850 7.10, 7.36
Mediana, The [1900] A.C. 113 15.16
Meering v. Grahame-White Aviation Co. (1919) 122 L.T. 44 6.20
Mehmet v. Perry [1977] 2 All E.R. 529 15.60
Meldrum v. Australian Broadcasting Commission [1932] Argus L.R. 432 18.37, 18.39
Melvin v. Reid (1931) 112 Cal.App. 285 19.05
Mendelssohn v. Normand Ltd [1970] 1 Q.B. 177 3.32
Mennie v. Blake (1856) 6 E. & B. 842 7.42
Menow v. Honsberger & Jordan House Ltd [1974] S.C.R. 239 1.03
Mentmore Manufacturing Co. Ltd v. National Machinery Co. Inc. (1978) 89 D.L.R. (3d) 195 3.06
Merchant Prince, The [1892] P. 179 13.04
Mercury Communications v. Scott-Garner [1984] 1 All E.R. 179 2.23, 21.01
Merivale v. Carson (1887) 20 Q.B.D. 275 18.63, 18.64, 18.67, 18.68
Merkur Island Shipping Corporation v. Laughton [1983] 2 All E.R. 189 21.01, 21.53
Merrick v. Nott-Bower [1965] 1 Q.B. 57 18.84
Merrington v. Ironbridge Metal Works Ltd [1952] 2 All E.R. 1101 12.02, 12.32, 13.20
Merry v. Green (1841) 7 M. & W. 623 7.07
Merryweather v. Nixan (1799) 8 T.R. 186 3.40, 4.04, 4.14
Mersey Docks & Harbour Board v. Coggins & Griffiths (Liverpool) Ltd [1947] A.C. 1 3.05
Mersey Docks & Harbour Board v. Proctor [1923] A.C. 253 14.22

Mersey Docks Trustees v. Gibbs (1866) L.R. 1 H.L. 93 2.02
Metalt und Rohstoff AG v. Donaldson Lufkin & Jenrette [1988] 3 All E.R. 116 H.C.; [1989] 3 All E.R. 14 C.A. 21.04, 22.18, 22.21
Metals and Ropes Ltd v. Tattersall [1966] 3 All E.R. 401 7.46
Metropolitan Asylum District Managers v. Hill (1881) 6 App.Cas. 193 8.55, 8.58
Metropolitan Bank v. Pooley (1885) 10 App.Cas. 210 22.20
Metropolitan Police District Receiver v. Croydon Corporation [1957] 2 Q.B. 154 15.37
Metropolitan Properties Ltd v. Jones [1939] 2 All E.R. 202 8.11
Metropolitan Railway v. Jackson (1877) 3 App.Cas. 193 12.114
Metropolitan Salvon Omnibus Co. v. Hawkins (1859) 4 H. & N. 87 2.17
Meyer v. General Exchange Insurance Corporation (1962) 31 D.L.R. (2d) 689 22.07
Middleton v. Fowler (1698) 1 Salk, 282 3.02
Midland Bank Ltd v. Hett, Stubbs & Kent [1979] Ch. 384 1.11
Midland Bank Trust Co. Ltd v. Green (No. 1) [1979] 3 All E.R. 28 A.C.; [1981] A.C. 513 18.29, 21.33
Midland Bank Trust Co. Ltd v. Green (No. 3) [1979)] 2 All E.R. 193; [1979] Ch. 496 affirmed [1982] Ch. 529 2.24, 21.08
Midland Bank Trust Co. Ltd v. Hett, Stubbs & Kemp [1979] Ch. 384 12.68
Midland Cold Storage Co. Ltd v. Steer [1972] Ch. 630 21.31, 21.52
Midwood v. Mayor of Manchester [1905] 2 K.B. 593 8.07, 8.09, 9.09, 9.13
Mighell v. Sultan of Johore [1894] 1 Q.B. 149 2.13
Migliore v. Gerard (1987) 42 D.L.R. (4th) 619 12.76
Miles v. Forest Rock Granite Co. (1918) 34 T.L.R. 500 9.14, 9.32
Miller v. Armstrong (The Bernina) (1883) 13 App.Cas. 1 13.30
Miller v. Decker [1957] S.C.R. 624 13.16
Miller v. Dell [1891] 1 Q.B. 468 7.40
Miller v. Jackson [1977] 3 All E.R. 338 8.09, 8.17, 8.47, **8.48**, 8.51, 8.70
Miller v. South of Scotland Electricity Board 1958 S.C. 20 14.16
Mills v. Baitis [1968] V.R. 583 13.45
Mills v. Brooker [1919] 1 K.B. 535 8.63
Mills v. Cooper [1967] 2 Q.B. 459 22.18
Mills v. Hawker (1874) L.R. 9 Ex. 309 2.19
Mills v. Winchester Diocesan Board of Finance [1989] 2 All E.R. 317 12.10, 12.38, 12.39
Minister of Health v. Belotti [1944] K.B. 298 5.01, 5.40
Ministry of Housing & Local Government v. Sharp [1970] 2 Q.B. 223 12.37, 12.38, 16.14
Ministry of Pensions v. Channell [1947] K.B. 250 12.116
Minories Finances Ltd v. Arthur Young [1989] 2 All E.R. 105 12.10
Mint v. Good [1951] 1 K.B. 517 8.44, 8.85
Minter v. Priest [1930] A.C. 558 18.83
Mintuck v. Valley River Bank No. 63A (1977) 75 D.L.R. (3d) 589 21.23, 21.53
Miraflores, The and The Abadessa; Miraflores v. Livanos (George) (Owners) [1967] 1 A.C. 826; [1967] 1 All E.R. 672 4.11, 13.41, **13.43**
Mirror Newspapers Ltd v. Jools (1986) 65 A.L.R. 174 18.103
Mitchell v. Ealing London B.C. [1979] 1 Q.B. 1 7.21
Moeliker v. Reyrolle & Co. Ltd [1977] 1 All E.R. 9 15.28
Moffatt v. Kazana [1969] 2 Q.B. 152 7.07, 7.35
Mogul Steamship Co. Ltd v. McGregor Gow & Sons (1885) 21 Q.B.D. 544 H.C.; (1889) 23 Q.B.D. 598 C.A.; [1892] A.C. 25 H.L. 1.21, 21.04, 21.11, 21.12, 21.14, 21.47
Moloney v. Lambeth Borough Council (1966) 64 L.G.R. 440 14.32
Monarch Steamship Co. Ltd v. A/B Karlshamns Oljefabriker [1949] A.C. 196 15.08

Monk v. Warbey [1935] 1 K.B. 75 16.02, 16.07, 16.10, 16.14
Monsanto plc v. T.G.W.U. [1982] 1 All E.R. 358 21.01
Monson v. Tussauds Ltd [1894] 1 Q.B. 671 18.12, **18.38**
Monte Rosa, The [1893] P. 23 13.33
Moon v. Towers (1860) 8 C.B.N.S. 611 2.30
Moore v. D.E.R. Ltd [1971] 3 All E.R. 517 15.12
Moore v. Lambeth County Court Registrar (No. 2) [1970] 1 Q.B. 560 7.13
Moore v. News of the World Ltd [1972] 1 Q.B. 441; [1972] 1 All E.R. 915 18.58, 19.01
Moore v. Palmer (1886) 2 T.L.R. 782 3.05
Moore v. R. Fox & Sons [1956] 1 Q.B. 596 12.93
Moore v. Robinson (1831) 2 B. & Ad. 817 7.32
Moorgate Mercantile Co. Ltd v. Finch [1962] 1 Q.B. 701 7.22
Moorgate Mercantile Co. Ltd v. Twitchings [1977] A.C. 890 7.24, 7.30
Moorgate Tobacco v. Phillip Morris (1984) 59 A.L.J.R. 77 21.76
Mordaunt v. Mordaunt (1870) L.R. 2 P. & D. 103 2.32
Moore v. Weaver [1928] 2 K.B. 520 18.80, 18.83
Morey v. Woodfield [1963] 3 All E.R. 533n 1.17
Morgan v. Aylen [1942] 1 All E.R. 489 12.30
Morgan v. Fry [1968] 2 Q.B. 710 21.20, **21.22**, 21.28
Morgan v. Hughes (1788) 2 T.R. 225 22.05
Morgan v. Odhams Press Ltd [1970] 2 All E.R. 544 A.C.; [1971] 2 All E.R. 1156 H.L. **18.23–25**, 18.28, 18.114
Morgans v. Launchbury [1973] A.C. 127 1.18, 3.02, 3.13
Moriarty v. McCarthy [1978] 2 All E.R. 213 15.33
Morison v. Moat (1851) 241 20.04
Morisson v. International Thomson Publishing Ltd [1989] 3 All E.R. 733 18.60
Morren v. Swinton & Pendlebury B.C. [1965] 2 All E.R. 349 3.04
Morris v. Beardmore [1981] A.C. 446 5.46, 6.45
Morris v. C.W. Martin & Sons Ltd [1966] 1 Q.B. 716 3.02, 3.22, 3.27
Morris v. Luton Corporation [1946] 1 All E.R. 1 12.16
Morris v. Redland Bricks Ltd [1967] 3 All E.R. 1 8.67
Morris v. W. Hartlepool Steam Navigation Co. Ltd [1956] A.C. 552 12.16
Morrison Holdings Ltd v. Manders Property Ltd [1976] 2 All E.R. 205 14.19
Morrison Steamship Co. Ltd v. Greystoke Castle [1947] A.C. 265 12.116
Morriss v. Marsden [1952] 1 All E.R. 925 2.32, 6.06
Morrisson Shipping Co. Ltd v. Greystoke Castle [1947] A.C. 265 12.46
Morton v. William Dixon Ltd 1909 S.C. 807 12.81
Mostyn, The [1928] A.C. 57 9.46
Motherwell v. Motherwell (1976) 73 D.L.R. (3d) 62 8.35, 19.01, 19.04
Mott v. Shoolbred (1875) L.R. 20 Eq. 22 8.50
Mount Carmel Investments Ltd v. Peter Thurlow Ltd [1988] 3 All E.R. 129 5.08
Mount Isa Mines Ltd v. Pusey [1971] A.L.R. 253 12.25
Mouse's Case (1609) 12 Co.Rep. 63 7.26
Muirhead v. Industrial Tank Specialities Ltd [1985] 3 All E.R. 705 12.47, **12.49**
Muirhead v. Timber Bros. (1977) 3 C.C.L.T. 1 8.11
Mulchahy v. R. (1868) L.R. 3 H.L. 306 21.03
Mulholland v. Mitchell [1971] A.C. 666 15.45
Mulholland & Tedd Ltd v. Baker [1939] 3 All E.R. 253 10.06, 10.08
Mullard v. Ben Line Steamers Ltd [1970] 1 W.L.R. 1414 13.41
Mullis v. United States Lines Ltd [1969] 1 Lloyd's Rep. 109 14.36
Munro v. Wilmott [1949] 1 K.B. 295 7.52
Munster v. Lamb (1883) 11 Q.B.D. 588 18.78
Murfin v. United Steel Companies Ltd [1957] 1 All E.R. 23 16.13
Murphy v. Culhinane [1976] 3 W.L.R. 458 6.39

Murray v. Hall (1849) 7 C.B. 441 5.15
Murray v. Haringay Arena [1951] 2 K.B. 529 13.05, 13.07
Murray v. Ministry of Defence [1988] 1 W.L.R. 692 6.20
Musgrove v. Pandelis [1919] 2 K.B. 43 9.19, 9.20, 10.02, 10.06, **10.08–09**
Mutual Life Assurance Co. Ltd v. Evatt [1971] A.C. 793 12.36, 12.78

N

Naismith v. London Film Productions Ltd [1939] 1 All E.R. 794 14.52
Nalder v. Ilford Corporation [1951] K.B. 822 5.51
Nance v. British Columbia Electric Railway Co. [1951] A.C. 601 13.26, 15.45
Nancollas v. Insurance Officer [1985] 1 All E.R. 833 3.18, 3.21
National Bank of Greece SA v. Pinios Shipping Co. (No. 1) [1989] 1 All E.R. 213 12.10, 12.70, **12.71**
National Coal Board v. England [1954] A.C. 403 13.44, 13.46
National Coal Board v. Evans [1951] 2 K.B. 861 5.11, 5.28, 6.07, 7.15
National Mercantile Bank v. Rymill (1881) 44 L.T. 767 7.23, 7.28, 7.29
National Phonographic Co. v. Edison-Bell Consolidated Phonograph Co. Ltd [1908] 1 Ch. 235 16.08
National Telephone Co. v. Baker [1893] 2 Ch. 186 9.20
National Union of General & Municipal Workers v. Gillian [1945] 2 All E.R. 593; Affirmed [1946] K.B. 81 2.17, 2.22, 18.03
Navarro v. Moregrand [1951] 2 T.L.R. 674 3.10
Naylor v. Genstar Ltd (1977) 76 D.L.R. (3d) 697 21.39
Nelles v. The Queen in Right of Ontario [1986] 21 D.L.R. (4th) 103; (1989) 60 D.L.R. (4d) 609 S.C. 22.26
Netherton v. Coles [1985] 1 All E.R. 227 3.21
Nesterczuk v. Mortimore (1965) 39 A.L.J.R. 288 12.85
Nettleship v. Weston [1971] 2 Q.B. 691 12.78, **13.14**
Neumann v. Bakeaway Ltd [1983] 2 All E.R. 929 7.22, 7.37
Nevill v. Fine Arts and General Insurance Co. [1897] A.C. 68 18.07, 18.17
New Zealand Shipping Co. Ltd v. A.M. Satterthwaite & Co. Ltd [1989] A.C. 154 12.38, 13.10
Newbigging v. Adam (1886) 34 Ch.D. 582 17.01
Newcastle-under-Lyme Corporation v. Wolstanton Ltd [1947] Ch. 92; [1947] Ch. 427 8.33, 8.49, 8.74
Newsby v. General Lighterage Co. Ltd [1955] 1 Lloyd's Rep. 273 12.61
Newstead v. London Express Newspapers Ltd [1940] 1 K.B. 377 18.06, 18.21, 18.54(a)
Newton v. Edgerley [1959] 3 All E.R. 337 2.30
Newton v. Harland (1840) 1 Man. & G. 644 5.48
Ng Chun Pui v. Lee Chicu Tat [1988] R.T.R. 298 12.93
Nicholls v. Bastard (1835) 2 C.M. & R. 659 7.09, 7.33
Nicholls v. Ely Beet Sugar Co. [1936] Ch. 343 1.04, **8.31**, 8.33, 8.49, 8.65
Nicholls v. Ely Beet Sugar Factory Ltd [1931] 2 Ch. 84 5.05, 5.13, 8.49, 8.74
Nichols v. F. Austin (Leyton) Ltd [1946] A.C. 493 16.18
Nichols v. Marsland (1875) L.R. 10 Ex. 255 9.47, 9.48, 9.49, 11.03
Nicholls v. Richmond (Township) (1983) 145 D.L.R. (3d) 362 21.35
Nicholson v. Atlas Steel Foundry & Engineering Co. Ltd [1957] 1 All E.R. 776 12.94, 12.103
Nicholson v. Revill (1836) 4 Ad. & E. 675 4.06
Nicholson v. Zoological Society (1960) The Times 26 February; [1960] C.L.Y. 2127 14.32
Nimmo v. Alexander Cowan & Sons Ltd [1968] A.C. 107 16.12
Noble v. Harrison [1926] 2 K.B. 332 8.40, 8.85, 9.09, 9.28
Nocton v. Lord Ashburton [1914] A.C. 932 12.35
North v. Wood [1914] 1 K.B. 629 11.03
North General Wagon & Finance Co. v. Graham [1950] 2 K.B. 7 **7.34**

Northwestern Utilities Ltd v. London Guarantee & Accident Co. Ltd [1936] A.C. 108 9.09, 9.13, 9.28, 9.41, 9.42, **9.45**, 12.19, 12.114
Norton v. Canadian Pacific Steamships Ltd [1961] 2 All E.R. 785 3.34
Nor-Video Services Ltd v. Ontario Hydro (1978) 19 O.R. (2d) 107 8.11
Nottingham v. Aldridge [1971] 2 Q.B. 739 3.13, 3.21
Nowsco Well Services Ltd v. Canadian Propane Gas & Oil Ltd (1981) 122 D.L.R. (3d) 228 12.98
Nugent v. Smith (1876) 1 C.P.D. 19, 423 **9.46**, 9.47
N.Z. Forest Products Ltd v. O'Sullivan [1974] N.Z.L.R. 80 9.14, 10.11
NWL Ltd v. Woods [1979] 3 All E.R. 614 21.01

O

Oakes v. Turquand & Hardy (1867) L.R. 2 H.L. 325 17.06
Oakley v. Lyster [1931] 1 K.B. 148 7.16, 7.25
Observer Ltd v. Gordon [1983] 2 All E.R. 945 7.22, 7.37
Ocean Accident & Guarantee Corp. v. Ilford Gas Co. [1905] 2 K.B. 493 5.16
Ocean Estates Ltd v. Pinder [1969] 2 A.C. 19 5.13, 5.19
O'Connell v. Jackson [1972] 2 Q.B. 270 13.26, 13.37
O'Connor v. Bray (1937) 56 C.L.R. 464 16.05
O'Connor v. British Transport Commission [1958] 1 All E.R. 558 14.32
O'Connor v. Waldron [1935] A.C. 76 18.80
Office Cleaning Services Ltd v. Westminster Window & General Cleaners Ltd (1946) 63 R.P.C. 39 21.70
Ogden v. Turner (1704) 6 Mod.Rep. 104 22.14
Ogwo v. Taylor [1987] 3 All E.R. 961 12.29, 12.32, 13.20
Old Gate Estates v. Toplis [1939] 3 All E.R. 209 12.35
Oliver v. Ashman [1962] 2 Q.B. 210 15.29
Oliver v. Birmingham & Midland Omnibus Co. [1933] 1 K.B. 35 13.30
Oliver v. Saddler & Co. [1929] A.C. 584 14.02, 14.14
O'Malley v. Sheppard & Sons [1962] 2 Lloyd's Rep. 221; [1963] 1 Lloyd's Rep. 189 14.18
Ontario (384238) Ltd v. The Queen in right of Ontario (1983) 8 D.L.R. (4th) 676 7.13
Orbit Mining & Trading Co. Ltd v. Westminster Bank Ltd [1963] 1 Q.B. 794 7.19
Ordog v. District of Mission (1980) 110 D.L.R. (3d) 718 14.11
O'Reilly v. National Rail & Tramway Appliances Ltd [1966] 1 All E.R. 499 3.20
Ormrod v. Crosville Motor Services Ltd [1953] 2 All E.R. 753 3.13
O'Reilly v. National Rail & Tramway Appliances Ltd [1966] 1 All E.R. 499 14.50, 14.52
Oropesa, The [1943] P. 32 12.11, 12.114
O'Rourke v. Schout [1976] 1 S.C.R. 57 1.03
Osborn v. Gillett (1873) L.R. 8 Ex. 88 2.36
Osborn v. Thomas Boulter & Son [1930] 2 K.B. 226 18.32, 18.39, 18.99
Osborn v. Veitch (1858) 1 F. & F. 317 6.15
Osborne v. Chocqueel [1896] 2 Q.B. 109 11.03
Osborne v. Milman (1886) 17 Q.B.D. 514 6.19
Otto v. Bolton & Norris [1936] 2 K.B. 46 12.53
Overseas Tankship (U.K.) Ltd—*see* Wagon Mound (Nos. 1 and 2)
Owen v. Knight (1837) 4 Bing.N.C. 54 7.33
Owners of Ship Philippine Admiral v. Wallem Shipping (Hong Kong) Ltd [1979] 1 All E.R. 78 2.13
Oxley v. Watts (1785) 1 T.R. 12 5.09
Oxley v. Wilkes [1898] 2 Q.B. 56 18.116

P

Pacific Associates Inc. v. Baxter [1989] 2 All E.R. 159 12.10, 12.37, 12.38, 12.39
Padbury v. Halliday & Greenwood Ltd (1912) 28 T.L.R. 4.94
Pain v. Rochester (1599) Cro. Eliz. 871 22.06
Paine v. Colne Valley Electrical Supply Co. [1938] 4 All E.R. 503 14.08
Paine & Co. Ltd v. St. Neots Gas Co. [1939] 3 All E.R. 812 8.49, 8.72, 8.74
Painter v. Liverpool Gas Light Co. (1836) 3 Ad. & El. 433 6.22
Pannett v. P. MacGuinness & Co. Ltd [1972] 2 Q.B. 599 14.44
Panorama Developments (Guildford) Ltd v. Fidelis Furnishing Fabrics Ltd [1971] 2 Q.B. 711 3.07
Pantam v. Isham (1701) 3 Lev. 54 10.02
Panton v. Williams (1841) 2 Q.B. 161 22.06
Paris v. Stepney Borough Council [1951] A.C. 367 **12.19**, 12.74, 12.80, 12.81, 14.51, 14.53
Parker v. British Airways Board [1982] 1 All E.R. 834 7.06, **7.07, 7.35**
Parker, v. London & North-Eastern Railway (1945) 175 L.T. 137 10.07
Parker v. Miller (1926) 42 T.L.R. 408 3.13, 12.88
Parker-Knoll Ltd v. Knoll International Ltd [1962] R.P.C. 265 21.70
Parkins v. Scott (1862) 1 H. & C. 153 18.07
Parrish v. Judd [1960] 3 All E.R. 33 8.82
Parry v. Cleaver [1970] A.C. 1 15.08, 15.36, 15.37
Parry v. Smith (1879) 4 C.P.D. 325 14.04
Parsons v. B.N.M. Laboratories Ltd [1964] 1 Q.B. 65 15.24
Parton v. Hill (1864) 10 L.T. 414 22.19
Parukey v. Parukey [1945] 4 D.L.R. 81 6.08
Pasley v. Freeman (1789) 3 T.R. 51 17.16
Pass of Ballater, The [1942] P. 112 16.21
Paterson Zochonis & Co. Ltd v. Merfahken Packaging Ltd [1986] 3 All E.R. 520 12.53
Patrick v. Colerich (1838) 3 M. & W. 483 5.33
Paul v. Summerhayes (1878) 4 Q.B.D. 9 5.12
Paxhaven Holdings Ltd v. Attorney-General [1974] 2 N.Z.L.R. 185 8.05
Payne v. Harrison [1961] 2 Q.B. 403 12.83
Payton v. Fraser [1981] R.T.R. 496 5.39
Peabody Donation Fund (Governors) v. Sir Lindsay Parkinson & Co. Ltd [1985] A.C. 210 12.06, 12.10, 12.44, 12.62
Peachdart Ltd, re [1983] 3 All E.R. 204 7.26
Pearce v. Round Oak Steel Works Ltd [1969] 3 All E.R. 680 14.51
Pearce v. Secretary of State for Defence [1988] 2 All E.R. 348 2.07
Pearson v. Coleman Bros. [1948] 3 K.B. 359 14.22
Perason v. Lambeth Borough Council [1950] 2 K.B. 353 14.17
Pearson & Son Ltd v. Dublin Corporation [1907] A.C. 351 17.13, 17.14, 17.15
Pedro v. Diss [1981] 2 All E.R. 59 6.14, 6.45
Peck v. Gurney (1873) L.R. 6 H.L. 377 17.12
Peerless Baker Ltd v. Watts [1955] N.Z.L.R. 339 18.84
Penfold v. Westcote (1806) 2 B. & P. (N.R.) 335 18.07
Penfold's Wines v. Elliott (1946) 74 C.L.R. 204 7.09
Penman v. Saint John Toyota Ltd (1972) 30 D.L.R. (3d) 86 15.16
Pennington v. Norris (1956) 96 C.L.R. 10 13.41
Penny v. Wimbledon U.D.C. [1899] 2 Q.B. 72 3.37, 3.38
Penruddock's Case (1598) 5 Co.Rep. 100b 8.61
Performance Cars v. Willoughby [1962] 1 Q.B. 33 4.02
Perera v. Peiris [1949] A.C. 1 18.71, 18.88, **18.89**, 18.97
Perera v. Vandiyar [1953] 1 W.L.R. 672 5.05
Performance Cars Ltd v. Abraham [1962] 1 Q.B. 33 12.100

Performing Right Society Ltd v. Ciryl Theatrical Syndicate Ltd [1928] 1 K.B. 1 3.06
Perkowski v. Wellington Corporation [1959] A.C. 53 14.16, 14.17
Perl (P.) (Exporters) Ltd v. Camden London Borough [1984] 1 Q.B. 342 12.53, 12.61, 12.119
Perry v. Clissold [1907] A.C. 73 5.19
Perry v. Kendricks Transport Ltd [1956] 1 W.L.R. 85 9.14, **9.33**, 9.44, 10.08
Perry v. Sidney Phillips & Son [1982] 3 All E.R. 705 12.113, 15.17, 17.18
Perry v. Truefitt (1842) 6 Beav. 66 21.65
Perry (Howard E.) Ltd v. British Railways Board [1980] 2 All E.R. 579 7.02, 7.17, **7.19**, 7.25, 7.46
Peruvian Guano Co. v. Dreyfus Bros. [1892] A.C. 166 7.52
Peters v. Prince of Wales Theatre Co. Ltd [1943] K.B. 73 9.22, **9.39**, 13.05
Petterson v. Royal Oak Hotel Ltd [1948] N.Z.L.R. 136 3.22
Pfizer Corporation v. Minister of Health [1965] A.C. 512 3.04
Philadelphia, The [1917] P. 101 15.13
Philco Radio v. Spurling [1949] 2 All E.R. 882 12.114
Phillips v. Britannia Hygienic Laundry [1923] 1 K.B. 539 9.20, 16.02, 16.07
Phillips v. Eyre (1870) L.R. 6 Q.B. 1 2.02
Phillips v. Ford Motor Company of Canada Ltd [1971] 2 O.R. 637 12.93
Phillips v. Homfray (1871) L.R. 6 Ch.App. 770 5.21
Phillips v. Homfray (1883) 24 Ch.D. 439 2.36
Phillips v. London & South Western Railway (1879) 5 C.P.D. 280 15.24, 15.59
Phillips v. Soloway (1957) 6 D.L.R. (2d) 570 2.32, 6.06
Phillips v. William Whiteley Ltd [1938] 1 All E.R. 566 12.78
Philpott v. Kelley [1935] 3 All E.R. 106 7.26
Phipps v. Rochester Corporation [1955] 1 Q.B. 450 14.31
Photo Productions Ltd v. Securicor Transport Ltd [1980] A.C. 827 3.27, 13.06, 13.10
Pickard v. Smith (1861) 10 C.B. N.S. 470 3.38
Pickering v. Rudd (1815) 4 Camp. 219 5.05, 5.23, 5.26
Pickett v. British Rail Engineering Ltd [1980] A.C. 136 2.38, 15.23, 15.29, 15.38, 15.45
Pickles v. National Coal Board [1968] 2 All E.R. 598 15.20
Pidduck v. Eastern Scottish Omnibuses Ltd [1989] 2 All E.R. 261 15.60
Piggot v. Eastern Counties Railway (1864) 3 C.B. 229 10.07
Pigney v. Pointers Transport Services [1957] 2 All E.R. 807 12.119
Pinchon's Case (1611) 9 Rep. 86b 2.36
Pirelli General Cable Works Ltd v. Oscar Faber & Partners [1983] 1 All E.R. 85 15.19, 18.103
Pitcher v. Martin (1937) 53 T.L.R. 903 11.04, 11.20
Pitman v. Southern Electricity Board [1978] 3 All E.R. 901 12.58
Plato Films Ltd v. Speidel [1961] 1 All E.R. 876 18.111
Playa Larga (Cargo Owners) v. I Congresso del Partido; Mable Islands (Cargo Owners) v. same [1981] 2 All E.R. 1064 2.13, 7.16, 7.37
Playa Larga and Marble Islands, The; Cubazucar v. Industria Azucarea Nacional S.A. (IANSA) [1983] 2 Lloyd's Rep. 171 7.16, 7.19
Plessey Co. plc v. Wilson [1982] I.R.L.R. 199 21.01
Plumb v. Cobden Four Mills [1914] A.C. 62 3.10, 3.25
Plumber v. P.B. Wilkins & Sons Ltd [1981] 1 All E.R. 91 15.24
Plummer v. Charman [1962] 3 All E.R. 823 18.98
Poland v. Parr & Sons [1927] 1 K.B. 236 3.14, 3.19
Polemis, Re [1921] 3 K.B. 560 12.111, 12.118, 12.121, 13.28
Polhill v. Walter (1832) 3 B. & Ad. 114 17.09
Pollen v. Brewer (1859) 7 C.B.N.S. 371 5.48
Polly Peck (Holdings) plc v. Trelford [1986] 2 All E.R. 84 18.58, 18.59
Pontadarwe R.D.C. v. Moore-Gwyn [1929] 1 Ch. 656 9.20, 9.21

Ponting v. Noakes [1894] 2 Q.B. 281 9.16, 9.20, **9.35**, 9.36–7
Poole v. Allen [1950] 1 All E.R. 476 2.21
Porky Packers Ltd v. Town of The Pas (1976) 65 D.L.R. (3d) 1 12.36
Porter v. Freudenberg [1915] 1 K.B. 857 2.08
Porter (J.B.) Co. Ltd v. Bell [1955] 1 D.L.R. 62 9.01, 9.28, 9.42
Portland Management Ltd v. Harte [1977] Q.B. 306 5.13
Porto Alexandre [1920] P. 30 2.13
Poslun v. Toronto Stock Exchange & Gardiner (1965) 46 D.L.R. (2d) 210 21.08, 21.39, 21.47, **21.48**
Post Office v. Norwich Union Fire Insurance Society [1967] 2 Q.B. 363 1.17
Potter v. Baker (1846) 3 C.B. 831 21.61
Poulton v. London & South-Western Railway (1867) L.R. 2 Q.B. 534 2.19
Poupard v. Lafortune [1973] S.C.R. 175 12.65
Povey v. Governors of Rysdale School [1970] 1 All E.R. 841 15.30
Powell v. Fall (1880) 5 Q.B.D. 597 9.13, 10.07
Powell v. Gelston [1916] 2 K.B. 615 18.29, 18.32
Prager v. Times Newspapers Ltd [1988] 1 All E.R. 300 18.57, 18.60
Pratt v. British Medical Association [1919] 1 K.B. 244 21.06, 21.49
Pratt v. Patrick [1924] 1 K.B. 488 3.13
Pretty v. Bickmore (1873) L.R. 8 C.P. 401 8.44
Price v. Helyer (1828) 4 Bing. 597 7.19
Pride of Derby and Derbyshire Angling Association v. British Celanese Ltd [1952] 1 All E.R. 1226 8.14, 9.40
Pridham v. Hemel Hempstead Corporation (1970) 69 L.G.R. 523 12.58
Priestley v. Fowler (1837) 3 M. & W. 1 14.46
Priestman v. Colangelo [1959] S.C.R. 615 12.65
Pritchard v. Briggs [1978] 2 W.L.R. 317 21.34
Pritchard v. J.H. Cobden Ltd [1987] 1 All E.R. 300 15.24, 15.27, **15.33**
Prosser (A.) & Sons Ltd v. Levy [1955] 3 All E.R. 577 9.39, 9.44
Pugliese v. National Capital Commission (1978) 79 D.L.R. (3d) 592; (1979) 97 D.L.R. (3d) 631 8.11, 8.18
Pullman v. Hill & Co. [1891] 1 Q.B. 524 18.29, 18.32, 18.95, 18.99
Purcell v. Sowler (1887) 2 C.P.D. 215 18.90
Purdy v. Woznesenski [1937] 2 W.W.R. 116 6.17
Pursell v. Horne (1838) 8 D. & El. 602 6.11

Q

Qualcast (Wolverhampton) Ltd v. Haynes [1959] A.C. 743 H.L.; *reversing* [1958] 1 W.L.R. 225 C.A. 14.51, 14.53
Quarman v. Burnett (1840) 6 M. & W. 499 9.04
Quartz Hill Consolidated Gold Mining Co. v. Beall (1882) 20 Ch.D. 501 18.118
Quartz Hill Gold Mining Co. v. Eyre (1883) 11 Q.B.D. 647 2.17, 22.14, 22.15, 22.17
Queen, The v. Jennings (1966) 57 D.L.R. (2d) 644 15.35, 15.42
Quinn v. Cameron & Robertson Ltd [1958] A.C. 9 16.15
Quinn v. Leathem [1901] A.C. 495 12.115, 21.04, 21.06, 21.11, 21.12, 21.30
Quinn v. Scott [1965] 1 W.L.R. 1004 8.85, 12.16

R

R. v. Adams (1884) 22 Q.B.D. 66 18.29, 18.41
R. v. Bishop [1975] Q.B. 274 18.11
R. v. Blamires Transport Services Ltd [1964] 1 Q.B. 278 21.08
R. v. Bottrill ex p. Kuechenmeister [1947] K.B. 41
R. v. Bradshaw (1874) 14 Cox C.C. 83 6.41
R. v. Buckinsky [1983] 1 S.C.R. 481 2.02

R. v. Burns (1886) 16 Cox C.C. 335 18.41
R. v. Churchill (No. 2) [1967] 2 A.C. 226 21.34
R. v. Clarke [1949] 2 All E.R. 448 6.31
R. v. Commissioners of Sewers for Essex (1885) 14 Q.B.D. 561 9.46
R. v. Coney (1882) 8 Q.B.D. 534 6.39, 6.41
R. v. Cotesworth (1705) 6 Mod. 172 6.11
R. v. Criminal Injuries Compensation Board ex p. Ince [1973] 3 All E.R. 808 12.122
R. v. Criminal Injuries Compensation Board ex p. Warner [1986] 2 All E.R. 478 1.08
R. v. Cross (1812) 3 Camp. 24 8.50
R. v. Deverell (1889) 86 L.T. Jo. 300 18.41
R. v. Donovan [1934] K.B. 458 6.39
R. v. Duffy [1967] 1 Q.B. 63 6.27
R. v. Fennell [1971] 1 Q.B. 428 6.27, 6.28
R. v. Grays Inn (1780) 1 Doug. K.B. 353 18.82
R. v. Holbrook (1878) 4 Q.B.D. 42 18.41
R. v. Howell [1982] Q.B. 417 6.47
R. v. Hull Prison Board of Visitors ex p. St. Germain [1979] Q.B. 425 6.19
R. v. Isitt [1978] R.T.R. 211 2.33
R. v. Jackson [1891] 1 Q.B. 671 6.31
R. v. James (1844) 1 C. & K. 530 6.15
R. v. Jones [1978] 3 All E.R. 1098 6.45
R. v. Labouchere (1884) 12 Q.B.D. 320 18.41
R. v. McDonnell (1966) 50 Cr.App.R. 5 21.08
R. v. Miller [1954] 2 Q.B. 282 6.31
R. v. Moore (1832) 3 B. & A. 184 12.114
R. v. Newport JJ. [1929] 2 K.B. 416 6.29
R. v. O'Brien [1974] 3 All E.R. 663 6.31
R. v. Pease (1832) 4 B. & Ad. 30 8.55
R. v. Pratt (1855) 4 E. & B. 860 5.12
R. v. Richardson and Adams [1948] S.C.R. 57 2.02
R. v. Risk [1937] 2 K.B. 375 18.90
R. v. Sadler [1970] 1 W.L.R. 416 6.20, 6.43
R. v. Spurge [1961] 2 Q.B. 205 2.33
R. v. Steele [1977] Crim.L.R. 290 6.31
R. v. Wicks [1936] 1 All E.R. 384 18.41
R. v. Williams [1923] 1 K.B. 340 6.38
R. v. Woodfall (1774) Lofft. 776 18.05
R.B. Policies at Lloyd's v. Butler [1950] 1 K.B. 76 7.40, 18.103
R.C.A. Corporation v. Pollard [1982] 3 All E.R. 771 16.07
Racine v. C.J.R.C. Radio Capitale Ltee (1978) 80 D.L.R. (3d) 441 19.01
Radford v. de Frobeville [1978] 1 All E.R. 33 12.113
Radley v. London & North Western Railway Co. (1876) 1 App.Cas. 754 13.32
Radstock Co-operative & Industrial Society Ltd v. Norton-Radstock U.D.C. [1968] Ch. 605 8.08
Rainham Chemical Works Ltd v. Belvedere Fish Guano Co. Ltd [1921] 2 A.C. 465 3.06, 9.13, 9.18, 9.20, 9.28, 14.04
Raleigh v. Goschen [1898] 1 Ch. 73 2.02
Ramburram v. Gurracharam [1970] 1 All E.R. 749 3.13
Randall v. Tarrant [1955] 1 W.L.R. 255 5.07
Randolph v. Tuck [1962] 1 Q.B. 175 4.11
Rands v. McNeil [1955] 1 Q.B. 253 11.22
Ratcliffe v. Evans [1892] 2 Q.B. 524 15.09, 18.43, 21.54, 21.55, 21.59, 21.64
Ravenga v. Mackintosh (1824) 2 B. & C. 693 22.08
Rayson v. South London Tramways Co. [1893] 2 Q.B. 304 22.14, 22.15
Razzell v. Snowball [1954] 1 W.L.R. 1382 3.04

Read v. Coker (1853) 13 C.B. 349 6.15
Read v. Edwards (1864) 17 C.B.N.S. 252 5.12
Read v. J. Lyons & Co. Ltd [1947] A.C. 156 1.31, 5.11, 8.06, 8.24, 8.32, 9.09, **9.12–13**, 9.14, 9.15, **9.16–18**, 9.19, 9.20, 9.21, 9.22, 9.24, 9.28, 9.31, 9.32, 9.33, 10.08, 12.78, 14.14
Read v. Friendly Society of Operative Stonemasons [1902] 2 K.B. 88 H.C.; [1902] 2 K.B. 732 C.A. 21.39, 21.47
Ready Mixed Concrete Ltd v. Minister of Pensions and National Insurance [1968] 2 Q.B. 497 3.05
Ready Mixed Concrete Ltd v. Yorkshire Traffic Area Licensing Authority [1970] 2 Q.B. 397 3.05
Reddaway v. Banham [1896] A.C. 199 21.65
Redland Bricks Ltd v. Morris [1969] 2 All E.R. 576 8.71
Redway v. McAndrew (1873) L.R. 9 Q.B. 70 22.05
Reed v. Nutt (1890) 24 Q.B.D. 669 6.13
Reedie v. London & N.W. Railway (1849) 4 Ex. 244 3.01
Rees v. Sinclair [1974] N.Z.L.R. 180 22.22
Reibl v. Hughes (1980) 114 D.L.R. (3d) 1; [1980] 2 S.C.R. 880 6.36, 13.17
Reichel v. Magrath (1899) 14 App.Cas. 664 22.18
Reid v. Croydon Corporation [1938] 4 All E.R. 631 16.09
Reid v. Fairbanks (1853) 13 C.B.N.S. 692 7.52
Reid v. Rush & Tompkins Group plc [1989] 3 All E.R. 228 12.42, 12.52, 12.70, 14.59
Rejnoldson v. Simmons (1982) 14 SasK.R. 257 11.05
Remorquage à Hélices (SA de) v. Bennetts [1911] 1 K.B. 243 12.46
Revesz v. Commonwealth [1951] S.R. (N.S.W.) 63 12.66
Rex v. Ball (1822) 1 L.J.K.B. (O.S.) 52 8.08
Rich v. Basterfield (1847) 4 C.B. 783 8.42
Rich v. L.C.C. [1953] 2 All E.R. 376 12.78
Richard v. Alberta Securities Commission (1988) 42 D.L.R. (4th) 300 12.43
Richards v. Easto (1846) 15 M. & W. 251 10.05
Richards v. Naum [1967] 1 Q.B. 620 18.85
Richards v. Redpath Brown & Co. Ltd [1944] A.C. 62 15.11
Richardson v. Atkinson (1723) 1 Stra. 576 7.26
Richardson v. West Lindsey D.C. [1990] 1 All E.R. 286 12.06, 12.10, 12.63
Riches v. D.P.P. [1973] 2 All E.R. 935 22.08, 22.12, 22.22
Riches v. News Group Newspapers Ltd [1985] 2 All E.R. 845 18.110
Richley v. Faull [1965] 3 All E.R. 109 12.90
Richman v. McMurtry (1983) 147 D.L.R. (3d) 748 22.26
Rickards v. Lothian [1913] A.C. 263 9.22, 9.25, 9.31, 9.39, **9.40**, **9.44**
Rickett v. Metropolitan Railway (1867) L.R. 2 H.L. 175 8.79
Ricketts v. Thomas Tilling Ltd [1915] 1 K.B. 644 3.25
Rickless v. United Artists [1987] 1 All E.R. 679 16.08
Riddick v. Thames Board Mills Ltd [1977] 3 All E.R. 677 3.02, **18.31**, 18.97, 18.99
Riding v. Smith (1876) 1 Ex.D. 91 21.54, 21.59
Rigby v. Chief Constable of Northamptonshire [1985] 2 All E.R. 985 5.31, 6.35, 9.10, 9.13, **9.50**
Rigby v. Hewitt (1850) 5 Ex. 240 12.116
Rimmer v. Liverpool City Council [1984] Q.B. 1 **12.45**, 14.08
Risk Allah Bey v. Whiteside (1868) 18 L.T. 615 18.90
River Wear Commissioners v. Adamson (1877) 2 App.Cas. 743 6.38
Rivers v. Cutting [1982] 3 All E.R. 69 3.34, 3.36
Riverstone Meat Co. Pty Ltd v. Lancashire Shipping Co. Ltd [1961] A.C. 807 3.34, 3.36
Rivtow Marine Ltd v. Washington Iron Works [1974] S.C.R. 1189 12.45
Robbins v. C.B.C. (1958) 12 D.L.R. (2d) 35 19.01
Roberts v. J. Hampson & Co. [1989] 2 All E.R. 504 12.37, 12.38

Roberts v. Ramsbottom [1980] 1 All E.R. 7 1.07, 2.33, 12.78
Roberts v. Roberts (1864) 5 B. & S. 384 18.43
Roberts v. Rose (1865) L.R. 1 Ex. 82 8.62
Roberts v. Smith (1857) 26 L.J. Ex. 319 14.46
Roberts v. Taylor (1845) 1 C.B. 117 5.37
Roberts v. Wyatt (1810) 2 Taunt, 268 7.33
Robertson v. LeStrange [1985] 1 All E.R. 950 15.59
Robertson v. Ridley [1989] 2 All E.R. 474 2.21
Robinson v. Balmain New Ferry Co. Ltd [1910] A.C. 295 6.19
Robinson v. Kilvert (1889) 41 Ch.D. 88 8.16
Robinson v. Ward (1958) 108 L.J. 491 18.53
Robson v. Hallett [1967] 2 Q.B. 939 5.39
Rodgers v. Ministry of Transport [1952] 1 T.L.R. 625 5.07
Rodgers (Joseph) & Son Ltd v. W.N. Rodgers & Co. (1925) 41 R.P.C. 277 21.66, 21.70
Rodrigue v. Penner (1970) 74 W.W.R. 96 13.45
Roe v. Minister of Health [1954] 2 Q.B. 66 3.04, 12.75, 12.76, 12.78, 12.85, 12.89, 12.91, 12.121
Roe d. Haldane v. Harvey (1769) 4 Burr. 2484 5.19
Roff v. British & French Chemical Manufacturing Co. [1918] 2 K.B. 677 18.32
Rogers v. Kenny (1846) 9 Q.B. 594 7.33
Rogers v. Secretary of State for Home Department [1973] A.C. 388 18.84
Rogers Sons v. Lambert & Co. [1891] 1 Q.B. 318 7.24
Roles v. Nathan [1963] 2 All E.R. 908 14.30, 14.33, 14.35
Roman Corporation Ltd v. Hudsons Bay Oil & Gas Co. Ltd [1973] S.C.R. 820 21.24
Romegialli v. Marceau [1964] 1 O.R. 407 22.04, 22.05
Rondel v. Worsley [1969] 1 A.C. 191 12.08, 12.39, 12.68
Rondos v. Wawrin (1968) 68 D.L.R. (2d) 658 13.45
Ronex Properties Ltd v. John Laing Construction Ltd [1982] 3 All E.R. 961 4.09
Rookes v. Barnard [1964] A.C. 1129 H.L. 1.08, 5.51, 6.13, 15.05, 15.06, 17.19, 18.109, 21.01, 21.10, **21.16–22**, 21.33, 21.25, 21.27, 21.28, 21.39, 21.44, 21.45
Rootes v. Shelton [1968] A.L.R. 33 13.07
Rose v. Buckett [1901] 2 K.B. 449 2.34
Rose v. Ford [1937] A.C. 826 15.40
Rose v. Groves (1843) 5 Man. & Gr. 613 8.75
Rose v. Miles (1815) 4 M. & S. 101 8.76
Rose v. Plenty [1976] 1 All E.R. 97 3.26
Rosenthal v. Alderton [1946] K.B. 374 7.40, 7.46, 7.49
Rosewall v. Prior (1701) 12 Mod. 635 8.36
Ross v. Associated Portland Cement Manufacturers Ltd [1964] 2 All E.R. 452 14.51, 16.16, 16.20, 16.21
Ross v. Caunters [1980] Ch. 297 12.37, **12.43**
Rouse v. Gravelworks Ltd [1940] 1 K.B. 499 9.28
Rouse v. Port of London Authority [1953] 2 Lloyd's Rep. 179 15.24
Rouse v. Squires [1973] Q.B. 889 4.02, 4.11, 12.119, 12.120
Rowling v. Takaro Properties Ltd [1988] 1 All E.R. 163 12.07, 12.66
Roy v. Prior [1970] 2 All E.R. 729 22.22
Royal Aquarium & Summer & Winter Garden Society Ltd v. Parkinson [1892] 1 Q.B. 431 18.80, 18.88, 18.101, 22,22
Royal Baking Powder Co. v. Wright, Crossley & Co. (1900) 18 R.P.C. 95 21.54
Royster v. Cavey [1947] K.B. 204 2.04
Rumsay v. Rawson (1669) 1 Vent. 18 11.35
Rusholme v. Polsue & Alfieri Ltd [1906] 1 Ch. 234; [1907] A.C. 121 8.13
Rushton v. National Coal Board [1953] 1 Q.B. 495 15.08

Rushton v. Turner Bros. Asbestos Co. [1959] 3 All E.R. 517 13.47, 16.20
Rushworth v. Taylor (1842) 2 Q.B. 600 7.20
Russell v. McCabe [1962] N.Z.L.R. 392 12.31
Russell v. Duke of Norfolk (1949) 65 T.L.R. 225 18.56
Rutherford v. Poole [1953] V.L.R. 130 21.39
Ryads v. Leader (1866) L.R. 1 Ex. 296 18.88
Ryan v. Clark (1849) 12 Q.B. 65 5.37
Ryan v. Fildes [1938] 3 All E.R. 517 6.29
Rylands v. Fletcher (1866) L.R. 1 Ex. 265; (1868) L.R. 3 H.L. 330 1.30, 1.31, 3.37, 5.01, 5.06, 6.02, **8.07**, 8.37, **Ch.9** *passim*, 10.01, **10.07–15**, 11.03, 11.04, 11.09, 11.23, 13.03, 13.05

S

S. v. Distillers Co. (Biochemicals) Ltd [1970] 1 W.L.R. 114 15.22, 15.30, 15.46
S. v. S. (or McC.); W. v. Official Solicitor [1972] A.C. 24 6.01, 6.12, 6.23
S. & K. Holdings Ltd v. Throgmorton [1972] 2 All E.R. 497 18.14, 18.59
S.C.M. Ltd v. Whittall Ltd [1971] 1 Q.B. 337 12.43
Sachs v. Miklos [1948] 2 K.B. 23 7.46, 7.50
Sadgrove v. Hole [1901] 2 K.B. 1 18.33
Said v. Butt [1920] 3 K.B. 497 21.08, 21.39
Saif Ali v. Sydney Mitchell & Co. [1980] A.C. 198 12.37, 12.68, 12.78, 22.22
St. Anne's Well Brewery Co. v. Roberts (1928) 44 T.L.R. 703 8.39, 8.40, 9.09, 9.28
St. Helens Colliery Co. Ltd v. Hewitson [1924] A.C. 59 3.17
St. Helens Smelting Co. v. Tipping (1865) 11 H.L.C. 642 1.31, 8.11, 8.12, **8.13**, 8.48
Salford City Council v. McNally [1976] A.C. 376 8.03, 8.05
Salmon v. Isaac (1869) 20 L.T. 895 18.90
Salmon v. Seafarer Restaurants Ltd [1983] 3 All E.R. 729 12.32, 14.22
Salsbury v. Woodland [1970] 1 Q.B. 324 3.35, 3.37, 3.38
Saltman Engineering Co. Ltd v. Campbell Engineering Co. Ltd [1963] 3 All E.R. 413 20.04
Saltpetre Case (1606) 12 Rep. 12 2.08
Salvanyagam v. University of West Indies [1983] 1 All E.R. 824 15.11
Salvin v. North Brancepeth Coal Co. (1873) 9 Ch.App. 705 8.15, 8.30
Salsbury v. Woodland [1970] 1 Q.B. 324 9.09
Sammy-Joe v. G.P.O. Mount Pleasant Office [1967] 1 W.L.R. 270 22.24
Sampson v. Hodson-Pressinger [1981] 3 All E.R. 710 8.39
Samson v. Aitchison [1912] A.C. 844 3.13
Samuel, re [1945] Ch. 408 7.23, **7.28**
Sanders v. Edwards [1987] 2 All E.R. 651 13.46
San Onofre, The [1922] P. 243 12.114
Sans Pareil, The [1900] P. 267 13.33
Santos v. Santos [1972] 2 All E.R. 246 11.19
Sarch v. Blackburn (1830) 4 C. & P. 297 11.03
Saskatchewan Wheat Pool v. Government of Canada (1983) 143 D.L.R. (3d) 9 1.31, 16.10, **16.14**
Saunders v. Anglia Building Society; Gallie v. Lee [1971] A.C. 1004 1.07
Saunders v. Edwards [1987] 2 All E.R. 651 17.01
Saunders v. Smith (1838) 2 Jur. 491 5.20
Savile v. Roberts (1698) 1 Ld. Raym. 374; Carth. 416; 1 Salk. 13; 3 Salk. 16; 5 Mod.Rep. 344; 12 Mod.Rep. 208; Holt K.B. 150, 153 22.13
Savory v. Holland & Hannen and Cubitts (Southern) Ltd [1964] 1 W.L.R. 1158; [1964] 3 All E.R. 18 3.05, 14.19
Sayers v. Harlow U.D.C. [1958] 2 All E.R. 342 6.18, 12.114
Scala Ballroom v. Ratcliffe [1958] 3 All E.R. 220 21.12

Scarff v. Wilson (1987) 39 C.C.L.T. 20 15.46
Scarsbrook v. Mason [1961] 3 All E.R. 767 3.13
Scavage v. Tatcham (1601) Cro. Eliz. 829 6.19
Schenck v. The Queen (1982) 20 C.C.L.T. 128 8.18
Schering Chemicals Ltd v. Falkman Ltd [1981] 2 All E.R. 321 19.01, 20.04, 20.09
Schiffman v. Order of St. John [1936] 1 All E.R. 517 9.20, 9.32
Schill v. Weimer (1980) 5 Sask.R. 112 13.45
Schneider v. Eisovitch [1960] 2 Q.B. 430 12.25
School Division of Assiniboine South No. 3 v. Hoffer (1971) 16 D.L.R. (3d) 703; [1973] 6 W.W.R. 765 2.30, 12.79
Schwan, The [1892] P. 419 13.02, 13.04
Science Research Council v. Nasse [1979] 3 All E.R. 673 19.05, 20.02
SCM (UK) Ltd v. W.J. Whittal & Sons Ltd [1970] 3 All E.R. 245 12.43, 12.46
Scott v. Green & Sons [1969] 1 W.L.R. 301 8.81
Scott v. London & St. Katherine Docks Co. (1865) 3 H. & C. 596 12.86, **12.87**
Scott v. Sampson (1882) 8 Q.B.D. 491 18.07, 18.111
Scott v. Shepherd (1773) 2 W.Bl. 892 5.10, 6.01, 6.02, 6.35, 12.114
Scott v. Stanfield (1868) L.R. 7 Ex. 220 18.76
Scott v. Tuff-Kots (Australia) Pty Ltd [1975] 1 N.S.W. L.R. 537 21.73
Scott v. Wakem (1862) 3 F. & F. 328 6.35
Scruttons Ltd v. Midland Silicones Ltd [1962] A.C. 446 12.38, 13.10
Seager v. Copydex Ltd [1967] 2 All E.R. 415 20.04
Seager v. Copydex Ltd (No. 2) [1969] 2 All E.R. 718 20.15
Seaman v. Nethercliff (1876) 2 C.P.D. 53 18.79
Searle v. Wallbank [1947] A.C. 341 **11.05**, 11.08, 11.09, 11.34, 12.53
Sedleigh-Denfield v. O'Callaghan [1940] A.C. 880 1.31, 8.05, 8.06, 8.11, 8.17, 8.24, 8.37, **8.38–40**, 8.44, 9.09, 9.25, 9.47
Semayne's Case (1604) 5 Co.Rep. 91a 5.44, 5.45
Semtex Ltd v. Gladstone [1954] 1 W.L.R. 945 4.11
Seneca College Governors v. Bhadauria [1981] 2 S.C.R. 181 16.03, 16.09
Seward v. Vera Cruz (1884) 10 App.Cas. 59 15.54
Seyfert v. Burnaby Hospital Society (1986) 27 D.L.R. (4th) 96 12.105
Seymour v. Maddox (1851) 16 Q.B. 327 14.46
Shapiro v. LaMorta (1923) 40 T.L.R. 39, 201 21.54
Sharp v. Slues (1909) 25 T.L.R. 336 18.32
Sharpe v. Avery [1938] 4 All E.R. 85 12.35
Sharpe v. E.T. Sweeting & Sons Ltd [1963] 2 All E.R. 455 12.56, 14.07
Sharrod v. London & North-Western Railway (1849) 4 Ex. 580 6.02
Shaw Bros. (Hong Kong) Ltd v. Golden Harvest (H.K.) Ltd [1972] R.P.C. 559 21.69, 21.73, 21.76
Shaw Savill & Albion Co. Ltd v. Commonwealth (1940) 66 C.L.R. 344 12.66
Shelfer v. City of London Electric Lighting Co. [1895] 1 Ch. 287 5.17, 8.11, 8.17, **8.67**
Shell Mex & BP Ltd v. Manchester Garages Ltd [1971] 1 W.L.R. 612 5.41
Shelley v. Paddock [1979] Q.B. 120 12.118, 17.19
Sheppard v. Glossop Corporation [1921] 3 K.B. 132 12.54
Sheppard Publishing Co. v. Press Publishing Co. Ltd (1905) 10 O.L.R. 243 21.59
Sherman v. Folland [1950] 2 K.B. 43 12.111
Sherrin v. Hagerty [1953] O.W.N. 962 5.30
Shiffman v. Order of St. John [1936] 1 All E.R. 557 9.14
Shipcott v. Magford (1619) 1 Ld.Raym. 187 5.05
Shore v. Ministry of Works [1950] 2 All E.R. 228 2.21
Short v. J. & W. Henderson Ltd (1946) 62 T.L.R. 427 3.05

Sidaway v. Bethlem Royal Hospital Governors [1985] 1 All E.R. 543; [1985] A.C. 871 12.80, **13.17**
Sidis v. F.-R. Publishing Corporation (1940) 113 F. (2d) 806 19.05
Sidmay v. Bethlem Royal Hospital Governors [1985] 1 All E.R. 643 6.08, 6.36
Sigerseth v. Pedersen [1927] S.C.R. 342 12.75, 13.02
Sigurdson (Martin) v. British Columbia Electric Railway Co. Ltd [1953] A.C. 291 13.32, 13.38
Silkin v. Beaverbrook Newspapers Ltd [1958] 2 All E.R. 516 18.67
Silverman v. Imperial London Hotels Ltd (1927) 137 L.T. 57 14.24
Sim v. Heinz [1959] 1 All E.R. 547 19.06
Sim v. Stretch (1936) 52 T.L.R. 669 18.08, 18.17, 18.20
Simaan General Contracting Co. v. Pilkington Glass Ltd (No. 2) [1988] 1 All E.R. 791 12.47, **12.50**
Simmons v. Pizzey [1979] A.C. 37 11.19
Simmons v. Heath Laundry Ltd [1910] 1 K.B. 549 3.05
Simmons v. Lillystone (1853) 8 Ex. 431 7.26
Simms, re [1934] 1 Ch. 1 7.50
Simms v. Leigh Rugby Football Club Ltd [1969] 2 All E.R. 923 13.07, 14.28, 14.41
Simpson v. Norwest Holst Southern Ltd [1980] 2 All E.R. 471 15.20, 15.48
Simpson v. Savage (1856) 1 C.B.N.S. 347 8.33
Simpson v. Weber (1925) 41 T.L.R. 279 5.01, 5.05
Simpson & Co. v. Thompson (1877) 3 App.Cas. 270 12.46
Sims v. Foster Wheeler Ltd [1966] 2 All E.R. 313 4.12
Singleton Abbey (SS) v. SS Paludina [1927] A.C. 16 12.114
Sirros v. Moore [1974] 3 All E.R. 776; [1975] 1 Q.B. 118 6.22, 18.76, 22.24, 22.25, 22.26
Six Carpenters' Case (1610) 6 Coke Rep. 146a 5.09
Skelton v. Collins (1966) 115 C.L.R. 94 15.42
Skinner v. London, Brighton & South Coast Railway (1850) 5 Ex. 787 12.90
Slade & Stewart Ltd v. Haynes (1969) 5 D.L.R. (3d) 736 21.49
Slater v. Clay Cross Co. Ltd [1956] 2 Q.B. 264 13.11, 13.13, 14.16, 14.40, 14.41
Slater v. Swann (1730) 2 Stra. 872 7.04
Slater v. Worthington Cash Stores Ltd [1941] 1 K.B. 488 8.40, 9.47
Slattery v. Haley [1923] 3 D.L.R. 156 12.78
Slavatych v. Baker (1975) 55 D.L.R. (3d) 224 18.97
Slazengers Ltd v. Gibbs & Co. (1916) 33 T.L.R. 35 18.11
Sley v. Tillotson & Sons (1898) 14 T.L.R. 545 18.116
Slim v. Daily Telegraph Ltd [1968] 2 Q.B. 157 18.15, 18.68
Slingsby v. District Bank Ltd [1932] 1 K.B. 544 3.02
Smart v. McCarty (1980) 33 N.B.R. (2d) 27 3.22
Smeaton v. Ilford Corporation [1954] Ch. 450 8.54, 9.40
Smith v. Austin Lifts Ltd [1959] 1 All E.R. 81 14.52, 14.53
Smith v. Badenoch [1970] S.A.S.R. 9 10.11
Smith v. Baker [1891] A.C. 321 13.05, 13.06, 13.13, 14.48, 14.49
Smith v. Baverstock & Co. [1945] 1 All E.R. 531 16.21
Smith v. Cammell Laird & Co. Ltd [1940] A.C. 242 3.36, 16.21
Smith v. Enright (1893) 69 L.T. 724 7.42
Smith v. Eric S. Bush [1989] 2 All E.R. 514 12.35, **12.36**, 12.37, 12.38
Smith v. Giddy [1904] 2 K.B. 448 5.01
Smith v. Great Western Railway (1926) 135 L.T. 112 9.20
Smith v. Jenkins (1970) 119 C.L.R. 397 13.45, 13.47
Smith v. Kenrick (1849) 7 C.B. 515 9.01, 9.03, 9.24
Smith v. Land & Home Property Corporation (1884) 28 Ch.D. 7 17.04
Smith v. Leech Brain & Co. Ltd [1962] 2 Q.B. 405 12.118
Smith v. Littlewoods Organisation Ltd [1987] 1 All E.R. 710 12.06, 12.10, 12.11, **12.13**, 12.53, 12.61, 12.119

Smith v. London & South Western Railway Co. (1870) L.R. 6 C.P. 14 12.111
Smith v. Morrison [1974] 1 W.L.R. 659 21.34, 21.44
Smith v. National Coal Board [1967] 2 All E.R. 593 14.52
Smith v. National Meter Co. [1945] K.B. 543 18.88, 18.102
Smith v. Scott [1972] 3 All E.R. 645; [1973] Ch. 314 8.42, **8.43**, 9.20
Smith v. Selwyn [1914] 3 K.B. 98 6.13
Smith v. Stages and Darbington Insulation Co. [1989] 1 All E.R. 833 3.17, 3.18, 3.21, 3.31
Smith v. Stone (1647) Style 65 5.34
Smith v. Streatfield [1913] 3 K.B. 764 18.102
Smith v. Vange Scaffolding and Engineering Co. Ltd [1970] 1 All E.R. 249 14.19
Smith v. Widdicombe [1987] 2 W.W.R. 480 10.11
Smith, Kline & French Laboratories plc v. Long [1988] 3 All E.R. 887 17.17
Smith (W.H.) & Son v. Clinton (1908) 99 L.T. 841 4.13
Smithies v. National Association of Operative Plasterers [1909] 1 K.B. 310 21.47, 21.49
Snook v. Mannion [1982] R.T.R. 321 5.39, 5.46
Sobieski, The [1949] P. 213 12.35
Sochaki v. Sas [1947] 1 All E.R. 344 12.90
Solloway v. McLaughlin [1938] A.C. 247 7.52
Solomons v. Gertzenstein Ltd [1954] 2 Q.B. 243 16.04
Somasundaram v. M. Julius Melchior & Co. [1989] 1 All E.R. 129 12.69
Sorrell v. Paget [1950] 1 K.B. 252 11.02
Sorrell v. Smith [1925] A.C. 700 21.04, 21.05, 21.06, 21.11
South Hetton Coal Co. Ltd v. N.E. News Association Ltd [1894] 1 Q.B. 133 2.17, 18.63, 18.64
South Staffs. Water Co. v. Sharman [1896] 2 Q.B. 44 7.35
South Wales Miners' Federation v. Glamorgan Coal Co. [1903] 2 K.B. 545 H.C.; [1905] A.C. 239 C.A. 21.30, 21.36, 21.37, 21.47, 21.49
Southam v. Guthro [1948] 3 D.L.R. 178 21.09
Southam v. Smout [1964] 1 Q.B. 308 5.45
Southern v. How (1618) Cro.Jac. 408 3.01, 3.02
Southern Portland Cement Co. v. Cooper [1974] A.C. 623 14.44
Southport Corporation v. Esso Petroleum Co. Ltd [1953] 3 W.L.R. 773; [1952] 2 All E.R. 1204 H.C.; [1954] 2 Q.B. 182 C.A.; *Subnom.* Esso Petroleum Co. v. Southport Corporation [1956] A.C. 218 H.L. 3.41, 5.06, 8.83, 13.04, 13.20
Southwark London Borough Council v. Williams [1971] Ch. 734 5.04, 5.18, 5.32, 6.34
Sovmots Investments v. Secretary of State for the Environment [1976] 3 All E.R. 720 5.20
Spackman v. Foster (1883) 11 Q.B.D. 99 7.19–20
Spalding (A.G.) & Bros. v. A.W. Gamage Ltd (1915) 32 R.P.C. 273 21.65, 21.66
Spanton v. Laviolette (1978) 19 O.R. (2d) 21 11.05
Sparham-Souter v. Town & Country Developments Ltd [1976] 1 Q.B. 858 15.19
Sparrow v. Fairey Aviation Co. Ltd [1964] A.C. 1019 16.18
Spartan Steel & Alloys Ltd v. Martin & Co. (Contractors) Ltd [1973] 1 Q.B. 21 12.43, 12.47
Speake v. Hughes [1904] K.B. 138 12.114
Speed v. Thomas Swift & Co. [1943] K.B. 557 14.53
Speed Seal Products v. Paddington [1986] 1 All E.R. 91 22.20
Spencer (David) Ltd v. Field [1939] S.C.R. 36 12.86
Spicer v. Holt [1977] A.C. 987 6.20, 6.43
Spicer v. Smee [1946] 1 All E.R. 485 8.06, 8.37, 8.42, 9.09, 10.13
Spill v. Maule (1869) L.R. 4 Ex. 232 18.101

Spittle v. Bunney [1988] 3 All E.R. 1031 15.59, 15.60
Springfield Spinning Co. v. Riley (1868) L.R. 6 Eq. 551 16.08
Spurling Ltd v. Bradshaw [1956] 2 All E.R. 121 13.10
Stafford v. Conti Community Services Ltd [1981] 1 All E.R. 691 12.90
Stamatopoulos v. Hagemeyer (Canada) Ltd (1983) 22 C.C.L.T. 310 22.17
Stanley v. Powell [1891] 1 Q.B. 86 1.31, 6.07
Stansbie v. Troman [1948] 2 K.B. 48 12.13, 12.114
Stanton v. Ewart F. Youldon Ltd [1960] 1 All E.R. 429 15.58
Stapeley v. Annetts [1980] 1 W.L.R. 20 22.03
Stapley v. Gypsum Mines Ltd [1953] A.C. 663 12.38, 13.41
Star v. Rookesby (1711) 1 Salk. 335 5.01
Star Industries Co. Ltd v. Yap Kew Kar [1976] 2 F.S.R. 256 21.65
Star Valley Tavern v. Nield (1977) 71 D.L.R. (3d) 439 12.43
Staveley Iron & Chemical Co. Ltd v. Jones [1956] A.C. 627 3.02, 3.41, 14.46, 14.56
Steel-Maitland v. British Airways Board 1981 S.L.T. 110 5.27
Stehlke v. Camenzind [1980] 4 W.W.R. 464 12.79
Stein v. Gonzales (1985) 14 D.L.R. (4d) 263 8.78
Stennett v. Hancock Peters [1939] 2 All E.R. 578 12.02, 14.04, 14.08
Stephen v. Garret [1898] 1 Q.B. 677 22.18
Stephen (Harold) & Co. Ltd v. Post Office [1978] 1 All E.R. 939 2.07
Stephen v. Anglian Water Authority [1987] 3 All E.R. 379 12.10
Stephens v. Avery [1988] 2 All E.R. 477 20.04, **20.08**
Stephens v. Elwall (1815) 4 M. & W. 259 7.28
Stephens v. Myers (1830) 4 C. & P. 347 6.15
Stern v. Prentice Bros. [1919] 1 K.B. 394 9.28
Stetler v. Stross Management Ltd (1978) 4 A.L.R. (2d) 386 11.05
Stevens v. Brodribb Sawmilling Pty Ltd (1985) 160 C.L.R. 16 3.37
Stevens v. Woodward (1881) 6 Q.B.D. 318 3.10
Stevens Jordan & Harrison Ltd v. Macdonald & Evans (1951) 69 R.P.C. 10; [1952] 1 T.L.R. 101 C.A. 3.04, 20.04
Stockdale v. Hansard (1839) 9 A. & E. 1 18.74
Stodden v. Harvey (1608) Cro.Jac. 206 11.02
Stone v. Taffe [1974] 3 All E.R. 1016 14.22
Stoneman v. Lyons (1975) 133 C.L.R. 350 3.37, 9.09
Stott v. Sir William Arrol & Co. Ltd [1953] 2 Q.B. 92 14.47
Stott v. Gamble [1916] 2 K.B. 504 21.48
Stott v. West Yorkshire Road Car Co. Ltd [1971] 2 Q.B. 651 4.08
Strand Electric & Engineering Co. v. Brisford Entertainments Ltd [1952] 2 Q.B. 246 5.50, 7.49
Strapazon v. Oliphant Munson Collieries Ltd [1920] 2 W.W.R. 793 9.15
Stratford (J.T.) & Son Ltd v. Lindley [1965] A.C. 269 21.14, 21.39, 21.41, 21.43, 21.44, 21.53
Street v. N.B.C. (1981) 645 F. (2d) 1227 19.05
Stretton's Brewery Co. v. Derby Coporation [1894] 1 Ch. 431 8.54
Stroud v. Bradley [1952] 2 All E.R. 76 5.04
Stuart v. Bell [1891] 2 Q.B. 341 18.95
Stubbs v. Mazure [1920] A.C. 66 18.17
Stupple v. Royal Insurance Co. Ltd [1971] 1 Q.B. 50 12.83
Sturge v. Hackett [1962] 3 All E.R. 166 10.02, 10.09, 10.12
Sturges v. Bridgeman (1879) 11 Ch.D. 852 8.13, **8.48**, **8.51–2**, 8.53
Sullivan v. Earl of Caithness [1976] Q.B. 966 7.06
Sullivan v. Sullivan (1961) 79 W.N. (N.S.W.) 615 13.45
Sultan of Johore v. Abubakar Tunku [1952] A.C. 318 2.13
Summers v. Salford Corporation [1943] A.C. 283 12.114
Summers (John) & Sons Ltd v. Frost [1955] A.C. 740 1.31, 16.12, 16.13
Sun Life Assurance Co. of Canada Ltd v. W.H. Smith Ltd (1934) 150 L.T. 211 18.06, **18.36**

Superintendent of Family & Children Services and Dawson, re (1983) 145 D.L.R. (3d) 610 — 6.38
Surok v. Mannion [1982] R.T.R. 321 — 6.45
Sutcliffe v. Holmes [1947] K.B. 147 — 11.02
Sutcliffe v. Pressdram Ltd [1990] 1 All E.R. 269 — 18.106
Sutcliffe v. Thackrah [1974] A.C. 727 — 12.37, 12.66, 22.23
Sutherland v. Stopes [1925] A.C. 47 — 18.62
Sutherland Shire Council v. Heyman (1985) 60 A.L.R. 1 — 12.06
Swadling v. Cooper [1931] A.C. 1 — 13.32, **13.34**
Swaffen v. Mulcahy [1934] 1 K.B. 608 — 7.42
Swaine v. Great Northern Railway (1864) 4 De G. J. & Sm. 211 — 8.67
Swales v. Cox [1981] Q.B. 849 — 5.46, 6.45
Swami v. Lo (1980) 105 D.L.R. (3d) 451 — 12.119
Swan v. Salisbury Construction Co. Ltd [1966] 2 All E.R. 138 — 12.92, 12.93
Swift v. Jewsbury & Goddard (1874) L.R. 9 Q.B. 301 — 17.08
Swire v. Leach (1865) 18 C.B.N.S. 479 — 7.51
Swiss Bank Corporation v. Lloyds Bank Ltd [1979] 2 All E.R. 853 — 21.34, **21.50**
Swordheath Properties Ltd v. Tabel [1979] 1 All E.R. 240 — 5.01, 5.50
Sycamore v. Ley (1932) 147 L.T. 342 — 11.23
Syeds v. Hay (1791) 4 T.R. 260 — 7.24
Szalatnay-Stacho v. Fink [1947] K.B. 1 — 18.81

T

T. v. T.; re T. [1988] 1 All E.R. 613 — 6.04, 6.36
Taff Vale Railway Co. v. Amalgamated Society of Railway Servants [1901] A.C. 426 — 2.22, 3.02
Taff Vale Railway Co. v. Jenkins [1913] A.C. 1 — 15.60
Taggart v. Innis (1862) 12 U.C.C.P. 77 — 6.06
Tai Hing Cotton Mill v. Liu Ching Hing Bank Ltd [1986] 1 A.C. 801 — 1.11, **12.71**
Tai Te Whatu v. Scandlyn [1952] N.Z.L.R. 30 — 5.50
Takara Properties Ltd v. Rowling [1978] 2 N.Z.L.R. 314 — 21.53
Tallow v. Tailfeathers [1973] 6 W.W.R. 732 — 13.45, 13.46
Tamlin v. Hannaford [1950] 1 K.B. 18 — 2.02
Tan Chye Choo v. Chang Kew Moi [1970] 1 All E.R. 266 — 16.10
Tancred v. Allgood (1859) 4 H. & N. 438 — 7.36
Tappenden v. Artus [1964] 2 Q.B. 185 — 7.24
Tarleton v. M'Gawley (1793) 1 Peake 270 — 21.16
Tarrant v. Webb (1856) 25 L.J.C.P. 261 — 14.46
Tarry v. Ashton (1876) 1 Q.B.D. 314 — 3.37, 8.85
Tart v. Chitty [1933] 2 K.B. 453 — 13.33
Tataryn v. Co-operative Trust Co. of Canada (1975) 54 D.L.R. (3d) 154 — 12.89
Tate & Lyle Industries Ltd v. Greater London Council [1983] 1 All E.R. 1159 — 8.03, 8.39, **8.58**, 8.75
Taunton v. Costar (1797) 7 T.R. 431 — 5.48
Taylor v. Bristol Omnibus Co. Ltd [1975] 2 All E.R. 1107 — 15.32
Taylor v. Ford (1873) 29 L.T. 392 — 22.05
Taylor v. O'Connor [1971] A.C. 115 — 15.27
Taylor v. Rover Co. Ltd [1966] 2 All E.R. 181 — 14.09
Taylor v. Sims & Sims [1942] 2 All E.R. 375 — 14.52
Taylor v. Whitehead (1781) 2 Doug. 745 — 5.30
Taylor (C.R.) (Wholesale) Ltd v. Hepworths Ltd [1977] 2 All E.R. 784 — 15.17
Temperton v. Russell [1893] 1 Q.B. 715 — 21.30, 21.39
Tempest v. Snowden [1952] 1 K.B. 130 — 22.07
Tetley v. Chitty [1986] 1 All E.R. 663 — 8.42, 8.69

Thackwell v. Barclays Bank plc [1986] 1 All E.R. 676 7.19, 13.46
Tharpe v. Stallwood (1843) 5 Man. & G. 760 7.06
Theaker v. Richardson [1962] 1 All E.R. 229 18.29, 18.30
Theobald v. Railway Passengers Assurance Co. (1862) 15 Jur. 583 15.39
Thermo King Corporation Ltd v. Provincial Bank of Canada (1981) 130 D.L.R. (3d) 256 21.34, 21.35, 21.48
Thomas v. Bradbury Agnew & Co. Ltd [1906] 2 K.B. 627 18.64, 18.66, 18.68
Thomas v. National Union of Mineworkers [1985] 2 All E.R. 1 2.23, 6.14, 8.02, 8.05, 21.01
Thomas v. Quartermaine (1887) 18 Q.B.D. 685 12.01, 13.13
Thomas v. Sawkins [1935] 2 K.B. 249 5.46
Thomas v. Sorrel (1673) Vaughan 330 5.40
Thomas v. Wignall [1987] 1 All E.R. 1185 15.26
Thomas v. Winchester (1852) 6 N.Y. 397 14.04
Thomas (Frank) Export Ltd v. Metropolitan Police Commissioner [1977] Q.B. 952 5.46, 7.14
Thompson v. Bankstown Municipal Council (1953) 87 C.L.R. 619 12.14, 14.16
Thompson v. British Medical Association (N.S.W. Branch) [1924] A.C. 764 18.88, 21.12
Thompson v. Brown Construction (Ebbw Vale) Ltd [1981] 2 All E.R. 296 15.49, **15.50**
Thompson v. Gibson (1841) 7 M. & G. 456 8.36
Thompson v. Park [1944] K.B. 408 5.40
Thompson v. Price [1973] 1 Q.B. 838 15.60
Thompson v. Smiths Shiprepairers (North Shields) Ltd [1984] Q.B. 405 12.80, 12.103
Thompson v. Toorenburgh (1973) 29 D.L.R. (3d) 608; (1975) 50 D.L.R. (3d) 717 12.119
Thompson v. Ward [1953] 2 Q.B. 153 5.13
Thompson v. Cremin (1941) 71 Ll.L.R.I; [1953] 2 All E.R. 1185 14.36
Thompson-Schwab v. Costaki [1956] 1 All E.R. 652 8.11
Thomson (D.C.) & Co. Ltd v. Deakin [1952] Ch. 646 21.32, 21.34, 21.37, **21.38–39**, 21.40, **21.41–43**, 21.52
Thorley v. Kerry (Lord) (1812) 4 Taunt. 355 18.07, 18.38, 18.45
Thorpe v. Brumfitt (1873) L.R. 8 Ch.App. 650 8.14
Thornton v. Broad of Trustees of School District No. 57 (1978) 83 D.L.R. (3d) 480 15.31
Thornton v. Kirklees Metropolitan Council [1979] 1 Q.B. 626 16.06
Thurgood v. Van den Berghs & Jurgens Ltd [1951] 2 K.B. 537 12.111
Thurman v. Wild (1840) 11 Ad. & E. 453 4.06
Thurston v. Charles (1905) 21 T.L.R. 659 7.05
Tidy v. Bateman [1934] 1 K.B. 319 13.33
Tillander v. Gosselin (1966) 60 D.L.R. (2d) 18 2.28, 6.06
Tillett v. Ward (1882) 10 Q.B.D. 17 7.15, 11.31
Tims v. John Lewis & Co. Ltd [1951] 2 K.B. 459 22.06
Tindale v. Tindale [1950] 4 D.L.R. 363 6.06
Tinsley v. Dudley [1951] 2 K.B. 18 7.18, 14.25, 14.27
Titchener v. British Railways Board [1983] 3 All E.R. 770 13.06, 13.10, 13.13, 13.22, 14.41
Tithe Redemption Commissioners v. Runcorn U.D.C. [1954] Ch. 383 5.07
Tobin v. The Queen (1864) 16 GB.N.S. 310 2.02, 2.03, 3.02
Todd v. Eastwood [1985] 1.C.R. 135 18.56
Todd v. Flight (1860) 9 C.B.N.S. 377 8.44
Todd v. Hawkins (1837) 8 C. & P. 88 18.96
Tolley v. Fry & Sons Ltd [1931] A.C. 333 18.13, 18.14, 18.20, 19.06, 19.09
Tomlinson v. Harrison [1972] 1 O.R. 670 13.45
Tomlinson (A.) (Hauliers) Ltd v. Hepburn [1966] A.C. 451 7.51

Toogood v. Spyring (1834) 1 Cr. M. & R. 181 18.95, 18.99, 18.101
Tool Metal Manufacturing Co. Ltd v. Tungsten Electric Co. Ltd [1955] 1 W.L.R. 761 5.40
Torette House v. Berkman (1940) 62 C.L.R. 637 9.09
Toronto Marlboro Major Junior "A" Hockey Club v. Tonelli (1971) 81 D.L.R. (3d) 407; (1979) 23 O.R. (2d) 193 21.32
Toronto Power Co. v. Paskawan [1915] A.C. 734 14.51
Toronto-St. Catherines Transport Ltd v. Toronto [1958] S.C.R. 61 16.05
Torquay Hotel Ltd v. Cousins [1969] 2 Ch. 106 21.38, 21.40, 21.43, 21.44, **21.52**
Tournier v. National Provincial & Union Bank of England [1924] 1 K.B. 461 18.08
Towerfield, The [1951] A.C. 112 13.29
Towers & Co. Ltd v. Gray [1961] 2 Q.B. 351 7.06
Townend v. Askery Coal Co. [1934] Ch. 463 5.51
Trapp v. Hnatuk (1976) 71 D.L.R. (3d) 63 12.79
Trapp v. Mackie [1979] 1 All E.R. 489 18.80
Travers v. Gloucester Corporation [1947] K.B. 71 12.53
Trawnik v. Gordon Lennox [1985] 2 All E.R. 368 2.02, 2.03
Treifus & Co. Ltd v. Post Office [1957] 2 Q.B. 325 2.07
Tremain v. Pike [1969] 3 All E.R. 1303 12.74, 12.118
Tremball (John) Ltd v. National Westminster Bank Ltd (1979) 39 P. & C.R. 104 5.01, 5.49
Trendtex Trading Corporation v. Central Bank of Nigeria [1977] 1 Q.B. 529 2.13
Treolar v. Nute [1977] 1 All E.R. 230 5.15
Trevett v. Lee [1955] 1 W.L.R. 113 8.48, 8.82
Trippett v. Cleaver [1973] W.A.R. 173 10.11
Trust Co. Ltd v. de Silva [1956] 1 W.L.R. 376 3.13
Truth (N.Z.) Ltd v. Holloway [1960] 1 W.L.R. 997 18.35
Tuberville v. Savage (1699) 1 Mod. 3 6.15
Tuberville v. Stamp (1697) 1 Ld.Raym. 264 3.01, 10.02, 10.03, 10.04
Tudor-Hart v. British Union for the Abolition of Vivisection [1938] 2 K.B. 329 18.62
Tuff v. Warman (1858) 5 C.B.N.S. 573 13.23, 13.32
Turner v. Ambler (1847) 10 Q.B. 252 22.11
Turner v. Ford Motor Co. Ltd [1965] 2 All E.R. 583 13.39
Turner v. Hockey (1887) 56 L.J.Q.B. 901 7.23, 7.29
Turner v. M-G-M Pictures Ltd [1950] 1 All E.R. 449 18.17, 18.20, 18.67, 18.69, 18.101
Turner v. Spooner (1865) 30 L.J. Ch. 801 8.73
Turpin v. Halifax-Dartmouth Bridge Commissioners (1956) 21 D.L.R. (2d) 623 9.42
Twine v. Bean's Express Ltd (1946) 62 T.L.R. 458 3.25

U

U.B.A.F. Ltd v. European American Banking Corp. [1984] Q.B. 713 17.08
U.S.A. v. Dollfus Mieg & Cie [1952] A.C. 583 2.12, 7.33
Ultramares Corporation v. Touche (1931) 255 N.Y. 170 12.37
Unident Ltd v. de Lacey (1982) 131 D.L.R. (3d) 225 21.32
Union Credit Bank v. Mersey Docks & Harbour Board [1899] 2 Q.B. 205 7.23
Union Transport Finance Ltd v. British Car Auctions Ltd [1978] 2 All E.R. 385 7.23, 7.34
United Africa Co. Ltd v. Saka Owoade [1955] A.C. 130 3.32
Universe Tankships of Monrovia v. I.T.W.F. [1982] 2 All E.R. 67 21.01
Unterreiner v. Wilson (1982) 142 D.L.R. (3d) 588 22.26

United Motor Services Inc. v. Hutson [1937] S.C.R. 392 12.93
Updale v. Bloomsbury Area Health Authority [1983] 2 All E.R. 522 2.27
Uren v. John Fairfax Pty Ltd (1967) 117 C.L.R. 118 1.08
Uxbridge Permanent Building Society v. Pickard [1939] 2 K.B. 248 3.15

V

Vacwell Engineering Co. Ltd v. B.D.H. Chemicals Ltd [1971] 1 Q.B. 88, 111 12.118, 14.01
Van Camp Chocolates v. Aulsebrooks [1984] 1 N.Z.L.R. 354 1.06, 21.53
Vanderpant v. Mayfair Hotel Co. [1930] Ch. 138 8.15, 8.77, 8.79
Vandyke v. Fender [1970] 2 Q.B. 292 3.21
Van Oppen v. Bedford Charity Trustees (Clerk to) [1989] 1 All E.R. 273; *affirmed* [1989] 3 All E.R. 389 12.05, 12.10, 12.36, 12.40, **12.43**, 12.52
Van Oppens v. Tredegar Ltd (1921) 27 T.L.R. 504 7.25
Vancouver General Hospital v. Fraser [1952] S.C.R. 36 12.78
Vancouver General Hospital v. McDaniel (1934) 152 L.T. 56 12.80
Vaughan v. Hampson (1875) 33 L.T. 15 5.42
Vaughan v. McKenzie [1969] 1 Q.B. 557 5.45
Vaughan v. Menlove (1837) 3 Bing. N.C. 468 9.02, 10.08, 12.73, 12.77
Vaughan v. Taff Vale Railway (1860) 5 H. & N. 679 8.55, 10.07
Vaughn v. Halifax-Dartmouth Bridge Commissioners (1961) 29 D.L.R. (2d) 253 8.34, 9.14
Veldhuizen v. Blakzyl [1977] 1 W.W.R. 526 15.32
Venafra v. Johnson (1833) 10 Bing. 301 22.06
Veness v. Dyson Bell & Co. (1965) The Times 25 May; *see* [1965] C.L.Y. 2691 14.50
Verbeek v. Stefura (1981) 26 A.R. 497 3.22
Vessey v. Douglas Bros. (1977) 13 Nfld & P.E.I.R. 129 13.03
Victoria Park Racing and Recreation Grounds Co. Ltd v. Taylor (1939) 58 C.L.R. 479 19.03, **19.09–10**, 21.69
Victorian Railway Commissioners v. Coultas (1888) 13 App.Cas. 222 12.25, 12.28
Videan v. British Transport Commission [1963] 2 Q.B. 650 12.32
Videto v. Kennedy (1981) 33 O.R. (2d) 497 13.17
Villiers v. Monsley (1769) 2 Wils. 400 18.49
Vine Products Ltd v. MacKenzie & Co. Ltd [1969] R.P.C. 1 21.73
Vitzelly v. Mudie's Select Library Ltd [1900] 2 Q.B. 170 18.06, 18.36
Volkswagen Canada Ltd v. Spicer (1978) 91 D.L.R. (3d) 42 21.41, 21.44
Volute, The [1922] 1 A.C. 129 13.32, 13.33
Vorvis v. Insurance Corp. of British Columbia (1989) 58 D.L.R. (4th) 193 1.12

W

W. v. Meah; D. v. Meah [1986] 1 All E.R. 935 6.13
W. v. W. [1964] P.67 6.01, 6.12
Wade v. C.N.R. [1978] 1 S.C.R. 1064 2.28, 12.79
Wade v. Martin [1955] 3 D.L.R. 635 6.39
Wagner v. International Railroad Co. (1921) 232 N.Y. Supp. 176 12.30
Wagon Mound (No. 1); Overseas Tankship (U.K.) v. Morts Dock Engineering Co. [1961] A.C. 388 1.18, 8.27, 7.74, **12.117–9**, 12.121, 12.123, 13.28, 14.11
Wagon Mound (No. 2); Overseas Tankship (U.K.) v. Miller Steamship Co. Pty [1967] 1 A.C. 617 **8.27–8**, 8.40, 8.41, 8.66, 8.83, 9.19, 12.117
Wah Tat Bank Ltd v. Chan Cheng Kun [1975] 2 All E.R. 257 3.06, 4.04, 4.05

Waite v. North Eastern Railway (1858) E.R. & E. 719 13.30
Waldron v. War Office [1956] 1 All E.R. 108 15.23
Walker v. Baird [1892] A.C. 491 2.10
Walker (John) & Sons Ltd v. Henry Ost & Co. Ltd [1970] 2 All E.R. 106 12.53, 21.73, 21.75
Walkley v. Premium Forging Co. Ltd [1979] 2 All E.R. 348 15.49
Wallace v. Newton [1982] 2 All E.R. 106 11.17–18
Wallis v. Hands [1893] 2 Ch. 75 5.13
Wallis's Cayton Bay Holiday Camp Ltd v. Shell Mex & BP Ltd [1975] Q.B. 94 5.15
Walmsley v. Humenick [1954] 2 D.L.R. 232 2.28, 6.06, 12.79
Walsh v. Ervin [1952] A.L.R. 650 8.76
Walsh v. Holst & Co. Ltd [1958] 2 All E.R. 33 12.89, 12.93
Walter v. Selfe (1851) 4 De. G. & Sm. 315 8.15
Walters v. W.H. Smith [1914] 1 K.B. 595 6.46
Wandsworth Board of Works v. United Telephone Co. (1884) 13 Q.B.D. 904 5.20, 5.23, 5.24
Wansborough v. Manton (1836) 4 A. & E. 884 7.25
Ward v. Cannock Chase District Council [1985] 3 All E.R. 537 12.61
Ward v. Evans (1703) 2 Salk. 442 3.02
Ward v. Hertfordshire County Council [1970] 1 All E.R. 535 C.A., *reversing* [1969] 2 All E.R. 807 14.28
Ward v. James [1966] 1 Q.B. 273 12.84, 15.46
Ward v. Macauley (1791) 4 T.R. 481 7.06
Ward v. Tesco Stores Ltd [1976] 1 All E.R. 219 12.86
Warder v. Cooper [1970] Ch. 495 16.14
Ware v. Garston Haulage Co. [1944] K.B. 30 8.02, 8.82
Ware & de Freville v. Motor Trade Association [1921] 3 K.B. 40 21.03, 21.06, 21.12
Warner v. Riddeford (1858) 4 C.B.N.S. 180 6.20
Warren v. Henleys Ltd [1948] 2 All E.R. 935 3.22, 3.33
Warren v. King [1963] 3 All E.R. 521 15.45
Warren v. Scruttons [1962] 1 Lloyd's Rep. 497 12.118
Warwick University v. De Graaf [1975] 1 W.L.R. 1126 5.15, 5.18
Wason v. Walter (1868) L.R. 4 Q.B. 73 18.89
Waters v. Sunday Pictorial Newspapers Ltd [1961] 2 All E.R. 758 18.111
Watmore v. Jenkins [1962] 2 Q.B. 572 2.33
Watson v. Buckley [1940] 1 All E.R. 174 14.08
Watson v. M'Ewan [1905] A.C. 480 18.81, 22.22
Watson v. Powles [1968] 1 Q.B. 596 15.02
Watson v. Wingate 1960 S.L.T. 321 15.19
Watt v. Hertfordshire County Council [1954] 2 All E.R. 368 12.16, 12.75, 13.20
Watt v. Kesteven County Council [1955] 1 Q.B. 408 16.09
Watt v. Longsdon [1930] 1 K.B. 130 18.73, 18.95, **18.96**
Watt v. Thomas [1947] A.C. 484 12.84
Watts v. Rama [1972] V.R. 353 2.25
Wauchop v. Mordecai [1970] 1 W.L.R. 317 12.83
Waugh v. James K. Allan Ltd [1964] 2 Lloyds Rep. 1 2.33
Weaver v. Commercial Press Co. (1947) 63 T.L.R. 466 4.11
Weaver v. Ward (1616) Hob. 134 1.31, 6.06, 6.07, 6.34, 9.05
Webb v. Beavan (1883) 11 Q.B.D. 609 18.46, 22.14
Webb v. Times Publishing Co. Ltd [1960] 2 All E.R. 789 18.88, 18.90–91, 18.97
Welbridge Holdings Ltd v.Metropolitan Corporation of Greater Winnipeg (1972) 22 D.L.R. (3d) 470 12.63
Weld-Blundell & Co. Ltd v. Camden London Borough Council [1984] Q.B. 342 12.13

Weld-Blundell v. Stephens [1920] A.C. 956 12.96, 12.111, 12.116, 12.122, 18.30
Weller & Co. Ltd v. Foot & Mouth Disease Research Institute [1966] 1 Q.B. 569 12.43, 12.46
Wells v. Cooper [1958] 2 Q.B. 265 12.78, 14.36
Wellway v. Courtier [1918] 1 K.B. 208 7.06
Wenman v. Ash (1853) 13 C.B. 836 18.29, 18.95
Wennhak v. Morgan (1888) 20 Q.B.D. 635 18.29
Wenz v. Royal Trust Co. [1953] O.W.N. 798 3.22
Wershaf v. Commissioner of Police for the Metropolis [1978] 3 All E.R. 540 6.14, 6.45, 6.46
West v. Bristol Tramways [1908] 2 K.B. 214 9.13
West (H.) & Son Ltd v. Shephard [1964] A.C. 326 15.08, 15.39, **15.42**
Western Counties Manure Co. v. Lawes Chemical Manure Co. (1874) L.R. 9 Ex. 218 21.54
Western Engraving Co. v. Film Laboratories Ltd [1938] 1 All E.R. 106 9.22, **9.39**
Western Stevedoring Co. Ltd v. Pulp, Paper & Woodworkers of Canada (1975) 61 D.L.R. (3d) 701 21.42
Westlake v. Smith's Transport Ltd (1973) 2 O.R. (2d) 258 12.93
Weston v. Lawrence Weaver Ltd [1961] 1 Q.B. 402 8.33
Westripp v. Baldock [1938] 2 All E.R. 779; [1939] 1 All E.R. 279 5.01, 5.05, 7.04
Westwood v. Post Office [1974] A.C. 1 13.29, 13.37, 16.20
Westwood v. Secretary of State for Employment [1985] A.C. 20 15.24
Wheat v. Lacon & Co. Ltd [1966] A.C. 552 14.19
Wheatley v. Lodge [1971] 1 W.L.R. 29 6.20, 6.43
Wheatley v. Patrick (1837) 2 M. & W. 650 3.13
Wheeler v. Copas [1981] 3 All E.R. 405 14.02, 14.16, **14.18**
Wheeler v. New Merton Board Mills Ltd [1933] 2 K.B. 669 16.19
Wheeler v. Sommerfield [1966] 2 Q.B. 94 18.12
Whitby v. Brock (1888) 4 T.L.R. 241 9.39
White v. Blackmore [1972] 2 Q.B. 651 13.10
White v. Jameson (1874) L.R. 18 Eq. 303 8.42
White v. John Warwick & Co. Ltd [1953] 2 All E.R. 1021 13.10
White v. London Transport Executive [1982] 1 All E.R. 410; [1982] Q.B. 489 2.38, 15.29
White v. Melling [1895] A.C. 154 21.54, 21.61
White v. Morris (1852) 11 C.B. 1015 7.06
White v. Pile (1951) 68 W.N. (N.S.W.) 176 6.06
White v. Power (1973) 4 N.S.R. (2d) 718 11.05
White v. Steadman [1913] 3 K.B. 340 11.03, 14.04
White v. Stone [1939] 2 K.B. 829 18.99
White v. Sweetland (1978) N. & P.E.I.R. 58 15.16
White v. Turner (1981) 47 O.R. (2d) 764 13.17
White v. White [(1950] P. 39 2.32
White (Arthur) (Contractors) Ltd v. Tarmac Civil Engineering Ltd [1967] 1 W.L.R. 1508 3.05
White Horse Distillers Ltd v. Gregson Associates Ltd [1984] R.P.C. 61 3.06
Whiteford v. Hunter [1950] W.N. 553 12.80
Whitehouse v. Jordan [1981] 1 All E.R. 267 12.73, 12.75, **12.76**, 12.84
Whiting v. Middlesex C.C. [1948] 1 K.B. 162 8.58
Whittaker v. Campbell [1983] 3 All E.R. 582 7.13, 7.37
Whittaker v. Minister of Pensions & National Insurance [1967] 1 Q.B. 157 3.04, 3.05
Whittome v. Coats [1965] 1 W.L.R. 1285 15.59
Wickham Holdings Ltd v. Brook House Motors Ltd [1967] 1 W.L.R. 295 7.50

Wieland v. Cyril Lord Carpets Ltd [1969] 3 All E.R. 1006 12.118
Wiffen v. Bailey and Romford U.D.C. [1915] 1 K.B. 600 22.14, 22.15
Wigley v. British Vinegars Ltd [1964] A.C. 307 16.15
Wilchick v. Marks & Silverstone [1934] 2 K.B. 56 8.44
Wilcox v. Kettel [1937] 1 All E.R. 222 5.21
Wilkes v. Hungerford Market (1835) 2 Bing. N.C. 281 8.75, 8.76, 8.77, 8.79
Wilkes v. London Passenger Transport Board [1947] 1 All E.R. 258 14.37
Wilkins v. Leighton [1932] 2 Ch. 106 8.39
Wilkinson v. Coverdale (1793) 1 Esp. 75 12.42
Wilkinson v. Downton [1897] 2 Q.B. 57 6.17, 12.24, 17.16
Wilks v. Cheltenham Home Guard Motor Cycle & Light Car Club [1971] 2 All E.R. 369 13.07
Wilkinson v. Howel (1830) Moo. & M. 495 22.05
Wilkinson v. Verity (1871) L.R. 6 C.P. 206 7.40
Williams v. Archer (1847) 5 C.B. 318 7.49
Williams v. Gesse (1831) 3 Ding. N.C. 849 7.20
Williams v. Holland (1833) 10 Bing. 112 6.02
Williams v. Home Office (No. 2) [1981] 1 All E.R. 1211 6.19
Williams v. Houlder Bros. & Co. [1962] 2 Lloyd's Rep. 199 14.35
Williams v. Jones (1736) Lee Temp. Hard. 298 6.04
Williams v. Jones (1865) 3 H. & C. 602 3.22
Williams v. Lardner (1798) 8 T.R. 72 11.02
Williams v. Milotin (1957) 97 C.L.R. 465 6.08
Williams v. Owne [1956] 1 All E.R. 104 10.06
Williams v. Peel River Land & Mineral Co. Ltd (1886) 55 L.T. 689 7.49
Williams v. Port of Liverpool Stevedoring Co. [1956] 1 W.L.R. 551 13.41
Williams Bros. Direct Supply Ltd v. Raferty [1958] 1 Q.B. 159 5.15
Willinski v. Anderson (1909) 19 O.L.R. 437 22.04
Willis v. Brooks [1947] 1 All E.R. 191 18.03
Willis (R.H.) & Son Ltd v. British Car Auctions Ltd [1978] 2 All E.R. 392 7.23, **7.29**, 7.30
Wills v. Bowley [1982] 2 All E.R. 654 6.45
Wilsher v. Essex Area Health Authority [1988] 1 All E.R. 871 H.L.; [1986] 3 All E.R. 801 C.A. 12.103, 12.105, **12.108**
Wilson v. Lombank Ltd [1963] 1 W.L.R. 1294 7.13
Wilson v. Pringle [1986] 2 All E.R. 440 1.27, 6.04, 6.06, **6.08**, 6.09, 6.23
Wilson v. Swanson [1956] S.C.R. 804 12.78
Wilson v. Tyneside Window Cleaning Co. [1958] 2 Q.B. 110 14.52
Wilson v. United Counties Bank Ltd [1920] A.C. 102 2.34, 13.31
Wilson v. Vancouver Hockey Club (1983) 5 D.L.R. (4th) 282 12.105
Wilson v. Waddell (1876) 2 App.Cas. 95 9.24
Wilsons Clyde Coal Co. Ltd v. English [1938] A.C. 57 3.36, 14.47, 16.13
Wiltshire v. Barrett [1966] 1 Q.B. 312 5.09
Wiltshire County Council v. Frazer [1986] 1 All E.R. 65 5.04, 5.15, 5.18
Wimpey (George) & Co. Ltd v. B.O.A.C. [1955] A.C. 169 4.08
Windrem v. Hamill [1978] 3 W.W.R. 684 11.05
Wing v. London General Omnibus Co. [1909] 2 K.B. 652 9.14, 9.32
Winkfield, The [1902] P. 42 7.33, 7.39, 7.48, 7.51, 15.12
Winter v. Banchs (1901) 84 L.T. 504 7.24
Winter Garden Theatre (London) Ltd v. Millennium Productions Ltd [1946] 1 All E.R. 678; [1948] A.C. 173 5.40, 5.42
Winterbourne v. Morgan (1809) 11 East 295 5.08
Winterbottom v. Earl of Derby (1867) L.R. 2 H.L. 175 8.76
Winterbottom v. Wright (1842) 10 M. & W. 109 1.28, 12.01, 14.04
Wise v. Kaye [1962] 1 Q.B. 638 15.39, 15.42
Wise Bros. v. N.S.W. Commissioner of Railways (1947) 75 C.L.R. 59 9.26, 10.11
With v. O'Flanagan [1936] Ch. 575 17.07

Withers v. Perry Chain Co. Ltd [1961] 3 All E.R. 676 14.53
Woadson v. Nawton (1727) 2 Stra. 777 7.11
Wood v. Leadbitter (1845) 13 M. & W. 838 5.01, 5.40, 5.42
Woodage v. Moss [1924] 1 All E.R. 584 7.06
Woodman v. Richardson [1937] 3 All E.R. 866 14.17
Woods v. Duncan; Duncan v. Cammell Laird & Co. [1946] A.C. 401 12.13, 12.92, 12.116
Woods v. Martins Bank [1959] 1 Q.B. 55 12.35
Woodward v. Begbie [1962] O.R. 60 12.65
Woodward v. Hutchins [1977] 1 W.L.R. 760 20.05
Woodward v. Mayor of Hastings [1945] K.B. 174 14.36
Woolerton & Wilson Ltd v. Richard Costain Ltd [1970] 1 All E.R. 483 5.25
Woolins v. British Celanese Ltd (1966) 1 K.I.B. 438 14.33, 14.35
Woolridge v. Sumner [1963] 2 Q.B. 43 6.36, 13.05, 13.06, 13.07
World Beauty, The; Andros Springs (Owners) v. World Beauty (Owners) [1969] P.12 H.C.; [1970] P. 144 C.A. 15.16
World Harmony, The [1967] P. 341 12.46
Wormald v. Cole [1954] 1 Q.B. 614 11.29, 12.111
Worsfold v. Howe [1980] 1 All E.R. 1028 12.85
Wotta v. Haliburton Oil Well Cementing Co. [1955] S.C.R. 397 12.85, 12.89
Wray v. Essex County Council [1936] 3 All E.R. 97 14.04
Wren v. Weild (1969) L.R. 4 Q.B. 730 21.54
Wright v. Bennett [1948] 1 All E.R. 227 21.05
Wright v. British Railway Board [1983] 2 All E.R. 773 15.22, 15.38
Wright v. Callwood [1950] 2 K.B. 515 11.05, 12.53
Wright v. Cheshire County Council [1952] 2 All E.R. 789 12.80
Wright v. Dunlop Rubber Co.; Cassidy v. same (1971) 11 K.I.R. 311 H.C.; (1972) 13 K.I.R. 255 14.49
Wright v. Ramscot (1667) 1 Wms. Saund. 84 7.04
Wright v. Tyneside Improvement Commissioners [1968] 1 All E.R. 807 4.12
Wright v. Wilson (1699) 1 Ld.Raym. 739 6.18
Wright, Layman & Umney Ltd v. Wright (1949) 66 R.P.C. 149 21.66, 21.70
Wringe v. Cohen [1940] 1 K.B. 229 8.40, 8.44, 8.85
Wuta-Ofei v. Danquah [1961] 1 W.L.R. 1238 5.15
Wyld v. Silver [1963] Ch. 243 1.22

X

X, re [1975] 1 All E.R. 697 19.05

Y

Yachuk v. Oliver Blais & Co. Ltd [1949] A.C. 386 2.24, 13.30, 14.07
Yarmouth v. France (1887) 19 Q.B.D. 647 13.13
Yaselli v. Goff (1926) 12 F. (2d) 396 22.24
Yates v. Lansing (1810) 5 John. N.Y. 282 22.24
Yepremian v. Scarborough General Hospital (1980) 110 D.L.R. (3d) 513 3.04, 3.41
Yianni v. Edwin Evans & Son [1982] Q.B. 438 12.37
Yorke v. Chapman (1839) 10 Ad. & El. 207 6.19
Yorkton Agricultural & Industrial Exhibition Association v. Morley (1967) 58 D.L.R. (2d) 282 12.79
Young v. Bankier Distillery [1893] A.C. 691 8.11
Young v. Edwards Box Co. Ltd [1951] 1 T.L.R. 789 3.25
Young v. Rank [1950] 2 K.B. 570 12.83
Young v. Sandford (1983) 61 N.S.R. (2d) 16 12.79
Yousoupoff v. M-G-M (1934) 50 T.L.R. 581 18.07, **18.08**, 18.15, 18.39
Yuen Kun-yeu v. Attorney-General of Hong Kong [1987] 2 All E.R. 705 12.05, 12.06, 12.07, **12.08**, 12.53, 12.66
Yuill v. B. & B. Fibres (Leigh) Ltd [1958] 2 Lloyds Rep. 596 3.06

Table of Statutes

Abortion Act 1967 2.26
Accident Compensation Act 1972 (New Zealand) 1.15, 9.07
Accidental Fires Act 1980 (Ontario) 10.01
Administration of Justice Act 1969
s. 22 15.23, 15.38
Administration of Justice Act 1982 2.38, 15.38, 15.52, 15.57
s. 1(1) 15.40
s. 2 1.03, 12.22, 15.32, 21.30
s. 2(c)(i) 2.02
s. 4 15.29
s. 4(1), (2) 2.37
s. 5 15.30
s. 6 15.02
s. 75(1) 2.38
Sch. 9 Pt I 2.38
Administration of Justice Act 1985
s. 57(2) 18.103
s. 57(4) 18.103
Agriculture (Safety, Health and Welfare) Act 1956 14.46
Animals Act 1971 9.32, 11.01
s. 1(1) 1.32, 11.07, 11.08
s. 2 11.07
s. 2(1) 11.13, 11.20
s. 2(2) 11.14, 11.15, 11.16, 11.18, 11.20
s. 3 11.08, 11.25, 11.26
s. 4 5.01, 11.08, 11.32
s. 4(1) 1.32, 11.28
s. 4(2) 11.28
s. 5 11.07, 11.08
s. 5(1) 11.22, 11.25, 11.30
s. 5(2) 11.22, 11.24
s. 5(3) 11.23, 11.24
s. 5(4) 11.25, 11.27
s. 5(5) 11.31
s. 5(6) 11.30
s. 6(2) 11.10
s. 7 11.28
s. 7(1) 11.02, 11.32
s. 7(2) 11.32
s. 7(3) 11.20, 11.32
s. 7(4) 11.20, 11.32
s. 7(5) 11.22
s. 7(6) 11.33
s. 7(7) 11.32
s. 8(1) 11.34, 12.55
s. 8(2) 11.35
s. 9 7.13, 11.08, 11.26
s. 9(1) 11.27
s. 9(2) 11.27
s. 9(3)–(5) 11.27
s. 10 11.13, 11.25, 11.29
s. 11 11.10, 11.13, 11.25, 11.26, 11.29, 11.30, 11.35
s. 12 11.07
s. 13(4) 11.07
Atomic Energy (Weapons Group) Act 1973 2.07

Bankruptcy Act 1914
s. 30 2.39
s. 30(1) 2.35
Bill of Rights 1689 18.74
art. 9 18.74
British Telecommunications Act 1981 2.07
s. 23 2.07

Cable and Broadcasting Act 1984
s. 28(1) 18.40
Chancery Amendment Act 1858 (Lord Cairns' Act) 8.67
Cheques Act 1957
s. 4 7.19
Children and Young Persons Act 1933
s. 1 6.29
s. 55 2.30
Children and Young Persons Act 1969 2.28
Civil Aviation Act 1949
s. 40(1) 5.27
s. 40(2) 5.11, 5.27, 9.07
Civil Evidence Act 1968
s. 11 12.83
Civil Liability Act 1961 (Rep. of Ireland)
s. 56 13.38
Civil Liability (Contribution) Act 1978 2.04
s. 1(1) 4.07
s. 1(2)–(5) 4.08
s. 1(6) 4.07
s. 2(1)–(3) 4.11
s. 3 4.05
s. 4 4.05
s. 7(3) 4.12
s. 9(1) 4.05
Sch. 2 4.05
Clean Air Acts 1956, 1968 8.03
Commons Registration Act 1965 12.55
s. 22(1) 11.35
Companies Act 1985
s. 35(1) 2.19

Congenital Disabilities (Civil Liability) Act 1976 2.25
s. 1 2.25
s. 1(5) 12.80
s. 2 2.25
s. 4(2), (3) 2.25
s. 4(5) 2.27
Consumer Credit Act 1974 14.01
Consumer Protection Act 1987 9.07
Pt I 14.01, 15.47
s. 4 15.47
s. 6(1) 15.48
s. 6(6) 15.19, 15.48, 15.49
Sch. 1 15.48, 15.49
Consumer Safety Act 1978
s. 6 16.05
Contributory Negligence Act 1924 (Ontario) 13.25
Control of Pollution Act 1974 8.03
Copyright Act 1956
s. 43 19.01
Copyright, Designs and Patents Act 1988
s. 77 19.01
Countryside Act 1968
ss. 16–19 5.44
County Courts Act 1984
s. 144 7.42
Sch. 1 7.42
Criminal Code 1970 (Canada)
s. 281.2 18.26
Criminal Justice Act 1982
s. 27 2.30
Criminal Law Act 1967
s. 2 6.46, 6.48
s. 3 6.27, 6.46
Criminal Law Act 1977 5.01, 5.48
s. 1 6.13
s. 6 5.48
s. 7(2) 5.48
s. 60 1.08
s. 65 18.41
Sch. 13 18.41
Crown Proceedings Act 1947 2.03, 2.04, 2.06, 2.07, 2.08
s. 2(1) 2.04
s. 4 2.04
s. 10(1), (2) 2.07
s. 11 2.08
Crown Proceedings (Armed Forces) Act 1987 2.07

Damages (Scotland) Act 1976
s. 1(4) 15.58
Data Protection Act 1984 19.01, 19.04
Defamation Act 1952 18.21, 18.35, 18.73
s. 1 18.40
s. 2 18.53
s. 3(1) 21.64
s. 4 18.06, 18.54, 18.117
s. 4(2) 18.55
s. 5 18.58, 18.63
s. 6 18.63, 18.66
s. 7(1) 18.92
s. 7(2) 18.89, 18.92
s. 7(3) 18.92
s. 7(4), (5) 18.92
s. 8 18.88
s. 9 18.40
s. 9(2) 18.88
s. 10 18.98
s. 12 18.113
s. 16 18.92
s. 17(2) 18.87
s. 18(3) 18.87
Sch. 18.92
Pt I 18.93
Pt II 18.94
Defamation Act 1970 (Manitoba)
s. 19 18.26
Defamation Act 1980 (Alberta)
s. 2(2) 18.01
Defective Premises Act 1972 12.44, 12.56, 12.57, 13.10, 14.15
s. 3 12.56
Deposit-Taking Companies Ordinance 1976 (Hong Kong) 12.08
Diplomatic Privileges Act 1964
s. 1 2.14
s. 2(1) 2.14
Sch. 1 2.14, 18.85
Disposal of Unsolicited Goods Act 1952 7.22
Distress for Rent Act 1689
s. 3 7.43
Distress for Rent Act 1737
s. 19 5.09
Dogs Acts 1906, 1928 11.01, 11.06
Domestic Violence and Matrimonial Proceedings Act 1976
s. 4 5.40

Education (Scotland) Act 1980 18.80
Employer's Liability (Defective Equipment) Act 1969 3.36, 14.47, 14.51
Employment Act 1980 2.23
s. 17 2.23, 21.01
s. 18 21.01
Employment Act 1982 21.01
s. 15 21.01
s. 15(2) (a), (b) 2.23
s. 15(4)–(6) 2.23
s. 16 2.23, 21.01
s. 17 2.23, 21.01

s. 18 21.01
s. 19 2.23, 21.01
Employment Protection Act 1975 21.01
European Communities Act 1972
s. 9(1) 2.19

Factories Act 1961 14.46, 14.52, 16.05, 16.06
Fair Trading Act 1973 14.01
Family Law Act 1986 (Ontario)
s. 61(1) 15.58
Family Law Reform Act 1969
s. 1 2.24, 6.06
s. 8(1) 6.38
ss. 20–3 6.33
Fatal Accidents Act 1846 2.36, 12.22, 15.52
Fatal Accidents Act 1976 2.36, 12.22, 15.27, 15.52
s. 1(1) 15.54
s. 1(2)–(5) 15.56
s. 1A 2.37, 15.57
s. 2(1)–(4) 15.53
s. 3(1)–(2) 15.58
s. 3(3)–(4) 15.60
s. 3(5) 15.58
s.4 15.60
s. 5 15.54
Fires Prevention (Metropolis) Act 1774
s. 86 10.05–06, 10.07, 10.08, 10.10, 10.12, 10.14

Guard Dogs Act 1975 11.24
s. 1 11.24
s. 5 11.24
Gulf Oil Refining Act 1965 8.56

Health and Safety at Work Act 1974 14.46
ss. 1, 11, 15, 47 9.07
Highways Act 1980
s. 58 8.81
s. 58(1), (2) 12.58
s. 59 3.37
Highways (Miscellaneous Provisions) Act 1961 12.58
s. 1 8.81
Hire Purchase Act 1964
Pt III 7.24

Industrial Relations Act 1971 2.22, 2.23, 21.01
Insolvency Act 1986
s. 382 2.39
International Organisations Act 1968
ss. 1, 2, 6, Sch. 1 2.14
Interpretation Act 1978
s. 5 11.10
s. 22(1) 11.10
Sch. 1 11.10
Sch. 2, paras. 4(2), 5(a) 11.10

Justices of the Peace Act 1979 22.24
Justices' Protection Act 1848
s. 1 22.24

Land Drainage Act 1930 8.54
Land Registration Act 1925
s. 56(3) 21.62
Latent Damage Act 1986 1.11, 15.19, 15.20, 15.21
ss. 1, 2(1), 3(1) 15.20
Law of Libel Amendment Act 1888
s. 3 18.86
s. 4 18.87
Law of Property Act 1925
s. 40(1) 5.37
Law of Property (Miscellaneous Provisions) Act 1989
s. 2 5.37
Law Reform (Contributory Negligence) Act 1945 2.04, 7.30, 11.13, 11.22, 11.25, 11.29, 13.25, **13.37**, 13.43, 14.40, 16.16
s. 1(1) 15.54
s. 1(6) 13.39
s. 3(1) 13.37
s. 4 13.37
Law Reform (Husband and Wife) Act 1962 2.24, 18.29
Law Reform (Married Women and Tortfeasors) Act 1935 2.24, 4.07
s. 6(1) 4.05
Law Reform (Miscellaneous Provisions) Act 1934 2.38, 3.01, 4.09, 15.47, 15.51, 15.59
s. 1(2), (4) 2.36, 2.37
s. 1(5) 2.38
s. 1(6) 2.39
Law Reform (Miscellaneous Provisions) Act 1970
s. 4 1.03, 2.37, 12.22
s. 5 2.37, 12.22
Law Reform (Personal Injuries) Act 1948 15.28, 15.35
s. 1(1) 14.46
s. 2 14.47
s. 2(1) 1.16, 15.24
s. 2(4) 15.30
Libel Act 1792
s. 1 18.20
Libel Act 1843
s. 1 18.112, 18.115
s. 2 18.05, 18.06, 18.115

Libel Act 1843—*cont.*
ss. 4–7 18.05
s. 6 18.41
Libel Act 1845
s. 2 18.05, 18.06, 18.115
Libel and Slander Act 1980 (Ontario)
s. 25 18.67
Limitation Act 1975 15.49
Limitation Act 1980 1.07, 1.11, 2.37, 7.40
s. 2 7.40, 15.19, 15.47
s. 3(1) 7.40
s. 3(2) 4.08
s. 4 7.40
s. 6A 18.103
s. 10 4.10
s. 11 15.20, 15.50
s. 11(1) 15.47
s. 11(1A) 15.48
s. 11(2) 15.47
s. 11(4) 15.19, 15.47
s. 11(5) 2.37, 15.47, 15.51
s. 11(6) 15.47, 15.51
s. 11A 15.47
s. 12(1)–(3) 15.55
s. 13(1)–(3) 15.55
s. 14 15.19, 15.48
s. 14(1)–(3) 15.48
s. 14A 15.20, 15.48
s. 14B 15.20
s. 28 15.19
s. 28A 15.20
s. 32 15.19
s. 32(1) 7.40
s. 32(3) 7.40
s. 32A 18.103
s. 33 15.49, 15.50, 15.55
s. 33(1) 15.49
s. 33(1A) 15.49
s. 33(3) 15.49
s. 33(4) 15.51
s. 38(1) 15.47
s. 38(2)–(4) 15.20
s. 39 15.55
Sch. 1, para. 3 15.19
London County Council (Improvements) Act 1962 8.58

Magistrates' Courts Act 1980
s. 33 6.48
s. 43 6.43
s. 125(3) 6.47
s. 150(1) 1.08
Maritime Conventions Act 1911 13.25, 13.32, 13.43
Married Women's Property Act 1882
s. 17 2.24
Matrimonial Causes Act 1973
ss. 21–16 2.24
Merchant Shipping Act 1894 7.55
Merchant Shipping Act 1970
s. 79 6.32
Mines and Quarries Act 1954 14.46
Misrepresentation Act 1967
s. 2(1) 17.14

National Insurance (Industrial Injuries) Act 1946 9.07
National Parks and Access to the Countryside Act 1949 14.21, 14.43
s. 60 5.04, 5.44, 14.20
Negligence Act 1980 (Ontario) 13.25
Newspaper Libel and Registration Act 1881
s. 1 18.86, 18.115
ss. 4, 5 18.41
Northern Ireland Emergency Powers Act 1978 6.45
Nuclear Installations Act 1965 9.07

Occupiers' Liability Act 1957 2.06, 2.21, 3.36, 7.18, 11.26, 13.10, 14.02, **14.15**, 14.22, 14.33, 14.40, 14.43, 14.44–5, 14.52
s. 1(2) 14.19, 14.20
s. 1(3) 14.17, 14.21, 14.25
s. 1(4) 14.20
s. 1(6) 14.22
s. 2(1) 14.28, 14.37
s. 2(2) 14.28
s. 2(3) 14.29
s. 2(4) 14.30, 14.34, 14.36, 14.42
s. 2(5) 14.34, 14.41
s. 3(1) 14.37, 14.42
s. 3(2)–(4) 14.42
s. 4 14.15
s. 4(4) 12.56
s. 5(1) 14.17, 14.20, 14.21, 14.25
s. 5(2) 14.17, 14.21
s. 5(3) 14.21
s. 6 14.19
Occupiers' Liability Act 1984 13.10, 14.15, 14.20, 14.45
s. 1(1) 14.20, 14.21, 14.44
s. 1(2) 14.20, 14.21
s. 1(3)–(6) 14.44
s. 1(7) 14.20
s. 1(8) 14.44
s. 2 14.38
Occupiers' Liability (Scotland) Act 1960
s. 2 14.44
s. 2(3) 13.10, 14.41
Offences against the Person Act 1861
ss. 42–44 6.13
s. 45 6.13
Offices, Shops and Railway Premises Act 1963 14.46

Parliamentary Papers Act 1840
s. 3 18.75
Partnership Act 1890
s. 24(2) 4.12
Performers' Protection Act 1963 16.08
Police Act 1964
s. 48 2.05
s. 51 6.14
Police and Criminal Evidence Act 1984
s. 24 6.47, 6.48
s. 25 6.47, 6.49
s. 26(1) 6.45
s. 27 6.45
s. 28 6.44, 6.50
s. 30(1) 6.50
s. 31 6.50
s. 32 6.50
s. 33 6.47
ss. 34–65 6.51
s. 47(8) 6.43
s. 121(1) 6.47
Sch. 7, pt 1 6.47
Post Office Act 1969 2.07
s. 6(5) 2.07
s. 29(1) 2.07, 7.37
s. 29(3) 7.37
s. 30 2.07
Powers of Criminal Courts Act 1973
ss. 35–38 1.08
Proceedings against Estates Act 1970 2.37
Public Health Act 1936 8.03
Public Order Act 1986
s. 4 18.41
Public Works Utilities Street Act 1950 8.57

Railways Fires Acts 1905, 1923 10.07
Rehabilitation of Offenders Act 1974
s. 8(3), (5) 18.58, 18.119, 19.01, 19.04
Restrictive Trade Practices Act 1956 21.44
Rights of Entry (Gas and Electricity Boards) Act 1954 5.44
Road Traffic Act 1930
s. 35 16.10
Road Traffic Act 1972 5.46
s. 148(3) 13.15
Road Traffic Act 1988 6.33, 16.10
s. 14 13.26
s. 143 16.10
s. 149 13.10, 13.15

Sale of Goods Act 1979 14.01
Slander of Women Act 1891
s. 1 18.50
Social Security Act 1975 9.07, 14.47, 15.24, 15.30
Social Security Pensions Act 1975 15.24
State Immunity Act 1978
s. 1(1) 2.13
s. 2(1) 2.13
ss. 5, 6, 10 2.13
s. 14(1), (2) 2.13
s. 17(1) 2.13
Statute of Frauds 1677
s. 4 5.37
Statute of Frauds Amendment Act 1828 12.37
s. 6 17.08
Statute of Limitations 1623
s. 5 5.10
Statute of Westminster II 1285 16.02
Statutes of Forcible Entry 1381, 1429, 1623 5.01, 5.44
Supply of Goods and Services Act 1982 14.01
Supply of Goods (Implied Terms) Act 1973 14.01
Supreme Court Act 1981
s. 19 8.67
s. 32A 15.02
s. 35A 15.23, 15.38
s. 69 18.19
s. 69(1) 18.106

Theatres Act 1968
s. 4(1) 18.40
s. 7 18.40
Theft Act 1968
s. 28 1.08
Tokyo Convention Act 1967
s. 3 6.32
Torts (Interference with Goods) Act 1977 7.02
s. 1 7.02, 7.19
s. 1(b) 7.15
s. 1(c) 7.44
s. 1(d) 7.10, 7.45
s. 2(1) 7.02, 7.45
s. 2(2) 7.02, 7.18
s. 3(1) 7.46
s. 3(2) 7.46, 7.49
s. 3(3) 7.46, 7.49
s. 3(4)–(7) 7.46
s. 4 7.42
s. 5(1) 7.55
s. 5(2)–(3) 7.55
s. 5(5) 7.55
s. 6 7.53
s. 7 7.51
s. 7(1)–(3) 7.39
s. 7(4) 7.39, 7.51
s. 8 7.20

Torts (Interference with Goods) Act 1977—*cont.*
s. 8(1) 7.11, 7.13, 7.24, 7.39
s. 9 7.39, 7.48
s. 10 7.32
s. 10(1) 7.11, 7.27
s. 10(3) 7.27
s. 11(1) 7.15, 7.30, 7.55
s. 11(2) 7.19
s. 11(3) 7.25
s. 12 7.22
s. 13 7.22
Sch. 1 7.22
Town and Country Planning Act 1971 12.63
Town Police Clauses Act 1847 6.45
Trade Descriptions Act 1968 14.01
Trade Disputes Act 1906 21.01, 21.12, 21.16, 21.17
Trade Disputes Act 1965 21.01
Trade Marks Act 1938 21.65
Trade Union Act 1871 2.22
Trade Union and Labour Relations Act 1974 18.03, 21.01
s. 2(1) 2.22
s. 13 2.23, 21.01
s. 17 21.01
s. 17(2) 21.01
s. 29 21.01
s. 143 21.01
Trade Union and Labour Relations (Amendment) Act 1976
s. 1 21.01
Trade Unions Act 1984
ss. 10, 11 21.01
Transport Act 1981
s. 27 13.26

Unfair Contract Terms Act 1977 12.38, 13.10
s. 1(3) 14.38
s. 2 14.38
s. 2(3) 13.13
s. 11 14.38
s. 12 14.01
Sch. 2 14.38
Union with Scotland Act 1706 11.10
Unsolicited Goods and Services Act 1971
s. 3 7.21
Unsolicited Goods and Services (Amendment) Act 1975
s. 2 7.21

Visiting Forces Act 1952
s. 9 2.15

War Damage Act 1965 2.08
Wireless Telegraphy Act 1949
s. 8 19.03
Workmen's Compensation Acts 1897–1925 9.07

Statutory Instruments

County Court Rules 1981 (SI 1981 No. 1687/L.20)
O.12 4.04
O.13, r. 4 7.39
O.13, r. 7 7.46
O.24 5.15, 5.18
Rules of the Supreme Court 1965 (SI 1965 No. 1776)
O.13, rr. 4, 5 5.50
O.15, r. 1 5.50
O.15, r. 6A 2.37
O.15, r. 10A 7.39
O.16 4.07
O.17, r. 8 7.37
O.21, r. 1(8) 15.38
O.22, rr. 1–7 18.112
O.22, r. 7 18.116
O.29, r. 1 18.118
O.29, r. 2A 7.46
O.33, r. 5 18.19
O.42, r. 1A 7.46
O.80, r. 2 2.24
O.80, r. 12 15.58
O.82, r. 3 18.13
O.82, r. 3(2) 18.62
O.82, r. 4(2) 18.116
O.82, r. 6 18.62
O.82, r. 7 18.114
O.113 5.15, 5.18

Conventions and Treaties

Brussels Convention on Immunity of State-Owned Ships 1926 2.13
European Convention on Human Rights 1950 19.01
International Covenant on Civil and Political Rights 1966 19.01
Treaty of Rome 1957
arts. 85, 86 1.35
Universal Declaration on Human Rights 1948 19.01
Vienna Convention on Diplomatic Relations 1961 2.14
art. 24 18,85

CHAPTER 1

The Nature of Tort Liability

1. INTRODUCTION

1.01 This book is about the law of torts. At the outset the question arises: What is a "tort"? Like all such definitional questions, it is not easy to answer. The purpose of a definition is, or ought to be, to provide the means by which the subject-matter of the definition can be identified. Where torts are concerned, the object of a definition should be to permit the differentiation of torts from other legal concepts. History reveals that, unlike some legal systems, the common law did not begin with a fixed idea of what constituted a tort, thereafter deducing from such definition different categories of tortious behaviour. Instead individual instances of tort were identified and dealt with by the courts, the jurisdiction of which would only be involved by the use of the appropriate writ.[1] Although it is no longer essential to identify a particular cause of action in a writ[2] today, after several centuries of evolution, we have a set of distinct instances of tortious liability. Each of them involves its own elements or ingredients. Each has its particular features. Each has evolved in its own manner from its early beginnings. Some have been modified or affected by modern legislation, designed to eradicate features which hinder the proper administration of justice as conceived in the twentieth century, by removing or changing aspects of such torts which seem archaic or outmoded. Others have gradually been adapted and improved by judicial action. Still others have been created by the courts to cope with situations previously not dealt with by any of the earlier writs. The manner in which the law of torts has evolved makes it difficult to locate some common principles of liability.

2. THE MEANING AND SCOPE OF TORTS

(a) The idea of wrong

1.02 The word "tort" is derived from the Norman-French that was used in the courts after the conquest and means "wrong". The law of torts is concerned with wrongdoing that merits recognition by the law and draws in its train some legal consequence. There are many different types of wrongdoing. Not all come within the purview of the law of torts. Hence it is inaccurate to identify the law of torts as "the law of wrongs". Some

1 Plucknett, *A Concise History of the Common Law*, 2nd ed. 1936, Book 2, Part I.
2 *Letang v. Cooper* [1965] 1 Q.B. 232 at 242–243; *Hesperides Hotels v. Aegean Turkish Holidays Ltd* [1977] 3 W.L.R. 656.

"wrongs" are not torts. Moreover some examples of wrongful conduct do not qualify as legal wrongs. They have no legal consequence. The law of torts concerns wrongful behaviour which has legal effects but is distinct from other types of wrongdoing.

(b) Legal and non-legal wrong

1.03 Torts must be differentiated from acts which, though harmful, are ignored by the law. Some acts may be immoral and yet not give rise to liability. For example if a women were seduced, by her consent, without the use of force or fraud, by a man, the woman could not sue the man in tort.[3] If a person ignored another's plea for assistance where the latter were drowning, the one who failed to come to the rescue of the other would not be guilty of any tortious behaviour.[4]

1.04 In the course of the evolution of the law there has been a gradual enlargement of the situations which are accepted as involving potential liability. For example, until the decision in *Donoghue v. Stevenson*,[5] it was not tortious for a manufacturer to be negligent in the manufacture of some article which was intended for ultimate sale by a retailer to a customer or for use by someone who had never purchased the article from a retailer. Until the decision in *Hedley Byrne v. Heller*,[6] it was not tortious for someone to give advice or information that was inaccurate to another, unless the person providing the information or advice had been fraudulent or was under a contractual or fiduciary duty to the party to whom the information or advice was given. Until the early part of this century it was not tortious to cause another person nervous shock, in the absence of any physical contact between the alleged wrongdoer and the victim.[7] Nor was it tortious until recently to inflict damage on an unborn child in the womb of its mother, although the act in question might involve liability to the mother.[8] Until the middle of the nineteenth century it was not tortious to induce one person to break his contract with another.[9] Nor was interference with the economic relations between two parties actionable, unless a

3 Until the Administration of Justice Act 1982, s. 2, the employer of the woman would have had an action based on loss of her services. In this devious way the father of the woman was enabled to bring an action. A husband might have had an action against the man, as an adulterer, on the ground of "criminal conversation". This was abolished by the Law Reform (Miscellaneous Provisions) Act, 1970, s. 4.

4 *Gautret v. Egerton* (1867) L.R. 2 C.P. 371 at 375; *Dorset Yacht Club v. Home Office* [1970] A.C. 1004 at 1027. Note the situation of one who attempts to rescue someone endangered by his own or another's act: below at 12.29. But the situation would be different if the danger had been created by the one who failed to effect a rescue: or if the latter owed a duty towards the one in danger, e.g. a policeman with respect to warning of hazardous conditions on the highway; *O'Rourke v. Schact* [1976] 1 S.C.R. 57, or the captain of a ship; *Horsley v. McLaren* [1972] S.C.R. 441 (both of which were decisions of the Supreme Court of Canada): cp the duty of a tavern owner towards a drunken customer: *Menow v. Honsberger & Jordan House Ltd* [1974] S.C.R. 239, another Canadian decision.

5 [1932] A.C. 562: below Chapter 14.

6 [1964] A.C. 465: below para 12.36.

7 Below paras 12.24ff.

8 Below paras 2.24ff

9 Below paras 21.30ff.

contract was breached in consequence, until some recent decisions.[10] In such situations there was "*damnum sine injuria*", i.e. damage without wrongdoing.[11]

1.05 Some misconduct, for various reasons, is still not tortious although it may be morally or socially wrongful. For example, one who commits perjury will not be liable to a person who alleges that he was convicted as a result of the jury's belief in the perjured testimony.[12] One who suffers economic loss as a consequence of a wrongful act committed by one person, A, against another B, may not have an action against A, unless the one suffering that loss can claim to be a dependent of B; under modern legislation that dates from 1846, the dependents of one who was killed by someone's wrongful act were first entitled to maintain an action, despite the old common law idea that death of a human being could not give rise to liability in tort.[13] An invasion of someone's "privacy" may still not be wrongful, unless it entails commission of some recognised tort such as trespass or nuisance.[14]

1.06 In spite of such limitations on the scope of tortious liability, it must be acknowledged that the ambit of this part of the law is still expanding, just as it has done in the past. In this respect a distinction can be made between "nominate" and "innominate" torts. The first expression refers to those torts which originated in the various writs issued by the Chancery in the middle ages. Innominate torts are those, of more recent origin and development, that do not fit under any of the historically recognised and accepted categories of tort liability, but have emerged in consequence of judicial action either by way of analogy with some pre-existing tort or as a spin-off from such a tort.[15] The legal concept of "wrong" is coming more and more to correspond to the more popular or general notion of what is "wrong". Increasingly the courts are broadening the scope of tortious liability, so as to take into accout what new social and moral developments make desirable.

10 Below paras 12.40ff.
11 There are still instances of this, e.g, where publication of a defamatory statement is privileged: below paras 18.71ff: where a person acts under statutory authority: below paras 8.54ff. Note that there may be "*injuria sine damno*", i.e. where the tortious behaviour causes no damage but is nonetheless actionable, e.g. trespass to land: *Nicholls v. Ely Beet Sugar Co.* [1936] A.C. 343.
12 *Hargreaves v. Bretherton* [1959] 1 Q.B. 45 where Lord Goddard L.C.J. thought that to allow such an action would let every criminal in England sue: it would "open the floodgates of litigation", a familiar, and specious, argument against permitting liability.
13 Below paras 2.36ff.
14 Chapter 19.
15 There is some judicial disagreement on the recognition of such innominate torts, viz., those founded on an intention to cause harm where to do so cannot be justified in law: contract *Beaudesert Shire Council v. Smith* (1969) 120 C.L.R. 145, *Canada Safeway v. Manitoba Food & Commercial Workers Union Local 832* (1981) 25 C.C.L.T. 1, *Van Camp Chocolates v. Aulsebrooks* [1984] 1 N.Z.L.R. 354 with *Dunlop v. Woollarha Municipal Council* [1982] A.C. 158, *Lonrho v. Shell Petroleum Ltd* [1982] A.C. 173, *British Airways Board v. Laker Airways* [1985] A.C. 58. See Fridman, "Civil Liability for Criminal Conduct" (1984) 16 Ottawa L.R. 34 at 52–55.

(c) Torts and other forms of legal wrong

1.07 A tort is therefore a type of wrongdoing in respect of which the law provides a remedy. That remedy is usually unliquidated damages by way of compensation for the injury inflicted on the plaintiff by the defendant. Unliquidated compensatory damages are, indeed, the hallmark of tortious liability.[16] However such damages are not exclusive to torts. Nor are such damages the only remedy available to the victim of tortious behaviour.[17] Hence it is not possible to differentiate torts from other types of wrongdoing by reference only to the award of unliquidated compensatory damages on proof of commission of a tort by the defendant against the plaintiff. Yet it is important to mark the distinction between these various forms of wrongdoing.[18] Sometimes statutes refer specifically to actions in tort, as distinct from other actions:[19] therefore it is necessary to identify a particular action as one in tort. Certain legal principles, e.g., those relating to remoteness of damage, apply to torts but not to other forms of wrongdoing which may be governed by different principles. Certain concepts, such as negligence, relate to torts but not, or not in the same way, to other types of wrongdoing.[20]

(i) Tort and crime

1.08 The law of torts provides compensation to the victim of wrongdoing, while the criminal law imposes punishment on wrongdoers.[21] In modern times that distinction is far too simplistic. In the first place statutes now permit courts to order convicted criminals to pay compensation to their victims, as well as undergo punishment.[22] Secondly, the Criminal Injuries Compensation Scheme enables victims of crime to claim compensation, from the state, in respect of harm suffered through the commission of a crime.[23] Such developments recognise that it may not be sufficient, where a crime is committed, to punish the criminal. Some measure of compensation is desirable for the victim, either from the criminal or from society at large, where the criminal is not amenable to suit, although he or

16 *Gouriet v. Union of Post Office Workers* [1978] A.C. 435; *Garden Cottage Foods Ltd v. Milk Marketing Board* [1984] A.C. 130. Hence (a) a public nuisance is not a tort except where an individual has suffered particular damage for which he can sue: below at p. 214: (b) conduct which leads to a clain for a liquidated sum, e.g. where money is paid under a mistake, is not a tort: below p. 7.

17 E.g., abatement or injunction in nuisance cases: below pp. 207, 211.

18 See, however, Hadden, "Contract, Tort and Crime" (1971) 87 L.Q.R. 240.

19 E.g., the Limitation Act, 1980. So, too, with respect to service out of the jurisdiction: *Matthews v. Kuwait Bechtel Corp.* [1959] 2 Q.B. 57.

20 E.g., in respect of the defence of *non est factum* to an action for breach of contract and the reply that the negligence of the signer of the contract estops him from pleading such defence: *Saunders v. Anglia Building Society* [1971] A.C. 1004. However, the standard of care in the tort of negligence is the same as that which is applied in the criminal law in relation to the offences of reckless driving and driving without due care and attention: *Roberts v. Ramsbottom* [1980] 1 All E.R. 7 at 13 *per* Neill J.

21 But the law of torts is historically connected with criminal law and procedure, and has a common origin in the ideas of revenge and deterrence: Fleming, *Law of Torts*, 7th ed. 1987, 1. Moreover some crimes are also torts, e.g., assault, libel, theft.

22 Powers of Criminal Courts Act 1973 ss. 35–38 amended by Criminal Law Act 1977 s. 60. See also Magistrates' Courts Act 1980 s. 150(1); Theft Act, 1968, s. 28.

23 *R. v. Criminal Injuries Compensation Board, ex parte Warner* [1986] 2 All E.R. 478.

she may have committed a tort as well as a crime. At the same time the law of torts sometimes permits courts to award punitive or exemplary damages to a plaintiff as well as damages to compensate for injuries or loss occasioned by the tort.[24] Such damages are designed to punish the wrongdoer, and perhaps aid in the deterrence of other potential wrongdoers. They are not meant as compensation. Indeed their amount may bear no relation to the harm suffered or the nature of the wrong perpetrated, in contrast with "aggravated" damages which are a true form of compensatory damages, having a relation to the way in which the tort was committed.[25] Admittedly, in consequence of the decision in *Rookes v. Barnard*[26] the role of punitive damages in English law, as contrasted with their role in other parts of the common law world such as Australia and Canada, is severely limited.[27] Nevertheless as long as the courts accept that such damages may be awarded in certain restricted instances, it cannot be said that the law of torts provides compensation not punishment.

1.09 Between criminal law and the law of torts there is a similarity that distinguishes both from, for example, the law of contract. Criminal and tort liability stem from the breach of a duty imposed by the law, not by consent or assumption of responsibility on the part of the wrongdoer. However, it is possible for a potential victim of tort to consent in advance to the commission of such tort upon him. Indeed the defence of *volenti non fit injuria* is a vital element in tort liability.[28] So, too, a victim of tort may be deprived of a remedy in total or in part by reason of his or her own neglect, i.e. contributory negligence.[29] However, consent is not generally a defence to criminal liability: nor is contributory negligence. A criminal cannot raise the victim's own conduct as a bar to the imposition of punishment for a criminal act. Since the law of torts is concerned with compensating the victim of wrongdoing which has caused harm, if the harm has been caused by the victim himself or the victim has given his consent to the possibility of insuring harm, there can be no compensation. The punitive aspect of damage awards in tort has not derogated from this basic principle.

(ii) Torts and breaches of contract[30]

1.10 The law of torts and the law of contract both provide for awards of unliquidated damages by way of compensation where a tort or breach of contract is committed. However where torts are concerned, the purpose of

24 *Rookes v. Barnard* [1964] A.C. 1129: below pp. 408, 514
25 *Rookes v. Barnard, supra* at 1221 *per* Lord Devlin: *Archer v. Brown* [1985] Q.B. 401.
26 *Supra.*
27 Fridman, "Punitive Damages in Tort" (1970) 48 Can. B.R. 373: see e.g. *Uren v. John Fairfax Pty Ltd* (1967) 117 C.L.R. 118, affirmed [1969] A.C. 590.
28 Below pp. 348–356.
29 Below pp. 356–369.
30 Markesinis "An Expanding Tort Law—The Price of a Rigid Contract Law" (1987) 103 L.Q.R. 354. Note that an action for breach of bailment, which is distinct from tort or contract, has certain features both of liability in tort and for breach of contract: but the burden of proof shifts to the bailee to explain how the loss occurred: *American Express v. British Airways Board* [1983] 1 All E.R. 557.

an award is to restore the plaintiff, so far as possible, to the position in which he or she was prior to the commission of the tort. In cases of contract, generally speaking, an award of damages is designed to provide the plaintiff with what he would have obtained had the contract been performed.[31] Some qualification of this should be noted. First, there are situations where the award is restitutionary in nature, not based on the plaintiff's expectancy. The plaintiff will recover what has been paid over to the defendant. Or the plaintiff will be entitled to recover what he has expended in reliance on the performance of the contract. Secondly, in some situations a plaintiff will be able to obtain specific performance of a contract, or an injunction to restrain its non-fulfillment instead of, or as well as damages. Remedies in contract are aimed at ensuring performance rather than making up for non-performance: whereas remedies in tort are designed to restore the plaintiff to the position he was in before to tort was committed, in other words to put the situation back to what it was. Tort, in other words, looks backwards, while contract is forward-looking.

1.11 There is another important difference between tort and contract. A tort involves the breach of a duty imposed by the law. Such duties are created by the courts, or by statute, for the purposes of regulating the relations between different persons, so as to ensure safety, security of person or property, or the harmonious conduct of business, trade or other affairs. Contracts give rise to duties agreed upon by the parties. Everyone is subject to the duties imposed under the law of torts, unless such a duty is excluded to the extent that the parties are permitted by the law to agree to such exclusion. Only those who are parties to a contract are subjected to its obligations, or may acquire rights thereunder. Indeed the doctrine of "privity of contract" had a great impact on the law of torts until recent times, and may still have certain important consequences.[32] However in some situations a contracting party may be subject both to a contractual and a tortious duty. The former arises from the agreement between the parties. The latter is imposed by the law in consequence of the relationship between them. An example is the solicitor-client relationship. Until recently it was considered that where a contract was in existence, the relationship in question was regulated in every respect by the terms of such contract, and no possible liability in tort could emerge from conduct which was a breach of such contract and at the same time amounted to a tort, such as the tort of negligence. It is now accepted that the victim of the misconduct can sue either for breach of contract, or for negligence.[33] In this respect, in such situations, the law of tort and the law of contract

31 Hence the principles of remoteness of damage differ as between tort and contract: see, generally, *The Heron II* [1969] 1 A.C. 350.
32 Below pp. 270–271.
33 *Midland Bank v. Hett, Stubbs & Kemp* [1979] Ch. 384. See also the decisions of the Supreme Court of Canada in *Central Trust v. Rafuse* (1986) 31 D.L.R. (4th) 481 and *C.P. Hotels Ltd v. Bank of Montreal* (1988) 40 D.L.R. (4th) 385. But see *Tai Hing Cotton Mill v. Liu Ching Hing Bank Ltd* [1986] 1 A.C. 801.

overlap. However liability in tort and liability in contract must be kept distinct.[34]

1.12 In contract only compensatory damages may be awarded. Punitive damages cannot be granted. In Canada such damages were awarded in certain cases of wrongful dismissal. But the Supreme Court of Canada has now held that this is not permissible.[35] However punitive damages for breach of contract are not unknown in the United States. Indeed it has been held that a breach of contract, if committed in bad faith, i.e. for an improper motive and not through accident or negligence, may constitute a tort, which would undoubtedly entitle the plaintiff to punitive as well as compensatory damages.[36] But damages for nervous shock may be awarded in contract cases, just as in appropriate instances of tort,[37] as long as they can be said to fall within the ambit of the principles governing the assessment and award of damages for breach of contract as laid down in *Hadley v. Baxendale.*[38]

(iii) Torts and restitution[39]

1.13 The modern law of restitution or unjust enrichment, which fulfills and expands the role once played by the law of quasi-contract, is based upon the idea that a defendant who has been unjustly enriched at the expense of the plaintiff must make restitution. Some instances of restitutionary recovery or unjust enrichment overlap with breaches of contract, torts, or breaches of trust. They involve deliberate or negligent wrongdoing. However a claim in restitution may validly be made even where the defendant was wholly innocent of any conscious or careless misconduct vis-a-vis the claimant. Restitution is not dependent on proof of "wrong" or wrongdoing. Nor, in a restitutionary claim, can the plaintiff recover damages at large based on injury or loss or expectancy. His claim is limited to the value of the enrichment of the defendant by his having received from the plaintiff or a third party money, goods, land, services or some other "benefit". In some situations, where a tort has been committed, the victim is allowed to "waive the tort" and sue in unjust enrichment or restitution. Where this is permitted the gravamen of the plaintiff's claim is not necessarily the commission of a tort, so much as the fact that the defendant has been unjustly enriched at his expense. Indeed

34 Prior to 1986 there might have been an important difference between tort and contract in relation to the time from which a statutory period of limitation began to run: see now the Latent Damage Act 1986 amendment to the Limitation Act 1980: below pp. 446–448.

35 *Vorvis v. Insurance Corp. of British Columbia* (1989) 58 D.L.R. (4th) 193.

36 Hill, "Breach of Contract as a Tort" (1974) 74 Col. L.R. 40. This idea has not been accepted in England: *Salmond & Heuston on the Law of Torts*, 19th ed. 1987, at 13.

37 Below pp. 283–286.

38 (1854) 9 Ex. 341. See Cheshire, Fifoot & Furmston, *Law of Contract*, 11th ed. 1986, 593 note 12: Treitel, *Law of Contract*, 6th ed. 1983 at 742–745.

39 Historically they are connected, since *assumpsit*, which was the writ that was used in conmtract cases, arose from trespass on the case, a tort action, and restitution, or quasi-contract, evolved from *assumpsit*.

it has been argued that in such situations, and others, tort is irrelevant.[40] Whether or not this is so, on historical or other grounds, it is plain that the law of torts is quite distinct from the law of restitution: and a claim founded on tortious liability is not the same in nature, scope or effect as one that is rooted in restitution.

(iv) Torts and breaches of trust

1.14 Like contracts, trusts are normally created by agreement with a trustee or trustees. Like torts, however, there are situations when a trust relationship, with some if not all of its consequential duties and obligation, is created by the law and imposed on a party without his or her consent. However the liability of a trustee, whether express, implied or constructive, is more like the liability of someone who has been unjustly enriched at another's expense than the liability of a tortfeasor. It is an obligation to disgorge any improper gains made by such trustee rather than a liability to pay damages at large so as to restore the plaintiff to his earlier position. Moreover the law of trusts is the creation of the Court of Chancery and its successor, the Chancery Division of the High Court of Justice. It is not common law in origin like the law of torts. It is more limited in scope, applying only to trustees, not to people generally. Third parties may become involved, however, where they improperly and with knowledge of the existence of a trust, acquire trust property. Where this occurs such third parties are treated as constructive trustees for the purposes of making them liable to reimburse the beneficiaries of the trust in respect of the trust property so acquired and any profits made in consequence. Once again the consequence of liability is not compensation but restitution. A breach of trust may be a "wrong", but it is a different kind of wrong which produces a different kind of remedy.

3. THE FUNCTION OF TORT LIABILITY

1.15 Definitions of tort emphasise that the fundamental consequence of such liability is the obligation to pay compensatory damages to the victim.[41] This suggests that the real aim, purpose or function of the law of torts is to provide for compensation of those against whom a tort is perpetuated. However the role of torts in providing compensation for injuries is not as unique as once it was. Modern developments have resulted in other methods whereby compensation can be obtained, without the need to establish guilt of tortious conduct on the part of anyone.[42] To such an extent has this come about that it has been argued that the law of

40 See, generally, Beatson, "The Nature of Waiver of Tort" (1978) 17 U. West. Ont. L.R. 1; Hedley, "The Myth of Waiver of Tort" (1984) 100 L.Q.R. 657; Friedmann, "Restitution of Benefits Obtained Through the Appropriation of Property or the Commission of a Wrong" (1980) 80 Col. L.R. 504.

41 E.g., *Salmond & Heuston on the Law of Torts*, 19th ed. 1987 at 15; *Winfield & Jolowicz on Tort*, 12th ed. 1984 at 3.

42 Harris, *Compensation and Support for Illness or Injury*, 1984; Atiyah, *Accidents, Compensation and the Law*, 4th ed. 1987.

torts is an old-fashioned, inefficient and outmoded way of providing compensation, which can be achieved much more cheaply and easily by other methods. In New Zealand this has led to the replacement of much of the law of torts by a comprehensive scheme of accident compensation.[43] In England, however, such a development was rejected by the Pearson Commission,[44] which reported on the law of personal injuries after an exhaustive examination of the law and practice in England and many other jurisdictions.[45]

1.16 However, despite the Pearson Committee's conclusions, there remain in modern English law several alternatives to claims founded on liability in tort. The older law of workmen's compensation, which dated from 1895, was replaced in 1946 by industrial injuries insurance. Under the governing legislation, claims for injuries resulting from industrial accidents or disease caused by working in industry do not depend on proof of commission of a tort, such as negligence or breach of statutory duty on the part of the employer. The fact of occurrence will be sufficient. Problems of proof can emerge. So can issues regarding the amount or duration of compensation. Disputes, whether of fact or law, are dealt with by tribunals, not by the courts of law. Other welfare legislation provides the means whereby those in need, through non-industrial sickness, or because of unemployment or redundancy, can obtain a measure of relief. This is not, strictly speaking, compensation. But it does serve to alleviate hardship and suffering caused by events out of the victim's control (much in the same way as the award of compensatory damages in cases of tort). It should be noted that, unlike some jurisdictions in which legislation on workmen's compensation or industrial accidents deprives the victim of a common law claim in tort even where a tort has been committed,[46] the English legislation preserves the victim's common law right of action. But the damages recovered may be reduced having regard to compensation awarded under the industrial injuries and similar legislation.[47] Extraneous payments may not always be relevant and taken into account where an action in tort is brought and damages are awarded. Not all "collateral benefits" as they are termed will operate to reduce the liability of a tortfeasor, even though the the effect will be to compensate the victim more than once for the same harm.[48] In this respect the law of torts does more than provide compensation based on actual loss.

43 Accident Compensation Act, 1972, as amended: see Harris, "Accident Compensation in New Zealand: A Comprehensive Insurance Scheme" (1974) 37 M.L.R. 361; Palmer, "Compensation for Personal Injury: A Requiem for the Common Law in New Zealand" (1977) 21 Am.J.Comp.L. 1.

44 *Report of Royal Commission on Civil Liability and Compensation for Personal Injury*, 1978, Cmnd, 7054.

45 On this see Fleming, "The Pearson Report: Its Strategy" (1979) 42 M.L.R. 249; Marsh, "The Pearson Report on Civil Liability and Compensation for Death or Personal Injury" (1979) 95 L.Q.R. 513; Allen, ed. *Accident Compensation After Pearson*, 1979.

46. E.g., Ontario.

47 Law Reform (Personal Injuries) Act 1948, s. 2(1): but not after 5 years: *Haste v. Sandell Perkins Ltd.* [1984] Q.B. 735.

48 Below pp. 424–425.

1.17 Compensation has been argued not to be the only aim, function or purpose of the imposition of tortious liability. Some have suggested that the law of torts serves a deterrent function or purpose.[49] By making a certain misconduct actionable, such as negligence, it is said, the law tries to prevent a tortfeasor from repeating his misconduct and discourages potential wrongdoers from acting in such a manner.[50] The sanction for such wrongdoing is the liability to pay damages. In this way the courts stipulate the standards of behaviour to be expected by everyone and enforce those standards. Indeed the possibility of an award of punitive damages in certain instances may be said to reinforce this view. However, various considerations call the deterrent function of torts into question. In the first place, the growth of insurance against liability has meant that in many instances, especially where negligence is the cause of action, not the actual tortfeasor but an insurance company will be called upon to pay the damages. Hence the knowledge that any damages will be paid by an insurance company will not operate to deter a potential tortfeasor or make him or her act with greater care.[51] On the other hand, such satisfaction of a judgment against the tortfeasor by the insurance company may lead to the tortfeasor having to pay a higher premium. Or all those insured against such liability may have their premiums raised in consequence of large monetary awards to plaintiffs discharged by insurance companies. This, for example, has led to the very high cost of medical insurance in the United States, where jury awards against negligent doctors have been large and highly punitive. A different factor is that in determining whether a defendant has been negligent courts will take into account the comparison between the cost of avoiding an accident and the potential costs involved in its occurrence. If the former is greater than the latter, the failure to take such precautions may not be negligence.[52] In other words, the existence of a tort of negligence does not operate as a deterrent in such cases, because it will be cheaper for the party whose conduct caused the injury to compensate the victim than to prevent his becoming a victim. On the whole it is questionable how far it may be legitimate and reasonable to regard the law of torts either as a means to deter the commission of wrongs or as a method whereby standards of conduct can be assured. Even the criminal law, which punishes in a very different way, can scarcely be treated as a satisfactory way of ensuring the observance of

49 Williams, "The Aim of the Law of Tort" [1951] C.L.P. 137 at 144. It has also been suggested that "tort law is an educator": Linden, *Canadian Tort Law*, 4th ed. 1988 at 11; or may "perform certain psychological functions", *ibid.* at 14.

50 A variation on this is "market deterrence", i.e. lowering accident costs by making the activities which are accident-prone more expensive by requiring them to bear the full costs of the mishaps they produce, which renders safe substitutes more attractive because they cost less: Linden, *op. cit.* at 17.

51 Hence it has also been suggested that the knowledge that a defendant is insured may lead to wider liability: especially since the fact of insurance, once said to be irrelevant to liability (see *Davie v. New Merton Board Mills* [1959] A.C. 609 at 627; *Lister v. Romford Ice & Cold Storage Co. Ltd* [1957] A.C. 555 at 572), has now been judically recognised: *Lamb v. Camden London Borough Council* [1981] Q.B. 625 at 638; *Morey v. Woodfield* [1963] 3 All E.R. 533n; *Post Office v. Norwich Union Fire Ins. Society* [1967] 2 Q.B. 363 at 368; *The Abidin Daver* [1984] A.C. 398 at 420.

52 Below pp. 314–316.

standards of behaviour. Much less satisfactory a mode of achieving such an end is provided by the law of torts.

1.18 Others have purported to discover the function of the law of torts in such ends as "economic efficiency", "wealth maximisation", or loss-distribution. There is no doubt that economic considerations play an important role in the calculation of damages to be awarded in tort cases. However, although courts may consider the consequences to society in general, not merely the particular litigants, of reaching a certain conclusion as to the governing legal principles in a case, those considerations are not necessarily confined to matters of economics, i.e. to the financial results of any such decision. Indeed, as pointed out by the House of Lords in *Morgans v. Launchbury*,[53] the courts are not the best forum in which such issues should be determined. They are not provided with all the essential information that would enable them to reach the most satisfactory solution: nor are they equipped to deal with conflicting policy issues that must be resolved in such instances. These matters should be discussed by law reform bodies and legislatures on the basis of a complete and thorough examination of all the relevant facts, arguments and policies. The courts are concerned with what is to be considered to be reasonable and fair having regard to the interests of plaintiffs and those of defendants. As the Privy Council explained in *The Wagon Mound (No. 1)*,[54] the limits of a defendant's liability for negligence were to be determined in light of what society would think was just and reasonable, rather than in terms of physical or scientific causation.[55] Logic and experience, reason and policy, all play a role in the formation of legal principles, including the determination of what conduct should be treated as tortious and how far liability for such tortious behaviour should extend. Economics may be a factor, but it is not the sole guiding or determining factor.

1.19 Such approaches to the development of the law may be termed "instrumentalist" in character. They emphasise the ultimate purpose or purposes to be served by the law of torts. A recent commentator has criticised such approaches,[56] arguing that there is an intrinsic legal ordering involved in the law of torts that differs from what he calls "conventional legal ordering". His conclusion is that the law of torts must be understood as not serving any higher or ulterior purpose, but as existing in its own right, as it were, much like the feeling or emotion of love, which can no more be explained or understood than the law of torts. This rarefied philosophical view, it is suggested, is difficult to comprehend or accept. Instead the law of torts may be said to fulfil a certain function that is necessary in any civilised society. It replaces the atavistic concept of revenge, as originally sublimated in Anglo-Saxon law by the idea of making a blood payment,[57] or in old Mosaic law of offering certain

53 [1973] A.C. 127.
54 [1961] A.C. 388.
55 Sere further below pp. 336–344.
56 Weinrib, "Understanding Tort Law" (1989) 23 Valparaiso U.L.R. 485.
57 Potter, *An Historical Introduction to English Law and Its Institutions*, 2d ed. 1943 at 306–308.

sacrifices to atone for wrongdoing, by a system of compensation based upon (a) the guilt and degree of involvement of the defendant as compared with other defendants and the plaintiff, and (b) the harm suffered by the plaintiff and the amount of money required to restore him to his original situation insofar as money can do this.

4. FUNDAMENTAL PRINCIPLES OF LIABILITY

1.20 Attempts have been made in modern times to identify a general theory of tortious liability. These attempts have centred around such concepts as causation;[58] fairness and reciprocity;[59] justice;[60] and conflicting interests;[61] as well as economic efficiency or wealth maximisation.[62] It cannot be said with any degree of confidence that there is any unanimity among commentators. What may be said, echoing the discussion of Holmes J. of more than a hundred years ago,[63] is that the various existing forms of tortious liability fall into one of three categories. They depend upon proof of (a) some intentional wrongdoing; or (b) negligence; or (c) the existence of a strict duty that has been broken without either an intention to do so or any negligence on the part of the tortfeasor. To understand liability in tort, therefore, it is necessary to discuss intention, negligence and strict liability. Consideration of these raises the question: how far is the law of torts based upon the idea of "fault"?

(a) Intention

1.21 Certain torts depend upon proof that the defendant acted with the intention and in the knowledge that damage would result to the plaintiff.[64] Indeed in such cases it will be insufficient to establish that the defendant acted carelessly, i.e. without any intention to cause harm but careless of the possibility that harm might follow from his acts. The underlying basis of liability is the defendant's manifest intent to cause harm. In the nineteenth century Bowen L. J. suggested that whenever someone intentionally caused harm without any lawful justification or excuse for his act,

58 Epstein, "A Theory of Strict Liability" (1973) 2 J.Leg.St. 151; *idem*, "Defences and Subsequent Pleas in a System of Strict Liability" (1978) 7 J.Leg.St. 165; *idem*, "Nuisance Law: Corrective Justice and Its Utilitarian Constraints" (1979) 8 J.Leg.St. 49. See also Kretzmer, "Transformations of Tort Liability in the Nineteenth Century: The Visible Hand" (1984) 4 Ox.J.Leg.St. 46.

59 Fletcher, "Fairness and Utility in Tort Theory" (1972) 85 H.L.R. 537.

60 Cane, "Justice and Justifications for Tort Liability" (1982) 2 Ox.J.Leg.St. 30.

61 Pound, "Interests in Personality" (1915) 28 H.L.R. 343; Machin, "Negligence and Interest" (1959) 17 M.L.R. 405; Lipstein, "Protected Interests in the Law" [1963] C.L.J. 85; Fleming, *Law of Torts*, 6th ed. 1983, at 3–4.

62 Posner, "A Theory of Negligence" (1972) 1 J.Leg.St. 29; Landes & Posner, "The Positive Economic Theory of Tort Law" (1981) 15 Geo.L.R. 851; Klevorick, "Legal Theory and the Economic Analysis of Torts and Crimes" (1985) 85 Col.L.R. 905.

63 Holmes, "The Theory of Torts" (1877) 7 Am.L.R. 652; Holmes, *The Common Law*, 1881, Chapters 3, 4. For criticism see Atiyah, "The Legacy of Holmes Through English Eyes" (1983) 63 Boston U.L.R. 341.

64 E.g., conspiracy, inducing breach of contract, intimidation: below Chapter 21.

liability should and would follow.[65] That statement did not represent the law at the time it was made. Even today, when developments have taken place having the effect of creating new forms of liability founded upon the intent to cause harm,[66] it remains too broad a proposition. Some acts may be perfectly lawful, even though they are performed with a view to causing injury to another and even if they are performed maliciously, from some spiteful motive.

1.22 Malice in this sense, which has been referred to as "malice in fact",[67] does not in general render an act otherwise lawful into something that is actionable.[68] In contrast malice in the sense of the intention to perform a harmful act, which has been termed "malice in law",[69] is accepted as an ingredient of several different kinds of liability.[70] Malice in fact, however, is relevant in some contexts for the purpose of disproving the right of the defendant to act as he did. For example, the plea of qualified privilege as a defence to an action for libel or slander may be defeated by proof that the defendant did not publish defamatory words in the legitimate exercise of a privilege but for the purpose of causing harm to the plaintiff, from a feeling of spite or ill-will towards him.[71] Similarly, in some instances of nuisance, proof of malice in fact will establish that the defendant was not making a reasonable use of his land. Once the defendant's use of his land can be held to be unreasonable, liability for nuisance can follow.[72] Malice in fact is also relevant in relation to malicious prosecution or the burgeoning tort of abuse of process.[73] Except in these special instances the law of torts is not concerned with the motive of the defendant but only in whether he acted intentionally, with knowledge of what he was doing.

1.23 Purpose, not motive, may sometimes be material. In the tort of conspiracy, for example, it has been decided that where an intended unlawful act is not committed by the conspirators, their liability will depend on the ultimate purpose of their combination.[74] If it was to injure the plaintiff, and was not justified in some way, they will be liable. In contrast, if their purpose can be regarded as legitimate and justified by the law, then, even if the result of their combination was, or would be likely to cause injury, they will not be guilty of a tort. Only where causing injury

65 *Mogul S.S. Co. Ltd. v. McGregor Gow & Sons* (1889) 23 Q.B.D. 598 at 613.
66 Below pp. 538–566.
67 *Bromage v. Prosser* (1825) 4 B. & C. 247 at 255 *per* Bayley J.
68 *Bradford Corp. v. Pickles* [1895] A.C. 587; *Allen v. Flood* [1898] A.C. 1: *Chapman v. Honig* [1963] 2 Q.B. 502; *Wyld v. Silver* [1963] Ch. 243. In England, unlike the continent, there is no doctrine of "abuse of rights". But there is a tort of misfeasance in public office, based on the malicious or negligent exercise of statutory powers by a statutory corporation or public officer: *Bourgoin S.A. v. Ministry of Agriculture* [1986] Q.B. 716; *Calveley v. Chief Constable of Merseyside Police* [1989] 1 All E.R. 1025. See also *Jones v. Swansea City Council* [1989] 3 All E.R. 162.
69 *Bromage v. Prosser, supra* at 255.
70 Fridman, "Malice in the Law of Torts" (1958) 21 M.L.R. 484.
71 Below pp. 505–573.
72 Below pp. 186–188.
73 Chapter 22.
74 Below pp. 538–544.

was the sole purpose of some, if not all the conspirators will liability ensue. The presence of malice in fact will not have any effect unless it indicates an unlawful or illegitimate purpose that dominates the combination.

1.24 Just as the fact that the defendant acted from an evil or improper motive will not necessarily make his conduct actionable, so the fact that he was actuated by a motive that might be regarded as good or laudable will not excuse him from liability if his act was tortious. The law is concerned with the legal not moral justification of his act. Thus in cases of trespass to the person, the defendant will be excused from liability if he was acting in self-defence.[75] He will not be similarly excused if the trespass was motivated by the desire to punish a wrongdoer who had caused him or another injury.[76] Punishment must be imposed by the law, not by individuals acting outside the law. Whatever feelings of moral indignation drove the defendant to his act, it will be inexcusable in law. If the defendant acted intentionally in committing a trespass he will be liable.

1.25 The line between malice and intention is a fine one. Although the courts have established and elaborated this distinction, it is not always easy to determine when the defendant's state of mind is relevant because it proves he was malicious. Proof of malice may reveal that the defendant acted with the intention of causing harm, where such an intention is a material factor in establishing liability. Absence of malice, on the other hand, will not necessarily disprove the relevant intention. But, as shown by cases on conspiracy, a party may act out of malice and yet not be liable because he also acted with a purpose or intention that was justifiable. It is not actionable to perform an act that is harmful but is justifiable in law merely because the actor enjoys the opportunity to inflict harm.

1.26 A further problem is that proof of intention to harm may be a matter of inference from the facts rather than capable of being established by a clear manifestation of such intent. In this respect the question is whether intention can be proved to exist by the application of the somewhat tarnished, misleading doctrine that "a man intends the natural and probable consequences of his acts".[77] The doctrine of constructive intent has been the subject of much criticism in the context of the criminal law. It may also be said to be of dubious utility and validity in relation to tortious liability. The view that appears to be most generally accepted at the present time is that the requisite intention should be proved by evidence that makes clear that the defendant actually, not constructively, was imbued by such intent.

75 Below pp. 127–128.
76 Even provocation of the defendant by the plaintiff will not excuse the defendant: below p. 128.
77 *Gollins v. Gollins* [1964] A.C. 644 at 664 *per* Lord Reid.

(b) Negligence

1.27 What began as an allegation in a pleading in the fourteenth century, justifying the granting of a writ of trespass *in consimili casu*, the beginnings of the action on the case,[78] has become in the twentieth century the focal point of a vital kind of liability. Indeed it might even be argued that the concept of negligence, like Aaron's rod, swallowed everything else in sight.[79] Not until then did negligence become a distinct tort in contrast with its being a mode of committing other torts.

1.28 Until then the law was restricted by the doctrine of "privity of contract". A negligent act that involved a breach of contract on the part of the defendant towards A could not be the basis of an action against the defendant by B, who was not a party to the contract but was injured in consequence of such breach.[80] Despite the evolution of various kinds of liability for negligence founded on the elaboration of different duties that were owed by virtue of certain relationships, e.g., those between an occupier and his visitors, a master and his servants, the scope of negligence was limited in the nineteenth century, and the earlier part of the twentieth, by the dominance of the "privity" doctrine. As long as that doctrine exercised its influence on the law, it was only possible to specify a restricted list of situations, historically derived, in which one party owed a duty of care to another, such that its breach by careless conduct falling short of the standards of the reasonable man could result in negligence liability.

1.29 This changed as a consequence of the decision in *Donoghue v. Stevenson*.[81] What that case decided will be considered elsewhere.[82] In the present context it is only necessary to explain that the attitude of the House of Lords was that negligence was more than a kind of conduct that could lead to liability in certain specific situations. Instead the House recognised the existence of a tort of negligence that was based on a breach of a duty of care owed by the defendant to the plaintiff: and such duty arose from the defendant's foresight as a reasonable man in his position of the likelihood of damage to the plaintiff if the defendant should fail to observe a reasonable standard of care and skill. In the more than fifty years since then the courts have been striving to define with greater accuracy and precision the nature of duties of care, and the elements of

78 Kiralfy, *The Action on the Case*, 1951, Appendix B, at 224–226. For the distinction between trespass and trespass on the case and its significance, see Winfield & Goodhart, "Trespass and Case" (1933) 49 L.Q.R. 359; Pritchard "Trespass, Case and the Rule in Williams v. Holland" [1964] C.L.J. 234; Milsom, "Not Doing is No Trespass" [1954] C.L.J. 105.

79 Hence the suggestion that there is no true distinction between trespass and negligence in modern law: *Berry v. British Transport Commission* [1962] 1 Q.B. 307 at 339; *Letang v. Cooper* [1965] 1 Q.B. 232 at 238. Cp. *Fowler v. Lanning* [1959] 1 Q.B. 426. But this is disputed: *S.C.M. Ltd v. Whittall Ltd* [1971] 1 Q.B. 337 at 357: *Wilson v. Pringle* [1986] 2 All E.R. 440.

80 *Winterbottom v. Wright* (1842) 10 M. & W. 109.

81 [1932] A.C. 562.

82 Below, Chapters 12, 14.

which the tort of negligence is compounded.[83] The tort of negligence has been developed to cover novel situations which, in previous centuries, were considered beyond the scope of legal intervention, if, indeed, they were considered at all. Liability for negligence, which once was limited by reference to such factors as physical injury to a person or property, and the existence of a special relationship between the parties arising from contract, ownership or occupation of property, or use of the highway, has now been extended to cover nervous shock, unborn children, verbal or written communications and economic loss unconnected to any physical damage. It may be said that there is no limit to the ultimate reach of this tort for, as Lord Macmillan said in *Donoghue v. Stevenson*:[84] "The categories of negligence are never closed".

1.30 The complexities of the tort of negligence will be discussed later. What is material here is that the evolution of this tort has had a profound effect on other forms of liability. Little by little the concept of negligence has become an integral part of other torts, such as trespass and nuisance.[85] It has even permeated the older stricter forms of liability such as that under the rule in *Rylands v. Fletcher*[86] or the doctrine of *scienter* in relation to harm caused by animals.[87] In its different forms, varieties or variations, negligence accounts for a major part of all tort liability in theory and considerably more in practice. It has become the universal tort.

(c) Strict liability

1.31 Although the law has never adhered to any doctrine that a man acts at his peril,[88] the idea of strict liability, by virtue of which the causation of harm by one's acts *prima facie* sufficed for guilt, may be said to have been an integral part of the law. From the seventeenth century onwards, particularly in relation to the law of trespass, there evolved a doctrine whereby a defendant who could prove he was "utterly without fault" might escape responsibility.[89] Nevertheless the view that causation or harm was enough lasted a long time,[90] as the nineteenth century decision in *Stanley v. Powell*[91] revealed, at least in respect of trespass to the person. Other forms of tort liability, such as nuisance, also illustrated the same attitude. Where damage was caused to the plaintiff's land by the defendant's use of his, no excuse based on lack of fault would be available to the latter to prevent his liability.[92] The ancient principle of cattle-

83 Below pp. 272–344.
84 *Supra* note 81 at 619.
85 Below pp. 87, 116, 190.
86 (1868) L.R. 3 H.L. 330: below pp. 221–222.
87 Below pp. 255–265.
88 Holmes, *The Common Law*, 1881, at 88–90; Winfield, "The Myth of Absolute Liability" (1926) 42 O.Q.R. 37.
89 *Weaver v. Ward* (1616) Hob. 134.
90 Cp. *Leame v. Bray* (1803) 3 East 593.
91 [1891] 1 Q.B. 86.
92 *St. Helen's Smelting Co. v. Tipping* (1865) 11 H.L.C. 642: cp. *Sedleigh-Denfield v. O'Callaghan* [1940] A.C. 880: below pp. 181–195.

trespass, under which an owner of cattle that strayed onto his neighbour's land would be liable even if their straying was not the result of any carelessness on his part, nor was intended by him, continued to operate.[93] Indeed, both nuisance and cattle-trespass were the sources of a newer rule of strict liability that was enunciated by Blackburn J., and approved by the House of Lords, in *Rylands v. Fletcher*[94] in the 1860's. All these doctrines, although perhaps modified and alleviated by the infusion of certain aspects of negligence, have survived well into the twentieth century,[95] a period when the idea of negligence has attained greater and greater importance and relevance, and when the law has seen the emergence of more forms of liability founded upon the intention to cause harm.

(d) Fault

1.32 It would be satisfying to be able to say that the law of torts rests firmly on the basis of the idea that there should be no liability without fault, in the sense of wrongful intention or culpable negligence: and that the true purpose and aim of the law of torts is to penalise such behaviour and compel the wrongdoer to compensate his victim. There are various reasons why this cannot be done. First, as previously noted, because of the rise in voluntary and compulsory insurance, the actual perpetrator of harm does not always provide the compensation. Second, the continued existence of strict liability makes it impossible to equate tort liability with fault. Third, even where fault is material to liability, especially in negligence, the test of what is "fault" for this purpose is not dependent on the standards of the actual tortfeasor but on those of the hypothetical reasonable man or woman. The law imposes an ideal standard of conduct,[96] which may not even vary where the tortfeasor is young, mentally incompetent, or otherwise lacking in judgment or experience.[97] Fourth, although through the medium of punitive damages some measure of punishment is involved in certain kinds of tortious liability, by and large punishment is not the real function of the law of torts. Compensation is its justification and end. Moreover, by virtue of the legal rules relating to remoteness of damage and assessment,[98] the amount of compensation awarded to a victim of tortious behaviour is not necessarily commensurate with the

93 *Ellis v. Loftus Iron Co.* (1874) L.R. 10 C.P. 10. This form of liability has been abolished and replaced by the provisions of the Animals Act 1971 ss. 1(1), 4(1): below pp. 266–267

94 (1866) L.R. 1 Ex. 265; (1868) L.R. 3 H.L. 330.

95 *Read v. J. Lyons & Co. Ltd.* [1947] A.C. 156. Note also the situation in respect of breach of statutory duty: *Galashiels Gas Co. v. O'Donnell* [1949] A.C. 275; *Carroll v. A. Barclay & Sons Ltd* [1948] A.C. 477; *John Summers & Sons Ltd v. Frost* [1955] A.C. 740: below Chapter 16. But in Canada it has been held that the breach of a statute does not obviate the need to prove negligence: *Saskatchewan Wheat Pool v. Government of Canada* (1983) 143 D.L.R. (3d) 9.

96 For some judicial expressions of what is to be understood by the "reasonable man" see *Hall v. Brooklands Auto Racing Club* [1933] 1 K.B. 205 at 224 *per* Greer L.J.; *Hawkins v. Coulsdon & Purley U.D.C.* [1954] 1 Q.B. 319 at 341 *per* Romer L.J.; *London Passenger Transport Board v. Upson* [1949] A.C. 155 at 173 *per* Lord Uthwatt, 176 *per* Lord Du Parcq; *A.C. Billings & Sons Ltd v. Riden* [1958] A.C. 240 at 255 *per* Lord Reid.

97 *Glasgow Corporation v. Muir* [1943] A.C. 448; see further below pp. 316–318.

98 Below, Chapter pp. 336–344, 418–432.

degree of "fault" attributable to the tortfeasor. Fifth, behind the notion that "fault" is the basis of liability stands the idea that the law of torts serves the purpose of deterring would-be tortfeasors by stating that those who are fault will be liable, and may also operate to educate people to behave properly by avoiding the deliberate or negligent infliction of harm. Once again these are not intrinsically the aims of the law of torts, albeit that sometimes awards of damages, for example in libel actions, may deter others from committing such a tort, and possibly the realisation that negligence or some other tortious behaviour can entail liability may induce people to be more circumspect and act accordingly. Such consequences are useful by-products. They are not the major concern of this part of the law.

1.33 A further consideration is that not all "faulty" behaviour leads to liability in tort. As previously noted, some improper conduct may be outside the ambit of the law. Admittedly, newly emergent torts, and new developments in older torts, have gradually extended the scope of conduct that becomes potentially actionable. Nevertheless, there is no congruence between faulty conduct and liability in tort. Nor is it likely that such congruence will ever completely come to pass.

1.34 It may be concluded, therefore, that it is highly unlikely that it will ever be possible to postulate the law of torts upon one basic, simple fundamental principle, namely that whenever someone behaves with the intention of causing harm or with negligence he or she will be liable in tort.

5. THE FUTURE OF TORT LIABILITY

1.35 The law of torts is not, and never has been static. It continues to undergo development.[99] Old torts have been revised, restated to fit new situations and changes in society. New torts gradually emerge to cope with relationships and situations hitherto not conceived of as coming within the ambit of the law. Sometimes such evolution is the product of judicial activity; at others legislation has been passed to deal with something that is not amenable to judicial development by reason of the strictness of the doctrine of precedent or because the courts do not consider they are qualified or sufficiently informed to determine.[100] The work of the Law Commission reveals the extent to which there is a constant need to rethink and reform the older common law. The work of commentators has also helped to expose areas where the law is out of touch with the facts of everyday life and requires alteration so as to make the law confirm more closely to what is needed to provide protection and a remedy where they

99 Perhaps some expansion is the consequence of the rigidity of the law of contract: Markesinis, (1987) 103 L.Q.R. 354.

100 Another potential source of tort liability is international treaty: *Garden Cottage Foods Ltd. v. Milk Marketing Board* [1984] A.C. 130 at 141, 144, dealing with the effect of undue restriction of competition, etc., under the Treaty of Rome, articles 85, 86.

are lacking or inadequate. It is unlikely that there will ever be a time when it is possible to say that the law of torts has reached perfection and no longer calls for development.

1.36 At the same time, however, certain social and economic changes have led to the replacement or augmentation of the law of torts. The advent of the welfare state has meant that those who were not, or were not adequately, protected by the existing law of torts have been provided with means whereby their plight can be alleviated. Industrial injuries insurance, unemployment and sickness insurance, welfare payments, criminal injuries compensation, have been introduced to cope with situations not covered, or not dealt with satisfactorily, by the common law. The creation of such new forms of what might be termed loosely as "compensation", and the rising cost of litigation, have caused some commentators and legislatures to seek the replacement of common law liability by various forms of administrative or governmental procedure which are considered to be less costly, more efficient and more productive of providing relief to those in need as a result of accidents, whether caused by another party's fault, such as negligence, or without any fault on the part of anybody. There remain some areas where the law of torts operates which do not seem quite so amenable to such treatment. For example, defamation, conspiracy, deceit, injurious falsehood, passing-off, even nuisance, are all examples of torts which do not appear to be capable of being remedied by some form of state or semi-governmental action in the same way as highway, industrial, or other accidents.

1.37 Indeed while some types of liability in tort have been replaced or affected by such extraneous modes of relief, new forms of tort liability are emerging, expanding the role played by the law of torts in society. Abuse of process, privacy, breach of confidence, for instance, provide examples of the way in which, in the twentieth century, there is still scope for further evolution.[101] It may be concluded, therefore, that, while the precise role and scope of the law of torts may alter in the future, there will be an important position for this branch of the law to occupy in the general scheme of the legal system. As long as this is so, it will be necessary to expound and explain the law of torts.

101 Below, Chapters 19, 20, 22.

CHAPTER 2

The Scope of Tort Liability

2.01 The law is concerned not only with the types of conduct that give rise to an actionable tort, but also with determining who can sue and who may be sued in consequence. This includes the conditions under which a person may sue or be sued. The right to sue is not confined to human beings. Nor are only human beings capable of being sued. Furthermore there have been, and still may be, restrictions on the right of a human being to sue, in general or in particular instances, or the liability of such a being to be sued. An associated issue is that of vicarious liability, whereby one person who has not performed the tortious act, however the term "person" is defined or understood, is the one who is liable. When the doctrine of vicarious liability applies, responsibility for a tortious act is extended to someone not personally guilty of any wrongful act. The rationale of this, and the circumstances in which such liability arises will be discussed elsewhere.[1] In the present context consideration will be given to the legal capacity, i.e. the right to sue and possible liabilities of various potential parties to an action in tort.

1. THE CROWN

(a) At common law

2.02 By "the Crown" in this context is meant the sovereign in his or her incorporated state, not personally. The Crown is considered to a corporation sole, a legal or juristic body or person distinct from the actual sovereign. At common law the Crown could maintain an action in tort against a party alleged to have been guilty of actionable conduct.[2] Such an action would lie where the Crown suffered loss by reason of such acts.[3] However, this idealised, fictitious legal person, at common law, was protected from liability in tort by the maxim that "the King can do no wrong", and by the principle that the sovereign could not be sued in his or

1 Chapter 3.
2 *Attorney-General v. Valle-Jones* (1935) 2 K.B. 209.
3 But the Crown was not able to sue in the action *per quod servitium amisit* for injuries to a member of the armed forces or a police officer, neither of whom were servants of the Crown: *Commonwealth v. Quince* (1944) 68 C.L.R. 227; *Attorney-General for New South Wales v. Perpetual Trustee Co.* [1955] A.C. 457. This action has been abolished in England by the Administration of Justice Act, 1982, s. 2(c)(i). It is still available in Canada and the Crown has been able to sue for loss caused by injuries to a member of the armed forces: *Attorney-General of Canada v. Jackson* [1946] S.C.R. 489; *R. v. Richardson and Adams* [1948] S.C.R. 57; *Attorney-General of Canada v. Nykorak* [1962] S.C.R. 331; *R. v. Buchinsky* [1983] 1 S.C.R. 481.

her own courts.[4] As a corollary of that, the Crown could not be considered to have authorised a wrong committed by its servant or agent.[5] In consequence, someone who alleged that a tort had been committed by the Crown, through the medium of a servant or agent of the Crown, could not sue the Crown. The injured party could only sue the tortious servant or agent insofar as that person was not protected from liability by some legal immunity. It was no defence that the act had been commanded or authorised by the Crown.[6] Only if a statute gave freedom from liability to the servant or agent in advance of the commission of the wrongful act[7] or *ex post facto*, by an Act of Indemnity,[8] or if the servant or agent could claim the defence of "Act of State",[9] would liability be excluded. A superior servant or agent of the Crown would not be made liable vicariously for the acts of a subordinate.[10] Only the one personally responsible could be sued. The reason for this was that they were all servants of the Crown: and on general principles one servant cannot be made vicariously liable, as opposed to his being personally liable for an act committed by himself, for the acts of another servant. Only the master can be made vicariously liable.[11] But a public corporation which acted under statutory authority for the benefit of the public could be made liable if its servants or agents committed a tort on its behalf.[12] Such public corporations were not considered to be or to represent the Crown. Therefore they could not avail themselves of the Crown's immunity from suit. It has also been held that nationalised industries or undertakings are not agents or servants of the Crown, and so could not invoke the Crown's immunity or exemption from legislation which excluded the Crown from its scope.[13]

2.03 The only mode of obtaining redress from the Crown in respect of a wrong committed by the Crown's agent or servant was by petition of right seeking compensation for the harm suffered. Such petitions could be brought only where land, goods or money had found their way into the hands of the Crown. Hence a petition of right could be brought in cases of conversion and possibly nuisance:[14] but would not be available where personal injuries were concerned.[15] Moreover it was a matter of discretion

4 *Viscount Canterbury v. Attorney-General* (1843) 1 Ph. 306 at 321; *Adams v. Naylor* [1946] A.C. 543 at 549–550, 555; *Trawnik v. Gordon Lennox* [1985] 2 All E.R. 368 at 372 *per* Lawton L.J.
5 *Tobin v. The Queen* (1864) 16 C.B.N.S. 310; *Feather v. The Queen* (1865) 6 B. & S. 257.
6 *Entick v. Carrington* (1765) 19 St.Tr. 1029, where general warrants were held to be illegal; *Feather v. The Queen, supra*; *Raleigh v. Goschen* [1898] 1 Ch. 73 at 77 *per* Romer J.; *Johnstone v. Pedlar* [1921] 2 A.C. 262 at 271 *per* Lord Finlay.
7 *Attorney-General v. Nissan* [1969] 1 All E.R. 629 at 653 *per* Lord Pearce, making it clear that such statutes will be strictly construed. See in respect of nuisance and statutory authority, below pp. 204–207.
8 *Phillips v. Eyre* (1870) L.R. 6 Q.B. 1.
9 Below pp. 24–25.
10 *Bainbridge v. Postmaster-General* [1906] 1 K.B. 178; *Raleigh v. Goschen, supra.*
11 See Chapter 3 dealing with the vicarious liability of principals, masters and others.
12 *Mersey Docks Trustees v. Gibbs* (1866) L.R. 1 H.L. 93.
13 *Tamlin v. Hannaford* [1950] 1 K.B. 18.
14 Holdsworth, *History of English Law*, vol. ix, at 40–43.
15 *Tobin v. The Queen, supra.*

whether the Crown would accede to the petition and permit compensation. The petitioner had no right *per se* to any redress. It appears that despite the alteration of the law by the Crown Proceedings Act 1947, the possibility of no redress in tort save possibly by petition of right will survive in cases where the 1947 Act does not apply. Such was the case in *Trawnik v. Gordon Lennox,*[16] where the claim under the 1947 Act was barred by a certificate of the Secretary of State given under the provisions of that Act to the effect that any liability of the Crown in the action arose otherwise than in respect of Her Majesty's Government in the United Kingdom. This case arose out of the intended use by the Crown of a military airfield occupied by the Crown in the British sector of Berlin. The plaintiffs were German nationals who wished to prevent this. In the circumstances the claim could not be made against the Crown because the 1947 Act did not apply and therefore the Crown could not be sued in tort, i.e. for nuisance. Nor could the plaintiffs seek a declaration because to grant this would entail a finding that the Crown had committed a legal wrong which at common law was impossible.

(b) Statutory change

2.04 The necessity for statutory amendment of the law was made clear by the decision in *Adams v. Naylor,*[17] which held that whatever voluntary action the Crown took to defend and satisfy a claim made against a Crown servant for personal injuries resulting from the negligence or other wrongful act of such servant, such an action was not available since there was no right to maintain an action against the Crown where a suit would have been allowed against a private citizen for the same misconduct. Hence the Crown Proceedings Act was passed in 1947. This made the Crown liable for the torts of its servants or agents,[18] for the breach of the duties owed by the Crown to its employees at common law, for the breach of duties attached by the common law to the ownership, occupation, possession or control of property, and for the breach of a statutory duty binding both on the Crown and its subjects.[19] The appropriate action must be brought against a Government department or, if there is doubt as to which department is responsible, against the Attorney-General. Various other statutes that pertain to actions in tort, viz., Law Reform (Contributory Negligence) Act, 1945 and the Civil Liability (Contribution) Act 1978 also apply to actions against the Crown under the 1947 Act.[20] Certain restrictions on liability must be noted.

2.05 The Crown will only be liable for the acts of a servant or agent, an officer of the Crown, if the officer in question is appointed by the Crown directly or indirectly and at the material time was paid in respect of his or

16 [1985] 2 All E.R. 368. See also *Franklin v. Attorney-General* [1974] Q.B. 185.
17 [1946] A.C. 543: see also *Royster v. Cavey* [1947] K.B. 204.
18 I.e. not statutory corporations or nationalised industries which are not servants or agents of the Crown: above notes 12, 13.
19 Crown Proceedings Act 1947 s. 2(1).
20 *Ibid.* s. 4: for these statutes see below pp. 76, 364.

her duties as an officer of the Crown wholly out of the Consolidated Fund, moneys provided by Parliament, or a fund certified by the Treasury as equivalent. This means that the Crown is not liable for the activities of the police. Police constables are not servants of the Crown.[21] Nor will the Crown be liable under the 1947 Act for anything done by any person while discharging judicial duties vested in him or responsibilities in connection with the judicial process.[22] Thirdly, an action will only lie against the Crown for the acts of a servant or agent if, apart from the Act, the act of the servant or agent would have given rise to an action against such servant or agent. This means that the Crown can avail itself of a defence that would be open to the wrongdoing servant or agent, as well as defences such as "act of state". But it may not mean that the Crown will be excluded from liability where, in the case of private citizens, a master will be liable even though the servant is immune from liability on some technical rule of law.[23]

2.06 So, too, the Crown will only be liable for breach of statutory duty if the statute applies to the Crown. Some statues expressly provide for this, e.g. the Occupiers' Liability Act 1957. If the statute makes no express provision, the general principle is that the Crown will not be bound, though the fact that nothing is stipulated in the Fatal Accidents Acts[24] has not been held to mean that they do not apply to the Crown. The reason for this is that, to fulfil the policy of the 1947 statute it is necessary to imply the application of legislation dealing with the rights of dependents to suits against the Crown. The failure to do so would mean the serious curtailment of the operation and effect of the 1947 Act.

2.07 The 1947 Act excluded the possible liability of the Crown for the acts of members of the armed forces when on duty, where such acts resulted in the death or injury of another member of the forces and where the death or injury was certified as attributable to service for pension purposes.[25] The Act also excluded the liability of the Crown for death or personal injury incurred by a member of the armed forces as a result of the nature or condition of land, premises, a ship, aircraft or vehicle used for the purposes of the armed forces or the nature or condition of equipment or supplies used for those purposes where the death or injury was pensionable.[26] This has now been repealed by the Crown Proceedings (Armed Forces) Act 1987. A further change has been effected by the Post Office Act 1969 and the British Telecommunications Act 1981. As a consequence of these enactments the Post Office is not a servant or agent

21 Nor of the police authority that appoints, pays and dismisses them: *Fisher v. Oldham Corp.* [1930] 2 K.B. 364. See however the Police Act 1964 s. 48 on the liability of the chief officer of police in any area.
22 For the position of judicial officers in the law of tort see below pp. 589–591.
23 Below p. 45.
24 Below pp. 433–438.
25 Crown Proceedings Act, 1947, s. 10(1) (which did not protect the Crown from liability incurred under the Atomic Energy (Weapons Group) Act 1973: *Pearce v. Secretary of Statute for Defence* [1988] 2 All E.R. 348).
26 *Ibid.* s. 10(2).

of the Crown.[27] Hence the Crown will not be liable for torts committed by the Post Office, its servants or agents. Nor will the Post Office itself be liable in tort (or bailment)[28] for loss suffered by anyone by reason of any acts or omissions in the postal or communications services.[29] In this respect it was held in *American Express Co. v. British Airways Board*[30] that a breach of statutory duty is a tort: therefore the Post Office could not be liable. Where the Post Office is not liable, neither will be its servant or agent, except to the Post Office itself,[31] which is a strange doctrine to justify, unless on the ground that, otherwise, the Post Office might be made indirectly to do what it cannot be made to do directly, namely pay damages to a party damaged by the acts of the Post Office's agent or servant.[32]

(c) Act of state

2.08 Before the passage of the Crown Proceedings Act 1947 the common law recognised the immunity of the Crown's servants or agents from liability when their conduct could be defended by the plea of act of state.[33] This was only available, however, where the plaintiff was an alien resident abroad and the act in question was not committed within the Crown's dominions but in foreign countries or on the high seas.[34] An alien would be able to sue a tortfeasor for an act committed within the jurisdiction unless the action were brought in time of war and the alien was an enemy, not a friendly alien.[35]

2.09 For this doctrine to apply there are three important conditions to be satisfied. First: the act in question must be characterised as an act of state. In *Attorney-General v. Nissan*[36] the House of Lords held that the actions of British forces on Cyprus, where they were present to maintain a truce, were not acts of state. The occupation of the hotel, which was the subject

27 Post Office Act, 1969, s. 6(5).

28 *American Express Co. v. British Airways Board* [1983] 1 All E.R. 557.

29 Post Office Act 1969 s. 29(1). See also the British Telecommunications Act 1981 s. 23.

30 *Supra*: cp. *Harold Stephen & Co. Ltd v. Post Office* [1978] 1 All E.R. 939; *Treifus & Co. Ltd v. Post Office* [1957] 2 Q.B. 325.

31 Nor is any contractual liability possible, since the sender of something by post has no contract with the Post Office: *Treifus & Co. Ltd v. Post Office, supra.*

32 But there is liability under s. 30 in respect of loss or damage to a registered inland postal packet when this is caused by the wrongful act, neglect or default of an officer, servant or agent of the Post Office: see *Building & Civil Engineering Holidays Scheme Management Ltd v. Post Office* [1966] 1 Q.B. 247.

33 Note also the legality of an act if it were performed in the course of an exercise of the royal prerogative: *Saltpetre Case* (1606) 12 Rep. 12. But this does not entitle the Crown to seize and destroy the property of a subject without compensation: *Attorney-General v. De Keyser's Royal Hotel* [1920] A.C. 508; *Burmah Oil Co. Ltd. v. Lord Advocate* [1965] A.C. 75. However rights to compensation may be affected by statute, as in the War Damage Act 1965. The prerogative of the Crown is preserved by the Crown Proceedings Act 1947 s. 11; without affecting the right of a subject to compensation in respect of property.

34 *Buron v. Denman* (1848) 2 Ex. 167; *Johnstone v. Pedlar* [1921] 2 A.C. 262 at 271 *per* Lord Finlay.

35 *Commercial & Estates Co. of Egypt v. Board of Trade* [1925] 1 K.B. 271; *R. v. Bottrill* [1947] K.B. 41. An alien may also be sued, even an enemy alien in time of war: *Porter v. Freudenberg* [1915] 1 K.B. 857.

36 [1969] 1 All E.R. 629.

of the action, was not a *sine qua non* of the performance of the treaty that was the basis for the action by the British forces.[37] However it is by no means clear what the expression "act of state" means.[38] It has been said that it covers the transactions of foreign states, with the effect that an English court will not adjudicate on such transactions. This principle was affirmed by the House of Lords in *Buttes Gas and Oil Co. v. Hammer (Nos. 2 and 3)*[39] where it was also held that such a principle was not a variety of the plea or principle of act of state but was a principle of judicial restraint or abstention.[40] It was not a discretionary principle but was inherent in the very nature of the judicial process.[41] Moreover it was distinct from the doctrine that an English court will not pronounce directly or indirectly on rights to immovable property situated abroad;[42] and the doctrine of sovereign immunity excluding actions concerning property that is in the ownership, possession or control of a foreign sovereign state or in which a foreign state claims an interest.[43]

2.10 Secondly, the plaintiff must be an alien.[44] Hence a British subject, at least if he is also a citizen of the United Kingdom and colonies, according to Lord Reid in *Attorney-General v. Nissan*,[45] can never be deprived of his right to redress by any assertion by the Crown or decision of the court that the acts of which he complains were acts of state.

2.11 Thirdly, the act in question must occur outside the realm of the Crown's dominions. Hence in *Johnstone v. Pedlar*,[46] although the plaintiff was an alien, an American who was Irish by birth, his arrest for illegal drilling took place in Ireland, at a time when this was part of the United Kingdom. Hence he was within the Crown's dominions and protection at the material time and the plea of act of state could not be raised even though his arrest was by order of the Crown.

2.12 It is clear that this doctrine survives the passage of the 1947 Act. But it will only be applicable in the circumstances and to those persons envisaged by the common law before 1947.

2. FOREIGN SOVEREIGNS

2.13 Foreign sovereigns, whether in their personal or public capacity, could always and may still bring an action in tort but they could not be sued at common law for a tort which they committed whether within or

37 *Ibid.* at 650 *per* Lord Pearce.
38 *Ibid.* at 645 *per* Lord Morris.
39 [1981] 3 All E.R. 616.
40 *Ibid.* at 628 *per* Lord Wilberforce.
41 *Ibid.*
42 *British South Africa Co. v. Companhia de Mocambique* [1893] A.C. 602; *Hesperides Hotels Ltd v. Muftizade* [1979] A.C. 508.
43 Below pp. 25–27.
44 *Walker v. Baird* [1892] A.C. 491.
45 [1969] 1 All E.R. 628 at 639.
46 [1921] 2 A.C. 262.

outside the juridsdiction.[47] Under the State Immunity Act 1978,[48] the immunity of a "state" from the jurisdiction of the courts of the United Kingdom extends to all foreign and commonwealth states and to the sovereign or other head of that state in his public capacity, the government of that state and any department of that government (unless that immunity is waived by submission to the jurisdiction). But it does not extend to any separate entity which is distinct from the executive organs of the government of the state and is capable of suing or being sued.[49] Such a separate entity will be immune, however, if the proceedings relate to anything done by it in the exercise of sovereign authority, and the circumstances are such that a state, or in the case of certain proceedings arising from the use of a ship for commercial purposes,[50] a state which is not a party to the Brussels Convention,[51] would have been immune.[52] The purpose of this latter provision is to codify the restricted immunity theory so that the activities of sovereign states which could equally be performed by a trading corporation or by private individuals will no longer enjoy immunity from the jurisdiction of civil courts in the United Kingdom.[53] However a state, as defined above, is not immune as respects proceedings for death or personal injury, or damage or loss of tangible property caused by an act or omission in the United Kingdom; nor in relation to proceedings relating to any interest of the state in, or its possession or use of, immovable property in the United Kingdom; nor any obligation of the state arising out of its interest in, or its possession or use of such property; nor in respect of certain actions *in rem* or *in personam* arising from the use of ships used for commercial purposes.[54]

2.14 The diplomatic representatives of a foreign state, although also imbued with capacity to sue in tort, were also immune from liability while such persons held their diplomatic status unless such immunity was waived by the tortfeasor or his superior who had the power to do so.[55] At common law such immunity extended not only to ambassadors and similar personages but also to the servants of an ambassador and the members of his diplomatic staff.[56] The old law on diplomatic immunity was replaced by

47 *Mighell v. Sultan of Johore* [1894] 1 Q.B. 149; *U.S.A. v. Dollfus Mieg & Cie.* [1952] A.C. 583; *Sultan of Johore v. Abubakar Tunku* [1952] A.C. 318. But immunity could be waived at common law.
48 Ss. 1(1), 2(1), 14(1).
49 *Ibid.* s. 14(1).
50 *Ibid.* s. 10.
51 Viz., the International Convention for the Unification of Certain Rules Concerning the Immunity of State-owned Ships, signed in Brussels in 1926; State Immunity Act 1978 s. 17(1). See Cmd 5672.
52 State Immunity Act 1978 s. 14(2).
53 For earlier decisions on this point see *The Porto Alexandre* [1920] P. 30; *The Christina* [1938] A.C. 485; *Owners of the Ship Philippine Admiral v. Wallem Shipping (Hong Kong) Ltd* [1979] 1 All E.R. 78; *I Congreso del Partido* [1981] 2 All E.R. 1064; *Czarnikow Ltd v. Rolimpex* [1979] A.C. 351. See also *Trendtex Trading Corp. v. Central Bank of Nigeria* [1977] 1 Q.B. 529.
54 State Immunity Act, 1978, ss. 5, 6(1), 10.
55 *Dickinson v. Del Solar* [1930] 1 K.B. 376.
56 *Engelke v. Mussman* [1938] A.C. 433.

the Diplomatic Privileges Act 1964,[57] which enacted the provisions of the Vienna Convention on Diplomatic Relations signed in 1961, which came into force in 1964. Similar immunities are conferred on representatives and officers of international organisations[58] under the provisions of the International Organisations Act 1968.[59]

2.15 The provisions of the Visiting Forces Act 1952 s. 9 regulate the settlement of claims against members of visiting forces from the Commonwealth and States which are parties to the North Atlantic Treaty.

3. CORPORATIONS

2.16 Since corporations are artificial persons, whose personality is the construction of the law, there are certain limitations on the right of such bodies to sue in tort, and some problems associated with the question whether such bodies can be made liable.

2.17 As plaintiffs, there are no restrictions in general on the right of a corporation to maintain an action in respect of a tort committed against it,[60] save that the tort must be one that is capable of being committed against a corporation. This means that a corporation will not be able to bring an action for personal injury of any kind, but may sue in respect of damage to its property. Defamation can be considered for some purposes a tort against property, which suggests that a corporation may be the victim of libel or slander in respect of which it can sue. However the defamation must relate in some way to the property of the corporation. This means that it must refer to the trading reputation of the corporation, where the latter is a trading corporation. Hence a statement that a company leased insanitary cottages to its employees,[61] or that a company illegally carried on a restaurant in breach of statutory orders made in wartime by the Ministry of Food,[62] were the kind of defamatory statements in respect of which the companies in question could sue. If the corporation is a local government corporation, the view that such a body could not sue for libel or slander[63] was rejected by Browne J. in *Bognor Regis Urban District Council*

57 Ss. 1, 2(1), Schedule 1, which protects (a) members of the diplomatic staff who have full immunity with certain exceptions; (b) members of the administrative, technical and service staff, who have full immunity for official acts but not for acts outside the course of their employment.

58 And to some extent their official staff and families.

59 Ss. 1, 2, 6, Schedule 1, Parts II, III, IV.

60 Just as a human person can sue for malicious prosecution (below Chapter 22), so a juristic person can sue for the malicious presentation of a winding-up petition: *Quartz Hill Gold Mining Co. v. Eyre* (1883) 11 Q.B.D. 647.

61 *South Hetton Coal Co. Ltd v. North Eastern News Association Ltd* [1894] 1 Q.B. 133.

62 *D. & L. Caterers Ltd. v. D'Anjou* [1945] K.B. 364.

63 *Manchester Corporation v. Williams* [1891] 1 Q.B. 94, in relation to a libel that accused the corporation of corruption: cp. *Metropolitan Saloon Omnibus Co. v. Hawkins* [1859] 4 H. & N. 87 at 90 *per* Pollock C.B.

v. Campion.[64] There a leaflet alleged that the local council had conducted its affairs in a dictatorial and undemocratic fashion and had exerted pressure on the editor of a local newspaper to repress free speech and a free press; that members of the council had personal axes to grind, which was why the council was not carrying out the wishes of the electors; and that the council's policy to destroy people's homes as unfit was dishonest. The council could maintain an action against those who published this attack. It was not a libel on individual members or officers of the council, but on the council itself. As a local government corporation the council had a "governing" reputation, similar to the "trading" reputation possessed by a business or trading corporation. This reputation the council was entitled to protect in the same way as any other corporation could protect not only its property but also its personal reputation.

2.18 The liability of a corporation, of whatever kind, is always vicarious. It depends on proof that the servants or agents of the corporation acted in a tortious manner for which, in accordance with the general principles of vicarious liability,[65] the corporation would be responsible in law. This means that the corporation will be liable for the acts of its members, as well as its employees, where the members act on the corporation's behalf. However a member will not be liable for torts committed by the corporation, through its servants or agents, unless that member has committed the tort in question. The corporation is a person in law distinct from those human persons who are its members. For this reason a corporation can commit a tort against a member of the corporation, such as the shareholder of a company, just as it can commit a tort against a stranger.[66]

2.19 For a corporation to be liable in tort it must have expressly authorised the commission of the wrongful act or given an agent or servant the opportunity to commit such wrongful act in the course of his employment. Nor does it matter what is the nature of the tort. A corporation can be held liable for any kind of tort, even one that requires proof of malice as an essential ingredient of liability. This includes liability for a libel where malice on the part of a corporation's servant or agent destroys the plea of qualified privilege.[67] In this instance, as in many others, the act in question was one that could be authorised by the corporation.[68] The problem that has caused considerable vexation and difficulty, however, is whether a corporation can be liable in respect of a tort committed by an agent or

64 [1972] 2 All E.R. 61 at 68, where it was said that the *Williams* case had been overruled by the *South Hetton Coal* case and by *National Union of General & Municipal Workers v. Gillian* [1945] 2 All E.R. 593, affirmed [1946] K.B. 81: and the *Williams* case was distinguished on the ground that the corporation consisted of the mayor, alderman and citizens, not, as in the *Campion* case of the chairman and councillors: [1972] 2 All E.R. 61 at 69.

65 Chapter 3.

66 But an action of deceit (Chapter 17) will not lie against the corporation at the suit of the shareholder unless his allotment of shares has been rescinded, i.e. he has ceased to be a member: *Houldsworth v. City of Glasgow Bank* (1880) 5 App. Cas. 317.

67 *Citizens' Life Assurance Co. v. Brown* [1904] A.C. 423.

68 *Ibid.* at 425–426 *per* Lord Lindley.

servant who was not expressely authorised to commit the act, and could not be so authorised because the act was one which the corporation could not legally authorise since it was outside the legal powers of the corporation. For example, in *Poulton v. London & South-Western Railway*,[69] the railway company's servant purported to arrest the plaintiff for non-payment of the fare of a horse. The company did not have the legal power to arrest in such circumstances. Hence the servant could not have been authorised to do so. The company was held not liable, because the act of the servant was outside his authority. However in *Campbell v. Paddington Corporation*,[70] a municipal corporation could be held liable for a tort committed when it ordered the erection of a stand that caused damage to the plaintiff, although the corporation had no legal right to erect such stand. The corporation was liable because the tort had been committed.[71] It might be argued that since a corporation never has legal power to order or authorise the commission of a tort, a tort committed by its servant or agent is always outside the power of the corporation, with the result that a corporation would never be liable for torts, whether committed in the course of some lawfully authorised act by its servant or agent or in the course of some non-legally authorised act.[72] This would seem to be a *reductio ad absurdum*. Despite the rule at common law that a corporation would not be liable for a contract made *ultra vires* the corporation,[73] there are valid reasons for making a corporation liable in tort for acts of any kind committed by a servant or agent acting within the course of employment, whether such acts were, or could legally have been authorised by the corporation. Logic and convenience dictate that a corporation should always be liable for a tort committed on its behalf by a servant acting in the course of his employment, whether or not the act in question, or the act in pursuance of which the tortious act was perpetrated, could lawfully have been authorised by the corporation.[74]

4. UNINCORPORATED BODIES

2.20 Many groups exist without being incorporated. Such bodies include members' clubs and trade unions. Without incorporation such groups do not possess legal personality, the lack of which causes both substantive and

69 (1867) L.R. 2 Q.B. 534.

70 [1911] 1 K.B. 869.

71 *Ibid.* at 878 *per* Lush J. Cp. the situation under the Merchant Shipping Acts, in respect of which it has been held that a corporation could be guilty of "actual fault": *The Lady Gwendolen* [1965] P. 294, where it was held that the company itself had been guilty of the relevant act or omission, since the traffic manager, who was head of the department to which the company had entrusted the management of a ship, was the *alter ego* of the company for such purpose; therefore his act or omission was the act or omission of the company: [1965] P. 294 at 342–345 *per* Willmer L.J., 355–356 *per* Winn L.J.

72 *Campbell v. Paddington Corporation* [1911] 1 K.B. 869 at 875 *per* Avory J.: cp. *Mills v. Hawker* [1874] L.R. 9 Ex. 309 at 322 *per* Kelly C.B.; affirmed (1895) L.R. 10 Ex. 92.

73 Cheshire, Fifoot & Furmston, *Law of Contract*, 11th ed. 1986, at 430–434. This doctrine has been substantially altered by the European Communities Act, 1972, s. 9(1), now contained in the Companies Act, 1985, s. 35(1).

74 Even if the employment of the servant or agent was under a contract that was *ultra vires* the corporation insofar as the doctrine of *ultra vires* survives changes in the law: *supra* note 73.

procedural problems in relation to the commission of a tort by or against such a group and its capacity to sue or be sued. This has been most troublesome, as well perhaps as most important, in regard to trade unions, which may own large amounts of money, can own or possess property, and, through the activities of their members either with or without the advice, encouragement or instruction of their officers, can perpetrate acts which are capable of inflicting substantial damage upon others such as employers or other workers.

2.21 Some clubs are incorporated, in which event the situation will be governed by what has been considered in the previous section. Others may be proprietary, when the property and funds of the club belong to a proprietor who may sue and be sued in his own name or that of the club, and may make someone liable or be liable for an appropriate tort.[75] If a club is neither proprietary nor incorporated, it will have no separate legal personality. Hence no tort can be committed against the club itself. If a tort is committed, e.g. nuisance or trespass, the action must be brought on behalf of the members of the club by those who can be considered to represent the members, normally the governing committee, by a representative action. Nor can the club commit a tort, either against a member or a stranger. If a tort is committed, for example, under the Occupiers' Liability Act 1957 or nuisance, there may be difficulties with determining who should be sued. The members of the committee of the club, if there is one, might be personally liable for a tort they have authorised or committed directly or through a servant or agent.[76] Trustees may be liable, if the property of the club is vested in trustees and the tort arises out of the ownership or control of property such as the club's premises. The members as a whole may be liable, if the tort is committed by the committee, or a servant or agent of the club for and on behalf of the club. In such a case a representative action is appropriate against, e.g. the members of the committee.[77]

2.22 Trade unions have been subjected to special treatment by both the common law and statute. Prior to 1871 trade unions were regarded as unlawful combinations in restraint of trade and they were not considered to have any legal personality. The Trade Union Act 1871, and its successors, recognised trade unions as lawful bodies, but maintained that they were unincorporated associations unable to sue in their own name or to be sued. In *Taff Vale Railway Co. v. Amalgamated Society of Railway Servants*[78] the House of Lords held that a trade union was a quasi-

75 On the basis of the normal rules of vicarious liability: Chapter 3.

76 *Brown v. Lewis* (1896) 12 T.L.R. 455. But not where the rules of the club did not state that certain officers were responsible for the condition of the club's premises; consequently they did not owe a duty of care to an individual member who was injured by the state of the driveway: *Robertson v. Ridley* [1989] 2 All E.R. 474. Cp. *Poole v. Allen* [1950] 1 All E.R. 476 and *Shore v. Ministry of Works* [1950] 2 All E.R. 228.

77 *Campbell v. Thompson* [1953] 1 Q.B. 445.

78 [1901] A.C. 426, applied to a registered Friendly Society in *Longdon-Griffiths v. Smith* [1951] 1 K.B. 295 and to a Trustee Savings Bank in *Knight & Searle v. Dove* [1964] 2 Q.B. 631, but not to an ordinary members' club.

corporation or a near corporation by virtue of its registration under the 1871 Act. Hence it was subsequently decided that a trade union could be defamed in its proper name, and could sue for defamation, as long as the defamation touched its reputation,[79] just as a corporation could sue for a defamation that touched its trading, or, as subsequently held, its governing reputation in the case of a municipal corporation.[80] That was the situation in the 1950s before the passage of the Industrial Relations Act 1971, which gave effect to the recommendations of a Royal Commission in 1965 that unions should be bodies corporate. However the Trade Union and Labour Relations Act 1974 repealed the statute of 1971 and enacted that "a trade union which is not a special register body shall not be or be treated as if it were, a body corporate".[81] As a result of this O'Connor J. held in *Electrical, Electronic, Telecommunications and Plumbing Union v. Times Newspapers Ltd*[82] that a trade union could not sue in tort (at least as long as it was not a special register body under the 1974 Act). Nor could it maintain an action for damages for defamation on behalf of each and every one of its individual members in the name of the union, without identifying any particular members or member. No representative action was available to a number of different individuals where the relief sought was damages, and the interest of those members was not the same because their individual reputations differed and the amount of damages would be different.[83]

2.23 However the effect of other legislation[84] was to render trade unions capable of being sued in tort, as decided by the House of Lords in 1901. Nonetheless, while trade unions are for some purposes equated with natural persons, the legislation also imposes certain restrictions on that liability. For example, where conspiracy or inducing breach of contract[85] are alleged against a union it will only be liable if the act was authorised or endorsed by a "responsible" person.[86] If sued for personal injury caused by negligence, nuisance or breach of duty, or in respect of the ownership or possession of property, there is no limit on the damages that can be awarded against the union. In other cases financial limits are imposed.[87] In any event damages are not enforceable as against certain "protected property", including a political fund not available for financing strikes, and a provident fund.[88] It must be noted however, that there still exist

79 *National Union of General & Municipal Workers v. Gillian* [1945] 2 All E.R. 593, affirmed [1946] K.B. 81.
80 Above p. 27.
81 Trade Union & Labour Relations Act, 1974, s. 2(1).
82 [1980] 1 All E.R. 1097.
83 *Ibid.* at 1104–1105.
84 Viz., Employment Acts, 1980, 1982.
85 Or interfering with contract or intimidation by threats to interfere with contract: Employment Act 1982, s. 15(2)(a), (b).
86 *Ibid.* s. 15. Who is a "responsible person" is defined in s. 15(4)–(6). In other instances the ordinary rules of vicarious liability apply: *Heatons Transport (St Helens) Ltd v. Transport & General Workers' Union* [1973] A.C. 15, a decision under the Industrial Relations Act 1971. Acts outside the rules of a union may still be authorised: *Thomas v. National Union of Mineworkers* [1985] 2 All E.R. 1 at 29 *per* Scott J.
87 Employment Act 1982 s. 16.
88 *Ibid.* at s. 17.

certain immunities from liability that are available to a union, despite the vicissitudes through which the law on this subject has gone in recent years. Such immunities depend on whether the act complained of was committed in furtherance or contemplation of a trade dispute, a phrase which entered the law in 1906 and has been part of it ever since.[89]

5. PERSONS UNDER DISABILITY[90]

(a) Minors[91]

(i) Actions by minors

2.24 A minor is fully capable of suing for all wrongs committed against him or her. Such an action must be brought by someone on behalf of the minor acting as the minor's best friend. Usually this is a parent.[92] A child born after the death of its father by the wrongful act of the defendant may sue under the Fatal Accidents Act[93] in respect of the loss resulting through such death.[94] A minor may be guilty of contributory negligence which will reduce or even remove the liability of the defendant.[95] Moreover a minor may be held to be *volens* to the negligent act of the defendant, even though, if an express contract were raised as a defence to the action, it would not be binding on the minor by reason of the fact that it was not for the minor's benefit.[96]

2.25 The issue that caused considerable difficulty until recent times was whether a minor, when born, could sue in respect of injuries inflicted on

89 See, e.g., *Mercury Communications Ltd v. Scott-Garner* [1984] 1 All E.R. 179; *Dimbleby & Sons Ltd v. National Union of Journalists* [1984] 1 All E.R. 751; cp. also Chapter 21 note 1. For the immunity of individual members or officers of a trade union see the Trade Union & Labour Relations Act 1974 s. 13, as amended by the Employment Act 1980 s. 17 and the Employment Act 1982 s. 19.

90 The position of spouses in law of tort has undergone considerable change. By the Law Reform (Married Women and Tortfeasors) Act 1935, a married woman can be sued for her torts committed against a stranger and is subject to the law of bankruptcy and the enforcement of judgments as if she were unmarried. Furthermore, her husband is not liable for her torts just because he is her husband, which was the situation at common law. He may be liable on ordinary principles of vicarious liability, viz., if she was acting as his servant or agent when she committed the tort. Hence spouses now seem to be liable for conspiring together: *Midland Bank Trust Co. Ltd v. Green (No. 3)* [1979] Ch. 496, affirmed [1982] Ch. 529.

More importantly, by the Law Reform (Husband & Wife) Act 1962 husband and wife can now sue each other in tort as if they were not married. This fundamentally alters the old common law. But the action may be stayed if no substantial benefit (viz., presumably, financial benefit) will accrue to either party by continuance of the proceedings: or if the issue can be more conveniently disposed of under the Married Women's Property Act 1882 s. 17, dealing with ownership and possession of property: see also the Matrimonial Causes Act 1973 ss. 21–26.

91 I.e. those under 18: Family Law Reform Act 1969 s. 1.

92 R.S.C. Ord. 80, r. 2.

93 Below Chapter 15, pp. 433–438.

94 *The George & Richard* (1871) L.R. 3 Ad. & E. 466.

95 *Jones v. Lawrence* [1969] 3 All E.R. 267; *Gough v. Thorne* [1966] 3 All E.R. 398. This is not easy to establish, especially in the case of a young child: *Yachuk v. Oliver Blais Co. Ltd* [1949] A.C. 386. See further below pp. 360–361.

96 *Buckpitt v. Oates* [1968] 1 All E.R. 1145.

the minor while still in its mother's womb.[97] This has now been resolved by the Congenital Disabilities (Civil Liability) Act 1976.[98] By this statute a child born alive and disabled may be able to sue someone, other than the child's mother, responsible for an occurrence which was the cause of the disablement.[99] The relevant occurrence is one that affected either parent of the child or his or her ability to have a normal, healthy child or one which affected the mother during pregnancy, or affected her or the child in the course of the birth so that the child is born with disabilities that would not otherwise have been present.[100] However the person responsible for this occurrence will only be liable to the child if that person was, or if sued would have been liable in tort to the parent.[101] The child's action, therefore, is derivative. It is dependent on an action being available, actually or hypothetically, to the parent. But the defendant will be liable to the child as long as there was a breach of duty to the parent, even if the parent suffered no injury that would have supported an action by the parent.[102] So, if the mother is unharmed, but the child *en ventre sa mère* is harmed, there will be an action by the child when born alive, as long as the defendant did something that was a breach of a legal duty owed to the mother, e.g. by running her down through the negligent driving of a car, or causing her to incur shock, in accordance with decisions on nervous shock,[103] with the result that the child in her womb was affected. There will be no liability if this occurred before conception if either or both parents knew the risk of their child being born disabled, i.e. the particular risk created by the occurrence.[104] This would cover the situation if the mother took some drug for any purpose and the drug inherently involved a risk in the event of subsequent pregnancy.[105] However if the defendant is guilty of the "occurrence" this provision will not afford him an answer, if sued by the child, where he knew the risk and the mother did not.[106] Where the defendant acted in a professional capacity in treating or advising the parent, he will not be answerable to the child if he took reasonable care having due regard to the received professional opinion applicable to the particular class of case. But he will not be liable merely because he departed from received opinion.[107] Liability to the child can be excluded or limited by contract made with the affected parent to the same extent and subject to the same restrictions as liability to the parent.[108] A term in a contract that could be set up by the defendant to an action by

97 Such an action was allowed in Canada: *Duval v. Seguin* [1972] 26 D.L.R. (3d) 418: and Australia, *Watts v. Rama* [1972] V.R. 353.
98 Based on a report by the Law Commission: "Injuries to Unborn Children", 1974 Law Comm. No. 60.
99 Congenital Disabilities (Civil Liability) Act 1976 s. 1(1). "Born" means "born alive": the moment of birth being when it first has a life separate from its mother: *ibid.* s. 4(2)(a).
100 *Ibid.* s. 1(2).
101 *Ibid.* s. 1(3).
102 *Ibid.*
103 Below pp. 283–286.
104 Congenital Disabilities (Civil Liability) Act 1976 s. 1(4).
105 Cp. *Distillers Co. (Biochemicals) Ltd v. Thompson* [1971] A.C. 458.
106 Congenital Disabilities (Civil Liability) Act 1976 s. 1(4).
107 *Ibid.* s. 1(5).
108 *Ibid.* s. 1(6).

the parent, to exclude or limit his liability, operates in favour of the defendant in an action by the child, in the same way and to the same extent.[109] Where a parent shares responsibility for the child being born disabled, damages will be reduced by an amount the court thinks just and equitable having regard to the parent's responsibility.[110] The action by the child is to be treated as if it were an action for personal injuries sustained by the child immediately after birth.[111] Although a mother, but not a father, is exempt from liability for a child's being born disabled under the provisions of the opening section of the Act, a mother who drives a motor vehicle when she knows, or ought reasonably to know, that she is pregnant, is under the same duty to take care for the safety of her unborn child as she owes to other people.[112] If she breaches that duty and in consequence the child is born with disabilities that otherwise would not have been present, those disabilities are regarded as damage resulting from her wrongful act and actionable at the suit of the child.[113]

2.26 The statute therefore recognises a duty to an unborn child, as long as there was a duty to the child's parent. However if the defendant's conduct did not cause the child's injury, there will be no liability under this Act. In this respect the law has not changed. In *McKay v. Essex Area Health Authority*,[114] which concerned a birth that was not within the statute, the child was born severely disabled. But it was shown that this was because the mother had contracted rubella in the early months of her pregnancy. Hence the doctor could not be liable to the child. No action of his had caused the injury: and he had not been guilty of any breach of duty to the mother or father. It was argued, however, that there was liability on an alternative ground: namely that, since the doctor had knowledge of the rubella and its likely consequences, he should have terminated the pregnancy. Therefore the child could sue for what has been called "wrongful life". The question before the Court of Appeal was whether at common law such an action would lie. The court rejected such a claim on the ground that public policy was against any suggestion that a doctor should terminate a pregnancy since this would violate the sanctity of human life. Although the doctor was under a duty to advise the mother of the fact that she had been infected and what the consequences might be of that infection, and to explain to her the desirability of terminating the pregnancy, and although the Abortion Act 1967 gave mothers the right to terminate the lives of their unborn children and made it lawful for doctors to help to abort them, it could not be deduced from such facts that a doctor was under any duty to the unborn child to prevent its birth in such circumstances. To allow an action founded on such a duty, said Ackner L.J.,[115] would raise complicated religious and philosophical points and

109 *Ibid.*
110 *Ibid.*s. 1(7).
111 *Ibid.* s.4(3).
112 *Ibid.* s. 2.
113 *Ibid.*
114 [1982] 2 All E.R. 771.
115 *Ibid.* at 787.

would have social implications in the potential disruption of family life and bitterness which it would cause between parent and child. Ackner L.J. also referred to the problem of calculating the compensation that could be awarded in any such action. Such compensation would have to be based on a comparison between the value of non-existence and the value of the child's existence in a disabled state. But, as the learned judge exlaimed, "How can a court begin to evaluate non-existence?"[116] No comparison is possible; therefore no damage can be established which a court could recognise. Stephenson L.J. admitted that judges had to pluck figures from the air in putting any imponderables into pounds and pence.[117] Loss of expectation of life produced difficulty that led to the fixing of a constant and arbitrary figure. "To measure loss of expectation of death would require a value judgment where a crucial factor lies altogether outside the range of human knowledge . . . ."[118]

2.27 The Act of 1976 makes it clear that no such liability for "wrongful life" can arise under the statute.[119] The only possible claim of an unborn child is that which is created and established by the statute, namely a claim founded on the breach of a legal duty to the parent of the child. In this respect it was held in *Updale v. Bloomsbury Area Health Authority*[120] that a woman had no action in negligence based on the birth of a child against a health authority when doctors employed by that authority had sterilised her, the operation was unsuccessful and she became pregnant, except for the pain, suffering, inconvenience, anxiety, and the disruption of the family's finances caused by the unexpected pregnancy. She could also claim for lost income. But she had no claim for the cost of carrying out extensions to the family home or the cost of bringing up the child. To allow such a claim was against public policy. It was not appropriate for a court publicly to declare that a child's life or birth was a mistake or a disaster, and that the child was unwanted or rejected. This would disrupt families and weaken the structure of society.[121] Moreover to calculate the damages a court would have to take into account the value of the child's life viewed from the mother's perspective, with the result that an uncaring mother would be entitled to higher damages than a mother who was loving. In the words of Jupp J., "virtue would go unrewarded: unnatural rejection of womanhood and motherhood would be generously compensated".[122] This would not be just. A further point was that to allow such an action would put medical men under pressure to encourage abortions to prevent actions against them. Finally, it was an assumption of our culture for time immemorial "that a child coming into the world, . . . is a blessing and an occasion for rejoicing".[123] With due respect for the learned judge,

116 *Ibid.*
117 *Ibid.* at 782.
118 *Ibid.*
119 Congenital Disabilities (Civil Liability) Act 1976 s. 4(5): see [1982] 2 All E.R. 771 at 786 *per* Ackner L.J.
120 [1983] 2 All E.R. 522.
121 *Ibid.* at 531 *per* Jupp J.
122 *Ibid.*
123 *Ibid.*

there is a touch of unreality about his reasoning insofar as it relates to the advantages of having children. Even his comments about caring and uncaring mothers seem immaterial, given the problems, both financial and otherwise, entailed in giving birth to additional children when the parents have tried to avoid this by valid, lawful and medically approved means. Moreover, the argument that doctors would be encouraged to counsel abortions for the purpose of precluding their liability to pay damages is both ungracious and cynical. However, if a mother were able to sue in such circumstances, then, based on the 1976 Act, a child might be able to sue for wrongful life, which may be the most acceptable reason for denying the mother an action in the kind of situation involved in the *Updale* case, although it was not raised by the judge.[124]

(ii) Actions against minors

2.28 The general principle is that minority of itself is no defence. The minor will be fully liable just like an adult.[125] In this respect the law of torts differs from the criminal law, under which the age of an accused may be relevant to the issue of criminal responsibility.[126] However there are some qualifications of the general principle. Where a mental state, such as the intent to commit fraud, is material for liability in tort, the age of the defendant may negate liability. A child may not be able to be malicious or to appreciate that he is being deceitful.[127] Secondly, where a question of degree of care arises, minority could be relevant because someone who is under age may not be expected to show an adult's standard of care. This will depend on the age of the defendant. The younger he or she is the less likely is it that a court will find that the child was negligent, just as where contributory negligence is in question, the fact that the plaintiff was a child may affect the result.[128] Where children are involved the standard of care for negligence or contributory negligence will be dependant on whether the child behaved in a manner that was unreasonable for a child of his age.[129]

2.29 The fact that a minor can be sued in tort will not permit the minor to be sued on a contract, when such a suit is not maintainable against a minor, by treating the minor's acts, where this is theoretically possible, as a tort rather than a breach of contract.[130] Thus if the minor conceals his true age so as to get the plaintiff to enter into a contract, no action in

124 Although he discussed and followed the judgments in the *McKay* case: see [1983] All E.R. 522 at 530–531.
125 *Gorely v. Codd* [1967] 1 W.L.R. 19.
126 Children & Young Persons Act 1969.
127 Cp. *McHale v. Watson* (1966) 155 C.L.R. 199 with *Tillander v. Gosselin* (1966) 60 D.L.R. (2d) 18. There appear to be no English cases in point.
128 Cp. the cases cited *supra* note 95. See also *Walmsley v. Humenick* [1954] 2 D.L.R. 232, a Canadian case.
129 *McEllistrum v. Etches* [1956) S.C.R. 787: *Wade v. C.N.R.* [1978] 1 S.C.R. 1064, both Canadian cases. See also *Heisler v. Moke* (1972) 25 D.L.R. (3d) 670 which applied a subjective test contrary to the objective test in *Gough v. Thorne* [1966] 3 All E.R. 398.
130 Otherwise the protection given to minors by the law of contract would be lost in many instances.

fraud will lie against the minor,[131] although restitution can be obtained of property that has been passed, provided that the minor is not obliged to repay money, since "restitution stops where repayment begins".[132] Nor can an action be brought in negligence for what is in effect a negligent breach of contract (which might be possible where the defendant is an adult).[133] However a negligence action can be brought where the minor's wrongful act was outside the scope of the contract. Thus if a minor hires a vehicle and damages it by careless driving, no action in contract or tort will lie.[134] But if the minor hires a vehicle and then uses it improperly, for example, by letting someone else have possession and use of it contrary to the terms of the contract, an action will lie against the minor.[135]

2.30 Where a minor has been guilty of a tort a parent or guardian[136] will not be liable for the wrongful act, except where the minor was acting as the servant or agent of the parent or guardian when committing the act in question.[137] Such liability arises under the normal principles of vicarious liability.[138] Moreover the parent or guardian will be liable if the parent or guardian was guilty of a wrongful act, such as negligence, the result of which was that the minor was able to cause harm to the plaintiff.[139] In a number of cases involving the use of weapons, such as airguns, or vehicles, a parent or guardian was held liable not for the negligence, if any, of the minor, but for the parent or guardian's own negligence in allowing the minor to have and use the gun or vehicle when the minor was too young or too incompetent to be trusted with its possession and use.[140]

(b) Mental incompetents

2.31 A tort that is committed against someone who is mentally incompetent in whatever degree will be as actionable as one perpetrated against a person of completely sound mind, even if the mental incompetent is unaware that a tort has been committed. Realisation that one has been wronged, and harmed, is not a *sine qua non* of the liability of the person who commits the wrong and inflicts the harm, although the awareness of the plaintiff has been considered in relation to the calculation of damages,

131 *Johnson v. Pye* (1665) 1 Sid. 258.
132 *R. Leslie Ltd v. Shiell* [1914] 3 K.B. 607 at 618 *per* Hamilton L.J.
133 See pp. 312–314.
134 *Jennings v. Rundall* (1799) 8 T.R. 335.
135 *Burnard v. Haggis* (1863) 14 C.B.N.S. 45 (negligence); *Ballett v. Mingay* [1943] K.B. 281 (conversion).
136 For the liability of school authorities see *Carmarthenshire County Council v. Lewis* [1955] A.C. 549, no liability just because a young child ran out of a school and caused an accident in which the plaintiff's husband was killed.
137 *Moon v. Towers* (1860) 8 C.B.N.S. 611.
138 Chapter 3.
139 For liability to pay compensation under the Criminal Justice Act 1982 s. 27 when a juvenile court makes a compensation order, see *Leeds City Council v. West Yorkshire Police* [1983] A.C. 29, where a local authority was not a guardian for the purpose of the similar earlier provisions of the Children & Young Persons Act 1933 s. 55.
140 Cp. *Dixon v. Bell* (1816) 5 M. & S. 198 with *Bebee v. Sales* (1916) 32 T.L.R. 413. See also *Donaldson v. McNiven* [1952] 2 All E.R. 692; *Newton v. Edgerley* [1959] 3 All E.R. 337. Cp. *School Division of Assiniboine South No. 3 v. Hoffer* [1973] 6 W.W.R. 765.

especially in personal injury cases where the plaintiff has been rendered a vegetable, unable to appreciate his or her condition as a consequence of the injuries inflicted by the defendant.[141]

2.32 More problematical, however, is the question of the tort liability of those who are insane or otherwise lacking in complete mental competence.[142] *Prima facie* insanity or some lesser degree of mental incompetence is not a defence to an action in tort.[143] The purpose of liability being to compensate the victim, not to punish the wrongdoer, as in the criminal law,[144] the mental state of the defendant ought not to be material to the issue of liability in tort, however relevant it may be in determining guilt of a criminal act.[145] As Stable J. said in *Morris v. Marsden*,[146] "I cannot think that, if a person of unsound mind converts my property under a delusion that he is entitled to do it or that it was not property at all, that affords a defence". In that particular case the defendant was sued for trespass by assaulting the plaintiff. He pleaded that he was insane, i.e. was suffering from a mental disease. Stable J. held the defendant liable even though he did not know what he was doing was wrong because he knew the nature of his act. He acted voluntarily.[147] The rationale of this decision is that the act in question was unlawful in itself, viz., an assault. There was no need to establish any state of mind on the part of the defendant. Hence his insantiy was not material. However it was suggested that where the defendant's state of mind is an ingredient of liability, the mental condition of the defendant would be relevant.[148] Hence where malice or intent to defraud is crucial to liability, the fact that the defendant lacked full capacity to understand what he was doing might relieve him of liability. In contrast where liability is strict, without the need to prove intention or negligence, insanity or anything similar ought not to be a defence, unless the state of the defendant's mind indicates that he was not acting voluntarily.

2.33 The mental state of the defendant may therefore be a factor in cases of negligence. Admittedly, the question whether the defendant has been negligent falls to be resolved in accordance with the standards of the resonable man, and is not dependent on the subjective state of the defendant.[149] However there might be some relevance in the fact that the defendant lacked full mental competence or capacity. His state could be such that he did not know or appreciate what was expected of him. Certainly if that state was such that he lacked any ability to control his

141 Below pp. 426–428.
142 Fridman, "Mental Incompetency" (1963) 79 L.Q.R. 502, (1964) 80 L.Q.R. 84, especially at 84–96.
143 *Mordaunt v. Mordaunt* (1870) L.R. 2 P. & D. 103 at 142 *per* Kelly C.B.
144 Above pp. 4–5.
145 *White v. White* [1950] P. 39 at 58 *per* Denning L.J.
146 [1952] 1 All E.R. 925 at 927: cp. *Phillips v. Soloway* [1957] 6 D.L.R. (2d) 570.
147 Cp. *Heffernan v. Hayes* (1899) 25 V.L.R. 156, defamation: *Donaghy v. Brennan* (1900) 19 N.Z.L.R. 289, trespass to the person.
148 *Supra* note 146 at 927–928.
149 Below pp. 316–318.

actions, he could not be held to be negligent.[150] In *Roberts v. Ramsbottom*,[151] the defendant was not insane but suffered a stroke. Nevertheless he was held liable in negligence because he continued to be in control of the vehicle which he was driving, in consequence of which there was an accident. Consistent with decisions dealing with the effects of automatism,[152] however, if the defendant was in such a mental state that he was incapable of knowing what he was doing or controlling his conduct, he might have a defence to an action for negligence. It has been held, however, that if the defendant knew or ought to have known that he was subject to attacks, such as epileptic fits, that deprived him of the ability to control his acts, by rendering him unconscious or incapable of controlling his actions, he would be guilty of negligence in entering a course of action that might lead to harm if he suffered such an attack. The same would apply to acts performed during self-induced intoxication. The negligence here is not the way he performed the relevant act, such as driving, but in undertaking to perform the act at all.[153]

(c) Bankrupts

2.34 On the declaration of someone as a bankrupt, rights of action vested in him would normally pass to the trustee in bankruptcy to be pursued for the benefit of the bankrupt's creditors. This is certainly true where the cause of action arises because of some wrongful act causing injury to the bankrupt's property, for example, trespass to goods, or land, or conversion.[154] If the cause of action concerns injury to the person or reputation of the bankrupt, the right to sue remains vested in the bankrupt.[155]

2.35 Until recently it was the law that a claim for unliquidated damages arising from a tort committed by someone who became bankrupt could not be proved as a debt in the bankruptcy.[156] By virtue of the Insolvency Act 1986 s. 382, where the cause of action accrued before the commencement of the bankruptcy, the unliquidated claim in tort becomes a bankruptcy debt and a person claiming that he suffered loss and damage becomes a creditor of the bankrupt.[157]

150 Cp. *Buckley v. Smith Transport Ltd* [1946] 4 D.L.R. 721; *Waugh v. James K. Allan Ltd* [1964] 2 Lloyd Rep. 1.
151 [1980] 1 All E.R. 7.
152 *Hill v. Baxter* [1958] 1 Q.B. 227; cp. *R. v. Isitt* [1978] R.T.R. 211, an epilepsy case: *R. v. Spurge* [1961] 2 Q.B. 205 at 210 *per* Salmon J.; *Watmore v. Jenkins* [1962] 2 Q.B. 572.
153 *Jones v. Dennison* [1971] R.T.R. 174; *Gordon v. Walker* (1973) 42 D.L.R. (3d) 342; *Roberts v. Ramsbotton, supra* at 14 *per* Neill J.
154 *Halsbury's Laws of England*, 4th ed. 1989, Vol. 3(2), para 424.
155 *Ibid.* See *Beckham v. Drake* (1849) 2 H.L.C. 576; *Rose v. Buckett* [19001] 2 K.B. 449; *Wilson v. United Counties Bank Ltd* [1920] A.C. 102. For the situation where the transaction involves damage to the person and to property, when the trustee in bankruptcy can sue for the latter and the bankrupt for the former, see Halsbury, *op. cit.* para. 425. The damages for personal injury etc., are not property the trustee can claim for the estate: *ibid.* para 427.
156 Bankruptcy Act 1914 s. 30(1): cp. with respect to claims against a company in liquidiation *Re Great Orme Tramways Co.* (1934) 50 T.L.R. 450; *Re Islington Metal & Plating Works Ltd* [1983] 3 All E.R. 318.
157 Halsbury, *op. cit.* para. 479, note 10.

6. PERSONAL REPRESENTATIVES

2.36 At common law death did not give rise to a cause of action and the death of a plaintiff terminated his action. Moreover, if the tortfeasor died the plaintiff's cause of action against him did not survive. Any action in tort had to be begun and terminated before the death of either plaintiff or defendant. If an action had been started prior to the death of the plaintiff or defendant and a judgment had been rendered, it accrued to the plaintiff's estate, if it was the plaintiff who died: or it became enforceable as a debt against the estate of the defendant where the latter had died. The rationale of this doctrine was: *actio personalis moritur cum persona.*[158] But it was never fully or properly explained why this should have been so.[159] In fact other forms of action, for example, actions based on contract,[160] were not extinguished by death. Although in 1846 the Fatal Accidents Act[161] first created a right of action in favour of certain dependents of someone who was killed through the wrongful act of another, such action was, and continues to be, independent of any cause of action that might have been available to the deceased immediately prior to his death, whether that death was caused by the defendant's act or otherwise. This statutory cause of action, explained Lord Diplock in *Gammell v. Wilson*,[162] replaced the action the deceased could have brought in his lifetime, where he died from his injuries before he could sue and recover judgment and he left a widow or dependent relatives who had looked to him for their support. The damages recoverable under the original and subsequent Fatal Accidents Acts, "were purely compensatory and were assessed according to the jury's estimate of the economic loss which the dependents had suffered and would continue to suffer in consequence of the withdrawal of the deceased's support".[163] Not until the passing of the Law Reform (Miscellaneous Provisions) Act 1934 did the personal representatives of the deceased have a cause of action for loss to the deceased's estate resulting from his premature death.

2.37 Unlike the Fatal Accidents Act, the 1934 Act, which abolished the maxim *actio personalis moritur cum persona*, did not create a new cause of action based on the death of someone by the wrongful act or omission of another. It enabled a cause of action which arose prior to that person's death, whether from the act of the defendant or otherwise and whether at

158 *Baker v. Bolton* (1808) 1 Camp. 493; *Osborn v. Gillett* (1873) L.R. 8 Ex. 88; *Admiralty Commissioners v. S.S. Amerika* [1917] A.C. 38; *Gammell v. Wilson* [1981] 1 All E.R. 578 at 582 *per* Lord Diplock.

159 One reason may have been the connection between the law of tort and the criminal law. Since liability to be punished ceased when the malefactor died, so, logically, should his liability to compensate the victim. And the death of the victim would make it unreasonable to expect the wrongdoer to compensate someone who had not been personally affected, e.g. by a trespass, as a result of the wrongdoer's act.

160 *Pinchon's Case* (1611) 9 Rep. 86b: and certain restitutionary claims, see *Phillips v. Homfray* (1883) 24 Ch.D. 439.

161 Now contained in the Fatal Accidents Act 1976; below pp. 423–438.

162 [1981] 1 All E.R. 578 at 582.

163 *Ibid.*

the time of the act or subsequently, to subsist after such death,[164] so that the deceased victim's executor, if he died testate, or administrator, is he died intestate,[165] could begin or continue the appropriate action.[166] The only exception to this still remaining after later amendment of the 1934 Act[167] is an action for defamation. Personal representatives cannot sue for a defamation which was published about the deceased. Nor can the plaintiff sue the estate of a deceased defamer.[168] However, other actions in tort can be brought, or continued against the estate of a tortfeasor who died after or at the same time as the act or omission which caused the plaintiff's injury, or before or at the same time that the damage was suffered which eventually would have given rise to an action against the decreased had he lived.[169] Although the action may be brought by the decreased's estate, no exemplary damages can be recovered,[170] even if the deceased, had he lived, might have been awarded such damages.[171] To this extent certain rights are still regarded as "personal" and not transmissible on death for the benefit of those who become entitled to the deceased's estate under his will or on his intestacy. Nor can the estate recover damages for loss of income for any period after the death of the victim.[172] It should also be noted that where the death of the party who would have been a plaintiff has been caused by the act which gave rise to the cause of action, e.g. negligence, the damages recoverable by his estate are to be calculated without reference to any loss or gain to his estate consequent on his death (except for a sum for funeral expenses).[173] This has been interpreted to mean a gain (or loss) such as an annuity, insurance money or something similar, that would have accrued on death to the deceased's

164 But not a right to claim under the Fatal Accidents Act 1976 s. 1A, in cases of bereavement: Administration of Justice Act 1982 s. 4(1); included by reason of recommendations made in the *Report of the Royal Commission on Civil Liability and Compensation for Personal Injuries* (the Pearson Report), 1978, Cmnd. Vol. I, para. 437.

165 The administrator must obtain a grant of administration before he can sue: *Ingall v. Moran* [1944] K.B. 160; *Hilton v. Sutton Steam Laundry* [1946] K.B. 65.

166 *Gammell v. Wilson* [1981] 1 All E.R. 578 at 592 *per* Lord Scarman. Originally there were special limitation periods applied to such actions. These were removed by the Proceedings Against Estates Act 1970. The ordinary law of limitations, under the Limitation Act 1980, applies whether the action is brought by or against an estate. But see the Limitation Act 1980 s. 11(5). In the event of no grant of probate or administration, proceedings can be started under R.S.C. Ord. 15, r. 6A.

167 By the Law Reform (Miscellaneous Provisions) Act 1970 ss. 4, 5.

168 The reasons given for this exclusion were (i) avoidance of controversial areas; (ii) the urgent need to deal with the effects of death in road accidents which were increasing in the 1930s: *Report of Faulks Committee on the Law of Defamation*, 1975, Cmnd. 5909, Chapter 15.

169 Law Reform (Miscellaneous Provisions) Act 1934 s. 1(4). This refers to the situation that arises where a defendant is negligent, for example in making a statement that is inaccurate, but the damage is suffered by the victim, e.g., when he acts on the statement, not until after the death of the defendant, or the defendant dies at the same time as the damage is suffered. Since damage to the plaintiff is an essential ingredient of an action for negligence (below p. 327), no cause of action would have arisen at the moment of the defendant's death.

170 Law Reform (Miscellaneous Provisions) Act 1934 s. 1(2)(a)(i); Administration of Justice Act 1982 s. 4(2): in consequence of recommendations in the Pearson Report: above note 164.

171 Below pp. 432–433.

172 Law Reform (Miscellaneous Provisions) Act 1934 s. 1(2)(a)(ii): Administration of Justice Act 1982 s. 4(2).

173 Law Reform (Miscellaneous Provisions) Act 1934 s. 1(2)(c).

estate regardless of the fact that the death was caused by personal injuries attributable to the fault of the defendant.[174]

2.38 The 1934 Act did not deprive the deceased's dependents of their statutory cause of action under the Fatal Accidents Act.[175] Indeed actions are frequently brought by the very same people, acting in different capacities, under both Acts. In the usual case, i.e. in which the deceased's dependents succeed beneficially to the estate, this seldom involves duplication of the damages recoverable, since the financial benefit accruing to the dependent from the estate falls to be deducted from compensation for loss of dependency awarded to them under the Fatal Accidents Act.[176] The damages that could be recovered under the 1934 Act were said to come under three heads, according to Lord Diplock,[177] before change in the law by the Administration of Justice Act 1982. These were: loss of earnings; pain and suffering; and loss of expectation of life. As he pointed out, damages for loss of expectation of life had become a moderate conventional sum by 1981,[178] when Lord Diplock was giving judgment in *Gammell v. Wilson*, and pain and suffering and loss of earnings were suffered only up to the time of death. Hence it was not often that, in cases of fatal injuries, the damages under the 1934 Act exceeded the amount of dependency. What the House of Lords held in that case was that the estate of a deceased victim of negligence was able to claim damages for loss of earnings for the years that the deceased was deprived of the ability to work and earn by reason of the defendant's negligence, the "lost years". This was because, as decided in an earlier case,[179] the deceased, had he lived, could have sued for such losses: therefore the right of action which the deceased enjoyed at the moment of his death passed to his estate.[180] In this respect the provision of the 1934 Act referred to above relating to loss or gain consequent on the death applied only to loss or gain directly consequent on death (viz., a payment under an insurance policy maturing on the death of the assured) and not to a loss or gain resulting from a right to recover damages which vested in the deceased immediately before his death and then passed to the beneficiaries of his estate, whether or not they were his dependents.[181] Lord Diplock discussed the anomalies of this

174 *Kandella v. British Airways Board* [1980] 1 All E.R. 341: but see *Gammell v. Wilson* [1981] 1 All E.R. 578 at 585–586 *per* Lord Edmund-Davies, 592 *per* Lord Scarman on the subject of annuities.

175 Law Reform (Miscellaneous Provisions) Act 1934 s. 1(5).

176 *Davies v. Powell Duffryn Associated Collieries Ltd (No. 2)* [1942] A.C. 601; *Gammell v. Wilson* [1981] 1 All E.R. 578 at 582 *per* Lord Diplock. But the effect of this latter decision was to permit a certain degree of duplication: below at note 184.

177 *Gammell v. Wilson, supra.*

178 Below p. 427.

179 *Pickett v. British Rail Engineering Ltd* [1980] A.C. 136: below pp. 421–422.

180 This was applied to the loss of the prospect of an inheritance, although that was to be taken into account with moderation, in *Adsett v. West* [1983] 2 All E.R. 985. It is open to question whether this decision survives the amendment, discussed below, made by the Administration of Justice Act 1982.

181 For other cases on this see *Kandella v. British Airways Board*, para. 237 *supra*; *White v. London Transport Executive* [1982] 1 All E.R. 410; *Benson v. Biggs Wall & Co. Ltd* [1982] 3 All E.R. 300; *Harris v. Empress Motors Ltd* [1982] 3 All E.R.. 306; *Clay v. Pooler* [1982] 3 All E.R. 570.

interpretation of the law, which was logical and based upon the exigencies of situations which had arisen before *Gammell v. Wilson* but which became unjust and difficult to apply.[182] As Lord Fraser of Tulleybelton stated: "It seems to me to be difficult to justify a law whereby the deceased's estate, which may pass to persons or institutions in no way dependent on him for support, can recover damages for loss of earnings or other income, which he would probably have received during the 'lost years' ".[183] The cause of this problem was the difference between the action under the 1934 Act and that under the Fatal Accidents Act. Damages received in the former went, and still go, to the beneficiaries under the will or intestacy of the deceased. Damages under the latter went, and still go, only to certain dependents.[184] The purposes of the different statutes are different. Their consequences ought to be different. But the logic of the legal principles developed under the Fatal Accidents Act and the 1934 Act led to the situation as described and discussed in *Gammell v. Wilson.* Hence statutory reform occurred in 1982.[185] It is no longer possible for lost income of this kind to be recovered under the 1934 Act. Only dependents claiming under the Fatal Accident Act suit will be able to obtain redress in this way.[186]

2.39 If the tortfeasor has died, the action against his estate will lead to the award of whatever damages the tortfeasor himself might have been ordered to pay had he been alive. His death will not affect the extent of his liability. If the tortfeasor dies insolvent any liability under the action which is maintainable by virtue of the 1934 Act is a debt provable in the administration of the deceased tortfeasor's estate.[187]

182 [1981] 1 All E.R. 578 at 582–583.

183 *Ibid.* at 588. Note also the argument that the estate *and* the dependents might be able to recover the same sum twice over under different statutes: *ibid.* at 587 *per* Lord Edmund-Davies.

184 Who might be the same people: hence the possible duplication of damages: *supra* note 183.

185 When the relevant words in the 1934 Act were repealed by the Administration of Justice Act 1982 s. 75(1), Sch. 9, Part 1.

186 Below pp. 433–438.

187 Law Reform (Miscellaneous Provisions) Act 1934 s. 1(6), which was intended to exclude the operation of the Bankruptcy Act 1914 s. 30: see now the Insolvency Act 1986 s. 382.

CHAPTER 3

Vicarious Liability

1. RATIONALE

3.01 In some instances one person may be held liable to be sued for the wrongful act or omission of another even if the specific act or omission was unknown to him at the time it occurred. This doctrine of vicarious liability or responsibility is deeply ingrained in the common law. Its origins may be found in early medieval law,[1] although it began to take on new and more important functions in the post-mediaeval period, especially as commerce grew.[2] The underlying idea behind the doctrine was that someone who employed and authorised another for certain purposes would be liable for wrongful acts which the latter committed.[3] To begin with no distinction appears to have been drawn between different classes of employees. Later a distinction was made between those who were referred to as servants and those who were termed agents.[4] From the late seventeenth century until the early part of the twentieth this differentiation became more and more marked. In the twentieth century, however, while this distinction may remain vital in relation to the question of liability on a contract made by another, it has virtually lost its significance in the context of the law of torts.[5] The crucial issue, as will be seen, is whether what was done by the actual perpetrator of the wrong was within the scope or course of what he undertook or what he was employed to do on behalf of the one subsequently sued as being vicariously responsible for the act in question.[6] The result of this development is the extension of the scope of liability in tort. Not only can someone be sued for what he or she has personally done or omitted to do: he or she can also be made liable for a tortious act committed by another, not, as in the case of personal representatives sued under the Law Reform (Miscellaneous Provisions) Act 1934,[7] when such liability is purely nominal and designed to overcome the objection to the continuation of liability after the death of the tortfeasor by substituting a living defendant for the actual but deceased wrongdoer, but also in a real

1 Holdsworth, *History of English Law*, vol. ii at 387.
2 *Ibid.* vol. iii at 382–387, vol. viii at 227–228: see *Tuberville v. Stamp* (1697) 1 Ld. Raym. 264.
3 *Barton v. Sadock* (1611) 1 Bulst. 103; *Southern v. How* (1618) Cro.Jac. 408.
4 Muller-Freinfels, "Legal Relations in the Law of Agency" (1964) 13. Am. J. Comp L. 193; Holdsworth, *op. cit.* vol. viii at 299.
5 *Lloyd v. Grace, Smith & Co.* [1912] A.C. 716. See, however, the earlier views of Holmes J. in "Agency" (1891) 4 H.L.R. 745, 5 H.L.R. 1.
6 *Reedie v. London & North Western Railway* (1849) 4 Ex. 244, replacing older ideas based on the notion of command or authority: see, e.g. *Bush v. Steinman* (1799) 1 Bos. & Paul 404.
7 Above pp. 40–43.

sense, by adding a second defendant to the one who has performed the wrongful act and is therefore *prima facie* liable for its commission.

3.02 Since this type of liability does not depend upon proof of any actual wrongdoing by the party to be held vicariously responsible,[8] although in some circumstances such might be the case, it is a form of strict liability. Vicarious liability cannot be escaped by proving absence of negligence or of any intention to cause harm. It is the fact of employment of the guilty party, plus the fact that the guilty party was acting in a certain way and for a certain purpose, that creates the liability. Over the course of time various reasons have been suggested for the imposition of such liability by the common law. It has been argued that such liability is justified because the servant's act is that of the master: therefore when the servant acts, it is exactly the same as if the master had done so himself.[9] This is sometimes expressed in the form of a maxim: *qui facit per alium facit per se*. Another reason given is that the superior party, the employer, put the inferior, the employee, in a position in which the mischief might be done: therefore it is only just and reasonable that the former should be held liable for the conduct of the latter.[10] This, too, has been expressed in the form of a maxim: *respondeat superior*. Both of these succinct statements have been the subject of criticism.[11] They have been said to be very uninformative and not true reasons for explaining the nature and true meaning of vicarious liability. A further suggestion is that unless such liability existed it would always be possible for someone to evade responsibility for breach of a duty that lay upon him by delegating its performance to someone else. In that way the one obliged by the law could shield behind his own lack of wrongdoing (unless it could be established that he was careless in his selection of a delegate, or that he ordered the one so delegated to perform the wrongful act). Perhaps the most generally accepted rationale in modern times is the need to ensure that someone able to satisfy the loss incurred by the plaintiff was liable to be sued, the idea of the "deep

8 Although the original idea was that the master was liable for having commanded the act that caused the harm: *Southern v. How, supra.* Note also the debate whether the employer is liable for his own breach of duty to the plaintiff or only because of the relationship between himself and the actual tortfeasor. Is it the tort of the servant or the tort of the master? See Glanville Williams, "Vicarious Liability: Tort of the Master or the Servant" (1956) 72 L.Q.R. 522. Cp., for example, *Broom v. Morgan* [1953] 1 Q.B. 597; *Morris v. C. W. Martin & Sons Ltd* [1966] 1 Q.B. 716. But see in contrast *Staveley Iron & Chemical Co. Ltd v. Jones* [1956] A.C. 627 at 639 *per* Lord Morton; *I.C.I. v. Shatwell* [1965] A.C. 656 at 676 *per* Viscount Radcliffe.

9 *Middleton v. Fowler* (1698) 1 Salk. 282; *Ward v. Evans* (1703) 2 Salk. 442; *Broom v. Morgan* [1953] 1 Q.B. 597; cp. *Morgans v. Launchbury* [1973] A.C. 127 at 140.

10 *Tobin v. The Queen* (1864) 16 C.B.N.S. 310 at 350 *per* Erle C.J.: cp. *Hern v. Nichols* (1701) 1 Salk. 289. Or that the master prospered by his servant's act: *Boulton v. Arlesden* (1697) 3 Salk. 324; *Taff Vale Railway Co. v. Amalgamated Society of Railway Servants* [1901] A.C. 426 at 429 *per* Farwell J.

11 *Riddick v. Thames Board Mills Ltd* [1977] 3 All E.R. 677 at 685–686 *per* Lord Denning: *Staveley Iron & Chemical Co. Ltd v. Jones* [1956] A.C. 627 at 643 *per* Lord Reid. The idea that one person is liable because he "enabled" another to cause harm was stated in *Lickbarrow v. Mason* (1787) 2 T.R. 63 at 70 *per* Ashhurst J. It was criticised as too wide in *Farquharson Bros. v. King* [1902] A.C. 325 at 340 *per* Lord Lindley: cp. *Slingsby v. District Bank Ltd* [1932] 1 K.B. 544 at 560 *per* Scrutton L.J.; *Armagas Ltd v. Mundogas SA* [1986] 2 All E.R. 385 at 392 *per* Lord Keith.

pocket".[12] This is inherent in the language of Lord Wilberforce in *Kooragang Ltd v. Richardson & Wrench Ltd*,[13] where he said:

> "The manner in which the common law has dealt with the liability of employers for acts of employees (masters for servants, principals for agents) has been progressive: the tendency has been toward more liberal protection of innocent third parties."

He was referring to the gradual extension of the scope of such liability. But his words suggest that behind the doctrine lies the aim of providing a source of liability for those injured by the acts of employees who, themselves, might not be worth suing. In terms of economics, therefore, there is a greater need and justification for liability in situations where, from the juristic point of view, there is less validity in its creation.

2. APPLICATION

3.03 For the purposes of imposing vicarious liability the law recognised two major categories of persons for whose wrongful acts another will be responsible: agents and servants. Those who, although employed by another, do not come within either of these categories are termed independent contractors. For their acts or omissions, in general, their employer will not be liable. However some circumstances may give rise to such liability, for reasons which do not appear consistent with the underlying doctrinal explanations of vicarious liability for the acts of agents or servants. These exceptional situations may be said to be based upon very different considerations, and, in effect, are not true instances of vicarious liability but examples of the personal liability of the employer of an independent contractor.

3.04 After the decision of the House of Lords in *Lloyd v. Grace, Smith & Co.*,[14] there has been little, if any, practical importance or relevance in the law of torts in drawing or maintaining a distinction between agents and servants. It can be said, in general, that an agent is usually employed for a particular purpose and is given authority by his principal to achieve that purpose, whereas a servant is employed to work more generally and often more continuously for his master and whether he is acting as such depends upon whether what he does is within the course of his employment. An agent may be subject to less actual control than a servant with regard to what is to be done and how it is to be effected. Both are to a certain extent under such directional control, in contrast with an independent contractor who is much freer in respect of how he performs the work he has contracted to do.[15] The test of control, in recent years, has become less material than it was in the nineteenth century, when it was for all

12 *Limpus v. London General Omnibus Co.* (1862) 1 H.C. 526 at 539 *per* Willes J.

13 [1981] 3 All E.R. 65 at 68. But this might also be taken as referring to the idea of social convenience and rough justice, as expressed by Lord Pearce in *I.C.I. Ltd v. Shatwell* [1965] A.C. 656 at 685.

14 [1912] A.C. 716.

15 *Honeywell & Stein Ltd v. Larkin Bros.* [1934] 1 K.B. 191 at 196.

practical purposes the mainstay of the definition of a servant.[16] The issue became complicated by the problem of deciding whether professionals, such as doctors, lawyers, engineers or the captain of a ship, could properly be described as servants when their employer could not realistically exercise that degree of control over the way they performed their work that was once deemed an essential feature of the legal concept of a servant. The courts accepted that in the case of such professionals the test of control would have less meaning and relevance than when dealing with unskilled workers, to which the doctrine originally applied. The question in such cases became whether the duties performed by the alleged servant were an integral part of the business or activity on which the employer was engaged or only accessory to it. If the former, then the professional could be a servant: if the latter, it was more probable that he was an independent contractor. The relation of master and servant could exist between an employer and a professional, despite the fact that the employer could exercise extremely little, if any control over the way that the professional's skill was used.[17]

3.05 The distinction drawn by the common law and still maintained is between a contract for services, that denotes the relationship of employer and independent contractor, and a contract of service, that signifies the relationship of master and servant or that of principal and agent.[18] Although such matters as the right to appoint,[19] the right to dismiss, duration of service, the nature of such service, and the method of payment, may be material factors in indicating a sufficient degree of control to

16 *Whittaker v. Minister of Pensions & National Insurance* [1967] 1 Q.B. 157. Cp. *Market Investigations Ltd v. Minister of Social Security* [1969] 2 Q.B. 173 at 185 *per* Cooke J. The fundamental test to be applied was whether the person who engaged himself to perform services performed them as a person in business on his own account or on account of the employer. In this respect who provided the tools and risked his capital, and whether profit depended in any significant degree on the way he was managed were important factors: cp. *Ferguson v. John Dawson & Partners (Contractors) Ltd* [1976] 1 W.L.R. 1213. See, e.g. *Global Paint Ltd v. Secretary of State for Social Services* [1972] 1 Q.B. 139, provision of tools and equipment and exercise of control over driver sufficient for relationship of master and servant although some features of contract for services present.

17 *Stevenson Jordan & Harrison Ltd v. Macdonald & Evans* [1952] 1 T.L.R. 101 at 111 *per* Denning L.J.; *Morren v. Swinton & Pendelbury B.C.* [1965] 2 All E.R. 349; *Whittaker v. Minister of Pensions & National Insurance, supra*: *Beloff v. Pressdram Ltd* [1973] 1 All E.R. 241 at 247–250. Hence the acceptance by the courts that surgeons and nurses employed by a hospital could be servants for the purposes of vicarious liability: *Gold v. Essex C.C.* [1942] 2 K.B. 293; *Collins v. Hertfordshire C.C.* [1947] K.B. 598; *Cassidy v. Ministry of Health* [1951] 2 K.B. 343; in contrast to the older view expressed in *Hillyer v. St. Bartholomew's Hospital* [1909] 2 K.B. 820. Hospital authorities will be liable for what is done in hospitals under their jurisdiction, at least where the permanent medical staff is involved: cp. *Pfizer Corporation v. Minister of Health* [1965] A.C. 512. As for visiting and consulting surgeons or physicians, there appears to be equal liability: *Roe v. Minister of Health* [1954] 2 Q.B. 66; *Razzell v. Snowball* [1954] 1 W.L.R. 1382. A diferent view of the liability of hospitals for negligence by doctors was taken by the majority of the Ontario Court of Appeal, in light of the different situation of the medical profession in Ontario, in *Yepremiam v. Scarborough General Hospital* (1980) 110 D.L.R. (3d) 513.

18 *Beloff v. Pressdram Ltd, supra* at 247 *per* Ungoed-Thomas J.

19 E.g., hiring and firing of workmen and direction of their operations by a general manager or works foreman of an industrial limited liability company did not make the workmen appointed by them their servants: nor did the appointment of pickets by a trade union's general secretary and executive committee make the pickets the servants of those persons: *Bird v. O'Neil* [1960] A.C. 907.

establish a principal/agent or master/servant relationship,[20] they are not conclusive.[21] Indeed the existence of a contract between the parties, whereby one is rewarded for his service as either agent or servant, is unnecessary. A person can be a gratuitous agent or servant and as such may make the principal or master vicariously liable.[22] Hence the problem has sometimes arisen of determining the correct party to hold responsible as a master when a servant normally employed as such by a particular employer, the "general" employer, is lent, under some contractual or other relationship, to another employer, the "transferred" employer, while acting for whom the transferred servant commits a tort. The test approved and applied by the House of Lords in *Mersey Docks & Harbour Board v. Coggins & Griffith (Liverpool) Ltd*[23] was that of control. Was the servant transferred or only the use and benefit of his work?[24] The question is whether the transferred servant has truly become an integral part of the transferred employer's organisation,[25] or remains part of the organisation of the general employer, while he is carrying out the orders of the transferred employer, who is permitted to give such orders in consequence of the arrangement between the two employers.[26] A relevant factor will be the nature of the work the servant is employed to do: whether it is skilled or unskilled.[27] Another, connected factor is whether the servant is transferred with, and for the purposes of operating equipment also lent by the general to the transferred employer, or is transferred alone so that his services may be utilised in the execution of the transferred employer's operations and the management of the latter's equipment.[28]

20 *Short v. J. & W. Henderson Ltd* (1946) 62 T.L.R. 427 at 429 *per* Lord Thankerton.

21 Nor is the label applied by the parties: *Ready Mixed Concrete Ltd v. Minister of Pensions & National Insurance* [1968] 2 Q.B. 497; *Ferguson v. John Dawson & Partners (Construction) Ltd, supra*; *Massey v. Crown Life Insurance Co.* [1978] 1 W.L.R. 676; *Davis v. New England College of Arundel* [1977] I.C.R. 6. In *Cassidy v. Ministry of Health, supra* at 352–353 Somervell L.J., quoting Buckley L.J. in *Simmons v. Heath Laundry Ltd* [1910] 1 K.B. 549 at 553, suggested that the test of a contract of service is whether there is such a contract within the meaning which an ordinary person would give to the words. This was applied in *Whittaker v. Minister of Pensions & National Insurance, supra*.

22 Hence the liability in cases when one person has lent his vehicle to another for certain uses: below pp. 53–54. But not all those who act gratuitously for another will be "servants" or "agents". The question of control may still be important.

23 [1947] A.C. 1 This involves issues of payment, dismissal, direction of services; but see *Garrard v. Southey & Co.* [1952] 2 Q.B. 174; and see *Ready Mixed Concrete Ltd v. Yorkshire Traffic Area Licensing Authority* [1970] 2 Q.B. 397, on the relevance of authority to control and direct the servant.

24 *Ready Mixed Concrete Ltd v. Yorkshire Traffic Area Licensing Authority, supra*; *Moore v. Palmer* (1886) 2 T.L.R. 782.

25 He had in *Arthur White (Contractors) Ltd v. Tarmac Civil Engineering Ltd* [1967] 1 W.L.R. 1508, by virtue of a contract between the employers. But this was for the purpose of determining the liability *inter se* of the two employers. This may not directly decide who is the employer for the purposes of vicarious liability: *Herdman v. Walker (Tooting) Ltd* [1956] 1 W.L.R. 209.

26 The onus of establishing the transfer is on the general employer and it is a heavy one: *Bhoomidas v. Singapore Harbour Authority* [1978] 1 All E.R. 956.

27 *Savory v. Holland & Hannen and Cubitts (Southern) Ltd* [1964] 1 W.L.R. 1158. A skilled man is less likely to become the servant of the "transferred" employer than an unskilled one.

28 *Arthur White (Contractors) Ltd v. Tarmac Civil Engineering Ltd, supra*: cp. *Garrard v. Southey & Co., supra*; *Denham v. Midland Employers Mutual Assurance Ltd* [1955] 2 Q.B. 437. Transfer with equipment generally indicates that the servant remains the servant of the general employer; but the contrary was held in *Donovan v. Laing Syndicate Ltd* [1893] 1 Q.B. 629, which might be decided differently today in light of the *Mersey Docks* case.

3.06 The control that is relevant is not that exercised by one servant or agent over an inferior. It is titular or theoretical control as explained in the "transferred servant" cases and those which concern the employment of skilled professionals. All servants or agents, whatever their position in the hierarchy of employees, are equally servants or agents and not vicariously liable for each other.[29] In *C. Evans & Sons Ltd v. Spritebrand Ltd*,[30] the plaintiff when suing a company for infringement of the plaintiff's copyright also sued the director whom the plaintiff claimed personally authorised, directed and procured the commission of the allegedly tortious acts, presumably by other servants or officers of the company. The Court of Appeal upheld the trial judge's dismissal of the director's application for an order striking out the claim against him, on the ground that it disclosed no reasonable cause of action. The court held that an action could not proceed against the director on the basis of any alleged vicarious liability for the acts of employees of the company[31] but only if he could be shown to have been personally guilty of a wrong.[32] This did not have to be proved by establishing any particular state of mind or knowledge on his part unless that was a necessary element of the tort alleged.[33] In the case of infringement of copyright, there was no obligation on the plaintiff to prove such a particular state of mind or knowledge, therefore the director could be liable personally. No matter how small the company and how powerful the director's control over its affairs, a director was not to be identified automatically with the company: to do so might diminish commercial enterprise and adventure.[34] So the only appropriate way of involving a director, or other senior employee or agent of a company of this kind, is by establishing his own personal responsibility for what happened, which can then lead to the vicarious liability of the company when this is appropriate and justified on general principles.[35]

3.07 Once it has been determined that the tortfeasor was under another's control at the time he committed the tort, the question becomes one of deciding that what he did is to be attributed to that other. Whether this will be so depends on what the tortfeasor was doing at the time he committed the tort. For vicarious liability to ensue it must be established that when the wrong was perpetrated the tortfeasor was acting within the scope of his authority or the course of his employment. Since 1912 those expressions, formerly applicable to agents and servants respectively, have come to mean the same thing. What would be authorised in the case of an

29 Cp. above p. 21, dealing with the situation of servants or agents of the Crown.
30 [1985] 2 All E.R. 415.
31 Cp. *Rainham Chemical Works Ltd v. Belvedere Fish Guano Co. Ltd* [1921] 2 A.C. 465 at 488 *per* Lord Parmoor; and *Performing Right Society Ltd v. Ciryl Theatrical Syndicate Ltd* [1928] 1 K.B. 1 at 14–15 *per* Atkin L.J.
32 *Ibid.*; *Wah Tat Bank Ltd v. Chan Cheng Kun* [1975] 2 All E.R. 257 at 260 *per* Lord Salmon.
33 *Supra* note 30 at 424 *per* Slade L.J., disagreeing with *Mentmore Manufacturing Co. Ltd v. National Machinery Co. Inc.* [1978] 89 D.L.R. (3d) 195, a decision of the Federal Court of Appeal of Canada; *White Horse Distillers Ltd v. Gregson Associates Ltd* [1984] R.P.C. 61, a passing-off case. See, e.g., *Fairline Shipping Corporation v. Adamson* [1975] Q.B. 181.
34 *Supra* note 30 at 424.
35 *Yuill v. B. & B. Fibres (Leigh) Ltd* [1958] 2 Lloyds Rep. 596.

agent will be within the course of a servant's employment. What is within the course of such employment will be authorised.[36] As Lord Wilberforce explained in *Heatons Transport (St Helens) Ltd v. Transport & General Workers' Union*,[37] whether a servant or agent is involved the test is the same: was the servant or agent acting on behalf of and within the scope of the authority conferred by the master or principal? A servant usually has a wider authority, because his employment is more permanent, he has a larger range of duties and he may have to exercise discretion in dealing with a series of situations as they arise, whereas an agent is ordinarily engaged to perform a particular task on a particular occasion and has authority to do whatever is required for that purpose, but no general authority. This does not mean that for the purpose of determining the responsibility of the master for the acts of a servant and that of a principal for the acts of an agent different tests are to be applied. It only means that the application of the same test may produce different results. In certain instances an agent who is not a servant may have authority of considerable generality, which was the situation in the *Heatons Transport* case, which was concerned with the acts of shop stewards. Agents of this kind, stated Lord Wilberforce,[38] who are elected or appointed to an office or post for a substantial period, may have to perform acts of several classes for the principal and may have to exercise discretion in dealing with various situations as they arise. The position of such agents, and the scope of their authority, are very similar to those of a servant.

2. AUTHORITY

(a) Meaning

3.08 The term "authority" refers to the power entrusted to an agent by a principal to act on the latter's behalf. It circumscribes the activities which the agent may perform for, and in the name of, the principal.[39] Such authority can be actual or ostensible. Actual authority refers to the authority which has been given or conferred on the agent by the express instructions of the principal, or can be implied or inferred as being inherent in, or necessary for the performance of his duties.[40] In this regard, an agent can be said to be invested by implication with the authority to do what is usual or customary for agents of his particular class. Ostensible authority refers to an authority which is not actual in the sense that the principal has expressly or by implication conferred it on the agent. It arises where the principal's conduct is such that a reasonable person can reasonably conclude that the agent has the authority to do what he did. Such authority is founded on the doctrine of estoppel. By holding out or

36 Cp. *Panorama Developments (Guildford) Ltd v. Fidelis Furnishing Fabrics Ltd* [1971] 2 Q.B. 711 on the position of a company secretary.
37 [1972] 3 All E.R. 101 at 109.
38 *Ibid.*
39 Fridman, *Law of Agency*, 5th ed. 1983, at 15–17; *Bowstead on Agency*, 15th ed. 1985, at 1–8, 92–97.
40 Fridman, *op. cit.* at 53–54; Bowstead, *op. cit.* at 98–119.

representing the agent as having certain authority, the principal is precluded from raising the defence that he did not authorise what the agent did.[41] Generally speaking, only if the agent's acts can be said to occur in pursuance, or in the exercise of, his actual or ostensible authority will he make his principal vicariously liable in tort. The exception or qualification of this is provided by the anomalous doctrine of ratification.[42] By this, a principal can make himself vicariously liable for an act that was unauthorised and would not have come within the scope of the agent's authority, if the principal subsequently ratifies, i.e. approves and adopts, the act after it has occurred.[43] For this to result, the principal must have full knowledge of what happened, or must be careless whether or not he knows the truth.[44] He must say or do something that indicates he has ratified the wrongful act of the agent, and the acceptance of knowledge or the means of knowledge that it was acquired tortiously.[45] Thirdly, the act which entails the commission of a tort must have been done by the agent on behalf of the principal even though it was unauthorised at the time.[46] When the doctrine of ratification applies, the situation is considered to be exactly the same as if the principal had authorised commission of the act in advance rather than *ex post facto*.

(b) Prohibitions

3.09 Although the idea of authority indicates that what has been done took place with the consent or approval of the principal, or, the case of ostensible authority, in circumstances that suggest such consent and approval, this does not necessarily mean that an act that is expressly or impliedly prohibited by the principal cannot be considered to have been committed without authority. A prohibition will not have that effect where the agent has performed an act for the benefit of the principal, although the agent acted mistakenly or improperly. In this connection particular problems have arisen with regard to negligence or fraud perpetrated by an agent. Since only rarely will an agent actually be authorised or instructed to act negligently or fraudulently, the liability of a principal for the negligent or fraudulent act of his agent falls to be determined on other bases. In *Kooragang Ltd v. Richardson & Wrench Ltd*,[47] Lord Wilberforce stated:

> "Negligence is a method of performing an act: instead of it being done carefully, it is done negligently. So liability for negligent acts in the course of employment is clear."

41 Fridman, *op. cit.* Chapter 6; Bowstead, *op. cit.*, at 90–1, 284–292.
42 Fridman, *op. cit.* Chapter 5; Bowstead, *op cit.* at 51–84.
43 *Buron v. Denmon* (1848) 2 Ex. 167.
44 *Freeman v. Rosher* (1849) 13 Q.B. 780; cp. *Briess v. Woolley* [1954] A.C. 333.
45 *The Bonita* (1861) 1 Lush. 252; but see *Hilbery v. Hatton* (1864) 2 H. &. C. 822, with which contrast *Lewis v. Read* (1845) 13 M. &. W. 834.
46 *Eastern Construction Co. Ltd v. National Trust Co.* [1914] A.C. 197; cp. *Keighley Maxsted & Co. v. Durant* [1901] A.C. 240 at 260.
47 [1981] 3 All E.R. 65 at 69.

Cases of fraud were different. Fraudulent acts in most cases are either directly forbidden or impliedly prohibited by the principal. Where the agent acted fraudulently for the benefit of the principal it was held in *Barwick v. English Joint Stock Bank*[48] that the principal would be liable. Not until *Lloyd v. Grace, Smith & Co.*[49] was the point finally decided that the principal would be liable even if the agent acted fraudulently in his (the agent's) own interest and for his benefit, as long as the act in question was done within the course of his employment, or scope of his authority. The only difference between these two situations, as Lord Wilberforce explained,[50] is that where the act is for the principal's benefit it is more easily concluded that the act was done in the course of employment. The converse was not true after *Lloyd's* case.

3.10 A prohibition may have some effect, however, if it restricts what the agent is employed to do so as to take the prohibited act outside the scope of the agent's authority.[51]

(c) Actual authority

3.11 The *Kooragang* case involved only actual authority. The issue was whether what the agent did in that case came within the scope of what he was expressly authorised to do by his employer, the principal. The agent was employed to carry out valuations of property. He carried out valuations on the property of the GB Group until the employers gave instructions that no such valuations were to be carried out in the future because the GB Group had not paid for those already completed. Some time later the agent became a director of a company in the GB Group. He subsequently prepared valuations on instructions from companies in the group. These valuations were performed at the offices of the group. But they were typed by a secretary of the agent's principal on headed paper of the principal and were signed by the agent with the name of the principal. A photocopy was sent to the finance company which was lending money on mortgage. On the photocopy the names of the valuers were cut off, so the mortgagee did not know who had performed the valuation. No record of the valuation was made with the principals, the agent's employers, contrary to the usual procedure that applied in the office: and no fee was ever charged by or paid to them. The mortgagees advanced money on the strength of these valuations, which had been prepared negligently, with the result that the mortgagees lost money. They sued the agent's employers. The issue was whether the act of the agent in making the

48 (1867) L.R. 2 Ex. 259.
49 [1912] A.C. 716.
50 *Supra* note 47 at 69.
51 Cp., in relation to servants, *Plumb v. Cobden Flour Mills* [1914] A.C. 62 at 67 *per* Lord Dunedin; *C.P.R. v. Lockhart* [1942] A.C. 591 at 599 *per* Lord Thankerton; *Ilkiw v. Samuels* [1963] 2 All E.R. 879 at 889 *per* Diplock L.J.; *Kay v. I.T.W.* [1968] 1 Q.B. 140 at 158 *per* Sellers L.J. See, e.g., *Stevens v. Woodward* (1881) 6 Q.B.D. 318. Cp. *Navarro v. Moregrand* [1951] 2 T.L.R. 674, a contract, not tort case. Note that dicta of Lord Denning at p. 680 were criticised by the House of Lords in *Armagas Ltd v. Mundogas SA* [1986] 2 All E.R. 385 at 393 *per* Lord Keith.

valuations was an act performed within the scope of his authority as an employee of the principals. The Privy Council, upholding the trial judge, held that it was not, so that the principals were not vicariously liable.

3.12 In coming to this conclusion the Privy Council distinguished between cases where a third party dealt with an agent or servant, which raised the question of ostensible authority, and cases concerning the use of motor vehicles.[52] The resolution of the issue of vicarious liability in the latter turned on whether the servant or agent, though performing acts of the class he was authorised or employed to do, departed so clearly from the scope of that employment that the principal or master was not liable for his acts.[53]Authority could not be inferred from the fact that the acts done were of a class which the master, or principal, could himself have done or could have entrusted to the servant or agent.[54] Although the agent in this case was performing valuations, a class of act which he could perform on behalf of his employers, the principals, this did not entitle the conclusion to be reached that any valuation he did, without any authority from the employers, not on their behalf but in his own interest, without any connection with the employers' business, was a valuation for which the employers must assume responsibility. Any such conclusion, said Lord Wilberforce,[55] "would strain the doctrine of vicarious responsibility beyond breaking point and in effect introduce into the law of agency a new principle equivalent to one of strict liability". In effect the Privy Council held that the agent's acts amounted to a clear case of departure from the course or scope of his employment.

3.13 From this decision, and the various cases concerning the liability of the owner of a motor vehicle for the acts of someone whom the owner has permitted to drive it, whether in the presence of the owner or otherwise, it is clear that vicarious liability will be involved only where the act was for the benefit of the principal or was connected with what the agent was engaged to perform. In the vehicle cases, for example, the distinction has been drawn between situations where the driver was using the vehicle, in part at any rate, for the purposes of the owner, for instance by driving it to a destination which the owner desired even if the driver was also interested in arriving there on his own account,[56] and those when he was driving it entirely for his own purposes.[57] What is stressed in all the decisions,

52 *Supra* note 47 at 70–71.
53 *Ibid.* at 70: cp. below pp. 64–66.
54 *Ibid.* at 71.
55 *Ibid.*
56 *Hewitt v. Bonvin* [1940] 1 K.B. 108; *Ormrod v. Crosville Motor Services Ltd* [1953] 2 All E.R. 753; *Wheatley v. Patrick* (1837) 2 M. & W. 650; *Samson v. Aitchison* [1912] A.C. 844; *Pratt v. Patrick* [1924] 1 K.B. 488; *Trust Co. Ltd v. de Silva* [1956] 1 W.L.R. 376; *Scarsbrook v. Mason* [1961] 3 All E.R. 767; *Parker v. Miller* (1926) 42 T.L.R. 408; *Carberry v. Davies* [1968] 2 All E.R. 817.
57 *Klein v. Caluori* [1971] 2 All E.R. 701; *Nottingham v. Aldridge* [1971] 2 Q.B. 739.

especially that of the House of Lords in *Morgans v. Launchbury*,[58] is that an owner who permits another person to drive the owner's car does not, from that giving of permission alone, become vicariously liable for a tort committed by the driver while in possession of the car. Just as the fact that the valuer in the *Kooragang* case did not make his employers liable when he used their time, their paper, their secretary and his services to do something on behalf of himself and another, viz., the group to which he was attached, so a driver who is negligent while driving a car belonging to another person does not make the latter responsible for his negligence merely because it involved the use of that other person's property. In other jurisdictions, for example Canadian provinces, this result has been achieved by statutory provision. And in the United States, a somewhat similar position has been reached in relation to what has been termed "the family car". A car that is commonly used by family members, although owned by, e.g., the husband and father, is a vehicle the use of which by any of them (or perhaps by their friends as long as this was the express or implied consent of the owner) may involve the owner in vicarious liability.[59] Lord Denning desired to incorporate this doctrine into English common law.[60] The House of Lords rejected the suggestion. If there was to be a significant change in the law, it was to be effected by Parliament after due and proper consideration of all the policy and other issues arising from such a change, for instance the impact of the broadening of vicarious liability upon the question of insurance.

(d) Ostensible authority

3.14 In the context of the law of contract the concept of ostensible, apparent authority is very familiar. Its application enlarges the scope of an agent's authority beyond that which he has been expressly authorised, or which he can be considered to have been impliedly authorised to perform. The latter may arise where what was done was necessary to be done in the pursuit of the undertaking for which the agent was employed. This has been invoked in cases involving servants, for example where a carter off-duty acted to protect his master's property from which he thought the plaintiff was going to steal, and in the course of doing so injured the plaintiff. The employer was liable on the ground that the servant's act was impliedly authorised.[61] Ostensible authority, however, only arises where the conduct of the principal has "held out" the agent as having the authority in question, although he was never expressly invested with such authority. As long as the agent appears to the outside world as being

58 [1973] A.C. 127: cp. *Ramburram v. Gurrucharam* [1970] 1 All E.R. 749; *Manawatu County v. Rowe* [1956] N.Z.L.R. 78; *Jennings v. Hannon* (1969) 89 W.N. (Part 2) N.S.W. 232. See generally Kodilinye, "The Rule in *Barnard v. Scully* in the Commonwealth" (1977) 26 I.C.L.Q. 487; Kodilinye, "Vicarious Liability of Vehicle Owners in the Commonwealth Carribean" (1977) 6 Anglo-Am. L.R. 18.

59 Fridman, "The Doctrine of the 'Family Car': A Study in Contrasts" (1976) 8 Texas Tech. L.R. 323.

60 [1971] 1 All E.R. 642 at 647–648.

61 *Poland v. Parr & Sons* [1927] 1 K.B. 236. The servant struck the plaintiff; it might have been different if he had injured the boy by an unreasonable act, e.g., shooting.

engaged on his principal's business, even though he does so by means of what Lord Keith called[62] "blundering attempts to promote the employer's business interests, involving negligent ways of carrying out the employee's work or excessive zeal and errors of judgment in the performance of it", the principal will be vicariously liable. Problems have arisen, as Lord Wilberforce explained in the *Kooragang* case,[63] where the agent has been guilty of fraud. This has now been the subject of detailed investigation by the Court of Appeal and the House of Lords in *Armagas Ltd v. Mundogas SA*.[64]

3.15 An agent asserted to a third party that he possessed the authority to enter into a certain transaction, when in fact he had no such authority, but was acting fraudulently so far as the principal was concerned and in his, the agent's, own personal interests for his own benefit at the expense of the business of the principal. It had been decided by the House of Lords in *Lloyd v. Grace, Smith & Co.*[65] that an agent's authority could be extended to cover what he was employed to do even though he performed this for his own benefit and to defraud the employer. This, in turn, depended on whether the words or conduct of the employer could lead a reasonable person to believe that the person with whom he transacted business was acting as the servant or agent of the employer at the material time. The necessary representations had to be made by the employer: and these could be inferred by his putting the employee in the position in which he could perform the relevant act, even though it was performed fraudulently and contrary to the interests of the employer. Proof that the employment gave the employee the opportunity to commit a tort will not suffice; there must be some authorisation of the employee, or some holding out of him as being authorised to transact the business which leads to the commission of the tort. A solicitor's clerk, therefore, who acted fraudulently with respect to a client he was empowered to deal with for his employers, could make them liable for his acts. Hence in the *Armagas* case no vicarious liability arose, because the employer of the agent had done nothing to induce in the third party the belief that the agent possessed the necessary authority. The representation had been made by the agent himself.[66] The act in question, namely entering into a three-year charterparty of a ship with the plaintiffs, was not one the agent was authorised to do, as the plaintiffs knew. Nor was it within the usual authority of an employee holding his position. The defendants had done nothing to cause the plaintiffs to believe that the agent had been authorised to extend his express or usual authority. Hence they could not be liable vicariously in tort for the deceit of the agent.

3.16 Ostensible authority can therefore be invoked to broaden the vicarious liability of a principal for acts performed by his agent, but only if

62 *Armagas Ltd v. Mundogas SA* [1986] 2 All E.R. 385 at 391.
63 [1981] 3 All E.R. 65 at 69.
64 [1985] 3 All E.R. 795; [1986] 2 All E.R. 385.
65 [1912] A.C. 716; see also *Uxbridge Permanent Building Society v. Pickard* [1939] 2 K.B. 248.
66 [1986] 2 All E.R. 385 ad 394 *per* Lord Keith.

it is possible to conclude that the principal was the one responsible for endowing the agent with the appearance of enjoying or possessing authority to perform the particular acts. Such authority must be differentiated from what has been expressly authorised by the principal as well as what is implicit as being usual or necessary for the performance of his task by an agent of the class involved or engaged in the work that is entailed in the circumstances.

4. THE COURSE OF EMPLOYMENT

(a) Meaning

3.17 The traditional way of describing the circumstances in which a master would be liable vicariously for a tort committed by his servant was by stating that this result would only follow if the wrong were committed by the servant while acting in the course of his employment. That expression has received considerable judicial attention. The fundamental principle, said Lord Goff in *Smith v. Stages*,[67] "is that an employee is acting in the course of his employment when he is doing what he is employed to do, to which it is sufficient for present purposes to add, or anything which is reasonably incidental to his employment". In *St Helens Colliery Co Ltd v. Hewitson*,[68] Lord Atkinson put this in other words:

> ". . . a workman is acting in the course of his employment . . . when he is doing something in discharge of a duty to his employer, directly or indirectly, imposed upon him by his contract of service."

The true ground on which the test is based is a duty to the employer arising out of the contract of employment, bearing in mind that the word "employment" covers and includes things belonging to or arising out of it.[69]

3.18 In determining whether a given act was committed in the course of a servant's employment, which involves deciding what was the employment and what is properly to be considered to be within its course, the factual picture as a whole must be looked at, and any approach based on the fallacious concept that any one factor is conclusive must be rejected. The facts are of crucial importance, and the addition or subtraction of one factor in a given situation may tip the balance, whereas in another situation the addition or subtraction of the same factor may make no difference.[70] But this does not indicate that there are no principles in the light of which a court can decide whether a servant was acting within the course of his employment at the material time when the tort was committed. To Lord Lowry, in *Smith v. Stages*,[71] there were guiding principles that could be deduced from the cases. But new social and economic factors create new situations to which the older authorities,

67 [1989] 1 All E.R. 833 at 836.
68 [1924] A.C. 59 at 70–71.
69 *Ibid.*
70 *Nancollas v. Insurance Officer* [1985] 1 All E.R. 833 at 840 *per* Donaldson M.R.
71 *Supra* at 845 *per* Lord Lowry.

though binding as to principle, did not always furnish a cut-and-dried solution.[72] Thus an examination of the multitude of decisions on the question of a servant's course of employment may lead to the inference of some general ideas and principles as to what that expression means: but each case must still be decided on the basis of its own peculiar and particular facts. The principle of what is meant by the course of employment, though easy to state, is difficult to apply to an individual case but it is important to keep it in mind.[73] Equally, the guiding principles to which Lord Lowry referred, although often straightforward, are also not always easy to apply to the facts of an individual case; but they, too, must be borne in mind when reaching a conclusion. When they are forgotten, misinterpreted or misapplied, a higher court can, and will, reverse the decision of a lower, as the Court of Appeal reversed the decision of the trial judge in *Smith v. Stages*. If the principles are understood and applied correctly, the decision will be affirmed, as the House of Lords did with respect to the decision of the Court of Appeal.

(b) Acts within the course of employment

3.19 What a servant does in the performance of his ordinary duties recognised as pertaining to the task for which the servant is employed will be considered as occurring in the course of his employment. Even a wrong method of doing an authorised act can be regarded in the same way, as long as it was done not for the servant's own purposes but in the master's interests.[74] Hence a railway company was liable for injuries incurred by a passenger when a porter employed by the company pulled the passenger out of a train in the mistaken belief that the passenger was on the wrong train. Part of the duty of such porters was to promote the comfort of passengers. Although the porter had erred, what he did was done to perform his duty.[75] Similarly in *Kay v. I.T.W. Ltd*,[76] an assistant storekeeper employed by the defendants caused injury to the plaintiff when he drove a forklift truck to clear a space for the truck where it was kept when not in use. It was the employee's duty to return the forklift truck to the warehouse. Since what he did was in the performance of his duty, it fell within the course of his employment, despite the fact that he acted negligently in the way he drove, without making any inquiry as to the whereabouts of a lorry driver whose lorry had backed up to a ramp leading to the warehouse, or of the plaintiff, the chief storekeeper at the warehouse. In *General Engineering Services Ltd v. Kingston & St. Andrew Corporation*,[77] however, the acts of the employees were unconnected with what they were authorised to do: therefore they were not acts for which

72 *Ibid.* at 850.
73 *Ibid.* at 836 *per* Lord Goff.
74 *Poland v. Parr & Sons* [1927] 1 K.B. 236 at 242 *per* Bankes L.J.
75 *Bayley v. Manchester, Sheffield & Lincolnshire Railway Co.* (1873) L.R. 8 C.P. 148; cp. *Aitchison v. Page Motors Ltd* (1936) 154 L.T. 128, destruction by servant of defendants of the plaintiff's car bailed to the defendants for repairs.
76 [1968] 1 Q.B. 140.
77 [1988] 3 All E.R. 867.

the employers were vicariously liable. The firemen employed by a local fire brigade were operating a "go slow" policy as part of industrial action in support of a pay claim. So, when called to a fire, they took 17 minutes to cover the distance of $1\frac{1}{2}$ miles instead of the normal $3\frac{1}{2}$ minutes. They drove slowly forward, stopped, moved slowly forward again, stopped, and continued in this fashion until they reached the scene of the fire, by which time the premises were completely destroyed. The Privy Council, affirming the decisions of the Supreme Court and Court of Appeal of Jamaica, held that this mode of driving to a fire was not a wrongful and unauthorised mode of doing an act authorised by the employers, but was for a purpose and reason unconnected with the employer's business.[78] Therefore it was conduct outside the fire brigade's course of employment.

3.20 Acts which are incidental to the performance of a servant's duties may also be treated as coming within the course of his employment, although they are not immediately and directly the kind of acts that the servant is normally engaged to perform. In *Hanson v. Michelin Tyre Co. Ltd*[79] it was said that in determining whether an employee was acting in the course of his employment the test is whether a reasonable man would say that the employee's act was part and parcel of his employment, in the sense of being incidental to it, even if unauthorised or prohibited by the employer, or was so divergent from the employment as to be plainly alien and wholly distinguishable from it. In that case the servant whose act caused the plaintiff's injury was engaging in horseplay at the time, by pushing a hand truck under the duckboard of a machine on which the plaintiff, an employee of the defendants, was standing at the time talking to a fellow employee. In other cases such conduct by an employee has been held to be in the course of their employment despite the fact that it was indulged in for amusement or entertainment rather than for the purposes of fulfilling the employee's duties.[80] The courts have regarded such behaviour as a negligent or otherwise improper or wrongful mode of performing such duties rather than as entailing acts which markedly deviate from such performance.[81]

3.21 In a number of cases the problem arose because what happened occurred while an employee was travelling to or from work. In most instances, as Lord Goff explained in *Smith v. Stages*,[82] an employee is not engaged in the course of his employment at such times, even though he has to travel to his place of work and is doing so at the material time. The reason is because he is not employed to travel to his place of work: he is employed to work at such place and so his duty is to arrive there in time

78 *Ibid.* at 868–870.
79 [1985] 1 All E.R. 918.
80 E.g., *Hudson v. Ridge Manufacturing Co. Ltd* [1957] 2 Q.B. 348; *Coddington v. International Harvester Co. of Great Britain Ltd* (1969) 6 K.I.R. 146.
81 Contrast *O'Reilly v. National Rail & Tramway Appliances Ltd* [1966] 1 All E.R. 499 with *Chapman v. Oakleigh Animal Products Ltd* (1970) 8 K.I.R. 1063. The distinction may be based on what the employer knew about the vicarious propensities of the mischievous employee: i.e., it is personal not vicarious liability that is involved.
82 [1989] 1 All E.R. 833 at 836.

for his working day. Nor is he in the course of his employment when travelling home after his day's work is done. The test applied by the Court of Appeal in that case, and approved by the House of Lords, was that proposed by Lord Denning in *Vandyke v. Fender*.[83] Where an employee is driving solely between his home and his normal place of work or vice-versa he is not in the course of his employment unless it is an obligation to travel in the way in which he is travelling. Such was the situation in the *Vandyke* case, where the employers provided the employee with a car and paid for petrol on condition that the employee would pick up other employees, including the one who was injured by the driver's negligent driving. The same will not apply, however, if the negligent employee was not driving a vehicle provided by the employer, although the employer paid a mileage and passenger allowance, because the negligent driver was under no duty to drive himself, or the other employee who had been injured, to the place of work.[84] The mode and time of travel were at his discretion and the employers had no right of control. So too in *Netherton v. Coles*[85] an employee was not in the course of his employment when travelling from a hospital where he had to work to his home. This was exactly the same as if the employee had been going from his normal place of work to his home. But if an employee is using his own vehicle to go to the place where his work required his presence in the employer's paid time, and to return to that place during a lunch break, such employee is acting in the course of his employment.[86] As long as the employee was obliged to travel to a place where he was required to work, such as was the case with the disablement resettlement officer in *Nancollas v. Insurance Officer*,[87] where the employee was driving from home to keep an appointment with a disabled person some distance from the employee's home town, the employee can be said to be acting in the course of his employment. In *Smith v. Stages*[88] the employees, who worked on a power station in the Midlands, were sent to work on a power station in Wales. They were paid for travelling time as well as the equivalent of the rail fare for the journey. But they were not told of any obligatory mode of travel. The employees travelled in the car of one of them and on the way back from Wales one of the employees was injured by the negligent driving of the other, the owner of the car. Reversing the trial judge, the Court of Appeal held that this incident occurred in the course of the negligent employee's employment. Their decision was affirmed by the House of Lords. Summarising the propositions of law that could be said with reasonable confidence to apply to such instances, Lord Lowry stated:[89] (1) normally travelling to and from an employee's residence to a regular place of work is not in the course of his employment whatever the means of transport, even if provided by the

83 [1970] 2 Q.B. 292.
84 *Nottingham v. Aldridge* [1971] 2 Q.B. 739.
85 [1985] 1 All E.R. 227.
86 *Harvey v. O'Dell Ltd* [1958] 2 Q.B. 78; *C.P.R. v. Lockhart* [1942] A.C. 591; *Blee v. London & North Eastern Rly. Co.* [1938] A.C. 126.
87 [1985] 1 All E.R. 833: cp. *Elleanor v. Cavendish Woodhouse Ltd* [1973] 1 Lloyds Rep. 313.
88 *Supra* note 82.
89 *Ibid.* at 851.

employer, unless by his contract of service the employee is obliged to use that transport (unless something is expressly provided in that contract to the contrary); (2) travelling in the employer's time between workplaces, regular or otherwise, or in the course of a peripatetic occupation, such as an inspector of gas meters, will be in the course of employment; (3) receipt of wages, but not of a travelling allowance, will indicate the employee is travelling in the employer's time and for his benefit, and is therefore in the course of his employment, even if the employee has discretion as to the mode and time of travelling; (4) an employee travelling in the employer's time from his residence to a workplace other than a regular workplace, or in the course of a peripatetic occupation or to the scene of an emergency is acting in the course of his employment; (5) a deviation from or interruption of a journey in the course of employment, unless incidental to the journey, will for the time being, including an overnight interruption, take the employee outside the course of employment. These propositions apply to return as well as outward journeys. But these propositions were subject to express arrangements between the employer and the employee or those representing the latter's interests, viz., a trades union. Nor did they apply to salaried employees.

3.22 There are many other illustrations of acts which are incidental or ancillary to the performance of the servant's duties such that they can be considered to be acts performed in the course of employment. Even smoking a cigarette while working has been held to be in the course of employment[90] (a decision which may perhaps not be followed today when smoking, particularly in the workplace, has become an outlawed activity). Assaults by servants, although plainly not the kind of conduct for which a servant is employed, unless he is engaged to act as a "bouncer" at the employer's premises,[91] can nevertheless come within the general scope of what the servant is employed to do where it is part of his duties to maintain order. This has been held to be the situation with respect to barmen in a tavern or public-house.[92] But such was not the case where the servant was a pump attendant at a garage and the assault he committed was not in the course of keeping customers in order but by way of revenge for the customer's act in calling a policeman to complain of the servant's behaviour and threatening to report the servant's conduct to his employers.[93] If the servant's act can be described as a spontaneous act of retribution,[94] not as part and parcel of the attempt to carry out the servant's instructions although an improper method of doing so, then the assault will not come within the course of the servant's employment.

90 *Century Insurance Co. Ltd v. Northern Ireland Road Transport Board* [1942] A.C. 509; *Jefferson v. Derbyshire Farmers* [1921] 2 K.B. 281: with which contrast *Williams v. Jones* (1865) 3 H. & C. 602.

91 *Brown v. Doe & Astor Hotel Ltd* (1980) 23 B.C.L.R. 30; *Verbeek v. Stefura* (1981) 26 A.R. 497; *Smart v. McCarty* (1980) 33 N.B.R. (2d) 27.

92 *Petterson v. Royal Oak Hotel Ltd* [1948] N.Z.L.R. 136; *Wenz v. Royal Trust Co.* [1953] O.W.N. 798; with which contrast *Brezinski v. Schultz* [1975] 3 W.W.R. 467; *Deaton's Pty Ltd v. Flew* (1949) 79 C.L.R. 370.

93 *Warren v. Henlys Ltd* [1948] 2 All E.R. 935.

94 *Daniels v. Whetstone Entertainments Ltd* [1962] 2 Lloyds Rep. 1.

3.23 A servant who acts with malice, in the sense of an improper motive, may therefore make his master liable for what he does, as long as his act can be described as falling within what is incidental to his employment. For example, the secretary of a club writing a letter on behalf of the committee may be actuated by malice towards the plaintiff. This will render him liable, even though the occasion may be privileged. If writing and sending the letter were necessary duties involved in the secretary's employment, his employers will be liable for defamation. But the servant who is not malicious cannot be held liable if he were innocent of malice but those for whom he wrote the letter were motivated by malice towards the plaintiff.[95]

3.24 Even fraud and theft on the part of the servant have been held to be within the course of his employment, where the acts in question were incidental to the task the servant was engaged to perform.[96]

(c) Prohibited acts

3.25 Even if the servant has been expressly prohibited from performing the act in question, it may nonetheless come within the course of his employment, as long as it satisfies the conditions considered above as to the relevance to the fulfilment of the servant's duties.[97] This was stated clearly in *Limpus v. London General Omnibus Co.*[98] where a bus driver raced the buses of a rival bus company although forbidden to do so, and caused damage to the other company's bus. He made his employers vicariously liable. This has been confirmed in other decisions.[99] It has come into prominence in cases involving a driver giving lifts to passengers in his employer's vehicle when expressly forbidden to do so. In two instances[100] vicarious liability was negated by the conclusion that the act of giving a free ride was outside the course of the driver's employment. It was for his, not the employer's purposes. The driver was not doing what he was employed to do when he gave lifts when not permitted to do so. He was

95 *Egger v. Chelmsford (Viscount)* [1965] 1 Q.B. 248.
96 Below pp. 62–64.
97 *Marsh v. Moores* [1949] 2 K.B. 208 at 215 *per* Lynskey J. The distinction drawn is between a prohibition that limits the sphere of employment and one that only deals with control within the sphere of employment: *Plumb v. Cobden Flour Mills Co. Ltd* [1914] A.C. 62 at 67 *per* Lord Dunedin; *Ilkiw v. Samuels* [1963] 2 All E.R. 879 at 889 *per* Diplock L.J.
98 (1862) 1 H. & C. 526.
99 *Bayley v. Manchester, Sheffield & Lincolnshire Rly. Co.* (1873) L.R. 8 C.P. 148 at 152 *per* Kelly C.B.: see *C.P.R. v. Lockhart* [1942] A.C. 591; *L.C.C. v. Cattermoles (Garages) Ltd* [1953] 2 All E.R. 582; *Ilkiw v. Samuels* [1963] 2 All E.R. 879. Contrast *Gwilliam v. Twist* [1895] 2 Q.B. 84, which Diplock L.J. ([1963] 2 All E.R. at 889) thought would be decided differently today, if properly argued.
100 *Twine v. Bean's Express Ltd* (1946) 62 T.L.R. 458; *Conway v. George Wimpey Ltd* [1951] 2 K.B. 266, where a gratuitous passenger was held to be a trespasser; with which contrast *Young v. Edward Box Co. Ltd* [1951] 1 T.L.R. 789, where the plaintiff was a licensee, not a trespasser, according to Somervell and Singleton L.JJ., or according to Denning L.J., giving a lift was in the course of the servant's employment. Compare the decision in *Ricketts v. Thomas Tilling Ltd* [1915] 1 K.B. 644 that the employer was not liable for the negligence of his conductor in driving the bus, since this was outside the scope of his employment: he was not permitted to drive.

not merely acting in an unauthorised manner, but was going outside the performance of his duty as a driver.

3.26 A different conclusion was reached on the facts of the case by the majority of the Court of Appeal in *Rose v. Plenty*,[101] although the dissenting judgment of Lawton L.J. seems to confirm the attitude that a driver in such a situation is performing an act of a class not authorised.[102] In *Rose v. Plenty* a milk roundsman paid the plaintiff, aged 13, to help him collect and deliver milk bottles on his round contrary to an express prohibition from his employers against the use of young persons in the performance of the employee's duty. The plaintiff was injured when he fell off the milk float by reason of the roundsman's negligent driving. The trial judge held that the employers were not liable for that negligence because the roundsman was not acting in the course of his employment in allowing the plaintiff to assist him and the plaintiff was a trespasser on the milk float. The Court of Appeal reversed this decision. Scarman L.J. held that the prohibition affected only the conduct of the employment: it did not define or limit the scope of the roundsman's duties. Therefore the roundsman was not acting outside the scope or course of his employment.[103] Lord Denning thought that in disregarding his instructions the roundsman was performing his employer's business wrongfully, but his actions were not for his own purposes but for those of the employer. Therefore the latter was liable because his acts were within the scope or course of his employment.[104] Although the Court of Appeal accepted the earlier cases which they distinguished, it is not easy to reconcile them, having regard to general principles.

(d) Acts not in the interests of the master

3.27 Whatever may have been the attitude of the law in the nineteenth century, it is clear since *Lloyd v. Grace Smith & Co.*[105] that a servant can make his master liable for acts committed in the course of employment even if those acts are intended to benefit the servant not the master, and may be against the business interests of the master. This has been taken to include such acts as fraud:[106] theft of property entrusted to the master and by him to the employee for the purposes of the work of the employee.[107] The fact that the wrongful act in question was solely to benefit the servant will not by itself render the act one which is performed outside the course or scope of the servant's employment. For the master to avoid vicarious liability for such an act it must be shown that the act was not something

101 [1976] 1 All E.R. 97.
102 *Ibid.* at 102.
103 *Ibid.* at 106.
104 *Ibid.* at 101.
105 [1912] A.C. 716.
106 *Lloyd v. Grace Smith & Co.*, *supra*; and arson: see *Photo Productions Ltd v. Securicor Transport Ltd* [1980] A.C. 827.
107 *John Carter (Fine Worsteds) Ltd v. Hanson Haulage (Leeds) Ltd* [1965] 2 Q.B. 495.

that was connected with the manner in which the servant was to undertake the duties entrusted to him by the master. In *Morris v. C. W. Martin*,[108] for instance, the plaintiff sent a mink coat to a furrier to be cleaned. With the plaintiff's consent the furrier sent the coat to the defendants, who were well known cleaners, for them to perform the work. While the coat was in the possession of the defendants one of their servants stole it. For this act the defendants were liable, although they personally had not been guilty of any neglect. The defendants owed a duty as bailees to protect the property of the plaintiff. They had delegated or entrusted that duty to the larcenous servant. Therefore they were answerable for the manner in which the servant carried out that duty. But in *Leesh River Tea Co. Ltd v. British India Steam Navigation Co. Ltd*[109] a different conclusion was reached. A servant of stevedores employed by the shipowners to load and unload cargo from a ship stole a brass plate used as a cover to give access to a steam valve on the ship. As a result the ship became unseaworthy: sea water could enter when the ship rolled. In heavy weather on the subsequent voyage water entered the hold and damaged part of the cargo. One issue in the case was the liability of the shipowners for the act of the servant of the stevedores. The Court of Appeal held that the thief's employment only provided him with the opportunity to steal the plate. The act was not done for the purpose of loading or unloading the ship. Therefore the thief was not the agent of the shipowners when he stole the plate. His fault, therefore, was not the fault of their agent for the purposes of the Hague Rules. Consequently, they were not liable. The damage had not been caused by their fault or that of their agent or servant.

3.28 In deciding whether the servant's act was within or outside the course of his employment when he was acting for himself rather than for his master, the language of Lord Wilberforce in the *Kooragang* case[110] is apposite. After referring to the progressive way in which vicarious liability has been developed, he went on:

> "At the same time recognition has been given by the law to the movement which has taken place from a relationship, akin to that of slavery, in which all actions of the servant were dictated by the master, to one in which the servant claimed and was given some liberty of action."

Thus employees supplemented their wages by independent use in their own interests of the skills, and sometimes the tools, which they used in their employment. Such activities could be legitimate or surreptitious. But these realities had to be taken into account. From this and the decision in that case it may be deduced that an act of a servant can be outside the course of his employment if it is totally for himself that he performs it, even where it is performed during the hours of employment in the employer's place of work or business and entails the use of the employer's equipment.

108 [1966] 1 Q.B. 716. On the question of the burden of proof of proving absence of negligence, cp. *Port Swettenham Authority v. T.W. Wu & Co.* [1979] A.C. 580.

109 [1966] 3 All E.R. 593, with which contrast *Hourani v. Harrison* (1927) 96 L.J. K.B. 1025; *Heyn v. Ocean Steamship Ltd* (1927) 137 L.T. 158.

110 [1981] 3 All E.R. 65 at 68.

But it will be within the course of the servant's employment if, despite the factor of the servant's own interests or purposes, it is nevertheless connected with what he was employed to do for and on behalf of the employer.

3.29 Everything depends on whether the master, by employing a fraudulent or larcenous servant, was only providing him with an opportunity to commit the tort (when no vicarious liability will arise), or whether he gave the servant a task to perform in the performance of which the servant acted in a wrongful manner (which will cause his act to be one committed in the course of his employment, even though it was an improper mode of carrying out that employment). In the latter event the master will be vicariously liable for the act. Where the first situation is the case, the master will be liable personally if he has been negligent in his choice or supervision of the servant, or in some way has by his own default helped to bring about the wrongful act of the servant. He will not be liable vicariously.[111]

(e) Acts outside the course of employment

3.30 In sharp contrast with the cases considered above are those where the servant's act is considered to be outside the course of his employment. For this conclusion to be reached it must be found that at the material time the servant was, in words employed in one decision,[112] "a stranger to his employer". In that case the defendant's servant left the lorry he was employed to drive parked in the road and walked across to a café on the opposite side. For the resultant collision with the plaintiff's vehicle it was held that the defendant was not liable. The test, which goes back to the early part of the nineteenth century, when this issue first gained prominence, is whether when the servant acted in the way which gave rise to the tort he was on a "frolic of his own".[113] This refers to his doing something having no connection with the master's interests or the servant's employment. The servant must be doing something remote from what he is employed to do, something that is totally beyond the normal or implicit duties for which he has been engaged.

3.31 Thus in *Beard v. London General Omnibus Co.*[114] a conductor was employed by the defendants. When the driver of the omnibus on which the conductor was employed was absent, the conductor drove the bus around the corner. In doing so he injured the plaintiff. The Court of Appeal held that the defendants were not vicariously liable for the conductor's negligence, because he was doing something he was not employed to do but was exercising a totally different function. Even the fact that the situation was one of emergency made no difference. This

111 *Abrahams v. Deakin* [1891] 1 Q.B. 516; *Hillen v. I.C.I. (Alkali) Ltd* [1936] A.C. 65.
112 *Crook v. Derbyshire Stone Co. Ltd* [1956] 1 W.L.R. 432.
113 *Joel v. Morrison* (1834) 6 C. & P. 501 at 503 *per* Parke B.
114 [1900] 2 Q.B. 530: cp. *Gwilliam v. Twist, supra* note 99.

decision contrasts with that in the *Limpus* case where the driver was doing what he was employed to do, namely drive a bus, although he was doing it in an improper, unauthorised, even prohibited manner. The decision may not be followed today on several grounds. First, at the date of that case it was unlikely that a bus conductor would be qualified to drive a vehicle, which is probably not the situation today. Secondly, the fact that an emergency had arisen might today induce a court to find that what the conductor did was necessarily incidental to the performance of his duties to the bus company.[115] Thirdly, given the very broad approach to vicarious liability signified by Lord Wilberforce in the *Kooragang* case,[116] there would appear to be more likelihood today that the act of the conductor could be regarded as coming within the course of his employment.

3.32 Similarly in *Cheshire v. Bailey*[117] the servant was a coachman hired out to the plaintiff with the coach of the defendant, for whom the servant worked, to deliver samples of silver goods on behalf of the plaintiff. The servant connived at the theft of the goods. The Court of Appeal held that the deliberate action of assisting the theft was not within the course of the coachman's employment, therefore the defendant was not liable. A different conclusion was reached where the theft was the result of a coachman's negligence, not his wilful and deliberate default.[118] Moreover, as later cases have indicated, even where the servant acted deliberately and with wilful intent, his act in stealing goods or assisting in their theft can still come within the course of his employment. In this respect the law may have undergone some development since 1905, especially in light of the 1912 decision in *Lloyd v. Grace Smith & Co.*[119]

3.33 The distinction that has been drawn is that between a "frolic", which takes the servant's act outside his employment and a "detour", which can be described as an improper and unauthorised manner of performing what is an unauthorised action. In *Hilton v. Thomas Burton (Rhodes) Ltd*,[120] for example, what occurred was not a detour but a frolic. The plaintiff and another man were employed at a site 30 miles from the employers' premises. They travelled to and from that site in a van owned by the employers. They were allowed to get their lunch at a café or restaurant, for which purpose the employers allowed them to use the van. One afternoon after they had visited a nearby restaurant for refreshments they set out later to have tea at a café 7 or 8 miles from the work site.

115 Compare the remarks of Lord Lowry in *Smith v. Stages* [1989] 1 All E.R. 833 at 851, with regard to an employee travelling in the employer's time to the scene of an emergency relating to his work or his workplace, which could be within, and not outside the scope of his employment.

116 [1981] 3 All E.R. 65 at 68.

117 [1905] 1 K.B. 237: cp. *United Africa Co. Ltd v. Saka Owoade* [1955] A.C. 130.

118 *Abraham v. Bullock* (1902) 86 L.T. 796.

119 [1912] A.C. 716, para. 3.27 *supra*; see *Morris v. C. W. Martin & Sons Ltd*, para. 3.27 *supra*; *John Carter (Fine Worsteds) Ltd v. Hanson Haulage Ltd*, para. 3.27 *supra*; *Mendelssohn v. Normand Ltd* [1970] 1 Q.B. 177.

120 [1961] 1 W.L.R. 705.

When they were almost there they realised it was late and went back to collect the other members of the workgang at the site, to take them back to the employers' premises. While on that journey the accident occurred in which the plaintiff was injured. This was caused by the negligent driving of the other employee. Diplock J. held that the driver of the van, although driving with the permission of the employers, was not doing what he was employed to do at the material time: therefore it did not occur in the course of his employment. The trip to the café was only to fill in time until they could draw their pay. It was a frolic of their own having nothing to do with what they were employed to perform. Similarly, although an employee may be required to commit tortious acts in the performance of his duties, for example, where he has to maintain order, in *Keppel Bus Co. Ltd v. Ahmad*[121] the bus conductor who struck a passenger was not acting in the course of his employment because there was no disorder among the passengers at the time of the assault nor was the passenger struck interfering with the conductor's performance of his duties by protesting against the latter's use of abusive language. The conductor's conduct in this instance was as much a "frolic" of his own as that of the pump attendant who struck the customer who complained of his behaviour.[122]

5. INDEPENDENT CONTRACTORS

3.34 The general principle is that no vicarious liability is imposed on the employer of an independent contractor for torts committed by that contractor or his servants acting in the course of their employment for him. However where the defendant is under a duty to use care he cannot get rid of his responsibility by delegating the performance of it to someone else, no matter whether the delegation be to a servant under a contract of service or to an independent contractor under a contract for services.[123] For this situation to arise the defendant must owe a direct duty to the person injured. The test is not whether the acts are so dangerous as to transfer to one person liability for another's negligence,[124] but whether there is imposed on the person by the nature of the act he is getting done a duty to people whom as a reasonable man he ought to foresee as being affected by the performance of those acts.[125]

121 [1974] 1 W.L.R. 1082. Contrast the cases referred to *supra* note 92.
122 *Warren v. Henlys Ltd* [1948] 2 All E.R. 935.
123 *Cassidy v. Ministry of Health* [1951] 2 K.B. 343 at 363 *per* Lord Blackburn. Cp. *Dalton v. Angus* (1881) 6 App.Cas. 740 at 829 *per* Lord Blackburn; *McDermid v. Nash Dredging & Reclamation Co. Ltd* [1987] 3 W.L.R. 212.
124 This is one example of liability for the misconduct of an independent contractor, viz., where the work delegated is inherently dangerous: *Rivers v. Cutting* [1982] 3 All E.R. 69 at 72 *per* Fox L.J.
125 Chapman, "Liability for the Negligence of an Independent Contractor" (1934) 50 L.Q.R. 71 at 76. Cp. *McArdle v. Andmac Roofing Co.* [1967] 1 All E.R. 583 at 592 *per* Edmund Davies L.J. See *Riverstone Meat Co. Pty Ltd v. Lancashire Shipping Co. Ltd* [1961] A.C. 807, involving liability for the acts of an independent contractor that made a ship unseaworthy, so as to exclude the protection given to carriers by the Hague Rules. Contrast *Norton v. Canadian Pacific Steamships Ltd* [1961] 2 All E.R. 785, where there was no such liability for the negligence of porters at a landing stage of a port on the part of the shipping company when passengers were assisted by the porters.

3.35 In *Salsbury v. Woodland*[126] the Court of Appeal stated that there were two instances in which a duty was owed such that the employers of an independent contractor could be liable for his misconduct. The first involved extra-hazardous acts, that is to say, acts commissioned by an employer that are so hazardous in their nature that the law has thought it proper to impose a direct obligation on the employer to see that care is taken. The second concerned dangers created by work done in or on a highway, when an employer had a duty to see that due care was taken for the protection of those who used the highway. In *Salsbury* vicarious liability could not be imposed, because the circumstances fell within neither exception. The occupier of a house employed a competent felling contractor to remove a large tree in the front garden of the house. The contractor did his work so negligently that the tree fell and broke telephone wires running across the front garden. These fell in front of the house. The plaintiff, watching out of curiosity, went into the road to remove the wires. While doing so he had to jump out of the way of a vehicle being driven by another person, in the course of which he was injured. Reversing the trial judge, the Court of Appeal held that the house occupier was not liable for the negligence of his contractor. The exceptions to the general principle did not cover the case of someone employing another to carry out acts in close proximity to the highway.

3.36 By statute, since the Occupiers Liability Act 1957, clarifying a point that was a matter of some dispute, an occupier will be liable for the acts of his independent contractor, in certain circumstances, and under certain conditions.[127] An employer's duty to his employees to ensure that reasonable care is taken of them cannot be discharged by delegation to an independent contractor. The liability remains on the employer.[128] This was the case at common law where the duty of care was to be performed on the employer's own premises. Where the injury occurred elsewhere, the employer might not have been liable.[129] However, under the Employer's Liability (Defective Equipment) Act 1969, the employer will now be liable, even if the defect that causes the injury is attributable to a third party, where the injury is the result of the supply of defective equipment to the employee.[130] In other situations the common law doctrine still applies. Such statutes are not the only ones that entail liability for the acts of an independent contractor. Whenever a statute imposes a duty on someone in such terms that the duty is absolute,[131] it cannot be fulfilled by delegation

126 [1970] 1 Q.B. 324.
127 Below pp. 394–395. See, e.g., *A.M.F. International Ltd v. Magnet Bowling Ltd* [1968] 2 All E.R. 789 at 803 *per* Mocatta J. for a situation where no vicarious liability was involved.
128 *Wilsons Clyde Coal Co. Ltd v. English* [1938] A.C. 57: below pp. 402–406.
129 Hence the non-liability of the employer under common law where he purchased a standard tool from a reputable supplier, when the tool suffered from a latent defect that the employer had no means of discovering: *Davie v. New Merton Board Mills* [1959] A.C. 604.
130 This reverses the effect of the decision in the *Davie* case, *supra*.
131 E.g., duties imposed under legislation dealing with safety in factories, etc.

to an independent contractor.[132] The employer of that contractor will be liable should the latter be guilty of a breach of the duty.[133]

3.37 Common law duties may also give rise to liability for the acts of an independent contractor. Under the doctrine of *Rylands v. Fletcher*,[134] the actual decision in which involved liability for the negligence of an independent contractor, and in cases of private nuisance,[135] or damage by fire,[136] a defendant cannot escape responsibility by proving that the harm was caused by the act of an independent contractor. In such instances liability is strict. However this kind of liability also arises more generally where extra-hazardous activities are being carried out by the defendant by the use of an independent contractor rather than personally or by his servants or agents, for whom vicarious liability would usually arise.[137] All such situations fall within the first exception discussed in *Salsbury v. Woodland*. The second exception accounts for those cases in which work has been done on or in the highway. For example, in *Penny v. Wimbledon U.D.C.*[138] a contractor employed by the defendants left an unlit heap of rubbish behind after repairing a highway. The defendants were liable when the plaintiff fell over the heap while walking in the dark. The older common law doctrine has been reinforced by the Highways Act 1980, by s. 58 of which in an action for damages arising from non-repair of highways or bridges it is irrelevant to prove that the local authority had employed an independent contractor to perform or supervise the maintenance of the highway or bridge in question, unless the authority gave proper instructions about such maintenance and the contractor carried out those instructions. At one time a distinction was drawn between non-feasance and misfeasance. For the former there was no liability: for the latter there was, whether this was the fault of the highway authority itself, its servants or agents or an independent contractor employed by the authority. By virtue of the 1980 Act this differentiation has disappeared from the law, in the circumstances envisaged in the statute.

132 *Donaghey v. Boulton & Paul Ltd* [1968] A.C. 1; *Smith v. Cammell Laird & Co. Ltd* [1940] A.C. 242; *Galashiels Gas Co. Ltd v. O'Donnell* [1949] A.C. 275; cp. *Riverstone Meat Pty Ltd v. Lancashire Shipping Co. Ltd, supra.*

133 It must be a *duty*, not a *power*: *Darling v. Attorney-General* [1950] 2 All E.R. 793. The obligation and liability of the employer will depend on the terms of the statute: see e.g., *Rivers v. Cutting, supra.*

134 (1866) L.R. 1 Ex. 265; (1868) L.R. 3 H.L. 330: Chapter 9.

135 *Matania v. National Provincial Bank* (1936) 155 L.T. 74: Chapter 8. Note also the liability of an occupier whose independent contractor performs work on the occupier's land that causes withdrawal of support from the land of a neighbour: *Bower v. Peate* (1876) 1 Q.B.D. 34; *Dalton v. Angus*, para. 3.34 *supra*; *Hughes v. Percival* (1883) 8 App.Cas. 443.

136 *Black v. Christchurch Finance Co.* [1894] A.C. 48; *Balfour v. Barty-King* [1957] 1 Q.B. 406: Chapter 10.

137 *Tarry v. Ashton* (1876) 1 Q.B.D. 314; *Brooke v. Bool* [1928] 2 K.B. 578; *Honeywell & Stein Ltd v. Larkin Bros.* [1934] 1 K.B. 191; *A.C. Billings & Sons v. Riden* [1958] A.C. 240. This was not accepted by the High Court of Australia in *Stevens v. Brodribb Sawmilling Pty Ltd* (1985) 160 C.L.R. 16; cp. *Stoneman v. Lyons* (1975) 133 C.L.R. 350 at 562–565, 574–575.

138 [1899] 2 Q.B. 72.

3.38 However, where liability for the acts of a contractor can arise, it will not do so if the negligence involved was "collateral", or casual.[139] There is some difficulty in regard to the explanation and application of this notion.[140] In *Padbury v. Halliday & Greenwood Ltd*,[141] a tool left on a casement by a workman erecting certain premises was blown off by the wind, causing injury to the plaintiff. The defendant who employed the contractor whose workman's negligence caused the accident was not liable. But in *Penny v. Wimbledon U.D.C.*[142] the act of leaving the heap of rubbish was not collateral. It is not easy to see any real distinction between these cases. One commentator explained the difference in this way:

> "I am not liable if my contractor in making a bridge happens to drop a brick, but I am liable if the bridge itself is defective, [for] I owe a duty to see that my bridge will open, but I owe no duty with regard to the disposition of bricks . . . in the course of construction."[143]

Even such an explanation leaves the differences between the *Padbury* and *Penny* cases questionable.

3.39 Although such liability is referred to as an example of vicarious liability, it might be more correct to explain it as a form of personal liability on the part of the employer of the contractor.[144] The wrongful act is not that of the employer, any more than it is in the case of the liability of a principal for an agent or a master for a servant. The employer is liable because his contractor was negligent or otherwise behaved tortiously, just as the principal or master is liable because the agent or servant committed a tort. The fact that liability for the acts of an independent contractor is only imposed where a personal duty on the employer was not fulfilled by him indicates a liability that is more personal in character. It is the employer's failure to conform to the standards required by the law that gives rise to liability, not just his relationship with the actually responsible party.[145] Hence the usual explanations of vicarious liability do not seem appropriate to such instances. Liability for the acts of a contractor appears to be growing and broadening in scope, doubtless because of the increased use of contractors and subcontractors in many situations.[146] In keeping with the rationale of vicarious liability suggested earlier, namely the need to ensure that there is a defendant capable of satisfying a judgment in favour of an injured party, it may be argued that the justification of the liability of the employer of an independent contractor, which was once viewed as being exceptional rather than the norm, is the same necessity. Perhaps, in view of this and the gradual extension of the reach of vicarious liability, the time may have come, or may come in the near future, when

139 *Pickard v. Smith* (1861) 10 C.B. N.S. 470 at 480 *per* Williams J.
140 *Salsbury v. Woodland*, para 3.35 *supra* at 348 *per* Sachs L.J
141 (1912) 28 T.L.R. 494.
142 *Supra*: cp. *Holliday v. National Telephone Co.* [1899] 2 Q.B. 392.
143 Chapman, *loc. cit.* note 125 *supra* at 81.
144 But see Barak, "Mixed and Vicarious Liability—A Suggested Distinction" (1966) 29 M.L.R. 160, indicating that the liability is neither truly vicarious nor truly personal, because the employer is still liable for an act committed by another person, not himself.
145 *Daniel v. Rickett, Cockerell Ltd* [1938] 2 K.B. 322 at 325.
146 Cp. *Cynat Ltd v. Landbuild Ltd* [1984] 3 All E.R. 513 at 521–523.

the entire doctrine is re-examined from the standpoint of eradicating some fine, even awkward distinctions between those for whose conduct such liability is imposed as well as the circumstances in which it can be imposed.

6. THE PERSONAL LIABILITY OF EMPLOYERS

3.40 Where vicarious liability exists the one who commits the tort and the one who is held vicariously liable are joint not several tortfeasors. At common law this had certain important consequences which have been changed by statute.[147] *Inter alia* this now means that even where at common law the principal, master or employer of an independent contractor could not have sued the actual wrongdoer for an indemnity in respect of the former's liability to the injured party, such indemnity, or partial contribution towards the damages, can now be ordered by a court.[148] However no claim can be made against the wrongdoing agent, servant, or other person if he or she is immune from suit by the injured party. In *Broom v. Morgan*,[149] before change in the law relating to the position of spouses in the law of torts,[150] it was held that a master could be liable vicariously for the act of his servant even though the servant could not have been sued by the injured plaintiff because, as in that case, the plaintiff was the wife of the negligent servant. By virtue of the then existing law, it would have been possible for the master to recover the damages paid to the plaintiff from the husband. With the abolition of the older law in 1962 there would appear to be no barrier to the right of the master in a *Broom v. Morgan* situation to sue the servant. Insofar as there may be other immunities from suit in tort that still exist, that immunity would seem to extend to an immunity to make contribution to or to indemnify a joint tortfeasor.

3.41 It must be borne in mind, however, generally and in relation to the issue of contribution or indemnity under recent statutory law, that a master, principal or employer of an independent contractor may be guilty of personal wrongdoing distinct from any vicarious liability.[151] Where this is the case his or her liability is founded on his or her own wrongdoing or breach of duty towards the plaintiff. Hence the liability of the principal or other person is founded upon a very different duty owed to the plaintiff from the duty owed by the wrongdoing agent, servant or other party.

147 Chapter 4.
148 E.g., *Harvey v. O'Dell* [1958] 2 Q.B. 78. Note also the possible common law claim of a master against his servant for breach of contract: *Lister v. Romford Ice & Cold Storage Co. Ltd* [1957] A.C. 555; unless the master has been guilty of fault, personally or through another servant, when the old common law doctrine of *Merryweather v. Nixan* (1799) 8 T.R. 186 will still apply, leaving the master with only the statutory remedy; below pp. 76–79.
149 [1953] 1 Q.B. 597.
150 Above at p. 32 note 90.
151 Or both vicariously and personally: *Fairline Shipping Corporation v. Adamson* [1975] Q.B. 180.

Personal and vicarious liability must be kept separate.[152] In *Yepremiam v. Scarborough General Hospital*,[153] a dissenting view, by reason of which the hospital would have been liable for the injuries caused by negligent diagnosis, was based on the idea that the hospital owed a duty of care to the patient and that duty extended to cover all aspects of the safety, health and welfare of the patient while under the care and within the jurisdiction of the hospital. In consequence the hospital's liability was not vicarious, and did not require consideration of such matters as whether the doctors were servants and whether what happened occurred within the course of their employment. That liability stemmed from the breach by the hospital of its primary obligation to take care of the patient. This may be an acceptable view in England:[154] but it was not so in Ontario where the case arose.[155] However, there may be situations in which an institution, such as a school, is under a direct duty to someone such as a pupil, and the liability of the institution will be personal, not vicarious.[156] If that is so, then it must be pleaded correctly, since amendment of the pleadings may not be permitted.[157]

152 *Staveley Iron & Chemical Co. Ltd v. Jones* [1956] A.C. 627.

153 (1980) 110 D.L.R. (3d) 513 at 560–579 *per* Blair J.A.

154 In view of the National Health Service: *Cassidy v. Ministry of Health* [1951] 2 K.B. 343 at 362–365 *per* Denning L.J.

155 Because of the difference in the situation of the medical profession and the supply of medical care and attentioon: *Aynsley v. Toronto General Hospital* (1969) 7 D.L.R. (3d) 193 at 208 *per* Aylesworth J.A., affirmed [1972] S.C.R. 435: contrast *Yepremiam v. Scarborough General Hospital*, *supra* at 565 *per* Blair J.A.

156 Cp. the liability of the school and the local authority which was responsible for the school to the plaintiff whose husband was killed in an accident caused by a child running out of the school premises onto the highway: *Carmarthenshire County Council v. Lewis* [1955] A.C. 549.

157 *Esso Petroleum Co. Ltd v. Southport Corporation* [1956] A.C. 218.

CHAPTER 4

Joint and Several Tortfeasors

1. NATURE OF THE DISTINCTION

4.01 Damage can be caused to a plaintiff by a number of different wrongdoers, whose acts may be successive or contemporaneous. They may produce different damage or their conduct may combine so as to result in one particular injury or loss. Where the acts of wrongdoers not only produce or help to produce the damage of which the plaintiff complains, but also are intended or in law are taken as intended to be one act or design, such wrongdoers are described as joint tortfeasors.[1] There is a connection between their acts.[2] The cause of action against them is the same.[3] For this to result, their respective shares in the commission of a tort must be done, or must be considered to be done in furtherance of a common design. Similarity of design is not enough: there must be concerted action towards a common end.[4] Sometimes such concerted action is actual. Parties have behaved together by express or tacit agreement, for example, by attacking the plaintiff in a fight. In *Arneil v. Paterson*[5] two dogs, owned respectively by the two defendants, acted in concert and attacked the plaintiff's sheep, killing some of them. The House of Lords held that the defendants were joint tortfeasors. The concerted action may also take the form of a joint breach by two or more defendants of a duty which is jointly owned by them to the plaintiff. This would be the case if the drivers of two vehicles on the highway both drove negligently, as for example where they were racing each other and drove at speeds beyond the legal limit, the consequence being that they collided and struck the plaintiff. The requisite concerted action or design may be constructive rather than actual. This will occur when an agent or servant commits a tort in circumstances that involve the principal or master in vicarious liability for the agent's or servant's acts.[6] The principal or master is considered to be jointly, as well as separately, liable along with the agent or servant.[7]

4.02 In contrast, tortfeasors who act independently are described as several tortfeasors. Their acts are quite separate and unconnected in

1 *The Koursk* [1924] P. 140 at 155 *per* Scrutton L.J.
2 *Ibid.* at 151 *per* Bankes L.J.
3 *Ibid.* at 155 *per* Scrutton L.J.
4 *Ibid.* at 159 *per* Sargant L.J.
5 [1931] A.C. 560.
6 Chapter 3 *supra*.
7 *Brooke v. Bool* [1928] 2 K.B. 578.

intention even though they lead to the same injury. In *The Koursk*,[8] two ships were being handled negligently, such negligence not being the result of a common design. In consequence the ships collided with the vessel of the plaintiff and sank it. The acts of negligence were held to be separate and distinct. Hence two separate causes of action arose. Similarly, although a parent may be liable if his child negligently injures someone, the liability of the parent may not be vicarious, as in the case of master and servant or principal and agent, unless the child was acting as the parent's agent or servant at the material time. It may be independent, founded on the parent's own negligence in allowing the child to do what he did, for example, use an airgun or drive a vehicle.[9] In such cases the two acts of negligence may be simultaneous. In other instances, however, in which the separate nature of the wrongdoing is clearer, the independent acts of the defendants occur at different times. For example, the first defendant may cause injury to the plaintiff by knocking him down. Subsequently, while the plaintiff is prone in the street, the second defendant, by his own act of negligence, may run over the plaintiff, thereby causing further, different injury. Where such is the situation, each defendant is liable for his own act of negligence in a separate cause of action and will be responsible only for the injury which that act of negligence caused.[10] But if the combined, though not simultaneous or contemporaneous, acts of the two defendants jointly produce the plaintiff's injury, such defendants will be joint tortfeasors.[11]

4.03 If it is necessary for liability to establish a particular intent, e.g., malice in cases of qualified privilege where defamation is the cause of action,[12] then, even though the defendants may have been involved in the same publication, as author, printer and publisher of a newspaper that contains a libel, they will not be joint tortfeasors.[13] Each individual defendant will be liable or not depending on whether the requisite malice can be proved on his or her part.[14] If such malice can be proved against all, then the common design that is an essential element in establishing that tortfeasors are joint not several, will be proved.[15]

2. IMPORTANCE OF THE DISTINCTION

4.04 The common law endowed the distinction between joint and several tortfeasors with great importance. Every joint tortfeasor could be sued by the injured party for the total amount of his damage or loss. It was not possible for the tortfeasor to excuse himself by proving that his part in the

8 [1924] P. 140.
9 *Bebee v. Sales* (1916) 22 T.L.R. 413.
10 *Performance Cars Ltd v. Willoughby* [1962] 1 Q.B. 33; *Baker v. Willoughby* [1970] A.C. 467.
11 *Rouse v. Squires* [1973] Q.B. 889.
12 Chapter 18 at pp. 505–513.
13 *Gardiner v. Moore (No. 2)* [1966] 1 All E.R. 365.
14 *Egger v. Chelmsford (Viscount)* [1965] 1 Q.B. 248.
15 *Gardiner v. Moore, supra* at 388 *per* Thesiger J.

causation of the ultimate loss suffered by the plaintiff was only a small one.[16] A several tortfeasor, on the other hand, could only be sued for that part of the plaintiff's damage or loss actually caused by the wrongful act of the particular tortfeasor. If tortfeasors were joint, therefore, the plaintiff was entitled to pick out one, for example the one most likely to be able to satisfy a judgment, and make him wholly responsible. Where independent tortfeasors were involved, the plaintiff would have to bring separate actions against each and every tortfeasor in order to recover the full amount of his loss. A plaintiff could, and still may, sue all joint tortfeasors together in one action, and execute the judgment he obtains against any one of them, since only one sum will be awarded.[17] Individual sums will be awarded against several tortfeasors, as long as the total amount awarded in the actions does not exceed the loss incurred by the plaintiff. At common law, therefore, whereas several tortfeasors could escape liability for loss other than that caused by their individual actions, a joint tortfeasor might find himself liable for more than the loss actually caused by his misconduct. The injustice of this situation was compounded by the refusal of the common law, with certain exceptions,[18] to allow contribution of indemnity from other tortfeasors,[19] a situation which has been changed, although only within the past fifty years, by statute.[20]

4.05 Secondly, an important difference existed as between joint and several tortfeasors in respect of the effect of a judgment against one of them. A judgment against one several tortfeasor, whether satisfied or not, did not affect the plaintiff's rights against other several tortfeasors. The causes of action were separate and distinct. But a judgment against one joint tortfeasor, whether satisfied or not, would bar any further action against any other joint tortfeasor, even though, at the time he sued, the plaintiff was unaware that he could have sued other joint tortfeasors.[21] The tort merged in the judgment.[22] Hence a plaintiff might be deprived of any recovery, by reason of a technical rule of law, despite his innocence and ignorance of material facts. The injustice of this doctrine was finally removed by the Law Reform (Married Women and Tortfeasors) Act

16 Unless the negligence of another tortfeasor was so extreme as to mean that the tortfeasor sued had no causative effect vis-à-vis the plaintiff's injury: *Rouse v. Squires, supra.*

17 *Wah Tat Bank Ltd v. Chan Cheng Kun* [1975] 2 All E.R. 257 at 263: *Cassell & Co. Ltd v. Broome* [1972] A.C. 1027.

18 Viz., (i) where the tort committed was illegal and the party claiming contribution believed his act was lawful; (ii) where the tort was illegal and the party claiming contribution was vicariously liable for the tort even though he had not authorised it and did not know it was being committed. Cp. below at p. 79, in connection with contracts of indemnity.

19 Joint tortfeasors: *Merryweather v. Nixan* (1799) 8 T.R. 186: several tortfeasors: *Howell v. London General Omnibus Co.* (1877) 2 Ex.D. 365.

20 Below pp. 76–79.

21 *Brinsmead v. Harrison* (1872) L.R. 7 C.P. 547. The reason given was to avoid multiplicity of actions: *Bryanston Finance Ltd v. de Vries* [1975] 2 All E.R. 609 at 618 *per* Lord Denning; which it did but at too high a price: *Wah Tat Bank Ltd v. Chan, supra* at 261 *per* Lord Salmon. The rule goes back to 1605: *Brown v. Wootton* (1605) Cro. Jac. 73; see *Wah Tat Bank Ltd v. Chan, supra* at 261 *per* Lord Salmon. But it did not apply in the U.S.A. where only full satisfaction of the judgment would have a similar effect: *Lovejoy v. Murray* (1866) 3 Wall 1.

22 *King v. Hoare* (1844) 13 M. & W. 494 at 504 *per* Parke B.

1935,[23] which is now replaced by the Civil Liability (Contribution) Act 1978.[24] The earlier statute only applied to actions in tort. As a result of criticism expressed in the Law Commission's Report on Contribution in 1977,[25] this has now been revised to include actions for any "debt or damage". It also covers not only successive actions against two or more tortfeasors or other persons liable for a debt or damage, but also a single action against two or more persons.[26] Judgment against one defendant will not bar an action or the continuance of an action against another person jointly liable for the same debt or damage. However, if more than one action is brought in respect of any damage against those liable in respect of the damage, whether liable jointly or otherwise, the plaintiff will be deprived of his costs or actions subsequent to the first one, unless the court thinks there were reasonable grounds for bringing such further actions.[27] By reason of the repeal of the previous provisions of the 1935 Act,[28] it would appear that a plaintiff can bring a subsequent action against other joint or several tortfeasors not only to obtain an award which he could not get satisfied from the first judgment, but also to increase the damages he originally claimed, for example, where he has discovered that he suffered more than he first thought he had. Presumably this will be discouraged by courts, through denial of costs, unless there was a valid reason for the plaintiff's inability to appreciate the true and complete loss he had incurred.[29]

4.06 The third vital effect of the distinction was in connection with the release of a tortfeasor. Where a plaintiff released a several tortfeasor, his cause of action against the others remained extant and viable. Release of a joint tortfeasor, however, had the effect of barring any further action against other joint tortfeasors.[30] Once again this was because the plaintiff's cause of action against each and every joint tortfeasor was one and indivisible. Nor did it matter whether the release were gratuitous, under seal or in the form of an accord and satisfaction, i.e. a settlement under which the tortfeasor in question agreed to pay money in return for his release from liability.[31] The courts drew a curious distinction, however, between a release and a covenant not to sue a particular tortfeasor, which did not affect the right to sue other joint tortfeasors.[32] Although described by Lord Denning on one occasion as "an arid and technical distinction

23 S. 6(1)(a): repealed by 1978 c. 47, s. 9(1), Sch. 2.
24 S. 3.
25 Law Commission No. 79.
26 Cp. *Bryanston Finance Ltd v. de Vries* [1975] 2 All E.R. 609 at 618 *per* Lord Denning.
27 Civil Liability (Contribution) Act, 1978 s. 4; replacing the Law Reform (Married Woman and Tortfeasors) Act, 1935 s. 6(1)(b).
28 S. 6(1)(b).
29 Cp. Lord Denning in *Bryanston Finance Ltd v. de Vries*, *supra* at 618, referring to the provisions of the 1935 Act.
30 *Cocke v. Jenner* (1614) Hob. 66; *Nicholson v. Revill* (1836) 4 Ad. & E. 675; *Duck v. Mayeu* [1892] 2 Q.B. 511; *Cutler v. McPhail* [1962] 2 Q.B. 292.
31 *Thurman v. Wild* (1840) 11 Ad. & E. 453.
32 *Hutton v. Eyre* (1815) 6 Taunt. 289; *Duck v. Mayeu*, *supra*; *Apley Estates Co. Ltd v. de Bernales* [1947] Ch. 217.

without any merits",[33] the distinction was clearly recognised. Indeed in *Gardiner v. Moore*[34] Thesiger J. went so far as to hold that where a plaintiff settled an action against certain defendants to a libel action who were being sued jointly, a reservation of the right to sue the others could be implied, so that the settlement operated as a covenant not to sue the defendants who were parties to the settlement and not as a release of the plaintiff's cause of action against the other defendants. The Acts of 1935 and 1978 have not affected these common law rules.[35] It will therefore still be of some importance, in this context, to determine whether tortfeasors are joint or several.

3. CONTRIBUTION BETWEEN TORTFEASORS

4.07 The old common law against any form of contribution or indemnity between joint tortfeasors was abrogated by the Act of 1935, which only applied to tortfeasors. The statute of 1978, which repealed the earlier legislation, now deals with contribution between all those liable in respect of "the same damage", whether jointly or otherwise.[36] Hence it applies to several as well as joint tortfeasors, and to those who may be liable to the plaintiff in contract or breach of trust as well as those liable in tort.[37] There were problems that emerged in litigation based on the provisions of the 1935 Act. In the 1978 statute they have been addressed and resolved. One concerned the right to claim contribution by a tortfeasor who has settled the claim against him, with or without an admission of liability. The other was whether contribution could be claimed from a defendant who had been sued and held not liable, for whatever reason, even though he would have been held liable if sued at another time or on another ground.

4.08 Now it does not matter whether the tortfeasor claiming contribution paid or was ordered to pay damages to the plaintiff, or agreed to make such a payment, provided he was liable to pay such damages immediately before he made, was ordered, or agreed to make the payment.[38] The fact that the claimant ceased to be liable as a result of the discharge of his prior liability by payment or compromise will not deprive

33 *Bryanston Finance Ltd v. de Vries, supra* at 619: "It is a trap into which the unwary fall but which the clever avoid": *ibid.*

34 [1966] 1 All E.R. 365.

35 Despite the view of Lord Denning in *Bryanston Finance Ltd v. de Vries, supra* at 619 that it should be discarded now that there were statutory provisions for contribution between joint wrongdoers.

36 S. 1(1). "Liability" throughout refers to actual or hypothetical liability in an action brought against someone claiming contribution by an injured party in England and Wales, even if the issue in such action was or could be determined by the law of some other country, in accordance with the rules of private international law: *ibid.* s. 1(6).

37 A plaintiff may sue all defendants together or may sue any one, who can thereupon make another tortfeasor a third party to the action with the same rights of defence as if he had been sued by the defendant: R.S.C. Ord. 16; C.C.R. Ord. 12. Assessment of the contribution should be made at the end of the trial: *Calvert v. Pick* [1954] 1 W.L.R. 456.

38 Civil Liability (Contribution) Act 1978 s. 1(2).

him of the right to claim contribution. Contribution may be claimed from someone who is no longer liable in respect of the damage in question, for example because the plaintiff's claim against him has been dismissed for want of prosecution,[39] unless he is no longer liable by reason of the expiry of a period of limitation on which the claim against him was based.[40] In this respect it is provided also that a judgment in any part of the United Kingdom by or on behalf of the party suffering damage against anyone from whom contribution is sought is conclusive in the action for contribution as regards any issue determined in favour of the person from whom contribution is sought.[41] Hence if in that action the party from whom contribution is now being sought was held not liable for any reason, it is not open to the one claiming contribution to upset or deny the validity of that original decision. Someone who has compromised or agreed to compromise in good faith a claim against him by an injured party, including where he has made a payment into court that has been accepted, can recover contribution, whether or not the party who compromises or pays into court was ever liable for the damage, as long as he would have been liable if the factual basis of the claim against him could have been established.[42] This provision was inserted to dispose of the point in *Stott v. West Yorkshire Road Car Co. Ltd*,[43] that a contribution claim made after settlement before judgment would fail unless it was established in those proceedings that the defendant claiming contribution was actually a tortfeasor.

4.09 In *Ronex Properties Ltd v. John Laing Construction Ltd*,[44] decided under the 1935 Act, it was held that a claim for contribution could still be brought even though the defendant claiming contribution had died. His personal representatives could maintain the third party proceedings against the other defendant. That claim did not survive under the Law Reform (Miscellaneous Provisions) Act 1934, which preserved rights of action subsisting and vested in a deceased at the time of his death,[45] because at the date when he died the defendant claiming contribution had not been held liable nor had he admitted liability to the plaintiff in the main action. Nevertheless the old common law doctrine *actio personalis moritur cum persona*, which had been abrogated by the 1934 Act in respect of vested rights of action, did not apply to this defined inchoate right under the 1935 Act.[46] That right, although arising out of tortious rights, viz.,

39 *Hart v Hart & Pickles Ltd* [1969] 1 Q.B. 405.
40 Civil Liability (Contribution) Act 1978 s. 1(3): cp. *George Wimpey & Co. Ltd v. B.O.A.C* [1955] A.C. 169. Note that most periods of limitation bar the remedy, not the right, hence the proviso will not be too inhibitory. However the expiration of the limitation period bars the plaintiff's right, not merely his remedy, where conversion is involved: Limitation Act, 1980, s. 3(2). Therefore a claim for contribution may be defeated where the original tort was conversion, if the first defendant delays too long before bringing his claim against other tortfeasor.
41 Civil Liability (Contribution) Act 1978 s. 1(5).
42 *Ibid.* s. 1(4).
43 [1971] 2 Q.B. 651.
44 [1982] 3 All E.R. 961.
45 See pp. 40–43.
46 *Ronex Properties Ltd v. John Laing Construction Ltd, supra* at 966–967 *per* Donaldson L.J.

those of the plaintiff in the main action, was not a claim in tort as between the party claiming contribution and the one from whom contribution was claimed: it was a right *sui generis*[47] which, according to Sir Sebag Shaw,[48] resembled a plaintiff's claim for money paid by him, i.e. the defendant, to a third party, i.e. the plaintiff in the main action, to the use of the defendant in the claim for contribution. Clearly the reasoning in this decision applies with equal force and logic to claims made under the 1978 Act.

4.10 Since the right to claim contribution is *sui generis*, not a cause of action in tort, it was held that such a claim had to be made within six years.[49] Under the Limitation Act 1980,[50] claims for contribution must be made within two years of the time that the right to claim contribution accrued to the tortfeasor making such claim.[51] The date when such right accrued depends on whether the tortfeasor making the claim for contribution was held liable by a civil judgment or arbitration award. If so, the date in point is the date of the judgment or award. In any other instance, i.e. where the party claiming contribution has admitted liability to the injured party, the relevant date is the earliest date on which the amount to be paid by him in discharge of his liability to the injured party is agreed by or on behalf of the tortfeasor and the injured party or parties.[52] A variation of a judgment or award on an appeal of the damages to be paid by the tortfeasor claiming contribution is to be disregarded in this context.

4.11 The amount recoverable in a claim for contribution is, in general, to be determined by the court on the basis of what is just and equitable having regard to the extent of the responsibility of the party from whom contribution is claimed for the damage in question.[53] The court can exempt any person from liability to make contribution, or direct payment of a complete indemnity.[54] Thus the court has a very wide discretion. After some debate on the question whether responsibility under this statute refers to causation or culpability, it would appear that the proper test for assessment of contribution is a combination of both causation and relative blameworthiness.[55] But in apportioning damages the court cannot take

47 *Harvey v. R. G. O'Dell Ltd* [1958] 2 Q.B. 78.
48 *Supra* note 46 at 968.
49 *Harvey v. R. G. O'Dell Ltd, supra.*
50 S. 10.
51 S. 10(3) makes a saving for cases of fraud, disability and mistake.
52 *Ibid.* s. 10(2).
53 Civil Liability (Contribution) Act 1978 s. 2(1). But the amount awarded by way of contribution cannot exceed the maximum for which the person from whom contribution is claimed would be liable to the plaintiff having regard to any financial limit on the amount of damages set by a statute or by a contract made with the plaintiff before that person's breach of duty, and having regard to contributory negligence on the part of the plaintiff: *ibid.* s. 2(3).
54 *Ibid.* s. 2(2): see, e.g., *Semtex Ltd v. Gladstone* [1954] 1 W.L.R. 945; *Jones v. Manchester Corporation* [1952] 2 Q.B. 852.
55 *Brown v. Thompson* [1968] 2 All E.R. 708; *The Miraflores and The Abadesa* [1967] 1 A.C. 826; *Baker v. Willoughby* [1970] A.C. 467. See also *Weaver v. Commercial Press Co.* (1947) 63 T.L.R. 466; *Randolph v. Tuck* [1962] 1 Q.B. 175. The applicable principle is similar to that applied in cases of apportionment of liability between plaintiff and defendant on the ground of the former's contributory negligence: cp. pp. 366–368.

into account the possible liability of a person not a party before the court.[56] An apportionment made by a trial judge will only be altered on appeal in exceptional instances, where it is clearly wrong, or there has been an error in principle or a mistake of fact.[57] But an appellate court can make its own assessment if it rehears a case *de novo*.[58]

4. CONTRACTS OF INDEMNITY

4.12 The statutory provisions supersede any rights to recover contribution, as distinct from indemnity, other than an express contractual right,[59] such as the right of joint contractors to recover contribution from each other (a matter which is outside the scope of the law of torts). However the statute does not affect express or implied contracts providing for any indemnity: or any express contract regulating or excluding contribution, as long as any such contract would be enforceable apart from the Act.[60] Nor does the statute make enforceable any contract for indemnity or contribution that would not be enforceable apart from the Act.[61] In this context it is necessary to consider instances of express[62] or implied[63] contracts of indemnity[64] in the light of the provisions of the 1978 Act.

4.13 Thus certain contracts of indemnity are unlawful, such as one by which an insured person claims that his insurers are obliged to indemnify him against the results of his criminal act, where that is intentional. But in *Gardner v. Moore*[65] the House of Lords held that this did not apply where it was the injured plaintiff who was claiming the benefit of the agreement between the Motor Insurers' Bureau and the Secretary of State under which the Bureau compensated the victims of uninsured drivers unable to satisfy a judgment against them. The plaintiff had been injured when the uninsured driver deliberately drove at him. Although this was a crime, the doctrine of public policy that a person was not entitled to profit by his own wrongdoing did not apply. The object of the agreement with the Bureau was the protection of innocent third parties.[66] However a contract to indemnify a party in respect of an act which is manifestly illegal or which

56 *Maxfield v. Llewellyn* [1961] 3 All E.R. 95.
57 *The MacGregor* [1943] A.C. 197; *Brown v. Thompson, supra*; *Rouse v. Squires* [1973] Q.B. 889.
58 *Hanson v. Wearmouth Coal Co. Ltd* [1939] 3 All E.R. 47.
59 Civil Liability (Contribution) Act 1978 s. 7(3).
60 *Ibid.*
61 *Ibid.*
62 See, e.g., *Wright v. Tyneside Improvement Commissioners* [1968] 1 All E.R. 807.
63 See, e.g., *Sims v. Foster Wheeler Ltd* [1966] 2 All E.R. 313, indemnity arising by way of a breach of warranty between contractors and sub-contractors as a result of which an employee of the contractors was injured. The contractors were held 25% liable. This was recoverable from the sub-contractors.
64 Rights to indemnity may also arise under statute, e.g. the Partnership Act 1890 s. 24(2), as between partners: or by a principle of law, e.g. as a consequence of the relationship of principal and agent.
65 [1984] 1 All E.R. 110.
66 *Ibid.* at 1105-1106 *per* Lord Hailsham L.C., citing and approving *Hardy v. Motor Insurers' Bureau* [1964] 2 Q.B. 745.

the party seeking indemnity knew to be unlawful at the time he committed it, such as a libel, will not be enforceable.[67] But if one person does something apparently legal at the request or instigation of another party, on the terms that he will be indemnified, that agreement to indemnify can be enforced even if the act was not legal, where judgment was given against the party seeking indemnity in respect of damage to a third party.[68] It would seem that, where a contract of indemnity is unlawful and unenforceable, a party who acted under the provisions of such contract may be able to claim contribution under the terms of the 1978 Act. However, he will only be able to recover whatever the court thinks just and equitable.[69] This may mean that the claimant receives nothing, where the court considers that his participation in a criminal or otherwise unlawful act, e.g. a tort, should deprive him of any claim.

4.14 In certain instances a right to indemnity is implied into the relationship between the parties.[70] For example, a principal who has authorised his agent to commit an illegal act, where the illegality was unknown to the agent, will be obligated to indemnify the agent for all liability the latter incurs.[71] So, too, a wrongdoing servant may be obliged to indemnify his master in respect of damages paid by the master to a third party because the master was vicariously liable for the servant's tort. This will depend on whether the servant was in breach of the terms of his contract of employment, e.g. by driving negligently when he was employed to drive a lorry.[72] But if the negligence was unconnected with his employment, although it occurred in the course of that employment, the situation will be different.[73]

67 *W. H. Smith & Son v. Clinton* (1908) 99 L.T. 841; cp. *Haseldine v. Hosken* [1933] 1 K.B. 822.
68 *W. Cory & Sons Ltd v. Lambton & Hetton Collieries Ltd* (1916) 86 L.J.K.B. 401; cp. *Burrows v. Rhodes* [1899] 1 Q.B. 816.
69 Above at p. 78.
70 Indeed such rights of indemnity anteceded the statutes and provided exceptions to the doctrine of *Merryweather v. Nixan* (1799) 8 T.R. 186: *supra* para 4.04 note 18.
71 *Adamson v. Jarvis* (1827) 4 Bing. 66.
72 *Lister v. Romford Ice & Cold Storage Co Ltd* [1975] A.C. 555.
73 *Harvey v. R. G. O'Dell Ltd* [1958] 2 Q.B. 78.

CHAPTER 5

Trespass to Land

1. ELEMENTS OF LIABILITY

(a) General Characteristics

5.01 The present law of trespass to land stems from the old writ of trespass *quare clausum fregit.* This was available when the defendant had perpetuated a forcible invasion of the plaintiff's land. Today a trespass is accomplished in various ways, for example, by entering upon the plaintiff's land;[1] remaining on it against the will of the plaintiff after an initial entry with permission;[2] or throwing or placing objects on the land without permission.[3] The act of the defendant must be wrongful and unjustified. This means that the conduct of the defendant must not be authorised or allowed by the common law or the provisions of a statute.[4] Trespass takes the form of a direct, as well as a forcible interference. Hence the alleged trespass must amount to an immediate invasion or intrusion upon the land of the plaintiff, not the consequential result of some other conduct.[5] But the degree of force employed by the defendant may be minimal. Any unauthorised and wrongful interference with another's land will be

1 Personally, or by the directed intrusion of some object (or by one's servant or agent or hounds: *League Against Cruel Sports Ltd v. Scott* [1985] 2 All E.R. 489). Note also the old tort of cattle trespass (now "straying livestock" under the Animals Act 1971, s. 4): below pp. 266–267.

2 *C.P.R. v. Gaud* [1949] 2 K.B. 239; cp. *Minister of Health v. Belotti* [1944] K.B. 298; *Wood v. Leadbitter* (1845) 13 M. & W. 838 (below pp. 102–105, dealing with licences); or acting outside the scope of the permission; *Hillen v. I.C.I. (Alkali) Ltd* [1939] A.C. 65. This can be very important where the liability of an occupier is concerned: below pp. 399–401. However a person originally lawfully in possession of land, as a lessee, will not be a trespasser if he holds over after the expiration of his term: *Hey v. Moorhouse* (1839) 6 Bing N.C. 52.

3 *Gregory v. Piper* (1829) 2 B. & C. 591; *Westripp v. Baldock* [1938] 2 All E.R. 779, affirmed [1939] 1 All E.R. 279; *Simpson v. Weber* (1925) 41 T.L.R. 279.

4 Below pp. 105–107.

5 If it is consequential, the resulting cause of action, if any, will be nuisance or negligence, e.g., where roots or branches of the defendant's tree project over or onto the plaintiff's land: *Smith v. Giddy* [1904] 2 K.B. 448; *Davey v. Harrow Corporation* [1958] 1 Q.B. 60: below pp. 178–193. Thus to fail to remove a decayed branch which then falls over a boundary onto the plaintiff's land will be trespass: *Star v. Rookesby* (1711) 1 Salk. 335. Note also the possibility of liability under the doctrine of *Rylands v. Fletcher* (1868) L.R. 3 H.L. 330, when damage to land results from an "escape" of dangerous object: below pp. 221–222.

regarded as a forcible trespass.[6] Trespass is actionable *per se*, without proof of any damage,[7] therefore an action may be maintained as soon as, and as long as an unauthorised, wrongful interference has occurred.[8] It will not be necessary for the plaintiff to establish any actual loss, although such loss will be recoverable,[9] as may aggravated, or possibly even punitive or exemplary damages in an appropriate instance.[10]

5.02 Trespass to land is a wrong against possession, not ownership. At an early stage in the history of the common law, protection was given to possession without any need to prove title. Indeed, eventually, through the development of the action of ejectment, which originally protected leaseholders, not owners, and was a variety of trespass *quare clausum fregit*, disputes about land could be litigated. The common law was concerned with better rights to possession rather than rights of ownership (although methods to establish such ownership were also available). Trespass was the appropriate procedural route to settle issues of possession. Hence the employment and development of the action for trespass not only in the context and for the purpose of determining liability for wrongful acts in respect of land, but also as a means of determining rival claims to land without the need to invoke the older forms of action with their undesirable modes of trial and technical rules.[11]

5.03 Trespass to land therefore involves three major features: (i) some kind of interference; (ii) with the plaintiff's possession; (iii) of land.

(b) Interference

(i) Acts of trespass

5.04 The essence of the tort of trespass to land is an act that touches or affects the land in question. To walk over someone else's land is a trespass, if no permission to do so has been granted by the party in possession of the

6 *Entick v. Carrington* (1765) 19 St. Tr. 1030 at 1066: "every invasion of property be it ever so minute is a trespass". Trespass may be a crime under the Criminal Law Act 1977 and other statutes (see Glanville Williams, *Textbook of Criminal Law*, 2d ed. 1983, 915–917). The Act of 1977 repeals and replaces the Statutes of Forcible Entry 1381, 1429 and 1623: below p. 108. Only certain trespasses are made criminal under the 1977 Act: viz., trespass with an offensive weapon, trespass on foreign diplomatic missions, refusing to leave premises when required to do so by a displaced residential occupier, and entering premises by violence (except as a displaced residential occupier): below pp. 000. For the possibility that an owner could forcibly eject a trespasser to his land under the old law, see *McPhail v. Persons Unknown* [1973] Ch. 447 at 456 *per* Lord Denning.

7 *Ashby v. White* (1703) 2 Ld. Raym. 938. Hence an injunction can be granted to stop a trespass even if damage is trival: *John Tremball Ltd v. National Westminster Bank Ltd* (1979) 39 P. & C.R. 104.

8 On "continuing" trespass, below pp. 85–86.

9 *Swordheath Properties Ltd v. Tabet* [1979] 1 All E.R. 240.

10 *Drane v. Evangelou* [1978] 2 All E.R. 437 at 440–441 *per* Lord Denning, 443 *per* Lawton L.J., 444 *per* Goff L.J.

11 Holdsworth, *History of English Law*, vol. iii 213–217, vol. vii, 4–23. Hence the modern use of ejectment, now termed the action for recovery of land, to regain possession when a plaintiff has been wrongfully dispossessed: below pp. 108–110.

land or by some statute (such as those which entitle various inspectorates[12] to enter for specific purposes[13]) or by the common law, as in the case of police officers who may be allowed to enter land or premises, even against the will of the occupier, to effect an arrest or for other purposes.[14] In *League Against Cruel Sports Ltd v. Scott*,[15] for example, it was a trespass on the part of the local hunt to enter onto unfenced areas of land on Exmoor, which the plaintiff had purchased for the purpose of providing sanctuaries for wild deer when hunted, after the plaintiff had refused to allow the hunt on such land. Squatters, who enter and occupy land that is, or appears to be, unoccupied at the time of such entry, are guilty of trespass, and may be evicted by appropriate legal action (or, in some instances, by dispossession).[16]

5.05 There need be no invasion of the plaintiff's land by a person or persons. Trespass may be committed through the medium of some object, as where the defendant allowed a pile of rubbish to touch the plaintiff's land:[17] or the defendant drove a "holdfast" into the plaintiff's wall;[18] or allowed a creeper to grow too far and extend onto the land of the plaintiff;[19] or placed a ladder or other objects against the plaintiff's property.[20] However, no trespass will be committed where the defendant extends a plank over the plaintiff's close, i.e. land, without touching the land itself[21] (even if the result is that damage may be caused to the land, for example, by rainwater being diverted from the defendant's land onto the plaintiff's).[22] In such circumstances the tort of nuisance may be committed: but not trespass.[23] So, too, if something was placed on the plaintiff's land lawfully, for example with his permission, a failure to remove it when requested by the plaintiff will not be a trespass.[24] Similarly to deprive the plaintiff of facilities will not be a trespass.[25]

5.06 In some common law jurisdictions it has been held that trespass will be committed when the defendant allows some harmful substance to come

12 Or the public: National Parks and Access to the Countryside Act 1949 s. 60.
13 An inspector or other person who exceeds his statutory, or common law power of entry will be a trespasser: *Darling v. Attorney-General* [1950] 2 All E.R. 793; *Stroud v. Bradley* [1952] 2 All E.R. 76.
14 Below pp. 106–107.
15 [1985] 2 All E.R. 489: below pp. 88–89.
16 *Southwark London Borough Council v. Williams* [1971] Ch. 734; *Wiltshire County Council v. Frazer* [1986] 1 All E.R. 65: see further below pp. 98–100.
17 *Gregory v. Piper* (1829) 9 B. & C. 591.
18 *Lawrence v. Obee* (1815) 1 Stra. 22.
19 *Simpson v. Weber* (1925) 41 T.L.R. 302. Or the boom of a crane: *Anchor Brewhouse Developments v. Berkeley House (Docklands) Developments* (1987) 38 Build.L.R. 82.
20 *Westripp v. Baldock* [1938] 2 All E.R. 779, affirmed [1939] 1 All E.R. 279.
21 *Pickering v. Rudd* (1815) 4 Camp. 219.
22 *Nicholls v. Ely Beet Sugar Factory Ltd* [1931] 2 Ch. 84 (water).
23 Below Chap. 8.
24 *Shipcott v. Mugford* (1696) 1 Ld. Raym. 187.
25 *Perera v. Vandiyar* [1953] 1 W.L.R. 672; but it may be a breach of contract or another wrong: *McCall v. Abelesz* [1976] Q.B. 585.

onto the plaintiff's land, such as gas[26] or oil which has jettisoned from a ship at sea.[27] Decisions of this kind are questionable. The distinction may be drawn between the deliberate (or, as will be seen, perhaps the negligent) driving of the deleterious substance onto the land of the plaintiff, so that it is caused to touch and affect that land, and an accidental escape of such a substance which ultimately comes onto that land. The former will be a direct, forcible interference with another's land: the latter will be an indirect, consequential interference, which, historically, would have been remedied by an action on the case, not by trespass, and, in modern times, should give rise to an action in negligence, nuisance, or under the doctrine of *Rylands v. Fletcher*.[28] Similarly if the defendant's "cattle" wrongfully come onto the plaintiff's land the defendant will be liable for cattle trespass: if some other animal belonging to, or kept by the defendant strays onto the plaintiff's land, the appropriate action will not be trespass but something else[29] (although trespass would be committed were the defendant to throw the animal in question onto the plaintiff's land). The distinction is important because historically trespass involved strict liability, that is to say liability without the need to show any intent to commit trespass,[30] whereas other forms of liability for damage, or interference with land required proof of an intent or negligence or, where the doctrine of *Rylands v. Fletcher* is involved, some dangerous activity or use of his land on the part of the defendant, or, where nuisance is the cause of action, some unreasonable use of land by the defendant. In trespass the courts were not, and are still not concerned with the nature of the use the defendant is making of his land. If he or his property directly touches or comes upon the plaintiff's land, the tort will be committed, unless the act in question can be justified or excused on some ground recognised by law.

5.07 It will be a trespass to walk or stand on the highway otherwise than for the purpose of some lawful use.[31] Against whom the trespass is committed will depend upon the person in whom the highway, i.e. the topsoil, is vested.[32] If the highway is public, no trespass will be committed against an occupier of land that is adjacent or adjoined to the highway. If the highway is privately owned, although open to the public, a trespass will be committed against the owner of the highway if it is used otherwise than for the purpose of legitimate transportation on foot or by some vehicle (unless a situation of necessity arises when the defendant may be

26 *McDonald v. Associated Fuels* [1954] 3 D.L.R. 775.
27 *Southport Corporation v. Esso Petroleum Ltd* [1953] 3 W.L.R. 773, [1954] 2 Q.B. 414, [1956] A.C. 242, where different views were expressed by different members of the various courts which dealt with the case.
28 Below Chaps. 8, 9, 12
29 Below Chap. 11.
30 *The Case of Thorns* (1466) Y.B. 6 Ed. IV 7, pl. 18.
31 But see *Randall v. Tarrant* [1955] 1 W.L.R. 255, leaving car parked in a narrow lane while occupants trespassed nearby was not a trespass to the highway.
32 Viz., a local authority or adjoining landowner but subject to a public right of way: *Tithe Redemption Commissioners v. Runcorn U.D.C.* [1954] Ch. 383 at 497 *per* Denning L.J.

entitled to remain stationary or use the highway differently).[33] In *Harrison v. Duke of Rutland*,[34] for example, the plaintiff came onto the defendant's highway to try to prevent the defendant from enjoying the shooting of grouse. He was ejected and sued for trespass to the person. The defendant was entitled to eject the plaintiff as he had done because the plaintiff was himself a trespasser on the defendant's land. His reason for being on the highway was not legitimate: it was to interfere with the defendant's lawful use of his own property. Similarly in *Hickman v. Maisey*[35] the defendant was held to be a trespasser on the highway which ran across the plaintiff's land, and was dedicated to public use, because the defendant's purpose in coming on the land was not to go to and from his destination but was to loiter on the highway, even though he walked up and down, taking notes of the trials of the plaintiff's racehorses on the plaintiff's land.

(ii) Continuing trespass

5.08 Trespass is a continuing wrong. As long as the interference lasts a trespass will be committed.[36] In *Konskier v. Goodman*,[37] for example, the defendant pulled down the upper storeys of a house and allowed rubbish to fall onto an adjoining property belonging to the plaintiff. The defendant did not remove the rubbish, which eventually choked a gully in the basement thereby producing a flood during a heavy storm. The defendant's act was considered to be a continuing trespass, with the result that the plaintiff, who came into possession after the original act of trespass, could sue and recover in trespass. As long as the trespass continues the plaintiff may have an action from day to day.[38] In *Holmes v. Wilson*[39] the plaintiff accepted a payment into court which had been made in respect of the wrongful erection by the defendant on the plaintiff's land of buttresses to support the defendant's road. Notwithstanding this, the plaintiff could bring another action for trespass in respect of the continuation of the interference by the defendant's buttresses with the plaintiff's land. There is a distinction, however, between a continuing trespass and the continuing

33 Or some other reasonable and ordinarily incidental use: *Rodgers v. Ministry of Transport* [1952] 1 T.L.R. 625; *Liddle v. Yorkshire (North Riding) C.C.* [1934] 2 K.B. 101. Not, however, depasturing cattle: *Dovaston v. Payne* (1795) 2 H.Bl. 527; picketing unless protected by statute: *Hubbard v. Pitt* [1976] Q.B. 142; nor just sitting down in the middle of the road when there is no emergency; *The Carlgrath* [1927] P. 93 at 107–108 *per* Scrutton L.J. On the use of tidal waters and the foreshore, see *Fowley Marine (Emsworth) Ltd v. Gafford* [1967] 2 Q.B. 808, [1968] 2 Q.B. 618; *Beckett Ltd v. Lyons* [1967] Ch. 449; *Blundell v. Catterall* (1821) 5 B. & Ald. 268.

34 [1893] 1 Q.B. 142.

35 [1900] 1 Q.B. 752.

36 *Hudson v. Nicholson* (1839) 5 M. & W. 437; *Bowyer v. Cooke* (1847) 4 C.B. 236. But a trespasser who remains in possession long enough, *viz.* twelve years under the Limitation Act 1980 s. 15(1), will acquire an immunity from suit and title by adverse possession; this may even be achieved by combination of two shorter periods of adverse possession by different squatters: *Mount Carmel Investments Ltd v. Peter Thurlow Ltd* [1988] 3 All E.R. 129.

37 [1928] 1 K.B. 421.

38 *Winterbourne v. Morgan* (1809) 11 East 295. Damages will be assessed only up to the date of the action, unless they are awarded in lieu of an injunction, in which event they will be regarded as compensating the plaintiff for past and future loss: *Masters v. Brent L.B.C.* [1978] Q.B. 841.

39 (1839) 10 M. & W. 503.

consequences of a trespass. Thus an omission by the defendant to rectify a wrong done by the defendant's original trespass will not itself be a trespass. In *Clegg v. Dearden*,[40] the defendant excavated on the plaintiff's land, when he undertook to mine coal. This resulted in the creating of an aperture through which water came causing damage to the plaintiff's coal mine. The defendant was liable in trespass for the original trespass: but leaving the hole through which the water came was not a continuation of the trespass: therefore the defendant was not liable for the consequential damage caused by the water.

(iii) Trespass ab initio

5.09 The curious doctrine of trespass *ab initio*, which appears to have fallen into disfavour, if not disuse, in recent times,[41] operated to render an originally lawful "interference" by the defendant a trespass as a result of the subsequent conduct of the defendant. This occurred where a defendant was given a licence by law to enter land, which meant that he was not a trespasser, but later abused the licence, thereby becoming a trespasser. This doctrine, which made the subsequent trespass relate back to the time when the licensee came onto the premises and caused him to become a trespasser *ab initio*, i.e. from the moment when he first entered, despite the original permission to enter, did not apply where the licence to enter was granted by the occupier. Nor did it operate where the alleged wrongful act by the defendant was an omission rather than a positive abuse of the licence. Such was the effect of the decision in the *Six Carpenters' Case*[42] in 1610. The defendants entered the plaintiff's tavern, to eat and drink, and then refused to pay for wine and bread. They were not trespassers *ab initio*, even though their original licence to enter was postulated on the basis that they were legitimate guests in the inn, and therefore entitled by law to come on to the plaintiff's premises, as long as they were intending to use them lawfully. By way of contrast, in *Oxley v. Watts*[43] the defendant took the plaintiff's horse as an estray, but afterwards worked it. This was a trespass *ab initio*, because the original lawful possession of the horse was abused. Similarly a landlord who took goods that were not subject to distraint in the course of a lawful distraint was a trespasser *ab initio*, but only as regards the goods improperly taken, not those which had been distrained lawfully.[44] The decline of the doctrine can be said to have been noted first in *Elias v. Pasmore*[45] in 1934. Police officers had a warrant for the arrest of the plaintiff. In pursuance of that warrant they entered the

40 (1848) 12 Q.B. 576.

41 See, however, *Cinnamond v. British Airports Authority* [1980] 1 W.L.R. 582 at 588, where Lord Denning M.R. applied the doctrine, though he had earlier regarded it unfavourably in *Chic Fashions (West Wales) Ltd v. Jones* [1968] 2 Q.B. 299, *infra*.

42 (1610) 8 Coke Rep. 146a.

43 (1785) 1 T.R. 12.

44 *Harvey v. Pocock* (1843) 11 M. & W. 740: cp. *Canadian Pacific Wine Co. v. Tuley* [1921] 2 A.C. 417. On the situation with respect to distress for rent see Distress for Rent Act 1737 s. 19.

45 [1934] 2 K.B. 164, although the decision might be justified on the ground that there was an independent reason for entry unaffected by the abuse, *viz.*, the right to enter premises to arrest the plaintiff.

plaintiff's premises and took certain documents. Some of these were not evidence against the plaintiff at his trial. In other words it was not necessary and therefore lawful for the police to take them. Horridge J. held that the police officers committed trespass to goods when they took the wrong documents. But they were not trespassers to the plaintiff's land under the doctrine of trespass *ab initio*. More recently in *Chic Fashions (West Wales) Ltd v. Jones*,[46] Lord Denning M.R. pointed out that the doctrine was a by-product of the old forms of action[47] and should be interred along with them. Hence it may be argued that it no longer matters whether the defendant entered under a licence from the plaintiff or under permission granted by the law; nor whether the wrongful conduct of the defendant was an omission or a positive act; nor whether the original entry was justified on some independent ground unrelated to the subsequent abuse. In any of these instances the defendant will only become a trespasser when he acts improperly and will only be a trespasser vis-a-vis the particular wrongful act he is alleged to have committed.[48]

(iv) The mental element

5.10 As far back as 1623 the Statute of Limitations[49] provided that there would be no liability for trespass to land that was negligent or involuntary, if the defendant disclaimed any title to the land. However in *Basely v. Clarkson*[50] the statute could not be pleaded as a defence where the defendant unintentionally mowed the plaintiff's grass. This was because the fact, i.e., the deed, was voluntary and the defendant's intention and knowledge were not traversable: they could not be known. If this decision had been followed to the letter it is possible that the statute of 1623 might have had no effect, and strict liability for trespass to land might have been the rule. Almost a century later, in *Beckwith v. Shordike & Hatch*,[51] Aston J. drew a distinction between voluntary and involuntary trespasses, a distinction that may have been ignored by De Grey C.J. in *Scott v. Shepherd*[52] when he said: "Actions of trespass will lie for legal acts when they become trespasses by accident." At this time, of course, the law still seemed to be that trespass to the person was actionable unless the defendant clearly proved that he was not at fault in any way: so that it might be possible to construe or interpret the language of De Grey C.J. as meaning that an

46 [1968] 2 Q.B. 299: *Wiltshire v. Barrett* [1966] 1 Q.B. 312 at 323 *per* Lord Denning. Contrast his remarks in *Cinnamond v. British Airports Authority*, *supra*, where taxi-drivers were barred from an airport because of their practice of picking up passengers and charging them extortionate fares: the ban was upheld, on the ground that the taxi-drivers became trespassers *ab initio*, since they had abused their right to enter the airport grounds. This seems to be inconsistent with the approach of Lord Denning to the situation in the *Chic Fashions* case, which is remarkable in view of the origins of the doctrine which lie in the desire and need to protect people from abuse of authority (an idea that is very dear to Lord Denning as a common lawyer).

47 I.e. to allow an action in trespass rather than in trespass on the case.

48 Unless the doctrine can be invoked to serve some other useful purpose, as in the *Cinnamond* case, *supra*.

49 S. 5: as long as the defendant offered sufficient amends.

50 (1681) 3 Lev. 37.

51 (1767) 4 Burr. 2093 at 2094.

52 (1773) 2 W.Bl. 892 at 899.

"accidental trespass" would nonetheless be actionable unless the accident had not been caused by negligence.

5.11 It will be seen that, eventually, trespass to the person became dependent on proof of intention or negligence with respect to the act that was alleged to be the trespass.[53] Cases on trespass to the highway in the latter part of the nineteenth and early part of the twentieth centuries[54] indicated that the intent of the defendant could be material in deciding whether or not such a trespass had been committed, although negligence was never in issue. Until 1951 it was still an open question whether it was necessary to establish negligence (or an intention to trespass) to found liability for trespass to land.[55] In that year, however, in *National Coal Board v. Evans*,[56] the Court of Appeal seem to have determined that some kind of fault had to be shown for such liability. The defendants struck the plaintiff's cable while the defendants were excavating land. This was involuntary and purely accidental, not negligent, because the defendants did not know, and had no reason to know, of the presence of the cable. In the absence of any fault there was no liability.[56a]

5.12 Support for this approach is to be found in the decision in *League Against Cruel Sports v. Scott*.[57] The issue was whether the joint masters of a local hunt were liable for trespasses alleged to have been committed when the hunt's hounds entered the plaintiff organisation's land. The defendants argued that a master of hounds was not liable for trespass by the hunt's hounds unless he intended that the hounds should trespass. The plaintiff organisation argued that neither intention nor any other kind of fault was an element in the tort of trespass to land; that only necessity or inevitable accident were defences, at least in the circumstances of this case; and that the only question relating to liability was whether the intrusion by the hounds was voluntary or involuntary. After considering several earlier decisions on liability for trespassing during fox-hunting[58] and damage done by dogs,[59] Park J. concluded by saying that "before a master of hounds may be held liable for trespass on land by hounds, it has to be shown that he either intended that the hounds should enter the land or by

53 Below pp. 116–117.
54 *Harrison v. Duke of Rutland* [1893] 1 Q.B. 142; *Hickman v. Maisey* [1900] 1 Q.B. 752: above p. 85.
55 Cp. *Read v. J. Lyons & Co. Ltd* [1949] A.C. 156 at 166 *per* Viscount Simon, to the effect that trespass is a wrong without question of negligence. But ignorance of the fact of trespassing is not a defence, as long as there was an intent to enter upon the plaintiff's land: *Conway v. George Wimpey & Co. Ltd* [1951] 2 K.B. 266 at 273–274.
56 [1951] 2 K.B. 861: strictly speaking this was an action for trespass to goods, but the language of the court seems to be applicable to trespass to land.
56a But there is no need to prove intention or negligence to establish liability under the Civil Aviation Act 1949 s. 40(2), which creates liability for loss or damage caused to any person or property by or by a person in or an article of person falling from an aircraft while in flight, taking off or landing: see also below p. 97.
57 [1985] 2 All E.R. 489.
58 *Paul v. Summerhayes* (1878) 4 Q.B.D. 9; *Calvert v. Gosling* (1887) 5 T.L.R. 185; *Baker v. Berkely* (1827) 3 C. & P. 32.
59 *Read v. Edwards* (1864) 17 C.B.N.S. 252; *Beckwith v. Shordike v. Hatch*, para 5.10 *supra*; *R. v. Pratt* (1855) 4 E. &. B. 860.

negligence failed to prevent them from doing so."[60] He expressed the law in these words:[61]

> "Where a master of staghounds takes out a pack of hounds and deliberately sets them in pursuit of a stag or hind, knowing that there is a real risk that in the pursuit hounds may enter or cross prohibited land, the master will be liable for trespass if he intended to cause hounds to enter such land or if by his failure to exercise proper control over them he caused them to enter such land."

The learned judge's analysis of the facts and the evidence led him to the conclusion, in this instance, that the masters' persistence in hunting in the vicinity of the plaintiff organisation's land, where hunting was prohibited, knowing that it was virtually impossible to prevent the hounds from entering the land, whatever precautions might be taken, and their indifference to the risk of trespass, could be construed as an intention that the hounds should trespass.[62] The masters were also vicariously liable for the acts and omissions of those hunt servants, agents and mounted followers over whose conduct they could exercise control.[63] The facts also indicated that the masters, or their servants and agents as well as followers of the hunt, were guilty of negligence. Damages, of small amounts, were awarded in respect of certain trespasses; and an injunction was also granted to restrain the masters of the hunt and servants, agents or mounted followers of the hunt, from entering or crossing the plaintiff's property.

(c) Possession

(i) The basis of the action

5.13 Possession is the hall-mark of trespass to land.[64] It is unnecessary for the plaintiff to establish that he was the owner of the land against which the trespass was committed.[65] But an owner out of possession who evinces the intention of regaining or obtaining possession may sue in trespass in respect of some wrongdoing by the defendant.[66] Even the slightest act which reveals such intention suffices on the part of the person who has title.[67] An owner who is out of possession, and is not at the time reclaiming

60 [1985] 2 All E.R. 489 at 494.
61 *Ibid.* at 494–495.
62 *Ibid.* at 495.
63 *Ibid.*
64 *Thompson v. Ward* [1953] 2 Q.B. 153 at 158–159. Unless two people both claim *de facto* possession, when legal possession, i.e. the right to sue for trespass will be in the party who can show a better right to possess, i.e. title: *Jones v. Chapman* (1849) 2 Ex. 803 at 821 *per* Maule J.
65 But exceptionally the plaintiff may be defeated by a plea of *jus tertii*, i.e. that someone else has ownership or the right to possess, and that the defendant acted under that person's authority and on his behalf: *Graham v. Peat* (1801) 1 East 244; *Chambers v. Donaldson* (1809) 11 East 65; *Nicholls v. Ely Beet Sugar Factory Ltd* [1931] 2 Ch. 84. The defendant may also succeed if he is the rightful owner: *Delaney v. T. P. Smith Ltd* [1946] K.B. 393 at 397: see below p. 101. As to the case where the plaintiff occupies Crown land with the Crown's consent, see *Harper v. Charlesworth* (1825) 4 B. & C. 574.
66 *Ocean Estates Ltd v. Pinder* [1969] 2 A.C. 19.
67 Or his predecessors: *Portland Management Ltd v. Harte* [1977] Q.B. 306; *Fowley Marine (Emsworth) Ltd v. Gafford* [1968] 2 Q.B. 618.

possession, cannot sue in trespass, although he may have other remedies in respect of injuries alleged to have been suffered by him as a result of another's trespass to the land.[68] Thus where land is leased to a tenant, the appropriate plaintiff is the tenant, not the landlord.[69]

5.14 There are two kinds of possession: possession in fact (*de facto* possession) and possession in law (posession *de jure*). Normally the former will also include and involve the latter. However it may be possible for someone to have possession in fact without having possession in law. Both forms of possession must be distinguished from the right to possess. This is the right to keep the possession one has or the right to obtain possession, and is an element of ownership, but is not a necessary ingredient of the right to sue for trespass.[70]

5.15 Possession in fact refers to custody, detention or occupation of the land in issue. It involves the power to use the land and the *animus possidendi*, the intention of excluding others.[71] One who possesses in fact may sue for trespass (unless the defendant can show a better right to possess based, for example, on ownership).[72] Possession in fact depends upon having actual or notional control over land. Thus one who is a squatter may possess in fact, even when he is physically absent from the land.[73] Possession in law involves the manifest intention to exclude everyone and claim the land as one's own. Thus a landlord who leases land to a tenant has surrendered possession in law to the tenant;[74] but a landlord who only licenses a lodger to use a room, or an owner who lets a room to a guest, has not divested himself of possession in law,[75] any more than a master who puts his servant in physical possession of premises makes his servant the possessor in law or those premises.[76] The importance of this lies

68 *Wallis v. Hands* [1893] 2 Ch. 75: see below p. 92.

69 *Attersoll v. Stevens* (1808) 1 Taunt. 183 at 190; unless there is damage to the landlord's reversionary interest: below p. 92.

70 See however below in respect of trespass by relation.

71 And the concomitant lack of *animus possidendi* and power to control on the part of others.

72 See *supra* note 65. Or a right to recover possession: *Wuta-Ofei v. Danquah* [1961] 1 W.L.R. 1238.

73 And so may sue for trespass, unless the "trespasser" is the owner or someone with a better right to possess. The reason usually given for the protection of "unlawful" possessors is the prevention of breaches of the peace. Appropriate action may be taken to evict a squatter, even one who comes later than an original possession order: *Wiltshire C.C. v. Frazer* [1986] 1 All E.R. 65 (under R.S.C. Order 113; or C.C.R. Order 24). See also, on identification of squatters, *Warwick University v. De Graaf* [1975] 1 W.L.R. 1126.

74 Hence the tenant can sue a stranger in trespass, and the landlord, unless the landlord was entering under the terms of the lease: *Lane v. Dixon* (1847) 3 C.B. 776.

75 *Allan v. Liverpool Overseers* (1874) L.R. 9 Q.B. 180 at 191–192 *per* Blackburn J. The use of land without exclusive possession is not sufficient to support an action for trespass: *Hill v. Tupper* (1863) 2 H. & C. 121. As to one who has a seat in a train, or a theatre, etc., see *Lane v. Dixon*, *supra* at 784. What if a lodger is given exclusive occupation of a room? And why should the occupant of a seat on a train, or in a threatre, not claim sufficient possession to sue in trespass, or oust one who seeks to dispossess him? Cp. *Hurst v. Picture Theatres Ltd* [1915] 1 K.B. 1; below p. 104. See also *Hounslow London Borough v. Twickenham Garden Developments* [1971] Ch. 233.

76 *Lotan v. Cross* (1810) 2 Camp. 464. Unless, perhaps, there is the intention to put the servant exclusively in control, e.g., a manager living on the employer's property as part of his duties of employment.

in the possibility that one who has possession in law, although not possession in fact, may be able to sue for trespass to the land.[77] In short, therefore, the law of torts protects one who possesses in fact,[77a] except where the defendant has a better right to possession; and will protect one who possesses in law, through an intermediary in actual physical possession, without possessing in fact.

(ii) Claims not based on possession: (1) *Trespass by relation*

5.16 Where the plaintiff had the right to possession at the time of the trespass and took possession afterwards, he is considered to have had possession from the moment that he first had or acquired the right to possess.[78] Therefore he will be able to sue the defendant for the trespass which was committed while the plaintiff lacked possession in fact or in law. This doctrine of relation back is "created by law for the purpose of preventing wrong from being dispunishable."[79] If no such doctrine were recognised by the law, the party in possession at the time of the trespass would probably not sue, since he would have no further interest in pursuing an action: and the party who did have an interest in bringing an action would lack the basis for a suit. In *Barnett v. Earl of Guildford*,[80] for example, the heir at law of a copyholder sued the lord of the manor in respect of the latter's wrongful occupation of the land before the heir at law's entry into possession. The action could be maintained on the basis of this doctrine. Similarly, a mortgagee who entered and took possession of the mortgaged property was able to sue a trespasser for a trespass committed prior to such entry in *Ocean Accident & Guarantee Corporation v. Ilford Gas Co.*[81] So a landlord who is entitled to recover possession of leased premises, but has not yet obtained such possession, may be enabled to sue a trespasser who commits the tort between the time the tenant left and the time the landlord took possession.[82] Conversely a tenant who is not yet in possession may be able to sue in respect of a trespass occurring before he took possession of the demised premises. The doctrine of relation back, which provides for a "constructive possession" of land for the purposes of an action,[83] is also relevant in connection with the action for mesne profits that may be brought as a result of a trespass.[84]

77 Hence the importance of intention: *Williams Bros. Direct Supply Ltd v. Raftery* [1958] 1 Q.B. 159: *Treloar v. Nute* [1977] All E.R. 230, which distinguished the *Williams Bros.* case; *Leigh v. Jack* (1879) 5 Ex.D. 264; and *Wallis's Cayton Bay Holiday Camp Ltd v. Shell-Mex & BP Ltd* [1975] Q.B. 94 (all of which were concerned with adverse possession and the acquisition of rights by squatters of one kind or another).

77a However a joint tenant or tenant in common of land cannot sue his co-tenant in trespass, or ejectment, unless the act of the defendant amounts to ouster of the plaintiff (or destructive waste of the property): *Murray v. Hall* (1849) 7 C.B. 441.

78 *Dunlop v. Macedo* (1891) 8 T.L.R. 43.

79 *Barnett v. Earl of Guildford* (1855) 11 Ex. 19 at 33 *per* Parke B.

80 *Supra.*

81 [1905] 2 K.B. 493.

82 Or even a tenant who wrongfully remains in possession after termination of the lease, but only if the landlord has done something to determine the lease after a breach of convenant by the tenant: *Elliott v. Boynton* [1924] 1 Ch. 236.

83 *Alicia Hosiery Co. Ltd v. Brown Shipley & Co. Ltd* [1970] 1 Q.B. 195 at 207 *per* Donaldson J.

84 Below p. 109.

(iii) Claims not based on possession: (2) *injuries to reversionary interests*

5.17 Ordinarily an owner out of possession cannot sue for trespass. Exceptionally he is allowed to do so if the trespass permanently injures the land in respect of which he holds a reversionary interest. This is because such a trespass will damage his reversion.[85] Hence no action was available in *Cooper v. Crabtree*.[86] The plaintiff's cottage was occupied by a weekly tenant. The defendant erected poles and a hoarding on the plaintiff's land. This did not cause substantial injury to the land and was not a permanent trespass; therefore the plaintiff could not sue. A permanent injury must be differentiated from a continuing injury. The former involves some damage which constitutes a completed wrong, for example, digging a hole in the land, the consequences of which will last until the reversioner takes possession.[87] A continuing injury is one which is in the process of being committed. This is of especial importance in relation to nuisance, which is also a tort that can be committed against a plaintiff with a reversionary interest in land, although currently out of possession.[88] It should be noted that if injury to a reversionary interest is caused by a tenant of the owner of the land, the appropriate remedy will probably be an action for waste, the law pertaining to which is part of the law of property rather than the law of torts. If such an injury is caused by a stranger, then trespass will be apposite.

(iv) Claims not based on possession: (3) *the right to possess: ejectment*

5.18 A plaintiff out of possession, but claiming an immediate right to possession, may also sue in trespass the person, who, in his view, wrongfully possesses the land in question. Indeed, historically, ejectment, a form of the action of trespass, was devised and utilised to enable disputes about title to land to be litigated without the need to have recourse to antiquated "real" actions, which involved undesirable methods of decision, such as trial by battle.[89] It involved various legal fictions which served to make it available to try title to freehold, although it was invented to protect leaseholders. Modern law has replaced these archaic forms by a simple action for recovery of land; and now also includes a summary procedure to obtain an order for possession and a writ for its enforcement against persons in occupation of the plaintiff's land who entered or remain there without his leave and consent, whether or not those persons are identifiable.[90]

85 *Baxter v. Taylor* (1832) 4 B. & Ad. 72.
86 (1882) 20 Ch.D. 589.
87 *Shelfer v. City of London Electric Lighting Co.* [1895] 1 Ch. 287 at 318.
88 Below pp. 193–194.
89 Holdsworth, *History of English Law*, vol. iii 214–217, vol. vii 4–23. Title to "foreign" land cannot be litigated through the medium of an action for trespass: *British South Africa Co. v. Companhía de Moçambique* [1893] A.C. 602; *Hesperides Hotels v. Muftizade* [1978] 2 All E.R. 1168.
90 R.S.C. Ord. 113; C.C.R. Ord. 24; *Southwark London B.C. v. Williams* [1971] Ch. 734; *Wiltshire C.C. v. Frazer* [1986] 1 All E.R. 65; *Warwick University v De Graaf* [1975] 1 W.L.R. 1126.

5.19 The present-day action, like its predecessor, may be maintained by a plaintiff who claims title to the land. Therefore, today, as was the case with the old action of ejectment, the plaintiff "must recover upon the strength of his own title and not by the weakness of the defendant's."[91] The way this was interpreted in relation to the older law and the modern law, it would seem that as long as the defendant shows possession in fact of the land that is in issue, he may be presumed to have title to the land, and it will be upon the plaintiff to prove a better title.[92] In this respect it may be possible for the defendant in such an action[93] to raise a plea of *jus tertii*.[94] By this the defendant pleads that title to the land is vested in some other person, neither plaintiff nor defendant.[95] There has been considerable debate on the question whether *jus tertii* is and should be a valid defence to an action of ejectment.[96] However, it would seem, despite *dicta* against the plea,[97] that the availability of such a plea is consistent with the view that the plaintiff can only succeed if he shows that as between himself and the defendant, he, the plaintiff, has a better right to the land. If the defendant can show that title is vested in some third party, that would appear to suffice to destroy any claim the plaintiff might otherwise have had as between the two parties to the litigation.

(d) Land

(i) Below the surface

5.20 In its origins trespass to land was concerned with invasions of the plaintiff's land which occurred on the surface. Developments since then have raised questions with respect to the extent of the plaintiff's possession for the purposes of trespass. The maxim *cuius est solum, eius est ad coelum et ad inferos*, coined in the thirteenth century,[98] has long been part of English law.[99] The idea enshrined in the maxim that whoever owns the soil owns all above and below it from heaven to perdition, has recently been stated

91 *Martin v. Tregonwell & Strachan* (1742) 5 T.R. 107n *per* Lee C.J.: *Roe d. Haldane v. Harvey* (1769) 4 Burr. 2484 at 2487 *per* Mansfield C.J.: *Danford v. McAnulty* (1883) 8 App. Cas. 456 at 460 *per* Lord O'Hagan, 462 *per* Lord Blackburn; *Emmerson v. Maddison* [1906] A.C. 569.

92 *Asher v. Whitlock* (1865) L.R. 1 Q.B. 1; *Perry v. Clissold* [1907] A.C. 73.

93 Not normally available in other actions of trespass: above note 65.

94 *Doe d. Carter v. Barnard* (1849) 13 Q.B. 954: *Asher v. Whitlock, supra.*

95 The plea is not available, however: (1) where the defendant acquired possession from the plaintiff or his predecessor in title: *Dalton v. Fitzgerald* [1897] 2 Ch. 86; *Doe d. Johnson v. Baytup* (1835) 3 Ad. & E. 188 (unless the plaintiff's title has expired or been lost: *Claridge v. Mackenzie* (1842) 4 Man. & Gr. 142, a form of estoppel); (2) where the defendant is a trespasser vis-a-vis the plaintiff, e.g. a squatter: *Davison v. Gent* (1857) 1 H. & N. 744; cp. *Fowley Marine (Emsworth) Ltd v. Gafford* [1968] 2 Q.B. 618.

96 Wiren, "The plea of *Jus Tertii* in Ejectment" (1925) 41 L.Q.R. 139; Hargreaves, "Terminology and Title in Ejectment" (1940) 56 L.G.R. 376; Holdsworth, "Terminology and Title in Ejectment—A Reply" (1940) 56 L.Q.R. 479. Holdsworth's view that *jus tertii* was a good defence was rejected by the High Court of Australia in *Allen v. Roughley* (1955) 94 C.L.R. 95; and see *Ocean Estates Ltd v. Pinder* [1969] 2 A.C. 19 at 25 *per* Lord Diplock.

97 *Asher v. Whitlock, supra* at 6; *Perry v. Clissold, supra* at 79–80.

98 By Accursius of Bologna, according to Griffiths J. in *Lord Bernstein of Leigh v. Skyviews & General Ltd* [1977] 2 All E.R. 902 at 905.

99 Blackstone's Commentaries on the Laws of England, II, 18; III, 217: Co.Litt. 4a.

by a Canadian judge to refer to ownership, not possession.[100] However, it has been used in cases of trespass to justify a plaintiff's action in trespass for invasions of the sub-soil and the airspace above the land he possesses. Although it has been termed "a fanciful phrase",[101] and its validity questioned,[102] there can be little doubt that it has been utilised.[103].

5.21 In one instance this was to allow a possessor of land to maintain an action in trespass in respect of things found under the ground, such as a prehistoric boat.[104] In another it was invoked to permit a plaintiff to sue in trespass defendants who were digging holes in his land.[105] Any entry below the surface, if wrongful, would be a trespass. However if the plaintiff has granted rights to the sub-soil he will not be able to sue in trespass anyone who intrudes therein. This will be the situation where the owner of the land has given mining rights to someone else. Should a stranger drill below the surface and enter the area over which the mining rights have been given, the trespass thus committed will be against the party who is the donee of the mining rights, not the owner of the land above the mines.[106] So, too, trespass to the highway is committed against the person in whom the highway is vested, who may be different from the one who owns, and therefore possesses, the sub-soil beneath the surface, i.e. below the highway.[107]

(ii) Above the ground

5.22 In respect of alleged trespasses to airspace, more serious problems have arisen: for the logic of the maxim suggests that any intrusion over the plaintiff's land, for whatever length of time and at whatever height, will be a trespass if it is direct, without the need to show any damage. Yet common sense, and sound reason, suggest to the contrary that it would be outrageous to permit the plaintiff to stop others from using the air above his land as long as such use did not cause or threaten any damage or loss to the plaintiff. The common law appears to have adopted the conclusion of common sense, to which legislation has added both certainty and definition where the intrusion is through the use of aircraft. It is convenient, therefore, to distinguish between intrusion by things other than aircraft and intrusion by aircraft.

100 Cavanagh J. in *Didow v. Alberta Power Ltd* (1986) 37 C.C.L.T. 90 (*reversed* [1988] 5 W.W.R. 606).

101 In *Wandsworth Board of Works v. United Telephone Co.* (1884) 13 Q.B.D. 904 at 915 *per* Brett M.R.

102 *Commissioner for Railways v. Valuer-General* [1974] A.C. 328 at 351, 352 *per* Lord Wilberforce: *Sovmots Investments v. Secretary of State for the Environment* [1976] 3 All E.R. 720 at 728 *per* Browne L.J.; cp *Lord Bernstein of Leigh v. Skyviews & General Ltd*, *supra*, at 907.

103 *Saunders v. Smith* (1838) 2 Jur. 491; *Corbet v. Hill* (1870) L.R.9 Eq. 76.

104 *Elwes v. Brigg Gas Co.* (1886) 33 Ch.D. 563: below p. 145.

105 *Cox v. Glue* (1848) 5 C.B. 533, where the plaintiff had given rights over his close to a third person to pasture his cattle: hence the defendant committed no trespass against the plaintiff in riding over his land, since the plaintiff was not in possession of the surface. See also *Glegg v. Dearden* (1848) 12 C.B. 576; *Wilcox v. Kettel* [1937] 1 All E.R. 222.

106 Cp. *Bulli Coal Mining Co. v. Osborne* [1899] A.C. 351; *Phillips v. Homfray* (1871) L.R. 6 Ch. App. 770.

107 Above p. 84.

5.23 That an owner has certain rights in the air space above his land is well established by authority.[108] A surface owner would seem to be entitled to the ownership of the air space within the limits of the area of ordinary user surrounding and attendant upon the surface and any erections on it. This applies to conduct by a defendant that amounts to a nuisance as well as to acts which could be construed as being trespasses, i.e. invasions or intrusions. It has been suggested to be a sound and practical rule to regard any intrusion into the air space at a height which may interfere with the ordinary user of land as a trespass (rather than a nuisance). Adjoining owners then know where they stand; they have no right to erect structrues overhanging or passing over their neighbours' land and there is no room for argument whether they are causing damage or annoyance.[109] Thus in *Pickering v. Rudd*[110] a defendant who allowed his plank to overhang the plaintiff's garden was not guilty of trespass. Lord Ellenborough did not think it was a trespass "to interfere with the column of air superincumbent on the close." Had damage resulted, however, an action on the case, for negligence or nuisance, would have been an appropriate remedy. Similarly, to permit a cornice to overhang the plaintiff's land and drip rainwater onto it was not a trespass, although it could be a nuisance.[111]

5.24 In these cases the courts were somewhat critical of the application of the maxim. So, if a defendant shot a bullet over the plaintiff's land it was queried whether this would be a trespass (assuming no property was damaged and no person was injured).[112] The addition of injury might make a difference, as in *Ellis v. Loftus Iron Co.*,[113] where a horse which leaned over the plaintiff's land bit the plaintiff's horse. The defendant, who owned the offending horse, was liable to trespass. But this might be explained on various grounds: (i) the invasion was only just above the surface of the land; (ii) the plaintiff's horse was harmed; (iii) the situation involved a form of cattle trespass.[114] Similarily, the construction of telephone wires over a street was not a trespass in *Wandsworth Board of Works v. United Telephone Co.*[115] because the existence of the wires did not create any danger to the plaintiffs who lived on the street in question. In that case, however, the defendants were a statutory company with ownership of the street, but not the land underneath the street.

5.25 A defendant who erected on his own land a sign which protruded over the plaintiff's land could be guilty of trespass because of the projec-

108 *Lord Bernstein of Leigh v. Skyviews & General Ltd, supra* at 905 *per* Griffiths J.; e.g. to lop branches of overhanging trees: *Lemon v. Webb* [1894] 3 Ch. 1; [1895] A.C. 1 (nuisance rather than trespass); or to cut a wire placed over his land: *Wandsworth Board of Works v. United Telephone Co., supra* at 927 *per* Fry L.J.

109 *Lord Bernstein of Leigh v. Skyviews & General Ltd., supra* at 906.

110 (1815) 4 Camp. 219

111 *Fay v. Prentice* (1845) 1 C.B. 828.

112 *Kenyon v. Hart* (1865) 6 B. &. S. 249. But there was liability for firing bullets over the plaintiff's land in *Clifton v. Viscount Bury* (1887) 4 T.L.R. 8. Was this really trespass? Or was it nusiance? See also a Canadian case, *Big Point Club v. Logan* [1943] 4 D.L.R. 136 and an Australian one, *Davies v. Bennion* (1927) 22 Tas. L.R. 52.

113 (1874) L.R. 10 C.P. 10; *Bridges v. Forest Protection Ltd* (1976) 72 D.L.R. (3d) 335 (aerial spraying).

114 Below pp. 255, 265.

115 *Supra.*

tion, regardless of damage.[116] It has been suggested that such cases are based on ownership of the air space not possession.[117] However it seems difficult to divorce the issue of ownership from that of possession (unless in any given instance the plaintiff had no rights of ownership in land, merely possession, for example as a squatter, and was seeking to complain of an intrusion into the air space above the land on which the plaintiff is squatting). Similarly in a case concerning the use of a large construction crane the jib of which overhung the plaintiff's premises 50 feet above roof level, the plaintiff's rights to exclude the defendants were recognised.[118] The plaintiff was in no fear; nor was there any inconvenience as a result of the intrusion. Nonetheless, he was *prima facie* in the right. However Stamp J. postponed the operation of an injunction, which had been sought by the plaintiff, until a date by which time the defendants would have finished with the crane. In that case, however, the defendants had offered compensation which had been rejected by the plaintiff; the intrusion was inadvertent, not wilful; and it was impermanent. So, although in a sense a technical trespass had been committed, the plaintiff was effectively denied any remedy. The tenor of this and other cases in modern times, whatever may have been the attitude in the nineteenth century, is that the idea contained in the maxim is far too wide in its scope. It is a sweeping, unscientific and impractical doctrine, and as such is unappealing to the common law mind.[119] What should be noted, however, is that where damage is caused or threatened, as a consequence of some intrusion, especially where it is not a temporary intrusion, there is a much greater willingness to grant the plaintiff a remedy based on nuisance.[120]

5.26 Where the intrusion is not at so low a level as was the case in these decisions, the attitute of the courts seems to have been, and to be still, much more downright and decisive. Once the intrusion occurs at a height which is far beyond the control of the plaintiff, and is not likely to disturb his enjoyment or use of the air space above the surface, the intrusion becomes less and less of a trespass. In 1815 Lord Ellenborough was not prepared to say that firing across a field *in vacuo*, no part of the contents touching the field, was a trespass. Nor, from his remarks, would an action lie against an aeronaut on the part of the occupier of every field over which the aeronaut's balloon passed in the course of a voyage.[121] Subsequent decisions have endorsed this view.[122] At common law it will not be

116 *Gifford v. Dent* [1926] W.N. 336; *Kelsen v. Imperial Tobacco Co. Ltd* [1957] 2 Q.B. 334.
117 *Didow v. Alberta Power Ltd, supra* at 97 *per* Cavanagh J. But his decision was reversed on appeal: [1985] 5 W.W.R. 606.
118 *Woolerton & Wilson Ltd v. Richard Costain Ltd* [1970] 1 All E.R. 483; cp. the Canadian case of *Lewvest Ltd v. Scotia Towers Ltd* (1981) 126 D.L.R. (3d) 239, where the injunction was granted without any postponement (in an attempt to force the parties to negotiate). See also *Anchor Brewhouse Developments v. Berkley House (Docklands) Developments* (1987) 38 Build.L.R. 82: trespass by the boom of a crane.
119 *Commissioner for Railways v. Valuer-General* [1974] A.C. 328 at 352 *per* Lord Wilberforce.
120 Below pp. 211–212.
121 *Pickering v. Rudd* (1815) 4 Camp. 219 at 221.
122 *Lacroix v. R.* [1954] 4 D.L.R. 470; *Atlantic Aviation v. Nova Scotia Light & Power Co.* (1965) D.L.R. (2d) 554. Note however the situation with respect to nuisance: below pp. 178–186.

a trespass for an aeroplane, or some other flying machine, to pass over another's land, as long as this passage is at a reasonable height above the land in question, and is a lawful flight. Above the reasonable height needed by the occupier of land for his use and enjoyment of it, such occupier has no greater rights in the air space than any other member of the public.[123] This does not necessarily mean that the occupier of the land has no ownership, such air space being *res omnium communis*, i.e., the property of everyone, the exclusive property of none.[124] But it does mean that, merely because a person is in occupation of land, such a person is not entitled to sue in respect of intrusions above a certain height. This was clarified by Griffiths J. in *Lord Bernstein of Leigh v. Skyviews & General Ltd.*[125] The defendant company, which was in the business of taking aerial photographs of properties and then offering them for sale to the owners, took a single photograph of the plaintiff's house from a height of several hundred feet. The plaintiff sued in respect of this entry into the air space above his land, claiming that this was a trespass (an invasion of his privacy).[126] The learned judge held that the plaintiff had no cause of action in trespass at common law. Because of the height at which the defendant company's aircraft entered the air space, there was no infringement of the plaintiff's rights. The action of the defendant company did not interfere with the plaintiff's actual or potential use of his land, or the air space above it. The taking of a photograph was not of itself wrongful, and not therefore actionable. For an action to lie there would have to be some other conduct on the part of a defendant amounting to a tort such as trespass or nuisance.

5.27 Griffiths J. also considered the provisions of the Civil Aviation Act 1949 s. 40(1), which has clarified the law so far as flights of aircraft are concerned. This precludes an action of trespass, or nuisance, where an aircraft flies over land at a height which, having regard to wind, weather, and all the circumstances in the case, is reasonable: or where what has happened occurred as an ordinary incident of such a flight.[127] However there is strict liability, without proof of negligence, intention, or other cause of action, if material loss or damage is caused to any person or property by a person in, or by an article or person falling from, an aircraft while in flight, taking off, or landing.[128] Griffiths J. relied on this provision in support of his construction of sub-section (1), which could not be restricted to providing protection to aircraft passing over land analagous to the limited right of a member of the public to pass over the surface of a highway.

123 *Lord Bernstein of Leigh v. Skyviews & General Ltd*, *supra* at 970.

124 The view of Fournier J. in the Canadian case of *Lacroix v. R.*, *supra* at 476: cp. Cavanagh J. in *Didow v. Alberta Power Ltd*, *supra* at 97–98. See, however, [1988] 5 W.W.R. 606.

125 *Supra.*

126 Below pp. 521–522.

127 Compliance is required with the provisions of Part II of the Act and Orders in Council made thereunder (see S.I. 1970, No. 289, applying the Act to civil aircraft belonging to or exclusively employed by the Crown).

128 Civil Aviation Act 1949, s. 40(2); *Blankley v. Godley* [1952] 1 All E.R. 436n; *Steel-Maitland v. British Airways Board* 1981 S.L.T. 110, applying the provision to damage caused *cumulatively* by a number of different aircraft.

2. DEFENCES

(a) Inevitable accident or mistake

5.28 Trespass to land, in the same way as all forms of trespass, involved strict liability. It was no defence for the defendant to plead that he committed the trespass accidentally or in error. This medieval approach to liability is out of place in the modern law of torts. As noted previously, it is probable that for a plaintiff to succeed in an action for trespass to land today he must establish that the defendant acted intentionally or negligently.[128a] Following the precedent set in cases of trespass to the person, this would mean that the onus is on the plaintiff to prove the requisite type of conduct by the defendant.[129] Hence the defendant may be able to rely on the plea of "inevitable accident". In consequence he will not be liable if what occurred was not foreseeable by the reasonable man, and could not have been prevented by taking reasonable precautions. For example, the facts might reveal that the defendant was thrown onto the plaintiff's land by an explosion for which he was not responsible, and in respect of which he had no forewarning and could have done nothing to prevent what happened. The same would be the case if a bolt of lightning struck the defendant's house causing a piece to fall onto the house of the plaintiff, with resultant damage.

5.29 It would seem that ordinarily a defendant cannot rely on error as a defence to trespass. Thus if the defendant believed that land belonged to, or was possessed by him, when in fact it was the plaintiff's, it is not open to him to plead that he had not trespassed on the plaintiff's land.[130] On the other hand, a mistake which affected the facts on which could be based an available defence to trespass, such as lawful entry or recaption of chattels,[131] might be relevant. In such circumstances the liability of the defendant could be determined not on the basis of the actual facts but by reference to those which were believed to exist, as long as such belief were reasonable.

(b) Necessity

5.30 Circumstances may arise in which the defendant is compelled by some urgent necessity to commit a trespass to the plaintiff's land. If someone blocks the highway, making it essential for those using the highway to deviate onto the land of an adjoining owner in order to get by the obstruction, it would seem likely that such deviations, although in a

128a Above p. 88.
129 *National Coal Board v. Evans* [1951] 2 K.B. 861.
130 *Basely v. Clarkson* (1681) 3 Lev. 37: above para 5.10. But the mistake might affect the question of damages. It might also negate intent, as in *National Coal Board v. Evans*, *supra*.
131 Below pp. 100–101, 105–107.

strict sense trespasses, would not be actionable.[132] Similarly, if the defendant broke into the plaintiff's house to save someone, or perhaps some property, endangered by a fire which had broken out, or caused by the negligence or other wrongful act of a stranger, it would be reasonable to conclude that no trespass had been committed by the defendant.[133]

5.31 The possibility that necessity might be a defence to trespass was recognised by Taylor J. in *Rigby v. Chief Constable of Northamptonshire.*[134] This involved the firing of a canister of CS gas into the plaintiff's shop to flush out a dangerous psychopath who had broken into the premises. The canister set the shop on fire, causing considerable damage to the plaintiff's property. In an action against the police brought by the plaintiff, alleging, *inter alia*, trespass, the defendants raised the plea of necessity. This defence was successful. It was pointed out that necessity could never be relied on as a defence by a defendant whose negligence had brought about the situation which gave rise to the necessity to trespass.[135] In this instance the police had not been negligent, either at the time of the incident or prior to its occurrence in not having available a new CS gas device, rather than the CS gas canister, although the newer device involved no fire risk.

5.32 Emergencies of this sort may substantiate a plea of necessity. They involve some sudden, unforeseen situation which calls for immediate action and does not permit any alternative but the acts which amount to the trespass of which complaint is made.[136] However the same is not true of a situation which is not susceptible to resolution by acts of trespass. Such situations are not of sudden occurrence, calling for emergency measures; they may arise out of an ongoing set of circumstances that can be, and perhaps should be remedied by some kind of action, but are dealt with, or attempted to be dealt with by acts which involve trespass. Here the defendants have acted precipitously, as well as unlawfully, because they are not prepared to wait, or to remedy the situation by methods which may take longer to achieve success. Wrongdoing cannot be justified or excused by such conduct, even if it can be explained by reference to the wearing out of patience, frustration with the slowness of the law or administrative action. Thus it was no excuse for squatters in *Southwark London Borough Council v. Williams*[137] that nothing had been done to alleviate the plight of homeless people. Although the defendants were in desperate need of housing accommodation and the plaintiff's property was empty and not being used by tenants, the defendants could not raise the plea of necessity as a defence to the action for trespass brought against them. It is not legitimate to take the law into one's own hands and

132 *Dwyer v. Staunton* [1947] 4 D.L.R. 293. But see *Taylor v. Whitehead* (1781) 2 Doug. 745, private right of way.
133 *Sherrin v. Hagerty* [1953] O.W.N. 962; cp. *Cope v. Sharpe No. 2)* [1912] 1 K.B. 496.
134 [1985] 2 All E.R. 985.
135 *Ibid.* at 994–995.
136 In determining whether the defendant's act was necessary, the state of things as they appeared at the time of the interference, not after the event, must be considered; *Cope v. Sharpe (No. 2), supra.*
137 [1971] Ch. 734.

endeavour to help oneself, if this entails the commission of a tort or other wrong against another, in the absence of some imediate pressing emergency that does not allow either time or space for any other form of action than self-help[138] (such as arises where a person being attacked defends himself by the use of force, or a highway user has to surmount an obstacle placed on the highway by another, or as in the *Rigby* case, the police have to deal with a dangerous person and not let him escape). For the law to adopt any other approach would be a surrender of legal ideals. It would encourage the breakdown of law and order and make control of unlawful conduct impossible.

(c) Recaption of chattels

5.33 One "limited" form of necessity which is recognised by the law[139] is where a defendant enters on another's land in order to recover chattels which belong to him and have been improperly taken or detained from him.[140] Thus in *Patrick v. Colerich*[141] the plaintiff had put the defendant's goods on the plaintiff's land. The defendant could enter the plaintiff's land and reclaim his goods without committing a trespass. But if the defendant cannot show the circumstances in which the chattel got on the plaintiff's land, he will have no defence to an action for trespass.[142]

5.34 The view has been expressed that this type of self-help, for that is what it amounts to, is not permitted where possession of the defendant's goods was originally obtained lawfully, and the defendant alleges that the plaintiff is detaining them unlawfully.[143] If the orginal taking of the defendant's goods was wrongful, a trespass has been committed against him, and this might justify his use of force, where it was reasonably necessary to do so to regain possession.[144] If the taking of the goods was lawful to start with but the plaintiff has acted improperly towards the goods subsequently, the defendant cannot claim interference with his possession, only a wrong against his right to possession. Hence, it is argued, the difference between two situations. In the latter case, self-help should not be allowed, and is not permitted. The defendant ought to have recourse to the appropriate legal action, as he should for example where he has bailed the goods to the plaintiff who refuses or neglects to return them. Decisions support both this view and the one stated earlier that the privilege or recapation may be exercised however the plaintiff originally obtained the goods.[145]

138 *Ibid.* at 743–744 *per* Lord Denning, on the limitations of the defence of necessity.
139 Bosanquet J. in *Anthony v. Haney* (1832) 8 Bing. 186 at 193.
140 *Blades v. Higgs* (1861) 10 C.B.N.S. 713, affirmed (1865) 11 H.L.C. 621. This may also be a defence to an action for trespass to goods or conversion: pp. 127, 148, 166 *infra*.
141 (1838) 3 M. & W. 483; cp. *Austin v. Dowling* (1870) L.R. 5 C.P. 534 at 539.
142 *Anthony v. Haney*, *supra*.
143 *Devoe v. Long* [1951] 1 D.L.R. 203; Fleming, *Law of Torts*, 7th ed. 1987.
144 It may be necessary to make a demand for peaceful return of the goods before the entry: *Blades v. Higgs*, *supra*.
145 *Devoe v. Long*, *supra*: *De Lambert v. Ongley* [1924] N.Z.L.R. 430.

5.35 Where the defendant's goods come onto the plaintiff's land otherwise than through the wrongful or subsequently wrongful act of the plaintiff, there may nonetheless be a limited right to enter the plaintiff's land to recover the goods, although in such situations, force may not be used. Thus goods coming accidently on the plaintiff's land,[146] or left there by some wrongdoer, not the plaintiff or those for whom he is responsible in law,[147] might be retaken in this way.[148] Of course if the plaintiff refused to hand over such goods, he might thereupon become a wrongdoer, thereby entitling the defendant to employ a reasonable amount of force if there is no other way by which he can recover his property. However, mere refusal to return a chattel left by a stranger on the plaintiff's land will not be treated as conversion of the chattel by the plaintiff, so as to justify what would otherwise be a trespass by the defendant: there must be some exercise of dominion over the goods.[149]

5.36 There are grave dangers in permitting someone to retake his chattels by force instead of pursuing a legal remedy in the courts. To prevent possible breaches of the peace this "privilege" should be curtailed, especially in modern times when, unlike the situation in the medieval period when this form of justification emerged, judicial remedies are more expeditious and more readily available. However there may be good reasons why the owner of chattels cannot and should not wait. He may lose title by some intervening act of the possessor of the land. He may require the goods urgently. He may not be able to obtain adequate compensation from the owner of the land were he to sue instead of reclaiming the goods. Hence, as long as excessive force is not used (when trespasses may be committed by a party otherwise justified in using self-help to retain his property), there may be less objection to this kind of conduct than might be considered at first sight to arise.

(d) Liberum tenementum

5.37 The defendant may be able to justify what would otherwise be a trespass if he can establish a right of possession in himself or in someone else by virtue of which his entry is lawful. This would be the case if the defendant were owner of the freehold in the property.[150] This plea, according to Patteson J. in *Ryan v. Clark*,[151] "admits such a possession as would maintain an action against a wrongdoer but asserts a freehold in the defendant with a right to possession." If the freehold is in someone else, the defendant may justify his trespass if he is that other's servant or agent. An example of this is provided by *Delaney v. T. P. Smith Ltd.*[152] The

146 *The Case of Thorns* (1466) Y.B. Ed. IV 7 p. 18.
147 *Higgins v. Andrewes* (1619) 2 Roll. Rep. 55: *Anthony v. Haney supra*.
148 But perhaps not goods lawfully acquired by the plaintiff, left on his premises when he took possession, by the defendant himself or someone else (not a wrongdoer).
149 *Capital Finance Co. Ltd v. Bray* [1964] 1 W.L.R. 323; *British Economical Lamp Co. v. Empire, Mile End* (1913) 29 T.L.R. 386.
150 *Roberts v. Taylor* (1845) 1 C.B. 117.
151 (1849) 12 Q.B. 65 at 71.
152 [1946] K.B. 393.

plaintiff entered a house clandestinely after the defendant had decided to sell, not let it to the plaintiff. The defendant ejected the plaintiff, who had no note or memorandum of his agreement with the defendant, as required under the Law of Property Act 1925[153] (replacing the provisions of the Statute of Frauds[154]). The plaintiff was held to have had possession of the premises as against a wrongdoer, but not as against a lawful owner, i.e. the defendant, since the plaintiff could not rely on his agreement with the defendant to found his right to possession. Consequently the defendant had not committed trespass in ejecting the plaintiff.

5.38 Such a plea is not the same as a plea of *jus tertii*. The latter asserts that the plaintiff is not entitled to the land in question, since someone else, neither plaintiff nor defendant, has a better title than the plaintiff. It has been seen previously that *jus tertii* is not a good defence to an action for trespass.[155] The defence now under discussion is based on the defendant's own better right to possession (or that of someone for whom he acts). Hence where validly raised it is a complete answer: because the defendant will than have a greater right to be in possession than the plaintiff.

(e) Leave and licence

5.39 If the plaintiff has licensed, that is permitted the defendant to enter his land, the latter will not be guilty of trespass.[156] Such a plea is in effect a variant of the defence *volenti non fit injuria.*[157] Problems have arisen, however, because of the different types of licence that may be granted. The legal situation is also complicated by the fact that a wrongful termination of a licence by the landowner may be a breach of contract, but yet the licensee might be a trespasser once his licence has been terminated. Whether the termination of a licence is a breach of contract will depend upon the kind of licence that has been granted by the plaintiff to the defendant. Whether the licensee becomes a trespasser should he stay on the land after his licence has been terminated is a vexed question.

5.40 Licences may be revocable at will or irrevocable. A licence is revocable at will even if the licence is contractual, i.e. given for consideration or under seal.[158] Irrevocable licences are created when the licence is coupled with the grant of an interest in land.[159] Thus if the owner of land grants someone the right to cut and take away wood from the land, and

153 S. 40(1) (now repealed and replaced by the Law of Property (Miscellaneous Provisions) Act 1989, s 2).
154 1677, s. 4.
155 Above p. 93.
156 The permission may be express or implied: *Robson v. Hallett* [1967] 2 Q.B. 939; *Armstrong v. Sheppard & Short Ltd* [1959] 2 Q.B. 384; cp. *Payton v. Fraser* [1981] R.T.R. 496; *Lambart v. Roberts* [1981] R.T.R. 113; *Snook v. Mannion* [1982] R.T.R. 321.
157 See pp. 000 *infra*.
158 *Thomas v. Sorrel* (1673) Vaughan 330; *Wood v. Leadbitter* (1845) 13 M. &. W. 838 at 846 *per* Alderson B.; *Thompson v. Park* [1944] K.B. 408.
159 *Thomas v. Sorrell, supra* at 351 *per* Vaughan C.J.; *Wood v. Leadbitter, supra*; *Jones & Sons Ltd v. Tankerville* [1909] 2 Ch. 440 at 442 *per* Parker J. There may also be statutory irrevocable licenses: cp. Domestic Violence and Matrimonial Proceedings Act, 1976, s. 4.

licences that person to come onto the land for the purpose of exercising the right in question, that licence is irrevocable until the wood that is comprehended within the original grant has been cut and removed. Clearly, in the case of a licence coupled with a grant, the attempt by the landowner to revoke the licence prior to the appropriate time will be invalid;[160] and the licensee will not thereupon become a trespasser. If a licence is revocable at will, however, the licensor may determine at any time the right of the licensee to enter or stay on the licensor's land. If the licensee is on the land when the licence is revoked, it has been held that he is entitled to a reasonable time within which he can leave and remove his goods before he becomes a trespasser,[161] unless reasonable notice of the intention to revoke is given in advance.[162] That is certainly the case where the licence has been revoked properly.[163] If the purported revocation of a contractual licence is not valid and correct, the licensee may not become a trespasser at such time, or even after a reasonable length of time has passed within which he would have been able to leave.[164]

5.41 The situation of the licensee, therefore, will depend upon a number of factors. First, whether or not the licence is revocable at will.[165] Second, if the licence is revocable, whether it has been granted under a valid, enforceable contract or has been given gratuitously. Third, if it has been granted by contract, whether the revocation involved a breach of the contract or was effected in accordance with the terms of the contract. Fourth, whether the fact that a licence was given contractually, although not involving or coupled with a grant of an interest in land, gives the licensee a right to remain on the land unless and until the licence has been revoked properly, in accordance with the terms of the contract, and until a reasonable time has elapsed within which the licensee can leave the land. In the context of the law of torts, and especially the law of trespass, the real issue is not whether the licensor's revocation is a breach of contact (important though that issue may be), it is whether the fact that a revocation amounts to a breach of contract *per se* means that it will be an ineffective revocation in the sense that it does not render the licensee a trespasser.

160 It may be restrained by injunction: *Frogley v. Lovelace* (1859) Johns. 333.

161 *Cornish v. Stubbs* (1870) L.R. 5 C.P. 234; *Canadian Pacific Railway v. R.* [1931] A.C. 414; *Minister of Health v. Bellotti* [1944] K.B. 289; *Tool Metal Manufacturing Co. Ltd v. Tungsten Electric Co. Ltd* [1955] 1 W.L.R. 761; *Isaac v. Hotel de Paris Ltd* [1960] 1 W.L.R. 239. This is so whether the license is gratuitous or contractual. But the licensee cannot treat the licence as still existing if no, or no sufficient notice of revocation is given: *Dorling v. Honnor Marine Ltd* [1964] Ch. 560, reversed on other grounds by [1965] Ch. 1.

162 *Winter Garden Theatre (London) Ltd v. Millennium Productions Ltd* [1948] A.C. 173. But see *Australian Blue Metals Ltd v. Hughes* [1962] 3 All E.R. 335 on the subject of notice.

163 The licensee must leave and not return: *Thompson v. Park* [1944] K.B. 408.

164 On the ground that an invalid revocation may be a breach of contract on the part of the licensor who cannot profit by his own wrong, viz., a breach of contract. If the licence is gratuitous, it can always be revoked at will, with the consequences set out in the text.

165 Or is not a licence at all but a lease, which gives the lessee greater rights: *Shell Mex & BP Ltd v. Manchester Garages Ltd* [1971] 1 W.L.R. 612. For the difficulties in distinguishing between a tenancy at will and a licence at will, see *Donald v. Baldwyn* [1953] N.Z.L.R. 313 at 319 *per* Adams J.

5.42 In *Wood v. Leadbitter*[166] the plaintiff was licensed to come onto the defendant's racecourse. He was asked to leave, that is to say his licence was revoked. When he refused to do so he was forcibly ejected. The issue was whether he could sue for assault: and this depended upon whether or not he was a trespasser. Because the plaintiff had only a bare licence, not coupled with the grant of any interest in the land, it was held that he became a trespasser once the licence was revoked (whether or not that revocation was a breach of the plaintiff's contract with the defendant). By way of contrast in *Butler v. Manchester, Sheffield & Lincolnshire Railway*,[167] the defendant could not revoke the licence of the plaintiff, a passenger on the railway, because the plaintiff failed to show a ticket or to pay his fare. Therefore the plaintiff did not become a trespasser and could not be ejected. The situation was complicated by the decision of the Court of Appeal in *Hurst v. Picture Theatres Ltd.*[168] The plaintiff purchased a ticket to see a picture at the defendant's theatre. During the showing of the picture the defendant ejected the plaintiff, wrongfully and improperly, under the belief that he had done something that would have entitled the defendant to terminate the licence, when in fact the plaintiff had done nothing wrong. This was clearly a breach of contract for which the defendant could be liable (although the damages were minimal). However the plaintiff sued for trespass to the person, which meant that it was material to determine whether or not he became a trespasser on the defendant's premises once his licence to see the picture had been revoked. Although no interest in land was given along with the licence, the court held that the licence in this instance was not revocable at will. The plaintiff had the right to stay to see the picture for which he had paid. Consequently his ejection was wrongful and an actionable trespass.[169] The effect of this case would appear to be that if there is some purpose associated with the grant of a licence, other than the grant of an interest in land, the licence is not revocable unless and until that purpose has been fulfilled (in the absence of some wrongful conduct on the part of the licensee that might justify the termination of the license, i.e the contract, and his subsequent ejection as a trespasser). Two factors seemed to have been of importance: first, the change in the law effected by the Judicature Acts, in consequence of which although the contract was oral, equity might treat that as having been done which ought to have been done, and so regard the oral contract as capable of being enforced, so as to entitle the licensee to compel the licensor to let him remain in the premises;[170] and secondly, the availability of an injunction from a court of equity by which a breach of contract could be restrained.[171] Notwithstanding such arguments, the decision in the *Hurst* case is questionable. If taken literally it would mean that licences

166 (1845) 13 M. & W. 838.
167 (1888) 21 Q.B.D. 207.
168 [1915] 1 K.B. 1.
169 Cp. *Vaughan v. Hampson* (1875) 33 L.T. 15, the right to attend a creditors' meeting.
170 But even if the licence had been under seal this should have made no difference: cp. Alderson B. in *Wood v. Leadbitter*, *supra* at 845.
171 But this is a discretionary remedy and is only available where damages would not be an adequate remedy, which is hardly the situation in cases like *Hurst v. Picture Theatres*.

would be irrevocable once they were given for consideration even though they conferred no interest or right in land along with the permission to enter the land in question. To admit this would be to abandon the long observed distinction between mere licences and those which were coupled with, and attached to grants of legal or equitable interests in land. It would amount to a confusion between contractual and proprietary rights which is fundamental to the law in general, as well as the law of trespass in particular. Not surprisingly therefore the decision in the *Hurst* case was not followed in Australia,[172] where, on facts similar to those in *Wood v. Leadbitter*, the licensee was considered a trespasser once his licence to come on the racecourse was revoked, on the ground that the licence was contractual, not proprietary in character, was therefore revocable at will, had been revoked, and in consequence the licensee had no further right to remain on the premises. Nevertheless, whatever the merits of the technical argument that suggests that the *Hurst* case is incorrect, the modern view would seem to be, as stated earlier, that a contractual licence issued for a particular purpose is not revocable at will once the licensee has entered the premises, until the purpose has been fulfilled (or some wrongful conduct is perpetrated by the licensee).[173]

5.43 Of course if a licensee acts otherwise than in accordance with the terms of the licence, if it is contractual, or outside the scope of the permission he has been given if it is gratuitous, he may be treated as no longer covered by the licence. In such circumstances he can clearly be treated as a trespasser, although it would seem reasonable to add that he should be given a reasonable time to leave the premises (unless his conduct makes such flexibility inappropriate, e.g. where the licensee, when asked to leave, flatly refuses to do so). Once this is the case there is no doubt that the licensor can use reasonable force to eject the ex-licensee. Such force must not be excessive, as is the case where any landowner seeks to invoke the idea of self-help to redress a situation in which a trespass to his land is being committed.[174]

(f) Lawful entry

5.44 The right to enter the land of another may be given by statute or the common law. Under some statutes, for example, the Rights of Entry (Gas and Electricity Boards) Act 1954, such entry can only be made with the consent of the occupier or by warrant, unless the situation is one of

172 In *Cowell v. Rosehill Racecourse Co. Ltd* (1936) 56 C.L.R. 605. Contrast *Donald v. Baldwyn* [1953] N.Z.L.R. 313 at 319 where Adams J. thought that *Wood v. Leadbitter, supra*, was no longer good law in the light of the decision in the *Winter Garden* case.

173 *Winter Garden Theatre (London) Ltd v. Millennium Productions Ltd* [1946] 1 All E.R. 678 at 685 *per* Lord Greene M.R.; [1948] A.C. 173 at 189 *per* Lord Simon, 202 *per* Lord Uthwatt; *Errington v. Errington* [1952] 1 All E.R. 149 at 155 *per* Denning L.J. *Bendall v. McWhirter* [1952] 2 Q.B. 466 at 479–480 *per* Denning L.J. See also *Ferris v. Weaven* [1952] 2 All E.R. 233.

174 Below pp. 107–108.

emergency. Where allowed, entry under such statute may even be forcible.[175] Under other statutes, conditions may be applied to the right to enter, as for example by virtue of legislation dealing with access to the countryside.[176] In modern times, during which administrative powers have been vested in many bodies and officials, it has become necessary to allow representatives of such authorities to come onto premises to inspect them with a view to determining whether the provisions of, for example, legislation dealing with safety, health or welfare have been fulfilled. To the extent to which legislation of this kind has proliferated, it is no longer true to say, as Coke C.J. did in *Semayne's Case*,[177] "an Englishman's home is his castle".

5.45 Even at common law there were, and still exist, some exceptional qualifications of this idea. Thus a landlord may enter demised premises in order to distrain for unpaid rent. A bailiff can come onto private premises in pursuance of some civil process, such as the seizure of property in execution of a judgment, as long as he does not break in to the premises in question.[178] Where the debtor's property is on the premises of somebody else, not the debtor, entry may be made thereon; but if such property is not there, the bailiff will be liable in trespass.[179] However, the most important instance of justified or legal entry without permission or consent, and indeed even against the will of the occupier, is the right of the police, and even private citizens, to enter premises for certain purposes of law enforcement.[179a]

5.46 Where entry by police officers is concerned, a distinction must be drawn between entry under a search warrant and other entries. Police who have a valid search warrant do not commit trespass when they come on to premises in pursuance of such warrant and seize goods, even if the goods seized are not covered by the warrant, as long as what is taken can be used as material evidence establishing commission of offences in respect of which the warrant was issued.[180] By exceeding the limits of the warrant, as noted previously, the police do not become trespassers *ab initio*, even if what is seized cannot be regarded as justified. The police may be guilty of trespass to goods in regard to the improperly seized goods, but not of trespass to the land.[181] At common law, unless police had a warrant to do

175 *Grove v. Eastern Gas Board* [1952] 1 K.B. 77; Feldman, *The Law Relating to Entry , Search and Seizure*, 1986, pp. 53ff.

176 National Parks and Access to the Countryside Act 1949 s. 60; Countryside Act 1968 ss. 16–19.

177 (1604) 5. Co.Rep. 91a: *Morris v. Beardmore* [1981] A.C. 446.

178 *Semayne's Case, supra*: *Southam v. Smout* [1964] 1 Q.B. 308; *Vaughan v. McKenzie* [1969] 1 Q.B. 557.

179 *Southam v. Smout, supra.*

179a Feldman, op. cit. supra, Chs. 2, 5–9 and 12. See Police and Criminal Evidence Act 1984 ss. 8, 15, 16, 17, 18 and 19.

180 *Chic Fashions (West Wales) Ltd v. Jones* [1968] 2 Q.B. 299; applied in *Frank Thomas Export Ltd v. Metropolitan Police Commissioner* [1977] Q.B.952. Cp. in relation to a search warrant under the Taxes Management Act 1970 s. 20C(1), *I.R.C. v. Rossminster Ltd* [1980] 1 All E.R. 80.

181 *Ibid.* See pp. 143–149.

so, they could not enter premises, after someone had been arrested, to take a car involved in the commission of a crime in respect of which the arrest had been made.[182] The power to enter has now been conferred on the police by statute.[182a] But police may enter premises to effect an arrest even wihout a warrant.[183] They may also enter if invited, and such invitation may be oral or by conduct.[184] In *Snook v. Mannion*[185] a notice saying "police keep out" was posted on a house. Nonetheless it was held that the police, like other citizens, had an implied licence to come inside if they had, or reasonably thought they had legitimate business with the occupier. The administration of a breath test to the occupier was such legitimate business. When the occupier used language which purported to exclude the police, the issue became whether what he said was a revocation of the licence or mere vulgarity. This was a question of fact (which was decided in favour of the police in this instance). If police have no legitimate business on the premises, and have no search or other warrant, their entry will be a trespass. Thus in *Morris v. Beardmore*,[186] where the police could not oblige the defendant to provide a sample of breath under the Road Traffic Act 1972 the entry of the police onto the defendant's premises was a trespass. Similarly, a police officer who enters premises without the prior permission of the occupier to investigate the safety of property will be a trespasser.[187] But if he enters to prevent a breach of the peace his entry will not be a trespass.[188]

5.47 Private citizens as such have no right of entry to the premises of another without permission, or statutory authority, unless, perhaps, they do so in order to arrest someone in circumstances which justify arrest by a private citizen without warrant, which, as seen elsewhere, may or may not still be possible.[189] But a private citizen may be able to enter premises without committing a trespass, in order to prevent a murder (and possibly other serious offences).[190]

3. REMEDIES

(a) Self-help

5.48 A person who has been dispossessed from his land may retake possession, without prior recourse to judicial decision, as long as he can do so peacefully and without force (even without the aid of a sheriff after a

182 *McLone v. Oxford* [1982] 2 W.L.R. 423.
182a Police and Criminal Evidence Act 1984 s. 18(1) and (2).
183 *Swales v. Cox* [1981] Q.B. 489.
184 *Faulkner v. Willetts* [1982] R.T.R. 159.
185 [1982] R.T.R. 321.
186 [1981] A.C. 446: cp. *Fox v. Chief Constable of Gwent* [1985] 1 All E.R. 230, affirmed by the House of Lords [1985] 3 All E.R. 392, where *Morris v. Beardmore* was distinguished on grounds that are not relevant here.
187 *Great Central Railway v. Bates* [1921] 3 K.B. 578.
188 *Thomas v. Sawkins* [1935] 2 K.B. 249.
189 See pp. 135–140.
190 *Handcock v. Baker* (1800) 2 Bos. & P. 260.

judgment of possession).[191] Forcible entries, even by those entitled to possession, were made criminal by Statutes of Forcible Entry,[192] the rationale for which was the need and desire to prevent breaches of the peace. Those earlier statutes have now been repealed and replaced by the Criminal Law Act 1977.[193] A number of new offences have been created, e.g., the use of threat of violence to secure entry onto premises against the known opposition of the occupier, unless the person attempting to regain possession is a "displaced residential occupier."[194] The new legislation may go further than the older statutes, since, under the old law, no offence was committed by the use of force unless the owner trying to regain possession had originally acquiesced in his dispossession.[195] Under the old law, although forcible entry was a crime, the guilty party could not be sued for trespass to the land,[196] nor could he be sued for any trespass to the person of the party forcibly ejected or for damage to any chattels on the premises as long as only a reasonable amount of force was used.[197] In this respect the law was the same as applied to situations where force was used to prevent a trespass, control someone who was on the land, or eject someone who had trespassed without claiming or exercising possession. If force were used against such a person, even by the lawful occupier of the land, a trespass to the person of the party prevented, controlled or ejected would be committed unless no more force was used than was reasonably necessary for the purpose, and in the circumstances.[198] The right to use force to defend land in one's possession from trespassers was, and is, akin to the right to use force in self-defence or in defence of certain others, e.g. a spouse or child.[199] In this context, as in that, the law is concerned lest people go too far in protection of their persons or property. Whether this will apply under the new law is still unresolved (though there would appear to be no reason why the same principles should not apply with respect to civil liability for forcible ejection, even though criminal liability may be imposed under the 1977 Act).

(b) Judicial remedies

5.49 Where a trespass is threatened, or is in progress and likely to continue, the occupier may obtain an injunction to restrain the occurrence or the repetition or continuation of the trespass: and it will not matter that

191 *Taunton v. Costar* (1797) 7 T.R. 431; *Aglionby v. Cohen* [1955] 1 Q.B. 558.
192 1381, 1429, 1623.
193 1977, c. 45.
194 *Ibid.*, s. 6: note also the concept of a "a potential residential occupier" in *ibid.* s. 7(2).
195 *McPhail v. Persons Unknown* [1973] Ch. 447.
196 *Pollen v. Brewer* (1859) 7 C.B.N.S. 371; *Clifton Securities v. Huntley* [1948] 2 All E.R. 283; because the ejector was seeking to recover possession and so had not infringed any "right" of the party ejected (unless the ejector used more force than was reasonably necessary). Breaking down doors or windows was force, but not lifting off the roof of a house: *Jones v. Foley* [1891] 1 Q.B. 730.
197 *Hemmings v. Stoke Poges Golf Club* [1920] 1 K.B. 720, overruling earlier decisions such as *Newton v. Harland* (1840) 1 Man. & G. 644; and *Bedall v. Maitland* (1881) 17 Ch.D. 174.
198 *Harrison v. Duke of Rutland* [1893] 1 Q.B. 142; *Green v. Goddard* (1702) 2 Salk. 641; *Dean v. Hogg* (1834) 10 Bing. 245; *Holmes v. Bagg* (1835) 1 E. & B. 782.
199 See pp. 127–128.

the amount of damage that was, or would be done by the trespass is minimal.[200] Injunctive relief is discretionary, and probably rare. The more usual remedies that can be obtained from a court are (i) an order for repossesssion, which is the modern version of the old action of ejectment; and (ii) damages. The former will be appropriate where the plaintiff has been dispossessed by the defendant.[201] Damages are the proper remedy where there has been interference with possession without any challenge to the plaintiff's occupation of the land or premises in question.

5.50 In an action for repossession, however, the plaintiff may also recover "mesne profits", i.e. the damage which the plaintiff suffered as a result of his having been dispossessed for any period of time.[202] What the plaintiff recovers is all that he has lost, not only any profits made by the defendant during the latter's unlawful occupation, but also any deterioration in the property and the costs incurred in regaining possession.[203] The plaintiff may sue for recovery of possession: or for recovery and mesne profits: or simply for mesne profits. This last action can be maintained where the plaintiff has already recovered possession, or his interest in land has terminated. Under the doctrine of trespass by relation,[204] the plaintiff will be considered to have been in possession for the entire period in respect of which he claims mesne profits. Usually, mesne profits means the value to the trespasser of the use of the property for the period of the trespass, which is normally the letting value of the property. In this respect it has been held that an owner claiming mesne profits by way of an action for trespass will be successful even without evidence that he could or would have let the property had he been in possession.[205] Other loss may also be recovered in such an action, such as loss of custom caused by the trespasser's closing down of the plaintiff's inn.[206] If the trespasser makes improvements in the land, it would seem that he cannot set-off the value of these against an action for mesne profits, unless perhaps where the plaintiff has allowed the improvements to be made in the knowledge that he was going to sue to recover possession, a form of estoppel.[207]

5.51 A trespass which does not involve the dispossession of the occupier gives rise to an action for damages representing the damage caused to the plaintiff, which will normally be the cost of the physical damage to the land. But this does not mean that the plaintiff can recover the cost of

200 *John Tremball Ltd v. National Westminster Bank Ltd* (1979) 30 P. & C.R. 104.
201 Above pp. 92–93.
202 R.S.C. Ord. 13, rr. 4, 5; Ord. 15, r. 1. Damages are assessable from the date of the writ in certain instances: *Elliott v. Boynton* [1924] 1 Ch. 236.
203 *Strand Electric Co. v. Brisford* [1952] 2 Q.B. 246; *Hall & Co. Ltd v. Pearlberg* [1956] 1 W.L.R. 244.
204 Above p. 91.
205 *Swordheath Properties Ltd v. Tabet* [1979] 1 All E.R. 240.
206 *Dunn v. Legge* (1783) 3 Doug. 335.
207 *Cawdor v. Lewis* (1835) 1 Y. & C. 427. But it has been suggested that no decision has been given with respect to set-off by a trespasser who has acted *bona fide*, e.g. under a mistaken belief that the land was his: *Salmond & Heuston on the Law of Torts*, 19th ed. 1987, at 624: *contra* Fleming, *Law of Torts*, 7th ed. 1987 at 46, citing a New Zealand case, *Tai Te Whetu v. Scandlyn* [1952] N.Z.L.R. 30.

restoring the land or premises into the former condition. The test is the diminution in value of the land, or, in appropriate instances, the cost of making good the damage done.[208] In certain cases of trespass, such as where a landlord unlawfully evicts a tenant, it may be possible to grant exemplary or aggravated damages, even where the plaintiff has not initially relied on trespass, if the court wishes to treat the facts as raising a claim in trespass.[209] Whether exemplary damages are appropriate depends on the application of the language used by the House of Lords in *Rookes v. Barnard*[210] to the effect that such damages may be awarded whenever it is necessary to teach a wrongdoer that tort does not pay.

208 *Nalder v. Ilford Corp.* [1951] K.B. 822; *Lodge Holes Colliery v. Wednesbury Corp.* [1908] A.C. 323. Prospective damage may be claimed: *Townend v. Askery Coal Co.* [1934] Ch. 463.
209 *Drane v. Evangelou* [1978] 2 All E.R. 437.
210 [1964] A.C. 1129 at 1227 *per* Lord Devlin. See further below pp. 515–516.

CHAPTER 6

Trespass to the Person

1. GENERAL CHARACTERISTICS

6.01 There are different forms of trespass to the person. All trace their origin to the writ of trespass *vi et armis*, which involved the direct application of force by the defendant to the plaintiff.[1] Trespass became actionable, as well as involving, as it still does, criminal liability, because a trespass entailed a breach of "the king's peace".[2] That medieval expression, archaic though it may be, nonetheless enshrines what continues to be recognised as the reason for making trespasses actionable. The importance of actions for trespass to the person today lies in the fact that the existence of such liability recognises and enforces the legal interest in personal safety and freedom.[3] That interest is at once personal and societal. It is personal in that everyone has an interest in his or her own freedom from personal harm or the infringement of personal liberty of action and movement. It is societal in that the community in general is concerned that individuals should be allowed to live free from fear of interference with their ability to act in a lawful manner and from fear of being subjected to physical or other injury.[4] Much has happened to the law of trespass since its early medieval beginnings. Nonetheless the fundamental principle, plain and uncontestable, as Goff L.J. said in *Collins v. Wilcock*,[5] is that every person's body is inviolate. The breadth of the principle reflects the funamental nature of the interest so protected. In Blackstone's words:[6] "The law cannot draw a line between different degrees of violence, and therefore totally prohibits the first and lowest stage of it; every man's person being sacred, and no other having a right to meddle with it, in the slightest manner".

6.02 Classical tort law drew a distinction between true cases of trespass, where the defendant himself struck or otherwise injured the plaintiff, from situations where the injury to the plaintiff was indirectly brought about by

1 *Scott v. Shepherd* (1773) 2 W.Bl. 892 at 899 *per* De Grey C.J.
2 Allen, *The Queen's Peace*, Hamlyn Lectures, 1953.
3 Which is protected by a legal duty, viz., a general duty to all the world not to trespass: *Long v. Hepworth* [1968] 1 W.L.R. 1299.
4 English law goes to great lengths to protect a person of full age and capacity from interference with is personal liberty: *S. v. McC. (S. v. S.)* [1972] A.C. 24 at 43 *per* Lord Reid: cp. *W. v. W.* [1964] P. 67, subjecting a person to a blood test against his will is an assault and battery and invasion of his personal liberty (unless allowed by statute to establish a child's paternity: *S. v. McC, supra*).
5 [1984] 3 All E.R. 374 at 378.
6 3 Blackstone's Commentaries 120.

an act of the defendant. The law differentiated immediate from consequential injury. Nonetheless the intervening act of a third party might not preclude a conclusion that the plaintiff's injury was directly, not consequentially caused by the defendant. Such was the opinion of the majority of the "squib" case, *Scott v. Shepherd.*[7] So, where vicarious liability was involved, the defendant would be guilty of trespass if he sat next to his servant while the latter were driving the vehicle which ran into and injured the plaintiff.[8] If the servant were on his own, though operating under the orders of the defendant, the defendant could not be sued in trespass, but would be liable, if at all, on an action on the case, forerunner of the modern law of negligence.[9] Trespass was defined as the personal act of the defendant.[10] Anything else would be remediable in negligence, nuisance, or some other action derived from the action on the case.[11] The old forms of action have now gone and the strict division between trespass and negligence has diminished. In the light of recent decisions it is no longer vital to determine whether the plaintiff's claim should be for trespass to the person or negligence. That is because the essential nature of liability for trespass has undergone development that goes beyond the mere abolition of forms of action. Such changes are procedural, rather than substantive.[12] There remains a valid doctrinal difference between trespass to the person and other torts resulting in personal injury. That difference is between direct and consequential infliction of personal harm. Direct contact between plaintiff and defendant can be trespass. Acts by the defendant that indirectly cause physical harm to the plaintiff will not support an action for trespass, but must be remedied by actions in, for example, negligence, nuisance, or under the doctrine of *Rylands v. Fletcher.*[13]

6.03 In the same way as directness has changed its meaning in the context of trespass, so the idea of force has undergone development and explanation. Assaults do not involve the application of force, only the threat that force may be used.[14] In cases of false imprisonment there may be such an absence of force that the plaintiff may be ignorant of what is happening.[15] Even where battery is involved, force, in the sense of some significant interference with, or attack upon the personal integrity of the plaintiff, may be lacking. In the early eighteenth century Holt C.J.

7 (1773) 2 W.Bl. 892.
8 *Chandler v. Broughton* (1832) 1 Cr. & M. 29. See also *Day v. Edwards* (1794) 5 T.R. 648; *Covell v. Laming* (1808) 1 Camp. 497; *Sharrod v. London & North-Western Rly.* (1849) 4 Ex. 580.
9 *Leame v. Bray* (1803) 3 East 593. Unless the harm inflicted was a direct consequence of the defendant's conduct and the servant's want of care: *Gregory v. Piper* (1829) 9 B. & C. 591.
10 *Leame v. Bray, supra* at 599 *per* Lord Ellenborough C.J.
11 But in *Williams v. Holland* (1833) 10 Bing. 112 it was ultimately decided that a plaintiff could sue in trespass or case if the injury, though immediate, was not wilful. This led to the greater use of case for various procedural reasons: Goodhart & Winfield, "Trespass and Negligence" (1933) 49 L.Q.R. 359; Pritchard, "The Rise of *Williams v. Holland*" [1964] C.L.J. 234.
12 Below p. 117.
13 Below Chap. 9.
14 Below p. 120.
15 Below p. 124.

pointed out that the least touching of a man in anger was a battery.[16] Anger may not be a prerequisite of liability for trespass, as the law has now evolved: but it is certainly true to say that very little force is necessary for the commission of trespass. More important than the degree of force is the nature of the intent that accompanies the act of the defendant. That intent may turn a minimal use of force into a trespass: just as the lack of any appropriate intent may render even a significant degree of force an innocent, non-trespassory act.

6.04 In *Wilson v. Pringle*,[17] the Court of Appeal held that an intention to injure was not an essential ingredient of an action for trespass to the person. The trespass itself was the offence. It is the act, rather than the injury which has to be intentional. The distinction is between an intentional and an accidental application of force. The distinction is also drawn between the intentional use of force in an unlawful way, or for an unlawful purpose, and the use of force in a manner which is regarded in modern times as acceptable. In this respect the degree of force used may be extremely relevant, despite the earlier language of Holt C.J. The use of only a slight degree of force is not a battery every time. The intention of the defendant and the degree of force used are both relevant. A slight degree of force is not battery if done by way of a joke, or in friendship.[18] There are many examples in everyday life where an intended conduct or touch is not actionable as a trespass. Hence it is important that the defendant not only intended the physical contact in question, but did so with what the court in *Wilson v. Pringle*[19] referred to as a "hostile" intent. Such hostility may be evinced by anger, by words or gesture. Sometimes the very act will speak for itself, as where somebody uses a weapon on another. The question to be answered is: what turns a friendly touching, which is not actionable, into an unfriendly one, which is?[20] In *Collins v. Wilcock*,[21] Goff L.J. purported to define the line between conduct which was actionable, and that which was not, in terms of whether the physical contact involved went beyond generally accepted standards of conduct. This attempt to rationalise the law suggested a method whereby various "defences" to an action for trespass to the person,[22] such as consent, self-defence, ejection of a trespasser, exercising parental authority, statutory authority (and, it may be added, lawful arrest) could be expressed under one umbrella of a general exception. In *Wilson v. Pringle*,[23] Croom-Johnson L.J. approved the broad approach of Goff L.J. on the grounds of convenience, and so as to avoid an attitude which resembled that adopted by the courts in the days of special pleading. At the same time he thought

16 *Cole v. Turner* (1704) 6 Mod. 149.
17 [1986] 2 All E.R. 440: cp. *T. v. T.* [1988] 1 All E.R. 613 at 622–625 *per* Wood J.
18 *Wilson v. Pringle* [1986] 2 All E.R. 440 at 443 *per* Croom-Johnson L.J., citing *Williams v. Jones* (1736) Lee temp. Hard. 298.
19 *Supra* note 17 at 444, 445, 447.
20 *Ibid.* at 445–446.
21 [1984] 3 All E.R. 374 at 378: cp. *T. v. T.*, *supra* at 622–4 *per* Wood J.
22 Below pp. 127–130, 135–141.
23 *Supra* note 17 at 447.

that the rationalisation of Goff L.J. did not provide a practicable way of defining battery (or, indeed, any other form of trespass). The true test of when a touching was wrongful and actionable was that of "hostility". Hostility was not to be equated with ill-will or malevolence. It was a question of fact. It could be established by proof of an expressed intention (though such intention did not suffice by itself). It could be imported from the circumstances. Thus it might be evident from the circumstances that a playful blow was struck in anger: or that taking hold of a woman's arm was more than was necessary to attract her attention, but was designed to restrain her when she was unwilling to be restrained.[24] Just as the law of negligence discriminates risks that are part and parcel of daily life from those which go beyond what a reasonable person is expected and obliged to accept,[25] so the law of trespass differentiates situations where the intent of the defendant was not to act unlawfully, beyond the boundaries of permitted behaviour, from those where the defendant intended to act unlawfully.[26]

6.05 The intent with which the act complained of is committed will therefore characterise the force that is used. Force that might otherwise not be wrongful may become so when applied with hostile intent. Force that appears at first sight to be wrongful may not be actionable if applied with a lawful, non-hostile intent. However, underlying the question of force is the notion of intention in another, but not altogether unrelated sense. Before there can be liability for trespass to the person it must be shown that the defendant perpetrated the act intentionally. That is to say he must have been aware that he was performing the act that constitutes the trespass, and must have intended such act. Investigation of this aspect of intent raises such issues as capacity to commit the tort of trespass and the distinction between trespass and accident.

6.06 Since an intent to commit the act that is a trespass is a prerequisite of liability, a person who is incapable of formulating the necessary intent cannot be liable. In this respect special note must be taken of the situation of minors and insane or mentally incompetent persons. A minor[27] is not *per se* incapable of forming the necessary intent.[28] Whether or not he can do or has done so is a question of fact. The younger the party the less likely is it that he will be able to appreciate what he is doing, so as to have attributed to him the required intent.[29] Age alone, however, is not a determinant. In the old common law phrase, "malice supplies intent". In

24 *Ibid.* at 447–448.
25 Below Chap. 12.
26 Cp. *Wilson v. Pringle*, *supra* note 19 at 448.
27 I.e. anyone under 18 years of age: Family Law Reform Act 1969 s. 1.
28 *McHale v. Watson* (1966) 115 C.L.R. 199.
29 *Tillander v. Gosselin* (1966) 60 D.L.R. (2d) 18; *Walmsley v. Humenick* [1954] 2 D.L.R. 232.

other words, proof of the motive or purpose behind the act in question may well entitle a court to conclude that the minor possessed the intent to commit the act (and did so from hostility).[30] There is no rule of law in torts, as there is in contract, that minority precludes liability. Someone who is insane[31] may also be capable of having the necessary intent.[32] The issue seems to be whether the defendant could form the intention to commit the act that was involved, i.e. whether his act was voluntary, not whether he knew that what he was doing was wrong.[33] The M'Naghten Rules are not relevant in the context of torts.[34] Hence someone who involuntarily does something which amounts to the infliction of force upon another may not be liable in trespass. Such would be the case when the one person seized another's arm by force and compelled him to strike the plaintiff. The one whose arm actually struck the plaintiff would not be guilty of trespass (but the one who used that arm would be liable).[35] In effect the arm was being used as a weapon in the same way as a stick. Lack of any voluntary quality in the alleged trespasser's act would also explain the immunity from suit of a person acting under hypnosis, while sleep-walking, or in a state of automatism.[36] Perhaps, too, this mode of thought underlies the approach of the court in *Wilson v. Pringle*.[37] One who acts involuntarily cannot be considered to have acted with any hostile intent. The notion of hostility is intimately connected with the whole issue of intent. Lack of hostility, as that word is explained in *Wilson v. Pringle*, may reveal that the defendant acted without intent. Because hostility does not necessarily involve either malice, i.e. spite or ill-will, or negligence, the underlying desires of the defendant are immaterial. The defendant must appreciate what he is doing. If his mind is capable of formulating the desire and intention to assault, as was the defendant's mind in *Morriss v. Marsden*,[38] despite its diseased state, the requisite intention will be present. The defendant's act will be voluntary. The line is being drawn between an act which was committed knowingly and deliberately and an act which occurred against the defendant's will, or in the absence of his knowledge or awareness of what was happening. The reason for this, perhaps strict

30 In *Wilson v. Pringle, supra*, for instance, the plaintiff and defendant were both schoolboys, aged 13. They were engaged in horseplay in a school corridor and the plaintiff was injured. The issue was whether the defendant should be given leave to defend on the ground that he alleged no hostile intent, even though he had admitted that he had indulged in the horseplay. The Court of Appeal reversed the judge who, reversing the decision of a registrar, had held that the plaintiff was entitled to enter judgment without trial. Leave to defend was given.

31 *A fortiori* someone who is not insane but lacks full mental competence.

32 *Morriss v. Marsden* [1952] 1 All E.R. 925. See also *Borrowdail v. Hunter* (1843) 5 Man. & Gr. 639 at 669; *Donaghy v. Brennan* (1901) 19 N.Z.L.R. 289; *Taggart v. Innis* (1862) 12 U.C.C.P. 77; *Tindale v. Tindale* [1950] 4 D.L.R. 363; *Phillips v. Soloway* (1957) 6 D.L.R. (2d) 570; *Beals v. Hayward* [1960] N.Z.L.R. 131. For a different view in Australia see *White v. Pile* (1951) 68 W.N. (N.S.W.) 176.

33 *Morriss v. Marsden, supra.*

34 Fridman, "Mental Incompetency" (1964) 80 L.Q.R. 84 at 87–95 for discussion and criticism of the legal situation created by the cases cited *supra* note 32.

35 *Weaver v. Ward* (1616) Hob. 134.

36 Cp. *Morriss v. Marsden, supra* note 32.

37 [1986] 2 All E.R. 925.

38 [1952] 1 All E.R. 925.

approach to liability for trespass, seems to be twofold.[38a] First, the law of torts is designed to compensate victims, not to punish those guilty of wrongdoing. Therefore appreciation of guilt is not relevant. Secondly, while there may be validity in excusing from liability someone who, through some deficiency such as age or unsoundness of mind, is incapable of realising the precise nature of what he is doing, there is no reason for granting such exemption from liability to someone who is well aware of what he is doing, while at the same time is unable to realise the consequences of what he is doing. In determining the limits of liability for trespass to the person the law recognises that it is impossible and unreasonable to provide protection or to allow compensation where injuries are inflicted accidentally: but it is neither impossible nor unreasonable to extend the scope of liability to situations where injury is inflicted deliberately, albeit by a defendant who for some reason cannot refrain from the act which inflicts the injury.

6.07 This discrimination between accident and trespass has been manifested by the common law for a long time. As long ago as 1616 it was held that an alleged trespass would not be actionable where the defendant showed that it occurred "utterly without his fault".[39] In the succeeding three hundred years the issue became whether the onus lay on the defendant to prove that what happened did so without his intent and without any negligence on his part, or whether it lay on the plaintiff to establish that the defendant committed a trespass intentionally or at the least negligently. Until 1959 the prevailing view would seem to have been that all the plaintiff had to allege and prove was that he had been injured by the direct act of the defendant, leaving it to the defendant to excuse himself by proving lack of intent, and the absence of negligence.[40] If there were no intentional application of force to the plaintiff by the defendant, the latter might still be liable in trespass unless he established that the plaintiff's injury resulted from an "inevitable accident". That meant establishing that the concatenation of events that produced the plaintiff's injury as a direct result of the defendant's act was something totally unforeseeable by the defendant as a reasonable man, and therefore was something against which he could not have been expected to guard by appropriate action or care before or when he acted.[40a] If the defendant failed to show that the incident occurred because of an inevitable accident, he would be liable in trespass because his act was intentional, in the sense that he knew what he was doing and intended to do it, even though he did

38a In addition it may be noted that other policy arguments have been put forward, viz: (i) where both parties are "innocent" he who caused the harm should bear the loss; (ii) the insane person's relations might exercise control over him; (iii) it is better to avoid the difficult problems of defining insanity and applying the notion of insanity to the law of torts.

39 *Weaver v. Ward* (1616) Hob. 134.

40 *Stanley v. Powell* [1891] 1 Q.B. 85: cp. *National Coal Board v. Evans* [1951] 2 K.B. 861 (a case of trespass to chattels); *Cook v. Lewis* [1951] S.C.R. 830.

40a *The Marpesia* (1872) L.R. 4 P.C. 212 at 220 *per* Sir James Colville.

not intend to cause injury to anyone, and especially the plaintiff, by what he did.

6.08 In *Fowler v. Lanning*,[41] however, Diplock J. held that the onus of proof was on the plaintiff to establish that the trespass committed against him, in that instance his being shot by the defendant, was perpetrated either intentionally or negligently. Subsequently, in *Letang v. Cooper*,[42] the Court of Appeal, at least in the judgment of Lord Denning, M.R.,[43] took the view that if personal injuries were inflicted negligently, not intentionally, even though by a direct act of the defendant, and not as a consequence of something done by the defendant, the plaintiff's recourse lay in an action in negligence, and not in an action for trespass.[44] The treatment of this case more recently by the Court of Appeal in *Wilson v. Pringle*,[45] would suggest that Lord Denning went too far when he said that unintentionally inflicted personal injuries were remediable only in negligence. In the more recent case the court stressed that no intention to injure was required for liability in trespass. But the act which caused the trespass had to be intentional. On that basis a negligent act would suffice. The act itself would be intended, even though the consequences would not. Proof of negligence would negate that what occurred did so through accident, that is to say, totally unintentionally.[45a]

6.09 This development has affected the issue of onus of proof in cases of trespass to the person. It has not altered the essential nature of the tort. As *Wilson v. Pringle* evidences, in trespass the distinction is drawn between an act and its consequences; whereas in negligence no such separation is made.[46] In trespass it is the act which determines liability; in negligence it is the consequences which are material in deciding whether the defendant should be held liable. Foresight of consequences is highly relevant when negligence is the issue. Such foresight is only material in cases of trespass when the defendant relies on a plea of accident or inevitable accident to excuse himself from what would otherwise be liability for what he has done.

41 [1959] 1 Q.B. 426; cp. *Beals v. Hayward* [1960] N.Z.L.R. 131.
42 [1965] 1 Q.B. 232.
43 *Ibid.* at 232–240.
44 For a different view see *Williams v. Milotin* (1957) 97 C.L.R. 465 (Australia), with which contrast *Kruber v. Grzesiak* [1963] V.L.R. 621. See also *Parukey v. Parukey* [1945] 4 D.L.R. 81; *Eisener v. Maxwell* [1951] 3 D.L.R. 345; *Hollebone v. Barnard* [1954] O.R. 236; *Dahlberg v. Naydiuk* (1970) 10 D.L.R. (2d) 319 (Canada). See Fridman, "Trespass or Negligence?" (1971) 9 Alberta L.R. 250.
45 [1986] 2 All E.R. 440 at 445.
45a However it has been suggested that for personal injuries inflicted by the negligent act of a doctor, assault and battery is an inappropriate cause of action; such a claim should be pleaded in negligence: *Chatterton v. Gerson* [1981] 1 All E.R. 257 at 266 *per* Bristow J.; *Hills v. Potter* [1983] 1 All E.R. 717 at 728 *per* Hirst J.; *Sidaway v. Bethlem Royal Hospital Governors* [1985] 1 All E.R. 643 at 650 *per* Lord Scarman.
46 Below pp. 340–343.

2. VARIETIES OF TRESPASS

(a) Battery

6.10 The law draws a distinction, in terms more easily understood by philologists than ordinary citizens, between an assault and a battery.[47] A battery is the actual infliction of unlawful force on another person.[48] Although it has been said that battery is included within the notion of assault,[49] and in many if not most instances a plaintiff will sue for assault and battery, because both forms of trespass have been committed, it is technically correct, though colloquially unusual, to differentiate battery from assault. A battery could be committed without any accompanying assault, for example where the defendant strikes the plaintiff from behind, without any forewarning or foreknowledge of the attack on the part of the plaintiff. In common parlance, as well as in the criminal law, however, the term assault is used to connote what is a battery as well as what is in law an assault.

6.11 Given the hostile intent to which reference has been made,[50] any infliction of force will suffice, for example, spitting in a man's face,[51] throwing water over the plaintiff,[52] taking hold of someone to remove her when the defendant believed that the plaintiff should give way before her as a matter of precedence.[53] Nor need the act of the defendant involve any physical contact with the plaintiff, as long as the physical injury is the direct result of what the defendant did.[53a] Thus it will be a battery to remove a chair from beneath a plaintiff as he is about to sit down, with the result that he falls and is injured.[54] So, too, if the defendant so threatens the plaintiff that the latter is compelled to jump from a window to escape violence at the hands of the defendant, and in consequence the plaintiff is injured, battery will have been committed.[55]

6.12 The infliction of force must be without the plaintiff's consent and without lawful excuse.[56] So, to subject a person to a blood test against his will, unless there is statutory authority for this, will involve a battery, as

47 *Collins v. Wilcock* [1984] 3 All E.R. 374 at 377 *per* Goff L.J.; cp. *Fillipowich v. Nahachewsky* (1969) 3 D.L.R. (3d) 544.
48 *Collins v. Wilcock, supra* at 377.
49 *Fagan v. Metropolitan Police Commissioner* [1969] 1 Q.B. 439 at 444 *per* James J.; cp. *Bettel v. Yim* (1978) 20 O.R. (2d) 617.
50 Above pp. 113–114.
51 *R. v. Cotesworth* (1705) 6 Mod. 172; or cutting his hair: *Forde v. Skinner* (1830) 4 C. & P. 239.
52 *Pursell v. Horne* (1838) 8 Ad. & El. 602.
53 *Ashton v. Jennings* (1672) 2 Lev. 133; but not touching a man to attract his attention: *Coward v. Braddeley* (1859) 4 H. & N. 478.
53a Or the causing of nervous or emotional shock by some deliberate act not involving touching: see below p. 121.
54 *Hopper v. Reeve* (1817) 7 Taunt. 698.
55 Cp. *Gray v. Barr* [1971] 2 Q.B. 554, no intention to hurt but only to frighten the deceased, but death resulted.
56 *Fagan v. Metropolitan Police Commissioner, supra* at 444; *Attorney General's Reference (No. 6 of 1980)* [1981] 2 All E.R. 1057 at 1058 *per* Lane C.J. See further below p. 131.

well as assault.[57] However a battery may occur even though the plaintiff is ignorant that it has taken place. The plaintiff may consent to an operation, and be anaesthetised. While unconscious the defendant may perform acts not within the scope of the plaintiff's consent, and not justified on grounds of necessity or otherwise.[58] In such circumstances the defendant is guilty of battery.

6.13 A defendant guilty of trespass to the person may also be liable criminally if the battery in question involved the commission of a crime, such as rape or indecent assault. At the present time the old rule[59] that a tort action could not be brought, if it also involved the commission of a felony, until the crime had been prosecuted, has been abolished.[60] Whether exemplary or punitive damages may be obtained in an action for battery may depend upon the nature of the circumstances. Such damages have been awarded in jurisdictions which recognise to a fuller extent the power of a common law court to award exemplary or punitive damages. In England, however, the decision of the House of Lords in *Rookes v. Barnard*[61] may preclude such awards, save in very exceptional instances, i.e. where the defendant's conduct has been in contumelious disregard of the plaintiff's rights.[62] Aggravated damages, however, may be awarded if the circumstances are such as to indicate that the battery was committed in some particularly atrocious form or inflicted more than normally grievous harm on the plaintiff. Thus in *W. v. Meah*[63] the plaintiffs were awarded a measure of aggravated damages when they suffered rape and sexual assault at the hands of the defendant, who had been sentenced to life imprisonment for these and other similar crimes. Despite the distressing and sensational circumstances of the plaintiffs' injuries, Woolf J. said that thc court must bear in mind that an award in this case should bear a proper relationship to awards made by the courts in more conventional personal injury cases.[64] As he pointed out, very often the physical injuries sustained by the victims of traffic accidents are more serious than the physical injuries suffered by the plaintiffs in the case in question.[65]

(b) Assault

6.14 An assault is an act which causes another person to apprehend the infliction of immediate, unlawful force on his person.[66] Although assault is

57 *W. v. W.* [1964] P. 67; *S. v. McC* [1972] A.C. 24.
58 Cp. below p. 130.
59 *Smith v. Selwyn* [1914] 3 K.B. 98.
60 Criminal Law Act 1967 s. 1. But prosecution for a summary offence of battery under the Offences Against the Person Act 1861 ss. 42–44 may bar subsequent civil proceedings: *ibid.* s. 45; see *Maspo v. Brown* (1876) 1 C.P.D. 97; *Dyer v. Munday* [1895] 1 Q.B. 742; *Reed v. Nutt* (1890) 24 Q.B.D. 669; *Ellis v. Burton* [1975] 1 All E.R. 395.
61 [1964] A.C. 1129.
62 Below pp. 515–516.
63 [1986] 1 All E.R. 935. See for the further consequences of this case, *Meah v. McCreamer (No. 2)* [1986] 1 All E.R. 943; below p. 342.
64 [1986] 1 All E.R. 935 at 942.
65 *Ibid.*
66 *Collins v. Wilcock* [1984] 3 All E.R. 374 at 377 *per* Goff L.J.

a distinct form of trespass to the person from battery, there is a noticeable tendency in several jurisdictions to assimilate assault to battery, such that the term assault is used, in the courts and elsewhere, to comprehend both an assault *stricto sensu* and a battery.[67] The technical legal distinction between the two is very clear. A battery denotes the actual infliction of force to the person of the plaintiff; an assault is committed when a battery is threatened, though not completed. As Scott J. said in *Thomas v. National Union of Mineworkers*,[68] assault is "an overt act indicating an immediate intention to commit a battery, coupled with the capacity to carry that intention into effect." The tort of assault, he continued, is not committed unless the capacity in question is present at the time the overt act is committed. In the case in question, which concerned picketing at colliery gates, the issue was whether this conduct was actionable as an assault on working miners who wished to break the strike and were brought to the colliery in vehicles. When this occurred the pickets subjected the vehicles to demonstrations accompanied by abusive and violent language. Because the working miners were in vehicles and the pickets were held back by the police from the vehicles, no assault had been committed. There was no possibility that the threats of violence could have been carried out by the pickets.

6.15 This decision brings out two very important aspects of assault. First, that there must be conduct which amounts to a threat of violence, i.e. the infliction of force upon the plaintiff, that would be likely to put a reasonable person in reasonable fear of attack. Hence, (a) the threat must be one which, in its form and given the surrounding circumstances, would be interpreted as involving the possibility of being carried out; and (b) the threat must be one which would affect the ordinary person, not one who was peculiarly or particularly susceptible to fear and apprehension. Thus, a statement that the defendant would run the plaintiff through, "if it were not Assize time", even when accompanied by the seemingly threatening gesture of putting a hand to the defendant's sword, was not an assault.[69] So, too, in *Gavely v. Codd*,[70] to point an airgun at the plaintiff was not an assault, because the defendant had not deliberately aimed the gun at the plaintiff with any wrong intent. To point a loaded gun at half-cock can be an assault.[71] But there will be no assault if the gun is not loaded,[72] or could not go off because it was improperly primed.[73] To advance on the plaintiff with a clenched fist is an assault where the defendant intended to strike.[74]

67 *Ibid.*: and see *Fillipowich v. Nahachewsky* (1969) 3 D.L.R. (3d) 544; *Gambell v. Caparelli* (1974) 54 D.L.R. (3d) 661; *Bettel v. Yim* (1978) 20 O.R. (2d) 617. So, too, in the criminal law, the term assault is used to describe what is in effect a battery, e.g., assaulting a constable in the execution of his duty, e.g. Police Act 1964 s. 51: *Pedro v. Diss* [1981] 2 All E.R. 59; *Wershof v. Commissioner of Police for the Metropolis* [1978] 3 All E.R. 540.
68 [1985] 2 All E.R. 1 at 20.
69 *Tuberville v. Savage* (1699) 1 Mod. 3.
70 [1967] 1 W.L.R. 19.
71 *Osborn v. Veitch* (1858) 1 F. & F. 317.
72 *Blake v. Barnard* (1840) 9 C. & P. 626.
73 *R. v. James* (1844) 1 C. & K. 530, a criminal case.
74 *Stephens v. Myers* (1830) 4 C. & P. 349.

It would be otherwise if he had no such intention. However, in such cases, if the plaintiff, as a reasonable person, reasonably believed that he was going to be struck, or that he was going to be shot, an assault would be committed.[75] Words alone may not constitute an assault,[76] for example, where insults are hurled at the plaintiff.[77] It is otherwise, however, if the words are of a more threatening kind, to the effect that the defendant was going to break the plaintiff's neck, and are uttered by a group of people who surround the plaintiff and tuck up their sleeves and aprons.[78] Inaction will be insufficient.[79] There must be some active measures taken by the defendant, for example, preventing the plaintiff from entering a room and taking his place at a meeting of a society of which the plaintiff was a member.[80]

6.16 Secondly, there must be present the ability to carry out the threat, or at the very least the reasonable belief by the plaintiff that the threat could be carried out. Hence the possibility that an assault could be committed by pointing an unloaded gun at the plaintiff, who was ignorant that it was unloaded. The same would be the situation if the gun were a toy gun, but its character was not obvious to the plaintiff, and would not have been obvious to any reasonable person in the situation of the plaintiff.

6.17 An assault is an inchoate battery.[81] However, whereas a battery could be committed without the plaintiff's knowing that he was the subject of attack, it is impossible for an assault to occur unless the plaintiff knows that he is being threatened. It is the plaintiff's state of mind that is a vital feature of assault. Hence, if the plaintiff is particularly susceptible to nervous or emotional shock, a threat which would have no effect on a person of ordinary susceptibilities may not constitute an assault if uttered to such a plaintiff. In cases in which it has been held a trespass to inflict a nervous shock on a plaintiff by uttering threatening or false words which cause a nervous reaction on the plaintiff,[82] it appears to have been assumed that the words in question would have such an effect on any reasonable person in the plaintiff's position.[83] Whether it is correct to describe such conduct as an assault (still less as a battery) is questionable. The decisions where liability has been imposed for such behaviour seemingly proceed on the basis of trespass to the person, rather than on negligence or deceit. To cause nervous or emotional shock by negligence

75 *Ibid.*
76 *Meade's & Belt's Case* (1823) 1 Lewin 184.
77 Handford, "Tort Liability for Threatening or Insulting Words" (1976) 54 Can. Bar Rev. 563 at 564–573.
78 *Read v. Coker* (1853) 13 C.B. 349.
79 *Innis v. Wylie* (1844) 1 C. & K. 257 at 263 *per* Lord Denman C.L.
80 *Innis v. Wylie, supra.*
81 Because no actual force is required, an assault may be committed without battery: *Jones v. Sherwood* [1942] 1 K.B. 127.
82 *Wilkinson v. Downton* [1897] 2 Q.B. 57; *Janvier v. Sweeney* [1919] 2 K.B. 316; cp. *Brelitski v. Obadiah* (1922) 65 D.L.R. 627; *Purdy v. Woznesensky* [1937] 2 W.W.R. 116; *Cant v. Cant* (1985) 49 O.R. (2d) 25.
83 Cp. *Bunyan v. Jordan* (1936) 57 C.L.R. 1.

or fraud is actionable on such basis, provided that the necessary ingredients of such torts are established, such as duty of care, negligent conduct, an intent to defraud rather than to cause shock.[84] To cause such harm by deliberately making a statement that was intended to cause such harm and calculated to do so is not easily regarded as trespass, in the form of assault.[85] If the shock results from the plaintiff's fear of personal injury, it may be reasonable to subsume such case under the rubric of assault. If, as was the case in the decisions that impose liability, the fear is for or about other persons, not the plaintiff, to consider such conduct as an assault on the plaintiff is doubtful on strictly doctrinal and logical grounds. Perhaps the attitude of the courts can be explained on the basis that such conduct is regarded as being reprehensible and worthy of being treated as actionable. Since such conduct approximates to the type of conduct that amounts to an assault, treatment of such conduct as a trespass appears legitimate.[86]

(c) False imprisonment

6.18 The adjective "false" does not mean untruthful in this context, but erroneous, wrongful or unjustified. This form of trespass involves totally restraining by force or show of authority the liberty of another person for any period, however short.[87] It will be actionable without proof of damage unless the defendant can establish that he acted in the exercise of some sufficient legal authority.[88] As Coleridge J. said in *Bird v. Jones*,[89] "it is part of the definition of freedom to be able to go whithersoever one pleases; but imprisonment is something more than the mere loss of this power; it includes the notion of restraint within some limits defined by a will or power exterior to our own." It is entire restraint upon the will that constitutes imprisonment.[90] Total restraint is necessary. Thus in *Bird v. Jones*, where the plaintiff was forced by the defendant to go back on the highway, no false imprisonment occurred. As long as there is a way out there will be no imprisonment, even if that way involves the plaintiff in committing a trespass on someone else's land.[91]

84 Below pp. 283–286, 254–256.
85 *Contra* in the United States: Prosser, "Insult and Outrage" (1956) 44 Cal. L.R. 40; Restatement of Torts (2d) para. 46.
86 As well it is the intention of the defendant that is material, not his motive: if he intends to bring about such a result the situation is more easily assimilated to assault.
87 Stephens, *Commentaries on the Laws of England*, Vol. 2, at 288.
88 But aggravated damages may be awarded in a suitable case, as may punitive or exemplary damages: *Cassell & Co. Ltd v. Broome* [1972] A.C. 1027.
89 (1845) 7 Q.B. 742 at 744. On the kind of limits that may be prescribed see *Kuchenmeister v. Home Office* [1958] 1 Q.B. 496 (the perimeter of certain airport buildings): cp. *British Airports Authority v. Ashton* [1983] 3 All E.R. 6.
90 (1845) 7 Q.B. 742 at 748 *per* Williams J.
91 *Wright v. Wilson* (1699) 1 Ld. Raym. 739. But the plaintiff may have had a special action on the case for infringement on his liberty. Would this be now an action in negligence? See *Sayers v. Harlow U.D.C.* [1958] 2 All E.R. 342, woman accidentally locked in a public lavatory. Note also the possibility of actions for other torts, e.g. defamation, malicious prosecution, infliction of mental distress or emotional harm, and the availability of the writ of *habeas corpus*.

6.19 The restraint in question must be unjustified. Thus if a person is lawfully arrested or incarcerated, no false imprisonment is committed. What amounts to lawful arrest will be considered in due course.[92] A very different kind of justification was present in *Robinson v. Balmain New Ferry Co. Ltd.*[93] The plaintiff had gone on a ferry boat and then changed his mind. The defendant would not allow the plaintiff to come off the wharf where the boat was moored, until the plaintiff paid a toll (of one penny). The plaintiff had contracted with the defendant to go on the wharf and stay there for the boat to carry him across. The Privy Council held that the toll was reasonable, and was legitimate in the circumstances, therefore no false imprisonment had occurred. A more recent, and important example is the decision in *Williams v. Home Office (No. 2)*.[94] The plaintiff was serving a prison sentence i.e. was being lawfully detained. However he was kept in a special cell and a special way. This was because the Secretary of State, exercising his discretion under statutory powers, had ordered this kind of treatment of the plaintiff. By reason of the statutory authority, this did not involve false imprisonment.[95] Nor did it come within the prescription of "cruel and unusual punishment" under the Bill of Rights. The detention of the plaintiff was lawful and could not become unlawful only because the nature, i.e. the conditions of the imprisonment changed.[96] There would have to be some alteration in the reason or basis for the detention. For example, if the plaintiff has appealed against his conviction, had succeeded, and had not been released, his continued detention in prison would have been tortious.

6.20 There must be some positive act on the part of the defendant to constitute imprisonment. Should the defendant fail to assist the plaintiff to get away from a situation not created by the defendant, the latter will not be guilty of the tort. In *Herd v. Weardale Steel Coal & Coke Co.*,[97] which the House of Lords regarded as an instance of the application of the maxim *volenti non fit injuria*,[98] the Court of Appeal decided against the plaintiff on the basis that no false imprisonment had occurred. There the plaintiff, who worked in a coal mine at the coal face, broke his contract with the defendants, the colliery owners, by refusing to work once he was down the mine. Instead of bringing the plaintiff back to the surface right away, the defendant left him down the mine until some time later, although the lift was available for use. To the Court of Appeal the plaintiff's breach of

92 Below pp. 135–141.
93 [1910] A.C. 295. See Tan, "A Misconceived Issue in the Tort of False Imprisonment", (1981) 44 M.L.R. 166.
94 [1981] 1 All E.R. 1211.
95 Cp. *R. v. Hull Prison Board of Visitors, ex parte St. Germain* [1979] Q.B. 425.
96 Unless the plaintiff was detained in the wrong place not authorised by law: *Scavage v. Tateham* (1601) Cro. Eliz. 829; *Yorke v. Chapman* (1839) 10 Ad. & El. 207; *Osborne v. Milman* (1886) 17 Q.B.D. 514; *Collett v. Gray* (1850) 4 Ex. 729 at 736 *per* Parke B.; all of which support the proposition that removing a prisoner from one part of a prison to another in which by law he ought not to be confined is *prima facie* a trespass: cp. *Arbon v. Anderson* [1943] K.B. 252, as interpreted by Tudor Evans J. in *Williams v. Home Office (No. 2)*, *supra* at 1226–1227.
97 [1913] 3 K.B. 771, [1915] A.C. 67: Tan, *loc. cit.* supra note 93.
98 [1915] A.C. 67 at 71–72 *per* Lord Haldane. On *volenti* see below pp. 131–135.

contract with his employer meant that the plaintiff could not compel the defendant to keep to its obligations under the contract, which included the duty to transport the plaintiff to the surface. The positive act of the defendant need not involve any immediate physical contact with the plaintiff. Thus, to arrest someone, and thereby deprive him of liberty of movement it may not be necessary to seize or touch him, as long as the conduct or language of the defendant makes it clear to the plaintiff that he is not free to move without the immediate response of some physical restraint or force.[99] At the other extreme, it has been suggested that a plaintiff may be falsely imprisoned even if he does not know that his freedom of movement has been removed. In *Meering v. Grahame-White Aviation Co.*[100] the plaintiff was kept in a waiting room to be arrested in due course on a charge of stealing. He was ignorant that he had been deprived of liberty of movement. Nonetheless it was held that he had been falsely imprisoned. This case was hard to reconcile with *Herring v. Boyle*,[101] in which it was indicated that the detention must be against the plaintiff's will, so that it would be impossible to hold a defendant guilty of falsely imprisoning the plaintiff unless the latter knew and objected to that fact, that he is being deprived of his liberty of movement. The view expressed by Lord Atkin in the *Meering* case has been endorsed by the House of Lords in *Murray v. Ministry of Defence*.[102] It is not actual physical contact but restraint that is the test of false imprisonment.

6.21 It is important to distinguish between false imprisonment and malicious prosecution, even though in many instances both torts may be committed when a plaintiff is improperly arrested and then subjected to prosecution. A plaintiff may be arrested but not subsequently prosecuted. The arrest may be lawful and not tortious, despite the later realisation that the plaintiff should not or cannot be prosecuted for any offence.[103] By way of contrast a plaintiff may be prosecuted under conditions that entitle him to sue for malicious prosecution[104] without ever having been arrested in such a way as to justify an action for false imprisonment. It is only where there is an arrest followed by such an invocation of the legal process as amounts to a prosecution for the purposes of the tort of malicious prosecution that it becomes necessary to differentiate the arrest aspects of the situation from the other.[104a] False imprisonment is a form of trespass to

99 *Warner v. Riddeford* (1858) 4 C.B.N.S. 180; *Alderson v. Booth* [1969] 2 Q.B. 216 at 220. It is not necessary that the person who is seized or touched should submit or be brought under control for an arrest to occur: *Hart v. Chief Constable of Kent* [1983] R.T.R. 484. The test is whether or not a person has been deprived of his liberty to go where he pleases: *Spicer v. Holt* [1977] A.C. 987 at 1000 *per* Lord Dilhorne; cp. *R. v. Sadler* [1970] 1 W.L.R. 416 at 423 *per* Winn L.J. As to the arrest of a deaf person which depends on what is reasonable in the circumstances see *Wheatley v. Lodge* [1971] 1 W.L.R. 29.

100 (1919) 122 L.T. 44, especially at 53–54 *per* Atkin L.J.: on which see Prosser, "False Imprisonment: Consciousness of Confinement" (1955) 55 Col.L.R. 847.

101 (1834) 6 C. & P. 496.

102 [1988] 1 W.L.R. 692 at 701–702 per Lord Griffiths. But the movements of the plaintiff will affect the amount of damages recoverable.

103 Below pp. 136–139.

104 Below pp. 580–587.

104a *Lock v. Ashton* (1848) 12 Q.B. 871

the person actionable without proof of damage. Malicious prosecution is a tort that stems from the action on the case: therefore damage must be established. False imprisonment is wrongful unless justified by some legitimate basis for the arrest. Malicious prosecution will not be actionable unless both lack of reasonable and probable cause for the prosecution and malice on the part of the prosecutor are proved. Malice is irrelevant to liability for false imprisonment.

6.22 False imprisonment is committed when the defendant either himself, or through some ministerial officer, such as a policeman acting under his direction or orders, wrongfully detains the plaintiff.[104b] If the detention of the plaintiff is the result of the intervention of a judicial officer, who orders the plaintiff to be taken or kept in custody, even though this is at the instance of instigation of the defendant, the latter will not be guilty of false imprisonment, although he may be liable for malicious prosecution, or some other form of abuse of the judicial process.[105] The action of a court is an independent act, not performed for and on behalf of the defendant who set the judicial process in motion. Therefore if the court orders the plaintiff to be kept in custody, the order of the court cannot be treated in the same way as the act of a policeman or other person who detains the plaintiff at the wish or on the orders or instructions of the defendant. It may well be that the reasonable belief of the defendant that the plaintiff could lawfully be arrested will excuse the defendant from liability for false imprisonment, or other kinds of trespass to the person, in much the same way as a reasonable and probable cause for prosecution will excuse a defendant from liability for malicious prosecution. However, the similarity ends there: and the kind of reasonable belief that is relevant in one tort may not be the same as in the other.

3. DEFENCES[105a]

(a) Accident

6.23 The plea of inevitable accident has previously been mentioned.[106] As a result of several centuries of development it is now clear that a completely accidental trespass to the person is not actionable. That means that a defendant will not be liable unless the plaintiff proves that the defendant acted either intentionally or negligently. The attitude of English

104b *Hopkins v. Crowe* (1836) 4 Ad. & El. 774; but not if the constable makes his own inquiries and then arrests: *Grinham v. Willey* (1859) 4 H. & N. 496.

105 *Austin v. Dowling* (1870) L.R. 5 C.P. 534 at 540 *per* Willes J.: see *Brown v. Chapman* (1848) 6 C.B. 368; *Lea v. Charrington* (1889) 23 Q.B.D. 45. Even if the court acted without jurisdiction in ordering the imprisonment of the plaintiff: *Painter v. Liverpool Gas Light Co.* (1836) 3 Ad. & El. 433. As for the liability of the court in such circumstances, see *Sirros v. Moore* [1975] 1 Q.B. 118: below p. 590.

105a Note the approach to "defences" by the court in *Collins v. Wilcock* [1984] 3 All E.R. 744 and *Wilson v. Pringle* [1986] 2 All E.R. 440: above p. 113.

106 Above pp. 98. For another use of the plea of accident see *Gray v. Barr* [1971] 2 Q.B. 554, where the trespasser was acquitted of a criminal offence but could not rely on his insurance policy when sued civilly because what happened was not an "accident".

courts, not those of other common law jurisdictions, is that trespass to the person involves some kind of fault on the part of the defendant. In reaching this conclusion the courts have been influenced by the development of the law of negligence and the fact that, where personal injuries are concerned, the tort of negligence has become far more important and relevant than trespass, except where the defendant has acted with the deliberate and unlawful intent to commit a trespass. This may be a valid pragmatic result, but it remains illogical in relation to the original concept of trespass as the direct infliction of force upon another. It was for the defendant to justify or excuse his act, rather than for the plaintiff to establish the wrongful nature of that act, once it was shown to have been direct and to involve the necessary infliction of force or threat of force. Although it is open to the House of Lords to reverse the views of lower courts and revert to more classical notions of trespass, it would seem unlikely that this will happen.[107]

6.24 Closely allied to the notion of accident is the plea of mistake. In general it may be said that it is not open to a defendant to allege that he committed a trespass by mistake (unless the circumstances indicate that, as a result of the mistake, the trespass was committed accidentally, in the sense just explained of without negligence on his part). Mistake may be a defence in appropriate circumstances in the criminal law.[108] It does not usually excuse a defendant from liability in tort. Certain mistakes would not be a defence in any event, as where the defendant strikes the plaintiff in the mistaken belief that he is someone else whom the defendant wished to strike. What in the criminal law is termed "transferred malice"[109] would operate. The intent to strike the other person would be considered an intent to strike the plaintiff, and would render his conduct actionable. If the defendant intended to strike a dummy and erroneously struck the plaintiff, in the belief that he was a dummy, or by an erroneous direction of his blow, it would be unlikely that the defence of mistake would apply. As long as there was the intent to strike, accompanied by the necessary hostility[110] and the absence of some lawful excuse or justification, the ingredients of trespass to the person would be present. However a mistake on the part of the defendant might be relevant where what is involved is some plea such as lawful arrest or self-defence. If the defendant mistakenly but reasonably believed that he had grounds for arresting the plaintiff, when in fact such grounds were lacking, he might still be able to rely on the defence of legality as an answer to a suit for trespass.[111] So, too, if the

107 It may be important to reassert the older law for several reasons: (i) there is a difference between trespass and negligence in respect to the proper tests of remoteness of damage, that in trespass being directness, that in negligence being foreseeability: (ii) there may be a difference as to the date when the cause of action arises: (iii) trespass is actionable *per se*, negligence is only actionable on proof of damage: (iv) punitive damages may be allowed in trespass, never in negligence: (v) contributory negligence is a defence to negligence, but it is uncertain whether it provides a defence to trespass.

108 Glanville Williams, *Criminal Law*, 2d. ed. 1961, Chap. 5: Smith & Hogan, *Criminal Law*, 6th ed. 1988, 207–209.

109 Glanville Williams, *op. cit.*, para. 46: Smith & Hogan, *op. cit.* 62–64.

110 Above pp. 113–114.

111 Below pp. 135–141. But mistake was not relevant in *Albert v. Lavin* [1981] 3 All E.R. 878.

defendant mistakenly, but reasonably believed that he was about to be attacked by the plaintiff, and struck the plaintiff by way of defence against this anticipated trespass upon him, the defendant might nonetheless be able to plead self-defence, although he was never under attack or threatened with attack.[112]

6.25 The difference between accident and mistake is clear and founded upon sound reason and policy. Since intent is an essential ingredient of trespass, anything that negates intent should be relevant to the question of liability. The fact that a trespass results from an inevitable accident obviously negates the requisite intent. But the fact that the defendant made a mistake does not necessarily have the same effect. Only if the mistake can possibly refute an allegation that the defendant acted intentionally, or negligently, might it be possible to invoke mistake as a basis for excusing the defendant from liability. Such might only be the case where the defendant's mistake relates to his awareness of what he is doing or to the legality of his conduct.

(b) Self-defence

6.26 A defendant may be privileged to commit a trespass to the person of the plaintiff if he is acting in defence of force that is used against himself[113] or his property.[114] The latter situations usually arise where a defendant is attempting to regain chattels which have been taken wrongfully by the plaintiff, or is ejecting a trespasser on his land. Accordingly those instances of justifiable trespasses to the person are considered in relation to wrongful interference with goods (which has now taken the place of the old torts of trespass to chattels, conversion and detinue)[115] and trespass to land.[116] The present discussion will be concerned with the legality of a trespass committed in personal self-defence.

6.27 There is no doubt that reasonable force can be employed to defend oneself, a spouse or other family members from the commission of a crime, especially, though perhaps not exclusively, one that involves an offence against the person.[117] It may even be correct to say that such force can be used to protect a stranger from being the victim of a crime.[118] Two features must be established before such a plea will be recognised. First, there must be the threat of imminent danger from the crime or other wrongful act, including the exercise of an unlawful restraint.[119] The danger in question must be of injury to the person (although, where an unlawful arrest is involved, it would seem that there need be no fear of personal injury; the

112 Below pp. 127–128.
113 *Cockroft v. Smith* (1705) 11 Mod. 43.
114 *Green v. Goddard* (1705) 2 Salk. 641.
115 Below pp. 142–168.
116 Above pp. 100, 107–108.
117 Criminal Law Act 1967 s. 3: *R. v. Duffy* [1967] 1 Q.B. 63.
118 *Aliter* in former times: *Leward v. Bosely* (1699) 1 Ld. Raym. 62.
119 *R. v. Fennell* [1971] 1 Q.B. 428.

fact that an arrest is improper will suffice, since every person is entitled to prevent himself being detained, restrained, or otherwise deprived of personal liberty, even though he may not be in danger of being physically hurt: the deprivation of liberty is itself a sufficient wrong or injury to make the general principle of self-defence applicable). Secondly, only reasonable force may be used.[120] If the defendant exceeds what is reasonable to effect the legitimate purpose of protection or the release of the threatened or detained party, he will be guilty of trespass. What is a reasonable degree of force depends on such matters as the nature of the threat that is involved, and perhaps the relationship between the defendant and the person who is threatened or detained. The closer that relationship, the greater the force that may be justified. So, too, the more force employed by the plaintiff, or the more violent or serious the crime that is being committed by the plaintiff, the greater the force that may be used by the defendant.[121]

6.28 The defendant need not wait until he is actually attacked before he can invoke the use of force by way of protection, as long as he has a reasonable belief that he is about to be attacked. Even if he is mistaken, and there is no attack, or no crime is being committed, or the arrest of either himself or another person to whose rescue he comes is not unlawful, the defendant may still be able to plead self-defence. In *R. v. Fennell*[122] it was held that where a person honestly and reasonably believed that he or his child was in imminent danger of injury, a genuine mistake of fact would not deprive him of the right to use reasonable force by way of defence.[123]

(c) Parental or Other Authority

6.29 At common law a parent was allowed to chastise his children within reasonable limits. Cruelty to children was, and remains, a criminal offence;[124] but to inflict punishment on a child for improper behaviour was not considered either criminal or tortious, as long as the punishment did not exceed the boundaries of what was reasonable and justified in the circumstances. This parental power was treated as delegable. Hence when a child was sent to school the parental privilege of punishment could be exercised by a schoolmaster in the same circumstances and to the same extent as it could be exercised by a parent, in respect of acts done by the child on school premises or while on the way to and from the school.[125] Thus it was not a trespass for a schoolmaster to punish a boy for smoking

120 Cp. *Hemmings v. Stoke Poges Golf Club* [1920] 1 K.B. 720.
121 *Cook v. Beal* (1697) 1 Ld. Raym. 176; *Lane v. Holloway* [1968] 1 Q.B. 379.
112 *Supra.*
123 Self-defence must be distinguished from provocation which may affect aggravated damages but not the issue of liability: *Lane v. Holloway* [1968] 1 Q.B. 379.
124 Children and Young Persons Act 1933 s. 1.
125 *Cleery v. Booth* [1893] 1 Q.B. 465; *Mansell v. Griffin* [1908] 1 K.B. 160, 947. The modern view seems to be different, namely that the schoolmaster's right to punish is based on the need to maintain order and discipline in the school. Would this survive the change that is mentioned below? Cp. the situation of ship captains and airline pilots.

in the street.[126] But a box on the ear was regarded as an excessive form of punishment in *Ryan v. Fildes*.[127]

6.30 In view of recent developments in the European Court of Human Rights,[128] it would now seem that any right of punishment that could have been exercised by schoolmasters, whether at common law or under statute, has been abrogated. Given the current situation, and modern views on corporal punishment generally, it may be suggested that the common law right of a parent to chastise a child may also have gone. If this is correct, any infliction of punishment on a child, whether by a parent or the delegate of a parent, such as a schoolmaster, would now be an actionable trespass to the person of the child.

6.31 Despite the language of Lord Halsbury in *R. v. Jackson*,[129] a husband would not now have any right to beat his wife, or keep her forcibly in custody, even if she were to commit marital misconduct or acts amounting to a proximate approach to such misconduct. Marital relationships have undergone considerable change since 1891 when that case was decided.

6.32 The captain of a ship, or the pilot of an aircraft, may have authority to commit trespasses, including the forcible restraint and imprisonment of someone, in order to protect the passengers or crew of the ship or aircraft while in the course of the voyage. Such authority may arise either at common law[130] or under statute[131] and may be justified on the ground of necessity.[132] For the safety of property and the persons of those who are travelling, it may be necessary for a captain or pilot to maintain order and security. In these days of terrorism and hijacking, there would appear to be even greater need for such officers to be empowered to act in an emergency without the possibility of subsequent liability. Even if the

126 *R. v. Newport Justices* [1929] 2 K.B. 416.
127 [1938] 3 All E.R. 517.
128 *Campbell & Cousans v. United Kingdom* (1982) 4 E.H.R.R. 293, holding that to administer corporal punishment was not subjecting a person to torture or inhuman or degrading treatment as provided in article 3 of the European Convention on Human Rights, but that refusal to allow a child to attend school because the parents objected to corporal punishment was a violation of article 2 of Protocol 1, which grants the right to education without prejudice to the religious or philosophical convictions of the children or parents.
129 [1891] 1 Q.B. 671 at 679: cp. *ibid.* at 683 *per* Lord Esher, M.R. Note that if a husband uses force or violence to exercise his "right" of intercourse he will not be guilty of rape, unless the parties are separated by decree of judicial separation, decree nisi or divorce, or there is an injunction against molestation or an undertaking in lieu thereof: *R. v. Clarke* [1949] 2 All E.R. 448; *R. v. O'Brien* [1974] 3 All E.R. 663: *R. v. Steele* [1977] Crim. L.R. 290. He will be guilty of criminal assault: *R. v. Miller* [1954] 2 Q.B. 282. Possibly therefore he could be sued in trespass, since husband and wife can now bring actions in tort against each other: see above p. 32 note 90. The situation is different in the United States, where forcible intercourse by a husband can be rape.
130 *Aldworth v. Stewart* (1866) 4 F. & F. 957. But it must be reasonable and may have to be preceded by an inquiry: *The Agincourt* (1824) 1 Hagg. Ecc. 271.
131 Merchant Shipping Act 1970 s. 79; Tokyo Convention Act 1967 s. 3.
132 Which is a question of fact: *Hook v. Cunard S.S. Co. Ltd* [1953] 1 All E.R. 1021 (where it was not justified to put a steward in confinement after an allegation that he had indecently assaulted a child passenger on the ship).

captain or pilot made a mistake, as long as it was honest and reasonable, and committed a trespass against the wrong person, or when, as it turned out, it was not necessary, he ought to be protected from liability towards the innocent party.

6.33 Other forms of trespass may also be authorised or justified by statute, such as the taking of a blood test to establish paternity,[133] or the taking of a sample of breath by a breathalyser to establish whether a driver had exceeded the statutory limit of alcohol.[134] In such instances the extent to which the defendant committing a battery or imprisonment of the plaintiff in order to administer the appropriate test will be liable to the plaintiff depends on the interpretation and application of the particular statute to the facts of an individual case.[135]

(d) Necessity

6.34 The law does not regard with favour the plea of necessity, whether it is raised as a defence in a criminal case or an action in tort.[135a] It is all too easy for a defendant, or an accused, to suggest that he was compelled by the acts of another, or by force of circumstances, to commit a tort against the plaintiff, or the crime with which he is charged. It can be pleaded, by way of answer to an action for trespass, that the defendant was compelled to commit the trespass by the physical act of another, for example if the defendant's hand was seized by another and made to strike the plaintiff.[136] In such a way the defendant had acted involuntarily. Threats of violence against the defendant, however, will not permit him to plead duress as a defence.[137] Necessity, therefore, should not be confused with duress. Nor should it be muddled with self-defence, which may only be raised where the defendant is attacked, or threatened with attack by the plaintiff. It may be necessary to commit a trespass to protect others for whom the defendant is responsible; but the circumstances must clearly justify such a measure as locking up a ship's steward. It it not enough that he is accused of an alleged indecent assault upon a child passenger.[138] However it is possible to plead necessity even if the situation has not been created by the plaintiff himself.

133 *S. v. McC* [1972] A.C. 24; Family Law Reform Act 1969 ss. 20–23.
134 Road Traffic Act 1988 ss. 6–8.
135 As to forcible feeding of persons lawfully detained in gaol, see *Leigh v. Gladstone* (1909) 26 T.L.R. 139; and on the administration of drugs to a prisoner so detained see *Freeman v. Home Office* [1984] 1 All E.R. 1036, which also involved questions of consent.
135a Cp. *Southwark London Borough Council v. Williams* [1971] Ch. 734. See also Glanville Williams, *Textbook of Criminal Law*, 2d ed. 1983, Ch. 26.
136 *Weaver v. Ward* (1616) Hob. 134: *Smith v. Stone* (1647) Style 65.
137 *Gilbert v. Stone* (1647) Aleyn 35.
138 *Hook v. Cunard S.S. Co.* [1953] 1 All E.R. 1021, though the case might be explained on other grounds: above para. 6.32.

6.35 There appear to be no instances where a plea of necessity has excused a trespass against the person,[139] although necessity has sometimes been raised successfully as a defence to other forms of trespass, namely to land or chattels.[140] From those authorities it may be deduced that, if necessity is to be an operative defence to trespass to the person, the danger that gives rise to the need to commit a trespass must actually exist, and not merely be believed to exist by the defendant.[141] Moreover it is the state of affairs at the time of the defendant's act that is the criterion of necessity, not the actual result.[142] Furthermore, the interference must be reasonably necessary, having regard to the situation that exists, and not be too excessive. Lastly, the defence of necessity will not be available where the situation has arisen through the negligence of the defendant.[143] Hence if a trespass is the result of the defendant's negligence, even though unintended, it would seem unlikely that the defendant could rely on necessity as an answer to an action.

(e) Consent

6.36 *Volenti non fit injuria* is an ancient maxim derived from the Roman law of slavery, according to which one who assented to his being sold as a slave could not subsequently demand his freedom.[144] In the modern law of torts the statement means that a person who has assented to being injured by another may not be allowed subsequently to sue that other in tort. A distinction can and should be drawn between torts involving an intent to commit a wrong and those founded on negligence. In cases where intent is an essential ingredient of liability, the plea of *volenti* involves consent to the alleged wrongdoing.[145] But where negligence is the basis of an action, the plea of *volenti* involves what has been termed "assumption of risk".[146] Consent may sometimes be a valid defence to trespass to the person, if the plaintiff agreed in advance, expressly or impliedly, to be the victim of what otherwise would amount to an assault, battery or false imprisonment. Assumption of risk is more appropriate where it is the risk of being injured, rather than the certainty of wrongdoing, that is taken into account by the plaintiff. For example, one who agrees to undergo an

139 See, however, dicta in *Scott v. Shepherd* (1773) 2 W.Bl. 892 at 900 *per* De Grey C.J., 898 *per* Gould J.: see also *ibid.* at 896 *per* Blackstone J. However there are decided cases on forcible feeding of convicted prisoners (*Leigh v. Gladstone*, *supra*) and restraining a dangerous lunatic (*Scott v. Wakem* (1862) 3 F. & F. 328). Moreover necessity might excuse a defendant who, as a surgeon, performs an operation in an emergency on an unconscious patient, incapable of giving consent to such operation; cp. on a slightly different point the discussion of "agency of necessity" in the Canadian case of *Matheson v. Smiley* [1932] 2 D.L.R. 787.

140 pp. 98, 148, 164.

141 *Cope v. Sharpe (No. 2)* [1912] 1 K.B. 496 at 508 *per* Kennedy L.J.

142 *Ibid.* at 507 *per* Kennedy L.J.

143 *Rigby v. Chief Constable of Northamptonshire* [1985] 2 All E.R. 985, where the defence of necessity was raised to the action for damaging the plaintiff's property: above p. 99.

144 *Woolridge v. Sumner* [1963] 2 Q.B. 43.

145 And so deprives the act of its tortious character: *Freeman v. Home Office* [1984] 1 All E.R. 1036 at 1044 *per* Donaldson M.R.

146 And so provides a bar to enforcing a cause of action without negating the cause of action itself. *ibid.*

operation that is reasonable and necessary at the hands of a qualified surgeon consents to what would have been a battery.[147] Hence, in recent years, the argument that liability in such situations should be founded on negligence, not on trespass.[148] One who accepts a free ride from a careless driver of a vehicle may be said to have assumed the risk that he might be hurt if the driver operates the vehicle negligently.[149]

6.37 Certain features of the *volenti* doctrine are common to both applications of the maxim: whether the plaintiff's consent or assumption of risk was genuine or was brought about by fraud, duress, mistake, or the force of circumstances; and whether it is sufficient to establish consent to prove that the plaintiff know what was going to happen, or the risk he was running when he undertook a certain course of action. These will be discussed in connection with liability for negligence, where they have given rise to greater problems and more judicial investigation.[150] The aspect of the *volenti* doctrine that has been the object of more concern in relation to trespass to the person is whether it was legally possible for the plaintiff to consent to the particular type of trespass that was alleged.

6.38 Trespass to the person may be committed either intentionally or negligently.[151] Non-intentional trespasses may now be remediable more appropriately by an action for negligence. In such situations consent, in the form of voluntary assumption of risk, may be more easily established. There are no policy objections that can be raised to the plea of *volenti*, as long as the reality and validity of the consent underlying the assumption of risk are established. Indeed this can be implied from the undertaking of certain activities such as using the highway. In the nineteenth century the courts decided that anyone who used the highway necessarily consented to being injured by other users acting normally and without negligence. It was an inherent risk of such use that one might be injured by other users. Extraordinary risks, however, were not assumed. Thus if one road user were negligent, this created an abnormal or extraordinary risk which would not automatically come within the scope of the consent or assumption of risk impliedly given or undertaken by other users of the highway. Only an express assumption on the part of the injured plaintiff to the particular risk that caused his injury would provide a defence to the

147 *Attorney General's Reference (No. 6 of 1980)* [1981] 2 All E.R. 1057 at 1059 *per* Lord Lane C.J. Note, however, the argument that such acts are not trespasses because they are not "hostile", which was not regarded by Wood J. in *T. v. T.* [1988] 1 All E.R. 613 as a sufficient defence or denial of liability.

148 *Chatterton v. Gerson* [1981] 1 All E.R. 257; *Hills v. Potter* [1983] 3 All E.R. 716 at 728 *per* Hirst J.; *Sidmay v. Bethlem Royal Hospital Governors* [1985] 1 All E.R. 643 at 650 *per* Lord Scarman.

149 Below p. 351; but see *Chatterton v. Gerson*, para. 6.08 *supra* on the irrelevance of the doctrine of "informed consent" in English law, as finally determined by the House of Lords in *Sidmay v. Bethlem Royal Hospital Governors*, *supra*, rejecting the decision of the Supreme Court of Canada in *Reibl v. Hughes* (1980) 114 D.L.R. (3d) 1: below pp. 353–354.

150 Below pp. 348–356.

151 Above pp. 116–117.

negligent defendant.[152] Intentional trespasses are treated differently. The law is more circumspect about permitting the defendant to raise the plea of *volenti* or consent.[153]

6.39 No person can licence another to commit a crime, said Swift J. in *R. v. Donovan.*[154] There are many acts in themselves harmless and lawful which become unlawful only if they are done without the consent of the person affected. As a general rule it is an unlawful act to beat another person with such a degree of violence that the infliction of bodily harm is a probable consequence and when such act is proved consent is immaterial. In that case, therefore, it was not a defence to a criminal charge, and would not have been to an action for assault and battery, that the person beaten by the defendant with a cane for his gratification consented to the act. Two distinct situations may be considered. In the first, the plaintiff and defendant are involved in mutual assaults, in a fight. It was thought at one time that if the parties consented to the fight neither could sue the other for assault, since both had consented to being hurt at the hands of the other. This only applied where parties decided to fight with their fists. If a weapon or something of that nature were employed, or excessive force was otherwise used, the situation would be different. The one who used the weapon or excessive force would be liable, and could not plead consent as a defence. So, too, if the particular form of fighting was itself illegal or unlawful, consent would not be a defence. These propositions could be deduced from the decision and judgments in *R. v. Coney.*[155] This, which was a criminal case, concerned the legality of prize fighting, and the question whether the fighters and those who watched the fight were guilty of committing or aiding and abetting criminal assaults. Various reasons were given by the different members of the court. A different approach was adopted in *Attorney General's Reference (No. 6 of 1980).*[156] The court rejected the view that an act, even if consensual, would be an assault if it occurred

152 *Holmes v. Mather* (1875) L.R. 10 Ex. 261 at 267 *per* Bramwell L.J.; *River Wear Commissioners v. Adamson* (1877) 2 App. Cas. 743 at 767 *per* Lord Blackburn: *Gayler & Pope v. Davies & Son* [1924] K.B. 75.

153 Hence the need to show that the consent was real, i.e. not vitiated by fraud: cp. *Hegerty v. Shine* (1878) 14 Cox C.C. 145; *R. v. Williams* [1923] 1 K.B. 340, a criminal case, and the Canadian criminal case of *Bolduc v. R.* [1967] S.C.R. 677; cp. the discussion in relation to criminal law in Glanville Williams, *Textbook of Criminal Law*, 2d ed. 1983, Ch. 25, especially at 559–568; or lack of capacity, on which see now the Family Law Reform Act 1969 s. 8(1) on consent to medical and dental treatment by a child between 16 and 18 years old. Consent may be dispensed with if a medical procedure is necessary and there is a lack of capacity through childhood or other inability such as unconsciousness: Skegg, "A Justification for Medical Proceedings Performed Without Consent", (1974) 90 L.Q.R. 512; Bates, "Consenting to the Necessary" (1972) 46 Austr.L.J. 73; and see Skegg, "Consent to Medical Proceedings on Minors" (1973) 36 M.L.R. 370. Such consent may be given against the wishes of the parents of a mongoloid child: *Re B. (a minor)* [1981] 1 W.L.R. 1421: cp. the Canadian case, *Re Superintendent of Family and Children Services and Dawson* (1983) 145 D.L.R. (3d) 610, and *Gillick v. West Norfolk and Wisbech Area Health Authority* [1986] A.C. 112.

154 [1934] K.B. 458 at 507.

155 (1882) 8 Q.B.D. 534: cp. *Wade v. Martin* [1955] 3 D.L.R. 635; *Murphy v. Culhinane* [1976] 3 W.L.R. 458; *Lane v. Holloway* [1968] 1 Q.B. 379. Note also the effect of the maxim, *ex turpi causa non oritur actio*: below p. 369.

156 [1981] 2 All E.R. 1057 at 1059. On which see Glanville Williams, *Textbook of Criminal Law* 2nd ed. 1983 pp. 582–593.

in public on the ground that it constituted a breach of the peace and was therefore itself unlawful. That approach belonged to the time when there was little by way of a police force and prize fights were a source of civil disturbance. Regular policing has produced a different state of affairs. Statutory offences and bylaws provide a sufficient sanction against true cases of public disorder. So do common law offences such as affray. The test today is whether the public interest favours or disfavours the kind of assault or trespass that is involved. Except where a minor struggle occurs, it is not in the public interest that people should try to cause or should cause each other actual bodily harm for no good reason. Whether the acts occur in public or in private is immaterial. If actual bodily harm is intended and/or caused, an assault will be committed. This means that most fights will be unlawful, regardless of consent. Although these remarks were made in what was a criminal law context, it would be surprising if the courts did not also apply them to tort situations where trespass to the person is alleged. Hence it may be said that, unless the occasion is too trivial to merit the application of the law, a party to a fight, whether using his fists or something else, will be guilty of trespass and will not be able to plead the consent of the injured party by way of defence.

6.40 The situation will be different, however, if the trespass occurs in the course of a properly conducted game or sport (just as it will be different if the trespass takes place by way of lawful chastisement or correction, reasonable surgical interference, or a dangerous exhibition). Such trespass may be justified as involving the exercise of a legal right, in the case of chastisement or correction, or as needed in the public interest, as in the case of surgical treatment.[157]

6.41 Thus the law differentiates between lawful and unlawful games and sports. Consent is easily implied to what would otherwise be batteries on the part of a person participating in a lawful game or sport, provided that the acts which cause the trespass are not unlawful in themselves, or contrary to the rules and practices of the game or sport.[158] It will be different, however, if the sport is in itself illegal, as was the prize fighting in *R. v. Coney*, or the act complained of occurred in contravention of the rules or practices of a lawful sport.[159] The public interest, as it was put in 1981, will not render legitimate and consensual trespasses of that nature: they are unwarranted and unnecessary for the proper performance of the sport or the attainment of the aims of the game.

6.42 A person may not be required to consent to what amounts to an assault and battery, unless statute makes the act necessary. Thus it has been held that a plaintiff could not be required to consent to a medical examination to determine his life expectancy, when the plaintiff was

157 [1981] 2 All E.R. 1057 at 1059.
158 *R. v. Bradshaw* (1874) 14 Cox C.C. 83.
159 A participant does not consent to illegal blows or acts e.g. hitting below the belt in a properly conducted boxing match, or a foul tackle in a rugby football game.

claiming damages from the defendant for a tort committed against him. Such an examination or test would be an invasion of the plaintiff's personal liberty; and is only justified where Parliament has imposed or authorised the imposition of such a requirement and has provided an appropriate sanction for non-compliance.[160] On the other hand, in *Freeman v. Home Office*[161] it was decided that a prisoner in gaol could, and did voluntarily consent to the administration of drugs to him by the prison doctor. The plaintiff was serving a term of life imprisonment in the highest security category. He had a severe personality disorder and had behaved in a disruptive way. In consequence injections of a drug were given to him to control his behaviour. The plaintiff argued that he had not submitted voluntarily to the administration of the drugs, which was negated by the evidence; and that in any event he could not freely give such consent as he was a prisoner subjected to constraint by prison officials. The court held that, while it might be difficult to establish that real consent had been given, there was no automatic barrier to the application of the doctrine of consent in such a case, as long as real, true consent could be shown, as it had been in this instance.

(f) Lawful arrest[161a]

6.43 Whether or not a person has been arrested depends not on the legality of the arrest but on whether he has been deprived of his liberty to go where he pleases.[162] A person may be arrested without his being actually seized or touched, as long as some form of words is used by the party arresting him and those words are calculated to, and do, bring to his notice that he is under compulsion, to which he submitted.[163] If the one being arrested is deaf, the arrester must do what is reasonable in the circumstances to bring home the fact of arrest. This will also be the situation if the person arrested cannot understand English.[164] The purpose of arrest has long been to secure the detention of someone who is suspected of committing a criminal offence "to dispel or confirm the reasonable suspicion by questioning the suspect or seeking further evidence with his assistance".[165] Arrest is also the first stage in the criminal process, whereby a suspected offender can be brought before a magistrate and charged with

160 *Baugh v. Delta Water Fittings* [1971] 3 All E.R. 258, with which contrast *Edwardes v. Thames Board Mills Ltd* [1969] 2 Q.B. 67, said in the later case to be wrongly decided. Cp. on the assessment of damages if the plaintiff unreasonably refuses to undergo corrective surgery, *Janiak v. Ippolito* [1985] 1 S.C.R. 146.

161 [1984] 1 All E.R. 1036.

161a Feldman, *The Law Relating to Entry, Search and Seizure*, 1986, Chs. 8, 9.

162 *Spicer v. Holt* [1977] A.C. 987 at 1000 *per* Lord Dilhorne; cp. *R. v. Sadler* [1970] 1 W.L.R. 416 at 423 *per* Winn L.J.

163 *Alderson v. Booth* [1969] 2 Q.B. 216; *Hussien v. Chong Fook Kam* [1970] A.C. 942 at 947 *per* Lord Devlin: ". . . where by words or conduct he makes it clear that he will, if necessary, use force to prevent the individual from going where he pleases."

164 *Wheatley v. Lodge* [1971] 1 W.L.R. 29.

165 *Holgate-Mohammed v. Duke* [1984] 1 All E.R. 1054 at 1059 *per* Lord Diplock.

the offence.[166] The power of arrest is therefore of considerable importance. Its abuse is considered a grievous wrong. As Lord Diplock pointed out in *Holgate-Mohammed v. Duke*,[167] "there is inevitably the potentiality of conflict between the public interest in preserving the liberty of the individual and the public interest in the detection of crime and the bringing to justice of those who commit it". The compromise which English common and statutory law has evolved for the accommodation of the two rival public interests while the police take the first steps of identification of offenders and obtaining sufficient evidence admissible in a court of law against persons suspected of committing offences is twofold. First: no person may be arrested without warrant, i.e. without the intervention of a judicial process, unless the constable arresting has reasonable cause to suspect him of being guilty of an arrestable offence. Such arrest is the only means by which a person can be compelled against his will to come to or remain in any police station. Secondly: a suspect so arrested and detained in custody must be brought before a magistrates' court as soon as practicable, generally within 24 hours. Otherwise, save in serious cases, he must be released on bail.[168]

6.44 Arrest is a continuing act and it continues until the person restrained is either released from custody or, having been brought before a magistrate, is remanded in custody by the magistrate's judicial act.[169] The mere act of taking a person into custody does not constitute an "arrest" unless that person knows, either at the time when he is first taken into custody or as soon thereafter as is reasonably practicable to inform him, on what charge or on suspicion of what crime he was being arrested.[170]

6.45 If a person is wrongly arrested, he or she will have an action in trespass against the arrester, whether the one perpetrating the arrest is a private citizen or a police officer. Moreover, if an arrest is wrongful it is lawful for the person arrested to resist arrest: and actions taken to resist an unlawful arrest are neither torts nor crimes (as long as the one resisting does not indulge in conduct that is excessive or unwarranted having regard to the nature of the threat posed by the attempt at unlawful

166 Unless the attendance of a suspected offender is secured by a summons issued by a magistrate on information laid before him (*Halsbury's Laws of England*, 4th ed. 1976, Vol. II, paras. 89–91); in which event no trespass will be committed, although, if the summons is issued improperly there may be liability for malicious prosecution on the part of the person laying the information: below pp. 580–581.

167 [1984] 1 All E.R. 1054 at 1059.

168 *Ibid.* See the Magistrates' Courts Act 1980 s. 43 as amended by the Police and Criminal Evidence Act 1984 s. 47(8).

169 *Holgate-Mohammed v. Duke*, *supra* at 1056 *per* Lord Diplock.

170 *Ibid.*: *Christie v. Leachinsky* [1947] A.C. 573: and see the Police and Criminal Evidence Act 1984 s. 28 on the information to be given by a private citizen or a police officer to the arrested person on arrest if the arrest is to be lawful (where the arrest is effected otherwise than by informing the arrested person that he is under arrest, or even, in the case of arrest by a constable, if the fact of arrest is obvious). See also *Abbassy v. Commissioner of Police of the Metropolis* [1990] 1 All E.R. 193. On subsection 3 of this section see *D.P.P. v. Hawkins* [1988] 3 All E.R. 673 on the powers of the police officer between the time of the arrest and the time when it becomes practicable for him to inform the arrested person of the reason for his arrest.

arrest).[171] Furthermore, if police attempt to enter premises in order to effect an unlawful arrest,[172] they may be guilty of trespass to land.[173] It is a matter of considerable importance, therefore, to distinguish lawful from unlawful arrest. In this regard two vital distinctions must be drawn. The first is between common law and statutory powers of arrest.[174] The second is between arrest without a warrant issued by a judicial officer, and arrest under such a warrant.

6.46 The Criminal Law Act 1967[175] preserved the common law power of arrest without warrant that existed in respect of breaches of the peace that were being committed in the presence of a private person or a police officer, or which were reasonably apprehended.[176] That Act also abolished the distinction between felonies and misdemeanours, with the result that the power of arrest in the case of felonies that could be exercised by citizens and police officers (with some differences as to when such power might be exercised)[177] disappeared. In place of the previous law, that Act drew a distinction between arrestable and non-arrestable offences. The result was that, without a warrant, private citizens and police officers were endowed with certain powers of arrest in the case of arrestable offences, as defined in that Act. The difference was that police officers could arrest on reasonable

171 I.e. he may rely on the plea of self-defence: *Pedro v. Diss* [1981] 2 All E.R. 59 at 64 *per* Lord Lane C.J., relying on *Kemlin v. Gardiner* [1967] 2 Q.B. 510; *Wershof v. Commissioner of Police for the Metropolis* [1978] 3 All E.R. 540; *R. v. Jones* [1978] 3 All E.R. 1098, where the defendant was entitled to use reasonable force to resist a forcible attempt to take his fingerprints at the wrong place (on fingerprinting of offenders see now the Police and Criminal Evidence Act 1984 s. 27). Contrast *Donnelly v. Jackman* [1970] 1 W.L.R. 562: *Kemlin v. Gardiner, supra.* But the defence was not open to the accused in *Albert v. Lavin* [1981] 3 All E.R. 878 because the accused was causing a breach of the peace and anyone, not only a police officer, could have detained him.

172 Or an unlawful seizure of goods without a warrant, even if someone has been arrested: *McCone v. Oxford* [1982] 3 W.L.R. 423; or an unlawful demand to take a breath sample, *Morris v. Beardmore* [1981] A.C. 446; cp. *Fox v. Chief Constable of Gwent* [1985] 1 All E.R. 230.

173 Not if the police have the power to enter and arrest without a warrant: *Swales v. Cox* [1981] Q.B. 849; nor if the police are recapturing an escaped prisoner: *Hart v. Chief Constable of Kent* [1983] R.T.R. 484; nor if the police are invited into the house: *Faulkner v. Willetts* [1982] R.T.R. 159; nor if the police have, or reasonably think that they have legitimate business with the occupier even if a notice tells the police to keep out: *Surok v. Mannion* [1982] R.T.R. 321.

174 Apart from the general statute considered below, certain statutes may give specific powers of arrest under certain conditions: e.g., the Northern Ireland (Emergency Powers) Act 1978, on which see *McKee v. Chief Constable for Northern Ireland* [1985] 1 All E.R. 1; Town Police Clauses Act 1847, on which see *Wills v. Bowley* [1982] 2 All E.R. 654 (this statutory power has now been revoked: Police and Criminal Evidence Act 1984 s. 26(1)).

175 1967, c. 58, s. 2.

176 See *Wershof v. Commissioner of Police for the Metropolis* [1978] 3 All E.R. 540 at 550 *per* May J.; *R. v. Howell* [1982] Q.B. 417 at 426. The onus of proving reasonable grounds for suspicion is on the person arresting: *Dallison v. Caffery* [1965] 1 Q.B. 348. This does not mean *prima facie* proof of the offence, so there is no need for such belief to be based on admissible evidence: *Hussien v. Chung Fooh Kam* [1970] A.C. 942; *Dumbell v. Roberts* [1944] 1 All E.R. 320; *McArdle v. Egan* (1934) 150 L.T. 412.

177 *Walters v. W.H. Smith* [1914] 1 K.B. 595; *Beckwith v. Philbey* (1827) 6 B. & C. 635; *Dumbell v. Roberts, supra.* A private person who arrests without a warrant has to take the arrested person before a magistrate or police officer as soon as reasonably practicable: *John Lewis & Co. v. Tims* [1952] A.C. 676. See, generally, Potts, "Common Law and the Legal Fiction of the Citizen Policeman" (1984) 13 Anglo-American L.R. 53.

suspicion of the commission of such an offence, even if no offence had been committed, as long as there were reasonable grounds for believing that it had been. They could also arrest someone who was reasonably suspected of being about to commit such an offence.[178] A private citizen could only arrest without warrant someone who was committing an arrestable offence or was reasonably suspected of committing such an offence.[179] Anyone who was effecting or assisting in the lawful arrest of offenders or suspected offenders was empowered under the statute to use such force as was reasonable in the circumstances.[180] That provision replaced the older common law on the question of justification of the use of force to effect an arrest.[181]

6.47 The section of the Criminal Law Act 1967 which dealt with "arrestable offences" and the power of arrest has now been repealed and replaced by the Police and Criminal Evidence Act 1984,[182] which was passed as a result of the Report of the Royal Commission on Criminal Procedure,[183] although the later statute has not affected the provision of the earlier Act dealing with the use of force while arresting. The result would seem to be that there are now no common law powers of arrest without warrant.[183a] The legality of an arrest without warrant depends on the provisions of the 1984 Act. Arrest under warrant[184] will also depend upon whether a warrant has been properly issued by a magistrate, and has been properly used by the police officer. Thus if a police officer acts under an invalid warrant, his arrest of the person named in the warrant will be a trespass.[185] If the police officer arrests the wrong person, although he acts under a valid warrant, he will be liable for trespass, i.e. false imprisonment.[186] But it may not be necessary for the police officer to have the warrant in his possession at the time he arrests the person named in the warrant.[187]

178 Criminal Law Act 1967 s. 2(4) and (5); they could also enter, if need be by force, and search any place where the person to be arrested was or was reasonably suspected to be: *ibid.* s. 2(6).
179 *Ibid.* s. 2(2) and (3).
180 *Ibid.* s. 3(1).
181 *Ibid.* s. 3(2).
182 1984, c. 60, s. 121(1), Schedule 7, Part I: brought into effect by S.I. 1985 No. 1934, as from 1 January 1986.
183 1981 Cmnd. 8092.
183a Unless they are preserved by s. 25 of the Police and Criminal Evidence Act 1984, which sets out the conditions under which a constable can arrest without warrant for a non-arrestable offence and then states, in s. 25(6): "this section shall not prejudice any power of arrest conferred apart from this section." Is this intended to deal with the common law power of arrest without warrant of a police officer and a private citizen? Or is it intended to make the provisions of s. 25 consistent with those of s. 24? The view has been expressed that it preserves the common law power of arrest for breach of the peace: Birch, "Powers of Arrest and Detention" [1985] Crim.L.R. 546 at 550 n. 43.
184 See *Halsbury's Laws of England*, 4th ed. 1976, Vol. II paras. 92–95.
185 *Horsfall v. Brown* [1932] 1 K.B. 358.
186 *Diamond v. Minter* [1941] 1 K.B. 656.
187 Magistrates' Courts Act 1980 s. 125(3) as amended by the Police and Criminal Evidence Act 1984 s. 33.

6.48 An arrestable offence means: (1) an offence for which the sentence is fixed by law; (2) an offence for which a person aged 21 or over (not previously convicted) may be imprisoned for 5 years, or might be so sentenced but for restrictions under the Magistrates' Courts Act 1980 s. 33; and (3) various other offences specifically set out in the Police and Criminal Evidence Act 1984 s. 24(2), conspiring to commit such offences, attempting to commit such offences, inciting, aiding, abetting, counselling or procuring the commission of such offences.[188] Anyone, not only a police officer, may arrest without warrant anyone committing an arrestable offence, or anyone he has reasonable grounds for suspecting to be committing such an offence.[189] Anyone, not only a police officer, may arrest without warrant anyone guilty of an arrestable offence, or anyone he has reasonable grounds for suspecting to be guilty of such an offence, provided that an arrestable offence has been committed.[190] A police officer may arrest without warrant anyone he has reasonable grounds for suspecting to be guilty of an arrestable offence, if he has reasonable grounds for suspecting that an arrestable offence has been committed.[191] He may also arrest without warrant anyone about to commit an arrestable offence, or anyone he has reasonable grounds for suspecting to be about to commit such an offence.[192] The old distinction between citizens and police officers has been maintained: the former can only arrest without warrant where an arrestable offence is being, or has been committed; whereas the latter may also arrest where there are reasonable grounds for believing that an arrestable offence has been, or is about to be committed.

6.49 Police officers also have wider powers of arrest without warrant, and without waiting for the service of a summons, in respect of non-arrestable offences. These may be invoked where the officer has reasonable grounds for suspecting that any such offence has been committed or attempted, or is being committed or attempted.[193] He may then arrest "the relevant person" i.e. anyone he has reasonable grounds for suspecting of having committed or attempted to commit the offence or being in the course of committing or attempting to commit it.[194] For such an arrest to be lawful it must appear to the officer that service of a summons is impracticable or inappropriate because any of what the Act terms "the general arrest conditions" are satisfied.[195] These relate to the impossibility of knowing or finding out the name of the person to be arrested; the failure or probable failure to discover the arrested person's address for service; the belief that arrest is necessary to prevent physical injury, loss or damage to

188 Police and Criminal Evidence Act 1984 s. 24(1), (2) and (3).
189 *Ibid.* s. 24(4). On the exercise of discretion by a police officer see *Holgate-Mohammed v. Duke* [1984] 1 All E.R. 1054, which dealt with the previous powers under the Criminal Law Act 1967 s. 2(4). A police officer need not specify a particular crime or a technical definition of the offence or refer to his power of arrest: *Abbassy v. Commissioner of Police of the Metropolis* [1990] 1 All E.R. 193.
190 Police and Criminal Evidence Act 1984 s. 24(5).
191 *Ibid.* s. 24(6).
192 *Ibid.* s. 24(7).
193 *Ibid.* s. 25(1).
194 *Ibid.* s. 25(2).
195 *Ibid.* s. 25(1).

property, the commission of an offence against public decency, or the unlawful obstruction of the highway; and the belief that arrest is necessary to protect a child or other vulnerable person from the one who is to be arrested.[196]

6.50 Where a person is arrested otherwise than by being informed that he is under arrest, the arrest will not be lawful unless the person arrested is informed that he is under arrest and the ground of the arrest as soon as practicable after the arrest, even if the fact and ground of arrest are obvious.[197] These obligations apply to arrests by police officers and citizens alike, unless it is not reasonably practicable to give such information because the person arrested escaped from arrest before the information could be given.[198] When arrested by a police officer, or taken into custody by a police officer after arrest by a citizen, the person arrested must be taken to a police station as soon as practicable.[199] Before being taken to a police station, the arrested person, and the premises where he was arrested or where he was immediately prior to the arrest, may be searched by the police officer.[200] This power of search, however, is subject to certain statutory restrictions with respect to removal of clothing, concealment of objects to assist an escape or providing evidence of an offence, and the area of the premises which may be entered and searched.[201] A person already arrested for one offence and held at a police station may be arrested for another offence, if he would be liable to arrest for such other offence if he were released from the original arrest.[202]

6.51 Once a person has been arrested for an offence, in accordance with what has been set out above, it must be noted that other provisions of the 1984 Act regulate such matters as detention of the arrested person at a police station, and the questioning and treatment of arrested persons by the police, including searches, intimate searches, fingerprinting, and the taking of intimate samples.[203] All these statutory provisions affect the law of trespass, since they legalise what would otherwise be batteries, assaults, and false imprisonment. The code of law governing the exercise of the powers of arrest and detention by the police is now a complex, detailed set of rules which will require earnest consideration by the police and the courts before its meaning and extent will be fully understood.[204] The necessity for such exactitude and detail stems from the great increase in

196 *Ibid.* s. 25(3): and see *ibid.* s. 25(4) and (5).
197 *Ibid.* s. 28(1)–(4): (on which see *D.P.P. v. Hawkins*, *supra* note 170).
198 *Ibid.* s. 28(5).
199 *Ibid.* s. 30(1).
200 *Ibid.* s. 32(1) and (2).
201 *Ibid.* s. 32(3)–(8); as to seizure of things found see *ibid.* s. 32(8)(a).
202 *Ibid.* s. 31.
203 *Ibid.* ss. 34–65.
204 See *ibid.* s. 66 and *Codes of Practice*, 1985, 1990, issued by the Home Secretary as required by that section.

crime and criminal activity, the need to give police much broader powers than they possessed before the Act, and, at the same time, the desire to set out with precision the limits of those powers and the rights of those arrested for or suspected of crimes. The age-old conflict between the need to control crime and the desire to protect personal liberty still continues. This statute is but the latest attempt to cope with the problem.

CHAPTER 7

Wrongful Interference With Goods

1. THE LEGISLATION OF 1977

7.01 At common law there were various torts that could be committed in respect of another person's goods. The most important of these were trespass of goods, conversion, and detinue. In addition, if goods were wrongfully seized in distress, the law recognised forms of action that were appropriate to provide the victim with remedy. These were actions for replevin, rescous and pound breach.[1] The history of these different wrongs is complex and full of archaic notions.[2] Its complexity stemmed from the technicalities of the older forms of pleading, the distinction between actions for trespass and actions on the case, and the disadvantages of the modes of trial employed in certain instances. Which action was appropriate for, and relevant to the kind of wrongdoing perpetrated by the defendant depended on whether the defendant had damaged goods, interferred with the possession of the plaintiff, destroyed the goods, disposed of the title of goods, detained or retained them against the will of the plaintiff, or taken the goods wrongfully in distress as a pledge for satisfaction of a debt in respect of which distress might be allowed. Success in an action might also turn on whether the defendant had committed some positive act of misfeasance, or only omitted to act. The title asserted by the plaintiff in support of his action was also material. Trespass was a wrong to possession; conversion a wrong against ownership (although, it may be stated, the plaintiff did not always have to establish that he was the owner of goods in order to sue in conversion). Different defences were available according to the nature of the wrong committed. Damages were calculated differently in respect of the diverse torts.

7.02 Although legislative reforms in the nineteenth century achieved some improvements by the abolition of fictions which underlay the action for conversion (in its older form of trover), and of trial by wager of law which made the action of detinue unattractive to litigants, no serious efforts were undertaken to simplify the substance of the law. It remained a

1 Replevin, originally a remedy for wrongful distress by a lord, became available for other forms of unlawful handling of goods in the fifteenth century: YB. 19 Hen. VI, 6, 65. In practice it has been limited to cases of unlawful distraint.

2 See, e.g. Holdsworth, *History of English Law*, vol. iii 285–287, 350–351, 450, 581–584; vol. vii 405–513, vol. viii 466–468; Milsom, "Not Doing is no Trespass" [1954] C.L.J. 105; Simpson, "The Introduction of the Action on the Case for Conversion" (1959) 75 L.Q.R. 364; Salmond, "Observations on Trover and Conversion" (1905) 21 L.Q.R. 43; Fifoot, *History and Sources of the Common Law*, Ch. 6; Ames, "History of Trover" (1898) 11 H.L.R. 277, 374.

collection of disparate remedies. The Law Reform Committee reporting in 1971[3] recommended revision of the law with a view to reducing the number of separate remedies that might be available; the clarification and simplification of the law of conversion; the elimination of anomalies; and the improvement of the law dealing with the liability of certain bailees. The consequence of the Law Reform Committee's Report of 1971 was the passage of the Torts (Interference with Goods) Act 1977.[4] This statute abolished detinue.[5] However it retained both trespass to goods and conversion, which, together with negligence and other torts in so far as they result in damage to goods or to an interest in goods, are now included in the tort of "wrongful interference" or "wrongful interference with goods".[6] The language of the statute also suggests that replevin, rescous and pound breach are also now forms of the "new" tort. Although some amendments of the older common law relating to these various torts have been effected by the Act, the basic concepts of the older law have not been altered. In consequence it remains necessary to consider distinctly, although with an eye on what the state has done, trespass, conversion, and the other wrongs set out above (with the exception of detinue).

2. VARIETIES OF WRONGFUL INTERFERENCE

(a) Trespass to goods

7.03 Trespass to goods, which stems from the old writ of trespass *de bonis asportatis*, consists of a wrongful interference by the defendant with another person's possession of goods. Like trespass to land and trespass to the person,[7] trespass to goods involves a direct, physical act which affects the goods in question. Unlike the tort of conversion, no attack upon the title of the plaintiff is required for trespass to be committed. As long as there is some interference with possession (which includes the causing of damage to the goods even without their being moved or otherwise affected) the tort will be committed, provided that the defendant's act is direct and immediate. Conversion, in contrast, may be indirect, without any immediate touching of the goods; but it requires some conduct which is a denial of the plaintiff's right to the goods. To constitute the tort of trespass to goods, there must therefore be (i) an interference; (ii) with possession of the goods; (iii) and such interference must be wrongful.

3 *Report on Conversion and Detinue*, 1971, Cmnd. 4774.
4 1977 c. 32: see Palmer, *Bailment*, Appendix 1.
5 1977 c. 32, s. 2(1). One of the shortest sub-sections in the statute book: *per* Megarry V.C. in *Howard E. Perry Ltd v. British Railways Board* [1980] 2 All E.R. 579 at 582. The one case which gave rise to an action in detinue but not also to an action in conversion, viz., where goods are lost or destroyed by a bailee in breach of his duty to the bailor, is now a wrong for which an action lies in conversion: 1977, c. 32, s. 2(2): Palmer, *op. cit.*, 1017–1019.
6 1977, c. 32, s. 1. "Goods" includes all chattels personal other than things in action and money: *ibid.*, s. 14(1). This excludes the operation of the Act from acts involving land, money, choses in action, good will, or intellectual property: but note that infringement of copyright is something like conversion: below note 68.
7 Chs. 5 and 6 *supra* respectively.

(i) Interference

7.04 Any injury to goods is sufficient, for example, scratching the panel of a car,[8] beating an animal,[9] or shooting pigeons.[10] Actual contact is not necessary. Thus shooting the plaintiff's animals in a field and preventing the plaintiff from having access to, and removing them, will be a trespass, as will driving them away from the plaintiff's field.[11] Even moving goods from one place to another, if not authorised or otherwise justified, will suffice.[12] It is the direct application of "force", which, as in other instances of trespass, need only be minimal, as long as it is unlawful, that constitutes a trespassory interference.[13] Even a negligent act will be a trespass, as long as it is direct, and not consequential.[14] Hence to drive a vehicle negligently so that another vehicle was struck was originally a trespass: but, for reasons which have been mentioned elsewhere, such acts became actionable in case, i.e. negligence, in the nineteenth century, and have remained so ever since[15] (though, presumably, now, they will be actionable as wrongful interferences with goods under the 1977 Act). There need not be any damage caused to the plaintiff by the interference.[16] Nor need damage be intended or even foreseen: mere inadvertent damage will support an action for trespass.[17]

7.05 There must be some positive act involving the touching of the goods. It is trespass to take a private letter and look at it.[18] But it is not trespass to look at such a letter without actually touching it.[19] Hence, the only way that privacy can be protected is, *inter alia*, if some trespass to goods can be established.[20] So, too, the interference must be direct. To poison an animal by giving it some harmful substance will be a trespass. To leave some poisoned food about so that the animal will eat it and die,

8 Cp. *Fouldes v. Willoughby* (1841) 8 M. & W. 538 at 549 *per* Alderson B. Or removing a tyre from a car: *G.W.K. Ltd v. Dunlop Rubber Co. Ltd* (1962) 42 T.L.T. 376, 593.
9 *Slater v. Swann* (1730) 2 Stra. 872; *Wright v. Ramscot* (1667) 1 Wms. Saund. 84.
10 *Hamps v. Darby* [1948] 2 K.B. 311; cp. *Creswell v. Sirl* [1948] 1 K.B. 241; *Gott v. Measures* [1948] 1 K.B. 234 (involving the killing of dogs).
11 Cp. *Farmer v. Hunt* (1610) 1 Brownl. 220; *Durant v. Childe* (1611) 1 Brownl. 221.
12 *Kirk v. Gregory* (1876) 1 Ex.D. 55.
13 The defendant may act through some agent such as an animal, e.g. where he trains or permits his dog to fetch the plaintiff's property: *Manton v. Brocklebank* [1923] 2 K.B. 212 at 229; cp. trespass to land by hunting hounds: *League Against Cruel Sports Ltd v. Scott* [1985] 2 All E.R. 489, para. 5.04 *supra*.
14 *Leame v. Bray* (1803) 3 East 593.
15 See p. 112.
16 *Leitch & Co. v. Leydon* [1931] A.C. 90 at 106: *cp.* trespass to land, *Westripp v. Baldock* [1938] 2 All E.R. 779, [1939] 1 All E.R. 279. But this has been denied in New Zealand: *Everitt v. Martin* [1953] N.Z.L.R. 298: cp. Fleming, *Law of Torts*, 6th ed. 1983 at 48; and elsewhere, such as the United States: Palmer, *op. cit.*, 118–119. Cp. the situation with respect to trespass to the person: *Letang v. Cooper* [1965] 1 Q.B. 232 at 244–245 *per* Diplock L.J. But this would leave unprotected art galleries and museums whose property was improperly touched, although no damage was caused. Presumably, the proper way to prevent unnecessary actions is by giving only nominal damages and making the plaintiff pay the costs.
17 *Covell v. Laming* (1808) 1 Camp. 497.
18 *Thurston v. Charles* (1905) 21 T.L.R. 659.
19 Or to listen to private conversations: *Malone v. Metropolitan Police Commissioner* [1979] Ch. 344 at 374–376 *per* Megarry V.C.
20 Or some form of trespass, e.g. to land, or a nuisance is committed: cp. *Lord Bernstein of Leigh v. Skyviews & General Ltd* [1977] 2 All E.R. 902: see paras. 5.26–5.27 *supra*.

will not be trespass (although it will probably amount to conversion as long as the animal is one that can be, and is, owned by the plaintiff).

(ii) Possession

7.06 Trespass is a tort against the possessor of goods.[20a] The plaintiff need not be the owner, as long as he has actual possession.[21] Possession, as noted in connection with trespass to land,[22] is either possession in fact or possession in law. *De facto* possession is not protected as such, but the apparent and actual possessor has rights against everyone except the true owner, or a person with a better right to possess.[23] For one to have possession in law he must have the manifest intention to exclude others and to claim as his own.[24] Is it necessary that he should know that he has physical custody of the goods? This has been a question that has troubled the courts for many years. The problem is that, since possession in law requires an intention, a person who is not aware of the existence and presence of some chattel in or on his land, or inside some chattel which is his, or is attached to the land, cannot logically be said to manifest any intention with respect to such chattel. How, then, can he be said to be in possession of it for the purpose of supporting an action for trespass against someone who finds the chattel? The same problem arises in relation to conversion, where questions of title are involved.[25] In the context of trespass, which is based upon possession, not title, it is important to determine who is in possession or such "unknown" objects, since only the possessor can sue (and one who finds the object may be entitled to claim possession, at least if his discovery was made honestly).[26]

7.07 The question has been litigated where goods were found in the street,[27] on land,[28] attached to land,[29] underground,[30] inside a chimney,[31]

20a For the difficulties inherent in the terms "possession" and "possessor" of chattels, see *Hall v. Cotton* [1986] 3 All E.R. 332 at 335–336 per Stocker L.J., citing *Towers & Co. Ltd v. Gray* [1961] 2 Q.B. 351; *Woodage v. Moss* [1924] 1 All E.R. 584; *Sullivan v. Earl of Caithness* [1976] Q.B. 966.

21 *Ward v. Macauley* (1791) 4 T.R. 481. It has been suggested that there are some exceptions, e.g., trustees in respect of goods in the hands of a beneficiary; executors and administrators in respect of trespasses committed before probate is granted or letters of administration are taken out; owners of a franchise in respect of trespasses before the owner of the franchise can take the goods in question. These are probably not real exceptions: see *White v. Morris* (1852) 11 C.B. 1015; *Tharpe v. Stallwood* (1843) 5 Man. & G. 760; *Bailiffs of Dunwich v. Sterry* [1831] 1 B. & Ald. 831. The various persons referred to may have "constructive possession". It has also been suggested that a right to immediate possession will suffice: *Hesperides Hotels Ltd v. Muftizade* [1978] 2 All E.R. 1168 at 1183 *per* Lord Fraser, where the issue was justiciability in respect of foreign hotels.

22 Pp. 90–91 *supra*.

23 *Armory v. Delamirie* (1721) 1 Stra. 505; *Graham v. Peat* (1801) 1 East 244.

24 *Wellaway v. Courtier* [1918] 1 K.B. 208.

25 Below pp. 164–165.

26 Cp. *Hibbert v. McKiernan* [1948] 2 K.B. 142, a case of larceny of golf balls by someone who was trespassing on the golf course. But see *Bird v. Fort Francis* [1949] 2 D.L.R. 791, where a different view is taken, "because of the need to avoid a free-for-all", *per* Donaldson L.J. in *Parker v. British Ariways Board* [1982] 1 All E.R. 834 at 837.

27 *Armory v. Delamirie, supra.*

28 *Bridges v. Hawkesworth* (1851) 21 L.J.Q.B. 75.

29 *South Staffordshire Water Co. v. Sharman* [1896] 2 Q.B. 44: *Hannah v. Peel* [1945] K.B. 509.

30 *Elwes v. Brigg Gas Co.* (1886) 33 Ch.D. 562.

31 *Moffatt v. Kazana* [1969] 2 Q.B. 152; cp. *Re Cohen* [1953] 1 Ch. 88; *London City Corporation v. Appleyard* [1963] 2 All E.R. 834.

or inside other chattels.[32] All these authorities were fully discussed by the Court of Appeal in *Parker v. British Airways Board*,[33] where a gold bracelet was found in the executive lounge of an airline at an airport belonging to the defendants. Donaldson L.J. summed up the law relating to the rights of a finder and those of the occupier of the land, building or chattel where the disputed chattel was found.[34] In the present context, the most relevant remarks are those which refer to the rights of the occupier. He has superior rights to those of the finder over chattels in or attached to the land or attached to the building, even if he is unaware of the presence of the chattel. Where the found chattel is on or in, but not attached to, the building occupied by the occupier, the latter will only have rights superior to the finder if, before the chattel is found, the occupier has manifested an intention to exercise control over the building and things which may be on or in it. Where the occupier manifests such intention he is obliged to take reasonable measures to ensure that lost chattels are found, and when found, whether by the occupier or someone else other than the owner, to acquaint the true owner of the finding and to care for the chattels in the meanwhile. The manifestation of the relevant intention may be express or implied from the circumstances, including, in particular, the circumstance that the occupier manifestly accepts or is obliged by law to accept liability for chattels lost on his premises. The examples given by Donaldson L.J. of this latter situation were the respective liabilities of innkeepers and carriers. Other examples of this manifestation of intention to exercise control over a building and the things on or in it, are where the occupier occupies a private house or a room to which access is strictly controlled.[35] The airport lounge, in this instance, was not such a place: therefore the defendants were not occupiers who could maintain that they had possession.[36]

7.08 Finders who are trespassers on the premises where the chattel is found, and thieves who come onto such premises in order to "find" goods, may not have possession in law such as will entitle them to sue for trespass anyone who interferes with the goods so found. Other wrongful possessors, however, even those who have stolen goods, may have sufficient possession to enable them to sue anyone who commits what amounts to a trespass against the goods, unless that alleged trespasser is the true owner of the goods, or has a better right to their possession. The reason for this is that even a wrongful possessor, such as a thief, not only has physical possession but also has the manifest intention to exclude others. In contrast, those who may have physical custody of goods perfectly lawfully may not be endowed with possession for the purposes of maintaining an action in trespass. An auctioneer of goods, for example, may not sue in trespass.[37]

32 *Merry v. Green* (1841) 7 M. & W. 623.
33 [1982] 1 All E.R. 834.
34 *Ibid.* at 843.
35 *Ibid.* at 846 *per* Sir David Cairns: cp. *ibid* at 845 *per* Eveleigh L.J.
36 Or title: below pp. 164–165.
37 *Davis v. Danks* (1849) 5 Ex. 435.

Indeed in certain situations auctioneers may themselves be liable for dealings with such goods that were lawfully in their custody.[38]

7.09 Where goods are bailed, for consideration and for a fixed period of time, e.g. in the case of hire, it is the bailee who will normally be regarded as having possession for the purposes of bringing an action in trespass.[39] Indeed, such a bailee may even sue the owner, should the latter attempt to interfere with the goods bailed during the term of the bailment.[40] If the bailment is gratuitious and is not for any fixed period of time, the bailee will not be regarded as being in possession so as to sue in trespass. The bailor will be the proper plaintiff.[41]

7.10 An owner out of possession, as in case of bailment for reward for a fixed period, is unable to sue in trespass, unless the trespass in question has permanently injured or damaged the goods so as to affect the bailor's reversionary interest.[42] This right to sue, for what is now wrongful interference with goods, is preserved by the 1977 Act.[43]

7.11 It should be noted that, under the 1977 Act,[44] it is now possible, which may or may not have been the case at common law, in an action for trespass[45] for the defendant to plead that someone else, not the plaintiff, had a better right to possession of the goods than the plaintiff. The rule of law sometimes called *jus tertii*, as the Act expresses it, is abolished. This is more relevant to conversion than trespass.[46] Nor is co-ownership any defence to an action for trespass, where the defendant, without the authority of the other co-owner, *inter alia*, destroys the goods, or does anything equivalent to the destruction of the owner's interest in the goods.[47]

(iii) Wrongfulness

7.12 Trespass to goods must be the result of an act either wilful or negligent.[48] This means that the defendant must have acted intentionally or negligently.

38 Below p. 161.
39 *Hall v. Pickard* (1812) 3 Camp. 186; Palmer, *Bailment* 177.
40 But the bailor cannot sue the bailee in trespass for an unauthorised use of the chattel bailed: *Penfold's Wines v. Elliott* (1946) 74 C.L.R. 204 at 226–228.
41 *Lotan v. Cross* (1810) 2 Camp. 464; *Ancona v. Rogers* (1876) 1 Ex.D. 285 at 292. Contrast *Nicholls v. Bastard* (1835) 2 C.M. & R. 659 at 660 *per* Parke B., suggesting that the bailee can also sue.
42 *Mears v. London & South Western Railway* (1862) 11 C.B.N.S. 850.
43 1977, c. 32, s. 1(d).
44 *Ibid.* s. 8(1).
45 Cp. *Woadson v. Nawton* (1727) 2 Stra. 777 with *Blades v. Higgs* (1865) 20 C.B.N.S. 214.
46 Below p. 166.
47 1977, c. 32, s. 10(1).
48 *Manton v. Brocklebank* [1932] 2 K.B. 212 at 229 *per* Atkin L.J. Contrast, however, *Ellis v. Loftus Iron Co.* (1974) L.R. 10 C.P. 10. But damage caused by animals may be treated differently: below pp. 258–269.

7.13 Where the act of the defendant is intentional, i.e. where he knows what he is doing and deliberately handles the goods in question, there will be strict liability unless the defendant can rely on a defence such as mistake, self-defence or necessity. These different defences to, or limitations upon liability for trespass have been considered in the context of other forms of trespass.[49] It may not be easy for a defendant to escape liability on one of these grounds. For example, a mistaken belief that the defendant is entitled to the goods will not relieve him from liability,[50] although, under the Torts (Interference with Goods) Act 1977 s. 8(1), such a defendant may be able to claim that a third party, not the plaintiff, had a better right to the goods, and that he acted, or believed that he was so acting, on behalf of such third party. Other mistakes might be more helpful to a defendant, such as the belief that he was acting under some lawful authority such as a search warrant which entitled him to seize the goods in question. A defendant who acts to save his own property, for example, by killing a dog which is attacking cattle belonging to the defendant, may be excused from liability, as long as there was a situation of emergency and no other method of protecting the defendant's property was available.[51] But if the defendant does not have title to the threatened property, no plea of necessity or defence of property will be open. Even a mistaken belief that the defendant owned the property that was being threatened, such as game, will not suffice.[52] But a mistaken belief that there is a situation in which only the causing of damage to the plaintiff's goods will be effective might permit the defendant to rely on the plea of necessity or defence of property. However, there must be a reasonable belief that the steps taken by the defendant were reasonably necessary in all the circumstances. Hence in *Kirk v. Gregory*[53] no such plea was successful. The defendant, a relative of a deceased person, removed jewellery from one room to another, in the honest belief that, when servants and others were around, the goods would be safer so disposed. The goods so moved were later stolen. The defendant was liable in trespass, and could not rely on necessity as a defence.[53a]

7.14 An intentional handling of another's goods will also not be wrongful if it is allowed by law, as where goods are seized under a valid search

49 Pp. 98 and 125 *supra*. Consent may also be a defence, and it has been stated in a *criminal* case that there is no general principle that fraud vitiates consent: *Whittaker v. Campbell* [1983] 3 All E.R. 582 at 585 *per* Goff L.J. If this is correct, then a defendant who obtains possession of another's goods by a fraudulent misrepresentation will not guilty of trespass, although he might commit the tort of deceit: below pp. 452–460.

50 *Wilson v. Lombank Ltd* [1963] 1 W.L.R. 1294; cp. *Moore v. Lambeth County Court Registrar (No. 2)* [1970] 1 Q.B. 560, taking of goods in belief that they were subject to execution: cf. *384238 Ontario Ltd v. The Queen in right of Ontario* (1983) 8 D.L.R. (4d) 676.

51 *Creswell v. Sirl* [1948] 1 K.B. 241; *Hamps v. Darby* [1948] 2 K.B. 311. See now the Animals Act 1971 s. 9: below pp. 265–266.

52 *Gott v. Measures* [1948] 1 K.B. 234.

53 (1876) 1 Ex.D. 55.

53a Note also the plea that the defendant acted as an "agent of necessity", in *China-Pacific S.A. v. Food Corp. of India* [1981] 3 All E.R. 688. But this is rarely a good defence: Fridman, *Law of Agency*, 5th ed. 1983, 120–124: cp. below p. 166.

warrant,[54] or damage is caused to the plaintiff's property when the plaintiff is being validly and lawfully arrested by a police officer using no more force than is reasonably necessary in the circumstances.[55]

7.15 Unintentional trespasses to goods may be actionable where the defendant was negligent. This raises the question whether the onus is on the defendant to disprove negligence, i.e. to plead inevitable accident, or is on the plaintiff to prove that the defendant, although not acting with any intent to damage the plaintiff's goods, acted negligently with the consequence that the goods were damaged. If the incident occurs on the highway, involving a collision between two vehicles, it is now clear that an action for trespass is not appropriate: the plaintiff must sue for negligence, just as in the case where personal injury is caused.[56] So, too, if damage is caused to the plaintiff's goods adjoining the highway, by the defendant's vehicle on the highway, negligence, not trespass, is the appropriate action. Thus if the defendant's car veers off the road onto the plaintiff's land and there damages the plaintiff's car, trespass is not the proper cause of action.[57] Under the 1977 Act, it would seem that in both situations the action is now for interference with goods, or wrongful interference with goods. In these instances it is clear the onus is on the plaintiff to establish the elements of a cause of action, including the defendant's negligence. In other cases, however, the law is not clear. If the precedent of trespass to the person is followed,[58] it would appear that where a trespass to goods is not intentional, the plaintiff must prove negligence, and, indeed, the cause of action is in negligence, not trespass.[59] This would mean that there can no longer be an action for unintentional trespass to goods. However, in the 1977 Act[60] it is provided that contributory negligence is not a defence to an action founded on intentional trespass to goods, while at the same time the Act draws no distinction between intentional and unintentional trespasses to goods, when it provides that wrongful interference or wrongful interference with goods means, *inter alia*, trespass to goods (without any distinction between intentional and unintentional trespasses).[61] Perhaps the better view is that the law still recognises that there can be unintentional, i.e. negligent trespasses to goods; and that, in such cases, the plaintiff must do more than establish that a trespass, i.e. an improper touching of the goods, was committed: he must prove that the defendant was negligent (and, it may be added, that in consequence some damage was caused to the goods, a factor that is not relevant where the trespass was intentional).[62]

54 Contrast *Ghani v. Jones* [1970] 1 Q.B. 693, no lawful seizure, with *Chic Fashions (West Wales) Ltd v. Jones* [1968] 2 Q.B. 299; *Frank Thomas Export Ltd v. Metropolitan Police Commissioner* [1977] Q.B. 952 (where seizure was lawful). Cp. *I.R.C. v. Rossminster Ltd* [1980] A.C. 952.
55 Above pp. 135–140.
56 Above pp. 116–117.
57 Cp. *Tillett v. Ward* (1882) 10 Q.B.D. 17; *Gaylor & Pope Ltd v. Davies* [1942] 2 K.B. 75.
58 *Letang v. Cooper* [1965] 1 Q.B. 232.
59 Cp. *National Coal Board v. Evans* [1951] 2 K.B. 861.
60 1977 c. 32, s. 11(1).
61 *Ibid.* s. 1(b).
62 Above p. 144.

(b) Conversion

(i) Definition

7.16 The tort of conversion, which is derived from the action of trover, involves some act which denies the title of the plaintiff. In *Fouldes v. Willoughby*[63] Rolfe B., dealing with what was then the action of trover, said that in every such case there had to be a taking with the intent of exercising over the chattel an ownership inconsistent with the real owner's right of possession. Alderson B. said that any asportation, i.e. carrying off, of a chattel for the use of the defendant or a third person amounted to a conversion, for it was an act inconsistent with the general right of dominion that the owner of the chattel has in it.[64] A mere taking,[65] it should be noted, will be insufficient to constitute the tort of conversion (although it would be trespass). As Lord Abinger C.B. said in the same case,[66] in which the distinction between trespass and conversion was of the utmost importance, a person who takes goods must intend some use to be made of them, by himself or by those for whom he acts, for the conduct to amount to conversion; alternatively, that because of the defendant's act, the goods are destroyed or consumed to the prejudice of the lawful owner. A more modern definition, uttered when the old writ of trover had become the modern tort of conversion (which is now one version of wrongful interference, or wrongful interference with goods under the 1977 Act), was provided by Atkin J. in *Lancashire & Yorkshire Railway Co. v. MacNicoll.*[67] Conversion is defined as "dealing with goods in a manner inconsistent with the right of the true owner . . . provided that it is also established that there is also an intention . . . in so doing to deny the owner's right or to assert a right which is inconsistent with the owner's right". He went on to say that where the act done was necessarily a denial of the owner's right or an assertion of a right inconsistent therewith, intention did not matter. Hence, as Lord Porter explained in *Caxton Publishing Co. Ltd v. Sutherland Publishing Co.*,[68] another way of reaching the same conclusion was to say that conversion consists in an act intentionally done inconsistent with the owner's right, though the doer may not know, or intend to challenge the property or possession of the true owner. A slightly different approach is found in the language of Bramwell B. in *Hiort v. Bott*,[69] where conversion is

63 (1841) 8 M. & W. 540 at 550. In this case the defendant took the plaintiff's horses off the defendant's ferry-boat and left them behind while the plaintiff was transported by the ferry. This was held to be a trespass not conversion: trover would not lie.
64 (1841) 8 M. & W. 540 at 548.
65 Without any intent with respect to the exercise of permanent or temporary dominion over the goods taken, as in *Fouldes v. Willoughby* itself.
66 *Ibid.* at 547.
67 (1919) 88 L.J.K.B. 601 at 605, approved by Scrutton L.J. in *Oakley v. Lyster* [1931] 1 K.B. 148 at 153; and by Lord Porter in *Caxton Publishing Co. Ltd v. Sutherland Publishing Co.* [1939] A.C. 178 at 201–202.
68 [1939] A.C. 178 at 202, a case which dealt with conversion when a copyright was infringed: on which see *Infabrics Ltd v. Laytex Ltd* [1981] 1 All E.R. 1057, where an action for damages for conversion did not lie because there had been no infringement of copyright since the defendants had not "published" the fabric design in question within the meaning of the Copyright Act 1956. See now Copyright, Designs and Patents Act 1988 s. 96(2).
69 (1874) L.R. 9 Ex. 86 at 89.

described as occurring "where a man does an unauthorised act which deprives another of his property permanently or for an indefinite time". By this last phrase, Bramwell B. obviously meant to refer to an act which indicated that the wrongdoer was exercising control over the chattel in such a way as to manifest to the outside world that he, and not the true owner, was the person entitled to exercise such control.[69a] For, as the statements referred to suggest, that idea is central to the definition and explanation of conversion.

7.17 As Megarry V.C. said more recently in a case which arose after the 1977 Act, *Howard E. Perry Ltd v. British Railways Board*,[70] there are a number of definitions or descriptions of the tort of conversion: and it is probably impossible to frame a definition which will cover every conceivable case. Prior to modern rules of pleading, perhaps even prior to the 1977 Act, it may have been necessary to distinguish carefully between conversion and other torts affecting goods, such as trespass, negligence, and replevin. It may not be quite as vital today to do so, although, even after the 1977 Act, which has abolished detinue (replacing it by the generic tort of wrongful interference), and has made inroads on the previous differences between trespass and conversion, it may be relevant to mark the distinction between conversion and such other types of wrongful conduct. Perhaps the most important way in which such distinction can affect the outsome of an action is in relation to the measure of damages.[71]

7.18 From what has been stated above it will be clear that conversion at common law could be committed in various different ways. This is still true, although the Act of 1977[72] has added one important instance when conversion will now be committed, when prior to the statute the act in question was actionable as detinue. This is the case where goods which were bailed to a bailee have been lost or destroyed in consequence of a breach of duty by the bailee, or if the bailee refuses to yield them up. In this situation there will now be liability for conversion although the defendant has not been guilty of some active interference with the goods, which was the requirement of the common law for liability for conversion.[73] The bailee, who formerly might have been liable for detinue, and

69a Hence even a temporary disposition of goods can be a conversion: *The Playa Larga* [1983] 2 Lloyd's Rep. 171: *I Congresso del Partido* [1981] 2 All E.R. 1064.

70 [1980] 2 All E.R. 579 at 583.

71 Below pp. 171–174.

72 1977 c. 32, s. 2(2).

73 Cp. *Ashby v. Tolhurst* [1937] 2 K.B. 242; *Tinsley v. Dudley* [1951] 2 K.B. 18, where cars were stolen from the defendants' car parks because of the negligence of the defendants' servants, but without any positive act by them. Contrast the case where the servant handed over the car to a thief, under a *bona fide* mistake: *Hollins v. J. Davy Ltd* [1963] 1 Q.B. 844, although an exemption clause protected the defendant from liability. A refusal to help the plaintiff obtain a substitute registration book for a car, which had been lost by the defendant, the lessee of the vehicle, except under certain unacceptable conditions, was held to be a deliberate interference with the property rights of the plaintiff, a positive act inconsistent with the plaintiff's ownership, and therefore a conversion, in *Bryanston Leasings Ltd v. Principality Finance Ltd* [1977] R.T.R. 45.

certainly for breach of bailment,[74] can now be sued for conversion, perpetrated by his negligent omission (as well as by some act of commission).[74a]

(ii) Acts of conversion

7.19 (1) *Taking possession of goods.* To take possession of another's goods will not be conversion unless it involves some permanent or temporary denial of the other person's right and title to the goods.[75] If such a taking is unauthorised it will be a trespass, as was the removal of the horses in *Fouldes v. Willoughby.*[76] Hence, if the goods cannot be replaced, for example because they have been stolen by a third party or destroyed by accident, the defendant who originally took the goods will still not be guilty of conversion, although he will be liable in trespass.[77] A principal or master may be liable in conversion, even though he did not take the goods or originally authorise the taking. Where the defendant's servant took goods from the plaintiff's ship, which was stranded off the coast of Africa, and this taking was unauthorised, the defendant became liable in conversion when he subsequently ratified the servant's act.[78] The original taking of the goods may be lawful, in which event neither trespass nor conversion is committed. A subsequent act with the requisite intent to deny the plaintiff's title will constitute conversion, for which the defendant who took the goods will be liable.[79] However the mere innocence of the recipient of goods[80] would not at common law excuse or exempt him from liability for conversion unless the recipient were protected by one of the

74 Such liability not being affected by the Occupiers' Liability Act 1957 (on which see pp. 382–398): *Fairline Shipping Corporation v. Adamson* [1975] Q.B. 180.

74a But this provision of the 1977 Act would not have affected the outcome on the facts in *Ashby v. Tolhurst, supra* and *Tinsley v. Dickey, supra*, because there was no bailment in those cases.

75 But if temporary it should probably be uncertain in length and of substantial duration: Megarry V.C. in *Howard E. Perry Ltd v. British Railways Board* [1980] 2 All E.R. 579 at 583. There the defendants refused to deliver steel to the plaintiffs, or let the plaintiffs collect it, although it belonged to the plaintiffs, because of a strike of steelworkers which was supported by a railway union, the NUR, thereby affecting the defendants. This was held to be a wrongful interference, i.e. a conversion, within the 1977 Act, s. 1. Cp. *The Playa Larga* [1983] 2 Lloyd's Rep. 171 at 181.

A cheque may be converted by the wrongful collection of the cheque and payment out under it by a bank: this is not conversion of the money, since no specific coins are involved, but of the chattel, the piece of paper, the cheque under which the money is collected: *Lloyds Bank v. Chartered Bank of India, Australia and China* [1929] 1 K.B. 40 at 56 *per* Scrutton L.J. The value of the chattel converted is the money paid out and received under it. However the bank might have a defence under the Cheques Act 1957 s. 4, as long as the bank was not negligent or if the plaintiff was party to a fraudulent transaction: *Thackwell v. Barclays Bank plc* [1986] 1 All E.R. 676.

For other documents see, e.g., *Building and Civil Engineering Holidays Scheme Management Ltd v. Post Office* [1966] 1 Q.B. 247 (trading stamps); credit cards, Cmnd. 4774, paras. 90–91; *Loosemore v. Radford* (1842), 9 M. & W. 657 (title deeds).

76 (1841) 8 M. & W. 540, para. 7.16 above; cp. *Price v. Helyer* (1828) 4 Bing. 597.

77 *Bushel v. Miller* (1718) 1 Stra. 128. However if the one who takes possession then does something to render it impossible to return the goods to the owner, conversion might be the appropriate cause of action: cp. below in respect of destruction of goods.

78 *Hilbery v. Hatton* (1864) 2 H. & C. 822.

79 *Balme v. Hulton* (1837) 9 Bing. 471 at 476 *per* Patteson J.

80 See, e.g. *Ingram v. Little* [1961] 1 Q.B. 31. Or a cheque: *Orbit Mining and Trading Co. Ltd v. Westminster Bank Ltd* [1963] 1 Q.B. 794; cp. *supra* note 75.

common law and statutory exceptions to the doctrine *nemo dat quod non habet*. By virtue of these, an innocent purchaser of goods who mistakenly acquired them *bona fide* and for value was, and still is, protected against liability for conversion at the hands of the original owner. Indeed such a party acquires ownership in the goods, which is the reason why he cannot be made liable in tort.[81] Receipt of goods by a *pledgee* who was in good faith did not amount to conversion, unless and until there was a demand for their return and a refusal to give them up. In *Spackman v. Foster*[82] the pledgee in such circumstances was treated as an honest, innocent finder. Under the Act of 1977,[83] however, receipt of goods by way of pledge will be conversion if the delivery of the goods is conversion. Thus, as with the case of sales by a person not an owner, when the purchaser will not be protected from liability if the sale is not within the exceptions to the *nemo dat* rule, so that the sale will be a conversion, a pledgee will be protected if the pledge comes within one of those exceptions, but will be liable if it does not. The illogicality of the decision in *Spackman v. Foster*, in which innocence was treated as a valid defence although in other instances it was not, has thus been removed by statute.

7.20 That case was also questionable on another ground. It held that no conversion was committed, in the case of the pledgee, until a demand and refusal. However "demand and refusal" was not, and is not still, a conversion in itself. It is only evidence of conversion.[84] Certainly it is unnecessary for the plaintiff to prove that he demanded the return of the goods and that his demand was refused by the defendant in order to maintain an action for conversion.[85] Admittedly proof of a demand and refusal indicates that the defendant's possession is wrongful. However this cannot be taken too far, because not every refusal will establish conversion, The refusal must be unjustified. Thus failure to deliver goods at the moment of the demand will not amount to conversion where there were valid reasons for the defendant to make inquiries before acceding to the plaintiff's demand. Such would be the situation where there was some question as to the plaintiff's right to the goods.[86] In view of the change in the law made by the 1977 Act,[87] as a result of which a defendant may now plead that a third party has a better right to the goods, it is abundantly clear that a defendant will not be guilty of conversion merely because he believes that there may be a better right to the goods than the right asserted by the plaintiff. It follows therefore that the defendant can legitimately make a qualified refusal to deliver the goods to the plaintiff without being *ipso facto* guilty of conversion. His liability will depend upon

81 Below pp. 161–162.
82 (1883) 11 Q.B.D. 99; *Miller v. Dell* [1891] 1 Q.B. 468.
83 1977 c. 32, s. 11(2): see Law Reform Committee, 18th Report, Cmnd. 4774, para 43.
84 *Clayton v. LeRoy* [1911] 2 K.B. 1031 at 1046 *per* Scrutton L.J.
85 Cp. *London Jewellers Ltd v. Sutton* (1934) 50 T.L.R. 193. The demand must be unconditional, specify the goods, and be brought to the notice of the defendant: *Rushworth v. Taylor* (1842) 2 Q.B. 699; *Abington v. Lipscomb* (1841) 1 Q.B. 776.
86 *Clayton v. LeRoy, supra*. Or the goods may no longer be in the defendant's possession: *Williams v. Gesse* (1831) 3 Ding. N.C. 849.
87 1977 c. 32, s. 8: below p. 167.

the reasonableness of the qualification.[88] So, if the defendant states that he will investigate the plaintiff's claim, or that the plaintiff must bring evidence that supports his assertion, before the defendant will surrender the goods, the defendant may not be liable.[89]

7.21 One who acquires possession of goods involuntarily is not guilty of conversion merely because he has had possession of goods belonging to a third party thrust upon him. Stolen goods may be left on premises without the knowledge of the owner or occupier of such premises. Goods may be sent by merchants to householders without any prior order or request. The problem of such "involuntary bailees" has exercised the courts for some considerable time. Legislation has now taken care of some egregious examples of this.[90] The recipient of unsolicited goods which were sent to the recipient with a view to his acquiring them, as long as the recipient did not have reasonable cause to believe that they were sent with a view to their being acquired for the purposes of a trade or business and as long as the recipient did not agree either to acquire or return them, can treat such goods as an unconditional gift after six months from their receipt or 30 days from notice to the sender (unless in the meantime the sender takes possession of them and the recipient does not unreasonably refuse to permit him to do so). This deals with one particular situation of involuntary bailment. Other situations have arisen, and may still arise. Goods may be sent by mistake or through a third party's fraud, without the prior knowledge, consent, or participation of the recipient. The latter will not be guilty of conversion unless he deals with the goods unreasonably, albeit honestly, and the true owner is thereby prejudiced. The involuntary bailee must act reasonably. He need not be excessively careful in respect of the condition of the goods. Thus he will not be liable if the goods are damaged[91] or lost[92] through negligence. But he may not destroy the goods wilfully.[93] And if he interferes with the goods unreasonably, with the result that there is loss to the owner of the goods, the involuntary bailee will be liable in conversion. In *Hiort v. Bott*[94] a rogue induced the mistaken transmission of an invoice for barley from the plaintiff to the defendant. The rogue then called on the defendant and asked him to endorse the invoice to him so that, without any fresh delivery order, he could collect the goods and send them back to the plaintiff. The defendant did so. The rogue collected the goods and improperly disposed of them. The plaintiff, thereby deprived of his goods and their value, claimed that the defendant

88 *Alexander v. Southey* (1821) 5 B. & Ald. 247.
89 Cp. *Clayton v. LeRoy*, *supra* with *Burroughes v. Bayne* (1860) 5 H. & N. 296. The defendant's conduct will be an excusable interference if there is a *bona fide* doubt as to the plaintiff's title: *Hollins v. Fowler* (1875) L.R. 7 H.L. 757 at 766 *per* Blackburn J.
90 Unsolicited Goods and Services Act 1971 s. 3, as amended by Unsolicited Goods and Services (Amendment) Act 1975, c. 13, s. 2.
91 *Lethbridge v. Phillips* (1819) 2 Stark. 544.
92 *Howard v. Harris* (1884) Cab. & Ell. 253.
93 Although he may be able to deal with them in an emergency, viz., if they are perishable and the sender cannot be found or does not collect the goods within a reasonable time.
94 (1874) L.R. 9 Ex. 86; see Burnett, "Conversion by an Involuntary Bailee", (1960) 76 L.Q.R. 36.

was liable in conversion. Although the defendant had acted innocently throughout, and only intended that the goods should be returned to the plaintiff, he was liable for having endorsed the delivery order without authority and occasion to do so. His action was not reasonable.[95] He had acquired title to the goods, albeit by mistake, and his behaviour with respect to the order and the goods amounted to wrongful action inconsistent with the plaintiff's title.[96] However, in contrast, the defendant was not guilty of conversion, because his conduct was not unreasonably negligent, in *Elvin & Powell Ltd v. Plummer Roddis Ltd.*[97] A rogue fraudulently induced the plaintiff to send goods to the defendant. The rogue then sent a telegram to the defendant stating that the goods were delivered in error and he was sending a van to collect them. The telegram was falsely signed with the plaintiff's name. Subsequently an associate of the rogue called at the defendant's premises, showed the plaintiff's card and took the goods, which were delivered into his possession. Here the defendant was asserting no title, nor had any passed to the defendant, even by mistake. The defendant was not denying the plaintiff's title. He had acted reasonably, and was not liable for conversion or for negligence as a bailee (in respect of which it was held that the plaintiff had been guilty of contributory negligence).[98]

7.22 (2) *Abusing possession of goods.* It will be an act of conversion to misuse another's goods. Thus in *Lancashire & Yorkshire Railway v. MacNicoll*[99] the defendant accepted drums of carbolic acid belonging to the plaintiff that had been delivered by mistake, and poured their contents into his (the defendant's) tank. This was a conversion of the contents of the drums. To give possession of the plaintiff's goods to a third party, without authority, is conversion. In the famous case of *Hollins v. Fowler*[100] the defendants, cotton brokers, bought the plaintiff's goods from a rogue who had obtained them by fraud from the plaintiff. The defendants received the goods believing them to be satisfactory for their clients, who ultimately bought them. This was held to be conversion (despite the innocence of the defendants).[101] A bailee who uses the goods bailed for an improper purpose will also be guilty of conversion, as where the defendant used the car borrowed from the plaintiff to smuggle watches, with the result that the car was confiscated by customs authorities.[102] Not every misuse of goods bailed will be conversion however, even though it might render the bailee liable for breach of bailment. Even loss of the goods will not be conversion

95 (1874) L.R. 9 Ex. 86 at 90 *per* Bramwell B.
96 *Ibid.* at 91 *per* Cleasby B.
97 (1934) 50 T.L.R. 158.
98 Which at that time would have barred an action for negligence: see pp. 356–364. Distinguish the involuntary bailee from the gratuitious, but voluntary bailee, who is liable if he fails to take reasonable care of goods and so cannot deliver them to the bailor at the stipulated date: *Mitchell v. Ealing London B.C.* [1979] 1 Q.B. 1, where the plaintiff, a squatter, could sue the local authority which stored his goods.
99 (1918) 88 L.J.K.B. 601.
100 (1875) L.R. 7 H.L. 757.
101 Below pp. 159–160.
102 *Moorgate Mercantile Co. Ltd v. Finch* [1962] 1 Q.B. 701.

(unless there is also some act which denies the bailor's title).[103] A wrongful disposition of the goods will be conversion, e.g. where a pledgee sells them, unless, now, the act of the bailee is protected by the 1977 Act,[104] which, replacing earlier legislation,[105] allows certain bailees[106] the power to sell goods left with the bailee, subject to certain conditions including giving notice to the bailor (where this is possible),[107] or under the authority of the court.[108] A sheriff who breaches the terms of a writ of *fieri facias* when he sells a debtor's goods may also be liable for conversion (unless protected by the provisions of Rules of Court).[109]

7.23 Whether such wrongful dispositions of goods are conversion depends on whether the one who dealt with, or handled the goods had "possession" of them. In *Hollins v. Fowler*[110] the brokers obtained possession of the goods before they disposed of them to their clients. But in *Union Credit Bank v. Mersey Docks & Harbour Board*,[111] the defendants, warehousemen, did not convert goods when they handed them over to a third party after the third party showed the defendants a delivery order signed by the plaintiff and handed to the third party, under which the third party had authority to fill in the blank space in the order specifying the number of hogsheads to be delivered. Here the defendant's possession was not independent: it was for and on behalf of the plaintiff, whose goods were stored with the defendants. It is this notion of independent possession that is crucial to the cases dealing with auctioneers. If the auctioneer has an independent possession of goods left with him for auction, and disposes of them wrongfully, albeit innocently, under a mistake, the auctioneer will be guilty of conversion.[112] If the auctioneer's act is merely "ministerial", i.e. it changes the position of the goods without affecting the property in them so that the auctioneer is a mere "conduit-pipe", his act in disposing of the goods will not be conversion.[113] Receiving goods in custody and then handling them over to another person to pass property to the transferree makes the auctioneer no mere conduit-pipe.[114] Even if the auctioneer

103 But it might have been detinue prior to the 1977 Act. Detinue has now become conversion, with the result that a bailee who does not return the bailed goods may possibly now be guilty of conversion: cp. above para. 7.19.
104 1977 c. 32, ss. 12, 13, Schedule 1.
105 Disposal of Uncollected Goods Act 1952.
106 If the bailor is in breach of an obligation to take delivery of the goods or to give directions as to delivery, if the bailment so provides: 1977 c. 32, s. 12(1)(a), (2), Schedule 1, Part I.
107 *Ibid.* s. 12(3), Schedule 1, Part II.
108 *Ibid.* s. 13.
109 *Neumann v. Bakeaway Ltd* [1983] 2 All E.R. 929; *Observer Ltd v. Gordon* [1983] 2 All E.R. 945.
110 *Supra.*
111 [1899] 2 Q.B. 205: cp. *Re Samuel* [1945] Ch. 408, where the solicitor was held to have acted "ministerially", not exercising an independent possession—a strange conclusion on the facts.
112 *Barker v. Furlong* [1891] 2 Ch. 172; *Consolidated Co. v. Curtis & Son* [1892] 2 Q.B. 495; *Cochrane v. Rymill* (1879) 40 L.T. 44. Cp. *International Factors Ltd v. Rodrigues* [1979] Q.B. 351.
113 *National Mercantile Bank v. Rymill* (1881) 44 L.T. 767: *Turner v. Hockey* (1887) 56 L.J.Q.B. 901. These expressions were regarded as unhelpful by Browne L.J. in *R.H. Willis & Son v. British Car Auctions, infra* at 398.
114 *Barker v. Furlong, supra* at 181 *per* Romer J.

believes that the party who has given him the goods to sell by auction is the owner, when he is a mere bailee, conversion will be committed.[115] So, too, will the auctioneer be liable in conversion if the sale was not under the hammer or by private treaty, but involved what is called the "provisional bid" procedure.[116]

7.24 There must be a delivery of possession to a third party. A contract of sale or an attempt to dispose of goods will not be conversion.[117] However a redelivery of possession may not be conversion, where the defendant has innocently received goods from someone be believes is their owner and, when required, gives them back (unless the defendant had notice of a claim from the true owner, in which event, to avoid possible liability, he should interplead).[118] For a delivery of possession by the defendant to a third party to amount to conversion it must be for some purpose, or under some contract or other agreement which is designed to pass title to the third party, or give such third party rights which are inconsistent with the true owner's right to immediate possession of the goods, for example by creating a lien in favour of the third party[119] (unless the defendant has the express or implied authority of the owner to create such a lien, e.g. in some instances of bailment).[120] The fact that the dispostion by the defendant may suffice to pass good title to the transferee of the goods, under a sale or pledge, will not render the defendant's act innocent. He will be guilty of conversion albeit that the transferee becomes owner of the goods, or is able to claim his interest as pledgee and is not himself liable in conversion to the original owner, the plaintiff. Such situations will arise under the Sale of Goods Act, the Factors Act, by virtue of the doctrine of estoppel,[121] or under the Hire Purchase Acts.[122]

7.25 Since some handling of the goods or delivery to a third person is a prerequisite of conversion, the mere refusal of the defendant to allow the plaintiff to get goods which are his but are in the defendant's possession (as long as that possession was not obtained unlawfully, i.e. by trespass) will

115 *Union Transport Finance Ltd v. British Car Auctions Ltd* [1978] 2 All E.R. 385.
116 *R.H. Willis & Son v. British Car Auctions Ltd* [1978] 2 All E.R. 392.
117 *Lancashire Waggon Co. v. Fitzhugh* (1861) 6 H. & N. 502; *Consolidated Co. v. Curtis & Son, supra.*
118 *Hollins v. Fowler, supra* at 767 *per* Blackburn J.: *Winter v. Banchs* (1901) 84 L.T. 504. Indeed a bailee is estopped from denying the title of his bailor and will be guilty of conversion if he refuses to redeliver (even if the bailor has no title—unless this is known to the bailee): *Biddle v. Bond* (1865) 6 B. & S. 225; *Rogers Sons v. Lambert & Co.* [1891] 1 Q.B. 318. Note in this respect the right of the defendant to plead that a third party has a better right than the plaintiff: Torts (Interference with Goods) Act 1977 s. 8(1). The bailee was not estopped if he had given possession to the true owner on demand, or was acting with or defending an action on behalf of, and with the authority of the true owner: *Kahler v. Midland Bank* [1950] A.C. 24.
119 *Syeds v. Hay* (1791) 4 T.R. 260 at 264 *per* Buller J.
120 *Tappenden v. Artus* [1964] 2 Q.B. 185. Cp. the shipmaster's agency of necessity: Fridman, *Law of Agency*, 5th ed. 1983, 118–119. But this agency of necessity cannot be invoked too widely: *ibid.* 120–124.
121 Carelessness of the plaintiff, the owner, will not estop him from claiming title or suing in conversion: *Moorgate Mercantile Co. v. Twitchings* [1977] A.C. 890.
122 Fridman, *Law of Agency*, 5th ed. 1983, 243–263: Hire Purchase Act 1964 Part III.

not be conversion.[123] However it is suggested, by Scrutton L.J. in *Oakley v. Lyster*,[124] following earlier case law,[125] that a mere denial of title would be a conversion, even if the defendant did not have either actual or construction possession of the goods. That statement was *obiter dicta*, because in that case the defendant had also used some of the plaintiff's goods, as well as refused to allow the plaintiff to get them off land which had been rented by the plaintiff and was now owned by the defendant. The Law Reform Committee in 1971 thought that this dictum was too wide, and was not consistent with other authority.[126] They held the view that mere denial of title should not amount to wrongful interference with goods. Hence the 1977 Act provides that denial of title is not of itself conversion.[127] But to deny the owner most of the rights of ownership, including the right to possession, for a period which is indefinite, whether short or long as long as it is uncertain, is one form of conversion, even if the defendant acknowledges the plaintiff's entitlement to the possession that is being denied.[127a]

7.26 (3) *Destruction of the goods.* Any act which completely destroys goods,[127b] or changes their identity[127c] will be a conversion of them, if unauthorised by common law or statute (for example in cases of necessity to preserve life or other goods, as where a shipmaster jettisons cargo to save the ship from disaster).[128] As Lord Abinger C.B. said in *Fouldes v. Willoughby*,[129] if the defendant had thrown the horses into the water so that they drowned, instead of leaving them ashore, he would have been guilty of conversion. Damage less than complete destruction of goods, with resultant loss of their identity, will be actionable, if at all, as trespass, not as conversion.[130] Obviously, the consumption of goods, for example food or drink, is conversion.[130a] So, too, will be the use of goods to make a new article (*specificatio* to the Roman lawyers) or the mixture of goods with the defendant's in such a way that it is no longer possible to identify which goods belong to the plaintiff and which to the defendant (*confusio* and *commixtio* in Roman law, depending on the kind of admixture that took place).[131] The goods may not be destroyed in the physical sense, as they

123 *England v. Cowley* (1872) L.R. 8 Ex. 126.
124 [1931] 1 K.B. 148 at 150.
125 Cp. *Wansborough v. Manton* (1836) 4 A. & E. 884; *Van Oppens v. Tredegar Ltd* (1921) 27 T.L.R. 504 at 505 *per* Darling J.
126 Cmnd. 4774, para. 45.
127 1977 c. 32, s. 11(3). Presumably, even after the Act, if the defendant wrongfully asserts ownership of the goods as well as denying the plaintiff's title, conversion will be committed: *Douglas Valley Finance Co. Ltd v. S. Hughes (Hires) Ltd* [1969] 1 Q.B. 738; cp. *Bryanston Leasings Ltd v. Principality Finance Ltd* [1977] R.T.R. 45.
127a *Howard E. Perry Ltd v. British Railways Board* [1980] 2 All E.R. 579 at 583–584 *per* Megarry V.C.
127b *Richardson v. Atkinson* (1723) 1 Stra. 576, *McLeod v. McGhue* (1841) 2 Man. & G. 771.
127c *Keyworth v. Hill* (1820) 3 B. & Ald. 685.
128 *Mouse's Case* (1609) 12 Co. Rep. 63 (which took place on an inland waterway: at sea the principle of general average may apply).
129 (1841) 8 M. & W. 540 at 547: cp. above.
130 *Simmons v. Lillystone* (1853) 8 Ex. 431.
130a *Philpott v. Kelley* [1935] 3 All E.R. 106.
131 Note also *accessio*, viz., using the plaintiff's goods and those of the defendant, or a third party, to make a new article, or adding the plaintiff's goods to those of the defendant, or a third party.

are when they are consumed or used to make something new that is different from the original goods (either by themselves or with other goods belonging to the defendant or a third party). They are lost to the plaintiff, however, since he cannot get them back. The result of the admixture may be to make plaintiff and defendant co-owners of the product.[132]

7.27 In this respect it should be noted that there may be conversion on the part of one co-owner vis-à-vis the other co-owner, even though both share ownership, as well as possession, of the goods co-owned. At common law this would occur where one co-owner, without the authority of the other, destroyed the goods, or disposed of them in a way giving good title to the entire property in the goods, or otherwise did anything equivalent to the destruction of the other co-owner's interest in the goods.[133] Thus a sale by one co-owner under the Sale of Goods Act or Factors Act provisions referred to earlier,[134] would be conversion if unauthorised by the other co-owner (but not a pledge, since this does not dispose of the entire property in the goods). This common law doctrine is restated in the 1977 Act,[135] which also makes an extension. Under the Act[136] a co-owner will also commit conversion if he purports to dispose of the goods owned in common in a way which would give a good title to the entire property in the goods if he was acting with the authority of all co-owners of the goods. This means that a co-owner will be guilty of conversion even if his disposition does not confer a good title on the party to whom the goods have been transferred under the purported disposition.

(iii) The mental element

7.28 Conversion can be committed intentionally and deliberately, with knowledge that the goods belong to someone else, and awareness that the act in question is wrongful. Conversion may also be committed unwittingly and unintentionally, in the belief that the defendant has a right to act in relation to the goods. A mistake on the part of the defendant will not excuse him from liability. This was determined in *Hollins v. Fowler*,[137] the facts of which have been given.[138] In that case the brokers were dealing on their own behalf, in order to sell the cotton to a purchaser from them, and with a particular purchaser in mind, namely their client. If they had been acting ministerially, i.e. not in an independent manner but on behalf of

132 *Gill & Duffus (Liverpool) Ltd v. Scruttons Ltd* [1953] 1 W.L.R. 1407. But a totally new article may belong to the plaintiff; see however *Gough v. Wood & Co.* [1894] 1 Q.B. 713 at 719 *per* Lindley L.J. Note also the importance of any contract between the parties, with terms dealing with reservation of title: *Aluminium Industrie Vaasen B.V. v. Romalpa Aluminium Ltd* [1976] 2 All E.R. 582; *Re Bond Worth Ltd* [1979] 3 All E.R. 919; *Borden (U.K.) Ltd v. Scottish Timber Products Ltd* [1979] 3 All E.R. 961; *Re Peachdart Ltd* [1983] 3 All E.R. 204; *Clough Mill Ltd v. Martin* [1984] 1 All E.R. 721; *Re Andrabell Ltd* [1984] 3 All E.R. 407; *Hendy Lennox (Industrial Engines) Ltd v. Grahame Puttick Ltd* [1984] 2 All E.R. 152; *Four Point Garage Ltd v. Carter* [1985] 3 All E.R. 12.

133 Or claimed a right to exclusive possession: *Baker v. Barclays Bank Ltd* [1955] 1 W.L.R. 822.

134 Fridman,, *Law of Agency*, above note 122.

135 1977 c. 32, s. 10(1)(a), (3). Subsection 10(1)(a) also applies to trespass to goods.

136 1977 c. 32, s. 10(1)(b). This also applies to trespass to goods.

137 (1875) L.R. 7 H.L. 757.

138 Above para. 7.22.

another, they might not have been held liable.[139] For this to be the result, the defendant must have been acting on behalf of someone who had control of the goods, in the belief that such a person was the owner, or had the right to deal with them: and the act of the defendant must have consisted simply in transferring custody of the goods, not a dealing with title. As Romer J. said in *Barker v. Furlong*,[140] "the general rule is that where an agent takes part in transferring the property in the chattel and it turns out that his principal has no title, his ignorance of this fact affords him no protection". The distinction is between obtaining an independent possession and passing such possession over, which grounds liability, and acting merely as agent, which does not. It is the difference between an interfering act and an intervening intention. The agent must be more than a mere conduit-pipe. This explains the distinction between cases that have been cited earlier.[141] In at least one instance, however, *Re Samuel*,[142] the characterisation of the defendant's act is questionable. The defendant, a solicitor, handed jewellery belonging to a bankrupt to the bankrupt's servant who, contrary to instructions, delivered the jewellery to the bankrupt. The bankrupt's trustee-in-bankruptcy brought an action against the defendant for conversion. The Court of Appeal held that the defendant was not liable, although he had dealt with the possession of the goods (believing it was safe to do so and without intending to cause loss to the trustee). His act in delivering the jewellery to the servant was only ministerial. This decision does not accord well with the old case of *Stephens v. Elwall*.[143] The defendant was the servant of a man in America. He bought goods belonging to a bankrupt after the bankruptcy and sent them to his master in America. When sued by the bankrupt's assignees in trover he pleaded that he acted innocently and as clerk for his master. Nonetheless he was held liable. Lord Ellenborough stated that "a person is guilty of conversion who intermeddles with my property and disposes of it, and it is no answer that he acted under authority from another who had himself no authority to dispose of it".[144]

7.29 Perhaps because of this decision, and that in *Hollins v. Fowler*,[145] the courts evolved the distinction between independent and ministerial acts. The decisions are by no means easy to reconcile, as may be evidenced by the discussion in *R.H. Willis & Son v. British Car Auctions Ltd*,[146] in which

139 *Hollins v. Fowler, supra*, at 766–767 *per* Blackburn J. (cp. at 787 *per* Cleasby B., 797 *per* Lord Cairns: contrast Brett J., dissenting, at 778–779). For example, a finder of goods moving them to a place of safety; a carrier who simply transports the plaintiff's goods under directions from a third party who has no authority to give such directions; or a wharfinger who looks after the owner's goods while under the belief that they belong to the one who deposited them with him.

140 [1891] 2 Q.B. 172 at 181–182.

141 *Supra* notes 111–116.

142 [1945] Ch. 408; cp. *National Mercantile Bank v. Rymill* (1881) 44 L.T. 767.

143 (1815) 4 M. & W. 259.

144 *Ibid.* at 261.

145 *Supra* para. 7.22.

146 [1978] 2 All E.R. 392 at 396.

Lord Denning questioned the correctness of some of them,[147] while applying others[148] which, in his view, were consistent with principles stated by Blackburn J. in *Hollins v. Fowler*[149] and accepted by the House of Lords. Auctioneers sold the plaintiff's car by an auction which followed the "provisional bid" procedure. Under this procedure, where there is a reserve price which is not reached at the auction a bid not very far short of the reserve price may be treated as a provisional bid. If the bidder in question is prepared to stand by his bid, it may be accepted by the auctioneer, not by the fall of the hammer but orally. The car in fact had been hired from the plaintiff by a third party who had brought it to the defendants to be auctioned, telling them that it was his. The auctioneers therefore acted in innocence and good faith. Nonetheless they were held liable in conversion. The sale had taken place as a result of their intervention: and this sufficed to render them liable.

7.30 Strict liability for conversion is imposed not only upon one who, albeit innocently and in good faith, transfers the true owner's goods to someone else, in the belief that he is validly disposing of the title to the goods. It extends also to the transferee. He, too, at common law will be guilty of conversion, although he acted innocently and in good faith. So strict is this liability that even carelessness on the part of the owner, in consequence of which an intermediary was enabled to perpetrate a fraud on the innocent transferee, will not remove the stigma of liability from such a transferee. The common law protected the property rights of the true owner and enforced them strictly as against anyone who dealt with the goods inconsistently with the dominion of the true owner. Even though the true owner may have been very negligent and the defendant may have acted in complete innocence, nevertheless the common law held him liable in conversion. Both the "innocent acquirer" and the "innocent handler" have been hit hard.[150] Statutes such as the Factors Act and the Hire Purchase Act have provided some protection for the innocent transferee of goods under certain conditions.[151] But the common law refused to go to the length of treating the owner's negligence as founding any kind of estoppel against him such as would preclude the innocent transferee's liability for conversion.[152] Suggestions that some apportionment of liability might be desirable and just as between an innocent owner and an innocent transferee, both of whom may have been the victims of a third person's criminal

147 E.g. *National Mercantile Bank v. Rymill, supra*; *Turner v. Hockey* (1887) 56 L.J.Q.E. 301.
148 *Cochrane v. Rymill* (1879) 40 L.T. 944; *Barker v. Furlong* [1891] 2 Ch. 172; *Consolidated Co. v. Curtis & Son* [1892] 1 Q.B. 495.
149 *Supra* at 766, 767.
150 *R.H. Willis & Son v. British Car Auctions* [1978] 2 All E.R. 392 at 395 *per* Lord Dening, M.R.
151 Cp. above notes 121, 122.
152 *Central Newbury Car Auctions Ltd v. Unity Finance Ltd* [1957] 1 Q.B. 371; *Moorgate Mercantile Co. Ltd v. Twitchings* [1977] A.C. 890. There have been some exceptions: but these are rare and depend on proof of some duty of care that could be shown to have been owed in the circumstances by the owner to the defendant, or the class of persons to which the defendant belonged.

behaviour, were rejected by the Law Reform Committee.[153] Under the 1977 Act, the prior approach of the common law has been endorsed. Contributory negligence is no defence in proceedings founded on conversion.[154]

(iv) The plaintiff's title

7.31 An action for conversion may be brought by someone who is the owner of the goods and in possession of them at the time of the act of conversion, or by a person who is in possession at the material time, or by someone with an immediate right to possession; or, in certain instances, by an owner without either possession or an immediate right to possession.

7.32 Ownership, coupled with possession,[154a] is quite obviously a legitimate basis for suing for conversion.[154b] Under the 1977 Act,[155] as previously noted,[156] if goods are owned by two or more persons, one co-owner can sue any other co-owner who commits conversion by destroying the goods, injuriously affecting the plaintiff co-owner's interest in the goods or purporting to disposing of the goods in a manner which would give good title to the entire property in the goods if the defendant were acting with the authority of all the co-owners. But this does not affect the law relating to enforcement or execution of judgments or the law of distress. Consequently a co-owner who subjects the goods to seizure under a judgment or by way of distress will not commit conversion.

7.33 Anyone who is in possession of goods as a bailee may sue whomever commits conversion.[157] But if the bailment is one which does not exclude the bailor from possession, both bailor and bailee may be able to sue.[158] Such would be the case where there is a simple bailment at will. Possession

153 12th Report, *Transfer of Title to Chattels*, 1966, Cmnd. 2958. Cp. also the possibility of apportionment under the Law Reform (Contributory Negligence) Act, 1945: *Lumsden v. London Trustee Savings Bank* [1971] 1 Lloyd's Rep. 114, which involved conversion of a cheque. Note also the relevance of the owner's contributory negligence in *Elvin & Powell Ltd v. Plummer Roddis Ltd* (1934) 50 T.L.R. 158, above para. 7.21; but (i) the defendant was not liable in conversion apart from any contributory negligence by the plaintiff; and (ii) such contributory negligence was applicable to the plaintiff's alternative claim for negligence by the defendant as bailee (which the jury negatived). In *Hiort v. Bott* (1874) L.R. 9 Ex. 86, above para. 7.21, the plaintiff might have been negligent, but this was not regarded as affecting the defendant's liability.

154 1977 c. 32, s. 11(1); and to an action founded on intentional trespass to goods (does this mean it might be applicable when the trespass was unintentional, i.e. negligent?): cp. above p. 149).

154a A master may possess "through" his servant and so sue for conversion; but if the servant is a bailee, with exclusive possession of the goods entrusted to him by his master, the servant may sue: *Moore v. Robinson* (1831) 2 B. & Ad. 817.

154b But a buyer of goods who has not yet obtained title or possession of goods cannot sue: *Leigh & Sillivan Ltd v. Aliakmon Shipping Co.* [1986] 2 All E.R. 145. An action can be brought in respect of goods located abroad: *Hesperides Hotels Ltd v. Muftizade* [1978] 2 All E.R. 1168.

155 1977 c. 32, s. 10.

156 Above p. 159.

157 *Burton v. Hughes* (1824) 2 Bing. N.C. 173. Even the bailor may be sued if he dispossesses the bailee during the period of the bailment, as long as it is not a bailment at will: *Roberts v. Wyatt* (1810) 2 Taunt. 268.

158 *Nicholls v. Bastard* (1835) 2 C.M. & R. 659.

of the goods passes to the bailee, which suffices to give him title to sue (since ownership of goods is not a prerequisite to bringing an action,[159] despite older cases which suggest that the plaintiff must have a right of property, viz., ownership, in the goods converted).[160] The bailor in such instances has a right to immediate possession, because he can terminate the bailment at will. By virtue of his right to immediate possession the bailor can exercise those possessory remedies which are available to the possessor.[161] Thus in *Manders v. Williams*[162] the plaintiff supplied someone with porter in casks on terms that the casks were to be returned when they were empty. As soon as the casks were empty the plaintiff could determine the bailment at will. He had an immediate right to possession. Therefore when the sheriff wrongfully took the casks in execution of a debt owed by the one to whom the casks had been bailed, the plaintiff could sue. But in *Bradley v. Copley*,[163] the bailor could not sue for conversion. Before he had an immediate right to possession he had to demand the return of the goods bailed.

7.34 The immediate right to possession of goods is therefore an important basis for bringing the action for conversion. This may be, but is not necessarily based on ownership. In *North General Wagon & Finance Co. v. Graham*,[164] the plaintiffs were selling a car on hire purchase. The contract provided that if it were broken the plaintiffs were entitled to terminate the hiring, and could retake possession of the car. The hire-purchase buyer, in breach of the agreement, placed the car with the defendant, an auctioneer, who sold it by auction. The plaintiffs were held able to sue in conversion, although they were out of possession at the time, because once the agreement was broken they had the right to immediate possession of the car. As Roskill L.J. said in a more recent case where the facts were similar, and the auctioneer was held liable to the owners who were selling a car on hire-purchase despite their innocence of wrongdoing,[165] *Union Transport Finance Ltd v. British Car Auctions Ltd*,[166] "an action for conversion depends on injury to the right to possession." Here the plaintiffs had an immediate right to possession, since they could terminate the hire-purchase contract both under the contract and at common law. A mere contractual right to goods is not sufficient.[167] The plaintiff must have a property right which he can assert with respect to the goods. This need not be legal ownership. It

159 *The Winkfield* [1902] P. 42; *Marquess of Bute v. Barclays Bank Ltd* [1955] 1 Q.B. 202. Hence a person who has a lien over goods may sue in conversion: *Rogers v. Kenny* (1846) 9 Q.B. 594 at 596 *per* Patteson J. Where an unpaid seller of goods has a lien for the unpaid purchase price, the buyer cannot sue for conversion by a third party: *Lord v. Price* (1874) L.R. 9 Ex. 54.

160 *Gordon v. Harper* (1796) 7 T.R. 9; *Bloxam v. Sanders* (1825) 9 B. & C. 941; *Owen v. Knight* (1837) 4 Bing. N.C. 54; *Bradley v. Copley* (1845) 1 Q.B. 685.

161 *U.S.A. v. Dollfus Mieg & Cie.* [1952] A.C. 582 at 605 *per* Earl Jowitt; cp. *ibid.* at 611 *per* Lord Porter: "where the bailor can at any moment demand the return of the object bailed he still has possession'.

162 (1849) 3 Ex. 339.

163 (1845) 1 Q.B. 685.

164 [1950] 2 K.B. 7.

165 Applying *Hollins v. Fowler, supra.*

166 [1978] 2 All E.R. 385 at 387.

167 *Jarvis v. Williams* [1955] 1 All E.R. 108.

can be an equitable title. Hence in *International Factors Ltd v. Rodriquez,*[168] the plaintiffs were able to sue in conversion in respect of cheques which, by agreement with a company of which the defendant was a director, were to be held in trust for the plaintiffs on receipt by the company. Although the cheques were made out to the company, conversion was committed by the director who paid them into the company's bank account because the company was in financial difficulties. Since the cheques were to be handed over to the plaintiffs, they were held in trust by the company as soon as they were received: and this equitable title formed the basis for the plaintiff's claim.

7.35 Since ownership is not necessary to found a right to sue for conversion, as long as there is possession or an immediate right to possession, it has been held that a finder of goods, as long as he is honest and *bona fide*, not one who "finds" goods by looking for them with the intent to steal them,[169] and as long as the owner cannot be traced, will have a right to sue anyone who commits conversion with respect to the goods.[169a] The rights of a finder were set out in some detail by Donaldson L.J. in *Parker v. British Airways Board,*[170] after a detailed analysis of the cases in which the competing rights of finders and occupiers of land where goods were found have been examined.[171] If goods have been abandoned or lost,[172] and the finder takes them into his care and control, the finder does not acquire any absolute property or ownership in them. But he does acquire a right to keep them against all but the true owner or those in a position to claim through the true owner or one who can assert a prior right to keep the goods which was subsisting at the time when the finder took the goods into his care and control. A servant or agent who finds goods in the course of his employment or agency and not wholly incidental and collateral thereto, and takes them into his care and control, does so on behalf of his employer or principal, who acquires a finder's rights to the exclusion of the actual finder, unless otherwise agreed between the actual finder and his employer or principal. A person who has finder's rights is obliged to take reasonable measures to acquaint the true owner of the finding and present whereabouts of the goods and to care for them in the

168 [1979] 1 All E.R. 17; cp. *Healey v. Healey* [1915] 1 K.B. 938.

169 Cp. *Hibbert v. McKienrnan* [1948] 2 K.B. 142. But in *Bird v. Fort Francis* [1949] 2 D.L.R. 791, a trespassing finder could keep the money he found, when the occupier made no claim to it.

169a The finder of "treasure trove" may now have rights to what is found, even if it is found on his own land; but the situation depends on whether what is found is indeed "treasure trove", that is to say objects of gold or silver containing a substantial amount of the metal: *Attorney General of Duchy of Lancaster v. G.E. Overton (Farms) Ltd* [1982] 1 All E.R. 524.

170 [1982] 1 All E.R. 834 at 843.

171 Viz., *Armory v. Delamirie* (1721) 1 Stra. 505 (where the dispute was not with the occupier of the land, since the goods were found in the street, but with the jeweller to whom the goods had been entrusted by the finder, but the principles are much the same); *Bridges v. Hawkesworth* (1851) 21 L.J.Q.B. 75; *Elwes v. Brigg Gas Co.* (1886) 33 Ch. D. 562; *South Staffs. Water Co. v. Sharman* [1896] 2 Q.B. 44; *London City Corp. v. Appleyard* [1963] 2 All E.R. 834. See above p. 145.

172 Goods that are hidden are not lost: *Re Cohen* [1953] 1 Ch. 88; nor are goods which are forgotten, rather than abandoned: *Moffatt v. Kazana* [1969] 2 Q.B. 152.

meanwhile. As an involuntary bailee, therefore, the finder will be bound to act reasonably, but not with any great degree of diligence: but he must not wilfully use or destroy the goods, else he will be liable for conversion to the true owner (or to trespass in appropriate circumstances).[173] Whether a finder of goods can assert these "rights" against the occupier of land or premises where the goods are found will depend on the "rules" relating to an occupier's rights with respect to found goods that have been considered in connection with trespass.[174] Much depends on where the goods were found, whether in the street, attached to or in land or a building, and on the occupier's intention to exercise control over the building and things on or in it.[175]

7.36 Ownership without either possession or the immediate right to possession is not usually a basis for bringing an action for conversion of goods. Such is the situation when goods are bailed for a fixed term.[176] The bailor cannot sue if the bailed goods are converted during the period of the bailment. Exceptionally, however, the bailor may bring an action if the effect of the conversion is to cause damage to the bailor's reversionary interest.[177] Thus if goods are destroyed by the defendant, so that, when the bailment ends the bailee cannot return them to the bailor (and the bailee was not guilty of negligence or breach of duty as a bailee so as to be liable to the bailor for the loss of the goods), the bailor will be able to sue the defendant.[178] Strictly speaking this was not an action for conversion but an action on the case for being deprived of the benefit of the reversionary interest. Presumably the same right of action is available to a buyer of goods, to whom ownership, though not possession, has passed, if the seller, or a third party converts the goods, for example as a consequence of a sale by the seller to a third party (though the latter would not be liable if the sale, or other disposition, passed title under the Sale of Goods or Factors Acts).[179]

(v) Defences

7.37 Many of the defences that may be pleaded by a defendant in action for trespass to goods[180] may also be raised as a defence to an action for conversion. Thus liability may be avoided by a successful plea of leave and

173 Above p. 148.
174 Above p. 146.
175 A non-occupier of land however will have no rights against the finder: *Hannah v. Peel* [1945] K.B. 509.
176 *Mears v. London & South Western Railway* (1862) 11 C.B.N.S. 850; contrast *Gordon v. Harper* (1796) 7 T.R. 9.
177 *Donald v. Suckling* (1866) L.R. 1 Q.B. 585 at 611–612 *per* Blackburn J.: cp. *Halliday v. Holgate* (1868) L.R. 3 Ex. 299 at 302. But he will not be able to sue for wrongful taking or detention of the bailed goods: *Tancred v. Allgood* (1859) 4 H. & N. 438.
178 1977 c. 32, s. 1(d).
179 Fridman, *Law of Agency*, above note 122.
180 Or trespass to land in appropriate instances.

licence (or consent);[181] recaption of chattels which were wrongfully taken from the defendant;[182] lawful authority, for example where goods may be seized by police acting under a search warrant or, in certain instances even without a warrant,[183] or by other persons acting under powers conferred on them by statute,[184] or under the protection of legislation, such as a sheriff enforcing a writ of *fieri facias*;[185] or necessity, under the peculiar doctrine of "agency of necessity".[186] Immunity from suit may be granted by statute, as in the case of the Post Office, or an air carrier.[187]

7.38 However, inevitable accident and mistake, which may be pleaded in cases of trespass,[188] are not defences to conversion. Anyone who interferes with another's title to goods does so at his peril.[189] It has been seen that the common law regarded conversion as a tort of very strict liability. Hence neither the innocence of the defendant nor the negligence of the plaintiff would affect the responsibility of the defendant where he committed an act of conversion.[190]

7.39 At common law there was considerable debate, and difficulty, surrounding the defence of *jus tertii*. Whether it was open to a defendant to plead this defence to conversion depended on whether the plaintiff relied on possession of the goods, when *jus tertii* would not be a defence,[191] or on the right to possess, when the defence might be available.[192] A bailee could not rely on the defence, however, against his bailor unless the bailee had been evicted by "title paramount", i.e. someone who had a better right to

181 See *Maynegrain Pty Ltd v. Campofine Bank* [1984] 1 N.S.W.L.R. 258 (P.C.). Consent may not be vitiated by fraud: *Whittaker v. Campbell* [1983] 3 All E.R. 582 at 585 *per* Goff L.J., a criminal case involving taking a car without the consent of the owner. The accused obtained possession of the car by a fraudulent misrepresentation and was not guilty. On this basis he would not be guilty of either trespass to goods or conversion. On leave and licence as a defence to trespass to land, see above pp. 102–105.

182 Above pp. 101–101. But not hived bees which swarm on to the plaintiff's land from which the defendant seeks to recover them: *Kearry v. Pattinson* [1939] 1 K.B. 471, such bees belong to nobody until again hived.

183 Above pp. 135–140. See, however, *Ghani v. Jones* [1970] 1 Q.B. 693, where police were held to have acted unlawfully in taking and detaining passports belonging to the owner of a house, his wife and daughter, after a search was made of the house without a warrant. Feldman, *The Law Relating to Entry, Search and Seizure* 1987, Ch. 10.

184 E.g. tax inspectors in *I.R.C. v. Rossminster Ltd* [1980] A.C. 952.

185 *Neumann v. Bakeaway Ltd* [1983] 2 All E.R. 935; *Observer Ltd v. Gordon* [1983] 2 All E.R. 945: the sheriff could be protected under R.S.C. Order 17, r. 8.

186 *China-Pacific S.A. v. Food Corp. of India Ltd* [1981] 3 All E.R. 688: cp. above para. 7.24 note 120.

187 *American Express Co. v. British Airways Board* [1983] 1 All E.R. 557, a decision under the Post Office Act 1969 s. 29(1), (3), which gives the Post Office immunity from actions in tort (not to be outflanked by suing for breach of bailment), including breach of statutory duty. Immunity may also be conferred by International Law, in the case of sovereigns: see *I Congresso del Partido* [1981] 2 All E.R. 1064.

188 Above p. 148.

189 Cp. *Marfani Co. Ltd v. Midland Bank Ltd* [1968] 1 W.L.R. 956 at 971 *per* Diplock L.J.

190 Above pp. 155, 159.

191 *Armory v. Delamirie*, para. 7.35 *supra*.

192 *Leake v. Loveday* (1842) 4 Man. & G. 972; because in conversion, unlike trespass to goods, title is in issue: *ibid.* at 985–986 *per* Maule J.

the goods than the bailor.[193] The bailee had to defend the action based on the right and title, and with the authority of the third person in question.[194] Under the 1977 Act,[195] the defendant, in an action for wrongful interference, which includes trespass, conversion, negligence, or any other tort resulting in damage to the goods or an interest in the goods,[196] may show, in accordance with rules of court, that a third party has a better right than the plaintiff as respects all or any part of the interest claimed by the plaintiff, or in right of which he sues. The *jus tertii* rule, to the contrary, has been abolished. Such rules of court[197] may require the plaintiff to give particulars of his title; or to identify any person who, to his knowledge, has or claims any interest in the goods; and may authorise the defendant to apply for directions as to whether any person should be joined with a view to establishing whether he has a better right than the plaintiff, or has a claim as a result of which the defendant might be doubly liable. On the failure of a party to appear on an application for such directions, or to comply with such directions when given by the court on an application, the court may be authorised by the rules to deprive that party of any right of action against the defendant either unconditionally or subject to such terms or conditions as may be specified. It should also be noted that under another provision of the Act,[198] where two or more claimants are parties to an action for wrongful interference, the relief given must avoid double liability on the part of the wrongdoer as between the claimants. Double liability arises where one of two or more rights of action is founded on a possessory title,[199] or where the measure of damages in an action founded on a proprietary title is or includes the entire value of the goods, although the interest is one of two or more interests in the goods. Other provisions require that a successful claimant may be liable to account over to another person having a right to claim:[200] and that a claimant who has been unjustly enriched as the result of enforcement of a double liability must reimburse the wrongdoer to the extent of that enrichment.[201] The Act gives the example of a converter of goods paying damages to a finder of the goods and subsequently to the true owner. The finder must account to the true owner, else he is unjustly enriched. The true owner will then be unjustly enriched, and so must reimburse the converter of the goods.

193 *Biddle v. Bond* (1865) 6 B. & S. 225.
194 *Ibid.* at 234: *Rogers & Son v. Lambert & Co.* [1891] 1 Q.B. 315; cp. *Kahler v. Midland Bank Ltd.* [1950] A.C. 24 at 38 *per* Lord Macdermott.
195 1977 c. 32, s. 8(1).
196 Quaere: does this include slander of title (below p. 566)?
197 R.S.C. Ord 15 r. 10A (inserted by S.I. 1978, No. 579, r. 7); C.C.R. Ord 13 r. 4.
198 1977 c. 32, s. 7(1), (2). Note also the provisions with respect to the situation where there are concurrent actions, i.e. two or more claims for wrongful interference, whether founded on the same wrongful act or relating to other goods as well: *ibid.* s. 9.
199 Which seems to preserve the rule that a plaintiff relying on a possessory interest, e.g. a bailee, can recover the full value of the goods converted, not just the value of his interest: *The Winkfield* [1902] P. 42. Such a claim might extinguish the right of the bailor: but the bailee must account to the bailor for the amount by which the damages exceed the bailee's own possessory interest: *Eastern Construction Co. Ltd v. National Trust Ltd* [1914] A.C. 197; *Hepburn v. A. Tomlinson (Hauliers) Ltd* [1966] A.C. 451.
200 1977 c. 32, s. 7(3).
201 *Ibid.* s. 7(4).

7.40 The plaintiff may also be defeated by a plea that he is out of time. Under the Limitation Act 1980[202] this means that a plaintiff will not succeed unless he sues within six years of the accrual of his cause of action.[203] However two matters are particularly material to the tort of conversion, and require mention. First of all, under the 1980 Act,[204] the passage of time not only extinguishes the plaintiff's right of action, it also determines his title to the goods that have been converted in respect of which he is suing. But a thief or any person claiming through him cannot rely on these provisions as a defence to an action or a barrier to the plaintiff's title.[205] Secondly, there may be problems when goods are converted by one party and then later acts of conversion are committed by the same or another party. Prior to the 1939 Act some decisions sugested that time did not run against the plaintiff until the last act of conversion,[206] or the act of conversion by the defendant who acted later than the original conversion.[207] This has been reversed by a provision of the 1980 Act.[208] Time will run from the original act of conversion, whether by the defendant himself or his predecessor in title[209] (unless the original conversion involved fraud, or the defendant has deliberately concealed facts relevant to the plaintiff's cause of action, when time does not run until the plaintiff has discovered the fraud or concealment or could have discovered it with reasonable diligence).[210] But a *bona fide* purchaser of property for valuable consideration or any person claiming through him will not be deprived of the protection of the limitation period by this provision.[211]

(c) Replevin, rescous and pound-breach

7.41 These antique causes of action presumably survive the 1977 Act and will not be instances of wrongful interference with goods.

7.42 Replevin deals with the recovery of goods wrongfully taken in distress for rent or rates, although in theory it applies to every situation in which one person has taken chattels out of the possession of another.[212]

202 1980, c. 58, s. 2.
203 Unless the defendant is a thief or one who claims through a thief (since theft and allied offences are "imprescriptable"): Limitation Act 1980 s. 4.
204 S. 3(2).
205 Limitation Amendment Act 1980 s. 4.
206 *Wilkinson v. Verity* (1871) L.R. 6 C.P. 206, conversion followed by detinue (which is now conversion under the 1977 Act).
207 *Miller v. Dell* [1891] 1 Q.B. 468, successive conversions.
208 S. 3(1), But this does not apply in favour of a thief or one claiming through a thief: Limitation Act 1980 s. 4(1).
209 *R.B. Policies at Lloyd's v. Butler* [1950] 1 K.B. 76; although it has been suggested that this does not affect the case of successive wrongful acts by the *same* party: *Beaman v. A.R.T.S.* [1948] 2 All E.R. 89 at 92–93 *per* Denning J. (on appeal [1949] 1 K.B. 150); cp. *Rosenthal v. Alderton* [1946] K.B. 374; i.e. that *Wilkinson v. Verity* is still good law.
210 Limitation Act 1980, s. 32(1).
211 Limitation Act 1980, s. 32(3): *Eddis v. Chichester Constable* [1969] 2 Ch. 345.
212 Including a bailee: *Swaffen v. Mulcahy* [1934] 1 K.B. 608.

The plaintiff may replevy goods immediately and provisionally on providing security that he will bring the action of replevin. This enables the plaintiff to recover his goods at once, without having to prove his title in action for conversion or trespass. To bring the action the plaintiff must show that he was the owner of the goods or entitled to possession of them, and that the goods were unjustly detained from him. The underlying theory of replevin is that the possessor of goods is their owner (and therefore should not have his possession interrupted, so that any interruption is *prima facie* illegal).[213] The 1977 Act now provides for a form of interlocutory relief where goods are detained, pending the determination of questions of title of rights to possession in an action for wrongful interference, i.e. conversion or trespass. Under rules of court made under the Act a party can apply for delivery of the goods which may be ordered on terms specified by the court.[214]

7.43 Rescous and pound-breach are torts (and seemingly criminal offences), in respect of which treble damages may be given,[215] committed by one who wrongfully "rescues" distrained goods. If the goods are retaken before they reach the pound, rescous is committed: if when at the pound, the proper cause of action is pound-breach. A person whose goods have been improperly or illegally distrained may have some appropriate remedy: but he may not exercise self-help. There must be knowledge that the goods have been impounded, i.e. taken by way of distress.[216] This means that there is some uncertainty as regards the position where goods are in the "walking possession" of a bailiff. Perhaps a person who takes those goods out of such "possession" may not realise that they have been distrained; in which event no tort may be committed.[217]

(d) Other wrongs

7.44 Negligence which results in damage to goods or to an interest in goods is now wrongful interference or wrongful interference with goods,[218] and will be subject to the provisions of the 1977 Act. What constitutes negligence with respect to goods or interests in goods is discussed in the context of negligence generally.[219]

7.45 The Act also applies to any other tort so far as it results in damage to goods or to an interest in goods (subject to the abolition of the tort of

213 *Mennie v. Blake* (1856) 6 E. & B. 842. The successful plaintiff keeps the property and gets damage for the loss caused by the seizure: *Smith v. Enright* (1893) 69 L.T. 724, annoyance in trade; see, however, *Dixon v. Calcraft* [1892] 1 Q.B. 458; the unsuccessful plaintiff must return the property and pay what is owed.
214 1977 c. 32, s. 4: R.S.C. Ord. 15 r. 10A (inserted by S.I. 1978, No. 579, r. 7): C.C.R. Ord. 13 r. 11A (inserted by S.I. 1978, No. 682); County Courts Act 1984 s. 144 and Sch. 1.
215 Distress for Rent Act 1689 s. 3.
216 *Abingdon R.D.C. v. O'Gorman* [1968] 2 Q.B. 811.
217 Contrast *Lavell & Co. v. O'Leary* [1933] 2 K.B. 200 with *Abingdon R.D.C. v. O'Gorman*, *supra*.
218 1977 c. 32, s. 1(c).
219 Chs. 12 and 14.

detinue by the Act).[220] Some torts directly affect goods or interests in goods, for example the tort that is variously termed "slander of goods", "slander of title", or "injurious falsehood".[221] Others, such as deceit,[222] may do so indirectly. Where such a tort is committed, therefore, and goods or interests in goods are affected, it will be necessary to take into account the provisions of the Act which have been considered earlier, as well as those which will be examined on subsequent pages.

3. REMEDIES

(a) Where goods are detained

7.46 Detinue has gone. Therefore the common law remedy of specific recovery or restitution of goods which were being detained unlawfully by an action in detinue has also disappeared.[223] However under the 1977 Act[224] where an action for wrongful interference is brought against someone who is in possession or control of goods,[224a] the court may order delivery of the goods and payment of any consequential damages; or delivery of the goods, giving the defendant the alternative of paying damages by reference to the value of the goods[225] (in either case with the addition of consequential damages); or damages, i.e. the value and the consequential loss.[225a] Only one remedy may be given.[226] Delivery of the goods is in the discretion of the court.[227] The plaintiff may choose as between the other possibilities.[228] If specific restitution has been ordered but not fulfilled, the court may revoke the order and make an order for

220 1977 c. 32, ss. 1(d), 2(1).
221 Ch. 21.
222 Ch. 17.
223 *General & Finance Facilities Ltd v. Cooke Cars (Romford) Ltd* [1963] 2 All E.R. 314. Detinue was the appropriate form of action for a person with an immediate right to possession as against a person who was in possession but on proper demand refused or failed to deliver the goods without lawful excuse: *Alicia Hosiery Co. Ltd v. Brown Shipley & Co. Ltd* [1970] 1 Q.B. 195 at 207 *per* Donaldson J.
224 1977 c. 32, s. 3(1) and (2). This will apply not only to what used to be detinue but also to cases of conversion where the defendant is still in possession or control of the goods. These expressions are used widely, not in any narrow technical sense: Halsbury, *Statutes of England*, 3rd ed. Continuation Vol. 1977, 1344–1345.
224a Or who was in possession or control of the goods at the time proceedings were commenced: *Hillesden Securities Ltd v. Ryjak Ltd* [1983] 2 All E.R. 184.
225 At common law the proper date for assessing the value of goods in detinue was the date of judgment: *Rosenthal v. Alderton* [1946] K.B. 374; in conversion it was the time of conversion: *Sachs v. Miklos* [1948] 2 K.B. 23; see below p. 173. As detinue is now conversion it would seem that the conversion rule should apply under s. 3 of the 1977 Act.
225a The law can also award commercial hire charges for the period that a profit-earning chattel was wrongfully in the defendant's possession: *Hillesden Securities Ltd v. Ryjak Ltd, supra.*
226 1977 c. 32, s. 3(3)(a).
227 *Ibid.* s. 3(3)(b). For rules of court made under s. 3(3) see R.S.C. Ord. 29, r. 2A, Ord. 42, r. 1A (inserted by S.I. 1978, No. 579) and C.C.R. Ord. 13, r. 7. The discretion will be exercised if damages would not be an adequate remedy, as in *Howard E. Perry Ltd v. British Railways Board* [1980] 2 All E.R. 579, see especially at 585–586 *per* Megarry V.C.
228 1977 c. 32, s. 3(3)(b).

payment of damages by reference to the value of the goods.[229] Where delivery of the goods is ordered it can be conditional, if the court so determines.[230] If damages by reference to the value of the goods would not have amounted to the whole of the value of the goods, the court may require an allowance to be made by the plaintiff to reflect the difference.[231] If an order has been made for delivery of goods with the alternative to the defendant of paying the value of the goods, the latter may satisfy the order by returning the goods before execution of the judgment: but this will not prejudice his liability to pay consequential damages to the plaintiff.[232]

(b) Damages

7.47 Damages are recoverable: (a) where goods are in the possession and control of the defendant; (b) where goods have been destroyed by the defendant; (c) where goods have been dealt with by the defendant in such a manner as to interfere with the plaintiff's title; (d) where goods have been damaged by the defendant, although they are still in the plaintiff's possession. Situation (a) corresponds to the old tort of detinue; situations (b) and (c) to what was, and still is, conversion; situation (d) and (and situation (b)) to what was, and remains, trespass to goods. Subject to two matters to which reference will be made, viz., improvements of goods and extinction of title on payment of damages, the Act of 1977 makes no changes in the common law relating to the measurement or calculation of damages payable in cases of conversion (including now detinue) or trespass.

(i) Trespass

7.48 The measure of damages depends on whether what has occurred is damage to the goods or deprivation of the plaintiff by, for example, their total destruction. In the first instance, the plaintiff's damages will be calculated on the basis of the loss he has suffered as a direct consequence of the trespass. In the second, the value of the goods is the proper measurement of the plaintiff's loss, subject to any interest the defendant might have in the goods.[233] Should the plaintiff have only a limited interest in the goods, for example as a bailee, he may nonetheless recover their full value,

229 *Ibid.* s. 3(4).

230 *Ibid.* s. 3(6): e.g., the court might order the defendant to return the goods to the plaintiff, by his own personal act, which would take care of the problem in *Metals and Ropes Ltd v. Tattersall* [1966] 3 All E.R. 401, viz., that the plaintiff might have to get them back himself at common law: 18th Report of the Law Reform Committee, 1971, Cmnd. 4774, para. 94.

If an improvement allowance is made under s. 6, below p. 174, payment of such allowance may be made a condition of delivery by the defendant: *ibid.* s. 3(7).

231 *Ibid.* s. 3(6): e.g. in an action by a bailor against a bailee the measure of damages might not be the full value of the goods; the court may order delivery of the goods but require the bailor to pay the bailee a sum reflecting the difference: *ibid.*

232 *Ibid.* s. 3(5). But the return of the vehicle in *Hillesden Securities Ltd v. Ryjak Ltd* made it impossible to assess damages on the basis of the value of the vehicle at the date of conversion plus interest.

233 *Blades v. Higgs* (1861) 10 C.B.N.S. 713; *Brierly v. Kendall* (1852) 17 Q.B. 937.

subject to his accountability to the owner for such damages as exceed the bailee's own interest.[234]

(ii) Conversion

7.49 If the conversion consists in wrongful detention of goods, which, prior to 1977 would have been actionable as detinue, the Act allows the payment of damages as a possible remedy instead of delivery of the goods.[235] Where this is done the damages are calculated by reference to "the value of the goods", with the addition of consequential damages.[236] At common law before the Act, it was determined that the date of judgment was the time when the value of the goods detained should be assessed in cases of detinue.[237] Since detinue has been abolished, presumably the test to apply is that applicable to conversion, viz., the date when the wrong was committed.[237a] In cases of wrongful detention this could be either the original wrongful taking or the time when the defendant's possession became wrongful, or the last moment of detention, viz., judgement. Where the chattel being detained was something hired, and capable of being hired out by the plaintiff if he had possession, the value of the chattel is the amount it would have produced by being hired during the period of the wrongful detention[238] (a measure of damages akin to mesne profits recoverable in cases of trespass to land).[239] The test of consequential damages in every case, however, was whether the plaintiff has suffered substantial loss by being deprived of the goods.[240] This idea was restated, after the 1977 Act, by the Court of Appeal in *Brandeis Goldschmidt & Co. Ltd v. Western Transport Ltd.*[241] Here copper purchased by the plaintiffs was detained by the defendants, who were transporting imported copper to the plaintiffs' refinery, in order to offset a debt owed to them by the plaintiffs' forwarding agents. Liability for wrongful detention was admitted by the defendants. The issue was whether the plaintiffs had suffered any damage by the detention. They claimed that they were entitled to damages based on the fall in the price of copper during the period of detention and additional interest paid by the plaintiffs on their bank overdraft during that period. On appeal both claims were rejected. There was no evidence of any lost profits from the sale of products of the refined copper which would have reduced the plaintiffs' overdraft by a particular date. Hence the plaintiffs could only claim nominal damages for infringement of their right to possession of the copper. There was no universally applicable rule for assessing damages for wrongful detention. It was for the plaintiffs to

234 *The Winkfield* [1902] P. 42. Note the provisions of the Torts (Interference with Goods) Act, 1977, s. 7 on "double liability": above para. 7.39.
235 1977 c. 32, s. 3(2)(b)(c), s. 3(3)(b).
236 *Ibid.* s. 3(2)(b).
237 *Rosenthal v. Alderton* [1946] K.B. 374.
237a Below.
238 *Strand Electric & Engineering Co. v. Brisford Entertainments Ltd* [1952] 2 Q.B. 246; *Hillesden Securities Ltd v. Ryjak Ltd* [1983] 2 All E.R. 184 at 188 *per* Parker J.
239 Above p. 109.
240 *Williams v. Peel River Land & Mineral Co. Ltd* (1886) 55 L.T. 689 at 692–693 *per* Bowen L.J.: cp. *Barrow v. Arnaud* (1846) 8 Q.B. 595; *Williams v. Archer* (1847) 5 C.B. 318.
241 [1982] 1 All E.R. 28.

prove that there was loss suffered by adverse interference with the course of their business operations. This they had not done.[242]

7.50 Where the act of conversion is one which would have been actionable as conversion before the Act of 1977, as well as thereafter, the common law principle was, and presumably remains, that damages are calculated by reference to the value of the goods at the date of conversion.[243] But consequential loss will be recoverable if it is not too remote,[244] for example the loss of work by a carpenter as a result of the conversion by the defendant of the carpenter's tools.[245] The value in question is the market value of the goods, if one is available.[246] If necessary, however, the highest value of the goods will be assumed as against a defendant liable for conversion.[247] Where goods are special, and have no market value that is ascertainable, the loss incurred by the plaintiff will be assessed by reference to the cost of replacement of the goods.[248] Where goods that have been converted were subject to a hire-purchase agreement, the Court of Appeal has held that the measure of damages is the market value of the goods or the amount that the plaintiff had failed to recover from the purchaser under the hire-purchase agreement, when this exceeded the market value of the goods at the material time.[249]

7.51 The fact that the plaintiff may have suffered no real loss because he was not liable over to a third party, such as a bailor, is irrelevant.[250] Equally irrelevant is the fact that the plaintiffs might be liable to account for damages recovered from the defendant to a third party. In *Chabbra Corporation Pte Ltd v. Jag Shakti*,[251] the plaintiffs were the indorsees for value of bills of lading on goods bought by buyers of edible salt shipped by the

242 *Ibid.* at 31–32 *per* Brandon L.J.

243 *Sachs v. Miklos* [1948] 2 K.B. 23; *Caxton Publishing Co. Ltd v. Sutherland Publishing Co. Ltd* [1939] A.C. 1789 at 192 *per* Lord Roche, 203 *per* Lord Porter; *Re Simms* [1934] 1 Ch. 1 at 17–18 *per* Lord Hansworth M.R.; *The Arpad* [1934] P. 189 at 205 *per* Scrutton L.J.: *Hillesden Securities Ltd v. Ryjak Ltd., supra* , at 188 *per* Parker J. Any increase in value of the goods between the date of conversion and the date of judgment can be recovered as part of the loss caused by the tort: *Sachs v. Miklos, supra* at 40–41 *per* Lord Goddard, C.J. But the plaintiff may not deliberately defer from claiming the goods and bring the action in order to get the benefit of a rise in their value: *ibid.* at 41.

244 *Hillesden Securities Ltd v. Ryjak Ltd supra* at 188 *per* Parker J.

245 *Bradley v. Reynolds* (1846) 8 Q.B. 779.

246 *The Arpad* [1934] P. 189.

247 *Armory v. Delamirie* (1721) 1 Stra. 505.

248 *Hall v. Barclay* [1937] 3 All E.R. 620.

249 *Chubb Cash Ltd v. John Colley & Son* [1983] 2 All E.R. 294; *Wickham Holdings Ltd v. Brook House Motors Ltd* [1967] 1 W.L.R. 295.

250 *Swire & Leach* (1865) 18 C.B.N.S. 479; *The Winkfield* [1902] P. 42. Hence even if the bailee has only a limited interest he can claim the full value of the goods for which he may be accountable over; cp. the case of insured goods: *A. Tomlinson (Hauliers) Ltd v. Hepburn* [1966] A.C. 451.

If others interested in the goods object to the plaintiff's action, can he still sue? Presumably not. Therefore if such others have sued, the bailee can only recover the value of his interest: and see 1977 c. 32, s. 7, above para. 7.39. A defendant who has paid a claim by a plaintiff with a limited interest is probably discharged from further liability, at least when s. 7 of the 1977 Act is applicable and has been applied, e.g. payment of damages to a finder: *ibid.* s. 7(4).

251 [1986] 1 All E.R. 480.

suppliers on the defendant's vessel. For reasons which are not relevant, the plaintiffs could sue the shipowners for breach of contract or conversion. The issue before the Privy Council was the proper measure of damages. It was held that the situation as between the plaintiffs and the buyers of the salt was *res inter alios acta*, not relevant to the dispute between the plaintiffs and the shipowners.[252] However the plaintiffs were unsuccessful before the Privy Council on an entirely different point, namely that the trial judge had incorrectly awarded the plaintiffs the market value of the salt on delivery when he should only have awarded the amount which had been expended by the party who had endorsed the bills of lading over to the plaintiffs when that party, as pledgee of the bills of lading, financed the sales transaction.[253]

(c) Improvement of the goods

7.52 At common law the defendant could be given credit for any amount spent by him on increasing the value of the goods, by some kind of improvement, as long as the defendant acted *bona fide*, i.e. in ignorance of the fact that he was committing conversion.[254] Nor would he be liable for any increase in the value of the goods converted due to any act of his, for example, where the defendant converted a half-finished ship belonging to the plaintiff and completed it: he was liable only for the value at the date of the original act of conversion.[255] He was liable, however, for any increase in the value of the goods not due to his act, but, for example, because of natural causes such as the birth of a foal, or economic reasons, such as the rise in value of shares. On the other hand he would gain nothing from a fall or loss in value: he was still liable for the value at the date of conversion.[256]

7.53 Under the 1977 Act, if an improver of goods acted in the mistaken but honest belief that he had good title to them, an allowance is to be made for the extent to which, at the time at which the goods fall to be valued in assessing damages (which in conversion is the date of the conversion and in what was detinue may be that date or the date of judgment),[257] the value of the goods is attributable to the improvement.[258] This applies only where the improver was a converter who believed he had acquired title. If the defendant is someone who in good faith has purported to purchase the goods from the improver, or is a subsequent

252 *Ibid.* at 484 *per* Lord Brandon.
253 *Ibid.* at 486–487.
254 *Munro v. Wilmott* [1949] 1 K.B. 295: he was "bona fide" in that he believed, wrongly as it turned out, that he could rely on the doctrine of "agency of necessity". This would also be the case in an action for detinue: *Greenwood v. Bennett* [1973] 1 Q.B. 195, where Lord Denning, M.R. preferred to base such a claim on the doctrine of unjust enrichment or restitution.
255 *Reid v. Fairbanks* (1853) 13 C.B.N.S. 692; *Peruvian Guano Co. v. Dreyfus Bros.* [1892] A.C. 166 at 174 *per* Lord Macnaghten; *Caxton Publishing Co. Ltd v. Sutherland Publishing Ltd* [1939] A.C. 178 at 192 *per* Lord Roche.
256 *Solloway v. McLaughlin* [1938] A.C. 247 at 257 *per* Lord Atkin.
257 Above pp. 170, 172.
258 1977 c. 32, s. 6(1).

purchaser in good faith, the allowance is to be made in respect of the earlier improvement.[259] If such purchaser or subsequent purchaser sues the improver or the seller to him for recovery of the purchase price for failure of consideration, or other proceedings founded on failure of consideration, the allowance is also to be made.[260] The foregoing provisions apply where what has taken place is a bailment or other disposition of goods instead of a sale of goods.[261]

(d) Extinction of title

7.54 Under the common law before the Act of 1977, judgement for the plaintiff in an action for converstion, if followed by satisfaction in the form of payment of the damages awarded, transferred the property in the goods that had been converted. If no such satisfaction took place, the judgment had no effect and the plaintiff could sue for further acts of conversion.[262]

7.55 The Act of 1977 extends the scope of the common law to all actions for wrongful interference, whether based on what was trespass, detinue or conversion. Where damages for wrongful interference are, or would fall to be assessed on the basis of compensation for the whole of the plaintiff's interest in the goods, or the whole of such interest subject to a reduction for contributory negligence (which will be possible where the cause of action is not conversion or intentional trespass to goods),[263] payment of the damages, or settlement of the claim for damages, extinguishes the plaintiff's title to the interest on which his claim was based.[264] This will not be the situation, however, where the damages paid are limited to some lesser amount than the whole of the plaintiff's interest in the goods by virtue of some enactment[265] or rule of law,[266] nor where the parties have agreed to the contrary, nor where the court otherwise orders.[267]

259 *Ibid.* s. 6(2).
260 *Ibid.* s. 6(3).
261 *Ibid.* s. 6(4).
262 *Ellis v. Stenning* [1932] 2 Ch. 81; *Brinsmead v. Harrison* (1871) L.R. 6 C.P. 584.
263 1977 c. 32, s. 11(1).
264 *Ibid.* s. 5(1); settlement includes where a plaintiff takes out of court a sum which has been paid into court by the defendant; and payment of a settlement or compromise, whether the claim is made in or out of court: *ibid.* s. 5(2). A third party's interest in goods will be extinguished when the plaintiff accounts over to the third party under s. 7(7); *ibid.* s. 5(5).
265 E.g. Merchant Shipping Act 1894; Carriage by Air Act 1961.
266 E.g., where there is a valid limitation of liability clause in a contract between the parties.
267 1977 c. 32, s. 5(3) and (5).

CHAPTER 8

Nuisance

1. THE FORMS OF NUISANCE

(a) The meaning of nuisance

8.01 In large measure the difficulties surrounding the law of nuisance stem from two factors. The first is the protean character of the expression "nuisance". The second is the way that different kinds of nuisance may be dealt with by the law. There are common features to these distinct varieties of nuisance.[1] There are also vital differences with respect to the nature and scope of liability,[2] that make elusive both precision and certainty in regard to general principles.

8.02 The term "nuisance" sometimes refers to a state of affairs or a condition that causes damage or harm to another. It can also refer to the actual causation of damage or harm. On other occasions the expression has been employed to refer both to the situation which gives rise to harm and the liability that flows therefrom. Yet a distinction ought to be made between what might be called "factual" nuisance, i.e. a situation which undoubtedly results in damage or harm to another, and "legal" nuisance, when a given situation involves the necessary elements of an action. Not every nuisance in fact amounts to a nuisance in law,[3] any more than every negligent act involves liability for the tort of negligence. From the larger mass of activities which are commonly described as "nuisances" the law has carved a smaller collection of situations in which the tort of nuisance is committed. Nuisance, for legal purposes, refers to some factual situation which satisfies the legal requirements of liability. The law must strike a balance between conflicting rights and interests.[3a]

(b) Varieties of nuisance

8.03 The law distinguishes different kinds of nuisance. The distinctions are sometimes based upon the scope of nuisance, sometimes upon the legal

1 E.g., the notion of "unreasonableness" in both private and public nuisance: *Harper v. Haden* [1933] 1 Ch. 298 at 320 *per* Romer L.J. (public nuisance): *Bamford v. Turnley* (1862) 3 B. & S. 66 at 82–84 *per* Bramwell B. (private nuisance).

2 E.g., the distinction between interference with one person or "the public", which may not mean more than a limited number of persons: *Attorney-General v. P.Y.A. Quarries* [1957] 2 Q.B. 169; the relevance of negligence in public as contrasted with private nuisance: below pp. 219–220.

3 Despite what is said in *Ware v. Garston Haulage Co.* [1944] K.B. 30.

3a *Thomas v. National Union of Mineworkers* [1985] 2 All E.R. 1 at 22 per Scott J.; cf. *Home Brewery plc v. Davis & Co.* [1987] 1 All E.R. 637 at 644.

basis of liability, sometimes upon the nature of the nuisance itself. Thus the difference between private and public nuisance turns upon the persons who may be affected. In private nuisance these are adjoining landowners or others with an interest in land.[4] In public nuisance the community or public at large may be affected. The defendant's wrongful conduct is against a more generalised group.[5] Private and public nuisance are common law forms of liability. The former gives rise to a civil action for damages or for injunctive relief. The latter is criminal, or quasi-criminal in nature. Additionally there may be civil liability but not at the suit of any individual,[6] because the wrong in question has been committed against the public, not any specific individual.[7] Under modern legislation there is also a class of "statutory nuisances" dealing with particular modern problems such as pollution,[8] or public health.[9] The categories of public and statutory nuisance sometimes overlap.[10] Lastly, some nuisances are more specifically defined in nature, such as nuisance on or to the highway and injuries to servitudes. The former are a type of public nuisance, although in some instances a nuisance of this kind can result in an action by a private individual who incurs particular loss or damage in consequence of the defendant's conduct.[11] The latter are more akin to private nuisance: but they concern conduct which relates to a particular and limited legal interest enjoyed by the plaintiff, namely a servitude, such as an easement, over the land of another.[12]

8.04 Most nuisances, of whatever kind, involve the use of land in a manner that causes harm or is potentially dangerous to others. That land may belong to the defendant himself: it may belong to another: it may be the highway. Where a nuisance occurs may be relevant to the variety of nuisance that is committed. What usually matters, however, is the form taken by the nuisance, whether it affects the public generally or only one or more private individuals, whether the kind of nuisance involved comes within the scope of some statute or is only dealt with by the common law. The remedies available also depend on the variety of nuisance that is involved. Private nuisance is remediable by an action for damages or an injunction (and, to a limited extent by self-help, i.e. abatement at the

4 Below pp. 193–195.
5 Below pp. 213–214. Hence it comprehends forms of conduct which do not readily or easily fit together with the more usual kinds of private nuisance. As Salmond says: "There is no generic conception which includes the crime of making a bomb-hoax and the tort of allowing one's trees to overhang the land of a neighbour": *Salmond & Heuston on the Law of Torts*, 19th ed. 1987 at 61 (note the change from "keeping a common gaming house" in the 18th ed.).
6 Save when particular damage has been incurred: *Gravesham B.C. v. British Railways Board* [1978] 3 All E.R. 853; *Tate & Lyle Ltd v. Greater London Council* [1983] 1 All E.R. 1159: below p. 214.
7 What is meant by "the public" is uncertain: *supra* note 2; below p. 213.
8 Control of Pollution Act 1974; Clean Air Acts 1956, 1968. See *A. Lambert Flat Management Ltd v. Lomas* [1981] 2 All E.R. 280; *London Borough of Hammersmith v. Magnus Automated Forecourts Ltd* [1978] 1 All E.R. 401.
9 Public Health Act 1936: see *Coventry City Council v. Doyle* [1981] 2 All E.R. 184.
10 But not always: *Salford City Council v. McNally* [1976] A.C. 376 at 390.
11 Below pp. 213–215.
12 Below pp. 212–213.

hands of the affected party).[13] Public nuisance may be remedied by a relator action brought by the Attorney-General or by a local authority to put an end to the nuisance by injunction, or by an indictment, since a public nuisance is a criminal offence.[14] Statutory nuisances are remediable by enforcement orders granted to a local authority under the provisions of the relevant statute, with a view to putting an end to the nuisance in question. Whereas private nuisances are dealt with by judicial remedies designed to provide compensation or relief from the consequences of wrongful conduct, and public nuisances are most frequently the subject of criminal proceedings designed to punish an anti-social offender, statutory nuisances involve administrative action, though the courts may be invoked to enforce administrative requirements. The modern tendency may be to oust the operation of private, civil law where nuisances are committed by some public action entailing the intervention of public authorities. However, in cases of individual damage, there is still scope for the common law of nuisance, i.e. the private law of torts.

2. PRIVATE NUISANCE[14a]

(a) Definition

8.05 Nuisance is a wrongful interference with another's enjoyment of his land or premises by the use of land or premises either occupied or in some cases owned by the tortfeasor. The occupier or owner is not an insurer. There must be more than the mere harm done to the neighbour's property to make the party responsible. Deliberate act or negligence is not an essential ingredient, but some degree of personal responsibility is required which is connoted by the word "use".[15] The gist of the action is the unreasonable and unjustified interference by the defendant in the use of his land with the plaintiff's right to enjoy his property.[16] An owner or occupier of land must so use it that he does not thereby substantially interfere with the comfortable enjoyment of their land by his neighbours.[17]

8.06 What distinguishes nuisance from other similar forms of tortious conduct is that the defendant's acts must relate to the use of land, whether the defendant's or another's, and must have consequences with respect to the land of the plaintiff by damaging that land, or what is on it, or by causing personal injury to the plaintiff while on his land, or by making his use of his land less pleasant or desirable. To cause personal injury or injury

13 Below para. 8.60.
14 Below pp. 213, 215.
14a Gearty, "The Place of Private Nuisance in a Modern Law of Torts" [1989] C.L.J. 214.
15 *Sedleigh-Denfield v. O'Callaghan* [1940] A.C. 880 at 896–897 *per* Lord Atkin.
16 *Ibid.* at 904 *per* Lord Wright; *Thomas v. National Union of Mineworkers* [1955] 2 All E.R. 1 at 22 *per* Scott J.
17 *Supra* note 15 at 912 *per* Lord Romer. The interference should emanate from outside the plaintiff's land: *Salford City Council v. McNally* [1976] A.C. 379 at 389. This view has been challenged in New Zealand: *Paxhaven Holdings Ltd v. A.-G.* [1974] 2 N.Z.L.R. 185; *Clearlite Holdings Ltd v. Auckland City Council* [1976] 2 N.Z.L.R. 729.

to personal property to another will not be a nuisance unless the injury resulted from the use by the defendant of his or someone else's land, and the personal or proprietary injury was suffered by the plaintiff himself, not someone else, while on the plaintiff's land.[18] Trespass and negligence are torts which may be committed against anyone, not necessarily an owner or occupier of land, and may have no connection with the place where the plaintiff or his property were situated at the material time. Nor need the trespassory or negligent act of the defendant occur on or in relation to the land where the defendant was located when he acted wrongfully. Nuisance is therefore a tort of more limited scope and application than trespass or negligence. Trespass involves a direct application of force by the defendant. Nuisance occurs when the injury to the plaintiff is an indirect consequence of the defendant's acts. Trespass is actionable *per se*, without the need to prove damage. Nuisance, being a derivative of the action on the case, is only actionable on proof of damage. In negligence the plaintiff must prove a duty of care, which is not so with nuisance. They are different in their nature in that a private nuisance arises out of a state of things on the defendant's property whereby his neighbour's property is exposed to damage. Negligence requires proof of some negligent conduct in breach of a duty.[19] Nuisance is not dependent upon proof of negligence,[20] although dicta suggest that negligence may be a relevant factor in respect of certain instances of liability in nuisance.[21] To the extent that negligence need not be established it can be said that liability for nuisance is "strict".[22] Insofar as it means that a defendant may be liable for the acts of third parties of which he was ignorant and in respect of which he was not personally responsible, it can also be said that liability for nuisance can sometimes be strict.[23] However, not every nuisance that is caused by the act of a third party will involve a defendant landowner or occupier of land in liability in nuisance, in the absence of negligence or other conduct by the defendant, even though the acts which constitute or give rise to the nuisance occurred on his land.[24]

8.07 Liability for nuisance greatly resembles liability under the doctrine of *Rylands v. Fletcher*.[25] Both depend upon the way a defendant has used land he owns or occupies. Both deal with damage to the land of a neighbour. Under *Rylands v. Fletcher*, however, liability depends upon a "non-natural" use of land, whereas nuisance is concerned with the "unreasonable" use of land. Liability under *Rylands v. Fletcher* results normally from a single unrepeated incident. Nuisance arises from the continuing state or condition of the defendant's land as a consequence of

18 Below pp. 193–195.
19 *Spicer v. Smee* [1946] 1 All E.R. 485 at 493 *per* Atkinson J.
20 *Sedleigh-Denfield v. O'Callaghan, supra* at 896–897 *per* Lord Atkin, 904 *per* Lord Wright.
21 *Bolton v. Stone* [1951] A.C. 850: below pp. 188–192.
22 *Sedleigh-Denfield v. O'Callaghan, supra* at 904 *per* Lord Wright: cp. *Read v. J. Lyons & Co. Ltd* [1947] A.C. 146 at 183 *per* Lord Simonds.
23 Below pp. 195–197.
24 Below pp. 197–201.
25 (1866) L.R. 1 Ex. 265; (1868) L.R. 3 H.L. 330.

which the damage to the plaintiff has occurred.[26] Nuisance and liability under the rule in *Rylands v. Fletcher* may be so intimately related that many cases involve liability for both. Yet they must be differentiated. *Rylands v. Fletcher* requires the "escape" of a dangerous thing which has been collected on his land for his own purposes by the defendant. Nuisance may not involve an escape. The damage or injury need not result from the use or collection of any dangerous thing by the defendant on his land. Nor are the purposes of the defendant in acting as he has done of any relevance to liability. Moreover the plaintiff need have no interest in land to maintain an action under *Rylands v. Fletcher*. He will not succeed in an action for nuisance unless he is the owner of land, or occupies it under some legal or equitable interest. Mere presence of the plaintiff on land is not sufficient to establish a basis for liability in nuisance. However both under the doctrine of *Rylands v. Fletcher* and the law of nuisance, a defendant will not be liable for the acts of a stranger unless the defendant was guilty of negligence.[27]

(b) Elements of liability

(i) A continuing state of affairs

8.08 The idea of "activity" connotes that the defendant has been doing something or allowing a state of affairs to exist over a period of time. The interference, generally speaking, must be for "a substantial length of time".[28] However what is not a nuisance to start with cannot become a nuisance merely by the lapse of time.[29] A sewer that had been laid properly and maintained, without being moved or altered by the defendant or anyone for whom the defendant was responsible in law, did not become a nuisance even though it obstructed the river with resulting damage to the plaintiff's property.[30] A nuisance that is only temporary, for example, saws making noise that affects the occupier of premises, will not be a nuisance with respect to the owner of the property: such interference is not the kind that continuously and substantially affects the owner.[31]

8.09 Consistently with this idea it has been held that one solitary act is insufficient to amount to a nuisance. In *Bolton v. Stone*,[32] for example, the plaintiff was struck, on one occasion, by a cricket ball that had been hit out of the ground by an overly successful batsman. The Court of Appeal said that this was not a nuisance: and the House of Lords confirmed their opinion. But if cricket balls had been continually hit out of the ground, with consequent danger to those living outside the area where cricket was

26 But not always; sometimes a single incident can amount to a nuisance, e.g. when accumulated gas explodes, causing damage to property: *Midwood v. Mayor of Manchester* [1905] 2 K.B. 593: below p. 181. It has been said that *Rylands v. Fletcher* is a special form of the ancient action for nuisance, and not fundamentally distinguishable: *Benning v. Wong* (1969) 43 A.L.J.R. 467 at 484 *per* Windeyer J.
27 Below pp. 195–196: cf pp. 243–244.
28 *Cunard v. Antifyre Ltd* [1933] 1 K.B. 441 at 557.
29 *Rex v. Ball* (1822) 1 L.J.K.B. (O.S.) 42.
30 *Radstock Co-operative & Industrial Society Ltd v. Norton-Radstock U.D.C.* [1968] Ch. 605.
31 *Jones v. Chappell* (1875) L.R. 20 Eq. 539.
32 [1950] 1 K.B. 201 at 208 *per* Jenkins L.J., affirmed [1951] A.C. 850.

played, a different legal result would follow.[33] Such was the situation with respect to golf balls in *Castle v. St. Augustine Links*.[34] The repeated slicing of golf balls by players so that they became a danger and hindrance to people on adjoining land did constitute a nuisance. What is crucial is whether the activity carried on by the defendant, or permitted to be carried on by others on his land, involved the continuing prospect of damage, even though actual injury or damage only occurred or was occasioned once. In *Midwood v. Mayor of Manchester*[35] a fire was caused by the fusing of a main which made bitumen turn into inflammable gas that exploded. The creation of this incident had taken some length of time. There was a gradual accumulation of the gas that ultimately resulted in the explosion and the consequent damage. To Collins M.R.[36] this was emphatically a nuisance.

8.10 Where the plaintiff alleges that his property was damaged by reason of the nuisance committed by the defendant, the courts may have been less concerned with the period over which the defendant was engaged in the offending activity.[37] Time seems more important where interference with comfort or enjoyment are in question. Nevertheless, as the *Midwood* case indicates, to support an action for nuisance, in contrast with actions for trespass, negligence, or under the doctrine of *Rylands v. Fletcher*, there must be some evidence that what happened was the product of a continuing condition of or on the defendant's premises.

(ii) Personal comfort or enjoyment of property

8.11 The tortious activity of the defendant must materially and substantially interfere with the personal comfort of the plaintiff or his ability to enjoy his property. This means that the interference must be sensible, not trivial or small.[38] As the House of Lords pointed out in *St. Helens Smelting Co. v. Tipping*,[39] there are two ways in which a defendant can interfere with another so as to commit an actionable nuisance. He can cause damage to the property of the plaintiff. Or he can prevent the plaintiff from enjoying the use of his property by producing something that makes life less comfortable for the plaintiff, such as noise, noxious vapours, smoke or the like.[40] The possibilities are virtually unlimited.[41] In addition to the more usual consequences of a defendant's use of his property, such as those enumerated above, and such others as fumes, offensive smells, vibrations,

33 *Miller v. Jackson* [1977] 3 All E.R. 338: below p. 185.
34 (1922) 38 T.L.R. 615.
35 [1905] 2 K.B. 597.
36 *Ibid.* at 605.
37 Just as they have been less concerned about the issue of quality or standard of life enjoyed by the plaintiff: *St Helens Smelting Co. Ltd v. Tipping* (1865) 11 H.L.C. 642: below.
38 *St Helens Smelting Co. Ltd v. Tipping* (1865) 11 H.L.C. 642 at 653 *per* Lord Wensleydale.
39 *Supra.*
40 *Cunard v. Antifyre Ltd* [1933] 1 K.B. 551. For examples see *Shelfer v. City of London Electric Lighting Co. Ltd* [1895] 1 Ch. 287 and *Metropolitan Properties Ltd v. Jones* [1939] 2 All E.R. 202 (noise): *St Helens Smelting Co. Ltd v. Tipping, supra* (vapours).
41 The forms of nuisance are protean: *Sedleigh-Denfield v. O'Callaghan* [1940] A.C. 880 at 903 *per* Lord Wright.

denial of support rendering the plaintiff's land liable to subsidence, deprivation or diminution of light, encroachment, or obstruction,[42] the courts have been prepared to hold that the comings and goings of prostitutes from premises used as a brothel could amount to a nuisance, in that their presence and that of potential customers could pose a threat to the morals of the plaintiff's family.[43] A similar attitude has been taken with respect to the use of premises as a sex shop and cinema in an area which included residential accommodation.[44] Vinelott J. held that there was a triable issue as to whether such use of property could constitute a nuisance, justifying the issuance of an interlocutory injunction pending the trial. Following the approach of the Court of Appeal in *Thompson-Schwab v. Costaki*,[45] the brothel case, the important factor was the knowledge by occupants and visitors of the open use of the defendant's property which was in itself a material interference with the comfortable enjoyment of the plaintiff's property.[46]

8.12 If damage to the plaintiff's property results from the defendant's activity, there is little difficulty in establishing the kind of interference that amounts to an actionable nuisance. As long as it is not of so trifling a nature as to be beyond the attention of a court, physical injury to land will suffice to create liability, since it results in the diminution of the plaintiff's enjoyment of the property, and nobody expects or is required to suffer physical damage to his property. Discomfort on the part of the plaintiff need not be shown.[47] Where the defendant's conduct causes personal

42 For examples see *Bone v. Seale* [1975] 1 All E.R. 787; *Halsey v. Esso Petroleum Co. Ltd* [1961] 2 All E.R. 145; *Adams v. Ursell* [1913] 1 Ch. 269; *Hoare & Co. v. McAlpine* [1923] 1 Ch. 167; *Manchester Corporation v. Farnworth* [1930] A.C. 171; *Davey v. Harrow Corporation* [1958] 1 Q.B. 60; *Dalton v. Angus* (1881) 6 App. Cas. 740; *Young v. Bankier Distillery* [1893] A.C. 691.

43 *Thompson-Schwab v. Costaki* [1956] 1 All E.R. 652. But it has been held that there was no right to receive television free from electrical interference; this was not so important a part of an ordinary householder's enjoyment of property: *Bridlington Relay Ltd v. Yorkshire Electricity Board* [1965] Ch. 436. Contrast the view taken by an Ontario court in *Nor-Video Services Ltd v. Ontario Hydro* (1978) 19 O.R. (2d) 107, though this was concerned with the relaying of television by the plaintiff to their customers rather than the reception of television by householders. Nor is there any right to have an aesthetic view undisturbed by the defendant's conduct or activity: cp. *Muirhead v. Timber Bros.* (1977) 3 C.C.L.T. 1, with which contrast *Lockwood v. Brentwood Park Investments Ltd* (1970) 10 D.L.R. (3d) 143 at 161 (see below note 46). On the issue of subsidence caused by dealing with underground water, see the judgment of the Ontario Court of Appeal in *Pugliese v. National Capital Commission* (1978) 79 D.L.R. (3d) 592, on appeal (1979) 97 D.L.R. (3d) 631.

44 *Laws v. Florinplace Ltd* [1981] 1 All E.R. 659.

45 *Supra* at 656 *per* Romer L.J.

46 *Supra* note 44 at 66. Is this a hint of a change with respect to the "right to a pleasing view"?

47 *St Helens Smelting Co. Ltd v. Tipping* (1865) 11 H.L.C. 642 at 650–651 *per* Lord Westbury. What if the effect of the nuisance is to diminish the value of the plaintiff's property in the market without causing any physical damage? *Winfield & Jolowicz on Tort*, 12th ed. 1986, at 391 note 95 suggest this will suffice: *Hammersmith Rly v. Brand* (1867) L.R. 1 Q.B. 130; L.R. 2 Q.B. 223; (1869) L.R. 4 H.L. 171; cp. *Halsey v. Esso Petroleum Co. Ltd* [1961] 2 All E.R. 145 at 151 *per* Veale J. This is very questionable, unless the economic loss is a consequence of other, more physical damage, or accompanies discomfort. To accept the other view is to alter the entire nature and underlying purpose of the law of nuisance, which is about damage to the personal well-being of the plaintiff, not his economic situation.

discomfort to the plaintiff without at the same time producing property damage, the approach of thc law is more flexible. Two important factors must be taken into account. The first is the nature of the locality where the alleged nuisance occurred. The second is the quality of the interference with the plaintiff's comfort or enjoyment of land.

8.13 (*1*) *Locality*. In *St. Helens Smelting Co. v. Tipping*[48] the House of Lords upheld a direction to the jury which drew attention, *inter alia*, to the locality where the parties' properties were situated. In that case the plaintiff bought a valuable estate close to the defendants' smelting works. As a result of extensive operations begun shortly afterwards the plaintiff's shrubs and trees were injured by vapours exhaled from the works. In affirming a verdict for the plaintiff Lord Westbury L.C. said:[49]

> "... the personal inconvenience and interference with one's enjoyment, one's quiet, one's personal freedom, anything that discomposes or injuriously affects the senses or the nerves, whether that may or may not be denominated a nuisance, must undoubtedly depend greatly on the circumstances of the place where the thing complained of actually occurs."

Whether anything is a nuisance or not is a question to be determined not merely by an abstract consideration of the thing itself but in reference to its circumstances.[50] Thus even in a noisy neighbourhood it may be a nuisance for a defendant to increase the noise so as to interfere with the plaintiff's comfort.[51]

8.14 Despite the importance of the character of the locality in determining whether or not the defendant is committing a nuisance, it is not open to a defendant to argue that, on his own, he would not have created a nuisance and that it is only because others are engaging in the same activity that a nuisance occurred.[51a] For example, in *Lambton v. Mellish & Cox*[51b] the two defendants independently caused noise by their merry-go-rounds and organs used for school treats. Together these constituted a nuisance although the use by only one defendant of the merry-go-round and organ would not have done so. Similarly in *LeFanu v. Malcholmson*[51c] the defendant could not be heard to say that his factory only created a nuisance because the emanations from his property when added to those from other factories caused discomfort to the plaintiff. Some inconsistency seems apparent. What the defendant does is or is not a nuisance depending on whether the locale where everything happens is of a certain character or quality which is affected or disturbed by the defendant's activity. Yet if others are engaging in a similar activity, which would indicate that the locality has accepted such activity as the normal state of affairs, the

48 *Supra.*
49 *Ibid.* at 650.
50 *Sturges v. Bridgeman* (1879) 11 Ch.D. 852 at 865.
51 *Rusholme v. Polsue & Alfieri Ltd* [1906] 1 Ch. 234; [1907] A.C. 121.
51a *Thorpe v. Brumfitt* (1873) L.R. 8 Ch.App. 650; *Pride of Derby v. British Celanese* [1952] 1 All E.R. 1226 at 1331–1333.
51b [1894] 3 Ch. 163.
51c (1848) 1 H.L.C. 637.

defendant cannot excuse himself from liability by saying that he was only doing what others were doing (without having previously generated complaint). Thus a defendant can commit a nuisance while simultaneously conforming to the character of the district. This paradox can perhaps be explained by saying that a defendant can behave in a manner that is consistent with the norms of the area in question; but he may not go beyond those norms, so as to produce greater inconvenience or harm. Subtleties of this sort are by no means unfamiliar in the law of nuisance.[51d]

8.15 (2) *Standards.* Whether the consequences of the defendant's activity amount to a nuisance will also depend on the standards of the reasonable person, not on those of the plaintiff insofar as they may depart from such objective standards. As Luxmore J. said in *Vanderpant v. Mayfair Hotel Co.*:[52]

> "In deciding whether . . . a nuisance has been caused, it is necessary to determine whether the act complained of is an inconvenience materially interfering with the ordinary physical comfort of human existence, not merely according to elegant or dainty modes and habits of living but according to plain and sober and simple notions obtaining among English people . . .".

This is an idea that has been reiterated many times. The standards to be applied are those of ordinary everyday people.[53] Special circumstances that cause something to be an annoyance to a particular person, will not be regarded and taken into consideration in order to make something into a nuisance that would not be offensive to the average person. There must be some visible, actual, substantial damage that would have been incurred by the ordinary reasonable person.[54] Hence in *Colls v. Home & Colonial Stores*,[55] there was no nuisance by interference with light because the degree of interference and deprivation of light would not have affected the ordinary, average person, although it did have a harmful effect so far as the plaintiff was concerned. Similarly, no nuisance occurred in *Salvin v. North Brancepeth Coal Co.*,[56] where the alleged nuisance took the form of smoke from collieries. In that case[57] James L.J. referred to the necessity of showing "by a plain witness to a plain jury" that the ordinary reasonable person would have suffered the damage incurred by the plaintiff. Failing such proof, there could be no liability.

8.16 Thus in *Robinson v. Kilvert*[58] the defendant was not liable in nuisance when the heat from his premises, emanating from a manufacturing process that required high temperatures, damaged the plaintiff's brown paper

51d A more pragmatic explanation may be that to force a plaintiff to identify precisely how he was harmed by the particular defendant's activity might be to impose too great a burden or hardship on the plaintiff.

52 [1930] Ch. 138 at 165–166; Cp. *Walter v. Selfe* (1851) 4 De G. & Sm. 315 at 322 *per* Knight-Bruce V.C.

53 *Halsey v. Esso Petroleum Co. Ltd* [1961] 2 All E.R. 145 at 151 *per* Veale J.

54 *Colls v. Home & Colonial Stores* [1904] A.C. 179 at 209 *per* Lord Lindley.

55 *Supra.*

56 (1873) L.R. 9 Ch.App. 705.

57 *Ibid.* at 709.

58 (1889) 41 Ch.D. 88.

which he sorted in a room let to the plaintiff by the defendant. The latter carried on his manufacturing in a cellar below the room leased to the plaintiff. What he did there would not have been harmful or injurious to ordinary personal comfort. It caused damage to the plaintiff only because of the peculiar susceptibility of the paper kept by the plaintiff. The plaintiff could not complain, said Lopes L.J.,[59] because his exceptionally delicate trade was injured by something inherently lawful that would not injure anything else. A plaintiff must prove that the nuisance was due to an act that was unlawful, or the doing of something that was unnecessary and unreasonable and therefore unjustifiable.[60]

8.17 In this respect the courts have long entertained the conception of "live and let live", or "give and take".[61] People must accept the compromises of social life. As long as the defendant acted reasonably and carried on his activity in a convenient manner, it may be incumbent upon the plaintiff to accept the discomfort that is entailed.[62] But everything depends on the question whether the defendant has gone too far and inflicted excessive harm upon the plaintiff. The fact that the public may benefit from what the defendant is doing will not in itself operate as an excuse, justifying the defendant and exonerating him from liability. The public interest should not prevail over private interest.[63] The true issue is whether the right of the defendant to do what he likes with his own property outweighs the plaintiff's right not to be interfered with. It is a question of balance. One test that has been suggested is what is reasonable according to the ordinary usages of mankind living in society, or in a particular society.[64] Thus in *Kennaway v. Thompson*[65] the plaintiff obtained an injunction to prevent the defendants from organising and conducting motor boat races and water skiing on a lake on to which the plaintiff's property abutted. Despite the public's interest in such activities, and their inherent legality, it was held that this was a nuisance. The court ordered that the defendant's club be permitted to hold such activities only for restricted periods in the year and to keep down the noise level of boats using the lake at other times. In *Miller v. Jackson*[66] Lord Denning M.R. thought that the playing of cricket on the village green did not constitute a nuisance, although damage to the plaintiff's property resulted in consequence. The other members of the Court of Appeal disagreed. Over the question of an appropriate remedy, there was a difference of opinion. It is the divergence of views with respect to the utility of the defendant's conduct that is interesting.

59 *Ibid.* at 97. But once ordinary enjoyment has become the subject of interference the plaintiff can recover damage for his extraordinary or sensitive use, as occurred with respect to the damage to the plaintiff's orchids in *McKinnon Industries Ltd v. Walker* [1951] 3 D.L.R. 577.

60 *Dwyer v. Mansfield* [1946] K.B. 437 at 440 *per* Atkinson J.

61 *Bamford v. Turnley* (1862) 3 B. & S. 66.

62 *Ibid.* at 80 *per* Pollock C.B., dissenting.

63 *Kennaway v. Thompson* [1980] 3 All E.R. 329, following *Shelfer v. City of London Electric Lighting Co.* [1895] 1 Ch. 287. But see *Miller v. Jackson* [1977] 3 All E.R. 338 below.

64 *Sedleigh-Denfield v. O'Callaghan* [1940] A.C. 880 at 903 *per* Lord Wright.

65 *Supra* note 63.

66 [1977] 3 All E.R. 338.

8.18 (*3*) *Utility*. Sometimes the utility of what the defendant is doing may have some relevance to the issue of nuisance. A prime example is the situation with respect to construction of buildings, during which there is inevitably some disturbance to adjoining landowners (as well, perhaps, to the public at large).[67] The mere fact that what the defendant is doing may be of value and advantage to others, even to the general community, will not of itself excuse him from liability should interference, and *a fortiori* damage, result. Indeed, were the attitude of the law different, there would be no necessity for the passage of legislation giving protection to certain forms of activity from liability for nuisance.[68] In a recent Canadian case, for example, although it was accepted that putting de-icing agents on highways in the depths of a Canadian winter was necessary and desirable for public safety and the clearance of roads essential, that did not excuse the defendant, the Crown of Ontario, from liability when the de-icing substance in question got onto the plaintiff's land and caused damage to his trees (and consequent economic loss).[69] Hence it was surprising to learn that the playing of cricket could be so beneficial that it might not attract liability in nuisance. That had not been the attitude of the House of Lords in *Bolton v. Stone*[70] (where the issue involved considerations of negligence). Nor has it ever been the approach of the courts to the playing of other games, such as golf, which are lawful and may be regarded as beneficial. On the whole, though some writers suggest that social utility is a factor to be taken into account in determining whether a defendant's activity can amount to a nuisance,[71] it may be argued that it is closer to the truth to state that the courts seek to protect private individuals from interference with their comfort and enjoyment of property, rather than to provide immunity from liability to those whose activities have caused the interference. A party who upsets the normal state of condition of a certain neighbourhood, and creates dangers or discomfort which did not arise or exist before, does so at his peril.

(*iii*) *Malice*

8.19 A proved intention to annoy may show that the defendant is not using his property in an ordinary and legitimate way such as good neighbours habitually tolerate. Thus while the lack of any intent to harm or annoy will not disprove nuisance, the presence of such intent can have the opposite effect. It is not wrongful to exercise one's rights, such as the right to use one's property for one's own advantage and profit. Even if his use of the property is "malicious", in the sense of designed to injure others, the defendant may not be guilty of any tortious behaviour, since a bad motive cannot turn an otherwise lawful act into an unlawful, and therefore

67 *Harrison v. Southwark Water Co.* [1891] 2 Ch. 409.
68 Below pp. 204–207.
69 *Schenck v. The Queen* (1982) 20 C.C.L.T. 128.
70 [1951] A.C. 850.
71 Fleming, *Law of Torts*, 7th ed. 1987 at 391–393; *Winfield v. Jolowicz on Torts*, 12th ed. 1984 at 391: cp. the suggestion that social utility may be relevant *per* Howland J.A. in *Pugliese v. National Capital Commission* (1977) 79 D.L.R. (3d) 592 at 618. Contrast *Salmond & Heuston on the Law of Torts*, 19th ed. 1987 at 79.

tortious one.[72] However the fact that the defendant acted out of a desire to injure, rather than for the purpose of exercising rights over his property, may indicate that his activity goes beyond the standards that are acceptable as between landowners. In the context of the law of nuisance, the defendant's motive can sometimes have an effect upon the legality or otherwise of this conduct.[73]

8.20 In *Bradford Corporation v. Pickles*[74] the House of Lords held that the defendant was not liable in nuisance when he interfered with the course of water percolating underground in undefined channels below his property, even though his motive or purpose in doing so was to compel the plaintiffs to buy his land so as to provide water for the City of Bradford. Some years earlier, in *Chasemore v. Richards,*[75] it had been held that such water could not be regarded in the same way as water above ground moving in a defined channel. Over such water riparian owners had certain rights. They could prevent owners of riparian land above stream from diverting, or otherwise interfering with the flow of the water to the deprivation of riparian owners downstream. Underground water in an undefined channel was different. Hence Pickles was the absolute owner of the water under his property. He could do with it what he liked. Even if what he did was actuated by some improper motive or purpose, he committed no wrong, i.e. he was not guilty of nuisance.

8.21 Yet in the earlier case of *Christie v. Davey,*[76] the motive for making noise was material in determining the issue of nuisance. The plaintiff, a music-teacher, and the defendant, an engraver, were adjoining occupants for several years of two parts of a semi-detached house. The plaintiff's students caused noise which offended the defendant. Consequently, he indulged in hammering on the wall whenever the plaintiff was giving a lesson. His purpose was not to engage in his legitimate occupation of engraving but to annoy and disturb the plaintiff. The plaintiff's claim for nuisance was successful and the counterclaim of the defendant was dismissed. The noise from the plaintiff's music lessons was not excessive; the sound of the hammering was. It was suggested that if the plaintiff had acted maliciously, i.e. to offend the defendant not to engage in her legitimate activity, a diferent view of her conduct would have been taken by the court.[77]

8.22 In *Hollywood Silver Fox Farm v. Emmett*[78] liability was imposed on the

72 *Allen v. Flood* [1898] A.C. 1. See further below pp. 541–544. In the United States there has developed the idea of "*prima facie* tort", which is committed when something otherwise lawful is done for the purpose of causing injury, i.e. economic loss. No such doctrine can be found in England: *Abbott v. Sullivan* [1952] 1 K.B. 189, i.e. it is necessary to find some actual, nominate tort that has been committed before there can be liability to compensate a plaintiff.

73 Fridman, "Motive in the English Law of Nuisance" (1954) 40 Virginia L.R. 583.

74 [1895] A.C. 587.

75 (1859) 7 H.L.C. 349; see also *Broadbent v. Ramsbotham* (1856) 11 Ex. 602. Note the duty to receive water flowing above ground: *Mason v. Hill* (1833) 5 B. & Ad. 1. See, generally, *Home Brewery plc v. Davis & Co.* [1987] 1 All E.R. 637 at 641–644.

76 [1893] 1 Ch. 316.

77 *Ibid.* at 328.

78 [1936] 2 K.B. 468.

defendant for nuisance when the discharge of firearms on his property caused damage to the plaintiff. The latter owned a fox farm on land adjoining that of the defendant, who believed that the presence of the farm would prejudice the building value of his own land. The defendant's son let of "black-powder" cartridges on the boundary between the two properties so as to frighten the plaintiff's vixens. Some of them ceased to breed, others miscarried, others ate their young, because of their reaction to the noise. The defendant argued that he was entitled to shoot guns on his property, especially for the purpose of killing rabbits. He was held liable, however, because his purpose in shooting and making noise was not to exercise the legitimate rights of a landowner but to cause harm to his neighbour. He had acted maliciously, with intent to damage.

8.23 There are many possible interpretations of these decisions, which appear at first sight to be inconsistent. One is that under the doctrine of "give and take, live and let live" pronounced in *Bamford v. Turnley*,[79] reciprocal nuisances, such as the noise of the music lessons and the hammering in *Christie v. Davey*, the presence of the foxes and the shooting in the *Emmett* case, would provide a defence to nuisance if the defendant's acts had been honest, i.e. carried out for legitimate reasons. The abuse of the right to perform certain acts on one's property by reason of malicious intent with which the acts are perpetrated deprives the defendant of the opportunity to argue that his conduct was reasonable, having regard to the obligation on others to accept some interference with comfort or the enjoyment of property resulting from the exigencies of everyday life. In the *Pickles* case what was involved was not the performance of certain acts on his property by the defendant but the use of the property itself, in that the defendant was altering the flow of water below ground. The right to use such property was absolute, not relative. The right to do certain things on one's land, such as make noise, is not absolute: it can only be exercised or enjoyed if it is a legitimate and necessary action for a defendant to undertake and is connected with the reasonable use of his property.[79a]

(iv) Negligence

8.24 Neither deliberate act nor negligence are an essential ingredient of liability.[80] Negligence, said Lord Wright in *Sedleigh-Denfield v. O'Callaghan*,[81] is not a necessary condition of a claim for nuisance. Liability for nuisance is said to be strict, i.e. without the need to show that the defendant acted negligently. If a man commits a legal nuisance, said Lord Simonds in *Read v. J. Lyons & Co.*,[82] it is no answer to his injured neighbour that he took the utmost care not to commit it. The liability is strict. Lord Simonds was contrasting nuisance involving injury to property

79 (1862) 3 B. & S. at 84 *per* Bramwell B.
79a *Home Brewery plc v. Davis & Co.* [1987] 1 All E.R. 637 at 646–8, discussing the right of a party receiving percolating, unchannelled water to take steps to stop up holes into which the water flowed, even though this resulted in damming the water, which then flooded the plaintiff's land.
80 *Sedleigh-Denfield v. O'Callaghan* [1940] A.C. 880 at 886–897 *per* Lord Atkin.
81 *Ibid.* at 904.
82 [1947] A.C. 156 at 183.

with personal injury where it was necessary to establish that the defendant had acted negligently, in breach of a duty of care. In *Sedleigh-Denfield v. O'Callaghan*, the House of Lords dealt with the different situation that arose where the activity constituting the nuisance was not that of the defendant or those for whom in law he is responsible but that of a trespasser. The position of a defendant whose own acts are not involved is not the same as that of a defendant whose own behaviour or those of those for whom he is legally responsible has caused the nuisance. Where the latter is concerned the remarks quoted above indicate it is the character of the activity that is determinative of liability in nuisance, not the quality of that activity. What the defendant does on his land is the basis of liability in nuisance, not whether he is behaving carefully, i.e. taking such reasonable care as ought to be required of a person in the defendant's situation performing the activity that is the subject-matter of complaint.

8.25 The reason for this attitude is that the concept of nuisance was fashioned by the courts to regulate standards of behaviour as between neighbours, in an effort to control the extent to which one landowner could put others in jeopardy of either property damage or interference with comfort and enjoyment. Before modern legislation on town and country planning (what is called in North America "zoning"), the law of nuisance operated as an elementary, unsophisticated, unbureaucratic method of achieving much the same object. To a certain extent it managed to differentiate commercial and industrial areas from those which were residential, agricultural or otherwise not subject to the increased dangers emanating from the propagation of noise, fumes, etc. Negligence played no role in this determination. The purpose of the law was not to compel entrepreneurs or others to exercise care, but to preclude their conducting harmful or potentially harmful operations in localities where such activities must unduly upset the character of the area (or to compensate injured parties in respect of the harm that such operations caused). Modern writers, eschewing what might be termed the political or sociological aspects of the law of nuisance, have suggested instead that it served to regulate economic relations between different kinds of landowners.[83] Perhaps a better way of regarding the older law of nuisance is as a means whereby the common lawyers sought to protect the environment in which people lived (a task that is often performed by statutes or delegated legislation in modern society).

8.26 With the onset of such legislation perhaps a subtle change has been effected in the law of nuisance. Some decisions appear to suggest that, at least in certain situations, whether the defendant was negligent could be a factor in determining whether he has committed nuisance. An early

83 Ogus and Richardson, "Economics and the Environment: A Study of Private Nuisance" (1977) 36 C.L.J. 284. See also Tromans, "Nuisance—Prevention and Payment" (1982) 41 C.L.J. 87. The *locus classicus* of the economic view is Coase, "The Problem of Social Cost" (1960) 3 J.Law & Econ. 1: on which see Epstein, "A Theory of Strict Liability" (1973) 2 J.Leg.Stud. 151; Fletcher "Fairness and Utility in Tort Theory" (1972) 85 H.L.R. 537.

indication of this altered attitude is to be found in *Bolton v. Stone.*[84] There the House of Lords held that there would not be liability for damage resulting from the playing of cricket unless it could be shown that such damage was foreseeable as a consequence, and the defendants had failed to take reasonable care to prevent its occurrence. Because there was no evidence that balls had been hit great distances on previous occasions, so as to endanger those living nearby, it could not be concluded that to maintain a cricket ground and permit the playing of cricket was a nuisance. It might be argued that all the House of Lords was saying was that where no danger to adjoining landowners could be expected, since the possibility of a ball leaving the ground was very remote in view of past experiences, it was not "unreasonable" for the defendants to carry on the activity of holding cricket matches on their ground. Because nuisance involves making an "unreasonable" use of one's land, involving risk to other landowners in the neighbourhood, it followed that the behaviour of the defendants did not amount to making such a use of their land.

8.27 The language of the Privy Council in *The Wagon Mound (No. 2)*,[85] a case concerned with public nuisance, in the form of nuisance to navigable waters, suggests that negligence may have a greater role to play in defining when conduct is a nuisance. Indeed it is not too strong a statement to say that the dicta of Lord Reid in that case have made the task of defining what can be a nuisance much more difficult and complex. What Lord Reid said in the course of delivering the opinion of the Privy Council was:[86]

> "Nuisance is a term used to cover a wide variety of tortious acts or omissions, and in many negligence in the narrow sense is not essential .... And although negligence may not be necessary, fault of some kind is almost always necessary and fault generally involves foreseeability ....
>
> It could not be right to discriminate between different cases of nuisance so as to make foreseeability a necessary element in determining damages in those cases where it is a necessary element in determining liability, but not in others. So the choice is between its being a necessary element in all cases of nuisance or in none. In their Lordships' judgment the similarities between nuisance and other forms of tort to which *The Wagon Mound (No. 1)*[87] applies far outweigh any differences."

Admittedly Lord Reid was talking in terms of "foreseeability" not "negligence in the narrow sense", i.e., presumably, by reference to a duty of care, breach and consequent damage.[88] Nevertheless the language of Lord Reid indicates some movement away from the idea that "fault", "foresight of consequences", or "negligence" in some broader, more general sense, are all irrelevant to liability in nuisance and towards the notion that the defendant did not act innocently or ignorantly. This was established as the situation where the nuisance resulted from the act of a trespasser, or a predecessor in title, even before *The Wagon Mound (No. 2)* in cases

84 [1951] A.C. 850: with which contrast *Miller v. Jackson, supra.*
85 [1967] 1 A.C. 617: below p. 197.
86 *Ibid.* at 639–640.
87 [1961] A.C. 388: see pp. 340–341.
88 Pp. 273–344.

concerned with the adoption or continuation of a nuisance, as opposed to its original creation by the defendant.[89] *The Wagon Mound (No. 2)* suggests that a similar approach may be legitimate where a plaintiff seeks to make the defendant liable for creating a nuisance.

8.28 However the language of Lord Reid is far from clear: and there is debate over the question whether he intended to introduce negligence as an element of liability in nuisance, beyond the sphere of public nuisance with which the case was concerned, or something quite different, namely, "fault".[90] A more recent decision of the Court of Appeal once again stresses that a plaintiff need not plead or prove negligence in order to succeed in an action for nuisance but, at the same time, reveals how the language of Lord Reid in *The Wagon Mound (No. 2)* may have been used to make further adaptations of the law. In *Leakey v. National Trust*[91] the nuisance in question took the form of a natural hazard, not something created by the defendant. The plaintiffs claimed an injunction to compel the defendant to act so as to prevent the situation of the defendant's land from causing damage to the property of the plaintiff. The defendant argued unsuccessfully that there was no obligation to do anything where the potentially dangerous situation came about by reason of the natural state of the land; and that to impose liability on the defendant the plaintiff would have to show that the defendant was negligent. On the defendant's land was a conical shaped hill composed of soil that would crack and slip when weathered. The plaintiffs owned houses at the base of the hill, beyond the boundary between the land of the defendant and that of the plaintiffs. Slides of soil, rocks, tree-roots and other debris had occurred in previous years. In the year in question a drought followed by a wet autumn aggravated the natural weathering of the soil and created a large crack in the bank of the hill above the house of one of the plaintiffs. She pointed this out to the defendant, who replied that there was no obligation to do anything as this was caused by the natural movement of the earth. A little later there was a large fall from the bank, i.e. the hill, onto the plaintiff's land. This fall of soil came right up to her house and put it in danger if there were further falls. When asked to do so the defendant, disclaiming responsibility for what had happened, refused to clear the fallen earth. As a result the plaintiffs sued for injunctions to require the defendant to remove the fallen soil and debris and prevent further falls of earth, etc., and for damages for nuisance. Negligence was not pleaded. At trial the plaintiffs were successful. The defendant's appeal was dismissed.

8.29 The lengthy, analytical judgment of Megaw L.J.,[92] adopts the decision of the Privy Council in *Goldman v. Hargrave*[93] as part of the law of

89 Below pp. 195–198.
90 Dias, "Trouble in Oiled Waters: Problems of *The Wagon Mound (No. 2)*" [1967] C.L.J. 62; Buxton, "The Negligent Nuisance" (1966) 8 Malaya L.R. 1; Buxton, "Nuisance and Negligence Again" (1966) 29 M.L.R. 676; Eekelaar, "Nuisance and Strict Liability" (1973) 8 Ir.Jur. 191.
91 [1980] 1 All E.R. 17 (followed and applied in *Bradburn v. Lindsay* [1983] 2 All E.R. 408: see also *Home Brewery plc v. Davis & Co.* [1987] 1 All E.R. 637b at 645–646).
92 *Supra* note 91 at 24–37.
93 [1967] 1 A.C. 645.

England, although it involved an appeal from Australia. As a consequence of that earlier decision, where a dangerous situation arose by operation of nature, not by some human act, the liability of the occupier of the land in nuisance was based on his neglect of remedial action in the face of something that might damage his neighbour. Hence all depended on whether the occupier knew of the danger. In this respect, therefore, a distinction could be drawn between patent and latent hazards or conditions. Once the condition was known to the occupier, or ought to have been known to him, there was a duty on the occupier to do what was reasonable in all the circumstances, but no more than what was reasonable to prevent or minimise the known risk of damage or injury to the occupier's neighbour or to his property.[94] It was recognised by the Court of Appeal in the *Leakey* case[95] that *Goldman v. Hargrave* was, in the words of Shaw L.J., "the climax of a movement in the law of England expanding that part of the law which relates to liability for nuisance". Thus, foresight of harm or fault or negligence in a broad, not narrow sense, has been utilised by the courts not as a means of alleviating the strictness of nuisance liability as might be thought, but as a method to extend or expand the scope of such liability.

(v) Damage

8.30 The modern tort of nuisance is based upon the old action on the case. Hence damage is the gist of the action. Damage must therefore be proved, not merely conjectured.[96] However it is sometimes possible for damage to be presumed, as, for instance, where damage is so likely that it would seem unnecessary to insist on strict proof that it has occurred. This would be the situation where damage to property is the essence of the plaintiff's claim in nuisance.[97] Where personal discomfort is involved it is necessary for the plaintiff to establish that he has been affected materially, and in a manner that would affect ordinary persons, not abnormally sensitive ones.

8.31 There are certain types of nuisance in respect of which damage will be presumed by the law. It was pointed out in *Nicholls v. Ely Beet Sugar Co.*[98] that disturbance of an easement or similar right is a wrong in the nature of a trespass and therefore actionable without allegation or proof of special, i.e. actual damage. The action was on the case only because trespass was technically impossible. In that case the defendants discharged refuse into a river in which the plaintiff owned fisheries. The Court of Appeal held that the action could be maintained without proof of actual

94 *Supra* note 91 at 35 *per* Megaw L.J.
95 *Ibid.* at 39. Shaw L.J. was very doubtful about the validity of this.
96 *Salvin v. North Brancepeth Coal Co.* (1873) L.R. 9 Ch.App. 705 at 709 *per* James L.J.
97 *Fay v. Prentice* (1845) 1 C.B. 828.
98 [1936] Ch. 343 at 349 *per* Lord Wright M.R.: and see *Pride of Derby and Derby Angling Association Ltd v. British Celanese Ltd* [1953] Ch. 149.

pecuniary loss, although, on the facts, the plaintiff was unsuccessful because he could not prove that his injury was caused by the defendants.

(c) Entitlement to sue

8.32 Originally nuisance was remedied by the assize of nuisance which could only be maintained by one freeholder against another. Later, when the action on the case for nuisance was more general, others could sue even if not freeholders. Some interest in the property wrongly interfered with had to be shown before the action would lie. That principle pervades modern English case law. In 1907 Gorell Barnes P. stated that no principle of law could be formulated to the effect that a person who has no interest in property, no right of occupation in the property sense of the term, could maintain an action for nuisance.[99] In order to maintain an action the plaintiff must show some title to the thing to which the nuisance is alleged to be.[100] In the language of Lord Simonds in *Read v. J. Lyons*:[101] "He alone has a lawful claim who has suffered an invasion of some proprietary or other interest in land."

8.33 Hence the owner of the land to which the nuisance is committed can bring an action.[102] This can include the owner of a semi-detached house built as a unit along with another semi-detached property. The owner of one part of the unit could sue for nuisance committed by the owner of the other part who had allowed his part to get into such a state of dereliction that damage could be caused to the plaintiff's property by the general state of the defendant's property as well as by dry rot emanating from the latter premises.[103] If the nuisance is a continuing nuisance, a person who subsequently acquires ownership may also sue in respect of what the defendant did prior to the acquisition of title to the affected property by the plaintiff. In *Masters v. London Borough of Brent*[104] the roots of a lime tree affected property in which the plaintiff's father held a leasehold. The plaintiff paid for repairs necessitated by the growth of the tree and later purchased his father's interest. He was able to recover the cost of the repairs, even though he had not been the owner of the leasehold at the time the repairs were carried out. If the nuisance causes damage that will permanently affect property, the owner of a reversionary interest in the property will be able to maintain an action in respect of the damage that has been caused to him.[105] A tenant, in virtue of his occupation of

99 *Malone v. Laskey* [1907] 2 K.B. 141 at 151.
100 *Cunard v. Antifyre Ltd* [1933] 1 K.B. 551 at 557.
101 [1947] A.C. 146 at 183.
102 Where the property consists of an easement or other incorporeal hereditament disturbance of the right is the basis of the action: *Nicolls v. Ely Beet Sugar Co.* [1936] 1 Ch. 343: *Weston v. Lawrence Weaver Ltd* [1961] 1 Q.B. 402.
103 *Bradburn v. Lindsay* [1983] 2 All E.R. 408.
104 [1978] 2 All E.R. 664.
105 *Jones v. Llanwrast U.D.C.* [1911] 1 Ch. 393; e.g. where vibrations caused substantial damage: *Colwell v. St Pancras B.C.* [1904] Ch. 707. But not noise or fumes causing tenants to leave or reducing the letting value of premises: *Simpson v. Savage* (1856) 1 C.B.N.S. 347; *Cooper v. Crabtree* (1882) 20 Ch.D. 589.

land or premises, even one which is only a weekly tenant, can also sue in nuisance.[106] Possession of land suffices.[107]

8.34 A person who is merely present on land, however, without some title or interest, will not be permitted to sue in nuisance[108] and will have to establish some other cause of action, such as negligence. The reason given for this exclusion by the court in *Cunard v. Antifyre Ltd*[109] was that "it would manifestly be inconvenient and unreasonable if the right to complain of such interference extended beyond the occupier or (in the case of injury to the reversion) the owner of such neighbouring property". Hence in that case the plaintiff's wife who was injured through the failure of the defendant to repair his premises was unable to recover in nuisance as she was not the occupier. In the earlier decision in *Malone v. Laskey*[110] the wife of a tenant could not be heard to complain of damage caused by vibrations produced by the defendant on his adjoining premises.

8.35 These authorities were not followed, however, by the Alberta Court of Appeal in *Motherwell v. Motherwell.*[111] There the basis of the claim for an injunction against the defendant was the defendant's constant telephoning of various members of the family living in one house. The true nature of the plaintiff's claim was "invasion of privacy".[112] But in the absence of a claim on such basis, the court was prepared to allow a remedy on the ground of nuisance. Not only was the actual tenant or owner of the house where the telephone calls were received causing harrassment and inconvenience: the court held that others equally offended and upset, even though lacking any proprietary or possessory interest, could also maintain an action. This case could be distinguished on a variety of grounds. It involved injunctive relief, not damages as the *Malone* and *Cunard* cases. It was essentially an action designed to protect privacy, a personal right comparable to personal rather than property rights. The injury suffered by the various plaintiffs was all of the same kind, namely disruption of peaceful life by reason of the constant telephoning, rather than different kinds of damage incurred by the spouses in the earlier English cases. However, if no such distinctions are truly capable of being drawn, the decision in this Albertan case suggests that some courts may be prepared to abandon the strict discrimination between landowners or tenants and others so far as private nuisance is concerned in the same way as the law has readily abandoned any such differentiation where private actions based on public nuisance are involved.[113] Since, in both instances, the

106 *Jones v. Chappell* (1869) L.R. 20 Eq. 539 at 544.
107 Even if unlawful: *Newcastle-under-Lyme Corporation v. Wolstanton Ltd* [1947] Ch. 92, reversed on other grounds [1947] Ch. 427: cp. *Fitzgerald v. Firbank* [1897] 2 Ch. 96.
108 *Malone v. Laskey, supra* at 154 *per* Fletcher-Moulton L.J.: cp. *Vaughn v. Halifax-Dartmouth Bridge Commissioners* (1961) 29 D.L.R. (2d) 523.
109 [1933] 1 K.B. 441 at 557.
110 *Supra* para. 8.32.
111 (1976) 73 D.L.R. (3d) 62. See also *Devon Lumber Co. Ltd v. MacNeill* (1988) 45 D.L.R. (4th) 300.
112 See below pp. 523.
113 Below pp. 213–216.

purpose is to compensate for personal injury, in contrast with damage to, or in connection with property, there seems nothing irrational in this development.

(d) Incidence of liability

(i) Creator of nuisance

8.36 Whoever is responsible for the actual creation of the situation that constitutes the nuisance will be liable. In most instances this person will be the occupier or owner (or owner/occupier) of the land from which the nuisance emanates. However there need be no evidence that the creator of the nuisance had any proprietary or possessory interest in the land in question.[114] If at the time the nuisance was created the creator did have such an interest, it will be no defence to an action for damages to say that, since the time the nuisance was created, he has lost or disposed of that interest so that he can no longer enter the land in order to abate or discontinue the nuisance.[115]

(ii) Occupier

8.37 The occupier of the land on which the nuisance is created will be liable if he has created the nuisance. Occupation can be as owner or otherwise. The ground of responsibility, said Lord Wright in *Sedleigh-Denfield v. O'Callaghan*,[116] is the possession and control of the land from which the nuisance proceeds. The occupier will be liable not only if he personally created the nuisance, or it was created by his servant or agent, but also if it was created by someone who is his licensee, for example gypsies allowed to camp on the defendant's land.[117] He will also be liable if the nuisance resulted from the acts of his independent contractor.[118] In this respect nuisance differs from negligence and other torts, and resembles liability under the doctrine of *Rylands v. Fletcher*.[119] The attitude of the law has been that the obligations of an occupier of land are sufficiently strict and onerous to entail responsibility for the behaviour of contractors, for whom, usually, employers are not vicariously liable.[120]

8.38 The scope of liability for nuisance extends even further. As the House of Lords held in *Sedleigh-Denfield v. O'Callaghan*,[121] an occupier will also be liable for nuisances created by a trespasser of whose presence and activities he was ignorant, if the occupier had reasonable means of knowledge of what the trespasser has done and a reasonable opportunity

114 As to the suggestion that the nuisance might be created on the plaintiff's land, see two New Zealand cases: *Baxhaven Holdings Ltd v. Attorney-General* [1974] 2 N.Z.L.R. 185; *Clearlite Holdings Ltd v. Auckland City Council* [1976] 2 N.Z.L.R. 729: cp. *supra* note 17.
115 *Thompson v. Gibson* (1841) 7 M. & G. 456: *Rosewall v. Prior* (1701) 12 Mod. 635.
116 [1940] A.C. 880 at 903.
117 *Attorney-General v. Stone* (1895) 12 T.L.R. 76.
118 *Spicer v. Smee* [1946] 1 All E.R. 489; cp. *Bower v. Peate* (1876) 1 Q.B.D. 321; *Dalton v. Angus* (1881) 6 App. Cas. 740; *Matania v. National Provincial Bank* [1936] 2 All E.R. 633.
119 (1868) L.R. 3 H.L. 330: see pp. 221–222.
120 Pp. 66–70 below.
121 [1940] A.C. 880, following the dissenting judgment of Scrutton L.J. in *Job Edwards v. Birmingham Canal Navigation Co.* [1924] 1 K.B. 341.

to deal with the nuisance in question. The fact that the occupier could have discovered the condition of his land and could have remedied the situation had he acted with reasonable care leads to his responsibility. In the *Sedleigh-Denfield* case a trespasser entered on to the defendants' land without the defendants' knowledge and blocked a pipe and a ditch by the erection of a culvert. The defendants' servants annually cleaned the ditch and knew about the culvert but did nothing about it. After some years a heavy rainfall choked the pipe with leaves and caused a flood which damaged the land of the plaintiff. The defendants were held liable in nuisance although they had not created the nuisance and knew nothing about it when it was first created. The defendants were liable for having "continued" the nuisance since they had knowledge or presumed knowledge of the existence of the culvert which constituted the nuisance and had failed to take reasonable care to bring it to an end.

8.39 The House of Lords distinguished between three ways in which a defendant could be liable for nuisance. The first was by its creation. Secondly, the defendant might continue a nuisance created by someone else. Thirdly the defendant could "adopt" a nuisance created by someone else.[122] Some members of the House differentiated continuation from adoption of a nuisance:[123] Lord Wright thought that these were but two ways of saying the same thing.[124] Either way, the essential point is that an occupier can be held responsible even though he was not directly or vicariously guilty of creation of a nuisance where he fails to abate a nuisance that is present on his land as a consequence of the activities of a stranger. As Singleton J. said in *Cunliffe v. Bankes*:[125]

> "A person is liable for a nuisance constituted by the state of his property (1) if he causes it, (2) if by the neglect of some duty he allowed it to arise, and (3) if, when it has arisen without his own act or default, he omits to remedy it within a reasonable time after he ought to have become aware of it."

This means also that an occupier can be held liable for a nuisance created by his predecessor in title if he knew or ought to have known of its existence at the time when he occupied the property.[126] Hence in *Sampson v. Hodson-Pressinger*[127] a person who purchased the freehold of a flat was liable for a nuisance committed by the tenant of the flat, since the purchaser knew of the existence of the state of affairs that constituted the nuisance at the time of the purchase. The state of affairs in question was

122 See *Tate & Lyle Industries Ltd v. Greater London Council* [1983] 1 All E.R. 1159, where the Port of London Authority was not liable for continuing or adopting a nuisance merely because they approved a plan of the Greater London Council to construct ferry terminals in the river, the construction of which caused sedimentation of the bed of the river affecting the plaintiff's raw sugar jetty.

123 [1940] A.C. 880 at 894 *per* Lord Maugham.

124 *Ibid.* at 904–905.

125 [1945] 1 All E.R. 459 at 465: cp. *Noble v. Harrison* [1926] 2 K.B. 332 at 338 *per* Rowlatt J.

126 *St Anne's Well Brewery Co. v. Roberts* (1928) 44 T.L.R. 703; *Wilkins v. Leighton* [1932] 2 Ch. 106; in neither of which the defendant had the required knowledge and no liability was imposed.

127 [1981] 3 All E.R. 710.

the result of the original construction, as a consequence of which when the tenant had guests the noise from the tenant's flat permeated the flat of the plaintiff in the floor beneath.

8.40 There are *dicta* which suggest that an occupier might be liable for a nuisance created by a predecessor in title even without knowledge of its existence or the means of removing it.[128] However the tenor of the judgment in the *Sedleigh-Denfield* case, and other decisions, before and later,[129] would indicate that some degree of fault is necessary before such an occupier can be held liable. The test of "foreseeability" propounded by Lord Reid in *The Wagon Mound (No. 2)*[130] and further considered and discussed by the Court of Appeal in *Leakey v. National Trust*,[131] points to the need to establish some degree of awareness and lack of reasonable care on the part of an occupier who was not the originator of the nuisance.

8.41 This has certainly been the situation where the nuisance emanated from natural causes, where some natural hazard developed on the occupier's land without the occupier's intervention, desire or knowledge. As noted earlier, the courts have taken the view that the occupier will be liable if and when he knew or ought to have known about the condition resulting from the operation of natural causes, could have remedied the situation by taking reasonable care, which means without involving himself in undue and unreasonable expenditures of money, and failed to do anything.[132] If the occupier lacks such knowledge, the situation will be different. In this way the element of negligence, in a broad sense, not as Lord Reid expressed it in *The Wagon Mound (No. 2)*,[133] "the narrow sense", enters into the discussion of liability in nuisance. The tempering of what would otherwise be a form of strict liability by the requirement of knowledge and reasonable care, where it is sought to hold an occupier liable for a nuisance which he has not himself created, has led some commentators to the point of view that nuisance and negligence are not as distinguishable as formerly they might have been.[134] However it might be said by way of response that an occupier who actually knows of the hazardous condition of his property, or fails to discover this when a reasonable person would have done so by taking ordinary, not extraordinary care, is not entirely without blame, and should not be permitted to excuse himself from liability merely by pleading ignorance or the fact that

128 *Sedleigh-Denfield v. O'Callaghan* [1940] A.C. 880 at 897 *per* Lord Atkin, 919, *per* Lord Porter: cp. *Wringe v. Cohen* [1940] 1 K.B. 229, the status of which is in doubt after *Sedleigh-Denfield*.

129 *Noble v. Harrison* [1926] 2 K.B. 332: *St Anne's Well Brewery Co. v. Roberts* (1928) 44 T.L.R. 703 at 706 *per* Scrutton L.J.; *Cushing v. Walker & Son* [1941] 2 All E.R. 700; *Slater v. Worthington Cash Stores Ltd* [1941] 1 K.B. 488; *Leanse v. Egerton* [1943] K.B. 323; cp. *Caminer v. Northern and London Investment Trust* [1951] A.C. 88.

130 [1967] 1 A.C. 617, above para. 8.27.

131 [1980] 1 All E.R. 17; above para. 8.28.

132 *Leakey v. National Trust, supra*; *Goldman v. Hargreave* [1967] 1 A.C. 645.

133 *Supra* note 130 at 639–640.

134 See the authorities cited *supra* note 90.

he did not originate the condition of his property.[135] It is control of property that is the basis of liability in nuisance. Occupation or control of property carries with it duties and responsibilities towards others such as adjoining occupiers.[136]

(iii) Landlord out of possession

8.42 That idea, namely that control of property entails responsibility for its state or condition, underlies the question of a landlord's or owner's liability for nuisances on his property even though the landlord or owner is out of possession of the property when the plaintiff incurs the damage or discomfort. If the property is let in a state that produces a nuisance, the landlord will be liable when nuisance occurs.[137] It is the landlord who has brought about the damage or inconvenience to the plaintiff by permitting his premises to be occupied by a tenant when in a hazardous or offensive condition. In such situations the landlord is liable by reason of his personal responsibility for what occurs. A landlord may also be personally responsible for a nuisance which results from the activity of his tenant where the landlord leases property for a purpose which involves the commission of nuisance.[138] Several different tests of liability were referred to by McNeil J. in *Tetley v. Chitty*.[139] First there was the proposition that where an occupier of land grants a licence to another to do certain acts on the land, and the licensee in doing them commits a nuisance, the occupier may be made a defendant to a suit to restrain the nuisance.[140] A second proposition was that the landlord could only be liable if what was done was done with his express or implied authority. It would be insufficient to show merely a likely consequence: a plaintiff to succeed must show a necessary consequence of the lease by the landlord for the purpose in question.[141] As Lush J. put it,[142] the nuisance must be "the ordinary and necessary" consequence of what the tenant or licensee was authorised to do on the property. The nuisance must be expressly authorised or must be certain to result from the purposes for which the property is let, as Pennycuick V.C. said in *Smith v. Scott*.[143] Applying this latter test, McNeil J. held in *Tetley v. Chitty* that the defendant council was liable in nuisance for noise resulting from the use of land let to a go-kart club to develop a go-kart trade.

8.43 Liability results in such situations from an extension of the idea of control. The landlord who knows or ought to know the use to which the

135 But he may excuse himself if to remedy the situation would cost more than it was reasonable to expect of him in his individual circumstances: *Goldman v. Hargrave, supra* at 663 *per* Lord Wilberforce. This is a subjective test, not the more usual objective test applied in the tort of negligence: see pp. 316–318.

136 Hence, perhaps the old maxim "*Sic utere tuo ut alienum non laedas*", which has been said to be misleading: *Bamford v. Turnley* (1862) 3 B. & S. 66 at 79, 83–84; *Bonomi v. Backhouse* (1867) L.R. 2 Q.B. 223 at 247 *per* Erle J.

137 *Spicer v. Smee* [1946] 1 All E.R. 489 at 493.

138 *White v. Jameson* (1874) L.R. 18 Eq. 303; *Rich v. Basterfield* (1847) 4 C.B. 783; *Johnson v. Jackson* (1889) 40 Ch.D. 71. Contrast *Smith v. Scott* [1972] 3 All E.R. 645.

139 [1986] 1 All E.R. 663 at 669–671.

140 *White v. Jameson, supra* at 305 *per* Jessel M.R.

141 *Harris v. James* (1876) 45 L.J.Q.B. 545 at 546 *per* Blackburn J.

142 *Ibid.* at 547.

143 *Supra* at 649.

leased property will be put notionally controls such use. He could refuse to lease the property for such purpose: he could in other ways require the tenant not to commit nuisances. That was the reason why the defendant council was not liable in *Smith v. Scott.*[144] Although the council had put a family likely to cause a nuisance into a house next door to the plaintiff, the council had done so on terms expressly prohibiting the commission of a nuisance. Pennycuick V.C. held that the council was not liable for the nuisance eventually committed by the family, i.e. the tenants, for the council had not authorised the nuisance: it had in fact attempted to prevent its occurrence. Control is also theoretically exercisable by a landlord who has the right or duty to repair premises which have been leased. Hence in many decisions a landlord out of possession has been held liable for a nuisance resulting from a state of disrepair into which premises had fallen by reason of the landlord's failure to fulfil his obligation.

8.44 Such was the decision in *Wringe v. Cohen,*[145] even though the landlord did not know, and could not be presumed to know, that the pointing on the chimney of the premises leased to a tenant had weathered so as to cause the chimney-breast to bulge and eventually fall and damage the adjoining shop of the plaintiff. The authority of this decision has been in some doubt since the case of *Sedleigh-Denfield v. O'Callaghan,*[146] which emphasised the element of knowledge or presumed knowledge.[147] However other decisions also suggest that regardless of whether the landlord was negligent in not dealing with a state of affairs of which he was aware or ought to have been aware, he will be liable if the nuisance complained of came about because the landlord failed to carry out his duties with regard to maintaining the leased premises in a state of repair.[148] In these cases the landlord expressly reserved a right, or duty, to repair in the lease. In *Mint v. Good,*[149] however, it was held that the same result would follow where the landlord impliedly reserved the right to repair. Here the defendant let a house on a weekly tenancy. He was held liable for injury caused by the collapse of a wall that was in a defective condition which could have been ascertained by a reasonable person. The plaintiff in that case was a passer-by on the highway, as in the cases referred to above, which may have made a difference. The judgment of the court seems to be concerned with the issue of liability for nuisance to the highway. But it can be argued that, logically, if a landlord is liable where he has expressly undertaken to keep premises in repair to adjoining occupiers who are affected by his failure to maintain the property, he ought to be liable equally if his duty or right to enter and repair is implied. Moreover, the liability described in these cases is based on the principle of "proximity", a principle which should

144 [1972] 3 All E.R. 645.
145 [1940] 1 K.B. 229.
146 [1940] A.C. 880.
147 Cp. *Todd v. Flight* (1860) 9 C.B.N.S. 377; *Gwinnell v. Eamer* (1875) L.R. 10 C.P. 658; *Pretty v. Bickmore* (1873) L.R. 8 C.P. 401.
148 *Wilchick v. Marks & Silverstone* [1934] 2 K.B. 56; *Heap v. Ind Coope & Allsopp Ltd* [1940] 2 K.B. 476.
149 [1951] 1 K.B. 517.

apply equally to neighbours at least as far as known dangers are concerned.[150]

8.45 A more recent case seems to take the law further. In *Brew Bros. Ltd v. Snax (Ross) Ltd*[151] a lease of premises placed the burden of repair on the tenants under an express convenant to repair. The flank wall of the premises subsequently tilted towards the plaintiff's neighbouring garage. The landlord, tenant and plaintiff all agreed to shore up the wall temporarily, thereby creating an obstruction to the forecourt of the garage. The reason for the tilting was that the foundations of the wall had shifted because of seepage from drains below the demised premises, probably because of wartime bomb damage. It was found as a fact that the landlord ought to have known at the date of the granting of the lease that the foundations of the wall were so defective that unless they were remedied the whole building was doomed and was liable to collapse onto the neighbouring property. It was held, *inter alia*, by two members of the Court of Appeal that the landlords were jointly responsible with the tenant for obstructing the forecourt, for damages resulting from the obstruction and the cost of the subsequent abatement of the nuisance (which the landlord had agreed to do). Two members of the court also considered that the landlord was not exculpated once the landlord knew or ought to have known of the dangerous state of the premises merely by the fact that the landlord had taken a full repairing convenant from the tenant. Both Sachs and Phillimore L.JJ. stressed that the liability of an owner of premises rests on control and foresight of harm to a neighbour. In the words of Sachs L.J.:[152]

> "If the nuisance arises after the lease is granted, the test of an owner's duty to his neighbour now depends on the degree of control exercised by the owner in law or in fact for the purpose of repairs . . . . As regards nuisances of which he knew at the date of the lease, the duty similarly arises by reason of his control before that date. Once the liability attaches I can find no rational reason why it should as regards third parties be shuffled off merely by signing a document which as between owner and tenant casts on the latter the burden of executing remedial work. The duty of the owner is to ensure that the nuisance causes no injury—not merely to get somebody's promise to take the requisite steps to abate it . . . .
>
> The owner of property . . . remains liable to third parties for the effects of a nuisance of which he has knowledge at the date of granting a lease unless excused by some further fact over and above taking a covenant to repair . . ."

The tenor of the judgments in this case, in which are discussed the earlier decisions dealing with the liability of owners out of possession by virtue of a lease of the property that is the source of the nuisance, is that the law regards the burden on a landowner as very heavy. His duty to avoid causing injury to a neighbour by the state of his property which he has leased remains unfulfilled if he leases the property in the dangerous condition, as long as he knows or ought to have known of this and if he

150 *Brew Bros. Ltd v. Snax (Ross) Ltd* [1970] 1 All E.R. 587 at 601 *per* Sachs L.J.
151 *Supra.*
152 *Ibid.* at 601.

expressly or impliedly undertakes the duty of keeping the property in repair. The fact that he is not the occupier will not exempt the owner from liability when he still has effective control over the situation at the time the nuisance comes into existence. In this sense, therefore, owners of property are considered by the law to be occupiers even though they do not enjoy physical or legal possession of the property.

(e) Defences

(i) Coming to the nuisance

8.47 It has long been held that it is no defence that the plaintiff came to the nuisance. The fact that the plaintiff leased or bought the property with knowledge of the condition of the defendant's land or premises, such that he was aware that a nuisance was in existence, will not afford the defendant any excuse or defence. In *Bliss v. Hall*[153] the defendant carried on the business of a tallow-chandler, which emitted smells, etc. The plaintiff bought the house next door knowing of the defendant's activity. He then complained of nuisance. He was successful. The plaintiff was entitled to enjoy the right to "wholesome air",[154] despite his foreknowledge that such air was sadly lacking. In other words the plea of *volenti non fit injuria*, which has been effective in other contexts to deny liability,[155] is not applicable in the law of nuisance.[156] However, at the same time, it is correct to say that the existing state of the land where a plaintiff decides to buy or lease may have relevance to potential liability for nuisance.

8.48 The distinction appears to be this. If the defendant's activity was not a nuisance to anyone prior to the advent of the plaintiff, it can become a nuisance vis-à-vis the plaintiff once the latter becomes an adjoining landowner or occupier. As Lane L.J. said in *Miller v. Jackson*:[157]

> ". . . it is no answer to a claim for nuisance for the defendant to show that the plaintiff brought the trouble on his own head by building or coming to live in a house so close to the defendant's premises that he would inevitably be affected by the defendant's activities, where no one had been affected previously."

This rule might work injustice, but the Court of Appeal was bound by authority, viz., *Sturges v. Bridgeman*,[158] to hold accordingly. In that case, the

153 (1838) 4 Bing. N.C. 183.
154 *Ibid.* at 186 *per* Tindal C.J.
155 Pp. 348–356 below.
156 But consent to the activity may be a defence if the defendant is not negligent: *Kiddle v. City Business Properties Ltd* [1942] 1 K.B. 268. In Canada there are cases which indicate that acquiescence in the defendant's activity might be a defence: Linden, *Canadian Tort Law*, 4th ed. 1988 at 516–517. But a plaintiff will not be deprived of the right to sue if his inconvenience is in part the result of his own use of his land, unless this produces "abnormal sensitivity": above pp. 184–185. Nor is the plaintiff expected to take steps to avert or minimise the consequences of a nuisance, when this could be burdensome, e.g., living behind shutters or staying indoors during the playing of cricket: *Miller v. Jackson* [1977] 3 All E.R. 338.
157 [1977] 3 All E.R. 338 at 349.
158 (1879) 11 Ch.D. 852: see also below p. 203.

fact that the defendants had been making noise with their pestle and mortar for more than 20 years before the plaintiff, who was a physician, built a consulting-room on his own land immediately adjoining the defendants' confectionary shop, did not provide them with a defence. Prior to the building of the consulting-room the defendants' use of their land was neither preventible nor actionable. It is otherwise if the activity of the defendant was already causing inconvenience to other occupiers or owners in the neighbourhood before the plaintiff came along. As seen earlier, the character of the locality where the plaintiff resides or carries on business, and complains of nuisance, is determinative in part of the issue of liability.[159] A neighbourhood that is noisy, smelly, suffused by smoke or fumes, etc., is treated differently by the law from one that is generally speaking free of such inconveniences. Hence a party who voluntarily comes to a neighbourhood of that kind is in no position to complain of nuisance. This approach however only applies where inconvenience is concerned. If the plaintiff's complaint is of damage to property, the previous character of the neighbourhood will not be relevant.[160,161]

(ii) Jus tertii

8.49 The question has been raised whether a defendant can plead that the plaintiff had no right to the land in respect to which the nuisance is committed. The plea that a third party had a better right to property than a plaintiff is one that was available, prior to recent legislation, to a defendant sued for conversion (though not to a defendant in an action for trespass to goods).[162] Trespass, whether to land or goods, is a wrong to possession: and it is clear that the possession need not be lawful, as long as it was possession *de jure* not *de facto*.[163] Since nuisance is a wrong against the occupier of land, rather than the owner, except in special circumstances,[164] it would seem logical to conclude that the legality of the plaintiff's occupation is not material to the defendant's liability. Such indeed was the conclusion reached by Farwell J. in *Nicholls v. Ely Beet Sugar Factory Ltd.*[165]

159 Above pp. 183–184.
160 *St Helens Smelting Co. v. Tipping* (1865) 11 H.L.C. 642; nor where there is obstruction of ancient lights: *Fishenden v. Higgs & Hill* (1935) 153 L.T. 128 at 140 *per* Romer L.J.; see also below pp. 212–213.
161 There are different views on whether contributory negligence is a defence to private nuisance (it can be a defence in cases of public nuisance: *Trevett v. Lee* [1955] 1 W.L.R. 113: *Gilson v. Kerrier D.C.* [1976] 1 W.L.R. 904; *Dymond v. Pearce* [1972] 1 Q.B. 496). *Salmond & Heuston on the Law of Torts*, 19th ed. 1987, at 78–79 say that it is not; *Winfield & Jolowicz on Tort*, 12th ed. 1986, at 415 say that it is (see also Winfield, "Nuisance as a Tort" (1930–32) 4 at 205 note 10). Fleming, *Law of Torts*, 7th ed. 1987, at 409, regards both views as incorrect "because both fail to take into account the dual function which the concept of nuisance plays in modern law and which in the context, as elsewhere, causes confusion." His point is that when nuisance regulates competing uses of land contributory negligence is irrelevant; but when nuisance has "intruded into the field of ordinary accident litigation, particularly in regard to personal injury suffered as a result of a public nuisance on the highway" contributory negligence will be relevant, lest the plaintiff is better off suing in nuisance than in negligence. With respect, is this not the same view as that of Salmond, if not Winfield?
162 Above para. 7.39.
163 Above para. 7.06.
164 Above p. 193.
165 [1931] 2 Ch. 84 (on appeal [1936] 1 Ch. 343), following *Fitzgerald v. Firbank* [1897] 2 Ch. 96 at 97 *per* Kekewich J.

This case dealt with pollution of a private fishery, the invasion of rights of property rather than physical damagc or inconvenience. It was an injury to a servitude. However it would seem to follow that if *jus tertii* is not a defence to such an action it should not be to nuisance in general. However the point is unsettled by authority.[166]

(iii) Prescription

8.50 If the defendant has maintained the activity that results in the nuisance for a period of twenty years, openly not secretly, against the will of the plaintiff not with his agreement, peacefully not by force, this may provide the defendant with a defence.[167] Such long enjoyment of his use of property by the defendant can never excuse or act as a defence to liability for physical damage to the plaintiff's property, only to nuisance in the form of discomfort or disruption of the plaintiff's enjoyment of his property.

8.51 The nuisance must be known to the plaintiff: it must affect him continuously throughout the period in question. Hence time will only begin to run against the plaintiff from the date that he is aware that there is a nuisance. In *Sturges v. Bridgeman*,[168] on which the Court of Appeal relied more recently in *Miller v. Jackson*,[169] the defendant caused noise for twenty years or more. However the plaintiff was not aware of such noise, and it did not affect him injuriously, until he built his consulting-room. When he sued for nuisance the defendant attempted to rely on the defence of prescription, pleading his twenty years of continuous activity creating the noise in question. The defence failed, because there was no actionable nuisance, and therefore the prescription period did not commence, until the plaintiff actually suffered in consequence of what the defendant was doing.

8.52 This right to commit nuisance gained by prescription relates only to a specific piece of property. It is not a right against the whole world to commit the nuisance in question. Moreover because the idea behind prescription is that a particular use of a particular piece of property may legitimise the acts of the defendant as against the adjoining landowner or occupier who has been affected for the necessary period of time, it would appear to follow that the period may be calculated by reference to the continuation of the activity by the current owner or occupier of the offending property following after the enjoyment of that activity by his

166 For views similar to this see *Newcastle-under-Lyme Corporation v. Wolstanton Ltd* [1947] Ch. 92 at 109–110 *per* Evershed J. (reversed on other grounds [1947] Ch. 427); cp. *Paine & Co. Ltd v. St Neots Gas Co.* [1939] 3 All E.R. 812 at 816–817 *per* Scott L.J.

167 *Liverpool Corporation v. H. Coghill & Son Ltd* [1918] 1 Ch. 307. But not as a defence to public nuisance, for that is an offence against the common law: *Dewall v. Sanders* (1618) Cro. Jac. 490; *R. v. Cross* (1812) 3 Camp. 24; *Mott v. Shoolbred* (1875) L.R. 20 Eq. 22. Why twenty years? There is no magic in the twenty years, but a fixed period does have the advantage of certainty: Ogus and Richardson, "Economics and the Environment: A Study of Private Nuisance" (1977) 36 C.L.J. 284 at 303.

168 (1879) 11 Ch.D. 863.

169 [1977] 3 All E.R. 338.

predecessor in title; whereas once a prescriptive right has been acquired by the defendant against a particular occupier of the neighbouring property it will not be valid against the occupier's successor in title. Only when that party begins to suffer the effects of the nuisance will the prescription period begin to run against him. Such is the meaning and effect of *Sturges v. Bridgeman.*

8.53 The situation will be different, however, if as a consequence of the passage of the prescription period the defendant acquires an easement (which he could have acquired by grant from the adjoining, i.e. servient, tenement, or on acquisition of his property were such easement attached to it). Such an easement would confer a proprietary right on the owner of the dominant tenement to commit the nuisance. However such easements are confined to forms of interference that can be turned into easements.[170] Thus it may be possible for a defendant to acquire the right to discharge rainwater onto the land of the adjoining owner,[171] or to pollute water,[172] or emit fumes through a flue.[173] It would seem impossible to acquire an easement to inconvenience an adjoining landowner by offensive smells, or noise, because there is no certainty or uniformity in respect of the measurement and determination of the amount of user by which the extent of the prescriptive right is acquired.[174]

(iv) Statutory authority

8.54 Where a statute authorises an act, i.e. requires it to be performed, there is no liability for damage caused by the performance of that act, even if it amounts to a nuisance.[174a] The only remedy is to claim such compensation, if any, as the statute provides.[175] Only if the duty imposed by the statute is fulfilled negligently will there be liability.[176] Where the nuisance is attributable to the exercise of a *power*, not a duty, conferred by statute, the body so empowered will be liable, even without negligence, if the statute expressly makes it liable, or not exempted from liability for nuisance.[176a] But if a statute gives immunity when a power is exercised, it

170 Fleming, *op. cit.* at 409, suggests that prescription is only possible where an easement can be obtained. This, it is suggested, is not correct. There is a distinction between a prescriptive right to commit a nuisance and an easement, a servitude.

171 *Harvey v. Walkers* (1873) L.R. 8 C.P. 162.

172 *Hulley v. Silversprings Bleaching Co.* [1922] 2 Ch. 268.

173 *Jones v. Pritchard* [1908] 1 Ch. 630.

174 *Hulley v. Silversprings Bleaching Co., supra* at 281 per Eve J. This would be another reason for denying the defendant's claim in *Sturges v. Bridgeman, supra.*

174a *Hammond v. St Pancras Vestry* (1874) L.R. 4 C.P. 3126; *Stretton's Brewery Co. v. Derby Corporation* [1894] 1 Ch. 431; *Smeaton v. Ilford Corporation* [1954] Ch. 450.

175 See, e.g., *Marriage v. East Norfolk Rivers Catchment Board* [1950] 1 K.B. 284, awarding compensation under the Land Drainage Act 1930, for flooding caused by dredging a river and interfering with the river's ordinary flood course. Here there was no negligence.

176 *Geddis v. Proprietors of Ban Reservoir* (1878) 3 App. Cas. 430 at 455–456 *per* Lord Blackburn: e.g. *Manchester Corporation v. Farnworth* [1930] A.C. 171, failure to use reasonable care to prevent emission of poisonous fumes from generating station erected under statutory powers; the defendant was liable in nuisance: see *ibid.* at 183 *per* Viscount Dunedin.

176a *Charing Cross Electricity Supply Co. v. Hydraulic Power Co.* [1914] 3 K.B. 772.

may be possible for the body in question to rely on the defence of statutory authority.

8.55 The availability of the defence of "statutory authority" was established by a series of nineteenth century cases concerned with the operation of railways under statutory powers.[177] This was finally confirmed by the House of Lords in *Hammersmith & City Railway Co. v. Brand.*[178] In the subsequent case of *Geddis v. Proprietors of Bann Reservoir,*[179] it was also established that the authority of Parliament to construct and use certain works does not relieve the undertakers from the obligation to take due care that their operations do not cause injury to neighbouring proprietors. So the defence of statutory authority, the application of which has been extended to a wide field of industrial activities, does not avail against a claim that the creation of a nuisance has been brought about by negligence.[180] The present state of the law was summarised by Lord Wilberforce in *Allen v. Gulf Oil Refining Ltd*[181] in these words:

> "It is now well settled that where Parliament by express direction or by necessary implication has authorised the construction and use of an undertaking or works, that carries with it an authority to do what is authorised with immunity from any action based on nuisance. The right of action is taken away .... To this there is made the qualification or condition, that the statutory powers are exercised without 'negligence', that word here being used in a special sense so as to require the undertaker, as a condition of obtaining immunity from action, to carry out the work or conduct the operation with all reasonable regard and care for the interests of other persons .... It is within the same principle that immunity from action is withheld where the terms of the statute are permissive only, in which case the powers conferred might be exercised in strict conformity with private rights."

8.56 In the *Allen* case the House of Lords held, by a majority, that the Gulf Oil Refining Act 1965 would provide Gulf Oil with the defence if they could prove that a nuisance was the inevitable result of constructing and operating on the site dealt with in the Act a refinery which conformed to the intentions of Parliament (but not necessarily inevitably resulting from the refinery which had in fact been constructed). If any actual nuisance caused by the refinery that had been constructed exceeded the nuisance which inevitably resulted from any refinery that might have been constructed on the site, Gulf Oil would not be able to rely on the defence of statutory authority and would be liable. Hence the House of Lords reversed the Court of Appeal, which had reversed the trial judge and given judgment for the plaintiff, who alleged nuisance by smell, noise and vibration. Since the proceedings were in the form of an order for the determination of a preliminary point of law, namely the availability of the defence, there had been no actual decision on whether a nuisance was

177 *R. v. Pease* (1832) 4 B. & Ad. 30; *Vaughan v. Taff Vale Rly* (1860) 5 H. & N. 679.
178 (1869) L.R. 4 H.L. 171.
179 (1878) 3 App. Cas. 430.
180 *Allen v. Gulf Oil Refining Ltd* [1981] 1 All E.R. 353 at 361 *per* Lord Keith, dissenting.
181 *Ibid.* at 356, citing *Hammersmith and City Railway Co. v. Brand, supra*; *Geddis v. Proprietors of Bann Reservoir, supra*; *Metropolitan Asylum District Managers v. Hill* (1881) 6 App.Cas. 193.

committed by Gulf Oil. The issue was solely as to the issue of the defence, if nuisance were established.

8.57 Not all statutes confer such immunity upon their proper construction. The Public Works Utilities Street Act 1950 did not do so in respect of the construction and maintenance of a water main running under a street, according to the House of Lords in *Department of Transport v. North West Water Authority*.[182] Hence the defendants were liable when the main burst and damaged part of the street if the common law of nuisance applied to their behaviour. This involved proof of negligence, failing proof of which the defendants were not liable. Hence the decision of the trial judge was reversed. Whether a statute has this effect depends on the object and terms of the particular statute, including the presence or absence of a compensatory clause, the nature of the act complained of and the nature of the resulting injury.[183]

8.58 However even if the statute does *prima facie* provide for immunity, the powers conferred by the statute and exercised under its authority must not be exercised negligently. This means without proper judgment and caution.[184] This means that statutory powers must not be exercised deliberately without taking care of people's rights.[185] However where the acts are incidental and necessary to the exercise of powers conferred by the statute the fact that they cause inconvenience and nuisance does not give rise to liability in the absence of negligence, in the sense explained.[186] In *Tate & Lyle Industries Ltd v. Greater London Council*,[187] The House of Lords, over the dissent of Lord Diplock, held that the London County Council (Improvements) Act 1962, did not relieve the Greater London Council of its elementary duty to design and construct ferry terminals in the River Thames, the effect of which was to interfere with the operation of the plaintiff's jetty by reason of siltation that affected the river bed, with all reasonable care for the interests of other persons and to cause no more harm than was necessary. The statute only gave immunity in respect of siltation that was inevitable, not in respect of additional siltation caused by the particular design chosen for the terminals.

8.59 English courts approach the question of immunity on the basis of statutory authority from a strict "constructionist" point of view. The speeches in the *Allen* and *Tate & Lyle* cases reveal a close attention to the detailed provisions of the relevant statute: and a built-in bias against any potentially broad interpretation of its provisions as would enlarge the

182 [1983] 3 All E.R. 273.
183 *Marriage v. East Norfolk Rivers Catchment Board*, para. 8.54 *supra* at 306 *per* Jenkins L.J.
184 *East Suffolk Rivers Catchment Board v. Kent* [1941] A.C. 74 at 90 *per* Lord Atkin.
185 *Metropolitan Asylum District Managers v. Hill, supra.*
186 *London & Brighton Railway v. Truman* (1885) 11 App.Cas 45. Cp. *Fisher v. Ruislip-Northwood U.D.C.* [1945] K.B. 584; *Whiting v. Middlesex C.C.* [1948] 1 K.B. 162; *Law v. Railway Executive* [1949] 65 T.L.R. 288 (negligence established) with *Lagan Navigation Co. v. Lambeg Bleaching Co.* [1927] A.C. 226; *Longhurst v. Metropolitan Water Board* [1948] 2 All E.R. 834 (no negligence).
187 [1983] 1 All E.R. 1159.

scope of the suggested immunity or release from liability. Similarly the language of Lord Fraser in *Department of Transport v. North West Water Authority*[188] suggests that, when construing statutory powers as contrasted with statutory duties[189] the courts must be careful not to extend the natural meaning of the words of the Act. Such statutes are enacted because what is to be done is regarded as of sufficient public utility and importance to entitle the bodies required or empowered to act in a certain way to some measure of protection from potential liability for nuisance (or, in some instances, other forms of liability in tort). Since the common law does not regard "utility" in general as a reasoon for excluding or limiting liability for nuisance, it has been deemed necessary to give effect to some notion of "utility" through the medium of legislation. Negligence, however, will take away the statutory protection. So, too, will the unnecessary causing of a nuisance (which, it may be argued, is a form of negligence).[190]

(f) Remedies

(i) Abatement

8.60 In the same way as other forms of self-help,[191] abatement has fallen into disfavour in modern times. Partly this is the result of improved access to the courts; partly it is because of the development of the idea that parties should be discouraged from acting on their own and thereby possibly creating breaches of the peace; and in part it is the consequence of the evolution of the remedy of the injunction.[192] However, in theory if not in practice, it is still possible to abate a nuisance, although abatement is not an advisable measure to adopt.

8.61 Abatement is the removal of the source of the nuisance, for example, cutting off the branch of a tree that overhangs the land of the neighbour who suffers from the effects of such nuisance.[193] If the victim of a nuisance pursues the remedy of abatement, the exercise of this privilege will destroy other rights, such as a claim for damages.[194] Hence to some extent the inadvisability of abatement unless the extent of damage is so small that a suit for damages would be unprofitable or expensive, or unless there is a threat of imminent danger.[195] A further inhibiting factor is that the privilege of abatement is regarded very jealously by the law such that its exercise is fraught with problems, especially where entry on another's land is required in order to abate. If the abator exceeds the limits of the privilege he may be liable. Thus unnecessary damage must not be caused

188 [1983] 3 All E.R. 273 at 276–277.
189 Cp. *East Suffolk Rivers Catchment Board v. Kent* [1941] A.C. 74: *Farnworth v. Manchester Corporation* [1929] 1 K.B. 533 at 557 *per* Lawrence L.J.
190 *Lagan Navigation Co. v. Lambeg Bleaching Co.* [1927] A.C. 226 at 243 *per* Lord Atkinson.
191 See pp. 107–108.
192 Below pp. 211–212.
193 Or severing encroaching roots even if no damage has occurred such as would support an action for nuisance: *Lemmon v. Webb* [1894] 3 Ch. 1; [1895] A.C. 1.
194 *Basten's Case* (1610) 9 Co.Rep. 53b; *Lagan Navigation Co. v. Lambeg Bleaching Co.* [1927] A.C. 226 at 224.
195 *Penruddock's Case* (1598) 5 Co.Rep. 100b.

by the abatement.[196] In *Lagan Navigation Co. v. Lambeg Bleaching Co.*,[197] for example, the defendants were liable when they cut away banks put in a canal by the plaintiffs in order to prevent a lock from being flooded. An injunction was issued against the defendants to preclude that activity. Here the plaintiffs were acting under statutory powers, and had not been guilty of negligence; hence no nuisance was committed by the plaintiffs that might have entitled the defendants to act as they did.

8.62 Interference by the party abating must be necessary: i.e. there must be a nuisance. It must also be carried out properly. If there are two ways of abating a nuisance, the less mischievous alternative, i.e. that less harmful to the creator of the nuisance, is the one that must be adopted. Nor may abatement effect the rights of third parties.[198] In *Roberts v. Rose*[199] the defendant revoked a licence given by him to the plaintiff to construct a watercourse and discharge water from the plaintiff's mines onto the defendant's land across the land of a third party. The plaintiff refused to discontinue the use of the watercourse. The defendant entered the land of the third party and obstructed the watercourse. It was held that if the defendant had stopped the watercourse on his own land this would have caused more damage to the third party and to the public at large. Hence the defendant's method of abatement was reasonable and justified, even though it involved going onto the land of the third party. Here the defendant had acted in the best interests of himself and the third party: he had exercised his privilege legitimately.

8.63 The purpose of abatement must be to put an end to some act of misfeasance being committed by the party on whose land the nuisance occurs. Abatement cannot consist of making good a non-feasance,[200] such as the failure to erect a bridge in order to keep up a right of way.[201] However some apparent acts of non-feasance may in effect be regarded as acts of misfeasance. Thus to permit the branches of a tree to overhang is a form of misfeasance, such as to entitle the owner of the land which is overhung to cut off the offending branches.[202]

8.64 As long as the abatement can be carried out by the offended party[203] on his own land, or without leaving his own land, no notice need be given to the offending party. The situation is different if, in order to abate, the offended party has to enter the land of the creator of the

196 *Lagan Navigation Co. v. Lambeg Bleaching Co.*, *supra* at 244–246. Nor unnecessary or unreasonable force: *Jones v. Williams* (1843) 11 M. & W. 176.
197 [1927] A.C. 226.
198 *Roberts v. Rose* (1865) L.R. 1 Ex. 82 at 89 *per* Blackburn J.
199 *Supra.*
200 *Earl of Lonsdale v. Nelson* (1823) 2 B. & C. 302 at 311 *per* Best J.
201 *Campbell Davys v. Lloyd* [1901] 2 Ch. 518.
202 *Lemmon v. Webb*, *supra.* But not to keep the branches, which would amount to conversion: *Mills v. Brooker* [1919] 1 K.B. 535.
203 I.e., the occupier or someone acting with his authority and on his behalf; in cases of public nuisance abatement is only possible if the party abating has suffered particular injury: cp. below p. 214. As to abatement of a nuisance on the highway, see *Dimes v. Petley* (1850) 15 Q.B. 276.

nuisance.[204] Failure to give such notice may involve the purported abating party in liability for trespass.

(ii) Damages

8.65 Monetary compensation, i.e. damages, can be awarded in an action for nuisance for the purpose of rectifying the loss or inconvenience caused to the plaintiff. Such damages will be granted and assessed up to the date of the action. If the nuisance continues, a fresh action for damages may be brought for each separate continuation. Damage must of course be proved since damage is the gist of an action for nuisance. However where the defendant's act interferes with a servitude,[205] or, if allowed to continue, might permit the defendant to acquire the right to commit a nuisance by prescription,[206] damages may be awarded even if no actual loss is established; though such damages will be nominal, rather than truly compensatory.

8.66 It was decided in *The Wagon Mound (No. 2)*[207] that damage must be foreseeable in order to be recoverable in an action in nuisance. Unforeseeable damage will be too remote. Such damage will include not only physical damage to property, such as land or chattels, but also damage for discomfort and inconvenience.[208] Under this heading it has been held that a plaintiff can recover damages for economic consequences of a nuisance. Thus if the defendant's emission of smoke, fumes or smells, for example, causes the value of the plaintiff's property to decline, or forces hotel guests to refrain from using the plaintiff's premises, such loss is part of the damage suffered by the plaintiff as a result of the nuisance. It will not be too remote. In *Dodd Properties (Kent) Ltd v. Canterbury City Council*[209] the Court of Appeal held that in a claim for repairs made necessary by the defendants' activities which resulted in serious structural damage to the plaintiff's building, the cost of the repairs was to be assessed on the principle of compensating the plaintiff, i.e., putting him in the position he would have been in had the injury not occurred. This meant that the assessment of the cost of repairs was to be made as at the earliest date at which the repairs could be undertaken, rather than at the date when the damage occurred. In this instance the plaintiffs would have been in straitened financial circumstances had they carried out the repairs when they first became necessary. It made commercial sense to postpone the repairs until the outcome of the action. Hence the correct date for assessing the cost of the repairs was the date of the action, not the date of the nuisance. Here the financial difficulties of the plaintiffs were not the

204 E.g., to demolish an inhabited house: *Davis v. Williams* (1851) 16 Q.B. 546; *Jones v. Jones* (1862) 1 H. & C. 1.

205 As in *Nicholls v. Ely Beet Sugar Co.* [1936] A.C. 343.

206 *Fay v. Prentice* (1845) 1 C.B. 828.

207 [1967] 1 A.C. 617: above paras 8.27–8.

208 In this respect it should be noted that "abnormal sensitivity" will be relevant to whether a nuisance has been committed; above pp. 184–185. But once there is liability the plaintiff can recover damages resulting from his particular sensitivity to the interference emanating from the defendant: *McKinnon Industries Ltd v. Walker* [1951] 3 D.L.R. 577 at 581 *per* Lord Simonds.

209 [1980] 1 All E.R. 928.

result of pre-existing impecuniosity or financial embarrassment; hence it was not an extraneous cause that was to be ignored in the measurement of damages.[210] In this decision, which involved a cause of action that was framed alternatively in nuisance and negligence, it is possible to see another illustration of the way in which the torts of nuisance and negligence have been coming together in modern times.

8.67 In consequence of Lord Cairns' Act,[211] the court may award damages in lieu of, or in addition to the granting of the injunction. The principles upon which an award of damages would be given in such situations were outlined by A.L. Smith L.J. in *Shelfer v. City of London Electric Lighting Co.*[212] Damages would be given instead of an injunction if:

> "(i) the injury to the plaintiff's legal rights is small; (ii) and is one which is capable of being estimated in money; (iii) and is one which can be adequately compensated by a small money payment; (iv) and the case is one in which it would be oppressive to the defendant to grant an injunction."

In that case the Court of Appeal reversed Kekewich J., who had not given damages, and instead granted an injunction against the use of engines which caused structural injury to the plaintiff's house. Similarly, in *Maberley v. Peabody & Co.*[213] an injunction was granted to prevent the piling up of earth against the plaintiff's wall, when chemical substances in the earth damaged the wall and the plaintiff's soil. Damages were not the appropriate remedy.

8.68 The power to award damages in lieu of an injunction to prevent the continuation of a nuisance has been said to amount to "a judicial power of expropriation".[214] For this reason it is a power that perhaps ought to be exercised sparingly. Its inherent dangers were increased by the decision of the House of Lords in *Leeds Industrial Co-Operative Society v. Slack.*[215] The plaintiffs sought a *quia timet* injunction to restrain in advance the defendants from building in such a way as to obstruct the plaintiff's ancient lights. The majority of the House of Lords held that, under Lord Cairns' Act, since damages could be awarded in lieu of an injunction, it was possible to make the defendants compensate the plaintiff in advance for potential injury to him, rather than compel the defendant to desist from his building. To Lord Sumner, on the other hand, it was incorrect to award damages before any wrong had been committed.[216] The minority

210 Contrast *Liesbosh v. Edison* [1933] A.C. 449, which was distinguished: see p. 338.
211 Chancery Amendment Act 1858; see now Supreme Court Act 1981 s. 19. On this see Jolowicz, "Damages in Equity—A Study of Lord Cairns' Act" [1975] C.L.J. 224.
212 [1895] 1 Ch. 287 at 322–327: see *Morris v. Redland Bricks Ltd* [1967] 3 All E.R. 1 at 12–13 *per* Sellers L.J.
213 [1946] 2 All E.R. 192. Contrast *Attorney-General v. Sheffield Gas Co.* (1853) 3 De G. M. & G. 304; *Swaine v. Great Northern Railway* (1864) 4 De G. J. & Sm. 211.
214 Fleming, *Law of Torts*, 7th ed. 1987 at 414. See also Tromans, "Nuisance—Prevention or Payment" [1982] C.J.J. 87. This raises questions of economic efficiency which have been widely debated in the United States: Coase, "The Problem of Social Cost" (1986) 3 J. Law & Econ. 1; Calabresi & Melamed "Property Rules, Liability Rules and Inalienability" (1972) 85 H.L.R. 1089.
215 [1924] A.C. 851.
216 *Ibid.* at 866–869.

view seems more logical, given the purpose of awards of damages. The majority opinion, however, would seem to be the law, and follows equally logically from the language of the statute.

(iii) Injunction

8.69 An injunction is an order of court restraining the commission or continuance of the wrongful act involving the nuisance, or the continuation of a wrongful omission.[217] It is a discretionary remedy, unlike damages which must be awarded if damage can be proved. An injunction will not be granted where damages would provide an adequate and appropriate remedy to the plaintiff.[218]

8.70 In *Miller v. Jackson*[219] the Court of Appeal refused to grant an injunction to restrain the defendants from playing cricket on the ground that the interests of the public at large outweighed the private interests of the plaintiffs, so that damages would be a satisfactory method of relieving the plaintiffs. Lane L.J. dissented and thought that an injunction was suitable although he was prepared to suspend its operation for one year to enable the defendants to see if they could find another playing ground by the use of which they would not harm the plaintiffs. The idea that the public interest is also a factor to be taken into account in deciding whether to grant an injunction or award damages is a novel one.

8.71 The classical general principles on which injunctions, particularly mandatory injunctions, would be granted were discussed by Lord Upjohn in *Redland Bricks Ltd v. Morris*.[220] That case involved the granting of an injunction to restrain the defendants from withdrawing their support from the plaintiff's land and a mandatory injunction ordering the defendants to take all necessary steps to restore the support to the plaintiff's land within six months. The House of Lords discharged the latter injunction on the ground that it did not inform the defendants what they had to do, even though there was a strong possibility that grave damage would ensue to the plaintiff in the future. Lord Upjohn pointed to several vital matters of which a court had to be satisfied before such an injunction could be granted. Not only was it necessary to show a very strong probability that grave damage would accrue to the plaintiff, and to take into account in

217 In the context of nuisance the main injunctions that are relevant are interlocutory, perpetual, prohibitory, mandatory and *quia timet*; on interlocutory injunctions see *American Cyanamid Co. v. Ethicon Ltd* [1975] A.C. 296; *Hubbard v. Pitt* [1976] Q.B. 142, where such an injunction was granted to prevent nuisance by picketing; *Attorney-General v. Manchester Corporation* [1893] 2 Ch. 87; *Hopper v. Rogers* [1975] Ch. 43; and *Fletcher v. Bealy* (1885) 28 Ch.D. 688.

218 E.g. *Kennaway v. Thompson* [1980] 3 All E.R. 329 (noise from motor boat races); and *Tetley v. Chitty* [1986] 1 All E.R. 663 (noise from go-kart races).

219 [1977] 3 All E.R. 338: see p. 185.

220 [1969] 2 All E.R. 576 at 579–580.

certain situations[221] the cost of the work needed to prevent or lessen the likelihood of future apprehended wrong (unlike the situation where a negative injunction was granted). It was also vital to show that damages would not be a sufficient or adequate remedy if the damage which the plaintiff feared did in fact occur. In this case no question of public interest or involvement in the activities of the defendant arose. Perhaps it is possible to distinguish such cases from those, like *Miller v. Jackson*, where the public are also interested in the situation as between the litigating parties.

3. INJURIES TO SERVITUDES

8.72 Servitudes are rights over the land of another person. An easement is a right to use the land of another without appropriating any part of the produce or substance of the servient land. A *profit à prendre* entitles the owner of the dominant land to take away and appropriate some part of the produce or substance of the servient land. A licence, which is contractual in nature in contrast to easements and profits which are forms of property, gives the licensee a right to enter on the land of the licensor or do something thereon which would otherwise be unlawful, e.g. make use of certain facilities on the land. In the present context, interference with, or disruption of an easement is material, since the only appropriate remedy in such instances is an action in nuisance.[222] One who interferes with a profit may be sued in trespass, even if the defendant is the occupier of the land in respect of which the profit has been granted.[223] One who prevents a licensee from enjoying his licence may be sued in trespass or breach of contract (if the licence has been granted for consideration and the defendant is the licensor).[224]

8.73 The interest that is the subject-matter of the alleged easement must be capable of forming the subject-matter of a grant. Hence there are no easements in respect of a right to an uninterrupted or aesthetic view from the windows of a house, or to a right to privacy.[225] Among recognised easements are rights of way, rights of entry for any purpose of the dominant land, rights of support for buildings or land, rights of light and air, rights in respect of water, rights to do something that would otherwise

221 When the defendant acted without regard to his neighbour's rights or tried to steal a march on him or tried to evade the jurisdiction of the court, i.e. acted wantonly and unreasonably, the defendant could be ordered to do positive work to restore the *status quo* at whatever cost, even if out of proportion to the advantage to the plaintiff. If the defendant acted reasonably, though wrongly, the cost of repairing by positive acts his earlier activities is important because: (i) no legal wrong may have occurred and might never do; and (ii) if the plaintiff incurs heavy damage he can still sue for damages at law as well as other equitable remedies.

222 Trespass is not maintainable: *Paine & Co. Ltd v. St Neots Gas Co.* [1939] 3 All E.R. 812 at 823.

223 *Mason v. Clarke* [1955] A.C. 778.

224 See pp. 102–105.

225 *McVittie v. Bolton Corporation* [1945] K.B. 281 at 283 *per* Scott L.J.; *Turner v. Spooner* (1865) 30 L.J. Ch. 801. On privacy see Chapter 19.

amount to a nuisance, and rights to place or keep something on the servient land.

8.74 Interference with an easement is actionable *per se*,[226] i.e. without any need to take into account such factors as locality, utility, reasonableness (except where the alleged infringement relates to the rights of a riparian owner to the continued flow of a stream in its natural condition).[227] Hence, possibly, the idea that infringement of an easement is a distinct wrong though it may resemble the tort of nuisance.[228] One point that seems to mark a difference relates to the question of entitlement to sue. In nuisance the occupier of land, whether a lawful or unlawful occupier, may sue for discomfort or inconvenience, or presumably also, damage to the property. His title to the land is not in issue. Where infringement of, or interference with an easement is concerned (and this would seem to apply to profits as well, insofar as nuisance is an appropriate cause of action in such instances), the plaintiff may have to prove his title to the easement or profit,[229] unless the servitude in question is a natural, not acquired one.[230] The distinction is between such rights as those of support for land on which there are no buildings, which are naturally appurtenant to land, and rights such as those of support for buildings which must be acquired by grant from the servient tenement owner to the dominant tenement owner.

4. PUBLIC NUISANCE

8.75 A public nuisance affects the public or community at large, i.e., a representative cross-section or a class of the public,[231] not any particular individual. The question whether a nuisance is sufficiently broad in its effects as to disturb the comfort of large numbers of Her Majesty's subjects, or to interfere with the rights of a large enough group,[232] is one of fact. At common law public nuisances were criminal offences: and remain so.[232a] However statutes have created special offences with respect to

226 *Colls v. Home & Colonial Stores Ltd* [1904] A.C. 179 at 182 *per* Lord Halsbury.

227 When unreasonable and unauthorised use of the water must be shown: *Embery v. Owen* (1851) 6 Ex. 353 at 369 *per* Parke B.

228 *Colls v. Home & Colonial Stores Ltd*, *supra* at 186 *per* Lord Macnaghten.

229 *Paine & Co. Ltd v. St Neots Gas Co.*, *supra* at 823. A New Zealand case suggests the contrary view: *Keegan v. Young* [1963] N.Z.L.R. 770.

230 *Newcastle-under-Lyme Corporation v. Wolstanton Ltd* [1947] Ch. 92; *Nicholls v. Ely Beet Sugar Factory* [1931] 2 Ch. 84.

231 *Attorney-General v. P.Y.A. Quarries Ltd* [1957] 2 Q.B. 169.

232 I.e., is so indiscriminate that it would be unreasonable to expect any one person to take proceedings to stop it: *Attorney-General v. P.Y.A. Quarries Ltd.*, *supra* at 190–191 *per* Denning L.J. Note also the older view that to allow many actions would expose the defendant to being punished many times for the same cause: Fleming, *Law of Torts*, 7th ed. 1987 at 382. But this is illogical since in other situations a defendant may be liable to many plaintiffs if he has caused harm to them all by his wrongful act, e.g., a manufacturer whose negligence in making a product brings about harmful consequences to a multitude of consumers of the product.

232a The abolition of the crime of public nuisance is advocated by Spencer, "Public Nuisance—A Critical Examination" [1989] C.L.J. 55.

certain forms of activity which affect the public generally, such as noise, smoke, and other kinds of pollution.[233] Insofar as all such nuisances, at common law or by statute, are dealt with by the criminal law, or by administrative action, they are irrelevant to the law of torts. However, a public nuisance can give rise to civil, tort liability if a private individual can establish that he or she has incurred some particular damage, over above and distinct from the harm suffered by the public generally.[234] As Tindal C.J. said in *Wilkes v. Hungerford Market*,[235] "the law has said from the yearbooks downwards that if a party has sustained any peculiar injury beyond that which affects the public at large, an action will lie for redress." That this continues to be the law was acknowledged by Lord Templeman in *Tate & Lyle Industries Ltd v. Greater London Council*,[236] where no public nuisance was held to have been committed: "An individual who suffers damage resulting from a public nuisance is, as a general rule, entitled to maintain an action."

8.76 Particular or special damage is not confined to actual pecuniary loss, or physical injury incurred by the plaintiff, although most instances involve some or the other. It can also consist of delay or inconvenience resulting from the acts of the defendant,[237] as long as such delay or inconvenience is substantial and direct.[238] In *Benjamin v. Storr*,[239] for example, the nuisance in question was obstruction of the light to the plaintiff's business and upsetting customers by the smells caused by horses allowed to stand close to the plaintiff's coffee-house. In *Bundy, Clark & Co. v. London & North Eastern Railway Co.*,[240] the defendant failed to perform its statutory duty and maintain a lock. When the lock collapsed, the plaintiffs, sand and gravel merchants, had to transport their goods by rail at greater expense. For this they were entitled to sue. But in *Harper v. Haden & Sons*[241] the scaffolding erected by the defendant was only a temporary obstruction: it was reasonable both as to quantum and duration. Hence the plaintiff could not sue. Nor could he succeed in *Dwyer v. Mansfield*.[242]

233 Control of Pollution Act 1974, Clean Air Acts 1956, 1968 and Public Health Act 1936: *A. Lambert Flat Management Ltd v. Lomas* [1981] 2 All E.R. 280; *London Borough of Hammersmith v. Magnus Automated Forecourts Ltd* [1978] 1 All E.R. 401; *Coventry City Council v. Doyle* [1981] 2 All E.R. 184.

234 *Iveson v. Moore* (1699) 1 Ld. Ray. 486. See Kolidiniye, "Public nuisance and particular damage in modern law", (1986) 6 Legal St. 102. A public nuisance may also involve a private one: *Rose v. Groves* (1843) 5 Man. & Gr. 613.

235 (1835) 2 Bing. N.C. 281 at 293.

236 [1983] 1 All E.R. 1159 at 1171. The plaintiff does not have to prove special damage, only particular damage: *Rose v. Groves, supra* at 616 *per* Cresswell J.

237 *Walsh v. Ervin* [1952] A.L.R. 650; on which case see Fridman, "The Definition of Particular Damage in Nuisance" (1953) 2 Ann. L.R. (West Aust.) 490.

238 Cp. *Rose v. Miles* (1815) 4 M. & S. 101; *Wilkes v. Hungerford Market* (1835) 2 Bing. N.C. 281, where the plaintiff was successful; *Winterbottom v. Earl of Derby* (1867) L.R. 2 H.L. 175, where there was no recovery (*Wilkes* being distinguished on the ground that the obstruction was unjustifiably extended in duration—but also doubted so far as its correctness was concerned: see Slade J. in *Gravesham B.C. v. British Railways Board* [1978] 3 All E.R. 853 at 870).

239 (1874) L.R. 9 C.P. 400: cp. *Fritz v. Hobson* (1880) 14 Ch.D. 542.

240 [1931] 2 K.B. 334: cp. *Hart v. Basset* (1681) T. Jones 156.

241 [1933] Ch. 298.

242 [1946] K.B. 437.

The defendant's attraction of queues to obtain rationed goods was neither a substantial nor a lengthy interference. More recently, in *Gravesham Borough Council v. British Railways Board,*[243] the plaintiff port authority had standing to sue when the railway board decided to curtail a certain ferry service. Obstruction or hindrance of the ferry was a public nuisance. The result of the changes to the service was that some of the authority's employees were prevented from using the ferries, which meant that the port authority incurred a substantial loss in having to train replacement employees. This was particular damage: and entitled the port authority to maintain an action (although, in the result, the action failed because Slade J. held that the change in the timetable for the ferries did not amount to a breach of the railway's common law duty to provide a ferry service at all reasonable hours: nor would it be permissible for the court to intervene by granting a mandatory injunction).

8.77 In *Benjamin v. Storr,*[244] Brett J. summed up these requirements for a private action based on public nuisance as follows: (i) particular injury; (ii) that was direct and not merely consequential; (iii) substantial and not fleeting or evanescent.[245] However there is some dispute on the question whether the expression "particular damage" means damage that is different in kind from that which is suffered by the public at large, or different in degree only. The generally accepted view is that the difference need only be one of degree not one of kind.[246] However the distinction between the two approaches is far from straightforward and the argument can be made that what has to be shown is some injury or loss that is completely different, virtually unique to the plaintiff.[247]

8.78 Another form of civil action that may be brought in cases of public nuisance is a claim for an injunction brought by the Attorney-General on the information of a member of the public: a "relator" action. Such proceedings may be brought if a criminal prosecution will not adequately sanction the misconduct of the defendant.[248] However the Attorney-General cannot be compelled to commence the necessary proceedings. It is

243 [1978] 3 All E.R. 853, following *Blundy, Clark & Co. v. L.N.E.R., supra* at 362–363, 365, *per* Greer L.J.

244 *Supra* at 406–407.

245 Hence in *Vanderpant v. Mayfair Hotel Ltd* [1930] 1 Ch. 138, the plaintiff failed because he did not show substantial obstruction to access to his house by the defendants' hotel which turned a quiet road into a busy street and caused congestion.

246 For a curious application of this see the Canadian case of *Hickey v. Electric Reduction Co. of Canada Ltd* (1970) 21 D.L.R. (3d) 368, where the economic loss to the plaintiffs, by pollution interfering with their ability to fish, was not different in kind because the public had the same fishing rights as the plaintiffs. Yet the decision seems to conflict with cases such as *Wilkes* and *Benjamin v. Storr.*

247 Fridman, "The Definition of Particular Damage in Nuisance" (1953) 2 Ann. L.R. (West Aust.) 490.

248 But it has been suggested in Canada that the Attorney-General may not be granted injunctive relief when he is really seeking to enforce the criminal law by equitable civil remedies: *Attorney-General of Nova Scotia v. Beaver* (1985) 32 C.C.L.T. 170, affirming (1984) 66 N.S.R. (2d) 419. This may be the peculiar result of the constitutional position in Canada where criminal law is federal and civil law is provincial. The proceedings arose out of attempts to regulate the activities of prostitutes: cp. *Stein v. Gonzales* (1985) 14 D.L.R. (4th) 263.

a matter for his discretion, for the failure to exercise which he cannot be called to account in court.[249] Although framed as if it were a claim in tort, such relator proceedings are administrative in nature, seeking to enforce standards of public behaviour rather than purporting to regulate the relations between private citizens. The fact that the Attorney-General is answerable only in the political sphere for his handling of such matters reinforces the argument that such actions are very different from suits for private nuisance or for particular damage stemming from a public nuisance.[249a]

5. NUISANCE TO THE HIGHWAY

(i) Obstruction causing loss to adjoining owners

8.79 Cases referred to in the previous section indicate that sometimes an obstruction to the highway can lead to a private civil action for damages. It is necessary to prove that the plaintiff has suffered "particular damage", as explained earlier. His loss must be different in some measure from the harm incurred by other users of the highway: for example, if the plaintiff trying to leave his house fell into a hole dug by the defendant and broke his leg, or was put to additional expense by having to take a roundabout route for his business purposes. The most extreme case of this type appears to be *Wilkes v. Hungerford Market.*[250] There the plaintiff complained that because of the defendant's obstruction of the highway passengers were diverted from the street where the plaintiff's business was situated, with the result that the plaintiff suffered loss of business. The case has been distinguished,[251] and criticised.[252] It may have applied the requirements of direct and substantial injury for such an action too broadly. In other decisions plaintiffs who complained of injury through obstruction of the highway involving disruption of access to their premises have not been successful.[253]

(ii) Disrepair

8.80 At common law an action for damages only lay in respect of failure by a public authority in the course of repairing the highway, where such failure resulted in damage. No action could be brought for injury resulting from a failure to repair. The law drew a distinction between misfeasance and non-feasance.[254] The issue in any case was to determine whether the defendant authority had failed to repair at all or had created a dangerous

249 Cp. *Gouriet v. Union of Post Office Workers* [1978] A.C. 435.
249a Spencer, *loc. cit. supra* note 232a at 81–83, also recommends the abolition of civil liability for damages for public nuisance.
250 (1835) 2 Bing N.C. 281: cp. *Benjamin v. Storr* (1874) L.R. 9 C.P. 400.
251 *Ricket v. Metropolitan Railway* (1867) L.R. 2 H.L. 175.
252 *Gravesham B.C. v. British Railways Board* [1978] 3 All E.R. 853 at 870.
253 *Harper v. Hayden & Sons* [1933] Ch. 298; *Vanderpant v. Mayfair Hotel Co.* [1930] 1 Ch. 128; *Dwyer v. Mansfield* [1946] K.B. 437.
254 *Cowley v. Newmarket Local Board* [1892] A.C. 345.

situation by performing the task of repairing negligently.[255] Thus to put land near a highway into a state of disrepair was misfeasance;[256] but allowing the highway to get into a state of disrepair was non-feasance, for which there would not be liability in the event of injury to the plaintiff.[257]

8.81 The law was changed by the Highways (Miscellaneous Provisions) Act 1961 section 1, which is now contained in the Highways Act 1980 section 58. This states that in any action against a highway authority for damage resulting from its failure to maintain a highway maintainable at the public expense it shall be a defence (without prejudice to any other defence such as *volenti*, or contributory negligence) to prove that the authority had taken such care as in all the circumstances was reasonably required to secure that the part of the highway to which the action relates was not dangerous for traffic.[258] To determine whether the defence is applicable, the court must have regard to the character of the highway and the traffic which was reasonably to be expected to use it; the standard of maintenance appropriate for a highway of that character and used by such traffic; the state of repair in which a reasonable person would have expected to find the highway; whether the highway authority knew, or could reasonably have been expected to know, that the condition of the part of the highway to which the action relates was likely to cause danger to users of the highway; and where the highway authority could not reasonably have been expected to repair that part of the highway before the cause of action arose, what warning notice of its condition had been displayed. The section also confirms the decision at common law[259] that the duty to repair is non-delegable. The authority will not be able to plead that it arranged for a competent person to carry out or supervise the maintenance of the relevant part of the highway unless it also proves that it gave that person proper instructions with regard to maintenance and he carried out such instructions. The Act does not create a duty to repair; that emerges from other legislation or the common law.[260] It provides immunity from liability for nuisance, negligence or breach of statutory duty, where the provisions of the statute are applicable. But it also abrogates the defence of non-feasance, as contrasted with misfeasance. However there have been contradictory decisions on whether the onus is on the plaintiff to prove lack of care or on the highway authority to establish that it has performed its statutory duty so as to entitle it to rely on the defence provided by the Act of 1961.[261]

255 See the different views of Latham C.J. and McTiernan J. in *Buckle v. Bayswater Road Board* (1936) 57 C.L.R. 259 on whether letting a drain get into disrepair was nonfeasance or misfeasance.

256 *Barnes v. Ward* (1850) 9 C.B. 392; cp. *Harrold v. Watney* [1898] 2 Q.B. 320, defective fence next to highway: plaintiff who leaned on the fence trying to get through it was hurt; held, the plaintiff could recover.

257 *Gorringe v. Transport Commission* (1950) 80 C.L.R. 357.

258 The test is reasonable foreseeability of danger: *Littler v. Liverpool Corporation* [1968] 2 All E.R. 343.

259 *Hardaker v. Idle D.C.* [1896] 1 Q.B. 335: see pp. 68–70.

260 *Scott v. Green & Sons* [1969] 1 W.L.R. 301; *Haydon v. Kent C.C.* [1978] 2 W.L.R. 485.

261 *Griffiths v. Liverpool Corporation* [1967] 1 Q.B. 374; *Haydon v. Kent C.C.*, *supra*.

(iii) Obstruction to users

8.82 To place something on the highway that results in injury to other road users may produce liability, even though the injured party has no proprietary interest in land adjoining the place where the obstruction has been put. In such circumstances the obstacle may amount to a nuisance, i.e. a public nuisance, and the injury incurred by the plaintiff will satisfy the requirement of "particular damage". However not every occasion when an obstacle is placed on the highway, or something is done, such as the excavation of a hole, to render the highway impassable or difficult to use, will amount to a nuisance so as to be potentially actionable. Road users are expected to accept and assume the normal inconveniences of use or risks of passage.[262] It is only when an unreasonable danger has been created by the defendant that there will be liability for ensuing damage. For an obstruction to become a nuisance it must be neither negligible nor reasonable in the circumstances and in its duration.[263] In *Maitland v. Raisbeck*,[264] where that remark was made, the light at the back of the defendant's lorry was extinguished, a fact of which the defendant was ignorant when he left the lorry parked in the road. The plaintiff was injured when his vehicle collided with the defendant's lorry. The defendant was held not liable in nuisance. He had not behaved unreasonably in the circumstances. In contrast to leave a lorry unguarded and without lights was held to amount to a nuisance in *Ware v. Garston Haulage Co.*[265] In *Dymond v. Pearce*[266] the defendant left his lorry parked in the road with the lights on for a long time. This was not because of some mechanical failure (as in earlier instances) but for the convenience of the driver. This was a nuisance by obstruction of the highway. It was held to be actionable if it caused damage to the public, in this case the plaintiff who was a passenger on a motorcycle that collided with the lorry.[267] However the defendant was not liable because the nuisance was not the cause of the plaintiff's injury. The negligence of the driver of the motorcycle brought about the plaintiff's injury. In order for an obstruction to amount to a nuisance, said Edmund-Davies L.J.,[268] there had to be an element of danger involved in the nature of the obstruction, which was in fact so in this instance.

8.83 Although the cases refer to the unreasonable nature of the obstruction, it does not seem to make this form of nuisance depend on negligence. However in a New Zealand case, *Everitt v. Martin*,[269] it was held that the basis of actions of this kind was negligence. The plaintiff's coat was damaged by being torn when it came into contact with the defendant's

262 E.g., vehicles parked while delivering goods, repair of gas mains, construction of buildings (which may be regulated by municipal by-laws).
263 *Maitland v. Raisbeck* [1944] K.B. 689 at 692 *per* Lord Greene N.R.: cp. *Harper v. Hayden & Sons* [1933] Ch. 298 at 308 *per* Lawrence L.J. See *Parrish v. Judd* [1960] 3 All E.R. 33.
264 *Supra.*
265 [1944] K.B. 30.
266 [1972] 1 Q.B. 496.
267 Cp. *Trevett v. Lee* [1955] 1 All E.R. 406.
268 *Supra* note 266 at 504–505.
269 [1953] N.Z.L.R. 298.

dilapidated car parked on the highway. The defendant was liable on the ground of negligence, without the need for the plaintiff to rely on nuisance. In cases where the law of negligence will suffice to determine liability, Adams J. said, the less heared of nuisance the better. It was a mistake to suppose that liability for nuisance is always independent of negligence. If these remarks were intended to refer to nuisance generally they must be considered inaccurate. However, if they were meant to apply to nuisance by obstruction on the highway, they are more legitimate. Indeed in *Southport Corporation v. Esso Petroleum Co.*,[270] at first instance, Devlin J. made it clear that where the nuisance alleged to be the cause of the plaintiff's injury was nuisance in public navigable waters, which were akin to a public highway, negligence was an essential ingredient. This was accepted and endorsed by the Privy Council in *The Wagon Mound (No. 2)*.[271] There the concept of "foreseeability" was made an integral part of liability for nuisance of this kind: and the relevance of negligence was emphasised. It would appear that this variety of nuisance is firmly involved with proof of negligence, and may indeed be nothing more than another form of negligence liability rather than liability in nuisance. Whether the relevance of negligence in such cases spills over into other kinds of nuisance, in particular private nuisance, as between adjoining landowners, is a much more debatable issue. Despite the language of Lord Reid in *The Wagon Mound (No. 2)*, it is probably still accurate to say that, unless adopting or continuing a nuisance is involved, there is no element of negligence in liability for nuisance of that kind.[272]

(iv) Projections over the highway

8.84 If something overhangs the highway, be it an artificial construction or some natural thing such as the branch of a tree, that will not of itself constitute a nuisance. It is different if the overhanging object projects over the land of another person, as long as there is some degree of inconvenience or interference with the enjoyment of the latter's land, or some actual property damage, for example if the branch of a tree were to break the window of an adjoining house. Once the object projecting over the highway causes damage, however, for example by falling onto a passer-by, the question of liability for nuisance arises.

8.85 The vexed question is whether the owner of the projecting object, or the occupier of the land from which it projects, is liable strictly for what has occurred or can only be held liable if he is at fault. That usually means that there must be proof that he was aware of the dangerous character of the projection, or as a reasonable man could and ought to have been aware of this, and could have taken reasonable steps to correct the situation but failed to do so. Cases dealing with natural projections, such as the branches of a tree, have held that knowledge or the means of knowledge and failure to take reasonable precautions are necessary before

270 [1952] 2 All E.R. 1204: on appeal see [1954] 2 Q.B. 182, C.A., [1956] A.C. 218 H.L.
271 [1967] 1 A.C. 617.
272 Above pp. 188–192, 195–198.

there can be liability. In other words negligence or something approaching negligence is an essential ingredient of actionability.[273] If the damage is caused by the disrepair of an artificially constructed object, such as a lamp, or a chimney on a house, there are conflicting decisions and dicta. Some judicial statements indicate that the liability of the occupier is strict;[274] others that it depends on knowledge and lack of care following such knowledge[275] (unless the projection when created was already dangerous to those using the highway).[276] In *Wringe v. Cohen*[277] the Court of Appeal appear to have settled on a rule of strict liability, i.e. liability in the absence of knowledge or the means of knowledge of the dangerous situation. They did exempt from this situations where the damage resulted from "a secret and unobservable operation of nature", or by the act of a trespasser.[278] Given those expectations, it is hard to see how the occupier could avoid being found guilty of negligence either in relation to discovery of the danger or failure to do anything to remedy the situation. The general attitude of the courts seems to be that if a structure falls into dangerous disrepair and so causes damage there must have been negligence or the failure to perform a duty such as the landlord's duty to repair.[279] The courts seem to have entrenched the distinction between natural hazards, when there must be positive proof of knowledge and negligence, and artificially created ones, when negligence may well be presumed from the fact of injury.[280]

273 *Noble v. Harrison* [1926] 2 K.B. 332; *Cunliffe v. Bankes* [1945] 1 All E.R. 459; *Brown v. Harrison* (1947) 177 L.T. 281; *Caminer v. Northern & London Investment Trust* [1951] A.C. 88; *British Road Services v. Slater* [1964] 1 W.L.R. 498; *Quinn v. Scott* [1965] 1 W.L.R. 1004.
274 *Tarry v. Ashton* (1876) 1 Q.B.D. 314 at 330 *per* Lush and Quain JJ.
275 *Ibid.* at 319 *per* Blackburn J.
276 *Barker v. Herbert* [1911] 2 K.B. 633 at 636–637 *per* Vaughan Williams L.J.
277 [1940] 1 K.B. 229.
278 *Ibid.* at 233.
279 Cp. *Mint v. Good* [1951] 1 K.B. 517: cp. above para. 8.44.
280 And the occupier will be liable for the acts of an independent contractor: *Tarry v. Ashton, supra.*

CHAPTER 9

The Rule in Rylands v. Fletcher

1. THE RULE STATED

9.01 Occupiers who in the course of using their land in some extraordinary way bring on to it some dangerous thing likely to cause harm if it escapes are liable for damage caused by the escape of the thing without any proof of negligence. Such is the famous rule or doctrine first pronounced in *Rylands v. Fletcher*.[1] The defendant in that case employed an independent contractor to construct a reservoir on the defendant's land. Unknown to either the defendent or his independent contractor there was a mine under the adjoining land of the plaintiff and there were workings of the mine connecting it with excavations made for the reservoir. As a consequence when the reservoir was filled the water flooded the plaintiff's mine. The defendant was held liable even though he was not personally negligent, was ignorant of the possibility that damage could be caused to the plaintiff by what was being done on the defendant's land, and had employed an independent contractor for whose actions the general principle was that the employer would not be responsible.[2] In the Court of Exchequer Chamber Blackburn J. stated:[3]

> "The true rule of law is that a person who for his own purposes brings on his land and collects and keeps there anything likely to do mischief if it escapes must keep it at his peril, and if he does not do so is *prima facie* answerable for all the damage which is the natural consequence of the escape."

Some limitations were accepted by Blackburn J. upon the broad scope of such liability, for example, the act of the plaintiff himself, or an "act of God". Subject to these qualifications, however, the court made quite clear the very strict nature of the liability that could result from the collection on one's land of a "dangerous" thing. When the case reached the House of Lords,[4] where Lord Cranworth said that "if a person brings or accumulates on his land anything which, if it should escape, may cause damage to

1 (1865) 3 H. & C. 744; (1866) L.R. 1 Ex. 256; (1868) L.R. 3 H.L. 330. The historical background is exhaustively assessed and discussed by Simpson, "Legal Liability for Bursting Reservoirs: The Historical Context of *Rylands v. Fletcher*" (1984) 13 J.Leg.Studies 209. He points out the circumstances behind the case and other instances of such reservoirs causing damage and concludes that only Thomas Fletcher ever actually employed the rule in *Rylands v. Fletcher* to recover damages for injury caused by a burst reservoir.

2 The facts are fully stated by Simpson, *loc. cit. supra* at 238–242; and the judgments at various levels are fully analysed *ibid.* 244–251.

3 (1866) L.R. 1 Ex. 265 at 279–280.

4 There has been some doubt about the composition of the House of Lords for the case. Only two opinions were delivered. It is not clear who, if anyone, was the third Law Lord necessary for a quorum: Heuston, "Who was the Third Lord in *Rylands v. Fletcher?*" (1970) 86 L.Q.R. 160; Simpson,*loc. cit. supra* note 1, at 250–251.

his neighbour, he does so at his peril",[5] a further ingredient appears to have been added by Lord Cairns.[6] The latter introduced the idea that, to produce this liability, the defendant must have been making what Lord Cairns called a "non-natural user" of his land. This concept of non-natural user might be implicit in the language of Blackburn J. The latter spoke of the defendant bringing something dangerous onto his land. Nonetheless it is customarily accepted that the speech of Lord Cairns complicated the original rule as set out by Blackburn J. by reason of his employment of the expression "a non-natural user of land." Hence it has been suggested[7] that there are really two rules in *Rylands v. Fletcher*. One is that stated by Blackburn J., who made no mention of the kind of user that would attract the operation of the rule. The other was stated by Lord Cairns and involves the necessity to prove that the use being made of his land by the defendant was in some way "non-natural". This would appear not to be a tenable view. In *Leakey v. National Trust*[8] Megaw L.J. pointed out that *Rylands v. Fletcher* "does not impose strict liability except where there has been some non-natural user of the land."

2. SOURCES OF THE RULE

9.02 The judgment of Blackburn J. purports to derive the rule that was propounded in the case from long-established decisions on cattle-trespass and nuisance through the escape of fumes and filth from a privy. Medieval common law took a strict view of liability as between adjoining land-owners. The harsh attitude of the common law towards damage done by trespassing cattle, fire, and other harmful objects that left the land of the defendant and caused damage on the land of the plaintiff survived the passing of the middle ages and became a recognised feature of the later common law of the seventeenth and eighteenth centuries.[8a] Although by the date of *Rylands v. Fletcher* negligence had emerged as a distinct form of action, and as a possible ingredient of other types of liability,[9] it had not displaced other actions where proof of negligence was not required for liability. The Court of Exchequer Chamber clearly accepted this and extended existing law by generalising into a novel principle those other situations where a defendant could be guilty of tort without being guilty of any deliberate or negligent wrongdoing. Whatever was potentially

5 (1868) L.R. 3 H.L. 330 at 340.
6 *Ibid.*, at 338–339.
7 By a Canadian judge, MacDonald J., in *J.P. Porter Co. Ltd v. Bell* [1955] 1 D.L.R. 62 at 66.
8 [1980] 1 All E.R. 17 at 30. Hence the contrast between *Rylands v. Fletcher* and the earlier case of *Smith v. Kenrick* (1849) 7 C.B. 515.
8a For a critical assessment of the view that responsibility was based on causation rather than fault at this time, see Kretzmer, "Transformation of Tort Liability in the Nineteenth Century: The Visible Hand" (1984) 4 Ox.J. Legal Studies 46.
9 *Vaughan v. Menlove* (1837) 3 Bing. N.C. 468: *Blyth v. Birmingham Waterworks* (1856) 11 Ex. 781; *Indemaur v. Dames* (1866) L.R. 1 C.P. 274; (1867) L.R. 2 C.P. 311.

dangerous was now to be kept at one's peril, not just cattle, sewage, fire, as in previous decisions.[10]

9.03 What is curious, however, is not the manner in which Blackburn J. broadened the scope of prior law, but the introduction in the House of Lords of the idea that only an "unnatural" or "non-natural" user would have this effect.[11] The reliance by Blackburn J. on cases of cattle or filth escaping from the defendant's land reveals that he did not have in mind any such distinction between "natural" and "unnatural" uses as affected Lord Cairns. Grazing of cattle is an old, and presumably by the nineteenth century natural use of land, certainly in the country if not in towns. The accumulation of sewage could also be said to result from other "natural" uses of land, whether in country or town. The reasoning of Blackburn J. might conceivably be considered logical and founded on secure historical considerations: that of Lord Cairns seems to depart from the innate sense of symmetry that is present in the argument of Blackburn J. Nonetheless it is Lord Cairns' statement of the rule that governs the modern law, not that of Blackburn J.

9.04 A further explanation of the principle in *Rylands v. Fletcher* may be found in the developing of law of vicarious liability.[12] Prior to the latter part of the eighteenth century and the early years of the nineteenth, it does not appear to have been necessary to make any sharp distinction between servants and independent contractors. The chief problem for the courts in this area was to identify those acts of a servant for which a master would be liable and those for which he would not. Social and economic change, stemming from the industrial revolution, produced a class of entrepreneurial actors whose relationship with those for whom they performed various tasks was very different from the relationship, during and after the medieval period, between a master and his servants. It became important to determine the limits of vicarious liability for the torts committed by such different "agents". The courts settled on the principle that there would not be liability for the negligence of an independent contractor, one who was an entrepreneur providing some special kind of services rather than the more general service supplied by a servant.[13] At a time when more and more such entrepreneurs were being used for a variety of tasks, such a resolution of the issue might have reduced the

10 For other explanations see: Bohlen, "The Rule in *Rylands v. Fletcher*" (1911) 59 U. Penn. L.R. 298, 373, 423, explaining everything in terms of a conflict between conservative landowners and commercial, industrial interests that challenged the older agricultural class; Molloy, "*Fletcher v. Rylands*—A Reexamination of Juristic Origins" (1942) 9 U.Ch.L.R. 266, which destroys the arguments of Bohlen; Fridman, "The Rise and Fall of *Rylands v. Fletcher*" (1956) 34 Can. B.R. 810; Epstein, "A Theory of Strict Liability" (1973) 2 J. Leg. Studies 151; Epstein, "Defences and Subsequent Pleas in a System of Strict Liability" (1974) 3 J. Leg. Studies 165; Simpson, *loc. cit. supra* note 1 at 216.

11 Derived, perhaps from *Smith v. Kenrick, supra* note 8: see Simpson, *loc. cit. supra* note 1 at 214 footnote 15; Newark, "Non-Natural User and *Rylands v. Fletcher*" (1961) 24 M.L.R. 557.

12 Chap. 3.

potential liability of landowners, particularly those engaged upon industrial activities, and thereby diminished the protection available to other landowners who could be affected injuriously by the performance of these tasks.

9.05 The previous broad liability of landowners might have been restricted just at the moment of time when it had become of even greater importance and relevance. *Rylands v. Fletcher* provided the courts with the opportunity to deal with the matter. The negligence, if any, was that of an independent contractor. The choice was between applying the distinction between servants and independent contractors in a logical manner (thereby exempting the landowner whose purposes gave rise to the damage) and refusing to apply that distinction when some hazardous activity was being carried out by a landowner to the detriment of his neighbours. The Court of Exchequer Chamber and the House of Lords made a choice that seemed reasonable and necessary at the time. Moreover their decision to hold the landowner responsible for what his independent contractor had done conformed to received notions of vicarious liability and the maintenance of a high standard of responsibility as between landowners, both of which had been inherited from the courts of previous centuries. At that time there was nothing inherently remarkable about a decision which placed liability for what happened as a consequence of one's use of one's own land upon the owner of that land, no matter who actually performed the act which caused the eventual harm.[14] Only if the landowner was "utterly without fault"[15] (to adopt a phrase from the earlier law of trespass)[16] might he escape liability. Such would be the case, as Blackburn J. pointed out, if the escape were the result of the intervention of a stranger, one over whom the landowner had no control and who had not been employed in any capacity by the landowner, or was the result of an "Act of God", unforeseeable and unpreventable by any reasonable man.[17] Similarly, the otherwise liable landowner would be relieved of liability were the incident the result of the plaintiff's own act, or the plaintiff had agreed in advance to what the defendant landowner was doing, so as to erase any possibility that he was injured against his will or involvement.

9.06 Thus the rule adopted by the courts in *Rylands v. Fletcher* may be derived in part from history and prior accepted legal doctrines, in part from the social and economic needs of the time, and in part from the views of the judges that responsibility should be placed on the shoulders of those

13 *Laugher v. Pointer* (1826) 5 B. & C. 547; *Quarman v. Burnett* (1840) 6 M. & W. 499.
14 Although it was viewed as an anomalous decision, "an atavistic decision, a throwback or a survival from more primitive times": Simpson, *loc. cit. supra* note 1 and 214. On the suggestion that the decision was counter to the growth of the fault principle in the period in question, see *ibid.* at 215.
15 *Weaver v. Ward* (1616) Hob. 134: see p. 116.
16 In this respect note the attempt by Bramwell B. to impose liability in *Rylands v. Fletcher* in the Court of Exchequer, on the basis of trespass: (1865) 3 H. & C. 744 at 789, relying on *Gregory v. Piper* (1829) 9 B. & C. 591; Simpson, *loc. cit. supra* note 1 at 246.

who upset the natural balance of danger as between adjoining landowners and increase the possibilities of harm in order to serve their own selfish ends.

3. CHARACTER OF THE RULE

9.07 *Rylands v. Fletcher* liability is "strict". That means that the defendant will be liable without proof of negligence or any deliberate intent to harm his neighbour, the plaintiff. It is not, however, absolute liability. There are limits on its extent; circumstances in which liability will not be imposed even though the defendant has collected onto his land for his own purposes a dangerous object which has escaped and caused damage. What those limits are will be considered later.[18] For the moment it suffices to say that their existence qualifies the otherwise stringent nature of the rule. Since the decision in that case courts have come to adopt a view of the law of tort that is more heavily weighted in favour of making responsibility depend upon fault, more especially negligence, whether in the form of the breach of a duty of care or in the broader sense of a failure to take reasonable care as demanded by the circumstances. Yet strict liability has not been disregarded or eradicated either by the courts or by legislation. Indeed in some ways it has been extended in scope,[19] for example by the way in which vicarious liability has been interpreted and applied,[20] and by the enactment of industrial injury insurance.[21]

9.08 The breadth and stringency of the rule in *Rylands v. Fletcher* have been affected by the way in which the courts have understood and applied the features of the rule as stated both by Blackburn J. and Lord Cairns. Its fundamental, inherent nature has not altered. When and where it applies it results in liability that is imposed simply by reason of the causation of some injury in consequence of what the defendant has done on his own land, however lawful that may have been in itself. Sometimes it has been suggested that in reality it is nothing more than a very stringent doctrine of negligence: that a defendant liable under *Rylands v. Fletcher* is guilty of a high degree of negligence (which may be presumed or inferred rather than

17 (1866) L.R. 1 Ex. 265 at 280.
18 Below pp. 239–246.
19 Cp. Linden, "Whatever Happened to *Rylands v. Fletcher?*" in Klar, ed. *Studies in Canadian Tort Law*, 1977, 325 at 326.
20 Chap. 3.
21 National Insurance (Industrial Injuries) Act 1946, replacing the Workmen's Compensation Acts 1897–1925: see now the Social Security Act 1975. See also Health & Safety at Work Act 1974 ss. 1, 11, 15, 47. Note also legislation dealing with damage by aircraft, Civil Aviation Act 1949 s. 40(2); nuclear energy, Nuclear Installations Act 1965. In New Zealand the Accident Compensation Act 1974 makes liability in all instances of "personal injury by accident" dealt with on a non-fault basis: Fleming, *Law of Torts*, 7th ed. 1987, 375–378. See also, for recommendations in England, the Law Commission's *Report on Civil Liability for Dangerous Things and Activities* (1976), the *Report of the Royal Commission on Civil Liability and Compensation for Personal Injury*, 1978, Cmnd. 7054, Vol. 1, Chap. 31, and the EEC Product Liability Directive, resulting in the Consumer Protection Act 1987, under which it is no longer necessary to prove negligence against manufacturers of defective goods.

required to be established in the same way as "ordinary negligence").[22] Notwithstanding the occasional overlap that can occur, *Rylands v. Fletcher* liability is a different order of liability from liability for negligence. It is founded upon totally different bases and policies.

9.09 In some instances a defendant may be liable in negligence as well as under the rule in *Rylands v. Fletcher*. This does not mean that negligence and the doctrine of *Rylands v. Fletcher* are the same, merely that a particular fact situation may give rise to both, neither, or only one of these two different kinds of liability.[23] Similarly, there are cases in which liability may arise both under the rule and by virtue of the law of nuisance.[24] Yet that does not make nuisance and the doctrine of *Rylands v. Fletcher* the same kind of liability, even though there is a close connection between them. As Lord Wright said in the *Northwestern Utilities case*:[25] "This form if liability" [viz. under *Rylands v. Fletcher*] "is in many ways analagous to a liability for nuisance, though nuisance is not only different in its historical origins but in its legal character and many of its incidents and applications. But the two causes of action often overlap." Nuisance and *Rylands v. Fletcher* liability have been said to be "related to one another as intersecting circles".[26] However, important differences exist.[27] Some nuisances, for example, obstruction of the highway, are not within the doctrine of *Rylands v. Fletcher*. Nuisance, but not *Rylands v. Fletcher*, applies only to injuries affecting the use and enjoyment of land. No escape of anything is necessary for nuisance, and a remedy in nuisance may be available when harm is only threatened. *Rylands v. Fletcher* requires that something escape from the defendant's land: and there can be no liability unless and until actual damage is incurred. Nuisance may be defeated by a plea of prescription. Such a defence is not available where *Rylands v. Fletcher* liability is involved. The defence of "Act of God", conversely, is available to a defendant sued under *Rylands v. Fletcher* but not to a defendant sued in nuisance. Non-occupiers can be liable in nuisance but not under *Rylands v. Fletcher*. A plaintiff who suffers damage because of his unusual sensitivity may be denied a remedy in nuisance, but such sensitivity is irrelevant to liability under *Rylands v. Fletcher*. Nuisance may be committed even where

22 Prosser, *Selected Topics on the Law of Torts*, Ch. 3; cp. the view that different rules apply to different types of conduct and these relate to the attribution of risk: Dunlop, "Liability for Damage Caused by Things" (1962) 40 Can. B.R. 240; Keeton, "Conditional Fault in the Law of Torts" (1959) 72 H.L.R. 401; Fletcher, "Fairness and Utility in Tort Theory" (1972) 85 H.L.R. 537; Ehrenzweig, "Negligence without Fault" (1966) 54 Calif. L.R. 1422; Linden, *Canadian Tort Law*, 4th ed. 1988, 481–484.

23 *Attorney-General v. Cory Bros.* [1921] 1 A.C. 521; *Northwestern Utilities Ltd v. London Guarantee & Accident Co. Ltd* [1936] A.C. 108.

24 *St. Anne's Well Brewery v. Roberts* (1928) 140 L.T. 1; *Noble v. Harrison* [1926] 2 K.B. 332; *Charing Cross Electricity Supply Co. v. London Hydraulic Power Co.* [1914] 3 K.B. 772 (relying on a case of nuisance: *Midwood v. Mayor of Manchester* [1905] 2 K.B. 597); cp. *Read v. J. Lyons & Co. Ltd.* [1947] A.C. 156 at 183 *per* Lord Simonds. Cp. the judgment of Megaw L.J. in *Leakey v. National Trust* [1980] 1 All E.R. 17 at 30 *et seq.*, in which he points out that *Rylands v. Fletcher* did not determine the issue which arose in that case as to the duty of a landowner to take care in respect of natural hazards.

25 [1936] A.C. 108 at 119; cp. Lord Wright in *Sedleigh-Denfield v. O'Callaghan* [1940] A.C. 880 at 904.

26 Winfield, "Nuisance as a Tort" (1932) 4 Camb. J. 189 at 195.

27 *Ibid*: see pp. 195–197.

the defendant's use of his land is "natural". *Rylands v. Fletcher* liability requires a "non-natural" user of land. Whatever the distinction be, it marks an important difference between the two causes of action. However, one difference that has been suggested between nuisance and *Rylands v. Fletcher* does not seem valid, namely that a defendant is liable for the acts of an independent contractor under *Rylands v. Fletcher* but not in nuisance. There are decisions which make an occupier liable in nuisance for the acts of his independent contractor.[28] Indeed, this extension of vicarious liability is one of the major features which make both the rule in *Rylands v. Fletcher* and nuisance causes of action involving "strict" liability.

9.10 Finally the rule in *Rylands v. Fletcher* must be differentiated from trespass. Situations within the rule may involve injuries to the person of a plaintiff as well as damage to land or property, just as there are various forms of trespass. To that extent trespass and *Rylands v. Fletcher* liability occupy the same ground. The difference is that trespass requires that the injury be inflicted directly,[29] whereas under *Rylands v. Fletcher* the consequence of an escape are indirect.[29a] Moreover, trespass seems to involve proof of a deliberate intent or some negligence on the part of the defendant;[30] *Rylands v. Fletcher* liability does not depend upon intention or negligence, but may be invoked where damage or injury is inflicted in the appropriate circumstances, viz., escape of a dangerous thing from the defendant's land.

9.11 Though situations may occur in which these various causes of action can be pursued simultaneously, the conditions or ingredients of liability differ with each distinct cause of action. Hence it is vital to ensure and maintain the difference between *Rylands v. Fletcher* liability on the one hand and trespass, nuisance and negligence on the other.

4. ANALYSIS OF THE RULE

(i) *Parties*

9.12 Originally the rule was conceived of as applying between adjoining occupiers of land. "The doctrine of *Rylands v. Fletcher*", said Lord Macmillan in *Read v. J. Lyons & Co. Ltd*,[31] ". . . derives from a conception

28 *Bower v. Peate* (1876) 1 Q.B. 321; *Matania v. National Provincial Bank* [1936] 2 All E.R. 633; *Spicer v. Smee* [1946] 1 All E.R. 489. Cp. cases of nuisance on the highway: *Hole v. Sittingbourne Railway* (1861) 6 H. & N. 488; *Holliday v. National Telephone Co.* [1899] 2 Q.B. 292; but the situation is different where the danger is created on private land and threatens users of the highway: *Salsbury v. Woodland* [1970] 1 Q.B. 324. Not all authorities agree that there is vicarious liability in nuisance for the acts of an independent contractor. *Salmond & Heuston on the Law of Torts*, 19th ed. 1987, at 549–550 take the view that both *Matania* and *Spicer* were special cases which do not support any such general view as stated in the text here: similarly Fleming points out (*Law of Torts*, 7th ed. 1987 at 363) that in Australia courts have not accepted such vicarious liability: *Torette House v. Berkman* (1940) 62 C.L.R. 637; *Stoneman v. Lyons* (1975) 133 C.L.R. 350.

29 Pp. 111–112.

29a Hence *Rylands v. Fletcher* is not appropriate where there has been the intentional or voluntary release of a dangerous thing: according to Taylor J. in *Rigby v. Chief Constable of Northamptonshire* [1985] 2 All E.R. 985 at 996.

30 Pp. 113–117.

31 [1947] A.C. 156 at 173.

of mutual duties of adjoining or neighbouring landowners and its origins are trespass and nuisance". In the same case Lord Uthwatt declared:[32] "I do not regard *Rylands v. Fletcher* as laying down any principle other than a principle applicable between occupiers in respect of their land." This was one reason, though not the only one,[33] for denying a remedy to the plaintiff in that case. She was an inspector who was injured while on the defendant's premises. Although a lawful visitor on the defendant's land, she had no right to sue under the rule because she was not an occupier of land injured as a result of, or by reason of her occupation of land.

9.13 Yet there are cases, queried though they were by Lord Simonds in *Read v. Lyons*,[34] in which the scope of the rule was extended to cover injuries caused by the escape of something dangerous although the defendant was not in occupation of land, or the land from which the thing escaped.[35] In *West v. Bristol Tramways*[36] the defendant's blocks, used to pave the highway, were coated with creosote, which gave off fumes that damaged shrubs on the plaintiff's nearby land. The defendant was liable under the rule. In *Charing Cross Electricity Supply Co. v. Hydraulic Power Co.*[37] the plaintiff owned electric cables placed under a public street and the defendant owned hydraulic mains situated by their side. The defendant's mains burst, damaging the plaintiff's cables. The defendant was liable under *Rylands v. Fletcher*, although both plaintiff and defendant were mere licensees of their respective sites and lacked any right of property in the soil where their cables and mains were located. Lord Sumner, relying on *Midwood v. Mayor of Manchester*,[38] a case of nuisance, stated that *Rylands v. Fletcher* was not limited to the case of adjacent freeholders.[39] An earlier instance is the decision of the Privy Council in *Eastern & S. African Telegraph Co. v. Cape Town Tramways*.[40] The defendant's electricity escaped and caused the disturbance of the plaintiff's submarine cables, which resulted in interference with their transmission of messages. The defendants were liable under the rule.

9.14 In these situations the plaintiffs were affected through their personal property and it was immaterial that such property was legitimately situated on or under land belonging to someone else and such land was not injuriously affected by the escape. In several instances, however, it was either suggested that a plaintiff might sue under the rule where he

32 *Ibid.* at 186.
33 Below p. 230.
34 *Supra* note 31 at 183.
35 Cp. the *Northwestern Utilities Case* [1936] A.C. 108, where it was assumed without deciding that *Rylands v. Fletcher* was applicable: below p. 244. The point was left open in *Rigby v. Chief Constable of Northamptonshire*, para 9.10 *supra*.
36 [1908] 2 K.B. 214; cp. *Powell v. Fall* (1880) 5 Q.B.D. 597.
37 [1914] 3 K.B. 772.
38 [1905] 2 K.B. 597.
39 *Supra* note 37 at 779; cp. *ibid.* at 784 *per* Kennedy L.J. and *Jones v. Festiniog Rly* (1868) L.R. 3 Q.B. 733, where the defendants were managers and occupiers of the railway.
40 [1902] A.C. 381; cp. *Rainham Chemical Works Ltd v. Belvedere Fish Guano Ltd* [1921] 2 A.C. 465 at 479 *per* Lord Sumner.

suffered personal injury while on the highway or the land of another person without having any right of occupancy on either the highway or such land.[41] Lord Porter, in *Read v. Lyons*,[42] would appear not to have accepted such suggestions because he referred to the plaintiff being injured or affected in or on "some place over which he has a measure of control". Nonetheless in *Halsey v. Esso Petroleum Co.*[43] Veale J. was prepared to apply *Rylands v. Fletcher* to a case where the plaintiff's car was damaged by sulphuric acid or harmful sulphate which escaped from the defendants' premises and alighted, in the form of smuts or oily drops, on the plaintiff's car which was located not on the plaintiff's land but on the public highway. *Rylands v. Fletcher* applied wherever such smuts or drops alighted, on washing hung out to dry as well as a motor car in the street. But the language of Veale J. indicates some confusion or close connection between nuisance and *Rylands v. Fletcher*, although the learned judge did not seem to draw any distinction between these two causes of action so far as the need to prove a proprietary interest in the land where the damage was incurred was concerned.

9.15 In short, therefore, while no decision is completely straighforward and dogmatic, and despite the dicta in *Read v. Lyons*, it would appear to be reasonable and legitimate to infer that the courts are prepared to apply the rule in *Rylands v. Fletcher*, in appropriate cases,[44] even though the plaintiff had no interest in land, as owner or tenant, at the time he was affected, and *a fortiori* in the land on which the plaintiff's loss, whether personal injury or property damage, was suffered. But it would still seem vital that the defendant was in occupation of the land from which the dangerous object escaped. *Rylands v. Fletcher* liability arises from the occupation of land.[45]

(ii) *Escape*

9.16 There must be an escape from the defendant's land. Hence if the plaintiff suffers damage while on the defendant's land there can be no

41 *Wing v. London General Omnibus Co.* [1909] 2 K.B. 652 at 665 *per* Fletcher-Moulton L.J. (plaintiff injured by skidding bus); *Miles v. Forest Rock Granite Co.* (1918) 34 T.L.R. 500; *Shiffman v. Order of St. John* [1936] 1 All E.R. 557 (strict liability was invoked so that a plaintiff, a visitor on land, could sue when he was injured by a pole placed by the defendant, a licensee, on the land of a third party); *Perry v. Kendricks Transport Ltd* [1956] 1 W.L.R. 85; *British Celanese Ltd v. A.H. Hunt (Capacitors) Ltd* [1969] 2 All E.R. 1252 at 1258 *per* Lawton J. Contrast the view of the Nova Scotia Court of Appeal in *Vaughn v. Halifax-Dartmouth Bridge Commissioners* (1961) 29 D.L.R. (2nd) 523 and a New Zealand court in *N.Z. Forest Products Ltd v. O'Sullivan* [1974] N.Z.L.R. 80 at 83.

42 *Supra* note 31 at 176.

43 [1961] 2 All E.R. 145 at 152.

44 Not when the damage was incurred on the defendant's land: *Read v. J. Lyons & Co. supra* note 31; cp. *Strapazon v. Oliphant Munson Collieries Ltd* [1920] 2 W.W.R. 793 (but note the contrary view expressed by Laidlaw J.A. in *Dokuchia v. Domansch* [1945] O.R. 141 at 146).

45 *Bridges Bros. Ltd v. Forest Products Ltd* (1977) 72 D.L.R. (3d) 335.

liability under *Rylands v. Fletcher*. This was the situation in *Cheater v. Cater*[46] where the plaintiff was the tenant of the defendant: he took the premises as he found them. In the absence of negligence or the breach of some express or implied term, there could be no liability. Similarly in *Ponting v. Noakes*[47] no liability arose under *Rylands v. Fletcher* when the plaintiff's horse died from eating the leaves of a yew tree that was wholly in the defendant's field. Nothing had escaped. In contrast in the older case of *Crowhurst v. Amersham Burial Board*,[48] the defendant's yew tree projected over a fence between his land and that of the plaintiff. The plaintiff's horse ate some leaves from the tree. Liability under *Rylands v. Fletcher* was established because the yew tree had "escaped" from the defendant's land. This seems to take the idea of escape a considerable distance from the original view in *Rylands v. Fletcher* itself. Not surprisingly, therefore, the plaintiff in *Read v. J. Lyons & Co.*[49] attempted to argue that the requirement of an escape was no longer necessary for liability under the rule. As long as the plaintiff was injured by some dangerous object that had got out of control, even though it never strayed from the defendant's land, that would suffice. Such has been the position where liability was imposed for the behaviour of animals *ferae naturae*, to which the rule in *Rylands v. Fletcher* could also apply, as well as the doctrine of *scienter*.[50] The House of Lords took a different view.[51]

9.17 In *Read v. J. Lyons & Co.* the plaintiff, an inspector of munitions, was present at the factory of the defendants where shells were manufactured when there was an explosion that caused injury to the plaintiff. There was no explanation of how or why the explosion occurred. The plaintiff did not allege negligence on the part of the defendants; nor was it possible to prove negligence. The House of Lords held that *Rylands v. Fletcher* was inapplicable because there had been no escape from the defendants' land.

9.18 This decision, and the restriction it placed upon the utility and scope of the rule in *Rylands v. Fletcher*, have been criticised on the ground that the House of Lords made it impossible to formulate any general principle or policy with respect to strict liability for damage done by ultrahazardous things or activities.[52] The attitude of the House of Lords is explicable, however, when it is recalled that where personal injuries are

46 [1918] 1 K.B. 247.
47 [1894] 2 Q.B. 281.
48 (1878) 4 Ex.D. 5.
49 [1947] A.C. 156.
50 P. 256.
51 *Supra* note 49 at 168 *per* Lord Simon, 173, 174 *per* Lord Macmillan, 178 *per* Lord Porter, accepting the views of Lewis J. in *Howard v. Houlder Lines* [1936] 2 All E.R. 781, in which there was no liability under *Rylands v. Fletcher* when a boiler burst injuring an invitee. Only if negligence were to be proved would there have been liability.
52 Fleming, *Law of Torts*, 7th ed. 1987 at 314–315.

concerned the courts have more and more come to the view that negligence is an essential feature of liability. Exceptional situtations may exist,[53] such as was the case where such injuries were inflicted by animals within the *scienter* doctrine,[53a] or as a result of some nuisance, or the doctrine of *Rylands v. Fletcher* itself. Consequently, to have removed the necessity for such an escape would have made the rule of much wider application than intended by the court which decided the original case. There is authority for the the proposition that the doctrine of *Rylands v. Fletcher* should not be extended too far beyond the legitimate principle of the case as far as strict logic might require, else it would be a very oppressive decision.[54] Restriction of *Rylands v. Fletcher* liability to instances where an escape has occurred is consistent with the law of nuisance, to which the doctrine is closely related. It is also consistent with the way the law of negligence has evolved in recent decades. It conforms to the view that the doctrine of *Rylands v. Fletcher* is extraordinary and stringent; hence it should not be invoked too easily or in circumstances which are questionable and not clearly within the spirit of the eponymous decision.

(iii) Dangerous things

9.19 The rule does not apply indiscriminately to everything that is brought by someone onto his land. According to Blackburn J. it has to be "anything likely to cause mischief if it escapes". So many different objects or things have been held to be dangerous and within the scope of the rule that it has been suggested that the test of whether something comes within the rule or not is variable.[55] A thing may be dangerous in some circumstances and not in others. Lord Porter harked back to the words of Blackburn J. when in *Read v. J. Lyons*[56] he said that an object could be classified as being dangerous in the sense that if it escapes it will do damage. Yet that seems to suggest an element of foresight that the object or thing is dangerous. In an earlier case[57] Bankes L.J. said: "A thing may

53 Fleming notes that "escape" is not required when a public utility introduces a dangerous substance such as gas into mains on or under the highway: but in fact there is always an escape into neighbouring premises or other cables, pipes, etc. He also argues that the defendant need not occupy the land from which the escape occurs as long as he introduced or controlled the dangerous substance which escaped. The latter point is questionable, even though Fleming relies on the argument that *Rylands v. Fletcher* is a species of the genus nuisance, and occupation by the defendant of the land where the nuisance emanates is not a prerequisite of liability: see pp. 195–201. For the view that occupation *is* required under *Rylands v. Fletcher*, see *Bridges Bros. v. Forest Products Ltd supra* note 45, distinguishing *Rainham Chemical Works Ltd v. Belvedere Fish Guano Co. Ltd* [1921] 2 A.C. 465, where the rule did apply to a licence of the tenant or occupier of the land; in *Bridges Bros.* the rule did not apply to a defendant who was flying over land subjected to aerial spraying. The case of *Gertsen v. Metro Toronto* (1973) 41 D.L.R. (3d) 646, also cited by Fleming in support of his proposition, was a special situation when a municipal body had statutory authority to acquire land or the right to dump garbage on another's land. It is not really possible to generalise from either the *Rainham* or *Gertsen* cases.

53a For the present situation with respect to damage caused by animals and the status of the *scienter* doctrine, see Chap. 11.

54 *Green v. Chelsea Waterworks* (1894) 70 L.T. 547 at 549 *per* Lindley L.J.

55 Stallybrass, "Dangerous Things and the Non-Natural Use of Land" (1929) 3 Camb. L.J. 376 at 382–389.

56 [1947] A.C. 156 at 176.

57 *Musgrove v. Pandelis* [1919] 2 K.B. 43 at 47.

be dangerous although the danger is unexpected." Hence in that case a motor car was a dangerous object within the rule, although the condition of the car which made it ultimately a source of danger and damage was unknown. If the test of whether something is within the rule so as to attract strict liability when it causes damage is put on the basis of "foreseeable" or "expectable" danger, then it might be possible to argue that *Rylands v. Fletcher* is nothing more than a special variety of negligence liability.[58] Yet the operation of the rule does not depend upon what is foreseeable by the reasonable man, or preventable. It seems to depend more upon the willingness of a court to declare that the thing or object which resulted in the damage to the plaintiff is capable of falling within Blackburn J.'s category of "dangerous things", things likely to cause mischief if they escape.[59]

9.20 It seems to be a question of fact subject to a ruling by the trial judge whether the particular object can be dangerous.[60] It has been held, in various decisions, that the following are dangerous objects within the meaning and scope of the rule: gas,[61] explosive substances,[62] electricity,[63] oil,[64] fumes,[65] acid smuts,[66] poisonous vegetation,[67] vibrations,[68] a flag pole,[69] even dwellers in caravans, i.e. human beings.[70] The rule has also been held to apply to a motor car with a tank full of petrol.[71] But it was not applied in *Giles v. Walker*[72] to thistles which grew on land as a

58 *Contra: Salmond & Heuston on the Law of Torts*, 19th ed. 1987 at 367–368, where it is said that foreseeability is not the same thing as negligence: cp. the position in the law of nuisance after *The Wagon Mound (No. 2)* [1967] 1 A.C. 617 (above paras 8.27–8): cp. *Benning v. Wong* (1969) 43 A.L.J.R. 467 at 494 *per* Windeyer J. who also equates nuisance and *Rylands v. Fletcher*.
59 *Rylands v. Fletcher* (1866) L.R. 1 Ex. 265 at 279–280.
60 *Read v. J. Lyons, supra* note 56 at 176 *per* Lord Porter.
61 *Batcheller v. Tunbridge Wells Gas Co.* (1901) 84 L.T. 765.
62 *Rainham Chemical Works Ltd v. Belvedere Fish Guano Co., supra.*
63 *National Telephone Co. v. Baker* [1893] 2 Ch. 186; *Eastern & S. African Telegraph Co. Ltd v. Cape Town Tramways* [1902] A.C. 381.
64 *Smith v. Great Western Railway* (1926) 135 L.T. 112.
65 *Charing Cross Electricity Supply Co. v. Hydraulic Power Co.* [1914] 3 K.B. 772.
66 *Halsey v. Esso Petroleum Co. Ltd* [1961] 2 All E.R. 145.
67 *Crowhurst v. Amersham Burial Board* (1878) 4 Ex. D. 5; *Ponting v. Noakes* [1894] 2 Q.B. 281. Or colliery spoil: *Attorney-General v. Cory Bros.* [1921] A.C. 521.
68 *Hoare & Co. v. MacAlpine* [1923] 1 Ch. 167. But there is Canadian authority both for and against the application of the rule to vibrations: *Aikman v. George Mills Co. Ltd* [1934] O.R. 597 and *Bauer v. Richardson Construction Ltd* [1938] 2 D.L.R. 309 are cases which hold that the rule applies to vibrations; while *Barrette v. Franki Compressed Pile Co. of Canada* [1955] 2 D.L.R. 665 is a decision which refuses to apply *Rylands v. Fletcher* on the ground that the defendant did not bring the vibrations on to the land: a strange view since the defendant indulged in the activity which produced the vibrations.
69 *Schiffman v. Order of St. John* [1936] 1 All E.R. 517.
70 *Attorney-General v. Corke* [1933] Ch. 89 (a case of nuisance really, which was not followed in New Zealand: *Matheson v. Northcote College* [1975] 2 N.Z.L.R. 106). Contrast with the *Corke* case *Smith v. Scott* [1973] Ch. 314: above para. 8.43.
71 *Musgrove v. Pandelis, supra*, but not to merely defective motor vehicles: *Phillips v. Britannia Hygienic Laundry* [1923] 1 K.B. 539. In certain instances the operation of *res ipsa loquitur* may amount very closely to strict liability: *Henderson v. Jenkins* [1970] A.C. 282: see paras 12.86ff
72 (1890) 24 Q.B.D. 656, discussed by Goodhart, "Liability for Things Naturally on the Land" (1930) 4 Camb. L.J. 13; *Essays in Jurisprudence and the Common Law*, Chap. 8.

consequence of the cultivation of the land by the defendant. Nor did the rule apply to an outcrop of rock.[73]

9.21 In this respect it is to be noticed that there are similarities and confusion between the idea of dangerous things within the rule and the requirement that the defendant be making a non-natural user of his land in order to attract the operation of the rule.[74] To bring a dangerous object on to land may in itself be to make a non-natural use of the land.[75] Conversely, things which are naturally on the land are not "dangerous".[75a] This does not mean that there might not be liability for damage resulting from the situation or use of such things on the defendant's land. As indicated by the Court of Appeal in *Leakey v. National Trust*,[76] where *Giles v. Walker* was overruled,[77] there could be liability in nuisance for what happens as a consequence of the natural condition of land, where the defendant could have done something to remove a dangerous situation the existence of which he was aware of. The judgment of the court in the *Leakey* case reveals clearly the difference between liability in nuisance, which may be broader now than it once was, and liability under the rule in *Rylands v. Fletcher*. The latter depends in part upon the concept of "dangerous things" and in part on the idea of "non-natural user". Nuisance can be committed even though the source of the nuisance is not something inherently dangerous or likely to cause mischief and even though the defendant is making a "natural" use of his land.[78]

9.22 *Rylands v. Fletcher* liability attaches to what have been termed "extra-hazardous" or "ultra-hazardous" activities.[79] Hence a distinction has been drawn between what is sometimes referred to as a "domestic" use of some substances such as water, gas or electricity, and some more extensive, industrial or commercial use of such substances bringing with it an increased risk of harm to others.[80] Water in a toilet in a house would not attract the operation of the rule;[81] but water in a reservoir would.[82] Gas used to heat a stove in a kitchen would not involve strict liability under the rule; but gas in a gasometer used by a public utility to store gas would undoubtedly attract the rule (in the absence of some defence of statutory authority).[83] Where such "domestic" use of potentially dangerous substances occurs, there will only be liability if through negligence of

73 *Pontadarwe R.D.C. v. Moore-Gwyn* [1929] 1 Ch. 656.
74 Stallybrass, *loc. cit. supra* note 55 at 395–396.
75 *Read v. J. Lyons, supra* note 56 at 76 *per* Lord Porter.
75a *Rylands v. Fletcher* applies only to things artificially brought on the land and has no application to things naturally there: *Bartlett v. Tottenham* [1932] 1 Ch. 114 at 131 *per* Lawrence L.J.
76 [1980] 1 All E.R. 17.
77 *Ibid.* at 34: the reasoning in *Pontadarwe R.D.C. v. Moore-Gwyn* was also rejected, although the decision in the case was upheld on the basis of nuisance.
78 To the contrary, *Salmond & Heuston, op. cit.* at 360–361. See above p. 226.
79 *Read v. Lyons* (1947) 62 T.L.R. 646.
80 *Rickards v. Lothian* [1913] A.C. 263.
81 *Ibid.* Contrast *Peters v. Prince of Wales Theatre Ltd* [1943] K.B. 73; *Western Engraving Co. v. Film Laboratories Ltd* [1938] 1 All E.R. 106.
82 *Rylands v. Fletcher* itself; *Box v. Jubb* (1879) 4 Ex.D. 76.
83 Below pp. 242–243.

some kind the substance has become, in this particular instance, a source of danger which otherwise it would not be. When this happens the liability of the defendant is really in negligence, not under the rule in *Rylands v. Fletcher*.

(iv) *Non-natural user*

9.23 Even if a dangerous thing is brought or kept on the defendant's land, the question remains whether such dangerous thing is there in the course of a natural use of the land.[84] Although in a dictum in *Barker v. Herbert*,[85] a case of nuisance, Fletcher-Moulton L.J. referred to "something of an unusual nature which is essentially dangerous in itself", it is clear that the issues of natural or non-natural use of the land and the dangerous character of the object that escapes and causes damage must be kept distinct.

9.24 In the judgment of Blackburn J. in *Rylands v. Fletcher* there is no explicit reference to the difference between natural and non-natural user of land. Indeed he derives the rule in part from the old law of cattle trespass which involved the "natural" use of land to graze cattle (since natural does not mean "primitive").[86] The distinction may have come from cases prior to 1868 concerned with the working of mines. In *Smith v. Kenrick*,[87] for example, the defendant's mine was worked in such a way that the plaintiff's mine was flooded. The defendant was not liable because the water which seeped into the plaintiff's property was naturally on the land of the defendant.[88] In *Baird v. Williamson*[89] however the defendant was liable because the defendant had interfered with the natural state of the land and caused water to come on the land when it was not naturally there.

9.25 Whatever the true source of the distinction made by Lord Cairns when *Rylands v. Fletcher* was decided in the House of Lords, the concept of non-natural user has been accepted and applied by courts ever since.[90] It cannot be said, however, that they have been successful in defining or explaining what the expression means. In *Rickards v. Lothian*[91] Lord Moulton attempted to give meaning to the expression:

> "It is not every use to which land is put that brings into play [the doctrine of *Rylands v. Fletcher*]. It must be some special use bringing with it increased

84 *Bartlett v. Tottenham* [1932] 1 Ch, 114 at 131 *per* Lawrence L.J.
85 [1911] 2 K.B. 633 at 642.
86 *Read v. J. Lyons* [1947] A.C. 156 at 187 *per* Lord Uthwatt.
87 (1849) 7 C.B. 515; discussed by Megaw L.J. in *Leakey v. National Trust* [1980] 1 All E.R. 17 at 31.
88 Cp. the later case of *Wilson v. Waddell* (1876) 2 App.Cas. 95, where the defendant was not liable when his working of his mine caused subsidence which prevented the flow of natural water to the plaintiff's land.
89 (1863) 15 C.B. (N.S.) 376.
90 Stallybrass, "Dangerous Things and the Non-Natural Use of Land" (1929) 3 Camb. L.J. 376; Goodhart, "Liability for Things Naturally on the Land" (1930) 4 Camb. L.J. 13; Newark, "Non-Natural User and *Rylands v. Fletcher*" (1961) 24 M.L.R. 557.
91 [1913] A.C. 263 at 280: cp. Lord Maugham in *Sedleigh-Denfield v. O'Callaghan* [1940] A.C. 880 at 888.

danger to others and must not merely be the ordinary use of the land or such a use as is proper for the general benefit of the community."

The last phrase has caused difficulty, and may be said to have been an inappropriate way of phrasing a qualification of the doctrine of *Rylands v. Fletcher* that is accepted and undeniable, namely, the situation where the activity of the defendant is carried on for the benefit of the plaintiff as well as of the defendant.[92] The earlier part of Lord Moulton's remarks have been seized upon by courts to provide some form of distinction between natural or ordinary uses of land and non-natural or extraordinary uses.

9.26 If electricity, water, gas, or other such substances are brought on to land in quantities sufficient and necessary for ordinary domestic purposes, as opposed to their presence in bulk, as for example in cables or reservoirs, then such use of potentially harmful substances is a natural use.[93] The principle of *Rylands v. Fletcher*, said Lord Wright in *Collingwood v. Home & Colonial Stores*,[94] "does not apply to what may be described as the reasonable or ordinary user of premises". Hence in that case, where the plaintiff's shop was destroyed by a fire caused through a defect in the defendant's electric wiring, the defendant was not liable under *Rylands v. Fletcher.* It could also be said that substances like gas, electricity, water, etc., when collected in similar quantities, for domestic purposes, are not "dangerous". Almost anything, if not anything, can be dangerous, in itself or within the meaning of Blackburn J.'s remarks in *Rylands v. Fletcher.* Even "domestic" quantities of gas, water, etc., could be dangerous. What the courts have done has been to declare that domestic quantities are not dangerous because they are reasonable and ordinary.

9.27 The idea that certain uses of land may be reasonable and therefore not attract the rule's operation is one that must be regarded carefully. If this is to be accepted as the test of liability, the connection between nuisance and *Rylands v. Flectcher* becomes more pronounced. In nuisance much may depend upon whether the defendant is making a "reasonable" use of his land.[95] Under the rule in *Rylands v. Fletcher* the test is whether the use is non-natural. A defendant's use of his land may be reasonable from one point of view and at the same time non-natural and potentially dangerous. When Lord Wright spoke of a "reasonable and ordinary" use he must be taken to have intended some use of land that was not, in the usual, ordinary course of things particularly dangerous or foreseeable as being dangerous: a use of the land that was consistent with everyday, domestic activities, not commercial, industrial, hazardous ones. He could not have been employing the expression "reasonable" in the same way as in the context of negligence or nuisance.[96]

92 Below pp. 240–241.
93 But so was the manufacture of flour in an Australian case; *Wise v. N.S.W. Commissioner of Railways* (1947) 75 C.L.R. 59.
94 [1936] 2 All E.R. 200 at 206. On fire see further Chap. 10.
95 Pp. 188–190.
96 But some writers also think that nuisance and *Rylands v. Fletcher* are not all that distinguishable: supra note 78: Goodhart, *loc. cit. supra* note 90.

9.28 What kinds of use of land are considered "natural" can truly only be discovered or identified by reference to decisions since 1868. A wall was not a non-natural use of land (even though it is obvious that the wall was not a natural growth on the land but had been constructed by men). Hence there was no liability under *Rylands v. Fletcher* when the wall collapsed and caused damage.[97] When a defendant kept heaps of bones, from which he made manure, on his land and this attracted rats that went onto the plaintiff's land and ate his corn, the defendant was not liable under the rule.[98] The rats were "naturally" on the land, even though they had come there in consequence of the defendant's collection of bones (which surely was not a "natural" use of land). Perhaps the underlying ground of the decision was that the collection of bones was not something that could be seen in advance as being likely to cause mischief to anyone. A tree growing on land is a natural use of the land.[99] So apparently is excavating for gravel which is naturally on land. Hence when water filled a gravel pit dug by the defendant and the water was blown onto the plaintiff's land and did damage by erosion and otherwise, the defendant was not liable under *Rylands v. Fletcher*.[100] But using land for a chair-o-plane ride at a fair was not a natural use of the land in *Hale v. Jennings Bros.*[101] Nor was keeping gas at high pressure in pipes under the ground in the *Northwestern Utilities* case.[102] Nor was the making of explosives, i.e. shells, during the war-time a natural use of land, albeit that the manufacture of such articles was a reasonable, indeed even an ordinary use of land when the country is engaged in a war and explosives and shells are of urgent necessity.[103] Hence the queries raised on this point by various members of the House of Lords in *Read v. J. Lyons*.[104] But the making of shells, etc. in peacetime has been declared a non-natural use of land by a Canadian judge.[105] Perhaps there is a distinction between peace and war for this purpose, although it is hard to justify any such differentiation in modern times.

9.29 The relationship between dangerous things and non-natural user of land has been mentioned. It is not difficult to see why the requirement that an object be dangerous should be confused with the requirement that the use of the land be non-natural. If an object that is brought on to land is dangerous there would be a tendency to draw the conclusion that the bringing of such object on the land was inevitably and indisputably a non-natural use of the land. The language of Lord Moulton that has been quoted hints at the merging of the two ingredients of liability: at the same

97 *St. Anne's Well Brewery v. Roberts* (1929) 140 L.T. 1.
98 *Stern v. Prentice Bros.* [1919] 1 K.B. 394.
99 *Noble v. Harrison* [1926] 2 K.B. 332 at 342 *per* Wright J.
100 *Rouse v. Gravelworks Ltd* [1940] 1 K.B. 489. The defendant did no more than use the land in a natural way: *ibid.* at 498 *per* Slesser L.J.
101 [1938] 1 All E.R. 579 at 585 *per* Scott L.J.
102 [1936] A.C. 108.
103 *Rainham Chemical Works Ltd v. Belvedere Fish Guano Co.* [1921] 2 A.C. 465.
104 [1947] A.C. 156 at 170 *per* Lord Simon, 174 *per* Lord Macmillan, 187 *per* Lord Uthwatt.
105 *J. B. Porter & Co. v. Bell* [1955] 1 D.L.R. 62.

time it also indicates a difference between the use in question and the object that is involved in the use. Only when the object is dangerous and the use to which the land is put produces an increase in the risk of harm to others will the rule be applicable. Thus, for example, a loaded rifle is a dangerous object. But merely to bring it onto land is not a non-natural use of land (as for instance where it is being kept to reduce the threat to livestock from foxes, wolves, or rabbits). Only when the rifle is used in a dangerous way that is not concerned with the protection of livestock will it possibly entail liability under *Rylands v. Fletcher*.

9.30 The requirements of non-natural user and that the object be dangerous share the quality of being flexible. By determining whether a use is or is not natural or an object dangerous within the meaning of the original rule as laid down by Blackburn J. and the House of Lords, modern courts can adapt the rule to changed social and economic conditions, can broaden its scope or narrow its applicability as they see fit, having regard to the extent to which it is reasonable to impose strict liability for certain activities which are not in themselves unlawful. There must be some minimal content to the ideas of non-natural user and danger. Beyond this there are no clear guidelines. The application of *Rylands v. Fletcher* will alter in accordance with changing judicial philosophies.

(v) Damage

9.31 The original decision was concerned with damage to property. As Lord Macmillan pointed out in *Read. v. Lyons*,[106] the duty not to cause harm by what one does on one's land (i.e. *sic utere tuo ut alienum non laedas*),[107] "is to refrain from injuring not *alium* but *alienum*". Where damage is caused to real or personal property in consequence of an escape that is within the rule, there is no difficulty about imposing liability. But the issue has been raised whether *Rylands v. Fletcher* can also be invoked to provide a remedy in cases of personal injury.

9.32 Prior to *Read v. J. Lyons* there were *dicta* which suggested that the rule was equally applicable to personal injuries as to injuries to property.[108] Those cases, however, either did not raise the issue squarely or could be considered to have been decided on the basis of negligence. At the same time such *dicta* could be regarded as unfounded in principle

106 [1947] A.C. 156 at 173.

107 Said in *Rickards v. Lothian* [1913] A.C. 263 at 271 *per* Lord Moulton to be the basis for the rule.

108 *Wing v. London General Omnibus Co.* [1909] 2 K.B. 652 at 665 *per* Fletcher-Moulton L.J.; *Miles v. Forest Rock Granite Co.* (1918) 34 T.L.R. 500; *Schiffman v. Order of St. John* [1936] 1 All E.R. 557; *Hale v. Jennings Bros.* [1938] 1 All E.R. 579. Note the connection between this issue and the question whether a plaintiff has to have an interest in the land on which he suffers harm in order to sue under *Rylands v. Fletcher*. For the *obiter* statement by Blackburn J. that *Rylands v. Fletcher* applies to chattels (as well as land) which might therefore indicate an exclusion of personal injury or entitle a court to make a legitimate extension to cover such injury, see *Cattle v. Stockton Waterworks Co.* (1875) L.R. 10 Q.B. 453 at 457.

because the rule in *Rylands v. Fletcher* had its origins in wrongs as between adjoining landowners and the case should not be extended beyond the legitimate principle on which it was decided, even if logic demands such extension, because the result might be to make the case into an oppressive decision.[109] Logic would indeed suggest that if a plaintiff can recover under *Rylands v. Fletcher* if his chattel is damaged by the escape of a dangerous thing brought by the defendant on to his land in the course of a non-natural user of such land, he should also be able to recover if he, the plaintiff, is personally injured at the same time as his chattel is damaged. Moreover, to deny liability for such personal injury may be to confuse resultant damage with a cause of action, a well-known fallacy.[110] If there is an escape, a cause of action arises once damage has been inflicted. As long as some damage to property has occurred, personal injury that accompanies such property damage ought also to be within the scope of the action. What if only personal injury is suffered? That is conceivable, even though there might be property damage of some kind, e.g. the tearing of the plaintiff's clothes. In such an event the issue would be raised whether an action lies under *Rylands v. Fletcher* where the only damage is in the form of personal injury. Liability under the *scienter* doctrine was imposed for personal injuries, in the absence of negligence.[111] There seems no valid reason why it should not also be imposed under *Rylands v. Fletcher*, particularly when it is remembered that the doctrine of *Rylands v. Fletcher* might be invoked where the defendant collected dangerous animals on his land and one or more of such animals escaped and harmed the plaintiff. It would indeed be curious if the plaintiff were precluded from claiming for his personal injuries in an action based on *Rylands v. Fletcher* and would have been compelled to rely on the *scienter* doctrine (before 1971)[112] in order to recover, when he might have sued on either ground in respect of property damage.

9.33 *Read v. Lyons*,[113] where personal injury was inflicted on the plaintiff, left the issue unresolved, because there was no liability under *Rylands v. Fletcher* for other reasons. Some members of the House of Lords thought that "negligence is an essential requirement in an action for personal injuries".[118] Others were content to leave it open.[119] In *Perry v. Kendricks Transport Ltd*,[120] where again liability was denied on other grounds, it was either assumed by the Court of Appeal or definitively stated that there would have been liability for personal injuries under *Rylands v. Fletcher* had the rule been applicable in the circumstances. It was not applicable by reason of the defence or plea of act of a stranger or third party.[121] In any event there was more than a suggestion of negligence in the case; and it

109 *Green v. Chelsea Waterworks Co.* (1894) 70 L.T. 547 at 549 *per* Lindley L.J.
110 *Bourhill v. Young* [1943] A.C. 92 at 109 *per* Lord Wright.
111 Pp. 256.
112 And enactment of the Animals Act 1971: below pp. 258–269.
113 [1947] A.C. 156.
118 *Ibid.* at 171 *per* Lord Macmillan, cp. *ibid.* at 180 *per* Lord Simonds.
119 *Ibid.* at 168–169 *per* Lord Simon, 178 *per* Lord Porter.
120 [1956] 1 W.L.R. 85; cp. *Benning v. Wong* (1969) 122 C.L.R. 249 at 274, 277, 317.
121 Below p. 243.

might have been decided on that ground, if the facts had supported the conclusion that the defendants had behaved negligently in leaving an abandoned old bus on their property with some petrol vapour in its fuel tank so that, when a mischievous boy threw a lighted match into the tank, there was an explosion which injured the plaintiff, another boy. Although no English case has arisen in which a claim under *Rylands v. Fletcher* has been successful and personal injuries were incurred, there is at least one Canadian case[122] in which the plaintiffs recovered damages for personal injuries and the doctrine was applicable. However perhaps the case is a weak authority since there was also liability on the basis of nuisance and negligence.

9.34 The choice ultimately is between acceding to the demands of common sense and allowing recovery for personal injury, so as not to diminish the effectiveness of the rule, and conforming to the innate logic and rationale of the rule, the consequence of which would be to deny recovery for personal injuries on the basis of the strict, narrow interpretation of the doctrine. The better choice, it is suggested, is the former. To adopt this might distort the original doctrine of Blackburn J. and the House of Lords: but it would be consistent with developments with respect to personal injuries since 1868.

5. QUALIFICATIONS TO THE RULE

(i) Act of plaintiff

9.35 A plaintiff who is himself a wrongdoer may not be able to recover. Blackburn J. in the Court of Exchequer Chamber spoke of "the plaintiff's default", i.e. that the plaintiff himself brought about the escape.[123] If the plaintiff, by trespassing, puts himself in the path of injury resulting from the escape, that would seem to come within the scope of Blackburn J.'s language[123a] For example, in *Ponting v. Noakes*,[123b] the plaintiff's horse ate leaves of the defendant's tree, as a consequence of which the horse died because the tree was poisonous. Liability was not imposed on the defendant; but this may have been because the tree had not "escaped": it was on the defendant's land when the plaintiff's horse ate the leaves. It was suggested that the decision might have been different if the tree had been a trap to lure the horse and cause its death.[124] In such circumstances the plaintiff's default is the very act which the defendant intends to occur.

122 *Aldridge v. Van Patter* [1952] 4 D.L.R. 93. Contrast *Deyong v. Kingston Speedway Ltd* [1954] O.R. 227, where *Rylands v. Fletcher* was not applied because there was no "escape".

123 (1866) L.R. 1 Ex. 265 at 279; see *Dunn v. Birmingham Canal Co.* (1872) L.R. 7 Q.B. 244.

123a Perhaps if the plaintiff is harmed by reason of his peculiar abnormal sensitivity: *Eastern & S. African Telegraph Co. Ltd v. Cape Town Tramways* [1902] A.C. 381. Contrast *Hoare & Co. v. MacAlpine* [1923] 1 Ch. 167. This, again, points to the strong links between nuisance and *Rylands v. Fletcher*: cf. pp. 226–227.

123b [1894] 2 Q.B. 281.

124 *Ibid.* at 256 *per* Charles J.

9.36 If the plaintiff's trespassory act, unlike that of the horse in *Ponting v. Noakes*, has no causal connection with the plaintiff's ultimate damage, save that the plaintiff would not have been harmed had he not been present on the land in question at the material time, it could be argued that the "default" of the plaintiff, vis-a-vis the owner or occupier of the land, is immaterial to the plaintiff's suffering of harm: therefore it should not deprive the plaintiff of a remedy. Such is the situation where the plaintiff's claim sounds in negligence.[125] There is no valid reason why the fact that the defendant's liability is strict should make any difference.

9.37 Another possibility is that the plaintiff may be guilty of contributory negligence which helped to bring about his eventual harm.[126] *Ponting v. Noakes* may be referred to not only as a case where the plaintiff's horse was wrongfully taking the defendant's property, viz. leaves, and therefore committing trespass against the defendant, but also as a case where the plaintiff might be considered to have been guilty of contributory negligence in that he failed to ensure that his horse kept away from the defendant's dangerous, because poisonous tree.

(ii) Consent of plaintiff

9.38 This is another instance of the general applicability of the maxim *volenti non fit injuria*.[127] As Viscount Finlay said in *Attorney-General v. Cory Bros.*,[128] "A plaintiff who is a consenting party to the accumulation cannot rely upon the escape of the accumulated material." For him to make the defendant liable he must prove negligence.

9.39 The necessary consent may be express or implied. If the dangerous thing is brought on to the defendant's land for the purposes of the common interest of the plaintiff and the defendant, that will be evidence of consent.[129] It will also effectively oust the operation of the rule because, as Blackburn J. stipulated in *Rylands v. Fletcher*, the collection of the dangerous thing must be for the defendant's own purposes. Once the thing is on the defendant's land for the common purposes of the parties, the collection or accumulation will no longer be for the exclusive benefit of the defendant or his sole purposes. In *Peters v. Prince of Wales Theatre Co.*[130] the plaintiff leased a shop from the defendant knowing that an automatic sprinkler system was fitted to the defendant's theatre above the shop and that the system extended to the shop. After a severe frost the sprinkler flooded the shop. The defendant was not liable under the rule in *Rylands v. Fletcher* because the plaintiff had consented to the risk of being harmed by the sprinkler system, of the existence of which he had knowledge. In other

125 Pp. 369–371.
126 On contributory negligence generally see pp. 356–369.
127 Pp. 348–356.
128 [1921] 1 A.C. 521 at 539.
129 *Peters v. Prince of Wales Theatre Co.* [1943] K.B. 73 at 78 *per* Goddard L.J.
130 *Supra.*

instances[131] the fact that the plaintiff was a tenant in premises on or in which there was a system of pipes to provide water for basins and toilets to be used by those occupying premises in the building, or their visitors, sufficed to establish that the plaintiffs in such instances had consented to the presence of the dangerous thing, i.e. water in large quantities. Hence there could not be strict liability for bringing such water onto the premises from which it escaped by the detriment of the plaintiff in his part of the building.[132] By way of contrast in *Western Engraving Co. v. Film Laboratories Ltd.*,[133] the defendant kept large quantities of water on its premises for its own purposes, namely the washing of film which it was manufacturing and producing. This accumulation of water was not for the common benefit of the defendant and the plaintiff, which also was a tenant in the building where the defendant's premises were located. When the water escaped and flooded the plaintiff's premises on the floor beneath the defendant, the latter was liable under *Rylands v. Fletcher*. However it does not appear in this case, unlike others, that the plaintiff knew of the risk resulting from the defendant's use of its premises at the time the plaintiff came into the building. Such lack of knowledge would suffice to make the defence of consent inapplicable, without reference to the niceties of the rule.

9.40 In *Rickards v. Lothian*[134] Lord Moulton suggested that there would not be liability under *Rylands v. Fletcher* for an escape if the accumulation was for the general benefit of the community. In the context in which this language occurs, the "community" that was involved was the small community of occupants of different parts of the same building. As that case and others indicate, if the various parties expressly or impliedly agree that the dangerous thing is to come onto the premises in which they all have various rights of occupany as tenants or owners because the presence of the dangerous thing is for their common benefit and purposes, the rule is excluded. However the words of Lord Moulton were taken by Denning L.J. in *Pride of Derby & Derbyshire Angling Association v. British Celanese Ltd*[135] to mean that the rule might be inoperative if what the defendant was doing in collecting the dangerous thing was for the good of the public at large:

131 *Rickards v. Lothian* [1913] A.C. 263; *A. Prosser & Sons Ltd v. Levy* [1955] 3 All E.R. 577; *Akerib v. Booth Ltd* [1960] 1 W.L.R. 454 at 458 (reversed on other grounds [1961] 1 W.L.R. 367). But coming to the nuisance is not a defence to nuisance; why should taking possession with knowledge of the presence of such danger be enough to deprive the plaintiff of a remedy if there is an escape? Here the link with nuisance, above note 123a, appears to have been broken.

132 But it is not confined to water in pipes: *Carstairs v. Taylor* (1871) L.R. 6 Ex. 257, rain water percolating into the plaintiff's part of a house because of guttering which had become defective because of rats. Nor is it confined to cases where different storeys of a building are occupied by different parties: *Kiddle v. City Business Properties* [1942] 1 K.B. 269 at 274.

133 [1936] 1 All E.R. 106: cp. *Whitby v. Brock* (1888) 4 T.L.R. 241, no consent to damage from the use of fireworks.

134 [1913] A.C. 263 at 280.

135 [1953] Ch. 149 at 189.

> "I doubt whether *Rylands v. Fletcher* applies in all its strictness to cases where a local authority, acting under statutory authority, builds sewers which afterwards overflow, or sewage disposal works which later pour out a polluting effluence, for the simple reason that the use of land for drainage purposes by the local authority is 'such a use as is proper for the general benefit of the community' and is on that ground exempt from *Rylands v. Fletcher*."

These words were not assented to by Evershed M.R.[136] Nor were they accepted by Upjohn J. in *Smeaton v. Ilford Corporation*.[137] Despite the view of Denning L.J., it seems never to have been held, in an English court,[138] that there is any such defence to liability under the rule in *Rylands v. Fletcher*, or qualification of that rule, based upon the notion of "general benefit to the community". Indeed were such a defence or qualification to exist, it might not have been necessary to invoke statutory authority, to which Denning L.J. refers in the passage cited, as a valid answer to potential liability. Such authority is conferred on bodies such as municipalities or public utilities in order to give them protection from possible liability, which might otherwise be imposed under the rule in *Rylands v. Fletcher* as well as in nuisance.

(iii) *Satutory authority*

9.41 The situation under the rule in *Rylands v. Fletcher* with respect to the defence of statutory authority is the same as in relation to nuisance.[139] The statute must provide for immunity or exemption from liability: and the body given power to act, or obliged to act under the statute, must have performed its duty or exercised its power without negligence (unless the statute confers absolute immunity upon the body in question).[140] Decisions as to the application of the defence clearly depend upon the language of a given statute. In *Green v. Chelsea Waterworks*[141] the statute that was material had the effect of exempting the defendants from liability when a water main burst and water escaped onto the plaintiff's land.[142] The relevant statute did not have the same effect in the *Charing Cross* case.[143]

9.42 Since the kinds of activity which usually require protection for those undertaking the activity from potential strict liability normally involve a high degree of risk, the duty of care which must be observed by the defendant in order to come within the umbrella of the relevant statute is extremely onerous. The defendant will be expected to take considerable

136 *Ibid.* at 176.
137 [1954] 1 All E.R. 923.
138 But it has in a Canadian court: *Danku v. Town of Fort Frances* (1977) 73 D.L.R. (3d) 377. To the contrary is *Lawrysysn v. Town of Kipling* (1965) 50 W.W.R. 430, affirmed (1966) 55 W.W.R. 108.
139 Cp. pp. 204–207.
140 *Northwestern Utilities Ltd v. London Guarantee & Accident Co.* [1936] A.C. 108 at 120 *per* Lord Wright.
141 (1894) 70 L.T. 547.
142 For the similar situation where a gas main burst see *Dunne v. North West Gas Board* [1964] 2 Q.B. 806.
143 *Charing Cross Electricity Supply Co. v. Hydraulic Power Co.* [1914] 3 K.B. 772; above para. 9.13.

measures to ensure the safety of the performance of the statutory undertaking.[144] Although the usually stated rule is that the defendant must prove that the appropriate care was taken, in order to make the statutory protection applicable,[145] there is an Australian decision, of a divided High Court,[146] which suggests that once the statute applies, e.g. because the causing of harm by an "escape" within the doctrine was a necessary incident of the activity expressly authorised by the statute, the onus is on the plaintiff to prove negligence. This may have been the effect of the legislation dealing with liability for fires that cause damage.[147] Such legislation is very specific and particular in its scope: and it would appear unreasonable to conclude that a similar attitude should be adopted wherever a situation within the rule in *Rylands v. Fletcher* is governed by statute.[148]

(iv) *Act of a stranger*

9.43 Although the defendant may have brought the dangerous thing onto his land, if it escapes through the intervention of someone over whom the defendant had no control, or against whose acts the defendant as a reasonable man could not have been expected to guard, the defendant will not be liable. In such circumstances strict liability is inappropriate. The defendant will be liable if he has been guilty of negligence. That could be the case if the defendant ought to have foreseen that a stranger would or might interfere and cause the escape in question: and the defendant could have adopted reasonable precautions to prevent this.

9.44 This limitation or qualification on the strictness of the rule in *Rylands v. Fletcher* was stated in *Box v. Jubb*.[149] The defendant's reservoir flooded and damaged the plaintiff's land. This occurred because a third party, who also had a reservoir located on land above that of the defendant, let his water flow into the defendant's reservoir. The defendant was not liable. In *Rickards v. Lothian*[150] one ground for holding the defendant not liable[151] was that the waste-pipe was plugged in the washroom, with the result that water in the system overflowed and damaged the plaintiff's premises below those of the defendant. It was no mere accident that this occurred. There was a deliberate act on the part of a malicious stranger who not only blocked the pipe but then turned on the water. There was no possibility that the defendant could have controlled the situtation and excluded the stranger, discovered in time what had

144 *Manchester Corporation v. Farnworth* [1930] A.C. 171.
145 *Northwestern Utilities Ltd v. London Guarantee & Accident Co., supra* at 119, 121, *per* Lord Wright.
146 *Benning v. Wong* (1969) 122 C.L.R. 249. The Canadian position is that of England not Australia: *J. B. Porter & Co. Ltd v. Bell* [1955] 1 D.L.R. 62; *Turpin v. Halifax-Dartmouth Bridge Commissioners* (1956) 21 D.L.R. (2d) 623.
147 Below Chap. 10.
148 It also places an unfair burden on the plaintiff who presumably is not in a position to be able to dissect the defendant's operation so as to establish the requiste lack of care.
149 (1878) 4 Ex. D. 76.
150 [1913] A.C. 263: cp. *A. Prosser & Sons Ltd v. Levy* [1955] 3 All E.R. 577.
151 See above para 9.40.

happened, or prevented its occurrence. In *Perry v. Kendricks Transport Ltd*,[152] the explosion in the fuel tank of an abandoned bus on the defendant's parking lot was the result of the malicious, uncontrollable, unforeseeable act of children who threw lighted matches into the tank. The defendant was not liable under *Rylands v. Fletcher* for the resultant injury to the plaintiff (although there would have been liability if the plaintiff had shown that the defendant had been negligent in some way for example in failing to keep strangers away).

9.45 The question of liability will be determined differently, however, if the third party whose act produces the escape and the damage is someone for whom the defendant is responsible in law, such as a servant, agent or independent contractor. This was the situation in *Rylands v. Fletcher* itself. It was also the position in *Balfour v. Barty-King*.[153] The defendant employed an independent contractor who used a blowlamp that started a fire which eventually damaged the plaintiff's property. Liability will also be imposed if the defendant knew or ought to have known of the presence of the stranger and failed to take due care to prevent the stranger's acts from causing damage. In *Northwestern Utilities Ltd v. London Guarantee & Accident Co.*,[154] a hotel insured by the respondent plaintiffs was burnt down as a result of an explosion. This was the result of leaks in the defendant's gas pipe under the highway, caused by subsidence after excavation conducted by the third party. Here the defendants were aware of the acts of the third party undertaking the excavation (or ought to have realised the possible dangers that such excavation entailed). The defendants were liable in negligence, although not under the rule in *Rylands v. Fletcher*. But it could also be said that, once the neglect of due care was proved, the defendants were deprived of the opportunity of relying on the plea of act of a stranger that would otherwise have ousted the operation of the rule. Negligence was also held to be the appropriate cause of action, although there were also hints of the application of *Rylands v. Fletcher*, in *Hale v. Jennings Bros.*[155] The defendants operated a chair-o-plane ride at a fairground. The plantiff was injured when one of the chairs flew off from the central pole. It did so because it had been loosened by a third party while riding on the chair-o-plane ride. Here the defendant was liable because the ride and those on it, including the stranger whose fooling around caused the chair to become loose, were within the orbit of the defendant's control.

(v) *Act of God*

9.46 In *Rylands v. Fletcher*[156] Blackburn J. suggested that a defendant could excuse himself by showing that the escape was due to *vis major* or act of God. What is meant by the expression "act of God" has been doubted. It has been said that it would probably never be capable of complete,

152 [1956] 1 W.L.R. 85.
153 [1957] 1 Q.B. 496.
154 [1936] A.C. 108.
155 [1938] 1 All E.R. 579.
156 (1866) L.R. 1 Ex. 265 at 280.

exact and unassailable definition.[157] But it has also been said that this "untheological expression" is well understood by lawyers.[158] Attempts to pin down the meaning of the expression were made in *Nugent v. Smith*,[159] a case involving the liability of a common carrier. Brett J. said it was "such a direct and violent and sudden irresistible act of nature as the defendant could not by any amount of ability foresee would happen, or if he could foresee that it would happen, could not by any amount of care and skill resist so as to prevent its effect".[160] Cleasby B. thought it was "unusual violence of nature against which . . . precautions would be considered unavailing and could not be expected to be taken".[161] James L.J. thought that an act of God was "any accident . . . that is due to natural causes directly and exclusively without human intervention and that could not have been prevented by any amount of foresight and pains and care reasonably to be expected".[162] The events, in other words, must be incapable of being foreseen, or if foreseeable, must be impossible to guard against.[163]

9.47 The emphasis is therefore upon (a) natural causes—in contrast with inevitable accident, where human agency is an element;[164] (b) unusual violence, both sudden and irresistable; (c) an occurrence not reasonably foreseeable; and (d) impossible to prevent by any reasonable precautions, i.e. practically impossible to resist. Storms, earthquakes and other convulsions of nature will be acts of God.[165] But a fall of snow is one of the ordinary operations of nature,[166] in the same way as rain. However, there might be a fall of snow, just as there could be a fall of rain, a storm, that was so exceptional that it should be regarded as an act of God.[167]

9.48 Rats chewing guttering have been regarded as *vis major*.[168] So has a storm causing the overflow of the defendant's artificial pools.[169] On the other hand in *Greenock Corporation v. Caledonian Railway & Glasgow & S.W. Railway*[170] a storm was not considered an act of God relieving the defendants from liability. The course of a stream had been interfered with, obstructing the natural flow of water. This resulted in overflowing, because of a rainfall of extraordinary violence. Such overflow would not

157 In *Greenock Corporation v. Caledonia Railway and Glasgow & S.W. Railway* [1917] A.C. 556 at 580 *per* Lord Shaw.
158 *The Mostyn* [1928] A.C. 57 at 93 *per* Lord Phillimore.
159 (1876) 1 C.P.D. 19, 423.
160 At p. 34.
161 At p. 442.
162 At p. 444.
163 *R. v. Commissioners of Sewers for Essex* (1885) 14 Q.B.D. 561 at 574 *per* Lord Coleridge C.J.
164 Pp. 98, 116.
165 *Nugent v. Smith* (1876) 1 C.P.D. 423 at 441 *per* Cleasby B.: *Nichols v. Marsland* (1875) L.R. 10 Ex. 255 at 258 *per* Bramwell B.
166 *Fenwick v. Schwartz* (1868) L.R. 3 C.P. 313 at 316 *per* Wills J.; cp. *Slater v. Worthington's Cash Stores* [1914] 1 K.B. 488 at 492 *per* Oliver J.
167 *Sedleigh-Denfield v. O'Callaghan* [1940] A.C. 880 at 889 *per* Lord Maugham.
168 *Carstairs v. Taylor* (1871) L.R. 6 Ex. 217 at 221 *per* Kelly C.B.
169 *Nichols v. Marsland* (1875) L.R. 10 Ex. 255, (1876) 2 Ex. D. 1.
170 [1917] A.C. 556.

have occurred without the disruption of the prior course of the stream: the rainfall would have been carried off by the stream as it was before the interference. The earlier decision in *Nichols v. Marsland*[171] was distinguished on the ground that it dealt with the accumulation of water in a reservoir, not with an alteration in the course of a stream.[172] But this too was an interference with nature of the kind that was the basis for the decision in the *Greenock Corporation* case.

9.49 The criticism of *Nichols v. Marsland* by some members of the House of Lords in the subsequent decision[173] suggests that the law is taking a stricter view of what is an act of God and the applicability of this defence. As Goddard L.J. said in *J. & J. Makin Ltd v. London & North-Eastern Railway*,[174] in which act of God was held not to be a defence to an action for breach of statutory duty, when a storm caused an embankment to collapse with consequent flooding of the plaintiff's land: "Every act of God which causes injury may be called an accident, though not every accident is an act of God". The defence will be of very limited operation in modern times.

(vi) *Necessity*

9.50 *Dicta* in the judgment in *Rigby v. Chief Constable of Northamptonshire*[175] indicate that necessity will be a good defence to an action based on the rule in *Rylands v. Fletcher*. On the facts of that case, as Taylor J. held, the rule did not have to be invoked. There the plaintiff sued when the police fired a gas canister into his property in order to force out a psychopath trespasser. The canister caused a fire which damaged the plaintiff's shop. It was open to question whether *Rylands v. Fletcher* applied because (i) the police were not in occupation of the land from which the alleged dangerous thing, the gas canister, "escaped"; and (ii) the "escape" was not accidental, but intentional or voluntary. Hence liability might be imposed on the basis of trespass, but not under the rule which applied only to involuntary, unintentional escapes.[176] If it did apply, then necessity was a good defence, on the facts of this case, although not normally appropriate to the involuntary escape situation, because it was logical to allow necessity as a defence on the same basis as it would be a defence to trespass, if cases of voluntary release or firing, such as in the instant cases, were to be considered within the rule in *Rylands v. Fletcher*.[177]

171 *Supra* note 169.
172 *Supra* note 170 at 573 *per* Lord Finlay.
173 *Ibid.* at 580 *per* Lord Shaw, 581 *per* Lord Parker.
174 [1943] K.B. 467 at 478.
175 [1985] 2 All E.R. 985: see p. 99.
176 *Ibid.* at 995–996.
177 *Ibid.* at 996.

CHAPTER 10

Fire

1. SOURCE OF LIABILITY

10.01 The modern law relating to liability for damage caused by fire is derived from various sources. First there is the original common law, dating back to medieval times. That was affected by legislation of the eighteenth century, which is still in force.[1] The earlier law inevitably was also affected by the rule in *Rylands v. Fletcher*,[2] to the extent to which fire, or things which cause fire, come within the scope of that doctrine. It is hardly surprising that, when regard is paid to these different potential bases for liability, the present law evidences the existence of what have been described as "vagaries in liability for the escape of fire".[3]

2. EARLY STRICT LIABILITY

10.02 The common law originally dealt with cases of damage caused by fire through the use of an action of trespass on the case *pur negligent garder son few* available against an occupier of premises for allowing his fire to escape from his premises so as to cause damage to others.[4] That writ recognised a customary special duty on an occupier to "keep his fire safe". Such a duty was a very strict one, not arising from contract or any lack of care, but imposed by the law, in the same way as the law imposed strict duties on innkeepers and common carriers.[5] It covered fires which were within the occupier's control, for example, one which was lit in his field,[6] but not one which resulted from the defendant's firing a gun at a fowl.[7] It was immaterial whether the fire was started by the occupier himself or his servant or guest: in each case the fire was within the control of the occupier.[8] But the situation was different if the fire were lit by a stranger

1 It has been copied in other jurisdictions, e.g. Ontario: Accidental Fires Act, R.S.O. 1980, c. 4. It is also in effect in other Canadian jurisdictions, e.g., British Columbia and Saskatchewan:. *Franks v. Sanderson* (1986) 35 C.C.L.T. 307; *Halleck v. Doroshuk* (1985) C.C.L.T. 81.

2 (1866) L.R. 1 Ex, 265, (1868) L.R. 3 H.L. 330; Chap. 9. Note also the relevance of the law of nuisance: below p. 253.

3 Ogus, [1969] C.L.J. 104.

4 *Ibid.* 104–105, citing *Rastell's Entries*, p. 8: Winfield (1926) 42 L.Q.R. 46–50, Winfield (1931) 4 C.L.J. 203–206: see *Balfour v. Barty-King* [1957] 1 Q.B. 496; *Sturge v. Hackett* [1962] 3 All E.R. 166 at 168; and *Mason v. Levy Auto Parts of England Ltd* [1967] 2 All E.R. 62 at 69 per Mackenna J.

5 *Tuberville v. Stamp* (1697) 1 Ld. Raym. 264.

6 *Ibid.*

7 *Anon.* (1582) Cro. Eliz. 10.

8 *Beaulieu v. Finglam* (1401) Y.B. 2 Hen. IV, f. 18.

over whom the occupier had no control, or by an act of God. It was argued by counsel in the modern case of *Sturge v. Hackett*[9] that the common law, when referring in the writ to "*ignis suus*" (his own fire) meant to indicate a fire controlled by the defendant. Diplock L.J.[10] held that authority[11] made it clear, despite the ambiguity of the term, that it was occupation of premises where a fire occurred that mattered, not control of the fire.[12] Hence the breadth of an occupier's liability, namely where a fire was started by an independent contractor employed by the occupier.[13]

10.03 Negligence was not a relevant factor, at least in the modern sense of that term, even though the writ used the expression "*tam negligenter ac improvide*" when describing the conduct of the defendant. The occupier acted at his peril in failing through default to fulfil his duty.[14] As long as a fire begun on the defendant's land spread and did damage, the defendant would be liable, even though the spread of the fire was as accidental as the original beginning of the fire. Only where the origin of the fire was outside the occupier's control, or the spreading of the fire came about through the act of a stranger or an act of God, would the defendant escape liability. The occupier would be liable at common law, and seemingly is still liable today, for the negligence of an independent contractor[15] or a guest.[16] He is liable because he is the occupier and responsible in that capacity for those who come by his leave and licence.[17]

10.04 Who was a stranger for this purpose was considered by Lord Denning in *H. & N. Emanuel Ltd v. Greater London Council*.[18] He referred to the remarks of Markham J. in *Beaulieu v. Finglam*[19] in which it was said that the occupier would not be responsible if a fire were started by "a man from outside my household". and those of Holt C.J. in *Tuberville v. Stamp*[20] to the effect that "if a stranger sets fire to my house and it burns my neighbour's house, no action will lie against me". Lord Denning then said that a stranger is "anyone who in lighting a fire or allowing it to escape acts contrary to anything which the occupier of the house could anticipate

9 [1962] 3 All E.R. 166.
10 *Ibid.* at 169.
11 *Pantam v Isham* (1701) 3 Lev. 54; *Musgrove v. Pandelis* [1919] 2 K.B. 43; *Balfour v. Barty-King, supra.*
12 Ogus, *loc. cit. supra* note 3 at 104 disagrees on the ground that the defences of act of stranger and act of God are available, making not only occupation but also control essential. However, possibility of such defences does not necessarily make occupation an insufficient basis of liability: they only qualify the extent to which the occupier would otherwise be liable strictly (the onus being on the occupier to invoke and establish such defences).
13 *Sturge v. Hackett, supra* at 169.
14 *Tuberville v. Stampe, supra.*
15 *Balfour v. Barty-King, supra.*
16 *Boulcott Golf Club Inc. v. Engelbrecht* [1945] N.Z.L.R. 556.
17 *H. & N. Emanuel Ltd v. Greater London Council* [1971] 2 All E.R. 835 at 838 *per* Lord Denning, M.R.
18 *Supra* at 838–839.
19 *Supra* note 8.
20 *Supra* note 5.

that he would do."[21] Even someone invited to the occupier's house could be a "stranger" for this purpose if his conduct in lighting a fire was so alien to the invitation that he should *qua* the fire be regarded as a trespasser.[22]

3. THE INTRODUCTION OF NEGLIGENCE

10.05 A change was made by a statute passed in 1707,[23] section 6 of which provided that "no action, suit or process, whatever, shall be had, maintained or prosecuted against any person in whose house or chamber any fire shall . . . accidentally begin, or any recompense be made by any such person for any damage suffered or occasioned thereby, any law, usage or custom to the contrary notwithstanding." Other statutes were also enacted making regulations for the prevention and control of fires.[24] The important, and still governing, enactment is that contained in section 86 of the Fires Prevention (Metropolis) Act 1774,[25] which, despite its name, applied and still applies beyond the confines of London.[26] This states:

> ". . .no action, suit or process whatsoever shall be had, maintained or prosecuted against any person in whose house, chamber, stable, barn or other building, or on whose estate any fire shall. . .accidentally begin, nor shall any recompense by made by such person for any damage suffered thereby, any law, usage or custom to the contrary notwithstanding. . . ."

The statute appears to have been ignored,[27] at least in and by reported decisions until 1843,[28] possibly even later. However in *Filliter v. Phippard*[29] it was held that the word "accidentally" in the statute meant not only "unintentionally" but also "without negligence". In other words, in order to make a defendant liable it was necessary to establish that the fire in question had begun because of the negligence of the defendant or his servant. It has been argued that the source of this interpretation of the statute was the fact that by 1847, when *Filliter v. Phippard* was decided, the modern law of negligence had taken shape and was being invoked and applied by the courts, albeit in a rudimentary form which still awaited its later, more mature development in the nineteenth and twentieth centuries.[30]

10.06 Subsequent, more modern decisions have shown that the statute had clearly altered the common law by which liability for escaping fire

21 *Emanuel v. G.L.C., Supra* note 17 to 639.
22 *Ibid.*, citing *The Carlgarth* [1927] P. 93 at 110 *per* Scrutton L.J.; *Erikson v. Clifton* [1963] N.Z.L.R. 705.
23 6 Anne c. 31; on which see Ogus, *loc. cit.*, at 107–109; and *Becquet v. MacCarty* (1831) 2 B. & Ad. 951.
24 7 Anne, c. 17; 11 Geo. 1, c. 28; 12 Geo. III, c. 73.
25 14 Geo. III, c. 78
26 *Richards v. Easto* (1846) 15 M. & W. 251.
27 Ogus, *loc. cit. supra* note 3 at 110.
28 *Viscount of Canterbury v. Attorney-General* (1843) 1 Phil. 306.
29 (1847) 11 Q.B. 347 at 357 *per* Lord Denman C.J.
30 Ogus, *loc. cit. supra* note 3 at 109–112.

was independent of negligence.[31] The purpose of the legislation, Lush J. explained in 1919,[32] was to remove the common law presumption that a fire which was not proved to have been caused by some other person was caused or kindled by the householder, and to free him from liability for fires accidentally begun. Hence in *Mason v. Levy Auto Parts of England Ltd*,[33] Mackenna J., despite the argument of counsel, held that the defendant in an action for damage caused by fire did not have to disprove negligence in order to come within the protection of the statute. It was for the plaintiff to establish that the fire had been started through the negligence of the defendant or his servants or agents (or, it may be added, his independent contractor[34]). If under the statue the householder was no longer presumed to have caused the fire, he could not be presumed, even rebuttably, to have caused it negligently.[35]

4. THE IMPACT OF RYLANDS v. FLETCHER

10.07 Not long after the decision in *Rylands v. Fletcher*, Blackburn J., the originator of the rule in that case, applied its principles to the situation where damage was caused by sparks emitted from a railway engine. Earlier decisions had placed responsibility for such accidents on the basis of negligence.[36] In *Jones v. Festingiog Railway*,[37] however, it was held that the rule in *Rylands v. Fletcher* could be made applicable, on the ground that the railway company had brought onto its land, viz., the track, something likely to do mischief if it escaped. Curiously enough it was not the locomotive that escaped and did damage but the sparks from the fire in the locomotive. Under the Act of 1774 it might have been considered that the fire ought to have been started negligently or allowed to escape through negligence. In other words that strict liability as intended and provided for under the rule in *Rylands v. Fletcher* was not applicable to such a case. However this does not appear to have concerned the courts which accepted the analysis and approach of Blackburn J.[38]

10.08 Rejection of the application of the 1774 Act to situations where the rule in *Rylands v. Fletcher* could be invoked was plainly stated by the Court

31 *Mulholland & Tedd Ltd v. Baker* [1939] 3 All E.R. 253 at 255 *per* Asquith J.; *Williams v. Owne* [1956] 1 All E.R. 104 at 107 *per* Finnemore J.
32 *Musgrove v. Pandelis* [1919] 1 K.B. 314 at 317.
33 [1967] 2 All E.R. 62 at 67–68.
34 *Balfour v. Barty-King* [1957] 1 Q.B. 496: *H. & N. Emanuel Ltd v. G.L.C.* [1971] 2 All E.R. 835.
35 *Mason v. Levy Auto Parts of England Ltd.*, *supra* at 68.
36 *Piggot v. Eastern Counties Railway* (1864) 3 C.B. 229; *Vaughan v. Taff Vale Railway* (1860) 5 H. & N. 679.
37 (1868) L.R. 3 Q.B. 733.
38 *Powell v. Fall* (1880) 5 Q.B.D. 597; *Gunter v. James* (1908) 24 T.L.R. 868; *Mansel v. Webb* (1918) 88 L.J.K.B. 323. Note the limited liability under the Railway Fires Acts 1905 and 1923: *Attorney-General v. Great Western Railway* [1924] 2 K.B. 1; *Langlands (Swanley) Ltd v. British Transport Commission* [1956] 1 W.L.R. 890. Common law defences are available: *Groom v. Great Western Railway* (1892) 8 T.L.R. 253; *Parker v. London & North-Eastern Railway* (1945) 175 L.T. 137.

of Appeal in *Musgrove v. Pandelis.*[39] A motor car with petrol in its tank was held to be a dangerous thing within the meaning of the rule and, more surprisingly, to involve by its presence in a garage attached to a house a non-natural use of the land. Hence the rule in *Rylands v. Fletcher* applied. Bankes L.J.[40] drew a distinction between the mere escape of fire, to which the statute might apply, and an escape of fire under *Rylands v. Fletcher*, which was not the subject of exemption under the Act of 1774 because the legislature did not intend such exemption to apply[41] (a remarkable decision in view of the fact that in 1774 the rule in *Rylands v. Fletcher* did not exist). The argument of Bankes L.J. was that *Rylands v. Fletcher* was merely an illustration of the old principle "*sic utere tuo ut alienum non laedas*" (as stated by Tindal C.J. in *Vaughan v. Menlove*).[42] This reasoning has been criticised;[43] indeed it was rejected by Mackenna J. in *Mason v. Levy Auto Parts of England Ltd.*[44] The application of *Rylands v. Fletcher* to a garaged motor car has been doubted by other judges.[45] However the decision in *Musgrove v. Pandelis* was followed in several decisions[46] and was held by Mackenna J. to be binding upon him.

10.09 The principle that was applicable was not exactly that of *Rylands v. Fletcher*, because in *Musgrove v. Pandelis* the car had not escaped from the land nor had the petrol in its tank (any more than the locomotive or the fire in the locomotive in the railway cases). The principle was the wider one stated by Romer L.J. in *Musgrove v. Pandelis*, the wider one of *sic utere tuo. . .*, on which *Rylands v. Fletcher* was based, although the rule in *Rylands v. Fletcher* was not an illustration of that principle, as Bankes L.J. suggested, but an outcome or development from that principle. Hence Mackenna J. would not apply one form of the relevant principle, viz., the one that would require the plaintiff to prove that the defendant had brought something on to his land likely to do mischief if it escaped, that he had done so in the course of a non-natural user of the land, and that the thing had ignited and that the fire had spread. He applied a different test. This involved holding the defendant liable if he brought onto his land things likely to catch fire, and kept them there under such conditions that if they did ignite the fire would be likely to spread to the plaintiff's land, that he did so in the course of some non-natural use, and the thing ignited and the fire spread. This was the more reasonable test, since to make the likelihood of damage if the thing escapes a criterion of liability, when the thing has not in fact escaped but has caught fire, would not be very

39 [1919] 2 K.B. 43.
40 *Ibid.* at 46–47.
41 *Mason v. Levy Auto Parts of England Ltd supra* at 69 *per* Mackenna J.
42 (1837) 3 Bing. N.C. 468; para. 9.31 *supra.*
43 *Ogus, loc. cit. supra* note 3 at 113–114.
44 [1967] 2 All E.R. 62.
45 *Collingwood v. Home & Colonial Stores Ltd* [1936] 3 All E.R. 200 at 208–209 *per* Romer L.J., 206 *per* Lord Wright; *Read v. J. Lyons & Co. Ltd* [1947] A.C. 156 at 176 *per* Lord Porter.
46 *Collingwood v. Home & Colonial Stores Ltd, supra; Mulholland & Tedd Ltd v. Baker* [1939] 3 All E.R. 253; *Balfour v. Barty-King* [1956] 2 All E.R. 555; *Perry v. Kenricks Transport Ltd* [1956] 1 All E.R. 154.

sensible.[47] In the *Mason* case liability was imposed when the defendants stored on their land various combustible materials, and a fire broke out in their yard, probably because of a workman's cigarette, and the fire spread, damaging the plaintiff's adjoining laurel hedge.

10.10 The two problems arising from the application of *Rylands v. Fletcher* to cases of damages caused by fire are (i) to determine whether the thing which causes the fire, or from which the fire emanates, is a dangerous thing within the meaning of the rule; and (ii) whether bringing the thing on to the land, or a fire which spreads and does damage, is a non-natural user of land. On a strict interpretation of *Rylands v. Fletcher* what should escape is a fire which the defendant has brought onto his land for his own purposes, not a fire that is the product or result of bringing something else on to his land. The former seems more logically to justify the application of the rule in *Rylands v. Fletcher*. English courts, however, have clearly indicated that they will apply the rule where it is not fire that has been brought onto land but some other object which produces the fire that escapes and causes damage. The Act of 1774 will not excuse the defendant from liability even though he was not guilty of negligence either in starting the fire or allowing it to spread. The basis for rejecting the defence of the statute, however, has been said not to be that a fire caused in this way is not an "accidental" fire, i.e. one "produced by mere chance or incapable of being traced to any cause"[48] (since under *Rylands v. Fletcher* that can be liability because or when the escape is through mere chance or without any provable cause). The statute will not apply to protect the defendant, it is said,[49] because the statutory defence was only relevant to liability based upon "the mere escape of fire" and under *Rylands v. Fletcher* it is not the mere escape of fire that is involved but the escape of a fire resulting from a "dangerous thing".

10.11 The second difficulty involves consideration of what is a non-natural user of land. The use of fire for domestic purposes has been held to be a natural use of land; therefore if such a fire causes damage, negligence must be proved in respect of the starting of the fire or its spreading to the land of another.[50] A fire which is begun by an explosion or a fuse will also involve liability under *Rylands v. Fletcher*, if the thing which exploded or fused was something that could not be termed a "domestic" object, for example if the fire started on a factory or other industrial or commercial premises.[51] The position with respect to railways has previously been mentioned. Clearly to use land for a railway is a non-natural user of land. But there have been conflicting decisions in parts of the Commonwealth on the question whether to start a fire on agricultural land for the normal

47 *Mason v. Levy Auto Parts of England Ltd supra* at 69–70; Cp. *Sturge v. Hackett* [1962] 3 All E.R. 166, where the fire that caused the damage was not the fire started by lighting a rag to get rid of a sparrow's nest, but the fire which got out of control subsequently.
48 *Filliter v. Phippard* (1847) 11 Q.B. 347 at 357 *per* Lord Denman C.J.
49 Ogus, *loc. cit. supra* note 3 at 116.
50 *Sochaki v. Sas* [1947] 1 All E.R. 344.
51 *Collingwood v. Home & Colonial Stores Ltd, supra.*

purposes of clearing the land is a natural or non-natural user of land. Such issue has not arisen in England: but it has caused difficulty in Australia[52] and Canada,[53] and may be said to be unresolved. The decision in the *Mason* case indicates that whenever a fire emanates from an industrial or commercial use of land the situation will come within the scope of the rule in *Rylands v. Fletcher*.

5. THE MODERN SITUATION

10.12 The combined effect of the old common law as modified by the legislation of 1774 and the doctrine of *Rylands v. Fletcher* is that liability for damage caused by fire is based upon negligence in starting or controlling a fire but is strict if the fire is the consequence of a non-natural user of land. Two of the three cases in the past twenty to thirty years that have been referred to earlier[54] were dealt with under the law of negligence; the third was resolved by applying *Rylands v. Fletcher*.[55]

10.13 However it must be noted that there have been decisions in which damage caused by fire has been remedied by an action for nuisance.[56] Whether the state of the defendant's land, as a result of which a fire began and spread to the property of the neighbouring plaintiff, was such as to amount to "unreasonable" use of the land, an essential requirement of liability for nuisance,[57] will be a different question from whether the defendant's use of his land was non-natural, as required under in *Rylands v. Fletcher*.[58] But in cases of nuisance, unlike the difficulty experienced with *Rylands v. Fletcher*, it is unnecessary to establish that what escaped was what was brought onto the land. Hence it does not matter how the fire came into being and affected the plaintiff as long as the fire was the product of some unreasonable use by the defendant of his land. For example to allow wiring to become defective so that a fire is started will give rise to nuisance

52 *Hazelwood v. Webber* (1934) 52 C.L.R. 268; *Handraft Co. v. Commissioner for Railways* (1959) 77 W.N. (N.S.W.) 84; *N.Z. Forest Products v. O'Sullivan* [1974] 2 N.Z.L.R. 80. Contrast *Smith v. Badenoch* [1970] S.A.S.R. 9; *Trippett v. Cleaver* [1973] W.A.L.R. 173; *Wise Bros. v. N.S.W. Commissioner of Railways* (1947) 75 C.L.R. 59; *Mackenzie v. Sloss* [1959] N.Z.L.R. 533. See also *Black v. Christchurch Finance Co.* [1894] A.C. 48.

53 *Gogo v. Eureka Sawmills Ltd* [1944] 3 W.W.R. 268, [1945] 3 W.W.R. 446 (within the doctrine); *Dahler v. Bruvold* [1981] 5 W.W.R. 706; *Smith v. Widdicombe* [1987] 2 W.W.R. 480 (not within the doctrine). For earlier decisions see *Dean v. McCarty* (1884) 5 O.R. 531; *Fortin v. Daw* (1920) 19 O.W.N. 14 (negligence required); with which contrast *Canadian Southern Rly Co. v. Philps* (1884) 14 S.C.R. 132, liability without negligence.

54 *Sturge v. Hackett* [1962] 3 All E.R. 166 which is actually concerned with liability under an insurance policy: *H. & N. Emanuel Ltd v. G.L.C.* [1971] 2 All E.R. 835, in which the issue was whether the persons who started a fire on the defendant's site were "strangers" for whose acts the defendant (the occupier of the site) would not be liable; liability was imposed because the men regularly lit fires to burn rubbish despite a prohibition against doing so.

55 *Mason v. Levy Auto Parts of England Ltd* [1967] 2 All E.R. 62.

56 *Spicer v. Smee* [1946] 1 All E.R. 489; *Collingwood v. Home & Colonial Stores Ltd, supra*; *Goldman v. Hargrave* [1967] 1 A.C. 645.

57 Pp. 184–190.

58 Pp. 234–237.

liability for damage resulting from such a fire.[59] In much the same way, even if the fire begins accidentally or by some natural event such as lightning, if the defendant fails to behave reasonably in respect of the control of the fire he will be liable in nuisance (as well, perhaps, as in negligence).[60]

10.14 It has been suggested[61] (i) that nuisance is of greater importance in modern law by reason of a decline in the relevance of *Rylands v. Fletcher*; (ii) that it is not clear whether a defendant will be liable in nuisance for the acts of his independent contractor which produce an unreasonable state of affairs and a fire; and (iii) that the statute of 1774 is really irrelevant and inappropriate at the present time and should be repealed. Liability ought to be founded upon negligence or nuisance, both being based upon the fault of the defendant or his employee, but not of his independent contractor.[62] Whether such suggestions will attract support is open to question. Although it is not always clear whether liability for fire is based upon negligence or simply upon the fact that a fire has resulted from the defendant's use of his land, there appear to be valid reasons why the present law does not require fundamental reform.

10.15 First, since liability may be imposed either for negligence, or by the application of *Rylands v. Fletcher*, or on the basis of nuisance, it would appear that all conceivable situations are covered. Secondly, the defendant will be liable, whoever was responsible for the starting or spread of a fire, unless the defendant can establish (i) no negligence by him or his servants or agents; (ii) an act of a stranger; (iii) an act of God; or (iv) such use of his land as excludes the rule in *Rylands v. Fletcher* and nuisance. But this seems to place the burden on the defendant when it is potential plaintiffs who usually, indeed normally, insure against the risk of fire. The risk ought therefore to be on those who suffer the loss, it is argued, not on those whose conduct has caused it or brought it about: strict liability is undesirable. This attitute seems to take an approach to tort liability that is founded more upon economics and "efficiency"[63] than upon classical notions of liability in tort. Liability for damage caused by fire is based upon neglect or control. The defendant ought to be liable, either because he has failed to take reasonable care to prevent harm to others, or because his dangerous use of land has brought increased risk to his neighbours. The original common law may have been modified: but its purpose and role have been vindicated.

59 *Spicer v. Smee*, *supra*.
60 *Goldman v. Hargrave* [1967] 1 A.C. 645; cp. *Leakey v. National Trust* [1980] 1 All E.R. 17, not a case of fire but involving natural hazards: discussed paras 8.29–9 *supra*.
61 Ogus, *loc. cit. supra* note 3 at 116–119.
62 *Ibid.* 119–121.
63 *Viz.*, loss distribution.

CHAPTER 11

Liability for Animals

1. THE COMMON LAW BEFORE 1971

11.01 Significant change was made to the law relating to liability for harm caused by animals by the Animals Act, 1971.[1] Prior to 1971 the law in effect was derived from medieval notions overlaid by some modern common law developments,[2] and statutory provisions dealing with liability for dogs.[3] There were three ways in which a defendant could be sued in respect of something done by his animal. The appropriate cause of action depended upon (a) the kind of animal involved; (b) how the harm was caused; and (c) whether the defendant was guilty of negligence or some other form of behaviour which rendered him susceptible to action.

11.02 The first, and oldest in origin was the action of cattle-trespass.[4] This lay when cattle, which included cows, horses, sheep, goats, swine, asses, geese, ducks, etc., strayed from their owner's land onto the land of someone else.[5] This action was not available if the straying animal was not considered "cattle", for example a dog or a cat,[6] a lion or an elephant.[7] Liability was strict, i.e. without proof of negligence or intent.[8]

1 1971, c. 22. This statute was based on the Law Commission's Working Paper No. 13, 1967. An earlier Report is that of the Committee on the Law of Civil Liability for Damage done by Animals, 1953, Cmnd. 8746. This recommended that: (a) liability should be based on negligence; (b) the law of cattle trespass should remain unchanged; (c) occupiers should be liable for damage caused to persons or chattels by an animal which escaped on to the highway because of a breach of duty, i.e. negligence, whether or not the animal was acting in accord with its nature; (b) the *scienter* doctrine, distinguishing between animals *ferae naturae* and those *mansuetae naturae* should be abolished; (e) the onus should be on the defendant to show that he acted without negligence, i.e. with reasonable care.

2 Glanville Williams, *Liability for Animals*, 1939. See now North, *The Modern Law of Animals*, 1971.

3 Dogs Acts 1906, 1928.

4 *Stodden v. Harvey* (1608) Cro.Jac. 206; *Dovostan v. Payne* (1795) 2 H.Bl. 527; *Williams v. Lardner* (1798) 8 T.R. 72.

5 *Cox v. Burbridge* (1863) 13 C.B.N.S. 431; *Lee v. Riley* (1865) 18 C.B.N.S. 722; *Ellis v. Loftus Iron Co.* (1874) L.R. 10 C.P. 10; *Manton v. Brocklbank* [1923] 2 K.B. 212.

6 *Brown v. Giles* (1823) 1 C. & P. 118; *Buckle v. Holmes* [1926] 2 K.B. 125; *Sutcliffe v. Holmes* [1947] K.B. 147 at 153 *per* Somervell L.J.

7 Which would be the kind of animals that presented a peculiar risk, not agricultural animals, and therefore would come within the *scienter* doctrine.

8 But might depend on the obligation to fence: *Jones v. Price* [1965] 2 Q.B. 618. Note that cattle caught trespassing could be seized by the victim under the doctrine of distress damage feasant, which has now been abolished in respect of animals, though not other things: Animals Act 1971 s. 7(1). For other instances see *Boden v. Roscoe* [1894] 1 Q.B. 608; *Sorrell v. Paget* [1950] 1 K.B. 252.

11.03 The second cause of action was available when an animal caused damage, whether on the land of the defendant or elsewhere. Liability did not depend on whether the defendant was guilty of negligence or any intent to cause harm. This was the *scienter* action, based on the early writ which alleged that the defendant knowingly (*scienter*) kept an animal that was dangerous.[9] The common law divided animals into two classes, those *ferae naturae* and those *mansuetae naturae*.[10] The former were animals that were wild and could not be treated as domestic[11] (even if individual animals had been tamed and put to domestic uses).[12] The latter were animals which normally were regarded as domestic and tame,[13] such as horses, cows or dogs.[14] For harm caused by an animal *ferae naturae* liability was strict (although there were defences of limitations on liability similar to those which applied to the rule in *Rylands v. Fletcher*, e.g. act of God, act of a stranger, act of the plaintiff).[15] For harm caused by an animal *mansuetae naturae* there was only liability if: (i) the animal possessed a dangerous propensity that was not usual to its species;[16] (ii) the indulgence by the animal in that propensity, not some other, caused the harm in issue;[17] and (iii) the defendant knew of the propensity in question.[18] Although liability in these circumstances was strict, comparable to liability for an animal *ferae naturae* and subject to the same possible defences,[19] this liability was closer to negligence than liability for animals *ferae naturae*, in that it depended upon knowledge.[20] However it was distinguishable from negligence liability in that it was unnecessary for the plaintiff to prove that the defendant was negligent in controlling his animal and such negligence resulted in the plaintiff's damage. Liability for both classes of animals was imposed on the keeper of the animal, (which included the occupier of premises where the animal was allowed to go). This might or might not be the owner.[21]

9 Jackson, "On the Origin of *Scienter*" (1978) 94 L.Q.R. 85.
10 *Mason v. Keeling* (1699) 12 Mod. 232.
11 E.g., monkeys (*May v. Burdett* (1845) 9 Q.B. 101); bears (*Besozzi v. Harris* (1858) 1 F. & F. 92); elephants (*Filburn v. People's Palace* (1890) 25 Q.B.D. 250).
12 E.g., an elephant in a circus: *Behrens v. Bertram Mills Circus* [1957] 2 Q.B. 1; a camel in a zoo: *McQuaker v. Goddard* [1940] 1 K.B. 687.
13 I.e. they were not "naturally mischievous": *Mason v. Keeling*, *supra* at 335 *per* Holt C.J.
14 But not a ram: *Jackson v. Smithson* (1846) 15 M. & W. 563.
15 *Nichols v. Marsland* (1875) L.R. 10 Ex. 255 at 260 *per* Bramwell B.; *Baker v. Snell* [1908] 2 K.B. 825; *Marlor v. Ball* (1906) 16 T.L.R. 239; *Lee v. Walters* (1940) 162 L.T. 89; *Sarch v. Blackburn* (1830) 4 C. & P. 297. See Chapter 9.
16 *Hudson v. Roberts* (1851) 6 Ex. 697; *Cox v. Burbridge* (1863) 13 C.B.N.S. 431; *Buckle v. Holmes* [1926] 2 K.B. 125; *Manton v. Brocklebank* [1923] 2 K.B. 212.
17 *Osborne v. Chocqueel* [1896] 2 Q.B. 109; *Clinton v. Lyons* [1912] 3 K.B. 198; *Glanville v. Sutton* [1928] 1 K.B. 571.
18 *Mason v. Keeling*, *supra* at 335 *per* Holt C.J.; *Cox v. Burbridge*, *supra* at 439 *per* Willes J.; *Buckle v. Holmes*, *supra* at 128 *per* Bankes L.J.; *McQuaker v. Goddard* [1930] 1 K.B. 698 at 695–696 *per* Scott L.J.
19 It was said that *scienter* liability was part of the rule in *Rylands v. Fletcher*: *Filburn v. People's Palace* (1860) 25 Q.B.D. 258 at 261 *per* Bowen L.J.: *MacQuaker v. Goddard*, *supra* at 699 *per* McKinnon L.J., although the animal need not have "escaped" for there to be a liability.
20 Cp. *May v. Burdett* (1845) 9 Q.B. 101 at 110 *per* Lord Denman C.J. As to what was "knowledge", see *White v. Steadman* [1913] 3 K.B. 340; *Baldwin v. Casella* (1872) L.R. 7 Ex. 325; *Appleby v. Percy* (1874) L.R. 9 Q.B. 647; *Knott v. L.C.C.* [1934] 1 K.B. 126.
21 *M'Kone v. Wood* (1831) 5 C. & P. 1; *North v. Wood* [1914] 1 K.B. 629; *Knott v. L.C.C.*, *supra*.

11.04 Quite apart from such liability for cattle trespass or under the *scienter* doctrine, a defendant would be liable if he acted negligently and so permitted his animal to cause damage, e.g., by allowing a dog's lead to trip up the plaintiff.[22] Or if he deliberately injured the plaintiff by his use of an animal, e.g. by throwing a cat at the plaintiff, or invaded the plaintiff's land with his animals, in which event the defendant would be guilty of trespass.[23] Or if he kept animals on his land under circumstances that amounted to nuisance.[24] Or if he collected dangerous animals on his land and they escaped and caused harm, when the rule in *Rylands v. Fletcher* might be applicable.[25] Questions of liability in such instances fell to be determined by the principles that pertained to the particular tort involved: they did not turn upon definitions of cattle, whether the animal was *ferae naturae* or *mansuetae naturae*, whether the defendant knew of a dangerous propensity, and so on.

11.05 One special variety of negligence concerned the situation where an ordinarily harmless animal, such as a horse or a cow, strayed onto the highway and there caused harm, e.g. physical injury. A distinction was drawn between an animal lawfully brought on the highway and there permitted, through the defendant's negligence, to cause harm and an animal which escaped from the defendant's land where it was kept and got onto the highway where it caused harm to the plaintiff. The former situation was governed by the normal principles of negligence. If the defendant failed to exercise reasonable care in the control of his animal, he would be liable.[26] The latter situation was regulated by the doctrine laid down by the House of Lords in *Searle v. Wallbank*.[27] There it was held that a landowner was under no duty to fence, or to maintain a fence around his property so as to prevent his domestic animals, i.e. horses and cows, from getting onto the highway and causing harm.[28] This doctrine, which was grounded in medieval ideas and the peculiar position of landowners in English law, has not been followed and accepted everywhere in the Commonwealth. The Supreme Court of Canada rejected the decision and held a landowner liable, if negligent, in the same way as where he brings his animal to the highway where it later gets out of control and does

22 *Pitcher v. Martin* (1937) 53 T.L.R. 903; cp. *Brackenborough v. Spalding U.D.C.* [1942] A.C. 310 at 320 *per* Lord Wright. See *Draper v. Hodder* [1972] 2 Q.B. 556, no knowledge of vicious propensity of dogs: liability in negligence for allowing the dogs to escape and severely injure the infant plaintiff.

23 The vice of the animal being immaterial: *Manton v. Brocklebank* [1923] 2 K.B. 212 at 220 *per* Lord Sterndale M.R. Cp. *League Against Cruel Sports Ltd v. Scott* [1985] 2 All E.R. 489: see para. 5.04.

24 *Aldred's Case* (1610) 9 Co. 57b; *Leeman v. Montagu* [1936] 2 All E.R. 1677; *Hannam v. Mockett* (1824) 2 B. & C. 943. See Chapter 8.

25 Chapter 9: cp. *supra* note 19.

26 *Deen v. Davies* [1935] 2 K.B. 282; *Wright v. Callwood* [1950] 2 K.B. 515; *Gomberg v. Smith* [1963] 1 Q.B. 25; *Ellis v. Johnstone* [1963] 2 Q.B. 8.

27 [1947] A.C. 341: see *Brock v. Richards* [1951] 1 K.B. 529.

28 Also to straying dogs: *Ellis v. Johnstone*, *supra*; *Gomberg v. Smith*, note 31 *infra*; unless the dog was known to be vicious or dangerous, e.g. had a habit of dashing out onto the highway like a missile.

damage.[29] The English rule was maintained, however, although it could be distinguished, as it was in cases involving "straying" children[30] or dogs.[31]

11.06 Cats and dogs did not come within the scope of the definition of "cattle" so as to involve their owners in liability for cattle-trespass.[32] Nor were they animals *ferae naturae*. There might be liability for what a cat or a dog did if the animal acted abnormally and its abnormal propensity was known about by the owner. However for a cat or a dog to stray was not abnormal: hence there was no liability for what such an animal did when it strayed. However legislation on dogs[33] did provide for specific liability where a dog attacked and killed or injured livestock.

2. THE LEGISLATION OF 1971

(a) General effect

11.07 The Animals Act 1971[33a] enacts provisions which replace the rules of the common law imposing strict liability in tort for damage done by an animal on the ground that the animal is regarded as *ferae naturae* or that its vicious propensities are known or presumed to be known.[34] The *scienter* doctrine has thus been eradicated from English law. In its place are statutory provisions dealing with liability for damage done by dangerous animals.[35]

11.08 The statute also replaces provisions of earlier legislation dealing with liability for dogs which caused injury to cattle or poultry.[36] The common law of cattle trespass is also replaced by statutory provisions dealing with trespassing livestock.[37] So, too, are the rules of the common law relating to the exclusion of liability for animals escaping onto the highway as a result of a failure to fence land, as established by *Searle v.*

29 *Fleming v. Atkinson* [1959] S.C.R. 513; although there have been provincial decisions which have not always followed the Supreme Court of Canada: compare and contrast *Rejnoldson v. Simmons* (1982) 14 Sask.R. 257; *Bettenson v. Johnson* 1980) 18 A.R. 343; *Windrem v. Hamill* [1978] 3 W.W.R. 684; *Eales v. Jones* (1979) 17 N. & P.E.I.R. 242; *Spanton v. Laviolette* (1978) 19 O.R. (2d) 21; *Lane v. Biel* (1971) 17 D.L.R. (3d) 632; *Cormier v. McCarthy* (1969) 1 N.B.R. (2d) 866; *White v. Power* (1973) 4 N.S.R. (2d) 718; *Stetler v. Stross Management Ltd* (1978) 4 A.L.R.(2d) 386; *Baty v. Parkdale Farms Ltd* (1986) 37 C.C.L.T. 9; *Gibbons v. MacDonald* (1985) 70 N.S.R. (2d) 441. For Scotland, see *Gardiner v. Miller* 1967 S.L.T. 29.

30 *Carmarthenshire County Council v. Lewis* [1955] A.C. 549.

31 *Gomberg v. Smith* [1963] 1 Q.B. 25.

32 *Buckle v. Holmes* [1936] 2 K.B. 125.

33 Dogs Acts 1906, 1928, especially s. 1(1)–(3) of the 1906 Act.

33a Which applies to the Crown but not in a private capacity: Animals Act 1971 s. 12. The Act does not apply to Scotland and Northern Ireland: *ibid.* s. 13(4).

34 Animals Act 1971, s. 1(1)(a).

35 *Ibid.* ss. 2, 5.

36 *Ibid.* ss. 1(1)(b), 3, 5.

37 *Ibid.* ss. 1(1)(c), 4, 5.

Wallbank.[38] A further important consequence of the statute is the regulation by its provisions[39] of the defence of necessity insofar as it may have applied to the killing or injuring of a dog that was worrying or attacking livestock.

11.09 The Act does not affect the general law of negligence, nuisance and *Rylands v. Fletcher* (save insofar as it removes the limitation of liability for negligence stated in *Searle v. Wallbank*).[39a] Consequently, without relying on the Act, a plaintiff may maintain an action in respect of harm caused by an animal or animals, provided he can establish negligence in the way the animal was handled or controlled, or conduct which amounts to an actionable nuisance, or the circumstances bring the plaintiff within the protection of the rule in *Rylands v. Fletcher.* There may be situations in which the way in which harm is caused by an animal is not within the scope of the 1971 Act (though this is difficult to envisage having regard to the very wide provisions of the statute). Should such be the case, an individual harmed in this way will be compelled to resort to the remaining common law principles.

(b) Dangerous animals

(i) Definition

11.10 A dangerous species is defined as a species (including a sub-species or variety) which is not commonly domesticated in the British Isles and whose fully grown animals normally have such characteristics that they are likely, unless restrained, to cause severe damage or that any damage they may cause is likely to be severe.[40] The British Isles, for this purpose, are the United Kingdom, Channel Islands, the Isle of Man and the Republic of Ireland.[41] The United Kingdom consists of England, Scotland and Wales and Northern Ireland.[42] The Channel Islands comprise the islands of Jersey, Guernesey, Alderney and Sark and their respective dependencies.

11.11 It would appear to be obvious that, by its definition of the expression "dangerous species" the statute was intending to denote the kind of animals that, prior to the Act, were usually thought of as being *ferae naturae.* Most, if not all animals formerly within that category would probably come within the scope of the statutory definition. But it is not necessarily the case that an animal that was *ferae naturae* before 1971 will automatically belong to a dangerous species after the Act: nor that an

38 [1947] A.C. 341. See Animals Act 1971 s. 8: below p. 268.
39 Animals Act 1971 s. 9.
39a [1947] A.C. 358; below paras. 11.28ff.
40 Animals Act 1971 ss. 6(2), 11.
41 Interpretation Act 1978 ss. 5, 22(1), Sched. 1. Sched. 2 para. 4(2).
42 *Ibid.* s. 5, Sched. 1; Union with Scotland Act 1706, preamble, art. 1; Interpretation Act 1978 s. 22(1), Sched. 2 para. 5(a).

animal that was not *ferae naturae* before 1971 will fall outside the scope of the statutory definition.

11.12 The Act draws a clear distinction between animals which belong to a dangerous species and those which do not, i.e. animals which are commonly domesticated in the British Islands and do not normally have dangerous characteristics as defined in the statute.

(ii) Liability

11.13 If damage is caused by an animal belonging to a dangerous species, any person who is a keeper of the animal is liable for the damage, unless excused or exempted from liability under the Act.[43] Damage includes the death of, or injury to any person, including disease and any impairment of physical or mental condition.[44]

11.14 If damage is caused by an animal not belonging to a dangerous species, a keeper of the animal will be liable (subject to exceptions or defences provided by the Act) only if three conditions are satisfied.[45]

11.15 The first is that the damage is of a kind which the animal, unless restrained, was likely to cause, or which, if caused by the animal, was likely to be severe.[46] What is meant by damage "likely to be severe" was discussed in *Cummings v. Granger*.[47] This concerned injuries inflicted by an Alsatian dog. Although, for other reasons,[48] liability was not imposed on the defendant for the conduct of his dog, it was held by the Court of Appeal that the animal came within the scope of this provision, in that any damage it might inflict was likely to be severe.

11.16 The second condition is that the likelihood of the damage or its being severe was due to characteristics of the animal which are not normally found in animals of the same species or are not normally so found except at particular times or in particular circumstances.[49]

11.17 In *Cummings v. Granger*[50] the Court of Appeal were prepared to find that if the dog did bite someone, not only was the damage likely to be severe but also that the characteristics of the dog, namely barking and running around to guard its territory especially when coloured people approached, were characteristics not normally found in Alsatian dogs

43 Animals Act 1971 s. 2(1). Damages for which the keeper is liable under this provision is treated as due to "fault" for the purposes of the Fatal Accidents Act 1976, the Law Reform (Contributory Negligence) Act 1945 and the Limitation Act 1980. Animals Act 1971 s. 10. "Fault" in the Animals Act 1971 has the same meaning as in the Law Reform (Contributory Negligence) Act 1945: Animals Act 1971 s. 11.
44 Animals Act 1971 s. 11.
45 *Ibid.* s. 2(2). Cp. *supra* note 43 on "fault".
46 Animals Act 1971 s. 2(2)(a).
47 [1975] 2 All E.R. 1129 H.C.; [1977] 1 All E.R. 104 C.A.
48 Below para. 11.24.
49 Animals Act 1971 s. 2(2)(b).
50 Above note 47.

except in circumstances where used as guard dogs.[51] It was due to those circumstances that the damage was likely to be severe if an intruder did enter on its territory. These words were also considered by Park J. in *Wallace v. Newton*.[52] The plaintiff was a groom employed by the defendant to look after several horses. One horse was known to have a nervous and unpredictable temperament. On one occasion, while the plaintiff was loading the horse onto a horse box trailer, the horse became violent and uncontrollable. It leapt forward and crushed the plaintiff's arm against a breast bar. When the plaintiff sued it became vital to determine whether the likelihood of damage was due to the characteristics of the horse which were not normally found in horses. It was argued that the language of the Act was to be interpreted to mean that the horse must be shown to have had a vicious tendency to injure people by attacking them (which would seem to throw the law back to the older common law *scienter* doctrine). On that test the plaintiff would have failed to win his action. The contrary view was argued that the words had to be given their ordinary natural meaning, that is that the horse in question had characteristics of a kind not usually found in horses. On this test the plaintiff would win. It was the latter meaning that was to be attributed to the statute, according to the learned judge.[53] Hence the horse being unpredictable and unreliable became dangerous. The injury to the plaintiff's arm was due to this characteristic not normally found in a horse. The plaintiff therefore succeeded, since the requirement of knowledge was also satisfied.

11.18 This refers to the third condition in the Act, namely that the characteristics referred to previously were known to the keeper of the animal or were at any time known to a person who at that time had charge of the animal as the keeper's servant or, where the keeper was the head of the household, were known to another keeper of the animal who was a member of the household under the age of sixteen.[54] In the *Wallace* case the head man in charge of the defendant's horses knew about the horse's unpredictability and unreliability and had warned the plaintiff about the horse.[55]

11.19 The statute does not define what is meant by a "household" for this purpose. It has been held to refer to people held together by a particular kind of tie, even if temporarily separated.[56] But the expression itself and the question of membership in a household are questions of fact and degree, without there being any certain indicia the presence or absence of which are conclusive.[57]

51 [1977] 1 All E.R. 104 at 108 *per* Lord Denning M.R.
52 [1982] 2 All E.R. 106.
53 *Ibid.* at 110.
54 Animals Act 1971 s. 2(2)(c).
55 *Supra* note 52 at 111.
56 *Santos v. Santos* [1972] 2 All E.R. 246 at 255.
57 *Simmons v. Pizzey* [1979] A.C. 37 at 59 *per* Lord Hailsham; *Hackney London Borough v. Ezedinna* [1981] 3 All E.R. 438.

(iii) Incidence of liability

11.20 Whether the animal belongs or does not belong to a dangerous species, liability for damage it causes will fall upon "a keeper of the animal".[58] This, of course, harks back to the older common law. But the statute provides some guidance on the question of who is a keeper. A person will be a keeper of an animal if either he owns the animal or has it in his possession; of if he is the head of a household of which a member under sixteen owns the animal or has it in his possession.[59] Thus the head of a household will be liable should his child under sixteen have a dog or other animal which caused damage under circumstances which come within the provision of the Act. However the statute goes further. If at any time an animal ceases to be owned by or in the possession of a person, any person who immediately before that time was a keeper of the animal under the provisions set out above, continues to be a keeper of the animal until another person becomes a keeper of the animal under those provisions.[60] Thus if X owned a tiger which escaped and was later abandoned by X, only to be taken into captivity and reduced into ownership or kept in possession by Y, X would be liable for damage caused by the tiger between the time it escaped from him and the time it became the property or was kept in possession by Y: the latter would be liable for damage caused thereafter. It is also provided that someone who captured the animal in order to prevent it from causing damage or in order to return it to its owner will not be a keeper of the animal within the meaning of the Act.[61] Such a person might be liable in negligence or nuisance for what happened while it was in his possession.[62]

11.21 Although the Act purports to settle some undecided questions and to resolve potential difficulties in advance, problems might arise under these provisions. Thus it is not altogether clear what is meant by "possession" for this purpose (subject to the subsection that deals with temporary custody for protective reasons or to return the animal to its rightful owner). Reference will have to be made to the common law relating to the ownership of "wild" animals, those which escape from custody of their owners and revert to their wild state, to solve a question that might arise under this part of the statute.

(iv) Exceptions from liability

11.22 The Act provides that someone ordinarily liable under the foregoing provisions will not be responsible for damage which is due wholly to the fault of the person suffering it.[63] Thus someone whose contributory negligence results in his injury will not be able to sue. Nor will there be

58 Animals Act 1971 s. 2(1)(2).
59 *Ibid.* s. 6(3).
60 *Ibid.*
61 *Ibid.* s. 6(4).
62 *Fardon v. Harcourt-Rivington* (1932) 146 L.T. 391 at 392 *per* Lord Atkin; *Pitcher v. Martin* (1937) 53 T.L.R. 903.
63 Animals Act 1971 s. 5(1). "Fault" means the same as in the Law Reform (Contributory Negligence) Act 1945: see p. 365.

liability for damage suffered by a person who has voluntarily accepted the risk of such damage.[64] In this respect where a person employed as a servant by a keeper of the animal incurs a risk incidental to his employment, he is not to be treated as accepting it voluntarily.[65] Does this provision enact in statutory form the defence of *volenti non fit injuria*[66] (and make it inapplicable between master and servant as contrasted with strangers)?[67] Lord Denning thought that the effect of the statute was to introduce the defence of *volenti*.[68] Indeed he referred back to an old common law decision, *Illott v. Wilkes*,[69] the case of spring guns set out to trap trespassers, when deciding in *Cummings v. Granger*[70] that the defendant could plead this defence because the plaintiff knew about the guard dog and was frightened of it. Ormrod L.J., in the same case, however, did not want to complicate the question of voluntary acceptance of risk by the doctrine of *volenti*.[71] This he stated had nothing to do with strict liability, whether at common law or under the 1971 Act. He did not want the statutory defence whittled down by fine distinctions. The statutory language consisted of "fairly simple English words", to be treated as such. It might be said that more problems have been caused for the courts by "fairly simple English words" than by others, more technical and less simple. It appears that to mark a distinction between the common law plea of *volenti* and the statutory defence of "voluntary acceptance of risk" is hardly justified. As Bridge L.J. pointed out,[72] to show that someone has voluntarily accepted the risk what must be proved are two matters: (1) that the person in question fully appreciated the risk; and (2) that the person in question exposed himself to it. This does not appear to differ in any significant way from the content of the plea of *volenti*.

11.23 A novel defence is contained in section 5(3) of the Act. There will not be a liability for damage caused by an animal kept on premises or structures, under the provisions of the Act relating to dangerous and non-dangerous animals,[72a] to a person trespassing on those premises or that structure,[73] provided that the defendant proves one of two things. He must establish either that the animal was not kept on the premises or structures for the protection of persons or property:[74] or, if the animal was kept for purposes of protection, that keeping it there for the purpose of protection was not unreasonable.[75] An example of the first exception is an animal in a

64 Animals Act 1971 s. 5(2).
65 *Ibid.* s. 6(5).
66 Pp. 348–356.
67 For the situation before the Act see *Barnes v. Lucille Ltd* (1907) 23 T.L.R. 393; *Rands v. McNeil* [1955] 1 Q.B. 253.
68 *Cummings v. Granger* [1977] 1 All E.R. 108.
69 (1820) 3 B. & Ald. 304.
70 *Supra* at 108–109.
71 *Ibid.* at 111.
72 *Ibid.* at 113.
72a Hence the defence will not be available to a defendant sued in nuisance or negligence or under the rule in *Rylands v. Fletcher*.
73 What amounts to "trespassing" will presumably be decided by the common law relating to trespass to land: see Chapter 5.
74 Animals Act 1971 s. 5(3)(a).
75 *Ibid.* s. 5(3)(b).

zoo, or a farmer taking inside a bull which he knows to be dangerous.[76] The second exception covers the ordinary guard dog situation.[77] That was illustrated by the decision in *Cummings v. Granger*.[78]

11.24 The plaintiff, a barmaid in a public house next door to the defendant's yard, was injured by the defendant's Alsatian. This had been trained as a guard dog and was kept in the yard where the defendant stored scrap metal to be sold to customers who came there. During the day the dog was confined to a cage; at night and at weekends it was allowed to run loose in the yard. The dog barked and ran in circles in the cage when people came near. On a gate to the yard the defendant had painted "Beware of the Dog" in large letters. The plaintiff's boyfriend kept a car in the yard and was permitted by the defendant to go into the yard at night. The plaintiff knew the dog was in the yard: she thought it was fierce and she was frightened of it. When, one night, the plaintiff's boyfriend went into the yard to fetch some tools from his car, the plaintiff followed him, although she was not authorised to do so. When she was in the middle of the yard the dog attacked and severely injured her. The plaintiff sued the defendant under the Animals Act. At trial the judge held that the plaintiff was a trespasser in the yard, but the defendant could not rely on the statutory defence in section 5(3) because he had not proved that keeping a guard dog to guard scrap metal was reasonable. Nor could the defendant rely on the defence of acceptance of risk under section 5(2) of the Act because mere knowledge of the dog's presence was insufficient to prove that the plaintiff had voluntarily accepted the risk. On appeal[79] that decision was reversed. The plaintiff voluntarily accepted the risk, because she knew the dog was loose in the yard and had seen the warning.[80] In addition the defendant could rely on section 5(3). The plaintiff was a trespasser: and it was not unreasonable for the defendant to use a guard dog to look after valuable scrap metal which could easily have been stolen from the yard. Although the case was decided under the terms of the 1971 Act, the Court of Appeal also considered the provisions of the Guard Dogs Act 1975,[81] which had been passed several years after the incident from which this case emerged. In 1971 "guard dogs had not acquired the bad reputation that they have today," as Ormrod L.J. said in 1977.[82] The 1975 Act makes it a criminal offence to keep a guard dog without a handler.[83] If there is no handler the dog must be chained up so that it is not at liberty to roam around.[84] The statute specifically provides that it

76 Law Commission Working Paper N. 13, para. 22.
77 On which see, before the Act, *Brock v. Coupland* (1794) 1 Esp. 203; *Sycamore v. Ley* (1932) 147 L.T. 342.
78 [1975] 2 All E.R. 1129.
79 [1977] 1 All E.R. 104.
80 If she had been a burglar or thief with knowledge of the presence of the guard dog she might also have been defeated by the plea *ex turpi causa non oritur actio*: [1977] 1 All E.R. 104 at 109 *per* Lord Denning M.R.: cp. pp. 368–370.
81 1975 c. 50.
82 [1977] 1 All E.R..104 at 111.
83 1975, c. 50, ss. 1(1), 5(1). There must be a warning that the dog is present: *ibid.* s. 1(3).
84 *Ibid.* s. 1(2).

does not confer a right of civil action if the Act is contravened.[85] However, as Lord Denning explained in *Cummings v. Granger*,[86] the 1975 Act may have an effect on civil proceedings. To have a guard dog roaming freely at night, without a handler, might make the defendant's use of such a dog "unreasonable" within the meaning of the 1971 Act, so as to deprive the defendant of a defence under section 5(3). However the defendant might still be able to rely on the defence of voluntary acceptance of a risk under section 5(2).

(c) Dogs which attack livestock

11.25 Where a dog causes damage by killing or injuring livestock, any person who is a keeper of the dog will be liable for the damage,[87] unless the damage was wholly the fault of the person who suffered the damage,[88] or the livestock was killed or injured on land on to which it had strayed and the dog belonged to the occupier of that land or (where the stock had not strayed) the presence of the dog on the land was authorised by the occupier.[89]

11.26 The meaning of "keeper" has been explained. "Livestock" means cattle, horses, asses, mules, hinnies, sheep, pigs, goats, and poultry (which, in turn, means the domestic varieties of fowls, turkeys, geese, ducks, guinea-fowls, pigeons, peacocks and quails).[90] The expression "livestock" also includes deer not in the wild state, and, for the purposes of the section now under consideration, viz. section 3, and the section which deals with the killing of dogs worrying livestock,[91] viz. section 9, the term also includes pheasants, partridges and grouse while in captivity. The statute does not define who is an "occupier" for its purposes, so presumably this expression must be given its ordinary meaning, which is not necessarily the meaning given the term by the Occupiers' Liability Act 1957, as explained in cases determined under that statute.[92]

11.27 These provisions replace legislation which formerly dealt with the situation when a dog attacked livestock. Where a dog was killed or injured by the owner of livestock which was attacked by the dog, the common law defence of necessity was potentially available, although its scope and content were not altogether clear.[93] The Animals Act now provides that where a civil action is brought for killing or causing injury to a dog it is a

85 *Ibid.* s. 5(2)(a).
86 *Supra*, at 109.
87 Animals Act 1971 s. 3. Damage for which he is liable is caused by his "fault" for the purposes of the Fatal Accidents Act, the Law Reform (Contributory Negligence) Act 1945 and the Limitation Act; *ibid.* s. 10. For the meaning of "damage" see *ibid.* s 11: above para. 11.13.
88 *Ibid.* s. 5(1).
89 *Ibid.* s. 5(4).
90 *Ibid.* s. 11.
91 *Ibid.*
92 Chapter 14.
93 Pp. 98, 130: see *Creswell v. Sirl* [1948] 1 K.B. 241.

defence to prove that the defendant acted for the protection of any livestock and was a person entitled to act for the protection of that livestock, and that notice of the killing or injuring of the dog was given by the defendant to the officer in charge of a police station within 48 hours.[94] A person is entitled to act for the protection of livestock only if the livestock or the land on which it is belongs to him (i.e. if he is the owner or possessor of the animal, or is the occupier of the land in question).[95] Furthermore, to avail himself of this defence, the keeper of the dog must have been liable for what the dog did in killing or injuring livestock. That is to say, the circumstances must show that the livestock had not strayed onto land occupied by the keeper of the dog (or occupied by someone who had authorised the presence of the dog on his land).[96] A person entitled to act for the protection of livestock will be considered to have acted for the protection of livestock only if the dog is worrying or is about to worry livestock and there is no other reasonable means of ending or preventing the worrying: or if the dog has been worrying livestock, has not left the vicinity and is not under the control of anybody and there are no practicable means of ascertaining to whom it belongs.[97] The Act further provides that these conditions will be satisfied if there was belief on the part of the defendant that the dog was worrying or had been worrying livestock, there was no other way to stop what was happening or that the dog was not controlled by anybody and it was not practicable to find out whose it was. But there must be reasonable ground for that belief.[98]

(d) Trespassing livestock

(i) Liability

11.28 In place of the old common law of cattle trespass the Animals Act provides that where livestock belonging to any person strays on to land in the ownership or occupation of another and damage is done by the livestock to the land or any property on it which is in the ownership or possession of the owner or occupier of the land, the person to whom the livestock belongs will be liable for the damage.[99] That person will also be liable if because of the straying of the livestock onto land owned or occupied by someone else expenses are reasonably incurred by the owner or occupier of the land (i) in keeping the livestock while it cannot be restored to the person to whom it belongs, or (ii) while it is detained in pursuance of provisions of the Act which have replaced the old law of distress damage feasant in relation to animals,[100] or (iii) in ascertaining to

94 Animals Act 1971 s. 9(1).
95 *Ibid.* s. 9(2)(a), (5).
96 *Ibid.* s. 9(2)(b), applying *ibid.* s. 5(4): above.
97 *Ibid.* s. 9(3).
98 *Ibid.* s. 9(4).
99 *Ibid.* s. 4(1)(a).
100 *Viz* s. 7: below para. 11.32.

whom the livestock belongs.[101] For all these purposes livestock "belongs" to the person in whose possession it is.[102]

11.29 The statutory meaning of "livestock" has already been explained. It does not include, in this context, pheasants, partridges or grouse in captivity.[103] "Damage" in this context does not include, as it does elsewhere by virtue of the statute,[104] the death of or injury to any person. It is restricted to damage to land or property, i.e. chattels.[104a] However damage caused by livestock within the meaning of this provision will be considered to have been caused by the defendant's "fault" for the purposes of the Fatal Accident Act, the legislation on contributory negligence, and the Limitation Act.[105]

11.30 There will be no liability under these provisions for any damage which is wholly due to the fault of the person suffering the damage.[106] In determining this the damage will not be treated as due to the fault of the person suffering it by reason only that he could have prevented it by fencing,[107] which includes the construction of any obstacle designed to prevent animals from straying.[108] But a defendant will not be liable under the provisions of the Act dealing with straying livestock where it is proved that the straying of the livestock on to the land would not have occurred but for a breach by any other person, having an interest in the land, of a duty to fence.[109] Thus a mere failure to fence will not deprive a plaintiff of a right to sue under this provision of the Act. But his, or someone else's failure to fulfill a *duty* to fence will have precisely that effect. It may therefore be very important to discover whether, and for what reasons, a landowner is under a duty to fence his property.

11.31 Nor will a person normally liable for straying livestock be liable where the livestock strayed from a highway on which their presence constituted a lawful use of it.[110] The old common law stated that animals of this kind that strayed from the highway onto adjoining land would not involve their owners or keepers in liability, in the absence of negligence.[111] This provision seems to indicate that exemption from liability will extend to situations where the premises affected by the animals do not adjoin the highway.

101 Animals Act 1971 s. 4(1)(b).
102 *Ibid.* s. 4(2).
103 *Ibid.* s. 11.
104 *Ibid.*
104a For the situation under cattle-trespass see *Wormald v. Cole* [1954] 1 Q.B. 614.
105 Animals Act 1971 s. 10.
106 *Ibid.* s. 5(1).
107 *Ibid.* s. 5(6).
108 *Ibid.* s. 11.
109 *Ibid.* s. 5(6). On duty to fence see *Jones v. Price* [1965] 2 Q.B. 618; *Crow v. Wood* [1971] 1 Q.B. 77.
110 Animals Act 1971 s. 5(5).
111 *Tillet v. Ward* (1882) 10 Q.B.D. 17; *Gayler & Pope Ltd v. Davies & Son* [1942] 2 K.B. 75.

(ii) Detention

11.32 An animal that strayed onto land not belonging to the owner of the animal could be seized and detained by the owner of the land under the doctrine of distress damage feasant. This has been abolished insofar as it concerned animals.[112] In place of the older common law the Animals Act makes provision for the detention and sale of trespassing livestock. This applies to livestock not under the control of any person.[113] The right to detain such animals lasts for only 48 hours, unless notice of the detention has been given to the police and to the person who owns the animals, if known by the detaining occupier of land.[114] The right to detain will also cease when the person to whom the animals belong tenders to the occupier of land who is detaining the animals a sum sufficient to satisfy any claim the latter might have in respect of damages or expenses resulting from the straying of the animals[115] (but not damages or expenses incurred before the straying in question, i.e. only the particular incident leading to the detention of the animals is relevant in this context).[116] If the occupier of the land has no such claim to damages or expenses, the right to detain also ends when the livestock is claimed by a person entitled to possession.[117] After fourteen days' detention the occupier of the land may sell the livestock at a market or by public auction unless there is pending an action for the return of the livestock or for a claim in respect of damages caused or expenses incurred by the occupier as a result of the straying of the animals.[118] Should the proceeds of such a sale exceed the amount that may be claimed for damages or expenses by the occupier of the land where the animals strayed, the excess is recoverable by the person entitled to the animals but for the sale.[119]

11.33 The occupier of land who is detaining animals under these provisions is liable for any damage caused to the animals by failure to treat them with reasonable care and supply them with adequate food and water while detained.[120]

(e) Animals on the highway

11.34 The Act removes from the law the exception laid down in *Searle v. Wallbank*[121] to the general principle of negligence that would otherwise have governed the situation where animals strayed from land onto the highway. In that decision, as previously noted, it was held that landowners owed no duty to users of the highway to fence or maintain existing fences on land adjoining the highway so as to prevent animals straying

112 Animals Act 1971 s. 7(1).
113 *Ibid.* s. 7(2).
114 *Ibid.* s. 7(3)(a).
115 I.e. under s. 4 of the Act: above; Animals Act 1971 s. 7(3)(b).
116 *Ibid.* s. 7(7).
117 *Ibid.* s. 7(3)(c).
118 *Ibid.* s. 7(4), i.e. a claim under s. 4 of the Act.
119 *Ibid.* s. 7(4).
120 *Ibid.* s. 7(6).
121 [1947] A.C. 341.

onto the highway and causing damage. There might be liability if the landowner knew of some peculiar behaviour of the animal as a result of which the damage or injury was inflicted, i.e. under the *scienter* doctrine.[122] Without such peculiarity and knowledge the landowner could escape liability. That will no longer be the case.[123] However the statute does not specifically put any duty to fence on landowners. What it does, by getting rid of *Searle v. Wallbank*, is to impose on landowners a duty to use reasonable care to prevent their animals from straying and causing damage on the highway. This may entail the erection or maintenance of fencing. Such fencing, however, is not obligatory unless it is the only way to exercise the duty.

11.35 However, no breach of duty will be committed by a person whose animals have caused damage after straying from unfenced land on which he put them if the land is common land, land situated in an area where fencing is not customary, or is a town or village green: as long as the person placing the animals on that land had a right to place the animals on that land.[124] It was held by the Court of Appeal in *Davies v. Davies*[125] that this provision protected not only the person who had the legal right to place animals on common land but also anyone licensed by the owner to put his animals there, as long as the lawful number was not exceeded.[126] In that case the defendant could rely on the 1971 Act although the farm where he worked belonged to his mother and she, as owner of the farm, not he, had the right to graze ten head of cattle and 100 sheep on the common. The sheep that caused damage to the plaintiff's car actually belonged to the defendant, not his mother (and numbered less than 100). In these circumstances the defendant came within the scope of the Act. The simple question was whether the man who placed the animals on the common was entitled to do so.[127] The defendant and his mother were farming together to all intents and purposes and he had some sheep. So it would be ludicrous in 1974, said Ormrod L.J.[128] "to hold that he had no right to use his mother's common rights within the meaning of the Animals Act 1971, no matter whether the conclusion might have been different if we were sitting in a manorial court in Glamorgan in 1270."

122 *Brackenborough v. Spalding U.D.C.* [1942] A.C. 310; *Fitzgerald v. E. D. & A. D. Cook Bourne (Farms) Ltd* [1964] 1 Q.B. 249.
123 Animals Act 1971 s. 8(1).
124 Ibid. s. 8(2): the expressions "common land" and "town or village green" mean the same as in the Commons Registration Act 1965 s. 22(1): Animals Act 1971 s. 11.
125 [1974] 3 All E.R. 817.
126 *Ibid.* at 819 *per* Lord Denning M.R., relying on *Rumsey v. Rawson* (1669) 1 Vent. 18; *Hoskins v. Robins* (1671) 2 Saund. 319.
127 *Davies v. Davies, supra* at 821 *per* Cairns L.J., who thought it was not necessary to go back to abstruse questions of ancient law dealing with rights appurtenant and appendant.
128 *Supra* note 125 at 822.

CHAPTER 12

Negligence

1. THE TORT OF NEGLIGENCE

12.01 Negligent behaviour has long been recognised as a basis for liability. Long before 1932 the courts accepted that one who was negligent in the manner in which he performed certain activities might be accountable to a person injured in consequence. For nineteenth century judges, to go back no further, negligence imported acting carelessly.[1] It denoted the absence of such care as it was the duty of the defendant to use.[2] But the circumstances in which such a duty of care arose were not given very wide application. The courts identified certain situations in which a duty of care lay upon someone in a particular relationship with another, for example, a master towards his servant, an occupier towards his visitor, a user of the highway towards another such user. Most important of all, a duty of care might emerge from a contractual relationship. All of these situations continue to be potential sources of liability for negligent behaviour.[3] In earlier periods of the history of the law, however, they were, if not the sole such situations, the most important and common. In the latter part of the nineteenth century some judges suggested a wider connotation and scope for negligence. They endeavoured to break out of the limitations imposed on the law by the pervasive doctrine of "privity of contract". This still vital aspect of the law of contract had the effect of denying that the breach of a contract between A and B, resulting from the negligence of A, could lead to A's liability to C, who might be injured as a result of that breach. This was firmly established in the earlier part of the century.[4] Towards its end, however, Lord Esher, among others, revealed an inclination to extend the law of negligence. In *Heaven v. Pender*[5] he stated: "there may be the obligation of such a duty", i.e. to use ordinary care or skill, "from one person to another although there is no contract between them with regard to such duty". He purported to elaborate on this suggestion in a passage that antedates the more famous influential language of Lord Atkin fifty years later:

> "Whenever one person is by circumstances placed in such a position with regard to another that every one of ordinary sense who did think would at

1 *Kettlewell v. Watson* (1882) 21 Ch.D. 685 at 706 *per* Fry J.
2 *Grill v. General Iron Screw Colliery Co.* (1866) L.R. 1 C.P. 600 at 612 *per* Willes J.
3 See pp. 132, 381, 400. Note that the negligent breach of a contract may now be remedied by an action in tort for negligence in some situations: above p. 6, below pp. 312–14.
4 By *Winterbottom v. Wright* (1842) 10 M. & W. 109. There was an exception in the case of dangerous chattels and another if a chattel was known to be dangerous: below pp. 374–5.
5 (1883) 11 Q.B.D. 503 at 507. Contrast *ibid.* at 516 *per* Cotton and Bowen L.JJ.

once recognise that if he did not use ordinary care and skill in his own conduct with regard to those circumstances he would cause danger of injury to the person or property of the other, a duty arises to use ordinary care and skill to avoid such danger."[6]

12.02 Not until the decision of the House of Lords in *Donoghue v. Stevenson*[7] in 1932, however, did this suggestion become part of the law. There the House of Lords, by a majority, recognised that a duty of care lay on a manufacturer whose product was intended for use or consumption by others than those with whom the manufacturer contracted for their supply. That duty was to take reasonable care to ensure that the product did not cause injury or damage to an ultimate consumer or his property. But that duty, as will be seen in greater detail elsewhere,[8] only arose where there was no reasonable prospect of an examination of the product that would reveal its defect prior to use or consumption. Viewed from this perspective, the decision merely added to the already existing list of situations or relationships that could give rise to a duty of care between the parties an additional, and novel one. However the language of those in the majority, especially of Lord Atkin, went beyond this narrow *ratio decidendi*[9] (although at least to begin with some judges considered that it should be confined thereto).[10] The broader meaning and effect of the decision was that there was a distinct tort of negligence, for which there could be liability, without the need to prove any other tort. For liability to be imposed for such tort it was necessary to show that the defendant had breached a duty of care owed by him to the plaintiff. The existence of such a duty depended in turn upon the notion of "proximity". That, too, was a term requiring elaboration and explanation. It denoted that the defendant, as a reasonable man, could and should have foreseen as a reasonable probability or likelihood the prospect of injury or damage to the plaintiff or his property if the defendant failed to exercise such care as a reasonable man would and ought to have shown in the circumstances. In this respect the categories of negligence were never closed.[11]

12.03 The effect of *Donoghue v. Stevenson* was summarised in these words by Lord Wright in *Lochgelly Iron & Coal Co. Ltd v. M'Mullen*:[12]

6 *Ibid.* at 509: cp. *Thomas v. Quartermaine* (1887) 18 Q.B.D. 685 at 694–695 *per* Bowen L.J.
7 [1932] A.C. 562.
8 Below pp. 377–8.
9 See *Grant v. Australian Knitting Mills* [1936] A.C. 85 at 103–105 *per* Lord Wright.
10 *Farr v. Butters Bros.* [1932] 2 K.B. 606 at 614 *per* Scrutton L.J.; *Chandler v. Crane, Christmas & Co.* [1951] 2 K.B. 164 at 192 *per* Asquith L.J.; *Merrington v. Ironbridge Works Ltd* [1952] 2 All E.R. 1101 at 1105 *per* Hallett J.; cp. Lord Atkin himself in *East Suffolk Rivers Catchment Board v. Kent* [1941] A.C. 74 at 88–94, suggesting that a duty was owed "to some people in some circumstances". But it was extended almost immediately beyond the situation of manufacturers to, e.g. repairers: *Stennett v. Hancock Peters* [1939] 2 All E.R. 578; *Haseldine v. Daw* [1941] 2 K.B. 343; and to other goods apart from consumables, e.g. a tombstone: *Brown v. Cotterill* (1934) 51 T.L.R. 21: a sidecar: *Malfroot v. Noxal* (1934) 51 T.L.R. 551; and to other activities, e.g. loading timber on a barge: *Denny v. Supplies & Transport Co. Ltd* [1950] 2 K.B. 374. In these and other cases emphasis was placed on the lack of any possibility of an intervening inspection, examination or intervention before the "thing" could be used and cause damage: cp. also *Dranfield v. Bristol Insulated Cables* (1937) 54 T.L.R. 11.
11 *Donoghue v. Stevenson* [1932] A.C. 562 at 619 *per* Lord Macmillan.
12 [1934] A.C. 1 at 25.

> "In strict legal analysis negligence means more than heedless or careless conduct whether in omission or commission: it properly connotes the complex concept of duty, breach and damage thereby suffered by the person to whom the duty was owing."

The original idea contained in the speeches in *Donoghue v. Stevenson*, notably that of Lord Atkin,[13] was that a duty of care was owed to one's "neighbour", who was a person who was or should have been in one's contemplation as being likely to be injured through lack of reasonable care such as a reasonable man would have foreseen was necessary to avoid injury to person or property. This wide proposition has been the subject of judicial analysis and exposition in the more than fifty years since that case was decided. In particular, the question of when a duty of care is owed, so as to bring into operation the doctrine of negligence and possible liability for the tort, has caused considerable debate. In brief, the effect of subsequent decisions has been to enlarge the scope of the tort of negligence, by recognising more and more situations that potentially may give rise to damage as supporting the existence of a duty of care,[14] although there are still some in which courts have refused to apply the Atkinian notion of a "neighbour".[15] Moreover, especially within the past few years, judicial statements have revealed the extent to which the language of Lord Atkin and other members of the House of Lords in *Donoghue v. Stevenson* has led to uncertainty about the underlying principles upon which a court should base its conclusion as to whether or not the defendant owed a duty of care to the plaintiff.[16]

12.04 The concept of duty of care is crucial to an understanding of the nature and scope of the tort of negligence. There are other aspects of the tort that have also been productive of problems and uncertainty. Among these is the issue of causation, which has entailed changes of view as to the issue of remoteness of damage,[17] and has given rise to difficulty with respect of burden of proof.[18] In addition, courts have been obliged to wrestle with the issue of standards of care in determining whether a defendant has breached whatever duty he owed the plaintiff;[19] and with the pre-*Donoghue v. Stevenson* doctrine of *res ipsa loquitur* and its consequences in relation to proof of negligent conduct.[20] Some of these matters are complicated by disagreement over the true nature of the particular problem and the factors that are relevant to its solution. For example, although duty of care, breach, and causation of damage may be looked upon as separate questions or issues to be resolved in any given instance, some authorities have taken the view that, ultimately, questions of duty, breach, and causation really turn upon the same question. They are part

13 [1932] A.C. 562 at 580.
14 Below pp. 283–309.
15 Below pp. 309–12.
16 Below pp. 273–6.
17 Below pp. 336–44.
18 Below pp. 320, 332.
19 Below pp. 314–20.
20 Below pp. 322–7.

and parcel of one issue before the court: was the defendant negligent?[21] It may be suggested that although there is a certain relationship between these questions, it is necessary to keep them separate and distinct for analytical purposes. Furthermore, if they are not kept separate and distinct, there is a danger that courts will come to view negligence not in the modern version that stems from *Donoghue v. Stevenson* but in a manner more consistent with nineteenth century attitudes towards negligence before the currently accepted tort came to be recognised.

2. THE DUTY OF CARE

(a) Relevant factors

12.05 In *Donoghue v. Stevenson* Lord Atkin stressed the importance of what was to be foreseen by the defendant as a vital element or factor in the determination of whether a duty of care existed. What could be foreseen affected the issue of proximity, which he stated was not confined to physical proximity but extended to "such close and direct relations that the act complained of directly affects a person to whom the person alleged to be bound to take care would know would be directly affected by his careless act".[22] As explained by Lord Keith more recently,[23] Lord Atkin clearly had in contemplation that all the circumstances of the case, not only the foreseeability of harm, were appropriate to be taken into account in determining whether a duty of care arose. Thus, as indicated in *Hedley Byrne & Co. Ltd v. Heller & Partners Ltd*,[24] assumption of responsibility could be material. *Dorset Yacht Co. Ltd v. Home Office*[25] revealed that there might be a special relationship between parties, such as that between prison officers and borstal boys, or parents and children,[26] that gives rise to a duty to control the other party to that relationship so as to prevent him from causing damage to the plaintiff.

12.06 Lord Keith referred to these specific cases because they formed a trilogy which was the basis for some remarks in *Anns v. Merton London Borough Council*,[27] in which Lord Wilberforce purported to summarise the factors that were relevant to establish that a duty of care arose in a particular situation. For such purpose it was not necessary to bring the facts of the situation within those of previous situations in which a duty of care had been held to exist. That was the position of the law before 1932. Since this trilogy of cases the question had to be approached in two stages.

21 *Roe v. Ministry of Health* [1954] 2 Q.B. 66 at 85 *per* Denning L.J.
22 [1932] A.C. 562 at 580.
23 In *Yuen Kun-yeu v. Attorney-General of Hong Kong* [1987] 2 All E.R. 705 at 711.
24 [1964] A.C. 465; below pp. 290–1.
25 [1970] A.C. 1004: below pp. 307–8.
26 Or, it may be added, between a school and its pupils in relation to their physical safety; but not in respect of damage to their economic welfare by failing to insure them against injury or advising their parents to insure (since a parent was under no duty to insure even if advised to do so): *Van Oppen v. Bedford Charity Trustees* [1989] 1 All E.R. 273; affirmed [1989] 3 All ER 389.
27 [1978] A.C. 728 at 751.

"First one has to ask whether, as between the alleged wrongdoer and the person who has suffered damage there is a sufficient relationship of proximity or neighbourhood such that, in the reasonable contemplation of the former, carelessness on his part may be likely to cause damage to the latter, in which case a *prima facie* duty of care arises. Secondly, if the first question is answered affirmatively, it is necessary to consider whether there are any considerations which ought to negative, or to reduce or limit the scope of the duty or the class of persons to whom it is owed or the damages to which a breach of it may give rise . . . ."

This statement was subject to criticism in the House of Lords in several subsequent cases,[28] as well as by the Privy Council in *Yeun Kun-yeu v. Attorney-General of Hong Kong*[29] and the High Court of Australia.[30] In Australia the view was expressed that foreseeability was not the exhaustive criterion;[31] if it were it would have to be subjected to a restrictive qualification such as that contained in Lord Wilberforce's second stage. It was preferable for the law to develop novel categories of negligence "incrementally". That development should take place by analogy with established categories, rather than by a massive extension of a *prima facie* duty of care restrained only by indefinable considerations which ought to negative or to reduce or limit the scope of the duty or the class of person to whom it is owed.[32] In the Privy Council case,[33] Lord Keith, speaking for the other members of the Board, thought that Lord Wilberforce's two-stage test had been elevated to a degree of importance greater than it merited and greater perhaps than Lord Wilberforce intended. The second stage would rarely have to be applied. It could only arise in a limited category of cases where, notwithstanding that a case of negligence was made out on the basis of proximity, public policy required there should be no liability. On the basis of the way the law had developed, the two-stage test in *Anns* was not to be regarded as in all circumstances a suitable guide to the existence of a duty of care. Foreseeability, although a necessary ingredient, was not the only one.[34]

12.07 The question whether it is appropriate that a duty of care should be imposed, Lord Keith stated in the subsequent Privy Council decision in *Rowling v. Takaro Properties Ltd*,[35] was one of an intensely pragmatic character, well suited for gradual development but requiring most careful

28 *Governors of the Peabody Donation Fund v. Sir Lindsay Parkinson & Co. Ltd* [1985] A.C. 210 at 239 *per* Lord Keith; *Leigh & Sillivan Ltd v. Aliakmon Shipping Co. Ltd* [1986] A.C. 785 at 815 *per* Lord Brandon; *Curran v. Northern Ireland Co-Ownership Housing Association Ltd* [1987] 2 All E.R. 13 at 17 *per* Lord Bridge; cp. *Business Computers International Ltd v. Registrar of Companies* [1987] 3 All E.R. 465 at 471–472 *per* Scott J.; *Jones v. Department of Employment* [1988] 1 All E.R. 725 at 735–736 *per* Glidewell L.J; *Richardson v West Lindsay D.C.* [1990] 1 All E.R. 296 at 304; *Clough v. Bussan* [1990] 1 All E.R. 431 at 433.

29 *Supra* note 23.

30 *Sutherland Shire Council v. Heyman* (1985) 60 A.L.R. 1.

31 Cp. *McLoughlin v. O'Brian* [1983] 1 A.C. 410 at 420 *per* Lord Wilberforce.

32 *Sutherland Shire Council v. Heyman* (1985) 60 A.L.R. 1.

33 *Yuen Kun-yeu v. Attorney-General of Hong Kong*, *supra* at 710.

34 *Ibid.* "Otherwise there would be liability in negligence on the part of one who sees another about to walk over a cliff with his head in the air and forbears to shout a warning"; *ibid. per* Lord Keith. Cp. the remarks of Lord Goff in *Smith v. Littlewoods Organisation Ltd* [1987] 1 All E.R. 710 at 735–736.

35 [1988] 1 All E.R. 163 at 172.

analysis. All common law jurisdictions could learn from each other, because they and their social conditions were not sensibly distinguishable. All, however, should be sensitive to each other's reactions: but all were searching for in the others, and striving themselves to achieve, a careful analysis and weighing of the relevant competing considerations. In that case the Privy Council did not have to determine whether a duty of care existed; but they commented on the "relevant considerations" that would have led to the conclusion that no such duty arose in the circumstances of that case, which concerned the giving of consent by a minister under a New Zealand statute dealing with overseas exchange transactions. Those considerations were: (i) that the only effect of a negligent decision was delay; (ii) the fact that only rarely would an error of law alleged to have been made by the minister or some other public authority be properly categorised as negligent; (iii) the danger of overkill resulting from imposing too high a standard so that civil servants and others would become too cautious, which might lead to considerable delay while a legal opinion was sought from a court; and (iv) the difficulty of identifying when a minister was under a duty to seek legal advice.[36] All these factors suggest that some of the "relevant competing considerations" to which Lord Keith referred in this case relate to aspects of public policy, which Lord Keith had played down in importance in the earlier decision in *Yeun Kun-yeu*.

12.08 This indicates that the issue of public policy may well be very relevant to the determination of the existence of a duty of care. In fact there are certainly some situations in which the courts have adverted to that issue and have invoked it with the result that no duty of care was owed in the particular circumstances. In the *Yuen Kun-yeu* case Lord Keith mentioned two: the first concerned the question of a barrister's liability for negligence in the conduct of proceedings in court;[37] the second involved the liability of a chief constable for failing to apprehend a murderer in time to prevent his causing the death of the daughter of the plaintiff.[38] But public policy was not as important a factor in relation to duty of care as Lord Wilberforce seems to have indicated. The primary and all-important matter for consideration in the *Yuen Kun-yeu* case, and seemingly in others, in view of Lord Keith's remarks about the two-stage test of Lord Wilberforce, is whether there existed between plaintiff and defendant "such close and direct relations" as would place the defendant, in the exercise of his activity, in that case as Commissioner of Deposit-taking Companies in Hong Kong exercising his functions under the Deposit-taking Companies Ordinance 1976, under a duty of care towards the plaintiff, in that particular case a would-be depositor. The Privy Council decided against the plaintiff. Although it was reasonably foreseeable that depositors in an uncreditworthy company which was allowed to remain on

36 *Ibid.* at 172–173.
37 *Rondel v. Worsley* [1969] 1 A.C. 191: below para. 12.69.
38 *Hill v. Chief Constable of West Yorkshire* [1987] 1 All E.R. 1173; below para 12.61. Cp *Clough v. Bussan, supra.*

the register would be at risk of losing their money, mere foreseeability of harm did not of itself create sufficient proximity between the commissioner and a would-be depositor for a duty of care to arise. The commissioner had no control over the day-to-day management of existing deposit-takers in deciding whether to deregister a particular company, as the plaintiff thought he should have done.

12.09 Foresight of harm, therefore, is a relevant, but not determinative factor. A close and direct relationship of proximity between the parties is also of significance. Although at first sight these two factors appear to be so closely connected that they amount to the same thing, analysis of the case law reveals their distinction. It is possible for harm to be foreseen by a defendant to various people in consequence of what he does or omits to do: it is also possible for the kind of harm to be foreseen. Yet there may be insufficient close and direct relations between the defendant and those to whom harm may be foreseen to justify the conclusion that the defendant owed a duty of care to such persons.

12.10 It is not enough to establish that as between the alleged wrongdoer and the person who has suffered damage there is a sufficient relationship of proximity or neighbourhood that in the reasonable contemplation of the former carelessness on his part may be likely to cause damage to the latter. Apart from considerations of public policy that may arise and be relevant, the court must be satisfied that it is "just and reasonable" for a duty of care to be owed to the person concerned. This requirement is really one of ordinary reason and common sense.[39] In deciding whether the factual situation merits the application or invocation of the concept of duty of care, therefore, a court must take into consideration not only foresight of harm, and proximity in a legal sense, but also, in addition to public policy, the question of what is just and reasonable in all the circumstances.[40] The application of this factor has resulted in the denial or negation of a duty to take care, although the possibility of harm was or ought to have been foreseen, in several instances in recent times.[41]

39 *Minories Finances Ltd v. Arthur Young* [1989] 2 All E.R. 105 at 110 *per* Saville J. Cp. *Governors of the Peabody Donation Fund v. Sir Lindsay Parkinson & Co. Ltd* [1985] A.C. 210 at 240–241 *per* Lord Keith. See *Richardson v. W. Lindsey C. C.* [1990] 1 All E.R. 296.

40 *Caparo Industries plc v. Dickman* [1989] 1 All E.R. 798 at 803 *per* Bingham L.J.: cp. *Banque Keyser SA v. Skandia (U.K.) Insurance Co Ltd* [1987] 2 W.L.R. 1300.

41 *Minories Finance Ltd v. Arthur Young*, *supra*; *Jones v. Department of Employment* [1988] 1 All E.R. 725; *Business Computers International Ltd v. Registrar of Companies* [1987] 3 All E.R. 465; *Leigh & Sillivan Ltd v. Aliakmon Shipping Co. Ltd* [1986] 2 All E.R. 145; cp. *Smith v. Littlewoods Organisation Ltd* [1987] 1 All E.R. 710; *D. & F. Estates Ltd v. Church Commissioners for England* [1988] 2 All E.R. 992; *National Bank of Greece SA v. Pinios Shipping Co. (No. 1)* [1989] 1 All E.R. 213; *Van Oppen v. Beford Charity Trustees* [1989] 3 All E.R. 389; *Pacific Associates Inc. v. Baxter* [1989] 2 All E.R. 159; *Mills v. Winchester Diocesan Board of Finance* [1989] 2 All E.R. 317; *Clough v. Bussan* [1990] 1 All E.R. 431. A duty of care may also be negated on other grounds, e.g. a landowner's absolute right to abstract subterranean water flowing in undefined channels under his land: *Stephens v. Anglian Water Authority* [1987] 3 All E.R. 379.

(b) Foreseeability

12.11 Although its importance may have been diminished by recent judicial comments, foreseeability, in other words what the reasonable man in the defendant's situation could and ought to have foreseen, nevertheless plays some role in the decision of whether a duty of care was owed. The test is whether what occurred was within the reasonable contemplation of the person doing the act.[42] If on the application of this test it cannot be said that what occurred was within such reasonable contemplation, then no duty was owed. For example, in *Glasgow Corporation v. Muir*,[43] the defendant's servant allowed tea to be carried in an urn through a public tea shop. Tea had been spilt on the floor though it was unknown how this occurred, with the result that the servant carrying the urn slipped which caused the plaintiff to be scalded. The House of Lords held that although the defendant's servant and those she allowed to carry the urn were bound to take reasonable care to avoid the risk of injury to persons they could reasonably foresee would be injured by the failure to take reasonable care, the defendant was not liable because carrying the urn involved no extra special danger such as would lead a reasonable person to foresee injury to the plaintiff. Lord Wright, for example, stressed the importance of what the hypothetical reasonable person would have foreseen.[44]

12.12 In *Bourhill v. Young*,[45] a pregnant woman suffered nervous shock when she heard, but did not see, a collision between the defendant and another road user. The House of Lords held that no duty of care was owed by the negligent defendant to the woman, although he owed a duty to the other negligent road user with whom he collided. The existence of the woman, and the possibility of her being affected through the collision, were not foreseeable by the defendant. Lord Russell, for instance, said:[46]

> "In considering whether a person owes another a duty of care, breach of which will render him liable to that other in damages for negligence, it is material to consider what the defendant ought to have contemplated as a reasonable man."

Lord Macmillan, who had been one of the majority in *Donoghue v. Stevenson*, said that the duty to take care is a duty "to avoid doing or omitting to do anything the doing or omitting to do of which may have as its reasonable and probable consequence injury to others".[47] It is to be noted, also, that the House of Lords laid great emphasis not only on the prospect of injury but also upon the importance of anticipation or contemplation of the person likely to be injured,[48] an aspect of negligence which will be further discussed.[49]

42 *Denny v. Supplies & Transport Co. Ltd* [1950] 2 K.B. 374 at 380 *per* Evershed M.R.
43 [1943] A.C. 448: cp. *Smith v. Littlewoods Organisation Ltd*, *supra*, especially at 720–721 *per* Lord Mackay.
44 [1943] A.C. 448 at 460: cp. Lord Macmillan, *ibid.* at 456–457.
45 [1943] A.C. 92: see further below para 12.20.
46 *Ibid.* at 101.
47 *Ibid.* at 104.
48 *Ibid.* at 102.
49 Below pp. 282–302.

12.13 Foreseeability may extend as far as the contemplation of an intervening act or event which, when added to the act or omission of the defendant, can be anticipated or contemplated as being likely to cause injury. In *Woods v. Duncan*,[49a] contractors' negligence in painting a submarine was held not to have been the cause of its sinking, although the concatenation of events resulted in the blocking of a test-cock connected with a torpedo tube, which allowed water to enter the vessel. The question in that case, said Lord Simonds, was "whether the assumed negligent actor ought reasonably to have foreseen the intervening act and having foreseen it to have provided for it or ignored it at this peril". It was on this basis that the House of Lords denied liability in *Smith v. Littlewoods Organisation Ltd.*[50] The owners of a cinema allowed it to remain empty and unattended, with the result that it was not lockfast and was being regularly entered by unauthorised persons. Eventually a fire was started in the cinema which affected debris that had accumulated outside the cinema. This resulted in damage to two adjoining properties which had to be demolished. The owners of the affected properties sued the owners of the cinema. The latter were held not responsible. Although they were under a general duty to exercise reasonable care to see that the condition of their premises was not a source of danger to neighbouring property,[51] they could not reasonably foresee the acts of vandals that caused the fire.[52] They did not know of vandalism in the area nor of previous attempts to start fires. Lord Mackay thought that where injury or damage was caused by an independent human agency, it was necessary to establish that there was a real risk of injury or damage, in the sense of it being a highly likely consequence of the alleged tortfeasor's act or omission rather than a mere possibility. The more unpredictable the intervening conduct, the less easy was it to affirm that any particular result was probable: it would be only a mere possibility, which was insufficient for liability.[53] Lord Goff considered that there was no general duty of care to prevent persons from harming others by deliberate conduct, even if this were foreseeable where a defendant did not take steps to prevent it.[54] Liability for such conduct could only be imposed where a special relationship existed between plaintiff and defendant,[55] or where the source of danger was negligently created by the defendant and it was reasonably foreseeable that a third party might intervene and cause damage by producing the danger,[56] or where the defendant had knowledge or the means of knowledge that a

49a [1946] A.C. 401 H.L.
50 [1987] 1 All E.R. 710.
51 *Ibid.* at 713 *per* Lord Brandon, 719 *per* Lord Mackay.
52 *Ibid.* at 713–714 *per* Lord Griffiths, stressing the importance of common sense in this matter.
53 *Ibid.* at 719–721 *per* Lord Mackay.
54 *Ibid.* at 728–729. The fundamental reason was that the common law did not impose liability for pure omissions: *ibid.* at 719; *Home Office v. Dorset Yacht Co. Ltd* [1970] A.C. 1004 at 1060 *per* Lord Diplock; cp. *Weld-Blundell & Co. Ltd v. Camden London Borough Council* [1984] Q.B. 342.
55 E.g., *Stansbie v. Troman* [1948] 2 K.B. 48; *Home Office v. Dorset Yacht Co. Ltd supra*; *London Passenger Transport Board v. Upson* [1949] A.C. 155; *Carmarthenshire County Council v. Lewis* [1955] A.C. 549.
56 *Haynes v. Harwood* [1935] 1 K.B. 146, on which see below para 12.30.

third party had created or was creating a risk of danger on his property and the defendant took no reasonable steps to abate it.[57]

12.14 Sometimes a defendant ought to foresee that the plaintiff himself will act in such a way that he comes into contact with something belonging to the defendant with the result that the plaintiff is injured. Such is the situation where children climb trees or other objects and thereby come to touch electric wires owned and controlled by the defendant. It has been held that such defendants owed a duty of care to the children because they ought to have foreseen that children would act in this way, because of the allurement that attracted the children to the area and to physical proximity with dangerous electric equipment.[58] Where the ultimate injury is caused not directly by the defendant's act or omission but in consequence of the intervention of the plaintiff or a third person or some non-human act or event which when combined with the defendant's negligence results in injury, the question whether a duty of care existed has sometimes become inextricably entwined, or even confused with the problems of remoteness and causation.[59] However, it should be remembered that it is more properly to be considered to be part of the question of foresight, which relates to the issue of duty of care, not to those of remoteness of damage or causation.[60]

(i) Risk

12.15 As well as the act complained of by the plaintiff, injury or the risk of injury to somebody must also have been foreseeable. In *Farndon v. Harcourt-Rivington*,[61] which was decided about the same time as *Donoghue v. Stevenson*, the distinction was drawn in this regard between "reasonable probabilities" and 'fantastic possibilities". A defendant was only responsible for the former, not the latter. Hence the defendant was not liable in negligence when the plaintiff was injured by a splinter from a window in the defendant's car that was broken by the dog that had been left in the vehicle. What occurred was not something that a reasonable person would have foreseen as being probable or likely. The House of Lords took up this issue in greater detail in *Bolton v. Stone*.[62] Here the plaintiff, standing outside the door of her home, was struck by a cricket ball that had been hit by a player on the defendants' cricket ground and sent so far outside the ground that it fell on the plaintiff a considerable distance away. Although such hits were not unknown in the history of the defendant cricket club, the likelihood of such a stroke hitting someone in the situation

57 *Goldman v. Hargrave* [1967] 1 A.C. 645.
58 *Buckland v. Guildford Gas Light & Coke Co.* [1949] 1 K.B. 410; cp. *Thompson v. Bankstown Municipal Council* (1953) 87 C.L.R. 619; cp. *British Railways Board v. Herrington* [1972] A.C. 877. See also *Hibberd's Foundry v. Hardy* [1953] N.Z.L.R. 14.
59 E.g., *Lamb v. Camden London Borough Council* [1981] 2 All E.R. 408.
60 Below paras 12.21ff.
61 (1932) 46 L.T. 391.
62 [1951] A.C. 850: with which compare *Hilder v. Associated Portland Cement Manufacturers Ltd* [1961] 3 All E.R. 709.

of the plaintiff was so small that the House of Lords held that there was no liability. Lord Porter explained the question in these words:[63]

> "In order that the act may be negligent there must not only be a reasonable possibility of its happening but also of injury being caused .... It is not enough that the event should be such as can reasonably be foreseen: the further result that injury is likely to follow must also be such as a reasonable man would contemplate before he can be convicted of negligence. Nor is the remote possibility of injury occurring enough; there must be sufficient probability to lead a reasonable man to contemplate it."

Lord Reid explained that the tendency was to base duty, i.e. a duty of care, "rather on the likelihood of damage to others than on its foreseeability alone".[64] The test to be applied, according to Lord Reid,[65] was whether the risk of damage, in this particular instance to a person on the road outside the cricket ground and not inside the ground itself, was so small that a reasonable man considering the matter from the point of view of safety would have thought it right to refrain from taking steps to prevent the danger.

12.16 In this respect it has frequently been said that a material factor is the relative cost of avoiding injury compared with the degree of risk of injury involved. A possible, even probable injury might well be prevented or avoided by taking certain steps and incurring certain expense. But the cost of this might be prohibitive: it might make performance of a given activity not economically or otherwise feasible. If the activity is one that is not necessarily for the general benefit of the community, then a court could decide that the risk of injury outweighed the cost of its prevention. Where the activity has, or may have some less personal benefit for the defendant and some utility for the public at large, then the factor of expense may incline a court to hold that, as against the risk of injury, the incursion of such expense or the practical or administrative inconvenience would be an unreasonable burden on the defendant. In such instances, although a certain degree of risk is present, failure or refusal to indulge in the administrative or financial obligations involved in reducing the risk or precluding its occurrence will not be regarded as unreasonable behaviour, entailing liability for negligence should injury result from the activity.[66]

12.17 Two matters have some relevance here. The first is the nature of the injury. There may be a risk of greater injury in some situations or with regard to some persons, than in others. The question is whether the risk of greater injury is as material as the greater risk of injury. Secondly, there is the closely connected question whether a defendant ought to have in mind

63 [1951] A.C. 850 at 858.
64 *Ibid.* at 865.
65 *Ibid.* at 867.
66 Some relevant authorities are: *Daborn v. Bath Tramways Motor Co.* [1946] 2 All E.R. 333 especially at 336; *Watt v. Hertfordshire County Council* [1954] 2 All E.R. 368; *Goldman v. Hargrave* [1967] 1 A.C. 645; *Marshall v. Gotham Co. Ltd* [1954] A.C. 360; *Morris v. West Hartlepool Steam Navigation Co. Ltd* [1956] A.C. 552, especially at 574, 579; *Morris v. Luton Corp.* [1946] 1 All E.R. 1 at 4; *Edwards v. National Coal Board* [1949] 1 K.B. 704 at 710; *Quinn v. Scott* [1965] 2 All E.R. 588; *Latimer v. A.E.C.* [1953] A.C. 643.

persons who are subject to some peculiar idiosyncrasy or susceptibility such that they are more likely to be injured.

12.18 In an Australian case, *Levi v. Colgate-Palmolive*,[67] the fact that the plaintiff was peculiarly susceptible to a substance in the defendant's bath salts and suffered from a skin disease by reason of his special susceptibility did not impose a duty of care on the defendants (in the absence of knowledge that the plaintiff might use their product). Even the fact that a percentage of the population could be affected in this way did not make any difference.[68] In the words of Jordan C.J.:

> "Special circumstances may give rise to a duty to take special precautions to avoid injury to particularly abnormal persons known to be likely to be affected by a particular act; but the mere fact that abnormal persons exist in the community does not alter the general standards by which rights and duties are established".

12.19 But in *Paris v. Stepney Borough Council*[69] the House of Lords held that although there was no greater risk of an accident happening because the plaintiff only had one eye, since there was risk of a greater injury to the plaintiff if he were injured by the defendants' failure to provide him with goggles, the defendants' duty to the plaintiff was higher than it would have been in respect of a two-eyed man. Therefore the defendants were negligent in not providing the plaintiff with goggles: and they were liable when a metal chip flew off and injured his other eye. Greater risk involved greater care.[70] The difference between these two cases lies in the fact that in the *Paris* case it was not a matter of special susceptibility to injury but to loss from injury. Perhaps the *Paris* case relates more to the standard of care to be expected in such cases, in that a higher degree of risk requires a higher degree of care where a duty is owed: the latter being proportionate to the former.[71]

12.20 However in *Haley v. London Electricity Board*[72] the House of Lords also took into account, when deciding whether a duty of care was owed to the plaintiff, the fact that he was blind and the percentage of blind persons in the community. Hence it was foreseeable by the defendants that if they left an unfenced or unprotected hole in the ground there was a risk that a blind person might be affected, even though someone with normal sight would notice the hole and would not fall into it as the plaintiff had done. A notable feature of this case is the manner in which the House of Lords was prepared to accept as relevant statistics about blind persons. It reveals

67 (1941) 41 S.R. (N.S.W.) 48.
68 *Ibid.* at 51–52 *per* Jordan C.J.
69 [1951] A.C. 367.
70 *Ibid.* at 381, 383 *per* Lord Normand, 384 *per* Lord Oaksey, 389–390 *per* Lord MacDermott. But Lord MacDermott confined the decision to cases of master and servant, to which category the situation belonged: *ibid.* at 388.
71 Cp. *Bolton v. Stone* [1951] A.C. 850 at 867 *per* Lord Reid; *Northwestern Utilities Ltd v. London Guarantee & Accident Co. Ltd* [1936] A.C. 108 at 126 *per* Lord Wright; *Glasgow Corporation v. Muir* [1943] A.C. 448 at 458 *per* Lord Macmillan.
72 [1965] A.C. 778.

that such sociological facts may be of considerable importance in determining the question of risk, and therefore the issue of duty of care. What can be said is that if a significant percentage of the population is affected by an especial susceptibility or idiosyncrasy, it is no longer something that the reasonable man need not anticipate or contemplate when he considers what he ought to do or not do in order to prevent the occurrence of injury to others. In this regard it may also be noted that the courts have altered their attitude towards the likelihood of emotional shock both to pregnant women and to family members as a consequence of injury caused by a defendant to another person. The approach of the House of Lords in *Bourhill v. Young*[73] was based on the idea that a user of the highway did not have to contemplate that his negligent behaviour on the highway might have an impact of a non-physical kind upon someone who was not within the area of foreseeable physical harm if he drove negligently. This appears to have changed.[74]

(ii) Foreseeable plaintiffs and foreseeable harm

12.21 A man is not liable for negligence in isolation.[75] Liability for negligence only arises where there is a duty to take care and where failure in that duty has caused damage. Such a duty only arises towards those individuals of whom it may be reasonably anticipated that they will be affected by the act which constitutes the breach.[76] The necessity for establishing the appropriate connection, i.e. the direct and close relationship, between the defendant's act or omission and the damage or injury suffered by the plaintiff, requires consideration of two important factors. The first is whether the plaintiff was someone whom the defendant ought to have had in mind when he acted. The second is whether the damage that was suffered was the kind of damage that the defendant ought to have contemplated as being likely to result.[77] These two issues are sometimes highly interconnected and integrated.

12.22 The law has undergone much development since 1932. The original decision in *Donoghue v. Stevenson* related to physical injury to the person or to property. At the same time the House of Lords indicated that liability was dependent on the question of "proximity". Such proximity was limited or restricted, at that time, to those who were likely to be affected physically and directly by the acts or omissions of the defendants, such as the consumer of the ginger-beer in that particular case. In 1932, as now, a statutory exception did exist: namely the liability of a negligent defendant to the dependents of someone killed because of his negligence, even though such dependents were never in any physical danger from the

73 [1943] A.C. 92, especially at 109–110 *per* Lord Wright.
74 Below pp. 283–6.
75 *Bourhill v. Young* [1943] A.C. 92 at 102; cp. *Donoghue v. Stevenson* [1932] A.C. 562 at 618 *per* Lord Macmillan.
76 Below pp. 283–302.
77 A corollary of this is whether the defendant ought to have foreseen the manner in which the damage would be incurred; and this relates to causation and remoteness of damage: below pp. 336–44.

behaviour of the defendant.[78] At common law other exceptions also existed; these related to the liability of a defendant to the master of a servant injured or killed by the defendant's negligence to compensate the master for loss of the servant's services, as well as the liability of a defendant to a husband for causing him to lose the consortium of his wife. These latter common law exceptions have now been abolished by statute.[79] But the liability to dependents continues to exist and to provide an important extension of the scope of liability for negligence. However this form of liability is a special statutory form of action, not the same as the deceased's action for causing his death (although the defendant's action can only be maintained if the deceased could have sued, i.e. it will not lie if the deceased was *volens* or participating in illegality, and the damages may be affected by the deceased's contributory negligence, if any).[80]

12.23 The dual and interwoven issues of foreseeable plaintiffs and foreseeable harm require consideration of the way the law has evolved in respect of a number of disparate matters.

(iii) Nervous shock

12.24 The expression "nervous shock" refers to psychiatric harm, not to grief or sorrow.[81] In order to sustain an action where the law recognises and permits an action for such damage, the plaintiff has to establish an illness caused by "the impact through the senses, of external events on the mind".[82] In *McLoughlin v. O'Brian*,[83] Lord Bridge referred to "emotional trauma" which caused the plaintiff's psychiatric or psychosomatic illness. Just as physical injuries can give rise to organic and psychiatric disorders, so "an acute emotional trauma, like psychical trauma, can cause a psychiatric illness in a wide range of circumstances and in a wide range of individuals whom it would be wrong to regard as having any abnormal psychological make-up".[84] This is a crucial point. At one time it seems to have been considered judicially that only abnormally susceptible people would be emotionally affected in such a way as to produce mental or emotional disorder, by incurring nervous shock in certain situations. In view of the attitude of the law towards liability in negligence to those who diverged from the norm of the hypothetical reasonable man or woman, it was not surprising that the courts were reluctant to admit liability where the injury incurred by the plaintiff was emotional or mental rather than physical. It has taken a long time for the law ultimately to realise that the former, as well as the latter, was damage that could be recognised and could form the basis for a cause of action. Damage for "nervous shock",

78 Under the Fatal Accidents Act 1846: see now the Fatal Accidents Act 1976.
79 Administration of Justice Act 1982 s. 2. For the abolition of other actions which formerly were available to a husband in respect of conduct affecting his wife, and his marraige, see the Law Reform (Miscellaneous Provisions) Act 1970 ss. 4, 5.
80 Below paras 13.23ff.
81 For this the law provides no damages: *McLoughlin v. O'Brian* [1982] 2 All E.R. 298 at 301 *per* Lord Wilberforce.
82 *Ibid.*: cp. *Hinz v. Berry* [1970] 2 Q.B. 40 at 43 *per* Lord Denning M.R.
83 *Supra* at 312.
84 *Ibid.*

i.e. for psychiatric illness occasioned by shock, is now regarded as a separate head of damage, distinct from damage for personal injury.[85] Liability for causing nervous shock is not a distinct tort, but is an example of liability for damage caused by negligence.[86] Hence, whether such liability exists will depend upon the application of the general principles of the tort of negligence.

12.25 Until the decision of the House of Lords in *McLoughlin v. O'Brian*[87] the law with respect to negligent infliction of nervous shock was comparatively haphazard and disorganised. In some instances liability was imposed: in others it was denied. In some situations liability was said to exist or not on the basis of whether the defendant owed a duty of care to the plaintiff to act with care so as to avoid the causation of shock.[88] In others the issue of liability turned on the question whether the shock, i.e. the damage, was too remote a consequence of the defendant's negligent act.[89] By reason of this diversity of rationales and approaches it is not surprising that inconsistent decisions were reached: or that distinctions were made on the ground of slight differences of fact. What can be said, however, is that from the nineteenth century, when liability for causing nervous shock was totally negated,[90] the law gradually developed. First it was held that a plaintiff who suffered shock through fear of immediate personal physical injury in consequence of the defendant's wrongful act, could maintain an action.[91] Next it was held that even if the fear concerned the safety of others to whom the plaintiff was related, such as the plaintiff's children, the plaintiff could sue in respect of such shock. For this to result it had to be established that the shock was the direct consequence of what the plaintiff saw and heard and was not produced by some intervening act, such as the plaintiff's being told of what happened by a third person when the plaintiff was not in the vicinity of the incident involving the plaintiff's children.[92] However, in some cases, seemingly in contradiction of what was held in the decisions referred to in the previous sentence, it was held that the plaintiff's physical proximity to the danger to the relative at the time the relative in question was injured or endangered so as to generate fear and shock on the part of the plaintiff, was unnecessary for liability to exist, as long as the plaintiff came to learn

85 *Attia v. British Gas plc* [1987] 3 All E.R. 455 at 457 *per* Dillon L.J.
86 Note, however, that there may be liability for intentionally inflicted nervous shock: *Wilkinson v. Downton* [1897] 2 Q.B. 57; *Janvier v. Sweeney* [1919] 2 K.B. 316. This raises different problems from those considered in the law of negligence: see pp. 121–2.
87 [1982] 2 All E.R. 298; on which see Teff, "Liability for Negligently Inflicted Nervous Shock" (1983) 99 L.Q.R. 100.
88 E.g., *Bourhill v. Young* [1943] A.C. 93; cp. *Schneider v. Eisovitch* [1960] 2 Q.B. 430.
89 E.g., *Hambrook v. Stokes Bros.* [1925] 1 K.B. 141; *King v. Phillips* [1953] 1 Q.B. 429. In the Canadian case of *Guay v. Sun Publishing Co. Ltd* [1953] 2 S.C.R. 216 the Supreme Court of Canada was divided as to whether the test of liability for nervous shock caused by a negligent misstatement was based on lack of duty or lack of causation.
90 *Victorian Railway Commissioners v. Coultas* (1888) 13 App. Cas. 222.
91 *Dulieu v. White* [1901] 2 K.B. 664.
92 *Hambrook v. Stokes Bros., supra*: cp. *Boardman v. Sanderson* [1964] 1 W.L.R. 1317; *Hinz v. Berry, supra*; *King v. Phillips, supra*. Contrast *Chester v. Waverley Municipal Council* (1939) 62 C.L.R. 1.

about the incident almost immediately after it occurred.[93] A further extension of this emerged in *Chadwick v. British Transport Commission.*[94] There a plaintiff who was involved in effecting a rescue after a train accident caused by the defendant's negligence recovered for the shock caused not by fear for himself nor for fear or horror on account of a relative, but because of the scenes of horror he saw when he assisted in the rescue operations. There was no danger apprehended to himself nor to anyone closely related to him. Indeed, the moment of actual or apprehended danger had past. Nevertheless liability was imposed for the shock suffered by the plaintiff.[95]

12.26 The problem in these actual, and some hypothetical instances (such as those outlined by Lord Bridge in the *McLoughlin* case)[96] is whether they ought to be determined on the basis of foreseeability or by the application of the doctrine of causation or on more general grounds of public policy in the sense of what would be consistent with fairness, justice, reason and what Lord Bridge referred to as "the good sense of the judge enlightened by progressive awareness of mental illness".[97] The cases before *McLoughlin v. O'Brian* reveal a variety of opinions and a diversity of approaches. That decision appears to have put the law relating to nervous shock on the solitary, if flexible foundation of "reasonable foreseeability". This was accepted by the Court of Appeal in the subsequent case of *Attia v. British Gas plc*,[98] where, for example, Bingham L.J. said:

> "The majority ratio of this decision is . . . that reasonable foreseeability of psychiatric damage to the plaintiff is a necessary condition of a successful claim, but . . . even where reasonable foreseeability of such damage is shown a right to recover may be denied on grounds of policy".[99]

The reason for the difficulty in such cases[100] is that they involve plaintiffs who were not at the material time within the area of foreseeable risk of physical harm to themselves, which the House of Lords stressed as vital in *Bourhill v. Young.*[101] Hence the issue for the courts was whether the area of foreseeable harm should be extended to those who could be affected emotionally although not immediately and directly physically; and, if so, how far that extension should be taken.

12.27 It now seems that the tort of negligence extends as far as to cover those who are not in immediate physical danger but suffer shock when

93 *Boardman v. Sanderson, supra*: cp. *Marshall v. Lionel Enterprises* (1971) 25 D.L.R. (3d) 141; *Benson v. Lee* [1972] V.R. 879.
94 [1967] 2 All E.R. 945.
95 Cp. *Dooley v. Cammell Laird & Co.* [1951] 1 Lloyd's Rep. 271; *Mount Isa Mines Ltd v. Pusey* [1971] A.L.R. 253. The test was whether a reasonable person would have been affected in this way. On the liability of a negligent defendant to "rescuers" see below paras 12.29ff.
96 [1982] 2 All E.R. 298 at 319–320.
97 *Ibid.* at 320.
98 [1987] 3 All E.R. 455.
99 *Ibid.* at 464.
100 Other than *Dulieu v. White, supra*, and, perhaps, on one view of the facts, *Hambrook v. Stokes Bros., supra.*
101 [1943] A.C. 92.

learning of actual injury or injury they believe has been incurred by those who are closely related, i.e. as parent and child or husband and wife. But the ordinary bystander is not necessarily excluded from recovery.[102] Cases involving less close relationships must be very carefully scrutinised. That does not mean they will never be admitted. The closer the tie, not only in relationship but in care, the greater the claim for consideration. However the claim has to be judged in the light of factors such as proximity to the scene in time and place and the nature of the accident.[103] Thus the plaintiff suffering shock must be proximate in time and space to the accident. This did not mean, in *McLoughlin v. O'Brian*, that the plaintiff was denied recovery because she was not at the scene of the accident in which her husband and some children were injured and one child was killed, so that she did not see or hear what happened. It sufficed that she learned of the accident in the immediate aftermath of its occurrence. Cases where by analogy with the "rescue" cases,[104] a person of whom it could be said that one would expect nothing else than that he or she would come immediately to the scene, were also to be regarded as being within the scope of foresight and duty. In summary, "the shock must come through sight or hearing of the event or of its immediate aftermath":[105] which leaves open whether there would be liability if the plaintiff saw and heard the incident through simultaneous television or something akin to such a means.[106]

12.28 As a consequence of this decision the Court of Appeal in *Attia v. British Gas plc*[107] allowed an action to proceed. The plaintiff complained of shock suffered when she saw her house and its contents destroyed by a fire caused by the negligence of the defendants. The issue to be determined at the trial was whether this consequence was reasonably foreseeable as a result of the negligence and whether, applying the test of causation that was relevant to cases of negligence,[108] it could be said that the shock was caused by that negligence, and not by some independent or intervening factor. If the latter were the case, as explained in *McLoughlin v. O'Brian*, there would not be the necessary proximity to permit liability to be imposed. Although the judgements in the *McLoughlin* case accept and recognise, without entirely specifying them in detail or depth,[109] that there must inevitably be limitations upon the scope of liability for nervous shock inflicted by negligence, it is clear that the law has advanced or progressed a great distance from the decision of the Privy Council in *Victorian Railways*

102 *McLoughlin v. O'Brian*, *supra* at 304 *per* Lord Wilberforce.
103 *Ibid.* The House of Lords appears to have differed in respect of the matter of limits on liability. Some thought that the issue of policy was "justiciable", along the lines indicated by Lord Wilberforce: see, e.g. *per* Lord Edmund-Davies at 308, *per* Lord Russell of Killowen at 310. Contrast Lord Scarman at 310–311, Lord Bridge at 319–320.
104 Below paras 12.29ff.
105 [1982] 2 All E.R. 298 at 305 *per* Lord Wilberforce.
106 *Ibid.*
107 *Supra* note 93.
108 Below paras 12.94ff.
109 See the references cited *supra* note 102.

Commissioner v. Coultas[110] that liability for nervous shock did not exist in the common law.

(iv) Rescuers

12.29 Like the person who suffers nervous shock by reason of what he or she sees or hears, although never in any danger of being physically injured in consequence of the defendant's negligent act, the rescuer, or would-be, although failed rescuer, is also someone who was not in the original path of the defendant's negligence, and would not have been injured if he or she had not attempted to save another endangered by that negligence. Whether rescuers should be able to sue the negligent defendant if injured in the course of trying to effect a rescue, is a question that has involved courts in considering the issues of consent, i.e. the doctrine of *volenti non fit injuria*,[111] contributory negligence,[112] and causation.[113] The last of these has loomed large in some decisions more than others.[114] Although it can be looked at as a distinct question, to be answered once it has been established that a duty of care was owed to the rescuer, its resolution also entails examination of the issue of the duty of care, especially since the test of causation approximates to, if it does not entirely equate with, that of duty.[115]

12.30 Looked at from the standpoint of duty, it becomes a question of deciding whether the reasonable man ought to foresee that if he endangers someone, another, previously unaffected person will probably attempt to save the endangered party. In an early case, *Brandon v. Osborne Garrett & Co.*,[116] thc problem was looked at entirely from the point of view of causation. But in *Haynes v. Harwood*[117] the Court of Appeal, as well as considering the issues of causation, contributory negligence and *volenti*, stated clearly that in appropriate instances one who came to the rescue of another would be someone to whom a duty of care was owed, as long as the prospect of rescue in such circumstances was reasonably probable. In that case a police officer who stepped in to save someone put in danger by the defendant's runaway horse could recover from the negligent owner of the horse. The police officer was someone who, by virtue of his office and duties, would be likely to act as he did: and the circumstances justified such intervention on his part. In *Morgan v. Aylen*,[118] this was held to extend to the act of a private person. However in *Cutler v. United Dairies*,[119] no duty was owed to someone who tried to halt a runaway horse not in a busy

110 Above note 89.
111 Below paras 13.05ff.
112 Below paras 13.23ff.
113 Below paras 12.94ff.
114 E.g., *Knightley v. Johns* [1982] 1 All E.R. 851.
115 Cp. *Knightley v. Johns*, *supra* with *Ogwo v. Taylor* [1987] 3 All E.R. 961.
116 [1924] 1 K.B. 548.
117 [1935] 1 K.B. 146, accepting the remarks of Cardozo J. in *Wagner v. International Railroad Co.* (1921) 232 N.Y. Supp. 176 at 180.
118 [1942] 1 All E.R. 489.
119 [1932] 2 K.B. 297 with which contrast *Haynes v. Harwood*, *supra* at 158 *per* Greer L.J., 163 *per* Maugham L.J., 167 *per* Roche L.J.

street, as in the earlier cases, but in a field away from people. The rescuer was *volens*.

12.31 In these, and subsequent decisions,[120] the rescuer was intervening in order to save human life. But in *Hyett v. Great Western Railway*[121] the principle seems to have been extended to apply to the case of a man trying to save property from damage as a result of the defendant's negligence. The plaintiff was not an employee of the owner of the property, which might have made the situation clearer and more emphatic; but he was on the property in a capacity connected with the property of the owner of the endangered chattel. It would seem likely that, in certain circumstances, it might be reasonable for someone to attempt to save property as contrasted with human life. If this is so, for example, where extremely valuable property is in danger, or some public interest is served by endeavouring to ensure that property is not damaged or destroyed, it would be reasonable for someone who acts negligently to foresee that another person might try to save what was endangered. Only where this was foreseeable by the reasonable man would it be legitimate to conclude that a duty of care was owed to the successful or would-be rescuer.

12.32 There is, in general, no affirmative duty to rescue at common law. One who refrains from attempting to rescue, even where to do so would be an easy matter, is under no liability to the person who is not rescued from danger, unless a duty to rescue arose from some statutory obligation of care that was imposed on the non-rescuer towards the party endangered, or the former had put the latter into a dangerous situation by his own negligence.[122] Whatever duty is owed to the rescuer is owed by the one who endangered the party to be rescued. That duty emerges from foresight of the likelihood of rescue. Such was the situation in *Videan v. British Transport Commission*,[123] where the stationmaster who tried to rescue his young son, who was wandering on a railway track, could recover damages for injuries he incurred in the course of the rescue. Although it was not foreseeable that the child might be on the track, it was foreseeable that a situation might arise in which the stationmaster by virtue of his office might be obliged to do something to rescue others. Similarly, although this is contained only in dicta,[124] it is conceivable that the party

120 Cp. *Chapman v. Hearse* (1961) 106 C.L.R. 112 (Australia); *Russell v. McCabe* [1962] N.Z.L.R. 392 (New Zealand); *Horsley v. McLaren* (1971) 22 D.L.R. (3d) 545 and *Corothers v. Slobodian* (1975) 51 D.L.R. (3d) 1 (Canada). In *Chadwick v. British Transport Commission* [1967] 2 All E.R. 945, the rescurer was engaged in helping *after* a train accident, not in trying to prevent the incident. He suffered nervous shock in consequence of what he saw. He was able to recover from the negligent defendants for such injury: cp. above para. 12.25.

121 [1948] 1 K.B. 345.

122 Or the rescuer was under some other kind of duty, e.g., contractual, to perform acts that involve rescue, e.g., in the case of firemen: *Ogwo v. Taylor*, para. 12.29 *supra*; *Merrington v. Ironbridge Metal Works Ltd* [1952] 2 All E.R. 1101; *Salmon v. Seafarer Restaurants Ltd* [1983] 3 All E.R. 729.

123 [1963] 2 Q.B. 650.

124 *Horsley v. McLaren*, *supra* at 558 *per* Laskin J.

rescued could be liable to the rescuer, if the former created the situation requiring his rescue as a result of his own negligence.

12.33 Whatever the cause of the original situation, which occasioned the need for a rescue, it must be shown that the plaintiff's intervention was not "wanton" or unnecessary, but was required and was a reasonable reaction to the situation.[125] A person who could not swim but dived into the sea to rescue someone would not be a person to whom the negligent party, whose conduct resulted in the rescued person's being in the water, owed a duty of care, because the negligent party could not foresee that a non-swimmer would attempt a rescue. The response of the rescuer must be reasonable, not rash nor so foolhardy as to amount to a wholly unreasonable disregard for his own safety.[126] It must be commensurate with the danger created by the negligence and the capacities of the rescuer. A doctor who went down a well to rescue men trapped therein and in danger of dying from poisonous gas did not act rashly or recklessly, it was held in *Baker v. T.E. Hopkins Ltd.*[127] To some extent this issue relates to questions of causation and contributory negligence.[128] It is also connected to the issue of duty, however, since an unreasonable response, in the sense of unnecessary action or action by someone not qualified or capable in respect of the rescue to be effected, is not something that the ordinary reasonable negligent party can or ought to be expected to contemplate as being likely to occur.[129]

12.34 Unquestionably there are difficulties involved in extending the notion of foreseeability and risk, and therefore the concept of a duty of care, to rescuers.[130] The approach of the law has been pragmatic and utilitarian, rather than logical. In order to encourage behaviour that is socially commendable and desirable, the law has taken the view that the liability of the negligent party can and should be extended to those who try to prevent or limit the harmful consequences of the negligent party's act. Whatever technical objections may be raised to this attitude, its general purpose and effect are neither objectionable nor unacceptable.

(v) Negligent mis-statements

12.35 The original scope of liability under the principle expounded in *Donoghue v. Stevenson* was damage to the person or to property.[131] The latter appeared to relate to personal property, chattels, and was not extended to

125 *Baker v. T.E. Hopkins & Sons Ltd* [1959] 3 All E.R. 225 at 241 *per* Willmer L.J., 233–234 *per* Morris L.J.
126 *Ibid.* at 244 *per* Willmer L.J.: cp. *Canadian Pacific Railway Co. v. Kelvin Shipping Co. Ltd* (1927) 138 L.T. 369 at 370 *per* Lord Haldane.
127 *Supra.*
128 Cp. *Knightley v. Johns*, para. 12.29 *supra* at 862–864 *per* Stephenson L.J.
129 *Ibid.* at 858–860.
130 *Horsley v. MacLaren, supra* at 558 *per* Laskin J.
131 Cp. *Old Gate Estates v. Toplis* [1939] 3 All E.R. 209 at 216–217 *per* Wrottesley J.

realty until some time subsequently.[132] In 1932 the courts did not have in mind the possibility that harm might be caused by negligence in making a statement or proferring advice. Indeed in the nineteenth century, in *Derry v. Peek*,[133] the House of Lords had held that for the tort of deceit to be committed it was insufficient that the defendant had negligently misled the plaintiff. Actual or constructive fraud was required. That opinion was confirmed by the majority of the Court of Appeal in *Candler v. Crane, Christmas & Co.*[134] over the dissent of Denning L.J. The majority took the view that *Donoghue v. Stevenson* had not changed anything with respect to liability for negligent misrepresentations or negligent misstatements.[135] It was not until the decision of the House of Lords in *Hedley, Byrne & Co. v. Heller and Partners*[136] in 1963 that the doctrine of *Donoghue v. Stevenson* was extended to take within its ambit situations involving negligently spoken or written words as well as negligent acts. That case held that there could be liability under the tort of negligence for such misconduct even where it did not result in physical damage to the person or to property. Prior to then it had been held that where a statement was inaccurate as a result of negligence, in contrast with fraud, only when that statement caused physical damage could there be the basis of an action in negligence.[137] *Donoghue v. Stevenson*, by eliminating the privity of contract doctrine from the law of negligence, opened the way for such a decision, in contrast with nineteenth century cases where fraud had to be shown before there could be liability even where physical harm to the person was the consequence.[138] Since the *Hedley Byrne* case, the law has developed in two directions. The first concerns situations in which there may be liability for an inaccurate statement. The second is in respect of "pure" economic loss, i.e. economic loss that is not consequent upon physical damage to the person or to property.[139]

12.36 The principle established in the *Hedley Byrne* case was that someone who provided information or advice in response to a request was under a duty to take reasonable care that his reply was accurate and not misleading provided that he knew or ought to have known that his statement was likely to be relied upon by the person to whom it was made

132 Below para 17.02.
133 (1889) 14 App.Cas. 337: below Chapter 17.
134 [1951] 2 K.B. 164, following the earlier decision in *Le Lievre v. Gould* [1893] 1 Q.B. 491, which had overruled *Cann v. Wilson* (1888) 39 Ch.D. 39. See Fridman, "Negligence by Words" (1954) 32 Can. B.R. 678.
135 Cp. the decision in the Canadian case of *Guay v. Sun Publishing Co. Ltd* [1953] 2 S.C.R. 216. Note that there might be liability if a contractual or fiduciary relationship existed between the parties: *Nocton v. Lord Ashburton* [1914] A.C. 932; *Woods v. Martins Bank* [1959] 1 Q.B. 55. This is still true.
136 [1964] A.C. 465.
137 *Sharpe v. Avery* [1938] 4 All E.R. 85; *The Sobieski* [1949] P. 213; *Clayton v. Woodman & Sons Ltd* [1962] 2 Q.B. 533: see the remarks of Rowlatt J. in *Humphrey v. Bowers* (1929) 45 T.L.R. 297 at 298–299.
138 E.g., *Langridge v. Levy* (1837) 2 M. & W. 519.
139 *Smith v. Eric S. Bush* [1989] 2 All E.R. 514 at 537 *per* Lord Jauncey. On economic loss see below paras 12.40ff.

and that such reliance might cause damage to that person.[140] In *Smith v. Eric S. Bush*,[141] Lord Griffiths posed the question in what circumstances should the law deem those who give advice to have assumed responsibility to the person who acts on the advice: in other words, in what circumstances should a duty of care be owed? His answer was:

> "... only if it is foreseeable that if the advice is negligent the recipient is likely to suffer damage, that there is a sufficiently proximate relationship between the parties and that it is just and reasonable to impose the liability".

The *Hedley Byrne* case resulted in no liability because the defendants, when giving their opinion about the financial position of the party about whom the plaintiffs had made inquiries, expressly disclaimed any responsibility for the accuracy of their statement.[142] However the decision clearly established that there could be liability for a statement that was inaccurate and misled the one to whom it was made. In the later Privy Council case of *Mutual Life Assurance Co. Ltd v. Evatt*,[143] the majority purported to restrict this to situations where the party making the statement was providing a professional service, as a result of which it was foreseeable that reliance would be placed on what he said. Hence in that case a company that gave advice on a subject that was not within the normal scope of its business was not liable when the advice turned out to be inaccurate and misleading, causing financial loss to the person to whom the statement was made. The minority disagreed with this: and the two members of the Board who constituted the minority had been members of the House of Lords in the original decision. The views expressed in the *Evatt* case have been disavowed by courts in other jurisdictions:[144] nor do they appear to have had much, if any influence on later English cases.[145] Indeed the broader attitude of the minority in the *Evatt* case may be considered to have become the basic principle. According to this, therefore, as long as the reliance on the statement made by the defendant is a reasonably foreseeable consequence of its being made, and it was the intention of the

140 One view of this is that there must be a commercial relationship between the parties that was possibly only a little short of privity of contract: *Junior Books Ltd v. Veitchi Bros.* [1983] 2 All E.R. 201 at 211. But this may be too narrow in view of what has happened to the decision in the *Evatt* case, below. This will exclude "purely social" relationships, but where the relationship of principal and agent exists, this evidences that the occasion on which the information or advice was given was not a purely social one: *Chaudhry v. Prabhaker* [1988] 3 All E.R. 718 at 722 *per* Stuart-Smith L.J., a case of gratuitous agency.

141 [1989] 2 All E.R. 514 at 536. On voluntary assumption of responsibility as the basis of a duty of care, see *Banque Financière de la Cité SA v. Westgate Insurance Co. Ltd* [1989] 2 All E.R. 952; *Van Oppen v. Clerk to Bedford Charity Trustees* [1989] 3 All E.R. 389. The factor of "proximity" was stressed by Millett J. in the subsequent case of *Al Saudi Banque v. Clark Pixley* [1989] 3 All E.R. 361 at 368–70.

142 Contrast *Smith v. Eric S. Bush, supra.*

143 [1971] A.C. 793.

144 See, e.g., *Porky Packers Ltd v. The Town of The Pas* (1976) 65 D.L.R. (3d) 1.

145 Cp. *Esso Petroleum Ltd v. Mardon* [1976] 1 Q.B. 801; *Howard Marine & Dredging Co. Ltd v. A. Ogden & Sons* [1978] Q.B. 534; *McInerney v. Lloyds Bank Ltd* [1974] 1 Lloyd's Rep. 246; *Box v. Midland Bank Ltd* [1979] 2 Lloyd's Rep. 391; *Argy Trading Development Co. v. Lapid Developments Ltd* [1977] 1 W.L.R. 444.

maker of the statement as well as that of the one to whom it was made that such reliance should be placed upon it, a duty of care will arise.

12.37 Duties of care have been placed upon accountants,[146] surveyors,[147] government officials,[148] and others.[149] There would seem to be no, or virtually no theoretical limit to the classes of persons who can be subject to a duty under the doctrine first stated in *Hedley Byrne v. Heller*. But at least one limitation, other than that resulting from a disclaimer of responsibility, has been indicated. The notion of proximity suggests that the person to whom the duty is owed must be someone directly and closely related to the person making or giving the statement or advice such that pecuniary loss to the latter was reasonably foreseeable.[150] It has been questioned whether this should be understood to mean the one to whom the statement is immediately given, or can be extended to someone to whom the statement will subsequently be given with the knowledge of the maker of the statement, or, more broadly, to any member of a class of persons to whom the statement might be relevant and might be given. For example, where an accountant is engaged to prepare the accounts of a company, does the accountant owe a duty of care, apart from the contractual obligation he owes to the company, to (a) a person the accountant knows is interested in investing in the company, because the accountant has been told of the existence of that person; (b) a member of the limited class of persons the accountant actually knows will use and rely on his statement on the accounts; (c) someone whom the accountant can foresee will use the financial statement and rely on it? In *Haig v. Bamford*[151] the Supreme Court of Canada accepted that actual knowledge of the specific person was too narrow, and the test of foreseeability was not a proper test to apply. The court preferred the test which involved actual knowledge of the limited class who would use and rely on the statement.[152] In that case, as in the English decision in *JEB Fasteners Ltd v. Marks Bloom & Co.*,[153] the auditor who prepared the accounts knew a person to whom they were going to be shown with a view to his purchasing shares in the company to which the accounts related. As Bingham L.J. said,[154] in relation to the facts in the *Haig* case, without that finding the plaintiff's

146 *Caparo Industries plc v. Dickman* [1989] 1 All E.R. 798.
147 *Roberts v. J. Hampson & Co.* [1989] 2 All E.R. 504; *Smith v. Eric S. Bush, supra*; cp. *Yianni v. Edwin Evans & Son* [1982] Q.B. 438.
148 *Ministry of Housing & Local Government v. Sharp* [1970] 2 Q.B. 223.
149 E.g., valuers, as long as they are not deciding a dispute as arbitrators: *Arenson v. Casson, Beckman Rutley & Co.* [1977] A.C. 405; *Sutcliffe v. Thackrah* [1974] A.C. 727; barristers and solicitors: *Saif Ali v. Sydney Mitchell & Co.* [1980] A.C. 198; *Ross v. Caunters* [1980] Ch. 297 (see further below pp. 311–12); bankers: *McInerney v. Lloyds Bank Ltd., supra*; insurance brokers: *Chevry Ltd v. Allied Insurance Brokers Ltd* [1978] 1 Lloyd's Rep. 274. See also *W.B. Anderson & Sons Ltd v. Rhodes (Liverpool) Ltd* [1967] 2 All E.R. 850 on the effect of negligence in relation to the Statute of Frauds Amendment Act 1828.
150 *Pacific Associates Inc. v. Baxter* [1989] 2 All E.R. 159 at 169–170 *per* Purchas L.J.; cp. *ibid.* at 186 *per* Gibson L.J.
151 (1977) 72 D.L.R. (3d) 68 at 75.
152 Lest there be liability in an indeterminate amount for an indeterminate time to an indeterminate class: *Ultramares Corporation v. Touche* (1931) 255 N.Y. 170 at 179.
153 [1983] 1 All E.R. 583.
154 In *Caparo Industries plc v. Dickman* [1989] 1 All E.R. 798 at 814.

claim would have failed for want of proximity. In *Caparo Industries plc v. Dickman*[155] the distinction drawn by the Court of Appeal between members of the public wishing to buy shares in a company and existing shareholders buying more shares was rejected by the House of Lords. In neither instance, they held, was there sufficient proximity between the auditors and purchasers of shares to give rise to a duty of care on the part of the former. Thus the appeal of the auditors against liability to the shareholders was allowed and the cross-appeal of the shareholders against the decision that no duty was owed to them as potential investors was dismissed.[156] What emerges from this and other cases, it would appear, is that before any duty of care of this kind can be said to be owed there must be more than a foreseeable prospect, however reasonable it may be, that someone might be caused loss by relying on the statement. It must be established that the party making the statement knew or had means of knowledge that a specific person or class or persons would in fact be relying on that statement, would act upon it, and might thereby incur loss.

12.38 What the defendant could reasonably have foreseen is one aspect of the issue of proximity. Another, also of importance, is the issue of reliance. The circumstances must be such that the defendant knew or, as a reasonable man, ought to have known or foreseen that the plaintiff would rely on the defendant's statement. In *Pacific Associates Inc. v. Baxter*,[157] Purchas L.J. said that the central question was whether, against the contractual structure of the contract into which the contractor was prepared to enter with the employer, it could be said that the contractor looked to the engineer by way of reliance for the proper execution of the latter's duties under the contract in extension of the rights which would accrue to the contractor under the contract against the employer. The answer being in the negative, no duty of care arose in that case. In *Mills v. Winchester Diocesan Board of Finance*,[158] which involved advice given by the Charity Commissioners to the board of finance at the instigation of the inhabitants of a village, Knox J. said that the *Hedley Byrne* principle was inapplicable because there was never any question of the plaintiff's relying on the Commissioners' advice which the plaintiffs had consistently opposed and resisted. But in *Roberts v. J. Hampson & Co.*[159] the decision was the other way. There was sufficient proximity because the defendants "undoubtedly knew from the very fact that a scheme 1 survey was being undertaken that it was highly unlikely that the plaintiffs were relying on some other professionally based information as to the property".[160] But in

155 [1990] 1 All E.R. 568 H. L., reversing [1989] 1 All E.R. 798 C. A., which was followed in *Al Saudi Banque v. Clark Pixley* [1989] 3 All E.R. 461, where, once again, auditors were not liable, this time to a bank which lent money to a company whose accounts were audited by the defendants.
156 Note also the question whether it was just and reasonable to impose such a duty on an auditor vis-a-vis such investors: below.
157 [1989] 2 All E.R. 159 at 171.
158 [1989] 2 All E.R. 317 at 332.
159 [1989] 2 All E.R. 504.
160 *Ibid.* at 512 *per* Kennedy J.

Caparo Industries plc v. Dickman[161] no duty was owed to shareholders, because their reliance on the auditors' report was too remote. There was no duty to potential investors either because within the auditors' contemplation there was no focus on any person or class of persons who might decide to invest. Foreseeability of reliance was conceded by the auditors, but the element of proximity was lacking: the auditors could not be expected to know who would be relying on their support. In this connection the existence of a disclaimer clause, or its equivalent, may be of great relevance. It will establish that the party seeking the information or advice was not purporting to hold the defendant responsible.[162] However it must be remembered that under modern legislation a disclaimer, exclusion or exception clause may be unreasonable, and therefore invalid and inoperative.[163] Moreover such a clause might only protect a party to the contract in which it appeared. The attitude of the courts to third party beneficiaries under contracts is such that only with difficulty will it be possible for one not a party to a contract to be able to rely on its terms.[164]

12.39 A third factor is also vital. This is the requirement that the imposition of a duty of care should be just and reasonable.[165] The cases reveal that the courts are much concerned with this particular aspect of the question whether a duty of care arises. It is a question of public policy.[166] The function of the court is to examine the probable effects of declaring that someone in the situation of the defendant is under a duty of care in relation to making a statement or giving an opinion or advice from the standpoint of the general public interest or the existence of some potentially conflicting duty or responsibility. Hence barristers,[167] an officer adjudicating on entitlement to unemployment benefit,[168] the Charity Commissioners,[169] an auditor providing information in a report to investors,[170] and others[171] have been held not to owe duties of care of this kind, on the ground that no public advantage, and possibly some public disadvantage, would flow from a decision to the contrary effect.

161 [1990] 1 All E.R. 568 H. L.
162 But this notion of reliance must not be confused with the test of duty based on "voluntary assumption of responsibility" which is contained in the *Hedley Byrne* case but has been rejected as the crucial and determining test of liability: see, e.g., *Ministry of Housing & Local Government & Sharp* [1970] 2 Q.B. 223; *Smith v. Eric S. Bush* [1989] 2 All E.R. 514; *Caparo Industries plc v. Dickman, supra.*
163 Under the Unfair Contract Terms Act 1977.
164 *Scruttons Ltd v. Midland Silicones Ltd* [1962] A.C. 446; *New Zealand Shipping Co. Ltd v. Satterthwaite* [1979] A.C. 154.
165 See, e.g. *Pacific Associates Inc. v. Baxter* [1989] 2 All E.R. 159 at 170 *per* Purchas L.J.
166 See further below pp. 309–12.
167 *Rondel v. Worsley* [1969] 1 A.C. 191.
168 *Jones v. Department of Employment* [1988] 1 All E.R. 725.
169 *Mills v. Winchester Diocesan Board of Finance* [1989] 2 All E.R. 317.
170 *Caparo Industries plc v. Dickman* [1989] 1 All E.R. 798; reversed on other grounds [1990] 1 All E.R. 568.
171 Cp. *Greater Nottingham Co-operative Society Ltd v. Cementation Piling & Foundations Ltd* [1989] Q.B. 71; *Pacific Associates Inc. v. Baxter* [1989] 2 All E.R. 159.

(vi) Economic loss

12.40 Before *Hedley Byrne* a plaintiff could only recover in tort for economic loss caused by negligence where: (a) the loss was the result of physical damage to his person or property; or (b) the loss was caused by the death of a family member on whom the plaintiff was dependent;[172] or (c) it was the result of the loss of a servant's services or, in the case of a husband, the *consortium* of his wife.[173] One important consequence of *Hedley Byrne* was the recognition that in an action for negligence a plaintiff might be able to recover "pure" economic loss, not the result of any of the foregoing situations, i.e. not consequent on personal injury or damage to property.[174] Since 1963 the courts have been concerned with the limits of such liability.

12.41 Where the defendant and plaintiff are in a relationship in which the defendant has the plaintiff directly in mind as being likely to be affected by his conduct in such a way as to incur economic loss, the issue does not present overmuch difficulty, once the question of liability for pure economic loss was resolved by *Hedley Byrne*. Cases of negligent misrepresentation made by the defendant to the plaintiff, and cases where the defendant acted gratuitously for the plaintiff, by providing him with a service which, if performed carelessly might result in pecuniary loss to the plaintiff, could be, and were determined on the basis that foresight of such loss gave rise to a duty of care, provided that there was a sufficient relationship of proximity between the parties and it was just and reasonable to impose such a duty in the circumstances. The real difficulty arose in cases where the defendant behaved in a careless manner which caused loss of some kind to a person, not the plaintiff, to whom the defendant owed a duty which arose under the law of tort, or by virtue of a contract, or in consequence of a public obligation, and the breach of such duty caused economic loss to the plaintiff. To hold the defendant liable to the plaintiff it was necessary to decide that (i) the loss to the plaintiff was foreseeable; (ii) there was a sufficient relationship of proximity between plaintiff and defendant; and (iii) it was just and reasonable to impose a duty of care on the defendant with respect to the plaintiff and the plaintiff's foreseeable loss. In a variety of cases the courts have struggled with this problem in the effort to distinguish between cases where the causation of such economic loss should give rise to liability and those where, for one reason or another, such liability should be negated.

12.42 The circumstances in which pure economic loss has been recovered have been limited.[175] One set of such circumstances consists of situations in

172 Under the Fatal Accidents Act: below pp. 432–7.
173 Both of which have now been abolished: above p. 253.
174 *Van Oppen v. Clerk to Bedford Charity Trustees* [1989] 1 All E.R. 273 at 287 *per* Boreham J; affirmed [1989] 3 All E.R. 389.
175 *Van Oppen*, para. 12.40 *supra*. See, e.g., *Reid v. Rush & Tompkins Group plc* [1989] 3 All E.R. 228: no liability of employer for economic loss of employee working overseas resulting from the lack of any personal accident insurance on the part of the employee in respect of special risks due to an overseas posting.

which the plaintiff relies on the acts of the defendant, there being no contract between them, and, in consequence, suffers economic loss through the defendant's carelessness. Such is the situation where the defendant is a gratuitous agent, or performs other services gratuitously for the plaintiff, including the provision of advice or information.[176] The negligent misrepresentation or misstatement cases discussed previously fall into this category. The other set of circumstances in which pure economic loss has been recovered has caused more difficulty. This involves situations where there is no reliance by the plaintiff on the defendant, but the latter could foresee that if he acted in a careless manner damage could be caused to the plaintiff. From time to time the attempt has been made to create liability for economic loss caused by a defendant's negligent act to the plaintiff, where the defendant has been negligent vis-a-vis a third party and the result of this has been the economic loss of which the plaintiff complains. In the majority of such instances the plaintiff has been unsuccessful. That lack of success was founded on the absence of a duty of care owed by the defendant to the plaintiff, in consequence of the decision that the reasonable man was not expected to foresee the loss in question, or, if it were foreseeable, there was no sufficient relationship of proximity between the parties to justify the conclusion that a duty of care existed. Put in the terms which have become more widely accepted in recent years, and were used by Boreham J. in *Van Oppen v. Clerk to the Bedford Charity Trustees*,[177] before any such duty can be imposed it must be determined, *inter alia*, that it would be just and reasonable to do so. In most situations where economic loss to the plaintiff is a direct, and perhaps even foreseeable consequence of causing physical damage to another person, the courts have determined that the imposition of such liability would not be just and reasonable.

12.43 For example, where economic loss to the plaintiff was caused by the destruction of property belonging to another,[178] or the endangering of other people's property through the escape of a disease from the defendant's property,[179] liability was denied, because no duty of care was owed. Even where physical damage to the plaintiff's property was caused by the defendant's negligence, and economic loss, *viz.*, loss of profit, was a consequence of such damage, there could not be liability for such loss despite the fact that the plaintiff was compelled to stop his operations, and, in consequence, incurred the loss.[180] In *Ross v. Caunters*,[181] a solicitor who was negligent in failing to warn the testator that the will should not

176 *Wilkinson v. Coverdale* (1793) 1 Esp. 75; *Hedley Byrne & Co. Ltd v. Heller & Partners Ltd* [1964] A.C. 465; cf *Chaudhry v. Prabhaker* [1988] 3 All E.R. 718.

177 *Supra* note 174 at 290.

178 *Electrochrome Ltd v. Welsh Plastics Ltd* [1968] 2 All E.R. 205. Canadian cases have raised the same problem and have been decided the same way: *Hunt v. T.W. Johnstone Ltd* (1976) 12 O.R. (2d) 623; *Star Valley Tavern v. Nield* (1977) 71 D.L.R. (3d) 439; *Richard v. Alberta Securities Commission* (1988) 42 D.L.R. (4th) 300; *B.D.C. Ltd v. Hofstrand Farms Ltd* (1986) 26 D.L.R. (4th) 1. But a different result was reached in *C.N.R. Co. v. Norsk Pacific Steamship Co Ltd* (1990) 65 D.L.R. (4th) 321.

179 *Weller & Co. Ltd v. Foot & Mouth Disease Research Institute* [1966] 1 Q.B. 569.

180 *Spartan Steel & Alloys Ltd v. Martin & Co. (Contractors) Ltd* [1973] 1 Q.B. 21, with which contrast *SCM (United Kingdom) Ltd v. W.J. Whittal & Sons Ltd* [1970] 3 All E.R. 245.

181 [1980] Ch. 297.

be witnessed by the spouse of a beneficiary, was liable to the beneficiary who lost what he would have inherited because the will was void. The judgment of Megarry V.C. in that case reveals that there was a relationship of sufficient proximity between the solicitor and the beneficiary to entitle the court to conclude that a duty of care existed. The existence of, and proposed disposition to the beneficiary were both known to the solicitor. He should have had in his contemplation the possibility of economic loss to the beneficiary if something were amiss with the will.[182] But in *Clark v. Bruce Lane & Co.*[183] a solicitor was not liable to an intended beneficiary under a will drawn up by the solicitor. Here there was no negligence in the manner in which the will was drawn and attested. The alleged negligence on the part of the solicitor consisted of his failure to advise the testator after the will was made in regard to a transaction by which the testator disposed of property to a third party for what was an uncommercial price to be paid on the death of the testator. That property had been left to the beneficiary. His argument was that the product of the sale was considerably less than it ought to have been; and his loss was the result of the solicitor's negligence. The Court of Appeal held that there was no cause of action. Whatever the relationship between a solicitor drawing a will and prospective beneficiaries under that will, there was no close degree of proximity between the solicitor and the beneficiary in respect of the post-testamentary disposition of the property. The benefit of the plaintiff, the beneficiary, was not the object of that transaction. The fact-situation in this case was sharply distinguished from that in *Ross v. Caunters*. Similarly, in *Van Oppen v. Clerk to the Bedford Charity Trustees*,[184] no duty of care was owed by a school to its pupils to insure them against accidental injury while at the school; nor was there such duty on the school to protect the pupils' economic welfare by insuring them. Nor did the school owe any duty of care to parents of pupils either to advise them of the dangers of rugby football, in the playing of which the pupil was injured, or of the need for personal accident insurance. To impose a duty of care towards the pupil in respect of insurance would have been to go beyond what was normally expected of a school, which was to educate its pupils. To impose a duty of care on the school vis-a-vis the parents would have been inapproriate because the school did not hold itself out as having expertise to advise on or deal with insurance. Moreover it would be unfair and unreasonable to put a school in peril for failing to do something which a parent did not have to do, namely insure, or could do carelessly with complete impunity because a parent was not under any comparable duty to the pupil.[185]

12.44 One suggestion that has been made in relation to liability for economic loss is that it should be determined by "the barrier of commercial sense and practical convenience".[186] Undoubtedly much will depend

182 *Ibid.* at 308–309.
183 [1988] 1 All E.R. 364.
184 [1989] 1 All E.R. 273; affirmed [1989] 3 All E.R. 389.
185 *Ibid.* at 290–291, 295–296; [1989] 3 All E.R. 389 at 410–12 *per* Balcombe L.J.
186 *Lambert v. Lewis* [1982] A.C. 225 at 267 *per* Stephenson L.J.

on the facts of a particular case, and the nature of the relationship between the defendant and the plaintiff. In this respect the decision of the House of Lords in *Junior Books Ltd v. Veitchi Bros.*[187] which, as will appear, seemed to have enlarged the scope of liability for economic loss, has been severely restricted by subsequent dicta. Similarly, the broad suggestions in *Anns v. Merton Borough Council*[188] and the later decision of the Court of Appeal in *Batty v. Metropolitan Property Realizations Ltd*,[189] as to the liability of a local authority or a builder for economic loss consequent upon negligence in supervising construction under statutory powers or duties on the one hand, or in the actual construction on the other,[190] have been rejected by the House of Lords in *D. & F. Estates Ltd v. Church Commissioners for England*.[191] In that case the House of Lords, while accepting that the *Anns* case involved an entirely new concept of the common law tort of negligence in relation to building cases, was not prepared to extend the scope of such liability to cover pure economic loss. To have done so in relation to realty, where it was not possible in relation to chattels, would have entailed the breakdown of any distinction between contractual and tortious liability. The issue in these cases was whether damages could be recovered for the cost of repairing a building which was defective by reason of the negligence of the builder or the local authority. Such cost might be incurred by the original owner, to whom the building was sold or for whom it was constructed: or by a subsequent purchaser, or lessee. To have allowed such liability would have involved a decision that could mean that builders and others would be bound by what was the equivalent of a contractual warranty in respect of the quality of the building. Moreover, insofar as such liability might be incurred towards someone other than the original purchaser with whom the builder was in a contractual relationship, it would have extended the scope of the tort of negligence too far, especially having regard to the provisions of the Defective Premises Act 1972.[192]

12.45 In consequence, although damages may be recovered for certain financial losses resulting from negligence by builders or local authorities, e.g., those which result from personal injuries or damage to property,[193] pure economic loss, unconnected with such damage, will not be recoverable, any more than in the case of a defective chattel; according to the majority of the Supreme Court of Canada in *Rivtow Marine Ltd v.*

187 [1983] A.C. 520.
188 [1978] A.C. 728.
189 [1978] Q.B. 554.
190 See further below pp. 304–7.
191 [1988] 2 All E.R. 992: *Department of Environment v. Thomas Baker & Sons Ltd* [1989] 1 All E.R. 1075. See also *Governors of Peabody Donation Fund v. Sir Lindsay Parkinson & Co. Ltd* [1985] A.C. 210; *Curran v. Northern Ireland Co-ownership Housing Association Ltd.* [1987] 2 All E.R. 13; *Greater Nottingham Co-operative Society Ltd v. Cementation Piling & Foundations Ltd* [1988] 2 All E.R. 971.
192 Below pp. 305–6. See *D & F Estates Ltd v. Church Commissioners for England, supra* at 996–1007 *per* Lord Bridge.
193 *Rimmer v. Liverpool City Council* [1984] Q.B. 1; *Anns v. Merton London Borough, supra.*

Washington Iron Works,[194] the cost of repairing the chattel was not recoverable, unless it could be shown that such loss emanated from reliance on a negligent misrepresentation, as contrasted with negligence in the manufacture of the chattel. The issue in these instances is part of the wider question whether someone who incurs economic loss by reason of the defendant's negligent breach of a contract between himself and a third party may bring an action in tort for negligence against the negligent contract-breaker. This is the question that was answered in the affirmative, on the facts of the case, by the majority of the House of Lords in the *Veitchi* case. Subsequent decisions seem to have limited the effect and scope of that decision: and to have indicated that, without the added factor of a negligent misrepresentation or some reliance to which the principle in *Hedley Byrne* can apply, there will be no such liability.

12.46 Prior to the decision in *Junior Books v. Veitchi Bros.*, the generally accepted and approved doctrine was that a plaintiff who was caused economic loss by reason of the defendant's wrongful act, whether a breach of contract or a tort, against a third party, could not maintain an action.[195] Even before the more recent statements already cited[196] that enunciate the requirement for a duty of foreseeability and proximity, and that imposition in the circumstances of a duty would be just and reasonable, the cases indicated that to open the door to liability for economic loss incurred by a plaintiff as a result of the breach of a duty owed to a third party by the defendant would create too wide a liability on the part of defendants. The scope of a defendant's liability for an act of negligence would reach to an indeterminate class of persons.[197] In cases after *Hedley Byrne* it was argued that the result of that decision was that the older rule, antagonistic to such broader liability for economic loss, had been breached; therefore further extension was not only possible but also desirable. In Australia the High Court did admit such a further extension by way of qualification of the older rule in *Caltex Oil (Australia) Pty Ltd v. Dredge Willemstad.*[198] The judgments in that case proceeded on different bases, as the Privy Council pointed out in *Candlewood Navigation Corporation Ltd v. Mitsui OSK Lines Ltd.*[199] Hence it was difficult to identify precisely what that case decided and on what principle the older rule should be considered to have been qualified or restricted in its scope. It might have been on the basis of the

194 [1974] S.C.R. 1189; see also *City of Kamloops v. Nielsen* (1984) 10 D.L.R. (4th) 641.
195 *Cattle v. Stockton Waterworks Co.* (1875) L.R. 10 Q.B. 483; *Simpson & Co. v. Thomson* (1877) 3 App.Cas. 270; *SA de Remorquage à Hélices v. Bennetts* [1911] 1 K.B. 243; *Elliott Steam Tug Co. Ltd v. Shipping Controller* [1922] 1 K.B. 127; *The World Harmony* [1967] P. 341. Cp. the cases referred to above in notes 177, 178, 179. Contrast *British Celanese Ltd v. A.H. Hunt (Capacitors) Ltd* [1969] 2 All E.R. 1252; *SCM (United Kingdom) Ltd v. W.J. Whittal & Sons Ltd* [1970] 3 All E.R. 245.
196 Above pp. 274–6.
197 Cp. *Weller v. Foot & Mouth Disease Research Institute* [1966] 1 Q.B. 569. See however *Morrison Steamship Co. Ltd v. Greystoke Castle* [1947] A.C. 265.
198 (1976) 136 C.L.R. 529, where liability was imposed for economic loss caused to the plaintiff, owner of an oil terminal, by the negligent act of the defendants in respect of another party, the owner of an oil pipeline that was broken by the negligence of the defendants' vessel. The breach of the pipeline resulted in no flow of oil to the terminal which caused loss of business to the owner of the terminal.
199 [1985] 2 All E.R. 935 at 943–945.

defendant's knowledge of the likelihood that the plaintiff individually would suffer economic loss. It might have been some concept of foreseeability or proximity. It might have been physical propinquity of the plaintiff's property to the incident that resulted in the loss. Nothing was clear or definite. More apposite was the decision of the House of Lords in *Junior Books*[200] where, as Lord Fraser acknowledged in the *Candlewood case*,[201] the scope of duty was "somewhat" extended. However, as he went on to state, "some limit or control mechanism has to be imposed on the liability of a wrongdoer toward those who have suffered economic damage in consequence of his negligence". The *Junior Books* case appeared to have pushed that limit too far. Later decisions have indicated that a more rigorous control must be exercised over this form of liability.

12.47 In the *Junior Books* case, the breach of a sub-contractor's contract with the contractor who was building a factory for the plaintiffs led to the later necessity for replacing a floor, which involved the closure of the factory for a period of reconstruction. This caused economic loss to the plaintiffs. The plaintiffs, who could presumably have sued the contractor for breach of contract, did not do so, for reasons which were never elucidated. Instead the plaintiff sued the sub-contractors. Such action could not be founded on contract. It was based on the tort of negligence. By a majority the House of Lords held that the action could proceed. The decision and the judgments in that case have been the subject of discussion in the Court of Appeal and the House of Lords in subsequent cases.[202] The view that emerges from those decisions is that the *Junior Books* case was a decision that was based upon, and ought to be restricted solely to its own special facts. It did not give rise to any new principle that would enure or entitle courts to overrule earlier decisions such as that in *Spartan Steel & Alloys Ltd v. Martin & Co. (Contractors) Ltd*,[203] and so overcome the earlier aversion of the common law to permitting an action for economic loss in the kind of circumstances exemplified in the *Junior Books* case. Indeed to have endorsed and accepted that decision more generally might have meant greater inroads on the current law of contracts or products liability. It might also have made reliance on contractual remedies virtually unnecessary. Although attempts were made to base the decision in that case on some rational ground such as that physical damage occurred as a consequence of which economic loss was suffered, or that there was close proximity between the parties, the opinion that appears to have been widely accepted is that which was voiced by Dillon L.J. in *Simaan General Contracting Co. Ltd v. Pilkington Glass Co. Ltd (No. 2)*:[204]

200 [1983] 1 A.C. 520.
201 *Supra* note 199 at 945.
202 *Muirhead v. Industrial Tank Specialities Ltd* [1985] 3 All E.R. 705; *Leigh & Sillavan Ltd v. Aliakmon Shipping Co. Ltd* [1986] 2 All E.R. 145; *London Congregational Union Inc. v. Harriss* [1988] 1 All E.R. 15; *Simaan General Contracting Co. v. Pilkington Glass Ltd (No. 2)* [1988] 1 All E.R. 791; *Greater Nottingham Co-operative Society Ltd v. Cementation Piling & Foundations Ltd* [1988] 2 All E.R. 971. See also *Candlewood Navigation Corporation Ltd v. Mitsui OSK Lines Ltd* [1985] 2 All E.R. 935.
203 [1973] Q.B. 27: above para 12.43.
204 [1988] 1 All E.R. 791 at 805.

"... the speeches of their Lordships have been the subject of so much analysis and discussion with differing explanations of the basis of the law that the case cannot now be regarded as a useful pointer to any developments of the law .... Indeed I find it difficult to see that any future citation from *Junior Books* can ever serve any useful purpose."

12.48 In a number of instances after *Junior Books*, in which resort to that decision was made by plaintiffs, claims for economic loss proved to be unsuccessful. In *Leigh & Sillavan Ltd v. Aliakmon Shipping Co. Ltd*[205] a buyer of goods, not yet their legal owner, who claimed in negligence against the carrier of the goods when they were damaged while en route to him, failed. Lacking either legal or equitable ownership in the goods there was no basis on which he could sue, even though the carrier's negligence caused him economic loss. In this the House of Lords followed the path shown by the Privy Council in the earlier *Candlewood* case,[206] where the plaintiffs, who were time charterers of a vessel, claimed for economic loss made up of hire they had had to pay while the vessel they had chartered was undergoing repairs because of a collision caused by the defendants' vessel. They also claimed loss of profits for that period. Both claims failed, on the ground that the plaintiffs were not the owners of the vessel, but were suing only for the loss of its use.

12.49 In *Muirhead v. Industrial Tank Specialities Ltd*[207] the plaintiff was a wholesale fish merchant who wished to store lobsters in a large tank during the summer and then sell them at Christmas so as to achieve a higher price for the goods. For this purpose he required pumps which were manufactured in France by the manufacturers' parent company. The pumps were then sold to a supplier who supplied them to the company which installed the plaintiff's tanks. Because the pumps were defective, the recirculation of water in the tanks was affected and the plaintiff lost his entire stock of lobsters. He sued, *inter alia*, the manufacturers, claiming the loss of the lobsters and economic loss including loss of profits on intended sales. The Court of Appeal held the manufacturers liable for the physical harm to the lobsters because this was reasonably foreseeable if the pumps failed. They were not liable for the economic loss. Such liability on the part of a manufacturer of defective goods would only arise where the ultimate purchaser placed real reliance on the manufacturer rather than the vendor who sold the goods to him. In such a situation there would be a very close proximity or relationship between manufacturer and ultimate purchaser.

12.50 A similar attitude was expressed by the Court of Appeal in *Simaan General Contracting Co. v. Pilkington Glass Ltd (No. 2)*.[208] The defendants manufactured glass panels to be used by contractors in installing certain units of glass to be incorporated in the curtain walling of a building to be erected by the contractors for the building owner. Those panels were constructed under a contract between the defendants and sub-contractors

205 [1986] 2 All E.R. 145: cp. *Margarine Union GmbH v. Cambay Prince Steamship Co. Ltd* [1967] 3 All E.R. 775.
206 *Supra* note 202.
207 [1985] 3 All E.R. 705.
208 [1988] 1 All E.R. 791.

with whom the contractors were in a contractual relationship. The glass panels were defective. In consequence the building owner withheld payment from the contractor. The latter sued the defendants for their economic loss. The action failed. The contractors had not relied on the defendants, nor had the latter voluntarily assumed direct responsibility to the contractors for the quality of the glass. There was no contractual relationship between these parties; nor was there physical damage to property owned by the contractor, nor was there sufficient proximity to entitle the latter to sue in negligence. Moreover it would not be just and reasonable to impose a duty of care on the defendants not to make the contractors' contract less profitable, because the contractors had a claim against the sub-contractors who, in turn, could claim against the defendants under the contract between them. Any of these liabilities would be affected in the light of exemption clauses, if any, that applied to each particular contract.

12.51 Somewhat similar facts, involving negligent work by a sub-contractor that ultimately caused economic loss to a building owner whose contractor had engaged the sub-contractors to do the work that was negligently performed, were the basis of the action in *Greater Nottingham Co-operative Society Ltd v. Cementation Piling & Foundations Ltd.*[209] Once again the Court of Appeal rejected the plaintiff building owner's claim. In order to establish liability for economic loss, what Purchas L.J. termed "the *Hedley Byrne* type of liability",[210] it had to be possible to cull from the close relationship of the parties the assumption by the tortfeasor of a duty not to cause pecuniary loss to the victim. For this to be the case, there had to be absent a contractual relationship between the parties that affected the issue of liability. In this instance there was a collateral contract between the building owner and the sub-contractors by which the latter were required to exercise reasonable care and skill in the design of the relevant works and the selection of materials. That contract defined exclusively the responsibility of the sub-contractors. Hence there was no scope for any conclusion that they had assumed any other responsibility.

12.52 The feature of these cases that is most pronounced is the unwillingness of the courts to admit liability for pure economic loss, of the kind that has been discussed, save in the most exceptional circumstances or in special cases. The extension of liability under *Donoghue v. Stevenson* to economic loss that was first broadly admitted or permitted by the decision in *Hedley Byrne v. Heller & Partners* will not be allowed to become so large and general that it will cause liability for negligence to reach out to cover harm to plaintiffs even if foreseeable, where to do so would entail too great a scope for such liability. Other decisions in recent years have revealed that it is not only in relation to economic loss that the courts have realised that the underlying principle of *Donoghue v. Stevenson*, if allowed to operate too widely, can lead to unjust, unreasonable or undesirable results. Hence

209 [1988] 2 All E.R. 971.
210 *Ibid.* at 984.

although there has been some application of the general theory of negligence to novel situations, including some that were not originally thought of as coming within the scope of *Donoghue's* case, at the same time there have been rejections by the courts of any such application.[210a]

(c) Extensions of duty

(i) Limitations

12.53 The purported generality of the doctrine expounded by the House of Lords, notably Lord Atkin, in *Donoghue v. Stevenson* was not, to begin with, as extensive as might have been thought. In several situations, apart from those previously considered, such as negligent misstatements,[211] where foreseeable harm was likely to a foreseeable plaintiff, the law excluded a duty of care. One of these was the situation that arose where cattle were able to get on the highway from the defendant's land and cause harm to a road user. In contrast with the strict liability of a landowner to his neighbour if the cattle strayed on to the latter's property, there was no duty to fence one's land so as to ensure that cattle did not stray onto the highway and cause harm.[212] Yet another concerned the liability of builders, vendors and landlords of real property towards those who had not purchased or leased such property. The situation of purchasers and lessees was governed by the terms of the contract with the builder, vendor or lessor. But the family or guests of the purchaser or lessee or a subsequent purchaser from the original purchaser, were unprotected by such contract. Nor could they claim the benefit of the law of negligence, before *Donoghue v. Stevenson* or afterwards.[213] The only way such persons could bring themselves within the ambit of negligence was if it could be shown that their injury was caused by a dangerous chattel[214] attached to, but not forming part of the realty.[215] A further limit on the scope of *Donoghue v. Stevenson* was in respect of omissions, as contrasted with negligent acts of commission. By this reference is meant not to the negligent performance of some duty by a failure to act, i.e. to take reasonable steps to prevent harm.[216] The term "omission" here refers to a

210a See, e.g., *Reid v. Rush & Tompkins Group plc* [1989] 3 All E.R. 228, discussed and applied by Balcombe L.J. in *Van Oppen v. Clerk to Bedford Charity Trustees* [1989] 3 All E.R. 389.

211 Above paras 12.35ff.

212 *Searle v. Wallbank* [1947] A.C. 341; *Brock v. Richards* [1951] 1 K.B. 329; cp. *Brackenborough v. Spalding Urban District Council* [1942] A.C. 310, no duty on market authority to public to provide pens for domestic animals, therefore no liability for death of plaintiff's husband killed by an escaping steer. If the animal was on the highway there was a duty owed to other road users: *Dean v. Davies* [1935] 2 K.B. 282; *Wright v. Callwood* [1950] 2 K.B. 515. Cp. also liability for dogs escaping onto the highway and causing harm: *Gomberg v. Smith* [1963] 1 Q.B. 25; *Ellis v. Johnstone* [1963] 2 Q.B. 8. See further Chapter 11.

213 *Cavalier v. Pope* [1906] A.C. 428; and *Bottomley v. Bannister* [1932] 1 K.B. 458 respectively.

214 *Davis v. Foots* [1940] 1 K.B. 116; *Travers v. Gloucester Corporation* [1947] K.B. 71; *Otto v. Bolton & Norris* [1936] 2 K.B. 46.

215 *Bottomley v. Bannister, supra* at 469–473 *per* Scrutton L.J.; *Ball v. L.C.C.* [1949] 2 K.B. 159; see further below paras 14.12ff, on things dangerous *per se*.

216 E.g., not shutting off steam to a train: *Kelly v. Metropolitan Railway* [1895] 1 Q.B. 947.

failure to act when there was no duty to act.[217] Even though harm could be foreseen to a particular person through such failure, there could be no liability in negligence. The introduction of the "neighbour" principle of Lord Atkin seemingly did nothing to alter this state of affairs.[218] Moreover unless the situation were one in which the doctrine of vicarious liability applied,[219] there was no duty of care to prevent harm to a plaintiff by reason of the act of a third party, where the defendant had no control over such third party. Even if the act of such a third party was foreseeable there was no duty of care in such circumstances.[220]

12.54 A further limitation on the scope of negligence through the breach of a duty of care was stated by the House of Lords in *East Suffolk Rivers Catchment Board v. Kent.*[221] There it was held that the plaintiff could only succeed in the event that a public body was negligent in its exercise of statutory powers if the damage caused was fresh or additional damage resulting from the statutory body's attempt to perform the duty. The plaintiff had to show that he suffered more harm than if nothing at all had been done.[222] In this respect there was a difference between the performance or non-performance of a statutory duty on the one hand and the performance or non-performance of a power or discretion on the other.[223]

(ii) Developments

12.55 *Animals.* The former doctrine with respect to cattle straying on the highway was abolished by the Animals Act 1971. Section 8(1) provides: "So much of the rules of the common law relating to liability for negligence as excludes or restricts the duty which a person might owe to others to take such care as is reasonable to see that damage is not caused by animals straying on to a highway is hereby abolished." The effect of this is that it will be a question for determination whether, in the circumstances, a duty was owed on the basis of what was foreseeable, and whether that duty was breached by the landowner. However in some

217 But there may be a duty to act if the relationship between the parties requires this, in which event an ommission will create liability: e.g. employer and employee: *Kasapis v. Laimos Bros.* [1959] 2 Lloyd's Rep. 378. Note also the Canadian cases of *Horsley v. MacLaren* [1972] S.C.R. 441 and *Jordan House v. Menow* (1973) 38 D.L.R. (3d) 105, involving respectively an obligation to rescue and an obligation to prevent a drunken customer of a tavern from being injured on the highway.

218 Cp. the remarks of Lord Keith in *Yuen Kun-yeu v. Attorney General of Hong Kong* [1987] 2 All E.R. 705 at 710: and of Lord Goff in *Smith v. Littlewoods Organisation Ltd* [1987] 1 All E.R. 710 at 735–736. See also the cases cited *supra* note 53.

219 Chapter 3.

220 E.g., a seller of goods which are used by the purchaser for an illegal and harmful purpose: see *Paterson Zochonis & Co. Ltd v. Merfahken Packaging Ltd* [1986] 3 All E.R. 520 at 529–530 *per* Oliver L.J., 538–542 *per* Goff L.J. Cp. *King v. Liverpool City Council* [1986] 3 All E.R. 344; *P. Perl (Exporters) Ltd v. Camden London Borough* [1984] 1 Q.B. 342. Contrast *John Walker & Sons Ltd v. Henry Ott & Co. Ltd* [1970] 2 All E.R. 106, where circumstances supported an inference of common design or commission of a tort by the supplier.

221 [1941] A.C. 74, a "much-battered case" according to *Winfield & Jolowicz on Tort*, 12th ed. 1984, at 82, note 93.

222 *Fellowes v. Rother District Council* [1983] 1 All E.R. 513 at 518 *per* Goff J. See also *Sheppard v. Glossop Corporation* [1921] 3 K.B. 132.

223 *Fellowes v. Rother District Council*, *supra* at 518 *per* Goff J.

situations no breach of duty will be committed by placing animals (which would seem to include dogs, cats and poultry, all of which were formerly outside the ambit of the operation of the law, by reason of the fact that there is no definition in the Act of the term) on unfenced land, from which they stray on to the highway and cause damage. For this exception to apply, the land must be common land or land in an area where fencing is not customary or a town or village green,[224] as long as the owner of the animals had a right to place them on the land.[225]

12.56 *Defective buildings.* The older approach to the liability of builders was abandoned as a result of several decisions[226] culminating in the case of *Anns v. Merton London Borough Council.*[227] There Lord Wilberforce explained that there was no valid reason why the principle of *Donoghue v. Stevenson* should not apply, where personal injury was the consequence of negligence in construction, to the builder, whether or not the owner of the building, so as to give a remedy to a subsequent purchaser of the building, who would not be in a contractual relationship with the builder.[228] That decision, however, did not directly deal with the liability of a vendor who was not the builder, nor with a lessor. The liability of the latter towards non-lessees was first created by the Occupiers' Liability Act 1957.[229] That provision has now been replaced by the Defective Premises Act 1972, which deals with the liability of builders, vendors and lessors. In effect this complex statute, which was based on the Law Commission's recommendations,[230] achieves four main effects. It creates a statutory duty to build dwellings properly. It abolishes the doctrine of *caveat emptor* in relation to work done on premises within the Act by making the duty of care apply not only to those "who might reasonably be expected to be affected by defects in the state of the premises created by the doing of the work", but also to anyone to whom the premises are subsequently disposed. The doctrine of *caveat emptor* was mentioned in the *Anns* case as perhaps the reason why the law had denied a duty and a remedy in the case of a subsequent purchaser.[231] A third consequence of the 1972 Act is to impose on a landlord a wide statutory duty of care, which covers not only his obligation to effect repairs carefully but also his liability for an omission to carry out repairs. The language of the relevant provision of the Act[232] also indicates that the landlord may be liable not only to visitors to a tenant but to others who might reasonably be expected to be affected by defects in the premises, for example, a neighbour or a passer-by: and that the obligations apply whether or not the landlord knows of the defect, and

224 Cp. Commons Registration Act 1965.
225 *Davies v. Davies* [1975] Q.B. 172.
226 *Gallagher v. McDowell Ltd* [1961] N.I. 26; *Sharpe v. E.T. Sweeting & Sons Ltd* [1963] 2 All E.R. 455; *Dutton v. Bognor Regis United Building Co. Ltd* [1972] 1 Q.B. 373.
227 [1977] 2 All E.R. 492.
228 *Ibid.* at 504.
229 S. 4(4).
230 Civil Liability of Vendors and Lessors of Defective Premises, Law Comm. No. 40, 1970.
231 *Supra* note 227 at 504.
232 *Viz.*, s. 3.

whether or not the landlord is under an obligation to the tenant to repair, as long as he has a right to enter the premises to effect repairs.

12.57 The builder's duty is to ensure that the dwelling will be fit for habitation when completed. It does not seem to entail, as the *Anns* principle does, that the building must not be a danger to person or property. Secondly, the builder's duty arises only in the case of a dwelling. The *Anns* principle applies to all buildings of any kind and for whatever purpose. The landlord's duty of care applies only to prevent personal injury or damage to property. This clearly and expressly excludes liability for pure economic loss. In relation to the liability of a builder or vendor, however, the language of the statute is not as plain. Does "fit for habitation" mean that liability under the Act will extend to pure economic loss, e.g., diminution in the value of the property? Does the duty of care owed to those who might reasonably be expected to be affected by defects in the state of the premises by the doing of work of construction, repair, etc., go so far as to protect such persons, whether the one who ordered their performance or a subsequent disponee of the premises, from pure economic loss? Perhaps the answers to these questions depend on whether, under the doctrine approved in the *Anns* case, there can be liability for negligence in producing, selling or leasing a defective building not only for personal injury or damage to property but also for pure economic loss unconnected with either personal injury, or the danger of such injury, or damage to property. As previously seen, the ultimate decision of the House of Lords, after other cases in which the matter was dealt with obliquely in relation to the liability of local authorities not builders or vendors, was that at common law there would be no liability for pure economic loss under the doctrine that emerged in the *Anns* case.[233] On this basis there would seem to be no justification for interpreting the 1972 statute so as to permit an action for pure economic loss caused by a breach of the statutory duties set out in the Act.

12.58 *Omissions.* One situation in respect of which an omission can now give rise to liability is in connection with the non-repair of highways. At common law a highway authority was under no liability for damage caused by its failure to repair a road, in contrast with damage resulting from misfeasance in the performance of such repairs. The Highways Act 1980, replacing earlier similar legislation,[234] now provides for such liability. Certain defences are available to such authority in an action for failure to maintain a highway where reasonable care was taken to secure that the relevant part of the highway was not dangerous for traffic.[235] What is relevant to the issue of reasonable care is set out in the statute.[236]

233 Above para 12.44.
234 Highways (Miscellaneous Provisions) Act 1961.
235 Highways Act, 1980, s. 58(1).
236 *Ibid.* s. 58(2). On the effect of these provisions see and compare: *Griffiths v. Liverpool Corporation* [1967] 1 Q.B. 374; *Pridham v. Hemel Hempstead Corporation* (1970) 69 L.G.R. 523; *Littler v. Liverpool Corporation* [1968] 2 All E.R. 343; *Pitman v. Southern Electricity Board* [1978] 3 All E.R. 901; *Haydon v. Kent County Council* [1978] Q.B. 343.

12.59 Common law decisions have also recognised that there may be situations where there may be a duty to act, such that failure to do anything can be negligence. Such instances appear to involve some control on the part of the defendant of the circumstances, such as his ownership of land on which a danger has emerged.[237] The *Anns* case may have also had an effect in this context. From that decision, and later ones, there arises the principle that where a local authority is empowered by statute to act in a certain way, the failure to do which might foreseeably cause harm to a plaintiff, the non-exercise of such power may constitute negligence. In other words there may be a duty to exercise the power. The *Anns* case and its successors were concerned with statutory powers connected with the erection of buildings.[238] In *Curran v. Northern Ireland Co-ownership Housing Association Ltd*,[239] Lord Bridge summarised the effect of the *Anns* case in these words:

> "First, the statutory power which the authority is alleged to have negligently failed to exercise . . . must be specifically directed to safeguarding the public, or some section of the public of which the plaintiff asserting the duty of care is a member, from the particular danger which has resulted; in the *Anns* case the danger of buildings being erected on inadequate foundations. Second, the power must have been such that its due exercise could have avoided the danger . . . . Third the non-exercise . . . of the power must have created a hidden defect which cannot subsequently be discovered and remedied before damage results."

12.60 Such decisions suggest that the common law is beginning to overcome its earlier reluctance to hold someone liable for an omission that is not a negligent manner of performing a positive obligation, for example by incorrectly diagnosing a disease.[240] Not every situation imposes a duty on someone to act, even where harm is foreseeable in consequence of a failure to act. There may be insufficient "proximity" between the parties. Or it may not be just and reasonable to compel the defendant to act in the circumstances. But sometimes there is sufficient proximity and it is just and reasonable to oblige the defendant to take reasonable steps to prevent the occurrence of harm that he can or ought to foresee as being a probable consequence of an omission.[241]

12.61 *Acts of third parties.* It is clear from some recent cases that, in general, there is no duty to take steps to prevent the occurrence of harm by the acts of third parties who are not the agents, servants or independent contractors of the defendant.[242] Sometimes this has been determined on the

237 *Goldman v. Hargrave* [1967] 1 A.C. 645. Or has knowledge of the risk from dishonesty: *Banque Keyser SA v. Skandia (U.K.) Insurance Co. Ltd* [1987] 2 W.L.R. 1300 at 1338 *per* Steyn J. (Reversed on appeal: [1989] 2 All E.R. 952.

238 Above paras. 12.56–7.

239 [1987] 2 All E.R. 13 at 19.

240 *Harnett v. Bond* [1924] 2 K.B. 517 at 541 *per* Bankes L.J.

241 In this regard the argument has been made in favour of a duty to rescue, even where the defendant has not brought about the situation necessitating rescue (as in *Johnson v. Rea Ltd* [1962] 1 Q.B. 373): Weinrib, "The Case for a Duty to Rescue" (1981) 90 Yale L.J. 247.

242 E.g., *Smith v. Littlewoods Organisation Ltd* [1987] 1 All E.R. 710.

ground that the defendant lacked the means of control over such a third party's act.[243] Sometimes the decision has been based on the doctrine of remoteness of damage.[244] But in at least one instance, *Home Office v. Dorset Yacht Co. Ltd*,[245] a duty to protect the plaintiff from the acts of third parties, not the defendant, was imposed so as to give rise to liability for damage inflicted by them. The Crown operated a Borstal institution on an island. By reason of the careless acts of the officers employed at the institution some of the juvenile delinquents housed in the institution escaped and caused damage to the plaintiff's yacht. There had been numerous other escapes in the past (in contrast with the rarity of a far-reaching hit of a cricket ball out of the ground in *Bolton v. Stone*).[246] The Crown was held liable in negligence in failing to exercise proper control so as to prevent the causation of harm to the plaintiff by the inmates of the Borstal.

> "A special relationship existed on the one hand between the prison officers and the borstal boys who were in their custody and on the other hand between the prison officers and the owners of yachts moored near the encampment. That the boys might seek to make use of a yacht in order to get away to the mainland and might damage it in the process was the very thing which the prison officers ought reasonably to have foreseen."

In the case in which these remarks were made by Lord Keith, *Hill v. Chief Constable of West Yorkshire*,[247] the House of Lords distinguished the *Dorset Yacht* case and would not impose a duty of care on the police to individual members of the public to identify and apprehend an unknown criminal, even though it was reasonably foreseeable that harm was likely to be caused to a member of the public if the criminal was not detected and apprehended. It might have been different if the criminal, the "Yorkshire Ripper", had been in custody from which he had escaped through police negligence. But he was not. Nor was the victim, whose mother was the plaintiff, an individual member of the public who was at a special distinctive risk in relation to the criminal's activities, like the owners of the yachts moored off the island in relation to the foreseeable conduct of the Borstal boys. The victim was one of a vast number of the female general public who might be at risk from the criminal's activities.[248] In these two cases, therefore, foreseeability was vital factor in whether or not a duty of care was owed.

12.62 *Statutory powers*. The attitude adopted in *East Suffolk Rivers Catchment Board v. Kent*[249] has been varied by the decision in *Anns v. Merton London*

243 *King v. Liverpool City Council* [1986] 3 All E.R. 544; *P. Perl (Exporters) Ltd v. Camden London Borough* [1984] Q.B. 342.
244 *Lamb v. Camden London Borough* [1981] Q.B. 625. Contrast *Ward v. Channock Chase District Council* [1985] 3 All E.R. 537, where liability was admitted: see *King v. Liverpool City Council* [1986] 3 All E.R. 544 at 548 *per* Purchas L.J.; and *Newsby v. General Lighterage Co. Ltd* [1955] 1 Lloyd's Rep. 273.
245 [1970] A.C. 1004.
246 [1951] A.C. 850: above para. 12.15.
247 [1988] 2 All E.R. 238 at 242.
248 *Ibid.* at 242–243. See also *Clough v. Bussan* [1980] 1 All E.R. 431 on the duty of the police.
249 [1941] A.C. 74.

Borough Council.[250] As Goff J. explained in *Fellowes v. Rother District Council*,[251] the principle of the earlier House of Lords case only applies where the body in question acted within the limits of its discretionary powers, and its action was *bona fide*. Liability for negligence can arise if the statutory body exceeded its discretion, there was sufficient proximity having regard to all the circumstances, including the legislation that created the power, to create a duty of care to avoid the type of damage complained of, and it was reasonably foreseeable by the defendant that the act complained of was likely to cause damage of the type in fact suffered by the plaintiff by reason of the act.[252] The underlying basis for such liability, said Goff J.,[253] was that citizens are entitled to expect that powers conferred on public authorities will be exercised and entitled therefore to expect that such powers will be exercised with due care.

12.63 However a distinction has been drawn, as discussed in the *Anns* case, between policy or planning decisions and operational decisions.[254] The question of policy is a matter for public law, not for the intervention of the law of negligence. Just as whether or not a legislative body has exercised a power to legislate, or has done so carefully, is not something that can be questioned by means of an action for negligence,[255] so a decision whether or not to adopt a particular policy is also not amenable to the jurisdiction of the courts by an action for damages. Such decisions may be open to judicial review, depending on the kind of issue in question.[256] However an operational decision may give rise to a common law duty to take reasonable care in the carrying out of the operation. So in *Davy v. Spelthorne Borough Council*[257] an action could be based on the local authority's negligence, through its lawyers, in advising the plaintiff of his rights under the Town & Country Planning Act 1971. This did not involve a matter of public law, as the making of an "enforcement notice" would have done. So in the *Anns* case, the decision on the number of building inspectors to appoint was a matter of policy, not justiciable by an action for negligence, and only to be questioned in an election. The carrying out of their functions was an operational matter for which the council could be vicariously liable if this was performed negligently, as occured in that case. However, as subsequent decisions indicate, though there may be liability in negligence for operational decisions that result in

250 *Supra* note 227: see also *Governors of Peabody Donation Fund v. Sir Lindsay Parkinson & Co. Ltd* [1986] 3 All E.R. 529: both applied in *Christos Industry Ltd v. South Bedford District Council* [1986] 1 Q.B. 1034.
251 [1983] 1 All E.R. 513 at 518–522.
252 *Ibid.* at 522.
253 *Ibid.*
254 See also *Dennis v. Charnwood Borough Council* [1982] 3 All E.R. 486; *Acrecrest Ltd v. W.S. Haskell & Partners* [1983] 1 All E.R. 17. See also *Richardson v. W. Lindsey D.C.* [1980] 1 All E.R. 296.
255 *Welbridge Holdings Ltd v. Metropolitan Corporation of Greater Winnipeg* (1972) 22 D.L.R. (3d) 470, a Canadian case.
256 *Davy v. Spelthorne Borough Council* [1983] 3 All E.R. 278.
257 *Supra.*

danger of physical injury to persons or property, there may not be such liability for economic loss.[258]

(iii) Exclusion of duty

12.64 The expansion of the scope of liability for negligence, by admitting the existence of duties of care in new situations, has not been limitless. Although "the categories of negligence are never closed"[259] in the sense that there is no *a priori* boundary to liability for negligence, this does not mean that there may not be rational bases for denying the possibility of a duty of care in a given situation so as to exclude potential liability for negligent conduct. In *Hill v. Chief Constable of West Yorkshire*,[260] for example, one reason for negating a duty of care in that case was public policy. It was not in the public interest to impose a duty of care on police in connection with the investigation and suppression of crime. In the words of Lord Keith, "the imposition of liability may lead to the exercise of a function being carried on in a detrimentally defensive frame of mind".[261] As Lord Templeman said: "The threat of litigation against a police force would not make a policeman more efficient".[262]

12.65 In *Calveley v. Chief Constable of the Merseyside Police*,[263] the plaintiffs were police officers who had been the subject of police disciplinary proceedings. The various complaints had been dismissed, quashed on appeal or discontinued. But the plaintiffs alleged that the proceedings had been misconducted with the result that they had suffered loss, although they had received full pay and allowances while they had been suspended pending the outcome of the investigation into the complaint made against them. They sued the chief constable for lost overtime pay and general damages for anxiety, vexation and injury to reputation. The actions were struck out by a trial judge, the Court of Appeal and the House of Lords. The relevant ground for this in the present context was that no such action could succeed on the basis of negligence: bad faith or possibly lack of reasonable cause had to be established. Mere negligence would not suffice, because no duty of care was owed under the principle in *Donoghue v. Stevenson*. Echoing the language in the *Hill* case, Lord Bridge said,

> "... it would plainly be contrary to public policy ... to prejudice the fearless and efficient discharge by police officers of their vitally important public duty of investigating crime by requiring them to act under the shadow of a potential action for damages for negligence by the suspect."[264]

Because no duty of care was owed to a suspect, therefore no such duty was owed by an officer investigating a suspected offence against discipline by a

258 Above paras 12.40ff. See generally Todd, "Negligence Liability of Public Authorities" (1986) 102 L.Q.R. 370.
259 *Donoghue v. Stevenson* [1932] A.C. 562 at 619 *per* Lord Macmillan.
260 [1988] 2 All E.R. 238, applied in *Clough v. Bussan, supra.*
261 *Ibid.* at 243.
262 *Ibid.* at 245. See however *Kirkham v. Anderton* (1990) The Times 4 January for a situation where the police *were* under a duty of care.
263 [1989] 1 All E.R. 1025.
264 *Ibid.* at 1030.

fellow officer. Similarly in *Marshall v. Osmond*[265] no duty of care was owed by a police officer driving a motor car in hot pursuit of persons he rightly suspected of having committed an arrestable offence, even though such a duty might be owed by a police officer to lawful and innocent users of the highway going about their lawful occasions.

12.66 Similarly those engaged in other public functions, such as adjudication, whether as judges on the bench or as arbitrators or under legislation dealing with social security, owe no duty of care to those who may be affected by the way they conduct themselves.[266] A similar attitude was expressed by the Privy Council in *Yeun Kun-yeu v. Attorney-General of Hong Kong*[267] in respect of the discharge of his functions by a commissioner under legislation dealing with deposit-taking businesses in Hong Kong: and in *Rowling v. Takaro Properties Ltd*,[268] in regard to the performance by a minister of the Crown of his duties and legislation dealing with the issue of shares to a foreign company. Some Australian cases also illustrate the fact that certain official acts do not involve a duty of care to those who may reasonably be expected to be affected by their negligent performance, such as the management of a naval vessel or the granting of an export license.[269]

12.67 The position of barristers and solicitors has also been the subject of consideration in recent years. There is an important distinction between these professions in England, although not in all other Commonwealth jurisdictions such as Canada.[270] Solicitors are in a contractual relationship with their clients, therefore they can be said to owe them a duty of care, which may be contractual or tortious, with the result that solicitors may be liable either for breach of contract or for the tort of negligence should a solicitor act negligently in the performance of his or her functions.[271] Indeed, as previously noted,[272] a solicitor may even owe such a duty to third parties, not his client, in certain circumstances. This has been held to extend to his client's opponent in hostile litigation where the solicitor stepped outside his role as solicitor for his client and accepted responsibilities towards his client's opponent. This occurred in *Al-Kandari v. J.R. Brown & Co.*[273] where the solicitors gave an undertaking with respect to a passport belonging to their client, a husband. When they failed to take

265 [1982] 2 All E.R. 610. Contrast the situation in Canada where it has been held that even when on duty e.g., chasing suspects, police may owe a duty of care to innocent bystanders: compare *Beim v. Goyer* [1965] S.C.R. 638 and *Woodward v. Begbie* [1962] O.R. 60 with *Priestman v. Colangelo* [1959] S.C.R. 615 and *Poupard v. Lafortune* [1973] S.C.R. 175.

266 *Sutcliffe v. Thackrah* [1974] A.C. 727; *Arenson v. Casson, Beckman, Rutley & Co.* [1977] A.C. 405; *Jones v. Department of Employment* [1988] 1 All E.R. 325: see also Chapter 22 at 589.

267 [1987] 2 All E.R. 705.

268 [1988] 1 All E.R. 163.

269 *Shaw Savill & Albion Co. Ltd v. Commonwealth* (1940) 66 C.L.R. 344; *Revesz v. Commonwealth* [1951] S.R. (N.S.W.) 63.

270 Cp. *Demarco v. Ungaro* (1979) 95 D.L.R. (3d) 385.

271 *Midland Bank Trust Co. Ltd v. Hett, Stubbs & Kemp* [1979] Ch. 384; cp. the Canadian case of *Central Trust Co. v. Rafuse* [1986] 2 S.C.R. 147.

272 Above at 296.

273 [1988] 1 All E.R. 833.

reasonable care of the passport and allowed the husband to have possession of it, which enabled him to kidnap the plaintiff, his wife, while he abducted the children and took them out of the country, the solicitors were held liable to the plaintiff. Such decisions relate to the performance by a solicitor of functions other than those of an advocate. In respect of his behaviour as an advocate, the situation of a solicitor resembles that of a barrister.

12.68 Barristers are not in contractual relations with their lay clients (nor, it may be added, with the solicitors who instruct them). The consequence of this was that in *Rondel v. Worsley*[274] the House of Lords held that a barrister could not be liable to a lay client for alleged negligence in the manner in which he handled the client's case in court. There was another reason for this denial of a duty of care. Barristers, as advocates, owe a duty to the court which is more important than any duty owed to the client. In this respect, therefore, public policy overcame any possibility of deducing from *Donoghue v. Stevenson* a duty of care towards a client. But in *Saif Ali v. Sydney Mitchell & Co.*[275] the House of Lords held that no such immunity from suit based on public policy grounds would apply where the alleged negligence took place in relation to non-contentious work unconnected with the administration of justice by the courts.

12.69 In the more recent case of *Somasundaram v. M. Julius Melchior & Co.*[276] the plaintiff sued his solicitors for alleged negligence in the way they conducted his defence on a criminal charge. They had arranged a conference with counsel who advised the plaintiff, on the basis of his revised story about what occurred, that he had no defence and should plead guilty, when he had previously instructed his solicitors to plead not guilty. The plaintiff's action was struck out on the ground that it involved an attack on the conviction by the Crown Court which had been upheld by the Court of Apeal. This was an abuse of process. In the course of the judgment it was stated that the immunity from suit which applied to barristers engaged in the conduct of litigation also applied to solicitors when acting as advocates, as long as what was involved was intimately connected with the conduct of a case in court. But that immunity did not apply when the solicitor had engaged a barrister to advise, unless the barrister had subsequently confirmed the solicitor's advice on a plea or the plea had resulted in a decision of the court.[277] Thus solicitors and barristers appear to be regarded in the same light when both are acting as advocates: they share an immunity. When they are acting in matters that do not involve the conduct of a case in court, they may equally be liable in negligence in appropriate circumstances. May L.J. explained in the *Somasundaram* case[278] that the courts were not willing to extend the

274 [1969] 1 A.C. 191.
275 [1980] A.C. 198.
276 [1989] 1 All E.R. 129.
277 *Ibid.* at 136–137.
278 *Ibid.* at 136.

immunity that protects barristers and advocates any further than is necessary in the interests of justice and public policy.

(d) Duty of care and contract

12.70 A duty to take reasonable care may arise under the express or implied terms of a contract between the parties. That was the situation prior to *Donoghue v. Stevenson*; it remains the situation today. The question that has engaged the attention of courts in England and elsewhere has been whether, in the event of negligence by the party contractually bound to exhibit reasonable care, the injured party is obliged to sue in contract or can bring an action in tort, for negligence, against the party guilty of the breach. It now appears that the plaintiff is free to choose which cause of action to pursue.[279] Which he will decide to bring may depend on the existence and nature of any exemption or exclusion clause in the contract; the issue of remoteness of damage; and the question whether the relevant statutory limitation period has expired.[280] However "it has never been the law that a plaintiff who has the choice of suing in contract or tort can fail in contract yet nevertheless succeed in tort".[281]

12.71 If that ever was the law it ceased to be since *Tai Hing Cotton Mill Ltd v. Liu Chong Hing Bank*.[282] In that case the Privy Council refused to imply a term into the contract between a bank and its customer that would result in a tortious duty of care arising when under the contract no such duty existed. Only if a term to such effect could be implied under the contractual doctrines applicable to the implication of term in a contract could a tortious duty arise. The parties' mutual obligations in tort could not be greater than those to be found expressly or by necessary implication in their contract. Similarly in *National Bank of Greece SA v. Pinios Shipping Co. (No. 1)*[283] no term could be implied into a contract between banker and customer to the effect that the bank was under a duty of care to see that the managing agent of a vessel did not under-insure a vessel being purchased by the shipowners under financial arrangements involving the bank as guarantors of promissory notes. The vessel was lost and the insurance proceeds failed to discharge the shipowners' indebtedness under the mortgage given the bank in return for the guarantee. When the bank sued the shipowners, the bank's claim could not be defeated by the plea

279 In a large class of cases he always was, e.g., actions against innkeepers and those exercising a common calling: *Brown v. Boorman* (1842) 3 Q.B. 511 at 525–526 *per* Tindal C.J., (1844) 11 Cl. & Fin. 1 at 44 *per* Lord Campbell; cp. *Esso Petroleum Co. Ltd v. Mardon* [1976] 2 All E.R. 5 at 15 *per* Lord Denning, M.R. See also *Banque Financière de la Cité SA v. Westgate Insurance Co. Ltd* [1989] 3 All E.R. 228; cp. *Bank of Nova Scotia v. Hellenic Mutual War Risks Association (Bermuda) Ltd* [1989] 3 All E.R. 628 at 670 *per* May L.J.

280 See further below pp. 416–18, 429–32.

281 *National Bank of Greece SA v. Pinios Shipping Co. (No. 1)* [1989] 1 All E.R. 213 at 223 *per* Lloyd L.J.

282 [1986] A.C. 80 (applied in *Bank of Nova Scotia*, note 279 *supra*): cp. the Canadian case of *Canadian Pacific Hotels Ltd v. Bank of Montreal* (1988) 40 D.L.R. (4th) 385, especially at 419–428, 432 *per* Le Dain J.

283 *Supra* note 281 (also applied in *Bank of Nova Scotia*).

that the bank had breached a duty of care which disentitled them to sue. The bank was under neither a contractual nor a tortious duty; therefore the shipowners could not appeal against the judgment which awarded the bank the amount still owing under the mortgage. Lloyd L.J. pointed out that the situation was different in a case where the contract and tort lay in different fields, e.g., where an employer gave his employee a lift home and injured him by careless driving. The contract of employment would not prevent the employee from successfully suing in negligence.[284]

12.72 However the existence of a contract between the parties may affect the issue whether a tortious duty of care under the law of negligence governed their relationship. In the first place, the contract may indicate that the parties' relationship was totally regulated by its terms. There would then be no scope for the addition of duties or liabilities.[285] Secondly, an express or implied term may operate to entitle the defendant to rely on the plaintiff's consent to the risk of being injured: this might entail a conclusion that, in the circumstances, the defendant owed no duty of care to the plaintiff.[286]

3. BREACH OF DUTY OF CARE

(a) Standard of care

12.73 Liability for negligence can only arise if the person subject to a duty of care has failed to observe the standard of care that is required by that duty. Generally speaking the applicable standard is that of the reasonable ordinary man or woman.[287] Negligence in law, said McNair J. in a judgment[288] that was later approved by the House of Lords,[289] means some failure to do some act which a reasonable man in the circumstances would do, or doing some act which a reasonable man in the circumstances would not do. The test of whether this act or failure is negligent is whether it would be adjudged so by the "man in the street". He is the ordinary man.

12.74 What ought to be done or not done by the ordinary man or woman will depend on various factors. The issue of risk is one of these. The standard to be adopted and maintained in any given set of circumstances will vary according to the degree of risk entailed in the operation that the

284 *Ibid.* at 223–224.
285 *Greater Nottingham Co-operative Society Ltd v. Cementation Piling & Foundations Ltd* [1988] 2 All E.R. 971 at 984 *per* Purchas L.J., 990–991 *per* Mann L.J. Contrast the situation in *Banque Keyser SA v. Skandia (U.K.) Insurance Co. Ltd* [1987] 2 W.L.R. 1300, where the contract did not preclude a common law duty of care to prevent damage from someone's dishonesty, with *Banque Financière de la Cité*, note 279 *supra*, where it was held that no duty was owed.
286 Below pp. 348–56.
287 *Vaughan v. Menlove* (1837) 3 Bing. N.C. 468; *Blyth v. Birmingham Waterworks Co.* (1856) 11 Ex. 781 at 784 *per* Alderson B.
288 *Bolam v. Friern Hospital Management Committee* [1957] 2 All E.R. 118 at 121.
289 In *Whitehouse v. Jordan* [1981] 1 All E.R. 267.

defendant is performing or undertaking. The greater the risk, the higher the standard of care required of the defendant. Reference to this has previously been made in relation to the question of foreseeability as it affects the existence of a duty of care.[290] Risk is also a material element in determining the care that must be taken. In this connection, as explained earlier, such matters as the seriousness of the injury or damage that might ensue if sufficient care is not taken,[291] and the likelihood of such injury or damage occurring,[292] are important. A risk of injury and a greater risk of injury are both material in assessing the standard of care in a particular situation. Foresight is therefore extemely relevant, as it is in connection with the imposition of a duty, and as it is in relation to the issue of remoteness of damage.[293] A person under a duty of care is not expected to foresee and therefore to guard against what is not a probable consequence of his act or failure to act. However this does not mean that he or she must foresee the particular consequence[294] or the particular way in which it happened,[295] any more than, save in special situations,[296] he or she is obliged to foresee the particular person, as opposed to the class of persons, who will be injured.[297] The subject of a duty of care will be expected to foresee the general type of injury or damage that will be a likely consequence of a failure to observe reasonable care.[298]

12.75 In assessing what ought to be done, or not done, in the light of the risk involved, it is pertinent to take into account, as explained previously,[299] the value to the general public of what the defendant is doing, i.e. what is the object to be achieved by his conduct.[300] It is also relevant to bring into the equation the relative cost and difficulty entailed in preventing harm. It is not expected of the reasonable person that excessive expense will be undertaken to prevent the occurrence of harm that is minimal. The question is whether the risk of injury, as well as the seriousness of the injury that might be expected to follow from negligent behaviour, outweighs the financial and administrative burdens that would have to be undertaken by the defendant in order to forestall the occurrence of that injury.[301] Nor is someone under a duty of care expected to guard against that which is inevitable, in the sense of being an occurrence

290 Above paras 12.15 *et seq.*
291 *Paris v. Stepney Borough Council* [1951] A.C. 367; above at para. 12.19.
292 *Bolton v. Stone* [1951] A.C. 850: above at para. 12.15.
293 Above at para. 12.11: below at para. 12.11b.
294 *Draper v. Hodder* [1972] 2 Q.B. 556.
295 *Hughes v. Lord Advocate* [1963] A.C. 837: below at para 12.118: cp. *Bradford v. Robinson Rentals Ltd* [1967] 1 All E.R. 267; contrast *Doughty v. Turner Manufacturing Co.* [1964] 1 Q.B. 518; *Tremain v. Pike* [1969] 3 All E.R. 1303: Fridman & Williams, "The Atomic Theory of Negligence" (1971) 45 Aust. L.J. 117.
296 E.g., where negligent misrepresentation is involved: above at para. 12.35; or nervous shock, above at para. 12.24.
297 *Grant v. Australian Knitting Mills Ltd* [1936] A.C. 85; *Haley v. London Electricity Board* [1965] A.C. 778.
298 *The Wagon Mound (No. 2)* [1967] 1 A.C. 617; below at para 12.117.
299 Above pp. 279–80.
300 E.g., saving life: *Watt v. Hertfordshire County Council* [1954] 2 All E.R. 368.
301 E.g., *Latimer v. A.E.C.* [1953] A.C. 643, risk of injury from slippery floor balanced against cost of closing the factory to prevent such injury.

that no reasonable man could expect to happen and against which no reasonable man could do anything reasonable to guard.[302] Certain things happen without anyone's fault and in circumstances that no reasonable person could be expected to foresee or in relation to which no reasonable person could be expected to take precautions.[303] The law distinguishes negligence from accident.[304] Such occurrences are events which everyone must accept as being part of normal everyday life. Only if a greater risk of harm is created by a failure to observe the appropriate degree of care will the conclusion be made that the one guilty of such failure is guilty of negligence. Thus accidents occur on the highway without a road user having been negligent:[305] and patients die[306] in operations despite the care taken by doctors and others who are engaged on such operations. Everything involves some degree of risk. Negligence consists in adding to that risk.

12.76 In this regard what was an error in judgment on the part of the defendant may or may not amount to negligence.[307] In the context of an action against a hospital registrar for negligence in delivering a child about to be born, *Whitehouse v. Jordan*,[308] the House of Lords indicated that an error of this kind can sometimes not negate a finding of negligence. Whether such an error is or is not negligent depends on the nature of the error. "If it is one that would not have been made by a reasonably competent professional man professing to have the standard and type of skill that the defendant held himself out as having," said Lord Fraser,[309] "then it is negligent. If, on the other hand, it is an error that a man acting with ordinary care might have made, then it is not negligence." In other words, if a defendant seeks to rely on the argument that his act or omission was an error, not the failure to observe the standard of the reasonable person in his situation, that argument will only succeed if, in all the circumstances, what occurred was not something that could have been prevented if the defendant had taken the kind of precautions that would have been taken by a reasonable person.

(b) Objectivity

12.77 The standard of care expected of a defendant is that which would be expected of a reasonable person in his or her situation, with his or her

302 Cp. *Griffiths v. Liverpool Corporation* [1967] 1 Q.B. 374 at 391 *per* Diplock L.J.
303 See further below paras 13.02ff, on the defence of "inevitable accident".
304 "Misadventure is not negligence": *Sigerseth v. Pedersen* [1927] S.C.R. 342 at 347 *per* Mignault J.
305 Cp. *Holmes v. Mather* (1875) L.R. 10 Ex. 261; *Gaylor & Pope v. Davies & Son* [1924] 2 K.B. 75.
306 Or suffer some injury: *Whitehouse v. Jordan* [1981] 1 All E.R. 267: cp. *Roe v. Minister of Health* [1954] 2 Q.B. 66 on the importance of the state of medical knowledge at the time harm was caused to the plaintiff.
307 Cp. two Canadian cases: *Armand v. Carr* [1926] S.C.R. 575, involving a collision between two vehicles, and *Migliore v. Gerard* (1987) 42 D.L.R. (4d) 619, involving the non-use of a safety-belt by children in a car driven by their parents. In the latter case emphasis was placed on the state of knowledge about the utility of safety-belts at the time of the accident: cp. *Roe v. Minister of Health, supra.*
308 [1981] 1 All E.R. 267.
309 *Ibid.* at 281.

experience and knowledge. The test is not variable in accordance with the particular knowledge or experience of the individual defendant whose conduct is in question.[310] It is not open to a defendant to argue that he did as well as he could, even if he acted *bona fide* and to the best of his judgment.[311] The personal equation is eliminated by the application of the standard of the reasonable man. Similarly whether that standard has been observed is not dependent on the idiosyncrasies of the defendant.[312] Someone who is more usually careless or neglectful or forgetful than the average will not be able to excuse himself on that ground.[313]

12.78 Though it is accepted that the standard will vary according to the nature of the risk involved,[314] so that one who is handling dynamite may be obliged to exercise more care than one who is dealing with butter,[315] this does not mean that the law recognises differing standards of care.[316] However someone who purports to exercise some special skill, e.g., a doctor, lawyer or other professional, must exhibit the standard of care to be expected of the reasonable person in such a profession. This may entail a higher degree of care than would be demanded of someone not exercising such a calling.[317] But that standard will depend on the operative standards and knowledge of the time at which the defendant acted. It is not possible to determine what should or should not have been done in the light of subsequent knowledge that establishes that what was done or

310 But special factors may change this, e.g. where the passenger in a vehicle was aware of the incompetence of the driver who was careless beyond the standard to be expected of one who was inexperienced: *Cook v. Cook* (1986) A.L.R. 353, an Australian case.

311 *Vaughan v. Menlove* (1837) 3 Bing. N.C. 468.

312 *Glasgow Corporation v. Muir* [1943] A.C. 448 at 457 *per* Lord Macmillan.

313 Conversely, someone who is above average in regard to the care he takes will not have to observe that standard, but only the standard of the reasonable man. English law, unlike Roman law, does not differentiate between different standards or degrees of care depending on the type of situation involved: *Houghland v. R.R. Low (Luxury Coaches) Ltd* [1962] 1 Q.B. 694; and contrast *Coggs v. Barnard* (1704) 2 Ld. Raym. 909. In Canada in certain instances a defendant will only be liable for "gross" negligence, requiring failure to observe a lower degree of care than that of the reasonable man: see Fridman, *Law of Torts in Canada*, Vol. 1, at 302–306. Such instances have been reduced in number by reason of the repeal of so-called "guest-passenger" legislative provisions, which negated liability to those being carried gratuitously in a vehicle unless the driver was guilty of gross negligence.

314 *Read v. J. Lyons & Co. Ltd* [1947] A.C. 156 at 173 *per* Lord Macmillan; *Goldman v. Hargrave* [1967] 1 A.C. 645 at 663 *per* Lord Wilberforce.

315 *Beckett v. Newalls Insulation Co.* [1953] 1 All E.R. 250 at 255 *per* Singleton L.J.

316 Cp. *Marshall v. Osmond* [1982] 2 All E.R. 610, above at para. 12.65; *I.R.C. v. Hoogstraten* [1985] Q.B. 1007.

317 *Bolam v. Friern Hospital Management Committee* [1957] 2 All E.R. 118 at 121–122 *per* McNair J.; cp. *Ashcroft v. Mersey Regional Health Authority* [1983] 2 All E.R. 245; *Hills v. Potter* [1983] 3 All E.R. 716; *Gold v. Haringey Health Authority* [1987] 2 All E.R. 888 (all of which concerned the liability of doctors): *Saif Ali v. Sydney Mitchell & Co.* [1980] A.C. 198, lawyers; *Mutual Life Assurance Co. Ltd v. Evatt* [1971] A.C. 793, accountants. Note that in Canada it has been held that a specialist may have to exercise a degree of skill above that of a general practitioner: *Wilson v. Swanson* [1956] S.C.R. 804; cp. *Duchess of Argyll v. Beuselinck* [1972] 2 Lloyd's Rep. 172, solicitors. But a novice or intern is not entitled to assert that a lesser standard of care is expected of him: *Vancouver General Hospital v. Fraser* [1952] 2 S.C.R. 36. A schoolmaster is expected to show his pupils the degree of care to be expected of a careful parent: *Rich v. L.C.C.* [1953] 2 All E.R. 376. But this is very dependent on the circumstances: cp. *Fryer v. Salford Corporation* [1937] 1 All E.R. 617 with *Camkin v. Bishop* [1941] 2 All E.R. 713.

omitted was careless. Hindsight is not a determinant of negligence. Only the foresight of the reasonable person in the shoes of the defendant may be used as the measure of the applicable standard.[318] One who purports to act in a certain capacity in some situations, even though he is not qualified to act in such a manner, may be expected to show the same degree of care as a person who normally holds himself out professionally as possessing the requisite skill.[319] For example, a person learning to drive must exhibit the same degree of care as any other driver.[320] Indeed, unless an emergency is involved, to undertake some activity for which a person is not qualified or specially trained, or for which he or she does not possess the necessary skill, may be negligence in itself, just as to drive a vehicle knowing that one is subject to epileptic fits may amount to negligence, even though the driver who causes an accident because of such a fit will not be held negligent if he or she was unaware of any susceptibility to such illness.[321]

12.79 However one class of persons may be tested according to a different standard of care than that which normally is applicable: children. There is no doubt that a child may be guilty of negligence, even one of 12 or 14[322] or a lower age,[323] in the same way as a child can be guilty of contributory negligence where this is relevant to liability.[324] At the same time the law appears to be willing to regard children, those under the age of legal minority but not yet sufficiently close to adulthood to qualify as fully capable of understanding the consequences of their acts, differently from both adults and minors who are mature enough to be treated for these purposes as if they were adults. The standard for such children is the degree of care to be expected of the child having regard to his or her youth and general intelligence.[325] What may be want of care in an adult or near-adult may not be considered so in the case of a child having regard to the

318 *Roe v. Minister of Health* [1954] 2 Q.B. 66.
319 *The Lady Gwendolen* [1965] P. 294.
320 *Nettleship v. Weston* [1971] 2 Q.B. 691 (on which see *Cook v. Cook* (1986) 68 A.L.R. 353, where the High Court of Australia admitted that special facts or knowledge might make a difference); cp. *Roberts v. Ramsbottom* [1980] 1 All E.R. 7, on the care expected of someone old and infirm but not unconscious. Contrast *Wells v. Cooper* [1958] 2 Q.B. 265, householder doing work on his own home not required to possess skill of professional carpenter; *Phillips v. William Whiteley Ltd* [1938] 1 All E.R. 566, jeweller piercing ears not expected to take precautions expected of a surgeon. But the situation may be different if an emergency is involved, e.g. non-medical person giving first-aid after a road accident.
321 Contrast *Boomer v. Penn* [1966] 1 O.R. 119, diabetic who lacked a supply of sugar was negligent because he did not prevent an insulin reaction, with *Slattery v. Haley* [1923] 3 D.L.R. 156 and *Gootson v. The King* [1948] 4 D.L.R. 33 and *Dessaint v. Carriere* [1958] O.W.N. 481.
322 *School Division of Assiniboine South No. 3 v. Hoffer* (1971) 16 D.L.R. (3d) 703, affirmed [1971] 4 W.W.R. 746, affirmed [1973] 6 W.W.R. 765.
323 Cp. Canadian cases on contributory negligence by children of tender years: *Larlee v. Cyr* (1970) 2 N.B.R. (2d) 50; *Trapp v. Hnatuk* (1976) 71 D.L.R. (3d) 63; *Young v. Sanford* (1983) 61 N.S.R. (2d) 16: with which contrast *Levesque v. St. Laurent* (1981) 35 N.B.R. (2d) 315; *Buck v. Conway* (1973) 9 N.B.R. (2d) 124.
324 Below para 13.30.
325 *Gough v. Thorne* [1966] 3 All E.R. 398; *Yorkton Agricultural & Industrial Exhibition Association v. Morley* (1967) 58 D.L.R. (2d) 282; *Walmsley v. Humenick* [1954] 2 D.L.R. 232.

child's capacity to understand and appreciate the nature of the activity in question.[326]

(c) Customary or general practices

12.80 In *Bolam v. Friern Hospital Management Committee*[327] McNair J. stated that a doctor would not be guilty of negligence if he acted in accordance with a practice accepted as proper by a reputable body of medical men skilled in that particular art, even if there was a body of opinion that took a contrary view. In this he was echoing the words of Lord Alness in *Vancouver General Hospital v. McDaniel*[328] who said that a defendant who shows that he has acted in accordance with general and approved practice can clear himself of negligence. But it does not follow that failure to conform to such a practice raises an inference of negligence.[329] Nor does it follow that pursuance of such a practice will negate negligence. If the practice itself involves a neglect of duty it will not cease to be a neglect of duty because it is repeated by other practitioners or the profession or business in question.[330] However the fact that something is normally done by those engaged in the same, or a similar undertaking may go to show that what was done was what ought to have been done by a reasonable person.[331] Under the Congenital Disabilities (Civil Liability) Act 1976,[332] indeed, a defendant will be held not liable if he took reasonable care having due regard to then received professional opinion. Although this refers particularly to the situation of medical practitioners, it appears to confirm and apply the common law approach with respect to what is customary, general or approved practice. However one who seeks to rely on this as a negation of negligence must show that he has kept up-to-date with the latest developments in the business or profession in question.[333]

326 Is the test subjective or objective? Or is it a combination of both? Cp. *Gough v. Thorne, supra*; *McHale v. Watson* (1966) 38 A.L.J.R. 267, an Australian case; *McEllistrum v. Etches* [1956] S.C.R. 787 and *Wade v. C.N.R.* [1978] 1 S.C.R. 1064 with *Heisler v. Moke* (1972) 25 D.L.R. (3d) 670. See *Stehlke v. Camenzind* [1980] 4 W.W.R. 464, where the test of the standard of a child of like age and intelligence (the objective test) and that of the capacities of the particular child (the subjective test) were both applied to negate negligence.

327 [1957] 2 All E.R. 118 at 122; applied in *Gold v. Haringey Health Authority* [1987] 2 All E.R. 888 and in *Maynard v. West Midlands Regional Health Authority* [1985] 1 All E.R. 635: and to the issue of advice as contrasted with diagnosis and treatment in *Sidaway v. Bethlem Royal Hospital Governors* [1985] A.C. 871, rejecting the American and Canadian doctrine of "informed consent": below pp. 353–4.

328 (1934) 152 L.T. 56 at 57.

329 *Brown v. Rolls Royce Ltd* [1960] 1 All E.R. 577. But see *Holmes v. Board of Hospital Trustees of City of London* (1977) 5 C.C.L.T. 1.

330 *Bank of Montreal v. Dominion Guarantee Co. Ltd* [1930] A.C. 659 at 666 *per* Lord Tomlin; *Carpenters Co. v. British Mutual Banking Co.* [1937] 3 All E.R. 811 at 820. See e.g., *Lloyds Bank v. Savory* [1933] A.C. 201; *Paris v. Stepney Borough Council* [1951] A.C. 367; *Cavanagh v. Ulster Weaving Co. Ltd* [1960] A.C. 145.

331 E.g., *Vancouver General Hospital v. McDaniel, supra*; *Whiteford v. Hunter* [1950] W.N. 553; *Wright v. Cheshire County Council* [1952] 2 All E.R. 789; *General Cleaning Contractors v. Christmas* [1953] A.C. 180. The decision whether or not adherence to such practice is negligence is a matter for the court, not expert witnesses, although the latter may be called to provide evidence about the practice.

332 S. 1(5); above at para. 2.25.

333 *Thompson v. Smiths Shiprepairers Ltd* [1984] Q.B. 405.

Thus it would be negligent for a lawyer not to have kept in touch with new judicial or statutory developments that may affect what lawyers do or how they perform their functions. Nor will the defendant be able to rely on such a practice unless it can be shown to exist;[334] or if he has been given precise instructions that contradict such practice;[335] or where the activity in question is reasonably foreseeable to be dangerous so that special precautions should be taken.[336]

12.81 Should the alleged negligence consist of a failure to do something, it has been said that this will not amount to non-observance of an applicable standard of care where there is no proof that a particular precaution is one usually taken by other persons in like circumstances, or was so obviously necessary that it would be folly in anyone to neglect to provide it.[337] By the expression "folly" here is meant that the conduct in question is "imprudent" or "unreasonable".[338]

12.82 Such practice may be relevant to the determination of the standard of care to be observed in a given instance; however it is still necessary for the plaintiff to establish what that standard of care demanded of the defendant. A plaintiff may be able to invoke evidence regarding such practices in support of his argument: but in the final analysis everything depends on what was to be expected by the reasonable man in the defendant's position having regard to the knowledge and appreciation of the risks involved that would be possessed by a reasonable man at the material time.

(d) Proof of breach

12.83 The onus of proof that a breach of duty has taken place is on the plaintiff. What the plaintiff has to do is to adduce sufficient evidence to prove that negligence occurred.[339] The legal burden of proof requires the plaintiff to establish his case on the balance of probabilities.[340] However this legal burden of proof is affected by two matters. First, by the Civil Evidence Act 1968,[341] it is now possible to introduce into a civil trial the fact that the defendant has been convicted of a criminal offence which may be relevant to guilt of negligence, e.g., where the defendant

334 *Lepine v. University Hospital Board* (1965) 50 W.W.R. 709, affirmed (1965) 54 D.L.R. (2d) 340, reversed on other grounds [1966] S.C.R. 565.

335 *James v. River East School Division No. 9* [1976] 2 W.W.R. 557; *Crits v. Sylvester* (1956) 1 D.L.R. (2d) 502, affirmed [1956] S.C.R. 991.

336 *Lloyds Bank Ltd v. Savory & Co.* [1933] A.C. 201 at 235 *per* Lord Wright.

337 *Paris v. Stepney Borough Council* [1951] A.C. 367 at 382 *per* Lord Normand; *Morton v. William Dixon Ltd* 1909 S.C. 807 at 809 *per* Lord Dunedin.

338 *Cavanagh v. Ulster Weaving Co. Ltd* [1960] A.C. 145 at 162.

339 And that the negligence caused his injury or damage: below pp. 327–8.

340 If the plaintiff does not do this, his action will fail: *Brown v. Rolls Royce Ltd* [1960] 1 All E.R. 577. In relation to the possible submission by the defendant of no case to answer, see *Payne v. Harrison* [1961] 2 Q.B. 403; *Young v. Rank* [1950] 2 K.B. 570.

341 S. 11, abolishing the common law rule to the contrary in *Hollington v. F. Hewthorn & Co. Ltd* [1943] K.B. 587.

committed a traffic offence that caused the accident on which the plaintiff's cause of action is based. Once the defendant is proved to have committed such offence, by the fact of conviction, he is presumed to have committed it unless the contrary is proved.[342] This means that in a traffic accident, the defendant convicted of a traffic offence will have to prove that, notwithstanding that conviction, he was not negligent. The legal burden of proof has shifted. Secondly, as will be seen, under the doctrine of *res ipsa loquitur* it may be necessary for the defendant to establish positively that he was not negligent. Normally such an onus is not on the defendant; it is for the plaintiff to prove affirmatively the fact of negligence. In *res ipsa loquitur* cases, however, the opposite may be the case.[343]

12.84 There must be evidence on which the case can go to the jury, where trial by jury still exists in actions for negligence,[344] or on which the judge can find as a fact that the defendant breached his duty of care. Unless the evidence is particularly strong, this is a matter of inference.[345] The court has to determine as a matter of law whether such an inference can be made, and then whether such an inference ought to be made. In the event of an appeal to a higher court it is clear that an appellate tribunal cannot question or disturb a judge or jury's finding of primary facts, e.g., that the defendant was travelling at 45 miles per hour. But an appellate tribunal is entitled to disagree with the lower court's inference from those facts. An appeal court can make its own evaluation of the evidence, in which respect it is as qualified as the trial judge, even though it is not in a position to evaluate the character of the witnesses and the value and credibility of their evidence.[346] However a decision of fact by a lower court, particularly a judge, will only be upset if it is clear that it was incorrect.[347]

12.85 A decision of a trial court on a question of fact must not be allowed to be translated into a proposition of law.[348] Thus there is no firm rule of law that determines what is to be the result where the evidence remains unclear as to which of two parties, viz., plaintiff and defendant, was the negligent one who caused the accident. If neither can be proved to be negligent, then neither should be able to sue the other.[349] However, it has been held in England[350] that in such a case, where an accident occurred on

342 On this see *Wauchop v. Mordecai* [1970] 1 W.L.R. 317; *Stupple v. Royal Insurance Co. Ltd* [1971] 1 Q.B. 50; *Hunter v. Chief Constable of West Midlands* [1981] 3 All E.R. 727 at 735–736 *per* Lord Diplock.
343 Below paras 12.86ff.
344 In personal injuries claims only in exceptional cases; *Ward v. James* [1966] 1 Q.B. 273.
345 Not conjecture: *Jones v. Great Western Railway* (1931) 142 L.T. 194 at 197 *per* Lord Buckmaster, 202 *per* Lord Macmillan.
346 *Benmax v. Austin Motor Co. Ltd* [1955] A.C. 370; *Watt v. Thomas* [1947] A.C. 484.
347 See, e.g., *Whitehouse v. Jordan* [1981] 1 All E.R. 267, where the House of Lords disagreed with the trial judge's finding of negligence by the surgeon.
348 See, e.g., *Worsfold v. Howe* [1980] 1 All E.R. 1028 at 1032 *per* Browne L.J.; *Garston Warehousing Co. Ltd v. O.F. Smart (Liverpool) Ltd* [1973] R.T.R. 377.
349 As in the Canadian cases of *Wotta v. Haliburton Oil Well Cementing Co.* [1955] S.C.R. 377; and *Gordon v. Trottier* [1974] S.C.R. 158.
350 *Baker v. Market Harborough Co-operative Society Ltd* [1953] 1 W.L.R. 1472. Contrast the view in the Australian case of *Nesterczuk v. Mortimore* (1965) 39 A.L.J.R. 288.

the highway, the proper or reasonable inference to be drawn is that both parties were negligent; therefore both should be held equally to blame. But if the only inference is that one or other of the parties was negligent, but it is unclear which, the correct conclusion should be the denial of liability.[351] Similarly, if there are two or more defendants and it is not clear from the evidence which was negligent, and, *a fortiori*, if both were negligent which one's negligence caused the plaintiff's injury, logic would indicate that the plaintiff cannot succeed. However in a Canadian case, *Cook v. Lewis*,[352] the Supreme Court held that in such a situation both of the defendants should be held liable, unless and until one of them disproves either that he was negligent or that his negligence caused the plaintiff's injury. English commentators appear to reject this as part of the common law in England.[353] The only qualification seems to arise in those situations where the plaintiff was injured in consequence of a concerted common design by the various defendants or where the defendants were otherwise joint tortfeasors because one was vicariously liable for the acts of the other.[354]

(e) Res ipsa loquitur

12.86 Despite the general proposition that negligence must be affirmatively proved by the plaintiff, there are situations in which a plaintiff may be relieved of this burden, and may be assisted in establishing the requisite negligence by the doctrine of *res ipsa loquitur*. This emerged as part of the common law in the nineteenth century,[355] perhaps as a corollary of the development of liability for negligence, in order to aid plaintiffs where the circumstances were such that it would be impossible for the plaintiff to obtain access to the information necessary to prove that the defendant was negligent. The maxim may be invoked, although it does not have to be pleaded specifically,[356] where all the facts are not known. If the evidence reveals all the facts, there is no scope for the application of *res ipsa loquitur*. The court must draw its own conclusions.[357] The utility and function of the maxim lie in the ability of a plaintiff to make use of it in order to persuade a court to draw an inference of negligence from the mere fact that the accident which injured or damaged him happened. Only when it is legitimate for that inference to be drawn will the maxim apply. Nor will it apply unless the inference of negligence is the sole inference that may

351 *Ibid.*
352 [1951] S.C.R. 830, on which see Hogan, "*Cook v. Lewis* Re-examined" (1961) 24 M.L.R. 331. See also below p. 329, on the issue of causation.
353 *Salmond & Heuston on the Law of Torts*, 19th ed. 1987 at 267; *Winfield & Jolowicz on Tort*, 12th ed. 1984 at 107.
354 *Cassidy v. Minister of Health* [1951] 2 K.B. 343 at 359; *Roe v. Ministry of Health* [1954] 1 Q.B. 66 at 80, 82, 88 cp. *Grant v. Australian Knitting Mills Ltd* [1936] A.C. 85 at 101.
355 *Christie v. Griggs* (1809) 2 Camp. 791; *Byrne v. Boadle* (1863) 2 H. & C. 722; *Scott v. London & St. Katherine Docks Co.* (1865) 3 H. & C. 596. See also *Ballard v. North British Co.* [1923] S.C. 43.
356 The contrary view has been expressed in Canada; at least where the plaintiff's allegations of negligence have failed: *David Spencer Ltd v. Field* [1939] S.C.R. 36.
357 *Barkway v. South Wales Transport Co.* [1950] 1 All E.R. 392 at 395.

reasonably be drawn. The facts must speak for themselves in a clear and unambiguous fashion.[358]

(i) Application

12.87 In *Scott v. London & St. Katherine Docks Co.*[359] Erle C.J. stated the rule or doctrine that is enshrined in the maxim in these words:

> "... where the thing is shown to be under the management of the defendant or his servants, and the accident is such as in the ordinary course of things does not happen if those who have the management use proper care, it affords reasonable evidence, in the absence of explanation by the defendants, that the accident arose from want of care."

This means that whatever caused the accident to happen must be under the control of the defendant or of someone for whom he is responsible in law; and what happened must be something that ordinarily would not occur unless someone had been negligent. If these conditions are satisfied, the result is that there is "reasonable evidence" of negligence. The cases indicate that *res ipsa loquitur* may be relied on by a plaintiff in an unlimited variety of circumstances where an accident occurs. Although there was at one time a belief that it should not be invoked in cases of alleged medical or dental malpractice, because this might have placed too heavy a burden on the defendant,[360] this is no longer so; and it is clear that the maxim may be applied even if professional negligence is involved.[361]

(ii) Control

12.88 Unless the situation was within the control of the defendant, his agents or servants, the maxim will not apply. If it is possible that some other hand might have been involved in causing the accident of which the plaintiff complains, then it is impossible to point solely to the defendant and say that he, or those for whom he is legally responsible, must have been negligent for what to occur to have happened. However it does seem that the notion of control in this context is very artificial. Actual physical custody or possession may be unnecessary.[362] What is important is whether the thing or situation which resulted in the injury was within the exclusive province of the defendant.[363] For example, in a Canadian case,[364] the issue was whether the defendants who were supposed to service and repair a furnace were in sufficient control for the purposes of the maxim to entitle the plaintiff to say *res ipsa loquitur*. In this regard the passage of time since the article left the physical possession of the defendant may or may not be

358 See the different views as to the application of the maxim in *Ward v. Tesco Stores Ltd* [1976] 1 All E.R. 219.
359 (1865) 3 H. & C. 596 at 601.
360 Or because it was not possible for courts to know what was the ordinary course of things: *Mahon v. Osborne* [1939] 2 K.B. 14.
361 *Cassidy v. Minister of Health* [1951] 2 K.B. 343: cp. *Holt v. Nesbitt* [1951] O.R. 601, affirmed [1953] S.C.R. 143, a Canadian case.
362 *Kirk v. McLaughlin Coal & Supplies Ltd* [1968] 1 O.R. 311 at 312.
363 I.e. the defendant had a right to control: *Parker v. Miller* (1926) 42 T.L.R. 408, so that there was no likelihood of some outside interference; cp. *Gee v. Metropolitan Railways* (1873) L.R. 8 Q.B. 161 with *Easson v. L.N.E. Railway* [1944] 2 K.B. 421; *Lloyd v. West Midlands Gas Board* [1971] 2 All E.R. 1240.
364 *Kirk v. McLaughlin Coal & Supplies Ltd supra.*

material. It depends on the condition the article was in at the time it came into the possession of the plaintiff.[365]

12.89 If there are two possible defendants, either of whom might have been responsible for what happened, the application of the doctrine is more difficult. There is no problem where the two parties are linked by the doctrine of vicarious liability. As long as it can be said that one is the servant or agent of the other, the maxim may be applied against one, which will make the other automatically liable.[366] If the parties are not joint tortfeasors by virtue of the doctrine of vicarious liability, but several tortfeasors, independent of each other, the application of *res ipsa loquitur* is questionable. The authorities are ambivalent. Sometimes it has been said that *res ipsa loquitur* can be invoked against all the potentially liable parties.[367] At others it has been argued that logically the maxim is inappropriate because it depends for its application upon there being only one possible cause of what happened, in other words only one possible defendant.[368] In this regard it would seem to be a matter of decision whether logic or practical necessity should govern. The rationale of the maxim indicates that as long as the plaintiff is at a disadvantage with respect to proof of his claim, since he is *ex hypothesi* ignorant of what occurred and must remain so by the very nature of the circumstances, the onus should be on the potential defendants to refute the allegation of negligence against each and every one of them. The logic of the maxim, on the other hand, suggests that it cannot be invoked where there is some ambiguity about the person whose conduct could have resulted in the plaintiff's injury.

(iii) An ordinary occurrence

12.90 The circumstances must be such that in the common experience of mankind what happened to the plaintiff does not happen unless there has been a lack of care, for example, a barrel falling from an upstairs window onto a passer-by in the street below,[369] a stone in a bun,[370] trains colliding,[371] scaffolding collapsing.[372] In some circumstances that a car

365 *MacLachlan & Mitchell Homes Ltd v. Frank's Rental & Sales Ltd* (1980) 106 D.L.R. (3d) 245.

366 *Walsh v. Holst & Co. Ltd* [1958] 2 All E.R. 33.

367 *Roe v. Ministry of Health* [1954] 2 K.B. 66 at 82 *per* Denning L.J.; *Baker v. Market Harborough Industrial Co-operative Society Ltd* [1953] 1 W.L.R. 1472: cp. *Interlake Tissue Mills Ltd v. Salmon & Beckett* [1948] O.R. 950; *MacLachlan & Mitchell Homes Ltd v. Frank's Rentals & Sales Ltd supra* at 257–258.

368 *Roe v. Minister of Health, supra* at 69–70 *per* McNair J.; cp. *Tataryn v. Co-operative Trust Co. of Canada* (1975) 54 D.L.R. (3d) 154; *Haverkate v. Toronto Harbour Commissioner* (1986) 30 D.L.R. (4th) 125. See e.g., *Wotta v. Haliburton Oil Well Cementing Co. Ltd* [1955] S.C.R. 377; *Gordon v. Trottier* [1974] S.C.R. 158.

369 *Byrne v. Boadle* (1863) 2 H. & C. 722.

370 *Chaproniere v. Mason* (1905) 21 T.L.R. 633.

371 *Skinner v. London, Brighton & South Coast Railway* (1850) 5 Ex. 787. Or an aeroplane crashing immediately after take-off: *Fosbrooke-Hobbes v. Airwork Ltd* [1937] 1 All E.R. 108 (*quaere*: is this necessarily so today when so many such accidents are the result of terrorist activity?); excess of sulphates in plants, *Grant v. Australian Knitting Mills Ltd* [1936] A.C. 85; explosion in hose carrying oxygen, *Colvilles Ltd v. Devine* [1969] 2 All E.R. 53.

372 *Kealey v. Heard* [1983] 1 All E.R. 973.

skidded may be evidence from which negligence can be presumed;[373] but not always.[374] There are events that occur without someone having been negligent, for example, losses in commodity futures trading.[375]

12.91 The suggestion that *res ipsa loquitur* does not apply to cases of medical negligence was also based in part on the notion that judges could not rule that such mischances in the common experience of mankind indicated negligence, because judges did not have the requisite experience.[376] This, too, seems too have been abandoned as a reason for denying the application of the maxim.[377] No matter what type of situation or what kind of accident is involved, the maxim may be invoked where the accident is such that the only reasonable inference to be drawn from the circumstances is that there was probably negligence, or else the accident would not have occurred. This means, therefore, that if there is evidence of some specific cause which could have generated the accident, e.g. the tyre on a car blowing out, the maxim cannot be relied on by the plaintiff.[378] Some initial reasonable explanation must be lacking, leaving the cause of the accident open to reasonable inference.

(iv) Effect of the maxim

12.92 Successful invocation of *res ipsa loquitur* means that there is reasonable evidence of negligence: a *prima facie* case has been made out by the plaintiff. He may not be non-suited: his case must be decided by the jury, if any, or the judge. Hence if the defendant offers no explanation by way of answer or defence, the plaintiff must succeed. The problem is to determine what kind of burden has shifted to the defendant as a result of the application of the maxim. There are two conflicting theories. One is that the legal burden of proof always remains on the plaintiff; therefore, once *res ipsa loquitur*, all the defendant has to do is to provide some explanation that is capable of establishing how the accident might have happened, which has the effect of shifting the provisional or evidentiary burden back to the plaintiff. The other is that a plaintiff sufficiently discharges the legal burden of proof that is initially upon him by establishing a case of *res ipsa loquitur*. This entails that the defendant must do more than put forward a reasonable explanation consistent with his having been negligent or having been careful. The defendant must prove on a balance of probabilities that he was not negligent. Of course if a defendant does affirmatively establish how the accident occurred, and this explanation proves he was not negligent, the plaintiff will fail in any event. Similarly if the defendant affirmatively proves that neither he nor his servants, agents or independent contractors for whom he is vicariously

373 *Richley v. Faull* [1965] 3 All E.R. 109.
374 *Laurie v. Raglan Building Co. Ltd* [1943] 1 K.B. 152 at 154 *per* Lord Greene M.R., suggesting that a skid is "neutral".
375 *Stafford v. Conti Community Services Ltd* [1981] 1 All E.R. 691; or a fire spreading from an ordinary domestic grate: *Sochaki v. Sas* [1947] 1 All E.R. 344.
376 *Mahon v. Osborne* [1939] 2 K.B. 14.
377 *Roe v. Minister of Health* [1954] 2 Q.B. 66.
378 *Barkway v. South Wales Transport Co. Ltd* [1950] 1 All E.R. 352; cp. *Hellenius v. Lees* (1971) 15 D.L.R. (3d) 147, affirmed (1971) 20 D.L.R. (3d) 369, a Canadian case.

liable were negligent, again the plaintiff will fail.[379] This leaves open, however, what is to be the consequence if the defendant can pursue neither of these courses although he can provide an explanation of what might conceivably have happened, without being able to establish positively that his explanation is a probable one capable of tipping the balance in his favour.

12.93 In Canada the cases support the proposition that the defendant need only offer an explanation that is not outlandish or merely scientifically or hypothetically plausible but is at least a valid and reasonable one, even if it is not the actual explanation of what occurred.[380] It must not be an improbable explanation, especially if the defendant has deviated from the approved practice in his profession.[381] In England, however, there are decisions which suggest that once *res ipsa loquitur*, the onus is on the defendant to disprove negligence on his part and on the part of those for whom he is responsible in law.[382] Admittedly, there are also dicta that support the alternative theory, that the legal burden of proof is not affected by the application of the maxim.[383] However, the statements to the opposite effect appear to have greater weight.[384] That some judges should adopt that approach is curious. In the first place, this would raise the status of the maxim to a rule of the law of evidence. It would create a presumption of great consequence and effect. Yet it has been stated judicially that the maxim is neither a rule of substantive law nor a rule of the law of evidence. It is at best or at most an example of the effect of circumstantial evidence. It operates as a guide to courts faced with the task of determining whether or not negligence has occurred in situations where it is difficult to attain the truth.[385] To require the defendant to disprove negligence would make a significant difference. Furthermore, if *res ipsa loquitur* had such effect, this would mean that a plaintiff who relied on the maxim would be in a better position, from the standpoint of proving his case, than one who provided evidence that set up a *prima facie* case of negligence. In the latter instance the defendant would only have to introduce evidence that cast sufficient doubt on the plaintiff's explanation or argument to make the balance of probabilities come down on the side of

379 *Ludgate v. Lovett* [1969] 2 All E.R. 1235; *Woods v. Duncan* [1946] A.C. 401; *Swan v. Salisbury Construction Co. Ltd* [1966] 2 All E.R. 138.

380 *United Motor Services Inc. v. Hutson* [1937] S.C.R. 392; *Phillips v. Ford Motor Co. of Canada Ltd* [1971] 2 O.R. 637; *MacLachlan & Mitchell Homes Ltd v. Frank's Rentals & Sales Ltd* (1980) 106 D.L.R. (3d) 245; *Cudney v. Clement's Motor Sales Ltd* (1969) 5 D.L.R. (3d) 3; *Jackson v. Miller* (1976) 59 D.L.R. (3d) 246; *Westlake v. Smith's Transport Ltd* (1973) 2 O.R. (2d) 258. Cp. *Government Insurance Officer of New South Wales v. Frederickberg* (1968) 118 C.L.R. 403, Australia.

381 *Holmes v. Board of Hospital Trustees of City of London* (1977) 5 C.C.L.T. 1.

382 *Moore v. R. Fox & Sons* [1956] 1 Q.B. 596; *Walsh v. Holst & Co. Ltd* [1958] 2 All E.R. 33; *Henderson v. Henry E. Jenkins & Sons* [1970] A.C. 282; *Swan v. Salisbury Construction Co. Ltd, supra*; cp. *Kealey v. Heard* [1983] 1 All E.R. 973.

383 *Colvilles Ltd v. Devine* [1961] 2 All E.R. 53.

384 But see *Lloyd v. West Midlands Gas Board* [1971] 2 All E.R. 1240 at 1246–1247 *per* Megaw L.J.; *Ng Chun Pui v. Lee Chieu Tat* [1988] R.T.R. 298, a decision of the Privy Council.

385 *Ibid.*

the defendant.[386] In view of the conflict that exists between different dicta, and the absence of any authoritative decision on facts which require determination of the effect of the maxim on the issue of proof, it would appear to be necessary at some time for the House of Lords to state with precision and certainty what is the true nature of the maxim and the real consequence of its application. Although it is legitimate for the common law to differ as between different jurisdictions in which it is applied, and although the greater likelihood of jury trials as contrasted with trial by judge alone in some Commonwealth jurisdictions make the theory that the legal burden does not shift more acceptable, it may be suggested that, in this particular regard, there is less reason for the existence of a significant difference between the common law in England and in other parts of the Commonwealth.

4. DAMAGE

(a) Causation and remoteness

12.94 Because the action for negligence was historically based on the action on the case, it is necessary for the plaintiff to prove that he has suffered damage before he can sue. Damage was the "gist" of the action on the case.[387] It remains an essential ingredient of the action for negligence. It can consist of damage to property, personal injury or economic loss.[388] However the damage must be proved to have been caused by the negligent act or omission of the defendant. Proof of the requisite causal connection involves two distinct elements. The first is that there was a sufficient factual relationship, the second that there was the necessary legal relationship, between the negligence and the damage. These two requirements are sometimes referred to as "cause in fact" and "cause in law".[389] The former is a question of causation in the strict sense. The second is a question of remoteness. In some situations the two become interwoven. The defendant may be held to have caused the plaintiff's injury or loss even though in a physical, direct sense the defendant did not actually cause what happened. This may have been the result of some intervening act or event, such that the defendant's negligent conduct combined with the intervention produced the harm of which the plaintiff complains. In such situations the issue to be determined is whether the defendant can be held as a matter of law to have caused that harm notwithstanding his

386 E.g. by proving that he acted reasonably in an emergency: *Ng Chiu Lui v. Lee Chieu Tat*, *supra*.

387 *Crofter Hand Woven Harris Tweed Co. Ltd v. Veitch* [1942] A.C. 435 at 439 *per* Viscount Simon L.C.

388 Including nervous shock: above paras 12.24ff. On liability for economic loss, see above paras 12.40ff. The calculation of damages for personal injuries, including the death of the victim, is discussed below in Chapter 15.

389 E.g., by Wright J. in the Canadian case of *Lomax v. Arsenault* [1986] 1 W.W.R. 68 at 74–75.

apparent isolation from the ultimate event.[390] In other instances the issue of causation does not involve any element of remoteness. Instead it falls to be determined solely on whether the plaintiff can prove on the balance of probabilities that the defendant's act was what caused his harm or loss. In the absence of such proof the plaintiff cannot succeed in his action despite his suffering harm. The onus is on the plaintiff to establish the necessary causal connection.[391]

12.95 In relation to both causation and remoteness it should be noted that the conduct of the plaintiff himself, as contrasted with that of a third party, may also be relevant. Where the plaintiff has also acted in such a way as to help in the occurrence of his harm, his conduct may be treated as contributory negligence, the effect of which will be considered in a later chapter:[392] or it may be relevant to determination of the issue whether the ultimate injury or harm suffered by the plaintiff was too remote a consequence of the defendant's original negligent conduct.[393]

12.96 Cause in fact is sometimes said to be determined by the application of the "but-for" test.[394] The distinction is drawn between a *causa causans* and a *causa sine qua non*.[395] The former is the effective, proximate cause of what happened. The latter is merely something that forms part of the general historical or physical background against which some other act or event operated so as to bring about the harm or injury that is in question. There may have been some default on the part of the defendant, but the plaintiff will not succeed in his action unless he can make out a sufficient causal connection, on the "but-for" test, between that default and his injury. Thus when the defendant has been negligent, if the plaintiff would have suffered the injury in question, for example he would have died, even if proper care had been taken, that injury cannot be attributed to the negligence of the defendant.[396] In other words if what happened would have happened whatever amount of care had been exercised or observed by the defendant in accordance with his common law or statutory duties,

390 See e.g., *Knightley v. Johns* [1982] 1 All E.R. 851, where, in the result, the injury to the plaintiff was held not to have been caused by one defendant's negligence because of the intervening act of another defendant: below at p. 342.

391 *Bonnington Castings Ltd v. Wardlaw* [1956] A.C. 613; *McWilliams v. Sir William Arrol & Co. Ltd* [1962] 1 All E.R. 623. See however *Nicholson v. Atlas Steel Foundry & Engineering Co. Ltd* [1957] 1 All E.R. 776; *McGhee v. National Coal Boad* [1972] 3 All E.R. 1008; below paras 12.103–09.

392 Below paras 13.23ff.

393 Below paras 12.110ff.

394 *Cork v. Kirkby Maclean Ltd* [1952] 2 All E.R. 402 at 406–407 *per* Denning L.J.; cp. *Madalena v. Kuhn* (1987) 35 D.L.R. (4d) 222, a Canadian case; see Strachan, "The Scope and Application of the 'But For' Test" (1970) 33 M.L.R. 386. Hence in *Meah v. McCreamer* [1985] 1 All E.R. 367 the negligent defendant was liable for the subsequent imprisonment of the injured plaintiff for sexual attacks on women. The accident changed the plaintiff's personality: "but for" that change, the plaintiff would not have been changed into an individual who would commit those offences: *ibid.* at 382 *per* Woolf J.

395 *Weld-Blundell v. Stephens* [1920] A.C. 956 at 984 *per* Lord Sumner. But other expressions have also been used: as have other tests: see Williams, "Causation in the Law" [1961] C.L.J. 62; Weinrib, "A Step Forward in Factual Causation" (1975) 38 M.L.R. 518.

396 *Barnett v. Chelsea & Kensington Hospital Management Committee* [1969] 1 Q.B. 428.

there will be no action for negligence.[397] An essential ingredient of such liability will be missing: viz., proof that the defendant's breach of duty caused the plaintiff's damage.

(b) Proof of causation

12.97 Three major problems have emerged in this connection. The first is the difficulty of establishing that the defendant's negligence caused the plaintiff's injury where there are two or more persons whose negligence might have been the cause. Secondly, there is the question of affixing responsibility in a causal sense on the defendant when there have been successive incidents resulting in the plaintiff's suffering greater harm than he would have incurred had only the one defendant been involved. The third is the problem of proving that some act or omission of the defendant is what caused the plaintiff's injury when the plaintiff has undoubtedly suffered the injury but it is difficult for the plaintiff to prove that the cause of the injury was attributable to the fault of the defendant.

(i) Several defendants

12.98 In connection with *res ipsa loquitur* it has previously been noted that where two or more persons have committed acts that can be considered negligent it may be impossible to determine with accuracy which party's negligence was the cause of the plaintiff's injury. This will not matter where the several potentially culpable parties are connected by virtue of the doctrine of vicarious liability. If they are independent, however, the issue of causation becomes more awkward. In *Cook v. Lewis*[398] the Supreme Court of Canada was faced with such a situation. Two hunters both fired at the same time. The plaintiff was hit by a shot, but it was not clear whose shot struck him. Rather than hold that the plaintiff could not succeed in his action for negligence because he could not identify which of the two was the one responsible for his injury, the court held that once he established that both were negligent the onus shifted to each of them to disprove that his particular act did not provide the cause. The rationale of this decision is not easy to explain. Given the insistence of the law upon the need for the plaintiff to prove that the defendant's negligence caused the plaintiff's harm, it seems strange that the court should hold that even in such eccentric circumstances the onus should move from the plaintiff to the defendants. The explanation proffered by one member of the Court was that it was the defendants' own misconduct that deprived the plaintiff of the opportunity to establish the necessary causal connection.[399] English dicta suggest that the underlying judicial philosophy of this decision does not form part of the common law in England.[400] What was held in *Cook v.*

397 *The Empire Jamaica* [1957] A.C. 386.
398 [1951] S.C.R. 830.
399 *Ibid.* at 833 *per* Rand J.; cp. Bayda J.A. in *Nowsco Well Services Ltd v. Canadian Propane Gas & Oil Ltd* (1981) 122 D.L.R. (3d) 228 at 247. The *Cook* case has been followed and distinguished in Canada: Fridman, *Law of Torts in Canada*, Vol. 1, at 341–342.
400 *Baker v. Market Harborough Industrial Co-operative Society Ltd* [1953] 1 W.L.R. 1472. But see *Hummerstone v. Leary* [1921] 2 K.B. 664.

Lewis might have been supported by the attitude adopted by the House of Lords in *McGhee v. National Coal Board*[401] with respect to the situation of a plaintiff who was in difficulties in respect of proving causation even where there was only one defendant. That case, as will be seen, may not have been as revolutionary as originally considered.[402] If that is so, then the approach adopted by the Canadian court may not be one that is acceptable in England.

(ii) Successive accidents

12.99 In contrast with the kind of situation that arose in *Cook v. Lewis*, where only one tort is committed, a plaintiff may be injured by one defendant and then, subsequently, injured by another. In cases involving successive accidents the plaintiff is the victim of two distinct torts. Had the plaintiff not been injured by one defendant in the first place, he would not have been in a situation or position to be further injured, or to have had his injuries exacerbated by the later act of the second defendant. That does not mean that the first defendant should be liable for all that ultimately occurred, nor that the later defendant should be liable for the prior injury or the increase of its harm, as well for what he himself actually caused. In this regard two decisions of the House of Lords provide discordant views.

12.100 In *Baker v. Willoughby*[403] the plaintiff was injured by the negligent driving of the defendant. This left him with an injured left leg and ankle. Three years later, while engaged in his employment, the plaintiff was the victim of a robbery in which he was shot. This inflicted further injuries to his leg, in consequence of which it was amputated. His disability was greater after the second injury, as a result of which he was fitted with an artificial limb. At trial it was held that the damages payable by the defendant in respect of the injury inflicted by him were not to be decreased by the fact of the second injury. The Court of Appeal held that those damages should be limited to whatever were the relevant damages for the period between the two injuries. This decision was reversed by the House of Lords, which held that the second injury was irrelevant to the assessment of the damages suffered by the plaintiff by reason of the first injury. Damages were not compensation for physical injury but for the loss suffered by reason of that injury. This meant inability to lead a full life, inability to earn as much as he used to earn. Those losses were not diminished by the second injury, but would continue as long as they would have done if the second injury had not occurred. Lord Reid referred to the law's recognition of two or more causes for the same injury: and held that

401 [1972] 3 All E.R. 1008.
402 Below paras 12.103ff.
403 [1969] 3 All E.R. 1528; which seems to contradict, or at least to be distinguishable from, *Performance Cars Ltd v. Abraham* [1962] 1 Q.B. 33, where the second defendant was not liable because the car was already damaged in a way that necessitated the same repairs as would have been required by the damage inflicted by the second defendants. This might be regarded as an instance of the application of the *talem qualem* rule: below para 12.113.

the later injuries were merely a concurrent cause of the disabilities caused by the injury inflicted by the defendant.[404] In the words of Lord Pearson,[405]

> "The supervening event has not made the apellant [i.e. the plaintiff] less lame nor less disabled nor less deprived of amenities. It has not shortened the period over which he will be suffering. It has made him more lame, more disabled, more deprived of amenities."

Hence he should not have had less damages through being worse off than might have been expected.

12.101 This decision was not followed in *Jobling v. Associated Dairies Ltd.*[406] Because of the employers' breach of statutory duty the plaintiff suffered a back injury and was thereafter only able to do light work. Before the trial of his action came on it was learned that the plaintiff was suffering from a spinal disease which was unrelated to the accident but made him wholly unfit for work. The House of Lords, affirming the decision of the Court of Appeal, which had reversed the trial judge, held that in assessing the damages to be paid to the plaintiff by his employers the supervening illness that was known about at the time of the trial, even though it was latent at the time of the earlier injury, was something that ought to be taken into account, as a known vicissitude of life.[407] There was no need to speculate about it, since it was known about at the trial. Therefore the employers were not liable for loss of earnings suffered by the plaintiff after the onset of the disease, which occurred about three years after the accident on which the plaintiff's action was based. The effect of the speeches in this case, in which *Baker v. Willoughby* was subjected to considerable criticism and doubt, is that the theory of concurrent causes espoused in the earlier case is not applicable where the second "cause" is what the House of Lords termed in the *Jobling* case a "vicissitude" of life. It is not clear from the various speeches in the *Jobling* case, however, whether the same would be true where the second injury was a successive tortious act by a third party. To some members of the House there was a distinction between a subsequent tortious injury and the illness in the *Jobling* case, which was a "vicissitude of life" that could be taken into account when assessing damages;[408] to others it was not in any way distinguishable from a subsequent tortious act which inflicted a new injury or increased the original one.[409] What appears to have concerned the House of Lords in the later case was the problem of steering a course between over-compensation of the victim and preventing the creation of a situation in which the plaintiff was deprived of compensation to which he was justly entitled. As Lord Wilberforce pointed out, there was a danger of producing either logical inconsistency or over- or under-compensation.[410] To Lord Wilberforece, therefore, it was impossible to state general, logical

404 [1969] 3 All E.R. 1528 at 1532.
405 *Ibid.* at 1535.
406 [1981] 2 All E.R. 752.
407 *Ibid.* at 754–755 *per* Lord Wilberforce.
408 *Ibid.* at 760 *per* Lord Russell, 763–764 *per* Lord Keith.
409 *Ibid.* at 767–768 *per* Lord Bridge.
410 *Ibid.* at 755.

or universally fair rules to cover, in a manner consistent with justice, cases of supervening events whether due to tortious, partially tortious, non-culpable or wholly accidental events.[411] The courts could only deal with each case as best they could in a manner so as to provide just and sufficient, but not excessive compensation, taking all factors into account.

12.102 Thus in cases involving multiple causes of this kind there appears to be no sure and clear guidance as to the proper way for a court to determine how the injuries of which the plaintiff complains, or the damge he has suffered, is to be attributed to a particular defendant. In such circumstances, the "but-for" test may be be appropriate or decisive.

(iii) The McGhee case and its aftermath

12.103 The onus of proving causation of the plaintiff's injury by the defendant's negligence is on the plaintiff. That onus was interpreted in a special way, where the plaintiff incurred an industrial disease, in *Bonnington Castings Ltd v. Wardlaw*.[412] The effect of that case, in which the plaintiff contracted pneumoconiosis from the inhalation of dust in the course of his employment, was said to be that:

> ". . . where it is proved that a wrongful act has made a material contribution to the plaintiff's injury, the law regards this as a sufficient discharge of the plaintiff's burden of proof on causation to render the defendant liable for the injury in full."[413]

In the cases which appear to have established this principle[414] the contribution made by the defendant to the risk was a contribution to the cause of the disease.[415] In these cases, therefore, it could have been said that there was a breach of duty that clearly did something to bring about the injury of which the plaintiff complained. In *McGhee v. National Coal Board*,[416] however, the House of Lords seems to have gone further and to have held that where a disease has been caused by a mechanism that is unclear, one can properly infer that a breach of duty which increased the risk of the disease thereby contributed to its cause.[417] In *McGhee* the plaintiff contracted dermatitis in consequence of the action of brick dust on his sweaty skin, the precise mechanism of which was a matter of conjecture. The defendants, his employers, were not at fault for his initial exposure to the dust. They were at fault for prolonging that exposure, because, in breach of duty, they had failed to provide him with washing facilities to

411 *Ibid.* at 759 *per* Lord Edmund-Davies.
412 [1956] A.C. 613.
413 *Thompson v. Smiths Shiprepairers (North Shields) Ltd* [1984] Q.B. 405 at 441 *per* Mustill J.
414 Including not only the cases referred to *supra* notes 412, 413, but also *Nicholson v. Atlas Steel Foundry & Engineering Co. Ltd* [1957] 1 All E.R. 7761; and *Bryce v. Swan Hunter Group plc* [1988] 1 All E.R. 659, applying this to a case of exposure to asbestos dust which caused the plaintiff to contract a particular disease. In light of later decisions, discussed below, this case may be taken to have been wrongly decided.
415 *Bryce v. Swan Hunter Group plc, supra* at 667 *per* Phillips J.
416 [1972] 3 All E.R. 1008, a Scottish case, but this does not appear to have made a difference.
417 Phillips J. in *Bryce v. Swan Hunter Group plc, supra* at 667, referring to the decision of the majority.

enable him to wash off the dust before he cycled home from work. Although the plaintiff failed to prove on a balance of probabilities that the additional exposure for which the defendants were responsible was the cause of his disease, the House of Lords held the defendants liable. The principle established by this case was subsequently expressed in these words:[418]

> "If it is an established fact that conduct of a particular kind creates a risk that injury will be caused to another or increases an existing risk that injury will ensue, and if the two parties stand in such a relationship that the one party owes a duty not to conduct himself in that way, and if the other party does suffer injury of the kind to which the risk related, then the first party is taken to have caused the injury by his breach of duty, even through the existence and extent of the contribution made by the breach cannot be ascertained".

12.104 It has been argued that the approach favoured in the *McGhee* case may have gone beyond the assistance provided for the plaintiff in *Cook v. Lewis*,[419] and may have obliged the defendant to prove that he did not cause the plaintiff's injury by his breach of duty, even where there is no question about the identity of the party whose conduct may have been responsible for what happened.[420] Moreover in *Cook v. Lewis* the defendant made it impossible for the plaintiff to prove his case; therefore the defendant was compelled to suffer the consequences. In *McGhee* the defendant had done nothing of the kind; the opportunity to prove causation was not impaired by the defendant: it was merely absent.[421]

12.105 In Canada subsequent cases indicated that the view of Lord Wilberforce in the *McGhee* case was that favoured as representing the effect of the decision.[422] Lord Wilberforce suggested that, in certain instances, the onus of proof shifted, so as to ensure justice for the plaintiff, and preclude the defendant's ability to ignore a legal duty he was obliged to fulfil.[423] That view was not the view of the majority of the members of the court in the *McGhee* case. Their approach was more limited in its nature and effect. However such an interpretation of the *McGhee* case has also been denied in Canada.[424] It has unquestionably been refuted by later decisions of the House of Lords. These decisions have involved not industrial injuries or diseases, as the earlier cases, but allegations of medical negligence.

418 *Ibid.* at 669, quoting Mustill L.J. in *Wilsher v. Essex Area Health Authority* [1986] 3 All E.R. 801 at 829. The decision in this case was later reversed by the House of Lords: below para. 12.108.
419 [1951] S.C.R. 830: above para. 12.98.
420 *Letnik v. Municipality of Metropolitan Toronto* (1988) 44 C.C.L.T. 69 at 94 *per* McGuigan J., a Canadian case.
421 *Ibid.*
422 Fridman, *Law of Torts in Canada*, Vol. 1 at 347 note 780.
423 *McGhee v. National Coal Board* [1972] 3 All E.R. 1008 at 1012–1013.
424 *Wilson v. Vancouver Hockey Club* (1983) 5 D.L.R. (4th) 282; *Seyfert v. Burnaby Hospital Society* (1986) 27 D.L.R. (4th) 96. See also *Gallant v. Fulkov* (1989) 69 O.R. (2d) 297 at 314–17, where *Wilsher v. Essex Area Health Authority* (below note 429) was applied.

12.106 *Kay v. Ayrshire and Arran Health Board*[425] involved a child suffering from meningitis. During treatment he was given an overdose of penicillin. The immediate effect of this was counteracted by remedial treatment. However after the child recovered from the meningitis, he was found to be suffering from deafness. At the trial expert evidence was to the effect that an overdose of penicillin had never been known to cause deafness; but deafness was a common sequela of meningitis. The trial judge found in favour of the plaintiff, who was suing by reason of the child's deafness. That decision was reversed on appeal. The plaintiff's appeal to the House of Lords was dismissed. Relying on *McGhee*, the plaintiff had argued that the overdose had created an increased risk of neurological damage, since deafness was a type of neurological damage: the causes of deafness was unclear; therefore the increased risk of neurological damage was sufficient to establish that the overdose had made a material contribution to the neurological damage that had resulted, i.e. the deafness. Therefore the defendants were liable. The House of Lords rejected this argument. Instead they held that where there were two competing causes of damage, in this instance the overdose and the meningitis, the law could not presume in the plaintiff's favour that the tortious cause was the one responsible for the damage, unless it was first proved that it was an accepted fact that the tortious cause, i.e. in this instance the overdose, was capable of causing or aggravating such damage. On the evidence this had not been established. Therefore the deafness had to be considered as resulting solely from the meningitis. The *McGhee* case could not assist the plaintiff because, as Lord Ackner pointed out,[426] in *McGhee* the absence of washing facilities was known to be a factor which increased the risk of dermatitis arising from the circumstances in which the plaintiff worked.

12.107 *Hotson v. East Berkshire Area Health Authority*[427] concerned a child whose hip had been injured in a fall. At the hospital the injury was not correctly diagnosed and the child was sent home. Subsequently, when he was in pain he returned to the hospital, when the nature and extent of his injuries became apparent and he was given emergency treatment. His injury was such that he was left with a severe condition causing deformity of the hip joint. He claimed for negligence, basing his claim on the delay in diagnosis. This the hospital admitted was a breach of duty. But the hospital argued that the resulting delay had not adversely affected the plaintiff's long-term condition. At the trial the judge held that even if the doctors at the hospital had correctly diagnosed the plaintiff's condition when he came the first time, there was still a 75% risk of the disability developing. The breach of duty had turned that risk into an inevitability, thereby denying the plaintiff a 25% chance of recovery. Therefore he gave the plaintiff 25% of the full value of the damages awardable for the plaintiff's disability. This decision was affirmed by the Court of Appeal.

425 [1987] 2 All E.R. 417.
426 *Ibid.* at 427.
427 [1987] 2 All E.R. 909. See Price, "Causation—the Lords' last chance?" (1989) 38 Int. & Comp. L.Q. 735; and Fleming, "Probabalistic causation in tort law" (1989) 68 Can. B.R. 661.

The House of Lords reversed this. They held that since the judge had held on a balance of probabilities, given the plaintiff's condition when he first attended the hospital, that even correct diagnosis and treatment would not have prevented the disability from occurring, the plaintiff had failed on the issue of causation. *McGhee's* case was discussed, but considered to be irrelevant to the circumstances in this case. However Lord Mackay did state that, until the House of Lords departed from *McGhee* it was not possible to affirm the propostion that "in no circumstances can evidence of loss of a chance resulting from breach of a duty of care found a successful claim for damages".[428]

12.108 The opportunity to reconsider the *McGhee* case was given the House of Lords in *Wilsher v. Essex Area Health Authority.*[429] The infant plaintiff was born prematurely, and suffered from various illnesses including oxygen deficiency. At the hospital a catheter was twice inserted into the baby's vein rather than an artery; each time the baby was given excess oxygen. It was later discovered that the baby was suffering from an incurable condition of the retina resulting in near blindness. This could have been caused by excess oxygen. However this condition also occurred in premature babies who were not given oxygen but suffered from five other conditions common in premature babies. All of these conditions had afflicted the plaintiff. At the trial of the baby's action for negligence the medical evidence was inconclusive on the issue whether the excess oxygen had caused the blindness. The trial judge held in the plaintiff's favour, applying the doctrine that since proper precautions had not been taken to prevent excess oxygen being administered to the plaintiff, and the plaintiff had suffered the injury against which such precautions were designed to be a protection, the burden of proof shifted to the defendant to establish not only no breach of duty but also that the damage did not result from the breach. Judgment was given for the plaintiff. This was affirmed by the Court of Appeal. The House of Lords reversed this decision and exonerated the hospital, on the ground that the plaintiff had not discharged the burden of proof as to causation. In coming to this decision the House stated that where a plaintiff's injury was attributable to a number of possible causes, one of which was the defendant's negligence, the combination of the defendant's breach of duty and the plaintiff's injury did not give rise to a presumption that the defendant's breach of duty had caused the injury. The burden remained on the plaintiff to prove the causation link between the defendant's negligence and his injury, although that link might legitimately be inferred from the evidence. In this particular case the evidence was far from conclusive. The plaintiff's condition could have been the result of a number of different agents or factors. Hence the burden of proof had not been discharged by the plaintiff. In the course of his judgment, Lord Bridge stated that, in the light of earlier decisions such as the *Bonnington Castings*[429a] case, the remarks of Lord Wilberforce in

428 *Hotson, supra.* at 916.
429 [1988] 1 All E.R. 871.
429a [1956] A.C. 613; para. 12.103 above.

McGhee as to the shifting of the burden of proof, were a minority opinion not supported by the other speeches in *McGhee*.[430] This did not mean that *McGhee* was wrongly decided. Lord Bridge pointed out the factual distinction between *McGhee* and the *Bonnington Castings* case, thereby manifesting the correctness of both decisions.[431] But he concluded that *McGhee* laid down no new principle of law. On the contrary it affirmed the principle that the onus of proving causation lies on the plaintiff.[432] What the House of Lords did in *McGhee* was to adopt "a robust and pragmatic approach to the undisputed primary facts of the case" to conclude that "it was a legitimate inference of fact that the defendant's negligence had materially contributed to the pursuer's injury".[433] It was "fruitless" to extract from *McGhee* some esoteric principle which in some way modified, as a matter of law, the nature of the burden of proof of causation which the plaintiff must discharge once he has established a relevant breach of duty.[434]

12.109 This judgment was concurred in by all the other members of the House, none of whom gave separate judgments. It must therefore be considered to be determined authoritatively that the erstwhile modification of the onus of proof of causation, that was thought by some judges to have resulted from the decision in *McGhee v. National Coal Board*, never took place. The law maintains its strict insistence upon proof that the defendant's breach of duty, once proved to have occurred, was "the" cause of the plaintiff's injury. The consequence of this latest pronouncement by the House of Lords suggests that the approach favoured by the Supreme Court of Canada to causation in *Cook v. Lewis* will not be acceptable to English judges.

(c) Remoteness of damage

(i) Introduction

12.110 The necessity for establishing a causal connection between the negligence of the defendant and the injury to the plaintiff has produced much difficulty not only in respect of the matters discussed in the foregoing pages, but also in relation to the question of attributing the kind or extent of harm suffered by the plaintiff to the defendant's wrongful act or omission. There is still difficulty, despite all the attention that has been devoted to this question by courts and commentators. There are two major problems. The first is whether the defendant should be held responsible for consequences that are different in kind or more extensive in nature than could have been expected to occur as a result of his wrongful conduct: where should his liability stop? The second is whether a negligent defendant should be held responsible for what happens in consequence of the combination of this conduct with some act on the part of another

430 [1988] 1 All E.R. 871 at 879.
431 *Ibid.* at 879–880.
432 *Ibid.* at 881.
433 *Ibid.* at 881–882.
434 *Ibid.* at 882.

person, including the plaintiff himself, or some event brought about by natural forces or the intervention of some non-human agency: for what consequences should the defendant be liable? Two major methods of resolving these problems have been suggested. One is to say that a defendant is liable for everything that is a direct, physical result of his negligence. The other is to say that defendant is only liable for what he ought to have foreseen as a reasonable man would be the probable consequence of his negligence. Each of these tests of remoteness appears at first sight to be straightforward and easily applicable. In truth both are complex and difficult to apply.

(ii) Direct consequences

12.111 Before 1961 judicial statements indicated that a defendant would only be liable for what was the natural and direct result of this wrongful act. As long as the damage of which the plaintiff compained was the direct result of the defendant's negligence, it was no answer to say that his negligence did much more than was expected.[435] That such damage was unforeseeable was irrelevant, as long as it was a direct consequence of his act.[436] The classical statement of this test or rule is contained in *Re Polemis*[437] in 1921. However later cases,[438] including decisions after *Donoghue v. Stevenson*,[439] confirmed that this was the correct test to apply, even though, in *Donoghue's* case, the House of Lords stressed the importance of foreseeability in determining whether a defendant had been guilty of negligence. The classical test of remoteness was summed up by Lord Wright in *The Oropesa*[440] in these words:

> "The question is not whether there was a new negligence but whether there was a new cause . . . . To break the chain of causation it must be shown that there was something which I will call ultraneous, something unwarrantable, a new cause which disturbs the sequence of events, something which can be described as either unreasonable or extraneous or extrinsic."

The language of Lord Wright indicates that the courts at this time were concerned with establishing a direct causal relationship, in the physical and historical senses, between the defendant's negligence and the plaintiff's injury.

12.112 Three important qualifications must be noted to the "direct consequences" test or rule.

12.113 First: a defendant took his victim as he found him. The defendant could not escape liability for consequences that were more serious or

435 *Smith v. London & South Western Railway Co.* (1870) L.R. 6 C.P. 14 at 22 *per* Blackburn J.
436 *Ibid.* at 21 *per* Channel B.
437 [1921] 3 K.B. 560. For earlier views to the same effect, see *HMS London* [1914] P. 72; *Weld-Blundell v. Stephens* [1920] A.C. 956 at 983–985 *per* Lord Sumner.
438 *Hambrook v. Stokes Bros.* [1925] 1 K.B. 141 at 156 *per* Atkin L.J.; *The Arpad* [1934] P. 189 at 222 *per* Maugham L.J.; *Sherman v. Folland* [1950] 2 K.B. 43; *Thurgood v. Van der Berghs & Jurgens Ltd* [1951] 2 K.B. 537; *Wormald v. Cole* [1954] 1 Q.B. 614.
439 [1932] A.C. 562: above at para. 12.53.
440 [1943] P. 32 at 39.

extensive than normal because the plaintiff's physical or emotional condition was such that he incurred greater harm than the ordinary reasonable man might be expected to suffer.[441] This doctrine of "*talem qualem*" applied for example to make a defendant liable for causing the death of someone who had an egg-shell skull (the classical illustration of the rule) which fractured when the defendant struck the plaintiff, although the blow in question would not have produced that result if the plaintiff's skull had been of usual strength and thickness.[442] The same result followed in respect of the economic state of the plaintiff. Hence if the defendant injured a wealthy man, so that he incurred greater economic loss through not being able to work for a period of time by reason of his injuries, the defendant could not argue that he did not know he was harming someone who would suffer more loss than the average person.[443] However in *Liesbosch Dredger v. Edison*[444] the House of Lords limited this. The economic condition of the plaintiff would not always be treated as an existing state which the defendant must accept as rendering the plaintiff susceptible of greater or more extensive loss than the ordinary reasonable man might be expected to incur. In this case the plaintiff was impecunious; therefore he could not afford to buy a vessel to replace the one sunk by the defendant's negligence. Instead he had to hire a replacement at an exorbitant rate. For this extra expense the defendant was not liable. The impecuniosity was an extrinsic cause of the loss. Although the case has never been overruled, it has been criticised;[445] and its rationale seems inconsistent with the doctrine of mitigation of damage,[446] under which the plaintiff ought to have been entitled to borrow money to lessen the effect of the loss caused by the defendant.[447] It should be noted in connection with physical, emotional and economic conditions of the plaintiff that a distinction was drawn between the strict application of the "*talem qualem*" rule and the principle that the peculiar physical, emotional or financial susceptibility of the plaintiff would not involve the defendant in a duty of care to him if no duty would have been owed to the ordinary reasonable person, unless the defendant knew, or ought to have known, that his conduct might affect someone in the position of the plaintiff, even though it would not effect someone not subject to such susceptibility or idiosyncrasy.[448]

441 *Dulieu v. White* [1901] 2 K.B. 669 at 679 *per* Kennedy J.; *Clippens Oil Co. v. Edinburgh & District Water Trustees* [1907] A.C. 291 at 303 *per* Lord Collins; *Bourhill v. Young* [1943] A.C. 92 at 109 *per* Lord Wright.

442 The same result might follow if the plaintiff's injuries were rendered worse by his abnormal condition or some external force operating subsequently, e.g., medical treatment, unless such treatment was a new, intervening cause: *Hogan v. Bentinck West Hartley Collieries* [1949] 1 All E.R. 588: cp. the Canadian case of *Fogg v. Kenora* [1941] 1 D.L.R. 100.

443 *Liesbosch Dredger v. Edison* [1933] A.C. 449 at 461 *per* Lord Wright.

444 *Supra.*

445 *Dodd Properties (Kent) Ltd v. Canterbury County Council* [1980] 1 All E.R. 928; *Perry v. Sidney Phillips & Son* [1982] 3 All E.R. 705; *Archer v. Brown* [1985] Q.B. 401.

446 Cp. *Radford v. De Frobeville* [1978] 1 All E.R. 33; cp. below note 450.

447 In any event there appear to be cases when "impecuniosity" or financial condition was not treated as making loss too remote: see e.g., *Compania Financiera Soleada SA v. Hamoor Tranker Corp. Inc.* [1981] 1 All E.R. 856, where the impecuniosity was produced by the defendant's negligent act; cp. the Australian case of *Fox v. Wood* (1981) 35 A.L.R. 607.

448 Cp. Lord Wright in *Bourhill v. Young* [1943] A.C. 92 at 109–110.

12.114 The second qualification of the *Polemis* directness of consequences test was that, in certain circumstances, consequences that were not direct might yet come within the scope of the defendant's liability if the defendant ought to have foreseen them as being likely. Hence the defendant could be liable even if the actual damage was caused in a physical sense by the behaviour of an animal, such as a horse left unattended for too long a time.[449] He could be liable where the plaintiff was the immediate cause of his own harm, in a physical or historical sense, but the plaintiff's behaviour was the result of his being under a legal or moral duty to act, as in the "rescue" cases;[450] or the plaintiff was a child who could not be expected to act otherwise than the way he did;[451] or the plaintiff's reaction to the situation produced by the defendant's negligence was foreseeable in the ordinary course of events or ought to have been foreseen[452] (which also affected the question of contributory negligence on the part of the plaintiff).[453] Thus if the plaintiff acted in the "agony of the moment", for example by jumping off a vehicle that was in danger of being the victim of a collision, and that danger was brought about by the defendant's negligence, the defendant would be liable for the plaintiff's injuries, even though the latter might not have been hurt had he stayed where he was instead of jumping.[454] Furthermore, even where a third party intervened and it was the intervening act that was the immediate cause of the plaintiff's injury, this might not result in the isolation of the defendant's negligence from the plaintiff's harm. This was the situation where the third party, the stranger, acted in excusable ignorance or alarm, much as the plaintiff in the "agony of the moment";[455] where the stranger acted in the exercise of his rights without any intent to injure, as in *Clarke v. Chambers*,[456] in which a third party moved an obstruction placed in the road by the defendant, by which obstruction the plaintiff was later harmed; or where the intervening act of the stranger was foreseeable in the ordinary course of events.[457] As long as this intervening act was foreseeable it was regarded as something against which the defendant should have guarded by taking appropriate precautions, or not performing the act which was the background to the intervention and led to its occurrence

449 *Aldham v. United Dairies* [1940] 1 K.B. 507.

450 See the cases cited above at paras 12.29ff; with which contrast *The San Onofre* [1922] P. 243. Or the plaintiff was seeking to minimise his damage: *Dee Conservancy Board v. McConnell* [1928] 2 K.B. 159.

451 *Lynch v. Nurdin* (1841) 1 Q.B. 29; contrast *Donovan v. Union Cartage Co.* [1933] 2 K.B. 71.

452 Which would make what happened part of an unbroken sequence: see *The Oropesa* [1943] P. 32. Cp. *The City of Lincoln* [1899] P. 15; *Summers v. Salford Corporation* [1943] A.C. 283. In such cases the hand of the original wrongdoer was said to be still heavy on the plaintiff or his property that was damaged: *SS Singleton Abbey v. SS Paludina* [1927] A.C. 16 at 27 *per* Lord Sumner. See also *The Guildford* [1956] P. 364.

453 Below pp. 359–60.

454 *Jones v. Boyce* (1816) Starke 493: cp. *The Bywell Castle* (1879) 4 P.D. 219; *Sayers v. Harlow District Council* [1958] 2 All E.R. 342. Contrast *Adams v. L. & Y. Railway* (1869) L.R. 4 C.P. 739.

455 *Scott v. Shepherd* (1773) 2 W.Bl. 892, the famous "squib" case.

456 (1878) 3 Q.B.D. 327.

457 *R. v. Moore* (1832) 3 B. & A. 184; *Northwestern Utilities v. London Guarantee & Accident Co. Ltd* [1936] A.C. 108; *Philco Radio v. Spurling* [1949] 2 All E.R. 882; *Stansbie v. Troman* [1948] 2 K.B. 48.

and causation of harm to the plaintiff. An unforeseeable act of intervention was treated by the law as a "*novus actus interveniens*". It made what ultimately happened too remote a consequence of the defendant's original negligent act or omission. Hence the defendant was not liable.[458] In all these various circumstances, therefore, foreseeability was a material factor in the determination of the scope or extent of the defendant's responsibility, despite the apparent reliance of the older law upon the doctrine of consequences.

12.115 The third qualification was that damage that was intended was never too remote.[459]

(iii) The rise of foreseeability

12.116 The directness test gave birth to, and encouraged the emergence of several different metaphors to describe and explain how the law functioned in regard to remoteness. Some were exotic and unusual; others were more common, such as "chains" or "nets" of causation. Such language, it may be suggested, indicated the lack of clarity on the part of the judges of the appropriate way to expound and justify the manner in which they differentiated situations when damage was too remote from those when it was not. The test of direct consequences, although espoused by the courts, was neither as all-embracing nor as simple as it seemed or was intended to be. Moreover the evolution of the tort of negligence by and after the decision in *Donoghue v. Stevenson* led to the development of the idea that it was impossible to conceive of liability for negligence except in terms of the foreseeable consequences of a negligent act or omission.[460] Conduct was only negligent insofar as it related to its probable results. In determining whether those results were foreseeable, regard was to be paid not only to what might normally be expected to occur, in the absence of extraneous intervention, or the extent of the damage that might be inflicted by such negligence, but also to what likely effect subsequent human or non-human acts or events might have in relation to such negligence. Even while the directness test was predominant, there were judicial suggestions that foreseeability was more appropriate.[461]

458 *SS. Singleton Abbey v. SS. Paludina* [1927] A.C. 16; *Cobb v. Great Western Railway* [1894] A.C. 419; *Metropolitan Railway v. Jackson* (1877) 3 App.Cas. 193; *Harnett v. Bond* [1925] A.C. 669. Cp. *Speake v. Hughes* [1904] K.B. 138, a defamation case. See also *The Calliope* [1952] A.C. 242, ship suffering heavy weather damage after having been damaged by collision with the defendant's negligently navigated vessel; defendants not liable for the weather damage.

459 *Quinn v. Leathem* [1901] A.C. 495 at 537 *per* Lord Lindley.

460 Above pp. 273–83.

461 Early remarks of this nature can be found in *Rigby v. Hewitt* (1850) 5 Ex. 240 at 243 *per* Pollock C.B.; *Greenland v. Chaplin* (1850) 5 Ex. 243 at 248 *per* Pollock C.B. See also *Ministry of Pensions v. Channell* [1947] K.B. 250 at 253 *per* Denning J.; *Morrison SS. Co. Ltd v. Greystoke Castle* [1947] A.C. 265 at 295–296 *per* Lord Porter, who had been one of the counsel for the unsuccessful party in *Re Polemis*. Lord Wright was the other. But the distinction made by Lord Sumner in *Weld-Blundell v. Stephens* [1920] A.C. 956 at 983–985 between culpability and compensation was echoed by Lord Porter in *Woods v. Duncan* [1946] A.C. 401 at 437.

12.117 Finally, in *The Wagon Mound (No. 1)*[462] the Privy Council held that foresight of consequences was the relevant test to be applied, where the ultimate results were wider in extent than might have been expected having regard to the knowledge of the defendant at the time of his negligent conduct. An act was only negligent in relation to its foreseeable consequences. Hence when the negligence of the defendants in performing repair work on a ship in harbour resulted in an extensive fire by reason of the presence of oil on the water, which was unknown to the defendants, there was no liability for such fire. The Privy Council stressed the importance of making the law relating to remoteness of damage consistent with what the reasonable man would consider to be a reasonable limit of liability for a negligent act.

12.118 The decision in *The Wagon Mound (No. 1)* has never been approved formally by an English court. However the authority of the Privy Council in this regard appears to have been accepted by the House of Lords[463] and the Court of Appeal,[464] although, in Canada, for example, there are decisions which apply or reject the test of foreseeability and adhere to, or repudiate the older test of directness in *Re Polemis*.[465] In England, therefore, it would seem that foreseeability has replaced directness as the general basis on which the remoteness or otherwise of damage or consequences is to be determined.[466] Some qualifications of this must be noted. In the first place the House of Lords held, in a Scottish appeal, *Hughes v. Lord Advocate*,[467] that it was unnecessary for the defendant to foresee precisely how the injury to the plaintiff would be inflicted as long as he ought to have foreseen the possibility of injury of the kind suffered by the plaintiff.[468] Secondly, even if damage is foreseeable, there will be no liability for its occurrence if the defendant was under no duty to guard against such damage on the part of the defendant, for example if a statute requires a defendant to take certain precautions to prevent consequence X, but it is consequence Y that occurs, in respect of which the statute was

462 [1961] A.C. 388: note that in *The Wagon Mound (No. 2)* [1967] 1 A.C. 617, a nuisance case arising from the same facts (above at paras 8.27–8), the Privy Council appear to have held that the fire that caused the harm was foreseeable, after having held it was not in *The Wagon Mound (No. 1)*.

463 In *Hughes v. Lord Advocate* [1963] A.C. 837: cp. *The Wagon Mound (No. 1)*, *supra* at 636 *per* Lord Reid; *Home Office v. Dorset Yacht Co. Ltd* [1970] A.C. 1004 at 1027; *C. Czarnikow Ltd v. Koufos* [1969] 1 A.C. 350 at 385–386 *per* Lord Reid, 422 *per* Lord Upjohn.

464 *Doughty v. Turner Manufacturing Co. Ltd* [1964] 1 Q.B. 518; and in many other cases by trial judges.

465 Fridman, *Law of Torts in Canada*, Vol. 1 at 328–329 where the relevant cases are collected.

466 See the discussion by Woolf J. in *Meah v. McCreamer (No. 2)* All E.R. 943 at 945–50. The effect of *The Wagon Mound (No. 1)* is criticised in, *inter alia*, Dias, "Remoteness of Liability and Legal Policy" [1962] C.L.J. 178; Dias, "Trouble on Oiled Waters" [1967] C.L.J. 62; Merrills, "Policy and Remoteness" (1973) 6 Ottawa L.R. 18; Davies, "The Road from Morocco" (1982) 45 M.L.R. 534.

467 [1963] A.C. 837. See also in relation to negligent mis-statement *Banque Financière de la Cité v. Westgate Insurance Co. Ltd* [1989] 2 All E.R. 952, especially at 981–8.

468 Cp. *Doughty v. Turner Manufacturing Co. Ltd* [1964] 1 Q.B. 518; *Bradford v Robinson Rentals Ltd* [1967] 1 All E.R. 267. Contrast *Tremain v. Pike* [1969] 3 All E.R. 1303. See Fridman & Williams, "The Atomic Theory of Negligence" (1971) 45 Austr. L.J. 117.

inapplicable.[469] Thirdly, decisions subsequent to *The Wagon Mound* (No. 1) have upheld the continued application of the egg-shell skull rule or doctrine to personal injuries, economic loss and damage to property.[470] It should also be noted that, outside the tort of negligence, the test of foreseeability in relation to remoteness may be irrelevant, for example, where liability is strict,[471] or is founded on deceit.[472]

12.119 It is in respect of harm that is the result, in part at any rate, of an intervening act or event as well as of the defendant's negligence that the foreseeability test achieves its greatest relevance and importance. Even prior to *The Wagon Mound (No. 1)*, as previously noted, foresight of such intervention was treated as sufficient to justify the conclusion that the ultimate harm to the plaintiff was a direct consequence of the defendant's negligence rather than a *novus actus interveniens*. This is obviously much more acceptable under the foreseeability test. Hence in a number of cases since 1961 it has been held, for example, that the act of strangers,[473] or the subsequent or contemporaneous act of the victim[474] does not necessarily isolate the defendant's conduct from the harm or damage that is the basis of the action against him. The "rescue" cases provide a striking illustration of when the plaintiff's intervention is foreseeable and when it is not.[475] Similarly if the victim of an accident later commits suicide because he or she cannot stand the pain which results from the injuries inflicted by the defendant, it has been held that the defendant will be liable for the death, not merely the pre-suicide injuries.[476] So, too, where the victim refused to undergo medical treatment because of certain fears, a Canadian court held that the seemingly voluntary and independent act of the plaintiff did not absolve the defendant from liability for injuries which might have been treated, with a certain percentage of success but a certain percentage of

469 *Gorris v. Scott* (1874) L.R. 9 Ex. 125: cp. below Chapter 16.

470 *Smith v. Leech Brain & Co. Ltd* [1962] 2 Q.B. 405; *Warren v. Scruttons* [1962] 1 Lloyd's Rep. 497; *Wieland v. Cyril Lord Carpets Ltd* [1969] 3 All E.R. 1006; *Malcolm v. Broadhurst* [1970] 3 All E.R. 508; cp. *The Despina R.* [1977] 1 Lloyd's Rep. 618 at 620, on appeal [1979] A.C. 685; *Vacwell Engineering Co. Ltd v. BDH Chemicals Ltd* [1971] 1 Q.B. 88. For Canadian cases on the same subject see Fridman, *op. cit.* at 329–330.

471 *The Wagon Mound (No. 1)* [1961] A.C. 388 at 426–427.

472 *Shelley v. Paddock* [1980] Q.B. 348.

473 *Rouse v. Squires* [1973] Q.B. 889; *Home Office v. Dorset Yacht Co. Ltd* [1970] A.C. 1004; with which contrast *Lamb v. Camden London Borough Council* [1981] Q.B. 625.

474 *The Calliope* [1952] A.C. 172; with which contrast *McKew v. Holland & Hannen & Cubitts (Scotland) Ltd* [1969] 3 All E.R. 1621. It will depend on whether the victim's reaction was reasonable; as in the "rescue" cases. In *Meah v. McCreamer (No. 2)* [1986] 1 All E.R. 947 the victim's subsequent criminal conduct, which led to his having to pay damages to the woman he attacked, did not entitle the victim to recover those damages a second time from the negligent driver. This was indirect loss: the driver who injured the victim owed no duty to the woman the victim assualted; this would have exposed defendants like the negligent driver to indefinite liability for an indefinite period.

475 Above paras 12.29ff.

476 *Pigney v. Pointers Transport Services* [1957] 2 All E.R. 807. For some contradictory Canadian cases see *Swami v. Lo* (1980) 105 D.L.R. (3d) 451; *Funk v. Clapp* (1984) 12 D.L.R. (4th) 62 (no liability); *Cotic v. Gray* (1981) 33 O.R. (2d) 356 (liability). On the duty to inform someone that the deceased was suicidal, which led to liability for the suicide, see *Kirkham v. Anderton* (1990) The Times 4 January.

risk of greater injury, had the plaintiff given his consent.[477] However, as seen earlier in the context of the discussion of duties of care,[478] there may be situations in which the intervention of third parties is foreseeable but the defendant is not held liable on the ground that a duty to prevent damage from such intervention was not owed as a matter of policy, i.e. it was neither just nor reasonable to impose such a duty on the defendant.[479]

12.120 The application of the foreseeability test to such instances of third party intervention may be illustrated by *Knightley v. Johns*.[480] The first defendant was negligent in causing a road accident near the end of a tunnel carrying two way traffic. The second defendant, a police inspector in charge of the scene of the accident, realised that he had forgotten to close the tunnel to oncoming traffic. He ordered a police officer, the plaintiff, to check the situation and close the tunnel. While he was doing so, the plaintiff was struck by an oncoming car, the driver of which was not guilty of negligence. The plaintiff was also not negligent in the manner in which he was performing his duty. When the first defendant was sued by the plaintiff, the first defendant argued that the inspector's action in ordering the plaintiff into the tunnel was a *novus actus interveniens* which made the first defendant not liable for the plaintiff's injuries. It was held that the inspector was negligent in not clearing the tunnel and in ordering his subordinate to do so. He had acted contrary to standard police procedures in ordering the plaintiff to go to the opening of the tunnel to close it off against oncoming traffic. In determining whether this act of negligence was a *novus actus interveniens*, the test was whether the damage that resulted was a natural and probable, and therefore a reasonably foreseeable, consequence. The question was whether what happened was likely to happen as a result of the first defendant's negligence, not whether what happened was a mere possibility that would not occur to the mind of the reasonable man. If the whole sequence of events was a natural and probable consequence of the first defendant's negligence and therefore a reasonably foreseeable result of that negligence, then none of the events in the sequence could be considered a *novus actus interveniens*. Mistakes and mischances that are to be expected when human beings have to cope with a crisis are part of the natural and probable consequences of negligence and do not constitute a *novus actus interveniens*. What happened here, however, was more than a mere mistake. It was an act of negligence. Therefore it was a *novus actus interveniens*.

(d) Directness versus foreseeability

12.121 The situation after *The Wagon Mound (No. 1)* may not be as different from what obtained under *Re Polemis* as might be considered at

477 *Janiak v. Ippolito* (1985) 16 D.L.R. (4th) 1. On the effect of intervening medical treatment compare two other Canadian cases: *Thompson v. Toorenburgh* (1973) 29 D.L.R. (3d) 608, affirmed (1975) 50 D.L.R. (3d) 717; and *David v. Toronto Transit Commission* (1976) 16 O.R. (2d) 248; Fridman, *op. cit.* at 332–334.

478 Above paras 12.73ff.

479 *P. Perl (Exporters) Ltd v. Camden London Borough Council* [1984] Q.B. 342; *Smith v. Littlewoods Organisation Ltd* [1987] 1 All E.R. 710.

480 [1982] 1 All E.R. 851; contrast *Rouse v. Squires, supra.*

first sight. Indeed even in the Privy Council decision the view was expressed that the emphasis on foreseeability would not result in any great change in the law or the way individual cases were decided.[481] Two reasons may be given for this. In the first place, foreseeability was frequently a factor to be taken into account in determining the issue of remoteness prior to *The Wagon Mound (No. 1)*. Secondly, before any question of remoteness could arise a court had to decide whether a duty of care was owed by the defendant to the plaintiff, in relation to which foresight of consequence was of vital concern.[482] Therefore, without having to rule on the issue of remoteness a court could impose or deny liability by determining the existence or absence of a duty. Indeed there has been judicial expression of the view that duty, remoteness and causation were merely aspects of the same fundamental question for the court;[483] and all were dependent on foreseeability of consequences, in other words the probability and nature of the risk of injury to the plaintiff.

12.122 In view of this it may be argued that recognition by the Privy Council of the predominant role of foreseeability amounted to nothing more than the express statement of what was implicit in the way the tort of negligence had evolved as a result of *Donoghue v. Stevenson* and its successors. Thus what was a "direct" consequence of a negligent act had a special, technical meaning, that was equated with what was foreseeable on the part of the defendant. Causation, for legal purposes, did not have the same connotation as it did in a philosophical, scientific or historical context. Lawyers were concerned with the meaning and application of the concept of causation for strictly practical legal purposes: to determine the nature, existence and extent of liability. They were not involved in deciding on philosophical or other grounds whether a causal connection could be found between an act and its consequences.[484] In determining this issue courts had to pay attention not only to the physical, scientific or historical meanings of causation but to questions of judicial or legal policy. Thus a consequence that might or might not be traceable to a negligent act in non-legal terms might or might not result in tortious liability, depending on whether to impose liability was in furtherance of the policy of the law with respect to such liability.[485]

12.123 It was suggested in *The Wagon Mound (No. 1)*[486] that the foreseeability test is simpler and fairer than the older test of directness. Given the way that directness was interpreted and applied before 1961, it may be questioned whether that argument has any sound basis. Certainly the

481 *The Wagon Mound (No. 1)* [1961] A.C. 388 at 422.
482 Above pp. 276–83.
483 *Roe v. Ministry of Health* [1954] 2 Q.B. 66 at 86 *per* Denning L.J.
484 *Weld-Blundell v. Stephens* [1920] A.C. 956 at 986 *per* Lord Sumner; *Liesbosch Dredger v. Edison* [1933] A.C. 449 at 460 *per* Lord Wright. See also *Barty-King v. Ministry of Defence* [1979] 2 All E.R. 80 at 89 *per* May J.; *R. v. Criminal Injuries Compensation Board ex parte Ince* [1973] 3 All E.R. 808 at 815 *per* Megaw L.J.
485 I.e. whether it was "just and reasonable" to impose a duty on the defendant: above pp. 275–6.
486 *Supra* note 481 at 422.

manner in which foreseeability has been applied in post-*Wagon Mound* cases suggests that there is little to choose between it and the older directness test. The truth appears to be that courts can, and do, manipulate both or either of these tests to achieve the kind of result or decision that they consider desirable having regard to the general nature of the tort of negligence, the aims and purposes it is designed to forward, and the interests in personal, property or financial safety it is designed to protect.[487]

487 There is also the point that to restrict the liability of a defendant on the *Wagon Mound* test may produce injustice or unfairness vis-à-vis the plaintiff: Glanville Williams, "The Risk Principle" (1961) 77 L.Q.R. 179 at 179–180. But the directness test, as it was interpreted and understood by the courts, may have been just as unfair to the plaintiff. Note the suggestion in *Lamb v. Camden B.C.* [1981] 2 All E.R. 408 at 421 *per* Watkins L.J. that "a robust and sensible approach" should be taken to this important area of the study of remoteness; and the possibility that public policy may also indicate the response of the court as in *Meah v. McCreamer (No. 2)*, note 474 *supra*, applying *Gray v. Barr* [1971] 2 Q.B. 554.

CHAPTER 13

Defences to Negligence

1. INTRODUCTION

13.01 It is always open to a defendant to deny or negate liability for negligence by arguing that no duty of care was owed to the plaintiff either on the basis of the facts, i.e. what was foreseeable, or on the ground that policy requires the denial of liability in the particular circumstances. Similarly, a defendant can seek to rely on proof that he had observed the requisite standard of care, or that he had not been guilty of negligence. He may successfully plead that his conduct did not cause damage to the plaintiff or that the damage which resulted was too remote a consequence of the defendant's act or omission. In addition there are various specific defences that can be raised. Apart from necessity, mistake, or insanity, all of which may be relevant to an action in negligence, as they are in respect of other torts, for example, trespass,[1] the following must be considered: inevitable accident: consent: contributory negligence: and the illegal activity of the plaintiff at the time he was injured by the defendant's negligence.

2. INEVITABLE ACCIDENT

13.02 This, in effect, is a denial of negligent behaviour. The assertion of the defendant is that what happened was something no reasonable person could foresee would occur and such that no reasonable person in the defendant's position could be expected to take precautions to prevent the occurrence, and indeed, no reasonable precautions could have been taken that would have precluded the occurrence.[2] What happened, therefore, must have been an accident, in the strict meaning of the word: and it must have been inevitable in the sense of not preventable by any reasonable person.[3] The law differentiates misadventure from misconduct.[4] The former is not a basis for liability, whereas the latter is. What the defendant is saying was inevitable was not the act which he committed but the

1 Above paras. 5.38–42.
2 *The Marpesia* (1872) L.R. 4 P.C. 212 at 220; *The Schwan* [1892] P. 419 at 429.
3 *J. & J. Makin Ltd v. London & North Eastern Railway* [1943] 1 All E.R. 362.
4 *Sigerseth v. Pedersen* [1927] S.C.R. 342 at 347.

consequence of that act. The latter could not reasonably have been avoided.

13.03 The relevance of the plea of inevitable accident in torts such as trespass has previously been considered.[5] Where it has been raised as an answer to a claim for trespass, especially trespass to the person, the issue has been whether the burden of disproving negligence was on the defendant, although normally the onus of establishing the elements of the defendant's liability is on the plaintiff. In cases of pure negligence, in contrast with actions where negligence is an element or factor in liability, the onus of proving that what happened was an inevitable accident is clearly on the defendant. It will be for him to prove that nothing he could have done as a reasonable man would have prevented the harm that was incurred by the plaintiff. In a Canadian case, *Vessey v. Douglas Bros.*[6] it was said that the defendant must prove the actual cause of what happened and that he was not responsible for it, or prove all the possible causes of the accident and that he was not responsible for any of them.

13.04 In *The Schwan*[7] Lord Esher indicated that the burden on the defendant relying on the plea of inevitable accident was to establish that what happened was beyond the control of the defendant and was unavoidable even by the exercise of the greatest care and skill. It has been suggested, however, that the onus on the defendant is the lesser one of proving the inevitability of what happened even if reasonable care had been exercised.[8] The English experience of the plea is limited. The Canadian experience suggests that it is by no means easy to determine in advance whether a court will be willing to accept the argument that what happened could not possibly have been the result of any act of negligence on the part of the defendant.[9] Perhaps, as has been suggested by at least one text,[10] the time has come to accept that in cases of negligence the plea of inevitable accident is nothing more than a denial of negligent behaviour, and that once the plaintiff has made out a *prima facie* case of negligence, in some instances by means of the doctrine of *res ipsa loquitur*,[11] the evidentiary burden passes to the defendant to adduce evidence from which it may be inferred that he was not negligent. In this regard, however, the division of opinion as to the location of the legal burden of proof in such cases[12] becomes relevant.

5 Above paras. 5.28ff. Note that it would not be a defence in torts of strict liability, e.g. under the rule in *Rylands v. Fletcher*, or in nuisance. But the plea of Act of God in some instances may resemble the plea of inevitable accident: see paras. 9.46ff.
6 (1977) 13 Nfld. & P.E.I.R. 129.
7 [1892] P. 419 at 429.
8 *Graham v. Hodgkinson* (1983) 40 O.R. (2d) 697.
9 Fridman, *Law of Torts in Canada*, Vol. 1, at 347–349, where relevant authorities are considered.
10 *Winfield & Jolowicz on Tort*, 12th ed. 1984 at 719.
11 Above paras. 12.86ff.
12 *The Merchant Prince* [1892] P. 179; *Southport Corporation v. Esso Petroleum Co. Ltd* [1956] A.C. 218 at 229–232: cp. above para. 8.83.

3. CONSENT

(a) Volenti non fit injuria

13.05 A fundamental principle of the law is that one who consents to being injured cannot make the one who causes his injury liable.[13] It has been seen that this applies to cases of trespass, subject to certain qualifications.[14] It is also relevant to liability for negligence. Where intentional harm is involved, for example in instances of battery or assault,[15] *volenti* means that the victim has consented to be injured. Where the plaintiff's claim is founded on the defendant's negligence, *volenti* more accurately means that the plaintiff voluntarily assumed the risk of being injured.[16] Hence the defence of consent or *volenti* in such cases is sometimes expressed in the form of assumption of risk. The courts continue to speak in terms of consent or of the plaintiff being *volens* although where a plaintiff is held to have consented or to be *volens*, in effect he has not agreed to be injured but to hold the defendant not liable should the defendant, through negligence, cause him injury. It is the risk of injury that he is accepting. This means not merely the physical risk of injury but the risk that, if injured, he will forfeit the right to sue that otherwise he would have enjoyed.

13.06 Although it has been said that the plea of *volenti* does not become relevant unless and until a tort has been committed by the defendant, or at least presumptively established,[17] it has also been argued that the plea of *volenti*, if successful, entails the conclusion that the plaintiff has relieved the defendant of a duty of care that otherwise would have been owed by the defendant to the plaintiff.[18] In such circumstances the defendant is not obliged to exercise reasonable care for the safety of the plaintiff. Under the first view the defence of *volenti* is a negation of liability, not of duty: in much the same way as in contract situations where there is an exception, exclusion or limitation clause, the party in whose favour such clause is inserted is obliged to perform the primary duties placed on him by the

13 *Smith v. Baker* [1891] A.C. 321 at 360 *per* Lord Herschell. See Dias, "Consent of Parties and *Volentas Legis*" [1966] C.L.J. 75; "*Volenti Non Fit Injuria*" [1985] C.L.J. 87. It originates in Roman law: Dig. 47, 10, 1.5. And it appears in English law as early as the 13th century. Theoretically the defence applies to damage to property as well as to personal injuries, but it has been of much greater relevance in relation to the latter.

14 Above paras. 6.36ff.

15 Or in defamation: *Chapman v. Lord Ellesmere* [1932] 2 K.B. 431. In cases of strict liability under *Rylands v. Fletcher*, the plaintiff's consent may also be of a defence: *Peters v. Prince of Wales Theatre Co. Ltd* [1943] K.B. 73: above para. 9.39.

16 See, e.g., *Hall v. Brooklands Auto Racing Club* [1933] 1 K.B. 205; *Murray v. Haringay Arena* [1951] 2 K.B. 529; cp. *Woolridge v. Sumner* [1963] 2 Q.B. 43, where negligence was not established; cp. also *I.C.I. Ltd v. Shatwell* [1965] A.C. 656, where the effect of the defence of *volenti* was to exclude the vicarious liability of an employer for the negligence of the plaintiff's fellow servant, to the risk of being injured by whom the plaintiff had consented.

17 *Smith v. Baker* [1891] A.C. 325 at 366 *per* Lord Herschell. Cp. *Woolridge v. Sumner* [1962] 2 All E.R. 978 at 982 *per* Sellers L.J., 990 *per* Diplock L.J.

18 *Buckpitt v. Oakes* [1968] 1 All E.R. 1145 at 1148; *Titchener v. British Railways Board* [1983] 3 All E.R. 770 at 776 *per* Lord Fraser. Cp. the similar view in Canada: *Ferris v. Stubbs* (1978) 89 D.L.R. (3d) 364 at 366 *per* Hughes C.J.N.B.; Fridman, *Law of Torts in Canada*, Vol. 1 at 353.

contract, but is relieved of the secondary liability to pay damages if guilty of non-performance.[19] Under the second view the argument that the plaintiff has consented to run the risk of being injured or has assumed such risk leads to the conclusion that the defendant is relieved of any duty. He may be as negligent as he likes as long as this negligence relates to the extent of the consent given by the plaintiff.[20]

13.07 It is important to ensure that a clear distinction is maintained between the question whether the defendant has been guilty of negligence and the question whether, in spite of such negligence, the defendant is not liable by reason of the fact that the plaintiff was *volens*, i.e. assumed the risk of being injured by negligence. In cases involving participants in, or spectators at sporting activities it has been indicated that the issue is not whether the maxim *volenti non fit injuria* applies in consequence of the participant's or spectator's voluntary involvement in the activity, but whether the defendant, a participant whose conduct is alleged to have been negligent, was in fact guilty of negligence.[21] In the latest of these decisions, *Condon v. Basi*,[22] the Court of Appeal considered two different views expressed in an Australian case, *Rootes v. Shelton*.[23] One approach was to take a generalised duty of care and modify it on the basis that the participants in a sport or pastime impliedly consent to take risks which would otherwise be a breach of duty of care. The other approach was to say that there was a general standard of care, namely that a person is under a duty to take all reasonable care taking account of the circumstances in which such a person is placed, so that in a game such as football, which was involved in the *Condon* case, the relevant circumstances are quite different from those which obtain when someone is going for a walk in the countryside.[24] The Court of Appeal preferred the latter approach. But it made no difference whether the tribunal of fact found that the defendant failed to exercise the degree of care appropriate in all the circumstances or that the defendant acted in a way to which the plaintiff cannot be expected to have consented. In either event there would be liability.[25]

13.08 In such situations the effect of the willing involvement of the plaintiff in the particular activity is to identify the scope and nature of the duty of care owed him by the defendant. In other instances such willing involvement on the part of the plaintiff has a different effect. It does not

19 *Photo Productions Ltd v. Securicor Transport Ltd* [1980] 1 All E.R. 556 at 567 *per* Lord Diplock.
20 Cp. the differing views expressed by various members of the High Court of Australia in *Insurance Commissioner v. Joyce* (1948) 7.C.L.R. 39.
21 *Woolridge v. Sumner*, *supra*: *Wilks v. Cheltenham Home Guard Motor Cycle & Light Car Club* [1971] 2 All E.R. 369. But the situation with regard to the liability of the occupier of premises where such an activity is being carried on might be different: see *Hall v. Brooklands Auto Racing Club* [1933] 1 K.B. 205; *Murray v. Harringay Arena* [1951] 2 K.B. 529; *Simms v. Leigh Rugby Football Club Ltd* [1969] 2 All E.R. 923.
22 [1985] 2 All E.R. 453.
23 [1968] A.L.R. 33.
24 *Supra* note 22 at 454 *per* Donaldson M.R.
25 *Ibid.*

regulate the standard of care expected of the defendant. Instead it negates liability for non-observance of an applicable standard of care that is required of the defendant under the general law of negligence.

13.09 Consent, or assumption of risk may occur as a result of an express agreement between the parties. This is the situation where the parties are in a contractual relationship, for example, a passenger travelling by train or aeroplane, and the contract contains an exclusion clause relieving the defendant from liability in the event of negligence on the part of himself, his servants or agents. In many instances of negligence the alleged consent or assumption of risk is founded on an implication that may be drawn from the behaviour of the plaintiff.

(b) Express consent

13.10 Agreement to run the risk of being injured has been given expressly in the absence of a contract between the parties.[26] The more usual situation is that a contract between the parties contains a term which amounts to acceptance by one party of the risks involved in some activity, and exempts the other party from liability that would normally follow from the latter's negligent act. Such terms are always strictly construed against the party in whose favour they are included.[27] Moreover legislation such as the Defective Premises Act 1972[28] or the Unfair Contract Terms Act 1977 may exclude the possibility of any such exemption or exclusion of liability or may restrict such exclusions or restrictions of liability to what satisfies a test of reasonableness.[29] Whether a clause of this kind is effective to exclude what would otherwise be liability for negligence is a matter for interpretation of a contract, possibly in the light of relevant statutory provisions.[30] This in turn involves discussion of the doctrine of fundamental breach of contract[31] and the extent to which such a clause can exempt from liability not only the party who entered into the contract but also the servants or agents of that party.[32] Mention should also be made of the notion of disclaimer, by virtue of which a party may purport to disclaim responsibility for his actions even though under a duty of care. This is sometimes prohibited by statute.[33] A disclaimer was permitted under the Occupiers' Liability Act 1957 in respect of the duty of

26 *Buckpitt v. Oakes, supra*; *Bennett v. Tugwell* [1971] 2 Q.B. 267; *Birch v. Thomas* [1972] 1 All E.R. 905: in all of which the plaintiff was a passenger in a car which he knew carried a notice stating passengers travelled at their own risk. Cp. the situation under the Occupiers' Liability Act: below pp. 397; cp. *Titchener v. British Railways Board, supra* at 776 on the provisions of the Occupiers' Liability (Scotland) Act 1960 s. 2(3).

27 *Spurling Ltd v. Bradshaw* [1956] 2 All E.R. 121.

28 Above pp. 305–6.

29 Cheshire, Fifoot & Furmston, *Law of Contracts*, 11th ed. 1986 at 172–188.

30 *White v. John Warwick & Co. Ltd* [1953] 2 All E.R. 1021; *White v. Blackmore* [1972] 2 Q.B. 651.

31 *Photo Productions Ltd v. Securicor Transport Ltd, supra*

32 *Scruttons Ltd v. Midland Silicones Ltd* [1962] A.C. 446; *New Zealand Shipping Co. Ltd v. A. M. Satterthwaite & Co. Ltd* [1975] A.C. 154; cp. *Dyck v. Manitoba Snowmobile Association* [1985] 4 W.W.R. 319.

33 Road Traffic Act 1988 s. 149: below para. 13.15.

care owed by an occupier to lawful visitors under the terms of that statute.[34] The effect of the Unfair Contract Terms Act 1977 and the Occupiers Liability Act 1984 is to allow an occupier to limit or exclude liability to recreational or educational visitors to his property if they are not charged a fee for entry and the occupier is a business occupier.[35]

(c) Implied consent

13.11 The situation more frequently met with is that which arises where the defendant seeks to establish that the plaintiff impliedly assented to assume the risk of being injured by the defendant's negligence.[36]

13.12 In such instances the voluntary assumption of risk on the part of the plaintiff will depend on two factors: (i) the knowledge of the plaintiff of the risks involved; and (ii) the reality of his consent to the assumption of those risks. Only if there is knowledge coupled with a true or real consent will the plaintiff be *volens* and the defendant's liability excluded.

(i) Knowledge

13.13 The plaintiff must know all the material facts on which his acceptance of the risk of injury could be based. In the absence of such complete knowledge there can be no valid consent on his part. Knowledge alone will not suffice, for as it has been said, the maxim is *volenti non fit injuria*, not *scienti non fit injuria*.[37] Knowledge of the dangerous state of things and the risk of injury at the hands of the defendant is a fundamental requirement for a successful plea of *volenti*: however it is not the sole basis for such success. Thus in cases involving employees injured by reason of the negligence of employers in relation to the conditions of work of the employee, it has been held, ever since *Smith v. Baker*[38] that the awareness of the employee that there was danger involved in his working under the existing conditions would not of itself entitle the employer to rely on the defence of *volenti*.[39] The same result has followed in other cases where the parties were not in the relationship of employer and employee.[40] To some

34 *White v. Blackmore, supra.*
35 Below p. 397.
36 Hence in *Slater v. Clay Cross Co. Ltd* [1956] 2 Q.B. 264 *volenti* was not an available defence because the plaintiff did not take the risk of negligence by the driver of the train, even though, walking along a narrow tunnel on a railway track, she voluntarily took the risk of damage from the running of the railway in the ordinary and accustomed way: *ibid.* at 271 *per* Lord Denning. Nor could *volenti* be relied on as a defence where a man in custody in a remand centre committed suicide while suffering from depression—his judgment had been impaired; see *Kirkham v. Anderton* (1990) The Times 4 January.
37 *Thomas v. Quartermaine* (1887) 18 Q.B.D. 685 at 696 *per* Bowen L.J.: cp. Unfair Contract Terms Act 1977 s. 2(3).
38 [1891] A.C. 321.
39 Cp. *Yarmouth v. France* (1887) 19 Q.B.D. 647; *Bowater v. Rowley Regis Corp.* [1944] K.B. 476. In *Titchener v. British Railways Board, supra* at 776 Lord Fraser said that the principle of *volenti* was less often relied on in industrial accident cases at the present time than formerly.
40 *Clayards v. Dethick* (1848) 12 Q.B. 439; *Letang v. Ottawa Electric Railway Co.* [1926] A.C. 725; *A. C. Billings & Sons Ltd v. Riden* [1958] A.C. 240: cp. *Slater v. Clay Cross Co. Ltd, supra.*

extent such decisions are based on the argument that knowledge of a risk is not enough to consitute acceptance of it. They also illustrate the extent to which the plaintiff's lack of freedom of choice inhibits his ability to give his consent so as to amount to a voluntary assumption of the risk entailed in a particular activity.[41]

13.14 The knowledge of the plaintiff may not operate to exclude the liability of the defendant even where it can be inferred that such knowledge indicated consent to the possible outcome of the defendant's conduct. In *Cook v. Cook*,[42] for example, the High Court of Australia held that the plaintiff's knowledge of the defendant's lack of experience as a driver sufficed to amount to consent to the risk that the plaintiff might be injured by a failure to observe the ordinary standard of care expected of a driver in view of the fact that, in the circumstances, the plaintiff could not expect this driver to maintain that standard. But it did not operate to exclude the liability of the driver for additional carelessness that was unrelated to his inexperience as a driver. This decision may be contrasted with the English case of *Nettleship v. Weston*,[43] where the plaintiff agreed to give driving lessons in the defendant's car to a defendant who was inexperienced. When the plaintiff was injured as a result of the defendant's driving, the plea of *volenti* was unsuccessful. To some members of the court this was because in such circumstances nothing short of an agreement could be the basis of the defence. To get into the car, even with the knowledge that the defendant was inexperienced, would not amount to consent or assumption of risk.[44]

13.15 Such instances, as well as those involving passengers in cars being driven by drunken drivers, may now be regulated by the provisions of the Road Traffic Act 1988.[45] This has the effect of rendering ineffective any antecedent agreement or understanding between a driver and a passenger, whether intended to be legally binding or not, restricting or negativing liability required to be covered by compulsory liability insurance. Furthermore no such agreement or understanding will be effective to impose any condition with respect to the enforcement of such liability. Nor will the fact that a passenger has willingly accepted as his the risk of negligence on the part of the driver be treated as negativing any such liability of the user of the motor vehicle. These provisions apply to any situation where a person uses a motor vehicle in circumstances where compulsory liability insurance is required.

13.16 Where that statute does not apply, or in the event that it is decided ultimately that these provisions do not deal with the situation of implied

41 Below pp. 355–6.
42 (1986) 68 A.L.R. 353.
43 [1971] 2 Q.B. 691.
44 *Ibid.* at 701 *per* Lord Denning M.R. and Megaw L.J. Salmon L.J. thought that the defence was not applicable because of a prior conversation about insurance which indicated no intention to assume the risk: *ibid.* at 704, 705.
45 S. 149; consolidating similar provisions in the Road Traffic Act 1972 s. 148(3).

volenti that was raised in the drunken driver cases,[46] it remains a question of fact in each case whether the conduct of the passenger who knows that the driver of the vehicle is under the influence of drink suffices to amount to consent to the possibility or risk of being injured. *Volenti* was rejected as a defence in *Dann v. Hamilton*,[47] a case that has been given rise to much controversy.[48] It was accepted as a defence by some of the judges of the High Court of Australia in *Insurance Commissioner v. Joyce*,[49] a decision that has recently come under attack by the same court.[50] In Canada the defence was considered in several decisions of the Supreme Court.[51] In the most recent decision[52] it was stated that this defence would only apply to motor vehicle accidents arising from negligence on the highway in unusual circumstances, namely, where the circumstances were such that it was clear that the plaintiff, knowing of the certain risk of harm, in essence bargained away his right to sue for injuries incurred as a result of the defendant's negligence. That was a necessary implication in many cases involving a drunken driver and a willing passenger. To make that implication, however, there had to be an awareness of the circumstances and the consequences of acts that was rarely present on the facts of such cases at the relevant time. Thus the plea of *volenti* would only rarely, if at all, be successful in such instances.

13.17 The extent of the plaintiff's knowledge of risks inherent in a course of conduct has been held relevant in Canada in cases where a patient was alleged to have given his or her consent to undergoing an operation or course of treatment. Unless the true nature of the risks involved have been explained to the patient so that he or she is capable of giving what has been termed an "informed consent", the position in Canada is that even if the patient has expressly agreed to undergo the operation or treatment, this will not relieve the doctor of liability should the undisclosed risk materialise to the patient's detriment.[53] Canadian courts draw a distinction between the actual operation or treatment and the agreement to undergo it. Consent may exclude liability for certain consequences of the operation or treatment, i.e. the battery or assault that it may involve. It will not affect liability for negligent behaviour in the performance of the operation.[54] However the patient's consent will not negate liability for

46 Contrast *Gregory v. Kelly* [1978] R.T.R. 426 with *Ashton v. Turner* [1981] Q.B. 137.
47 [1939] 1 K.B. 509.
48 See Gordon, "Drunken Drivers and Willing Passengers" (1966) 82 L.Q.R. 62: cp. the comments of Stable J. in *Dawrant v. Nutt* [1960] 3 All E.R. 681 at 682. In *Meah v. McCreamer* [1985] 1 All E.R. 367 the acceptance of a lift by the plaintiff, who was also affected by drink, amounted to contributory negligence.
49 (1948) 77 C.L.R. 39; see also *Loggenkamp v. Bennett* (1950) 80 C.L.R. 292.
50 *Cook v. Cook, supra.*
51 *Car & General Insurance Corp. Ltd v. Seymour & Maloney* [1956] S.C.R. 322; *Miller v. Decker* [1957] S.C.R. 624; *Lehnert v. Stein* [1963] S.C.R. 35; *Eid v. Dumas* [1969] S.C.R. 668.
52 *Dube v. Latour* (1986) 27 D.L.R. (4d) 653 at 658–659 *per* Estey J.
53 *Hopp v. Lepp* [1980] 2 S.C.R. 192; *Reibl v. Hughes* [1980] 2 S.C.R. 880; *White v. Turner* (1981) 47 O.R. (2d) 764, affirming (1981) 31 O.R. (2d) 773; *Videto v. Kennedy* (1981) 33 O.R. (2d) 497. This has been extended to manufacturers of drugs prescribed for and used by patients: *Buchan v. Ortho Pharmaceuticals (Canada) Ltd* (1986) 25 D.L.R. (4th) 658.
54 Cp. above pp. 131–2.

consquences that have not been disclosed with sufficient detail and clarity to enable the pateint to make a reasoned, sensible choice whether or not to undergo the operation or treatment having regard to the attendant risks. In *Sidaway v. Bethlem Royal Hospital Governors*[55] the House of Lords considered this plea of "informed consent" and held that the Canadian and American doctrine was inapplicable in England. The only duty on a doctor was to perform his functions with reasonable care and skill. He was not obliged to inform the patient, in the same way as a doctor in Canada, of the attendant risks. Therefore the patient's consent would negate any liability for consequences of treatment, as long as there was no negligence on the part of the doctor in providing it or performing the operation involved. A patient who agreed to such treatment or operation would be *volens*, even though he did not appreciate what its consequences might be. Of course, as in all cases where consent, assumption of risk or *volenti* is pleaded, the consent must have been given in the absence of fraud or misrepresentation on the part of the doctor. If fraud or misrepresentation was employed by the doctor in order to obtain the necessary consent, it would vitiate such consent. In other instances, however, the express consent of the patient to the operation or treatment will have the effect of an implied consent to the normal risks inherent therein, as long as these have not been created or exacerbated by negligence on the part of the doctor.

(ii) Consent

13.18 As noted in connection with consent as a defence to trespass, any consent to a risk can only be effective insofar as it is lawful for the plaintiff to agree to the assumption of such risk. The activity must be lawful.[56] Hence there can be no valid consent to participation in some unlawful activity, such as an illegal surgical operation, or a sport that is prohibited by law.[57] Where, through negligence, some harm is inflicted on the plaintiff in such situations, the question may arise whether the plaintiff's participation in an unlawful activity bars his right to sue.[58]

13.19 The plaintiff's consent must be real, i.e. it must be given in consequence of the plaintiff's awareness of the true state of affairs, which means that consent obtained by fraud will not be effective: it must be freely given, which means that consent obtained by duress or coercion will also be ineffectual. What this means is that although the plaintiff may be in a condition to accept the physical risk of being injured, he will not be considered to have accepted or assumed the legal risk of injury, which would relieve the defendant of liability for negligence, unless the plaintiff

55 [1985] 1 All E.R. 643. For earlier cases see *Freeman v. Home Office* [1983] 3 All E.R. 589; and *Hills v. Potter* [1983] 3 All E.R. 716. But *Chatterton v. Gerson* [1981] 1 All E.R. 257 appears to have adopted a contrary view.
56 Cp. above paras. 6.36ff.
57 *Dann v. Hamilton* [1939] 1 K.B. 509 at 516: cp. *Bravery v. Bravery* [1954] 3 All E.R. 59.
58 Below para. 13.45: cp. *Hegarty v. Shine* (1878) 4 L.R.Ir. 288, an assault case.

was fully and freely capable of giving his agreement to such a result.[59] In *Crocker v. Sundance Northwest Resorts Ltd*,[60] the Supreme Court of Canada held that a plaintiff who was drunk at the material time, when he undertook to participate in a race on inflated rubber tyres, had not assumed the legal risk involved in this activity, even if, which itself was doubted, he had assumed the physical risks. Although the courts had not required that all the necessary elements of a contract be present to constitute a valid agreement to accept a risk or risks,[61] nevertheless they seem to require that the allegedly consenting plaintiff manifests his free and clear agreement in this respect. There must be something akin to a bargain between the parties, even if no consideration has been given by the defendant for the assumption of risk or waiver of liability.[62].

13.20 Hence if there are factors which preclude such free granting of consent or waiver, there can be no valid plea of *volenti*. As previously noted, where a plaintiff is obliged or compelled to accept a known risk by reason of his employment, *volenti* will not be available as a defence to a negligent employer who has created the risk.[63] However someone who undertakes dangerous employment will be regarded as having accepted the normal risks of such employment, for example, a fireman who realises that there is danger in fighting fires. That implicit consent does not extend to risks which are additional to those normally to be found in this type of work and have been created by the negligence of the employer or someone else, for example the occupier of the premises where the fire occurs.[64] In the same way it was held in the nineteenth century[65] and accepted since that a user of the highway accepts the normal risk inherent in such use. But he is not thereby *volens* to any additional risk created by the negligence of another road user.[66]

13.21 Lack of freedom of choice whether or not to accept or assume a risk may also exist in other situations, for example, where a plaintiff wishes to exercise a right such as to enter or leave his premises, and finds that the defendant has created a dangerous situation. The fact that the plaintiff exercises his right, notwithstanding the risk of injury it entails, will not constitute an implied consent or assumption of risk.[67] Nor will such consent be implied where the plaintiff acts as a "rescuer" in consequence of a

59 See, e.g., *I.C.I. Ltd v. Shatwell* [1965] A.C. 656, where there was no economic pressure on the workman who employed a dangerous method of work that caused his injury: cp. *ibid.* at 681 *per* Lord Hodson, 686 *per* Lord Pearce.
60 (1989) 51 D.L.R. (4th) 321 at 322.
61 Thus it will not matter that the plaintiff is a minor: *Buckpitt v. Oakes* [1968] 1 All E.R. 1145.
62 *Bennett v. Tugwell* [1971] 2 Q.B. 267.
63 Above at p. 351.
64 *Merrington v. Ironbridge Metal Works Ltd* [1952] 2 All E.R. 1101; *Ogwo v. Taylor* [1987] 3 All E.R. 961. Cp. *Hartley v. Mayoh & Co.* [1954] 1 Q.B. 383; *Watt v. Hertfordshire County Council* [1954] 2 All E.R. 368.
65 *Holmes v. Mather* (1875) L.R. 10 Ex. 261.
66 The situation of a person whose property adjoins the highway is the same: *Esso Petroleum Co. Ltd v. Southport Corporation* [1956] A.C. 218 at 244.
67 *Claywards v. Dethick* (1848) 12 Q.B. 439; *A. C. Billings & Son v. Riden* [1958] A.C. 240.

situation brought about by the negligence or other wrongful act of the defendant. In such instances not only has it been held that a duty of care may be owed to the rescuer,[68] it has also been held that such a rescuer is not *volens*, nor will he be guilty of contributory negligence, as long as his intervention was necessary, reasonable, and not reckless having regard to the danger involved and the capacities of the rescuer.[69]

(d) The decline of consent

13.22 A successful plea of *volenti* bars any action for negligence against the defendant. In this respect *volenti* is very different from the present law of contributory negligence.[70] Formerly a successful plea of contributory negligence on the part of the plaintiff might have negated his right to sue the defendant for negligence. That is not necessarily so today. Instead responsibility may be apportioned. Hence the conduct of the plaintiff may be less harmful to his claim if it can be construed as amounting to contributory negligence rather than consent or assumption of risk. Not surprisingly, therefore, courts prefer to interpret the behaviour of the plaintiff as contributory negligence rather than as supporting the plea of *volenti*. It enables them to permit the plaintiff some remedy by way of damages, while at the same time allowing them to take the plaintiff's conduct into account. This is undoubtedly true of Canada, where the defence of *volenti* has fallen into disfavour in recent years, its role being taken by contributory negligence. It may also be true in England.[71]

4. CONTRIBUTORY NEGLIGENCE

(a) Historical survey

13.23 At the beginning of the nineteenth century, just at the time when the foundations of modern law of negligence were being laid, there emerged the idea that a plaintiff who was guilty of neglect of his own safety should be held responsible for what happened to him. One man's being at fault does not excuse another from looking after himself was the attitude expressed by judges of the period.[72] In consequence it became the law that a defendant would not be liable, even if he were guilty of negligence, where the plaintiff so far contributed to the misfortune that occurred to him by his own negligence that but for such negligence on his part the misfortune would never have happened.[73] The plaintiff had to look after himself: he could not rely on the fault of the defendant; and

68 Above pp. 12.29ff.
69 Below pp. 361.
70 Below paras. 13.37ff.
71 But in *Titchener v. British Railways Board* [1983] 3 All E.R. 770 at 776 Lord Fraser said that certainly in relation to the Occupiers' Liability (Scotland) Act 1960, there was no room for the argument that the principle of *volenti* is out of date or discredited.
72 *Butterfield v. Forrester* (1809) 11 East 60.
73 *Tuff v. Warman* (1858) 5 C.B.N.S. 573 at 585 *per* Wightman J.; *C.P.R. v. Frechette* [1915] A.C. 871 at 878.

whether the plaintiff was guilty of contributory negligence depended on whether he could reasonably have avoided the consequences of the defendant's negligence.[74]

13.24 There may have been some moral or even practical justification for the doctrine that the plaintiff's own behaviour should not be excluded from consideration when determining the liability of a negligent defendant. However the common law went too far in holding that a plaintiff guilty of contributory negligence could recover nothing. The harshness and sometimes injustice of this approach led to strange developments. To avoid the conclusion that the plaintiff should recover nothing by reason of his contributory negligence, the courts went to extraordinary lengths to hold that the plaintiff had not been guilty of contributory negligence: by finding that he was not negligent, or by finding that his negligence, though a *causa sine qua non* of the plaintiff's harm was not a *causa causans*, in other words it was not contributory. In this respect reference must be made to the so-called rule of "last opportunity", by which a party who had the last possible chance or opportunity to avoid the consequences of the other party's negligence would be solely responsible for what happened.[75]

13.25 Prior to the change in the law that occurred in 1945,[76] it was probably immaterial whether a defendant relied on *volenti non fit injuria* or contributory negligence as a defence to an action for negligence. If either were successful the result would be the same; the plaintiff would be denied any recovery. Since 1945, however, when the law relating to negligence on land was brought closer to the law relating to negligence at sea, which had been regulated by the Maritime Conventions Act 1911, there is a significant distinction between the plea of *volenti* and that of contributory negligence. Only the former will always operate to bar the plaintiff's recovery. The latter may sometimes do so. Whether or not this will be the case depends on how the statute which introduced apportionment to the law relating to negligence on land is properly to be interpreted and applied. In particular the question is raised as to the status of the "last opportunity" rule in the modern law of negligence.

(b) The common law doctrine

(i) Not dependant on duty

13.26 At one time whether a plaintiff was guilty of negligence was thought to depend on whether the plaintiff had broken a duty of care owed by him to the defendant, in the same way that a defendant could only be liable for negligence if his conduct was a breach of duty owed to the plaintiff. But most, if not all, cases where contributory negligence is

74 *Grayson v. Ellerman Lines Ltd* [1920] A.C. 468 at 477 *per* Lord Parmoor.
75 *Davies v. Mann* (1842) 10 M. &. W. 546: below para. 13.32.
76 Law Reform (Contributory Negligence) Act 1945: statutory changes had been effected in other jurisdictions much earlier, e.g. in Ontario by the Contributory Negligence Act, S.O. 1924 c. 32, see now Negligence Act, R.S.O. 1980 c. 315.

raised do not involve a situation where the plaintiff owed a duty of care to the defendant, or to anyone else. The issue in those instances is not whether the plaintiff was neglecting some legal duty but whether he was acting as a reasonable man and with reasonable care.[77] To establish contributory negligence it was enough to show lack of reasonable care by the plaintiff for his own safety. The Privy Council made this plain in *Nance v. British Columbia Electric Railway Co.*[78] The trial judge had directed the jury that they must find that the plaintiff owed a duty of care to the defendant and that he had broken it before contributory negligence could be found. This was a case in which the plaintiff, on a highway, was knocked down by the defendants' tram which was driven negligently by the defendants' servant. The direction of the trial judge was held to have been incorrect. The only question was whether the plaintiff in his own interest took reasonable care of himself and contributed by this want of care to his own injury.[79] However the Privy Council did recognise that sometimes a plaintiff might owe a duty of care to others, including the defendant. Thus where two parties are so moving in relation to one another as to involve the risk of collision, each owes the other a duty to move with due care. Similarly, when a man stepped from the kerb onto the roadway he owed a duty to traffic which is approaching him with risk of collision to exercise due care.

(ii) Negligence which causes or contributes to the damage

13.27 The approach of the common law was that contributory negligence was a question of causation rather than responsibility.[80] As in cases where the liability of the defendant was in issue, negligence was not relevant unless it was a cause of the damage that occurred as a result of it. However it was pointed out, in a case after 1945, that foreseeability was also important and material. In *Jones v. Livox Quarries*[81] the plaintiff, employed at the defendant's quarry, wrongly and against orders stood at the back of the defendant's excavator, riding it like a coachman. A dumper ran into the back of the excavator and the plaintiff was injured. The Court of Appeal held that, in standing at the rear of the excavator, the plaintiff unreasonably and improperly exposed himself to the particular risk and was a cause operating to produce his damage. Prior to 1945 this would have barred his remedy. Since this decision came subsequently to the change in the law, the plaintiff was held to be 20% to blame and his

77 *Davies v. Swan Motor Co. (Swansea) Ltd* [1949] 2 K.B. 291 at 324–325 *per* Denning L.J. The test of contributory negligence is therefore subjective, not objective, i.e. whether the plaintiff took reasonable care for his own safety.

78 [1951] A.C. 601.

79 *Ibid.* at 611 *per* Viscount Simon. E.g., by failing to wear a crash helmet when driving a motorcycle: *O'Connell v. Jackson* [1972] 2 Q.B. 270: cp. *Capps v. Miller* [1989] 2 All E.R. 333; or not wearing a safety belt while driving a car: *Froom v. Butcher* [1976] Q.B. 286. The wearing of safety belts is now compulsory: Road Traffic Act 1988 s. 14, replacing Transport 1981 s. 27.

80 *British Columbia Electric Railway Co. Ltd v. Loach* [1916] 1 A.C. 719 at 727, 728 *per* Lord Sumner; *Caswell v. Powell Duffryn Associated Colleries Ltd* [1940] A.C. 152 at 165 *per* Lord Aitkin; *Lewis v. Denys* [1940] A.C. 921; *The Boy Andrew* [1948] P. 140 at 148 *per* Viscount Simon (a case under the 1911 Act).

81 [1952] 1 T.L.R. 1377.

damages were reduced accordingly. Denning L.J. expressed the law as follows:[82]

> "Just as actionable negligence requires the foreseeability of harm to others, so contributory negligence requires the foreseeability of harm to oneself. A person is guilty of contributory negligence if he ought reasonably to have foreseen that if he did not act as a reasonably prudent man he might hurt himself, and in his reckonings he must take into account the possibility of others being careless . . . . Foreseeability is not the decisive test of causation. It is often a relevant factor, but it is not decisive."

Thus contributory negligence which would have operated as a defence if one result of negligence had occurred might not do so if another sort of negligence brought about the damage. The plaintiff's failure to exercise reasonable care for his own safety does not raise the defence unless the injury results from the particular risk to which his conduct has exposed him.

13.28 In this respect the law relating to contributory negligence seemed to have a close resemblance to the law on remoteness of damage laid down later in *The Wagon Mound (No. 1)*[82a] rather than to the test of remoteness set out in *Re Polemis*.[83] Thus in *Jones v. Livox Quarries*,[84] Singleton L.J. posited the example of a man sitting on an unsafe wall but being injured not through the collapse of the wall, brought about the negligence of the owner of the wall, but a collision between a negligently driven car and the wall. The man sitting on the wall might not be guilty of contributory negligence, although in one sense he was clearly guilty of neglect for his own safety. Denning L.J. was not so sure. He thought in accordance with *Re Polemis* that the distinction between the plaintiff's being crushed in the collision and being thrown off the wall by its collapse was too fine.[85] In view of the later case of *Hughes v. Lord Advocate*,[86] it would appear that it would not matter how the man in question were injured as long as he was on the wall at the material time. Just as in cases concerning the liability of a defendant for negligence, so in the context of contributory negligence the balancing of directness and foreseeability in relation to causation is by no means simple and straightforward. Although it may not now be as vital to the successful recovery by the plaintiff of damages for his injuries whether he was or was not guilty of contributory negligence, it is still somewhat material to decide this issue carefully since it will have some effect on the extent to which the plaintiff will be entitled to recover in full. Hence it may be very important to determine whether the plaintiff should be considered to have contributed to his injury on the basis of directness, i.e. pure causation, or foreseeability, i.e. causation as a matter of law and fact.

82 *Ibid.* at 1383.
82a [1961] A.C. 338.
83 [1921] 3 K.B. 560; above pp. 336–7.
84 *Supra* note 81 at 1380.
85 *Ibid.* at 1383–1384.
86 [1963] A.C. 837: above at para. 12.118.

(iii) Negligence not considered contributory

13.29 *(1) Defendant obliged to protect plaintiff.* In certain instances the plaintiff's act, albeit apparently entailing negligence on his part, may be one against which the defendant was under a duty to provide. The defendant should have been prepared for the plaintiff to be careless of his own safety and taken adequate precautions. Where such is the case the defendant cannot plead that the plaintiff ought to have foreseen that the defendant would be negligent, and should have acted in such a manner as to prevent his own injury. For example, in *Grant v. Sun Shipping Co. Ltd*[87] ship repairers left a hatch uncovered and unlit. The plaintiff, while working on the ship, fell down the hatch. The House of Lords held that he was not guilty of contributory negligence. If the repairers had fulfilled their duty the plaintiff could have acted without the slightest danger.[88]

13.30 *(2) Where the plaintiff was a child.*[89] The wrongful act of the defendant, not the carelessness of a child plaintiff, was treated as the cause of the damage if it led the child to act as he did with the result that the child was harmed. In *Lynch v. Nurdin,*[90] for example, the defendant negligently left an unattended horse and cart in the street. The seven-year-old plaintiff got on the cart to play. Another child led the horse on, in consequence of which the plaintiff was thrown and hurt. It was held that the plaintiff was not guilty of contributory negligence. The defendant had caused the injury. This was because the child was tempted or allured and could not be expected to exercise much care on his own behalf.[91] As noted in another context,[92] the age and intelligence of a child are material to determine whether a child can be negligent. Those factors are equally relevant to the issue of contributory negligence by a child. A child is not expected to act like an adult. Hence it is unlikely that a child's act will be construed as constituting contributory negligence.[93] There may be situations in which a child can be, and has been held guilty of such negligence.[94] But the conduct and expectations of the defendant may be relevant in determining whether the child has behaved improperly. This was emphasised by the Privy Council in *Yachuk v. Oliver Blais & Co.*[95]

87 [1948] A.C. 549: cp. *Westwood v. Post Office* [1974] A.C. 1.
88 [1948] A.C. 549 at 565 *per* Lord Du Parcq. See also *Gee v. Metropolitan Railway* (1873) L.R. 8 Q.B. 161; *Lord Passenger Transport Board v. Upson* [1949] A.C. 155; *The Towerfield* [1951] A.C. 112; *Almaroth v. Chivers* [1948] 1 All E.R. 53; *Lang v. London Transport Executive* [1989] 3 All E.R. 609.
89 Note that the old doctrine of "identification", by which a child in the charge of an adult was identified with that adult so that the negligence of the adult would be considered contributory negligence on the part of the child (and the same was held true of a passenger in a vehicle the driver of which was guilty of negligence), was abolished in *Miller v. Armstrong: The Bernina* (1883) 13 App.Cas. 1; *Oliver v. Birmingham & Midland Omnibus Co.* [1933] 1 K.B. 35; cp. *France v. Parkinson* [1954] 1 All E.R. 739. The earlier law is stated in *Waite v. North Eastern Railway* (1858) E.B. & E. 719.
90 (1841) 1 Q.B. 29; contrast *Donovan v. Union Cartage Co.* [1933] 2 K.B. 71.
91 Cp. *Harold v. Watney* [1898] 2 Q.B. 320.
92 Above p. 318.
93 Cp. *Gough v. Thorne* [1966] 3 All E.R. 398, thirteen-year-old girl not guilty of contributory negligence in crossing road without seeing if a vehicle was wrongly overtaking a halted lorry.
94 For Canadian cases to this effect see Fridman, *Law of Torts in Canada*, Vol. 1, at 373.
95 [1949] A.C. 386.

There the plaintiff, aged 9, obtained petrol from the defendants' servant by deceit, telling the servant it was wanted for his mother's motor car. In fact the child wanted it to make torches for a game. He used it by dipping bullrushes in a pail of petrol and lighting them. The petrol caught fire and the plaintiff was burned. The defendants' servant was held to have been the sole cause of the injuries. The boy was not contributorily negligent. "To put a highly inflammable substance into the hands of a small boy," said Lord Du Parcq,[96] "is to subject him to temptation and the risk of injury, and this is no less true if the boy has resorted to deceit in order to overcome the supplier's scruples."[97]

13.31 *(3) Where the plaintiff acted in the agony of the moment.* This may be expressed more generally in terms of the plaintiff's acting in a situation involving a dilemma or an emergency. If the defendant places the plaintiff in a position of extreme danger and the plaintiff reacts in a manner that produces his injury, the latter will not necessarily be held to have caused his injury, even though, in a physical, historical sense, the act of the plaintiff was the immediate cause of his injuries.[98] As Lord Atkinson said in a case of a very different kind, *Wilson v. United Counties Bank*:[99]

> "If one man inflicts an injury upon another, the resort by the sufferer to reasonable expedients for the *bona fide* purpose of counteracting, curing or lessening the evil effects of the injury done him, does not necessarily absolve the wrongdoer, even though the sufferer's efforts should, in the result, undesignedly aggravate the result of the injury."

It is on this basis that in the "rescue" cases,[100] the conduct of the plaintiff in placing himself in the path of danger when he could have stayed away from the possibility of incurring a risk and being injured has not been considered to amount to contributory negligence. The defendant, having created the dangerous situation, cannot be heard to say that the plaintiff caused his own injury by not staying away but attempting to protect or save someone, or someone's property, jeopardised as a consequence of the defendant's original negligence. This will only be the result where the plaintiff has acted reasonably, not rashly or recklessly, and his intervention was necessary. Unnecessary intervention or intervention that is unrelated to the exigencies of the situation or to the capacities of the plaintiff will be treated as involving the defence of *volenti* or as constituting contributory negligence.

(iv) The doctrine of "last opportunity" or "last clear chance"

13.32 The need to temper the severity or the common law doctrine of contributory negligence and its effects led to the development of the last

96 *Ibid.* at 394.
97 *Ibid.* at 395–396, where Lord Du Parcq said that the servant was negligent "because he ought to have recognised that a boy of the age of the infant appellant not only lacked knowledge and expertise but was likely to have mischievous propensities. These defects being characteristic of the normal boy, it was impossible . . . to impute to this boy . . . any failure to take reasonable care for his own safety."
98 See, e.g., *Jones v. Boyce* (1816) 1 Starke 493; *The Bywell Castle* (1879) 4 P.D. 219; *Claywards v. Dethick* (1848) 12 Q.B. 439.
99 [1920] A.C. 102 at 125.
100 Above paras. 12.29ff.

opportunity or last clear chance rule.[101] which, as Denning L.J. pointed out in *Davies v. Swan Motor Co. (Swansea) Ltd*,[102] was not a principle of law but a test of causation. Under this a defendant might still have been able to avoid the accident, despite the plaintiff's simultaneous or subsequent negligence. The defendant would be solely responsible if, by exercising ordinary care and causation, he might have avoided the consequences of the plaintiff's negligence.[103] The original decision in which this was enunciated was *Davies v. Mann*.[104] There the plaintiff left his hobbled donkey on the highway. The defendant, driving a wagon, collided with it. The plaintiff was not deprived of a remedy on the basis of contributory negligence. The underlying rationale of this case was applied in many later decisions. In one, *The Volute*,[105] where emphasis was placed on common sense principles,[106] the distinction was drawn between a subsequent and severable act of negligence, which would be the sole cause of an accident, and a situation where the negligence of one party was so much mixed up with the negligence of the other that it would be impossible to differentiate them, with the result that the plaintiff would fail on the ground of his having been guilty of contributory negligence.[107] The last act of negligence was not necessarily or even presumably the effective, proximate or direct cause of the accident: and it was this cause which was the subject of search by courts.[108] Hence if the plaintiff could have avoided the collision, in a case involving a collision between two vehicles, by the exercise of reasonable care, then the plaintiff failed because his injury was due to his own negligence in failing to take reasonable care.[109] Only if one party could have avoided the accident would that party be solely responsible.

13.33 The rules which regulated the application of this doctrine of last opportunity or last clear chance were set out by Greer L.J. in *The Eurymedon*,[110] only a few years prior to the passage of the 1945 Act. First: if one of the parties actually knew from observation of the negligence of the other party he would be solely responsible if he failed to exercise reasonable care towards the negligent other party, e.g. the plaintiff. This would

101 *Davies v. Swan Motor Co. (Swansea) Ltd* [1949] 2 K.B. 291 at 318 *per* Evershed L.J., 322 *per* Denning L.J.
102 *Ibid.* at 321.
103 *Tuff v. Warman* (1958) 5 C.B.N.S. 573 at 585 *per* Wightman J.; *Radley v. London & North Western Railway Co.* (1876) 1 App.Cas. 754 at 759 *per* Lord Penzance. For criticisms of this "rule of thumb" see *Alford v. Magee* [1952] A.L.R. 101 at 106 *et seq.*
104 (1842) 10 M. &. W. 546.
105 [1922] 1 A.C. 129. This was a case under the 1911 Act and it was not necessary to invoke the last opportunity rule because the statute provided apportionment in admiralty cases.
106 [1922] 1 A.C. 129 at 144: cp. *Marvin Sigurdson v. British Columbia Electric Railway Co. Ltd* [1953] A.C. 291 at 299.
107 *Supra* note 105 at 136, 144. See *Anglo-Newfoundland Development Co. v. Pacific Steam Navigation Co.* [1924] A.C. 406. The principles in these cases, applicable under the 1911 Act, were applied to accidents on land by *Swadling v. Cooper* [1931] A.C. 1. See below.
108 *The Eurymedon* [1938] P. 41 at 59 *per* Scott L.J.
109 *Swadling v. Cooper* [1931] A.C. 1 at 8 *per* Lord Hailsham: but contrast *Alford v. Magee*, note 103 *supra* at 109.
110 [1938] P. 41 at 49.

be a subsequent, severable and independent act of negligence.[111] In such an instance the negligent plaintiff might be "*functus culpa*".[112] Secondly, if one party was not in fact aware of the other's negligence but by the exercise of reasonable care could have become aware of it and, by exercising reasonable care could have avoided causing damage to the other negligent party, the one who could have become so aware would be solely responsible.[113] Thirdly, if the negligence of both parties continued right up to the moment of impact, both parties were to blame: and if the negligent act of one party was such as to make the other party make a negligent mistake that otherwise he would not have made, then both would be equally to blame.

13.34 The first limb of this third "rule" was exemplified in *Swadling v. Cooper*.[114] The plaintiff's deceased husband in his vehicle came to a crossroads without warning. The defendant, in his vehicle, hooted and applied his brakes, but he failed to swerve and as a result collided with and killed the plaintiff's husband. The defendant was first aware of the deceased husband's vehicle when it was only a few yards away, which allowed only a second to avoid impact. The House of Lords held that both were to blame and there was no need to put "last opportunity" to the jury. Lord Hailsham explained that there were cases "in which the negligence of the parties is contemporaneous or so nearly contemporaneous as to make it impossible to say that either could have contributed to the accident".[115] The second limb of the third "rule" is illustrated by the facts of *The Eurymedon* itself. One ship, the Eurymedon, coming up the Thames was negligent in failing to reduce speed on sighting lights ahead. These proved to be the anchor lights of another ship. Because of the negligence of this second ship in straddling the river, the lookout on the first ship reasonably failed to recognise them as anchor lights until it was too late to avoid an accident. The Court of Appeal held both ships to blame as the negligence of the second ship continued to affect the judgment of the Eurymedon's lookout.

13.35 To these "rules" another had to be added, in consequence of the decision of the Privy Council in *British Columbia Electric Railway Co. v. Loach*.[116] This is the idea of "notional" last opportunity. If one party would have been able to avoid the accident but for a prior act of negligence which prevented him from making use and taking advantage of what

111 *The Volute*, *supra* at 136: cp. *Alford v. Magee*, *supra* at 115: *The Monte Rosa* [1893] P. 23. The situation was illustrated by a number of cases involving accidents on the highway: *Maclean v. Bell* (1932) 112 L.T. 262; *Tart v. Chitty* [1933] 2 K.B. 453; *Baker v. Longhurst* [1933] 2 K.B. 461; *Tidy v. Bateman* [1934] 1 K.B. 319; *Henley v. Cameron* (1948) 65 T.L.R. 17.

112 *Davies v. Swan Motor Co. (Swansea) Ltd*, *supra* at 317 *per* Evershed L.J., 323 *per* Denning L.J.

113 *The Sans Pareil* [1900] P. 267; *Grand Trunk Railway v. McAlpine* [1913] A.C. 808; *Grayson v. Ellerman Lines Ltd* [1920] A.C. 468 at 472.

114 [1931] A.C. 1.

115 *Ibid.* at 10. See also *The Volute*, *supra*; *The Boy Andrew* [1948] A.C. 140.

116 [1916] 1 A.C. 719.

would otherwise have been the last opportunity of avoiding the accident that party will be solely responsible. In *Loach's* case, the driver of the defendants' train would have been able to avoid the collision, despite the plaintiff's negligence in being on the crossing, if the defendants had not allowed the brakes on their locomotive to be defective. Hence the defendants alone were responsible for what occurred.

13.36 Plainly these complex rules or tests of causation were capable of producing great confusion and uncertainty, especially where, as was the situation prior to 1945, juries were frequently involved in making determinations about negligence and contributory negligence. It is hardly surprising therefore that ultimately the law was altered by statute, so as to make contributory negligence no longer an absolute defence, but to permit apportionment between the responsible parties. The question is whether, and if so to what extent, this statuory change has made a difference to the common law position.

(d) The effect of the statute

(i) In general

13.37 By the Law Reform (Contributory Negligence) Act 1945, it is provided:

> "Where any person suffers damage as the result partly of his own fault and partly of the fault of any other person or persons, a claim in respect of that damage shall not be defeated by reason of the fault of the persons suffering the damage, but the damages recoverable in respect thereof shall be reduced to such extent as the court thinks just and equitable having regard to the claimant's share in the responsibility for the damage."

The defence of contributory negligence which was once a defence *in toto* is now a defence *pro tanto*.[117] But it must still be pleaded by the defendant:[118] and the burden of proving contributory negligence lies on him.[119] The common law rule has been brought into line with the rule obtaining in admiralty since 1911, although the 1945 Act does not apply where the Maritime Conventions Act applies.[120] The problem in admiralty and "common law" actions must be approached broadly, avoiding those fine distinctions which were apt to be drawn when some slight act of negligence on the part of the plaintiff might defeat his claim altogether.[121] However, apart from its consequences on the "last opportunity" or "last clear chance" rule, the Act of 1945 has not affected the rules for establishing whether contributory negligence has been proved.[122] In view of the possibility of apportionment, however, it may be that a broader, more flexible approach has been adopted by the courts. It should be noted that

117 *London Passenger Transport Board v. Upson* [1949] A.C. 155 at 167 *per* Lord Wright.
118 *Fookes v. Slaytor* [1979] 1 All E.R. 137.
119 *Hernager v. S.S. Diamond* [1939] A.C. 94 at 104 *per* Lord Wright.
120 Law Reform (Contributory Negligence) Act 1945 s. 3(1).
121 *The Boy Andrew* [1948] A.C. 140 at 155 *per* Lord Porter.
122 *Davies v. Swan Motor Co. (Swansea) Ltd* [1949] 2 K.B. 291 at 310.

the term "damage" in the statute includes loss of life and personal injury.[123] This has meant that the statute applies not only to the actual accident in which the plaintiff has been injured but also the extent of the plaintiff's injury. Hence if those injuries would have been less extensive had he used a precaution such as a safety belt or a crash helmet, the provisions as to contributory negligence can be applied to reduce the amount recoverable by the plaintiff.[124] "Fault" in the Act means "negligence, breach of statutory duty or other act or omission which gives rise to a liability in tort or would, apart from this Act, give rise to the defence of contributory negligence".[125] However this does not mean that proof of some such act will automatically amount to proof of contributory negligence.[126]

(ii) Last opportunity

13.38 A number of different views have been expressed as to the result of this statute with respect to the last opportunity or last clear chance rule. It has been said that there never was such a rule, therefore the Act of 1945 could not abolish it.[127] It has been said that the rule was defunct apart from, and before the passing of the Act.[128] It has also been stated that the Act abolished the rule and rendered it obsolete, because it was not necessary to go to extreme lengths to avoid the conclusion that the plaintiff would fail because of contributory negligence.[129] An alternative way of expressing this is by saying that as a practical matter the rule will not be of great importance after the Act.[130] But it has also been suggested that the rule is unaffected by the Act and is still a necessary part of the law although in a limited way and sense, namely, where there is actual knowledge of the dangerous situation created by the other party and a reasonable opportunity to avoid it, which is not taken.[131] As Lord Porter said in *Stapley v. Gypsum Mines Ltd*,[132] the abolition of the rule that any contributory negligence, however small, on the part of the plaintiff defeated his claim has no effect on causation. Courts may have to seek less strenously to find some ground for holding the plaintiff free from blame, or for concluding that the plaintiff's conduct played no part in his ultimate injury. What was the cause of an event, however, leads to an inquiry of the

123 Law Reform (Contributory Negligence) Act 1945 s. 4.

124 *O'Connell v. Jackson* [1972] 1 Q.B. 270; *Capps v. Miller* [1989] 2 All E.R. 333. Cp. the Canadian decisions, which have gone in the same direction: Fridman, *Law of Torts in Canada*, Vol. 1, at 377–380.

125 *Supra* note 123. But does it apply to breach of contract? This is a vexed, and unresolved question.

126 *Westwood v. Post Office* [1974] A.C. 1.

127 *The Boy Andrew* [1948] A.C. 140 at 148 *per* Viscount Simon: cp. *Alford v. Magee*, *supra*.

128 *Davies v. Swan Motor Co. (Swansea) Ltd*, *supra* at 318 *per* Denning L.J. This was also the view in Australia: Fleming, *Law of Torts*, 7th ed. 1987, at 252–3.

129 *Jones v. Livox Quarries* [1952] 1 T.L.R. 1377 at 1383 *per* Denning L.J.; *Harvey v. Road Haulage Executive* [1952] 1 K.B. 120 at 126; cp. *Winfield & Jolowicz on Tort*, 12th ed. 1984 at 158 note 62.

130 *Grant v. Sun Shipping Co. Ltd* [1948] A.C. 549 at 563–564 *per* Lord Du Parcq.

131 This was the view of Goodhart (1949) 65 L.Q.R. at 239, 246, 255; cp. Asquith L.J., dissenting in *Henley v. Cameron* (1948) 65 T.L.R. 17 at 20.

132 [1953] A.C. 663 at 677: cp. *Marvin Sigurdson v. British Columbia Electric Railway Co. Ltd* [1953] A.C. 291 at 303–304 *per* Lord Tucker.

same nature as existed before the change in the law. The doctrine has been abolished by statute in some jurisdictions, viz., Ireland[133] and Prince Edward Island.[134] Its abolition has been recommended elsewhere.[135] Until such time as this is achieved by legislation, however, despite the views of some writers,[136] it may be argued that, albeit in an attenuated version and with a more limited scope, the doctrine survives the apportionment legislation of 1945.[137]

(iii) Apportionment

13.39 The statute provides for the reduction of a plaintiff's damages to the extent that the court thinks just and equitable having regard to the plaintiff's share in the responsibility for the damage. The effect of contributory negligence, once it is established as a matter of law that this has occurred, is a question of fact.[138] The court has complete discretion as to how to make the apportionment.[139] That discretion must be exercised in accordance with general legal principles: and an appellate court may disturb the original findings of a trial judge in cases where he has erred in principle or has failed to take into account a factor that was relevant.[140]

13.40 The issue that has produced the greatest difficulty in regard to the interpretation and application of the statute is whether the apportionment that is made should be based upon causation or blameworthiness. It is obvious that the two do not always coincide. The older law of contributory negligence was firmly founded on the notion of causation, rather than responsibility (although the last opportunity or last clear chance rule suggests a possible moral foundation derived from the issue of culpability for the determination of whether certain conduct was contributory negligence.) The newer law is more concerned with achieving a just result in terms of the compensation of the plaintiff and the correct distribution of liability between two negligent litigants based upon the comparative effects of their respective acts or omissions. It is noteworthy in this regard that American courts and writers refer to the subject of apportionment on the basis of contributory negligence as "comparative negligence".[141]

133 Civil Liability Act 1961 s. 56.

134 S.P.E.I. 1978, c. 3, s. 4, as amended by S.P.E.I. 1980, c. 17, s. 1.

135 E.g. in Alberta, Report of the Alberta Institute of Law Research and Reform, No. 31, *Contributory Negligence and Concurrent Tortfeasors*, 1979, at 10; in Ontario, Report of the Ontario Law Reform Commission on *Contribution Among Wrongdoers and Contributory Negligence*, 1988 at 259.

136 E.g., *Salmond & Heuston on Torts*, 19th ed. 1987 at 575–576; contrast *Winfield & Jolowicz on Torts*, 12th ed. 1984 at 152–153.

137 E.g., in Canada, apart from Prince Edward Island: Fridman, *op. cit.* at 380–382.

138 To be determined by a jury if there is one; 1945 Act, s. 1(6).

139 By looking at the matter broadly: *Gregory v. Kelly* [1978] R.T.R. 426; even if the plaintiff's employer is not a party to an action in which it is sought to be pleaded that the plaintiff was not wearing a safety helmet as instructed by his employer while working at the defendant's premises: *Turner v. Ford Motor Co. Ltd* [1965] 2 All E.R. 583.

140 See e.g., *Capps v. Miller* [1989] 2 All E.R. 333, below. But not on the ground that the appellate tribunal would have made a different apportionment: *Owners of British Columbia Electric Railway Co. Ltd* [1953] A.C. 291; *Kerry v. Carter* [1969] 3 All E.R. 723.

141 See e.g., Turk, "Comparative Negligence on the Move" (1950) 28 Chi-Kent L.R. 189; Schwartz, "Contributory and Comparative Negligence: A Reappraisal" (1978) 87 Yale L.J. 697; Fleming, "Comparative Negligence At Last–By Judicial Choice" (1976) 64 Calif. L.R. 239. Cp. the American Uniform Comparative Fault Act.

13.41 Causation and responsibility as bases for apportionment have both been advanced. Yet both have their shortcomings. To rely on causation as a method of assessing apportionment may lead to the return of some of the more egregious defects of the old system: and can also involve contemplation of degrees of causation which has been described as a nightmarish conception.[142] To choose blameworthiness[143] as the foundation for apportionment may result in denial of recovery if the plaintiff has been guilty of some breach of duty based on strict liability, entailing no factually faulty behaviour.[144] To avoid such undesirable consequences, which might emasculate the protection given by the creation of strict statutory duties through the side-wind of apportionment,[145] it seems clear now, as a result of several decisions,[146] that both causation and blameworthiness must be considered when assessing apportionment. Somehow, although not on a mathematical basis,[147] nor by concentrating solely on either causation or responsibility, i.e. blameworthiness, the court must arrive at what is a "just and equitable" conclusion.

13.42 Whatever principles apply to determination of involvement of the parties in the happening of the accident in which the plaintiff was injured, also apply with equal force and effect to the apportionment of liability for the actual injury suffered. Thus the issue of contributory negligence has been raised where there was no question as to causation of the collision, but the question was whether the plaintiff, by failing to take proper precautions, may have produced greater or more extensive injury than otherwise would have resulted, for example by not wearing a safety belt (which is now compulsory, so that a plaintiff's failure to do so may amount to a breach of statutory duty, i.e legal fault as defined in the 1945 Act, on his part). In *Froom v. Butcher*[148] it was held that there should be a "conventional" 25% reduction if the injury would have been avoided completely had the belt been worn: and 15% if the injuries would have been less severe.[149] However in *Capps v. Miller*[150] the Court of Appeal distinguished between a case where the plaintiff was not wearing a safety belt at all (or a crash helmet as in that instance, which the court indicated was equivalent to a safety belt since both were the subject of compulsory use as a result of statutory regulations) and a case where the belt or helmet was worn but not properly fastened. *Capps v. Miller* was an instance of the

142 Chapman, (1948) 64 L.Q.R. 28.
143 I.e. the degree of departure from the standards of the reasonable man, rather than moral blameworthiness: *Pennington v. Norris* (1956) 96 C.L.R. 10.
144 *Lavender v. Diamints Ltd* [1948] 2 All E.R.249 at 252 *per* Denning L.J.
145 *Mullard v. Ben Line Steamers Ltd* [1970] 1 W.L.R. 1414 at 1418 *per* Sachs L.J.
146 *Davies v. Swan Motor Co. (Swansea) Ltd* [1949] 2 K.B. 291; *Stapley v. Gypsum Mines Ltd* [1953] A.C. 663; *The British Aviator* [1965] 1 Lloyd's Rep. 271; *The Miraflores and The Abedesa* [1967] 1 All E.R. 672; *Brown v. Thompson* [1968] 2 All E.R. 708; *Kearney v. British Railways Board* [1968] 2 All E.R. 532.
147 *Connor v. Port of Liverpool Stevedoring Co.* [1953] 2 Lloyd's Rep. 606; *Williams v. Port of Liverpool Stevedoring Co.* [1956] 1 W.L.R. 551.
148 [1976] Q.B. 286.
149 For the Canadian approach see Fridman, *op. cit.* at 379. On the seat-belt defence generally *ibid.* at 377–378.
150 [1989] 2 All E.R. 333.

second situation. The trial judge had held that the negligent defendant's responsibility for the plaintiff's injuries had not been reduced to any significant extent; therefore the plaintiff's damages would not be reduced. The Court of Appeal reversed this decision. In doing so Croom-Johnson L.J. pointed out that there was no rule that if the plaintiff's contributory negligence was less than 10% there should be no apportionment.[151] On the contrary, where the plaintiff was in breach of a statutory duty, as here, it was wrong to ignore his contribution to his injuries. Nor was this a case for the application of the *de minimis* principle. Hence there was contributory negligence that should be taken into account. On the issue of how much should be attributed to the plaintiff, Croom-Johnson L.J. accepted the guidelines suggested by Lord Denning in *Froom v. Butcher*, but decided that in the circumstances of this case the lower figure of 15% should be reduced to 10%. Glidewell L.J. agreed with this on the ground that "where a crash helmet is worn but not properly fastened, the whole scale of reduction, because of the lesser blameworthiness, should to an extent be less".[152] May L.J. agreed with this.[153]

13.43 An additional complication may be caused by the fact that there have been successive accidents, as well as contributory negligence by the plaintiff. For example, the plaintiff may be struck first by a car driven by one defendant and then by a car driven by a second defendant, as in *Fitzgerald v. Lane*.[154] In *The Miraflores and Abedesa*,[155] a case which fell to be determined under the apportionment provisions of the Maritime Conventions Act 1911, two tankers collided. To avoid becoming involved in that collision a third tanker ran aground and sustained damage. The owners of this third tanker sued the owners of the other two tankers. The owners of one of those tankers also sued the owners of the other one in respect of their collision. These two actions were heard together, when it was held that in respect of the collision tanker 1 was one third and tanker 2 two-thirds to blame. In regard to the grounding action, the judge held that the tanker that ran aground was also negligent. He treated the collision causing negligence as one unit and the grounding negligence as another unit. He could not distinguish between the degrees of fault of the two units. Therefore he held that the tanker that ran aground was 50% to blame, which meant that its owners could recover the other 50% of the cost of the damage sustained from the owners of the other two tankers in proportion of one-third and two-thirds respectively. The House of Lords held that this "unit" approach was wrong. The 1911 Act contemplated individual assessment of each vessel liable for the damage. Hence the House of Lords could reassess apportionment. They therefore allotted two-fifths of the liability to one of the two colliding tankers, one-fifth to the other, and two-fifths to the tanker that ran aground. In *Fitzgerald v.*

151 *Ibid.* at 340, discussing the unreported case of *Johnson v. Tennant Bros. Ltd* (1954), which had been said to be the basis for the rule.
152 *Supra* note 150 at 343.
153 *Ibid.*
154 [1988] 2 All E.R. 961.
155 [1967] 1 All E.R. 672.

Lane,[156] Lord Ackner pointed out that the scheme of the 1911 Act was not the same as that of the 1945 Act, which specifically provides that the legislation on contribution between two or more tortfeasors[157] applies where two or more persons are liable or would, if sued, be liable under the 1945 Act in respect of damage suffered by any person. Hence Lord Ackner preferred the statement by Denning L.J. in *Davies v. Swan Motor Co. (Swansea) Ltd*[158] to one by Lord Pearce in the *Miraflores* case.[159] Denning L.J. said that the 1945 Act contemplated that if the plaintiff's own fault was one of the causes of the accident, his damages were to be reduced by the self-same amount as against any of the others whose fault was a cause of the accident, whether the plaintiff sued one or more of them, and the defendants bore the amount so reduced in the appropriate proportions as between themselves. The result of this examination of the statutes and the case-law was that under the 1945 Act in such circumstances the incidents were to be regarded as a unit and the various degrees of contribution sorted out as one calculation. Hence in *Fitzgerald v. Lane* the House of Lords agreed with the Court of Appeal,[160] which had reversed the trial judge and held that the plaintiff was only entitled to recover half, not two-thirds of the damages awarded. Two issues appear to have been settled by this decision in relation to cases involving more than one defendant, where those defendants had a claim for contribution *inter se*. First, apportionment of that contribution was a separate issue to be considered after apportionment of liability and contributory negligence between plaintiff and defendants. Second, in determining contributory negligence between the plaintiff and the defendants the plaintiff's conduct was to be contrasted with the totality of the defendant's tortious conduct rather than the extent to which each defendant's fault contributed to the damage.

5. THE PLAINTIFF'S ILLEGALITY[161]

13.44 It has been suggested, and in one instance the suggestion was adopted and acted upon,[162] that a plaintiff who was involved in criminal activity at the time he was injured by the negligence of the defendant should be disqualified from successfully maintaining an action, on the ground that it is against public policy to permit someone to sue when he

156 [1988] 2 All E.R. 961 at 968–969.
157 Above Chapter 4.
158 [1949] 2 K.B. 291 at 325.
159 *Supra* note 155 at 677.
160 [1987] 2 All E.R. 455.
161 Gibson, "Illegality of Plaintiff's Conduct as a Defence" (1969) 47 C.B.R. 89; Wienrib, "Illegality as Tort Defence" (1976) 26 U.T.L.J. 28; Fridman, "The Wrongdoing Plaintiff" (1972) 18 McGill L.J. 275; Crago "The Defence of Illegality in Negligence Actions" (1964) 4 M.U.L.R. 534.
162 *Ashton v. Turner* [1981] Q.B. 137.

himself was acting criminally at the material time.[163] Just as no action can be brought on a contract that is illegal, so, it is argued, an action in tort should not be available to a participant in some illegal behaviour which produces his injury. *Ex turpi causa non oritur actio*, a maxim which originally applied to contracts, has been invoked in this context to deny an action.

13.45 The relevance of the plaintiff's illegal activity to an action by him for assault has previously been examined.[164] Where negligence is concerned there appears to be less authority in England, although the matter has been considered on several occasions by the Canadian and Australian courts.[165] In many instances the plaintiff's action could be denied on the basis of *volenti* or perhaps his contributory negligence. In one English case[166] the plaintiff failed to recover on the ground that the police officer who struck the car in which the plaintiff was travelling was not negligent. Hence it was unnecessary to consider the effect, if any, of the fact that the car in which the plaintiff was a passenger had been taken without the consent of the owner. In *Ashton v. Turner*,[167] however, the plaintiff's claim was specifically rejected on the ground that, because he was a participant in a crime being committed at the time by the allegedly negligent defendant, the defendant owed the plaintiff no duty of care.

13.46 There are many problems entailed in attempting to frame a rule which would differentiate situations where the plaintiff's illegal activity at the material time should disentitle him to sue from those where it would be unreasonable to achieve such a result. One is the issue of causation. The question is the extent to which the criminal act of the plaintiff was relevant to, and a factor in, the occurrence of his injury.[167a] Some acts clearly are the cause of the plaintiff's harm: for example, where two thieves are blowing open a safe and the carelessness of one results in an explosion in which the other is hurt. Some acts are not: for example, where, on the way to commit a crime, one participant drives so carelessly that there is an accident in which the other is injured. Secondly, the question is raised whether the basis for denial of recovery is public policy in general or

163 *National Coal Board v. England* [1954] A.C. 403 at 429 *per* Lord Asquith. But this did not apply where the deceased committed suicide in a remand centre. Suicide is no longer a crime and the public would no longer be shocked by allowing a widow to recover damages for the negligence of the police in not informing the remand centre of his suicidal tendencies; *Kirkham v. Anderton* (1990) The Times 4 January. But see the cases cited at note 167a *infra*.

164 Above pp. 133–4.

165 Canada: *Tallow v. Tailfeathers* [1973] 6 W.W.R. 732; *Funk v. Clapp* (1984) 12 D.L.R. (4th) 62; *Rondos v. Wawrin* (1968) 68 D.L.R. (2d) 658; *Tomlinson v. Harrison* [1972] 1 O.R. 670; *Bond v. Loutit* [1979] 2 W.W.R. 154; *Schill v. Weimer* (1980) 5 Sask. R. 112; *Rodrigue v. Penner* (1970) 74 W.W.R. 96. Australia: *Sullivan v. Sullivan* (1961) 79 W.N. (N.S.W.) 615; *Boeyen v. Kidd* [1963] V.R. 235; *Bonarenko v. Sommers* (1967) 69 S.R. (N.S.W.) 269; *Mills v. Baitis* [1968] V.R. 583; *Smith v. Jenkins* (1970) 119 C.L.R. 397; *Jackson v. Harrison* (1978) 19 A.L.R. 129.

166 *Marshall v. Osmond* [1983] Q.B. 1034.

167 *Supra* note 162.

167a That is, the issue of the proximity of the tort: cp. *Thackwell v. Barclays Bank* [1986] 1 All E.R. 676; *Sanders v. Edwards* [1987] 2 All E.R. 651; *Euro-Diam v. Bathurst* [1988] 2 All E.R. 23, which establishes that the *ex turpi* defence is not confined to criminal conduct: *Kirkham v. Anderton supra* note. 163.

something more specific. Thus, the crime may be trivial or relatively insignificant: for example, as in an Australian case, *Jackson v. Harrison*,[168] driving a vehicle while disqualified. The issue in such instances is whether the mere fact of criminality, to whatever degree, should suffice to disentitle the plaintiff. It seems clear that the plaintiff's breach of a statutory provision relating to industrial safety will not thereby automatically disqualify him from recovery.[169] Only if that misconduct on his part can be regarded as making him *volens*, or as constituting contributory negligence, will his breach of a statutory duty placed on him have any effect upon his right to sue in respect of his employer's negligence or breach of statutory duty, or the negligence of a fellow-employee for which the employer will be liable vicariously.[170] Thirdly, the issue has been raised whether to admit a defence of *ex turpi causa* is to negate the existence of a duty altogether, or whether it is better to say that although a duty was owed in such circumstances, the plaintiff will not be permitted to sue because to allow him to do so would be an improper use of the jurisdiction of the court.[171]

13.47 Canadian courts, which have not been too happy about the invocation and use of the plea that the plaintiff was acting illegally when he was injured, have set out certain elements of the defence that must be established before it can be maintained.[172] These are: (i) a necessary causal connection between the criminal act and the injury; (ii) the existence of a common intention between the parties, i.e. their execution of a common illegal purpose at the time; and (iii) the plaintiff's kmowledge that a criminal offence was being committed. In the absence of any one of these, the defence of illegality will not succeed. So far as the law in England is concerned, however, it must be stressed that whatever the final outcome of the discussion of this problem, the mere fact that the plaintiff was a wrongdoer will not of itself constitute a valid answer to an action for negligence.[173] When it will, however, remains unsettled.

168 *Supra* note 165: cp. the views of Clement J. A. in *Tallow v. Tailfeathers* [1973] 6 W.W.R. 732 at 742 as to the distinction between infringement of the Canadian Federal Criminal Code and commission of a crime under provincial or municipal law (which relates to less serious offences).

169 *National Coal Board v. England, supra.*

170 Cp. *I.C.I. Ltd v. Shatwell* [1965] A.C. 656; *Cakebread v. Hopping Bros. (Whetstone) Ltd* [1947] K.B. 641.

171 *Smith v. Jenkins, supra* note 165; cp. *Hillen v. I.C.I. (Alkali) Ltd* [1934] 1 K.B. 455 (reversed on appeal on other grounds: [1936] A.C. 65); *Danluk v. Birkner* [1946] 3 D.L.R. 172.

172 Fridman, *The Law of Torts in Canada*, Vol. 1 at 350–352.

173 Cp. *Henwood v. Municipal Tramways Trust* (1938) 60 C.L.R. 438 at 446 *per* Latham C.J. Although it may very well make the plaintiff's injuries too remote a consequence of the defendant's act: *Ginty v. Belmont Building Supplies Ltd* [1959] 1 All E.R. 414; *Rushton v. Turner Bros. Asbestos Co.* [1959] 3 All E.R. 517; *Boyle v. Kodak* [1969] 2 All E.R. 439 at 446 *per* Lord Diplock.

CHAPTER 14

Some Varieties of Negligence

1. LIABILITY FOR CHATTELS

(a) The immediate transferee

(i) Under contract

14.01 Where a chattel is transferred under a contract, the question whether any duty of care is owed by the transferor to the transferee and, if so, the nature and content of such a duty, involves matters to be determined by reference to the type of contract concerned and its terms. The duties of a seller of goods, for example, depend on the express and implied terms of the contract, including, where applicable, such terms as are implied under the Sale of Goods Act 1979.[1] In such situations no negligence or other fault need be proved as long as the condition of the goods was such as to entail a breach of the terms of the contract, whether expressly agreed by the parties, implied at common law, or by virtue of the legislation.[2] However, unless prohibited by statute,[3] the parties are free to exclude any otherwise applicable terms or to modify them in any way. The effect of any such exclusion or modification will depend on the application of contractual doctrines such as the doctrine of fundamental breach of contract.[4] Other contracts involving the transfer of chattels, similar to contracts of sale of goods, such as contracts of hire purchase, are also regulated by terms implied at common law or under statute.[5] Where contractual liability arises for the transfer of goods that do not fulfill the requirements of the contract, the liability of the transferor includes liability for personal injury or damage to property caused by such goods[6] as well as economic loss resulting from the breach, e.g., the cost of repairing the chattel or making it accord with the contractual requirements, the greater cost of a replacement chattel, or consequential loss

1 Viz., those relating to correspondence with description, merchantable quality, fitness for purpose and title.
2 Note also the possibility of offences in connection with the supply of defective goods under the Trade Descriptions Act 1968, the Fair Trading Act 1973 and the Consumer Protection Act 1987, Part I (enacting the product liability Directive of the EEC dated 25 July 1985).
3 E.g. Unfair Contract Terms Act 1977 s. 12.
4 Cheshire, Fifoot & Furmston, *Law of Contract*, 11th ed. 1986, at 164–171, 526–532.
5 Viz., Supply of Goods (Implied Terms) Act 1973, as amended by the Consumer Credit Act 1974; Supply of Goods and Services Act 1982.
6 *Grant v. Australian Knitting Mills* [1936] A.C. 85; *Andrews v. Hopkinson* [1957] 1 Q.B. 224; *Godley v. Perry* [1960] 1 All E.R. 36 (personal injury): *Vacwell Engineering Co. Ltd v. B.D.H. Chemicals Ltd* [1957] 1 Q.B. 88 (damage to property).

arising from the breach such as damages paid to a third party. These issues are matters for the law of contract, not the law of torts.

14.02 If the transfer is effected under a contract of bailment, such as a contract of hire or deposit, the common law recognises that the bailor for consideration owes the bailee a duty of care. In *Blakemore v. Bristol & Exeter Railway Co.*,[7] Coleridge J. said that the lender must be taken to lend for the purpose of a beneficial use by the borrower. Therefore, just as the borrower was not responsible for reasonable wear and tear of the chattel, but was liable for negligence, for misuses, or for gross want of skill in the use of the chattel, so, on the other hand,

> "as the lender lends for beneficial use, he must be responsible for defects in the chattel with reference to the use for which he knows the loan is accepted, of which he is aware, and owing to which directly the borrower is injured."

This statement was cited more recently by Chapman J. in *Wheeler v. Copas*,[8] where approval was given to the principle that there is a duty on a bailor for reward within the ambit of negligence to take reasonable care to see that what he is lending is, so far as reasonable care can secure it, made safe for the purpose. What is said in these cases about the hire of chattels would seem to be applicable, *mutatis mutandis*, to other instances of bailment for reward.[9] The common law duty of such a bailor may be made more onerous or may be modified or excluded by the terms of a contract, insofar as the law of contract permits such an alteration to relieve the bailor in part or in whole of his duty or his liability for breach.

(ii) Where there is no contract

14.03 A chattel may be transferred outright by way of gift, or possession may be transferred gratuitously by a bailment without reward, as in the case of a loan not for consideration. In such situations the common law took took the view that, unless fraud were established, as where the transferor knew that the chattel was dangerous and did not reveal this to the donee or bailee,[10] the transferor would not be under any duty in respect of dangers of which he was unaware. He was not obliged to discover whether the chattel was dangerous and might injure the transferee.[11] In *Gautret v. Egerton*,[12] a case that was concerned with the liability of an occupier of land or premises towards a licensee, in which the law

7 (1858) 8 E. & B. 1035 at 1050–1051; see also *McCarthy v. Young* (1861) 6 H. & N. 329; *Oliver v. Saddler & Co.* [1929] A.C. 584.

8 [1981] 3 All E.R. 405 at 408–409, where negligence was relied on as an alternative to liability under the Occupiers' Liability Act 1957 when a ladder collapsed and injured the plaintiff who was working on the defendant's land.

9 But in cases of simple custody it has been suggested that the bailor is only responsible for non-disclosure of a known danger that might cause damage to other goods stored with the bailee: Paton, *Bailment in the Common Law*, at 172. Consignment of goods to a common carrier involves the consignor (bailor) in giving notice that goods are dangerous or in warranting that the goods are fit for carriage: *ibid.* at 262.

10 *Langridge v. Levy* (1837) 2 M. & W. 519, where the injured party was not the purchaser of the chattel but the son of the purchaser, i.e. fraud entitles a non-contracting party or other ultimate transferee to sue.

11 Paton, *op. cit.* at 113, 151–153.

12 (1867) L.R. 2 C.P. 371 at 375.

relating to gratuitous transfer of chattels was equated to the law at that time governing the liability of occupiers towards non-contractual visitors to their property,[13] Willes J. said:

> "The principle of law as to gifts is that the giver is not responsible for damage resulting from the insecurity of the thing unless he knew its evil character at the time and omitted to caution the donee. There must be something like fraud on the part of the giver before he can be made answerable."

Thus in *Coughlin v. Gillison*[14] the defendant allowed workmen, including the plaintiff, to use a donkey engine to move a ship. The boiler of the engine exploded, injuring the plaintiff. The Court of Appeal held that the plaintiff could not sue the defendant, who did not know of the defects in the engine. There was no negligence on his part, nor any concealment of a material fact. To this there was an exception. If the chattel belonged to the category of chattels dangerous *per se*, because its character was such that it would normally be a potential source of danger and injury, the transferee was under a duty to warn the transferor of that dangerous character. The law distinguished between such chattels and one which was not normally dangerous in character but, on this particular occasion, was dangerous because of a defect that was hidden and rendered the particular chattel potentially dangerous. For example, in *Farrant v. Barnes*[15] the chattel in question was a carboy that contained nitric acid. Of this fact the defendant was aware, though the plaintiff was not. In the circumstances it was held that there could be liability for an injury caused by the carboy, because the defendant ought to have warned the plaintiff of the inherently dangerous character of the thing with which he was dealing.

(b) Ultimate transferees and others

(i) Before Donoghue v. Stevenson

14.04 A chattel may be transferred by the original transferee, who acquired ownership or possession of the chattel under the contract with the original transferor, to another party. Unless such transfer entailed the creation of a contractual relationship between the ultimate transferee and the original transferor,[16] the latter owed no duty to the former. Nor was any duty owed by such a transferor to anyone else injured by reason of the dangerous condition of the chattel. A breach of the contract between the original transferor and tranferee gave no right of action for negligence against the transferor to a third person, not a party to the original contract, such as that party's spouse,[17] the consumer of a product purchased from a retailer who had obtained it from a manufacturer,[18] the

13 Below paras. 14.28ff.
14 [1899] 1 Q.B. 145.
15 (1862) 11 C.B.N.S. 553.
16 Cp. the chain of contracts in *Lambert v. Lewis* [1982] A.C. 225.
17 *Longmeid v. Holliday* (1851) 20 L.J. Ex. 430; but contrast *George v. Skivington* (1869) L.R. 5 Ex. 1. Contrast *White v. Steadman* [1913] 3 K.B. 340, which concerned a dangerous horse hired by the plaintiff's husband; the defendant knew of its vicious propensities.
18 *Bates v. Batey* [1913] 3 K.B. 351; *Blacker v. Lake & Elliott* (1912) 106 L.T. 533.

passenger in a vehicle on which a defective wheel had been placed by a repairer,[19] or a passer-by in the street injured when the wheel came off and struck him.[20] The same situation was the case where the original transfer had occurred under a gratuitous bailment or a gift. Liability might be imposed on the original transferor, however, if he had been guilty of fraud in concealing a defect of which he was aware and which he knew rendered the chattel dangerous.[21] Similarly, if the chattel could be considered to be dangerous *per se*, e.g. loaded firearms, poisons, explosives, liability might be imposed even where the injured party was neither the immediate transferee nor in a contractual relationship with the original transferor.[22] The distinction between chattels dangerous *per se* and other chattels became of great importance.[23]

14.05 A radical transformation of the law took place as a result of the decision of the House of Lords in *Donoghue v. Stevenson*.[24] In consequence the former division of chattels into two categories, those dangerous *per se* and others, may no longer have any relevance.[25] Furthermore, although this is more debatable, the distinction between liability for economic loss caused by defective goods by virtue of the law of contract and liability for personal injury or damage to property under the law of bailment or the law of tort may also have disappeared.[26] In *Donoghue v. Stevenson*, the decision of the majority of the House of Lords settled the question of a manufacturer's duty to those who used his product in a manner that overruled earlier decisions on the same point and opened the way for a more general, far-reaching concept of liability for negligence in the absence of a contractual relationship between plaintiff and defendant. It created a duty of care in respect of danger of which the transferor was unaware.

(ii) The decision in Donoghue v. Stevenson

14.06 The defendants were manufacturers of ginger beer that was bottled in opaque, stoppered bottles so that the contents of the bottle could

19 *Winterbottom v. Wright* (1842) 10 M. & W. 109; *Earl v. Lubbock* [1905] 1 K.B. 263.
20 *Stennett v. Hancock Peters* [1939] 2 All E.R. 578.
21 *Langridge v. Levy, supra* note 10.
22 *Dominion Natural Gas Co. v. Collins* [1909] A.C. 640; *Dixon v. Bell* (1816) 5 M. & S. 198; *Parry v. Smith* (1879) 4 C.P.D. 325; *Rainham Chemical Works Ltd v. Belvedere Fish Guano Co. Ltd* [1921] 2 A.C. 465. See also *Anglo-Celtic Shipping Co. Ltd v. Elliott* (1926) 42 T.L.R. 297. Cp. the American case of *Thomas v. Winchester* (1852) 6 N.Y. 397, where the bottle contained poison not dandelion. Contrast *Wray v. Essex County Council* [1936] 3 All E.R. 97; *Bell v. L.C.C.* [1949] 2 K.B. 159.
23 Knowledge of the dangerous nature of the chattel that is not normally dangerous would involve the transferor in a duty to warn: in such circumstances the chattel virtually becomes something dangerous *per se*: cp. *Barnes v. Irwell Valley Water Board* [1939] 1 K.B. 21; *Howard v. Furness Houlder Ltd* [1936] 2 All E.R. 781. But if the thing was dangerous *per se*, lack of knowledge of its danger would not exclude the defendant's liability: *Burfitt v. Kille* [1939] 2 K.B. 743. But the plaintiff's knowledge of the danger would: *Bottomley v. Bannister* [1932] 1 K.B. 458.
24 [1932] A.C. 562.
25 Below paras. 14.12ff.
26 Below pp. 379–80.

not be examined before the bottle was opened.[27] The offending bottle had been supplied by the manufacturers to a retailer who had sold it to a customer by whom it had been given to a friend. The latter poured out some of the ginger beer and drank it. On pouring out more of the ginger beer the plaintiff discovered that it contained the decomposed remains of a snail. This caused the plaintiff to become ill, in the contemplation of the possibility that she had consumed some of the snail. These allegations of fact were assumed to be correct for the purposes of the action[28] since, under Scots procedure, the case came before the House of Lords for the purpose of resolving the issue whether, on those facts, the plaintiff had a cause of action in negligence against the manufacturer. Over the dissent of two members of the House, the majority held that:

> "A manufacturer of products which he sells in such a form as to show that he intends them to reach the ultimate consumer in the form in which they left him with no reasonable possibility of intermediate examination and with the knowledge that the absence of reasonable care in the preparation or putting up of the products will result in an injury to the consumer's life or property owes a duty to the consumer to take reasonable care."[29]

This was what is sometimes referred to as the "narrow" *ratio decidendi* of the case. The wider impact and effect of the decision, in respect of the general nature of liability for negligence, has previously been considered.[30] What is material in the present context is the effect of *Donoghue v. Stevenson* in relation to the non-contractual liability of a person who transfers a chattel that ultimately causes harm to another where the transferor was negligent, not fraudulent.

(iii) Extension of the decision

14.07 The original decision was restricted to manufacturers. Subsequent cases have extended the scope of the duty of care created by *Donoghue v. Stevenson* to repairers,[31] erectors,[32] assemblers,[33] even suppliers of goods such as a dealer who sold a car to a finance company which then transferred the car to the plaintiff under a hire-purchase agreement (in other words to the usual case of a buyer of a car when the purchase is financed by the borrowing of money).[34] It would seem that any person dealing with a chattel in a way that entails its transfer to someone otherwise than under a contract with that person (even though the original transfer was effected

27 But this was rejected as not material to the decision by the court in *Clay v. Crump Co. Ltd* [1964] 1 Q.B. 533 at 558.
28 Cp. *Alder v. Dickson* [1954] 1 W.L.R. 1482; *Freeman v. Home Office* [1984] 1 Q.B. 524. The action was compromised so the issue of facts was never tried.
29 *Supra* note 24 at 599 *per* Lord Atkin.
30 Chapter 12.
31 *Malfroot v. Noxal* (1934) 51 T.L.R. 551; *Herschel v. Stewart & Arden* [1940] 1 K.B. 155; *Haseldine v. Daw* [1941] 2 K.B. 343.
32 *Brown v. Cotterill* (1934) 51 T.L.R. 21.
33 *Howard v. Furness Houlder Ltd* [1936] 2 All E.R. 781; and builders: *Sharpe v. E.T. Sweeting & Son Ltd* [1963] 2 All E.R. 455.
34 *Andrews v. Hopkinson* [1957] 1 Q.B. 229; and those who let out goods in hire: *Astley Industrial Trust Ltd v. Grimley* [1963] 2 All E.R. 33; in other words to anyone who produces something or does something active to create the danger. This may now include those who inspect and certify, e.g. a building: *Anns v. Merton London Borough Council* [1978] A.C. 728: above Chapter 12 at paras. 12.56–7.

under or as a result of a contract) is under a duty to use care to ensure that the ultimate user or consumer of the chattel is not injured. That duty may involve taking reasonable care to ensure that the chattel is reasonably safe. Or it may only require that an adequate warning is provided such as will enable the user or consumer to be guarded against potential harm.[35] In one Canadian case,[36] for example, the manufacturer of a product issued a warning in very general terms. The Supreme Court of Canada held that the warning should have been more specific or detailed so as to reveal to the consumer that certain precautions were to be taken or certain uses to be avoided. Similarly, it has been held in Canada that not only must doctors prescribing a drug warn patients of the potential effects of the drug but also manufacturers of the drug are under a duty to provide a suitable warning, even though they can expect that the patient will be advised by a doctor about such drug. To inform the doctor of the drug's actual or potential effects will not be sufficient where the inherent dangers of the drug are such that it is possible that, if advised thereof, the patient might choose not to take it. To escape liability it must be proved that, despite such warning, the patient would nevertheless have used the drug.[37]

14.08 *Donoghue v. Stevenson* involved an article of food or drink. Later cases have extended the application of the duty to chattels generally.[38] Moreover it is not only a user or consumer of the chattel to whom the duty is owed. Anyone who comes within physical proximity to the chattel, such that he or she can be affected injuriously by it, is also owed the same duty of care.[39] The duty is also owed in respect to containers, packages, or other means whereby the product is distributed as well as labels, directions and instructions for use that relate to and accompany it.[40]

14.09 The underlying rationale of the duty expounded in *Donoghue v. Stevenson* is the lack of any reasonable opportunity for the user or consumer to examine the chattel prior to use. Liability is postulated on the negligence of the transferor being the cause of the ultimate harm. This has two aspects. First: there must be no possibility that the harm was caused by someone else's act, whether or not negligent, or some intervening event that insulates the original negligence from the subsequent injury. For

35 *Homes v. Ashford* [1950] 2 All E.R. 76. Unless the warning would be insufficient, e.g. where the transferee is a child: *Burfitt v. Kille, supra*; *Yachuk v. Oliver Blais & Co. Ltd* [1949] A.C. 386.

36 *Lambert v. Lastoplex Chemicals Co.* [1972] S.C.R. 569; cp. *Distillers Co. (Biochemicals) Ltd v. Thompson* [1971] A.C. 458.

37 *Buchan v. Ortho Pharmaceuticals (Canada) Ltd* (1986) 52 O.R. (2d) 92; see Fridman, *Law of Torts in Canada*, Vol. 1, at 294–295.

38 *Paine v. Colne Valley Electrical Supply Co.* [1938] 4 All E.R. 503; *Brown v. Cotterill, supra*; *Watson v. Buckley* [1940] 1 All E.R. 174; *Hasledine v. Daw, supra*: *Herschel v. Stewart & Arden, supra*; *Grant v. Australian Knitting Mills* [1936] A.C. 85. It also includes land and buildings: *Rimmer v. Liverpool City Council* [1984] Q.B. 1; above Chapter 12 at para 12.45; statements, *ibid.* para. 12.35.

39 *Brown v. Cotterill, supra*; *Stennett v. Hancock* [1939] 2 All E.R. 578; cp. *Barnett v. Parker* [1940] 3 All E.R. 575.

40 *Barnes v. Irwell Valley Water Board* [1938] 2 All E.R. 650; *Watson v. Buckley, supra; Homes v. Ashford, supra.*

example, if a sufficient lapse of time has occurred between the manufacture of the product and the harm to the plaintiff, it may be that something other than negligent manufacture caused the product to be harmful. Similarly, if some other person has been involved in the preparation of the chattel for use, there is the possibility that such other person acted in a negligent way, and damaged the product so that it was not in its original, safe state.[41] The user may have employed the product in the wrong manner, capable of causing harm, instead of the proper way, when it would have been harmless.[42] Thus for liability to be imposed on the transferor, whether manufacturer or otherwise, it must be clear that nothing intervened to change the article or product between the time when the chattel was first transferred for the purpose of reaching the ultimate user or consumer and the time when it was used or consumed and caused injury. Secondly: liability will only ensue where there was no reasonable possibility or likelihood of an intermediate examination that would have revealed the danger.[43] Hence there will be no breach of duty and no liability where the plaintiff was aware of the danger but disregarded it[44] (unless such conduct on the part of the plaintiff was foreseeable by the defendants);[45] where an adequate warning was not given by a third party who knew of the danger and ought to have acted thereon but did not do so;[46] or where a third party knew of the danger and should have prevented the chattel from reaching other hands.[47] The test is whether an intermediate examination should have been foreseen by the defendant and would have been sufficient to reveal the danger.[48] However the fact that no intermediate examination was carried out may be more relevant to questions of causation or contributory negligence than to the primary issue whether a duty of care existed. It is one thing to say that the possibility of such an examination negates a duty of care and another to say that a duty to take reasonable care that the chattel was reasonably safe for use was imposed on the transferor, but that his neglect of proper performance of that duty was not the cause, or not the sole cause, of the plaintiff's injury. As noted in the context of negligence generally, there are situations in which the intervening neglect of others, including the plaintiff, may be the very danger against which the defendant ought to have guarded in view of what he ought to have foreseen as being probable.[49]

41 *Grant v. Australian Knitting Mills, supra*; *Evans v. Triplex Safety Glass Co. Ltd* [1936] 1 All E.R. 283; *Mason v. Williams & Williams Ltd* [1955] 1 All E.R. 808. Cp. the Canadian case of *MacLachlan & Mitchell Homes Ltd v. Frank's Rentals & Sales Ltd* (1980) 106 D.L.R. (3d) 245, which concerned the possible application of *res ipsa loquitur*: above Chapter 12 at paras. 12.86ff.

42 *Griffiths v. Arch Engineering Co. Ltd* [1968] 3 All E.R. 217: this may involve questions of contributory negligence.

43 E.g., washing pants before use: *Grant v. Australian Knitting Mills, supra*. But a careless examination may not exempt the manufacturer, etc.: *Clay v. Crump & Co. Ltd* [1964] 1 Q.B. 533.

44 *Farr v. Butters Bros & Co.* [1932] 2 K.B. 606.

45 *Denny v. Supplies & Transport Co. Ltd* [1950] 2 K.B. 374.

46 *Kulbach v. Hollands* [1939] 3 All E.R. 907.

47 *Taylor v. Rover Co. Ltd* [1966] 2 All E.R. 181.

48 *Griffiths v. Arch Engineering Co. Ltd., supra*.

49 Chapter 12 at pp. 341–2.

14.10 Finally, in one other respect the original decision in *Donoghue v. Stevenson* may have undergone development and extension. That case was concerned with personal, i.e., physical injury, as well as the possibility of damage to property. The decision was about chattels that were dangerous, not those that were defective without being dangerous. The duty of a manufacturer, and those in respect of whom it was subsequently held the duty could also apply, was not a duty to prevent the possibility of pure economic loss by taking reasonable care.[50] It has been said that later evolution of the law of negligence has made it possible to invoke this tort in certain situations where the only foreseeable harm that might result from negligent conduct was economic loss. By and large, except where negligent misstatement or negligent misrepresentation was involved, the courts have not been favourably disposed towards the argument that the tort of negligence can cover pure economic loss.[51] However, in *Junior Books Ltd. v. Veitchi Co. Ltd*[52] the majority of the House of Lords accepted that the narrow *ratio decidendi* of *Donoghue v. Stevenson* could apply to a situation where the foreseeable loss resulting from negligence in supplying a chattel could only have been economic. Sub-contractors, engaged by a general contractor who was building a factory, negligently installed a floor that was defective but not dangerous. This meant that the floor had to be replaced, during which time the factory was closed. This caused economic loss to the owners of the factory. That loss was recoverable, in tort, from the subcontractors, with whom the owners were not connected by a contract. On the particular facts of this case it was held that there was sufficient proximity between the parties to permit the imposition of a tort duty of care on the sub-contractors vis-à-vis the owners of the factory. It is doubtful, however, whether this decision could be used to generate a wider form of *Donoghue v. Stevenson* liability in respect of pure economic loss as between manufacturers, repairers, suppliers, etc., and ultimate users and consumers to whom the former are not contractually bound. The decision has been severely criticised and restricted to its special circumstances, in language which indicates that it will not have general application.[53]

14.11 Admittedly there have been decisions in which the suggestion has been made, independently of the *Junior Books* case, that an action in negligence may be brought against a negligent manufacturer, to recover the cost of repairing a dangerous chattel which is the product of negligent manufacture,[54] by the ultimate owner or hirer of the chattel who has incurred that economic loss. Also, where a negligent breach of contract causes economic loss, it is now possible for one contracting party to sue the

50 Cp. the Canadian case of *Ital-Canadian Investments Ltd v. North Shore Plumbing & Heating Co. Ltd* [1978] 4 W.W.R. 289, with which contrast *Maughan v. International Harvester Co. of Canada Ltd* (1981) 112 D.L.R. (3d) 243.

51 Chapter 12 at paras. 12.40ff.

52 [1983] A.C. 520: see Chapter 12 at paras. 12.45–47.

53 Chapter 12 at para. 12.51.

54. *Batty v. Metropolitan Property Realisations Ltd* [1978] Q.B. 554; *Anns v. Merton London Borough Council* [1978] A.C. 728. Cp. *City of Kamloops v. Nielsen* (1984) 10 D.L.R. (4d) 641; *Smith v. Melancon* [1976] 4 W.W.R. 9; *Ordog v. District of Mission* (1980) 110 D.L.R. (3d) 718.

other negligent one in tort as well as contract.[55] Such decisions suggest that there is no great impediment to the bringing of a tort action for negligence in the fact that thereby the restrictions of the law of contract may be outflanked by the plaintiff. One of the arguments against the view adopted by the majority of the House of Lords in the *Junior Books* case was that it enabled someone who was not privy to a contract to sue for the negligent breach of such contact, thereby contradicting a fundamental principle of contract law, namely the doctrine of privity.[56] One problem that could emerge in such situtations relates to the effect of an exemption or exclusion clause in the contract upon the tort liability to a third party of the contract-breaker. If the innocent party to a contract sues in tort rather than contract, the terms of the contract may be relevant to the issue of liability. Indeed they may have the effect of negating any such tort liability as an alternative to liability under the contract. But there is no logical or even practical reason why the terms of a contract between A and B should affect the issue of possible tort liability by B to C, a non-party. What is really at stake here is not the logic of the law of negligence or the law of tort generally, but the question of policy. Post-*Junior Books* cases indicate that the courts are reluctant to extend *Donoghue v. Stevenson* liability in relation to dangerous or defective chattels which are transferred by the defendant and used or consumed by someone not contractually bound to the transferor too far beyond the confines of personal injury or damage to property.[57] The reason for this may be to preserve the distinction between contractual relations and those which arise under the law of torts. It may be because to open up the scope of liability for pure economic loss could lead to onerous responsibility for negligence, which the Privy Council declared was not in the general interest in the context of *The Wagon Mound (No. 1)*,[58] in that it was neither socially nor morally acceptable. Or it may be because it would involve the interpretation of "proximity" in ways which would make that expression vague, uncertain and ultimnately useless as a basis for distinguishing between legitimate causes of action and those where the imposition of liability for negligence would be counterproductive.

(iv) The demise of chattels dangerous per se

14.12 The distinction made before *Donoghue v. Stevenson* between chattels dangerous *per se* and other chattels was made necessary by the refusal of the law to accept a general concept of negligence, and in particular a generalised idea of negligence in relation to the transfer of chattels otherwise than under or by virtue of a contract. Whether it remains necessary or justifiable to make any such distinction after 1932 has been questioned.

14.13 Where a chattel is particularly dangerous in character there seems little doubt that a higher standard of care must be observed by the

55 Above at pp. 312–14.
56 But this was the argument against liability in negligence prior to *Donoghue v. Stevenson.*
57 Above Chapter 12 at pp. 298–302.
58 [1961] A.C. 388: above, Chapter 12 at p. 340.

defendant than in the case of chattels not normally dangerous but dangerous on a given occasion because of the defendant's negligence.[59] This does not mean that such normally dangerous chattels are the subject of a special duty or liability. Even before *Donoghue v. Stevenson* the concept of chattels dangerous *per se* was criticised as being too vague.[60] Since *Donoghue v. Stevenson*, if not before, the elasticity of reasonable care has been recognised, making it less important to make the earlier distinction. Indeed since the law has now accepted the possibility that there can be liability in negligence, in the absence of a contractual relationship between the parties, where the injury was the result of a defect in a chattel that was part of realty, it has become even less vital to classify such a chattel as dangerous *per se*, in order to overcome the earlier refusal of the law to provide a remedy where the injured party was not the purchaser of the realty or a tenant.[61]

14.14 Admittedly some post-*Donoghue v. Stevenson* dicta suggest (a) that the distinction persists and (b) that where a chattel is not dangerous *per se* negligence must be proved before there will be liability, whereas with dangerous chattels there will be liability unless the danger is removed by taking necessary precautions.[62] Such remarks give the impression that where a thing is dangerous by nature a special responsibility exists to take care to ensure that the thing does not cause harm. The more acceptable view today is that, whatever the nature of the thing, negligence in its handling must be established. However there are indications that the more dangerous the thing the more easily will a conclusion of negligence be reached.[63] This should not be considered as imposing something akin to strict liability where dangerous things are involved. The obligation on the defendant may be more onerous: and the plaintiff, by the invocation of the doctrine of *res ipsa loquitur*, may be able more easily to prove negligence on the part of the defendant. But the liability remains liability for negligence, i.e. breach of the duty of care that was owed by the defendant. As seen earlier, the doctrine of *res ipsa loquitur* may be, and has been, relied on by plaintiffs where proof of negligence would be hard, if not impossible for the plaintiff to obtain, as long as the situation was one that entitled a court to infer that there probably was negligence by the defendant or his servants or agents; else what occurred would never have happened.[64] Subject to what has been said previously with respect to the effect of the maxim when it is applicable, it may be suggested that in appropriate cases liability for negligence in the handling of a dangerous chattel may have become more like strict liability for injuries caused by such a thing. The more inherently

59 *Donoghue v. Stevenson* [1932] A.C. 562 at 595–598 *per* Lord Atkin.
60 *Hodge v. Anglo-American Oil Co.* (1922) 12 Ll.L.R. 183 at 187 *per* Scrutton L.J.
61 *Ball v. L.C.C.* [1949] 2 K.B. 156; with which contrast the pre-*Donoghue v. Stevenson* case of *Bottomley v. Bannister* [1932] 1 K.B. 458.
62 *Glasgow Corporation v. Muir* [1943] A.C. 448 at 463–464 *per* Lord Wright; *Read v. J. Lyons & Co. Ltd* [1947] A.C. 156 at 172 *per* Lord Macmillan.
63 *Burfitt v. Kille* [1939] 2 K.B. 743: cp. the pre-*Donoghue v. Stevenson* cases of *Dominion Natural Gas Co. v. Collins* [1909] A.C. 640 at 646 *per* Lord Dunedin; and *Oliver v. Saddler & Co.* [1929] A.C. 584 at 599 *per* Lord Dunedin.
64 Chapter 12 at pp. 322–7.

dangerous the thing, the more onerous the responsibility of the defendant and, consequently, the stricter his potential liability. In that sense, and to that extent, there may still be some merit and point to the prior distinction between chattels dangerous *per se* and other chattels. Apart from this, however, the distinction has been rendered obsolete and irrelevant by *Donoghue v. Stevenson* and its aftermath.

2. OCCUPIERS' LIABILITY

(a) The common law

14.15 Long before *Donoghue v. Stevenson*[65] the common law acknowledged that one who occupied premises might owe a duty of care to those who entered thereon. Independently of the evolution of a general tort of negligence, there emerged a considerable body of law which regulated the obligations and liabilities of occupiers. The matters which were the subject of development were: (a) the characterisation of the premises in respect of which duties were owed; (b) the definition of the term "occupier"; (c) the classification of entrants or visitors into several distinct categories; (d) the evolution of the duties owed by an occupier towards these various categories of visitors; and (e) the circumstances under which these duties might be excluded or modified or the occupier's liability might not arise. The multitude of decisions produced fine distinctions, conflicting opinions, uncertainty and, to some extent, injustice. Eventually it became evident that there was need for a radical overhaul that could be undertaken only by legislative action. In consequence of a report by the Law Reform Committee in 1954,[66] the Occupiers' Liability Act 1957 was enacted. This replaced the common law with respect to certain classes of visitors (as well as making other changes in the law in relation to the obligations of landlords).[67] The 1957 Act did not deal with the prior common law dealing with an occupier's liability towards trespassers, those on his land without his permission. After the enactment of the legislation the courts themselves made inroads on the previous law,[68] notably by the decision of the House of Lords in *British Railways Board v. Herrington*.[69] In 1984, by the passage of another Occupiers' Liability Act, the situation of trespassers was brought into the general statutory scheme.[70] At the same time the more recent legislation provided for the obligations of an occupier with regard to those exercising private rights of way and those exercising public rights of access, thereby changing the law that was left unaffected by the 1957 legislation.[71] The modern law relating to the liability of an occupier

65 [1932] A.C. 562.
66 Cmnd. 9305: its recommendations are summarised in North, *Occupiers' Liability*, 4–11.
67 S.4, since repealed by the Defective Premises Act, 1972: above para. 12.56.
68 On which see *Addie & Sons (Collieries) Ltd v. Dumbreck* [1929] A.C. 358; *Commissioner for Railways v. Quinlan* [1964] A.C. 1054.
69 [1972] A.C. 877: see also *Videan v. British Transport Commission* [1963] 2 Q.B. 650.
70 Occupiers' Liability Act 1984; below paras. 14.43ff.
71 *Greenhalgh v. British Railways Board* [1969] 2 Q.B. 286; *Holden v. White* [1982] 2 All E.R. 328; *Gautret v. Egerton* (1867) L.R. 2 C.P. 371.

therefore requires consideration of the statutes and the manner in which they have been interpreted and applied by the courts. However, in certain respects pre-1957 decisions may be invoked to illustrate or explain some of the terminology.

14.16 Originally the common law was concerned with the liability of an occupier for the static condition of his premises, whether land or something that was erected or built on land. This might include the condition of a chattel located on the premises, insofar as the chattel could be treated as part of the premises for this purpose. If the chattel were not in the occupation of the person who occupied the premises, liability for a defect in the chattel that caused injury was determined by reference to the law relating to dangerous chattels, not the law concerned with dangerous premises, i.e. occupiers' liability. This will still be the case under the modern, statutory law.[72] However, prior to 1957 a distinction was drawn between injury resulting from the static condition of premises or chattels thereon which were in the occupation and control of the defendant and injury caused by some activity being performed on the premises, whether by the occupier of the premises or someone else for whom the occupier was not responsible in law. Injuries of the latter type were dealt with under the general law of negligence, before and after *Donoghue v. Stevenson*, without regard to the classification of visitors that had emerged in relation to the liability of an occupier, with the exception of the distinction between those lawfully on the premises where the activity caused the injury and trespassers, those who were there unlawfully.[73] The 1957 Act abolished this distinction in relation to visitors affected by its provisions.[74] By virtue of the 1984 Act the distinction between static conditions and activity duties has now been abolished in respect of trespassers and other visitors referred to in that enactment. The present law of occupiers' liability covers the static condition of premises and the way activities are conducted on them.[75]

(a) The statutory law

(i) Scope of the Acts

14.17 *(1) Premises.* There is no definition of "premises" in the statutes. It is provided that the rules contained in the statute apply to regulate the obligations of an occupier or person having control over "any fixed or

72 *Wheeler v. Copas* [1981] 3 All E.R. 405.

73 See e.g., *Thompson v. Bankstown Municipal Council* (1953) 87 C.L.R. 623; *Commissioner for Railways v. Quinlan, supra*; *Slater v. Clay Cross Co. Ltd.* [1956] 2 Q.B. 264; *Miller v. South of Scotland Electricity Board* 1958 S.C. 20; *Perkowski v. Wellington Corporation* [1959] A.C. 53; *Commissioner for Railways v. McDermott* [1967] 1 A.C. 169; *Cooper v. Southern Portland Cement Ltd* [1974] A.C. 623; *Buckland v. Guildford Gas Light & Coke Co.* [1949] 1 K.B. 410.

74 Contrary views are expressed by North, *op. cit.* at 80–82, whose argument is rejected by *Salmond & Heuston on the Law of Torts*, 19th ed. 1987 at 295–296: see also *Winfield & Jolowicz on Tort* 12th ed. 1984 at 207.

75 So far as the occupier's liability is concerned (which might include liability for the acts of third parties in some circumstances: *Cox v. Coulson* [1916] 2 K.B. 177, with which contrast *Glasgow Corporation v. Muir* [1943] A.C. 448), but not the liability of a third party, which would be imposed and regulated on general grounds of negligence.

moveable structure, including any vessel, vehicle or aircraft."[76] Except for this, what is within the ambit of the legislation is left to the prior common law, and to later development by the courts. Before the Act it was clear that the term referred to more than land. It embraced "places and structures of all sorts to which persons may be invited to come".[77] All kinds of structures were held to be premises, for example a public urinal,[78] scaffolding on a ship that was situated in a dockyard for repairs,[79] stagings,[80] grandstands,[81] and not only immovable property but also movables such as taxicabs or railway carriages.[82] Nor did it matter whether the structure was permanent such as a diving board,[83] or temporary, such as a builder's ladder.[84] All such structures were at least attached in some way or other to land or to buildings themselves attached to land. It was not inappropriate to extend the meaning of premises to them. The language of the 1957 Act suggests that there may be a difference between this common law extension of "premises" and the "structures" referred to in the statute. Indeed in another provision,[85] dealing with the obligation of an occupier to visitors under a contract with the occupier, it is stipulated that the provision applies "to fixed and moveable structures as it applies to premises", which may indicate the statute's intention to confine fixed and moveable structures in the earlier provision only to those structures which would have been premises at common law. This interpretation would mean that a car on a highway did not come within the Act; whereas a car in a garage of a house would. The other interpretation, more broad in nature, would result in a car on a highway being premises for the purposes of the Acts. Such a result, it is suggested, would be inconsistent with the general idea of occupiers' liability, whether at common law or under the Acts. Hence the better interpretation is that the statute never meant the concept of "premises" to be extended so far as to bring within its scope chattels not attached to an occupier's land, even though under the control of the defendant.[86]

14.18 It is curious that instead of defining "premises" to include fixed and moveable structures, etc., the Act says that the obligations of an occupier or one in control of the structure, etc., will be governed by the same rules as apply to an occupier of premises and his visitors. However the object which caused the plaintiff's injury must be in the occupation or control of the occupier.[87] Hence a chattel hired by an occupier of land and erected by someone else is not within the Act: so that if it is defective the

76 Occupiers' Liability Act 1957 s. 1(3)(a).
77 *Glasgow Corporation v. Muir, supra* at 461 *per* Lord Wright.
78 *Pearson v. Lambeth Borough Council* [1950] 2 K.B. 353.
79 *London Graving Dock Co. v. Horton* [1951] A.C. 737.
80 *Heaven v. Pender* (1883) 11 Q.B.D. 503.
81 *Francis v. Cockerell* (1870) L.R. 5 Q.B. 501.
82 *Foulkes v. Metropolitan District Railway Co.* (1880) 5 C.P.D. 157; or aeroplanes: *Fosbrooke-Hobbes v. Airwork Ltd* [1937] 1 All E.R. 108.
83 *Perkowski v. Wellington Corporation* [1959] A.C. 53.
84 *Woodman v. Richardson* [1937] 3 All E.R. 866.
85 Occupiers' Liability Act 1957 s. 5(2), affecting s. 5(1): below p. 386.
86 Cp. North, *op. cit.* at 44–45; *Bunker v. Charles Brand & Son Ltd* [1969] 2 Q.B. 480.
87 *Kearney v. Eric Waller Ltd* [1967] 1 Q.B. 29.

appropriate law to apply is the law relating to dangerous chattels, not the law of occupiers' liability.[88] For example, in *Wheeler v. Copas*,[89] the plaintiff was hired to work on the defendant's farm. The farmer agreed to provide building materials and equipment necessary for the work. For this purpose the defendant lent the plaintiff a ladder which gave way with the result that the plaintiff was injured. Chapman J. held that the Occupiers' Liability Act was not applicable. Although a ladder came within the scope of moveable structures, such as vessels, vehicles and aircraft, this ladder was not "occupied" by the farmer once he had handed it over to the plaintiff. Instead the law relating to dangerous chattels was invoked, as seen earlier,[90] to impose liability on the farmer for negligence.

14.19 *(2) Occupiers.* For the purposes of the rules enacted by the 1957 statute, "the persons who are to be treated as an occupier . . . are the same . . . as the persons who would at common law to be treated as an occupier. . . ."[91] This means that it is necessary to refer to earlier decisions to understand the incidence of liability under the Acts. The expression "occupier" in this context appears to mean the person who has control over the premises or structure that is involved, sufficient control, that is, to put him under a duty of care.[92] Occupancy does not depend on ownership, although in many instances the owner will be the occupier for the purposes of the Act. The test is the possibility of permitting, inviting or excluding persons from the premises or structure.[93] Hence in a pre-1957 case licensees of the owner were held to be in occupation, even though they had no estate or interest in the land.[94] The liability of an occupier of land arises from the fact of his occupancy, as well as of some action of his while occupying. Hence an owner in possession will be an occupier. An owner out of possession may still be an occupier if the actual occupier is his servant or agent. But an owner who has demised the premises to a tenant and parted with possession will not be an occupier under the Act.[95] However, as explained by the House of Lords in *Wheat v. Lacon & Co. Ltd*,[96] control, which is the basis of occupancy for the purposes of the

88 *O'Malley v. Sheppard & Sons* [1962] 2 Lloyd's Rep. 221; [1963] 1 Lloyd's Rep. 189.
89 [1981] 3 All E.R. 405.
90 Above para. 14.02.
91 Occupiers' Liability Act 1957 s. 1(2). Note that the Crown is bound by the Act: *ibid.* s. 6; North, *op. cit.* at 34–36.
92 *Wheat v. Lacon & Co. Ltd* [1966] A.C. 552 at 577 *per* Lord Denning.
93 *Duncan v. Cammell Laird* (1944) 171 L.T. 186 at 190 *per* Wrottesley J., which can be broadly interpreted; *Harris v. Birkenhead Corporation* [1976] 1 All E.R. 341; *Morrison Holdings Ltd v. Manders Property Ltd* [1976] 2 All E.R. 205.
94 *Excelsior Wire Rope Co. v. Callan* [1930] A.C. 404.
95 Thus a landlord out of possession is not an occupier even if he is contractually bound to repair: *Cavalier v. Pope* [1906] A.C. 428. But he may be in possession of certain common areas, such as staircases, lifts, etc.: *Haseldine v. Daw* [1941] 2 K.B. 343; cp. *Fairman v. Perpetual Investment Building Society* [1923] A.C. 74. On the position of the landlord of a shopping centre with respect to the parking lot, cp. *Jacobs v. L.C.C.* [1950] A.C. 361.
96 *Supra* note 92; cp. *Fisher v. C.H.T. Ltd* [1966] 2 Q.B. 475. Contrast *Smith v. Vange Scaffolding & Engineering Co. Ltd* [1970] 1 All E.R. 249 on the situation where contractors are working on a building site. See also *Savory v. Holland & Hannen and Cubitts (Southern) Ltd* [1964] 3 All E.R. 18.

statute, may be shared between two or more persons.[97] Both will be subject to the provisions of the Act with regard to duty of care: but the duties of each may differ in respect of their requirements.[98]

14.20 *(3) Visitors.* For the purpose of defining the duty owed by an occupier to those who entered his premises, the common law distinguished between (a) contractees, those who came onto another's land under a contract with the occupier; (b) invitees, those who came on with the permission of the occupier and for a common or business purpose in which the occupier had an interest, or for their mutual benefit (which was not necessarily financial or economic); (c) licensees, those who entered with permission but solely for their own purposes, and not in any way for a purpose in which the occupier had an interest; and (d) trespassers, those who came on without any permission, and possibly even for an unlawful purpose. The lines of differentiation between invitees and licensees and between licensees and trespassers became blurred. The statute of 1957 made such differentiation obsolete so far as invitees and licensees are concerned.[99] It applied the same rules to those entering under a contract, save to the extent that the express terms of the contract might make a difference.[100] The Act of 1984 maintains the distinction between trespassers and lawful visitors (on whatever basis such people came onto the land); but, as will be seen, it makes provision for an obligation of care which did not exist prior to the 1957 Act.[101] The 1984 Act also imposed that obligation on an occupier with respect to other non-visitors under the provisions of the 1957 Act, viz., those exercising certain private or public rights of entry.[102]

14.21 Thus in place of the older classification of entrants to whom an occupier might owe some kind of duty, there has been installed the following, as a result of the cumulative effects of the 1957 and 1984 statutes, viz. (a) those having a contractual right to enter or use, or bring or send goods to premises (or fixed or movable structures to which the relevant provisions of the Act apply as they do to premises);[103] (b) those

97 *Hartwell v. Grayson Rollo & Clover Docks Ltd* [1947] K.B. 901. But in such a case a visitor may be a lawful visitor of one occupier and a trespasser with respect to the other: *Ferguson v. Welsh* [1987] 3 All E.R. 777 at 785 *per* Lord Goff.

98 An occupier may not owe the statutory duty of care to the employee of a contractor employed to carry out work on the occupier's premises: *Ferguson v. Welsh* [1987] 3 All E.R. 777.

99 Occupiers' Liability Act 1957 s. 1(2).

100 *Ibid.* s. 5(1).

101 Below paras. 14.43ff.

102 Occupiers' Liability Act 1984, s. 1(1), (2), viz., persons entering land subject to an access agreement or order in force under the National Parks and Access to the Countryside Act 1949 s. 60(1): see Occupiers' Liability Act, 1957, s. 1(4). And persons excercising a private right of way (dealing with the situation covered in *Holden v. White* [1982] 2 All E.R. 328). But the 1984 Act does not extend the operation of the 1957 Act to persons using a highway whether or not maintained at the public expense: Occupiers' Liability Act, 1984, s. 1(7); cp. *Greenhalgh v. British Railways Board* [1969] 2 Q.B. 286.

103 Occupiers' Liability Act, 1957, s. 5(1), (2). But this does not affect obligations imposed by or by virtue of certain contracts, e.g. hire, carriage for reward, bailment: *ibid.* s. 5(3). See, generally, North, *op. cit.* at 152–161.

who would at common law have been treated as the occupier's invitees or licensees;[104] and (c) those who were not visitors within the meaning of the 1957 Act, i.e. (i) trespassers; (ii) those using a public or private right of way; (iii) those entering premises in exercise of rights conferred by an access agreement or order under the National Parks and Access to Countryside Act 1949.[105] Those within category (c) are owed a different duty under the 1984 Act from the duty owed to those who were, and remain, "visitors" under the 1957 Act.

14.22 Visitors, as defined in the 1957 Act, include those who enter with the implied, but not express permission of the occupier[106] and those (other than entrants under an access agreement or order made under the National Parks and Access to the Countryside Act 1949) who enter premises for any purpose in the exercise of a right conferred by law.[107] The latter are treated as if they had been permitted by the occupier to be on his premises for that purpose.[108] Hence in *Salmon v. Seafarer Restaurants Ltd*[109] a fireman who was on premises for the purposes of fighting a fire came within the protection of the 1957 Act and was owed the appropriate duty of care. This class of visitors would also include within its scope police executing a search warrant, or a gas inspector reading a meter in the course of his duties. The problem of implied licenses or implied permission is one that has bedevilled the law for a considerable length of time. It was perhaps more important when there was a marked distinction between licensees and trespassers so far as the liability of the occupier for injury to them was concerned. Especially was this the case where the injured party was a child. It may no longer be necessary to go to extreme lengths in order to provide an injured child with a remedy. However it is still necessary to differentiate the case of someone who has genuinely been allowed to enter, by virtue of an implied permission, and one who has not. Although, as will be seen,[110] an occupier owes some duty towards a trespasser, i.e., one who has not obtained either express or implied permission to enter, that duty is not the same nor is it as onerous as the duty owed to a visitor within the meaning of the 1957 Act. Hence a visitor within that Act who exceeds the scope of the permission to enter given him by the occupier, by going to an unpermitted part of the premises,[111] or

104 *Ibid.* s. 1(2). But the employee of a contractor employed by the occupier may not be owed the statutory duty of care; if a duty is owed, it might not be as an occupier: *Ferguson v. Welsh* [1987] 3 All E.R. 777.
105 Occupiers' Liability Act 1984 s. 1(1), (2).
106 This is the effect of the older common law on who were licensees: see, e.g. *Edwards v. Railway Executive* [1952] A.C. 737; *Dunster v. Abbott* [1953] 2 All E.R. 1572; *Lowery v. Walker* [1911] A.C. 10.
107 By virtue of Occupiers' Liability Act 1957 s. 2(6).
108 Whether or not actual permission was received.
109 [1983] 3 All E.R. 729.
110 Below paras. 14.43ff.
111 *Mersey Docks & Harbour Board v. Procter* [1923] A.C. 253; *Hillen v. I.C.I. (Alkali) Ltd* [1936] A.C. 65. Unless it is foreseeable that he may do so: *Pearson v. Coleman Bros.* [1948] 3 K.B. 359, where the plaintiff was a child in search of a lavatory, which may have made a difference.

doing something which entitles the occupier to exclude or eject him,[112] will cease to come within the protection of the 1957 Act (although he may still come within the Act of 1984). Similarly, one who enters without any permission of any kind may have difficulty in proving that the occupier implicitly allowed him to enter. Knowledge on the part of the occupier that the unpermitted entrant is there, and even knowledge that such entries have been made in the past, will not suffice. Nor will the failure to take steps to exclude the person in question, although such steps might have been taken. In the final analysis it is a question of fact whether the requisite implication can be drawn from the circumstances considered as a whole.[113]

14.23 One great advance or improvement brought about by the 1957 Act is the removal of the necessity for agonising over whether a particular visitor or entrant was an invitee or a licensee. Before 1957 the distinction was vital and relevant because of the way the law regarded the duty owed by the occupier towards these two different classes of visitors. A higher, more demanding duty was originally owed by occupiers to invitees than to licensees.[114] However the decision of the House of Lords in *London Graving Dock Co. v. Horton*,[115] in which it was held that no duty of care of any kind was owed to an invitee who was aware of the danger that caused his injury, virtually abolished the rationale for any distinction between invitees and licensees. This decision was the prime reason for the investigation of the law by the Law Reform Committee and the eventual passage of the 1957 Act. Since then neither the formal differentiation of lawful, i.e. permitted visitors into two categories nor any differentiation of the duty owed to them has been part of the law.

14.24 *(4) Damage.* At common law and under the Acts an occupier will be liable for personal injuries caused by his breach of duty. It would appear from cases decided prior to the statutes, that this would include liability for disease caused by the state of the premises,[116] or for damages caused by an animal on the premises in question (as long as the animal was there with the permission of the occupier and for the occupier's purposes, e.g. as a guard dog).[117] Apart from any possible liability under the modern law relating to damage caused by animals,[118] the occupier could also be liable for breach of his duty as an occupier. Although no decisions exist that are directly in point, there is no reason why an occupier should not also be liable for nervous shock caused by the state of his premises, or something being done thereon, where the situtation is one

112 But only after he has been told to leave and was warned in advance when he must go: *Stone v. Taffe* [1974] 3 All E.R. 1016. On the right to eject, see para. 5.48.
113 *Edwards v. Railway Executive, supra.*
114 As settled in *Indemaur v. Dames* (1866) L.R. 1 C.P. 274, affirmed (1867) L.R. 2 C.P. 311.
115 [1951] A.C. 737.
116 *Lindsey County Council v. Marshall* [1937] A.C. 97; *Silverman v. Imperial London Hotels Ltd* (1927) 137 L.T. 57.
117 *Clarke v. J. Lyons & Co. Ltd* [1912] 3 K.B. 198.
118 Chapter 11.

in which such liability can arise in accordance with the general principles of negligence and remoteness of damage.[119]

14.25 Whatever the position at common law,[120] it is now clear that the occupier can also be liable for property damage,[121] whether this accompanies physical injury or is quite independent of such injury. The 1957 act provides that the rules it enacts with respect to the duty of care owed by an occupier apply to regulate the obligations of the occupier in respect of damage to property, including the property of persons who are not themselves his visitors.[122] Thus if a visitor within the meaning of the Act brings property onto the premises, the occupier's duty of care will be owed in respect of such property as well as with respect to the person of the visitor. That is one interpretation of the Act. However it has been pointed out that the statutory provision is framed in these words: that the rules the Act enacts apply "in like manner and to the like extent as the principles applicable at common law to an occupier of premises and his invitees or licensees would apply to regulate" obligations in respect of damage to property. Hence the suggestion has been made that the distinction between the duty owed an invitee and that owed a licensee might still continue to have effect in relation to property damage.[123] Secondly, when dealing with liability in contract,[124] the Act speaks of "goods" not property in general. It also refers to goods that have been brought or sent to the premises of the occupier. This indicates that the plaintiff need not have brought the goods onto the premises himself. Nor need he be there at the crucial moment when the goods are damaged through the state of the premises or something being done on them.[125] It is suggested that the ultimate intent of the 1957 Act was to provide the same protection for a visitor's property, of whatever kind, as the Act provides for the visitor himself. Hence whatever the form of words employed by the Act, the better view is that the statutory duty applies, not the pre-1957 duties dependent on the status of the visitor. Moreover, where goods are brought or sent into premises under a contract with the occupier, that contract need not be between the owner of the goods and the occupier (although if it is then its terms may affect questions of duty and liability). In the absence of any applicable terms, the statutory tort duty will be owed in respect of such goods.

14.26 Lastly, although "property" is used in one context and "goods" in another, it would seem reasonable to conclude that the statute did not

119 Chapter 12 at paras. 12.110ff; cp. *Dooley v. Cammell Laird & Co.* [1951] 1 Lloyds Rep. 271.

120 *Tinsley v. Dudley* [1951] 2 K.B. 18, which seems to distinguish between damage to property anicllary to personal injury and such damage in the absence of personal injury: North, *op. cit.* at 95–100, where the issue is fully discussed.

121 And economic loss consequent thereon: *A.M.F. International Ltd v. Magnet Bowling Ltd* [1968] 2 All E.R. 789.

122 Occupiers' Liability Act 1957 s. 1(3)(b).

123 North, *op. cit.* at 99.

124 Occupiers' Liability Act 1957 s 5(1).

125 North, *op. cit.* at 100.

intend to restrict the meaning of property in the context of tort liability to the narrower term "goods" used in the context of contractual liability. Hence if currency is damaged or destroyed by the neglect of the occupier, the visitor whose currency it was will have an action under the Act as long as the currency was with him at the time. If the currency was sent with a third person, no action will lie under the provision dealing with liability in contract. However, in view of the language of the statute when talking about damage to property, it would appear that if a visitor happened to have with him currency belonging to a third party, and that currency were destroyed, the owner of the currency would have an action under the Act where the destruction was caused by the occupier's neglect of duty. The suggestion has been made that this will only be the case where such property was brought onto the premises with the occupier's permission. Presumably this entails that the occupier knows or ought to have foreseen that a third party's property would be brought onto the occupier's premises. If he does not, then the visitor alone will be able to sue, possibly on the ground that he, the visitor, might be liable to the owner of the property for such loss, because the visitor was the bailee of the property and accordingly liable to the owner, the bailor. However this might not be appropriate if the visitor has obtained the third party's property unlawfully, for example by theft.[126]

14.27 The 1957 Act refers only to "damage" to property whether belonging to the visitor or to a third person. It does not cover the loss of such property, e.g. by theft committed by the occupier's servant or agent or by a stranger. At common law there was no liability for such loss on the basis of any tort duty.[127] However, it has been suggested that there may be some situations in which liability for loss could be imposed on an occupier, viz., where the occupier is an innkeeper, or a boarding-house keeper or is the bailee of the goods, or there is an implied contract between the owner of the goods and the occupier.[128]

(b) The occupier's duty

(i) The common duty of care

14.28 *(1) Contents of the duty.* In place of the various duties which at common law were owed by an occupier to the different categories of visitors to his premises, the Acts create a single, all-embracing duty, "the common duty of care". This is owed to all visitors within the meaning of the 1957 Act, except in so far as the occupier is free to and does extend, restrict, modify or exclude his duty to any visitor or visitors by agreement or otherwise.[129] The common duty of care is not owed to non-visitors who

126 *Ibid.* at 101–105 for a general discussion.

127 *Tinsley v. Dudley, supra; Edwards v. West Herts Group Hospital Management Committee* [1957] 1 All E.R. 541. Nor will an employee be able to sue for breach of the employer's duty of care when the employee's property is stolen: *Deyong v. Shenburn* [1946] K.B. 227: below para. 14.49.

128 North, *op. cit.* at 108–112.

129 Occupiers' Liability Act 1957 s. 2(1). On the effect of agreement see below.

are outside the scope of that statute. Such non-visitors, however, may be owed a duty under the provisions of the 1984 Act.[130] The common duty of care is as follows:[131]

> "a duty to take such care as in all the circumstances of the case is reasonable to see that the visitor will be reasonably safe in using the premises for the purposes for which he is invited or permitted by the occupier to be there."

The statutory duty, therefore, although it replaces the common law duty[132] is nothing more than a normal duty of care owed in any situation where negligence can give rise to liability. Everything depends on what a reasonable man would do or refrain from doing to ensure that the visitor is reasonably safe while on the premises.[133] In this respect two matters should be noted. First: the occupier is only obliged to take steps to prevent a foreseeable risk of harm to the visitor. Only probable, not improbable, risks must be guarded against by the occupier.[134] Secondly: the occupier's duty is owed only in respect of the vistor's use of the premises for the purpose for which he was invited or permitted to enter. If and when the visitor does something else on the premises, he may cease to be a visitor within the meaning of the 1957 Act, and may turn into a trespasser, to whom the only duty owed is under the 1984 Act, and not the common duty of care. Even if he does not become a trespasser, such a visitor is no longer entitled to the protection of the common duty of care.

14.29 An additional point to be noted is brought out in the 1957 Act. There it is provided that the circumstances to be taken into account in determining what the occupier should or should not do:

> "include the degree of care, and of want of care, which would ordinarily be looked for in such a visitor. . . ."[135]

This means that, subject to what is also set out in the same subsection, to be considered below, the visitor may be expected to take steps to ensure his own safety. An occupier is not charged with the sole responsibility for the safety of his lawful visitors. In appropriate situations he may rely on their being able to take care of themselves. The language set out above relates to the existence and scope of the duty of care: it is not intended to affect the issue of contributory negligence, which will be a defence where relevant.[136] Thus a visitor who neglects his own safety may be denied any relief, on the ground that the duty of care was not breached by the occupier, having regard to the occupier's legitimate expectation that the visitor will look after himself; or he may have his damages reduced on the ground that, although the occupier was in breach of the common duty of care, because he was not expected to rely on the visitor's care for himself,

130 Below pp. 400–401.
131 Occupiers' Liability Act 1957 s. 2(2).
132 Cp. *British Railways Board v. Herrington* [1972] A.C. 877 at 941.
133 See, e.g., *Ward v. Hertfordshire County Council* [1969] 2 All E.R. 807, reversed on appeal [1970] 1 All ER. 535.
134 *Simms v. Leigh Rugby Football Club Ltd* [1969] 2 All E.R. 923, where the risk was foreseeable but improbable.
135 Occupiers' Liability Act 1957 s. 2(3).
136 Below pp. 397.

the visitor was guilty of such contributory negligence that his claim should be reduced, or even negated entirely, in accordance with the general principles governing the nature and effect of contributory negligence.[137]

14.30 The Act gives examples, which are only illustrations and do not purport to describe the only relevant circumstances,[138] of what the occupier ought to look for in relation to the visitor's care for his own safety.[139]

> "In proper cases", [a phrase which leaves the matter very wide open]
> "(a) an occupier must be prepared for children to be less careful than adults; and
> (b) an occupier may expect that a person, in the exercise of his calling, will appreciate and guard against any special risks ordinarily incident to it, so far as the occupier leaves him free to do so."

These specific examples of factors which may influence the common duty of care require separate discussion.

14.31 *(2) Children.* Before the 1957 Act the position of child visitors or entrants was confused and complex. Sometimes, where a child was a trespasser in the same way as an adult would have been, it was argued that some duty of care was owed to the child when it would not have been to the adult. Sometimes a child was treated as an implied licensee when an adult would have continued to be considered a trespasser, especially where the child came onto the premises by reason of a "trap" or "allurement" that was situated thereon. Sometimes, where a child was a true licensee, not an imputed or fictional one, the duty owed was framed in a special way especially in the light of the particular physical and mental susceptibilities of a child. Sometimes very young children caused particular difficulty in view of their obvious inability to appreciate danger and the fact that almost anything can be dangerous to someone extremely young. Hence the suggestion that no duty was owed to such children, or would be breached, unless the child were accompanied by an adult or other responsible person. That view was rejected by Devlin J. in *Phipps v. Rochester Corporation*,[140] a pre-1957 case. The learned judge considered that the true rule was that in measuring the duty of a licensor to young children the habits of a prudent parent in relation to little children could be taken into account. Therefore in some circumstances the licensor was entitled to expect that a young or little child would not be allowed to go on the licensor's premises unless properly accompanied and guarded.

14.32 From post-1957 decisions it appears that the law after the Act in regard to an occupier's duty towards children who come within the ambit of the Act's provisions will be much the same as it was before the statute.[141]

137 Above paras. 13.23ff.
138 *Roles v. Nathan* [1963] 2 All E.R. 908 at 912 *per* Lord Denning, M.R. Cp. the use of "for example" in Occupiers' Liability Act, 1957, s. 2(4) discussed in North, *op. cit.* at 143.
139 Occupiers' Liability Act 1957 s. 2(3).
140 [1955] 1 Q.B. 450.
141 *O'Connor v. British Transport Commission* [1958] 1 All E.R. 558; *McCullie v. Butler* [1959] C.L.Y. 2207; *Nicholson v. Zoological Society* [1960] C.L.Y. 2127; *Moloney v. Lambeth Borough Council* (1966) 64 L.G.R. 440.

This means that the age of the child must be taken into account when determining the content or performance of the common duty of care vis-à-vis a child visitor: and that where a child is very young or small the occupier may be entitled to expect that such a child will be accompanied, so that the occupier's duty may be fulfilled if what he does is sufficient to enable the accompanying adult or older child to look after the child and prevent injury.

14.33 *(3) Knowledgeable visitors.* The 1957 Act recognises that a visitor who enters in pursuance of his calling of employment is expected to appreciate and guard against special risks that are usually incidental to such calling or employment.[142] Hence no duty of care was owed in *Roles v. Nathan*[143] to chimney sweeps who died from carbon monoxide poisoning incurred in the course of cleaning flues, when the sweep hold had not been properly sealed as required by a heating expert who considered the boiler being cleaned to be dangerous. This was the kind of special risk that was normally incidental to a sweep's calling. When a specialist is called in to deal with a defective installation on a householder's premises, the householder "is not bound to watch over him to see that he comes to no harm".[144] There have been several decisions in which such a risk was involved.[145] In other instances, however, the risk was not regarded as incidental to the visitor's calling, as contrasted with an ordinary risk incidental to the premises themselves.[146]

(ii) Discharge of the duty

14.34 *(1) Warnings.* Whether the common duty of care has been discharged is a question of fact, once it has been determined what was the content of that duty in light of the relevant circumstances, including, for example, those referred to in the preceding sections. The Act provides that to decide this question "regard is to be had to all the circumstances".[147] Again, by way of example only and not with any intention of being exclusive, two situations are specifically mentioned. The first is the effect of a warning. The common law eventually decided that, as regards a licensee, a warning of danger might suffice by way of performance of the licensor's duty.[148] Now, under the 1957 Act,[149]

> "Where damage is caused to a visitor by a danger of which he had been warned by the occupier, the warning is not to be treated without more as absolving the occupier from liability, unless in all the circumstances it was enough to enable the visitor to be reasonably safe."

142 This was the situation at common law: *Bates v. Parker* [1953] 2 Q.B. 231; *Christmas v. General Cleaning Contractors Ltd* [1953] A.C. 180.
143 *Supra* note 138.
144 *Ibid.* at 913 *per* Lord Denning.
145 North, *op. cit.* at 65.
146 Viz., *Woollins v. British Celanese Ltd* (1966) 1 K.I.R. 438; *Bird v. King Line Ltd* [1970] 1 Lloyds Rep. 349.
147 Occupiers' Liability Act 1957 s. 2(4).
148 *London Graving Dock Co. v. Horton* [1951] A.C. 737.
149 S. 2(4)(a).

Just as the provision about a visitor expected to look after himself does not replace the doctrine of contributory negligence, so this provision does not affect the general principles relating to the defence of *volenti* (which is specifically incorporated into the Act).[150]

14.35 In *Roles v. Nathan*[151] the warning given by the heating expert of the dangers inherent in the boiler and the flue was sufficient to exonerate the occupier. It would have enabled the deceased sweeps to avoid danger if they had taken notice of it. Although the Act states that the warning must be given by the occupier, it will be enough for the purposes of the Act if the warning is given by the occupier's agent, as in *Roles v. Nathan*, or his servant. If no warning is given this may be evidence of negligence, i.e. breach of the duty of care.[152] The same may be the case if the warning is inadequate to protect the visitor.[153] However it is not clear whether the warning must relate to the defect in the premises or the risks or peril consequent on the dangerous state of the premises. Moreover, a warning might not suffice, especially if it is only a verbal warning. The occupier may have to place some safeguards on the premises, such as a handrail on a cliff-path. Everything depends on the particular kind of danger and the person who is potentially the victim.

14.36 *(2) Independent contractors*. The 1957 Act deals with an issue that was much discussed in the earlier case law, viz., the extent to which an occupier would be liable for the negligence of an independent contractor. As noted in connection with vicarious liability, the general principle was that the employer of such a contractor would not be liable for negligence on his part or on the part of the contractor's servants. To this there were, and still exist, certain exceptions.[154] In respect of the liability of an occupier there were decisions which made the state of the law confused. In one instance an occupier was not liable for the negligence of his contractor:[155] in another he was.[156] The difference between these cases may have been that one involved the work of a skilled contractor, engineers engaged to service and maintain a lift; the other an unskilled contractor, employed to sweep the steps of the occupier's premises and keep them clear of snow.[157] In a subsequent decision from Scotland, *Thomson v. Cremin*[158] The House of Lords appear to have held that, where the visitor was an invitee (perhaps in contrast with the situation where the visitor was licensee), there would be liability for negligence by any independent contractor, because the invitor's duty was personal and could not be performed merely by delegating to such a contractor, even if reasonable

150 *Ibid.* s. 2(5): below, para. 14.41.
151 *Supra* note 138.
152 *Williams v. Houlder Bros. & Co.* [1962] 2 Lloyd's Rep. 199; *Bunker v. Charles Brand & Sons Ltd* [1969] 2 Q.B. 480.
153 *Woollins v. British Celanese Ltd., supra.*
154 Chapter 3 at pp. 46, 66, where the term is explained.
155 *Haseldine v. Daw* [1941] 2 K.B. 343.
156 *Woodward v. Mayor of Hastings* [1945] K.B. 174.
157 *Green v. Fibreglass Ltd* [1958] 2 Q.B. 245; *Wells v. Cooper* [1958] 2 Q.B. 265.
158 (1941) 71 Ll.L.R. 1; but not reported elsewhere until [1953] 2 All E.R. 1185.

care were taken to select a contractor who was competent. The 1957 Act contains the following provision:[159]

> "Where damage is caused to a visitor by a danger due to the faulty execution of any work of construction, maintenance or repair by an independent contractor employed by the occupier, the occupier is not to be treated without more as answerable for the danger if in all the circumstances he had acted reasonably in entrusting the work to an independent contractor and had taken such steps (in any) as he reasonably ought in order to satisfy himself that the contractor was competent and that the work had been properly done."

Three requirements must therefore be satisfied before an occupier can rely on the fact that any negligence was that of an independent contractor. First: that it was reasonable to employ an independent contractor to do the work in question.[160] Secondly: that the occupier exercised reasonable care to choose a contractor who was competent. Thirdly: the occupier must take reasonable care to see that the work has been properly done.[161] In any event the occupier will only be liable, where he has failed to satisfy any one or more of these requirements, if the work was executed faultily, which would appear to include non-feasance as well as misfeasance on the part of the contractor.[162] Moreover the work must be work of construction, maintenance or repair. This may not include demolition or the use by a contractor of the premises for some purpose other than construction, maintenance or repair. In one instance this language was held not to include stowage of timber.[163] In another it excluded stowage of cargo.[164] But in *Clayton v. Woodman & Son (Builders) Ltd*,[165] the wording of the Act was held to accommodate the delegation of supervisory work to an architect. Hence the suggestion that there are some situations involving employment of an independent contractor where the Act does not govern. In those situations, the older common law applies: and the occupier is *prima facie* liable. In situations under the Act the occupier is *prima facie* not liable, unless and until the requirements of the Act are shown not to have been fulfilled.[166]

(iii) Exclusion of the duty

14.37 The 1957 Act states that an occupier can "extend, restrict, modify or exclude" his duty to any visitor or visitors, by agreement or otherwise in so far as he is free to do so.[167] Prior to the Act an occupier who allowed a visitor to enter under contract could stipulate in the contract for the exclusion of any duty to the visitor. As long as the term was one that would be effective to achieve this result, and would be upheld and

159 Occupiers' Liability Act, 1957, s. 2(4)(b).
160 *Gibson v. Skibs A/S Marina etc.* [1966] 2 All E.R. 476.
161 *A.M.F. International Ltd v. Magnet Bowling Ltd* [1968] 2 All E.R. 789.
162 *Ibid.*.
163 *Gaffney v. Aviation & Shipping Co. Ltd* [1966] 1 Lloyd's Rep. 249.
164 *Mullis v. United States Lines Ltd* [1969] 1 Lloyd's Rep. 109.
165 [1962] 2 Q.B. 533.
166 North, *op. cit.* at 143–144.
167 Occupiers' Liability Act 1957 s. 2(1): see for an example of such restriction on the occupiers' freedom, *ibid.* s. 3(1): below para. 14.42.

enforced by the courts, in accordance with principles of the law of contract, the occupier would be successful in freeing himself of any obligation to the visitor. Where the visitor entered not under contract but with the consent of the occupier it was held that permission to enter could be given conditionally, i.e. under the condition that the occupier was not to be liable for injury to the visitor. In *Ashdown v. Samuel Williams & Sons Ltd*[168] a licence to use the occupier's premises as a method of going from one place to another was held to be conditional upon the terms of a notice prominently displayed by which the occupiers exempted themselves and their servants from liability to those using the premises. The notice would operate to protect the occupier from liability for breach of "occupancy" duties and "activity" duties.[169] Although such a notice might serve to exempt the occupier from liability for his negligence, it might not have had the same consequence with respect to the occupier's servants or agents, although mentioned in the notice. Under the doctrine of "privity of contract" such an exemption when contained in a contract would not generally serve to protect non-parties to the contract.[170] In pre-1957 cases involving a free pass on transport, not an occupier's liability, the privity of contract doctrine was successfully invoked by the plaintiff to negate the operation of an exemption in favour of the servant of the party granting the pass.[171] It has been argued that the same doctrine should apply to licenses to enter land, both before the 1957 Act and thereafter.[172] On this basis, therefore, the occupier can exclude his liability under the Act by contract, or an agreement short of contract, or by a notice: but such exclusion will not protect the occupier's negligent servant or agent whose conduct has caused the visitor to be injured.

14.38 It should be noted, however, that in some situations exclusion of duty or liability is prohibited by statute or regulations. As a result of section 2 of the Unfair Contract Terms Act 1977, no contract can exclude or restrict the occupier's liability for death or personal injury resulting from negligence: and where other loss or damage is concerned, such exclusion or restriction of liability for negligence is only possible if the term or notice satisfies the statutory requirement of reasonableness.[173] By the 1977 Act, these provisions only applied where the duty arose from things done in the course of a business or from the occupation of premises used for the business purposes of the occupier.[174] The distinction between business and other purposes remains important. The Occupiers' Liability Act 1984

168 [1957] 1 Q.B. 409.
169 *Ibid.* at 420 *per* Singleton L.J., 429–430 *per* Parker L.J.
170 Cheshire, Fifoot & Furmston, *Law of Contract*, 11th ed. 1986, at 158–164. There are some exceptions to and qualifications of this.
171 *Cosgrove v. Horsfall* (1945) 62 T.L.R. 140; *Genys v. Matthews* [1965] 3 All E.R. 24; *Gore v. Van der Lamm* [1967] 2 Q.B. 31. Contrast, however, *Wilkes v. London Passenger Transport Board* [1947] 1 All E.R. 258, where the court held that a pass was a revocable licence subject to the condition of not giving rise to a right to sue; therefore the plaintiff could not bring an action.
172 North, *op. cit.*, at 129.
173 Set out in the Unfair Contract Terms Act 1977 s. 11, and Schedule 2: Cheshire, Fifoot & Furmston, *op. cit.* at 177–181.
174 Unfair Contract Terms Act 1977 s. 1(3).

amended the 1977 Act by enacting that where an occupier admits persons to his premises for recreational or educational purposes his liability towards such persons is not a business liability unless granting such access for the purposes concerned falls within the business purposes of the occupier.[175] Where there is no business liability, the occupier is free to exclude or restrict his liability; he will not be hampered by the 1977 Act. Thus where recreational or educational purposes are involved in a visit, as long as no charge is sought from the visitor, the occupier can exclude or restrict liability despite the 1977 Act. If any charge is imposed, the provisions of the 1977 Act apply to regulate his freedom in this respect.

(iv) Defences to liability

14.39 Apart from the giving of a warning that satisfies the provisions of the Act, or the exclusion or modification of the statutory duty of care to the extent that this is permissible and has been accomplished, there are other possible defences available to the occupier if sued for breach of the duty.

14.40 Before the Act of 1957 it was held in *Slater v. Clay Cross Co. Ltd*[176] that the defence of contributory negligence could be raised to an action by a licensee or invitee against an occupier. The Act makes no specific mention of the defence of contributory negligence, but it appears to be accepted that this defence can be raised so as to reduce damages under the Law Reform (Contributory Negligence) Act 1945. There have been decisions in which apportionment under the statute has been allowed in claims based on the 1957 Act.[177] Contributory negligence on the part of the visitor is distinguishable from the requirement of the 1957 Act that in determining the standard of care expected of the occupier the degree of care of the visitor for his own safety is a relavant factor.[178] This indicates that the conduct of the visitor may affect the care to be shown by the occupier. But it does not exclude the possibility that, where the visitor has not shown sufficient care for his own safety, he might be found guilty of contributory negligence and have his damages reduced in accordance with the provisions of the 1945 Act.

14.41 Another possible defence is *volenti non fit injuria*, or assumption of risk.[179] The 1957 Act states:[180]

> "The common duty of care does not impose on an occupier any obligation to a visitor in respect of risks willingly accepted as his by the visitor (the question whether a risk was so accepted to be decided by the same principles as in other cases in which one person owes a duty to another)."

175 Occupiers' Liability Act 1984 s. 2.
176 [1956] 2 Q.B. 264.
177 E.g., *Foley v. Enso-Gutzeit* [1962] 1 Lloyd's Rep. 247; *Bunker v. Charles Brand & Son Ltd* [1969] 2 Q.B. 480; *Bird v. King Line Ltd* [1970] 2 Lloyd's Rep. 349.
178 Above para. 14.33.
179 Chapter 13 at paras. 13.05–09.
180 Occupiers' Liability Act 1957 s. 2(5).

It is clear that this provision is distinct from other provisions of the Act relating to the effect of a warning and the effect of a notice excluding liability. Thus in *Simms v. Leigh Rugby Football Club Ltd*,[181] one ground for rejecting the plaintiff's claim founded on his injury in a game was that the plaintiff had accepted the risks incidental to playing a contact sport such as rugby football, as long as what happened occurred while players were obeying the rules of the game or on a field which satisfies the by-laws of the governing body of the sport (since the accident happened when the plaintiff was hurled towards a wall beyond the playing field). The equivalent language of the Occupiers' Liability (Scotland) Act 1969[182] was considered by the House of Lords in *Titchener v. British Railways Board*.[183] Accepting the remarks by Lord Reid in an earlier decision[184] to the effect that this provision merely puts into words the principle of *volenti non fit injuria*, the House held that because the visitor fully appreciated the risk she took crossing a railway line in order to take a short cut,[185] and since the train which injured her had not been driven negligently,[186] the risk which caused her injury was one of the risks she had accepted when she came onto the land.[187]

(v) Duty to those entering under contract with third parties

14.42 The 1957 Act deals with the situation of someone who enters an occupier's premises by virtue of a contract between the occupier and someone else, not the visitor. For example a tenant might agree with his landlord to permit workmen to enter the tenant's premises; an occupier might contract with a company for work to be done on his premises and the company sends its employees to the premises for that purpose. There are innumerable possibilities. The contract might stipulate for the exemption of the occupier from liability to those who used the premises. At common law this was valid and prevailed over other rights of the entrant.[188] The 1957 Act provides[189] that in this situation, where the entrant is a "stranger to the contract" as defined in the Act,[190] the occupier cannot restrict or exclude the duty of care owed to the visitor.[191] On the contrary, the duty owed to such a visitor includes the duty to perform the occupier's obligations under the contract, whether undertaken for the protection of such a visitor or not, to the extent that those

181 [1969] 2 All E.R. 923.
182 s. 2(3).
183 [1983] 3 All E.R. 770.
184 *M'Glone v. British Railways Board* 1966 S.C. 1 at 13.
185 Unlike the boy in *M'Glone's* case, *supra*.
186 Unlike the train in *Slater v. Clay Cross Co. Ltd*, *supra*.
187 *Supra* note 183 at 776 *per* Lord Fraser.
188 *Fosbrooke–Hobbes v. Airwork Ltd* [1937] 1 All E.R. 108 at 112.
189 Occupiers' Liability Act 1957 s. 3(1).
190 *Ibid.* s. 3(3): "a person not for the time being entitled to the benefit of the contract as a party to it or as the successor by assignment or otherwise of a party to it." It includes a party to the contract who has ceased to be so entitled.
191 This is extended by s. 3(4) to tenancies (including statutory tenancies not amounting to a tenancy at common law) where the landlord or the tenant is bound to permit persons to enter or use the premises of which he is the occupier. But a landlord may contractually extend or limit his liability to the *tenant*, e.g. for injuries incurred on a common staircase in the landlord's occupation.

obligations exceed the obligations otherwise involved in the occupier's duty of care, i.e. the common duty of care. Thus the occupier may be obliged to do more than would be required by the common duty of care in such cases.[192] That depends on what the contract in question specifies by way of additional protection for such a visitor. But no contract of this kind will make an occupier liable for dangers due to faulty execution of construction, maintenance or repair or any similar operation undertaken by an independent contractor, unless the contract provides to the contrary, and as long as the occupier has taken all reasonable care.[193]

(vi) Duty to trespassers

14.43 The 1957 Act excluded from its scope trespassers and certain others.[194] Of these the most important group are probably those who did not fall within the ambit of those entering under a contract with the occupier, invitees or licensees. Such non-visitors within the meaning of the 1957 Act were, and remain trespassers. Because they were not dealt with in the 1957 Act it was plain that the common duty of care was not owed to them. Indeed at common law prior to 1957, an occupier owed no duty of care to a trespasser.[195] He was not allowed to do an act with the deliberate intention of doing harm to the trespasser, nor, perhaps, to act with reckless disregard for the presence of the trespasser.[196] Because of the stringent view taken by the common law of the trespasser's position vis-à-vis the occupier, there was a tendency in the courts to find that someone was not a trespasser even though that person had not been given any express permission by the occupier to enter the premises. Hence tacit licences were sometimes inferred from the facts: and this was particularly the case where the injured person was a child. However, even a visitor who entered with permission, either as licensee or invitee, could become a trespasser if he or she went beyond the scope of the permission granted by the occupier, e.g., by going onto a part of the premises not within the ambit of the permission, or by doing something that could lead to the termination of the permission.

14.44 Between 1957 and 1984 the House of Lords radically altered the law relating to an occupier's duty with respect to trespassers. The decision in *British Railways Board v. Herrington*[197] resulted in the creation of a duty of common humanity being owed by an occupier towards his trespassers. That duty was less than the duty of reasonable care based on foresight of harm that was the essence of negligence. Moreover it was subjective rather

192 And could do less: so that a tenant's visitor is always entitled to the benefit of the common duty of care on the part of the landlord. The justice of making the occupier do more has been questioned: North *op. cit.* at 150. But the visitor may assume risks or may be warned of them so as to come within the provisions of s. 2(4)(a), (b) of the 1957 Act.

193 Occupiers' Liability Act, 1957, s. 3(2).

194 Viz., visitors under the National Parks and Access to the Countryside Act 1949 and persons exercising rights of way: above, para. 14.21.

195 For the older law see North, *op. cit.* Chapter 11.

196 *Addie & Sons (Collieries) Ltd v. Dumbreck* [1929] A.C. 358 at 365.

197 [1972] A.C. 877. Contrast the provisions of the Occupiers' Liability (Scotland) Act 1960 s. 2.

than objective. It depended on the particular occupier, as well as on the state of the premises.[198] To resolve the problems raised by this decision, and to put the law on a sounder, more stable basis, the Occupiers' Liability Act 1984 was passed. This now provides for a duty to be owed by an occupier within the meaning of the 1957 Act towards persons other than the occupier's visitors as defined in that statute. The duty in question relates to the risk of entrants within the scope of the 1984 Act suffering injury on the occupier's premises by reason of any danger due to the state of the premises or to things done or omitted to be done on them.[199] Thus the 1984 Act, like that of 1957, refers to occupancy duties and activity duties.[200] A duty will be owed by the occupier to entrants covered by the 1984 Act if three conditions are fulfilled.[201] These are:

(i) The occupier must be aware of the danger or have reasonable grounds for believing that it exists.
(ii) The occupier must know or have reasonable grounds for believing that the entrant is in the vicinity of the danger concerned, or may come into the vicinity of the danger (whether or not the entrant is lawfully entitled to be in that vicinity).
(iii) The risk is one against which, in all the circumstances, the occupier may reasonably be expected to offer the entrant some protection.

The duty that is owed by the occupier is a duty to take such care as is reasonable in all the circumstances to see that the entrant does not suffer injury on the premises by reason of the danger in question.[202] That duty relates only to personal injury. A breach of the duty will not entail liability for loss of or damage to property[203] (unlike the situation under the 1957 Act).[204] The duty can be discharged by taking reasonable steps to warn of the danger in question or to discourage persons from incurring the risk.[205] Thus a sign that sufficiently clearly indicates, for example, thin ice, or rickety stairs, might be an adequate discharge of the duty. But, as under the 1957 Act, no duty will be owed where the entrant is *volens*, i.e. has willingly accepted the risk in consequence of which he is injured. The usual principles apply to determine whether or not the entrant was *volens* as regards any particular risk.[206]

14.45 The requirements of the duty may differ according to the character of the entrant, i.e. the trespasser. Thus an occupier may have to take more care with respect to a child trespasser than in relation to a burglar. The financial resources of the occupier, stressed in the *Herrington* case, will

198 *British Railways Board v. Herrington, supra* at 889 *per* Lord Reid. See, e.g. *Southern Portland Cement Co. v. Cooper* [1974] A.C. 623; *Pannett v. P. MacGuinness & Co. Ltd* [1972] 2 Q.B. 599.
199 Occupiers' Liability Act 1984 s. 1(1)(a).
200 Above p. 383.
201 Occupiers' Liability Act 1984 s. 1(3).
202 *Ibid.* s. 1(4).
203 *Ibid.* s. 1(8).
204 Above pp. 388–9.
205 Occupiers' Liability Act 1984 s. 1(5): cp. above pp. 393–4.
206 Occupiers' Liability Act 1984 s. 1(6): cp. above pp. 395–8.

no longer be relevant. A difference of opinion has been expressed, however, on whether the duty under the 1984 Act to trespassers is the same, or similar to the common duty of care under the 1957 Act, or is distinguishable.[207] In view of the remarks of Lord Goff in *Ferguson v. Welsh*[208] on the possibility that where there are two occupiers an entrant onto premises may be a lawful visitor within the 1957 Act vis-à-vis one occupier and a trespasser within the 1984 Act vis-à-vis the other, it may be argued that different duties are owed by occupiers under these statutes. Moreover, having regard to the language of the Act of 1984 laying down the conditions under which the duty arises, it may be said that the occupier is not under an absolute duty to take reasonable care for the safety of the entrant, as he is under the 1957 Act. He is only obliged to take such care when he knows or has reasonable grounds for knowing there is danger and the danger is near the entrant. Nor is the occupier obliged to do more than guard against a risk against which he can reasonably be expected to protect the entrant. Clearly there are important differences between the two statutes, even though the later Act may have ameliorated the situation with respect to trespassers, and conversely burdened the occupier beyond the obligations formerly placed on him by the common law.

3. EMPLOYER'S LIABILITY

14.46 By the middle of the nineteenth century it was accepted that a master or employer owed a duty of care with respect to the safety of his servant or employee.[209] Although this had been denied in early cases, in which the infamous doctrine of "common employment" was introduced to reduce the possible liability of a master, if not negate it entirely,[210] later decisions clearly established the master-servant relationship as one in respect of which a personal duty of care to avoid negligence existed,[211] long before *Donoghue v. Stevenson.*[212] The "common employment" doctrine has now been abolished by statute.[213] Moreover there is a host of statutes, some originating in the nineteenth century, by virtue of which employers in particular industries or occupations are under detailed, specific obligations

207 Cp. *Salmond & Heuston on Torts*, 19th ed. 1987, at 321 with *Winfield & Jolowicz on Tort*, 12th ed. 1984 at 227.
208 [1987] 3 All E.R. 777 at 785: above note 97.
209 *Bartonshill Coal Co. v. Reid* (1858) 3 Macq. 266: this obligation arises from an implied term in the contract of employment.
210 *Priestley v. Fowler* (1837) 3 M. & W. 1; *Farwell v. Boston & Worcester Railroad Corporation* (1842) 4 Metcalf 49; *Seymour v. Maddox* (1851) 16 Q.B. 327.
211 *Bryden v. Stewart* (1855) 2 Macq. 30; *Tarrant v. Webb* (1856) 25 L.J.C.P. 261; *Roberts v. Smith* (1857) 26 L.J. Ex. 319. But not vicarious liability for the negligence of a fellow servant.
212 [1932] A.C. 562.
213 Law Reform (Personal Injuries) Act 1948 s. 1(1). Hence the employer can be liable vicariously *and* for breach of his personal duty: *Staveley Iron & Chemical Co. v. Jones* [1956] A.C. 647.

with regard to the health, safety and welfare of their employees.[214] However the master's common law duty of care to his servants still persists,[215] and it is with this duty that the remainder of this chapter is concerned.

(a) The common law duty

14.47 Over and above any responsibilities imposed on an employer by statute, the employer is under a duty at common law to take reasonable care for the safety of his employees.[216] Distinct from the rights of an employee to benefits for industrial or sickness provided under insurance legislation,[217] the employee has a right at common law to sue the employer if, by reason of the employer's breach of duty, the employee has suffered injury in the course of his employment.[218] The employer's duty, and consequent liability, is separate from the liability of an occupier should an employee of someone other than the occupier be injured by reason of the state of the occupier's premises or something being done thereon. Thus it may arise that an injured employee will have one action against his employer for breach of the employer's duty at common law, and another against an occupier of premises where the employee was injured for breach of the occupier's common duty of care.[219] Moreover an employer might be liable to an employee both as employer and as occupier, although the duty of an employer may be a more stringent duty than the duty of an occupier. As seen earlier, an occupier may be able to discharge his obligations to visitors by delegation to a competent independent contractor.[220] An employer however cannot escape liability for breach of the duty to take reasonable care of employees by delegation, even to a contractor who is competent.[221] The employer's duty is personal. However the duty is not absolute, as are many statutory duties imposed for the benefit of employees. The common law duty involves the employer in acting with reasonable care and skill as required by the circumstances. It is an example of negligence liability.

214 E.g. Factories Act 1961; Health & Safety at Work, etc. Act 1974; Mines & Quarries Act 1954; Offices, Shops & Railway Premises Act 1963; Agriculture (Safety, Health & Welfare) Act 1956: see Fridman, *The Modern Law of Employment*, 1963, Chapters 16–23. On breach of statutory duty, see Chapter 16 below.

215 For a recent statement see *McDermid v. Nash Dredging & Reclamation Co. Ltd* [1987] 2 All E.R. 878: generally, Fridman, *op. cit.* 186–209.

216 Hence compliance with a statutory duty may not suffice to discharge the employer's common law duty of care: *Bux v. Slough Metals Ltd* [1973] 1 W.L.R. 1358.

217 See now Social Security Act 1975.

218 Damages recovered may be reduced by reference to the compensation awarded under industrial injuries legislation: Law Reform (Personal Injuries) Act 1948 s. 2: *Stott v. Sir William Arrol & Co. Ltd* [1953] 2 Q.B. 92; *Flowers v. George Wimpey & Co. Ltd* [1956] 1 Q.B. 73; *Hultquist v. Universal Pattern & Engineering Co. Ltd* [1960] 2 Q.B. 467.

219 But see *Ferguson v. Welsh* [1987] 3 All E.R. 777 for limitations on the occupiers' duty when the employee is making use of an unsafe system of work.

220 Above at para. 14.36.

221 *Wilsons Clyde Coal Co. Ltd. v. English* [1938] A.C. 57; *McDermid v. Nash Dredging & Reclamation Co. Ltd, supra.* The qualification of this in relation to provision of tools purchased from a reputable supplier, as set out in *Davie v. New Merton Board Mills Ltd* [1959] A.C. 6054, has been removed by the Employer's Liability (Defective Equipment) Act, 1969: above at para. 3.36.

(b) Nature of the duty

14.48 The employer's duty may arise under the contract of employment. Even if there is no express term in such contract to that effect, there will be implied into a contract of employment, unless excluded by its provisions, a duty of taking reasonable care to provide proper appliances, and to maintain them in a proper condition, and so to carry on the operations as not to subject those employed by the employer to unnecessary risk.[222] An employer cannot make employment, even dangerous employment, more dangerous by failing to take adequate precautions to prevent the occurrence of injury from risks which the employer knew or ought to have known as a reasonable man existed and against which he could have guarded by taking such precautions. Although this duty may be contractual, it is also accepted that the duty of an employer arises under the law of torts. Hence an injured employee may sue the employer either for breach of contract or in tort, for negligence. On which basis the employee sues will depend on which form of action is more advantageous to him.[223] In most instances the employer's liability is founded on tort, rather than on contract. In this regard an employer's liability falls to be considered in connection with the tort of negligence.

(c) Content of the duty

14.49 The employer's duty is "to take reasonable care to protect" his employee "from dangers to safety or health of which he", the employer, "knew or ought to have known".[224] That involves a number of subsidiary obligations: the provision of adequate and safe equipment, the provision of adequate and safe premises and the provision of a system of working so designed as to reduce to as low a degree as is reasonably possible the risk of any harm.[225] The proper performance of these obligations requires that the employer takes steps to keep himself informed of developments and increased knowledge in the sphere in which he operates and his use of such information to keep his own system and equipment reasonably up to date and abreast of the times.[226] For this reason, in *McCafferty v. Metropolitan Police Receiver*,[227] the employer was liable to an employee, a former detective-inspector working in a laboratory on experimental work on firearms, for breach of duty, in failing to take competent advice about precuations to take to avoid substantial damage to the employee's hearing. Although the employer's duty is sometimes divided into various categories, viz., those relating to equipment, premises, and a safe system of working, it is clear that these are merely facets of the duty, which is unitary and all-embracing.[228] It is a general duty of care: it covers every aspect of the

222 *Smith v. Baker* [1891] A.C. 321 at 362 *per* Lord Herschell.
223 *Matthews v. Kuwait Bechtel Corporation* [1959] 2 Q.B. 57.
224 *McCafferty v. Metropolitan Police Receiver* [1977] 2 All E.R. 756 at 773 *per* Lane L.J.
225 *Ibid.*
226 *Ibid.* at 773–774.
227 *Supra.*
228 *Smith v. Baker* [1891] A.C. 325 at 362 *per* Lord Herschell.

employee's work and working conditions.[229] For convenience, the different aspects of the duty may be considered separately.

(i) Competent staff

14.50 This does not appear to be as important as it used to be. By alleging that the employer had breached his duty by employing incompetent workmen, an injured employee was able to escape the barrier to recovery provided by the now defunct doctrine of common employment. Hence if a fellow servant is negligent while acting in the course of his employment, the employer will be liable vicariously, even if the employer has not been guilty of negligence in his selection of the negligent servant.[230] However, there have been some instances of the employer's direct liability for breach of his personal duty to an employee arising from an act of horseplay or similar conduct on the part of one employee, the result of which was injury to another. Such liability will only arise, however, if the employer was negligent in employing someone whom he knew or ought to have known possessed the propensity to act in such a way.[231] An employer might not be liable vicariously for such conduct, since it would probably be considered to be committed outside the course of the misbehaving employee's employment.[232]

(ii) Plant, equipment and premises

14.51 The employer must take reasonable care to ensure that the plant and equipment provided for the use of his employees are adequate for the performance of the work in question.[233] It must also be reasonably safe for use by the employee, which may entail that the employer keep himself up-to-date on the latest developments with respect to equipment and plant.[234] Plant and equipment must be maintained so that they are safe for use.[235] Apart from statutory provisions dealing with safety equipment and protective devices, the employer must ensure that such means are present to

229 E.g., provision of medical assistance in cases of illness or injury not attributable to the employer's negligence: *Kasapis v. Laimois Bros* [1959] 2 Lloyd's Rep. 378; warning employees to have medical examinations when past working conditions have caused dangers of disease: *Wright v. Dunlop Rubber Co.* (1971) 11 K.I.R. 311. But *not* the safety of the employee's property: *Deyong v. Shenburn* [1946] K.B. 227; *Edwards v. West Hertfordshire Group Hospital Management Committee* [1957] 1 All E.R. 451: Fridman, *op. cit.* 209–210. Nor economic loss resulting from the absence of, or failure to provide, personal accident insurance in respect of special risks involved in the employee's working overseas for the employer: *Reid v. Rush & Tompkins Group plc* [1989] 3 All E.R. 228.

230 Chapter 3.

231 *Hudson v. Ridge Manufacturing Co.* [1957] 2 Q.B. 348; *Veness v. Dyson Bell & Co.* [1965] C.L.Y. 2691; *Coddington v. International Harvester Co. of G.B. Ltd.* (1969) 6 K.I.R. 146.

232 *O'Reilly v. National Rail & Tramway Appliances Ltd* [1966] 1 All E.R. 499.

233 *Ross v. Associated Portland Cement Manufacturers Ltd* [1964] 2 All E.R. 452; *Lovell v. Blundells & Crompton & Co.* [1944] 1 K.B. 502.

234 *McCafferty v. Metropolitan Police Receiver, para.* 14.49 *supra.* Does this conflict with what was said by Sir Arthur Channell in *Toronto Power Co. v. Paskawan* [1915] A.C. 734 at 738? Note the employer's duty in respect of plant and equipment of a third party: *Gledhill v. Liverpool Abattoir Utility Co.* [1957] 3 All E.R. 117.

235 Merely inspecting the plant may not suffice: *Pearce v. Round Oak Steel Works Ltd* [1969] 3 All E.R. 680 at 681 *per* Lord Denning, M.R.: cp. *Henderson v. Henry E. Jenkins & Son* [1969] 1 All E.R. 401.

avoid the possibility of foreseeable injury.[236] Hence the need to provide goggles for a one-eyed man,[237] or something to prevent a hearing disability from noise experienced in working.[238] However an employer does not warrant the safety of the plant or equipment, although under the Employer's Liability (Defective Equipment) Act 1969[239] the former defence available to an employer that he obtained the faulty equipment from a reputable supplier and that the defect which caused the employee's injury was latent and not discoverable by the exercise of reasonable care by the employer,[240] is no longer available.

14.52 The employer is also obliged to see that the place of work,[241] and perhaps even the access to work,[242] is reasonably safe for use by the employee.[243] However the employer's duty extends only to foreseeable risks against which he could have taken reasonable, not unreasonable precautions.[244] This duty is more onerous than the duty of an employer as occupier of premises, under the provisions of the Occupiers' Liability Act 1957:[245] but it is probably not as strict nor as heavy as the duties imposed by statutes such as the Factories Act 1961.[246] It is also now clear, though formerly this was doubted,[247] that the employer's liability does not cease merely because the employee is sent to work on premises occupied by a third party.[248] The employer may be obliged to ensure that it is reasonably safe for the employee to work on the premises in question, although this would not extend to his having to visit the premises and see for himself that they were safe. However, there might be circumstances in which the requirement of reasonable care could involve precisely such action on the part of the employer,[249] e.g. so as to see that a safe system of work is in operation.[250]

(iii) Safe system of work

14.53 This, more general obligation has been described as involving reasonable care for the safety of the employee in relation to "the physical

236 *Lovelidge v. Anselm Odling & Sons Ltd* [1967] 2 Q.B. 351; *Qualcast (Wolverhampton) Ltd v. Haynes* [1959] A.C. 743.
237 *Paris v. Stepney Borough Council* [1951] A.C. 367.
238 *McCaffery v. Metropolitan Police Receiver, supra.*
239 See para. 3.36.
240 Successfully pleaded in *Davie v. New Merton Board Mills Ltd* [1959] A.C. 604.
241 *Naismith v. London Film Productions Ltd* [1939] 1 All E.R. 794; *Davidson v. Handley Page* [1945] 1 All E.R. 235.
242 *Hurley v. Sanders & Co. Ltd* [1955] 1 All E.R. 833 at 835; *Smith v. National Coal Board* [1967] 2 All E.R. 593. I.e. if this is private property not the public highway.
243 But not when the place has become unsafe through exceptional circumstances: *O'Reilly v. National Rail & Tramway Appliances Ltd* [1966] 1 All E.R. 499.
244 *Latimer v. A.E.C. Ltd* [1953] A.C. 643.
245 Above pp. 14.15.
246 *Latimer v. A.E.C. Ltd, supra.*.
247 *Taylor v. Sims & Sims* [1942] 2 All E.R. 375; *Cilia v. H.M. James & Sons* [1954] 2 All E.R. 9.
248 *Wilson v. Tyneside Window Cleaning Co.* [1958] 2 Q.B. 110; *Smith v. Austin Lifts Ltd* [1959] 1 All E.R. 81. But it may be enough to warn the employee: *ibid.*
249 *Wilson v. Tyneside Window Cleaning Co., supra* at 121–122 *per* Parker L.J.
250 *General Cleaning Contractors Ltd. v. Christmas* [1953] A.C. 180. On the occupier's duty to require a safe system of work to be used, see *Ferguson v. Welsh* [1987] 3 All E.R. 777. See also, with respect to the occupier's duty in such situations, *Bates v. Parker* [1953] 2 Q.B. 231.

lay-out of the job—the setting the stage so to speak—the sequence in which the work is to be carried out, the provision in proper cases of warnings and notices and the issue of special instructions".[251] Much may depend on whether the work is regular or routine or involves a single act of a particular kind.[252] It may also depend on the particular individual involved, as for instance where he has only one eye:[253] and upon the foresight by the employer of the possibility that an employee may be careless of his own safety.[254] But, as Lord Simonds said in *Smith v. Austin Lifts*,[255] the relation of employer and employee should not be treated as equivalent to that of a nurse and an imbecile child. Nor is it the equivalent of the relation of matron and patient[256] or schoolmaster and pupil.[257] The standard expected of the employer is the standard of the ordinary prudent employer. He must ensure that a suitable system of protection is kept in operation. But he may not have to enforce that system. He can expect employees who are skilled and experienced to be sensible enough to avoid dangers of which they have been warned.[258] So, proof that a workman was provided with protective clothing but was not instructed to wear it is not of itself sufficient to prove negligence on the part of the employer.[259]

(d) Defences

(i) Lack of causation

14.54 The onus is on the injured employee to prove that the employer was in breach of his duty, perhaps by proving that an alternative system of work would have been safer,[260] and that such breach caused the injury. It has previously been seen that this has given rise to some difficult problems and contradictory decisions.[261]

(ii) Volenti

14.55 The fact that an employee undertook dangerous work will render the employer not liable for dangers inherent in the type of work;[262] but it will not permit him to escape liability for additional risks created by negligence, i.e. a breach of the employer's duty. Nor will the fact that the employee continued to work in the knowledge of a particular danger's existence amount to consent to run the risks involved therein. There must be a real, freely given consent.[263]

251 *Speed v. Thomas Swift & Co.* [1943] K.B. 557 at 563–564 *per* Lord Greene M.R.
252 Though even in the latter instance the employer may have to organise the work: *Boyle v. Kodak Ltd* [1969] 2 All E.R. 439.
253 *Paris v. Stepney Borough Council, supra.*
254 *General Cleaning Contractors Ltd v. Christmas, supra*; *Smith v. National Coal Board* [1967] 2 All E.R. 593.
255 [1959] 1 All E.R. 81 at 85.
256 *Haynes v. Qualcast Ltd* [1958] 1 W.L.R. 225 at 230.
257 *Withers v. Perry Chain Co. Ltd* [1961] 3 All E.R. 676 at 680 *per* Devlin L.J.
258 *Qualcast (Wolverhampton) Ltd. v. Haynes* [1959] A.C. 743; contrast *General Cleaning Contractors Ltd. v. Christmas, supra.*
259 *Qualcast (Wolverhampton) Ltd. v. Haynes, supra* at 760 *per* Lord Denning.
260 But not always: *Dixon v. Cementation Co. Ltd* [1960] 3 All E.R. 417.
261 Chapter 12 at paras. 12.83ff.
262 *Hurley v. Sanders & Co. Ltd* [1955] 1 All E.R. 833.
263 Chapter 13 at paras. 13.05ff.

(iii) Contributory negligence

14.56 However, the conduct of the employee who continues to work when he is aware of the dangers involved may amount to contributory negligence.[264] This will be the case where the work is not of a repetitive kind performed under strain for long hours at dangerous machines.[265] The employee is expected to observe the standards of a reasonable man in relation to his own safety, where the common law duty of the employer is the basis for the employee's action. However the type of employment may soften the standard expected of the employee. Nevertheless there are situations in which the carelessness of the employee may be blamed on the exigencies of the employment rather than on the lack of the employee, in which event the employee will be less likely to be found guilty of contributory negligence.[266]

264 Chapter 13 at paras. 13.23ff.
265 *Staveley Iron & General Co. Ltd v. Jones* [1956] A.C. 627.
266 *Machray v. Stewarts & Lloyds Ltd* [1964] 3 All E.R. 716

CHAPTER 15

Damages for Negligence

1. INTRODUCTION

(a) The only remedy

15.01 Where negligence is the cause of action the only possible remedy available to the plaintiff is an award of damages. Certain torts may result in the granting of an injunction to restrain the commission of the wrongful conduct alleged to have been committed by the defendant, or alleged to be about to be committed by him. Nuisance,[1] and sometimes defamation,[2] are torts of this kind. Other torts can be remedied by the restitution of property that has been taken or withheld by the defendant: for example, what formerly was detinue and is now the tort of wrongful interference with goods.[3] Other situations may permit the plaintiff to adopt some form of self-help, for example, the abatement of a nuisance,[4] the recaption of chattels which have been acquired by a trespasser,[5] or the use of force to repel an attack on oneself, or to eject a trespasser.[6] In most instances of such torts, however, the suitable, realistic and desirable remedy is an award of damages. In the case of negligence causing loss of, or damage to property, or personal injury or death, the only relief available to the plaintiff is monetary compensation.[7]

15.02 A plaintiff will only have one cause of action in respect of all his damage, whether such damage has already occurred at the time of the action or is likely to occur in the future.[8] Hence the plaintiff must recover in one action all past, present and potentially future loss stemming from

1 Chapter 8 at pp. 211–12.
2 Chapter 18 at pp. 519–20.
3 Chapter 7 at pp. 170–1.
4 Chapter 5 at pp. 207–9.
5 Chapter 5 at pp. 100–1.
6 Chapter 6 at pp. 127–8.
7 Damages may now be awarded in the currency in which the loss was sustained: *The Despina R.* [1979] A.C. 685; *Hoffman v. Sofaer* [1982] 1 W.L.R. 1250.
8 *Fitter v. Beale* (1701) 1 Ld. Raym. 339, 692; *Watson v. Powles* [1968] 1 Q.B. 596; *Fletcher v. Autocar & Transporters Ltd* [1968] 2 Q.B. 322. This means not only that successive actions cannot be brought on the same facts, but also that the court cannot award periodical payments, but must give the plaintiff a once-for-all lump sum: see, however, the Supreme Court Act 1981 s. 32A, added by the Administration of Justice Act 1982 s. 6, which does allow for "provisional" awards and the power to award further damages in certain cases of personal injuries which eventually produce a serious disease or serious physical or mental deterioration. Reform of the law in this respect was rejected by the Ontario Law Reform Commission, in its *Report on Compensation for Personal Injuries and Death*, 1987, Chapter 5. See generally, Fleming, "Damages: Capital or Rent" (1969) 19 U. Tor. L.J. 295.

the defendant's negligence, in respect of which, by virtue of the doctrines of remoteness and causation,[9] the defendant can be held liable. Some exceptions to this exist: but they are not truly exceptions, rather situations where the plaintiff has two distinct causes of action in regard to separate violations of his rights,[10] or where there are separate wrongful acts by the defendant. A further exception, namely, where the plaintiff's cause of action is a continuing one,[11] is irrelevant in the context of negligence, being more pertinent to trespass to land and nuisance.[12]

(b) Kinds of damages

15.03 The law distinguishes between (a) contemptuous damages; (b) nominal damages; (c) exemplary or punitive damages; (d) aggravated damages; and (e) compensatory damages.

15.04 Contemptuous damages are awarded to show that, although the plaintiff has a right which has been violated, his claim should never have been brought. He, or his claim, was unmeritorious. He is undeserving of a real amount of money. The award is designed to be derisory, such as an award of a shilling (in the days when shillings existed) in an action for libel. Such awards may result in the plaintiff's loss of his costs of the action even though he is technically the successful litigant. Such damages are unlikely in a negligence action. Nominal damages are those which recognise that the plaintiff's right has been infringed or violated, but he has not suffered any real loss. Such will be the case where the plaintiff's right to sue is founded on a tort that is actionable *per se*. Again this may affect the issue of costs. Negligence is not a tort actionable *per se*: actual damage must be proved to have been caused by the defendant's wrongful act.

15.05 Exemplary or punitive damages are those which are intended to penalise the defendant, not to compensate the plaintiff in respect of his loss. They are awarded, when permissible, over and above compensatory damages. In *Rookes v. Barnard*[13] the House of Lords held that such damages were only to be awarded in three types of case: (1) where permitted by statute; (2) where the servants of the Crown had been guilty of oppressive, arbitrary or unconstitutional action;[14] (3) where the defendant's conduct had been calculated by him to make a profit for himself which could exceed the amount of compensatory damages payable to the plaintiff. The last category is illustrated by libel actions.[15] It would seem that negligence

9 Chapter 12 at pp. 327–44.
10 *Brunsden v. Humphrey* (1884) 14 Q.B.D. 141, distinguished by the Supreme Court of Canada in *Cahoon v. Franks* (1967) 63 D.L.R. (2d) 274.
11 *Konsiker v. Goodman* [1928] 1 K.B. 421.
12 Chapter 5 at pp. 85–6; Chapter 8 at pp. 180–1.
13 [1964] A.C. 1129 at 1226–7 *per* Lord Devlin. See also *Cassell & Co. Ltd v. Broome* [1972] A.C. 1072.
14 *Attorney-General of St Christopher, Nevis & Anguilla v. Reynolds* [1980] A.C. 637; *Holden v. Chief Constable of Lancashire* [1986] 3 All E.R. 836.
15 Chapter 18 at pp. 515–16; but for a case of trespass to land, see *Drane v. Evangelou* [1978] 2 All E.R. 437.

does not fall within any one of these three accepted categories. Certainly in England no case has ever been reported in which such damages were awarded for negligence. The very concept of negligence contradicts the principles on which exemplary damages can now be granted in England after the speech of Lord Devlin in *Rookes v. Barnard*. However, as recognised by the House of Lords subsequently in *Cassell & Co. Ltd v. Broome*,[16] the same attitude towards such damages need not be expressed by courts in Commonwealth countries. Canadian courts have been more flexible in regard to the award of such damages.[17] Indeed there is at least one recent decision in which such damages were awarded where the plaintiff sued the defendant for negligence in the conduct of medical treatment. The basis for such an award was that the defendant surgeon had deliberately inflicted on the plaintiff a course of treatment to support and promote the defendant's theories rather than to cure the plaintiff; and had done so in the teeth of professional opposition to his views.[18] It is highly unlikely that an English court would adopt a similar attitude, even though, it has been suggested,[19] the speech of Lord Devlin may not have entirely closed the door to awards of damages where the defendant's motives are suspect.

15.06 In *Rookes v. Barnard*,[20] the distinction was drawn between exemplary damages and aggravated damages. The latter can clearly be awarded in cases of negligence. Their function is not to punish the defendant but to compensate the plaintiff where his injury has been aggravated by the conduct of the defendant. In such instances the motives of the defendant may be material (which indicates that in the Canadian case referred to above the appropriate decision should have been to award aggravated rather than exemplary damages). Such aggravated damages are intended to compensate the plaintiff for injury to his feelings of dignity and pride.[21] In some circumstances, therefore, it is arguable that such damages could be awarded by way of addition to other damages in an action for negligence, where damages are at large. However, in *Kralj v. McGrath*,[22] a case of medical negligence, Woolf J. thought that aggravated damages were wholly inappropriate. To have allowed such damages in a case where a doctor did not treat his patient in accordance with his duty would have meant that such damages could be granted by extension to cases of personal injury in respect of driving. A higher award of damages would therefore be appropriate in cases of reckless driving which caused injury than in cases of careless driving causing such injury. That was inconsistent with the general approach to damages in that area, which is to compensate the plaintiff for the loss actually suffered. The law did not treat

16 *Supra* note 13.
17 Fridman, "Punitive Damages in Tort" (1970) 48 Can. B.R. 373; Fridman, *Law of Torts in Canada*, Vol. 1, at 80, 112–113, 406–408.
18 *Coughlin v. Kuntz* (1987) 42 C.C.L.T. 142.
19 *Mafo v. Adams* [1970] 1 Q.B. 548 at 558 *per* Widgery L.J., a case of breach of contract and deceit.
20 *Supra* note 13 at 1228.
21 *Clerk & Lindsell on the Law of Torts*, 15th ed. 1986, at 242–243, cited by Woolf J. in *Kralj v. McGrath* [1986] 1 All E.R. 54 at 60.
22 [1986] 1 All E.R. 54 at 61.

compensatory damages as a matter which reflected the degree of negligence or breach of duty of the defendant.

5.07 It follows, therefore, that only compensatory damages are relevant in the law of negligence. The task of the court, once liability has been established for the consequences of a wrongful act or omission on the part of the defendant,[23] is to assess or measure the amount of such damages that ought to be awarded the plaintiff in accordance with the principles of law that govern such awards.

(c) Compensation

15.08 The underlying principle and rationale of awards of damages is to compensate the plaintiff for the injury or loss suffered by him so as to put the plaintiff back to the position in which he was prior to the wrong, to the extent that this is possible by an award of money. *Restitutio in integrum* is the key idea.[24] By obliging the defendant to pay damages the court attempts to ensure that the plaintiff is in the position he was in before he was affected by the conduct of the defendant. In some instances of negligence, for example those involving loss of, or damage to property, this may be practically as well as theoretically possible. Where personal injuries are concerned, and *a fortiori* where the action is brought by dependants within and under the Fatal Accidents Act after the defendant has caused the death of the one on whom the plaintiffs were dependent,[25] *restitutio in integrum* is more a pious statement of intention than an end that can be achieved by any action of the court. An award of damages may adequately compensate the plaintiff for expenses and loss of earnings:[26] but it can hardly be said that money takes the place of a lost limb, physical or mental disability, or loss of a life. In a real, though not a technical sense, awards of damages in such instances are more a "solatium" to assuage the suffering and disappointment of the plaintiff than true compensation for what has been lost by him.[27]

15.09 In relation to compensatory damages the distinction has been made between "general" and "special" damages.[28] Originally this distinction marked the difference between torts where damages was presumed, e.g., libel, and those where actual damages had to be established by the plaintiff in order to found a cause of action, viz., actions on the case where

23 Above Chapter 12 at pp. 327–44.
24 *Liesbosch Dredger v. Edison* [1933] A.C. 449 at 463 *per* Lord Wright; *Monarch S.S. Co. Ltd v. Karlshamns Oljefabriker* [1949] A.C. 196 at 221 *per* Lord Wright; *General Tire & Rubber Co. Ltd v. Firestone Tyre & Rubber Co. Ltd* [1975] 2 All E.R. 173 at 177 *per* Lord Wilberforce.
25 Below pp. 432–7.
26 Below pp. 418–23; see *British Transport Commission v. Gourley* [1956] A.C. 185; *Parry v. Cleaver* [1970] A.C. 1.
27 Cp. *Rushton v. National Coal Board* [1953] 1 Q.B. 495 at 502 *per* Romer L.J.; *H. West & Son Ltd v. Shephard* [1964] A.C. 326 at 346 *per* Lord Morris; *Fletcher v. Autocar & Transporters Ltd* [1968] 2 Q.B. 322.
28 Jolowicz, "The Changing Use of 'Special Damage' and its effect in the law" [1960] C.L.J. 214.

damage was the gist of the action, or actions for slander.[29] However the difference between the two kinds of damage which existed for pleading purposes has become part of the substantive law of damages.[30] The difference is now between damages capable of precise and exact pecuniary assessment, such as loss of earnings prior to the date of a trial, and damages which are not, such as future loss of earnings.[31] Because "special damages" in the original sense were required to be pleaded strictly, it has become necessary for "special damage" in the modern sense also to be pleaded and proved with the same strictness.[32]

(d) Mitigation of loss

15.10 In cases of torts, as in breach of contract situations, the plaintiff is expected to mitigate his loss. This entails that the plaintiff takes reasonable steps to prevent the harm caused by the defendant from being exacerbated and to do whatever is reasonable to lessen the effect of such harm. A plaintiff is not expected or required to act unreasonably in this respect; indeed, since the defendant's wrongful conduct is the primary cause of the plaintiff's injury or loss, the onus on the defendant will be a heavy one to establish that the plaintiff would not have suffered as badly had the plaintiff taken certain measures in consequence of what had occurred. It must be remembered, however, that the issue of mitigation is distinct from remoteness of damage, contributory negligence, or consent. These relate to the question whether the defendant is, or should be, held liable for the harm suffered by the plaintiff. Mitigation is pertinent to the assessment of the damages for which the defendant can, and should be, held responsible.

5.11 Mitigation in relation to personal injuries rarely arises. However there have been cases in which a defendant has argued that the injury suffered by the plaintiff was made worse or not alleviated by the plaintiff's refusal to undergo medical treatment. In one instance, the Privy Council held that the trial judge had been right in his approach to this issue and the West Indian Court of Appeal had been wrong.[33] The plaintiff had refused to have surgery required as a consequence of injuries suffered by reason of the defendants' negligence, because he knew the risks of infection which he, as a diabetic, would run. The trial judge considered that this was reasonable. The appellate court reversed this on the ground that the plaintiff had behaved unreasonably in refusing to undergo the operation which, if successful, would probably have regained for him within a few months most of his earlier mobility. The Privy Council allowed the plaintiff's appeal. In doing so it was stated[34] that the burden of proving

29 *Ratcliffe v. Evans* [1892] 2 Q.B. 524.
30 See *The Lord Citrine v. The Hebridean Coast* [1961] A.C. 545.
31 *British Transport Commission v. Gourley* [1956] A.C. 185 at 206 *per* Lord Goddard.
32 *Perestrillo Ltd v. United Paint Co. Ltd* [1969] 3 All E.R. 479; *Domsalla v. Barr* [1969] 1 W.L.R. 630. But if not established, general damages can be awarded: *The Lord Citrine v. The Hebridean Coast*, *supra*.
33 *Salvanyagam v. University of the West Indies* [1983] 1 All E.R. 824.
34 *Ibid.* at 827: cp. *Fazlic v. Milingimbi Community Inc.* (1981) 38 A.L.R. 424, an Australian case.

reasonableness was on the plaintiff in such a case. This rule was based on a plaintiff's duty to act reasonably so as to mitigate his damage. The question was one of fact. Though medical advice received will always be a major factor for consideration, the true question is always whether in all the circumstances, including particularly the medical advice received, the plaintiff acted reasonably in refusing surgery.[35] A similar approach, leading to a comparable decision, was adopted by the Supreme Court of Canada in *Janiak v. Ippolito*[36] where, again for good reason, the injured plaintiff refused to undergo surgery otherwise deemed to be advisable as a result of the injuries inflicted on him by the negligent defendant. Here it was said that mitigation was not like contributory negligence, which reduced the defendant's liability, but more in the nature of determining whether the behaviour of the plaintiff was *novus actus interveniens*. If it were, i.e. in situations when the plaintiff acted not in accordance with what was reasonable and in his own best interests, then the conclusion could be reached that the damage in question was caused not by the defendant but by the plaintiff's own stubbornness or other attitude. A relevant factor in making such a determination was whether the plaintiff had adopted one of several courses recommended by his doctor.[37] Others were the degree of risk involved in the surgery, the gravity of the consequences of refusing the surgery, the potential benefits to be derived therefrom, and possibly the psychological condition of the plaintiff at the time. A defendant has to take his victim as he finds him: which means not only that the defendant cannot complain if the plaintiff suffers greater injury than the ordinary person because of the plaintiff's "thin skull",[38] but also that the defendant will not be able to argue that an ordinary person would have undergone surgery in the circumstances where the plaintiff he injured was psychologically incapable of undergoing such surgery.

2. PROPERTY

(a) Loss

15.12 Since the fundamental principle is *restitutio in integrum*, in cases where the plaintiff's chattel has been lost or destroyed by the defendant's negligence the normal measure of damages is the value of the chattel at the time the negligence occurred.[39] This, generally speaking, will be the replacement cost of the chattel.[40] However this may not suffice to effect *restitutio*, for example, where the plaintiff has to hire an alternative chattel until a true replacement can be obtained. As long as such consequential losses are not too remote, they will also be recoverable.[41] Even the loss of

35 *Richards v. Redpath Brown & Co. Ltd* [1944] A.C. 62.
36 (1985) 16 D.L.R. (4th) 1.
37 *Ibid.* at 14.
38 Above Chapter 12 at pp. 337–8.
39 Cp. *The Winkfield* [1902] P. 42.
40 *Liesbosch Dredger v. Edison* [1933] A.C. 449: see also *Bacon v. Cooper (Metals) Ltd* [1982] 1 All E.R. 397.
41 *Moore v. D.E.R. Ltd* [1971] 3 All E.R. 517.

profits which would have been obtained by the use of the destroyed chattel may be recovered where those lost profits are normally expected in the course of business.[42] But extraneous losses, resulting from some economic peculiarity of the particular plaintiff, such as his impecuniosity, are too remote and may not be counted in the recoverable damages.[43]

15.13 It has been stated that, in calculating the market value of the chattel, care must be taken not to add on thereto the loss of profits incurred as a result of its destruction, where the chattel was profit-earning. To do this might result in the plaintiff's being compensated twice over in respect of the same loss.[44] However in some situations, e.g., where a ship was under charter at the time of loss, and in consequence the plaintiffs, the owners of the ship, lost the charter, or lost part of the profits from such a charter, such loss or profits was recoverable as well as the market value of the vessel.[45]

5.14 Where land or buildings have been lost, rather than damaged, by the negligence of the defendant, similar principles apply. In the case of land complete loss may be inconceivable, except possibly, where the plaintiff is deprived of the land which he believed he would acquire by virtue of a negligent misrepresentation on the part of the defendant. If a building is destroyed, for example by a negligently caused fire, the issue may be whether it is more reasonable to award the plaintiff the cost of rebuilding rather than the cost of removing the business elsewhere.[46]

(b) Damage

15.15 If a chattel is damaged, not destroyed or lost, the normal measure of damages is the amount by which its value has been diminished in consequence of the defendant's negligence. This usually means the cost of repair.[47] However it may happen that the cost of repair does not represent the reduction in the value of the chattel, for example, where the chattel was en route to be scrapped. In such a case the real measure of damages is the value of the chattel as scrap.[48] Moreover if the cost of repair should be greater than the total market value of the chattel, the latter will be recoverable not the former, unless the chattel can be described as irreplaceable or unique.[49]

15.16 Loss of earnings or profits that would have been obtained by the plaintiff during the period the chattel is undergoing repair may also be recovered where the chattel was normally a profit-earning chattel. Should

42 *Liesbosch Dredger v. Edison* [1933] A.C. 449.
43 *Ibid.*
44 *Ibid.*
45 *The Philadelphia* [1917] P. 101; *The Fortunity* [1961] 1 W.L.R. 351.
46 *Harbutt's Plasticine Ltd v. Wayne Tank & Pump Co. Ltd* [1970] 1 Q.B. 447.
47 *The London Corporation* [1935] P. 70.
48 *Ibid.*
49 *Darbyshire v. Warran* [1963] 3 All E.R. 310.

the plaintiff be obliged to hire a replacement chattel for the relevant time, the cost of such hire may be recovered where it was incurred to avoid loss of profits.[50] The actual cost of such hire may be too high or too low, depending on whether the chattel that was being replaced was operating at a loss or had been contracted to a third person at a rate that exceeded the current market price of the hiring or letting out of such chattels.[51] However it seems that even if a chattel is normally not profit-earning, there may be recovery of damages for loss of its use despite lack of evidence of any actual pecuniary loss.[52] The plaintiff is being deprived of the opportunity of using the chattel, for which it appears he is entitled to be compensated.[53] However usually the cost of hiring a reasonable substitute will be the measure of damages where the chattel was not employed to earn profit.[54] If an alternative is not hired then interest on the capital value of the chattel will be allowed, plus any depreciation and expenses incurred during the period when the chattel could not be used.[55]

5.17 As in the case of total loss, so in respect of damage, the same principles are applied wherever applicable to damage to land or buildings.[56] Only reasonable costs of repair will be allowed, nor, for example, the cost of such repair as will improve the quality or utility of the property.[57] Nor will the cost of repairs be allowed when the plaintiff has no intention of having them performed. In such an instance only diminution of value may be claimed.[58]

(c) Date of assessment

15.18 The general rule is that the time and place of destruction of the property are the relevant factors. The same will be the case where property is damaged. It is the value, or the cost of repair, at that time which must be considered. However a problem arose when these amounts differed substantially as between the date of the negligence and the date of the trial (which might have taken place some years after the original

50 As long as this was reasonable or the cost was reasonable: *Penman v. Saint John Toyota Ltd* (1972) 30 D.L.R. (3d) 86, a Canadian case. If the plaintiff's position is improved thereby, this must be taken into account: *The World Beauty* [1969] P. 12, reversed on other grounds [1970] P. 144.

51 *The Bodlewell* [1907] P. 286; *The Argentino* (1889) 14 App. Cas. 519.

52 *The Mediana* [1900] A.C. 113 at 117 *per* Lord Halsbury L.C.

53 Contrast a Canadian case where this was denied: *White v. Sweetland* (1978) 29 N. & P.E.I.R. 58, vehicle used only for pleasure. This is not the situation where, e.g., the plaintiff loses a limb: he will not be awarded damages in respect of a use of the limb, such as playing games, which he never enjoyed: below p. 427.

54 *The Mediana, supra.*

55 *The Lord Citrine v. The Hebridean Coast* [1961] A.C. 545.

56 E.g., (i) reinstatement or repair where this exceeds the diminution in value of the property, when the latter will be recoverable: *Jones v. Gooday* (1841) 8 M. & W. 146; *C.R. Taylor (Wholesale) Ltd v. Hepworths Ltd* [1977] 2 All E.R. 784; contrast *Harbutt's Plasticine Ltd v. Wayne Tank & Pump Co. Ltd* [1970] 1 Q.B. 471; (ii) loss of rental or profits recoverable: *Dodd Properties Ltd v. Canterbury City Council* [1980] 1 All E.R. 928.

57 *Dodd Properties Ltd v. Canterbury City Council, supra.*

58 *Perry v. Sidney Phillips & Son* [1982] 3 All E.R. 705, a case of negligent misrepresentation with respect to the condition of property: the plaintiff was also awarded damages for vexation.

wrongful act). Hence it was held in *Dodd Properties Ltd v. Canterbury City Council*[59] that in appropriate circumstances a different date might be selected, namely, the time when the repairs could first reasonably be undertaken by the plaintiffs. This might be affected by the financial situation of the plaintiff. In this respect, therefore, the economic condition of the plaintiff was material,[60] where it had to be disregarded in *Liesbosch Dredger v. The Edison*[61] because the impecuniosity of the plaintiffs affected their ability at the time of the incident to replace the damaged chattel. In this respect, therefore, the courts gave consideration to the ravages of inflation.

(d) Limitation of actions

15.19 Actions for negligence must be brought within the appropriate limitation period. Where loss or damage to property by negligence is concerned this is six years from the date on which the cause of action accrued.[62] This normally means that the appropriate date is the time when the damage on which the action for negligence is based occurred, since no action for negligence can be maintained unless and until damage results from the alleged act of negligence.[63] Statutory provisions have long dealt with the situation where the defendant concealed material facts, or the plaintiff was under a disability viz., infancy or unsoundness of mind.[64] A problem that emerged in more recent times as being troublesome was the calculation of the date when a right of action accrued where the damage only became apparent after the expiration of the limitation period as calculated from the time the negligence occurred. This is the problem of "latent damage". In cases of personal injury that was dealt with by the Limitation Act 1963,[65] passed as a consequence of a decision of the House of Lords that highlighted the issue.[66] Where property damage was involved, however, the courts struggled with different views as to the appropriate time from which the period should run[67] until its resolution by the Latent Damage Act 1986.

59 *Supra* note 56: see also *London Congregational Union Inc. v. Harriss & Harriss* [1985] 1 All E.R. 335, reversed on appeal on other grounds [1988] 1 All E.R. 15.
60 Cp. *Perry v. Sidney Phillips & Son, supra.*
61 [1933] A.C. 449: see Chapter 12 at pp. 337–8.
62 Limitation Act 1980 s. 2.
63 Cp. *Watson v. Wingate* 1960 S.L.T. 321.
64 See now Limitation Act 1980 ss. 28, 32.
65 See now Limitation Act 1980 ss. 11(4), 14 (as amended by the Consumer Protection Act 1987 s. 6(6)), Schedule 1, para. 3 in relation to actions under the Act where death is caused by a defective product).
66 *Cartledge v. E. Jopling & Sons Ltd* [1963] A.C. 758.
67 See *Sparham-Souter v. Town & Country Developments Ltd* [1976] 1 Q.B. 858; *Foster v. Outred & Co.* [1982] 2 All E.R. 753; *Pirelli General Cable Works Ltd v. Oscar Faber & Partners* [1983] 1 All E.R. 85; *Dove v. Banham Patent Locks Ltd* [1983] 2 All E.R. 833; *Investors in Industry Commercial Properties Ltd v. South Bedfordshire District Council* [1986] 1 All E.R. 787; *Jones v. Stroud District Council* [1988] 1 All E.R. 5; *London Congregational Union Inc. v. Harriss & Harriss* [1988] 1 All E.R. 15; *Ketteman v. Hansel Properties Ltd* [1988] 1 All E.R. 38.

15.20 The amendments made by this statute to the governing Limitation Act 1980 have the effect of making the limitation period for actions of the kind now being considered either 6 years from the date the cause of action accrued or three years from what is termed the "starting date", where this exceeds the six years that is the norm.[68] However no action for negligence causing property damage can be brought more than fifteen years from the last act or omission which constituted the negligence alleged by the plaintiff and to which the damage in question is said to be attributable.[69] The starting date is "the earliest date on which the plaintiff or any person in whom the cause of action was vested before him first had both the knowledge required for bringing an action for damages in respect of the relevant damage and a right to bring such action".[70] The "knowledge" referred to here means knowledge of material facts about the damage in respect of which the action is brought and other relevant facts.[71] The other relevant facts are: (a) that the damage was attributable in whole or in part to the conduct that is said to constitute negligence; (b) the defendant's identity;[72] (c) the identity of someone else alleged to be the perpetrator of the conduct that was negligent as well as additional facts supporting an action against the defendant.[73] Knowledge that conduct did not as a matter of law involve negligence is irrelevant for this purpose.[74] But knowledge does include knowledge which someone might be reasonably expected to acquire from facts observed or ascertainable by him; or from facts ascertainable by him with the help of appropriate expert advice which it is reasonable for him to seek.[75] But no one will be deemed to have knowledge of a fact ascertainable only with the help of expert advice as long as he has taken all reasonable steps to obtain and, where appropriate, act on that advice.[76] The expression "material facts about damage," knowledge of which is therefore made vital to the possibility of extending the limitation period, means such facts about the damage that would lead a reasonable person suffering such damage to consider it sufficiently serious to justify the institution of an action against a defendant who did not dispute liability and was able to satisfy a judgment.[77] This new period of limitation in cases of negligence not involving personal injury is subject to another provision,[78] also introduced by the 1986 Act,[79] relating to the effect of the disability or death of the person entitled to sue.[80] Another

68 Limitation Act 1980 s. 14A(4), inserted by the Latent Damage Act 1986 s. 1. This applies only to negligence actions otherwise than for personal injuries under s. 11 of the 1980 Act; and the provision of s. 2 of the 1980 Act, stipulating 6 years as the limitation period in tort, is in these circumstances rendered inapplicable: *ibid.* s. 14A(1)(2).
69 *Ibid.* s. 14B, inserted by the Latent Damages Act 1986 s. 1.
70 *Ibid.* s. 14A(5).
71 *Ibid.* s. 14A(6).
72 See *Simpson v. Norwest Holst Southern Ltd* [1980] 2 All E.R. 471.
73 Limitation Act 1980 s. 14A(8).
74 *Ibid.* s. 14A(9).
75 *Ibid.* s. 14A(10). e.g., advice from a trade union representative: *Pickles v. National Coal Board* [1968] 2 All E.R. 598.
76 Limitation Act 1980 s. 14A(10).
77 *Ibid.* s. 14A(7).
78 *Ibid.* s. 28A.
79 In s. 2(1).
80 " 'Disability' means infancy or unsoundness of mind": Limitation Act 1980 s. 38(2), as explained by *ibid.* s. 38(3), (4).

section of the 1986 Act[81] stipulates that if a successive owner obtains an interest in property that has been damaged by negligence, after the date when the original cause of action arose but before material facts about the damage have become known to the previous owner or person with an interest in the property, a fresh cause of action in respect of the negligence accrues to the new owner on the date when he acquires his interest. That new date is the date that is to be taken into consideration when calculating the expiration of a limitation period under the revised provisions of the 1980 Act (apart from the provisions of the 1980 Act dealing with disability or death).

15.21 This enactment makes it no longer necessary to consider the notion of property that was "doomed from the start", as a result of negligence, an idea that evolved and was elaborated in the decisions referred to earlier.[82] The plaintiff's right to sue, notwithstanding the passage of more than six years from the original negligent conduct of the defendant, now depends on whether he knew, or could reasonably have known, about the damage which is the basis for the action.

3. NON-FATAL PERSONAL INJURIES

(a) Pecuniary and non-pecuniary loss

15.22 As a result of negligence inflicting personal injury on the plaintiff, he or she may suffer financial loss that is capable of being measured and compensated for by a monetary award, and other loss, not of a financial kind, that is not truly amenable to measurement in monetary terms. For pecuniary loss there can be true *resitutio in integrum*: for non-pecuniary loss *restitutio* is really impossible; what courts do is to attempt to compensate for such losses by awards of money designed to enable the plaintiff to live a satisfactory life insofar as this may be attainable having regard to the injuries. Although the distinction is therefore drawn between *restitutio* in its strict sense and compensation, awards for pecuniary and non-pecuniary loss may be characterised either as *restitutio* or as compensation, having regard to the underlying rationale of damage awards, namely to restore the plaintiff as far as possible to the situation in which he or she was prior to the damage caused by the negligence of the defendant.[83]

15.23 At one time it was the practice to make a global award, giving one lump sum for all the various losses suffered by the plaintiff.[84] This now

81 Viz., s. 3(1).
82 *Supra* note 67.
83 The amount to be awarded is a question of fact: *Waldron v. War Office* [1956] 1 All E.R. 108; and the court must do its best to assess what should be awarded: *Wright v. British Railways Board* [1983] 2 All E.R. 773. The court must assess what is fair and reasonable compensation, not only for the plaintiff but also for the defendant: *S. v. Distillers Co. (Biochemicals) Ltd* [1970] 1 W.L.R. 114 at 123 *per* Hinchliffe J.
84 To avoid overlapping and an excessive award: *Fletcher v. Autocar & Transporters Ltd* [1968] 2 Q.B. 322.

seems to be inappropriate in view of statutory provisions regarding the award of interest on personal injury damages.[85] In any event the law distinguished between different types of loss, within each category of pecuniary and non-pecuniary losses; and for analytical, as well as practical reasons, it is necessary and convenient to adhere to those differentiations.

(b) Pecuniary loss

(i) Lost earnings

15.24 The plaintiff is entitled to be awarded the lost wages, salary or profits[86] that he would have earned between the date when he was incapacitated by reason of the injuries received through the defendant's negligence and the date of the trial, or the date when he ceased to be incapacitated (if this occurred before the trial).[87] However from the gross amount of these lost earnings there must be deducted the income tax and social security contributions which the plaintiff would have made during that period.[88] If the plaintiff has received unemployment benefit during that period, this, too, must be deducted.[89] The purpose of the award is to make restitution of what has been lost: therefore such deductions and such benefits affect what has been lost by the plaintiff and must be brought into account. Under the Law Reform (Personal Injuries) Act 1948 section 2(1),[90] in assessing damages for personal injuries in respct of loss of earnings, the court must take into account one-half of the value of certain social security benefits[91] which accrue to the plaintiff for the five years beginning with the time when the cause of action accrued. This may extend beyond the period between the date of the accident and date of the trial (and therefore will affect the plaintiff's claim for future lost earnings).[92] But it unquestionably affects the plaintiff's claim for earnings, etc.,

85 Supreme Court Act 1981 s. 35A, replacing Administration of Justice Act 1969 s. 22: see *Cookson v. Knowles* [1979] A.C. 556; *Pickett v. British Rail Engineering Ltd* [1980] A.C. 136; *Wright v. British Railways Board, supra*. Earlier guidelines were set out in *Jefford v. Gee* [1970] 2 Q.B. 130.

86 *Lee v. Sheard* [1956] 1 Q.B. 192.

87 *Harris v. Bright's Asphalt Contractors Ltd* [1953] 1 Q.B. 617; *Cookson v. Knowles* [1979] A.C. 556; wage increases must be taken into account. But if a plaintiff would not have continued earning at the same rate, if he had not been injured, this will reduce the amount of his claim: *Phillips v. London & South Western Railway* (1879) 5 C.P.D. 280 at 291; *Rouse v. Port of London Authority* [1953] 2 Lloyd's Rep. 179. The date of the trial is the appropriate date on which to determine actual loss of earnings to that date: *Pritchard v. J. H. Cobden Ltd* [1987] 1 All E.R. 300.

88 *British Transport Commission v. Gourley* [1956] A.C. 185; *Cooper v. Firth Brown Ltd* [1963] All E.R. 31. And contributions to a compulsory pension scheme: *Dews v. National Coal Board* [1986] 2 All E.R. 769.

89 *Parsons v. B.N.M. Laboratories Ltd* [1964] 1 Q.B. 65 (affirmed by the House of Lords in *Westwood v. Secretary of State for Employment* [1985] A.C. 20). See also *Plummer v. P. B. Wilkins & Sons Ltd* [1981] 1 All E.R. 91.

90 As amended by the Social Security (Consequential Provisions) Act 1975, the National Insurance Act 1971, the Social Security Pensions Act 1975 and the Social Security Act 1975: see *Jackman v. Corbett* [1987] 2 All E.R. 699 at 700 *per* Fox L.J.

91 Viz., sickness benefit, invalidity benefit, non-contributory invalidity pension, injuries benefit, disablement benefit: cp. also *Gaskell v. Preston* [1981] 3 All E.R. 427 (family income supplement).

92 Below.

lost prior to the trial. In *Jackman v. Corbett*[93] the Court of Appeal held that the statute must be interpreted strictly. No deductions under this provision can be made for the period after the stipulated five years. The language of the Act did not mean that its provisions only applied to the first five years and that thereafter the total amount of social security benefit was to be deducted from the otherwise recoverable damages.

15.25 Damages cannot be awarded under this heading in respect of lost earnings not attributable to the defendant's negligence, for example, where the injury accelerated, but did not cause the plaintiff's absence from work.[94]

(ii) Future earnings

15.26 The major difficulties arise in connection with the assessment of damages where the plaintiff is rendered incapable of working in the future, or his earning capacity is reduced in one of two ways, either (i) because he has to take up other, less remunerative work or (ii) the injury results in loss of expectation of life which means that he will not work for as long as he might have done had he not been injured. The task or aim of the court is to calculate in reasonable terms the sum which must be awarded in order to guarantee to the plaintiff the income he would have made for the relevant period. In this respect the prospect of inflation is not a material factor that influences judicial thinking.[95] At the same time the prospect of a rise in interest rates may counterbalance inflation such that the capital sum awarded at the trial will produce sufficient interest to make up for what would otherwise be the ravages of inflation.[96]

15.27 The basic approach is to multiply the "multiplicand", i.e. the plaintiff's net annual loss, by the "multiplier", i.e., a number of years' purchase calculated on the likely duration of the disability.[97] The net annual loss of the plaintiff as seen above is his gross annual income less deductions for income tax and social security contributions he would be obliged to make. Loss of future earnings may not need to be pleaded specially, but it has been said that such pleading is advisable.[98] Where

93 [1987] 2 All E.R. 699: affirming *Haste v. Sandell Perkins Ltd*; *Denman v. Essex Area Health Authority* [1984] Q.B. 735.

94 *Cutler v. Vauxhall Motors Ltd* [1971] 1 Q.B. 418.

95 *Mallett v. McMonagle* [1970] A.C. 166; *Cookson v. Knowles, supra*; *Lim v. Camden Area Health Authority* [1980] A.C. 174; *Hodgson v. Trapp* [1988] 3 All E.R. 870. But this has been criticised: *Winfield & Jolowicz on Tort*, 12th ed. 1984 at 634–635; cp. Pearson Commission, Cmnd. 7054, Vol. I, Chapter 5. High rates of taxation may be relevant: *Thomas v. Wignall* [1987] 1 All E.R. 1185.

96 Hence the denial of a claim for damages for lost future capital payments such as a pension right in *Auty v. National Coal Board* [1985] 1 All E.R. 930.

97 The date of the trial is the appropriate date on which to determine the future loss of earnings based on a multiplier and multiplicand ascertained from the facts as they were at that date: *Pritchard v. J. H. Cobden Ltd* [1987] 1 All E.R. 300, pointing out the difference from Fatal Accidents Act cases: *ibid.* at 303–307 *per* O'Connor L.J. On the non-use of actuarial evidence and methods of calculation, see *Taylor v. O'Connor* [1971] A.C. 115. For a case where the normal method was inappropriate see *Joyce v. Yeomans* [1981] 2 All E.R. 21.

98 *Chan Wai Jong v. Li Ping Sam* [1985] 2 W.L.R. 396.

there are special circumstances which tend to prove that the plaintiff has sustained a future loss beyond what would normally be expected, it appears that those special circumstances must be pleaded to give the other side notice of the case to be answered.[99] Since only lump sum payments are awarded at the end of a trial, it has been suggested that the difficulties of prophesying what is likely to happen, both as regards the value of the money and as respects the future situation of the injured plaintiff, make it desirable to allow courts to order periodical, and therefore adjustable, payments in place of a lifetime, single award.[100] Apart from the slight change to which reference has been made,[101] this has not thus far received statutory endorsement.

15.28 Two issues have arisen in connection with the assessment of damages in respect of lost future earnings. One is the question of loss of earning capacity, that is to say the extent to which the plaintiff's injuries make it possible that he will not be able to obtain employment at some time in the future. The second is the issue of compensation of loss of earnings during what have been called the "lost years", i.e. the years of life of which the plaintiff has been deprived by the injuries, the consequence of which has been to reduce his life expectancy. As regards the first issue, it appears that courts are prepared in a proper case to award a sum to take into account the loss of the chance to earn in the future, as long as this loss is real or substantial and not merely speculative.[102] When it comes to estimating loss of earning capacity (or for a handicap in the labour market) there is no such thing as a conventional approach. There is no rule of thumb that can be applied. In each case the trial judge has to do his best to assess the plaintiff's handicap, as an existing disability. It is a matter of weighing up risks and chances in all the circumstances of a particular case.[103] It is not clear whether loss of earning capacity is a distinct head of damages from loss of future earnings.[104] But, in any event, it does not seem to matter because loss of earning capacity will not normally give rise to an award of damages unless there is at least some prospective loss of earnings.[105] Hence the award of damages for lost earning capacity is subject to the deduction specified in the Law Reform (Personal Injuries) Act 1948,[106] as long as the prospective loss of earnings, due to loss of earning capacity, is probable or certain or somewhere in between. However as pointed out in *Jackman v. Corbett*,[107] those deductions

99 *Domsalla v. Barr* [1969] 3 All E.R. 487.
100 Pearson Commission, Cmnd. 7054, Vol. I, Chapter 14.
101 Above p. 408.
102 *Moeliker v. Reyrolle & Co. Ltd* [1977] 1 All E.R. 9.
103 *Foster v. Tyne & Wear County Council* [1986] 1 All E.R. 567 at 570 *per* Lloyd L.J.
104 Contrast *Fairley v. John Thompson (Design & Contracting Division Ltd* [1973] 2 Lloyds Rep. 40 with *Clarke v. Rotax Aircraft Equipment Ltd* [1975] 3 All E.R. 794. The views of the Pearson Commission were that loss of earning capacity was not distinguishable from loss of future earnings: Cmnd. 7054, para. 338; cp. Law Commission, *Report on Personal Injuries Litigation, Assessment of Damages*, Law Comm. No. 56, para. 204.
105 *Foster v. Tyne & Wear County Council*, *supra* at 572 *per* Lloyd L.J.
106 Above para. 15.24.
107 [1987] 2 All E.R. 699.

relate only to five years from the date the cause of action accrued and cannot be continued beyond that time.

15.29 Following decisions of the House of Lords on the subject of claims for loss of earnings during the "lost years",[108] it was held that an infant plaintiff could recover damages for lost earnings during those years subject to proof of loss.[109] Such a claim should not be limited to the exceptional case of an infant who was already earning money at the time of the negligence which inflicted injury.[110] However in the particular case in question the infant's claim was assessed as nil. In another case the Court of Appeal agreed that such a claim could be made, and held that in the particular instance it should be assessed as nil.[111] However the majority also allowed the infant plaintiff to claim for loss of future earnings on the ground that a gravely injured child who was going to live for many years required care and attention and that could only be provided for by an award for loss of such earnings (since the award for future care[112] would not provide a sufficient sum to permit the infant to go to a residential home to be cared for at all times).

(iii) Expenses

15.30 The plaintiff can claim necessary expenses incurred prior to the trial. This will include medical expenses, if any, the cost of nursing or other care, board and lodging.[113] However deductions must be made from loss of income where the injured plaintiff has been maintained at the public expense in a hospital, nursing home or other institution.[114] Deductions must also be made, from damages in respect of both past and future expenses of providing for the care of the plaintiff, to take into account attendance and mobility allowances payable to the plaintiff under the Social Security Act 1975.[115] To allow the plaintiff to have those benefits and the damages would be to allow double recovery at the expense of

108 *Pickett v. British Rail Engineering Ltd* [1989] A.C. 136, overruling *Oliver v. Ashman* [1962] 2 Q.B. 210. This was extended to claims for the benefit of the deceased injured party's estate in *Gammell v. Wilson* [1982] A.C. 27: above Chapter 2 at para. 2.38. See now the Administration of Justice Act 1982 s. 4, prohibiting recovery of damages for loss of income in respect of a period after a person's death where the claim is made by the victim's estate, not the injured person while still alive.

109 *Connolly v. Camden & Islington Area Health Authority* [1981] 3 All E.R. 250. Certain deductions for living expenses may have to be made: *Harris v. Empress Motors Ltd* [1983] 3 All E.R. 561. But not deductions for expenditures on dependants: *White v. London Transport Executive* [1982] Q.B. 489.

110 *Connolly v. Camden & Islington Area Health Authority*, *supra*: e.g., it might also extend to a child who would have joined his or her father in a prosperous business, or a child who would have inherited a capital sum had the shortening of life not occurred.

111 *Croke v. Wiseman* [1981] 3 All E.R. 852.

112 Below at p. 423.

113 *Cunningham v. Harrison* [1950] 2 K.B. 43. Even if the medical expenses could have been dealt with by treatment under the National Health Service: Law Reform (Personal Injuries) Act 1948 s. 2(4). The cost of special equipment is also recoverable: *S v. Distillers Co. (Biochemicals) Ltd* [1970] 1 W.L.R. 114; *Povey v. Governors of Rysdale School* [1970] 1 All E.R. 841. Note that such expenses are special damages which must be specifically pleaded.

114 Administration of Justice Act 1982 s. 5.

115 *Hodgson v. Trapp* [1988] 3 All E.R. 870.

taxpayers and insurers, which as Lord Bridge pointed out in *Hodgson v. Trapp*,[116] was incapable of justification on any rational ground.

15.31 Damages may also be awarded to cover the cost of future care of the plaintiff, e.g. where he or she is rendered a vegetable.[117] However there should not be duplication of damages where a claim for those expenses is joined with a claim for loss of earnings. This requires deduction from the amount awarded for care of a sum representing "domestic" care, viz., food, laundry, etc, which would be expenses incurred in any event, whether the plaintiff were injured or not.[118] Such amounts, however, may be sufficiently small not to make any significant difference to the final, total amount awarded.

15.32 In *Donnelly v. Joyce*[119] it was held that the injured plaintiff could claim the wages lost by his mother when she gave up her employment in order to nurse him following his being injured by the defendant. It appears, therefore, that no contractual obligation to pay for those services need exist for the injured plaintiff to be able to recover their cost. It follows also that expenses incurred by a third person for the benefit of the plaintiff may also be recovered by the plaintiff, for example the cost of making visits to the hospital intended to aid the recovery of the plaintiff. Another expense which appears to be recoverable is the replacement cost of gratuitous services formerly rendered by the plaintiff in the household.[120] Although the action for loss of *consortium* has now been abolished,[121] the attitude of the courts to such expenses seems to make up for its absence. The difference is, however, that the claim is now made by the victim, the injured plaintiff, not by the victim's husband: and is available to men and women, not restricted (as the older action was) to men only.

15.33 Other consequential expenses stemming from the injury caused by the defendant's negligence may also be recovered: e.g. loss of board and lodging provided by the employer,[122] or the use of a car;[123] loss of pension rights where the plaintiff had to give up pensionable employment;[124] or

116 *Ibid.* at 876.
117 The principles relating to this were exhaustively discussed by the Supreme Court of Canada in a famous "trilogy" of cases: *Andrews v. Grand & Toy Alberta* (1978) 83 D.L.R. (3d) 492; *Thornton v. Board of Trustees of School District No. 57* (1978) 83 D.L.R. (3d) 480; *Arnold v. Teno* (1978) 83 D.L.R. (3d) 609.
118 *Lim v. Camden Area Health Authority* [1980] A.C. 174.
119 [1974] Q.B. 454; see also *Taylor v. Bristol Omnibus Co. Ltd* [1975] 2 All E.R. 1107: followed in Canada in *Veldhuizen v. Blakzyl* [1977] 1 W.W.R. 526 in preference to earlier authority, viz., *Greenaway v. C.P.R.* [1925] 1 W.W.R. 667: see Fridman, *Law of Torts in Canada*, Vol. I, at 399–400. The money so recovered has been held to be held in trust for the provider of the services: see, e.g., *Coderre v. Ethier* (1978) 85 D.L.R. (3d) 621.
120 *Daly v. General Steam Navigation Ltd* [1980] 3 All E.R. 696.
121 Administration of Justice Act 1982 s. 2.
122 *Liffen v. Watson* [1940] 1 K.B. 556.
123 *Clay v. Pooler* [1982] 3 All E.R. 570, a fatal accident case but the principles appear to be the same.
124 *Judd v. Board of Governors of the Hammersmith, West London & St. Mark's Hospitals* [1960] 1 All E.R. 607: cp. *Dews v. National Coal Board* [1986] 2 All E.R. 769 at 781 *per* Woolf L.J.; *Croke v. Wiseman* [1981] 3 All E.R. 852 at 860 *per* Griffiths L.J.

loss of marriage prospects where a woman was badly disfigured.[125] In *Jones v. Jones*[126] it was held that a man could claim the awards he would have to make to his wife and children in the event of the dissolution of his marriage where it could be proved that the breakdown of the marriage was caused by the defendant's negligence. In *Pritchard. v. J. H. Cobden Ltd*,[127] however, the Court of Appeal denied the plaintiff's claim for the extra expense he would incur as a result of his divorce which he alleged had been brought about as a result of his injuries. The reason given was that financial orders made in matrimonial proceedings did not represent a loss in the usual sense: such orders amounted to a redistribution of the combined assets of the parties. Furthermore the financial consequences of a divorce were too remote to be recoverable; or should be excluded as being indirect economic loss; or should be disallowed on the ground of public policy.[128] The *Jones* case was not followed, and possibly was disapproved.

15.34 A more original claim for expenses based on the defendant's negligence was made in *Meah v. McCreamer (No. 2)*.[129] Here the plaintiff committed sex offences for which he was prosecuted, convicted and sentenced to imprisonment and in respect of which he paid damages to the victims, as a result of the injuries incurred because of the defendant's negligence. The damages paid to the victims by the plaintiff were not a recoverable expense. Three reasons were given by Woolf J.: first, that such damages were too remote; secondly, that to allow such damages to be recovered would expose defendants in this and other cases to an indefinite liability for an indefinite duration; and third, that it was against public policy to permit a plaintiff to be indemnified for his crimes.

(iv) Deductions

15.35 It has been noted previously that in calculating the total amount of damages to be awarded the plaintiff in respect of pecuniary losses, such as lost past and future earnings, income tax payable by the plaintiff must be deducted from the final award. This was decided by the House of Lords in *British Transport Commission v. Gourley*,[130] a case that has been criticised on various grounds[131] and has not been followed in Canada.[132] By statute, viz., the Law Reform (Personal Injuries) Act 1948 and other social

125 Or otherwise injuriously affected: *Moriarty v. McCarthy* [1978] 2 All E.R. 213; the loss is economic, i.e. pecuniary.
126 [1985] Q.B. 704, varying [1983] 1 All E.R. 1037.
127 [1987] 1 All E.R. 300.
128 *Ibid.* at 317 *per* Sir Roger Ormrod.
129 [1986] 1 All E.R. 943.
130 [1956] A.C. 185; so is an income tax rebate: *Hartley v. Sandholme Iron Co.* [1975] Q.B. 602.
131 E.g., that the defendant profits from the fact that the plaintiff is in a high tax bracket; that the courts tax when the Revenue does not; that a plaintiff who loses his earning capacity is really losing a capital asset, which is not normally taxable. But the reality is that the plaintiff has only lost a net sum, and should not be awarded a gross sum.
132 *The Queen v. Jennings* (1966) 57 D.L.R. (2d) 644. But it *has* been followed in Australia: *Cullen v. Trappel* (1980) 29 A.L.R. 1 overruling *Atlas Tiles v. Briars* (1978) 21 A.L.R. 129.

security legislation,[133] other deductions must be made in respect of various kinds of benefit obtained by the plaintiff for a period of five years, which has been held to mean that such benefits beyond the five years are not deductible.[134] Rationalisation of this position was recommended by the Pearson Commission, which would have made all benefits deductible, although the deductions would be made in respect of different categories of benefit in relation to different categories of damage awards.[135]

15.36 Other "collateral benefits" accruing to the injured plaintiff in consequence of his injuries may also have to be taken into account by the court when assessing the amount to be paid by the defendant. Two principles seem to be in conflict, with the result that different approaches, i.e. different policies, have been adopted in regard to different kinds of collateral benefits. On the one hand the purpose of an award is to compensate the plaintiff for what has been lost in a financial sense. Insofar as some financial benefits result from the injuries, the plaintiff has not lost that amount.[136] To ignore those benefits in the calculation might result in overcompensation or double recovery. However, to allow the defendant to subtract those benefits from the damages payable by him might mean that the defendant is benefitted by chance, and that the loss is thereby borne by some other person or institution.

15.37 If the plaintiff receives money under a contract of insurance, that money is not deducted from the damages recoverable from the defendant. His right to such money is contractual: so far as the defendant is concerned it is *res inter alios acta*.[137] Sick pay paid by the employer, or wages which are paid under the employer's contractual obligation are deductible, because the plaintiff's loss is thereby reduced.[138] But a disability pension is not deductable, whether it is discretionary or not and whether it is contributory or non-contributory.[139] Payments made to the plaintiff by a charity are not deductible. To do so might result in the termination of such payments in the future on the ground that their being made was detrimental to the plaintiff's interests.[140]

(vi) Interest

15.38 The Administration of Justice Act 1969 section 22, which is now contained in the Supreme Court Act 1981 section 35A, as added by the

133 Above at p. 419: see also the cases cited *supra* notes 90, 91: and *Foxley v. Olton* [1965] 2 Q.B. 306; *Lincoln v. Hayman* [1982] 2 All E.R. 819; *Hodgson v. Trapp* [1988] 3 All E.R. 870.

134 *Jackman v. Corbett* [1987] 2 All E.R. 699; see para. 15.24 above.

135 Cmnd. 7054, Vol. I, Chapter 13, referring to compensation for loss of income, compensation for expenses, compensation for non-pecuniary loss.

136 *Parry v. Cleaver* [1970] A.C. 1.

137 *Bradburn v. Great Western Railway* (1874) L.R. 10 Ex. 1.

138 *Receiver for Metropolitan Police District v. Croydon Corporation* [1957] 2 Q.B. 154. Unless paid on condition of repayment in the event of a successful claim for damages: or possibly when such payments are *ex gratia*: *Dennis v. London Passenger Transport Board* [1948] 1 All E.R. 779.

139 *Parry v. Cleaver, supra.*

140 *Ibid.*

Administration of Justice Act 1982, permits courts to award interest on damages for which judgment has been given. Different rates are appropriate for different items of damage, viz., special damages, loss of future earnings, pain, suffering and loss of amenities.[141] Under R.S.C. Ord. 22, r. 1(8) no payment into court will be fully effective unless it includes interest. The purpose of these provisions is to compensate the plaintiff where there has been delay in the settlement or determination of his claim for the "use value" of the money to which he is entitled. In this respect there is a distinction between such loss and the loss that may result from inflation (i.e. the "risk" aspect of interest).[142]

(c) Non-pecuniary loss

(i) Pain and suffering

15.39 It is now accepted that a sum of money may be awarded in respect of the pain and suffering incurred by the plaintiff in consequences of the injuries inflicted by the defendant's negligence.[143] This includes an award for the mental consequences of the medical treatment required by those injuries, as well as the concern of the plaintiff regarding the effects of the injuries on his or her life. Also possibly relevant in this respect are worry about the resolution of the claim[144] and nervous shock,[145] but not mere disappointment or grief caused by the injuries and their consequences such as the ruin of a holiday.[146] However it must be shown that the pain and suffering were caused by the defendant's wrongful act.[147] Moreover the plaintiff must be aware that he is suffering the pain. Hence if the result of the defendant's conduct is to render the plaintiff unconscious and therefore incapable of appreciating that he is undergoing pain and concomitant suffering, no award can be made under this head.[148] What will be awarded naturally depends on the nature of the injuries and their consequences in terms of pain and suffering.[149] In *Croke v. Wiseman*,[150] for example, the trial judge awarded £35,000 for pain and suffering. The Court of Appeal did not interfere with this. It was not so high in proportion to the injuries or the total award to make it necessary to lower it to the sum of £20,000

141 See *Jefford v. Gee* [1970] 2 Q.B. 130; *Cookson v. Knowles* [1979] A.C. 556; *Pickett v. British Rail Engineering Ltd* [1980] A.C. 136; *Wright v. British Railways Board* [1983] 2 A.C. 773.
142 See *Birkett v. Hayes* [1982] 2 All E.R. 710.
143 Contrast the views of Pollock C.B. in *Theobald v. Railway Passengers Assurance Co.* (1862) 15 Jur. 583 at 586.
144 *James v. Woodall Duckham Construction Ltd* [1969 2 All E.R. 794.
145 *Hinz v. Berry* [1970] 2 Q.B. 40: cp. above Chapter 12 at paras. 12.24ff. Including such shock in the future: *Heaps v. Perrite Ltd* [1937] 2 All E.R. 60.
146 *Ichard v. Frangoulis* [1977] 2 All E.R. 461; but such loss is recoverable as part of the general damages, if reasonably foreseeable.
147 *Cutler v. Vauxhall Motors Ltd* [1971] 1 Q.B. 418, where the operation alleged to have caused his suffering was inevitable in any event.
148 *Wise v. Kaye* [1962] 1 Q.B. 638; *H. West & Son Ltd v. Shephard* [1964] A.C. 326: on this see below.
149 There must be evidence of physical suffering: *Bishop v. Cunard White Star Ltd* [1950] P. 240: but the fact that the plaintiff, because wealthy, may be able to assuage his suffering more easily than a poor persons should be irrelevant: cp. *Fletcher v. Autocar & Transporters Ltd* [1968] 2 Q.B. 322 at 340, 361.
150 [1981] 3 All E.R. 852: cp. *Walker v. John MacLean & Sons Ltd* [1979] 2 All E.R. 965.

which had been mentioned by Lord Scarman in *Lim v Camden Area Health Authority*[151] as appropriate in the circumstances of that case. Lord Scarman was not laying down that £20,000 was an appropriate standard amount,[152] a view which Lord Denning, dissenting, adopted subject only to raising the amount of £25,000 in view of inflation since the *Lim* case.[153]

15.40 Although damages for loss of expectation of life, which were formerly recoverable,[154] have been abolished by the Administration of Justice Act 1982,[155] it remains possible for an award to be made in respect of the mental suffering caused to the plaintiff by his or her awareness that life expectancy has been shortened by reason of the injuries.[156] Under the prior law the true benefit of such an award went to those entitled to claim on the death of the victim, as a form of damages for bereavement. That is now dealt with in other ways.[157]

(ii) Loss of amenities

15.41 An injured plaintiff may also recover damages in respect of loss of amenity or loss of a faculty,[158] the consequences of which is to reduce his or her enjoyment of life. Such is the case where the plaintiff loses a leg which prevents his playing football as he used to do,[159] or suffers intensive brain damage.[160] The amount to be awarded under this heading of damage depends quite obviously on the nature and seriousness of the injury and the extent to which it has caused interference with the plaintiff's previous way of life, and hence his or her ability to enjoy subsequent existence.[161]

15.42 The problem that has exercised the minds of judges in several common law jurisdictions, and has produced different resolutions,[162] is whether an award of damages for loss of amenities should be made to a plaintiff who has been rendered totally or partially incapable of appreciating such loss, for example, as in *H. West & Son Ltd v. Shephard*,[163] where the plaintiff was partially unconscious and totally paralysed because of her injuries. The English solution, as stated by the majority of the House of Lords in the *West* case[164] and subsequently approved and followed in *Lim*

151 [1980] A.C. 174.
152 *Croke v. Wiseman, supra* at 859 *per* Griffiths L.J.
153 *Ibid.* at 858.
154 *Flint v. Lovell* [1935] 1 K.B. 354; *Rose v. Ford* [1937] A.C. 826; *Benham v. Gambling* [1941] A.C. 157.
155 S. 1(1)(a).
156 S. 1(1)(b).
157 Below p. 435.
158 *Andrews v. Freeborough* [1967] 1 Q.B. 1 at 18 *per* Davies L.J.
159 *Heaps v. Perrite Ltd* [1937] 2 All E.R. 60.
160 *Lim v. Camden Area Health Authority* [1980] A.C. 174.
161 In *Croke v. Wiseman, supra*, for example, £35,000 was awarded for causing a 21 months old child to become blind, unable to speak and paralysed in all four limbs.
162 E.g., in Australia, *Skelton v. Collins* (1966) 115 C.L.R. 94; in Canada, *The Queen v. Jennings* (1966) 57 D.L.R. (2d) 644 (but see Fridman, *Law of Torts in Canada*, Vol. 1, at 404).
163 [1964] A.C. 326.
164 See also *Wise v. Kaye* [1962] 1 Q.B. 638, affirmed in the *West* case.

v. Camden Area Health Authority,[165] is to allow such damages and not to reduce the award because of the plaintiff's inability to realise that he or she has lost something of value.[166] What appears to be the situation is that more will be awarded a plaintiff for loss of amenities where the plaintiff is aware of what has happened than in cases where no such awareness is possible. There is no conventional sum, as there was in the case of loss of expectation of life before recent legislation abolished such a claim.[167] As pointed out in the Court of Appeal in *Croke v. Wiseman*,[168] the language of the House of Lords in the *Lim* case should not be interpreted as laying down any upper limit for such awards.

15.43 It is to be stressed that an award for loss of amenities is not an award of damages based on diminution of the plaintiff's subjective happiness: it is founded on the plaintiff's deprivation of some aspect of life that was of value to the particular plaintiff, albeit that to evaluate such loss may be an almost impossible task for the court. It is also vital to recollect that the courts seek to differentiate between a plaintiff who is still alive, even if rendered a vegetable or virtually incapable of appreciating that he or she is alive, and a negligence victim who is dead. Perhaps in the end the benefit of such an award accrues to the plaintiff's dependents, rather than the plaintiff. Nevertheless the loss that is being compensated is a loss incurred and suffered by the plaintiff.

(iii) The injury

15.44 What should be awarded to the plaintiff in respect of the particular injury, apart from its consequences in terms of pain, suffering and loss of amentities, is a matter for the court to determine by reference to the nature and extent of the injury. Something like a judicial "tariff" has emerged by reference to which courts can endeavour to make awards more or less consistent. Hence unless something about a particular case indicates that a different level of compensation is justifiable, it would seem that like injuries will receive the same amount of compensation in every instance.

(iv) Assessment of the award

15.45 Damages for non-pecuniary loss are "at large". This means that the court is entitled to award whatever it thinks fair and reasonable having regard to the nature of the plaintiff's injuries and their effects and insofar as an award is consistent with awards in similar cases.[169] While inflation

165 *Supra.*
166 No change was recommended by the Law Commission, No. 56, para. 31; but a change was suggested by the Pearson Commission in cases of permanent unconsciousness: Cmnd 7054, Vol. I, para. 398.
167 Above para. 15.40.
168 *Supra* note 162 at 859.
169 Where there was no jury the appellate tribunal can rehear the case and correct an erroneous judgment: *Warren v. King* [1963] 3 All E.R. 521. To reverse the finding of a trial judge on the issue of damages it must be shown that the judge applied a wrong principle of law or that the amount is so unusually high or low as to be erroneous estimate of the damage: *Nance v. British Columbia Electric Railway Co.* [1951] A.C. 601; *Pickett v. British Rail Engineering Ltd* [1980] A.C. 136. It is possible for an appellate court to have regard to post-trial facts: *Mulholland v. Mitchell* [1971] A.C. 666.

may not be a factor in the calculation of amounts to be awarded in respect of pecuniary loss,[170] it is clear that awards for non-pecuniary loss should be made taking into account the changes in the value of money over the years so that an award for a particular injury or loss of amenity in 1990 is roughly equivalent in value to a similar award in 1980.[171]

15.46 In the final analysis, however, it is extremely difficult for courts to compare different kinds of injury and different types of amenity that have been lost as a result of the defendant's negligence. As noted previously, the court must decide not only what is reasonable having regard to the interests of the plaintiff but also what is reasonable with respect to those of the defendant,[172] which, these days, probably means the defendant's insurer. In Canada an upper limit has been placed by the Supreme Court on awards for non-pecuniary losses.[173] This was $100,000 in 1978 values: it has now been increased so as to take into account the effects of inflation.[174] This has not been done in England as yet. Perhaps the same result may have been achieved by the consensus that has emerged among judges, since the time when awards of damages were assessed by juries (these being no longer as common in personal injuries cases, since they are invoked only in "exceptional" cases).[175]

(d) Limitation of actions

15.47 An action for damages for personal injuries must be brought within three years of the date on which the cause of action accrued, or three years from the date of knowledge of the person injured, if that is later.[176] This is the limitation period whether the claim is founded on negligence, nuisance or breach of contractual, statutory or other duty. The normal limitation period of six years for tort[177] is not applicable.[178] However, if the injured person dies before the expiration of the relevant three year period, claims made for the benefit of his or her estate under the Law Reform (Miscellaneous Provisions) Act 1934[179] must be brought within three years of the later of the injured party's death or the date of the personal representative's knowledge.[180] The term "personal representative" includes anyone who is or has been a personal representative of the

170 *Cookson v. Knowles* [1979] A.C. 556.
171 *Pickett v. British Rail Engineering Ltd, supra.*
172 *S. v. Distillers Co. (Biochemicals) Ltd* [1970] 1 W.L.R. 114.
173 *Andrews v. Grand & Toy Alberta Ltd* (1978) 83 D.L.R. (3d) 452; *Dhalia v. Jodrey* (1985) 16 D.L.R. (4th) 732.
174 *Hatton v. Henderson* (1981) 126 D.L.R. (3d) 50; *Scarff v. Wilson* (1987) 39 C.C.L.T. 200.
175 *Ward v. James* [1966] 1 Q.B. 273.
176 Limitation Act 1980 s. 11(1)(4). "Personal injuries" includes any disease and any impairment of a person's physical or mental condition: *ibid.* s. 38(1). If the action is brought under the Consumer Protection Act 1987 Part I, the similar provisions of s. 11A of the Limitation Act 1980 apply: note that this action can be brought after 10 years from the "relevant time" as defined in s. 4 of the 1987 Act: Limitation Act 1980 s. 11A(3).
177 *Ibid.* s. 2.
178 *Ibid.* s. 11(2).
179 Above Chapter 2 at paras. 2.36ff.
180 Limitation Act 1980 s. 11(5).

deceased, including an executor who has not proved the will (but not someone appointed as a special personal representative in relation to settled land).[181] Regard must be paid to knowledge acquired by a person within this definition while he or she is a personal representative or previously.[182] Thus someone who has the requisite knowledge before becoming a personal representative will be treated as having had that knowledge for the purposes of the limitation period.

15.48 The crucial question is what is meant by the "date of knowledge". This is defined in the Act.[183] The date of knowledge is the date on which a person first had knowledge (i) that the injury in question was significant; (ii) that it was attributable in whole or in part to the act or omission alleged to constitute the negligence; (iii) of the defendant's identity; and (iv) of the identity of any other person alleged to be responsible for the relevant act or omission, as well as of additional facts supporting the bringing of an action against the defendant.[184] In this regard knowledge that an act or omission did or did not, as a matter of law, involve negligence is irrelevant.[185] An injury will be significant if the person whose date of knowledge is in question would reasonably have considered it sufficiently serious to justify his instituting proceedings for damages against a defendant who did not dispute liability and was able to satisfy a judgment.[186] "Knowledge" in this context includes knowledge which the person in question might reasonably have been expected to acquire from facts observable or ascertainable by him: or from facts ascertainable by him with the help of medical or other appropriate expert advice which it is reasonable for him to seek.[187] In this latter instance, however, he will only have such knowledge as long as he has taken all reasonable steps to obtain, and where appropriate act upon, that advice.[188]

15.49 The effect of these provisions is to permit extension of the limitation period in cases of personal injuries where the effect of such an injury is "latent", just as such extension has been allowed in cases of latent damage to property.[189] Indeed the alteration of the law with respect to

181 *Ibid.* s. 11(6).
182 *Ibid.*
183 *Ibid.* s. 14: cp. what is provided in relation to damage to property in *ibid.* s. 14A: above at para. 14.20.
184 *Ibid.* s. 14(1): where the action is brought under the Consumer Protection Act 1987 s. 6(1)(a) the provisions are separate but similar: Limitation Act 1980 s 11(1A), added by the Consumer Protection Act 1987 s. 6(6), Sch. 1, para. 3. On the identity of the defendant in relation to this provision, see *Simpson v. Norwest Holst Southern Ltd* [1980] 2 All E.R. 471. The identity of another person would be relevant in a case of vicarious liability.
185 Limitation Act 1980 s. 14(1): see for earlier views to like effect *Central Asbestos Co. Ltd v. Dodd* [1973] A.C. 518.
186 Limitation Act 1980 s. 14(2): see on what is "significant" *McCafferty v. Metropolitan Police Receiver* [1977] 2 All E.R. 756, at 769–770 *per* Megaw L.J. 775 *per* Lane L.J.: cp. *Buck v. English Electric Co.* [1978] 1 All E.R. 271.
187 Limitation Act 1980 s. 14(3).
188 *Ibid.* Thus the failure of an expert to discover relevant facts did not affect the plaintiff's right to sue in *Marston v. British Railways Board* [1976] I.C.R. 124.
189 Above para. 15.20.

personal injuries was much earlier than the same alteration in connection with damage to property. However, in regard to personal injuries, another provision of the 1980 Act, namely section 33,[190] permits even further extension of time in certain instances.[191] This may be done if a court thinks it would be equitable to proceed with an action where to adhere to the provisions set out above would prejudice the plaintiff or anyone he represents (but the possibility of prejudice to the defendant or those he represents is also relevant).[192] In such situations the court may direct that the provisions set out earlier shall not apply to the action or a specified cause of action.[193] The circumstances of the case must be taken into account,[194] particularly the delay in suing and its reasons; the effect of such delay on the cogency of evidence; the conduct of the defendant after the cause of action arose (including his reaction to request for information or inspection to ascertain facts relevant to the plaintiff's cause of action); the duration of any disability of the plaintiff arising after the accrual of the cause of action; the promptness or otherwise of the plaintiff once he knew whether or not the act or omission of the defendant might be capable of supporting an action; and the steps taken by the plaintiff to obtain medical, legal or other expert advice, and the nature of such advice. Thus great power has been vested in the courts to dispense with the strict periods of limitation as laid down in other sections of the Limitation Act 1980.

15.50 This provision was considered by the House of Lords in *Thompson v. Brown Construction (Ebbw Vale) Ltd.*[195] The injured plaintiff failed to bring his action within the three-year limitation period because of the negligence of his solicitors. When the court was asked to exercise this statutory discretion and allow the action to proceed, by "disapplying" the otherwise relevant and applicable statutory provisions, the judge refused, holding that he was bound by authority to hold that he had no jurisdiction to make a direction. This was because the plaintiff would not be prejudiced if the usual limitation period continued to apply since he had an incontestable case in negligence against the solicitors, by which he would recover at least as much as he would have recovered against the parties whose negligence caused the plaintiff's injury. The House of Lords allowed

190 Originally contained in the Limitation Act 1975 which amended the Limitation Act 1939.

191 But the provisions will not permit a court to "disapply" other provisions relating to limitation of actions under the Consumer Protection Act 1987: Limitation Act 1980 s. 33(1A), added by the Consumer Protection Act 1987 s. 6(6), Sch. 1, para. 6.

192 Limitation Act 1980 s. 33(1): on the prejudice of the defendant, e.g., by his experiencing difficulty in conducting his affairs with the prospect of an action hanging indefinitely over his head, see *Biss v. Lambeth, Southwark & Lewisham Area Health Authority* [1978] 2 All E.R. 125.

193 Limitation Act 1980 s. 33(1): see *Conry v. Simpson* [1983] 3 All E.R. 369; *Firman v. Ellis* [1978] Q.B. 886; *Thompson v. Brown Construction (Ebbw Vale) Ltd* [1981] 2 All E.R. 296. But see *Walkley v. Premium Forging Co. Ltd* [1979] 2 All E.R. 348; *Deerness v. John R. Keele & Son (Brantham)* [1983] 2 Lloyd's Rep. 260.

194 Limitation Act 1980 s. 33(3). The circumstances of the case include factors which subconsciously prevent the plaintiff from litigating: *McCafferty v. Metropolitan Police Receiver*, *supra*: *Buck v. English Electric Co. Ltd*, *supra*.

195 [1981] 2 All E.R. 296.

the plaintiff's appeal and remitted the case to the judge for further consideration. The conduct of the parties as well as the prejudice that would be suffered by one or the other had to be considered. Moreover, the potential claim by the plaintiff against his solicitor was offset by the fact that he would be prejudiced by having to being a fresh action against the solicitor. In arriving at this conclusion, Lord Diplock, with whose speech the other members of the House agreed, explained the history and purposes of these provisions. The situation was summarised thus:[196]

> ". . . when the court makes a direction under [what is now s. 33] that the provisions of [what is now s. 11] should not apply to a cause of action, it is making an exception to a general rule of law that has already catered for delay in starting proceedings that is due to excusable ignorance of material facts by the plaintiff as distinct from his lack of knowledge that the facts which he does know may give him a good cause of action in law. The onus of showing that in the particular circumstances of the case it would be equitable to make an exception lies on the plaintiff; but, subject to that, the court's discretion to make or refuse an order if it considers it equitable to do so is, in my view, unfettered. The conduct of the parties as well as the prejudice one or the other will suffer if the court does or does not make an order are all to be put in the balance in order to see which way it falls."

The history of the law relating to limitation of actions reveals that there has been a gradual change from reducing the period of limitation to allowing it to be extended to provide for difficult cases where injustice might result if the policy of the law were adhered to with rigour and without the prospect of any flexibility. However a consequence of this may be to place defendants in a difficult situation, that of not knowing whether or not a valid claim may still subsist against them. In this instance perhaps the legislation illustrates the old maxim: hard cases make bad law.[197]

2. DEATH

(a) Survival of actions

15.51 Should the plaintiff, or the defendant, die before the commencement or completion of an action for negligence, or one for breach of statutory duty, the action can continue in favour of or against the estate of the deceased party. This means that the plaintiff's personal representatives may sue, and those of the defendant may be sued. In an earlier chapter this change in the law brought about in 1934 has been examined and discussed.[198] It is only necessary here to refer to the provisions of the Limitation Act 1980,[199] by which the limitation period may be extended where the injured party dies before the expiration of the lengthier period

196 *Ibid.* at 303.
197 Cp. Ormrod L.J. in *Firman v. Ellis* [1978] Q.B. 886 at 911: "Parliament has now decided that uncertain justice is preferable to certain injustice."
198 Above Chapter 2 at paras. 2.36ff. It has been suggested that, for many purposes, there is no valid reason why a claim under the Law Reform (Miscellaneous Provisions) Act 1934 should be available where the beneficiary under the will or intestacy of the deceased can claim under the Fatal Accidents Act, discussed below.
199 S. 11(5), (6): cp. above para. 15.47.

provided for in cases of excusable ignorance on the part of the injured party. It will then become three years from the injured party's death or three years from the date of the personal representative's knowledge (a phrase that has previously been explained[200]). Where there has been delay in bringing an action, and the injured party dies after the expiration of the lengthier limitation period, the reason for the delay may be taken into account by the court when deciding whether or not to extend the limitation period by "disapplying" the usual statutory provisions, as stated in section 33 of the 1980 Act.[201]

(b) Dependants' claims

(i) The Fatal Accidents Act

15.52 Because originally no action could be brought against a person who by negligence or other wrongful act caused the death of another, those who were economically affected by that death had no recourse against the wrongdoer. Since the estate of the deceased also could not sue the tortfeasor,[202] this had the effect of depriving widows and orphans of any means of support once their husband and father had been killed, or had died as a result of the defendant's negligence. The Fatal Accidents Act 1846 sought to change this and introduce the idea that there could be an action for what has been termed in recent years "wrongful death". The current legislation is contained in the Fatal Accidents Act 1976, as amended by the Administration of Justice Act 1982.

(ii) The right to sue

15.53 The appropriate action under the Act must be brought by and in the name of the executor or administrator of the deceased.[203] But if there is no executor or administrator or if the action is not brought within six months of the death by the executor or administrator, the action can be brought by and in the name of all those for whose benefit the executor or administrator could have sued.[204] Only one action will lie in respect of the same subject-matter, i.e. the claims of all those entitled to benefit under the Act must be brought together and disposed of at the same time.[205]

200 Above para. 15.48.
201 Limitation Act 1980 s. 33(4).
202 A situation that has only changed in 1934. See Chapter 12.
203 Fatal Accidents Act 1976 s. 2(1). All references to this Act are to the Act of 1976 as altered by the Act of 1982.
204 Fatal Accidents Act 1976 s. 2(2). The plaintiff must provide the defendant or his solicitors with full particulars of those for whom and on whose behalf the action is brought, and the nature of the claim for which damages are sought: *ibid.* s. 2(4).
205 *Ibid.* s. 2(3). Hence someone omitted has no claim (except possibly against the executor or administrator or other person: *Avery v. London & North Eastern Railway* [1938] A.C. 606 at 613 *per* Lord Atkin). Intervention by an unmentioned dependant may be possible: *Cooper v. Williams* [1963] 2 Q.B. 567.

15.54 The statutory right of action, which is *sui generis* and entirely new in its character,[206] may be brought only if the defendant's wrongful act, negligence or default would have entitled the injured person, whose death resulted from that act or default, to sue the defendant.[207] This means, therefore, that the statutory action can only succeed if there would have been no impediment to an action by the deceased had he lived and himself sued the defendant. Hence if the defendant could have escaped liability on the basis of the doctrine of *volenti non fit injuria*, or the illegal activity of the victim at the material time,[208] or if there is some other reason why the injured party would have failed in his action, such as remoteness of damage, lack of causation, or failure to prove negligence, then no action will lie under the Act. If the deceased's claim would have been affected, by being denied or reduced, in consequence of his contributory negligence,[209] that contributory negligence will have the same effect on the statutory claim. This is specifically provided in the Act.[210]

15.55 An action under the Act cannot be maintained if the death occurred when the injured person would no longer be able to maintain an action and recover damages because of a statutory time limit or some other reason.[211] Where an action by the injured person would have been barred by the passage of the extended time limit in the 1980 Act, viz., the special time limit for personal injuries,[212] the court must not take into account the possibility of that time limit being overridden by the provisions of the Act which give the court a discretion to disapply the other provisions of the Act.[213] The only time limits applicable to Fatal Accidents Act claims are those set out in Act, viz., three years from the date of death or the date of knowledge of the person for whose benefit the action is brought, whichever is the later.[214] That period may be affected by other provisions of the 1980 Act dealing with extension in cases of disability; new claims in pending actions; and, most importantly, the discretionary power of the court under s. 33 of the Act to disapply the ordinary and extended time periods.[215]

206 *Seward v. Vera Cruz* (1884) 10 App.Cas. 59 at 70–71 *per* Lord Blackburn.
207 Fatal Accidents Act 1976 s. 1(1). The deceased's right of action is hypothetical: *British Columbia Electric Railway Co. v. Gentile* [1914] A.C. 1034 at 1041 *per* Lord Dunedin.
208 Above Chapter 13 at paras. 13.44ff.
209 *Ibid.* at paras. 13.23ff.
210 Fatal Accidents Act 1976 s. 5. Otherwise to do so would be illogical, since the dependants' action is distinct from that of the deceased. But if the *dependant* is negligent it is questionable whether the law of contributory negligence applies, because the dependant's loss is not "damage" within the meaning of the Law Reform (Contributory Negligence) Act 1945 s. 1(1). But see *Dodds v. Dodds* [1978] Q.B. 543.
211 Limitation Act 1980 s. 12(1).
212 Above paras. 15.47–8.
213 Limitation Act 1980 s. 12(1), referring to s. 33 of that Act: above para. 15.49.
214 Limitation Act 1980 s. 12(2): but note s. 12(3) applying the provisions of s. 39 which relate to other limitation enactments. What is meant by "the date of knowledge" is explained above at para. 15.48. Where there are several dependants the provisions of the subsection relating to the date of knowledge apply to each of them separately: Limitation Act 1980 s. 13(1). This may lead to the exclusion of some of those for whose benefit the action is brought: *ibid.* s. 13(2), unless the action is brought exclusively for that person and would not be defeated by a defence of limitation: *ibid.* s. 13(3).
215 Limitation Act 1980 s. 12(3): cp. above p. 431.

(iii) Beneficiaries of the action

15.56 An action under the Act is for the benefit of the dependants of the deceased.[216] Dependants in this context is given statutory definition.[217] It refers to: the spouse or former spouse[218] of the deceased; anyone living with the deceased in the same household immediately before the death, as long as he or she had been living for at least two years and was living during all of that period as husband or wife of the deceased; any parent or other "ascendant"[219] of the deceased; any person treated by the deceased as his or her parent; any child[220] or other descendent of the deceased; anyone not a child of the deceased, who was treated by the deceased as a child of the family in relation to a marriage to which the deceased was at any time a party; and any brother, sister, uncle or aunt of the deceased or the issue of such relative. For all these purposes a relationship of affinity is to be treated as a relationship of consanguinity: a relationship of the half blood is to be treated as a relationship of the whole blood; a persons's stepchild is to be treated as his or her child; an illegitimate person is to be treated as the legitimate child of his mother and reputed father.[221]

(iv) Recoverable damages

15.57 *(1) Bereavement.* Under the new provision inserted by the Administration of Justice Act 1982, an action under the Fatal Accidents Act may now consist of or include a claim for damages for bereavement.[222] Such a claim may not be for more than £3500.[223] Moreover it is available only for the benefit of the spouse of the deceased or, if he or she was an unmarried minor, his or her parents, if he or she was legitimate, or mother if he or she was illegitimate.[224] A claim for both parents is to be divided equally between them.[225] The sum specified as claimable damages may be varied by statutory instrument made by the Lord Chancellor,[226] which would presumably come about if and when inflation made the original statutory sum outmoded.

15.58 *(2) Loss of support.* The more usual claim, and the one that was the original basis for an action, is for loss of support, i.e. for the pecuniary loss

216 Fatal Accidents Act 1976 s. 1(2): except for damages for "bereavement": below.
217 Fatal Accidents Act 1976 s. 1(3).
218 Including a person whose marriage to the deceased has been annulled or dissolved: Fatal Accidents Act 1976 s. 1(4).
219 The expressions "ascendant" and "descendant" appear to refer to lineal, not collateral ascendants and descendants; e.g., grandparents are included, great uncles are not: *Halsbury's Statutes*, 4th ed. 1987, Vol. 31 at 204–205.
220 Including a posthumously born child: *The George & Richard* (1871) L.R. Ad. & Ecc. 466.
221 Fatal Accidents Act 1976 s. 1(5).
222 *Ibid.* s. 1A(1).
223 *Ibid.* s. 1A(3).
224 *Ibid.* s. 1A(2).
225 *Ibid.* s. 1A(4).
226 *Ibid.* s. 1A(5).

suffered by the dependants in consequence of the death of the deceased.[227] The claim for bereavement is intended to provide some sort of comfort or solace for the particular dependants for whom such a claim can be made. It resembles the Scottish "solatium".[228] The chief claim was, and remains, the claim in respect of financial loss. This will include a claim for funeral expenses incurred by a dependant in respect of the deceased.[229]

15.59 There must be some financial loss resulting from the loss of the continued life of the deceased, i.e. based on the earnings that would have been made by the deceased,[230] as long as what was earned was earned lawfully and not by a life of crime.[231] Such a claim will be in two parts.[232] The first relates to the loss estimated as having been sustained by the dependants from the date of the death till the date of the trial, pre-trial loss. The second part consists of the pecuniary loss which it is estimated they will sustain from the trial onwards, the future loss. The latter will be a matter of conjecture; the former can be deduced from available facts which reduce, though do not entirely eliminate, reliance on conjecture. For the purpose of calculating the future loss the "dependency" used as a multiplicand should be the figure to which it is estimated the annual dependency would have amounted by the date of the trial. The multiplier should be calculated as from the date of death, not the date of the trial (and the number of pre-trial years for which special damages were awarded should then be deducted from the multiplier).[233] In calculating the multiplier it should not be assumed as certain that the deceased would have continued without interruption to make as valuable a contribution, in real terms, to the support of his family as he was making at the date of death right up to retiring age. A discount must be allowed for the

227 The Act refers only to "injury resulting from the death to the dependants respectively": Fatal Accidents Act 1976 s. 3(1). This has long been taken to mean the reasonable expectation of pecuniary benefit as of right, or otherwise, from the continuance of the life: *Franklin v. South Eastern Railway* (1858) 3 H. &. N. 211 at 213–214 *per* Pollock C.B. After deducting costs not recovered from the defendant, the damages recovered, except for bereavement, are divided among the dependants in such shares as the court directs: Fatal Accidents Act 1976 s. 3(2). As to the damages awarded to minors, see R.S.C. Ord. 80, r. 12.

228 Replaced by a claim for "non-patrimonial benefit": Damages (Scotland) Act 1976 s. 1(4). Cp. the award of damages for loss of "guidance, care and companionship" under the Ontario Family Law Act, S.O. 1986, c. 4, s. 61(1), replacing the older Fatal Accidents Act: Fridman, *Law of Torts in Canada*, Vol. I, at 418–419.

229 Fatal Accidents Act 1976 s. 3(5). Such expenses must be reasonable: *Hart v. Griffiths-Jones* [1948] 2 All E.R. 729: see, e.g., *Stanton v. Ewart F. Youldon Ltd* [1960] 1 All E.R. 429.

230 If in regular employment; but taxed down by having due regard to uncertainties: *Davies v. Powell Duffryn Associated Collieries Ltd (No. 2)* [1942] A.C. 601 at 617 *per* Lord Wright. The aim of the court is to estimate the loss of reasonable expectation of pecuniary benefit, which will be in most cases a matter of speculation or conjecture. A pure arithmetical calculation will not always lead to a just result where there are so many inponderables. The question of damages for loss of support is essentially a jury question, i.e. a matter of fact, to be dealt with on broad lines. Mathematical calculation can never lead to a precisely accurate estimate for the loss suffered: *Kassam v. Kampala Aerated Water Co. Ltd* [1965] 1 W.L.R. 668 especially at 674 *per* Lord Guest.

231 *Burns v. Edman* [1970] 2 Q.B. 541.

232 *Cookson v. Knowles* [1979] A.C. 556, which also discusses the element of interest; see also *Spittle v. Bunney* [1988] 3 All E.R. 1031 at 1041–1044.

233 *Graham v. Dodds* [1983] 2 All E.R. 953.

vicissitudes of life which might falsify that assumption.[234] Inflation must be disregarded, here as elsewhere.[235] But, just as in the case of a claim for loss of future earnings, where the plaintiff lives and sues on his or her own behalf, a deduction must be made for the deceased's own living expenses.[236] In addition under the Fatal Accidents Act, regard must be paid to the deceased's expectation of working life at the date of death and the duration of dependency of the dependants.[237]

15.60 The financial benefit that has been lost as a result of the death must arise from the relationship of the parties.[238] But there may be a loss of such benefit even though the dependant has no legal claim to support from the deceased.[239] It has also been held that the deceased need not have been earning anything or giving gratuitous help, as long as there was a reasonable probability that the deceased would have done so had he or she lived.[240] A child has been held able to claim damages under the Act for loss of a mother's care, not only as a housekeeper but also as someone who would instruct the child vis-à-vis the child's upbringing.[241] Where a wife and husband were separated at the time of the death, she was not awarded damages because it could not be shown that there was a reasonable probability of reconciliation in the future: hence she had really lost nothing that could have counted for the purposes of the Fatal Accidents Act.[242] It is also provided in the 1976 Act that, where a person is claiming by virtue of having lived with the deceased as husband and wife without being married, the court must take into account, as one of the relevant factors, the fact that the dependant had no enforceable right to financial support from the deceased as a result of their living together.[243] Where a wife is claiming it is now no longer open to a court to take into account the

234 *Ibid.* at 959 *per* Lord Bridge; *Phillips v. London & South Western Railway* (1879) 5 C.P.D. 280 at 291 *per* Brett L.J.

235 *Cookson v. Knowles, supra*; *Robertson v. Lestrange* [1985] 1 All E.R. 950. But tax must be taken into account: *British Transport Commission v. Gourley* [1956] A.C. 185.

236 *Harris v. Empress Motors Ltd* [1983] 3 All E.R. 561, which shows that such expenses differ according to whether the claim is under the Fatal Accidents Act or the Law Reform (Miscellaneous Provisions) Act. Under the Fatal Accidents Act no deductions are to be made for expenditures for the joint benefit of the deceased and the dependants.

237 *Gilbertson v. Harland & Wolff Ltd* [1966] 2 Lloyd's Rep. 190; *Whittome v. Coats* [1965] 1 W.L.R. 1285. A period of 16 years as a multiplier may be the upper limit; *Graham v. Dodds, supra.*

238 *Burgess v. Florence Nightingale Hospital for Gentlewomen* [1955] 1 Q.B. 349; *Maylon v. Plummer* [1964] 1 Q.B. 330. Thus a father may be able to claim loss of earnings when he gave up employment on the death of his wife to look after the children: *Mehmet v. Perry* [1977] 2 All E.R. 529.

239 *Franklin v. South Eastern Railway* (1858) 3 H. &. N. 211; *Berry v. Humm* [1915] 1 K.B. 627.

240 *Taff Vale Railway v. Jenkins* [1913] A.C. 1; *Kandalla v. British Airways Board* [1981] Q.B. 158. But a child could not recover for merely "pocket money" dependency: *Benson v. Biggs Wall & Co. Ltd* [1982] 3 All E.R. 300. There had to be genuine dependency: but the widow's damages could not include an amount for the son's upkeep: *ibid.*

241 *Hay v. Hughes* [1975] Q.B. 790: cp. *Mehmet v. Perry, supra.* But a child becomes more independent as he or she gets older, therefore damages should be reduced where based on the "nanny" idea: *Spittle v. Bunney* [1988] 3 All E.R. 1031 at 1035–1041 *per* Croom-Johnson L.J.

242 *Davies v. Taylor* [1974] A.C. 207.

243 Fatal Accidents Act 1976 s. 3(4).

remarriage of the widow or her prospects of re-marriage.[244] However, this only refers to a widow's claim. Hence it does not apply to: (a) a claim by a widower; (b) a claim by a woman living with, but not married to a man; or (c) a claim by a child, whose mother may remarry.[245] It is also now provided that in assessing the damages under the Act "benefits which have accrued or will or may accrue to any person from his estate or otherwise as a result of his death shall be disregarded".[246] This removes a problem that formerly bedevilled the courts.

244 *Ibid.* s. 3(3).
245 *Thompson v. Price* [1973] 1 Q.B. 838.
246 Fatal Accidents Act 1976 s. 4. In *Pidduck v. Eastern Scottish Omnibuses Ltd* [1989] 2 All E.R. 261, a pension and widow's allowance from an employer's pension fund were "benefits" and therefore to be disregarded under this section.

CHAPTER 16

Breach of Statutory Duty

1. INTRODUCTION

16.01 Statutes create duties which must be fulfilled. Failure to observe the requirements of a statute can have various consequences, including criminal penalties, invalidity of transactions, or the possibility of judicial review which may lead to the avoidance of an administrative procedure. It has long been held that the breach of a statute can also result in a civil action for the recovery of damages in respect of loss incurred to a particular individual.[1] Such an action for breach of statutory duty is an action in tort.[2] Hence it is appropriate to consider the circumstances in which a civil action for damages may be brought in respect of a breach of statute, even though other legal results may also follow from such breach.

16.02 Originally the common law adopted the view that such an action could be maintained whenever a statutory duty was breached and damage resulted.[3] During the nineteenth century the courts began to impose limitations on the availability of a civil action for damages in such situations.[4] At the present time, therefore, only when the statute in question can be construed or interpreted in such a way as to show that the intention of the legislature was to permit the possibility of a tort action for its breach can such an action be maintained.[5]

1 Williams, "The Effect of Penal Legislation in the Law of Torts" (1960) 76 L.Q.R. 240; Fridman, "Civil Liability for Criminal Conduct" (1984) 16 Ottawa L.R. 34. Cp. Morris, "The Relation of Criminal Statutes to Tort Liability" (1932) 46 H.L.R. 453; Morris, "The Role of Criminal Statutes in Negligence Actions" (1949) 49 Col. L.R. 21; Thayer, "Public Wrong and Private Action" (1913) 27 H.L.R. 317. Note that inducement of a breach of statutory duty exists as a head of tortious liability: *Meade v. Haringey L.B.C.* [1979] 2 All E.R. 1016; *Associated British Ports v. T.&G.W.U.* [1989] 3 All E.R. 796; reversed on other grounds [1989] 3 All E.R. 822.

2 *American Express Co. v. British Airways Board* [1983] 1 All E.R. 557.

3 *Anon* (1704) 6 Mod. 25; *Ashby v. White* (1703) 2 Ld Ray. 938; *Couch v. Steel* (1854) 3 E. & B. 402. This goes back to the Statute of Westminster II, 1285, 13 Ed. I, c. 50. Cp. *ex parte Island Records* [1978] Ch. 122; overruled by the House of Lords in *Lonrho Ltd v. Shell Petroleum Ltd* [1981] 2 All E.R. 456: below para. 16.06.

4 *Atkinson v. Newcastle & Gateshead Waterworks Co.* (1877) 2 Ex. D. 441; *Gorris v. Scott* (1874) L.R. 9 Ex. 125; see also *Groves v. Lord Wimborne* [1898] 2 Q.B. 402; *Phillips v. Britannia Hygienic Laundry Ltd* [1923] 2 K.B. 832; *Monk v. Warbey* [1935] 1 K.B. 75.

5 Thus the statute may indicate that only the Attorney General can take appropriate action; in which event a private citizen can do nothing. Only a political sanction can be applied against the Attorney-General, not a legal one: *Gouriet v. Union of Post Office Workers* [1978] A.C. 435.

2. CONSTRUCTION OF STATUTES

(a) The role of the courts

16.03 Whenever a plaintiff seeks to rely on an alleged breach of statute as the foundation for an action in tort for damages caused by such breach, it is the primary task of the court to determine whether the statute in question can be interpreted to mean that the legislation has permitted the possibility of such an action.[6] In *Cutler v. Wandsworth Stadium*,[7] the House of Lords held that to make such a determination it was necessary to look at the language, meaning and intent of the statutory provision invoked by the plaintiff. The issue was one of construction. In that particular case the plaintiff alleged that he had been deprived of the opportunity to pursue his business as a bookmaker at a dog stadium because the defendants had failed to fulfil their statutory obligation to provide him with appropriate space on the premises. After examining the statute in question it was held that the plaintiff had no civil cause of action. Similarly in *Board of Governors of Seneca College of Applied Arts and Technology v. Bhadauria*,[8] the Supreme Court of Canada rejected the plaintiff's claim to sue for damages for breach of an Ontario statute which prohibited discrimination. The statute concerned provided for a comprehensive system and procedure for dealing with accusations of discrimination, and contained provisions that stipulated the remedies available to someone against whom discrimination had been practised. There was no scope for construing the statute as granting the right to bring a civil action for damages based on breach of its provisions.

16.04 A fundamental issue in such instances, as explained by Morris J. in *Clarke & Wife v. Brims*,[9] is whether the intention of the Act was to make the duty a public duty or to make the duty one owed as well to the party aggrieved. This has been put differently as the distinction between a statutory duty imposed for the general welfare on the one hand or the interests of individuals or of a defined or definable class of the public on the other.[10] The fact that breach of the statute was made a crime punishable by imprisonment or fine would not of itself conclude the issue. On the contrary, although the primary purpose of the legislation might be to inflict a penalty on anyone who infringed its provisions, that did not exclude the possibility that, in addition to criminal liability, there might not also be civil liability to anyone particularly injured or affected by the breach.

6 A similar problem arises under the EEC Treaty, for breach of art. 86 of which it appears to have been held that an action for breach of statutory duty could be maintained, though not for damages, only for an injunction to prevent future loss: *Garden Cottage Foods Ltd v. Milk Marketing Board* [1983] 2 All E.R. 770.

7 [1949] A.C. 398.

8 [1981] 2 S.C.R. 181.

9 [1947] K.B. 497 at 505. This has been criticised on the ground that it assumes what has to be decided: *Winfield & Jolowicz on Tort*, 12th ed. 1984, at 165.

10 *Solomons v. Gertzenstein Ltd* [1954] 2 Q.B. 243 at 265 *per* Romer L.J.

16.05 A statute may expressly provide for the granting of a civil action for its breach.[11] Where there is no such express provision it might be argued that the omission reveals that the legislation intended that no such action should be available—*expressio unius est exclusio alterius.*[12] However, it is clear that, even in the absence of an express provision of this kind, a statute can be interpreted to mean that there was an intention on the part of the legislature that enacted the statute to allow aggrieved individuals to bring a private action for damages. Despite the difficulty involved in discovering the intention of a legislature,[13] where nothing specific in the legislation provides a clue to that intent, the courts gradually evolved a number of rules or tests, by the application of which a determination could be made that, even in the absence of express statements with respect to civil or private law remedies, a particular statute or provision of a statute could be understood to mean that the legislature had not foreclosed the possibility of such an action.[14]

(b) Rules of construction

16.06 In *Lonrho Ltd v. Shell Petroleum Ltd*[15] Lord Diplock began his discussion of the principles that were to be applied when considering whether a civil action could be brought for breach of a statute by referring to what he termed the "general rule" that where an Act created an obligation and enforced its performance in a specified manner, that performance could not be enforced in any other manner.[16] When the statute provided for enforcement by prosecution for a criminal offence of failing to perform the statutory obligation or contravention of the statutory prohibition created by the statute, which was the situation in the *Lonrho* case, there were two classes of exception to the general rule.[17] The first was where, on the true construction of the Act, it was apparent that the obligation or prohibition was imposed for the benefit or protection of a particular class of individuals. He illustrated this by reference to the Factories Act and similar legislation.[18] The second exception was where the statute created a public right, i.e. a right to be enjoyed by all those who wished to avail themselves of it, and a particular member of the public suffered "particular, direct and substantial damage other and

11 E.g., Consumer Safety Act 1978 s. 6.
12 See *Toronto-St. Catherines Transport Ltd v. Toronto* [1958] S.C.R. 61.
13 "The will-o-the-wisp of non-existent intention": Harper & James, *The Law of Torts*, at 995; "a barefaced fiction": Fleming, *Law of Torts*, 7th ed. 1987, at 114. It has been said that it is not the meaning of the instrument but judicial policy that is the determining factor: *O'Connor v. Bray* (1937) 56 C.L.R. 464 at 477–478, an Australian case.
14 It does not matter whether the duty imposed takes the negative form of a prohibition of particular kinds of conduct rather than the positive form of an obligation to do particular acts; as, for example, is evidenced by the way in which the Factories Act or regulations made thereunder have been interpreted and applied: *Garden Cottage Foods Ltd v. Milk Marketing Board* [1983] 2 All E.R. 770 at 775–776 *per* Lord Diplock.
15 [1981] 2 All E.R. 456 at 461.
16 *Doe d. Bishop of Rochester v. Bridges* (1831) 1 B. & Ald. 847 at 859 *per* Lord Tenterden C.J.
17 *Supra* note 15.
18 See, e.g. *Groves v. Lord Wimborne* [1898] 2 Q.B. 402; *Boyle v. Kodak Ltd* [1969] 2 All E.R. 439.

different from that common to the rest of the public".[19] This was chiefly illustrated by cases dealing with infringements of public rights existing at common law, particularly in respect of the use of highways. As previously seen this was the basis of an individual's right to sue for damages resulting from the commission of a public nuisance.[20] In general such nuisances involved a breach of the common law; but there were examples of statutory nuisances, the breach of which could give rise to a private action.[21]

16.07 Thus, for a statute to create or permit a private right of action, it had to be one which (a) was intended to benefit a particular class of persons, not the public generally; or (b) was intended to benefit the public generally and its breach caused particular damage to an individual. Although the first exception is one that has been emphasised in many decisions,[22] it would appear that there are other relevant considerations. One of these is whether the obligation is to be performed in a particular manner.[23] Another is the severity of the penalty.[24] The way the obligation is to be performed may indicate that the statute has in mind the public at large rather than members of a particular class or section of the public. For example, a statute that stipulates that certain dangerous machinery be fenced clearly is intended to look after the safety of those employed on such machinery, and not the public generally; a statute that provides for non-obstruction of the highway would seem to be directed more at the public at large rather than any specific section of the community. As far as penalties are concerned, the less serious the punishment for the statutory offence, the more likely is it that the statute contemplated the possibility of a civil action where an individual was personally, and seriously, affected by its breach.[25]

16.08 In *Ex parte Island Records Ltd*,[26] decided before the *Lonrho* case, the Court of Appeal had suggested that the right to sue did not depend on the scope and language of the statute; and that whenever a lawful business was carried on by one individual which suffered damage as a consequence of a contravention by another individual of a statutory prohibition, the former had a civil right of action against the latter for such damage. This was rejected by the House of Lords in the *Lonrho* case. Subsequently, in

19 *Benjamin v. Storr* (1874) L.R. 9 C.P. 400 at 407 *per* Brett J. A public law duty, when performed, may give rise to private law duties the breach of which can be actionable: *Cocks v. Thanet District Council* [1982] 3 All E.R. 1135; cp. *Thornton v. Kirkless Metropolitan Council* [1979] 1 Q.B. 626.
20 Chapter 8 at paras 8.75ff.
21 *Boyce v. Paddington Borough Council* [1903] 1 Ch. 109.
22 E.g., *Phillips v. Britannia Hygienic Laundry Ltd* [1923] 2 K.B. 832; *Monk v. Warbey* [1932] 1 K.B. 75; *R.C.A. Corporation v. Pollard* [1982] 3 All E.R. 771.
23 *Cutler v. Wandsworth Stadium* [1949] A.C. 398 at 411 *per* Lord Du Parcq.
24 *Cutler v. Wandsworth Stadium* [1948] 1 K.B. 291 at 301 *per* Somervell L.J.; see e.g. *Groves v. Lord Wimborne, supra.* But see *Atkinson v. Newcastle & Gateshead Waterworks Co.*, (1877) 2 Ex.D. 441, where the absence of provision for compensation in the legislation was an argument against, not for, civil liability.
25 Another consideration is the nature and adequacy of the remedies under the statute or at common law.
26 [1978] Ch. 122.

R.C.A. Corporation v. Pollard,[27] the Court of Appeal considered both decisions and held that the House of Lords had overruled the *Island Records* case on this point. Hence in the *Pollard* case, the plaintiffs could not claim an injunction in respect of alleged breaches of the Performers' Protection Act. The plaintiffs had an exclusive right under contract to recordings made by a musical performer. The defendants were trading in "bootleg" records of the performer's performances. The property right of the plaintiffs could not be protected by an action under the relevant statutes because those statutes did not confer on the plaintiffs a private right of action for breaches of the Act although the plaintiffs had suffered special damage in consequence, and the Act did not create any duty of permission or omission for the benefit of performers or recording companies, an illegal interference with which could give rise to an action for breach of statutory duty at the suit of a recording company. The property rights of the plaintiffs were not sufficient to support any such action despite the language in the *Island Records* case, because that language had been disavowed in the *Lonrho* decision. In the *Pollard* case, therefore, the principles stated by Lord Diplock in *Lonrho Ltd v. Shell Petroleum Ltd* were accepted as representing the present law with respect to the right to bring a civil tort action for breach of a statute that created a criminal offence. Whether or not the decision in the *Island Records* case could have been justified by orthodox reasons, such as that the statute in question was passed for the protection of a particular class of persons, viz., performers,[28] the wider doctrine of a cause of action arising whenever damage has been suffered propounded in that case has been rejected both by the House of Lords and the Court of Appeal.[29]

16.09 In the light of what was said in the *Lonrho* case, there are two factors that tend to indicate that a statute does not create any civil right of action. The first is the idea of "exclusivity". The contents of the statute may reveal that its purpose was to make the penalties indicated therein the exclusive consequence of a breach.[30] This may be achieved by making the penalty sufficiently severe as to show that the legislature considered that no other legal remedy was needed to punish the defendant for his breach. Or the statute may provide a comprehensive scheme whereby breaches of its provisions were to be dealt with, such as by setting up a body to investigate alleged breaches and provide a remedy or remedies that would cope with the harm incurred by a victim of such breach. This was the situation in the *Bhadauria* case,[31] where the human rights legislation set up

27 [1982] 3 All E.R. 771 at 778 *per* Lawton L.J., 785 *per* Slade L.J. See also *Rickless v. United Artists* [1987] 1 All E.R. 679: *CBS Songs Ltd v. Amstrad Consumer Electronics plc* [1987] 3 All E.R. 151: *Associated British Ports,* note 1 *supra.*

28 *Lonrho Ltd v. Shell Petroleum Ltd, supra* at 462 *per* Lord Diplock.

29 Since the *Pollard* case it is a matter of debate how far a civil action may be brought for "injury to property" as a result of a crime: *R.C.A. Corp. v. Pollard, supra* at 785 *per* Slade L.J., who referred to *Emperor of Austria v. Day & Kossuth* (1861) 3 De G.F. & J. 217; *Springfield Spinning Co. v. Riley* (1868) L.R. 6 Eq. 551; *National Phonographic Co. v. Edison-Bell Consolidated Phonograph Co. Ltd* [1908] 1 Ch. 235.

30 As in the *Lonrho* case itself, where the breach of statute was deliberate.

31 Above note 8.

a commission which had powers to investigate and make orders in respect of alleged discrimination.[32]

16.10 The second factor is that of "neutrality". This means that the statute does not set out a standard of conduct against which the tortious character of the defendant's conduct can be measured. The breach may involve criminal liability, but it does not of itself constitute tortious behaviour. Thus if a statute requires someone to do something, failure to do which is an offence, this may not indicate that any standard of behaviour is to be observed. But if a statute requires someone to act with reasonable care in doing something, this may suggest that a tort standard is to be observed, such that failure to do so may entail tortious liability. This approach has been adopted in England, where decisions under legislation dealing with safety in various forms of employment, for example, have held that a statute that requires the employer to act in a certain manner can more easily give rise to the interpretation that the person on whom the obligation was placed had to act in a way that was akin to the standard of behaviour expected of someone where a common law duty of care existed as between the defendant and the injured party.[33] Not surprisingly, therefore, English decisions have referred to this kind of liability as "statutory negligence".[34] In Canada, in consequence of a recent decision of the Supreme Court,[35] this view is no longer tenable. In England, however, it may still be possible to base a conclusion on the effects of a statute by reference to the neutrality or otherwise of its language.

3. ELEMENTS OF LIABILITY

(a) A duty owed to the plaintiff

16.11 This, as already discussed, is the fundamental primary issue. Its resolution depends on construction of the relevant statutes. In the *Lonrho* case, the House of Lords rejected the suggestion in the Australian case of *Beaudesert Shire Council v. Smith*[36] that there was a novel innominate tort in the nature of an action for damages on the case available to someone who suffered harm or loss as the inevitable consequence of the unlawful,

32 Cp. *Atkinson v. Newcastle & Gateshead Waterworks Co.* (1877) 2 Ex.D. 441; contrast *Reid v. Croydon Corporation* [1938] 4 All E.R. 631; *London Passenger Transport Board v. Upson* [1949] A.C. 155. But the absence of any sanction may not indicate that civil liability was intended: *Watt v. Kesteven County Council* [1955] 1 Q.B. 408.

33 See also *Monk v. Warbey* [1935] 1 K.B. 75, a case on the right of an injured passenger to sue the owner of a car under the Road Traffic Act 1930 s. 35 when the driver was not insured: (seemingly approved by the Privy Council in *Tan Chye Choo v. Chang Kew Moi* [1970] 1 All E.R. 266, where the duty was held to be public, and not to give rise to a personal action for its breach). Cp. *Martin v. Dean* [1971] 2 Q.B. 208. See now the Road Traffic Act 1988 s. 143.

34 *David v. Britannic Merthyr Coal Co.* [1909] 2 K.B. 164 at 164 *per* Fletcher-Moulton L.J.; *Lochgelly Iron & Coal Co. v. M'Mullan* [1934] A.C. 1; see further below pp. 445–6.

35 *Saskatchewan Wheat Pool v. Government of Canada* (1983) 143 D.L.R. (3d) 9.

36 (1966) 120 C.L.R. 145.

intentional and positive acts of another. Not only had this been rejected by the Privy Council in a later case,[37] but the High Court of Australia meanwhile had already held[38] that the term "unlawful" in this context did not include every breach of statutory duty that caused damage to the plaintiff. To what the expression did extend was uncertain.[39] The only proposition possibly acceptable is that no civil liability will arise as a result of the breach of a statute unless the statute creates a duty owed to the plaintiff as a member of the class intended to be benefited or protected by the statute[40] (except where the plaintiff, as a member of the public to which the duty is owed, suffers particular damage in consequence of the breach of statute).[41]

(b) Breach of the duty

16.12 This is a vexed point. It raises the question whether statutory duties are "absolute" or involve proof of some kind of fault, i.e. negligence or the intention to cause harm. Once again everything depends on the construction of the statute. It will be for the court to determine by an examination of the statutory language whether the intention of the Act was to require the defendant to do something regardless of whether it was reasonable for him to do so, or required the defendant to use due care in its performance such that if he is guiltless of lack of due care he will not be liable for a breach. Thus even if the statute can be construed as giving rise to civil liability, it remains open to question whether the circumstances that occurred bring the situation within the scope of such liability.[42]

16.13 In many instances, however, particularly those involving breaches of legislation designed to promote the safety, health and welfare of employees in different classes of employment, the language of the statute has been construed as involving reasonable foresight of harm on the part of the employer.[43] It has also been said that a breach of the statute constitutes personal negligence on the part of the employer,[44] even if the actual negligent act, the disregard of the statutory duty, was the act of the employer's servant, or independent contractor, to whom the employer, in

37 *Dunlop v. Woollahra Municipal Council* [1981] 1 All E.R. 1202.
38 *Kitano v. The Commonwealth* (1973) 129 C.L.R. 151; cp. *Hull v. Canterbury Municipal Council* [1974] 1 N.S.W.L.R. 300.
39 *Lonrho Ltd v. Shell Petroleum Ltd* [1981] 2 All E.R. 456 at 463.
40 Cp. *Hartley v. Mayoh & Co.* [1954] 1 Q.B. 383; *Canadian Pacific Steamships Ltd v. Bryers* [1958] A.C. 485; *Herbert v. Harold Shaw Ltd* [1959] 2 Q.B. 138; *Gutek v. Sunshine Village Corporation* (1990) 65 D.L.R. (4th) 406, a Canadian case.
41 *Lonrho Ltd v. Shell Petroleum Ltd* [1981] 2 All E.R. 456 at 461; above paras 16.06–07.
42 *Carroll v. Andrew Barclay & Sons Ltd* [1948] A.C. 477; *Brown v. National Coal Board* [1962] A.C. 574; *Greenwood v. Central Service Co.* [1940] 2 K.B. 447 at 461. See, e.g., *Galashiels Gas Co. Ltd v. Millar* [1949] A.C. 275: an absolute duty. Even if its fulfilment made machinery unusable: *John Summers & Sons Ltd v. Frost* [1955] A.C. 740. Contrast other legislation which requires what is "reasonably practicable": *Jenkins v. Allied Ironfounders Ltd* [1969] 3 All E.R. 1609; or what is necessary: *Brown v. National Coal Board, supra.* The onus may be on the defendant to prove impracticability or lack of necessity: *Nimmo v. Alexander Cowan & Sons Ltd* [1968] A.C. 107.
43 *John Summers & Sons Ltd v. Frost* [1955] A.C. 740.
44 *Lochgelly Iron & Coal Co. v. M'Mullan* [1934] A.C. 1 at 13 *per* Lord Warrington.

many instances a corporation, had delegated the task of fulfilling the statutory requirements.[45] Even if the duty is considered to be absolute, the attitude of the courts has been that the degree of care required is the fulfilment of the statutory obligation. If it be not fulfilled the person on whom the duty is imposed is negligent.[46] Thus, however the statutory duty was phrased, its non-observance was *per se* an act of negligence for which the party on whom the duty was placed would be liable.[47] Hence the view that breach of statute was "statutory negligence".[48] That opinion has been contradicted.[49] Indeed there are various bases for arguing that there is a distinction between common law negligence, e.g. breach of the employer's duty of care, and breach of statutory duty. They are separate causes of action.[50] Different defences may be raised.[51] Standards of care are fixed differently, by the common law notion of what is reasonably foreseeable on the one hand, by the language of the statute on the other.[52] Proof of breach of statute is not, without more proof, to be taken as proving a case of common law negligence; and *vice-versa*.[53]

16.14 This was taken a stage further by the Supreme Court of Canada in *Saskatchewan Wheat Pool v. Government of Canada*.[54] There the appellants had been guilty of breach of the Canada Grain Act, in that a shipment of wheat was insect-infested. This was not the result of negligence on the part of the appellants, who were unaware of the situation. Negligence was not pleaded or proved against the appellants. The respondent plaintiff argued that the breach of the statute, without more, entitled the plaintiff to sue. The appellants successfully argued that, notwithstanding the statute, before an action for damages could be maintained, the plaintiff would have to prove that the appellants had been negligent and so had broken their statutory duty. In a summary of the law as it seemed correct to the Canadian court, it was said that the true position was as follows:[55]

> "1. Civil consequences of breach of statute should be subsumed in the law of negligence.

45 *Ibid.*; *Wilsons Clyde Coal Co. Ltd v. English* [1938] A.C. 57.
46 *Riddell v. Reid* [1943] A.C. 1 at 31 *per* Lord Porter.
47 *Lochgelly Iron & Coal Co. v. M'Mullan, supra* at 13 *per* Lord Warrington.
48 *David v. Britannic Merthyr Coal Co.* [1909] 2 K.B. 146 at 164 *per* Fletcher-Moulton L.J.; *Lochgelly Iron & Coal Co. v. M'Mullan, supra* at 22–23 *per* Lord Wright; *Lewis v. Denys* [1940] A.C. 921 at 924–925 *per* Viscount Simon.
49 *Caswell v. Powell Duffryn Associated Collieries Ltd* [1940] A.C. 152 at 177–178 *per* Lord Wright; *ibid.* at 167 *per* Lord Macmillan; *London Passenger Transport Board v. Upson* [1949] A.C. 155 at 168 *per* Lord Wright.
50 *Murfin v. United Steel Companies Ltd* [1957] 1 All E.R. 23. Indeed the obligation involved in a statute may not indicate any standard of care, as in negligence: cp. the cases cited *supra* note 42.
51 E.g., *volenti* may not be a defence to breach of statutory duty, whereas it will be in negligence: below p. 449.
52 The language of a statute is crucial both as regards its application, i.e. whether the Act or regulation relates to the place in question: *Longhurst v. Guildford Water Board* [1963] A.C. 265; and its scope, i.e. the nature of the duty: *Chipchase v. British Titan Products Co.* [1956] 1 Q.B. 545.
53 See, e.g., *Kelly v. W.R.N. Contracting Ltd* [1968] 1 All E.R. 369; *Denyer v. Charles Skipper & East Ltd* [1970] 2 All E.R. 382.
54 (1983) 143 D.L.R. (3d) 9.
55 *Ibid.* at 25.

2. The notion of a nominate tort of statutory breach, giving a right to recovery merely on proof of breach and damage, should be rejected, as should the view that unexcused breach constitutes negligence *per se* giving rise to absolute liability.

3. Proof of statutory breach, causative of damages, may be evidence of negligence.

4. The statutory formulation of the duty may afford a specific and useful standard of reasonable conduct."

From this it appears that Canadian courts, unlike those in England, will not accept that the breach of a statute by itself creates a cause of action, even where the statute can be construed as permitting civil liability for its breach. The breach may evidence negligence, where negligence is the true cause of action. But if it does not, then actual negligence must be established. This makes breach of statutory duty, apparently in all instances, a part of the law of negligence, whereas in England it is a distinct type of liability, perhaps akin to or closely related to negligence, but nonetheless separate.[56] Moreover, although authority seems to be lacking for this proposition, it might be conceivable that an action could lie for the deliberate breach of a statute, where negligence is not involved. If the statute creates a private law liability and the conduct is intentional, the action for breach of statutory duty is founded on the breach, not on any conclusion that negligence has been committed.[57]

(c) Causation of damage

16.15 Where an action is brought for breach of statutory duty, the plaintiff must prove that the breach caused his damage in the same way as he must where his action is based on common law negligence.[58] However, as seen earlier in connection with negligence,[59] some decisions have significantly affected the issue of burden of proving causation, especially where the alleged breach consists of an omission, i.e. a failure to provide certain safety or health facilities, rather than an act of commission.[60]

16.16 Should the breach of duty actually be committed by the plaintiff himself, as in *Ginty v. Belmont Building Supplies Ltd*,[61] the defendant on whom the duty to comply with legislation was imposed may be able to escape liability. However once a breach has been shown and damage ensues, then, even though the damage was not foreseen as being occasioned in precisely the manner in which it occurred,[62] there will be *prima facie*

56 Indeed there may be a statutory duty where no common law duty of care exists: e.g., *Monk v. Warbey* [1935] 1 K.B. 75; *Ministry of Housing & Local Government v. Sharp* [1970] 2 Q.B. 223; *Warder v. Cooper* [1970] Ch. 495.

57 Perhaps the only example of this might be where a conspiracy to breach a statute was entered into with the express intention to injure the plaintiff: see the *Lonrho* case. On conspiracy, see below Chapter 21 at pp. 538–45.

58 *Bonnington Castings Ltd v. Wardlaw* [1956] A.C. 613; *McWilliams v. Sir William Arrol & Co.* [1962] 1 All E.R. 623; *Wigley v. British Vinegars Ltd* [1964] A.C. 307. The test is that of a balance of probabilities: *Quinn v. Cameron & Robertson Ltd* [1958] A.C. 9.

59 Chapter 12 at pp. 332–6.

60 *McGhee v. National Coal Board* [1972] 3 All E.R. 1008.

61 [1959] 1 All E.R. 414.

62 *Donaghey v. Boulton & Paul Ltd* [1968] A.C. 1.

liability: from which the defendant can only escape by proving that only the plaintiff's act or default caused the breach.[63] Hence, as long as the defendant is to some extent at fault, even though that fault would not suffice to found an action for breach of statute, the defendant will be liable,[64] subject to the possible reduction of the plaintiff's damages by reason of his own contributory negligence (bearing in mind the statutory definition of "fault" in the Law Reform (Contributory Negligence) Act 1945).[65]

(d) Injury within the scope of the statute

16.17 Since the nineteenth century, when *Gorris v. Scott*[66] was decided, it has been said that the damage suffered by the plaintiff must be the kind of damage envisaged by the statute as being likely to occur if the statutory duty is disobeyed. In that case a statute required shipowners to provide pens for cattle being carried on board ship to lessen the possibility of disease among the cattle. The defendant failed to provide such pens. In consequence the plaintiff's sheep were swept overboard in a storm. The defendant was not liable, at least on the basis of breach of statute (although the decision might have been different had the plaintiff sued, as he did not, for negligence or breach of contract). The damage incurred was not the sort of loss within the purview and intent of the statute.

16.18 However, as long as the damage suffered by the plaintiff is the kind of damage which, in general, is contemplated by the statute in question, the fact that it was not caused in precisely the way covered by the statute, or was more extensive than might have been foreseen as being a likely consequence, will not relieve the defendant from liability.[67] In this respect the law relating to breach of statutory duty resembles the modern law of negligence after recent decisions.[68] On the other hand, the language of the statute is all-important. Hence, as in *Close v. Steel Co. of Wales Ltd*,[69] if machinery has to be fenced in in order to keep workmen employed on such machinery from coming into contact with it and being injured, the defendant employer will not be liable on the basis of breach of statutory duty when, as a result of lack of adquate fencing, a piece of the machinery flies off and strikes the workman.

63 *Boyle v. Kodak Ltd* [1969] 2 All E.R. 439.
64 *Ross v. Associated Portland Cement Manufacturers Ltd* [1964] 2 All E.R. 452; *Boyle v. Kodak Ltd, supra*; *Leach v. Standard Telephones & Cables Ltd* [1966] 2 All E.R. 523; *Donaghey v. Boulton & Paul Ltd, supra*; *Barwick v. Brighton Corporation* [1949] 1 K.B. 339.
65 Chapter 13 at para. 13.37.
66 (1874) L.R. 9 Ex. 125: see *Donaghey v. Boulton & Paul Ltd, supra.*
67 *Johnson v. F.E. Callow Ltd* [1971] A.C. 335. See, generally, *Grant v. National Coal Board* [1958] A.C. 649; *Donaghey v. Boulton & Paul Ltd, supra.*
68 Above Chapter 12 at pp. 340–1.
69 [1962] A.C. 367; cp. *Sparrow v. Fairey Aviation Co. Ltd* [1964] A.C. 1019; *Nichols v. F. Austin (Leyton) Ltd* [1946] A.C. 493.

4. DEFENCES

(a) *Volenti*[70]

16.19 Generally speaking the defence of *volenti non fit injuria* is not available in an action for breach of statutory duty.[71] To allow *volenti* as a defence would permit an employee to contract out of a statutory obligation imposed on his employer. Whether this should be the case where the duty is not one concerned with employment is another question, on which there appears to be no authority. However, even where the injured plaintiff is an employee, the employer may raise the defence if the duty was imposed on the employer and not the workman. In *I.C.I. Ltd v. Shatwell*[72] two workmen were both under a statutory duty. They embarked on an undertaking in breach of that duty, in the course of which one was injured. Here it was held that *volenti* was a good defence. Otherwise an injured workman would be able to claim for breach by himself of his statutory duty as long as he had been joined in its commission by another workman, for whose breach of duty the employer would ordinarily be liable vicariously.

(b) Contributory negligence

16.20 The plaintiff's own default will be a defence to the action,[73] although since 1945 this may only result in the apportionment of liability between the parties.[74] However where statutory duties to protect employees are concerned, the courts have made it clear that too high a standard is not expected of the employee in respect of his own safety.[75] He is entitled to assume that statutory obligations have been fulfilled.[76] Moreover the employee will be guilty of contributory negligence probably only where he has acted totally improperly and in a manner that was "a crazy thing to do".[77] Even if the employee was also guilty of breach of duty, as noted earlier, this may not displace the employer's liability, unless the employee's conduct can be regarded as evidence of his own carelessness for his own safety.[78] Once the damage has been shown to be the consequence of the breach of statute, the onus is on the defendant to establish that the plaintiff's conduct was a material factor in what happened to him.[79]

70 Chapter 13 at pp. 348–56.
71 *Wheeler v. New Merton Board Mills Ltd* [1933] 2 K.B. 669.
72 [1965] A.C. 656.
73 *Caswell v. Powell Duffryn Associated Collieries Ltd* [1940] A.C. 152.
74 Chapter 13 at paras 13.39ff.
75 *Lewis v. Denys* [1940] A.C. 921.
76 *Westwood v. Post Office* [1974] A.C. 1.
77 *Rushton v. Turner Bros. Asbestos Co. Ltd* [1959] 3 All E.R. 517.
78 *Ross v. Associated Portland Cement Manufacturers Ltd, supra.*
79 *Caswell v. Powell Duffryn Associated Collieries Ltd, supra.*

(c) Delegation

16.21 Delegation to another person of the performance of a statutory duty is not a defence. Such duties are personal to the party on whom they are placed by the statute.[80] However it was thought at one time that delegation of performance of the statutory duty to the plaintiff himself might be a defence, where the plaintiff's own breach of the duty brought about his injury.[81] This now seems to have been abandoned or declared obsolete.[82]

80 *Lochgelly Iron & Coal Co. v. M'Mullan* [1934] A.C. 1; *Smith v. Cammell Laird & Co. Ltd* [1940] A.C. 242; *The Pass of Ballater* [1942] P. 112 at 117 *per* Langton J.; *Donaghey v. Boulton & Paul Ltd, supra.*

81 *Smith v. Baverstock & Co.* [1945] 1 All E.R. 531; *Barwick v. Brighton Corporation* [1949] 1 K.B. 339.

82 *Ross v. Associated Portland Cement Manufacturers Ltd, supra.* The question is really whose conduct caused the accident: *ibid.* at 455 *per* Lord Reid. See, e.g., *Leach v. Standard Telephones & Cables Ltd, supra.*

CHAPTER 17

Deceit

1. FRAUD

17.01 The tort of deceit is based on fraudulent representations that induce another to act to his detriment. The kind of representation that will entitle the victim to sue in tort is exactly the same as a fraudulent misrepresentation that would permit the other contracting party to avoid the contract.[1] In both contexts the law is interested in actual fraud, not misrepresentation caused by negligence and *a fortiori* not a completely innocent misrepresentation, where the representor does not know, and has no reason to know, that his statement or statements are untrue. The difference between fraud that justifies an action in tort and fraud that allows a contracting party to escape from his obligations is that the tort may be committed where the result of the fraud is not the making of a contract between the representor and the victim of the representation, whereas the contractual situation only arises where a contract was agreed between the parties as a consequence of the fraud that is in issue. It is accepted, however, that wherever a contracting party may rescind for fraudulent misrepresentation he may also sue for damages for deceit.[2]

17.02 Fraud entails deliberate deception, the existence of "a wicked mind".[3] In *Derry v. Peek*[4] the House of Lords held that fraud might be committed if the defendant made a representation without caring whether or not it was true, in other words if the representor did not believe the statement to be true. Reckless behaviour could amount to deliberate misconduct. In arriving at this conclusion the House of Lords rejected the idea that someone who by negligence misrepresented the truth could be liable for the tort of deceit. It took a further eighty years for this rejection of liability for a negligent misrepresentation itself to be rejected and for negligence in making a statement of fact to be capable of grounding liability in the absence of any special statutory provisions or the existence

1 Cheshire, Fifoot and Furmston, *Law of Contract*, 11th ed. 1986, 265–267; Treitel, *Law of Contract*, 6th ed. 1983, 262–263. Hence the possibility that the participation of the plaintiff in an illegal contract, which was entered into as a result of the defendant's fraud, might operate as a defence to the plaintiff's action for deceit (just as it might affect the contractual rights of the plaintiff): *Saunders v. Edwards* [1987] 2 All E.R. 651.

2 *Newbigging v. Adam* (1886) 34 Ch.D. 582. But to sue for damages he may have to rescind the contract first, viz., in the case of shares purchased by a subscriber in consequence of fraud: *Houldsworth v. City of Glasgow Bank* (1880) 5 App.Cas. 317.

3 *Le Lievre v. Gould* [1893] 1 P.B. 491 at 498 *per* Lord Esher.

4 (1889) 14 App.Cas. 337.

of a fiduciary or contractual duty of care.[5] Developments in the law of negligence have not affected the basic requirement of the law of deceit with respect to intentional wrongdoing. Carelessness alone will not constitute deceit.

17.03 Although there may be a moral basis for imposing liability for fraud, such that the legal idea of fraud corresponds to the moral concept, liability is imposed not because of the moral wrongdoing of the defendant in speaking or writing untruths, but by reason of the harm suffered by the plaintiff in consequence of the defendant's conduct. Without proof that the plaintiff has incurred damage or loss as a direct result of the alleged fraud there can be no liability in deceit.[6] The object of the law is not to punish a wrongdoer, unless his conduct also amounts to a criminal offence. The law of torts is concerned with the compensation of the victim. In the absence of damage or economic loss there is no victim to be compensated.

2. ELEMENTS OF LIABILITY

(a) A false statement of fact

17.04 Deceit is concerned only with false statements of fact. The notion of "fact" for this purpose may include everything except a promise. It has been held that a statement of opinion, if not honestly held, can be regarded as a mis-statement of fact.[7] Similarly, a statement of a party's intention as to the future might be treated as a statement of fact, where it is clear that the party in question states his intention of doing something when he has no such intention.[8] In *Edgington v. Fitzmaurice*[9] a company issued a prospectus asking for subscriptions for debentures, saying that the money so raised would be used to develop the company's trade, purchase horses and vans, and complete certain building alterations. The real object of the debentures was to enable the directors to pay off pressing liabilities. The plaintiff advanced money on the strength of these statements. When he discovered the truth he sued, and the directors were held liable in deceit.

17.05 A statement of fact must be distinguished from a statement of law. Since everyone is presumed to know the law, a mis-statement of law, even if deliberate and intended to deceive, does not constitute deceit.[10] The problem, however, is to determine whether a particular statement is one of

5 *Hedley Byrne & Co. Ltd v. Heller & Partners Ltd* [1964] A.C. 465: see para. 12.36. At common law and under statute there were, and still are situations in which negligence alone could result in liability: *ibid.*
6 *Diamond v. Bank of London & Montreal Ltd* [1979] Q.B. 337.
7 *Smith v. Land & Home Property Corporation* (1884) 28 Ch.D. 7; *Brown v. Raphael* [1958] Ch. 636. Contrast *Bisset v. Wilkinson* [1927] A.C. 177.
8 *Angus v. Clifford* [1891] 2 Ch. 449 at 470 *per* Bowen L.J.; *British Airways Board v. Taylor* [1976] 1 All E.R. 65 at 68 *per* Lord Wilberforce.
9 (1885) 29 Ch.D. 459.
10 Unless it is a misrepresentation of foreign law, which is a misrepresentation of fact: *André & Cie. S.A. v. Ets. Michel Blanc & Fils* [1979] 2 Lloyd's Rep. 427.

law or fact. To state that the law is such-and-such, when it is not, would be a mis-statement of law.[11] To say that such-and-such is the case when this is based on the representor's understanding of the factual and legal situation, which is not set out in detail, would be a mis-statement of fact.[12] It is drawing a conclusion as to a state of affairs based upon the law. For example, if a man who knew that his first marriage was valid were to hold himself out to be a bachelor, believing that his first marriage was a nullity, on the ground that he had married his first cousin, he would be making an untrue statement of fact. If he were to state that the law was such that men who married their first cousins were not validly married, he would be making an untrue statement of law.[13]

17.06 Non-disclosure of a fact is not a mis-statement amounting to deceit,[14] unless such non-disclosure makes whatever else has been stated false.[15] In *Legh v. Legh*[16] a husband's payment of money under an agreement to give the wife half his income involved a false statement of fact because his income was greater than the amount on which he had based his payment. Therefore he was liable in deceit. In contracts with insurance companies, which are regarded as contracts *uberrimae fidei*, not to disclose a material fact that would affect the issuance of a policy is fraud, even though everything that has been disclosed is true.[17] The reason for this is because in determining whether or not to undertake the policy of insurance the company must be aware of all circumstances that affect the nature and extent of the risk against which the policy is being taken out by the applicant for insurance. Failure to disclose a past criminal conviction, or some physical defect that might influence the granting of a policy of insurance would be fraud that would entitle the insurer to avoid the contract and, in appropriate circumstances, sue for deceit.

17.07 A statement might be true or might be believed true at the time when it is first made, only later discovered to have been, or to have become, untrue. If such is the situation, can it be said that the maker of the statement is guilty of deceit? At the time he first made the statement no such conclusion could have been reached. In several decisions it was held that failure to reveal the truth when it became known amounts to deceit, at least where the omission to correct the original statement results in a substantial alteration of the truth of that statement.[18] The reason why such changes can turn a statement for which there would not have been

11 *Beattie v. Lord Ebury* (1872) L.R. 7 Ch.App. 777 at 802; *Beesley v. Hallwood Estates Ltd* [1960] 2 All E.R. 314 at 323.
12 *Eaglesfield v. Marquis of Londonderry* (1876) 4 Ch.D. 693.
13 *Ibid.* at 702–703 *per* Jessel M.R.
14 *Fox v. Macreth* (1788) 2 Cox Eq. Cas. 320 at 321 *per* Lord Thurlow; *Bell v. Lever Bros.* [1932] A.C. 161 at 227 *per* Lord Atkin.
15 *Oakes v. Turquand & Hardy* (1867) L.R. 2 H.L. 325 at 342–343.
16 (1936) 143 L.T. 151.
17 Cheshire, Fifoot and Furmston's *Law of Contract*, 290–292; Treitel, *op. cit.* 304–305.
18 *Incledon v. Watson* (1862) 2 F. & F. 841; *Brownlie v. Campbell* (1880) 5 App.Cas. 925 at 950 *per* Lord Blackburn; *Arkwright v. Newbould* (1881) 17 Ch.D. 301 at 318 *per* Jmes L.J. 320 *per* Collins L.J.; *With v. O'Flanagan* [1936] Ch. 575; *Bradford Building Society v. Borders* [1941] 2 All E.R. 205 at 220 *per* Lord Wright.

liability in deceit into one for which such liability arises is because a false statement is not actionable unless and until it is acted upon by the party to whom it is made. The crucial moment of time, as Lord Tucker made clear in *Breiss v. Woolley*,[19] is the time when the alleged misrepresentation is acted upon by the representee. It is then that the tortious act is complete, provided that the statement is false at that date. Hence if the statement is false when it is made but becomes true by the time it is acted upon, there is neither misrepresentation nor deceit.

17.08 A false statement of fact that will entitle the plaintiff to sue for deceit may be made orally or in writing. However in one situation no action can be brought unless the statement has been put into writing. This is where the statement concerns the character, conduct, credit, trade or other dealings of another person to the intent or purpose that such other person may obtain credit, money or goods. For an action in deceit to be brought against the representor the statement must be in writing and signed by the person who made the statement.[19a] This enactment only applies to fraudulent statements, not to statements which are untrue but are made negligently.[19b] However it applies as long as the intent of the defendant was to procure the granting of credit to the person named, whatever other, ulterior motives the defendant may have had in mind.[19c]

(b) Knowledge of falsity

17.09 Before a defendant can be held liable for deceit it must be proved that he knew the statement he made was false or that he made the statement without an honest belief in its truth, not caring whether it was true or false.[20] In the words of Lord Wright, "fraud involves deliberate intent which is called *mens rea*."[21] Hence in *Derry v. Peek*[22] the defendants were not liable in deceit, because when they made representations in the prospectus of the company of which they were directors they were not guilty of any deliberate deception. The directors believed that consent to the use of steam or mechanical power, instead of animal power, to move their trams would automatically be given. Hence they asserted that the company had the right to use steam power instead of horses. On this basis the plaintiff bought shares in the company. His action for deceit failed although he proved that he had lost money as a result of reliance on the statement in the prospectus and that the statement was untrue in fact. The necessary intent or recklessness was lacking. But in the earlier case of

19 [1954] A.C. 333 at 353.
19a Statute of Frauds Amendment Act 1828 s. 6; *Diamond v. Bank of London & Montreal Ltd* [1979] Q.B. 333 at 347 *per* Lord Denning, 349 *per* Stephenson L.J.
19b *Swift v. Jewsbury & Goddard* (1874) L.R. 9 Q.B. 301; *W.B. Anderson & Sons Ltd v. Rhodes (Liverpool) Ltd* [1967] 2 All E.R. 850. See also *UBAF v. European American Banking Corporation* [1984] Q.B. 713.
19c *Clydesdale Bank Ltd v. Paton* [1896] A.C. 381.
20 *Edgington v. Fitzmaurice* (1885) 29 Ch.D. 459 at 479 *per* Cotton L.J., 481–482 *per* Bowen L.J.
21 *Bradford Building Society v. Borders* [1941] 2 All E.R. 205 at 220.
22 (1889) 14 App.Cas. 337.

Polhill v. Walter[23] the defendant was liable when he accepted a bill of exchange by procuration of the drawee in the belief that his acceptance would be sanctioned by the drawee who would pay the amount indicated in the bill. He knew he had no authority to act on behalf of the drawee of the bill. However, the fact that the defendant had no reasonable or sufficient grounds for believing the statement to be true is not enough to establish the fact that he knew the statement was untrue, or that he was indifferent in respect of its truth.[24] Mere negligence, or even so-called "gross negligence" in respect of the truth or falsity of the statement will not amount to such misconduct as will entitle the plaintiff to succeed. To make the defendant liable, where he had not deliberately misled the plaintiff, it must be proved that the defendant was conscious of the possibility that the statement might be false *and* careless whether it was true or false.[25] Thus the honest belief of the defendant will exonerate him from liability. In this respect the question is not whether the defendant honestly believed the statement he made to be true in the sense assigned to it by the court on an objective consideration of the statement's truth or falsity. The question is whether the defendant honestly believed the statement to be true in the sense in which he intended it to be understood, however erroneously, at the time it was made.[26] For fraud to be proved, therefore, the defendant must have intended the statement to be read in a certain way, a way that was misleading to the knowledge of the defendant.[27]

17.10 The standard of proof to be applied in determining the guilt or innocence of the defendant is the civil standard, not that applicable in criminal cases, even though fraud is, or can be, a criminal offence. The guilt of the defendant may be established on a balance of probabilities, not beyond all reasonable doubt. But there is no absolute standard of proof. The degree of probability is commensurate with the occasion and proportionate to the subject-matter.[28]

(c) The defendant's intent

17.11 It is not enough that the defendant knowingly made a false statement. His purpose in doing so must have been to produce some act on the part of the plaintiff, the person to whom the statement was made. In *Levy v. Langridge*[29] the defendant represented that a gun had been safely made, for the purpose of inducing the plaintiff's father to buy the gun. When the plaintiff who used the gun was injured because the gun was faulty and burst, the defendant was liable in deceit, because he knew and intended that the plaintiff would rely on the representation and use the

23 (1832) 3 B. & Ad. 114.
24 *Angus v. Clifford* [1891] 2 Ch. 449.
25 *Ibid.* at 471 *per* Bowen L.J.
26 *Akerhielm v. De Mare* [1959] A.C. 789 at 805 *per* Lord Jenkins.
27 *Gross v. Lewis Hillman Ltd* [1970] 1 Ch. 445.
28 *Hornal v. Neuberger Products Ltd* [1957] 1 Q.B. 247.
29 (1837) 4 M. & W. 337.

gun. At a time in the history of the development of the law of torts when mere negligence might not have resulted in liability to a party with whom the defendant had not contracted, the fraud of the defendant affixed him with responsibility.

17.12 The false statement must be made to the plaintiff directly by the defendant, so as to prove the requisite intent on the part of the latter. In *Andrews v. Mockford*[30] the defendant issued a prospectus that contained fraudulent misrepresentations. Some time later the plaintiff bought shares in the company in respect of which the prospectus was issued. He did so partly on the strength of what was contained in the prospectus and partly in reliance on statements in a newspaper. The defendant was liable for deceit. In *Peek v. Gurney*,[31] however, no such liability was imposed. The plaintiff bought shares from the original allottee of shares issued under a prospectus that contained misstatements that were made fraudulently. In these circumstances there was no causal connection between the fraud in the prospectus and the ultimate purchase of the shares by the plaintiff. What these decisions illustrate is the need for some causal link between the fraud that is the basis of the action and the action on the part of the plaintiff that leads to his loss. The fact that there was an intermediate party between the fraud and the plaintiff's action may isolate the fraud from the ultimate consequence of harm to the party who wishes to sue. If the plaintiff in *Peek v. Gurney* had been moved to buy the shares from his vendor in consequence of having read and believed the statements in the prospectus, as did the plaintiff in *Andrews v. Mockford*, it might then have been determined that his loss was brought about by reliance on the fraud and not as a consequence of his own independent decision to buy the shares in question.

17.13 In one situation, however, the fact that an intermediary is responsible for inducing the plaintiff to act may result in the defendant being liable. This is so where the statement is made to the plaintiff by the defendant's agent. If the principal authorises his agent to make a statement which both principal and agent know is untrue, both are liable in deceit. If the principal is innocent of any fraud, but his agent knows that the statement is untrue, both will again be liable in deceit: the agent because he has made a false statement knowing it to be false, the principal because the agent was acting on his behalf (as long as the agent was acting within the scope of some express or apparent authority entrusted to him by the principal).[32] If the agent is acting in an unauthorised way, only the agent will be liable. If the principal knows that a particular statement is untrue but deliberately conceals that fact from the agent with the intention that the agent should innocently represent the statement as true, the

30 [1896] 1 Q.B. 372.
31 (1873) L.R. 6 H.L. 377.
32 *Armagas Ltd v. Mundogas S.A.* [1985] 3 All E.R. 795, affirmed [1986] 2 All E.R. 385; cp. *Pearson & Son Ltd v. Dublin Corporation* [1907] A.C. 351 at 354 *per* Lord Loreburn

principal will be liable for deceit, but the agent will not. In *Ludgater v. Love*[33] the defendant's son was selling the defendant's sheep on his behalf. The defendant knew the sheep were not in good condition, but he authorised his son to state that the sheep were all right. The son was ignorant of the truth. The son was innocent but the defendant was held liable.

17.14 The situation is more complex where the principal knows that a particular statement is untrue but is unaware that his agent is making the statement, while the agent, who makes the statement, is unaware that it is untrue. In *Cornfoot v. Fowke*[34] the plaintiff sought rescission of a lease, not damages for deceit, where he discovered that the premises he was leasing were next door to a brothel. The agent who negotiated the lease did not know that the premises next door were a brothel (which the principal knew). He stipulated that the leased premises were satisfactory for the plaintiff. Rescission was not allowed. In *Pearson & Son Ltd v. Dublin Corporation*[35] some members of the House of Lords held that the division of incorrectness between the principal and agent did not make any difference to liability as long as there was a misstatement somewhere. Principal and agent were one person for this purpose.[36] Hence deceit could be commited in this way. Other courts held that only if the principal had the requisite "guilty knowledge" could there be liability for deceit when his agent innocently misrepresented the truth.[37] It was decided, however, by Devlin J. and the Court of Appeal in *Armstrong v. Strain*[38] that an innocent agent could not make his (presumably) innocent principal liable for deceit. Of course it is a matter of debate whether in such circumstances the principal can be described correctly as "innocent". If his lack of awareness of what is happening can render him guiltless of fraud, then the decision in *Armstrong v. Strain* would seem to be reasonable. If, as might be the case, the principal ought to have been more alert to what was occurring, it might be argued that his conduct was reckless within the meaning of that expression as expounded in *Derry v. Peek*, in which event he might be considered a guilty principal and so liable for deceit. In the context of contract, rather than the tort of deceit, the situation has probably been clarified by the provisions of the Misrepresentation Act 1967.[39] These provisions only apply where the consequence of a misrepresentation is to induce the plaintiff to enter into a contract with the representor (or the principal of the representor).

33 (1881) 44 L.T. 695.
34 (1840) 6 M. & W. 358.
35 [1907] A.C. 351 at 354 *per* Lord Loreburn, 359 *per* Lord Halsbury.
36 See *London County Freehold Properties Ltd v. Berkeley Properties & Investment Co. Ltd* [1936] 2 All E.R. 1039 at 1047 *per* Slesser L.J., 1050 *per* Romer L.J.
37 *Anglo-Scottish Beet Sugar Corporation Ltd v. Spalding U.D.C.* [1937] K.B. 607 (a case of mistake, not fraud); *Gordon Hill Trust Ltd v. Segall* [1941] 2 All E.R. 379.
38 [1951] 1 T.L.R. 866, [1952] 1 K.B. 232.
39 1967, c. 7, s. 2(1): Cheshire, Fifoot & Furmston's *Law of Contract*, 271; Treitel *op. cit.* 265–267.

(d) Reliance by the plaintiff

17.15 Liability for deceit depends on whether the plaintiff acted on the false statement that was made to him. If the plaintiff incurs loss or damage because of his own failure to realise that there was something wrong, he may not be able to sue for deceit. That was the situation in *Horsfall v. Thomas*,[40] where the alleged fraud on the part of the plaintiff was pleaded by way of defence to an action for the price of goods purchased by the defendant from the plaintiff. The defect in the goods, of which the plaintiff was aware and in respect of which the plaintiff failed to give notice or information to the defendant, was a defect that was patent. It could have been seen by the defendant if he had inspected the goods. In this instance the plaintiff's conduct did not constitute the kind of actionable fraud that could be used as a defence to the action for the price. However the decision in *Central Railway Co. of Venezuela v. Kisch*[41] throws some doubt on this. The plaintiff purchased shares in a company after having read statements in a prospectus that in fact were untrue and were misrepresentations. When sued for fraud, the defendants pleaded that the plaintiff could have discovered the truth had he inspected the books of the company and other reports which would have revealed that the statements in the prospectus were not true. Here it was held that the plaintiff was entitled to rely on the honesty of the defendant.[42] This must surely be the situation in every case even if the mis-statement is so glaring and obvious that no reasonable man could be held to have relied on it as the basis for the action taken that resulted in damage or loss. As long as it can be shown that the plaintiff relied on the statement in issue, there should be liability for deceit, since this is precisely what the defendant intended.

(e) Damage

17.16 A false representation must be effective, else there will be no tort.[43] In this respect deceit resembles defamation, where publication is necessary before the defamatory statement can be held to be libellous or slanderous. The false representation has to cause damage in order for it to be actionable.[44] This means not only that it has to be acted upon, but that the result must be the suffering of harm or loss. Whoever proves that he suffered damage by relying on the false representation can sue.[45] A distinction must be drawn between the commission of the tort and question of actionability. As soon as anyone has suffered damage the tort will be complete and committed.[46] For an individual plaintiff to be able to sue in respect of the tort, however, that plaintiff must prove that he has suffered damage. The necessity for proving damage stems from the origins

40 (1862) 1 H. & C. 90.
41 (1867) L.R. 2 H.L. 99.
42 See *Pearson & Son Ltd v. Dublin Corporation* [1907] A.C. 351.
43 *Diamond v. Bank of London & Montreal Ltd* [1979] Q.B. 337 at 349 *per* Stephenson L.J.
44 *Ibid.*
45 *Brown Jenkinson & Co. Ltd v. Percy Dalson (London) Ltd* [1957] 2 Q.B. 621 at 632 *per* Morris L.J. 638 *per* Pearce L.J.
46 *Diamond v. Bank of London & Montreal Ltd, supra* at 349 *per* Stephenson L.J.

of the modern tort of deceit in the action on the case.[47] The damage suffered may take the form of physical injury,[48] or damage to property.[49] More frequently it is economic or financial loss.

17.17 Where an action lies, the measure of damages is not the same as in the law of contract. In an action for breach of contract, based on fraud, the plaintiff is entitled *inter alia* for loss of foreseeable profits on the contract in question. Where a plaintiff sues for the tort of deceit, he can reover all damage directly flowing from the tortious act of fraudulent inducement as long as such damage is not rendered too remote by the plaintiff's own conduct, whether or not the damage so caused was foreseeable by the defendant.[50] The position of the plaintiff before and after the representation must be compared.[51] The object of an award of damages in an action for deceit is to put the plaintiff back into the position he was in prior to the making of the representation and the reliance on it by the plaintiff. Damages for deceit are not intended to compensate the plaintiff for lost expectations; they are meant to compensate him for his reliance losses, and to provide him with restitution of his expenditures.[51a] Damages are recoverable in deceit as well as rescission of any contract entered into by the plaintiff in consequence of the defendant's fraud. The fact that rescission is possible is not a reason for denying the plaintiff his remedy by way of damages.[52]

17.18 In *Archer v. Brown*[53] the plaintiff was allowed to recover the interest he had paid a bank on a loan which he had taken out from a bank in order to make the contract that was induced by the defendant's fraud. Such interest was recoverable because the defendant knew how the plaintiff was going to obtain the money that was needed. The defendant had put the plaintiff in the position in which he found himself, including the impecuniosity that resulted from deceit. Therefore the interest charged by the bank was a direct consequence of the defendant's misconduct.[54] The fraud involved the sale to the plaintiff of shares in a company which the defendant had already sold several times over. As a result of his belief that he was a shareholder in the company, the plaintiff signed a service agreement with the company and left his previous employment. He was

47 *Pasley v. Freeman* (1789) 3 T.R. 51.
48 *Levy v. Langridge* (1837) 4 M. & W. 377. Including mental suffering: *Wilkinson v. Downton* [1897] 2 Q.B. 57.
49 *Burrows v. Rhodes* [1899] 1 Q.B. 816; e.g. loss of a regulated tenancy: *Mafo v. Adams* [1970] 1 Q.B. 548.
50 *Doyle v. Olby (Ironmongers) Ltd* [1969] 2 Q.B. 158 at 167 *per* Lord Denning.
51 *Ibid.* at 168 *per* Winn L.J.
51a If a plaintiff has been permanently deprived of his goods by the defendant's deceit, he is entitled to recover the market price of the goods, not the cost of replacing them, just as if he was suing in conversion: *Smith, Kline & French Laboratories plc v. Long* [1988] 3 All E.R. 887 at 892–894 *per* Slade L.J.; cp. *The Jag Shakti; Chabbra Corporation Pte Ltd v. Owners* [1986] A.C. 337 at 345.
52 *Archer v. Brown* [1984] 2 All E.R. 267.
53 *Supra.*
54 *Supra* note 52 at 276–277, distinguishing *Liesbosch Dredger v. Edison* [1933] A.C. 449 and relying on *Dodd Properties (Kent) Ltd v. Canterbury City Council* [1980] 1 All E.R. 928; *Perry v. Sidney Phillips & Son* [1982] 3 All E.R. 705.

entitled to damages for loss of employment and to the expenses he incurred in searching for new employment after he discovered about the fraud. But he was not entitled to loss of prospective earnings from future employment with the company. There was a difference between compensating the plaintiff for actual loss and compensating him for prospective loss. But damages for inconvenience or annoyance may be recovered in an action for deceit.[55]

17.19 So, too, can aggravated damages. If the plaintiff has suffered injured feelings, it is possible to compensate him by means of an award of aggravated damages. However such an award, it was said in *Archer v. Brown*,[56] should be moderate. Whether it is possible to award exemplary or punitive damages in an action for deceit is an open question. In *Mafo v. Adams*[57] it was said that this might be possible, since any tort could give rise to exemplary damages, even after *Rookes v. Barnard*,[58] if the circumstances justified making it clear to the defendant that he should not be permitted to make a profit from his tort, or there was arrogance or similar intolerable behaviour on his part. This was *obiter*, since, on the facts in *Mafo v. Adams*, no such damages could properly be awarded. Nor could they be on the facts in *Archer v. Brown*, since the defendant had already been punished for his wrongdoing by serving a sentence in prison. However *dicta* elsewhere throw some doubt on the proposition that exemplary damages are recoverable in a deceit action.[59] But, as Pain J. said in *Archer v. Brown*,[60] the door was open on this question.

55 *Mafo v. Adams* [1970] 1 Q.B. 548.
56 *Supra* note 52 at 283; cp. *Shelley v. Paddock* [1979] Q.B. 120, damages for mental suffering.
57 [1970] 1 Q.B. 548 at 554–555 *per* Sachs L.J., 558–589 *per* Widgery L.J.
58 [1964] A.C. 1129; above pp. 409–10.
59 *Cassell & Co. Ltd v. Broome* [1972] A.C. 1027 at 1078–1079 *per* Lord Hailsham L.C., 1130–1131 *per* Lord Diplock.
60 *Supra* note 52 at 281.

CHAPTER 18

Defamation

1. DEFINITION AND RATIONALE

18.01 Defamation, which takes the form of either libel or slander,[1] involves the publication of a defamatory statement about the plaintiff[2] to some person or persons other than the plaintiff himself without lawful justification or excuse.[3] Damage to the plaintiff need not be shown to have been caused as a result of the publication in cases in libel, but must be proved where slander is alleged, except in certain specific situations at common law or under statute.[4] A defamatory statement is one that affects the reputation or good name of the plaintiff in respect of his business, trade, profession or calling, or in regard to his personal character. Personal injury does not have to be shown, although psychological consequences of defamation may be taken into account in the assessment of damages. Nor is damage to property involved. Loss of wealth in consequence of defamation may occur and will be accounted for by an appropriate award of damages. Nonetheless defamation differs from other torts in that it concerns wrongful acts which do not necessarily affect the plaintiff's person or his property.[5]

18.02 A party who alleges that he has been defamed asserts that he has been attacked and harmed in respect of something that is neither tangible nor immediately assessable in terms of money (although one effect of such attack may be to cause the plaintiff monetary loss). In granting an action for such harm the law appears at first sight to be going beyond what are legitimate boundaries of legal protection and intervention. It might be thought that the law should not be involved or concerned with something so nebulous and "unreal" (in the very literal sense of lacking the substance of a *res*) as a person's character. Such a form of injury pertains more to the moral than the legal aspects of personality. An award of damages in respect of defamation seems to amount to compensation for injured feelings perhaps akin to emotional distress, which has only recently become the subject of legitimate concern by the courts, rather than for

1 Below paras 18.37ff.
2 *Hayward v. Thompson* [1981] 3 All E.R. 450 at 456–457 *per* Lord Denning.
3 For what amounts to lawful justification or excuse see below paras 18.54ff.
4 Below pp. 482–7. But in some common law jurisdictions, damage is presumed whether libel or slander is involved: e.g., Alberta, Defamation Act, R.S.A. 1980, c. D-6, s. 2(2).
5 But defamation must be distinguished from injurious falsehood, also called by other names, which involves an attack upon some property of the plaintiff by false statements occasioning financial loss. Defamation is about the character of the plaintiff, not the character or nature of the plaintiff's property: below pp. 566–71.

actual harm. In recognising defamation as actionable, the law seems to have "reified" a person's character. It has been conceived of either as an extension of his physical person, so that an attack on character is viewed as being similar to an attack on his person, or as a facet of his property, having a value that is diminished as a consequence of the attack.

2. REQUIREMENTS OF LIABILITY

(a) Capacity to be defamed

18.03 The plaintiff must have a legal personality capable of being defamed. Hence there can be no defamation of a dead person.[6] For the same reason, an action for defamation could not be maintained by a trade union which was not a special register body within the meaning of the Trade Union and Labour Relations Act 1974. Such a trade union had no legal personality.[7] But a body corporate does have such personality.[8] Hence in *Bognor Regis U.D.C. v. Campion*[9] a local government corporation could sue, since it possessed not only personality but also a "governing" reputation which was protectable by the law in the same way as the personal reputation of an individual or the trading reputation of a trading company.[10]

(b) Falsity

18.04 To be actionable, a defamatory statement must be untrue. There is nothing tortious about publishing a statement that is clearly defamatory of the plaintiff if the statement is true.[11] Indeed it is always a defence to an action for defamation that the statement of which complaint is made is true.[12]

6 Nor will an action for defamation survive the death of the party defamed (or the alleged defamer): above p. 41. The relatives of the deceased also may not sue unless the defamatory matter is defamatory of them as well as the deceased. No change in the law was recommended by the Porter Committe's *Report on Defamation* in 1948, Cmnd. 7536: but change was recommended by a majority of the Faulks Committee on Defamation in 1975, Cmnd. 5909, para. 421; see Symmons, "New Remedies Against Libellers of the Dead? A Look at the Recommendations of the Faulks Committee on Defamation" (1980) 18 U.W.O.L.R. 521. It was suggested that certain relatives should be able to sue for a declaration that the statement was false and an injunction to prevent further repetition within five years of the death, with costs but no damages.

7 *E.E.P.T.U. v. Times Newspapers Ltd* [1980] 1 Q.B. 585. Other trade unions can sue: *N.U.G.M.W. v. Gillan* [1946] K.B. 81; *Willis v. Brooks* [1947] 1 All E.R. 191.

8 But the defamatory matter must cause actual damage to the corporation in respect of its property or business: *D. & L. Caterers Ltd v. D'Ajou* [1945] K.B. 364.

9 [1972] 2 Q.B. 169.

10 For a corporation to sue the libel must affect its property, i.e. its business reputation: *Manchester Corporation v. Williams* [1891] Q.B. 94. The Faulks Committee, *supra* note 6, recommended that such corporations should have to prove special damage: Cmnd. 5909, para. 342.

11 But this may amount to the offence of criminal libel: below para. 18.41.

12 Below paras 18.58ff.

18.05 It is not sufficient for the defendant to say that he honestly believed that his allegations were true.[13] Liability stems from the fact of defamation, not upon proof of malice, i.e. a deliberate intention to defame,[14] although in earlier times it was essential for the plaintiff to plead and prove that this was the case.[15] Malice, in this sense, is now imputed or implied from the fact of publication. However, in relation to the defence of qualified privilege it is necessary for the plaintiff to plead and prove "express" malice, i.e. knowledge and intent, if the defence is to be overcome.[16] Since the defendant's lack of either knowledge of the untruth of his allegation or any intent to defame are irrelevant to liability (although such matters might be material in assessing damages,[17] especially possible liability to pay exemplary or punitive damages[18]), it will not be open to the defendant to say that he received the information from someone else, even though he was entitled to rely on the source of his knowledge; nor that he was merely repeating what he had heard or read elsewhere without realising that he was defaming the plaintiff. However it has been held that in the absence of proof that an allegation was made dishonestly or maliciously and that the defendant maliciously or dishonestly proposed to say or publish information that he knew was untrue, an injunction would not be issued to restrain further publication of an alleged defamation in respect of which the plaintiff was bringing an action.[19]

18.06 Nor was it possible in general at common law for the defendant to plead that he had not acted negligently in publishing a defamatory allegation.[20] It is not necessary for the plaintiff, at common law, to prove that the defendant failed to take reasonable care to ensure that his allegation against the plaintiff was true. Defamation is a wrong of strict liability. As will be seen later, this applies both to the defamatory nature of the statement and the issue of its reference to the plaintiff. In several leading decisions the courts held that it was not open to a defendant to plead that he had not behaved negligently in publishing a statement that subsequently turned out to be, and to be taken as being, defamatory of the particular plaintiff who sued.[21] Under the Defamation Act 1952 section 4, a defence has been made available, in certain circumstances, in consequence of which it may be possible for a defendant within the scope of the

13 *Bromage v. Prosser* (1825) 4 B. & C. 247.
14 *R. v. Woodfall* (1774) Lofft. 776 at 781 *per* Lord Mansfield; *Cassidy v. Daily Mirror Newspapers Ltd* [1929] 2 K.B. 331 at 354 *per* Russell L.J.
15 But the malicious publication of a defamatory libel knowing it to be false is an offence punishable by imprisonment and fine: Libel Act 1843 ss. 4–7.
16 Below paras 18.99ff.
17 Libel Act 1843 s. 2, dealing with libels in a newspaper or other periodical publication, as long as there was an apology published or offered to be published, and a payment into court as amends: Libel Act 1845 s. 2.
18 Below pp. 515–16.
19 *Harakas v. Baltic Mercantile & Shipping Exchange Ltd* [1982] 2 All E.R. 701.
20 Negligence, or its lack, would be relevant under the Libel Act 1843 s. 2 and the Libel Act 1845 s. 2: *supra* note 17.
21 *Hulton v. Jones* [1910] A.C. 20; *Cassidy v. Daily Mirror Newspapers Ltd* [1929] 2 K.B. 331; *Hough v. London Express Newspapers Ltd* [1940] 2 K.B. 507; *Newstead v. London Express Newspapers Ltd* [1940] 1 K.B. 377.

Act to establish that he acted without negligence.[22] In one situation at common law negligence is relevant to liability. A distinction has been drawn between the publisher of a defamatory statement and a mere "distributor", for example, a vendor of newspapers.[23] The former will be liable whether or not he was negligent in determining the truth of the statement he published (unless the Defamation Act 1952 defence applies); the latter will not be liable unless he was negligent in not appreciating that he was guilty of distributing something defamatory of the plaintiff.[24]

(c) A defamatory allegation

(i) The meaning of "defamatory"[24a]

18.07 Judges have shrunk in the past, not without good reason, from the task of defining with precision the meaning of the word "defamatory".[25] The distinction has long been drawn between general abuse, which is not remediable, and defamation, which is.[26] The former is regarded as something that everyone must accept in the sense that others will not give credence or pay attention to language that is quite obviously excessive, vulgar, and not to be taken seriously by those who hear or read it.[27] The conventional test of defamation was that defamatory words are such as expose the plaintiff to hatred, ridicule and contempt.[28] But in *Nevill v. Fine Arts and General Insurance Co.*,[29] Lord Halsbury added the words "or to cause him damage", which indicates what has been asserted above, namely that the law was concerned with the financial or economic effects of defamation rather than its emotional consequences.

18.08 The conventional test is now generally accepted as being too narrow.[30] It is not sufficient to say that matter is defamatory if it brings the plaintiff into hatred, ridicule or contempt by reason of some moral

22 Below pp. 487–8.
23 *Emmens v. Pottle* (1885) 16 Q.B.D. 354.
24 *Vitzelly v. Mudie's Select Library Ltd* [1900] 2 Q.B. 170; *Sun Life Assurance Co. of Canada Ltd v. W.H. Smith* (1934) 150 L.T. 211.
24a This is an essential and truly preliminary question: *Stubbs Ltd v. Russell* [1943] A.C. 386 at 400 *per* Lord Shaw.
25 *Drummond-Jackson v. British Medical Association* [1970] 1 All E.R. 1094 at 1105 *per* Sir Gordon Willmer.
26 *Thorley v. Lord Kerry* (1812) 4 Taunt. 355 at 360 *per* Mansfield C.J.; *Parkins v. Scott* (1862) 1 H. & C. 153. But such abuse might be actionable if it causes emotional distress: see pp. 121–2.
27 However, the way the abuse is uttered may render it defamatory: *Penfold v. Westcote* (1806) 2 B. & P. (N.R.) 335; or conversely, may render something defamatory into mere abuse, as where a woman was called "a tramp" in a fit of temper: *Field v. Davis* [1955] C.L.Y. 1543. Written abuse may be defamatory: since such statements are not made in heat or anger, nor will readers appreciate the background against which such words are written.
28 Cave J. in *Scott v. Sampson* (1822) 8 Q.B.D. 491 at 503: "a false statement about a man to his discredit", quoted with approval by Scrutton L.J. in *Yousoupoff v. M-G-M* (1934) 50 T.L.R. 581 at 584.
29 [1897] A.C. 68 at 72.
30 *Drummond-Jackson v. B.M.A., supra* at 1105 *per* Sir Gordon Willmer; *Tournier v. National Provincial & Union Bank of England* [1924] 1 K.B. 461 at 477 *per* Scrutton L.J., 487 *per* Atkin L.J.

discredit on his part. It will also be defamatory if it tends to make the plaintiff be shunned and avoided, even without moral discredit on his part.[31] Hence it was possible for the Court of Appeal in *Yousoupoff v. Metro-Goldwyn-Mayer*[32] to hold that it was defamatory to say of a woman that she had been raped. This was comparable to an allegation of insanity or disease involving no moral responsibility. It is the effect of the language of the defendant upon the plaintiff's situation in society that is the essence of defamation. In this regard, as Slesser L.J. noted in the *Yousoupoff* case,[33] there can be judicial notice of loss of social reputation. The issue, as Lord Atkin explained in the subsequent case of *Sim v. Stretch*,[34] is whether the words in question would tend to lower the plaintiff in the estimation of right-thinking members of society generally. It is not necessary to establish that hatred, ridicule or contempt followed upon the publication of the defamation, as long as its effect was to diminish the standing of the plaintiff. Hence it is important to consider the person, or class of persons, whose reaction to the publication should be the test of the wrongful character of the words used.[35] In the *Yousoupoff* case the milieu in which the plaintiff moved was such that her social equals would regard her distastefully when they learned of the alleged rape by Rasputin. In *Sim v. Stretch*, however, it was not defamatory to suggest by telegram that the plaintiff had borrowed money from a domestic servant, which was an imputation that the plaintiff was in financial difficulties. Reasonable people would not think less of the plaintiff in the light of that allegation.[36]

18.09 In determining the potential effect of alleged defamatory matter, it has been said,[37] the courts have to consider the *arbitrium boni*, the view which would be taken by the ordinary good and worthy subject. The persons whose opinion of the plaintiff is important are ordinary reasonable folk, presumably, though it is not altogether clear why this should be so, of the same class, status, socio-economic group, as the plaintiff. In *Byrne v. Deane*[38] the words in question suggested that the plaintiff should be punished. Those words did not mean that the plaintiff was guilty of disloyalty to the club, nor that he had informed about a criminal offence, viz., allowing gambling, committed by the club.[39] To say of a man that he has put in motion the proper machinery for suppressing crime was a thing which could not on the face of it be defamatory.[40] The members of the golf club, in these circumstances, could not be viewed as belonging to the class of ordinary, reasonable people who would naturally and legitimately regard the plaintiff less favourably in consequence of an allegation that he

31 *Yousoupoff v. M-G-M* (1934) 50 T.L.R. 581 at 487 *per* Slesser L.J.
32 (1934) 50 T.L.R. 581.
33 *Supra* at 587 *per* Slesser L.J.
34 (1936) 52 L.T.R. 669 at 670.
35 *Drummond-Jackson v. B.M.A.*, *supra* at 1105–1106 *per* Sir Gordon Willmer.
36 This was a matter of etiquette; but if business ethics were involved the result would be different: *Angell v. Bushell & Co. Ltd* [1968] 1 Q.B. 813.
37 *Byrne v. Deane* [1937] 1 K.B. 818 at 833 *per* Slesser L.J.
38 [1937] 1 K.B. 818.
39 *Ibid.* at 834 *per* Slesser L.J.
40 *Ibid.*, at 840 *per* Greer L.J.

had merited some form of punishment because of what he had done. In contrast in *Drummond-Jackson v. British Medical Assocation*,[41] the defendants had attacked a technique of anaesthesia developed by the plaintiff for use in dentistry. The plaintiff was an experienced dental surgeon, and the article complained of related to dentistry. It was circulated to members of the profession, and clearly could affect how they viewed the plaintiff. The language in issue involved an attack on the plaintiff's professional reputation as a dentist and would have a deleterious effect upon him in the eyes of the class of persons whose reaction to the publication was to be considered.

18.10 A defamatory statement, therefore, means some statement about the plaintiff that, in the eyes of ordinary reasonable people to whom the statement is made, lowers or would naturally tend to lower their opinion of him or would cause them to shun or avoid him. The effect of the statement must be such as would, or actually does, have a harmful result so far as concerns the position of the plaintiff in normal everyday society. Thus whether matter is defamatory cannot be determined in relation to some atypical, special social background, such as a golf club, a gang of thieves, a group of psychopaths, but only insofar as it would be likely to have consequences in the context of the community at large or some segment of society that can be regarded as representative of a recognised and recognisable group within the community at large. Defamation is not to be viewed or considered against some unusual, abnormal societal background, but only in connection with, in the phrase used by Lord Atkin and quoted with approval by Sir Gordon Willmer in the *Drummond-Jackson* case, "right-minded members of society generally". The law is concerned with how the reasonable man would react to the alleged defamatory statement, not with how some person of eccentric views might respond to the allegations against the plaintiff that are in issue.[42]

18.11 However what is offensive and defamatory may depend upon the period when the alleged defamatory statement is made, as well as the social situation applicable at the material time. An allegation that can affect the reputation of another at one time and in one particular social context may not be regarded by "right-minded" people as defamatory to another time when society's views have changed with respect to the kind of allegation in question. Political, social and moral views alter with the times: and the effect of a statement must be looked at in the context of the time and place when and where it was made.[43] For example, an allegation of homosexuality against a man would certainly have been defamatory fifty years ago. In more recent times such as allegation might not have

41 [1970] 1 All E.R. 1094.

42 Cp. Lord Denning in *Drummond-Jackson v. B.M.A.*, *supra* at 1100: "Libel . . . is a lowering of the man himself in the eyes of right-thinking people generally".

43 E.g., to call a man a German in the First World War was defamatory: *Slazengers Ltd v. Gibbs & Co.* (1916) 33 T.L.R. 35; but presumably would not be today. So, too, with the allegation that the plaintiff was a Communist: *Braddock v. Bevins* [1948] 1 K.B. 380.

been.[44] With the arrival of the acquired immunity deficiency syndrome ("AIDS"), such an allegation would seem to be clearly defamatory since it might cause the party accused of homosexuality, rightly or wrongly, to be shunned or avoided by others.

18.12 The time or period when allegedly defamatory matter is published is not the only material factor. Where the publication takes place, in the sense of the precise location of what is alleged to be defamatory, may also have relevance. Thus, to put an otherwise innocent representation in wax of the plaintiff outside the "Chamber of Horrors" at a waxworks, indicating that the plaintiff, though not convicted of murder, was tantamount to a murderer, could be defamatory.[45] However a newspaper was not guilty of defamation when it published a non-defamatory article about the plaintiff in the same newspaper, although in different issues, as other articles attacking dishonest businessmen.[46] Nor was it defamatory to print an article which identified the plaintiff as Mr. X, about whom defamatory articles had appeared in other newspapers, not the one published by the defendants.[47] To put different things together in order to produce something defamatory it must be shown that a reasonable man, seeing the things together, would necessarily conclude that a defamatory allegation had been made against the plaintiff.[48]

(ii) Innuendo

18.13 A statement may be innocent on its face, but have an underlying defamatory meaning. This could be the result of the circumstances surrounding the publication of the statement, or the mode of publication itself.[49] When defamation has to be established in this manner, the plaintiff proves his case by innuendo. What he is doing is saying that a seemingly innocent statement is defamatory by implication, as a result of extrinsic facts giving words or other forms of statement a meaning which they might not have had. Innuendo is the explanation of the statement that is given by the plaintiff and alleged by him to make the statement defamatory. This implied sense of the statement must be specifically pleaded and proved by the plaintiff.[50] The test of whether the alleged implication can be made is what is reasonable in the circumstances.

44 *Contra*: *Salmond & Heuston on the Law of Torts*, 19th ed. 1987 at 158 note 45, citing *R. v. Bishop* [1975] Q.B. 274.
45 *Monson v. Tussauds Ltd* [1894] 1 Q.B. 671.
46 *Wheeler v. Sommerfield* [1966] 2 Q.B. 94.
47 *Astaire v. Campling* [1965] 3 All E.R. 666.
48 This resembles, if it is not the same as proving an innuendo: *infra*.
49 *Capital & Counties Bank v. Henty* (1882) 7 App.Cas. 741 at 771 *per* Lord Blackburn; *Tolley v. Fry & Sons Ltd* [1931] A.C. 333 at 338 *per* Lord Atkinson.
50 R.S.C. Ord. 82, r. 3: *Supreme Court Practice*, 1985, at 1185. Even if innuendo is not pleaded the plaintiff must set out in his pleadings what he alleges is the defamatory meaning borne by the statement of which he complains. The reasons for this are: (i) the defendant is entitled to know the case he has to meet and to decide whether to plead justification or fair comment, or to apologise; (ii) so that the trial can be conducted properly, by enabling the judge to rule whether the statement was reasonably capable of bearing the meaning alleged: *Allsopp v. Church of England Newspaper* [1972] 2 All E.R. 26; cp. *DDSA Pharmaceuticals Ltd v. Times Newspapers Ltd* [1973] Q.B. 21.

18.14 There are potentially separate causes of action based upon the statement and the innuendo. One cause of action arises from the defamation itself, based on whatever imputations or implications can reasonably be derived from the statement. Another, different cause of action, namely the innuendo, is based not merely on the statement itself but on an extended meaning created by conjunction of the statement with something outside it. This latter cause of action cannot come into existence unless there is some extrinsic fact to create the extended meaning.[51]

18.15 In support of the allegation of innuendo, the plaintiff must also set out particulars of the extrinsic facts on the basis of which he asserts that the innuendo can be established. Such facts must exist at the time of the publication of the alleged defamatory statement. Subsequent events cannot relate back so as to prove that the statement had the meaning which is attributed to it by the plaintiff.[52] Thus in *Capital & Counties Bank v. Henty*,[53] the fact that customers of the bank demanded the return of their deposits, causing a "run" on the bank, after the publication of the allegedly defamatory statement by the defendant that he would no longer accept payment of his bills by cheques drawn on the plaintiff bank, could not be relied on by the bank to establish the innuendo that the bank was insolvent and incapable of honouring its liabilities to customers.

18.16 In *Lewis v. Daily Telegraph Ltd*,[54] the House of Lords, following earlier indications in the Court of Appeal, explained that there was a distinction between what were termed "false" innuendoes[55] and what were "true" or "legal" innuendoes. A statement may have more than one meaning, even without reference to extrinsic circumstances.[56] It was considered at one time that such implicit meanings were also innuendoes, which could form the basis of a separate cause of action.[57] As Holroyd Pearce L.J. said in *Grubb v. Bristol United Press Ltd*:[57a]

51 *Grubb v. Bristol United Press Ltd* [1962] 2 All E.R. 380 at 390 *per* Holroyd Pearce L.J.; *Fullam v. Newcastle Chronicle & Journal Ltd* [1977] 3 All E.R. 32 at 35 *per* Lord Denning; *Grappelli v. Derek Block (Holdings) Ltd* [1981] 2 All E.R. 272 at 274 *per* Lord Denning. Even if the defendant was ignorant of the facts: *Cassidy v. Daily Mirror Newspapers Ltd* [1929] 2 K.B. 331; *Tolley v. Fry & Sons Ltd* [1931] A.C. 333. If the plaintiff does not plead an innuendo, he can only rely on the natural and ordinary meaning of the words, and the jury are entitled to put their own meaning on the words; so they are entitled to look at the whole article, including parts omitted by the plaintiff: *S. & K. Holdings Ltd v. Throgmorton* [1972] 2 All E.R. 497.

52 *Grappelli v. Derek Block (Holdings) Ltd*, *supra* at 274–275 *per* Lord Denning, 279 *per* Dunn L.J.

53 (1882) 7 App.Cas. 741; for criticism of which see *Yousoupoff v. M-G-M* (1934) 50 T.L.R. 581 at 584 *per* Scrutton L.J.; *Slim v. Daily Telegraph Ltd* [1968] 2 Q.B. 157 at 168 *per* Salmon L.J.

54 [1963] 2 All E.R. 151.

55 Though Lord Devlin did not like the expression and preferred the term "popular" innuendo in contrast with "legal" innuendo: [1963] 2 All E.R. 151 at 170.

56 *Ibid.* at 169–170 *per* Lord Devlin; cp. Lord Denning in *Fullam v. Newcastle Chronicle & Journal Ltd* [1977] 3 All E.R. 32 at 35.

57 *Grubb v. Bristol United Press Ltd* [1962] 2 All E.R. 380 at 383–389: *Loughans v. Odhams Press Ltd* [1962] 1 All E.R. 404 at 408–409 *per* Diplock L.J.

57a [1962] 2 All E.R. 380 at 391.

> "The word 'innuendo' has given rise to confusion in that it was, and sometimes is, used in a general sense embracing not only the genuine innuendo supported by extrinsic facts but also any implication that leads to identification of the libel with the plaintiff, and, more loosely, any alleged implication of the words themselves . . . . But the genuine innuendo which provides a separate cause of action is that which alleges an extension of the meaning of the words used and it must be supported by evidence of facts extrinsic to the words themselves."

In the *Lewis* case[58] Lord Devlin explained the historical and pleading reasons why what he called "rhetorical" innuendoes developed, largely for the purpose of ensuring that the plaintiff's case was properly presented. However he and the other members of the House of Lords clarified the difference between such improperly, or colloquially, termed innuendoes and the correct legal use of the expression. The former referred to a meaning that was capable of being detected in the language used by the defendant, and was deemed part of the ordinary meaning. The latter referred to a meaning that could only be put upon words when supported by extrinsic facts. Thus there could be three distinct allegations in an action for defamation. First the defamatory words might speak for themselves. If not, a second allegation could set out those innuendoes or indirect meanings that went beyond the literal meaning of the words but were inherent in them. Thirdly, there could be a secondary meaning or legal innuendo supported by particulars as required under the Rules of the Supreme Court.[59]

18.17 However if there are several possible inferences to be drawn from a statement that is the subject of an action, it is not legitimate to seize upon the defamatory interpretation to the exclusion of the others.[60] The test, as Lord Selborne said in *Capital & Counties Bank v. Henty*,[61] "is whether under the circumstances in which the writing was published reasonable men to whom the publication was made would be likely to understand it in a libellous sense." Defamatory meanings should not be given by inventing facts.[62] Hence the words in the *Henty* case were not defamatory. Nor was the statement that the plaintiff's agency at the defendant's office had been closed by the directors in *Nevill v. Fine Art & General Insurance Co.*[63] Nor was the statement that the plaintiff had borrowed money from a domestic servant in *Sim v. Stretch*.[64] However in *Stubbs v. Mazure*,[65] the false publication of the plaintiff's name in a weekly list of persons against whom decrees had been made *in absentia* in Small Debts Courts did mean that the plaintiff was a person lacking in credit despite a note appended to the publication saying that the decrees in such courts did not imply inability

58 *Supra* note 54 at 169–170.
59 *Ibid.* at 171.
60 *Capital & Countires Bank v. Henty* (1882) 7 App.Cas. 741 at 789–791 *per* Lord Bramwell: *Nevill v. Fine Art & General Insurance Co. Ltd* [1897] A.C. 68 at 73 *per* Lord Halsbury.
61 *Supra* at 745.
62 *Sim v. Stretch* (1936) 52 L.T.R. 669 at 672 *per* Lord Atkin.
63 *Supra.*
64 *Supra*: nor a statement that a film critic was out of touch with public taste: *Turner v. M-G-M Pictures Ltd* [1950] 1 All E.R. 449.
65 [1920] A.C. 66.

to pay. Hence the statement was defamatory. In *Lewis v. Daily Telegraph Ltd*[66] a statement in a newspaper that the London Fraud Squad was investigating the affairs of the plaintiff company and its subsidiaries did not entitle the jury to find that the statement was defamatory of the company or its chairman, who also sued. The ordinary reasonable man would not infer guilt of fraud merely from the existence of an inquiry.[67]

18.18 It may be sufficient to prove that there are persons who knew special facts capable of giving the statement a defamatory meaning.[68] It would appear that if this is the situation the plaintiff must not only plead the special meaning he attributes to the statement, but also must identify in his pleadings the person or persons who knew the special facts which enabled them to understand the innuendo. The identity of such persons is a material fact to the plaintiff's cause of action.[69]

(iii) Functions of judge and jury

18.19 Defamation actions are still open to trial by jury, unlike many other civil actions.[70] Hence it is important to make clear the distinct functions of judge and jury in such actions.

18.20 Under the Libel Act 1792,[71] the question whether a publication is or is not a libel is a matter for the jury. The jury must therefore decide whether the statement of which complaint is made was or was not defamatory. However it is for the judge to decide, as a matter of law, not fact, whether the statement is capable of bearing a defamatory meaning.[72] Hence it is possible for an appellate court to upset the verdict of the jury on the ground that the statement was incapable of bearing the defamatory meaning attributed to it in that verdict.[73] In this respect, as Lord Devlin pointed out in the *Lewis* case,[74] it is vitally necessary to identify the various meanings asserted by the plaintiff as being attributable to the statement, so that it can be clarified which meaning or meanings were left by the

66 *Supra* note 54.
67 A new trial was ordered.
68 But this might amount to defamation even if the person to whom the statement was made did not understand it in that sense or believe it; the question is whether reasonable people who knew the circumstances might understand the statement in that sense: *Hough v. London Express Newspapers Ltd* [1940] 2 K.B. 507 at 515 *per* Goddard L.J.
69 *Fullam v. Newcastle Chronicle & Journal Ltd* [1977] 3 All E.R. 32. This is especially true when the publication is limited and to a limited number of persons. There is no exception in the case of a newspaper: *Grappelli v. Derek Block (Holdings) Ltd* [1981] 2 All E.R. 272.
70 R.S.C. Ord. 33, r. 5; Supreme Court Act 1981 s. 69: *Supreme Court Practice* 1985, 520–522. However, the jury may be dispensed with if the trial would require prolonged examination of documents or accounts: *Goldsmith v. Pressdram Ltd* [1987] 3 All E.R. 485; *Viscount de l'Isle v. Times Newspapers Ltd* [1987] 3 All E.R. 499. Or if the trial involves a scientific or local investigation which cannot conveniently be made by a jury.
71 32 Geo. III, c. 60, s. 1.
72 *Capital & Counties Bank v. Henty* (1882) 7 App.Cas. 741 at 759, 762 *per* Lord Penzance; *Tolley v. Fry & Sons Ltd* [1931] A.C. 333 at 342 *per* Lord Dunedin; *Sim v. Stretch* (1936) 52 T.L.R. 669 at 670 *per* Lord Atkinson.
73 *Capital & Counties Bank v. Henty*, *supra* at 776 *per* Lord Blackburn; cp. *Lockhart v. Harrison* (1928) 44 T.L.R. 714 with *Broome v. Agar* (1928) 44 T.L.R. 339.
74 [1963] 2 All E.R. 151 at 174–175.

judge to the jury for decision as being capable of bearing a defamatory meaning. Since the judge must determine the potential legal effect of a statement, in one or all of its meanings, it is possible for the judge to withdraw a case from the jury on the ground that there is clearly no defamatory meaning, whether the statement is given its plain, ordinary everyday meaning, some legitimate innate inference, or some meaning founded on a legal innuendo.[75] Such a decision, naturally, can be the basis for an appeal, as it is a question of law not fact.[76]

(d) Reference to the plaintiff

18.21 The statement complained of must be shown to be directed at the plaintiff so as to make him the one in the public's gaze. As Lord Denning said in *Hayward v. Thompson*,[77] "... the plaintiff should be aimed at or intended by the defendant." The reference need not be express, as long as the plaintiff is the person identifiable as the person defamed. In the nineteenth century case of *Le Fanu v. Malcolmson*[78] a statement about "cruelty in some Irish factories" was referable to the plaintiff's factory although no express statement about the plaintiff was made. Lord Campbell suggested that the particular individual to whom the words applied could be pointed out by innuendo.[79] This use of innuendo, although supported by more recent decisions,[80] has been criticised, on the ground that it confuses a genuine innuendo supported by extrinsic facts, as previously explained, with "any implication that leads to identification of the libel with the plaintiff".[81] It may be strictly correct to refer to the identification as an innuendo, but particulars must be given of the facts supporting the identification: for the identification is a material fact precedent to the whole cause of action.[82] This language itself is ambivalent, like the use of the term "innuendo". What seems to be indicated is that it is unnecessary for the plaintiff to establish more than that reasonable people who know the plaintiff would take the plaintiff as the one meant by the statement in issue.[83] Lord Denning expressed the position pithily in *Hayward v. Thompson*:[84]

> "If the defendant intended to refer to the plaintiff he cannot escape liability simply by not giving his name. He may use asterisks or blanks. He may use his initials or words with a hidden meaning. He may use any other device.

75 Indeed probably he is obliged to do so, although courts will not normally dispose of a matter on an application to strike out an action: *Drummond-Jackson v. B.M.A.* [1970] 1 All E.R. 1094. But he must do so if a jury could reasonably find a defamatory meaning in the statement: *Turner v. M-G-M* [1950] 1 All E.R. 449 at 454 *per* Lord Porter: and see *Broome v. Agar, supra*.

76 *Brearley v. London & North Western Railway* (1899) 15 T.L.R. 237.

77 [1981] 3 All E.R. 450 at 457.

78 (1848) 1 H.L.C. 637.

79 *Ibid.* at 668.

80 *Hulton v. Jones* [1910] A.C. 20; *Bruce v. Odhams Press Ltd* [1936] 1 All E.R. 287; *Newstead v. London Express Newspapers Ltd* [1940] 1 K.B. 377; Symmons, "The Problem of Hidden Reference in Defamation" (1974) 3 Anglo-American L.R. 98 at 102–104.

81 *Grubb v. Bristol United Press Ltd* [1962] 2 All E.R. 380 at 391 *per* Holroyd Pearce L.J.

82 *Ibid.*

83 *Bourke v. Warren* (1826) 2 C. & P. 307 at 309 *per* Abbott C.J.

84 *Supra* note 77 at 457.

> But still, if he intended to refer to the plaintiff, he is liable . . . . The law goes further. Even if he did not aim at the plaintiff or intend to refer to him, nevertheless if he names the plaintiff in such a way that other persons will read it as intended to refer to the plaintiff, then the defendant is liable."

This is the reason why, in *Hulton & Co. v. Jones*,[85] although the defendants believed that the defamatory article was about a fictitious person, they could be liable since reasonable people took the article as referring to the plaintiff. So, too, in *Newstead v. London Express Newspapers Ltd*,[86] the defendants had in mind another Camberwell barber named Harold Newstead, not the plaintiff (who was also a barber in Camberwell with that name). The intended person was guilty of the accusation made in the newspaper; the plaintiff was not. Despite their lack of intention to defame the plaintiff, the defendants were held liable. This situation is one of those now dealt with by the provisions of the Defamation Act 1952, to which reference has been made, and of which more will be said.[86a]

18.22 The attitude adopted by the law is illustrated by *Hayward v. Thompson*.[87] The defendants, in a national newspaper, published an article which stated that the names of two or more people connected with an alleged murder plot had been given to the police, one of them being a wealthy benefactor of the Liberal Party. In a subsequent article the newspaper named the plaintiff in connection with the investigations. One issue before the Court of Appeal, after the jury had found in favour of the plaintiff, was whether the jury could look at the second article in order to establish that the defendants had identified the plaintiff as the person defamed by the first article. It was held that this was permissible. The first article was clearly defamatory. In it the defendants intended to refer to the plaintiff, although they argued that they did not know his name at that time. The second article could be admitted in evidence to prove that in first article the defendants were aiming at the plaintiff and intended to refer to him. In coming to this conclusion the court distinguished *Grappelli v. Derek Block (Holdings) Ltd*.[88] There it was held that reference could not be made to subsequent facts, occurring after the publication of the alleged defamation, in order to prove that the original publication was defamatory. Lord Denning accepted counsel's argument that this decision only related to establishing the defamatory nature of a statement. The issue of identification of the plaintiff was different.[89] As Sir George Baker explained, once it was accepted that the original article was not "innocent", but on the contrary was defamatory, it was not only possible but inevitable that those who read the second article would identify the plaintiff as the party who had been defamed in the first.[90]

85 [1909] 2 K.B. 444; [1910] A.C. 20.
86 [1940] 1 K.B. 377.
86a Para. 18.06 *supra*; para. 18.54 below.
87 [1981] 3 All E.R. 450.
88 [1981] 2 All E.R. 272.
89 *Hayward v. Thompson*, *supra* at 456.
90 *Ibid.* at 461–464.

18.23 Prior to these more recent cases an attempt was made by Lord Denning, in the Court of Appeal in *Morgan v. Odhams Press Ltd*,[91] to suggest that before an implied reference to the plaintiff could be utilised to establish that the plaintiff had been identified as the victim of defamation, there had to be "some key or pointer in the article itself indicating that it refers to the plaintiff". This was not accepted by the House of Lords.[92] Even those members of the House who dissented from the majority agreed that there was no such requirement. "What has to be decided", said Lord Reid,[93] "is whether it would have been unreasonable for a hypothetical sensible reader who knew the special facts proved to infer that this article referred to the plaintiff". Once the judge was of the opinion that a jury could come to the conclusion that reasonable readers would understand the words as referring to the plaintiff, it then became a matter of fact for the jury to decide whether some readers (knowing certain circumstances) would reasonably understand that the article referred to the plaintiff.[94] The necessity for a "key or pointer" in the publication itself referring to the plaintiff cannot be justified if extrinsic evidence is admissible to connect the plaintiff with the words of the article.[95] Just as extrinsic evidence is admissible to import a defamatory meaning to words otherwise innocent, so extrinsic evidence is admissible to connect the plaintiff with the person referred to in the article.[96] Where the plaintiff is not named or indicated in the libel he may call persons to say that in the light of their knowledge of extrinsic facts they understood the publication to be defamatory of him.[97]

18.24 In the *Morgan* case the newspaper article referred to a girl likely to be a key witness in a dog-doping scandal. The girl (M) was said to have left her lodgings at Shepherds Bush and was alleged to have been kidnapped by members of the gang when they heard she had made a statement to the police. She was kept at a house in Finchley and eventually allowed to leave. The plaintiff was not named, but M stayed at her flat in Willesden for a certain period. The plaintiff alleged that, because certain witnesses had seen her with M at a material time, she had been the subject of the article, in consequence of which the plaintiff had been defamed, since those witnesses would have been entitled to conclude that the plaintiff was a member of the gang involved in the dog-doping and the kidnapping. The jury found for the plaintiff. That decision was overturned by the Court of Appeal, which held that the case should not

91 [1970] 2 All E.R. 544 at 549; cp. *James v. Rutlech* (1599) 4 Co. Rep. 17a, 17b; *Bourke v. Warren, supra* note 80 at 110–111.
92 [1971] 2 All E.R. 1156, on the ground that it was inconsistent with *Cassidy v. Daily Mirror* [1929] 2 K.B. 331, where the defendants were liable even though they had not stated, but only inferred, that the plaintiff who was the wife of Cassidy was his mistress. In this case the plaintiff had not been named at all: any reference to her was by implication without any "key or pointer" in the article in question.
93 [1971] 2 All E.R. 1156 at 1163.
94 *Ibid.* at 1170 *per* Lord Morris.
95 *Ibid.* at 1175 *per* Lord Guest, dissenting.
96 *Ibid.*
97 *Ibid.* at 1179 *per* Lord Donovan, dissenting.

have gone to the jury. The House of Lords, by a majority, restored the original decision in favour of the plaintiff.

18.25 The effect of this decision, as is evident from the more recent cases to which reference has been made, is that the more liberal, broader interpretation of "reference to the plaintiff" in a defamatory statement has been adopted by the courts.[98]

(e) Defamation of a class

18.26 The common law does not recognise group or class defamation.[99] Only an individual, whether a natural or juristic person, can be defamed. Hence if an alleged defamatory statement is about a group of people, e.g. all the members of a named society, all the detectives in the X police force, it is not possible for those involved to sue as a group, claiming that they have been defamed collectively.[100] Any one member of the group concerned must prove that the defamation in question "referred" to him in the sense explained above. The issue in such instances is another example of "hidden" reference in cases of defamation.[101]

18.27 If the class or group is large it will not usually be possible for a plaintiff to establish the necessary connection between the defamation and himself. The allegations will be too broadly made to enable a judge to rule and a jury to decide that the words were capable of referring to the plaintiff and did refer to him. The smaller, more concentrated the class or group, the easier the task of the plaintiff, and the more likely that a conclusion in his favour will be both conceivable and reached.[102] The test is whether reasonable people would understand the plaintiff as being the object of the defamation. Can the necessary connection be made in terms of how right-thinking people would interpret the statement in question? The same general rules as to reference apply to class, as to non-class defamation. This is made abundantly clear by the House of Lords in *Knuppfer v. London Express Newspapers Ltd.*[103] There the plaintiff was unable to show that a reference to a group called "Young Russia", to which he belonged, could entail an implied, hidden reference to himself personally.

98 This is welcomed by Symmons, *loc. cit. supra* note 80 at 114, as being in step with developments in England, the U.S.A., Australia and Canada, and as simplifying at least one part of the tortuous law of defamation.

99 There has been change in some jurisdictions: see, for example, the Manitoba Defamation Act, R.S.M. 1970, c. D-20, s. 19, on which see *Courchene v. Marlborough Hotels Ltd* (1971) 20 D.L.R. (3d) 109; (1971) 22 D.L.R. (3d) 157. Furthermore the crime of seditious libel involves allegations against a group or class of citizens, although the gravamen of the offence is that it will tend to stir up hatred between different classes of subjects and cause a breach of the peace: cp. Canadian legislation on "hate propaganda": Criminal Code, R.S.C. 1985, c. 46, s. 319.

100 *A fortiori* if the allegation is of the kind "all lawyers are thieves", unless something points to a particular lawyer as being intended: *Eastwood v. Holmes* (1858) 1 F. & F. 347 at 349 *per* Willes J.: cp. *Le Fanu v. Malcolmson* (1848) 1 H.L.C. 637: above para. 18.21.

101 Symmons, *loc. cit. supra* note 80 at 107–108.

102 E.g. *Foxcroft v. Lacey* (1613) Hob. 89; *Browne v. D.C. Thomson* 1912 S.C. 359.

103 [1944] A.C. 116.

18.28 The reason why a defamation published of a large or indeterminate number of persons described by some general name generally fails to be actionable, said Lord Atkin,[104] is the difficulty of establishing that the plaintiff was, in fact, included in the defamatory statement. The habit of making unfounded generalisations "is ingrained in ill-educated or vulgar minds, or the words are occasionally intended to be a facetious exaggeration". Even so, in some cases words may be used which enable the plaintiff to prove that the words complained of were intended to be published of each member of the group, or at any rate, of himself. This latter situation arose in the Australian case of *Lee v. Wilson & Mackinnon.*[105] The defamatory statement referred to a detective named Lee in a particular police force. There were three detectives with that name in that force. It was held by the High Court of Australia that all three could sue the defendant provided that a reasonable man would understand that the allegation of bribery made by the defendant referred to each of them.[106] It is questionable whether the *Lee* case was a genuine "class" case. In *Morgan v. Odhams Press*[107] the fact that there were references to "two men", "a gang" and "Finchley" did not make the facts involve a "class" situation. What the *Lee* case shows is that in a suitable, appropriate instance the scope of the defamatory allegations may be sufficiently narrow to entitle a court to conclude that reasonable people would make the required connection between the statement and the plaintiff (even if another person not the one who sues was actually intended by the defendant).

(f) Publication

18.29 A defamatory statement must be published before it can be the subject of an action. Publication is "the making known of the defamatory matter after it has been written to some person other than the person of whom it is written".[108] For the purposes of establishing liability it does not matter how widely or narrowly the defamation is published, although this may have some effect on the damages that may be awarded to the plaintiff in light of the extent of the harm he has suffered. What is essential is that the statement be made or shown to someone other than the plaintiff.[109] A publication by the defendant to his or her spouse is not publication at common law, since husband and wife were regarded as being one person under the common law fiction of the unity of spouses.[110] Alteration of the law with respect to the inter-liability of spouses[111] may have had the effect

104 *Ibid.* at 122.
105 (1934) 51 C.L.R. 276.
106 *Ibid.* at 287–295 *per* Dixon J.
107 [1971] 2 All E.R. 1156.
108 *Pullman v. Hill & Co.* [1891] 1 Q.B. 524 at 527 *per* Lord Esher M.R. If the plaintiff consents to the publication, this may entitle the defendant to rely on the defence of *volenti non fit injuria*: *Champman v. Lord Ellesmere* [1932] 2 K.B. 431: on that defence see paras 13.05ff and 18.56.
109 *Wennhak v. Morgan* (1888) 20 Q.B.D. 635; *Powell v. Gelston* [1916] 2 K.B. 615. Though it might suffice for criminal proceedings: *R. v. Adams* (1882) 22 Q.B.D. 66.
110 *Wennhak v. Morgan, supra.*
111 By the Law Reform (Husband & Wife) Act 1962.

of making it possible to conclude that, for the purposes of the law of defamation, i.e. in relation to publication, spouses may be considered to be separate individuals. Such has been the suggestion with regard to conspiracy: prior to the new legislation husband and wife could not conspire, but this may have been changed in consequences of the alteration of the law relating to actions between spouses.[112] If this is correct with respect to conspiracy, there seems no reason why it should not also be applicable to defamation. Whatever the situation with regard to publication by the defendant to his or her spouse, publication of defamatory matter to the spouse of the party defamed will be sufficient publication for an action to be brought.[113] For this purpose, even at common law, husband and wife were distinct and different persons.[114] There would appear to be some illogicality about the common law situation. If spouses are separate where publication to the plaintiff's spouse is involved, then they ought to be separate where publication by the defendant to his or her spouse is concerned.

18.30 Since publication is the act of making "public" some defamatory matter, a person who for example writes something defamatory of another and secrets it in a drawer of a desk will not have committed actionable defamation. Even if a third party, fortuitously, comes across the matter in question and reads it, no publication will have occurred, unless it was foreseeable by the original maker of the defamatory statement that some third party would come across and read it, or, of course, if that occurrence were intended by the maker of the statement.[115] Thus if a defendant sends a defamatory letter by post in a sealed envelope, which is opened by someone other than the addressee, and the letter is read, there will be no publication by the defendant to such party.[116] However if defamatory matter is sent on a postcard, not contained in a sealed envelope, there is a presumption that unauthorised persons will read what is written on the postcard.[117] In some situations it may even be foreseeable as a natural and probable consequence that someone other than the addressee of a sealed envelope will open it and read the contents. In *Theaker v. Richardson*[118] this was the situation with regard to the husband of the plaintiff, to whom the defamatory letter had been addressed.

112 *Midland Bank Trust Co. v. Green (No. 1)* [1979] 3 All E.R. 28 at 35 *per* Lord Denning: reversed on other grounds [1981] A.C. 513 H.L.
113 *Wenman v. Ash* (1853) 13 C.B. 836. Hence there is publication if a natural and probable consequence of the defendant's conduct was that the plaintiff's spouse would hear or read the defamatory statement, e.g. by opening and reading a letter that was defamatory of the plaintiff: *Theaker v. Richardson* [1962] 1 All E.R. 229.
114 *Wenman v. Ash, supra* at 844–845 *per* Maule J.
115 *Weld-Blundell v. Stephens* [1920] A.C. 956. So if the defendant was careless as to whether a statement made to the plaintiff himself would be overheard by others, and it was, publication would have taken place even though only the plaintiff was the intended and obvious recipient of the defamation. *Aliter* if the presence of a third party was unknown and unforeseen: cp. Sheridan, *School for Scandal*, Act IV, scene 3.
116 *Huth v. Huth* [1915] 3 K.B. 32.
117 *Ibid.* at 41 *per* Lord Reading C.J.
118 [1962] 1 All E.R. 229.

18.31 In *Riddick v. Thames Board Mills Ltd*[119] the Court of Appeal had to consider another aspect of the problem of publication. If one member of a corporation publishes defamatory matter about a plaintiff to another member of the corporation, the question arises whether, in fact, there has been any publication, since the situation may be said to resemble what occurs when a defendant speaks or writes to himself, and no one else hears or reads what is said. That was the conclusion of Lord Denning where a defamatory memorandum was authorised to be written and to be sent to specific officers of a corporation of which the plaintiff was an employee. The memorandum concerned the behaviour of the plaintiff as an employee. Applying the law of master and servant,[120] Lord Denning held that the act of one servant in making the report was the act of the master and the act of the other servant in receiving and reading it was also the act of the master. So the master had published to himself. "No one can be made liable for a libel published only to himself, any more than a man is liable for writing a defamatory letter and keeping it in his desk, showing it to no one."[121] The other members of the court disagreed, although coming to the same conclusion as Lord Denning on the basis of the defence of qualified privilege.[122]

18.32 If a publication is privileged, then publication of a defamatory statement may not be actionable.[123] However it is clear that, to rely on that defence, the defendant must not publish the statement to others except those to whom the publication will be privileged.[124] If he intends a wider audience or public, he will no longer be protected by privilege. If he did not have such an intention but the defamatory matter is read by someone in respect of whom its publication was not privileged, the defendant will not be liable: this will not amount to publication. Such will be the situation where the intervention by a third party was unforeseen and unexpected, as where a letter was addressed to the business office of the plaintiff (the only address known to the defendant) and the letter was opened and read by the plaintiff's partner and a clerk in the firm.[125] In *Pullman v. Hill & Co.*,[126] however, a defamatory letter was dictated by the defendant to a shorthand typist clerk and the letter was read by the plaintiff's employees in the ordinary course of business. This was a publication and it did not come within the scope of privilege.[127] However if dictating a letter is a normal mode of conducting business, then such dictation to a typist, clerk or similar employee may not be publication that

119 [1977] 3 All E.R. 677.
120 Pp. 46–64.
121 *Supra* note 119 at 685.
122 *Ibid.* at 691–692 *per* Stephenson L.J., 698–699 *per* Waller L.J.
123 Below paras 18.71ff.
124 *Powell v. Gelston* [1916] 2 K.B. 615.
125 *Sharp v. Slues* (1909) 25 T.L.R. 336.
126 [1891] 1 Q.B. 524.
127 Cp. *Boxsius v. Goblet Frères* [1894] 1 Q.B. 842: *Bryanston Finance Ltd v. de Vries* [1975] Q.B. 703.

will support an action i.e. will be privileged.[128] However it seems to be concluded that publication, albeit privileged, occurs in such instances. Hence the reasoning of Lord Denning in the *Riddick* case may be contrary to such decisions.

18.33 If the identity of the plaintiff remains concealed in the statement, and is not discoverable in any way internally to the statement or extrinsically by the addition of facts known, or knowable by the reasonable person who would be expected to read or hear the statement, there is no publication for the purposes of liability, however open the manner in which the statement is conveyed or communicated. In *Sadgrove v. Hole*,[129] for example, there was no name mentioned on the postcard: hence a reader of the postcard could not associate the defamatory statement thereon with the plaintiff. No publication of a defamatory statement occurred.

18.34 Failure to remove a defamatory statement, even though such statement was not originally made public by the defendant, may be publication.[130] Thus if something defamatory of the plaintiff is carved or painted on a wall, or a defamatory statement is written by X and affixed to a wall, the defendant who owns the wall, and was not the maker of the statement in the first place, will be liable for the publication of the statement where he could have done something to remove the offensive matter and failed to do so.[131] The test seems to be one of responsibility for the continued presence of the offensive statement, in much the same way as an occupier of land on which someone has done something amounting to a nuisance may be liable to a plaintiff affected by the nuisance if the occupier could have abated the nuisance but unreasonably failed to do so.[132] He has made the nuisance his own. Similarly, a defendant who does not remove or eradicate a defamatory publication when he could do so, may be considered to have published the statement by a process of adoption or continuation.

18.35 Publication occurs not only when the original producer of a defamatory statement makes it known to a third party or third parties. Everyone who repeats, distributes or disseminates a defamation is guilty of publishing a defamatory statement.[132a] Where this is done knowingly, i.e. with knowledge that the statement is defamatory, no problems arise. Even

128 *Osborn v. Thomas Boulter & Son* [1930] 2 K.B. 226, where the issue was raised, but not determined, whether if this was publication it would be of a libel or a slander. See also *Edmondson v. Birch & Co. Ltd* [1907] 1 K.B. 371: *Roff v. British & French Chemical Manufacturing Co.* [1918] 2 K.B. 677.

129 [1901] 2 K.B. 1.

130 *Byrne v. Deane* [1937] 1 K.B. 818 at 829–830 *per* Greer L.J.: to the contrary Slesser L.J. at 834–836.

131 *Ibid.* at 838 *per* Greene L.J.

132 Paras 8.37ff. *supra*.

132a *"Truth" (N.Z.) Ltd v. Holloway* [1960] 1 W.L.R. 997; *Cutler v. McPhail* [1962] 2 Q.B. 292. Hence every such act is a further publication and creates a separate, fresh cause of action: on consolidation of such actions see Law of Libel Amendment Act, 1881, s. 5: Defamation Act 1952 s. 13.

if defamation was unintended, there will be liability, on general principles, in the absence of any defence under the Defamation Act 1952.[133] If the statement is published in the sense of disseminated or distributed, by someone who is ignorant that what he is distributing contains something defamatory, the situation is more complex. This may occur when the defendant sells or lends a newspaper or book which contains defamatory matter of the existence of which the defendant is ignorant. A distinction is drawn between those who publish a defamation and those who merely distribute it. The former include the printers and proprietors of a newspaper containing something defamatory of the plaintiff written by a contributor to the newspaper such as a journalist or the writer of a letter to the editor.[134] The latter are exemplified by newsvendors.

18.36 In *Emmens v. Pottle*[135] a newsvendor was not liable for a libel contained in newspapers that he sold from his shop or stand, in the absence of proof that he actually knew the papers contained the libel. Innocence is thus a good defence in such cases. But negligence will destroy a plea of innocence. Hence if the defendant ought as a reasonable man to have ensured that what he distributed did not contain defamatory matter, he would be liable even though he were ignorant of the existence of such matter in what he distributed.[135a] In *Vitzelly v. Mudie's Select Library Ltd*,[136] the proprietor of a circulating library failed to disprove negligence in not knowing that a book in his library contained matter defamatory to the plaintiff. He was liable for publication of a libel. Similarly in *Sun Life Assurance Co. of Canada Ltd v. W.H. Smith Ltd*[137] the defendants, newsvendors and booksellers, displayed a poster containing a libel on the plaintiff. The defendants were negligent in not putting the poster away out of sight of the public once they knew of the circumstances. In this instance, however, the defendants' liability might have been based more on failure to remove something defamatory put on the defendant's property by a third party than on negligence in not ensuring that something disseminated by the defendant was not defamatory.

3. LIBEL AND SLANDER

(a) Nature of the distinction

18.37 There are two kinds or types of defamation, the distinction between which is of practical importance. They are libel and slander. There appears to be no convincing explanation for so irrational a matter

133 Above para. 18.21; below para. 18.54.
134 *Lyon v. Daily Telegraph Ltd* [1943] K.B. 746; *Chernesky v. Armadale Publications Ltd* [1979] 1 S.C.R. 1067.
135 (1885) 16 Q.B.D. 354.
135a On onus of proof see the remarks of Lord Denning, *obiter*, in *Goldsmith v. Sperrings Ltd* [1977] 2 All E.R. 566 at 572–573.
136 [1900] 2 Q.B. 170, especially at 180 *per* Romer L.J.; *Bottomley v. F.W. Woolworth Ltd* (1932) 48 T.L.R. 521.
137 (1934) 150 L.T. 211.

as the distinction between these two forms or varieties of defamation,[138] although various attempts have been made to find one.[139] Indeed it was said by an Australian judge[140] that there was no discernible principle underlying the distinction. Yet it undoubtedly exists and continues to have vital consequences in the law. Whatever the historical origins of the difference, the idea lying at the root of the distinction, said Lord Herschell in 1892,[141] was that it would never do to permit actions to be brought in respect of every word spoken which might reflect on the character or conduct of another.

18.38 The difference seems to be in the permanence of the defamatory matter.[142] A defamatory statement that is permanent in form will be a libel. One that is transient will be slander. A libel, however, need not be in writing, although, most frequently it is. In *Monson v. Tussauds Ltd*[143] the libellous statement was in the form of an effigy of the plaintiff placed in a room adjoining the "Chamber of Horrors", the implication from this juxtaposition being that the plaintiff, although obtaining a verdict of "Not proven" from a Scottish jury, was nevertheless guilty of murder with which he had been charged. Slander is usually committed through the spoken word, or by the making of a gesture that conveys a defamatory meaning. Skywriting, for example, would probably amount to slander, as would writing a defamatory statement with "invisible" ink that appeared only when treated in a certain way and then disappeared within a short time.

18.39 Difficulties have arisen where there is a transitory representation of a permanent form, for example, where the defendant reads a defamatory letter aloud, without allowing others to read the letter for themselves. The written letter would be a libel, if published by letting someone else read it. But the actual defamation is spoken, not read. Hence it is a debatable matter whether the defamation is libel or slander.[143a] The same situation would occur if the defamatory matter were recorded on a gramophone record, or compact disc, but the defamation only became public when the record or disc were played, which would entail the hearing of the words

138 Kaye, "Libel and Slander—Two Torts or One?" (1975) 91 L.Q.R. 524 at 524.
139 Fisher, "A Chapter in the history of the law of libel" (1894) 10 L.Q.R. 158; Carr, "The English law of Defamation" (1902) 18 L.Q.R. 255, 388; Veeder, "The History of the law of Defamation" in *Select Essays in Anglo-American Legal History*, 1900, vol. iii, 446; Holdsworth, "Defamation in the Sixteenth and Seventeenth Centuries" (1924) 40 L.Q.R. 302, (1925) 41 L.Q.R. 31; Holdsworth, *A History of English Law*, 2nd ed. 1937, vol. viii, 361–367; Donnelly, "History of Defamation" [1949] Wisconsin L.R. 99; Fifoot, *History & Sources of the Common Law*, 132–133; Milsom, *Historical Foundations of the Common Law*, 1969, 343–344; Kaye, *loc. cit. supra*.
140 Mann J. in *Meldrum v. Australian Broadcasting Commission* [1932] Argus L.R. 432 at 436.
141 *Alexander v. Jenkins* [1892] 1 Q.B. 797 at 800.
142 *De Libellis Famosis* (1605) 5 Co. Rep. 125a; *King v. Lake* (1668) Hardr. 470; *Thorley v. Lord Kerry* (1812) 4 Taunt. 355; cp. *Mingey v. Moodie* and *Bolton v. Deane*, cited in *Austin v. Culpeper* (1683) 2 Show. K.B. 313.
143 [1894] 1 Q.B. 671: above para. 18.12.
143a *Hebditch v. MacIlwaine* [1894] 2 Q.B. 54 at 58; *Osborn v. Thomas Boulter & Son* [1930] 2 K.B. 226 at 231 *per* Scrutton L.J., 237 *per* Slesser L.J. (slander), 236 *per* Greer L.J. (libel).

not their communication in some permanent form. In *Yousoupoff v. M.G.M.*[144] the Court of Appeal assumed, without having to decide, since an allegation of unchastity against a woman was involved,[145] that where defamation was contained in a "talking" film, libel, not slander, was the appropriate tort. Slesser L.J. did suggest that the spoken words of the dialogue were part of the circumstances and surroundings in which the picture was exhibited, therefore were part of the permanent material.[146] On the other hand, reading a defamatory script over the wireless was publication of slander not libel, according to an Australian decision.[147] But this conflicts with other, English authority to the effect that even though the words are read, libel may have been committed as long as other people could have read the defamatory matter for themselves.[148] The test would seem to be, therefore, whether notionally it was possible for the defamation to have been published in a permanent form to other people, in other words they knew it was permanent though revealed through the spoken word. In the case of a letter, for example, this would be the situation, since the letter could be passed to those to whom it was read. With a record or compact disc, or a broadcast script, on the other hand, it would not be possible or likely that others to whom the contents were revealed orally or in a transitory manner would be able to have the defamatory material in a more permanent form.

18.40 The problem of broadcasting through radio and television was of such importance that it has been dealt with by statute. Some jurisdictions have made the whole question otiose, by considering all forms of publication of defamatory matter as defamation, without any distinction between libel and slander.[149] In England the difference has been maintained.[150] However the broadcasting of words by means of wireless telegraphy is treated as publication in permanent form, for the purposes of the law of libel and slander.[151] So will the publication of words in the course of a programme included in a cable programme service.[152] So, too, will the publication of words in the course of performance of a play.[153]

(b) Its effect

(i) Criminal law

18.41 One difference between libel and slander does not relate to liability in tort but to the criminal law. The crime of libel is not committed

144 (1934) 50 T.L.R. 581: above para. 18.08.
145 Below para. 18.50.
146 *Supra* note 144 at 587.
147 *Meldrum v. Australian Broadcasting Commission*, *supra* note 140.
148 *Fawcett v. Tyrrell* (1893) 9 T.L.R. 257.
149 Australia in some States: Fleming, *Law of Torts*, 7th ed. 1987 at 520 footnote 94; Canada, in Alberta, Manitoba, New Brunswick and Prince Edward Island; and New Zealand.
150 Despite recommendations to the contrary by the Faulks *Committee on Defamation*, Cmnd. 5909, 1975, Chapter 2.
151 Defamation Act 1952 s. 1. But some defences are available: *ibid.* s. 9: below paras. 18.75, 18.78 and 18.92.
152 Cable and Broadcasting Act 1984 s. 28(1).
153 Theatres Act 1968 s. 4(1), subject to certain exceptions: *ibid.* s. 7.

where defamatory words are spoken, or otherwise published in a transitory form. However spoken words may have consequences in the criminal law. If sufficiently objectionable they may result in guilt of minor offences involving insulting behaviour.[154] If the words would tend to cause hatred of the Crown, the government or the constitution, or to excite subjects to overthrow society, or produce feelings of ill-will between different classes of subjects, they may constitute sedition.[155] At one time it was considered that a criminal libel could only be committed if the defamatory words used by the defendant of the complainant were such as would tend to provoke a breach of the peace. It was not the insult or attack on the complainant's character that was the gravamen of the offence, but the likelihood that some disturbance that would offend the public might occur in consequence.[156] That has now been accepted as being outmoded.[157] A criminal libel must be a serious libel.[158] All libels have the tendency to create animosities and to disturb the public peace.[159] The essential feature of a criminal libel is the publication of a grave, not trivial libel.[160] In this context the important issue is whether there is sufficient public interest in the publication to warrant a prosecution rather than a civil action for damages.[161] This aspect of criminal libel is emphasised, according to the House of Lords in *Gleaves v. Deakin*,[162] by the fact that, in criminal libel, it is not enough for the defendant to plead and prove by way of defence that the statement he made was true; he must also show that publication was for the public benefit.[163] In this respect the crime of libel significantly differs from the tort.[164]

(ii) Law of torts

18.42 *(1) Proof of damage.* From the standpoint of civil liability, the difference between libel and slander is important in that libels are actionable *per se*, without proof of special damage, whereas slanders are

154 Public Order Act 1986 s. 4.
155 Stephen, *Digest of Criminal Law*, 2nd ed. Art. 93; *R. v. Burns* (1886) 16 Cox C.C. 335.
156 *R. v. Holbrook* (1878) 4 Q.B.D. 42; *R. v. Labouchere* (1884) 12 Q.B.D. 320; *R. v. Adams* (1884) 22 Q.B.D. 66; *R. v. Deverell* (1889) 86 L.T. Jo. 300.
157 *R. v. Wicks* [1936] 1 All E.R. 384; *Goldsmith v. Pressdram Ltd* [1977] 2 All E.R. 557; *Goldsmith v. Sperrings Ltd* [1977] 2 All E.R. 566.
158 *Gleaves v. Deakin* [1979] 2 All E.R. 497 at 502 *per* Viscount Dilhorne.
159 *Blackstone's Commentaries*, 16th ed. 1825, vol. iv. at 150–151, para. 13, quoted by Wien J. in *Goldsmith v. Pressdram, supra* at 560; and see *Gleaves v. Deakin, supra* at 508 *per* Lord Scarman.
160 *Gleaves v. Deakin, supra* at 509 *per* Lord Scarman.
161 *Ibid.* at 501 *per* Lord Dilhorne, 505 *per* Lord Edmund-Davies, 508 *per* Lord Scarman.
162 [1979] 2 All E.R. 497.
163 Libel Act 1843 s. 6; and see Newspaper Libel & Registration Act 1881 s. 4, dealing with newspapers, providing that on committal proceedings magistrates may receive evidence as to truth, public benefit and other matters of defence and may dismiss the case if of opinion that a jury would very probably acquit. Criminal libels are now triable on indictment: Criminal Law Act 1977 s. 65 and Sch. 13, repealing s. 5 of the 1881 Act. In *Gleaves v. Deakin* the House of Lords thought that prosecutions for criminal libel should not be brought without the leave of the Attorney-General or the Director of Public Prosecutions.
164 Below pp. 489–91.

only actionable if some special damage is proved to have occurred (except in certain instances).[165]

18.43 "Special damage" in this context means the loss of some definite material advantage, some financial loss actually proved in court.[166] In the language of Coleridge C.J. in *Chamberlain v. Boyd*,[167] "where words spoken . . . are not actionable in themselves they can become actionable only when they have been followed by pecuniary or temporal damage." In that particular case the publication of slander against the defendant resulted in the latter's being kept out of a club. This was not special damage (nor was it the direct result of the words spoken of the plaintiff). In *Lynch v. Knight*,[168] where the House of Lords seem to have decided the case on the issue of remoteness of damage, a husband's loss of consortium as a consequence of slanderous words was not special damage entitling him to bring an action. Nor was the loss of the company of neighbours by reason of allegations of unchastity in *Roberts v. Roberts*;[169] nor the subsequent illness of a wife, and its resultant expense to the husband, in consequence of allegations of adultery, in *Allsop v. Allsop*.[170] However where the plaintiff lost the hospitality of friends because of slanderous words spoken of him, it was held in *Davies v. Solomon*[171] that the friends' refusal to provide the plaintiff with meals did amount to special damage: it was "temporal loss".

18.44 Some of these decisions are not as persuasive or as clear as might be thought at first sight. Cases involving allegations of unchastity against women have now been dealt with by statute;[172] hence the authority of earlier decisions dealing with such allegations is open to question. Secondly, it has always been stressed that the special damage that is of concern to the law must be the direct result, not merely a possible risk, of the spoken words.[173] This has been expressed differently by different judges. Such loss must be the "natural or necessary result",[174] a "natural and probable consequence".[175] The consequence must be such, said Lord Wensleydale in *Lynch v. Knight*,[176] as "might fairly and reasonably have been anticipated and feared would follow from speaking the words." This language, appearing as it does in a case concerned with loss of consortium, which formerly was, but now no longer is, the basis of a possible action in

165 Below. For discussion of the historical basis on which actions for slander were allowed, see Kaye, *loc. cit. supra* note 138 at 526–528. On damages for slander, see Helmholz, "Damages in actions for slander at common law" (1987) 103 L.Q.R. 624.
166 Cp. the situation in cases of injurious falsehood or slander of title: *Ratcliffe v. Evans* [1892] 2 Q.B. 524 at 531–533; below paras. 21.54ff.
167 (1883) 11 Q.B.D. 407 at 412.
168 (1861) 9 H.L.C. 577.
169 (1864) 5 B. & S. 384.
170 (1860) 4 H. & N. 534.
171 (1871) L.R. 7 Q.B. 112.
172 Below para. 18.50.
173 *Chamberlain v. Boyd, supra* at 416 *per* Bowen L.J.
174 *Allsop v. Allsop, supra* at 539 *per* Martin B.
175 *Lynch v. Knight, supra* at 591 *per* Lord Campbell: cp. *Chamberlain v. Boyd, supra* at 414 *per* Brett L.J.
176 *Supra* at 600.

tort,[177] could be looked upon as archaic and inapplicable in more modern times, especially in view of changes in the view taken of when damage is too remote.[178]

18.45 *(2) Exceptions.* Four particular kinds of allegations will render slander actionable *per se*, without the need to prove "special damage" in the sense discussed above.[178a]

18.46 *1. Imputation of a criminal offence punishable with imprisonment.* The offence need not be one that is triable on indictment.[179] Any offence will suffice, as long as it is punishable by imprisonment, not the infliction of a fine, or the possibility of being bound over to keep the peace.[180] The words of which complaint is made must be "capable of being understood by the hearers as imputing a crime,"[181] although there is no need for the defendant to have the intention of imputing that a crime was committed. In *Marks v. Samuel*,[182] for example, words which accused the plaintiff of bringing a blackmailing action were actionable *per se*. The plaintiff was not said to have committed the crime of blackmail: but the imputation that the kind of action he brought was blackmailing in nature sufficed to lead those hearing the words to draw the conclusion that he must have acted criminally.

18.47 Where a corporation is the subject of alleged slander, it would appear that if the accusation against the corporation is of an offence that would entail imprisonment for a natural person if such a person had committed the offence, the fact that the corporation could not be imprisoned for that offence would not matter.[183] The words would be actionable *per se*. However the words must reflect upon the business character or reputation of the corporation (or its activities as a governmental corporation).[184] Words which attack personal reputation will not be actionable. An allegation of corrupt practices on the part of a corporation was

177 Pp. 294.
178 Pp. 336–44.
178a The explanation is historical. Originally all defamation had to be based on damage because the remedy was an action on the case for defamatory words when the common law absorbed the jurisdictions over defamation of ecclesiastical and local courts. But most allegations were of such a kind that damage could be and was presumed. To counteract this and reduce the number of cases, courts held that if at all possible words would be construed in a non-defamatory sense—the *mitiori sensu* rule: see *Holt v. Astrigg* (1608) Cro. Jac. 184. This rule disappeared at the end of the seventeenth century. But by then it had become accepted that, save in exceptional cases, damage had to be proved. Libels were held actionable *per se* as a result of the decision in *Thorley v. Lord Kerry* (1812) 4 Taunt. 355, interpreting the earlier decision in *King v. Lake* (1668) Hardr. 470, which really dealt with the character of the particular libel in that case but was understood to apply to all written defamation: Kaye, *loc. cit. supra* note 138.
179 *Webb v. Beavan* (1883) 11 Q.B.D. 609.
180 *Hellwig v. Mitchell* [1910] 1 K.B. 609.
181 *Marks v. Samuel* [1904] 2 K.B. 287 at 290 *per* Vaughan Williams L.J.
182 *Supra.*
183 *D. & L. Caterers Ltd v. D'Ajou* [1945] K.B. 210 at 213 per Slade J.: the point was left open by the Court of Appeal: [1945] K.B. 364.
184 Above p. 462.

therefore not actionable *per se*, because only the members of the corporation, not the corporation itself, could be guilty of corrupt practices.[185]

18.48 It is not clear whether the basis for making such allegations actionable *per se* is the social ostracism that would tend to follow from such statements[186] or the fact that an allegation of such crimes might jeopardise the plaintiff and possibly result in his being charged with the offence and running the risk of conviction and imprisonment.[187] In *Gray v. Jones*,[188] the allegation was that the plaintiff was a convicted man, i.e. that he had already served his sentence and was no longer liable to be imprisoned. Atkinson J. held that this was actionable *per se*, without the need to prove special damage. This seems a questionable decision. The obloquy that follows the making of such an allegation would be more relevant to the defamatory nature of the statement than to its effect. The learned judge made a comparison with the situation where slanderous words impute certain diseases, where the basis for holding that such words are actionable *per se* is the social ostracism that would tend to follow. However this is a separate category of slander actionable without proof of special damage, and there is no logical or practical reason why the accepted basis for permitting actionability without proof of special damage in one instance should be the same as in another.

18.49 *2. Imputation of a contagious or infectious disease.* It is by no means clear what kind of disease is intended in this context. No doubt allegations that a plaintiff is suffering from a venereal disease are actionable *per se*.[189] The same would seem likely to be true today where an allegation of "AIDS" is involved. However, imputations that the plaintiff is suffering from other, non-venereal but infectious or contagious diseases might also come within the scope of this exception.[190] If the basis for allowing liability without proof of special damage in these cases is that the allegation would result in social ostracism, which necessarily involves a presumption that damage will be suffered by the plaintiff, there is no logical reason for differentiating non-venereal from venereal diseases, as long as both kinds may be communicated by contact of some sort with the plaintiff.

18.50 *3. Imputation of unchastity to a woman.* Prior to 1891 an allegation of unchastity against a woman, for example by indicating that a married

185 *Mayor of Manchester v. Williams* [1891] 1 Q.B. 94. But see *Bognor Regis U.D.C. v. Campion* [1975] 2 All E.R. 61, above pp. 27–8, where it was said that *Williams* had been overruled. Cp. above p. 462.

186 *Gray v. Jones* [1939] 1 All E.R. 798.

187 *Carslake v. Mapledoram* (1788) 2 T.R. 473 at 474 *per* Ashhurst J.

188 *Supra*: cp. *Fowler v. Dowdney* (1838) 2 Moo. & Rob. 119; see also *Gainsford v. Tuke* (1619) Cro. Jac. 536; *Boston v. Tatam* (1621) Cro. Jac. 623; *Heming v. Power* (1842) 10 M. & W. 564.

189 *Bloodworth v. Gray* (1844) 7 Man. & Gr. 334: in olden times this also included plague and leprosy.

190 Older cases to the contrary may be regarded as turning upon archaic principles of liability such as the *mitiori sensu* rule, above note 178a: viz. *James v. Rutlech* (1599) 4 Co. Rep. 17a; *Villers v. Monsley* (1769) 2 Wils. 400: see Kaye, *loc. cit. supra* note 138 at 536–538.

woman had committed adultery, was not actionable unless it was in writing or gave rise to special damage. Sir Frederick Pollock criticised this state of the law, saying that the law had gone wrong from the beginning in making the damage and not the insult the cause of action. It is still true in respect of men that slanderous allegations of unchastity, such as the commission of adultery by a married man, will not be actionable unless special damage is proved.[191] The situation of women was altered by the Slander of Women Act 1891,[192] by virtue of which special damage is not required before an action may be maintained in cases where words imputing unchastity or adultery to a woman or girl are spoken and published. However in such actions the plaintiff may not recover more costs than damages unless the judge certifies that there was a reasonable ground for bringing the action. It has been held that to impute lesbianism to a plaintiff is an allegation of unchastity which brings the case within the statute.[193]

18.51 *4. Imputation against the fitness of the plaintiff in his profession, office or business.* This refers to "words spoken of a person following a calling and spoken of him in that calling, which impute to him unfitness for or in that calling."[194] There is no need to show that the office is one of profit, i.e. one in respect of which the plaintiff is paid. In such instances, however, the allegation must be of conduct that would justify the removal of the plaintiff from that office.[195] If the office in question is an office of profit, "the mere imputation of wan't of ability to discharge the duties of that office is sufficient".[196]

18.52 At common law there had to be something said of the plaintiff in the office or business that would damage him; or something which related to some quality that would show he was incapable by reason of want of ability or honesty of being fit to hold the office or carry on the trade, business or profession. The basis of liability *per se* was the law's presumption of the probability of pecuniary loss arising from such an imputation. In *Jones v. Jones*,[197] for example, words imputing adultery to a schoolmaster, even though the adultery was alleged to have been committed with a worker at the school, were not actionable *per se* because they had nothing to do with his performance as a schoolmaster (and were not otherwise actionable *per se* since they involved an imputation of adultery or unchastity against a man, not a woman). In *Hopwood v. Muirson*[198] words that alleged that the plaintiff, a solicitor, was "a pimp", that his reference was "worthless" and that "his very calling as a solicitor makes

191 *Jones v. Jones* [1916] 2 A.C. 481.
192 54 & 55 Vict. c. 51, s. 1.
193 *Kerr v. Kennedy* [1942] 1 K.B. 409: *quaere* whether this would still be the same today, i.e. whether this might impute "unchastity" to a woman.
194 *Jones v. Jones, supra* at 500 *per* Lord Sumner.
195 *Alexander v. Jenkins* [1892] 1 Q.B. 797. But a duty must be distinguished from an office, e.g. firewatching during the second World War: *Cleghorn v. Sadler* [1945] K.B. 325.
196 *Alexander v. Jenkins, supra* at 800 *per* Lord Hershell.
197 *Supra.*
198 [1945] K.B. 313; cp. *Doyley v. Roberts* (1837) 3 Bing. N.C. 835.

him write whatever suits his client best" were spoken of the plaintiff as a man, not in respect of his profession. Therefore they were not actionable *per se*. But in *Bull v. Vazquez*[199] the plaintiff, who was an M.P. and a soldier, complained of words spoken during the war that reflected on his conduct, i.e. his reason for being in England not abroad. They were actionable *per se* because they were spoken of him in relation to his profession as a soldier, not in his capacity as an M.P.

18.53 Because of the difficulties that accompanied establishing the application of this exception to the general rule in slander cases, the law was changed in 1952. Under the Defamation Act, section 2 the task of a plaintiff is no longer as difficult as it used to be:

> "In an action for slander in respect of words calculated to disparage the plaintiff in any office, profession, calling, trade, or business held or carried on by him at the time of the publication, it shall not be necessary to allege or prove special damage, whether or not the words are spoken of the plaintiff in the way of his office, profession, calling, trade or business."

Had this provision been part of the law at an earlier date, it is possible that decisions in cases such as *Jones v. Jones* and *Hopwood v. Muirson* might have been different. However, when an office of honor not profit is involved it is still necessary for the words to impute some want of integrity, or corrupt or dishonest conduct in the discharge of the office.[200] Moreover, in *Bridgman v. Stockdale*[201] it was held, after the Act, that words alleging cheating in an examination to qualify for a professional position were not said of the plaintiff in the way of his profession or business. He had not yet become a member of the profession.

4. DEFENCES

(a) Unintentional defamation

18.54 Although in general a defendant's lack of any intention to defame is irrelevant to his liability for libel or slander,[202] under the Defamation Act 1952 section 4, there is the possibility of relying on such lack of intention, provided that the circumstances come within the scope of the provision. To come within the scope of this defence, the following requirements must be satisfied:

(a) The defamation must be published "innocently".[203] This means that the publisher did not intend to publish the defamatory words of and concerning the plaintiff; and did not know of circumstances by virtue of which the words might be understood to refer to him[204] (which deals with the *Hulton v. Jones*[205] type of situation); or the words were not defamatory

199 [1947] 1 All E.R. 334.
200 *Robinson v. Ward* (1958) 108 L.J. 491.
201 [1953] 1 All E.R. 1166.
202 Above paras. 18.05–06.
203 Defamation Act 1952 s. 4(1).
204 *Ibid.* s. 4(5)(a).
205 [1910] A.C. 20: above para. 18.21.

on their face and the publisher did not know of circumstances by virtue of which they might be understood to be defamatory of the plaintiff[206] (which deals with the situation that arose in *Cassidy v. Daily Mirror Newspapers Ltd*,[207] and *Newstead v. London Express Newspapers*).[208]

(b) The publisher, his servants or agents concerned with the publication must have exercised reasonable care in relation to the publication.[209]

(c) The publisher must make an "offer of amends".[210] Such an offer must be made for the purposes of the Act and must be accompanied by an affidavit specifying the facts which indicate the innocence of the publication.[211] The offer must be to publish or join in the publication of a suitable correction of the words complained of and a sufficient apology to the plaintiff.[212]

(d) If the offer is accepted and duly performed, the plaintiff who accepts the offer can no longer sue or continue to sue for libel or slander the party who makes the offer in question. He may still sue anyone else responsible for the publication who has not made such an offer of amends.[213]

(e) If the offer is not accepted by the plaintiff, then the publisher who has made the offer of amends can prove, by way of defence to an action for libel or slander brought by the plaintiff, that the words were published "innocently" in relation to the plaintiff (in the sense previously explained); that the offer was made as soon as practicable after the defendant received notice that the words were or might be defamatory of the plaintiff; and that the offer has not been withdrawn.[214]

Where the publisher is not the author of the words, then, to take advantage of this defence, he must also prove that the words were written by the author without malice.[215] This would appear to concern most specifically the printer and publisher of a newspaper. It might be difficult for such parties to establish that the author of a letter to the editor, for example, was writing without malice. However the onus is clearly on them in such instances.

18.55 Where this defence is relied on by a publisher, the only evidence admissible to prove that the words were published innocently are the facts set out in the affidavit accompanying the offer of amends as they relate to the innocence of the publication.[216]

206 Defamation Act 1952 s. 4(5)(b).
207 [1929] 2 K.B. 331: above para. 18.23.
208 [1940] 1 K.B. 377: above para. 18.21.
209 Defamation Act 1952 s. 4(5).
210 *Ibid.* s. 4(1).
211 *Ibid.* s. 4(2).
212 *Ibid.* s. 4(3)(a); and where copies of a document or record containing the defamatory words have been distributed by or with the knowledge of the defendant making the offer, the offer must include an offer to take reasonably practicable steps to notify those to whom the offending statement has been distributed that the words are alleged to be defamatory of the plaintiff: *ibid.* s. 4(3)(b).
213 *Ibid.* s. 4(1)(a). As to the questions of fulfilment of the offer and costs, see *ibid.* s. 4(4)(a)(b).
214 *Ibid.* s. 4(1)(b).
215 *Ibid.* s. 4(6).
216 *Ibid.* s. 4(2).

(b) Consent

18.56 The plaintiff may assent to the publication of a defamatory statement about him. If he does so, then the defendant can rely on the defence of *volenti non fit injuria*,[217] as he may in other situations where a plaintiff has consented to being injured or to run the risk of injury at the hands of the defendant.[218] Consent must not be confused with a plea of privilege.[219] The former arises by agreement between the parties, the latter as a matter of law, and the parties cannot agree to confer any privilege upon the defendant.[220]

18.57 It was held in *Cookson v. Harewood*[221] that such assent by the plaintiff can be implied as well as express, and can relate not only to the obvious meaning of words published as a result of such consent but also to innuendoes which arise from that publication. There the plaintiff had submitted to the rules of the Pony Turf Club, controlled by the defendants. One rule was that the stewards could warn off any person at their absolute discretion. This might result from negligence by someone who was dealt with in this way or as a consequence of corrupt or dishonest activity. The defendants published a true statement that the plaintiff had been warned off all pony racing courses under their control. The plaintiff argued that this involved the innuendo that he had acted improperly, not merely negligently, and he had never consented to this. The Court of Appeal held that this argument was unsound. Once he submitted to the jurisdiction of the Club he was bound by what they did, even if readers of the publication put a different shade of meaning on the publication from what was expected.

(c) Justification

18.58 Truth is no libel, according to the old maxim. Therefore it is always open to the defendant to plead[221a] and prove that the words written or spoken of the plaintiff were true.[221b] At common law to justify a

217 *Chapman v. Ellesmere* [1932] All E.R. Rep. 221 at 233–234 *per* Slesser L.J.
218 Paras 13.05ff. No such consent could be implied into an employment contract in *Todd v. Eastwood* [1985] I.C.R. 135.
219 Though in *Chapman v. Ellesmere*, *supra*, some confusion seems to have taken place.
220 *Russell v. Duke of Norfolk* (1949) 65 T.L.R. 225 at 232 *per* Denning L.J.
221 [1932] 2 K.B. 478n.
221a Even, in appropriate circumstances, by a late amendment of his pleadings: *Atkinson v. Fitzwalter* [1987] 1 All E.R. 483, where the defendant was unsuccessful; see also *Prager v. Times Newspapers Ltd* [1988] 1 All E.R. 300.
221b But under the Rehabilitation of Offenders Act 1974 s. 8(5) it will not be sufficient for the defendant to prove that the plaintiff was convicted, if the conviction is "spent" under the Act. The defendant will be liable if the publication was made with malice. On malice for this purpose see *Herbage v. Pressdram Ltd* [1984] 2 All E.R. 769, below para. 18.119, which holds that it has the same meaning as in the context of qualified privilege: below para. 18.101. Defendants may also rely on the defences of fair comment and qualified privilege: Rehabilitation of Offenders Act 1974 s. 8(3). The purpose of the Act is to rehabilitate offenders by restricting or forbidding the disclosure of convictions which have been "spent: i.e. offences involving not more than 30 months' imprisonment when five to ten years (depending on the offence) have elapsed since the conviction. In a sense this is a protection of "privacy": below Chap. 19.

defamation involved proving that the words in question were substantially true without their having to be exactly true.[222] However if there was some inaccuracy in the statement that had the effect of making the statement sufficiently untrue to amount to defamation the defendant could not escape liability by arguing that what was untrue did not have a great effect upon the plaintiff's character and reputation.[223] Under the Defamation Act 1952, however, the position of defendants pleading justification has been eased.

> "In an action for libel or slander in respect of words containing two or more distinct charges against the plaintiff, a defence of justification shall not fail by reason only that the truth of every charge is not proved if the words not proved to be true do not materially injure the plaintiff's reputation having regard to the true remaining charges."[224]

The defence under this provision of the Act must be specifically pleaded.[225]

18.59 Where justification is relied upon by the defendant as a defence to libel or slander, the plea of justification must answer some meaning which a jury might put on the words in question.[226] When the defendant gives particulars of the facts on which he relies to establish his plea he can therefore include particulars which justify some part of the statement which he made on which the plaintiff is not relying to support his cause of action. Since the jury can look at the entire statement in order to determine whether the natural and ordinary meaning of the words was defamatory, the defendant is entitled to rely on the whole article in order to justify what he wrote. So, where an article was alleged to mean that the plaintiffs had been guilty of improper accountancy practices, the defendants were entitled to give particulars justifying not only the paragraphs of the article in question, on which the plaintiff relied on his statement of claim, but also of a paragraph which was not referred to by the plaintiff although it was part of the article.[227] The jury were entitled and bound to put their own meaning on the words, because the plaintiff did not plead any innuendo, despite the fact that he should have done so. For that purpose

222 *Alexander v. North Eastern Railway Co.* (1865) 6 B. & S. 340: plaintiff had been convicted of riding without payment of a fare; he was ordered to forfeit £9 in costs or face a term of imprisonment; the defendant alleged he had been ordered to pay a fine of £9 including costs or face three months' imprisonment; this was not defamatory since it was substantially true.

223 *English & Scottish Co-Operative Properties Mortgage & Investment Co. Ltd v. Odhams Press Ltd* [1940] 1 K.B. 440.

224 Defamation Act 1952 s. 5. On this see *Polly Peck (Holdings) plc v. Trelford* [1986] 2 All E.R. 84.

225 *Moore v. News of the World Ltd* [1972] 1 All E.R. 915.

226 *Waters v. Sunday Pictorial Newspapers Ltd* [1961] 2 All E.R. 758; *Cadam v. Beaverbrook Newspapers Ltd* [1959] 1 All E.R. 453. On the issue of what evidence may be introduced in support of a plea of justification, viz. other facts capable of justifying defamatory words in a wider sense than that pleaded, and on the possibility of introducing fresh evidence at a new trial, see *Williams v. Reason* [1988] 1 All E.R. 262. Note also *Bookbinder v. Tebbitt* [1989] 1 All E.R. 1169: a defence to a general charge—squandering public funds—could not stand when the alleged libel was later changed to refer to a particular charge.

227 *S. & K. Holdings Ltd v. Throgmorton Publications Ltd* [1972] 3 All E.R. 497 applied in *Polly Peck v. Trelford, supra.*

the jury were entitled to look at the whole article including the omitted paragraph, which might lead them to conclude that the article did mean that the plaintiffs were guilty of improper accountancy practices. On that meaning the particulars were certainly admissible: hence they could be pleaded.[228]

18.60 A defamatory statement may have more than one defamatory meaning.[229] If justification is relied on by the defendant he is obliged to justify each and every such meaning. As a result of the decision of the House of Lords in *Lewis v. Daily Telegraph*,[230] it has become the settled practice for a plaintiff, where the meaning of the words complained of is not clear and explicit, to plead the meanings which he says the words bear. This is to enable the defendant to know the case he has to answer. In *Lucas-Box v. News Group Newspapers Ltd*,[231] the Court of Appeal held that the reverse of the coin was also true. A defendant who pleads justification must state the meaning which he seeks to justify. "A defendant who is relying on a plea of justification must make it clear to the plaintiff what is the case which he is seeking to set up. The particulars themselves may make this quite clear, but if they are ambiguous then the situation must be made unequivocal."[232] Hence in that case the defendants were ordered to add paragraphs to their particulars of the defences of justification which they sought leave to add by amending their original defences two years after the latter were served.[232a]

(d) Fair comment

(i) Nature of the plea

18.61 By the defence of fair comment the defendant alleges not that the defamatory allegation in his statement was true but that the statement is not actionable because it amounts to what is a fair comment on a matter of public interest. As Cockburn C.J. said in *Campbell v. Spottiswode*:[233]

> "Where the public conduct of a public man is open to animadversion and the writer who is commenting upon it makes imputations which arise fairly and legitimately out of his conduct, so that a jury shall say that the criticism was not only honest but well founded, an action is not maintainable."

In that case the defendant alleged that that plaintiff's scheme was to promote the sale of his own paper. This was not fair comment because it

228 *Ibid.* at 500 *per* Lord Denning.
229 Above para. 18.17.
230 [1963] 2 All E.R. 151 especially at 166 *per* Lord Hodson, 171–172 *per* Lord Devlin. See also *Allsopp v. Church of England Newspaper Ltd* [1972] 2 All E.R. 26; *DDSA Pharmaceuticals Ltd v. Times Newspapers Ltd* [1972] 3 All E.R. 417.
231 [1986] 1 All E.R. 177. On which see *Viscount de l'Isle v. Times Newspapers Ltd* [1987] 3 All E.R. 499 at 505 *per* May L.J., 507 *per* Mustill L.J.; *Prager v. Times Newspapers Ltd* [1988] 1 All E.R. 300 at 304–307 *per* Purchas L.J., 310–311 *per* Nicholls L.J. In relation to the defence of fair comment, this case was followed in *Control v. New English Library Ltd* [1989] 3 All E.R. 577.
232 [1988] 1 All E.R. 177 at 183 *per* Ackner L.J.
232a Cp. *Morrell v. International Thomson Publishing Ltd* [1989] 3 All E.R. 733.
233 (1863) 3 B. & S. 769 at 777.

reflected upon the plaintiff's character, not merely on his conduct or works. The distinction is clear, if not always easy to apply. An attack upon a man's character can never be defended by a plea of fair comment. An attack upon his public acts or statements may be. The reason for the defence is that it is in the public interest to have free discussion of matters of public interest.[234]

18.62 Because it is necessary that comment to qualify as fair comment must be based upon true facts,[235] there came into being what was termed "the rolled-up plea". In *Sutherland v. Stopes*[236] the defendant pleaded: "In so far as the words complained of consist of statements of fact they are true in substance and fact, and in so far as they consist of expressions of opinion they are fair comment made in good faith and without malice upon the said facts which are a matter of public interest." This was, and still remains a plea of fair comment, not a plea of justification, i.e. truth. However it was severely criticised judicially, on the ground that the defendant could not be compelled to give particulars and state what was fact and what was comment.[237] Hence reform was recommended by the Porter Committee on Defamation in 1948.[238] Under Order 82, rule 3(2) of the Rules of the Supreme Court, replacing earlier provisions,[239] when this plea is relied on by the defendant, "he must give particulars stating which words complained of he alleges are statements of fact and of the facts and matters he relies on in support of the allegations that the words are true." However when the general plea of fair comment is relied on, not the rolled-up plea, the defendant need only give particulars of the basic facts on which he relies in support of his plea: he is not obliged to differentiate between words alleged to be statements of fact and words which are expressions of comment.[240]

18.63 Prior to 1952, if any of the facts on which the defendant relied in support of his plea of fair comment were untrue, the whole defence failed, unless the untrue facts were a minute part of those facts[241] (in much the

234 *Lyon v. Daily Telegraph Ltd* [1943] K.B. 746 at 752 *per* Scott L.J.
235 *Kemsley v. Foot* [1952] A.C. 345; *Grech v. Odhams Press Ltd* [1958] 2 All E.R. 462; *Digby v. Financial News Ltd* [1907] 1 K.B. 502 at 507 *per* Collins M.R.
236 [1925] A.C. 47.
237 *Aga Khan v. Times Publishing Co.* [1924] 1 K.B. 675 at 682 *per* Scrutton L.J.; *Tudor-Hart v. British Union for the Abolition of Vivisection* [1938] 2 K.B. 329 at 336, citing Atkin L.J. in *Hobbs v. Peoples Newspaper Publishing Co.*, 1926.
238 Cmnd. 7536.
239 R.S.C. 1883 Ord. 19, r. 22A, introduced in 1949 as a result of the Porter Report.
240 *Lord v. Sunday Telegraph Ltd* [1970] 3 All E.R. 504 at 507 *per* Lord Denning. Cp. *Aga Khan v. Times Publishing Co., supra*; *Cunningham Howie v. Dimbleby & Sons Ltd* [1950] 2 K.B. 882; *London Artists Ltd v. Littler* [1969] 2 Q.B. 375 at 390, 391 *per* Lord Denning. The defendant cannot be compelled to disclose his sources of information when fair comment (or privilege) is pleaded: this was formerly only applicable to newspapers but is now of more general application: R.S.C. Ord. 82, r. 6. But it only applies to interrogatories: *British Steel Corporation v. Granada Television* [1981] 1 All E.R. 417 at 440 *per* Lord Denning, 476–478 *per* Lord Fraser of Tulleybelton.
241 *Merivale v. Carson* (1887) 20 Q.B.D. 275; *South Hetton Coal Co. v. North-Eastern News Association* [1894] 1 Q.B. 133; *Kemsley v. Foot* [1952] A.C. 345.

same way as such failure would affect a plea of justification).[242] Corresponding to the loosening of the requirement in pleas of justification made by the statute,[243] the Defamation Act provides that a defence of fair comment will not fail by reason only that the truth of every allegation of fact is not proved if the expression of opinion is fair comment having regard to such of the facts as are proved.[244] This provision does not make the defence a plea of justification: it is still a plea of fair comment. Hence if any of the statements of fact on which the defence is based contain a defamatory sting, the defendant is obliged to rely on a plea of justification, not one of fair comment.[245]

(ii) Essential elements

18.64 (1) *Public interest.* Only matters which are of public interest may be the legitimate subject of fair, if defamatory comment. The test is usually whether the public's attention has been invited by the plaintiff. This would include representations on the stage or in films, as well as books, speeches or public behaviour of other kinds.[246] Even the conduct of the management of a play could be the subject of fair comment, as the comment in question, which accused the plaintiffs of conspiracy to force the end of a successful play, was on a matter of public interest in which people at large were legitimately interested. In the case in point, *London Artists Ltd v. Littler*[247] Lord Denning agreed that there was no definition in the books as to what is a matter of public interest, only a list of examples, coupled with the statement that it is for the judge not the jury to decide what is a matter of public interest. However he would not have confined it within narrow limits.

> "Whenever a matter is such as to affect people at large, so that they may be legitimately interested in, or concerned at, what is going on; or what may happen to them or to others; then it is a matter of public interest on which everyone is entitled to make fair comment."[248]

In *South Hetton Coal Co. Ltd v. North-Eastern News Association*[249] it was held that a reflection on the sanitary condition of cottages let by the plaintiff colliery company to its workmen was a matter of public interest. It was a matter with which the public were concerned. In the *Littler* case the public were legitimately interested. The public is interested in what happens in the theatre. The stars welcome publicity; producers are also interested in publicity. "When three top stars and a satellite all give notice to leave at the same time—thus putting a successful play in peril—it is to my mind a matter of public interest on which everyone, press and all, are entitled to

242 Above para. 18.59.
243 Defamation Act, 1952, s. 5: above para. 18.58.
244 *Ibid.* s. 6.
245 *Broadway Approvals Ltd v. Odhams Press Ltd* [1964] 2 Q.B. 683, reversed on other grounds [1965] 2 All E.R. 523.
246 E.g., *Merivale v. Carson, supra*, criticism of a play; *Thomas v. Bradbury, Agnew & Co. Ltd* [1906] 2 K.B. 627.
247 [1969] 2 All E.R. 193.
248 *Ibid.* at 198.
249 [1894] 1 Q.B. 133.

comment freely."[250] In the final analysis, however, it is for the judge, not the jury, to determine whether the matter in issue on which the comment was based could be a matter of public interest for the purposes of the defence of fair comment.

18.65 (2) *Opinion not fact.* In *Hunt v. Star Newspaper Co. Ltd*, which involved a defamatory statement about the conduct of a town clerk with respect to the performance of his duties as a returning officer, Fletcher-Moulton L.J. said:[251]

> "... comment in order to be justifiable as fair comment must appear as comment, and must not be so mixed up with facts that the reader cannot distinguish between what is report and what is comment .... The justice of this rule is obvious. If the facts are stated separately and the comment appears as an inference drawn from those facts, any injustice that it might do will be to some extent negatived by the reader seeing the grounds upon which the unfavourable inference is based. But if fact and comment be intermingled so that it is not reasonably clear what portion purports to be inference, he will naturally suppose that the injurious statements are based on adequate grounds known to the writer, though not necessarily set out by him."

Thus a statement that a plaintiff acted "dishonestly" and "corruptly" cannot be said to be comment. Such allegations are allegations of fact. Any matter which does not indicate with a reasonable clearness that it purports to be comment and not statement of fact cannot be protected by the plea of fair comment.[252] Assertions of fact must be distinguished from expressions of opinion.[253]

18.66 The facts on which the comment is based must be true, not false (subject to the protection given now by the Defamation Act 1952 section 6) or if not true, published on a privileged occasion.[254] The comment should be a reasonable inference from those facts. As seen above, where the plea is relied upon certain particulars must be provided by the defendant: and, if the plea is not a general plea of fair comment but the rolled-up plea set out earlier, more specific particulars have to be provided.[255]

18.67 *(3) Fairness.* To qualify for the purposes of this defence the comment must be "fair". What this term means has been the subject of judicial exegesis on more than one occasion. In *McQuire v. Western Morning News Co.*,[256] a case involving the defence of fair comment in relation to the publication of a criticism of a play in a newspaper, Collins M.R. stated

250 *Supra* note 249 at 198.
251 [1908–10] All E.R. Rep. 513 at 517, citing *Andrews v. Chapman* (1853) 3 C. & K. 286, and rejecting what was said in *Lefroy v. Burnside* (1879) 4 L.R. Ir. 566.
252 [1908–10] All E.R. Rep. 513 at 517.
253 *London Artists Ltd v. Littler*, *supra* at 201 *per* Edmund Davies L.J. See *Control Risks Ltd v. New English Library Ltd* [1989] 3 All E.R. 577.
254 *Ibid.* at 201: cp. above para. 18.63 on the Defamation Act 1952 s. 5: below paras. 18.71ff on privileged occasions. See also *Mangena v. Wright* [1909] 2 K.B. 958; *Thomas v. Bradbury Agnew & Co. Ltd* [1906] 2 K.B. 627 at 628.
255 Above para. 18.62.
256 [1900–1903] All E.R. Rep. 673 at 675.

that the jury had no right to substitute their own opinion of the literary merits of the article for that of the critic, or to try the "fairness" of the criticism by any such standard. "Fair" in this context did not mean what the ordinary reasonable man would think a correct appreciation of the work that was being criticised. "I think 'fair' embraces the meaning of honest and also of relevancy," said Collins M.R.[257] The view expressed must be honest and must be such as can fairly be called criticism.[258] Prejudice or exaggerated views will not make comment unfair if the reasonable man regards the views as fair.[259] The question is not whether the comment is justified in the eyes of judge or jury but whether it is the honest expression of the commentator's real view and not mere abuse or invective under the guise of criticism.[260] In his charge to the jury in *Silkin v. Beaverbrook Newspapers Ltd*,[261] Diplock J., quoting the earlier remarks of Bray J. in an unreported case, pointed out that strong, exaggerated views were not necessarily unfair comment. The test was one of honesty, not whether the jury agreed with the comment.[262] Hence if there is no evidence that the writer of the comment honestly held those views, it is possible to hold that a comment is unfair. In a leading Canadian case,[263] the effect of which was subsequently altered by legislation,[264] the Supreme Court of Canada held that the defence of fair comment was not available to the publishers of a newspaper in which a letter to the editor had appeared when the letter defamed the plaintiff. The writers of the letter were not available as witnesses and the editor could not tell whether their views as expressed in the letter were honestly held. There was evidence though that the newspaper did not hold the same views as the writers of the letter. Hence the decision, by a majority, over the powerful dissent of Dickson J, that the defence of fair comment could not be relied on by the publishers of the newspaper.[265]

18.68 Malice is not an essential part of unfairness in this context. But an intention to injure the plaintiff will make comment unfair.[266] And comment that is clearly malicious cannot be fair.[267] In this regard evidence may be given to show that a critic was actuated by malice and then the court or jury might find that the critic's unfavourable criticism was

257 *Ibid.*
258 *Ibid.*
259 *Merivale v. Carson* (1887) 20 Q.B.D. 275 at 281 *per* Lord Esher M.R. The relevant date is the date of *publication* of the comment. Hence evidence of the plaintiff's enhanced or undiminished reputation at the time of the trial is inadmissible, but evidence relating to the time of publication of the libel is: *Cornwall v. Myskow* [1987] 2 All E.R. 504.
260 *Turner v. M-G-M* [1950] 1 All E.R. 449 at 461 *per* Lord Porter; on onus of proof, *ibid.* at 461–462.
261 [1958] 2 All E.R. 516 at 518.
262 Nor whether other people read more into the statement than the writer intended. Cp. *Slim v. Daily Telegraph Ltd* [1968] 1 All E.R. 497 at 503 *per* Lord Denning.
263 *Chernesky v. Armadale Publications Ltd* [1979] 1 S.C.R. 1067.
264 Libel and Slander Act, R.S.O. 1980, c. 237, s. 25 (as introduced by S.O. 1980, c. 35, s. 2).
265 Contrast *Lyon v. Daily Telegraph Ltd* [1943] K.B. 746, where the newspaper did honestly hold the same views as the writer of the letter.
266 *Merivale v. Carson, supra* at 281 *per* Lord Esher M.R.
267 *Thomas v. Bradbury, Agnew & Co. Ltd* [1906] 2 K.B. 627.

inspired not by an honest belief, but by a desire to gratify his malice.[268] Thus an attack upon a plaintiff's character will make comment unfair.[269] For if the private character of a person criticised is involved, what is written will cease to be fair comment.[270] However the fact that a statement is made anonymously will not necessarily make any comment it contains into unfair comment. In *Lyon v. Daily Telegraph*[271] the newspaper published a letter criticising the plaintiff's radio show. The letter was signed, but it was later discovered that the name appended to the letter was fictitious. Hence it was, in fact, an anonymous letter. Since the contents of the letter also represented the views of the newspaper, the fact that the writer was unknown did not take away from its fairness.

18.69 Thus evidence of malice will negate what might otherwise be a valid defence of fair comment. However it was suggested by Sellers L.J. in *Broadway Approvals Ltd v. Odhams Press Ltd*,[272] that it was open to the House of Lords to decide whether this was correct. Although it is true that no decision at this level has ever firmly pronounced on the relevance of malice, or the relationship between malice and fair comment, it may be deduced from such cases as *Turner v. M-G-M*,[273] in which Lord Porter discussed both the meaning of fair comment and the onus of proof in cases where this defence was relied upon by a defendant, that the issue of malice does play a part in determining whether comment qualifies as fair. In this context "malice", or "express malice", in contrast with the idea of malice as implicit in the publication of a false defamatory statement,[274] has the connotation of "spite", "ill-will", or an intention to harm the plaintiff. What is involved is some intrinsic aspect of the statement, or some external circumstances which reveal the true nature and purpose of the statement, the effect of which will be to refute the contention of the defendant that all he was doing was honestly expressing an opinion about the matter in question, viz., the play, the book, the speech, or other utterance of the plaintiff.

18.70 The fact that malice, in this sense, will destroy a plea of fair comment, as it will in certain cases of privilege,[275] has led some judges to suggest that fair comment is a kind of privilege, namely the public right of fair comment.[276] Others have avoided the use of the term "privilege" in this context, as it would entail using a word which according to its

268 *Lyon v. Daily Telegraph Ltd*, *supra* at 755 *per* Scott L.J. Evidence of the plaintiff's undiminished or enhanced reputation at the time of the trial is not admissible or relevant to the issues of fair comment and malice, nor to the issue of damages where fair comment is the defence: *Cornwall v. Myskow* [1987] 1 W.L.R. 630.
269 *Merivale v. Carson*, *supra* at 283 *per* Bowen L.J.
270 *Lyon v. Daily Telegraph Ltd*, *supra* at 752 *per* Scott L.J.: e.g. *Campbell v. Spottiswode* (1863) 3 B. & S. 769.
271 *Supra*.
272 [1965] 2 All E.R. 523 at 534.
273 [1950] 1 All E.R. 449.
274 Above para. 18.05.
275 Below para. 18.101.
276 *McQuire v. Western Morning News Co.* [1900–1903] All E.R. Rep. 673 at 676 *per* Collins M.R. See *Henwood v. Harrison* (1872) L.R. 7 C.P. 606.

technical etymology denotes the special right of an individual as extending to cover the common rights of the whole community at large. As Collins M.R. pointed in *McQuire v. Western Morning News Co.*,[277] the expression "fair comment" co-existed with the doctrine of "privileged occasion". The comment in order to be within the protection of the privilege had to be fair, i.e. not such as to disclose in itself actual malice. It also had to be relevant; otherwise it never was within it, and the judge could hold as a matter of law that the privilege did not extend to it (in which event the only defence was truth). These factors were intended to be covered compendiously by the epithet "fair". It was intended to exclude those elements which took the comments out of, or prevented it from falling within the privilege of the occasion. In more modern times it would appear to be the better view that the defence of fair comment is not an aspect of privilege but a distinct issue. Whether an occasion is privileged is a question of law, and, as will be seen, the occasions on which a communication is privileged are limited.[278] The idea of "fair comment" is more general, and is limited only by the factors of "public interest", "comment" and "fairness", all of which depend upon the precise facts that are in issue.

(e) Privilege

(i) Nature of privilege

18.71 Certain occasions on which statements are made are the subject of privilege.[279] Occasions of privilege arise as a result of common law and statutory rules designed to serve the public interest or the common convenience of society.[280] Although a statement made on a privileged occasion may be false, and defamatory, the attitude of the law is that greater harm to the public good would arise from penalising a person who makes such a statement on a privileged occasion than would emerge from stifling freedom of speech or information. Other methods exist for controlling the extent to which a privilege may be exceeded: for example, the procedures of Parliament; the power of judges to discipline counsel, solicitors, witnesses and others; the Press Council.

18.72 Privilege is of two varieties: absolute and qualified. Absolute privilege entails what the expression would suggest, namely that the privilege attaches absolutely and cannot be defeated or destroyed by the state of mind of the maker of the statement who claims the privilege. However even such privilege may be exceeded, if the defendant makes his defamatory statement outside the bounds of the privilege. Thus a statement made inside either House of Parliament when the House in question

277 [1900–1903] All E.R. Rep. 673 at 676–677.
278 Below paras 18.74ff.
279 "The occasion is privileged: the communication is protected": *Adam v. Ward* [1917] A.C. 309 at 348 *per* Lord Shaw of Dunfermline.
280 *Perera v. Peiris* [1949] A.C. 1 at 20 *per* Lord Uthwatt: on which see *Blackshaw v. Lord* [1983] 2 All E.R. 311 at 339 *per* Fox L.J.

is sitting and the statement is made during the proceedings is the subject of absolute privilege,[281] while a similar statement made outside the confines of the House, for instance in casual conversation, or by way of comment on wireless or television, is not absolutely privileged (although it might fall within the scope of some variety of qualified privilege). Qualified privilege refers to those privileged occasions when the maker of a defamatory statement will be protected from liability unless it can be shown that he acted with "express malice".[282] In this respect an excessive mode or extent of publication may establish malice, and so destroy the privilege: or it may defeat a claim of privilege on the ground that the occasion was only privileged if the maker of the statement published it to a certain person or group of persons and not to a wider audience or readership.[283]

18.73 The situations in which absolute privilege arises have long been fixed and determined by statute or, in some instances, by the common law. Where qualified privilege is concerned, although there are some situations dealt with by statute, for example those contained in the Defamation Act 1952,[284] the main instances of privilege arise at common law. As explained in *Blackshaw v. Lord*[285] by Dunn L.J., in the eighteenth century privilege afforded no defence to a defamatory publication. During the nineteenth century judges used the word "privilege" as meaning the existence of a set of circumstances in which the presumption of malice was negatived. In one case[286] it was said that instead of the expression "privileged communication" it would be more correct to say that the communication was made on an occasion which rebutted the presumption of malice. The judges having to face the problem of what would be the circumstances in which the presumption of malice would be negatived went on two lines, duty and interest, and the public good and for the public interest. By the end of the nineteenth century certain categories of documents by their very nature rebutted the presumption of malice, and publication of them was privileged. These included fair and accurate reports of judicial proceedings and of proceedings in Parliament. The courts stressed that the categories were not closed and in each case it was necessary to determine not only whether the occasion was privileged but also its status and whether that gave rise to a duty to publish. It is now clear that whether an occasion is privileged, in the sense of qualified privilege, is a question of law for the judge, not of fact for the jury.[287] It may be difficult to decide.[288] But the principles upon which such a decision is to be made are clear and undisputed: unless some

281 Below para. 18.74.
282 In contrast to the malice that is "implied" by law on the publication of defamatory matter: above para. 18.05. See *Horrocks v. Lowe* [1975] A.C. 135 at 149 *per* Lord Diplock for the rationale of qualified privilege.
283 Below para. 18.101.
284 Below para. 18.92ff.
285 [1983] 2 All E.R. 311 at 332.
286 *Gilpin v. Fowler* (1854) 9 Ex. 615 at 623–624.
287 *Adam v. Ward* [1917] A.C. 309 at 320 *per* Lord Loreburn, 340 *per* Lord Atkinson: *Watt v. Longsdon* [1930] 1 K.B. 130 at 153 *per* Greer L.J.
288 *Macintosh v. Dun* [1908] A.C. 390 at 400 *per* Lord Macnaghten, as to the need to determine which interest is at stake; *London Association for Trade Protection v. Greenlands* [1916] 2 A.C. 15.

statute has determined the issue, the resolution of the question turns on the issues of duty and interest.[289]

(ii) Cases of absolute privilege

18.74 *(1) Statements made in Parliament.* The principle as to the privilege of Parliament comes from article 9 of the Bill of Rights 1689 which provides: "That the freedom of speech and debates or proceedings in Parliament ought not to be impeached or questioned in any court or place out of Parliament."[290] This applies to other legislatures as well as the British Parliament. In *Chenard & Co. v. Joachim Arisol*[291] defamatory statements made in the legislative council of the Seychelles were not actionable. The same absolute privilege applies to all competently created colonial legislatures because it is necessary for the exercise of their functions just as it is necessary for those of the British Parliament. As was made clear in *Stockdale v. Hansard*[292] and *Bradlaugh v. Gossett*,[293] as well as in Blackstone's Commentaries,[294] the proceedings of each House of Parliament must be entirely free and unshackled, so that whatever is said or done in either House is not liable to examination elsewhere. No action for defamation can be brought in respect of anything said in the House of Commons or the House of Lords. However in *Church of Scientology of California v. Johnson-Smith*[295] the question arose whether evidence of something said or done in Parliament could be admitted to support a cause of action in respect of something said by the defendant during a television interview, not in the House of Commons, although he was an M.P. Brown J. held, applying the general principles referred to in the authorities cited above, that they meant that such evidence was inadmissible. Nor is it possible to enquire into the validity of a select committee of the House of Commons on which an article alleged to be defamatory of the plaintiff has been partly based. The plaintiff in *Dingle v. Associated Newspapers Ltd*[296] tried to argue that there was a procedural defect in the proceedings of the committee. However it was held that the privilege of Parliament precluded any reference to, or investigation of, such matters.

18.75 *(2) Parliamentary papers.* Under the Parliamentary Papers Act 1840, which resolved a long dispute relating to the privilege of *Hansard*, in which Parliamentary debates were reported, it was provided that such documents are also absolutely privileged. However extracts or abstracts enjoy only qualified privilege.[297] Command papers, though published by

289 Below pp. 508–11.
290 *Church of Scientology of California v. Johnson-Smith* [1972] 1 All E.R. 378 at 379 *per* Brown J.
291 [1949] A.C. 127.
292 (1839) 9 A. & E. 1 at 114 *per* Lord Denman, 162 *per* Littledale J., 209 *per* Patteson, J., 233 *per* Coleridge J.
293 (1884) 12 Q.B.D. 271.
294 17th ed. 1830, vol. i at 163.
295 [1972] 1 All E.R. 378.
296 [1960] 2 Q.B. 405: for further proceedings see [1961] 2 All E.R. 897, [1962] 2 All E.R. 737: below para. 18.111.
297 Parliamentary Papers Act 1840 s. 3.

and with the authority of Parliament, are not included within the scope of this enactment: but they would probably enjoy qualified privilege at common law.[298]

18.76 *(3) Judicial proceedings.* Judges of all courts are protected from actions in respect of acts done or words spoken in their judicial capacity in the court of justice over which they preside.[299] There appears to be no distinction between judges of superior and judges of inferior courts. Whatever difference there may be relates to the difference in jurisdiction. Since judges of superior courts have an unlimited jurisdiction, there is no reason why they are not absolutely protected. Judges of inferior courts have a more limited jurisdiction, and if they act outside this they may be liable, even if they act in good faith and in the belief that they acted within their jurisdiction.[300] This latter condition would hardly seem to apply to cases of defamation, unless the judge believed that in making the comment he was acting within his powers as a judge in the particular instance.

18.77 The purpose of this immunity from suit, which extends beyond the field of defamation and so is perhaps more than a privilege, is so that the public can benefit. It is in the public interest that judges be not constrained in their actions but are free to make whatever comments are deemed necessary for the proper administration of justice. It is the quality of the judiciary and their sense of what is appropriate that can act as protection for those who fear defamation. A judge is unlikely to make defamatory statements unless such statements are pertinent to the disposition of the case in question.[301]

18.78 For the same reason counsel, and solicitors when acting as advocates in court, will also be protected from liability in defamation where an alleged defamatory statement is made in court, even if the statement is irrelevant or malicious.[302] The court will control the behaviour and statements of counsel and solicitors in such instances, by disciplining the lawyer for contempt. In *Munster v. Lamb*,[303] for example, the suggestion by a solicitor that the prosecutor kept drugs was not actionable as it was made in the course of proceedings at petty sessions.

18.79 Witnesses are also subject to the same protection.[304] It is also in the public interest that a witness should not fear litigation as a consequence of

298 Below para. 18.89.
299 *Scott v. Stanfield* (1868) L.R. 7 Ex. 220 at 223 *per* Kelly C.B.
300 *Sirros v. Moore* [1974] 3 All E.R. 776 at 781–785 *per* Lord Denning, 786–787 *per* Buckley L.J., 795–796 *per* Ormrod L.J. (a case of assault and false imprisonment, not defamation).
301 In the event that a judge acts improperly there are procedures to obtain his removal from office, depending on the rank of the judge, e.g. by address of both Houses of Parliament in the case of a High Court judge.
302 *Munster v. Lamb* (1883) 11 Q.B.D. 588 at 599–605 *per* Brett M.R.
303 *Supra.*
304 *Seaman v. Nethercliff* (1876) 2 C.P.D. 53, even though the defamatory statement was made of the witness's volition, after counsel had asked all his questions.

anything said in court. However a witness who is recalcitrant may be dealt with by the court for contempt. One who tells lies may be prosecuted for perjury, but no civil action for damages will be available against a witness who is alleged to have told lies while under oath. To permit this might be to open the floodgates of litigation and allow every convicted criminal to sue any witness whose evidence may have aided in his conviction.[305] Nor can any other action be based on what a witness says in court, or for the preparation of his evidence.[306]

18.80 The privileges and immunities which have been set out above will attach not only to courts of justice in the traditional sense, whatever the level of the court, but also to quasi-judicial proceedings, for example a court of inquiry instituted by the army under the Articles of War, as long as the statement in question was not made outside the terms of the inquiry.[307] This absolute immunity or privilege has also been held to apply to proceedings before the disciplinary committee of the Law Society established under the statute dealing with solicitors.[308] In *Trapp v. Mackie*[309] the House of Lords held that the privilege of a witness also applied where a tribunal of enquiry was set up under the Education (Scotland) Act by the Secretary of State for Scotland to enquire into the reasons for the plaintiff's dismissal from his post of headmaster of a school. The privilege or immunity extends to tribunals acting in a manner similar to courts of justice, with attributes similar to those of a court of justice.[310] Such a tribunal must be "recognised by law". The absolute privilege does not extend to purely domestic tribunals.[311] Tribunals recognised by law are not confined to those constituted or recognised by Act of Parliament; but the description embraces all that are.[312] Provided the tribunal is recognised by law there is no single element the presence or absence of which will be conclusive in showing whether the tribunal has attributes sufficiently similar to those of a court of law to create absolute privilege.[313]

18.81 If a tribunal is recognised as belonging to this category, evidence or matters produced for or in connection with the proceedings of such tribunal will be absolutely privileged.[314] Hence in *Hasselblad (GB) Ltd v.*

305 *Hargreaves v. Bretherton* [1959] 1 Q.B. 45.
306 *Marrinan v. Vibart* [1962] 3 All E.R. 380.
307 *Dawkins v. Lord Rokeby* (1873) L.R. 8 Q.B. 255; (1875) L.R. 7 H.L. 744; *More v. Weaver* [1928] 2 K.B. 520 at 522 *per* Scrutton L.J.
308 *Addis v. Crocker* [1960] 2 All E.R. 629.
309 [1979] 1 All E.R. 489. This was an action for giving false evidence, but what was said was of general application.
310 *Ibid.* at 491 *per* Lord Diplock; cp. *O'Connor v. Waldron* [1935] A.C. 76 at 81 *per* Lord Atkin; *Royal Aquarium & Summer & Winter Garden Society Ltd v. Parkinson* [1892] 1 Q.B. 431.
311 [1979] 1 All E.R. 489 at 492 *per* Lord Diplock.
312 *Ibid.*
313 *Ibid.* at 499 *per* Lord Fraser of Tullybelton.
314 *Watson v. M'Ewan* [1905] A.C. 480; *Lilley v. Ray* (1892) 61 L.J.Q.B. 727; but not if what is published is too remote from the proceedings: *Szalatnay-Stacho v. Fink* [1947] K.B. 1. See *Lincoln v. Daniels* [1961] 3 All E.R. 740 at 745 *per* Sellers L.J., 751–753 *per* Devlin L.J.

Orbinson,[315] a letter sent to the European Communities Commission in respect of proceedings being brought against the plaintiffs for breach of provisions of the EEC Treaty was sufficiently closely connected to the process of giving evidence for it to be covered if evidence given by the defendants directly to or before the Commission would be covered by absolute privilege. However such privilege did not attach to the functioning of the Commission. The procedure of the Commission and the fact that its decisions were reached by commissioners who had not attended the hearing on the basis of advice from representatives of member states who were not directly concerned indicated that the Commission acted in a manner dissimilar to that of a court of justice under both civil and common law. However the majority of the Court of Appeal also held that the public interest in favour of assisting the Commissioners to carry out their duties required that the court refuse the letter in issue to be produced in the libel action.

18.82 The need to show that the communication that was the subject of an action for defamation was made by way of evidence to, or in preparation of evidence to a judicial or quasi-judicial body which would be recognised by law for the proceedings was made clear by the Court of Appeal in *Lincoln v. Daniels*.[316] There a letter to the Bar Council did not come within the scope of absolute privilege. The Bar Council did not act judicially in respect of complaints about members of the Bar. Only the Benchers of an Inn of Court did that.[317] Hence a letter of complaint about the behaviour of a member of the Bar should have been sent to the Benchers of the barrister's Inn of Court, not to the Bar Council. The latter was not a judicial body recognised by law. The Benchers of an Inn of Court, when acting in disciplinary proceedings, were such a court.

18.83 *(4) Communications between solicitor and client.* In *More v. Weaver*[317a] the Court of Appeal held that such communications were privileged provided that they were "germane to the occasion". However it is not clear whether this privilege is absolute or qualified. The issue was raised but left undecided by the House of Lords in *Minter v. Priest*[317b] because the court held that the relationship of solicitor and client did not exist at the time of the alleged slander in issue. Therefore there was no privileged occasion that might have given protection to the defendant. Two requirements would seem to be essential for this privilege to apply. First, there must be the appropriate professional relationship in existence at the time the statement in issue is made. Secondly, the statement must be relevant to the professional purposes involved or the business in hand at the time it was made.

315 [1985] 1 All E.R. 173.
316 [1961] 3 All E.R. 740.
317 As delegates of the judges: *R. v. Grays Inn* (1780) 1 Doug. K.B. 353 at 354 *per* Lord Mansfield.
317a [1928] 2 K.B. 520.
317b [1930] A.C. 558.

18.84 *(5) Official communications by one officer of state to another in the course of official duty.* Certain categories of state documents have been made the subject of absolute privilege. The court must take into account the position occupied by the sender and the recipient and the nature and subject-matter of the communication. However the precise boundaries of the protection have yet to be established.[318] In *Chatterton v. Secretary of State for India in Council*[319] a dispatch by the Secretary of State to an under-secretary concerning the removal of the plaintiff to the half-pay list was privileged. In *M. Isaacs & Sons Ltd v. Cook*,[320] so too was a report by the Australian High Commissioner to the prime minister on commercial matters involving the interests of the Commonwealth. A report with respect to military duty was similarly protected in *Dawkins v. Lord Paulet*.[321] But in an Australian case[322] no such privilege extended to the report of an inspector made in the course of duty to a superior officer and containing a defamatory reference to a subordinate.

18.85 The rationale of cases such as *Chatterton v. Secretary of State for India in Council* is that the direct interests of the community in the United Kingdom demand that an officer of a certain status should be able to communicate candidly on certain subjects without running the risk of being brought before the courts as defendant or witness, and examined on the honesty or accuracy of what he has written.[323] In *Fayed v. Al-Tajir*[324] the Court of Appeal held that such privilege also attached to an inter-departmental memorandum prepared in the embassy of a foreign country while the defendant was acting as ambassador, though not formally holding the post. The memorandum criticised the conduct of the plaintiff, a national of the foreign country in question. Questions of international comity, as dictating public policy, and the law of nations, as reflected in art. 24 of the Vienna Convention on Diplomatic Relations as incorporated by the Diplomatic Privileges Act 1964 Sch. 1, required embassy documents to be treated as inviolable. Hence the same privilege attached to such documents as to those of the *Chatterton* variety.[325]

18.86 *(6) Fair and accurate reports of judicial proceedings.* By the Law of Libel Amendment Act 1888,[326] a fair and accurate report in any newspaper (as

318 *Fayed v. Al-Tajir* [1987] 2 All E.R. 396 at 402 *per* Mustill L.J.
319 [1895] 2 Q.B. 189; cp. *Merrick v. Nott-Bower* [1965] 1 Q.B. 57; *Rogers v. Secretary of State for Home Department* [1973] A.C. 388; cp. *Hasselblad (G.B.) Ltd v. Orbinson* [1985] 1 All E.R. 173, above, which really dealt with privilege attaching to judicial proceedings.
320 [1925] 2 K.B. 391.
321 (1869) L.R. 5 Q.B. 94.
322 *Gibbons v. Duffield* (1923) 47 C.L.R. 520; cp. *Jackson v. McGrath* (1947) 75 C.L.R. 293; *Peerless Bakery Ltd v. Watts* [1955] N.Z.L.R. 339.
323 *Fayed v. Al-Tajir* [1987] 2 All E.R. 396 at 402.
324 *Ibid.* at 403 *per* Mustill L.J.
325 But it was not certain nor did it have to be resolved whether such privilege attached to memoranda from middle or lower tanks in the secret service or to visiting forces of a friendly foreign power: *Richards v. Naum* [1967] 1 Q.B. 620.
326 51 & 52 Vict. c. 64, s. 3.

defined in the Newspaper Libel and Registration Act 1881)[327] of proceedings publicly heard before any court exercising judicial authority will be privileged, if it is published contemporaneously (unless the matter published is blasphemous or indecent).[328]

18.87 Although the statute does not make clear whether the privilege is absolute or qualified, the better view is that the statute creates an absolute privilege: certain decisions indicate this without actually coming to a firm decision;[329] under another provision of the 1888 Act, now repealed,[330] reports of public meetings were privileged unless published or made maliciously (which suggests that the statute was marking a clear distinction between two kinds of reports); and at common law fair and accurate reports of judicial proceedings, even though not contemporaneous, will be protected by qualified privilege unless prohibited by the court or blasphemous, seditious or obscene.[331]

18.88 Only courts come within this provision. It would seem that the protection of this statute does not extend to reports of quasi-judicial proceedings, even though established by law, since such proceedings are not heard by courts exercising judicial authority.[332] Thus the privilege did not apply to the report of a proceedings before a medical referee.[333] In *Chapman v. Ellesmere*[334] Romer L.J. stated that reports of domestic tribunals were excluded from this privilege because the public were not entitled to attend such proceedings, and therefore they were not entitled to be informed of what took place in their absence. In the case of courts exercising judicial authority, since they are open to the public, save in exceptional circumstances, the public have a right to know what occurred therein: and that right may be enjoyed directly, by attendance, or indirectly, by a newspaper report. Hence the need for contemporaneity in the report if it is to be absolutely privileged in this way. Although a report of proceedings in a foreign court may be granted qualified privilege in certain circumstances,[335] it would appear that it could not claim to be within the protection of the 1888 statute. That enactment applies only to

327 44 & 45 Vict., s. 60, s. 1; viz., "any paper containing public news, intelligence or occurrences, or any remarks or observations thereon printed for sale and published in England or Ireland periodically or in parts or numbers at intervals not exceeding 26 days between the publication of any two such papers parts or numbers."

328 *Burnett & Hallamshire Fuel Ltd v. Sheffield Telegraph & Star Ltd* [1960] 2 All E.R. 157: and to a report of a defamatory statement made by a member of the public from the body of the court: *Farmer v. Hyde* [1937] 1 K.B. 728.

329 *Farmer v. Hyde* [1937] 1 K.B. 728; *McCarey v. Associated Newspapers Ltd* [1964] 2 All E.R. 335, reversed on other grounds [1964] 3 All E.R. 947 C.A.

330 Viz. s. 4, repealed by the Defamation Act 1952 ss. 17(2), 18(3).

331 Below para. 18.90.

332 *Royal Aquarium & Summer & Winter Garden Society Ltd v. Parkinson* [1892] 1 Q.B. 431 at 447 *per* Fry L.J.: *ibid.* at 451 *per* Lopes L.J. See for a county court, *Hope v. W.C. Leng & Co. Ltd* (1907) 2 T.L.R. 243; a coroner's court, *McCarey v. Associated Newspapers Ltd*, *supra*; a Registrar in Bankruptcy, *Ryals v. Leader* (1866) L.R. 1 Ex. 296.

333 *Smith v. National Meter Co.* [1945] K.B. 543. But it did apply to the General Medical Council: *Thompson v. British Medical Association (N.S.W. Branch)* [1924] A.C. 764.

334 [1932] 2 K.B. 431 at 475.

335 *Webb v. Times Publishing Co. Ltd* [1960] 2 All E.R. 789: below para. 18.91.

proceedings in courts in the United Kingdom.[336] It will also apply to reports of the same kind, i.e. fair, accurate and contemporaneous, which are broadcast by wireless or television.[337]

(iii) Cases of qualified privilege

18.89 *(1) Privileged reports: 1. Common law.* At common law, even before statutory intervention, a newspaper was entitled to claim qualified privilege in respect of reports of Parliamentary proceedings.[338] This common law privilege subsists and is not limited or abridged by statute.[339] In certain circumstances, as seen earlier, the privilege enjoyed by newspapers is absolute.[340] Where a publication does not come within the statutory definition, or there is a lack of contemporaneity about the report, the publisher must rely on this common law qualified privilege (the right to publish a defamatory report as long as malice is absent). It has been said that such privilege is based on the element of public interest in such matters.[341] On this ground the Judicial Committee of the Privy Council, in *Perera v. Peiris*[342] held that a similar privilege attached to a report of extracts from the Official Report of a Bribery Commission set up by the Governor of Ceylon. The public interest of Ceylon demanded that the contents of the Report be widely communicated.[342a] This was criticised, however, by Dunn L.J. in *Blackshaw v. Lord*[343] as being too wide. From what was said in that case,[344] it would appear that the newspaper's privilege to report fairly and accurately what took place in Parliament, in either House or a committee thereof, would seem to be a specific example of a wider principle that a publication made in pursuance of a legal, social or moral duty to persons with a corresponding interest or duty to receive it will be protected by qualified privilege.[345] Hence in that case, the Court of Appeal, while admitting that the issue whether the article in question was a fair and accurate report of the plaintiff's resignation from the Civil Service could be left to the jury, also held that neither the common law nor the Defamation Act 1952 protected the article. The defendants had suggested that the plaintiff had resigned for personal reasons. At the time the article was written no allegation of incompetence against the plaintiff had been made good. The public at large therefore had no legitimate interest in receiving a statement by a press officer of the government department or the speculations of the writer of the article. Thus while fair

336 Defamation Act 1952 s. 8. For the previous situation see *Anderson v. Gorrie* [1894] 1 Q.B. 618; *Perera v. Peiris* [1949] A.C. 1.
337 Defamation Act 1952 s. 9(2).
338 *Wason v. Walter* (1868) L.R. 4 Q.B. 73; see *Cook v. Alexander* [1974] Q.B. 279, the writer was entitled to select those parts of the proceedings which in his view were of public interest as long as the selection was made fairly, honestly and without malice.
339 Defamation Act 1952 s. 7(4).
340 Above para. 18.87.
341 *Wason v. Walter, supra* at 88–89 *per* Cockburn C.J.; cp. *Allbutt v. General Council of Medical Education* (1889) 23 Q.B.D. 400 at 412; *Perera v. Peiris* [1949] A.C. 1 at 21 *per* Lord Uthwatt.
342 [1949] A.C. 1.
342a *Ibid.* at 21.
343 [1983] 2 All E.R. 311 at 339.
344 *Ibid.* at 327 *per* Stephenson L.J., 332–334 *per* Dunn L.J., 338–339 *per* Fox L.J.
345 Below paras. 18.95ff.

and accurate reports of certain matters occurring in Parliament may be covered by common law qualified privilege, this privilege does not extend beyond those narrow confines, unless the wider doctine can be made applicable.

18.90 A similar common law qualified privilege may be claimed in respect of newspaper reports of judicial proceedings, as long as such reports are fair and accurate.[346] The immunity from suit of participants in such proceedings is absolute.[347] To claim privilege for a newspaper report of such proceedings, however, an absence of malice must be shown. The scope of this privilege is much the same as the scope of the absolute privilege already considered. The proceedings in question must be those of a court recognised by English law. Hence no privilege attaches to a report, even one that is fair and accurate, of proceedings in a tribunal which does not qualify as a court, in the sense previously examined; nor to those of a domestic tribunal to which the public is not admitted,[348] for example, a hearing by the Jockey Club.[349] As Lord Denning said in *Boston v. W.S. Bagshaw & Sons*:[350] "The case of *Chapman v. Ellesmere* made it very difficult for a newspaper to claim privilege." Hence the changes made in the Defamation Act 1952.[351] In *Webb v. Times Publishing Co. Ltd*,[352] Pearson J. held that a claim of qualified privilege could be made by a newspaper reporting a judicial proceeding in a foreign country, where the subject-matter of the litigation could be said to be of interest to the public at large in England. The topic reported had to be of genuine public concern, not just the subject of idle curiosity or a desire for gossip.[353] However Pearson J. stated the principle too widely, according to Fox L.J. in *Blackshaw v. Lord*,[354] when he said:

> "As the administration of justice in England is a matter of legitimate and proper interest to English newspaper readers, so also is this report [viz., of foreign proceedings] which has so much connection with the administration of justice in England."

18.91 It may be necessary to a satisfactory law of defamation that there should be privileged occasions. But the existence of privilege involves a balance of conflicting pressures. On the one hand there is the need of the press to be able to publish fearlessly what is necessary for the protection of the public. On the other hand there is the need to protect the individual

346 *Allbutt v. General Council of Medical Education, supra*: *McCarey v. Associated Newspapers Ltd* [1964] 2 All E.R. 335; *Kimber v. Press Association* [1893] 1 Q.B. 65; *Risk Allah Bey v. Whiteside* (1868) 18 L.T. 615; *Andrews v. Chapman* (1853) 3 C. & K. 286; *Salmon v. Isaac* (1869) 20 L.T. 895.
347 Above para. 18.87.
348 *Kimber v. Press Association, supra*: cp. *Purcell v. Sowler* (1877) 2 C.P.D. 215, no privilege for report of meeting of poor law guardians.
349 *Chapman v. Ellesmere* [1932] 2 K.B. 431.
350 [1966] 2 All E.R. 906 at 910, quoted by Stephenson L.J. in *Blackshaw v. Lord* [1983] 2 All E.R. 311 at 326.
351 Below paras. 18.92ff.
352 [1960] 2 All E.R. 789.
353 *Ibid.* at 805, quoting Lord Hewart C.J. in *R. v. Risk* [1937] 2 K.B. 375 at 380.
354 *Supra* note 350 at 339.

from falsehoods. There are cases where the test of "legitimate and proper interest to English newspaper readers" would tilt the balance to an unacceptable degree against the individual. It would protect persons who disseminate untrue defamatory information of apparently legitimate public interest provided only that they honestly believed it and honestly thought it was information the public ought to have.[355] This went too far, in the view of Fox L.J. Hence it may be said that the general statement of principle in the *Webb* case, in contrast with the actual decision in the case on its facts, must not be taken too literally or too far. The decision was that of a single judge, who, admittedly, was breaking novel ground: as such it cannot be regarded as overly authoritative, especially in light of the more recent comments in the Court of Appeal.

18.92 *2. Statutory.* The Defamation Act 1952[356] provides that the publication in a newspaper of certain stipulated reports will be privileged unless the publication is proved to be made with malice. For this purpose a "newspaper" means any paper containing news or observations thereon, or consisting wholly or mainly of advertisements, printed for sale and published in the United Kingdom either periodically or in parts or numbers at intervals of not more than 36 days.[357] The statute differentiates two classes of such reports. Some statements are privileged, subject to proof of malice, without any kind of qualification. Others will enjoy that privilege unless the defendant has been requested by the plaintiff to publish a reasonable letter or statement by way of explanation or contradiction and the defendant has refused or neglected to do so or has done so inadequately having regard to the circumstances.[358] The fact that the statute creates this privilege in respect of certain reports does not throw doubt on the common law privilege already discussed. Indeed the statute expressly provides that it does not affect any privilege existing at common law.[359] But it does indicate that beyond the narrow confines of the common law qualified privilege of Parliamentary or judicial proceedings in the United Kingdom, there may not exist any other instances of qualified privilege at common law. Hence the need to make provision by statute.

18.93 The following are privileged statements not requiring explanation or contradiction.[360] They consist of fair and accurate reports of:

(1) proceedings in public of the legislatures of any dominion outside Great Britain;

(2) proceedings in public of an international organisation of which the United Kingdom or the Government is a member, or of any international conference to which the government sends a representative;

(3) any proceedings in public of an international court;

355 *Ibid.*, quoting Cantley J. in *London Artists Ltd v. Littler* [1968] 1 All E.R. 1075 at 1081.
356 S. 7(1), Schedule: this applies also to broadcasting by wireless or television: *ibid.* s. 16.
357 *Ibid.* s. 7(5).
358 *Ibid.* s. 7(2).
359 *Ibid.* s. 7(4). But it will not protect publications prohibited by law or publications not of public concern and not for the public benefit: *ibid.* s. 7(3).
360 Defamation Act 1952, Schedule, Part I.

(4) any proceedings before a court exercising jurisdiction throughout any part of the Queen's dominions outside the United Kingdom, or a court martial held outside the United Kingdom under the appropriate statutes;

(5) any proceedings in public of a body or person appointed to hold a public inquiry by the government or legislature of any part of the Queen's dominions outside the United Kingdom.

In addition fair and accurate copies or extracts from any register kept in pursuance of any Act of Parliament which is open to inspection by the public, or any other document required by the law of any part of the United Kingdom to be open to inspection by the public is also protected. So is a notice or advertisement published by or on the authority of any court within the United Kingdom or by any judge or officer of such court.

18.94 The following are protected subject to the possibility of an explanation or contradiction:[361]

(1) A fair and accurate report of the findings or decisions of various associations, their committees or governing bodies: viz. associations formed in the United Kingdom for promoting or encouraging art, science, religion or learning, or for promoting or safeguarding the interests of trade, business, industry or profession, or any game, sport, or pastime to the playing or exercise of which the public are invited or admitted, and empowered to exercise control over or adjudicate on matters of interest or concern to the association or the actions or conduct of those subject to its control or adjudication;

(2) A fair and accurate report of the proceedings at any public meeting held in the United Kingdom, i.e. a meeting *bona fide* and lawfully held for a lawful purpose, for the furtherance or discussion of matters of public concern, whether or not admission is restricted:

(3) A fair and accurate report of the proceedings at any meeting or sitting in the United Kingdom of local authorities, justices, or justices of the peace when not acting judicially, commissions, tribunals, committees or persons appointed to hold inquiries by Act of Parliament, the Queen, or a Minister, appointees of a local authority holding a local enquiry under Acts of Parliament, tribunals, boards, committees, or other bodies constituted by or under, and exercising, statutory powers (as long as the press and public are not excluded from such meetings);

(4) A fair and accurate report of proceedings at a general meeting of any public company created under an Act of Parliament or by Royal Charter;

(5) A copy or fair and accurate report or summary of any notice or other matter issued for the information of the public by or on behalf of a government department,[362] officer of state, local authority, or chief officer of police.

361 *Ibid.*, Schedule, Part II.

362 This did not cover the situation in *Blackshaw v. Lord*, para. 18.90 *supra*, because the information obtained by the writer of the article from the press officer of the government department involved was not of a formal nature issued by or under the authority of the department. It was obtained over the telephone as a result of pressure on the officer in question.

18.95 *(2) Statements which the maker had an interest or a legal, social or moral duty to make and the recipient had a corresponding interest or duty to receive.*[363] There must be an interest in the recipient and a duty to communicate in the speaker or an interest to be protected in the speaker and a duty to protect it in the recipient. In cases of common interest there may also be a common or reciprocal duty.[364] The interest in question is an interest material to the affairs of the recipient of the information such as would for instance assist in the making of an important decision or the determination of a particular course of action.[365] The duty in issue may be a legal duty. More often it is a moral or social duty.[366] Such a duty, in words of Lindley L.J.,[367] which have been cited with approval by other judges,[368] means "a duty recognised by English people of ordinary intelligence and moral principle, but at the same time not a duty enforceable by legal proceedings whether civil or criminal." The question is whether the great mass of right-minded people in the position of the defendant have considered it their duty, under the circumstances, to make the communications.[369]

18.96 In *Watt v. Longsdon*[370] the defendant, who was the director of a company of which the plaintiff was the foreign managing director, was sent a letter about the plaintiff's immorality, drunkenness and dishonesty. This came from X, the foreign manager of the company. Without obtaining confirmation, the defendant showed the letter from X to the chairman of the board of directors of the company and to the plaintiff's wife. The defendant also wrote to X with the comment that he, the defendant, held similar beliefs about the plaintiff. The Court of Appeal held that the publications to X and the chairman of the board of directors were protected by qualified privilege, but the publication to the plaintiff's wife was not. However the privilege that applied was destroyed by malice. Hence the defendant was liable for all the publications. In this instance the various officers of the company had a common interest and the appropriate duty arose as regards both X and the defendant. With respect to the plaintiff's wife, however, there was no duty on the part of the defendant to inform her husband. There would seen to be no duty on anyone to communicate what he thinks is the nature of a spouse's behaviour or moral character. Perhaps such a duty may exist where the maker of a statement

363 *Toogood v. Spyring* (1834) 1 Cr. M. & R. 181 at 193 *per* Parke B.; *Wenman v. Ash* (1853) 13 C.B. 836 at 846 *per* Maule J.; *Pullman v. Hill & Co.* [1891] 1 Q.B. 524 at 528 *per* Lord Esher M.R.; *Adam v. Ward* [1917] A.C. 309 at 334 *per* Lord Atkinson.

364 *Watt v. Longsdon* [1930] 1 K.B. 130 at 147 *per* Scrutton L.J.

365 *Austin v. Mirror Newspapers Ltd* [1986] 2 W.L.R. 57 at 62 *per* Lord Griffiths. See e.g., *Angel v. H.H. Bushell & Co. Ltd* [1968] 1 Q.B. 813, where the writer of the letter and the plaintiff, about whom the defamatory letter was written, were involved in a business way with the recipient of the letter.

366 Even if the obligation involved is imperfect: *Davies v. Snead* (1870) L.R. 5 Q.B. 608 at 611 *per* Blackburn J. On moral duties see *Stuart v. Bell* [1891] 2 Q.B. 341.

367 *Stuart v. Bell* [1891] 2 Q.B. 241 at 350.

368 Buckley L.J. in *Adam v. Ward* (1915) 31 T.L.R. 279 at 304; Greer L.J. in *Watt v. Longsdon, supra* at 153; Fox L.J. in *Blackshaw v. Lord* [1983] 2 All E.R. 311 at 338.

369 *Watt v. Longsdon, supra* at 153 *per* Greer L.J. Contrast Lopes L.J. in *Boxsius v. Goblet Frères* [1894] 1 Q.B. 842 at 946, suggesting that it was impossible to define a privileged occasion and each case must depend on its own facts.

370 [1930] 1 K.B. 130.

is the father, mother or other close relative of the spouse in question. A stranger does not have the same privilege.[371]

18.97 Privilege may attach if a statement is made for the protection of some lawful interest of the person who makes it, for example the protection of his own property.[372] It may attach if the statement is made for the protection of some lawful interest of the recipient, for example, where a reference is given about a potential employee,[373] or about the performance of an actual employee,[374] such as the conduct of a University professor who is being considered for the granting of tenure.[375] An allegation of improper or negligent conduct against a public servant may be privileged if made to persons having an interest to receive it, such as the police or senior officials.[376] In *Blackshaw v. Lord*,[377] the Court of Appeal considered the situation where an article in a newspaper discussed the conduct of a civil servant and his reasons for resigning. The defendants pleaded, *inter alia*, common law privilege. For this to attach to the publication it was necessary to establish that the newspaper had a duty to publish the information to the public at large and an interest in the public at large to receive the publication: a section of the public was not enough. The subject-matter must be of public interest; its publication must be in the public interest. The nature of the matter published and its source and the position or status of the publisher distributing the information must be such as to create the duty to publish the information to the intended recipients.[378] Where damaging facts have been ascertained to be true, or have been made the subject of a report, there may be a duty to report them, provided the public interest is wide enough. Where damaging allegations or charges have been made and are still under investigation or have been authoritatively refuted, there can be no duty to report them to the public. However, there may be extreme cases where the urgency of communicating a warning is so great, or the source of the information so reliable, that publication of suspicion or speculation is justified. Such would be the case where there is danger to the public from a suspected terrorist or the distribution of contaminated food or drugs.[379] It is insufficient, however, to argue that privilege of this sort extends to "fair information on a matter of public interest". Hence followed the criticisms of the decision in *Webb v. Times Publishing Co.*[380] that publication of judicial proceedings in a foreign country could come within the scope of qualified privilege, if the report were fair and accurate; and of the decision in *Perera*

371 *Todd v. Hawkins* (1837) 8 C. & P. 88. But even this is not clear: *Watt v. Longsdon, supra* at 149–150 *per* Scrutton L.J., who suggests there might sometimes be such a duty, 154 *per* Greer L.J. who takes a contrary view.
372 *Blackshaw v. Lord* [1983] 2 All E.R. 311 at 339 *per* Fox L.J.
373 *Jackson v. Hopperton* (1864) 16 C.B.N.S. 829.
374 *Riddick v. Thames Board Mills Ltd* [1977] 3 All E.R. 677: above para. 18.31.
375 *Slavutych v. Baker* (1975) 55 D.L.R. (3d) 224.
376 *Blackshaw v. Lord, supra* at 339 *per* Fox L.J.: see, e.g., *Andrews v. Nott-Bower* [1895] 1 Q.B. 888.
377 [1983] 2 All E.R. 311; above para. 18.89.
378 *Ibid.* at 327 *per* Stephenson L.J.
379 *Ibid.*
380 [1960] 2 All E.R. 789; above para. 18.90.

v. Peiris[381] that there was a duty to publish a report of a Commission on Bribery. It was the fact that nothing had actually been decided in respect of the conduct of the plaintiff that made it impossible for the defendant to argue that this publication was covered by the qualified privilege at common law pleaded in *Blackshaw v. Lord.* There was no duty on him to publish speculation about the plaintiff; and no interest on the part of the public at large to receive such speculative reports.

18.98 At common law the statements contained in an election address of one candidate for Parliament or other public office concerning the opposing candidate and his supporters were privileged in the absence of express malice, provided they were relevant to the matters which the electors would have to consider in deciding how to vote.[382] This has now been altered by the Defamation Act 1952 section 10, which removes any such privileges.[383]

(iv) Loss of qualified privilege

18.99 It is the occasion that is privileged, not the publication. As Lord Shaw said in *Adam v. Ward*:[384] "The occasion is privileged, the communication is protected." The publication on a privileged occasion must be a reasonable mode of publication, else it will not fall within the scope of the privilege.[385] In some instances the question has been raised whether the publication by dictation of a letter was covered by privilege when, although the letter might have been the subject of privilege if published to the addressee, e.g. another businessman, its contents were not subject to such privilege when published to, e.g. a clerk or a secretary.[386] The resolution of this issue depends on: (a) whether the method adopted was in accordance with normal business practices; or (b) in other instances whether the contents of the statement could have been seen or overheard by someone other than the person in respect of whom publication was privileged (and this was known to or foreseeable by the maker of the statement).[387] The privileged occasion can only arise when the publication is made to a person, other than the plaintiff, to whom the speaker has a duty or interest to make it and the hearer has a corresponding duty or interest to receive it.[388] This appears to conflict with decisions which hold that publication to a typist could still be privileged, although the typist had neither duty nor interest in relation to the defamatory statement.[389] In these situations the typist has been said to have an *original* privilege, like

381 [1949] A.C. 1: above para. 18.89.
382 *Braddock v. Bevins* [1948] 1 K.B. 580.
383 *Plummer v. Charman* [1962] 3 All E.R. 823.
384 [1917] A.C. 309 at 348: cp. *ibid.* at 328 *per* Lord Dunedin, 334 *per* Lord Atkinson.
385 *Edmondson v. Birch & Co. Ltd* [1907] 1 K.B. 371 at 380 *per* Collins M.R.
386 *Pullman v. Hill & Son* [1891] 1 Q.B. 524; *Boxsius v. Goblet Frères* [1894] 1 Q.B. 842; *Edmondson v. Birch & Co., supra*; *M. Isaacs & Sons Ltd v. Cook* [1925] 2 K.B. 391; *Osborn v. Thomas Boulter & Son* [1930] 2 K.B. 226; *Riddick v. Thames Board Mills Ltd* [1977] 3 All E.R. 677: above para. 18.95.
387 *White v. Stone* [1939] 2 K.B. 827.
388 *Ibid.* at 835 *per* McKinnon L.J.
389 *Bryanston Finance Ltd v. de Vries* [1975] Q.B. 703 at 719 *per* Lord Denning, 736–738 *per* Lawton L.J. Cp. Lord Diplock, dissenting, at 727.

the party dictating, or an ancillary privilege derived from that of the dictator. Two different principles seem to be involved according to the type of circumstances. The first is the idea that how publication occurs can affect the application of privilege. The second is the fact that publication beyond the true scope of the privilege destroys or can destroy the privileged occasion. As Parke B. explained in *Toogood v. Spyring*,[390] to say defamatory things of someone before a stranger might not be going outside the privilege, but going out of one's way to make a charge before a stranger might be evidence of malice, the effect of which would be to destroy the privilege. In *Adam v. Ward*,[391] publication to the Army Council of defamatory matter about the plaintiff, an M.P. who had made a speech in the House of Commons defamatory of a third party, was not an unreasonably wide publication and therefore neither excessive nor actionable. Nor in *Chapman v. Ellesmere*[392] was publication in the Racing Calendar of the results of an inquiry an excessive publication so as to permit an action by the plaintiff who had been the subject of the inquiry by the stewards.

18.100 Publication to persons other than those in respect of whom the publication will be privileged is not the only way that privilege may be lost. The same will be the result if extraneous matter is introduced, i.e. matter which does not deal with subjects involved in the interest or duty that gives rise to the privilege. Anything that is not relevant and pertinent to the discharge of the duty or the exercise of the right or the safeguarding of the interest which creates the privilege will not be protected.[393]

18.101 Malice also destroys privilege.[394] The expression "malice" in this context denotes the ideas of ill-will, or the intention of causing harm.[395] If the privileged occasion is not used honestly or is abused, the privilege is lost.[396] The occasion must be used *bona fide*, not for any indirect or wrong motive.[397] Malice may be shown by the extravagance of the language used;[398] or by the breadth of the language employed by the defendant, in the sense that such language was unnecessary for the purpose of protecting the material interest of fulfilling the duty otherwise governing the situation; or by the mode of publication, for example, if the statement is communicated deliberately to a stranger, one to whom publication would not be protected by privilege.[399] However, even if the defendant is *reckless*

390 (1834) 1 Cr. M. & R. 181 at 194.
391 [1971] A.C. 309.
392 [1932] 2 K.B. 431.
393 *Adam v. Ward* [1917] A.C. 309 at 320–321 *per* Lord Loreburn, 339 *per* Lord Atkinson, 348 *per* Lord Shaw.
394 See *Turner v. M-G-M Pictures Ltd* [1950] 1 All E.R. 449 for a discussion of malice.
395 Cp. above para. 18.68, in relation to fair comment.
396 *Royal Aquarium and Summer & Winter Gardens Ltd v. Parkinson* [1892] 1 Q.B. 431 at 443 *per* Lord Esher M.R.
397 *Ibid.* at 454 *per* Lopes L.J.
398 *Adam v. Ward* [1917] A.C. 309 at 326 *per* Lord Dunedin, 335 *per* Lord Atkinson: cp. *Spill v. Maule* (1869) L.R. 4 Ex. 232; *Turner v. M-G-M Pictures Ltd* [1905] 1 All E.R. 449 at 455 *per* Lord Porter.
399 *Toogood v. Spyring*, *supra* note 390.

in respect of the nature of his remarks or the occasion when they are made, this may not amount to malice so as to prevent or overcome an otherwise valid claim of qualified privilege, for example when the statement was made by one council member of another at a meeting of the council.[400]

18.102 Where there are several publishers, each one of whom has an interest or duty that would give rise to privilege, the malice of one publisher will not impair the privilege of the others. This was formerly a matter of some dispute.[401] However in *Egger v. Viscount Chelmsford*,[402] the Court of Appeal resolved the issue. A letter was written to the secretary of the dog club by the assistant secretary of the Kennel Club on behalf of the committee. The plaintiff sued for libel, saying that the contents of the letter, in which the plaintiff's application to be a judge of Alsatians for the Kennel Club was not approved, were defamatory. The jury found that five members of the Kennel Club committee acted with malice, but the other three members and the assistant secretary did not. On this evidence the Court of Appeal held that the members of the committee who acted from malice could be liable, despite the otherwise valid plea of qualified privilege, but the other three members of the committee, and the assistant secretary, were not liable. Each publisher had to be considered separately.[403] Moreover the malice of a principal or master, such as the guilty members of the committee, was not to be imputed to an agent or servant, the assistant secretary in this instance.

5. REMEDIES

(a) Damages

(i) Assessment

18.103 In an action for defamation the wrongful act is damage to the plaintiff's reputation.[403a] The injuries that he sustains may be classified under two heads. First there are the consequences of the attitude adopted

400 *Horrocks v. Lowe* [1975] A.C. 135.
401 *Smith v. Streatfield* [1913] 3 K.B. 764; *Smith v. National Meter Co.* [1945] K.B. 543; *Longdon-Griffiths v. Smith* [1951] 1 K.B. 295.
402 [1964] 3 All E.R. 406.
403 *Ibid.* at 412 *per* Lord Denning, 417 *per* Davies L.J.
403a Each publication of repetition of a defamation is actionable in respect of the damage such publication causes. Hence in *Culter v. McPhail* [1962] 2 All E.R. 474 the defendant was liable for the letter he sent to the editress of a journal, even though the plaintiff had released *other* defendants from liability, viz., those responsible for the publication of the letter in the journal. Since the repetition of the libel by the letter's publication in the journal was intended by the defendant, the damage from the repetition flowed from the original publication to the editress and could be taken into account in assessing damages recoverable for the original libel. The action must be brought within three years from the date when the cause of action accrued (i.e. the publication of the libel or the date of the damage in cases of slander not actionable *per se*, even if the plaintiff was unaware of the identity of the tortfeasor): Limitation Act 1980 s. 6A, inserted by the Administration of Justice Act 1985 s. 57(2): *R.B. Policies at Lloyd's v. Butler* [1950] 1 K.B. 76; *Pirelli General Cable Works v. Oscar Faber & Partners* [1983] 1 All E.R. 65. But note the possible extension of the term where the plaintiff lacks certain knowledge by virtue of the Limitation Act 1980 s. 32A, inserted by the Administration of Justice Act 1985 s. 57(4).

to him by other persons as a result of the diminution of the esteem in which they hold him because of the defamatory statement. Secondly, there is the grief or annoyance caused by the defamatory statement to the plaintiff himself.[404] The first heading relates to the compensation awarded to the plaintiff in respect of the damage to his character. Damages under the second heading, which also involves compensating the plaintiff for harm caused him by the defendant, may be "aggravated" by the manner in which or the motives with which the statement was made or persisted in by the defendant.[405]

18.104 Lord Hailsham pointed out in *Cassell & Co. Ltd v. Broome*[406] that in defamation actions, as well as other actions where damages for loss of reputation are involved, the principle of *restitutio in integrum*, i.e. of compensating the plaintiff for his loss which is the basic underlying idea behind awards of damages, has an even more highly subjective element than in other actions, such as those for personal injuries. Actions for loss of reputation

> "involve a money award which may put the plaintiff in a purely financial sense in a much stronger position than he was before the wrong. Not merely can he recover the estimated sum of his past and future losses, but, in case the libel, driven underground, emerges from its lurking place at some future date, he must be able to point to a sum awarded by a jury sufficient to convince a bystander of the baselessness of the charge."

18.105 The award must include factors for injury to the feelings, the anxiety and uncertainty undergone in the litigation, the absence of apology, or the reaffirmation of the truth of the matters complained of, or the malice of the defendant. All these are factors which may increase the damages to be awarded or may lead to a significant reduction in what might otherwise be awarded by a jury. Hence in *Cornwall v. Myskow*[407] a new trial was ordered on the issue of damages because the case for the defendant had not been put properly to the jury. It was not made clear that, by reason of lack of suggestion of financial loss, lack of damage to reputation and the fact that the plaintiff's hurt feelings resulted not from the defamation but from her views as to her performance in a play, which had been the subject of the alleged defamatory remarks, she had properly become entitled only to nominal damages. These take the form of a small sum to recognise the infringement of the plaintiff's right to reputation, at the same time indicating that the plaintiff had not really suffered damage either of a financial or emotional kind.

18.106 The bad conduct of the plaintiff may also enter into the question of calculating damages where the plaintiff has provoked the libel, or has libelled the defendant in reply. What is ultimately awarded is a figure

404 *McCarey v. Associated Newspapers Ltd* [1964] 3 All E.R. 947 at 959 *per* Diplock L.J. See e.g. *Mirror Newspapers Ltd v. Jools* (1986) 65 A.L.R. 174, damages for loss of professional standing of a medical practitioner, injury to his feelings and the effects on his health.

405 *McCarey, supra* at 959.

406 [1972] 1 All E.R. 801 at 824.

407 [1987] 2 All E.R. 504.

which cannot be arrived at by any purely objective computation.[408] For this reason the decision of the jury, unless a jury has been dispensed with at the request and with the consent of the parties,[409] will be final unless there has been a misdirection by the judge on the issue of damages or the award was out of all proportion to the injury or damage suffered by the plaintiff under either of the two heads mentioned above.[410]

18.107 The first head may consist of actual pecuniary loss, such as loss of practice by a doctor, loss of employment, or inability to obtain fresh appointments. But it may be purely social and lie in the attitude shown to the plaintiff by persons with whom he comes into social or professional contact. Neither this kind of injury (under the first head), nor grief and annoyance caused to the plaintiff (under the second head) involves pecuniary loss. But a money value must be put on these kinds of injury, even though this necessitates an attempt "to equate the incommensurable".[411]

18.108 Purely compensatory damages, awarded under the first head, and aggravated damages, awarded under the second, must be differentiated from "exemplary" or "punitive" damages. The difference between compensatory and exemplary damages, to use the expression favoured by Lord Hailsham in *Cassell & Co. Ltd v. Broome*,[412] is clear. The former are designed to make restitution: the latter to punish the defendant. Lord Hailsham considered that the expressions "vindictive" and "retributory" damages ought to be avoided.[413] Even when a purely punitive element was involved, vindictiveness was not a good motive for awarding punishment. "Retributory" was objectionable because it was ambiguous. It could be used to cover both aggravated damages to compensate the plaintiff because his injury was actually greater and as a result of the conduct of the plaintiff exciting the indignation of the court demanded a more generous solatium. It could also be used to cover punitive or exemplary damages purely to punish the defendant or hold him up as an example.

18.109 Exemplary damages may be awarded in defamation actions (and indeed other types of tort action).[414] However in *Rookes v. Barnard*[415] Lord Devlin, who appears to have spoken for the entire House of Lords on this

408 *Cassell & Co. Ltd v. Broome, supra* at 824.
409 Note, however, the court's power to refuse a jury when prolonged examination of documents or accounts or a scientific or local investigation cannot conveniently be made with a jury: Supreme Court Act 1981 s. 69(1). The Faulks Committee, Cmnd. 5909, 1975, did not recommend abolition of jury trials for defamation, but did suggest that juries should be allowed only at the discretion of the judge; also that the power of juries over damages should be limited to determining which category of damage should be allowed, leaving it to the judge to fix the amount.
410 *Broadway Approvals Ltd v. Odhams Press Ltd* [1965] 2 All E.R. 523; *Cassell & Co. Ltd v. Broome, supra* at 819 *per* Lord Hailsham, 845 *per* Lord Morris, 878 *per* Lord Kilbrandon. See also *Sutcliffe v. Pressdram Ltd* [1980] 1 All E.R. 269 at 281–3 *per* Lord Donaldson M.R., 288–9 *per* Nourse L.J., 290–3 *per* Russell L.J.
411 *McCarey v. Associated Newspapers Ltd* [1964] 3 All E.R. 947 at 959 *per* Diplock L.J.
412 [1972] 1 All E.R. 801 at 826.
413 *Ibid.* at 825–826.
414 *Ibid.*
415 [1964] A.C. 1129.

issue, limited the situations where such damages could be awarded. Although that decision has not been followed in this respect in other Commonwealth countries where the common law applies, such as Australia and Canada,[416] it was reaffirmed by the House of Lords in *Cassell & Co. Ltd v. Broome*,[417] over the view of the Court of Appeal[418] that Lord Devlin had spoken *per incuriam*. It is now settled that exemplary damages may only be awarded: (1) where statute allows; (2) where there has been oppressive, arbitrary, or unconstitutional action by the servants of the government, not the servants of private individuals, (though Lord Hailsham thought that this might be extended to others not servants of the government in the strict sense, e.g. the police, and to abuses of power without warrant by persons purporting to exercise legal authority);[419] or (3) where the defendant's conduct has been calculated by him to make a profit for himself which may well exceed the compensation payable to the plaintiff (i.e. under the two heads previously mentioned).

18.110 The last of these three categories is usually the one applicable to defamation actions (although the second, if not the first, is not entirely without potential relevance). This is the category that has been applied in several decisions[420] which themselves were approved and applied by the House of Lords in *Cassell & Co. Ltd v. Broome*.[421] The jury's award of £25,000 in that case was upheld on the basis of the principles stated by Lord Devlin because there was ample evidence that the defendants had calculated that they would make a profit out of publishing the book which defamed the plaintiff by indicating that he had behaved improperly while in command of a convoy going to Russia during the Second World War. Nor had there been any misdirection of the jury by the judge: so that it was not reasonable for the court to interfere with the jury's award in the absence of proof that such award was manifestly so large that no reasonable jury, properly directed, could possibly have reached such figure. This was an exceptionally high award of exemplary damages; but it was not impossible for a reasonable jury to reach that sum.[422]

(ii) Mitigation

18.111 A defendant may always tender evidence in mitigation of the compensatory damages that might otherwise be awarded to the plaintiff.

416 See *Cassell & Co. Ltd v. Broome*, *supra* at 860–861 *per* Lord Wilberforce, 871 *per* Lord Diplock.

417 *Supra.*

418 [1971] 2 All E.R. 187.

419 *Cassell & Co. Ltd v. Broome* [1972] 1 All E.R. 801 at 829–830.

420 *McCarey v. Associated Newspapers Ltd*, *supra*: *Broadway Approvals Ltd v. Odhams Press Ltd*, *supra*; *Fielding v. Variety Incorporated* [1967] 2 All E.R. 497; cp. *Manson v. Associated Newspapers Ltd* [1965] 2 All E.R. 954, where the jury did not award exemplary damages.

421 What should be done where there are several plaintiffs claiming such damages and the way the jury should be directed were discussed in *Riches v. News Group Newspapers Ltd* [1985] 2 All E.R. 845. The appropriate award is a single amount divided amongst the plaintiffs, not separate amounts for each plaintiff.

422 Contrast *Riches v. News Group Newspapers Ltd*, *supra*, where the Court of Appeal held that the trial judge had misdirected the jury on the question of exemplary damages and no reasonable jury, properly directed, would have intended to punish the defendants to the extent in question, viz., £250,000. A new trial was ordered on this issue.

At common law such evidence is concerned with the character or reputation of the plaintiff.[423] Its purpose is to prove that the plaintiff is not entitled to claim that he had a good reputation that was harmed or affected by the defamation published by the defendant. Such evidence may be admitted as showing that the plaintiff had a bad reputation in a sector of life relevant to the alleged defamation. Evidence of specific instances of misconduct or tending to show what character the plaintiff ought to have in public estimation (not the character that he does have) is inadmissible in mitigation of damages.[423a] The character of the plaintiff that is relevant in this context is not his disposition but the character that the plaintiff bears in public estimation, i.e. his reputation.[424] In this respect the House of Lords explained in *Associated Newspapers Ltd v. Dingle*[425] that the relevant reputation of the plaintiff is his reputation prior to the publication of the libel that is in issue. Hence other contemporaneous publications of the same libel were inadmissible to prove that the plaintiff did not have a reputation that could be tarnished by the defendant's publication of the libel. "When one speaks of a plaintiff's 'actual' reputation or 'current' reputation . . . one means his reputation as accumulated from one source or another over the period of time that precedes the occasion of the libel that is in suit."[426] Lord Denning distinguished between evidence from those who knew the plaintiff, had dealings with him and could judge his worth, and rumours or reports, often spread by busybodies who know nothing of the plaintiff or indulged in by newspapers for the benefit of their circulation which they have no material to justify.[427] In *Waters v. Sunday Pictorial Newspapers Ltd*,[428] however, it was held permissible to introduce evidence that the plaintiff had already been brought into public odium by judgments in earlier criminal and civil proceedings. Hence the defendants could plead those proceedings by way of mitigation of the damages sought by the plaintiff. That plea did no more than direct attention to the relevant sector of the plaintiff's life in respect of which he was alleged to be of bad reputation, viz., as being dishonest and fraudulent. Although the criminal conviction had been quashed for misdirection, and the civil proceedings by a company in which the plaintiff was interested had been dismissed, in these proceedings, as well as another civil action, there had been comments about the honesty of the plaintiff and his companies.

18.112 Under the Libel Act 1843,[429] a defendant, after giving written notice of his intention to do so, may give in evidence in mitigation of

423 *Scott v. Sampson* (1882) 8 Q.B.D. 491; *Hobbs v. Tinling* [1929] 2 K.B. 1.
423a But in mitigation any evidence properly before the jury, including evidence of specific acts of misconduct, or other evidence in support of an unsuccessful plea of justification, can be relied on by the defendant: *Pamplin v. Express Newspapers Ltd (No. 2)* [1988] 1 All E.R. 282.
424 *Plato Films Ltd v. Speidel* [1961] 1 All E.R. 876.
425 [1962] 2 All E.R. 737.
426 *Ibid.* at 747 *per* Lord Radcliffe.
427 *Ibid.* at 755.
428 [1961] 2 All E.R. 758.
429 6 & 7 Vict. c. 96, s. 1. Payment into court is not necessary, but is possible under R.S.C. Ord 22 r. 1–4. Such payment must not be disclosed until questions of liability and damages have been decided: R.S.C Ord. 22 r. 7.

damages that he made or offered an apology to the plaintiff before the commencement of the action or as soon as possible afterwards as he had opportunity to do so, if the action was commenced before he had an opportunity to make or offer such apology.

18.113 Under the Defamation Act 1952,[430] the defendant can give evidence in mitigation of damages that the plaintiff has recovered damages, or has brought an action for damages, for defamation in respect of the publication of words to the same effect as the words on which the action is founded, or has received or agreed to receive compensation in respect of any such publication. If the same defamation has been published by more than one defendant the jury should take into account how far the damage alleged by the plaintiff can be attributed solely to the defamation with which they are concerned and how far it ought to be regarded as the joint result of the various publications.[431]

18.114 Facts which tend to disprove malice on the part of the defendant[432] may also be given in evidence, as long as particulars of the matters which the defendant intends to give in evidence are provided to the plaintiff at least 7 days before the trial (unless the leave of the judge is given dispensing with such prior notification).[433] This provision of the Rules relates to evidence-in-chief, not cross-examination: and it deals with evidence of the circumstances under which the defamation was published, i.e. the issue of malice, and the character of the plaintiff, i.e. his lack of good reputation.

(b) Apology

18.115 A specific defence is provided for newspapers and other periodical publications by the Libel Act 1843.[434] Such defendants can plead that the libel was inserted without actual malice and without gross negligence; and that before commencement of the action, or at the earliest opportunity afterwards, the defendant inserted in the newspaper or other periodical a full apology for the libel, or, if the newspaper or other periodical was ordinarily published at intervals greater than one week, had offered to publish the apology in any newspaper or periodical selected by the plaintiff.[435] By the Libel Act 1845[436] it was provided that no such plea can

430 15 & 16 Geo. VI & 1 Eliz. II c. 66, s. 12.
431 *Lewis v. Daily Telegraph Ltd* [1963] 2 All E.R. 151.
432 E.g., no intention to refer to the plaintiff or that words should be honest belief of defendant that statement was true: *Campbell v. Spottiswoode* (1863) 3 B. & S. 769 at 781; honest belief that statement was vague and not believed by readers: *Morgan v. Odhams Press Ltd* [1971] 2 All E.R. 1156.
433 R.S.C. Ord. 82, r. 7.
434 6 & 7 Vict. c. 96, s. 2.
435 "Newspaper" is not defined in the Act, but is defined in the Newspaper Libel and Registration Act 1881 s. 1. A "periodical" is a work that comes out from time to time and is miscellaneous in its articles: *Brown v. Cooke* (1846) 16 L.J. Ch. 140 at 142 *per* Shadwell V.C.
436 8 & 9 Vict. s. 2; R.S.C. Ord. 22 r. 1.

be made unless the defendant also pays into court at the same time a sum of money by way of amends.[437]

18.116 The plaintiff can deny the whole or a part of the plea.[438] If the statutory defence fails in one particular, the payment into court cannot be relied on as a payment into court under the Rules of the Supreme Court,[439] so the plaintiff, if he recovers less than the amount paid in under this defence, will still be entitled to his costs.[440] Although generally payment into court must not be pleaded,[441] this is not the case where the defence of apology is involved.[442]

18.117 In view of the provisions of section 4 of the Defamation Act 1952, dealing with unintentional defamation,[443] it is probable that this defence is no longer of such utility to defendants in respect of whom this statutory defence was first introduced.

(c) Injunction

18.118 The originally equitable, discretionary remedy of an injunction,[444] for the purpose of preventing the defendant from publishing, or continuing to publish matter that is defamatory of the plaintiff, is obtainable in theory at the suit of the plaintiff. However the courts are reluctant to grant such a remedy since it necessarily involves interference with freedom of speech.[445] It will not be granted even when it can be shown by the plaintiff that irreparable harm, not compensable by any amount of damages, would be caused to him if the defamation is published.[446] The court will not usually grant an injunction in respect of a libel when it is said by the defendant that the words are true and he is going to justify them.[446a] Similarly, when an occasion is protected by qualified privilege the court will not grant an injunction to restrain the publication of defamation, so as to prevent the defendant from exercising the privilege, unless the plaintiff shows that what the defendant proposes to say is known by him to be untrue, so that it is clearly malicious. So long as he proposes to say what he honestly believes to be true, no injunction will be

437 Contrast the situation under the Libel Act 1843 s. 1, para. 18.112 *supra*, dealing with an apology in mitigation of damages.
438 *Chadwick v. Herapath* (1847) 3 C.B. 885.
439 *Oxley v. Wilkes* [1898] 2 Q.B. 56.
440 *Sley v. Tillotson & Sons* (1898) 14 T.L.R. 545.
441 R.S.C. Ord. 22 r. 7.
442 R.S.C. Ord. 82 r. 4(2).
443 Above para. 18.54.
444 See now R.S.C. Ord. 29, r. 1; Supreme Court Practice, 1985, vol. 1, 454–465.
445 *Herbage v. Pressdram Ltd* [1984] 2 All E.R. 769 at 771 *per* Griffiths L.J.; cp. *Fraser v. Evans* [1964] 1 All E.R. 8 at 10 *per* Lord Denning M.R.
446 *Herbage v. Pressdram, supra per* Griffiths L.J., refusing to apply *American Cyanamid Co. v. Ethicon Ltd* [1975] A.C. 396.
446a Unless the material is published in pursuance of a conspiracy with the sole or dominant purpose of injuring the plaintiff: *Gulf Oil (G.B.) Ltd v. Page* [1987] 3 All E.R. 14.

granted.[447] In *Harakas v. Baltic Mercantile Shipping Exchange Ltd*,[448] therefore, the sought for injunction was refused. The maritime bureau of the International Chamber of Commerce, which published a notice in the Baltic Exchange stating that it had information about the plaintiffs that would be made available to those contemplating business with them, was not enjoined from publishing such further information. The bureau had reasonable grounds for honestly believing that the information in question, which related to fraud, to obtain information and warn of which was the function of the bureau, was true.

18.119 The same principles were applied by the Court of Appeal in *Herbage v. Pressdram Ltd*[449] to a case involving the Rehabilitation of Offenders Act 1974. Under this statute to publish a "spent conviction" is defamatory.[450] The defendant cannot rely on the plea of justification if the publication is proved to have been made with malice.[451] Hence in that case an injunction to restrain the defendants from publishing the facts about the plaintiff was refused because there was no evidence that the defendants were acting from some "irrelevant, spiteful or improper motive".[452] That was the meaning of the expression "malice" in the statute, just as it was where a defendant acted on a defence of qualified privilege.[453]

447 *Harakas v. Baltic Mercantile Shipping Exchange Ltd* [1982] 2 All E.R. 701 at 703 *per* Lord Denning, M.R.; *Quartz Hill Consolidated Gold Mining Co. v. Beall* (1882) 20 Ch.D. 501; *Bonnard v. Perryman* [1891] 2 Ch. 269; *Herbage v. Pressdram Ltd*, *supra* at 771 *per* Griffiths L.J.
448 *Supra*.
449 *Supra*.
450 Above para. 18.58, note 221a.
451 Rehabilitation of Offenders Act 1974 s. 8(5).
452 *Supra* note 445 at 772 *per* Griffiths L.J.
453 *Ibid.*: see above pp. 18.101.

CHAPTER 19

Privacy

1. A QUESTIONABLE CONCEPT

19.01 There is no agreement on what is meant by the term "privacy" nor upon what is comprehended by the expression "invasion of privacy".[1] The classic definition of an American judge of the nineteenth century is "the right to be let alone".[2] This was taken up and expanded in a famous article in the *Harvard Law Review* in 1890, in which the authors, Warren and Brandeis, argued on the basis of older English authorities that the common law did recognise a person's right to privacy and that any improper invasion of that privacy could be dealt with by an appropriate remedy.[3] In the century that has elapsed since that article was published courts in America have developed doctrines which may loosely be referred to as creating a right of action in certain circumstances for conduct that is not otherwise within the scope of some existing, nominate tort, such as defamation, trespass or nuisance; and some American legislatures have passed statutes which, to a degree, put into effect what was contended for by Warren and Brandeis.[4] In Canada several provincial legislatures have passed Privacy Acts, which, without defining what is meant by the expression, allow an aggrieved party to sue in tort for certain types of conduct.[5] Apart from such legislation Canadian courts have provided a plaintiff with relief where what occurred was something that caused him or her distress, such as constant telephone calls that disturbed his peace,[6] or inviting the public to telephone the plaintiff and complain about his conduct;[7] or has amounted to what has been called "appropriation of personality",[8] where the defendant has sought to make a profit out of the use of the plaintiff's face, figure, reputation or public recognition, without

1 Seipp, "English Judicial Recognition of a Right to Privacy" (1983) 3 Ox. J. Leg. St. 325 at 328–335. See also Gavison, "Privacy and the Limits of the Law" (1980) 89 Yale L.J. 421. For arguments against the inclusion of such a concept in English law, see Wacks, "The Poverty of Privacy" (1980) 96 L.Q.R. 73; Wacks, *The Protection of Privacy*, 1980.
2 Cooley, *Law of Torts*, 2nd ed. 1888 at 29.
3 Warren & Brandeis, "The Right of Privacy" (1890) 4 H.L.R. 193.
4 See "Developments in the Law" (1982) 95 H.L.R. 1324; note "The Right to Privacy in Nineteenth Century America" (1981) 94 H.L.R. 1892.
5 British Columbia (R.S.B.C. 1979, c. 336); Manitoba (R.S.M. 1970, c. 74); Newfoundland (S.Nfld. 1981, c. 6); Saskatchewan (R.S.S. 1979, c. P–24).
6 *Motherwell v. Motherwell* (1976) 73 D.L.R. (3d) 62.
7 *Robbins v. C.B.C.* (1958) 12 D.L.R. (2d) 35.
8 Frazer, "Appropriation of Personality—A New Tort?" (1983) 99 L.Q.R. 282.

first obtaining the plaintiff's consent to such use.[9] In Canada and the United States, therefore, something which may be referred to as a "right of privacy" may be said to have been accepted by the courts and the legislatures, limited in scope though this right may be.[10] In contrast, in England, no such development has occurred. Several times, in consequence of committee reports and other similar interest, attempts have been made to secure the passage of legislation by Parliament that would give protection against conduct that could be called an invasion of privacy akin to what is covered by common law decisions or legislation elsewhere.[11] Nothing ever came of such efforts. It is therefore to the common law that one must look for any possible relief where the complaint is that the private life of the plaintiff has been invaded or interfered with by the conduct of the defendant.[12]

19.02 What this means is that the plaintiff must be able to show that the conduct of the defendant amounts to the commission of some recognised tort in respect of which the plaintiff has a cause of action. The nature of that tort will obviously depend upon the kind of misconduct that is involved and the way in which that misconduct impinges upon the life of the plaintiff. Hence it is necessary to identify some, at least, of the ways in which a defendant may behave in a manner that constitutes an invasion, infringement or attack upon the privacy, the private life, of the plaintiff. This, in turn, necessitates some examination of what is, or may be included within the scope of a person's private life.

2. THE SCOPE OF PRIVACY

19.03 To begin, this clearly includes his or her right to be physically undisturbed in his or her home or place of business or work. Everyone has the right to go about their daily lives without physical interference. Conduct which amounts to such interference may constitute trespass to the person, to land, or to goods.[13] But to allow the plaintiff an action it must

9 *Racine v. C.J.R.C. Radio Capitale Ltée* (1978) 80 D.L.R. (3d) 441; *Athans v. Canadian Adventure Camps Ltd* (1978) 80 D.L.R. (3d) 583; *Heath v. Weist & Barron School of Television (Canada) Ltd* (1981) 18 C.C.L.T. 129; *Darrell v. Mengen Institute* (1983) 72 C.P.R. (2d) 238. But contrast *Krouse v. Chrysler Canada Ltd* (1974) 40 D.L.R. (3d) 15, reversing (1972) 25 D.L.R. (3d) 49.

10 It is also recognised internationally in the Universal Declaration on Human Rights 1948; the International Covenant on Civil and Political Rights 1966; and the European Convention on Human Rights 1950; (see *Schering Chemicals Ltd v. Falkman Ltd* [1981] 2 All E.R. 321 at 333 *per* Lord Denning).

11 Right of Privacy Bill 1961; Right of Privacy Bill 1967; Right of Privacy Bill 1969. See the Report of the Committee on Privacy, 1972, Cmnd. 5012. However some protection is given by the Copyright Designs and Patents Act 1988 s. 77, in cases of false attribution of authorship (see on s. 43 of the 1956 Act *Moore v. News of the World Ltd* [1972] 1 Q.B. 441); the Rehabilitation of Offenders Act 1972, on which see para. 18.58; and the Data Protection Act 1984.

12 For the opinion that some judicial pronouncements come close to recognition of a general privacy interest protected at common law as one of the rights of every English subject, see Seipp, *loc. cit.* at 326 note 11.

13 See Chapters 5–7.

be possible to hold that a trespass has been committed. Hence to eavesdrop may not be actionable, as long as the eavesdropper has not come on to the plaintiff's land to do so. Nor will it be a trespass to listen in to another's telephone conversation, as long as this does not entail committing a trespass to the plaintiff's property.[14] But there may be a right to maintain the confidentiality of a telephone conversation, such that the defendant could be liable to be restrained from using taped material which he acquired by tapping the plaintiff's telephone and listening to his conversations.[15] Even if the defendant had no lawful reason, justification or excuse for surveillance of the plaintiff or his property, which might be the case where the surveillance is undertaken by the police under certain circumstances, the defendant will not be guilty of trespass unless he can be said to have invaded the plaintiff's property. In *Bernstein of Leigh v. Skyviews & General Ltd*,[16] the plaintiff was unsuccessful in his attempt to claim that the defendants' conduct was actionable. They had flown low over the plaintiff's property and taken pictures which they offered to sell to him. For reasons which are considered elsewhere,[17] the defendants were not guilty of trespass to the plaintiff's land. Hence the action failed. Although the plaintiff legitimately claimed that his privacy had been invaded, the court held that without proof that a trespass had been committed he could not succeed. The approach taken in this case indicates that before conduct that may be said to constitute an invasion of privacy in this fashion can become actionable it must satisfy the requirements of an action for trespass.

19.04 Similarly, where the interference is indirect rather than direct, in order for it to be actionable it must amount to a nuisance in the legal sense. This involves fulfillment of the essential elements of the tort of nuisance.[18] It also means, or should mean, that only someone who has a proprietary interest on the land on which he was when the alleged invasion of privacy/nuisance was committed can sue. However an Alberta court in *Motherwell v. Motherwell*[19] held that someone who was neither the owner nor the tenant of the property where the harassing telephone calls were received, but was the wife of the owner, could be a plaintiff in an action which sought injunctive relief, rather than damages, in respect of the distress and inconvenience caused by the defendant's continuous telephoning. Such an attitude indicates that some courts are prepared to broaden the scope of the tort of nuisance in order to cope with the problem of privacy. The stricter view of the law by English courts suggests that a

14 *Malone v. Commissioner of Police of the Metropolis (No. 2)* [1979] 2 All E.R. 620 at 642–644 *per* Megarry V-C. But a criminal offence may be committed under the Wireless Telegraphy Act 1949 s. 8.
15 *Francome v. Mirror Group Newspapers Ltd* [1984] 2 All E.R. 408.
16 [1978] Q.B. 479.
17 See paras. 5.26–27.
18 Chapter 8; cp. *Victoria Park Racing and Recreation Grounds Co. Ltd v. Taylor* (1939) 58 C.L.R. 479: below paras. 19.09–10.
19 Above note 6.

similar relaxation of the technical rules of nuisance might not occur on this side of the Atlantic.

19.05 The second major way in which invasions of privacy might occur is by the publication of information about the plaintiff. If false information is conveyed to others, this might constitute defamation, if the untrue statements are defamatory.[20] It might entail commission of the tort of injurious falsehood.[21] If the information misleads others and causes them harm or loss, not the person about whom the information is given, no wrong would seem to have been committed against the latter, only against those who relied on the information.[22] If the information is correct, no defamation has been committed.[23] Nevertheless the publication of the truth about the plaintiff may be embarrassing or even harmful. It has long been argued that to publish embarrassing, harmful or otherwise damaging true information about someone should be actionable when there is no valid reason for doing so, such as the protection of the public, or the invitation of the plaintiff to make such knowledge public by virtue of the plaintiff's own conduct, for example where the plaintiff has sought out publicity or engaged in some public activity such as acting or politics. The common law in England does not provide for any such liability.[24] Indeed in *Re X*[25] the Court of Appeal held that to enjoin the publication of the unpleasant truth about someone in a biography of him after his death could not be prevented even though it was admitted that knowledge of her father's character might have detrimental psychological effects upon the daughter of the deceased. The argument in favour of censorship, which is what was involved, was based on the fact that the daughter was a ward of court and the function of the court was to protect the interests of the ward. Notwithstanding this vital aspect of the courts' jurisdiction over minors, the court held that freedom of speech was an overriding consideration. There was no right to inhibit the publication of the truth. Nevertheless, it would appear from other decisions that, if the public interest is sufficiently great and important, there may be occasions when courts can order that something not be published or disclosed.[26] Such decisions usually relate to the disclosure of information relating to the conduct of litigation, such as the source of information on which proceedings were commenced. However, it has been held on several occasions that there is no right on the part of a journalist to conceal and not reveal the name of those who provided information on which he writes a column or article for the

20 Chapter 18.
21 Chapter 21 at paras. 21.54ff.
22 Viz., deceit: Chapter 17. But the law now provides some protection in the case of certain data collected for purposes of creditworthiness: Data Protection Act 1984.
23 But see the Rehabilitation of Offenders Act 1972 s. 8: see para. 18.58.
24 The situation may be different in the United States: *Melvin v. Reid* (1931) 112 Cal.App. 285. As to the denial of an action for public figures see *Sidis v. F.-R. Publishing Corporation* (1940) 113 F. (2d) 806; *Street v. N.B.C.* (1981) 645 F. (2d) 1227.
25 [1975] 1 All E.R. 697; and see *Re F* [1977] Fam. 58, 98; *Barritt v. Attorney-General* [1971] 1 W.L.R. 1713.
26 *D v. N.S.P.C.C.* [1978] A.C. 171; *Science Research Council v. Nassé* [1979] 3 All E.R. 673.

newspaper.[27] Only if the public interest is better served by concealment than revelation will the courts uphold a party's claim to refrain from making known the private source of his or her information.[28]

19.06 A third important type of infringement of privacy is appropriation of personality.[29] In effect the defendant makes use of certain attributes of the plaintiff, without the plaintiff's consent, and without in any way committing trespass, nuisance, defamation or some other tortious act. What is occurring is a sort of theft of something intangible belonging to the plaintiff, something which the plaintiff could, and perhaps was intending to use to his or her economic advantage, but because of what the defendant did might not be able to do so, or to do so as profitably. Several examples of this may be found in Canadian decisions.[30] It does not appear to have been accepted in England. In *Sim v. Heinz*,[31] the plaintiff sought an injunction to restrain the defendants from using a voice very similar to the distinctive voice of the plaintiff to advertise their wares. Unlike the famous decision in *Tolley v. Fry & Sons Ltd*,[32] where the use of the plaintiff's caricature was defamatory because it alleged that he was not an amateur golfer but was making money from his expertise at the game, the use of the plaintiff's voice in the *Sim* case could not be defamatory because he was a professional actor. Nor was it any other tort, such as injurious falsehood or passing-off. The Court of Appeal rejected the plaintiff's claim for an injunction. However it was left open whether he might have been successful had he sought damages. On the analogy of the Canadian cases there would be a good case for such a claim because by suggesting that the plaintiff had "sold" his voice to the defendants the defandants had made it difficult, if not impossible, for the plaintiff to enter into such a contract for the "sale" of his voice with any other party seeking to make similar use of the plaintiff's public image in the promotion of their product. Hence he had suffered actual, or potential, economic loss. The opportunity was missed to provide some guidance as to the possible emergence of tortious liability in consequence of such impropriety.[33] In any event, despite the decisions in which conduct of this kind has led to liability to compensate the plaintiff, it is difficult to consider such conduct as an invasion of privacy. It is more in the nature of "conversion" of the personal tributes of the plaintiff. The American scholar Prosser[34] considered such instances as typifying one sort of invasion of privacy: and the Canadian statutes, building on common law decisions, include it in their exposition of the kind of behaviour that will entail tortious liability.[35]

27 *Attorney-General v. Clough* [1963] 1 All E.R. 420; *Attorney-General v. Mulholland* [1963] 2 Q.B. 477; *British Steel Corporation v. Granada Television Ltd* [1981] 1 All E.R. 417.
28 *Harman v. Secretary of State for the Home Department* [1982] 2 W.L.R. 338.
29 Some statutory protection is provided under the law governing trade names, trade marks and copyright, as well as the law relating to passing off: see Chapter 21 at p. 571.
30 See the cases cited *supra* note 9.
31 [1959] 1 All E.R. 547.
32 [1931] A.C. 333; cp. *Dunlop Rubber Co. Ltd v. Dunlop* [1921] A.C. 367. Contrast *Corelli v. Ward* (1906) 22 T.L.R. 532; *Dockwell v. Dougall* (1899) 80 L.T. 556.
33 The correctness of this decision was left open by Lord Denning M.R. in *Fraser v. Evans* [1969] 1 All E.R. 8 at 11.
34 Prosser, "Privacy" (1960) 48 Calif. L.R. 383 at 389.
35 They are cited *supra* note 5.

3. DIFFERENT TYPES OF WRONGDOING

19.07 Such developments suggest that there are two aspects of privacy. One is concerned with the personal side of an individual's life, his freedom from interference, his character, his reputation, his integrity, his ability to relate personally and commercially with others. The other is concerned with the economic side of an individual's life, his freedom and ability to make use of his personality, repute, standing or individuality for the purpose of financial gain. They are widely different. Invasions of privacy of the first kind seem at first sight to be more amenable to the intervention of the law, in the sense that conduct of that kind approximates so very closely to such well-established torts as trespass, nuisance, defamation and injurious falsehood, that it would not be unreasonable to extend the scope of such torts to include the type of conduct in question. The courts have been reluctant to do so in England. Parliament with some limited exceptions[36] has not been able or willing to achieve what the courts have not done. Perhaps the unwillingness of the courts to enlarge existing torts so as to take into the account the kind of conduct that has been considered is the result of the concern felt by the courts not to carry the boundaries of tort so far in order to protect someone from certain kinds of harm that the rights of others become unduly limited.[37] A delicate balancing act is involved. At the moment the balance has come down on the side of restricting liability.

19.08 Where the alleged invasion of privacy relates to the economic aspects of the plaintiff's life rather than his freedom from embarrassing, inconvenient or distressing attacks upon his daily activities or character, the issues that are involved are different. There is a strong argument in favour of recognition of some tort of "appropriation of personality", although this might not be a suitable name to describe what is entailed. Such a tort is very closely related to existing forms of liability, such as injurious falsehood or the emergent tort of wrongful interference with trade or business.[38] What is more, to accept the existence of such a tort would not require the courts to make any vital decisions as between competing rights, viz., freedom from interference on the one hand versus freedom of speech, freedom of action, or the right to use one's own property on the other. The courts have accepted that interference with another's freedom to make use of his skills, expertise, abilities, or professional qualifications is wrongful: it may be a tort in certain circumstances; it may involve the invalidity of a contract on the ground of restraint of trade in others. There is not a big gap between such forms of liability and acceptance of the argument that to employ the personal attributes of someone without his or her agreement for the purposes of advancing one's own interests should be wrongful and actionable at the suit of the person whose attributes have been misused in this way.

36 See *supra* note 11. See also Seipp, *loc cit.*, 349–350 for some other statutory references.
37 But note the discussion of judicial initiatives by Seipp, *loc. cit.* at 353–362.
38 See pp. 565–566.

19.09 It is more questionable, however, whether this should be subsumed under the heading of "invasion of privacy".[39] Such behaviour is far removed from the original contention of Warren and Brandeis in 1890. They were more concerned with misconduct of the first type. Conduct falling within the second category can be regarded as a form of invasion of privacy only by arguing that it may embarrass or harass the plaintiff, or lead to his being regarded less favourably, as the plaintiff contended, successfully, in *Tolley v. Fry*,[40] rather than that it caused him financial loss. In this respect it is worthy of note that in *Victoria Park Racing and Recreation Grounds Ltd v. Taylor*,[41] fifty years ago, the High Court of Australia refused to allow an action where the defendant did not affect the plaintiff's land injuriously except by making it less likely that the plaintiff would obtain financial gain from the use of his land. The defendants did not trespass on the plaintiff's land; nor did they do anything on their land that could be treated as constituting what usually occurs in cases of nuisance. The defendants overlooked the plaintiff's racetrack from the defendants' land, and broadcast the races. The effect of this, argued the plaintiff, was that those who would normally pay to come onto the plaintiff's land to view the races would not need to do so. They could learn what happened by listening to the defendants' broadcast. On the application of the strict, technical rules of nuisance, no tort had been committed. The fact that economic loss or injury had been inflicted on the plaintiff by the defendant was not reason enough to treat the plaintiff's conduct as tortious.

19.10 Although it may be argued, in the present climate of legal opinion, that the defendants' behaviour ought to have been regarded as tortious, nevertheless what was done here cannot be spoken of as an invasion of privacy except by a gross distortion of the ordinary meaning of the expression. It is much more closely related to the Canadian decisions and statutory provisions that deal with the appropriation of other's personal attributes. It is even more closely related to wrongful interference with trade or business. However that tort depends upon the use of some wrongful means.[42] To look over a fence would not appear to be wrongful. Hence what was done by the defendants in the *Taylor* case might still not be sufficient to entitle a court to declare that the defendants had "wrongfully" interfered with the plaintiff's trade or business. Until such time as the courts are prepared to conclude that to make a profit at the expense of another party, without the latter's consent, is wrongful in itself,[43] there is little likelihood that such conduct will be tortious. The appropriation of personality cases may evidence some movement towards such a conclusion. If that is so, then the commission of some recognised nominate tort such as nuisance or trespass will not be necessary for the imposition of liability in such instances. Whatever that liability may be, however, it will not be an invasion or infringement of privacy.

39 Seipp, *loc. cit.* at 362–370 would not seem to have any difficulty in this respect.
40 *Supra* note 32.
41 (1939) 58 C.L.R. 479.
42 *Lonrho plc v. Fayed* [1989] 2 All E.R. 65.
43 But it might constitute an equitable wrong: Goff & Jones, *Law of Restitution*, 3rd ed. 1986, Chapter 34.

CHAPTER 20

Breach of Confidence

1. A NEW TORT?

20.01 Although privacy is not a concept that is recognised by English law, confidentiality is: and though invasion of privacy is not actionable as such, breach of confidence can give rise to remedies appropriate to the circumstances.[1] The courts do take notice of conduct that can be regarded as occasioning a breach of confidence.[2] When this occurs, they will grant the aggrieved party, whose confidence has been betrayed, suitable relief, including an award of damages.[3] Whether the general effect of this is to constitute breach of confidence a new tort is more questionable.[4] The Law Commission, in its report on the subject,[5] recommended the creation of a new statutory tort of breach of confidence since the courts had not done so.

20.02 The manner in which liability for breach of confidence has emerged, and the requirements for such liability, give support and credence to the idea that this form of wrongdoing can and should sometimes, but not always, be treated as a novel kind of tort. In the first place, it seems clear that what is involved is some intentional misconduct based upon the defendant's knowledge that a confidence has been entrusted to him and on his deliberate betrayal of such confidence to his own ends or for his own purposes and gain. Secondly, many of the situations in which relief has been granted for breach of confidence concern the transmission of trade or business information by the plaintiff to the defendant, which makes breach of confidence in such situations closely resemble wrongful interference with trade or business.[6] Other situations are not business-oriented, but relate to personal information or to matters of public concern. Thus there are two different sorts of breach of confidence, distinct from the previously mentioned category where trade interests are being or would be threatened by the misuse of confidential information. The first is where personal information about the plaintiff

1 Privacy and breach of confidence are distinguished by the Law Commission, *Report on Breach of Confidence*, 1981, Cmnd. 8388 at 5–7.
2 The history of this development, originally equitable in character, is set out in the Law Commission's report, at 10–18.
3 The present position is summarised in the Law Commission's report, Part IV at 18–25. See also Goff & Jones, *Law of Restitution*, 3rd ed. 1986, Chapter 35.
4 This was the suggestion by North, "Breach of Confidence: Is there a New Tort?" (1972) 12 J.S.P.T.L. 149. North was one of the Law Commissioners who produced the 1981 Report.
5 *Supra* note 1, Part V, at 100–164.
6 On which see Chapter 21.

has been given to the defendant who proposes to use it for a personal gain or advantage.[7] This situation seems to resemble certain cases of "invasion of privacy".[8] The second is where the disclosure relates to information which, for reasons of public policy, should not be revealed. This latter category is less a matter of tort than the others. It concerns the troublesome issue of the public's right to know as against the interests of the comments at large that the knowledge in question should be concealed.[9] What is at stake is not the resolution of the competing interests of private individuals or corporations, and the regulation of their rights as between themselves, but the problem of how far freedom of speech, freedom of the press or the rights of litigants should be upheld when to do so might endanger other legitimate and desirable ends or purposes.[10]

20.03 It is with the private aspects of breach of confidence that the law of torts is concerned. Consequently, for the purposes of the law of torts it is only necessary to consider (a) breach of confidence relating to trade or business and (b) breach of confidence relating to information about the personal life of the plaintiff.

2. THE MEANING OF CONFIDENCE

20.04 In essence what the law is concerned with are situations where one party has voluntarily given to another information that the former would normally keep to himself or herself under conditions or in circumstances that indicate that the confidant was entrusted with such information for a specific purpose or on the understanding that the information would not be misused, misappropriated or otherwise dealt with in a manner contrary to the interests of the one who imparted the information.[11] Where these requirements are satisfied the law considers that a fiduciary relationship arises between the parties. The confidant is therefore under a duty not to

7 E.g., *Duchess of Argyll v. Duke of Argyll* [1967] Ch. 302.

8 Chapter 19. Cp. Lord Keith in *Attorney-General v. Guardian Newspapers Ltd (No. 2)* [1988] 3 All E.R. 545 at 634: "The right to personal privacy is clearly one which the law should in this field seek to protect."

9 *Attorney-General v. Jonathan Cape Ltd* [1976] Q.B. 752: cp. *D. v. National Society for Prevention of Cruelty to Children* [1978] A.C. 171; *Science Research Council v. Nassé* [1979] 3 All E.R. 673. See also the European Convention on Human Rights, 1953; The Law Commission's Report, Cmnd. 8969; and *Attorney-General v. B.B.C.* [1980] 3 All E.R. 161.

10 *Attorney-General v. Guardian Newspapers Ltd* [1987] 3 All E.R. 316; *Attorney-General v. Guardian Newspapers Ltd (No. 2)* [1988] 3 All E.R. 545.

11 However there may also be liability if the information has come into the hands of a third party and that information was subject to an obligation of confidence which was known to the third party: *Prince Albert v. Strange* (1849) 1 Mac. & Gr. 25; *Morison v. Moat* (1851) 9 Hare 241; *Stevens Jordan & Harrison Ltd v. Macdonald & Evans* (1951) 9 R.P.C. 10, reversed on other grounds [1952] 1 T.L.R. 101.

behave in any way with respect to the information that is detrimental to the party who has disclosed the information.[12]

20.05 This entails that the information in question should be private to the one who imparts it. Whatever is public knowledge or in the public domain,[13] cannot be the subject of confidence.[14] So, too, information which could be, even if it was not immediately, available to the public at large is not confidential. The knowledge must be such that the only way the defendant could learn of it would be by the voluntary disclosure of it by the plaintiff. Only secret information can be the subject-matter of a confidence.

20.06 The information must be imparted or disclosed on the express or tacitly understood condition that it is intended to be kept secret unless and until the plaintiff authorises its disclosure or use by the defendant.[15] Or it may be transmitted to the defendant for use in a certain way or for a certain period and not otherwise. If it is given without any restriction on its use by the defendant, then no situation of confidence arises. It is a question of fact in every instance whether the necessary conditions for confidence exist, just as it is a question of fact whether the information was private knowledge that was capable of being the subject of a confidence.

3. THE SCOPE OF PROTECTION

20.07 For the most part the proposition that a breach of confidence will lead to liability relates to the disclosure of one party to the other of information that is of commercial interest and value. Trade secrets or knowledge that can be used for commercial purposes that are inimical to the interests and advantage of the one confiding the information have concerned the courts in large measure. It may be said that the origins of relief for breach of confidence can be found in decisions that involve the possibility of economic loss to the plaintiff as a result of the breach of proposed breach of a confidence on the part of the defendant.[16] However it is now clear that this type of liability is not confined to such instances. It may be involved, for example, to protect a plaintiff from having his *idea*

12 *Saltman Engineering Co. Ltd v. Campbell Engineering Co. Ltd* [1963] 3 All E.R. 413; *Coco v. A. N. Clark (Engineering) Ltd* [1969] R.P.C. 41 at 47 *per* Megarry J.; *Stephens v. Avery* [1988] 2 All E.R. 477 at 479 *per* Browne Wilkinson V-C. See also *Seager v. Copydex* [1967] 2 All E.R. 415 at 417 *per* Lord Denning M.R.; *Schering Chemicals Ltd v. Falkman Ltd* [1981] 2 All E.R. 321 at 328–329 *per* Lord Denning M.R. The duty may be contractual or equitable.

13 *Woodward v. Hutchins* [1977] 1 W.L.R. 760: Law Commission *Report on Breach of Confidence* at 27–38.

14 But see *Schering Chemicals Ltd v. Falkman Ltd, supra.*

15 This may be the result of a contract or in consequence of a relationship between the parties which gives rise to an equitable obligation of confidence: Law Commission, *Report*, at 18–21.

16 Goff & Jones, *op. cit.* at 659–661.

used by the defendant against the plaintiff's wish or in breach of the defendant's agreement or understanding with the plaintiff.[17]

20.08 Disclosure of personal information about the private life of the plaintiff, although perhaps such conduct might be considered to be an invasion or infringement of privacy, has also been controlled by the courts by the action for breach of confidence. This has been held to include matters relating to the matrimonial life of the parties[18] and, in *Stephens v. Avery*,[19] details of the sexual conduct of the plaintiff, including her lesbian relationship with a woman who had been killed by her husband. In that case, although it was argued that information about immoral behaviour was not protected and its discussion was mere gossip, it was held that the fact that the information related to matters which had a grossly immoral tendancy would not preclude the existence of a legally enforceable duty of confidence where it would be unconscionable for the recipient of the information on the express basis that it was confidential to reveal that information to another party. The defendant, who was a friend of the plaintiff and had been told about the conduct in question, passed it on to other defendants who were the editor and publishers of a newspaper in which the information was published. Browne-Wilkinson V-C upheld the decision of the master that the plaintiff's statement of claim disclosed a reasonable cause of action and confimed his dismissal of the defendants' application to have the statement of claim struck out.

20.09 Information of an economic or commercial nature is therefore not the only kind of material that may be the subject of a breach of confidence. There may also be liability if the information concerns matters which pertain to conduct or behaviour that has not been transmitted in the course of some potential commercial or industrial negotiations, although it may relate to the manner in which the party who provided the information conducts his, her or its affairs.[20] So, too, political information may be a matter of confidence, for example, the way in which members of the Cabinet talked to each other at meetings.[21] However, in such circumstances there may be a defence to liability or, to put this another way, there may be a limit on the extent to which the party to whom the information relates can restrict the publication of such information. This is because there may be a legitimate public interest in its dissemination, and that interest supersedes or overrides the private interest of the party in question that the confidentiality or privacy of the information be maintained.

17 *Fraser v. Thames Television Ltd* [1983] 2 All E.R. 101.
18 *Argyll v. Argyll, supra.*
19 [1988] 2 All E.R. 477.
20 *Lion Laboratories Ltd v. Evans* [1984] 2 All E.R. 417; *Schering Chemicals Ltd v. Falkman Ltd, supra.*
21 *Attorney-General v. Jonathan Cape Ltd* [1976] Q.B. 752.

4. DEFENCES

20.10 It has been suggested that a person who buys the information from the confidant, without knowledge that it was given or imparted in confidence, may be exempt or immune from liability for breach, and may be able to make use of such information.[22] Whether this is so has yet to be determined authoritatively. Similarly, the fact that an innocent party may have changed his position in reliance on the information, received without notice that it was confidential, has also been argued to provide a good defence.[23] But the most important, and seemingly judicially accepted, defence to an action for breach of confidence is that the public had an interest in the disclosure of the information.

20.11 In the words of Stephenson L.J. in *Lion Laboratories Ltd v. Evans*:[24]

> "There is confidential information which the public may have a right to receive and others, in particular the press, now extended to the media, may have a right and even a duty to publish, even if the information has been unlawfully obtained in flagrant breach of confidence and irrespective of the motive of the informer."

However, as he went on to explain,[25] there is a wide difference between what is interesting to the public and what it is in the public interest to make known: the media have a private interest of their own in publishing what appeals to the public, and this must not be confused with the public interest; sometimes it is in the public interest that such matters should not be disclosed to the public at large via the press but to the police or some other responsible body. A further relevant point was that "there is no confidence as to the disclosure of iniquity".[26] What was iniquity in 1856, when that remark was uttered by Page Wood V-C, was said in 1967 to be possibly too narrow or too wide;[27] and by 1984 it extended to serious misdeeds or grave misconduct, which will destroy the duty of confidence or excuse the breach of it.[28] Hence in the *Lion Laboratories* case the defence succeeded, because it was in the public interest to make known the accuracy and reliability of an approved device on which depended the liability of a person to disqualification, fine or imprisonment for a drink-driving offence. Such an instrument, manufactured by the plaintiffs, was the subject-matter of the disclosure made by some ex-employees of the plaintiffs. Those former employees were providing the information to national newspapers. The plaintiffs' attempt to restrain the newspapers by an interlocutory injunction failed in the end because the defendants successfully applied to have discharged an *ex parte* injunction originally granted to the plaintiffs.

22 Goff & Jones, *op. cit.* at 674.
23 *Ibid.* at 674–675.
24 *Supra* at 422.
25 *Ibid.* at 423.
26 *Gartside v. Outram* (1856) 26 L.J. Ch. 113 at 114.
27 *Initial Services v. Putterill* [1967] 3 All E.R. 145 at 151 *per* Salmon L.J.
28 *Lion Laboratories Ltd v. Evans, supra* at 423 *per* Stephenson L.J.

20.12 It is not clear, however, how far this defence reaches and to what situations, or in what circumstances, it will be available.[29] Decisions and dicta leave many questions unanswered. If breach of confidence does eventually become a recognised form of liability in tort, it will be necessary to define with greater care and precision when the defendant will be able to escape from such liability by a plea that his misconduct was excusable by reason of the public interest he served in behaving as he did or as he proposed to behave.

5. REMEDIES

20.13 In view of the hybrid nature of the present action for breach of confidence, it is not surprising that there are several different remedies which may be granted to the plaintiff.[30] Some of these are more consonant with the restitutionary aspect of the action than to its being treated as a means of providing protection against a tortfeasor. However the granting of injunctions to restrain the confidant from disclosing the confided matter and the award of damages in respect of the breach of duty not to disclose the confidence, although derived from the equitable aspects of the wrong, are also consistent with its being considered a tort.[31]

20.14 Injunctive relief may be appropriate where the secret information is of a private rather than a commercial nature;[32] in respect of the latter damages may be an adequate remedy. An injunction may not be granted where the defendant acted innocently as contrasted with a defendant who knowingly and deliberately breaks another's confidence. But proof of damage or detriment if the defendant is not enjoined may not be essential. It would seem that the attitude of the courts with respect to the granting of an injunction in such cases resembles their approach in cases of defamation or nuisance.[33] Whether or not breach of confidence is a tort, the granting of injunctive relief may depend upon considerations that are relevant in actions that are founded upon tortious behaviour.

20.15 Even more striking is the attitude of the courts with respect to awards of damages in such cases. As stated by the Court of Appeal in *Dowson & Mason Ltd v. Potter*,[34] the principle to be applied is that which

29 Goff & Jones, *op. cit.* at 682.
30 Law Commission *Report*, at 64–82; Goff & Jones, *op. cit.* at 667–674.
31 When it is not a breach of contract.
32 *Argyll v. Argyll, supra.*
33 Above pp. 519–520.
34 [1986] 2 All E.R. 418 at 421 *per* Sir Edward Eveleigh, quoting Lord Wilberforce in *General Tire & Rubber Co. Ltd v. Firestone Tyre & Rubber Co. Ltd* [1975] 2 All E.R. 173 at 177.

obtains in the case of "economic" torts, that is that the measure of damages is to be, so far as possible, that sum of money which will put the injured party in the same position as he would have been if he had not sustained the wrong. In that case the confidential information relating to the plaintiff's manufacture of an article had no special features and could have been obtained by the defendant from other sources than the plaintiff. Nevertheless the measure of damages was not limited to the value of the information without regard to loss of profits by the plaintiff by reason of the defendants' wrongful use of the information. Hence the position of the plaintiff had to be considered. If the plaintiff never intended to manufacture the article but to license others to use it in return for royalties, loss of manufacturing profits was not a suitable basis for the assessment of damages. If the plaintiff was a manufacturer intending to manufacture the article himself, his loss of manufacturing profits stemming from the defendant's wrongful use of the information by manufacturing a competing article was a relevant consideration in assessing damages. In this instance the original decision was that the proper basis for assessment was the plaintiff's loss of profits from the wrongful disclosure and use of the confidential information. That decision was upheld by the High Court and the Court of Appeal. The defendant's contention that only the value of the information was relevant, founded on the views expressed in *Seager v. Copydex Ltd (No. 2)*,[35] which analogised the situation in some breach of confidence cases to the tort of conversion, was unsuccessful. But that did not mean that the decision in the *Seager* case was incorrect: only that the circumstances in that case were different, which resulted in a different method of calculating or assessing the appropriate damages. It would appear, however, that in cases of breach of confidence where damages are claimed as the appropriate remedy, there is a close resemblance between the wrong committed by the defendant and certain kinds of torts, such as conversion, infringement of patents or copyright. That view indicates the strong possibility that, whether by statute or as a result of judicial activity, breach of confidence may come to be another tort.

20.16 Reference should be made to the recent Canadian decision in *LAC Minerals Ltd v. International Corona Resources Ltd.*[36] The case concerned a claim for breach of confidence and breach of fiduciary duty arising out of the imparting of certain information about mineral deposits on land by the plaintiffs to the defendants. The latter purchased the land, which became very profitable. In the event the Supreme Court of Canada, affirming the lower courts, held the defendants liable. The majority thought that the plaintiffs were entitled to the land (subject to certain cross-payments). Sopinka and McIntyre JJ., who thought that only breach of confidence had occurred, and not breach of fiduciary relationship, considered that an award of damages, rather than the transferance of the land, was the

35 [1969] 2 All E.R. 718.
36 (1989) 61 D.L.R. (4th) 14.

appropriate remedy.[37] Sopinka J., citing *Dowson & Mason Ltd v. Potter*,[38] said:[39]

> "In a breach of confidence case, the focus is on the loss to the plaintiff and, *as in tort actions*, the particular position of the plaintiff must be considered. The object is to restore the plaintiff monetarily to the position he would have been in if no wrong had been committed." (emphasis supplied)

37 *Ibid.* at 74–80.
38 *Supra.* note 34
39 *LAC Minerals*, *supra*, at 76–77 (emphasis supplied).

CHAPTER 21

Wrongful Interference with Trade, Business or Employment

1. INTRODUCTION

21.01 Various torts provide protection from improper or unfair interference with a plaintiff's trade or business activities, or the free deployment of his labour and skills. The past hundred years have seen the evolution of older torts, such as conspiracy, and the development of newer ones such as intimidation or inducing a breach of contract to deal with such actual or projected interference. Some of the torts to be considered in this chapter, namely injurious falsehood and passing-off, deal with attempts at unfair competition between traders by making tortious the dissemination of false information about goods or property, thereby inflicting economic loss on the plaintiff. The torts of conspiracy, intimidation and inducing or procuring a breach of contract can also be invoked to deal with trade rivalry that exceeds the bounds of legitimate acceptable behaviour as between business competitors. In these instances, however, it is not falsehoods that are the basis of liability, but other improper acts. These torts have also been relevant in situations involving industrial conflict between management and labour, as well as between different trade unions or the members of a trade union. These have given rise to concerns of a more political nature. The courts responded by developing the fundamentals and the limits of liability, by reference to classical notions of tort. The concern of the courts has been with the refinement of the idea of responsibility for intentionally inflicted economic harm, as contrasted with physical or proprietary damage: and with the relevance or otherwise of malice in fact, in contrast with what has been described as malice in law. Statutory provisions applicable to trade unions and to industrial disputes do not affect the common law conceptions of conspiracy and other torts, although they provide for exemption or immunity from liability for such torts in certain cases. Those exemptions or immunities have not sprung from the intrinsic nature of the torts themselves but from political, economic and social necessity.[1]

21.02 A matter of some debate, in the courts and among commentators, is whether the law has progressed beyond the stage of creating and defining particular distinct torts, the nature and scope of which are dependent on proof of certain specific elements. The question raised by the decisions which elucidate the elements of these torts is whether some

1 The granting of immunity from tort liability where acts are committed in contemplation or furtherance of a trade dispute (as well as the conferment of immunity on trade unions) has been the subject of considerable change over the years. The original legislation was the Trade Disputes Act 1906, which was amended by the Trade Disputes Act 1965, passed as a consequence of the decision in *Rookes v. Barnard* [1964] A.C. 1129: below pp. 545–546. Both statutes were repealed and replaced by the Industrial Relations Act 1971, which in turn was repealed and replaced by the Trade Union and Labour Relations Act 1974. Immunity for individuals was provided by s. 13 of that statute where the acts concerned were committed in furtherance or contemplation of a trade dispute, as defined by s. 29 (later amended by the Employment Act 1982 s. 18). On what is within this provision as being a "trade dispute", see *NWL Ltd v. Woods* [1979] 3 All E.R. 614; *Express Newspapers Ltd v. MacShane* [1980] 1 All E.R. 65; *Dupont Steels Ltd v. Sirs* [1980] 1 All E.R. 529; *Universe Tankships of Monrovia v. I.T.W.F.* [1982] 2 All E.R. 67; *Mercury Communications Ltd v. Scott-Garner* [1984] 1 All E.R. 179. The language of s. 13 of the 1974 Act was amended by the Trade Union and Labour Relations (Amendment) Act 1976, s. 1. It was further amended by the Employment Act 1980 ss. 17, 18. Section 18 of that statute dealt with the removal of immunity in cases of "secondary action": see *Marina Shipping Ltd v. Laughton* [1982] 1 All E.R. 481; *Hadmor Productions Ltd v. Hamilton* [1982] 1 All E.R. 1042; *Merkur Island Shipping Corporation v. Laughton* [1983] 2 All E.R. 189; *Dimbleby & Sons Ltd v. National Union of Journalists* [1984] 1 All E.R. 751; *Thomas v. N.U.M.* [1985] 2 All E.R. 1. By the Trade Unions Act 1984 s. 10, immunity under s. 13 of the 1974 Act (as amended) was limited to situations where a secret ballot was held prior to industrial action: see also *ibid.* s. 11 as to the nature and requirements of such ballots; and *Monsanto plc v. T.G.W.U.* [1987] 1 All E.R. 358.

Immunity for trade unions (and employers associations) was provided by the Trade Union and Labour Relations Act 1974 s. 143 (subsection (2) of which was repealed and replaced by the Employment Act 1982 s. 15: see also *ibid.* ss. 16, 17 on the limitation of awards against trade unions and the recovery of such awards against unions and employers' associations).

Two further points should be noted. First, the Act of 1974, in s. 13(2) gave immunity from liability for acts which interfered with trade, business or employment or the right of another to dispose of his capital or labour. In consequence of certain decisions, suggesting that there was no such tort liability, viz., *Hadmor Productions Ltd v. Hamilton, supra*; *Plessey Co. plc v. Wilson* [1982] I.R.L.R. 199, this provision was repealed by the Employment Act 1982 s 19. Secondly, s. 17 of the 1974 Act provided for the issuance of *ex parte* injunctions to restrain threatened industrial action. No injunction would be issued if the defendant claimed the protection of s. 13 of the Act, except in certain circumstances, and under certain conditions. This provision was changed by the Employment Protection Act 1975 and the Employment Act 1982. These enactments added a sub-section to s. 17 of the 1974 Act (sub-section (2)) which requires the court in exercising discretion whether to grant an interlocutory injunction to have regard to the likelihood of the defendant's success at the trial of action in maintaining a defence under other provisions of the 1974 Act, including those of s. 13. The discretion involved is that of the trial judge, who hears the application for an injunction, not that of a court of appeal. Moreover the judge must have regard not only to the principles enunciated by the House of Lords in *American Cyanamid Co. v. Ethicon Ltd* [1975] A.C. 396, which altered the older law dealing with the issuance of such injunctions by making it necessary for plaintiffs to show not a *prima facie* case but simply that there was a serious case to be tried and that on the balance of convenience an injunction should be issued. The judge must bear in mind the peculiarities of the statutory scheme put in place by the 1974 Act. On the meaning and application of these provisions reference should be made to *NWL Ltd v. Woods, supra*; *Express Newspapers Ltd v. MacShane, supra*; *Dupont Steels Ltd v. Sirs, supra*; *Mercury Communications Ltd v. Scott-Garner, supra*; *Dimbleby & Sons Ltd v. National Union of Journalists, supra.*

common features can be extracted such as would make it possible to state that there is in truth one broad, general tort of wrongful interference with contractual or other business relations, the effect of which would be to make it unnecessary for a plaintiff to specify any variety of tortious behaviour. Were this to be the state of the law, there might then be an all-embracing tort of intentional injury to the economic life of another, in much the same way as there is now a general tort of negligence causing physical, proprietary, emotional, and even financial loss.[1a]

2. CONSPIRACY

(a) Definition and scope

21.03 The classical definition of conspiracy is that of Willes J. in *Mulchahy v. R.*,[1b] a criminal case, in which it was said that "a conspiracy consists not merely in the intention of two or more, but in the agreement of two or more to do an unlawful act or to do a lawful act by unlawful means." The modern tort of conspiracy stems from the criminal offence of conspiracy, which has a long history. The criminal offence consists of the agreement of two or more persons to affect any unlawful purpose, whether as their ultimate aim, or only as a means to it. The crime is complete if there is such an agreement, even though nothing is done in pursuance of it.[2] The gist of the civil tort of conspiracy, "a highly anomalous cause of action", as Lord Diplock said in *Lonrho Ltd v. Shell Petroleum Ltd*,[3] is damage to the plaintiff. So long as it remains unexecuted, the agreement, which alone constitutes the crime of conspiracy, causes no damage. It is only acts done in execution of the agreement that are capable of doing that. So the tort, unlike the crime, consists not of the agreement but of concerted action taken pursuant to the agreement.[4]

21.04 The civil tort of conspiracy in its modern form has a history that begins with the judgment of Lord Coleridge C.J. at first instance in *Mogul Steamship Co. v. McGregor Gow & Sons*,[5] continues through the decisions of the House of Lords in that case,[6] *Allen v. Flood*,[7] *Quinn v. Leathem*,[8] *Sorrell v. Smith*[9] and the *Crofter case*,[10] culminating in the most recent decision of the

1a Carty, "Intentional Violation of Economic Interests: The Limits of Common Law Liability" (1988) 104 L.Q.R. 250.
1b (1868) L.R. 3 H.L. 306 at 317; cp. *Ware & De Freville v. Motor Trade Association* [1921] 3 K.B. 40 at 70 *per* Scrutton L.J.
2 *Crofter Hand Woven Harris Tweed Co. Ltd v. Veitch* [1942] A.C. 435 at 439 *per* Lord Simon.
3 [1981] 2 All E.R. 456 at 463.
4 *Ibid.*
5 (1885) 21 Q.B.D. 544.
6 [1892] A.C. 25.
7 [1898] A.C. 1.
8 [1901] A.C. 495.
9 [1925] A.C. 700.
10 *Supra* note 2.

House of Lords in *Lonhro Ltd v. Shell Petroleum Ltd.*[11] In the course of this evolution the tort has developed its present-day characteristics, in particular the extent to which a combination of two or more persons to act in a certain way can be actionable if they do not use unlawful means to effect their purpose. As Lord Diplock pointed out, the idea that an act done by two people in pursuance of their agreement is actionable even though the same act if done by one of them alone would not be actionable is an idea that was accepted in earlier decisions.[12] The rationale for this was that a combination might make oppressive or dangerous that would be otherwise if it proceeded only from a single person.[13] That notion received its quietus in the *Lonhro* case. In modern law the tort of conspiracy involves combinations that seek to effect acts that are unlawful *per se*: or acts that are lawful but are done with the express purpose of injuring the plaintiff by causing him economic loss.[14]

21.05 One difficulty that has plagued the law results from the fact that a conspiracy to commit a tort which is actually put into effect will not usually be sued upon as conspiracy. An averment of conspiracy in such circumstances is mere surplusage.[15] Indeed it has been held that in such instances the plaintiff must decide whether to sue for the tort in question or for conspiracy. Two separate actions may not be brought on the same facts.[16] Hence it is probably only where conspiracy does not involve unlawful means but is entered into for the purpose of injuring the plaintiff, that an action can successfully be brought.

(b) Elements of liability

(i) Agreement and combination

21.06 There must be an agreement between two or more persons leading to a combination between them, although there will be no liability until the conspiracy is carried into effect.[17] It is the combination to injure that

11 *Supra*, note 3. Cp. Lord Diplock in *Hadmor Productions Ltd v. Hamilton* [1982] 1 All E.R. 1042 at 1052. It has been queried whether this decision is the "culmination" of the development, in particular whether this decision is consistent with *Buttes Gas & Oil Co. v. Hammer (No. 2)* [1982] A.C. 888 and what is its effect on *Belmont Finance Corporation v. Williams Furniture (No. 2)* [1980] 1 All E.R. 393; see *Dedy & Co. Ltd v. Weldon (No. 3)* [1989] 3 All E.R. 118.

12 *Supra* note 3 at 464.

13 *Mogul Steamship Co. v. McGregor Gow & Co.* (1889) 23 Q.B.D. 598 at 616 *per* Bowen L.J.

14 Cp. *Canada Cement LaFarge Ltd v. B. C. Lightweight Aggregate Ltd* (1983) 145 D.L.R. (3d) 385. The suggestion that conspiracy was limited to cases where the predominant purpose of the conspirators was to impose another party's interest was made by Hirst J. in *Allied Arab Bank Ltd v. Heffer (No. 2)* [1988] 3 All E.R. 103. But in *Metall- und Rohstoff AG v. Donaldson Lufkin & Jenrette* [1988] 3 All E.R. 116 Gatehouse J. reiterated the view that there were two types of conspiracy as stated in the text: *ibid.* at 122–123. This decision was reversed on appeal, [1989] 3 All E.R. 14, and the purpose of injuring the plaintiff restored in importance; see *Lonrho plc v. Fayed* [1989] 2 All E.R. 65 at 68 *per* Dillon L.J.

15 *Sorrell v. Smith* [1925] A.C. 700 at 716 *per* Lord Dunedin.

16 *Greenhalgh v. Mallard* [1947] 2 All E.R. 255; *Wright v. Bennett* [1948] 1 All E.R. 227.

17 *Crofter* case [1942] A.C. 435 at 439 *per* Lord Simon.

makes an act unlawful.[18] If such an act would not be a tort if committed by one person, the fact that two or more have agreed to perform it in combination might make it actionable, but only now, as a result of the *Lonhro* case, if the purpose or aim of those combining was to injure the plaintiff.

21.07 The true rationale of conspiracy is that the tort lies for the abuse of an individual's right or privilege to combine with others to achieve ends that are communally desired. Such abuse occurs when the parties concerned intend to achieve their ends by the use of unlawful means or the end in question is itself unlawful, i.e. lacks justification.

21.08 An agreement here means not a contract but a consensus that the combiners will act together to achieve a common purpose. Hence, presumably, it is not necessary to prove that the defendants all had contractual capacity, as long as they were capable of appreciating what they were doing and intended to act together, in concert.[19] It is clear that a combination may exist between corporations, or between corporations and natural persons.[20] At common law a conspiracy between husband and wife was probably impossible, since they were not regarded by the law as being two persons for many purposes. Since changes in the law with respect to the liability in tort of husbands to wives and vice-versa,[21] it has been suggested that an actionable conspiracy between husband and wife would be possible.[22]

(ii) Unlawful means

21.09 This presents no unusual problems. Whether or not the end to be achieved by the combination is lawful in itself, it is tortious to endeavour

18 I.e. when the act would be unlawful if committed by one person: *Ware & De Freville Ltd v. Motor Trade Association* [1921] 3 K.B. 40 at 90–91 *per* Atkin L.J. The earlier view expounded in *Quinn v. Leathem* [1901] A.C. 495 at 537 *per* Lord Lindley and in *Pratt v. B.M.A.* [1919] 1 K.B. 244 at 260 *per* McCardie J. that the tort can be committed by *one* person must be treated as inaccurate: cp. *Sorrell v. Smith* [1925] A.C. 700 at 719–722 *per* Lord Dunedin.

19 Cp. *Posluns v. Toronto Stock Exchange & Gardiner* (1965) 46 D.L.R. (2d) 210 at 336, affirmed (1966) 53 D.L.R. (2d) 197, affirmed [1968] S.C.R. 330; *Fraser v. Board of Trustees of Central United Church* (1983) 38 O.R. (2d) 97; *Maguire v. Calgary* [1983] 4 W.W.R. 342. Lack of knowledge of the illegality of the agreement will mean that the one who is so ignorant will not be guilty of conspiracy: *Belmont Finance Corporation Ltd v. Williams Furniture Co.* [1979] 1 All E.R. 118.

20 *R. v. Blamires Transport Services Ltd* [1964] 1 Q.B. 278; but see *R. v. McDonnell* (1966) 50 Cr.App.R. 5 ("one-man" company). But not master and servant: *Said v. Butt* [1920] 3 K.B. 497; or partners and directors, if they are the "alter ego" of the firm or corporation: *Lehndorff Canadian Pension Properties Ltd v. Davis & Co.* (1987) 10 B.C.L.R. (2d) 342 at 350–351. But simply because the defendants were directors of the plaintiff company did not mean that their knowledge could be imputed to the company: *Belmont Finance Corporation Ltd v. Williams Furniture Ltd* [1979] 1 All E.R. 118.

21 P. 32.

22 *Midland Bank Trust Co. v. Green (No. 3)* [1979] 2 All E.R. 193, affirmed on other points [1981] 3 All E.R. 744.

to bring it about by unlawful means, such as a crime or a tort.[23] As seen earlier, however, in such instances, it is probable, indeed it may be mandatory, that the plaintiff will sue for the substantive tort that is involved rather than in conspiracy.

21.10 How far does the concept of "unlawful means" extend? This is by no means clear. Acts which are immoral without being either criminal or tortious would probably not come within its scope. If such acts are contemplated by the combiners, the plaintiff will probably have to fall back on the other category of actionable conspiracies, those involving an intent to injure, if he wishes to sue. Since the decision of the House of Lords in *Rookes v. Barnard*,[24] a breach of contract or a threat to break a contract may be regarded as unlawful means for the purposes of the law of conspiracy. Previously it was thought that such conduct, although actually or potentially actionable at the suit of the other contracting party, would not be "unlawful". It was held in *Rookes v. Barnard*, however, that for the purposes of affixing liability for the tort of intimidation, a breach or threatened breach of contract could be considered to involve the employment of unlawful means. There seems no reason why the same approach should not be adopted in a case of conspiracy.

(iii) Unlawful purpose

21.11 A conspiracy will be actionable, even though no unlawful means are used or contemplated to achieve its object, if the purpose that is proposed to be achieved by the combination is unlawful, that is to say without legal justification. The idea that a combination may be unjustified was recognised as early as the *Mogul* case,[25] in which traders combined to drive another trader out of business. Thirty years later, in *Sorrell v. Smith*,[26] Lord Cave summarised the effect of that decision and others when he stated:

> "(1) A combination of two or more persons wilfully to injure a man in his trade is unlawful and and if it results in damage to him is actionable.
>
> (2) If the real purpose of the combination is not to injure another but to forward or defend the trade of those who enter into it, then no wrong is committed and no action will lie, although damage to another ensues."

The distinction was drawn between combinations to promote or protect one's trade interests and those designed purely and simply to injure another trader. In *Quinn v. Leathem*[27] the House of Lords refused to apply a similar approach to trade union activities, even though these were

23 Or a breach of statute which is not itself a cause of action: *Southam v. Guthro* [1948] 3 D.L.R. 178 at 187; contrast *Lonrho Ltd v. Shell Petroleum Ltd* [1981] 2 All E.R. 456, where it was held that in such cases an intent to injure was necessary. A breach of the rules of natural justice might suffice: *Evaskow v. International Brotherhood of Boilermakers* (1969) 9 D.L.R. (3d) 715. There must be an intent to employ the unlawful means; but knowledge that the means are unlawful may not be necessary as long as the intent is present: *Churchill v. Walton* [1967] 2 A.C. 227.

24 [1964] A.C. 1129: below p. 545.

25 *Supra* note 6.

26 [1925] A.C. 700 at 711–712.

27 *Supra* note 8.

intended to promote or protect trade union interests. This had to be done by legislation.[28] However forty years later in *Crofter Hand Woven Harris Tweed Co. v. Veitch*,[29] the House of Lords extended the same shelter from liability as applied in the case of rival traders to the situation as between trade unions and employers. In that case the House of Lords stated the modern law of conspiracy in terms which indicated that, outside of the situation where unlawful means were used by the conspirators, liability would only be imposed where the purpose or object of the combiners was one of which the law did not approve and in respect of which the law said the conspirators were unjustified.

21.12 The "purpose" or "object" of the conspirators is the test.[30] The plaintiff is obliged to prove the wrongfulness of the defendants' object.[31] It is for the courts to stigmatise certain objects as unlawful or lawful. The touchstone of liability is the legitimate interest of the defendants. What, therefore, is justified or justifiable as an object or purpose to be achieved by a combination is both difficult and nebulous. At various times, in decisions and dicta, several objects or purposes have been held or considered to be unjustified and therefore unlawful and capable of supporting an action for conspiracy. One such instance is the wilful exercise of economic power by a trade union against an employer, i.e. a naked assertion of power for its own sake, not in order to advance the reasonable and legitimate interests of a trade union or its members.[32] A wanton display of power or of dislike for the plaintiff will suffice to make the purpose or object of a combination unlawful.[33] It is also unlawful to combine merely for the purpose of enforcing a debt, even if the debt is owed to the defendants, for example, a threat of a strike if the plaintiff were not dismissed, for the purpose of getting the plaintiff to pay his union dues.[34] So, too, it was unlawful to combine in order to achieve professional or social ostracism of the plaintiff:[35] but not if the purpose is to protect professional standards or interests.[36] Other suggestions have been that it would be unlawful to combine to benefit union funds by a bribe;[37] or to promote religious animosity, racial discrimination, political rivalry, or a colour bar.[38] In the words of an Australian judge, it would be unlawful to combine merely out of what he termed "disinterested malevolence".[39] Other purposes, however, have been held or said to be legitimate, for

28 Trade Disputes Act 1906. For the subsequent history see *supra* note 1.
29 [1942] A.C. 435.
30 *Ibid.* at 440, 445 *per* Lord Simon.
31 *Ibid.* at 469, 471–472 *per* Lord Wright: cp. *Sorrell v. Smith* [1925] A.C. 700 at 741–742 *per* Lord Dunedin.
32 *Quinn v. Leathem* [1901] A.C. 495 at 514–515 *per* Lord Shand, 527–528 *per* Lord Brampton: cp. *Ware & De Freville v. Motor Trade Association* [1921] 3 K.B. 40 at 60–61 *per* Atkin L.J.
33 *Huntley v. Thornton* [1957] 1 All E.R. 234.
34 *Giblan v. National Amalgamated Labourers' Union* [1903] 2 K.B. 600.
35 *Pratt v. British Medical Association* [1919] 1 K.B. 244.
36 *Thompson v. British Medical Association (N.S.W. Branch)* [1924] A.C. 764.
37 *Crofter* case, *supra*, at 446 *per* Lord Simon.
38 *Ibid.* at 451 *per* Lord Maugham.
39 Evatt J. in *McKernan v. Foster* (1931) 46 C.L.R. 343 at 397.

example, the maintenance of trade union discipline or the advancement of trade union policy;[40] the limitation of competition or protection of lawful business interests;[41] the furtherance of morality or religion;[42] the discouragement or prevention of the operation of a colour bar.[43] What is lawful or unlawful will clearly depend on the social, political, cultural and moral standards of the times. In this respect the operation of the law is at once both settled and flexible.

21.13 What is settled are the general principles applied to determine what is improper. The point was made emphatic by the House of Lords in the *Lonrho* case.[44] In regard to injury to a plaintiff's commercial interests it was accepted that the civil tort of conspiracy would be committed where the predominating purpose of the agreement and the acts done in its execution which caused damage to the plaintiff was the causing of such injury. Injury to the plaintiff and not the self-interest of the defendants must be the predominant purpose of the agreement, in the execution of which the damage-causing acts were done. The House made it clear that this, and this alone, was the test of civil conspiracy, where no means unlawful *per se* were used. It was not enough that two or more combined to perform acts which had the effect of causing injury. The combiners had to have the intention of causing injury to the interests of the plaintiff, and not the intention of protecting their own interests.[44a] Hence, in the *Crofter* case, even though the defendants were alleged to have broken a penal law, the effect of which, the plaintiffs contended, was to harm them economically, since the defendants did not have injury to the plaintiffs in mind, but only the promotion of their own economic interests, no liability for conspiracy could be imposed.[45]

21.14 Other vital matters were also stated by the decision in the *Crofter* case.[46] The purpose of the conspirators may be putative, that is they may honestly believe that is the purpose without such actually being the case. However the subjective element is important as showing or disproving the *bona fides* of the defendants. The test of "motive" or "purpose" is objective: but the intention to harm destroys *bona fides*, that is legitimacy or purpose.[47] What this entails is that malice, in the sense of spite or ill-will, is not the test of unlawfulness of purpose, though it may affect the issue of *bona fides* by establishing that the defendants had a wrongful object in

40 *McKernan v. Foster, supra*: *Sorrell v. Smith, supra*; *Crofter case, supra*.
41 *Mogul Steamship Co. v. McGregor Gow & Co., supra*; *Ware & De Freville v. Motor Trade Association, supra*; *British Motor Trade Association v. Salvadori* [1949] Ch. 556.
42 *Brimelow v. Casson* [1924] 1 Ch. 302.
43 *Scale Ballroom v. Ratcliffe* [1958] 3 All E.R. 220.
44 [1981] 2 All E.R. 456 at 464 *per* Lord Diplock.
44a Does the defendants' self-interest have to be reasonable to qualify as legitimate? This is unclear: *Crofter* case [1942] A.C. 435 at 435, 447 *per* Lord Simon, 453 *per* Lord Maugham, 469, 477 *per* Lord Wright.
45 On the issue of civil liability for breach of criminal statute, see pp. 439–444.
46 [1942] A.C. 435.
47 *Ibid.* at 445 *per* Lord Simon, 469, 471 *per* Lord Wright: cp. *McKernan v. Foster, supra* at 362 *per* Dixon J.

mind, or excluding a legitimate one.[48] In this regard malice may make a combination unlawful where the presence of malice on the part of a defendant acting alone will be irrelevant where his act is lawful.[49] The conduct of the combination may establish the unlawfulness of the object; what the conspirators do may reveal that they had the intention to injure, and not some other, legitimate aim in mind.[50] So, too, a disproportionate injury to the plaintiff may cast doubt on the *bona fides* of the conspirators, and reveal an intention to harm.[51] Where several purposes emerge as being the aims of the combination, the predominating one counts.[52] If the motives or purposes of the defendants are mixed, as where one is actuated by spite or malice, the situation is unclear. Lord Maugham suggested that hate or vindictive spite on the part of one conspirator would probably upset any defence of justification.[53] However this has been doubted,[54] on the ground that the test is objective, especially if no disproportionate damage has been caused to the plaintiff. In such circumstances can it be said that there has been an abuse of the right or privilege of combination?[55]

21.15 An issue that has never been resolved is whether the onus is on the plaintiff in cases of this kind to establish the unlawfulness of the purpose or object of the conspirators or is on the defendants to excuse themselves from liability by proving that their object or purpose was legitimate once the plaintiff has proved the elements of liability, i.e. combination and agreement, the intent to injure and resultant injury from the acts of the conspirators. If the attitude is adopted that conspiracy where no unlawful means are employed is only actionable if there was an intent to injure, it would appear more logical and consistent with principle to hold that the plaintiff should establish such intent as part of his case.[56] However, it may be that the necessary intent can be presumed, or deduced from the conduct of the conspirators viewed in the context of all the circumstances. In this regard note should be taken of the decision of the Supreme Court of Canada,[57] adopting and applying the decision in the *Lonhro* case, that the intent to injure necessary for liability where no unlawful means are used may be a "constructive intent". In other words where injury to the

48 *Crofter* case, *supra* at 471, 472 *per* Lord Wright.
49 *Allen v. Flood* [1981] A.C. 1.
50 Cp. *Mogul Steamship Co. v. McGregor Gow & Co.* [1892] A.C. 25 at 52, 57 *per* Lord Field, 60 *per* Lord Hannen; *Sorrell v. Smith* [1925] A.C. 700 at 741 *per* Lord Sumner.
51 *Crofter* case, *supra* at 447 *per* Lord Simon.
52 *Ibid.* at 445 *per* Lord Simon.
53 *Ibid.* at 453.
54 *Ibid.* at 445 *per* Lord Simon.
55 *Ibid.* at 450 *per* Lord Maugham, 471–472 *per* Lord Wright, 488 *per* Lord Porter; *J. T. Stratford & Son Ltd v. Lindley* [1965] A.C. 269 at 298 *per* Lord Salmon; Heydon, "The Defence of Justification in Cases of Intentionally Caused Economic Harm" (1970) 20 U.Tor. L.J. 139 at 150.
56 *Crofter* case, *supra* at 439 *per* Lord Simon.
57 *Canada Cement LaFarge Ltd v. B.C. Lightweight Aggregate Ltd* (1983) 145 D.L.R. (3d) 385: applied in *Canadian Training & Development Group Inc. v. Air Canada* (1987) 39 C.C.L.T. 72.

plaintiff was foreseen or foreseeable as a consequence of the defendants' acts in concert, they may be held as a matter of construction, i.e. inference, to have been actuated by the appropriate necessary intent.[58]

3. INTIMIDATION

(a) Emergence of the tort

21.16 In earlier centuries cases can be found which were used in more recent times to prove that a tort of intimidation existed at common law.[59] Whether such decisions really established that the idea of a wrong termed intimidation can be discovered embedded in the law is questionable. It does not matter, however, because in *Rookes v. Barnard*[60] the House of Lords determined conclusively that such a tort was known to the law and could be invoked to provide a remedy in appropriate cases. In *Rookes v. Barnard* the issue was important because the defendants would have been protected by the provisions of the then applicable legislation, i.e. the Trade Disputes Act 1906,[61] unless it could be shown that they had committed a tort that was independent and distinct from acts which interfered with the business or employment of another person. The statutory immunity granted the defendants by that Act was overcome by proof that the defendants had been guilty of the tort of intimidation.

21.17 The plaintiff was employed by B.O.A.C. as a draughtsman. He had quarrelled with, and then resigned from, the union which represented employees of B.O.A.C. In consequence several union officers informed the employer that, unless the plaintiff's employment were terminated, the other employees would come out on strike. B.O.A.C. thereupon terminated the plaintiff's employment by giving him the requisite amount of notice, in other words, the plaintiff lost his job but not by reason of a breach of contract on the part of his employer. The union in question had a collective agreement with B.O.A.C. under the terms of which the union would not indulge in strike action during the lifetime of the agreement. In threatening to strike unless the plaintiff were dismissed the officers of the union itself were threatening to break, or induce the breach of, a contract. The defendants relied on the provisions of the 1906 Act, by which conduct in pursuance of a combination or agreement that interfered with the employment of the plaintiff was protected if it occurred in contemplation or furtherance of a trade dispute. The plaintiff countered by saying that the statute gave protection "unless the act, if done without such agreement or combination, would be actionable". The defendants also relied on other provisions of the 1906 Act which protected acts in contemplation of

58 This makes the tort of civil conspiracy in Canadian law significantly wider: *Lehndorff Canadian Pension Properties Ltd v. Davis & Co.* (1987) 10 B.C.L.R. (2d) 342 at 347.

59 *Garrett v. Taylor* (1620) Cro. Jac. 567; *Tarleton v. M'Gawley* (1793) 1 Peake 270; *Keeble v. Hickersgill* (1760) 11 East 547n; *Carrington v. Taylor* (1809) 11 East 571.

60 [1964] A.C. 1129.

61 *Supra* note 1.

furtherance of a trade dispute even if the acts induced a breach of contract of employment or were an interference with the employment of another person or the right of another person to dispose of his labour. The plaintiff's response to this was that the language of the statute (viz., shall not be actionable on the ground "only" that it induces . . .) did not protect the defendants because they were guilty of a distinct, independent tort, namely the tort of intimidation, which took their action outside the scope of the statutory immunity. Thus, if there were such a tort, and if the defendants were guilty of its commission, the provisions of the 1906 Act would be inapplicable, and the immunity thereby granted the defendants would not operate.

21.18 Such indeed was the decision of the House of Lords. Modern in origins it may have been, but the tort of intimidation existed and was known to the law. It occurred when a person used unlawful means to achieve his object, even though that object may have been lawful in itself. Thus if the defendants had persuaded B.O.A.C. to dismiss the plaintiff, after proper notice, by arguments directed towards the utility or desirability of the plaintiff's being dismissed, the plaintiff would not have been able to sue. It is not wrongful to endeavour to persuade by peaceful and legitimate means, such as rational argument or an appeal to the listener's self-interest. Persuasion becomes wrongful when illegal means are employed to persuade. In effect it ceases to be persuasion and becomes coercion, which the law regards as improper and actionable. However the question remains: what are unlawful or illegal means, the use of which makes conduct actionable, on the basis of intimidation? Furthermore, can the tort of intimidation apply to the situation where the defendant coerces the plaintiff to act in a way that the plaintiff might not otherwise have done, or does it only apply where the defendant coerces a third party to act to the detriment of the plaintiff, although without committing a wrongful act with respect to the plaintiff? *Rookes v. Barnard* was a case of the latter type. Subsequent decisions have been of a similar kind. Hence the issue has never been resolved in England, although it has given rise to considerable debate.[62] In Canada, however, one case did raise the applicability of the tort of intimidation where the defendant acted directly upon and for the purposes of influencing the plaintiff.[62a] In the event the question did not need to be resolved, because it was held that no illegal means had been employed, and the defendant had not acted with intent to injure the plaintiffs but as a civil servant carrying out government policy as set in a statute and regulations made by a provincial legislature.

21.19 The decision in *Rookes v. Barnard*, therefore, opened the way for courts to hold that the use of illegal means to achieve one's objective was actionable provided that: (i) such means were employed against a third party; (ii) to coerce that party to act in a certain way; (iii) the effect of

62 See *infra* para. 21.26.
62a *Central Canada Potash Co. Ltd v. Government of Saskatchewan* (1976) 57 D.L.R. (3d) 7; (1977) 79 D.L.R. (3d) 297; (1979) 88 D.L.R. (3d) 609.

which was detrimental to the plaintiff; and (iv) in respect of which acts the plaintiff had no remedy against the third party because the latter had committed no wrong against him. In England it would appear very little use has been made of this development in the law of torts. In Canada, on the other hand, several cases have resulted in success for plaintiffs who were able to establish acts of intimidation on the part of defendants. Indeed these decisions suggest that from the tort of intimidation as set out in *Rookes v. Barnard* broader principles of liability can be created and applied.[63]

(b) Unlawful means

21.20 To coerce another person into acting to his or a third party's detriment is not intimidation unless the coercion involves the use of unlawful, or illegal means. Much of the discussion in *Rookes v. Barnard* was concerned with the exposition of what can amount to unlawful or illegal means for this purpose. The House of Lords, agreeing with the judge at first instance but reversing the decision of the Court of Appeal, held that a threat to break a contract was unlawful or illegal means for this purpose. In this respect the decision was innovative. Prior to this case unlawful or illegal means clearly included acts which amounted to crimes or torts, or threats to commit crimes or torts. To break or threaten to break one's contract in order to compel someone to act in a certain way was not thought of as unlawful or illegal, even if a breach or threat of a breach of contract could have led to some form of action, whether for damages for breach or an injunction to restrain a breach. Lord Denning later explained the decision in *Rookes v. Barnard* in the following terms:[64]

> ". . . the tort of intimidation exists, not only in threats of violence, but also in threats to commit a tort or breach of contract. The essential ingredients are these: there must be a threat by one person to use unlawful means (such as violence or a tort or breach of contract) so as to compel another to obey his wishes; and the person so threatened must comply with the demand rather than risk the threat being carried into execution. In such circumstances the person damnified by the compliance can sue for intimidation."

The rationale for accepting in this context that a threat to break a contract can be unlawful or illegal seems to be that, in Lord Hodson's words, "a breach of contract is unlawful in the sense that it involves the violation of a legal right . . ."[65] In the context of the facts of *Rookes v. Barnard*, which involved a threatened strike, Lord Hodson considered that such a threat was a more powerful weapon that a threat of violence. The injury and suffering caused by strike action was often very widespread as well as devastating and a threat to strike would be expected to be certainly no less serious than a threat of violence.[66]

63 Below pp. 548, 565.
64 *Morgan v. Fry* [1968] 2 Q.B. 710 at 724.
65 *Rookes v. Barnard* [1964] A.C. 1129 at 1201.
66 *Ibid.*

21.21 The language of the various members of the House of Lords in *Rookes v. Barnard*[67] suggests that there were two grounds upon which a threat to break a contract, or its breach, could be regarded as unlawful or illegal means for the purposes of the tort of intimidation. First, on what might be termed analytical grounds, the actual or threatened breach of a contract could be regarded as just as unlawful, in legal terms, as an actual or threatened crime or tort. The reason for this is that the essence of the tort is coercion, as long as the form of coercion is wrong. The test of what is wrongful coercion is whether the party threatened can or cannot legally resist what is threatened by the other party. To threaten to break a contract is to threaten an illegal injury. Therefore a plaintiff who suffers by the aversion of the illegally threatened act can fairly claim that he has been illegally injured.[68] The second ground might be termed the practical or realistic ground. This turns on whether what is threatened would have dire consequences for the party who is threatened, thereby forcing him to comply with the demands of the party making the threat. Since a breach of contract would be harmful to the party to whom the threat is conveyed, especially where, as in the *Rookes* case, it would involve not merely one contracting party but several, namely all those who would come out on strike, a threat to break a contract must be treated by the law as just as serious a threat, leading to the conclusion that coercion has occurred, as a threat to commit a crime or a tort. Looked at in this way the conclusion by the House of Lords that a threat to break a contract would be regarded as coercion so as to invite the determination that it involved the tort of intimidation is not only justified by reference to earlier dicta and decisions, as the House held, but is also supported by arguments of principle and reason.

21.22 The limits of unlawful or illegal means are illustrated by the subsequent decision of the Court of Appeal in *Morgan v. Fry*.[69] Here the defendants stated that unless their demands were met they would all leave their employment on a certain date. What they were doing was giving notice that they would terminate their contracts on that date. Under the terms of their contracts of employment such notice would be sufficient to end the contracts in question. Hence the defendants were not threatening to break their contracts with the employer, as were the defendants in *Rookes v. Barnard*; they were intimating that they were intending to terminate their contracts, which it was lawful for them to do. In consequence they were not threatening to do anything unlawful or illegal in order to persuade the employer to accede to their wishes. Hence the tort of intimidation was not committed in this instance. The problem is that in effect in *Morgan v. Fry* the defendants were stating that they would go on strike if the employer did not do as they wanted. In technical terms, however, they were informing the employer of their projected strike action

67 [1964] A.C. 1120 at 1168–1169 *per* Lord Reid, 1181–1182 *per* Lord Evershed, 1198–1201 *per* Lord Hodson, 1206–1210 *per* Lord Devlin, 1234–1235 *per* Lord Pearce.
68 *Ibid.* at 1217 *per* Lord Devlin.
69 [1968] 2 Q.B. 710.

in a way that did not involve any breach of contract. Though in practical terms they were doing what the defendants had done in the *Rookes* case, in legal terms they were behaving differently.

21.23 An example of threats to break a contract in a situation not involving industrial action is provided by a dictum of Lord Denning in *D. & C. Builders Ltd v. Rees*,[70] when he said that if a debtor threatened his creditor that he would pay no part of the sum owed by the debtor unless the creditor agreed to accept a lesser sum in settlement of the debt such threat would be illegal and would amount to intimidation. This was *obiter*, since the decision in that case could be reached on other grounds more pertinent to the law of contract than the law of tort. However in other decisions, Canadian, not English, various other acts have been considered to involve unlawful or illegal means capable of supporting an action for intimidation. In some of these cases the conduct of the defendant was clearly intimidation, and would have been regarded as such even before *Rookes v. Barnard*, for example, harrassment of the plaintiff, physical abuse and threats of death.[71] In another instance the conduct was more questionable, for example, acting outside statutory powers conferred on a marketing board for the express purpose of forcing an employer to dismiss the plaintiff, with whom the marketing board had a quarrel and in respect of whom the board was actuated by malice in the sense of spite or ill-will.[72] Perhaps in that case the basis for the decision was the employment of its powers by the board for the purpose of causing injury, and not for the legitimate control of a particular industry or trade.

21.24 A more difficult issue was raised in another Canadian decision which concerned what was alleged to be the use of legislation said to be *ultra vires* a provincial legislature in order to compel the plaintiffs to cut back on their production of potash to their ultimate detriment. [73] In the event the defendant was considered not to have acted with any intent to injure the plaintiffs, unlike the marketing board in the other instance, but for the purpose of carrying out government policy which, as a civil servant, he was obliged to do. But the case leaves it open for courts to hold that an act which is *ultra vires* the defendant may be regarded as an unlawful or illegal act if its performance is threatened in order to compel someone to act to his, or a third party's disadvantage and detriment. However it is arguable whether an *ultra vires* act, such as the passage of legislation that is not within the competence of a legislature, or the making of delegated legislation outside the legal powers of a minister of the Crown, can be looked upon as an illegal act in the same way as a breach or

70 [1966] 2 Q.B. 671 at 625, relied on by Disbery J. at first instance in *Central Canada Potash Co. Ltd v. Government of Saskatchewan* (1976) 57 D.L.R. (3d) 7 at 118.

71 *Mintuck v. Valley River Band No. 63A* (1977) 75 D.L.R. (3d) 589; *Boychuk v. Northwest Territories Housing Corp.* (1985) 33 C.C.L.T. 28.

72 *Gershman v. Manitoba Vegetable Producers' Marketing Board* [1976] 4 W.W.R. 406.

73 *Central Canada Potash Co. Ltd v. Government of Saskatchewan, supra* note 62a. But to threaten an act which induces breach of a statute was the use of unlawful means in *Canadian Ironworkers Union No. 1 v. Int. Association of Bridge, etc. Union, Local No. 97* (1970) 73 W.W.R. 172, affirmed on other grounds [1972] S.C.R. 295.

threatened breach of contract. If the reason why the latter is illegal is because it is a violation of another's rights, can it be said that the passage of *ultra vires* legislation or delegated legislation is a violation of any individual's rights? Undoubtedly the tort of intimidation cannot be invoked to restrain Ministers of the Crown from introducing legislation into a Parliament where such legislation, if passed, would have a harmful effect upon the plaintiff. Nor may the courts be used in order to control the way in which Ministers of the Crown or legislatures act or intend to act in the public interest, whether or not they are misguided in their beliefs.[74] Should the true purpose of such projected legislation be to cause harm to a particular individual, or to compel such individual to act in a stipulated manner so as to avoid the passage of the legislation, it becomes easier to question whether the conduct of the Ministers or the legislators concerned can be regarded as unlawful or illegal. Is it open to the courts to question the motives of Ministers and other legislators? The answer to that question raises difficult problems of constitutional law that transcend the law of torts.

(c) Varieties of intimidation

21.25 The speeches in *Rookes v. Barnard* recognise two different forms of intimidation, although only one was relevant on the facts of that case. These may be categorised as two-party and three-party intimidation. The first occurs where the defendant intimidates the plaintiff to act in a way which rebounds to the detriment of the plaintiff, by requiring him to do something he can choose not to do, or not to do something which he may legally do. The second arises where the defendant intimidates another person to do something, or refrain from doing something which he may legally do or not do, with intent to injure a third party, with the result that such third party incurs economic loss.

21.26 As far as the first, two-party category is concerned, some doubt has been expressed in England whether such a form of the tort truly exists.[75] The reason for such uncertainty is that the threat which the intimidator makes to compel or coerce the plaintiff to act in a manner harmful to himself may well constitute a wrongful act in itself, namely, a crime, a tort or a threat to break a contract, such as would support an action of some kind without any need to invoke the independent, distinct tort of intimidation. This may be true in general: but in some situations there may not be any action for damages if the plaintiff acceeds to the demands made by the defendant. Thus, a threat of violence may result in criminal liability on the part of the defendant; but it might not give rise to liability in tort unless a case of assault could be made out by the plaintiff. A threat to break a contract may also not be actionable, unless and until the contract is

74 *Roman Corporation Ltd v. Hudson's Bay Oil & Gas Co. Ltd* [1973] S.C.R. 820.
75 Wedderburn, "Tort Out of Contract: Transatlantic Warnings" (1970) 33 M.L.R. 309; Hamson, "A Further note on *Rookes v. Barnard*" [1964] C.L.J. 159; Hoffman, "*Rookes v. Barnard*" (1965) 81 L.Q.R. 116.

broken, which will only occur if the plaintiff does not do what is demanded of him by the defendant (in which event intimidation will not have occurred). Hence there may be good reasons for providing a remedy where the defendant's conduct brings about what he requires of the plaintiff, and the consequence is that the plaintiff incurs loss, e.g. by discontinuing his business in response to threats of violence by the defendant, or a threat that the defendant will break a contract which he has with the plaintiff. Canadian decisions provide illustrations of such two-party intimidation, largely where the conduct of the defendant has involved acts of violence, harrassment, or similar behaviour, resulting in the abandonment by the plaintiff of some projected activity which would have been to his advantage, thereby causing him loss.[76] Not all such claims have been successful, since much depends upon whether the law recognises the conduct of the defendant as involving the use of unlawful or illegal means. The invocation of legislation, or a threat of prospective legislation, have not been held to be unlawful or illegal means in this context.[77] Moreover in the absence of an intent to injure the plaintiff, the defendant's conduct may not be treated as constituting intimidation. Apart from any issue of justification, which must be considered separately,[78] it might be argued that a defendant who has other purposes in mind than to cause injury to the plaintiff is not acting unlawfully or illegally as long as he does not commit or threaten to commit a crime, a tort, or a breach of contract.[79]

21.27 Three-party intimidation is the variety of the tort that has more frequently attracted the attention of the courts. It was subjected to considerable analysis and discussion in *Rookes v. Barnard*, particularly in the speech of Lord Devlin. The problem is that to allow a plaintiff an action founded on a threat made to someone else, not himself, especially if the threat is of the breach of a contract between the defendant and the third party, is tantamount to permitting an action based upon the actual or threatened commission of a wrong to someone else, a proposition that has been rejected by the law in other contexts. Thus an action cannot be founded on damage caused to A by reasons of B's breach of a tort duty to C. It must be shown that B owed such a duty to A himself. An action cannot be brought by A in respect of the breach of a contract between B and C, even if the result of such breach is damage to A. The "privity" rule has been attenuated in the context of liability in tort, but only by postulating an independent duty owed to A, where harm was also contemplated to C, e.g., where A attempts to rescue C from dangers created by B's negligence, or where A suffers nervous shock as a result of B's negligence towards C.[80] The doctrine of privity is still very strong in the law of contract, although qualifications have arisen, e.g., under the law of

76 See the cases cited *supra* note 71.
77 See the cases cited *supra* notes 73, 74.
78 Below para. 21.28.
79 Or a breach of statute: *supra* note 73.
80 Pp. 283, 287.

agency, trusts, and negotiability.[81] Lord Devlin dealt with such comments, especially with respect to the situation under the law of contract, by stating that A's cause of action arises because of the action which C has taken to avert a breach of contract and that where a threatened breach of contract is involved, what is material to A's cause of action is the threat and C's submission to it.[82] What Lord Devlin is saying, and what other members of the House of Lords were also clarifying in *Rookes v. Barnard*, was that the gravamen of the plaintiff's cause of action in cases of intimidation is not the tort or threatened tort vis-à-vis C, nor the breach of contract or threat to break a contract with C that occurs on the part of B, but the use of such acts or threats by B in order to cause harm to A. It is the threat that is vital, since submission to the threat is what results in the intended harm to the plaintiff.

(d) Justification

21.28 In various dicta the possibility of defending an action for intimidation by pleading justification has been accepted.[83] Thus far, however, no such plea has met with success. This is hardly surprising, in view of the essential nature of the tort, which involves the intentional infliction of injury upon the plaintiff either by intimidating him or by intimidating a third party who acts in a way that causes loss to the plaintiff. It seems unlikely that a defendant will be able to "justify" threats of tort or breach of contract, and even less likely that justification of acts of violence, torts or breaches of contract, can ever be regarded as possible in the eyes of the law. Despite judicial language that hints at justification as a possible answer, it is suggested that the likelihood of this occurring is remote.

21.29 What has happened in some, Canadian not English, cases is that the court has accepted the argument that the conduct of the defendant was not aimed at the plaintiff, nor designed to cause him injury *per se*. It was perpetuated, or proposed, for other, legitimate purposes, such as the promotion of Government policy, or the effectuation of legislation. It might be argued that this is a form of justification, in that conduct that injures, or might injure a plaintiff, to the knowledge of the defendant, may not be actionable if there is a valid reason why such conduct takes place. If this is correct, the situation with respect to intimidation may be analagous to that which obtains in cases of conspiracy.[84] The main purpose or object of the combination is the test of liability in conspiracy. So, too, the main purpose of the alleged intimidation may be the test of whether the tort has

81 Trietel, *Law of Contract*, 6th ed. 1983, 478–485; Cheshire, Fifoot & Furmston's *Law of Contract*, 11th ed. 1986, 439–448.

82 *Rookes v. Barnard* [1964] A.C. 1129 at 1207–1209.

83 *Ibid.* at 1206 *per* Lord Devlin; *Morgan v. Fry* [1968] 2 Q.B. 710 at 729 *per* Lord Denning; *Cory Lighterage Ltd v. T. & G.W.U.* [1973] 14 K.I.R. 463 at 483–484 *per* Lord Denning. Cp. *C.P.R. Co. v. Building Material Construction & Fuel Drivers Union Local 213* [1971] 5 W.W.R. 1 at 50.

84 Above pp. 542, 543.

been committed. A similarity would also exist between the tort of intimidation and that of procuring or inducing a breach of contract.[85] In such instances, also, it may be possible for the defendant to justify what he has done, even if *prima facie* it is actionable. Such an attitude would make the law relating to these three distinct, but interrelated torts consistent.

4. INDUCING BREACH OF CONTRACT

(a) Origins

21.30 Long before the decision in *Lumley v. Gye*[86] in 1853, the common law recognised that interference with certain relationships could be tortious.[86a] Prior to that decision it was thought that only when a defendant caused a servant to leave his employment, or otherwise made it impossible for him to perform his functions, would a tort be committed. Such liability stemmed from the Statute of Labourers of the fourteenth century. Vestiges of this liability persisted in modern law to the extent that disruption of the relationship of master and servant, for example by negligently causing injury or the death of a servant so that temporarily or permanently he could not fulfil his contract of service, gave rise to liability under the action *per quod servitium amisit*.[87] This and other older law, dealing with the enticement of servants and the harbouring of servants who left their employment in breach of a contract of service, has now gone.[88] The judgment in *Lumley v. Gye* extended the scope of the older law, and in more recent times has become of greater importance. There it was held that it was actionable to procure or induce the breach of any contract for services, not only one between a master and his servant. The contract in that case was one by which an opera singer undertook to perform exclusively at a particular theatre for an impresario. A rival impresario persuaded the singer to perform at his theatre, thereby breaking her contract with the plaintiff. For this act the rival was held liable in tort. From this crucial decision evolved a broader liability, since later decisions extended the scope of *Lumley v. Gye* to cover all contracts, not only contracts of or for services.[89] The theoretical basis for such liability is that it is an actionable wrong knowingly to violate a legal right.[90] Once a contract has been made between two parties, each has a right to performance of the contractual obligations on the part of the other party. Hence to interfere so as to prevent such performance will be wrongful if it is done deliberately, without justification, with knowledge of the existence of the

85 Below.
86 (1853) 2 E. &. B. 216.
86a Note, "Tortious Interference with Contractual Relations in the Nineteenth Century; The Transformation of Property, Contract, Tort" (1980) 93 H.L.R. 1510.
87 Still maintainable in Canada. Fridman, *Law of Torts in Canada*, Vol 2, Chap. 5.
88 Administration of Justice Act 1982, s. 2: above p. 20.
89 *Bowen v. Hall* (1881) 6 Q.B.D. 333; *Temperton v. Russell* [1893] 1 Q.B. 715; *Quinn v. Leathem* [1901] A.C. 495; *South Wales Miners' Federation v. Glamorgan Coal Co.* [1905] A.C. 239.
90 *Quinn v. Leathem* [1901] A.C. 495 at 510 *per* Lord MacNaghten, 534–535 per Lord Lindley.

contract in question, with intent to cause economic loss, and with the effect of causing loss.[90a]

(b) Elements of liability

(i) A contract

21.31 There must have been a contract between the plaintiff and a third party. It is interference with this contract, in the form of an act or acts which induce or procure its breach, or would result in such breach if the act or acts in question are not enjoined by an injunction, that is the essence of liability. This tort is not committed where the defendant induces someone not to enter into a project contract with the plaintiff, even if the result is that the plaintiff suffers economic loss.[91]. If unlawful means are employed to prevent the conclusion of a contract, the tort of intimidation may be committed.[92] If two or more defendants act together by agreement in order to cause someone not to contract with the plaintiff, they may commit the tort of conspiracy.[93] If unlawful means are not employed, nor any combination to achieve this end, it would seem that no tort is committed by a person who induces or persuades another not to contract with the plaintiff.

21.32 The contract which is the subject of the actual or intended breach must be valid even if the terms are not clear.[94] It is not actionable to procure the breach of a void or illegal contract.[95] Nor will it be actionable to induce someone to break a contract which he could in law have terminated or avoided, for example on the ground that it was entered into as a result of fraudulent misrepresentation, or was entered into by a minor and was not binding on him by reason of his minority.[96] Where the contract is valid but unenforceable, there are inconsistent decisions.[97] On principle there is no reason why the tort may not be committed where the breach of an unenforceable contract is induced by the defendant. Unenforceable contracts are valid although no action may be brought on them unless certain conditions are satisfied. Hence they are contracts that may be broken, albeit perhaps with impunity so far as actions for breach are

90a *Grieg v. Insole* [1978] 3 All E.R. 449 at 484–485 *per* Slade J. Hence it has been extended to cover inducement of a breach of statutory duty, i.e. interference with rights generally: *Associated British Ports v. T.G.W.U.* [1989] 3 All E.R. 796 at 806, 812, 816 (reversed by the House of Lords on other grounds: [1989] 3 All E.R. 822).

91 *Midland Cold Storage Co. Ltd v. Steer* [1972] Ch. 630: see below pp. 565–6.

92 Above pp. 545–553.

93 Above para. 21.03.

94 *Daily Mirror Newspapers Ltd v. Gardner* [1968] 2 Q.B. 762 at 780 *per* Lord Denning M.R.

95 *Joe Lee Ltd v. Lord Dalmeny* [1927] 1 Ch. 300; *Greig v. Insole* [1978] 3 All E.R. 449 at 492 *per* Slade J.

96 *Grieg v. Insole*, *supra* at 485 *per* Slade J., citing *D. C. Thomson & Co. Ltd v. Deakin* [1952] Ch. 646 at 702 *per* Morris L.J.; *Emerald Construction Co. Ltd v. Lowthian* [1966] 1 All E.R. 1013 at 1019 *per* Diplock L.J. See, for example, a Canadian case involving a contract made by a minor: *Toronto Marlboro Major Junior "A" Hockey Club v. Tonelli* (1971) 81 D.L.R. (3d) 407, affirmed (1979) 23 O.R. (2d) 193.

97 In Canada, viz., *Brown v. Spamberger* (1960) 21 D.L.R. (2d) 630; *Unident Ltd v. De Lacy* (1982) 313 D.L.R. (3d) 225. English authority is lacking.

concerned. If they can be broken, then, presumably, their breach can be induced by a third party. In such an event it seems logical to say that the tort has been committed.

(ii) Knowledge of its terms

21.33 It is not actionable to induce the breach of a contract of which the defendant is ignorant. The defendant must be aware that there is a contract between the plaintiff and a third person. However it may not be necessary for the defendant to have precise knowledge of the terms of such contract. If he has the means of knowledge of the existence of a contract or its terms but recklessly proceeds without caring whether what he does will induce the breach of such contract or its terms, that will suffice.[98] It is unlawful for a third person to procure a breach of contract knowingly or recklessly indifferent whether it is a breach or not.[99] Hence to induce a vendor to sell land when there is knowledge of a binding option given to someone else will amount to the tort of inducing a breach of contract.[100]

21.34 An essential element of liability is that the defendant should have acted "knowingly", which means with realisation that what he is doing will, or very likely may, bring about a breach of contract. Since the tort consists in knowingly interfering with another's rights, then if a person does not know either of those rights or of the fact that he is interfering with them, even if he ought to have known, he will not be liable.[101] It would appear to follow from this that a defendant who is careless in not knowing or discovering that a contract is in existence between the plaintiff and a third party, or that his conduct may cause a breach of that contract, will not be liable for this tort. It is one thing to hold that a person may have constructive notice of the existence or terms of a contract. It is another to say that without such knowledge, but on proof that a defendant "ought" to have known of the existence or terms of a contract, there can be liability. It has been held, in Canada,[102] that this tort can be committed where the defendant ought to have foreseen that a breach of a contract between the plaintiff and a third party would be a necessary consequence of his conduct. It has also been held that without proof of an intention to injure, based upon knowledge of the existence of a contract or its terms, there can be no liability for the tort of inducing a breach of contract.[103] Having regard to the importance placed by the courts upon a defendant's awareness of the contractual relations with which he is interfering by his

98 *Emerald Construction Co. Ltd v. Lowthian* [1966] 1 All E.R. 1013; *Grieg v. Insole* [1978] 3 All E.R. 449 at 487–488 *per* Slade J.

99 *Emerald Construction Co. Ltd v. Lowthian, supra*, at 1017 *per* Lord Denning M.R.; *Daily Mirror Newspapers Ltd v. Gardner* [1968] 2 Q.B. 762.

100 *Midland Bank Trust Co. v. Green (No. 1)* [1980] Ch. 590 at 626 *per* Eveleigh L.J.

101 *Pritchard v. Briggs* [1978] 2 W.L.R. 317 at 342 *per* Walton J.; cp. *Smith v. Morrison* [1974] 1 W.L.R. 659. Contrast the fact situation in *Swiss Bank Corporation v. Lloyds Bank Ltd* [1979] 2 All E.R. 853. Criminal conspiracy is different; *R. v. Churchill (No. 2)* [1967] 2 A.C. 226 at 237 *per* Lord Dilhorne.

102 *Thermo King Corporation Ltd v. Provincial Bank of Canada* (1981) 130 D.L.R. (3d) 256.

103 *D. C. Thomson & Co. Ltd v. Deakin* [1952] Ch. 646; *Dirassar & Jones v. Kelly Douglas & Co.* (1967) 59 D.L.R. (2d) 452.

conduct, it would seem to be the better view that a defendant must be more than negligent with respect to knowledge of a contract: he must be fully cognisant of the contract and what his actions will do, or he must be, in Lord Denning's phrase,[104] "indifferent" to the possibility that he will be causing a breach.

(iii) Intention

21.35 The requirement of knowledge of the contract that is broken, or that the defendant wants to have broken, emphasises the fact that the tort of inducing breach of contract is one that can only be committed intentionally. Despite Canadian decisions that seem to suggest the contrary,[105] the tenor and rationale of this tort seem to be that the defendant has intentionally acted in violation of contractual rights enjoyed by the plaintiff. A defendant cannot have acted intentionally if either negligently or accidentally he caused a breach of a contract between the plaintiff and a third party. Therefore no action should lie against someone who accidentally, neither intentionally nor as a result of negligence, has caused one party to a contract to break it.[106] Indeed, although it may be wrongful for a defendant to act in a manner that induces a person who has already broken his contract (not because of any inducement on the part of the defendant) to continue to be in breach of that contract,[107] this conduct would also necessarily have to be deliberate, intentional, and in the knowledge that the contract had been broken.

21.36 At the present time, therefore, the better view is submitted to be that the law does not recognise or accept an action based upon negligently bringing about a breach of contract. It has been said that liability for this tort may be imposed where the defendant has acted with recklessness or as a result of "wilful blindness", which amounts to recklessness.[108] The man who is indifferent whether or not he causes a breach is like a man who turns a blind eye to the situation.[109] Such behaviour is a far cry from negligence, which is established by facts and inferences that are very different from those relevant to a determination of recklessness. The latter state of mind closely approximates to a deliberate intention. Neglience depends upon conduct that falls below the standards of the reasonable man, but does not invite the conclusion that the defendant set out to injure the plaintiff. The tort of inducing a breach of contract is founded upon an intention to injure the plaintiff by causing such a breach,[110] or, at the very least, reckless disregard for such a possibility.[111]

104 *Emerald Construction Co. Ltd v. Lowthian, supra* at 1017.
105 *Thermo King Corporation Ltd v. Provincial Bank of Canada, supra*; *Nicholls v. Township of Richmond* (1983) 145 D.L.R. (3d) 362.
106 But see *McLaren v. D.C. Institute of Technology* (1978) 94 D.L.R. (3d) 411.
107 *Fraser v. Board of Trustees of Central United Church* (1983) 38 O.R. (2d) 97 at 104; to the contrary *Jones Bros. (Hunstanton) Ltd v. Stevens* [1955] 1 Q.B. 275.
108 *Jones Bros. (Hunstanton) Ltd v. Stevens, supra* at 280 *per* Goddard L.C.J.
109 *Emerald Construction Co. Ltd v. Lowthian, supra* at 1017 *per* Lord Denning M.R.
110 But a man may be presumed to intend the reasonable consequences of his acts: *South Wales Miners' Federation v. Glamorgan Coal Co.* [1905] A.C. 239 at 244 *per* Lord Halsbury; *Grieg v. Insole* [1978] 3 All E.R. 449 at 489 *per* Slade J.
111 *Daily Mirror Newspapers Ltd v. Gardner* [1968] 2 Q.B. 762.

21.37 Although some dicta refer to malice on the part of the defendant, it is clear that, in this context, the expression does not mean spite or ill-will, sometimes called malice in fact. It refers to the intention of the defendant to injure, "malice in law".[112] In this respect the tort of inducing breach of contract resembles conspiracy. In both it is the object or intention of the defendant that is material to liability, not the motive by reason of which the defendant committed the actionable behaviour. However, in this context, as in cases of conspiracy, the conduct of the defendant may be justifiable, if his intention to bring about a breach of contract, to the damage of the plaintiff, was actuated by a legitimate purpose.[113] Hence malice, in the sense of spite or ill-will, may be relevant as indicating that the defendant did not act from any legitimate purpose but solely in order to cause injury to the plaintiff.[114]

(iv) Inducement

21.38 It is now accepted, since the decision of the Court of Appeal in *D. C. Thompson & Co. Ltd v. Deakin*,[115] that the tort can be committed by direct or indirect interference on the part of the defendant.[116] There are important differences between the two forms of conduct.

21.39 *(1) Direct.* This takes the form of speech or conduct that directly persuades, procures, or compels someone to break his contract with the plaintiff.[117] This is what occurred in *Lumley v. Gye*.[118] Unlike the tort of intimidation, the conduct of the defendant need not be illegal or unlawful in character. Even peaceful, reasoned, persuasion will suffice, as long as it can be shown that the acts of the defendant caused the contract-breaker to break his contract.[119] But if the contract-breaker makes up his or her own mind, as a consequence of advice from the defendant, no tort will be committed. Similarly, if the contract-breaker is affected by other considerations, not those put forward by the defendant, the latter will not be liable. In *D. C. Thompson & Co. Ltd v. Deakin*,[120] for example, the suppliers who refused to send paper to the plaintiffs did so not because of the speeches of the defendant calling upon the supplier's employees not to handle goods designated for delivery to the plaintiffs, but for other reasons. The courts

112 *South Wales Miners' Federation v. Glamorgan Coal Co.* [1905] A.C. 239 at 250–251 *per* Lord James; *D. C. Thomson & Co. Ltd v. Deakin* [1952] Ch. 646 at 676 *per* Evershed M.R.
113 Below pp. 562–5.
114 But good faith and absence of malice or a mistaken belief as to the defendant's legal rights will not provide a defence: *South Wales Miners' Federation v. Glamorgan Coal Co.*, *supra* at 246 *per* Lord MacNaghten; *Greig v. Insole*, *supra* at 485 *per* Slade J.
115 [1952] Ch. 646.
116 *Grieg v. Insole*, *supra* at 484 *per* Slade J., citing *Torquay Hotel Co. Ltd v. Cousins* [1969] 2 Ch. 106 at 138 *per* Lord Denning M.R.
117 *J. T. Stratford & Son Ltd v. Lindley* [1965] A.C. 269 at 333 *per* Evershed M.R.; *Greig v. Insole*, *supra* at 486 *per* Slade J. But the act of a servant which causes his employer to break his contract with a third party does not make the servant liable to such third party: *Said v. Butt* [1920] 3 K.B. 497; *Rutherford v. Poole* [1953] V.L.R. 130; *Naylor v. Genstar Ltd* (1977) 76 D.L.R. (3d) 697.
118 (1853) 2 E. & B. 216.
119 *Posluns v. Toronto Stock Exchange & Gardiner* (1965) 46 D.L.R. (2d) 210 at 266 *per* Gale J.
120 [1952] Ch. 646.

distinguish advice from pressure or direct persuasion.[121] Thus to bring about a breach of contract by threats, even threats to do something lawful, will result in liability.[122] Naturally there will be liability if the threat is to do something that is unlawful for the defendant to do, e.g., come out on strike in breach of contract, as in *Rookes v. Barnard*,[123] or in breach of a statute.[124]

21.40 Direct inducement can also occur in other ways. If the defendant performs an act that forces a party to a contract to break it against his will, there will be liability. This would occur if the defendant confined someone so as to prevent his performing a contract with the plaintiff; or stole an employee's tools;[125] or stole tyres which the plaintiff had agreed would be displayed on a car manufactured by a third party, the object of such display being to advertise the plaintiff's tyres.[126] Even though the third party might not have been liable to the plaintiff for breach of contract, the defendant could be liable for inducing or procuring a breach of the contract in issue. More recently, in *Torquay Hotel Ltd v. Cousins*,[127] the Court of Appeal held that it was actionable as inducement of a breach of contract for defendants to cause union members to stop the delivery of oil to the plaintiff's hotel in breach of a contract by which the oil company agreed to supply such oil, even though the hotel company could not have sued the oil company for breach of contract because under its terms what occurred was not actionable. There are many problems arising from the judgments in this case. However, it appears to have been accepted by the court as a whole that there could be liability for the tort of inducing a breach of contract, even though (a) there was no direct persuasion of the oil company to break its contract, but only acts by the union members that made it impossible for the oil company to perform or fulfill its contractual obligations; and (b) the result was that no actionable breach of contract had taken place because of an exemption clause under which the oil company was prohibited from liability.

21.41 *(2) Indirect.* This occurs where the intervener, without speaking or writing or publishing words or doing other acts which amount to pressure or persuasion on one of the contracting parties, nevertheless procures or attempts to procure a situation which will or may result in a breach of the contract.[128] Indirect inducement of a breach of contract is thus more tenuous and difficult to establish than the more obvious direct interference

121 *Ibid.* at 656 *per* Evershed M.R.
122 *Temperton v. Russell* [1893] 1 Q.B. 715; *Read v. Friendly Society of Operative Stonemasons* [1902] 2 K.B. 732.
123 [1964] A.C. 1129.
124 *Mark Fishing Co. Ltd v. United Fishermen's & Allied Workers' Union* (1972) 24 D.L.R. (3d) 585.
125 *D. C. Thompson & Co. Ltd v. Deakin, supra* at 678 *per* Evershed M.R., 695 *per* Jenkins L.J., 702 *per* Morris L.J.
126 *G.W.K. Ltd v. Dunlop Rubber Co. Ltd* (1926) 42 T.L.R. 376.
127 [1969] 2 Ch. 106.
128 *J. T. Stratford & Son Ltd v. Lindley* [1965] A.C. 269 at 337 *per* Lord Pearce; *D. C. Thomson & Co. Ltd v. Deakin, supra* at 678 *per* Evershed M.R.; *Grieg v. Insole, supra* at 486 *per* Slade J.

discussed above. Such a means of committing the tort was recognised by the Court of Appeal in *D. C. Thomson & Co. Ltd v. Deakin.*[129] There the issue arose because the defendants, trade union officers, were making speeches encouraging members of a union to refuse to drive vehicles for their employers because those employers had supply contracts with the plaintiffs. Another union was involved in a trade dispute with the plaintiffs: and the object of the defendants was to promote solidarity with the striking union by bringing about "sympathetic" industrial action. In the event the plaintiffs were denied the injunction they sought on the basis of an actual or attempted inducement of breach of contract, on the ground that there was no sufficient causal connection between the acts of the defendants and the failure by the suppliers to fulfil their contract with the plaintiffs. In the course of the judgments, however, the tort of inducing or procuring a breach of contract was extensively discussed and its main elements illuminated.

21.42 Two important points emerge from the discussion of indirect interference or inducement. The first is the issue of causation. There must be evidence that the defendant intended and deliberately brought about the breach, as a result of his actions, and that the breach was not the consequence of some independent action of a third party. In the *Thomson* case the suppliers made their own determination not to supply the paper they were obliged to deliver under their contract with the plaintiffs. Admittedly their decision was based upon the refusal of their drivers to operate vehicles intended to go to the plaintiffs. However, the court held that this was not a direct and necessary consequence of the defendants' acts in urging members of their union, to which the drivers belonged, to act in support of the members of the other union to which employees of the plaintiffs belonged. Clearly cases of indirect inducement will be difficult to establish by reason of the problem of making the essential causal connection between the acts alleged to constitute the interference or inducement and the ultimate breach of contract that gives rise to the action. The intervening will or decision of the contracting party who fails to perform his contract seems to stand between the acts of the defendant and the breach, because the decision to break the contract is not immediately brought about by the defendant's acts but as a result of the acts of others operating on the mind of the contract breaker. Although the acts of such others may be brought about or influenced by the conduct of the defendant, there is an element of remoteness in such situations that tends to disrupt the necessary connection between the defendant's conduct and the consequential damage to the plaintiff. Nevertheless, in some Canadian decisions,[130] involving breaches of statute, secondary picketing, or acting without a proper directors' resolution, such indirect interference has been

129 *Supra.*
130 *International Brotherhood of Teamsters v. Therien* [1960] S.C.R. 265; *Mark Fishing Co. Ltd v. United Fisherman's & Allied Workers' Union* (1972) 24 D.L.R. (3d) 585; *Western Stevedoring Co. Ltd v. Pulp, Paper & Woodworkers of Canada* (1975) 61 D.L.R. (3d) 701; *Volkswagen Canada Ltd v. Spicer* (1978) 91 D.L.R. (3d) 42.

held to give rise to liability for inducing a breach of contract. In those instances the required causal link could be established.

21.43 The second point established in the *Thomson* case is the need for proof that the defendant employed "unlawful means" to get the third party to act on or in respect of the contract breaker, so as to induce the latter to break the contract.[131] In other words, it is not actionable to use lawful means to persuade someone to act on another person with a view to getting that other to break a contract. The rationale of this distinction between lawful and unlawful means in the context of indirect interference, when it is irrelevant in cases of direct interference, has been variously expressed. One basis for the distinction is that a lawful act does not become unlawful by reason of a bad motive (for which there is ample authority in English law).[132] A second is that the distinction enables the courts to be flexible in their approach to liability for this tort. The courts can decide whether the conduct of the defendant in a case of indirect interference is deserving of being treated as wrongful, by reference to the reason for his actions, without having to decide as a matter of course that any indirect interference becomes actionable. A third reason is that unless the distinction were drawn the scope of the tort would be extended beyond reasonable and legitimate limits. Nobody would ever know when seemingly lawful and proper conduct might become tortious if, as a consequence, someone, not the person with whom the defendant was immediately dealing, were to break a contract made with another party, the eventual plaintiff.[133]

21.44 It is important to determine what are "unlawful means" for this purpose. According to Lord Denning, this expression refers to an act which the defendant is not at liberty to commit.[134] Obviously this includes criminal or tortious acts: and, in light of decisions previously discussed, it must also include an actual or threatened breach of contract.[135] Some decisions indicate that the expression goes beyond this. For example, it was held in *Daily Mirror Newspapers Ltd v. Gardner*[136] that the defendants had employed unlawful means when they recommended to the members of a federation of newsagents to stop ordering a certain newspaper. That recommendation was equivalent to a restriction contrary to the public interest under the Restrictive Trade Practices Act 1956. In *Brekkes v.*

131 *Daily Mirror Newspapers Ltd v. Gardner* [1968] 2 All E.R. 163 at 168 *per* Lord Denning M.R.; *Torquay Hotel Ltd v. Cousins* [1969] 2 Ch. 106 at 138 *per* Lord Denning M.R.; *Grieg v. Insole* [1978] 3 All E.R. 449 at 484 *per* Slade J.

132 But it would be unlawful indirectly to influence someone to break his contract if there is no sufficient justification for the interference: *Daily Mirror Newspapers Ltd v. Gardner*, *supra* at 168 *per* Lord Denning M.R.; *J. T. Stratford & Son Ltd v. Lindley* [1965] A.C. 269 at 330 *per* Lord Radcliffe.

133 Lord Denning expresses contradictory views as to the validity of the distinction in the *Daily Mirror* case and the *Torquay Hotel* case.

134 *Torquay Hotel Co. Ltd v. Cousins* [1969] 2 Ch. 106 at 139; cp. *Acrow (Automation) Ltd v. Rex Chainbelts Inc.* [1971] 3 All E.R. 1175 at 1181.

135 Cp *J.T. Stratford & Son Ltd v. Lindley* [1965] A.C. 269. Unlawful means were not used in *Grieg v. Insole* [1978] 3 All E.R. 449 at 484 *per* Slade J.

136 [1968] 2 All E.R. 163.

Cattel,[137] a resolution that was in restraint of trade was considered to involve unlawful means so as to invite the conclusion that the tort had been committed or threatened, even though the Restrictive Practices Court has not yet held that it would be void, since there was no reasonable doubt that such a decision would be made (in view of the fact that the resolution was contrary to the public interest and would not be exempted under the Act). In such situations the defendant procures the breach in question by an act which is not unlawful in the sense that it is criminal or tortious, nor unlawful in that it involves breaches or potential breaches of a contract between the defendant and a third party, but because the act of the defendant contravenes the policy of some statute, although that contravention does not entail any penalty in the form of a fine or imprisonment. The attitude of the law is that whatever is not permitted by the law is unlawful. Hence the decision in a Canadian case.[138] The defendants made a statement about changes with regard to signing authority that was not correct because the makers of the statement had not obtained necessary approval by resolution of the board of directors validating their representation about such authority. The result of this was that the bank did not honour cheques, which in turn caused the company of which the defendants were officials to break its contract with another company. This was held to amount to inducing a breach of contract by indirect, and unlawful means. Decisions such as these suggest that the concept of "unlawful means", which received a broad interpretation in *Rookes v. Barnard* in the context of the tort of intimidation,[139] has now been given an even wider connotation for other purposes. It may now mean anything that is unjustifiable, i.e. done without lawful justification.[140] How far this will extend is hard to conceive. It must be agreed that, at this stage, the notion of unlawful means has been given a broad meaning that may have extended the scope of the tort of inducing a breach of contract a long way from its original application in *Lumley v. Gye*.

(v) Damage

21.45 If the plaintiff is suing for damages in respect of an actual breach of contract resulting from the defendant's conduct, he must prove that he has suffered special damage, that is more than nominal damage.[141] Where the plaintiff is seeking a *quia timet* injunction, to restrain the defendant from carrying out his proposed course of action, which would result in a breach of contract as between the plaintiff and a third party, the plaintiff must show the likelihood of damage to him resulting if the act of interference is successful.[142] It is not open to the defendant who deliberately attempts to procure the breach of a contract between two other

137 [1971] 1 All E.R. 1031.
138 *Volkswagen Canada Ltd v. Spicer* (1978) 91 D.L.R. (3d) 42.
139 Above paras. 21.20ff.
140 Hence the honest belief of the defendant's solicitor excluded the finding of unlawful means in *Smith v. Morrison* [1974] 1 W.L.R. 659.
141 *Grieg v. Insole* [1978] 3 All E.R. 449 at 485 *per* Slade J.; *Rookes v. Barnard* [1964] A.C. 1129 at 1212 *per* Lord Devlin.
142 *Grieg v. Insole, supra* at 485 *per* Slade J.; *Emerald Construction Co. Ltd v. Lowthian* [1966] 1 All E.R. 1013 at 1019 *per* Diplock L.J.

parties to plead that his attempts are unlikely to succeed. All the plaintiff needs to do is to show the likelihood of more than nominal damage resulting if the attempt is unsuccessful.[143]

21.46 Once a cause of action is established damages are at large.[144] This means that the court must calculate the plaintiff's losses as a matter of impression.[145] The court can award whatever is appropriate, including an amount for intended and for reasonably foreseeable consequences.[146]

(c) Justification

21.47 Good faith and absence of malice, in the sense of spite or ill-will, on the part of the defendant will not provide a defence.[146a] The defendant may escape liability, however, if in the particular circumstances he can show sufficient "justification" in law for what he did.[147] When this is the situation the effect is to grant the defendant a privilege of interfering with a contract.[148] However it is by no means clear when justification can be relied on as an answer to an action for inducement of a breach of contract, although it has been suggested that the plea should be flexible, not confined to a narrow straitjacket.[149] It is difficult, even if it were possible, to give a complete and satisfactory definition of sufficient "justification".[150] The following factors have been suggested as being relevant to a determination whether sufficient justification is present in any given case: viz., the nature of the contract broken; the position of the parties to the contract; the grounds for the breach; the means employed to procure the breach; the relation of the person procuring the breach to the person who breaks the contract; and the object of the person in procuring the breach.[151] That the breach was to the advantage or interest of the defendant and the party who was induced to break the contract will not be enough of itself.[152] Nor will the fact that the defendant acted from impersonal and disinterested motives.[153] Nor can the use of illegal means to procure a breach ever be justified.[154]

143 *Grieg v. Insole, supra* at 490 *per* Slade J.
144 *Exchange Telegraph Co. Ltd v. Gregory & Co.* [1896] 1 Q.B. 147.
145 *Cassell & Co. Ltd v. Broome* [1972] A.C. 1027 at 1072.
146 *Lumley v. Gye* (1853) 2 E. & B. 216 at 233–234; *British Motor Trade Association v. Salvadori* [1949] Ch. 556; e.g. loss of profits foreseen by the defendant: *Jones v. Fabbi* (1973) 37 D.L.R. (3d) 27.
146a *Smithies v. National Association of Operative Plasterers* [1909] 1 K.B. 310; *South Wales Miners' Federation v. Glamorgan Coal Co. Ltd* [1905] A.C. 239.
147 *Grieg v. Insole, supra* at 491 *per* Slade J.
148 *Posluns v. Toronto Stock Exchange* (1965) 46 D.L.R. (2d) 210 at 261, 270–272 *per* Gale J.
149 *Grieg v. Insole, supra* at 493 *per* Slade J.
150 *Glamorgan Coal Co. Ltd v. South Wales Miners' Federation* [1903] 2 K.B. 545 at 573 *per* Romer L.J.: cp. *Mogul Steamship Co. Ltd v. McGregor Gow & Co.* (1889) 23 Q.B.D. 598 at 618–619 *per* Bowen L.J.
151 *Glamorgan Coal Co. Ltd v. South Wales Miners' Federation, supra* at 574–575 *per* Romer L.J.
152 *Ibid.*; *Read v. Friendly Society of Operative Stonemasons of England, Ireland and Wales* [1902] 2 K.B. 88 at 97 *per* Darling J., [1902] 2 K.B. 732 at 737 *per* Collins M.R.
153 *Grieg v. Insole, supra* at 492 *per* Slade J., disagreeing with Gale J. in *Posluns v. Toronto Stock Exchange, supra* at 270.
154 *Posluns v. Toronto Stock Exchange, supra* at 270.

21.48 The existence of a contractual right to act as the defendant acted under the terms of an agreement between the various parties may suffice, as in *Posluns v. Toronto Stock Exchange.*[155] There the defendants procured the dismissal of the plaintiff from the firm of stockbrokers by which he was employed. This was because the plaintiff had breached the rules of the Exchange. In consequence the defendants were entitled to terminate the plaintiff's membership in the Exchange which inevitably resulted in his loss of the employment. The fact that the defendants are fulfilling a public policy as enunciated in a statute will be enough to justify their acts.[156] There are some Canadian decisions which suggest that legitimate self-interest may suffice,[157] although this does not appear to have been accepted in England.

21.49 The furtherance of legitimate trade union or professional objects may not suffice,[158] unless the conduct of the defendant is protected by statute.[159] An honest belief in the existence of a duty to act will not be enough, as in *Camden Nominees v. Forcey*,[160] where the defendants persuaded other tenants to refuse to pay their rent for the purpose of displaying their displeasure at the fact that the landlord had not fulfilled certain of his contractual obligations. Indeed it is not justification to say that the plaintiff induced the breach because the third party once broke a contract between himself and the defendant.[161] Whether a belief that what the defendants are doing is for the public good and promotes a worthy end is questionable. In an English decision, *Brimelow v. Casson*,[162] where the defence succeeded, the defendants justified their procurement of breaches of contracts between a theatrical company and the theatre where the company was to perform by arguing that the conditions of employment of the members of the company were such that the chorus girls were compelled to resort to immorality to maintain themselves. The defendants, officers of the actor's union, were held to be fulfilling their duty to their members and to the public by endeavouring to raise the standards of the employees. In a Canadian case, the defendants sought to justify their persuasion of the plaintiff's employees not to handle grapes imported from parts of the United States by saying that they were endeavouring to promote the cause of grape farmers who were attempting to unionise to improve their working conditions. This was rejected as sufficient justification for the otherwise tortious behaviour.[163]

155 (1965) 46 D.L.R. (2d) 210, affirmed (1966) 53 D.L.R. (2d) 193, affirmed (1968) 67 D.L.R. (2d) 165.
156 *Stott v. Gamble* [1916] 2 K.B. 504; *Bank of Nova Scotia v. Gaudreau* (1985) 27 B.L.R. 101 at 144–146.
157 *Dirassar & Jones v. Kelly, Douglas & Co. Ltd* (1966) 59 D.L.R. (2d) 452; *Thermo King Corporation Ltd v. Provincial Bank of Canada* (1981) 130 D.L.R. (3d) 356. Contrast *Klein v. Jenoves* [1932] O.R. 504.
158 *South Wales Miners' Federation v. Glamorgan Coal Co. Ltd* [1905] A.C. 239; *Pratt v. B.M.A.* [1919] 1 K.B. 244.
159 Above note 1.
160 [1940] Ch. 352.
161 *Smithies v. National Association of Operative Plasterers* [1909] 1 K.B. 310.
162 [1924] 1 Ch. 302.
163 *Slade & Stewart Ltd v. Haynes* (1969) 5 D.L.R. (3d) 736.

21.50 No justification could be found in *Greig v. Insole*[164] for the defendants' conduct in interfering in the contracts between the individual plaintiffs, who were well-known cricketers, and the company for whom they had undertaken to play cricket. The defendants attempted to justify by arguing that they had acted out of impersonal and disinterested motives, for the protection of cricket in England. This was rejected by Slade J. as a sufficient answer. In this he was fortified by the fact that the defendants had not taken the trouble to see the contracts with which they were interfering by their resolutions about entitlement to play in test and county cricket matches. Nor in *Swiss Bank Corporation v. Lloyds Bank Ltd*[165] was there justification for the defendant bank's conduct in applying the proceeds of the sale of certain securities to discharging a debt owed by a third party to the bank. The bank converted the dollars from the sale into sterling instead of applying the dollars to the discharge of a debt owed by the third party to the plaintiffs. In this instance the charge on which the bank founded its claim was held to be void because it infringed exchange control legislation. Hence it was not open to the bank to rely on justification because they were seeking to act illegally and, in effect, in a manner contrary to public policy. The bank knew that what they were doing would probably interfere with the plaintiff's rights. Nonetheless they acted as they did. This was not a case where a defendant could plead that he acted in the honest belief that he was legally entitled to act. In such instances it would appear that, although there is no justification, the defendant may succeed on the ground that he was unaware that he was interfering with a contract unlawfully. Where this is the situation, the tort is not committed. Hence there is no necessity for the defendant to rely on justification.

21.51 But justification may exist if the defendant has an equal or superior right which could justify his interfering with the plaintiff's contractual rights with a third party, as in *Edwin Hall & Partners v. First National Finance Corporation.*[165a] There the finance company could justify their procurement of the dismissal of the plaintiffs as architects for a development which the defendants were financing by a substantial loan.

(d) The importance of breach

21.52 The principle in *Lumley v. Gye*[166] applies to situations where the defendant induces or procures a breach of contract, or his conduct would be likely to do so if it were not enjoined. The need to prove an existing contract that would be broken in this way was stressed by the Court of Appeal in *D. C. Thomson v. Deakin.*[167] Hence it was held in *Midland Cold Storage Ltd v. Steer*[168] that no action would lie for attempting to prevent the

164 [1978] 3 All E.R. 449.
165 [1979] 2 All E.R.853.
165a [1988] 3 All E.R. 801.
166 (1853) 2 E. &. B. 216.
167 [1952] Ch. 646.
168 [1972] Ch. 730.

conclusion of a projected contract between the plaintiff and a third party.[169] However it was also considered that no action would lie for any conduct that interfered with the performance of an existing contract without actually causing a breach or being intended to cause a breach. That the law did not go so far as to provide a remedy in such instances was thought by Lord Denning to be a serious limitation on the effectiveness of the principle in *Lumley v. Gye*. He considered that the time had come for the law to be extended to cover "deliberate and direct interference with the execution of a contract without that causing any breach". In the case where this comment was made, *Torquay Hotel Ltd v. Cousins*,[170] the defendants were held liable for inducing a breach of contract even though the contract-breaker could not be sued for breach of contract because the contract contained a clause that exempted or excluded liability in the circumstances that were involved, namely industrial action that prevented the delivery of the oil by the third party to the plaintiffs' hotel. Lord Denning was prepared to hold that there might be liability under *Lumley v. Gye* whether the contract was broken, or merely frustrated, without the failure to fulfil its terms being actionable at the suit of the plaintiff. He required that three conditions be satisfied.[171] The first was interference in the execution of a contract. The second was that such interference be deliberate. The third was that such interference be direct. Indirect interference, which might support an action where a breach occurred, would not suffice. He further indicated that the interference should involve the use of "unlawful means".[171a]

21.53 His suggestion received support in other English decisions,[172] although the issue was left open by the House of Lords in *J. T. Stratford & Son Ltd v. Lindley*.[173] Since then, in New Zealand[174] and in Canada,[175] there have been decisions which clearly indicate that, in those jurisdictions, the language and the ideas of Lord Denning have fallen on receptive ears. Those cases hold that there can be liability at common law for a deliberate interference short of causing a breach with the contract of a plaintiff, where unlawful means are used to attain that end. The important elements of that liability are those indicated by Lord Denning, namely,

169 Cp. above p. 554.
170 [1969] 2 Ch. 106 at 138.
171 *Ibid.*: cp. *Acrow (Automation) Ltd v. Rex Chainbelts Inc.* [1971] All E.R. 1175.
171a See also *Hadmor Productions Ltd v. Hamilton* [1981] 2 All E.R. 724, reversed on appeal [1982] 1 All E.R. 1042.
172 See *Merkur Island Shipping Corporation v. Laughton* [1983] A.C. 570 at 607, 609–610 *per* Lord Diplock; *Dimbleby & Son Ltd v. National Union of Journalists* [1984] 1 All E.R. 751; *Esso Petroleum Co. Ltd v. Kingswood Motors Ltd* [1973] 3 All E.R. 1057 at 1068 *per* Bridge J.
173 [1965] A.C. 239.
174 *Takara Properties Ltd v. Rowling* [1978] 2 N.Z.L.R. 314; *Van Camp Chocolates v. Aulsebrooks Ltd* [1984] 1 N.Z.L.R. 354.
175 *Einhorn v. Westmount Industries Ltd* (1969) 5 D.L.R. (3d) 71; (1970) 11 D.L.R. (3d) 509; *Gershman v. Manitoba Vegetable Producers' Marketing Board* (1975) 65 D.L.R. (3d) 181, affirmed (1976) 69 D.L.R. (3d) 114; *Lambair Ltd v. Aero Trades (Western) Ltd (No. 2)* [1977] 6 W.W.R. 212; *Mintuck v. Valley River Band No. 63A* (1977) 75 D.L.R. (3d) 589; *Boychuck v. Northwest Territories Housing Corp.* (1985) 35 C.C.L.T. 28; *Garry v. Sherritt Gordon Mines Ltd* (1988) 42 C.C.L.T. 241.

the necessary intent, the awareness of the consequences, and the employment of unlawful means. In many if not all of those cases the defendant could have been, or was, held liable on other grounds, so that it might be argued that it was unnecessary for the court to pronounce on this issue. Nevertheless this growing body of authority, in other common law jurisdictions indicated the willingness of the courts to extend the scope of the principle in *Lumley v. Gye* as suggested by Lord Denning. This has now come about. The judgment of the English Court of Appeal in *Lonrho plc v. Fayed*[175a] seems to reveal that there now exists in English law a tort of wrongful interference in trade or business which does not require a breach of contract, but does require proof of an unlawful act directed against the plaintiff or undertaken with the intention of harming the plaintiff. Proof of a predominant purpose to injure the plaintiff is not essential. Nor is proof that a tort was actually committed as between the defendant and a third party.

5. INJURIOUS FALSEHOOD

(a) Nature of the liability

21.54 The modern tort of injurious falsehood as it emerged in the nineteenth century[176] emanated from earlier law which recognised the possibility of an action on the case for words spoken or published by the defendant about some aspect of the plaintiff other than his character or reputation.[177] Earlier varieties of this tort were called "slander of goods" or "slander of title". These involved allegations that the plaintiff's goods were unsatisfactory, with the result that they could not be sold by him;[178] or that property owned by the plaintiff was really the property of the defendant, or of someone else, with the result that the plaintiff's rights as an owner were seriously jeopardised because other parties would not treat the plaintiff as an owner.[179] The tort of injurious falsehood, however, can be committed whenever the defendant makes a false statement about another person that reflects on the latter's material, economic interests.

175a [1989] 2 All E.R. 65. See the discussion in *Associated British Ports v. T.G.W.U.* [1989] 3 All E.R. 796 at 806–807, 813–814, 817–819 (reversed on other grounds by the House of Lords, [1989] 3 All E.R. 823).

176 *Wren v. Weild* (1969) L.R. 4 Q.B. 730; *Western Counties Manure Co. v. Lawes Chemical Manure Co.* (1874) L.R. 9 Ex. 218; *Riding v. Smith* (1876) 1 Ex.D. 91; *Ratcliffe v. Evans* [1892] 2 Q.B. 524.

177 *Pennycuick v. Roberts* (1596) Cro. Eliz. 427; *Gerrard v. Dickenson* (1588) Cro. Eliz. 196; *Holland v. Hopkins* (1600) Cro. Eliz. 787; *Hargrave v. LeBreton* (1769) 4 Burr. 2422; *Maloney v. Soper* (1836) 3 Bing. N.C. 371.

178 *White v. Melling* [1895] A.C. 154; *Alcott v. Millar's Karri & Jarah Forests Ltd* (1904) 21 T.L.R. 30; *Barrett v. Associated Newspapers Ltd* (1907) 23 T.L.R. 666; *Royal Baking Powder Co. v. Wright, Crossley & Co.* (1900) 18 R.P.C. 95; *British Railway Traffic & Electricity Co. v. C.R.C. Co.* [1922] 2 K.B. 260. "Slander of goods" must be differentiated from mere "puffing" i.e. promoting the goods of the defendant by comparing them favourably as against the goods of the plaintiff and without denigrating the latter: *White v. Melling*, *supra*.

179 *Halsey v. Brotherhood* (1881) 19 Ch.D. 386; *Dunlop Pneumatic Tyre Co. v. Maison Talbot* (1904) 20 T.L.R. 579; *Shapiro v. LaMorta* (1923) 40 T.L.R. 39, 201.

21.55 In this respect injurious falsehood differs from defamation, although its progenitors, slander of title and slander of goods, suggest that what is involved is something akin to defamation. The expression "slander" was and, to the extent that it is still material, is being used by analogy. That analogy is erroneous and misleading. In the first place the tort of injurious falsehood may be committed by either oral or written statements, whereas slander in its strictly defamatory sense refers only to oral or similar publications.[180] Secondly, injurious falsehood does not necessarily denote a defamatory allegation: it occurs whenever a harmful untrue statement is made about the plaintiff as property owner or trader in relation to his property or trade, not his personal reputation.[181]

21.56 Injurious falsehood must also be differentiated from deceit, although both torts involve the making of false statements. In cases of deceit the defendant makes a false statement to the plaintiff, with the result that the plaintiff acts thereon to his detriment.[182] Injurious falsehood occurs when the defendant makes a false statement about the plaintiff's property or business to third parties, with the result that those parties act in a way that is to the detriment of the plaintiff, such as refusing to deal with the plaintiff, or buy his goods, his house or his land.

21.57 Finally this tort must also be distinguished from passing-off, which it resembles in some respects. The tort of passing-off concerns conduct by the defendant that is intended to deceive the public into believing that goods belonging to or manufactured by the defendant are really goods that are the property or product of the plaintiff.[183] The intent of the defendant is not so much to harm the plaintiff, as in cases of injurious falsehood, as to promote the business of the defendant by taking advantage of the good name of the plaintiff or the plaintiff's product.

(b) Instances of liability

21.58 Perhaps the most important instances of injurious falsehood continue to be those which have been described as slander of title and slander of goods. At one time, it would appear, both versions of this wrong were regarded as amounting to slander of title, even though, in the latter instance, no attack on the title of the plaintiff was intended or conveyed.[184] The more modern distinction between the two versions of the tort has led some commentators, notably in the United States, to regard this part of the law as dealing with what is more appropriately described as "commercial disparagement".[185] The idea behind this is the recognition of this tort

180 Chapter 18.
181 E.g., by a false statement that the plaintiff has gone out of business: *Ratcliffe v. Evans*, *supra*; or that the plaintiff's house is haunted: *Manitoba Free Press Co. v. Nagy* (1908) 39 S.C.R. 340.
182 Chapter 17.
183 Below paras. 21.65ff.
184 Wood, "Disparagement of Title and Quality" (1942) 20 C.B.R. 296, 430.
185 Note (1953) 63 Yale L.J. 65; Note, "Developments in the Law: Competitive Torts" (1964) 77 H.L.R. 890.

as providing a remedy in cases of unfair, improper commercial competition. What American writers and courts have in mind is the protection of business interests from interference that is unlawful and actionable. This may be the effect of the development of the tort of injurious falsehood in modern times. It is not what the courts originally conceived as being its function and effect.

21.59 This point is emphasised by the fact that although many of the decisions before, during and since the nineteenth century, have concerned attacks on the quality of or title to goods, others have involved situations in which neither the quality of the plaintiff's goods nor his title to them have been mentioned. Two of the classic cases of the nineteenth century illustrate this. In *Riding v. Smith*[186] the defendant said that the plaintiff's wife, who assisted in the plaintiff's business, had committed adultery at the place of business. In consequence the plaintiff's business suffered. The plaintiff was able to sue in this action because he could show that his economic loss was a direct consequence of the defendant's statement. Yet that statement was not an attack on the quality of the plaintiff's goods. Nor did it suggest any lack of title. In *Ratcliffe v. Evans*,[187] the defendant stated that the plaintiff had ceased to carry on business as an engineer and boilermaker. This resulted in loss to the plaintiff, since it was not true. The defendant was held liable even though his statement was not an attack on the quality of the plaintiff's work or goods, nor a suggestion that he lacked title to property. Some Canadian decisions further exemplify the broader application of this tort, since they imposed liability for statements that indicated that the plaintiff infringed the defendant's patent rights,[188] or lacked the right to prescribe narcotics;[189] or that the plaintiff's son had committed suicide, which resulted in nervous shock on the part of the mother.[190] A more recent English case, *Fielding v. Variety Inc.*[191] involved an allegation that the plaintiff's musical play had been a disastrous flop in New York. In this instance, as in Canadian decisions, what occurred could hardly be described as an attack on the quality of goods. Yet, in all these situations, harm was suffered by the plaintiff in consequence of the defendant's statement.

(c) Elements of liability

(i) A false statement

21.60 The defendant must have made a false statement of fact concerning the plaintiff's goods, property, business or other activities that

186 (1876) 1 Ex. D. 91; cp. *Casey v. Arnott* (1876) 2 C.P.D. 24, statement that ship was uninsured: crew refused to go to sea in her.

187 [1892] 2 Q.B. 524: cp. *Sheppard Publishing Co. v. Press Publishing Co. Ltd* (1905) 10 O.L.R. 243.

188 *Alberta Geophysical Products Ltd v. Geo. E. Failing Supply Co. Ltd* (1964) 43 D.L.R. (2d) 681.

189 *Bresden v. Johnson* [1945] 1 W.W.R. 273.

190 *Bielirski v. Obadiski* (1922) 65 D.L.R. 627: this would surely be dealt with differently today: pp. 283–286.

191 [1967] 2 Q.B. 841.

relate to his economic or material condition. In true cases of defamation once it is established that the defendant published the offending statement it is presumed to be untrue and the onus lies on the defendant to justify it.[192] The position is different in injurious falsehood. Whatever the nature of the alleged false statement, the onus is on the plaintiff to prove its falsity.

(ii) Malice

21.61 Whether malice is an essential ingredient of liability for injurious falsehood, and what the expression means in this context, have been hotly debated.[193] One approach is that the plaintiff need only prove that the defendant published the false statement intentionally, knowing that what he was stating was false and would cause harm to the plaintiff.[194] Another approach is that which requires the plaintiff to prove that the defendant acted from spite or ill-will.[195] The difference is vital. On the first approach, the defendant would be able to escape liability, even for an untrue statement, if he had a reasonable or probable cause for publishing the statement, e.g., that certain regulations required the defendants to describe a hired car as theirs although they knew that the car was owned by the plaintiffs.[196] On the second approach, the plaintiff would have to show not only knowledge of the statement's falsity, but also an intent to injure for no good reason. The onus would lie on the plaintiff to prove that there was no justification for the making of the statement. If this is the situation, it would make the tort approximate more closely to true cases of defamation, in that the defendant would be relying on some privilege to make a statement about the plaintiff's goods, property, business, etc. and the plaintiff would need to establish express malice in order to show that an abuse of privilege had occurred.[197]

21.62 Many decisions directly or by implication indicate that malice is an essential element in liability: and that malice here denotes an improper motive or reason for making an untrue statement of the kind of question.[198] It is not an absence of reasonable and probable cause, which alone will not render the defendant liable, any more than it would in cases of malicious prosecution.[199] It is the presence of *mala fides*, an intent to injure, not an intent to exercise some right or privilege such as a claim to property which one believes belongs to oneself, or in respect of which one believes one has

192 Above para. 18.58.
193 Newark, "Malice in Actions on the Case for Words" (1944) 60 L.Q.R. 366; Wood, *loc. cit. supra* at 308–320, 431–435.
194 *British Railway Traffic & Electricity Co. v. C.R.C. Co.* [1922] 2 K.B. 260 at 267–272 *per* McCardie J.: *White v. Melling* [1895] A.C. 154 at 160 *per* Lord Herschell.
195 *Balden v. Shorter* [1933] Ch. 427 at 430 *per* Maugham J.; *Potter v. Baker* (1846) 3 C.B. 831.
196 *British Railway Traffic Co. v. C.R.C. Co., supra.*
197 Cp. pp. 497–513.
198 *Balden v. Shorter, supra*; *Re Lewis's Declaration of Trust* [1953] Ch. 423; *Fielding v. Variety Inc.* [1967] 2 Q.B. 841. But not if the plaintiff's cause of action arose under statute, e.g. Land Registration Act 1925 s. 56(3): see *Clearbrook Property Holdings Ltd v. Verrier* [1973] 3 All E.R. 614.
199 Chapter 22.

certain rights such as those of a personal representative.[200] The fact that malice in this sense is required indicates that the tort of injurious falsehood is not one that can be committed by mere negligence. Such, indeed, was the decision of Maugham J. in *Balden v. Shorter*.[201] The defendant carelessly, but without any intention of causing injury, stated that the plaintiff was employed by the defendant, which he was not. This caused damage to the plaintiff. The action would not lie, however, because malice, in the sense of "some dishonest or improper motive", was lacking. By way of contrast, in the Canadian case of *Manitoba Free Press v. Nagy*,[202] which concerned a statement that the plaintiff's house was haunted, liability could be imposed, in the view of the Supreme Court of Canada, on the ground that the statement was made recklessly without regard for its consequences, which were serious for the plaintiff in that he could not sell the house. This was sufficient to establish an absence of good faith on the part of the defendant. That absence of good faith was necessary for liability.[203]

(iii) Damage

21.63 At common law the plaintiff had to prove special damage as a result of the publication of the false statement.[204] In the absence of such damage no action would lie, although in one instance a declaration could be made to the effect that the defendant's allegation was untrue and he had no right to certain investments as the personal representative of his deceased sister, such investments really belonging to the plaintiff who was their nominal owner.[205]

21.64 By the Defamation Act 1952 section 3(1) it is no longer necessary to allege or prove special damage if the words on which the action is founded are calculated to cause pecuniary damage to the plaintiff and are published in writing or other permanent form.[206] Thus for spoken false statements that amount to injurious falsehood it is still necessary for the plaintiff to satisfy the old common law test, for example by showing that previous customers have abandoned his business, which could be established, as *Ratcliffe v. Evans*[207] indicated, by evidence of a general loss of business (unless the false statement were published only to a select group of possible users of the plaintiff's product). Where a statement is written, however, the Act eases the task of the plaintiff. He must show that the words are calculated to cause pecuniary damage, which should not be troublesome in most instances. If the attack is on the quality of the plaintiff's goods, his title, his continuance of business, his right to do certain things, it will be almost inevitable that pecuniary damage will

200 *Re Lewis's Declaration of Trust, supra.*
201 [1933] Ch. 427.
202 (1908) 39 S.C.R. 340.
203 *Langdon's Coach Lines Ltd v. Toronto Transit Commission* [1956] O.R. 45.
204 *Fielding v. Variety Inc.* [1967] 2 Q.B. 841 at 850 *per* Lord Denning M.R.
205 *Re Lewis' Declaration of Trust, supra.*
206 Cp. the situation in respect of certain types of slander: pp. 486–487.
207 [1892] 2 Q.B. 524: cp. *Glo-Klen Distributors Ltd v. B.C. Chemicals Ltd* (1959) 14 D.L.R. (2d) 635.

follow. But the question will remain: what pecuniary damage has the plaintiff suffered? As Lord Denning M.R. pointed out in *Fielding v. Variety Inc.*,[208] on this head of claim the plaintiff can recover only damages for his probable money loss, not for his injured feelings. In that case, therefore, the plaintiffs could only recover a nominal sum for the injurious falsehood published in America. There was no proof of any loss in England, where the musical play continued to be successful. Nor was there any evidence that the chances of a successful production in the United States had been adversely affected.

6. PASSING-OFF

(a) Nature and development of the action

21.65 What has been referred to as the action for passing-off in its classic form[209] arose in the nineteenth century out of the use in connection with his own goods by one trader of the trade name or trade mark of a rival trader so as to induce in potential purchasers the belief that his goods were those of the rival trader. This developed into a broader action that could be brought when one trader represented his goods as the goods of somebody else. At first it was confined to cases of the deceptive use of trade names, marks, letters or other indicia. The principle became: "A man is not to sell his own goods under the pretence that they are the goods of another man."[210] Fifty years later it was said that the action for passing-off did not protect the proprietary right of the trader in the mark, name or get-up improperly used.[211] Indeed statutes have intervened to deal with such proprietary matters.[212] The common law was stated in classic form in *Reddaway v. Banham*.[213] There it was held that the use by a trader of a term which accurately described the composition of his own goods ("camel-hair belting") would amount to the tort of passing-off if that term were understood in the market in which the goods were sold to denote the goods of a rival trader. Subsequently, in *A. G. Spalding & Bros. v. A. W. Gamage Ltd*,[214] the House of Lords identified the right the invasion of which is the subject of passing-off actions as the property in the business or goodwill likely to be injured by the misrepresentation.

21.66 Goodwill in law is a broad concept that means the benefit and advantage of the good name, reputation and connection of a business. It is

208 [1967] 2 Q.B. 841 at 850.
209 *Erven Warnink BV v. J. Townsend & Sons (Hull) Ltd* [1979] 2 All E.R. 927 at 929 *per* Lord Diplock.
210 *Perry v. Truefitt* (1842) 6 Beav. 66 at 73 *per* Lord Langdale M.R.; cp. *Croft v. Day* (1984) 7 Beav. 84; *Leather Cloth Co. v. American Leather Cloth Co.* (1865) 11 H.L.C. 523 at 538 *per* Lord Kingsdown.
211 *Reddaway v. Banham* [1896] 199.
212 See, e.g., Trade Marks Act 1938.
213 *Supra.*
214 (1915) 32 R.P.C. 273 at 284 *per* Lord Parker of Waddington; *Star Industries Co. Ltd v. Yap Kew Kar* [1976] 2 F.S.R. 256 at 269 *per* Lord Diplock.

the attractive force that brings in custom.[215] That goodwill can be injured in a number of ways, not only by representing one's own goods as those of another.[216] The same effect can be achieved by selling goods correctly described as being made by their actual manufacturer but of an inferior class or quality yet misrepresented as being of a superior class or quality.[217] It can also be injured where, although the plaintiff and defendant are not competing traders in the same line of business, a false suggestion by the defendant that their businesses are connected with one another would damage the reputation and thus the goodwill of the plaintiff's business.[218]

21.67 Thus misrepresenting one's goods as the goods of someone else is not a separate genus of actionable wrong but a particular species of wrong included in a wider genus.[219] This, in turn, is a form of unfair trading which is actionable at the suit of other traders who thereby suffer loss of business or goodwill by various actions.[220] One is conspiracy to injure a person in his trade or business.[221] Another is slander of goods (or injurious falsehood).[222] The most protean, in Lord Diplock's words,[223] is that which is generally and nowadays perhaps misleadingly described as passing-off.

21.68 There are five characteristics that must be present in order to create a valid cause of action for passing-off: (1) a misrepresentation; (2) made by a trader in the course of trade; (3) to prospective customers of his or ultimate consumers of goods or services supplied by him; (4) which is calculated to injure the business or goodwill of another trader (in the sense that this is a reasonably foreseeable consequence); and (5) which causes actual damage to a business or goodwill of the trader by whom the action is brought or (in a *quia timet* action, for an injunction) will probably do so.[224] However because all passing-off actions present these characteristics, it does not follow that all factual situations that present these characteristics will give rise to an action for passing-off. There may be what a moral code would censure as dishonest trading, based on deception of customers and consumers of a trader's wares. Our economic system, which relies on competition to keep down prices and the improvement of products, provides underlying practical reasons for the policy of the common law not to run the risk of hampering competition by giving a civil remedy to everyone competing in the market who has suffered damage to

215 *I.R.C. v. Muller & Co's Margagine Ltd* [1910] A.C. 217 at 223 *per* Lord MacNaghten.
216 See e.g., *F. Hoffman-La Roche & Co. AG v. DDSA Pharmaceuticals Ltd* [1972] R.P.C. 1; *Lee Kar Choo v. Lee Lian Choon* [1967] 1 A.C. 602.
217 *A. G. Spalding & Bros. v. A. W. Gamage Ltd., supra.*
218 *Harrods Ltd v. R. Harrod Ltd* (1923) 41 R.P.C. 74; *Biba Group Ltd v. Biba Boutique* [1980] R.P.C. 413. Contrast *Jay's Ltd v. Jacobi* [1933] Ch. 411; *Wright, Layman & Umney Ltd v. Wright* (1949) 66 R.P.C. 149; *Joseph Rodgers & Son Ltd v. W. N. Rodgers & CO.* (1925) 41 R.P.C. 277; *Granada Group Ltd v. Ford Motor Co. Ltd* [1972] F.S.R. 103.
219 *Erven Warnink BV v. J. Townsend & Sons (Hull) Ltd* [1979] 2 All E.R. 927 at 932 *per* Lord Diplock.
220 *Ibid.* at 931.
221 Above pp. 538–545.
222 Above paras. 21.54ff.
223 *Supra* note 219 at 931.
224 *Ibid.* at 932–933 *per* Lord Diplock.

his business or goodwill as a result of inaccurate statements made by rival traders about their own wares:

> "The market in which the action for passing-off originated was no place for the mealy mouthed: advertisements are not an affidavit: exaggerated claims by a trader about the quality of his wares, assertions that they are better than those of his rivals, even though he knows that to be untrue, have been permitted by the common law as venial 'puffing' which gives no cause of action to a competitor even though he can show that he has suffered actual damage in his business as a result."[225]

Thus there are limits to the common law liability of a rival trader.

21.69 Meanwhile, on a parallel rather than on a diverging course, Parliament has imposed on traders a higher standard of commercial candour for the protection of consumers, not rival traders. Those enactments do not give rise to a civil cause of action for breach of statutory duty to competing traders even though they have sustained actual damage as a result.[226] The common law has confined itself to providing remedies for unfair trading by the various methods mentioned above, including the action for passing-off, which, in recent years, has undergone extension.[227]

(b) Classical passing-off

21.70 The essence of passing-off is the representation of the defendant's goods as being those of the plaintiff. One way this may occur is if the defendant uses a name which resembles that of the plaintiff:[228] or gives the impression that the plaintiff is involved in the business enterprise.[229] Indeed even the use of one's own name may be enjoined by injunction on the ground of passing-off, if confusion results or is calculated to result from such use.[230] Another way in which the relevant representation may occur is by means of the way goods are presented or packaged. In *F. Hoffman La-Roche & Co. AG v. DDSA Pharmaceuticals Ltd*,[231] the plaintiffs manufactured

225 *Ibid.* at 933.

226 *London Armoury Co. Ltd v. Ever Ready Co. (Great Britain) Ltd* [1941] 1 K.B. 742; *Cutler v. Wandsworth Stadium Ltd* [1949] A.C. 398.

227 But it has not created a tort of "unfair competition" *per se*, as has emerged in the United States: *International News Service v. Associated Press* (1918) 248 U.S. 215 at 241–242 *per* Pitney J.; criticised in *Cheney Bros. v. Doris Silk Corporation* (1929) 35 F. (2d) 279; *Victoria Park Racing & Recreation Grounds Co. Ltd v. Taylor* (1939) 58 C.L.R. 479; *Cadbury Schweppes Pty Ltd v. Pub Squash Co. Pty Ltd* [1981] 1 All E.R. 213 at 219 *per* Lord Scarman. Cp. a Hong Kong case: *Shaw Bros. (Hong Kong) Ltd v. Golden Harvest (H.K.) Ltd* [1972] R.P.C. 559.

228 *Joseph Rodgers & Sons Ltd v. W. N. Rodgers & Co* (1925) 41 R.P.C. 277. But small differences in a competitor's trade name will render the competitor immune from action: *Office Cleaning Services Ltd v. Westminster Window & General Cleaners Ltd* (1946) 63 R.P.C. 39 at 42 *per* Lord Simonds. This is because there is always the risk of confusion by a blundering public: *ibid.* at 43; *Hornsby Building Information Pty Ltd v. Sydney Building Information Centre* (1978) 52 A.L.J. L.R. 312 at 396–397 *per* Stephen J.

229 *Eastman Photographic Materials Co. Ltd v. The John Griffiths Cycle Corporation Ltd* (1898) 15 R.P.C. 105; *Parker-Knoll Ltd v. Knoll International Ltd* [1962] R.P.C. 265; *Annabel's (Berkeley Square) Ltd v. G. Schock* [1972] F.S.R. 261.

230 *Wright, Layman & Umney Ltd v. Wright* (1949) 66 R.P.C. 149 at 153 *per* Lord Greene. Contrast *Jay's Ltd v. Jacobi* [1933] Ch. 41.

231 [1972] R.P.C. 1.

and marketed a certain drug under the registered name of Librium in distinctive black and green capsules with the name "Roche" on each one. The defendant obtained a compulsory licence to manufacture the plaintiffs' drug, which they marketed and advertised in black and green capsules identical to those of the plaintiffs except that they had the letters "DDSA" instead of the plaintiffs' name on them. The Court of Appeal upheld an injunction that had been granted on the ground that the public associated the black and green capsules with the plaintiffs, even though the public did not know the identity of the plaintiffs. The get-up of the plaintiffs' product had produced goodwill which the defendants realised it was to their commercial advantage to use.[231a] This representation need not be made fraudulently.[232] As long as it is made and does, or is likely to, cause damage to the plaintiff, the tort will be committed. However the complete innocence of the defendant making the representation or pretence may be a reason for limiting the account of the profits made by the defendant through its use to the period subsequent to the date when he became aware of the true facts.

21.71 The representation must be made in the course of business. Usually this will mean that the goods in question are sold to the public in the normal way, i.e. in shops or otherwise over the counter. That is not important, however, as long as the public could be misled into thinking that they were acquiring the goods from the same original and reliable, if unknown, source as before. Hence in the Librium case,[233] it made no difference to liability that the medicine was not sold in shops and the public had little or no choice over the medicine they were to take in certain situations. It is important, however, that the business of the defendant and that of the plaintiff should involve a common or related field of activity. Thus in *Granada Group Ltd v. Ford Motor Co. Ltd*[234] the plaintiffs were unsuccessful in their passing-off action. They operated television and similar activities under the name "Granada". The defendants manufactured a car called the "Granada". There was not the necessary connection between the two types of commercial activity to justify the conclusion that the public would confuse the two products or two businesses. However in *Biba Group Ltd v. Biba Boutique*[235] the injunction sought was granted. The plaintiffs had a considerable reputation in the name "Biba" in the fields of clothing, fashion accessories and cosmetics. The defendants carried on a boutique business under the name "Biba

231a Passing off can also be committed by making use of slogans or visual images associated through advertising with the plaintiff's product, e.g., by using the same suggestion of masculinity as had been utilised by the plaintiffs in their television campaign for a soft drink: *Cadbury Schweppes Pty Ltd v. Pub Squash Co. Pty Ltd* [1981] 1 All E.R. 213. But note that the remarks with respect to confusion about names, *supra* note 228, apply with equal force to other distinguishing marks: [1981] 1 All E.R. 213 at 218 *per* Lord Scarman.

232 *Habib Bank Ltd v. Habib Bank AG Zurich* [1981] 2 All E.R. 650 at 658 *per* Oliver L.J., quoting Lord Parker in *A. G. Spalding Bros. Ltd v. A. W. Gamage Ltd, supra.*

233 *Supra* note 231.

234 [1972] F.S.R. 103.

235 [1980] R.P.C. 413.

Boutique". In these circumstances there was the likelihood of confusion. Nor could the defendants escape liability on the basis that the boutique was called Biba because the proprietor's nickname was Biba. As noted earlier even one's own name cannot be used in certain circumstances: and this applies even more stringently to the use of a nickname.

21.72 The crux of the matter is whether the use of the name, get-up, or other means of describing the defendant's goods constitutes an attack on the goodwill of the plaintiff as established by his earlier use of the name, get-up or other description. It is even possible that a foreign plaintiff can have created such goodwill or reputation abroad that the use of the same name as that of the plaintiff's business can amount to passing-off.[236] But where a local company is formed in England as part of an international business, the reputation and goodwill of the international business continues to belong to that business. It is not the exclusive property of the local branch. Instead the reputation and goodwill in question attach to the local business set up in England.[237] Injury to goodwill may occur even if the plaintiff has ceased business. It has been held that a trader retains goodwill for some time after he ceases to trade: it is an asset which is entitled to exploit in the future and cannot be said to have been abandoned. Therefore he is entitled to have it protected.[238] It is possible for there to be passing-off even if the defendant does not infringe a trade mark owned by the plaintiff: the test is whether the public would be confused into thinking that the goods being purchased were those of the plaintiff by reason of the label used by the defendants.[239] Whenever this happens or is likely to occur, there is actual or potential injury to the goodwill and reputation of the plaintiff.

(c) Modern extension

21.73 Classical passing-off was given an extended form and application in *Bollinger v. Costa Brava Wine Co. Ltd*,[240] the Champagne case. It was subsequently adopted as correct in a case concerning sherry[241] and another involving Scotch whisky.[242] Those decisions were all at first instance.[243] But the newer version of passing-off was accepted by the House of Lords in *Erven Warnink BV v. J. Townsend & Sons (Hill) Ltd*,[244] which concerned

236 *Maxim's Ltd v. Dye* [1977] 1 W.L.R. 1155.
237 *Habib Bank Ltd v. Habib Bank AG Zurich* [1981] 2 All E.R. 650.
238 *Ad-Lib Club Ltd v. Granville* [1972] R.P.C. 673; contrast *Norman Kark Publications Ltd v. Odhams Press Ltd* [1962] 1 All E.R. 636.
239 *Lee Kar Choo v. Lee Liam Choon* [1967] 1 A.C. 602.
240 [1960] Ch. 262.
241 *Vine Products Ltd v. Mackenzie & Co. Ltd* [1969] R.P.C. 1.
242 *John Walker & Sons Ltd v. Henry Ost & Co. Ltd* [1970] 2 All E.R. 106.
243 But the Champagne case was approved in the Court of Appeal in *H. P. Bulmer Ltd and Showerings Ltd v. J. Bollinger SA & Champagne Lanson Père et Fils* [1978] R.P.C. 79; in New South Wales: *Scott v. Tuff-Kots (Australia) Pty Ltd* [1975] 1 N.S.W.L.R. 537; and in Hong Kong: *Shaw Bros. (Hong Kong) Ltd v. Golden Harvest (H.K.) Ltd* [1972] R.P.C. 559.
244 [1979] 2 All E.R. 927.

advocaat. According to Lord Diplock in the latter case,[245] two factors distinguished the Champagne case from all previous cases of passing-off. The first was that the element in the goodwill of the plaintiff in that case represented by his ability to use without deception the word "Champagne" to distinguish his sparkling wines, made by the *champénois* process from grapes produced in the Champagne district of France, was not exclusive to himself but was shared with every other shipper of sparkling wine to England whose wines could satisfy the same conditions. The second was that the class of traders entitled to the proprietary right represented by the ability without deception to call their wines "Champagne" was capable of continuing expansion. In previous decisions of shared goodwill the goodwill protected by a passing-off action had been shared by two traders.

21.74 The champagne case accepted the principle, for the first time in England, that parties who did not have an exclusive right to use a particular trade name, but who were some members of a class consisting of all those who had a right to use the name, were entitled to protect the name by a passing-off action. The novelty of the case, and its importance, lay in the nature of the misrepresentation against which the plaintiffs were held entitled to protection. The misrepresentation was not that the goods of the defendants were those of the plaintiffs. It was not even that the goods came from France. It was that "Spanish Champagne" was wine of the kind that enjoyed the reputation and goodwill that attached to genuine Champagne, in which the plaintiffs had a property right.[246] The case was rightly decided, said Lord Fraser in the advocaat case,[247] because it was soundly based on the principle of earlier passing-off actions, namely that the plaintiff is entitled to protect a right of property in the goodwill attached to a name which is distinctive of the product or class of product sold by him in the course of his business. The law has moved from a right of property in a name to a right of property in goodwill, and reputation (as pointed out by Lord Diplock earlier in the same case).[248] To establish a cause of action for passing-off it was necessary for the plaintiff to prove a number of factors including (1) that his business consisted of, or included, selling in England a class of goods to which the particular trade name applied; (2) that the class of goods was clearly defined, and that in the minds of the public, or a section of the public, in England the trade name distinguished that class from other similar goods; (3) that because of the reputation of the goods there was goodwill attached to the name; and (4) that the plaintiff, as a member of the class of those who sold the goods, was the owner of goodwill in England that was of substantial value.[249] The other main factor was the suffering or likelihood of suffering substantial damage to the plaintiff's property in goodwill.

245 *Ibid.* at 934.
246 *Ibid.* at 941 *per* Lord Fraser of Tullybelton.
247 *Ibid.* at 943.
248 *Ibid.* at 931–932.
249 *Ibid.* at 943–944 *per* Lord Fraser of Tulleybelton.

21.75 In the champagne case the descriptive term referred to the geographical provenance of the goods: and the class entitled to goodwill in the term was those supplying on the English market goods produced in that locality.[250] The same was more or less true in the sherry case. In the Scotch whisky case the product was blended whisky and the class entitled to the goodwill in the term "Scotch whisky" was extended to suppliers of blended whisky wherever the blending process took place, provided that the ingredients consisted exclusively of whiskies distilled in Scotland. Geographical connotations, as occurred in these cases, are not a key element. If the marketing of a product of a particular character or composition has been effected under a descriptive name, and the product under that name has gained a public reputation that distinguishes it from competing products of different composition, the goodwill in the name of those entitled to make use of it should be protected by the law against deceptive use of the name by competitors, if it denoted a product the ingredients of which came only from a particular locality; but not if the ingredients, however narrowly identified, are not restricted as to their geographical provenance.[251] Hence in the advocaat case, the plaintiffs were entitled to an injunction to protect their use of the name "advocaat" in respect of a drink made from a mixture of eggs and spirits. The defendants produced an alcoholic drink out of dried eggs and Cyprus sherry, properly called egg-flip, but marketed as "Old English Advocaat". The injunction was granted because the plaintiffs had acquired a substantial reputation and goodwill for their product. Even though other manufacturers produced the same drink as the plaintiffs, the latter's claim was upheld. Whatever the name advocaat meant in other countries, the plaintiffs had property in the goodwill attaching to that name in England. It was their reputation that was involved, not the reputation or meaning of the name elsewhere.

21.76 The decision in the *Warnink* case[252] makes two points very clear. The first is that the tort of passing-off now incorporates misrepresentations about another trader's goods which take the form of attacking a reputation derived from that trader's description of his goods, whatever the nature of the description, whether it relates to the name of the goods, their presentation or get-up, their contents, or their geographical provenance. It also applies even though there may be more than one trader who manufactures the goods in question (although as Lord Diplock pointed out,[253] it is necessary to be able to identify with reasonable precision the members of the class of traders of whose products a particular word or name has become so distinctive as to make their right to use it truthfully as descriptive of their product a valuable part of the goodwill of each of them). The second point is that despite some suggestion that this was the

250 *Ibid.* at 935 *per* Lord Diplock.
251 *Ibid.*
252 [1979] 2 All E.R. 927.
253 *Ibid.* at 937.

effect of the champagne case and its successors,[254] there is no general tort of "unfair competition" known to English law.[255] Liability depends on proof of a misrepresentation that the competitors' goods are goods of a definite class with a valuable reputation, and that such misrepresentation is likely to cause damage to established traders who own goodwill in relation to that class of goods.[256] The "new-fangled" tort of unfair trading or unfair competition is not really a new-fangled tort at all but part of the old tort of passing-off.[257].

254 *Shaw Bros. (Hong Kong) Ltd v. Golden Harvest (H.K.) Ltd* [1972] R.P.C. 559 at 560, where Huggins J. says that this was argued by the plaintiffs.

255 *Ibid.* at 562. Cp. *Moorgate Tobacco v. Phillip Morris* (1986) 59 A.L.J.R. 77. See Adams, "Is there a Tort of Unfair Competition?" [1985] J.B.L. 26.

256 *Erven Warnink BV v. J. Townsend & Sons (Hull) Ltd* [1979] 2 All E.R. 927 at 944 *per* Lord Fraser of Tulleybelton. See the remarks of Oliver L.J. in *Anheuser-Bush Inc. v. Budweiser Budvor Brewery* [1984] F.S.R. 431 at 463.

257 *Shaw Bros. (Hong Kong) Ltd v. Golden Harvest (H.K.) Ltd*, *supra* at 562 *per* Huggins J.

CHAPTER 22

Abuse of Process

1. MALICIOUS PROSECUTION

(a) The nature of the action

22.01 Malicious prosecution is the improper commencement of criminal proceedings against another person. To enforce the criminal law it is necessary to charge those accused of an offence and thereby bring them to trial. The privilege of instituting such proceedings in various ways appropriate to the particular offence that is involved is one that may be enjoyed by private citizens, the police, or other officials. As long as that privilege is exercised in a reasonable and legitimate manner the party who commences a prosecution will not be liable to the innocent accused; but should the prosecutor invoke the criminal process for a purpose other than the proper enforcement of the law, he may be held liable in an action for malicious prosecution. The law does not penalise a prosecutor who made a genuine mistake. The law does penalise someone who employs the criminal process for his own improper purposes.

22.02 The rationale of the tort of malicious prosecution is that the use of criminal procedure to achieve a personal aim other than the conviction and punishment of an undoubted offender is objectionable. It is to subject the law to abuse. Just as the privilege of speech may not be enjoyed in order deliberately to cause harm to others by making untrue defamatory statements, so the right, indeed the duty, to prosecute someone believed to have committed an offence may not be exercised solely to cause harm. Not every unjustified prosecution will give rise to an action for malicious prosecution. Were that the case, the bringing of criminal proceedings would be fraught with danger to those who considered that a prosecution was legitimate in the circumstances. That might lead to the failure or refusal of citizens or officials to undertake such prosecutions for fear of the consequences. Such a situation would not be in the public interest. The law has to maintain a balance between encouraging the prosecution of suspected offenders, even where it turns out that the prosecution cannot be sustained, and preventing unnecessary and unjustified prosecutions by visiting on the prosecutor liability in tort where his behaviour in starting such proceedings was without satisfactory justification.

22.03 In consequence the law lays down stringent conditions before a successful action for malicious prosecution can be brought. Unless those conditions are satisfied, the plaintiff will not be able to sue the party who initiated the proceedings in question. Before an action will succeed the plaintiff must establish: (1) that he is innocent of the crime charged against him; (2) that there was an absence of reasonable and probable cause for the prosecution; and (3) that the defendant was actuated by malice, namely, the presence in mind of the defendant of some indirect or improper or unlawful motive in instituting the criminal proceedings.[1] The onus is on the plaintiff to establish each and every part of these propositions.[2]

(b) Elements of liability

(i) Favourable end to prosecution

22.04 There must be a prosecution of the plaintiff. This usually means the laying of a charge before a court and the subsequent trial of the plaintiff. However it is not necessary for matters to proceed that far.[3] It has been held that to lay an information before a magistrate, even if it is not taken further but is kept in the magistrate's possession without any proceedings being brought, is to commence a prosecution for the purposes of a subsequent action for malicious prosecution.[4] What is required is some act on the part of the defendant that indicates that he is seeking the conviction of the plaintiff for an offence.[5] The distinction is drawn between arresting the plaintiff, which may be the basis for an action of false arrest or imprisonment, and commencing criminal proceedings against him. Once the plaintiff is brought before a magistrate, or a court is involved in the situation even without any actual seizure of the plaintiff, the defendant who has made this occur cannot be accused of false imprisonment, even if the consequence is the arrest and incarceration of the plaintiff. But he might be held liable for malicious prosecution if the circumstances warrant such an action. It is the intervention of a judicial officer, as contrasted with the employment or assistance of a policeman, that marks the difference between the improper institution of the criminal law and the improper detention of the plaintiff that would constitute false imprisonment.[6] Hence a pathologist and toxicologist who reported to the police, who then on the basis of that report might institute a prosecution, could not be sued for

1 *Abbott v. Regufe Assurance Co. Ltd* [1962] 1 Q.B. 432 at 453 *per* Upjohn L.J.; cp. Bowen L.J. in *Abrath v. North Eastern Railway Co.* (1883) 11 Q.B.D. 440 at 455.

2 *Abrath v. North Eastern Railway Co.* (1883) 11 Q.B.D. 440, affirmed (1886) 11 App.Cas. 247. In *Stapely v. Annetts* [1970] 1 W.L.R. 20 the plaintiff sought further and better particulars of the defendant's grounds for making a decision to prosecute the plaintiff for theft. His request for such particulars from the Director of Public Prosecutions was denied because the onus was on the plaintiff to prove both malice and lack of reasonable and probable cause.

3 E.g. where a charge was preferred and later withdrawn: *Romegialli v. Marceau* [1964] 1 O.R. 407.

4 *Casey v. Automobiles Renault Canada Ltd* [1965] S.C.R. 607.

5 E.g., giving evidence that results as a natural and probable consequence in the indictment of the plaintiff: *Fitzjohn v. Mackinder* (1861) 9 C.B.N.S. 505, distinguished by a Canadian court in *Willinsky v. Anderson* (1909) 19 O.L.R. 437.

6 *Austin v. Dowling* (1870) L.R. 5 C.P. 534 at 540 *per* Willes J.

malicious prosecution. The pathologist and toxicologist did not set the criminal law process in motion. The police or the Director of Public Prosecutions made the decision whether to charge someone with a crime on the basis of the findings and evidence of the scientists.[7]

22.05 Whether the proceedings go beyond the laying of an information or never proceed further than the appearance of the defendant before the magistrate for the purpose of beginning the process of the criminal law, the attempt to charge the plaintiff must terminate in his favour. This means the acquittal of the plaintiff,[8] or the withdrawal of the prosecution.[9] Should the plaintiff be convicted at trial but subsequently acquitted on appeal, this will be regarded as termination in his favour.[10] But a conviction followed by an absolute discharge is not favourable termination. Nor can the plaintiff sue for malicious prosecution if he has been bound over to keep the peace as a consequence of the prosecution.[11]

(ii) Lack of reasonable and probable cause

22.06 This is an objective question to be decided on the evidence, not on how the circumstances appear to the prosecutor at the time of the prosecution.[12] Whether reasonable and probable cause existed for the commencement of the proceedings is a question of law, not of fact.[13] However, facts must be found on the basis of which can be determined the issue of reasonable and probable cause.[14] The onus of proving absence of such cause for the prosecution is always on the plaintiff.[15] Where only part of the prosecution can be justified on the basis of reasonable and probable cause, the plaintiff can still succeed in his action if the shows that the substantial part of the charge was not justified by any reasonable and probable cause.[16]

7 *Evans v. London Hospital Medical College* [1981] 1 All E.R. 714: contrast *Fitzjohn v. Mackinder, supra.*

8 *Morgan v. Hughes* (1788) 2 T.R. 225; *Goddard v. Smith* (1795) 6 Mod. 252; *Castrique v. Behrens* (1861) 3 E. & E. 709; *Redway v. McAndrew* (1873) L.R. 9 Q.B. 70; *Taylor v. Ford* (1873) 29 L.T. 392. An acquittal is *prima facie* evidence that the prosecution was without foundation: *Wilkinson v. Howel* (1830) Moo. & M. 495.

9 *Romegialli v. Marceau, supra*; *Casey v. Automobiles Renault Canada Ltd, supra*: or a plea of *nolle prosequi*. But not the abandonment of the proceedings as a result of a compromise or arrangement between the complainant and the accused: *Baxter v. Gordon Ironsides & Fares Ltd* (1907) 13 O.L.R. 598.

10 *Herniman v. Smith* [1938] A.C. 305 at 315.

11 *Everett v. Ribbands* [1952] 2 Q.B. 198.

12 *Tims v. John Lewis & Co. Ltd* [1951] 2 K.B. 459 at 472 *per* Lord Goddard C.J. But it may become a subjective question if the prosecutor knows the prosecution is groundless and it was in fact groundless: *Leibo v. Buckman Ltd* [1952] 2 All E.R. 1057 at 1064 *per* Denning L.J.

13 *Pain v. Rochester* (1599) Cro. Eliz. 871; *Panton v. Williams* (1841) 2 Q.B. 161; *Hailes v. Marks* (1861) 7 H. & N. 56; *Lister v. Perryman* (1878) L.R. 4 H.L. 521.

14 *Venafra v. Johnson* (1833) 10 Bing. 301; *Hinton v. Heather* (1845) 14 M. & W. 131; *Heddick v. Haslop* (1844) 12 Q.B. 267; *Glinski v. McIver* [1962] 1 All E.R. 696.

15 Which means that the plaintiff must prove a negative: a very unusual situation.

16 *Leibo v. Buckman Ltd* [1952] 2 All E.R. 1057.

22.07 For reasonable and probable cause for a prosecution to exist usually entails that there is, in the words of Hawkins J. in *Hicks v. Faulkner*:[17]

> "an honest belief in the guilt of the accused based upon a full conviction, founded upon reasonable grounds of the existence of a state of circumstances which, assuming them to be true, would reasonably lead any ordinarily prudent and cautious man, placed in the position of the accuser to the conclusion that the person charged was probably guilty of the crime imputed."

In a subsequent case[18] Cave J. in directing the jury, asked them to consider two questions in relation to the issue of reasonable and probable cause. The first was whether the defendant took care to inform himself of the facts of the case. The second was whether the defendant honestly believed in the case. If these questions of fact were decided in favour of the defendant, the consequence would be, as a matter of law, that the defendant would have had reasonable and probable cause for bringing a prosecution. Although objectively determined honest belief in the guilt of the plaintiff has been stated to be the test only in some cases,[19] that seems to negate the whole idea of reasonable and probable cause. What the law is seeking to discover, by insistence on the validity of the prosecution, is whether the defendant prosecuted the plaintiff from a genuine belief that he was guilty, or without any legitimate basis for making the accusation. As Hodson L.J. said in *Leibo v. Buckman*:[20] "lack of honest belief destroys the defence of reasonable and probable cause." Hence in *Malz v. Rosen*[21] the defendant was not liable. He instituted a prosecution of the plaintiff after the police had told him that the conduct of the plaintiff constituted an offence, and after the police encouraged and asked him to prefer a charge. When he did so, and the plaintiff was acquitted, the latter sued. The defendant was held to have had reasonable and probable grounds for bringing the charge.

22.08 In some instances a charge has been brought only after the defendant sought the advice and opinion of a lawyer. Where this is the case, it may well be held that the prosecution was based on reasonable and probable grounds, unless the opinion of the lawyer was founded on an inaccurate statement of the circumstances by the defendant, or the defendant deliberately withheld information from the lawyer that would have made a difference to the latter's opinion and advice. In addition the lawyer whose opinion is sought must be experienced in the kind of work

17 (1878) 8 P.B.D. 167 at 171, approved by Lord Atkin in *Herniman v. Smith* [1938] A.C. 305 at 316. See the criticism of Lord Denning in *Glinski v. McIver* [1962] 1 All E.R. 696 at 709–710. Cp. the remarks of Tindal C.J. in *Broad v. Ham* (1839) 5 Bing. N.C. 722 at 725.

18 *Abrath v. North Eastern Railway Co.* (1883) 22 Q.B.D. 440 at 443.

19 *Tempest v. Snowden* [1952] 1 K.B. 130 at 136–137 *per* Evershed M.R.: *ibid.* at 140 *per* Denning L.J., both of whom say that honest belief is more relevant to the issue of malice.

20 [1952] 2 All E.R. 1057 at 1072.

21 [1966] 1 W.L.R. 1008: cp. the Canadian case of *Meyer v. General Exchange Insurance Corporation* (1962) 31 D.L.R. (2d) 689.

that is involved.[22] However it is not to be forgotten that it is the belief of the prosecutor in the charge against the plaintiff, not the belief of the legal advisor, that is the final test of liability.[23]

22.09 The belief of the defendant need not be that the plaintiff is guilty. It is enough if the defendant believes in the validity of the prosecution. The prosecutor has only to be satisfied that there is a proper case to lay before a court. However it is perfectly proper to ask whether the prosecutor was actuated by "belief in guilt", "belief in the case laid", or "belief that the facts amounted to the offence charged."[24] Reliance on the opinion or advice of a lawyer may be extremely relevant. This would tend to show that the defendant not only believed the facts that led to the prosecution being brought, but also believed, as a result of his request for advice, that those facts constituted the offence with which the plaintiff was charged.

22.10 The question of reasonable and probable cause is distinct from the issue of malice. In this respect the statement of Hawkins J. has been criticised on the ground that it suggests that to have reasonable and probable cause for a prosecution the prosecutor must bring to bear an open mind before he makes the charge, i.e. that he is free from malice.[25] It may be possible for a prosecutor to have reasonable and probable cause for a prosecution, on an objective basis, even though he lacks an open mind, in the sense that he is looking for the possibility of charging the plaintiff. The honesty of the prosecutor's action in bringing the prosecution will not prove or disprove that he had reasonable and probable cause, although proof of such cause may negate malice, just as malice may negate the presence of reasonable and probable cause.[26] What is important is whether there were facts on which a reasonable prudent, and cautious man could hold the belief that there were grounds for a prosecution. An honest belief will be useless and irrelevant to liability if the grounds for that belief were "flimsy and inadequate".[27]

(iii) Malice

22.11 Proof that the defendant lacked reasonable and probable cause for a prosecution will not suffice. The plaintiff must also establish that the defendant acted out of "malice". In this context malice means a "wrong or indirect motive".[28] It can connote spite or ill-will towards the plaintiff. But it goes further than such purely subjective issues. It involves the

22 *Abbott v. Refuge Assurance Co. Ltd* [1962] 1 Q.B. 432; *Hewlett v. Crutchley* (1813) 5 Taunt. 277; *Ravenga v. Mackintoosh* (1824) 2 B. & C. 693. But was the prosecution caused by the legal advice or some improper motive? See *Bradshaw v. Waterlow & Sons Ltd* [1913] 3 K.B. 527. Counsel is not an instrument of the person who initiates the prosecution: *Abbott v. Refuge Assurance Co. Ltd, supra.*

23 *Glinski v. McIver* [1962] 1 All E.R. 696. The fact that a prosecution was brought by the Director of Public Prosecutions did not itself establish that there was reasonable and probable cause for the prosecution: *Riches v. D.P.P.* [1973] 2 All E.R. 935.

24 *Glinski v. McIver, supra* at 708 *per* Lord Radcliffe.

25 *Ibid.* at 709–710 *per* Lord Denning.

26 *Johnstone v. Sutton* (1786) 1 T.R. 493 at 545.

27 *Glinski v. McIver, supra* at 710 *per* Lord Denning.

28 *Brown v. Hawkes* [1891] 2 Q.B. 718 at 722 *per* Cave J.

conclusion that the defendant brought the prosecution not to assert his belief in the guilt of the plaintiff, nor from the desire to enforce criminal law. It means that the defendant acted in order to achieve some end other than the entirely proper and appropriate one of bringing a criminal to justice. This does not mean that a defendant who has been personally affected by the alleged acts of the plaintiff, such as theft or fraud, is acting maliciously if he vindictively pursues the conviction of the plaintiff. A person will not be acting maliciously if he acts from the desire to have revenge for an offence committed against him. He will be acting maliciously if he prosecutes the plaintiff from some ulterior motive such as the desire to get rid of the plaintiff as a tenant, by proving him guilty of removing and selling some of the landlord's fixtures.[29] Similarly in *Glinski v. McIver*[30] it was suggested, but never decided because the case was determined on the issue of reasonable and probable cause, that the police prosecuted the plaintiff for one crime because he had given evidence on behalf of another criminal in another trial with the result that the criminal in question had been acquitted, to the annoyance and chagrin of the police. The motive of the police in charging the plaintiff, therefore, was alleged to be the desire to "even the score" as it were, by making the plaintiff suffer for something which he had not done as a punishment for something he had done, of which the police had not approved.

22.12 Lack of reasonable and probable cause may show malice.[31] But it is clear law that such want of reasonable and probable cause cannot be used as a basis for determining that the defendant acted maliciously. On the contrary, it has been held since 1786,[32] if not before, that the existence of malice cannot be inferred merely from lack of reasonable and probable cause for a prosecution. The presence of malice is a separate question. Hence it is possible for a court to decide that there was no reasonable and probable ground for a prosecution and yet find in favour of the defendant on the ground that he was not actuated by malice because he had an honest, but mistaken belief that the charge should be made.[32a]

(iv) Damage

22.13 Before an action for malicious prosecution can succeed, the plaintiff must prove that he has suffered damage. The historical reason for this was that the action was an action on the case *in consimili casu* to the action brought on the writ of conspiracy.[33] What kind of damage would suffice for this purpose was settled by Holt C.J. in *Savile v. Roberts*,[34] where it was

29 *Turner v. Ambler* (1847) 10 Q.B. 252.
30 [1962] 1 All E.R. 696.
31 *Brown v. Hawkes* [1891] 2 Q.B. 718 at 726 *per* Lord Esher M.R.; *Broad v. Ham* (1839) 5 Bing. N.C. 721.
32 *Johnstone v. Sutton, supra.*
32a A prosecutor, such as the Director of Public Prosecutions, is not ordinarily responsible for any malice that there might be on the part of prosecuting counsel: *Riches v. D.P.P.* [1973] 2 All E.R. 935 at 940 *per* Stephenson L.J.
33 *Berry v. British Transport Commission* [1960] 3 All E.R. 322 at 325 *per* Diplock J.
34 (1698) 1 Ld. Raym. 374: also reported in Carth. 416; 1 Salk. 13; 3 Salk. 16; 5 Mod. Rep. 344; 12 Mod. Rep. 208; Holt K.B. 150, 193.

said that three sorts of damages would be sufficient ground to support the action:[35]

> "1. The damage to a man's fame, as if the matter whereof he is accused be scandalous . . . . 2. The second . . . are such as are done to the person, as where a man is put in danger to lose his life, or limb or liberty . . . . 3. The third . . . is damage to a man's property, as where he is forced to expend his money in necessary charges, to acquit himself of the crime which he is accused . . . ."

The latter was appropriate in the case before Holt C.J., whereas the first two were not.

22.14 The first two categories were subjected to close scrutiny by Diplock J. in *Berry v. British Transport Commission.*[36] He pointed out that in Holt C.J.'s time "scandalous" was used as a synonym for "slanderous", in the sense of an imputation which, if spoken, was at that date slander actionable *per se*, and that actual loss of liberty by arrest on mesne process or final process in civil actions or by imprisonment pending trial or as a punishment in criminal cases had to be proved to substantiate Holt C.J.'s second head of damages that would support the action for malicious prosecution. Cases in the latter half of the seventeenth century and in the eighteenth century established that Holt C.J.'s first category referred to crimes the oral accusation of which constituted slander actionable *per se*, and was limited to such crimes. This meant that the crime was one which was punishable corporeally, not merely one which gave rise to an "infamous" or "villainous" punishment, as had been thought by some judges in the seventeenth century.[37] In the nineteenth century the comparison was drawn between slander which was actionable *per se* and malicious prosecution.[38] Both causes of action were dependent on an accusation of a crime punishable corporeally. But this pattern was disturbed first by the Court of Appeal in *Rayson v. South London Tramways Co.*[39] and then by the same court in *Wiffen v. Bailey & Romford Urban District Council.*[40] Any charge of a criminal offence, even if not punishable corporeally but only by a monetary penalty, was sufficient to found an action for malicious prosecution: which meant that there was a distinction between that action and slander actionable *per se.* Such was the effect of *Rayson's* case. In the subsequent decision the court determined that Holt C.J.'s first head of damages was satisfied if the crime charged conveyed an imputation of the plaintiff's "fair fame", while the second head was satisfied if the crime charged were punishable by imprisonment, even if the plaintiff had not been imprisoned. Diplock J. considered these cases had misinterpreted Holt C.J.'s judgment and were a departure from the old law. But he was bound by them and so had to apply them to the circumstances of the *Berry* case. This

35 (1698) 1 Ld. Raym. 374 at 378.
36 [1960] 3 All E.R. 322 at 325–329.
37 *Ogden v. Turner* (1704) 6 Mod. Rep. 104; *Low v. Berdmore* (1665) T. Raym. 135; *Henley v. Burstal* (1657) T. Raym. 180.
38 *Quartz Hill Gold Mining Co. v. Eyre* (1883) 11 Q.B.D. 674; cp. *Webb v. Beavan* (1883) 11 Q.B.D. 609. On slander actionable *per se* see paras 18.37ff.
39 [1893] 2 Q.B. 304.
40 [1915] 1 K.B. 600.

entailed a finding that the plaintiff who was charged with an offence punishable by fine only, not even potentially by imprisonment, could not sue for malicious prosecution unless the crime in question was one that injured his "fair fame".

22.15 In the *Berry* case the plaintiff had been charged with pulling the communication cord on a train without reasonable and sufficient cause. This was a statutory offence punishable by fine. The plaintiff was convicted by a magistrate's court but on appeal to quarter sessions her conviction was quashed. She sued for malicious prosecution. For the reasons already discussed she could not succeed under Holt C.J.'s second head of damages. Therefore Diplock J. had to consider whether the charge in question injured the plaintiff's "fair fame". That expression, which was not a term of art with a precise legal meaning, was borrowed by the court in the *Wiffen* case from the judgments in *Quartz Hill Gold Mining Co. v. Eyre.*[41] There it might have been used to indicate an analogy with slander actionable *per se*. That analogy was no longer tenable in view of the decision in *Rayson v. South London Tranways Co.*[42] Hence Diplock J. had to find his own meaning for the expression. He did so by saying that the test which must have been intended by the Court of Appeal in *Wiffen v. Bailey* was whether the charge was "defamatory" of the plaintiff.[43] But the issue was to be put in a negative way: viz., was the statement that the plaintiff was charged with the offence in question capable of a non-defamatory meaning? Therefore he had to see whether there might be facts which, if stated of the plaintiff, would not be defamatory of her, that is, lower her in the estimation of right-thinking members of society, although she could be convicted of the offence. On that test the plaintiff's fair fame had not been injured by a false accusation of pulling the communication cord without reasonable and sufficient cause.

22.16 However the third category of damage mentioned by Holt C.J. in *Savile v. Roberts* had to be considered. Although the plaintiff had been awarded costs by the recorder at quarter sessions, the amount in question was insufficient to cover her actual costs of defending herself at trial and on appeal. That difference measured her actual expense incurred as a result of the prosecution. Diplock J. thought that this did not come within Holt C.J.'s third category of damage that could sustain the action. The discretionary award of costs by the recorder acting under statutory powers fully compensated the plaintiff for expenses properly incurred by her in securing her ultimate acquittal.[44] On this point the Court of Appeal reversed the decision of Diplock J.[45] Unlike the latter, the Court of Appeal considered that there was a difference between an award of costs in a civil action and an award of costs in a criminal case. The effect of the

41 *Supra* note 38.
42 *Supra* note 39.
43 On what is defamatory see Chapter 18.
44 *Berry v. British Transport Commission* [1960] 3 All E.R. 322 at 329–331.
45 [1961] 3 All E.R. 65.

legislation on costs in criminal cases was that such an award was not intended by the legislature necessarily to compensate the successful appellant.[46] Hence the plaintiff in this case had suffered damage in the sense of incurring expense in necessary charges to acquit herself, and therefore her action could proceed.

22.17 As a result of the discussion in this case, there would now seem to be some degree of certainty as to the types of damage which will support the action for malicious prosecution. The plaintiff must now prove one of the three possibilities: (a) an accusation that endangers his liberty (by potentially leading to imprisonment) or his person, in the sense of causing physical harm or emotional disturbance;[47] (b) an accusation that is defamatory, in that it injures his fair fame; or (c) an accusation that puts him to expense to clear himself of the charge in question.[48]

2. OTHER IMPROPERLY INSTITUTED PROCEEDINGS

22.18 The tort of malicious prosecution is designed to provide a remedy in the event of the improper commencement of criminal proceedings. If a party has instituted other, non-criminal proceedings in circumstances in which they were unjustified, the normal method of penalising that party, and compensating the innocent party for expenses incurred in defending himself, is by an award of costs. However the common law also developed an action for abuse of process that can be called upon to provide an action for damages.[48a] The rationale of this was described by Lord Denning in *Goldsmith v. Sperrings Ltd*:[49]

> "In a civilised society, legal process is the machinery for keeping order and doing justice. It can be used properly or it can be abused. It is used properly when it is invoked for the vindication of men's rights or the enforcement of just claims. It is abused when it is diverted from its true course so as to serve extortion or oppression; or to exert pressure so as to achieve an improper end. When it is so abused, it is a tort . . . . The judges can and will intervene to stop it. They will stay the legal process if they can, before any harm is

46 *Ibid.* at 69 *per* Ormerod L.J.
47 *Wiffen v. Bailey, supra.*
48 But not an accusation that affects the plaintiff's credit rating: *Quartz Hill Gold Mining Co. v. Eyre* (1883) 11 Q.B.D. 647; *Wiffen v. Bailey, supra*: *Corbett v. Burger Warren & Ridgley Ltd* (1932) 48 T.L.R. 626; cp. *Stamatopoulos v. Hagemeyer (Canada) Ltd* (1983) 22 C.C.L.T. 310
48a But there is probably no general tort of maliciously instituting civil proceedings: *Metall- und Rohstoff AG v. Donaldson Lufkin & Jenrette* [1989] 3 All E.R. 14 at 51.
49 [1977] 2 All E.R. 557 at 574.

done.[50] If they cannot stop it in time, and harm is done, they will give damages against the wrongdoer."

22.19 The origins of this tort are to be found in *Granger v. Hill*.[51] Here the defendants sued out a writ of capias in order to compel the plaintiff to repay a debt before it was due. The result was that, under threat of being imprisoned, the plaintiff surrendered the register of a ship which had been mortgaged as security for the debt. In consequence the plaintiff lost voyages which he could not undertake because of the loss of the register. He sued for damages and for the return of the register. His action was successful. Liability was based on the fact that the defendants had employed the process of the law not for the legitimate purpose of recovering a debt that was due to them but to extort property from the plaintiff. This was a distinct action from what Tindal C.J.[52] referred to as malicious arrest, i.e. false arrest or imprisonment, and from malicious prosecution. Hence it was irrelevant for the plaintiff to have to allege want of reasonable and probable cause for their action.

22.20 This cause of action has been invoked in cases where the defendant has improperly commenced bankruptcy proceedings against the plaintiff,[53] or winding-up proceedings against a company.[54] It has been invoked when the purpose of the defendant was not to pursue a legitimate claim but to achieve some ulterior end, such as the limitation of competition within a certain industry.[55] In *Speed Seal Products Ltd v. Paddington*,[56] the defendants sought to amend their pleadings by adding a counterclaim alleging abuse of process of the court on the ground that the plaintiff's action for an injunction with respect to the use and disclosure of alleged confidential information was really brought for the ulterior motive of damaging the defendant's business, rather than for the protection of the legitimate interests of the plaintiffs. This was allowed by the trial judge and his decision was affirmed by the Court of Appeal.

22.21 The basis for allowing such an action is the general rule that court proceedings may not be used or threatened for the purpose of obtaining for the person so using or threatening them some collateral advantage to himself and not for the purpose for which such proceedings are properly

50 E.G. *Hunter v. Chief Constable of West Midlands* [1981] 3 All E.R. 727, which involved an attempt to raise again a matter that had previously been litigated; cp. *Stephen v. Garrett* [1898] 1 Q.B. 677; *Reichel v. Magrath* (1889) 14 App.Cas. 665. This must be distinguished from the case of estoppel *per rem judicatam*: *Mills v. Cooper* [1967] 2 Q.B. 459 at 468–469 *per* Diplock L.J.; and from "issue estoppel", which has no place in English criminal law: *D.P.P. v. Humphrys* [1977] A.C. 1.
51 (1838) 4 Bing. N.C. 212; see also *Parton v. Hill* (1864) 10 L.T. 414; *DeMedina v. Grove* (1847) 10 Q.B. 172.
52 (1838) 4 Bing. N.C. 212 at 221.
53 *Re Marjory* [1955] Ch. 600: *Metropolitan Bank v. Pooley* (1885) 10 App.Cas. 210; *Flame Bar-B-Q Ltd v. Hoar* (1980) 106 D.L.R. (3d) 438. Or an unfounded claim for a mechanic's lien: *Guildford Industries Ltd v. Hankinson Management Services Ltd* (1974) 40 D.L.R. (3d) 398.
54 *Re Bellador Silk Ltd* [1965] 1 All E.R. 667.
55 *Atland Containers Ltd v. Macs Corporation Ltd* (1975) 7 O.R. (2d) 107.
56 [1986] 1 All E.R. 91.

designed to exist.[57] If an action is brought to exert pressure so as to achieve an end which is improper in itself, then it is a wrong that is known to the law.[58] Malice, in the sense in which that expression is used in the context of malicious prosecution, is irrelevant. What is material is the genuineness or otherwise of the defendant's use of the legal process.

3. NON-LIABILITY FOR ABUSE OF PROCESS

22.22 Witnesses enjoy an absolute immunity with respect to anything said in court. This means that they cannot be sued for defamation[59] or perjury.[60] Nor can a witness be sued in respect of a statement made in preparation of a proof for trial[61] or a statement made in a report to the Director of Public Prosecutions.[62] If a statement or conduct is such that it can fairly be said to be part of the process of investigating a crime or a possible crime with a view to a prosecution or a possible prosecution in respect of the matter being investigated, then the maker of the statement or person whose conduct is in question is protected by absolute immunity from civil suit.[63] Hence in *Evans v. London Hospital Medical College*,[64] a pathologist and two toxicologists could not be sued in respect of a *post mortem* report on the plaintiff's infant son in which it was said that they had found morphine in the organs examined by them. The plaintiff was subsequently charged with the murder of the son by morphine poisoning. She was acquitted and wished to sue the pathologist and toxicologists. Her action was struck out on several grounds, including the defendants' right to rely on their absolute immunity from civil proceedings. However in *Roy v. Prior*[65] the House of Lords held that an action would lie in respect of the arrest of the plaintiff on a warrant issued by a trial judge. The defendant was a solicitor acting for an accused person. The plaintiff was issued a summons to attend as a witness at the trial. He failed to attend. The warrant was issued because the solicitor stated on oath that the plaintiff was evading service of the summons. The defendant argued that he was protected by the immunity that attached to statements made in court. The House of Lords held, however, that the plaintiff's action was for abuse of process, not for something said by the defendant in court. An action not brought in respect of evidence given in court but brought in respect of an alleged abuse of court will not necessarily be defeated, said Lord Morris,[66]

57 *Re Marjory*, *supra* at 623 *per* Evershed M.R.
58 *Goldsmith v. Sperrings Ltd*, *supra* at 574 *per* Lord Denning. But the conduct of a defendant in *defending* an action cannot be an abuse of process: *Metall- und Rohstoff AG v. Donaldson Lufkin & Jenrette* [1988] 3 All E.R. 116 at 125 *per* Gatehouse J.; nor was giving false evidence: *ibid.* on appeal, [1989] 3 All E.R. 14 at 48–52.
59 *Royal Aquarium & Summer & Winter Garden Society Ltd v. Parkinson* [1892] 1 Q.B. 431.
60 *Hargreaves v. Bretherton* [1959] 1 Q.B. 45.
61 *Watson v. M'Ewan* [1905] A.C. 480.
62 *Marrinan v. Vibart* [1962] 1 All E.R. 869 at 871 *per* Salmon J.
63 *Rees v. Sinclair* [1974] N.Z.L.R. 180 at 187, cited with approval in *Saif Ali v. Sydney Mitchell & Co.* [1980] A.C. 198.
64 [1981] 1 All E.R. 715.
65 [1970] 2 All E.R. 729.
66 *Ibid.*at 733.

if one step in the course of the abuse of the process of the court involved or necessitated the giving of evidence. The plaintiff's action therefore could not be struck out as being improper.

22.23 Judges also enjoy immunity with respect to their conduct in court. That immunity extends to arbitrators and to what the House of Lords referred to as "quasi-arbitrators".[67] It does not extend to valuers.[68] These propositions were laid down in the context of disputes between parties.[69] Judges owe no duties to the parties with respect to skilful performance of their judicial office. Their duty is to the state.[70] Hence there can be no civil liability where negligence is alleged against a judge or similar official. However it is possible for a judicial officer to act maliciously or to misinterpret his powers or authority and act unlawfully. The question then arises whether a litigant or accused who has likely incurred loss can bring an action for abuse of process.

22.24 As long as a judge is acting within his jurisdiction, i.e. in the discharge of the judicial function, he will be excempt from all civil liability for what he says or does in his judicial capacity.[70a] A judge who wrongly convicts an accused may not be sued for malicious prosecution or abuse of process, even if the conviction is subsequently quashed or reversed, and even if the judge acted maliciously. Such immunity from suit does not extend to situations where the judge was not acting judicially. Judicial immunity is granted because such immunity tends to ensure zealous and fearless administration of justice.[71] There are other ways of controlling improprieties by a judge, for example by dismissal after an address to such effect from both Houses of Parliament. The crucial question is whether the judge knowingly acted outside his jurisdiction. As long as a judge acts in the honest belief that what he does is within his jurisdiction, he is not liable to an action. He may be mistaken in fact. He may be ignorant of the law. What he does may be outside his jurisdiction—in fact or in law— but, as Lord Denning explained in *Sirros v. Moore*,[72] as long as he honestly believes it to be within his jurisdiction he should not and will not be liable. The courts will not entertain an action even if the judge is alleged to have acted maliciously or with ill-will or bias towards a party.

22.25 Prior to the decision in *Sirros v. Moore* it was thought that a distinction could be drawn between judges of superior courts and those of

67 *Arenson v. Casson, Beckman, Rutley & Co.* [1977] A.C. 405.
68 *Sutcliffe v. Thackrah* [1974] A.C. 727.
69 Cp. pp. 310–311.
70 *Arenson v. Casson, Beckman, Rutley & Co., supra* at 431 *per* Lord Kilbrandon.
70a *Mackay v. Attorney-General of Trinidad & Tobago (No. 2)* [1979] A.C. 385.
71 In *Bosada v. Pinos* (1984) 5 D.L.R. (4th) 334 at 337 an Ontario judge, Pennell J., referred to two American cases as authority: *Yates v. Lansing* (1810) 5 John. N.Y. 282: *Yaselli v. Goff* (1926) 12 F. (2d) 396.
72 [1974] 3 All E.R. 776 at 785: cp. *Sammy-Joe v. G.P.O. Mount Pleasant Office* [1967] 1 W.L.R. 270: magistrates protected by statute, Justices' Protection Act 1848 s. 1 (subsequently replaced by the Justices of the Peace Act 1979), where they issued a maintenance order at the request of a woman who falsely claimed to be the wife of the plaintiff.

inferior courts. The former could claim complete immunity whether acting within or outside their jurisdiction. The latter would only be protected if they were acting with jurisdiction at the material time, or had the honest belief that they were acting within their jurisdiction. It was also suggested that a judge of a court which was not a court of record could be liable if he acted maliciously and without reasonable and probable cause.[73] This form of liability has now been said to be obsolete, at least in England and Wales.[74] Hence in *McC v. Mullan*[75] magistrates were not liable for the consequences of an unlawful sentence they imposed, subsequently quashed for irregularity, as long as the magistrates had jurisdiction to enter on the proceedings and acted within their jurisdiction when imposing the sentence. But magistrates could be liable for imposing a sentence which they had no power to impose on the offender for the offence in question, on the ground that magistrates so acting were acting without or in excess of their jurisdiction. The sentence in this case was one of detention at a young offenders centre. It was imposed without the magistrates first having informed the offender of his right to apply for legal aid. The offender had been convicted of failing to comply with an order to attend an attendance centre, imposed on him as a result of a previous offence. The detention order was quashed by the Divisional Court in Northern Ireland on the ground of the irregularity and the offender was released from detention. He sued the magistrates for false imprisonment. The issue then arose whether the magistrates were capable of being sued. By statute no action would lie against magistrates unless they acted "without jurisdiction or in excess of jurisdiction". This was tried as a preliminary issue. In the House of Lords the magistrates' appeal from a decision that they had acted outside their jurisdiction was dismissed.

22.26 That decision seems to take care of the situation with respect to judges of courts that are not courts of record. Everything depends on whether such judges acted within or outside or in excess of their jurisdiction. In *Sirros v. Moore*,[76] however, it was suggested that as regards courts of record it did not make any difference whether such courts were superior or inferior courts. In either case a judge should be protected even if he acted outside his jurisdiction. The rationale of this was, in the words of Lord Denning,[77] the need to ensure that judges may be free in thought and independent in judgment. Each judge should be able to do his work in complete independence and free from fear. That view was rejected by Lord Bridge, *obiter*, in *McC v. Mullan*,[78] on the ground that the distinction between courts of superior and inferior jurisdiction was deeply rooted in the law and could only be changed by legislation. Indeed legislation, of

73 Thompson, "Judicial immunity and the protection of justices" (1958) 21 M.L.R. 517 at 528.
74 *McC. v. Mullan* [1984] 3 All E.R. 908 at 916 *per* Lord Bridge, 929 *per* Lord Templeman: *dubitante* Lord Keith of Kinkel at 910.
75 *Supra.*
76 *Supra.*
77 *Supra* note 72 at 785.
78 *Supra* note 74 at 923.

the kind that was involved in that case, made it clear that such a distinction did exist. In consequence the situation in English law at the present time is not clear. Outside England, in Canada, the judgment of Lord Denning in *Sirros v. Moore* has been approved.[79] Statute has made significant changes to the common law position in Canada.[80] Hence the limited Canadian judicial approval of the attitude expressed in *Sirros v. Moore*, may not be conclusive in light of the later English criticism made in the House of Lords.[81]

79 *Re Glendenning & Board of Police Commissioners for City of Belleville* (1976) 75 D.L.R. (3d) 33 at 37.

80 Feldthusen, "Judicial immunity: In search of an applicable limiting formula" (1980) 29 U. of New Brunswick L.J. 73 at 88–89.

81 The Attorney-General and the Director of Public Prosecutions or prosecuting counsel, it would seem may be sued for malicious prosecution, if the circumstances justify such a cause of action. That a prosecution is initiated and pursued by the D.P.P., or the Attorney-General has given his fiat, does not conclusively negate the existence of malice or prove that there was reasonable and probable cause for the prosecution: *Riches v. D.P.P.* [1973] 2 All E.R. 935 at 941 *per* Stephenson L.J. However in Canada a catena of authority suggested that such officials might be immune from suit on the ground that they enjoy the same immunity as judges, at least unless it could be shown that the official in question was acting from personal motives and not in the normal course of his official functions: *Unterreiner v. Wilson* (1982) 142 D.L.R. (3d) 588; *Richman v. McMurtry* (1983) 147 D.L.R. (3d) 748; *Bosada v. Pinos* (1984) 5 D.L.R. (4th) 334; *Levesque v. Picard* (1986) 34 C.C.L.T. 276; *Nelles v. The Queen in Right of Ontario* (1986) 21 D.L.R. (4th) 103. This has now been altered in consequence of the majority decision of the Supreme Court of Canada when the *Nelles* case came before them: (1989) 60 D.L.R. (4th) 609. The Attorney-General and his agents are not immune from suit. Note also that the Supreme Court of Canada has also held that judges cannot be called before a Royal Commission of Inquiry to give evidence on the reasons why they arrived at a particular decision in a case involving the reversal of a conviction for murder that had occurred several years previously: *Mackeigan v. Hickman* (1989) 61 D.L.R. (4th) 688.

Index

Abatement
  private nuisance, remedy for, 8.57-8.61
Abuse of process
  malicious prosecution,
    liability, elements of,
      damage, 22.13-22.17
      favourable end to
        prosecution, 22.04-22.05
      malice, 22.11-22.12
      reasonable and probable cause, lack
        of, 22.06-22.10
    nature of action, 22.01-22.03
  non-liability for, 22.22-22.26
  other improperly instituted
    proceedings, 22.18-22.21
Accident
  defences,
    land, trespass to, 5.28
    person, trespass to, 6.23-6.25
  inevitable,
    negligence, defence to, 13.02-13.04
    trespass to land, defence to, 5.28
  successive, proof of causation of
    damage, 12.98-12.101
  trespass distinguished from, 6.07
Accountant
  care, duty of, 12.37
Act of state
  Crown, liability of, 2.08-2.12
  meaning, 2.09
Agent
  corporation, of, liability, of, 2.19
  Crown, of,
    immunity of, 2.08
    liability for act of, 2.04-2.05
    wrong committed by, 2.03
  gratuitous, 3.05
  servant distinguished from, 3.01, 3.04
Alien
  act of state, liability of Crown, 2.08,
    2.10
Amenities
  loss of, 15.41-15.43
Anger
  trespass, prerequisite of liability
    for, 6.03
Animals
  cats, liability of owners for, 11.06
  cattle, meaning, 11.02
  common law before 1971, 11.01-11.06
  dangerous,
    liability,
      exceptions from, 11.22-11.24
      generally, 11.13-11.19
      incidence of, 11.20-11.21
    meaning, 11.10-11.12
  dogs,
    liability for, 11.06
    livestock, which attack, 11.25-11.27
  highway, on, 11.34-11.35
  keeper, meaning, 11.20
  legislation of 1971,
    dangerous animals,
      liability,
        exceptions from, 11.22-11.24
        generally, 11.13-11.19
        incidence of, 11.20-11.21
      meaning, 11.10-11.12
    general effect, 11.07-11.09
    highway, animals on, 11.34-11.35
    livestock,
      dogs which attack, 11.25-11.27
      trespassing,
        detention, 11.32-11.33
        liability, 11.28-11.31
  negligence, duty of care relating
    to, 12.55
Apology
  defamation, remedy for, 18.115-18.117
Apportionment
  contributory negligence, 13.39-13.43
Armed forces
  Crown, liability of, 2.07
  visiting, claim against member of, 2.15
Arrest
  trespass to person, defence to, 6.43-6.51
Assault
  nature of, 6.14-6.17
Authority
  actual, 3.11-3.13
  meaning, 3.08
  ostensible, 3.14-3.16

Authority—*cont*
prohibition, effect of, 3.09
statutory,
private nuisance, defence to, 8.51-8.56
Rylands v. Fletcher, rule in, 9.41-9.42

Bankrupt
liability, scope of, 2.34-2.35
Barrister
care, duty of, 12.67, 12.68
Battery
nature of, 6.10-6.13
Bereavement
recoverable damages, 15.57
Breach
confidence, of. *See* Confidence
contract, of. *See* Contract
statutory duty, of. *See* Statutory duty, breach of
Breathalyser
breath sample, taking of, as trespass to person, 6.33
Bridge
non-repair of, 3.37
Building
defective, duty of care relating to, 12.56-12.57
Business
wrongful interference with. *See* Wrongful interference

Captain of ship
trespass to person, defence to, 6.32
vicarious liability, application of, 3.04
Care, duty of. *See* Negligence
Cats
liability for, 11.06
Cattle
meaning, 11.02
See also Animals
Causation
damage, of. *See* Negligence
employer's liability, 14.54
liability, fundamental principle of, 1.20
Chattels
dangerous *per se*, old doctrine of, 14.12-14.14
liability for,
immediate transferee,
under contract, 14.01-14.02
where no contract, 14.03
ultimate transferees and others,
demise of chattels dangerous *per se*, 14.12-14.14
Donoghue v. Stevenson,
before, 14.04-14.05
decision in, 14.06
extension of decision, 14.07-14.11
recaption of, defence to trespass to land, 5.33-5.36
Child. *See* Minor
Class
defamation of, 18.26-18.28
Club
legal personality of, 2.21
liability, scope of, 2.20-2.21
Common law
animals, liability for, 11.01-11.06
contributory negligence,
damage, negligence causing or contributing to, 13.27-13.28
negligence not considered contributory,
last clear chance, doctrine of, 13.32-13.36
last opportunity, doctrine of, 13.32-13.36
plaintiff,
agony of moment, acting in, 13.31
child as, 13.30
defendant obliged to protect, 13.29
not dependant on duty, 13.26
statute, effect of,
apportionment, 13.39-13.43
generally, 13.37
last opportunity, 13.38
Crown, liability of, 2.02-2.03
employer's liability, 14.47
independent contractor, liability for act of, 3.37
joint and several tortfeasors distinguished, 4.04
occupier, liability of, 14.15-14.16
Compensation
collateral benefits, liability reduced by, 1.16
function of tort, 1.15
negligence, damages for, 15.08-15.09
Confidence
breach of,
defences, 20.10-20.12
new tort, as, 20.01-20.03
protection, scope of, 20.07-20.09
remedies, 20.13-20.16
meaning, 20.04-20.06
Conflicting interests
liability, fundamental principle of, 1.20
Congenital disability
minor, action by, 2.25
Consent
defamation, to, 18.56-18.57
negligence, defence to. *See* Negligence
plaintiff, of, rule in *Rylands v. Fletcher*, 9.38-9.48
trespass to person, defence to, 6.36-6.42
See also Volenti non fit injuria

Conspiracy
intention, effect on liability, 1.23
liability, elements of,
agreement and combination, 21.06-21.08
unlawful means, 21.09-21.10
unlawful purpose, 21.11-21.15
meaning, 21.03
scope, 21.03-21.05
Construction of statutes
courts, role of, 16.03-16.05
rules of, 16.06-16.10
Contract
breach of,
importance of, 21.52-21.53
inducing,
justification, 21.47-21.51
liability, elements of, 21.31-21.46
origins, 21.30
tort and, 1.10-1.12
care, duty of, and, 12.69-12.71
chattels, liability for, 14.01-14.02
indemnity, of, 4.12-4.14
privity of, 1.11, 1.28
Contract for services and of service distinguished, 3.05
Contractor. *See* Independent contractor
Contribution
tortfeasors, between, 4.07-4.11
Contributory negligence. *See* Negligence
Conversion
acts of,
goods,
abusing possession of, 7.22-7.25
destruction of, 7.26-7.27
taking possession of, 7.19-7.21
damages, 7.49-7.51
defences, 7.37-7.40
meaning, 7.16-7.18
mental element, 7.28-7.30
petition of right in case of, 2.03
title of plaintiff, 7.31-7.36
Corporation
liability, scope of, 2.16-2.19
Court
statutes, construction of, 16.03-16.05
Crime
tort and, 1.08-1.09
Criminal Injuries Compensation Scheme
victim of crime, claim by, 1.08
Crown
liability, scope of,
act of state, 2.08-2.12
common law, at, 2.02-2.03
statutory change, 2.04-2.07

Damage
causation. *See* Negligence
deceit, liability for, 17.16-17.19
injurious falsehood, liability for, 21.63-21.64
malicious prosecution, action for, 22.13-22.17
occupier's liability, 14.24-14.27
private nuisance, liability for, 8.28-8.29
property, to, 15.15-15.17
public nuisance, 8.73
Rylands v. Fletcher, rule in, 9.31-9.34
Damages
aggravated, 15.03, 15.06
compensatory, 15.03, 15.07
contemptuous, 15.03, 15.04
defamation, for,
assessment, 18.103-18.110
mitigation, 18.111-18.114
exemplary, 15.03, 15.05
goods, wrongful interference with,
conversion, 7.49-7.51
generally, 7.47
trespass, 7.48
liability, function of, 1.17
negligence, for. *See* Negligence
nominal, 15.03, 15.04
private nuisance, remedy for, 8.62-8.65
punitive, 15.03, 15.05
Dangerous things
Rylands v. Fletcher, rule in, 9.19-9.22
Death
dependants' claims,
beneficiaries of action, 15.56
Fatal Accidents Act, 15.52
recoverable damages,
bereavement, 15.57
support, loss of, 15.58-15.60
right to sue, 15.53-15.55
survival of actions, 15.51
See also Non-fatal personal injury
Deceit
fraud, 17.01-17.03
liability, elements of,
damage, 17.16-17.19
defendant's intent, 17.11-17.14
false statement of fact, 17.04-17.08
falsity, knowledge of, 17.09-17.10
plaintiff, reliance by, 17.15
Defamation
corporation, liability of, 2.17
defences,
consent, 18.56-18.57
fair comment,
essential elements,
fairness, 18.67-18.70
opinion not fact, 18.65-18.66
public interest, 18.64
nature of plea, 18.61-18.63
justification, 18.58-18.60
privilege, absolute, cases of,
judicial proceedings, 18.76-18.82, 18.86-18.88

Defamation—*cont*
defences—*cont*
privilege—*cont*
official communications, 18.84-18.85
Parliament, statement made to, 18.74
Parliamentary papers, 18.75
solicitor and client, communications between, 18.83
nature of, 18.71-18.73
qualified, cases of,
loss, 18.99-18.102
privileged reports, 18.89-18.94
statement, 18.95-18.98
unintentional defamation, 18.54-18.55
liability, requirements of,
capacity to be defamed, 18.03
class, 18.26-18.28
defamatory allegation,
defamatory, meaning, 18.07-18.12
innuendo, 18.13-18.18
judge, functions of, 18.19-18.20
jury, functions of, 18.19-18.20
falsity, 18.04-18.06
plaintiff, reference to, 18.21-18.25
publication, 18.29-18.36
libel and slander,
effect of distinction,
criminal law, 18.41
tort,
damage, proof of, 18.42-18.44
exceptions, 18.45-18.53
nature of distinction, 18.37-18.40
meaning, 18.01-18.02
rationale, 18.01-18.02
remedies,
apology, 18.115-18.117
damages,
assessment, 18.103-18.110
mitigation, 18.111-18.114
injunction, 18.118-18.119
slander. *See* libel and slander *above*
trade union, of, 2.22
unintentional, 18.54-18.55
Defective buildings
negligence, duty of care relating to, 12.56-12.57
Defences to actions in tort
confidence, breach of, 20.10-20.12
conversion, action for, 7.37-7.40
defamation. *See* Defamation
employer's liability,
causation, lack of, 14.54
contributory negligence, 14.56
volenti, 14.55
land, trespass to,
chattels, recaption of, 5.33-5.36
inevitable accident, 5.28
lawful entry, 5.44-5.47
leave and licence, 5.39-5.43
liberum tenementum, 5.37-5.38
mistake, 5.29
necessity, 5.30-5.32
occupier's liability, 14.39-14.41
person, trespass to,
accident, 6.23-6.25
authority, 6.29-6.33
consent, 6.36-6.42
lawful arrest, 6.43-6.51
necessity, 6.34-6.35
parental authority, 6.29
self-defence, 6.26-6.28
private nuisance,
coming to nuisance, 8.44-8.45
jus tertii, 8.46
prescription, 8.47-8.50
statutory authority, 8.51-8.56
statutory duty, breach of,
contributory negligence, 16.20
delegation, 16.21
volenti, 16.19
Defendants
deceit of, liability for, 17.11-17.14
several, proof of causation of damage, 12.97
Definitions. *See* Words and phrases
Delegation
statutory duty, breach of, 16.21
Dependent
claim by. *See* Death
Detention
trespassing livestock, of, 11.32-11.33
Detour
frolic distinguished from, 3.33
Diplomatic representative
immunity of, 2.14
Directness
foreseeability versus, 12.120-12.122
Director
vicarious liability of, 3.06
Disability. *See* Person under disability
Disrepair
highway, nuisance to, 8.77-8.78
Doctor
vicarious liability, application of, 3.04
Dogs
liability for, 11.06
livestock, which attack, 11.25-11.27
Duty of care. *See* Negligence

Earnings
future, 15.26-15.29
lost, 15.24-15.25
Economic efficiency
liability, function of, 1.18

Economic loss
  foreseeability of, 12.40-12.52
  legal and non-legal wrong, 1.05
  recovery of, 12.45-12.52
Ejectment
  possession, claim not based on, 5.18
Employer
  liability of,
    common law duty, 14.47
    content of duty,
      competent staff, 14.50
      equipment, 14.51
      generally, 14.49
      plant, 14.51
      premises, 14.52
      safe system of work, 14.53
    defences,
      causation, lack of, 14.54
      contributory negligence, 14.56
      volenti, 14.55
    generally, 14.46
    nature of duty, 14.48
    personal, 3.40-3.41
  personal liability of, 3.40-3.41
  reasonable care, duty of, 3.36
  vicarious liability of. *See* Vicarious liability
Employment
  course of,
    act within course of, 3.19-3.24
    acts outside, 3.30-3.33
    master, acts not in interest of, 3.27-3.29
    meaning, 3.17-3.18
    prohibited acts, 3.25-3.26
  wrongful interference with. *See* Wrongful interference
Engineer
  vicarious liability, application of, 3.04
Enjoyment of property
  private nuisance, liability for,
    generally, 8.11-8.12
    locality, 8.13-8.14
    standards, 8.15-8.17
    utility, 8.18
Entry
  trespass to land, defence to, 5.44-5.47
Equipment
  defective, supply of, 3.36
  employer's liability, 14.51
Escape of dangerous things
  Rylands v. Fletcher, rule in, 9.16-9.18
Expenses
  pecuniary loss, 15.30-15.34
Extra-hazarous act
  vicarious liability, 3.35

Fact
  malice in, 1.22
Fair comment
  essential elements,
    fairness, 18.67-18.70
    opinion not fact, 18.65-18.66
    public interest, 18.64
  nature of plea, 18.61-18.63
Fairness
  liability, fundamental principle of, 1.20
  nature of, 6.18-6.22
False imprisonment, 6.18-6.22
Falsehood. *See* Injurious falsehood
Fatal accident
  minor, action by, 2.24
  personal representative, liability of, 2.36-2.39
Fault
  liability, fundamental principle of, 1.32-1.34
Fire
  liability,
    early strict, 10.02-10.04
    modern situation, 10.12-10.15
    source of, 10.01
  negligence, introduction of, 10.05-10.06
  Rylands v. Fletcher, impact of, 10.07-10.11
Force
  intentional and accidental application distinguished, 6.04
  person, trespass to, use in case of, 6.03-6.05
Foreign sovereign
  liability, scope of, 2.13-2.15
Foreign state
  diplomatic representative of, immunity of, 2.14
Foreseeability
  care, duty of,
    economic loss, 12.40-12.52
    foreseeable harm, 12.21-12.23
    foreseeable plaintiff, 12.21-12.23
    generally, 12.11-12.14
    negligent misstatement, 12.35-12.39
    nervous shock, 12.24-12.28
    rescuers, 12.29-12.34
    risk, 12.15-12.20
  damage, remoteness of, 12.115-12.119
  directness versus, 12.120-12.122
Fraud
  minor, action against, 2.28, 2.29
  nature of, 17.01-17.03
  prohibition, 3.09
Frolic of one's own
  detour, distinguished from, 3.33

Goods
  destruction of, 7.26-7.27
  improvement of, 7.52-7.53

Goods—*cont*
possession of,
abusing, 7.22-7.25
taking, 7.19-7.21
title,
extinction of, 7.54-7.55
plaintiff, of, 7.31-7.36
wrongful interference with,
legislation of 1977, 7.01-7.02
remedies
conversion 7.49-7.51
generally, 7.47
trespass, 7.48
extinction of title, 7.54-7.55
goods detained, where, 7.46
improvement of goods, 7.52-7.53
varieties of,
conversion,
abusing possession of goods, 7.22-7.25
acts of, 7.19-7.27
damages, 7.49-7.51
defences, 7.37-7.40
destruction of goods, 7.26-7.27
meaning, 7.16-7.18
mental element, 7.28-7.30
taking possession of goods, 7.19-7.21
title of plaintiff, 7.31-7.36
other wrongs, 7.44-7.45
pound-breach, 7.43
replevin, 7.42
rescous, 7.43
trespass to goods,
generally, 7.03
interference, 7.04-7.05
possession, 7.06-7.11
wrongfulness, 7.12-7.15
Government official
care, duty of, 12.37

Harm
foreseeable, 12.21-12.23
Highway
animals on, 11.34-11.35
non-repair of, 3.37
nuisance to,
disrepair, 8.77-8.78
obstruction,
adjoining owners, causing loss to, 8.76
users, to, 8.79-8.80
projections over highway, 8.81-8.82
projections over, 8.81-8.82
work done in or on, 3.35
Hostility
trespass to person, characteristic of, 6.04
Household
meaning, 11.19
Husband
trespass to person, defence to, 6.31

Illegality
plaintiff, of, 13.44-13.47
Imprisonment
false, as trespass to person, 6.18-6.22
Indemnity
contracts of, 4.12-4.14
Independent contractor
meaning, 3.03
occupier's liability, 14.36
vicarious liability of,
bridge, non-repair of, 3.37
causal negligence, 3.38-3.39
collateral negligence, 3.38-3.39
common law, 3.37
defective equipment, supply of, 3.36
extra-hazardous acts, 3.35
fire, damage by, 3.37
general principle, 3.34
highway,
non-repair of, 3.37
work done in or on, 3.35
misfeasance, non-misfeasance distinguished from, 3.37
negligence, 3.37
nuisance, 3.37
occupier, liability of, 3.36
reasonable care, duty of, 3.36
Inevitable accident. *See* Accident
Injunction
defamation, remedy for, 18.118-18.119
private nuisance, remedy for, 8.66-8.68
Injurious falsehood
liability,
elements of,
damage, 21.63-21.64
false statement, 21.60
malice, 21.61-21.62
instances of, 21.58-21.59
nature of, 21.54-21.57
Injury
immediate, distinguished from consequential injury, 6.02
intention to injure, 6.04
non-fatal personal. *See* Non-fatal personal injury
servitudes, to, 8.69-8.71
Innominate tort
distinguished from nominate, 1.06
Insane person
trespass to person, characteristics of, 6.06
Intention
constructive intent, doctrine of, 1.26
liability, fundamental principle of, 1.21-1.26
malice distinguished from, 1.25

Interference
land, trespass to,
act of trespass, 5.04-5.07
continuing trespass, 5.08
mental element, 5.10-5.12
trespass *ab initio*, 5.09
wrongful. *See* Wrongful interference
Intimidation
emergence of tort, 21.16-21.19
justification, 21.28-21.29
unlawful means, 21.20-21.24
varieties of, 21.25-21.27

Joint tortfeasors
contracts of indemnity, 4.12-4.14
contribution between tortfeasors, 4.07-4.11
meaning, 4.01
release of tortfeasor, 4.06
several tortfeasors distinguished from,
importance of distinction,
common law, 4.04
judgment against one of them, effect of, 4.05
release of tortfeasor, 4.06
nature of distinction, 4.01-4.03
Judge
care, duty of, 12.66
defamation action, functions relating to, 18.19-18.20
Judgment
joint tortfeasors, against, effect of, 4.05
several tortfeasors, against, effect of, 4.05
Jury
defamation action, functions relating to, 18.19-18.20
Jus tertii
private nuisance, defence to, 8.46
Justice
liability, fundamental principle of, 1.20
Justification
defamation, defence to, 18.58-18.60
inducing breach of contract, 21.47-21.51
intimidation, for, 21.28-21.29

King's peace
trespass entails breach of, 6.01

Land
above ground, 5.22-5.27
below surface, 5.20-5.21
nuisance. *See* Nuisance
trespass to,
defences,
chattels, recaption of, 5.33-5.36
inevitable accident, 5.28
lawful entry, 5.44-5.47
leave and licence, 5.39-5.43
liberum tenementum, 5.37-5.38
mistake, 5.29
necessity, 5.30-5.32
liability, elements of,
general characters, 5.01-5.03
interference,
act of trespass, 5.04-5.07
continuing trespass, 5.08
mental element, 5.10-5.12
trespass *ab initio*, 5.09
land,
above ground, 5.22-5.27
below surface, 5.20-5.21
possession,
basis of action, 5.13-5.15
claim not based on, 5.16-5.19
remedies,
judicial, 5.49-5.51
self-help, 5.48
Landlord
possession, out of, 8.40-8.43
Last clear chance
doctrine of, 13.32-13.36
Last opportunity
doctrine of, 13.32-13.36
statute, effect of, 13.38
Law Reform Committee
interference with goods, report on, 7.02
Lawful arrest. *See* Arrest
Lawful entry. *See* Entry
Leave and licence
trespass to land, defence to, 5.39-5.43
Liability
abuse of process. *See* Abuse of process
animals, for,
common law before 1971, 11.01-11.06
legislation of 1971,
dangerous animals,
liability, 11.13-11.24
meaning, 11.10-11.12
dogs which attack livestock, 11.25-11.27
general effect, 11.07-11.09
highway, animals on, 11.34-11.35
livestock,
dogs which attack, 11.25-11.27
trespassing, 11.28-11.33
chattels, for. *See* Chattels
conspiracy. *See* Conspiracy
deceit, for,
damage, 17.16-17.19
defendant's intent, 17.11-17.14
false statement of fact, 17.04-17.08
falsity, knowledge of, 17.09-17.10
plaintiff, reliance by, 17.15
defamation. *See* Defamation
employer, of. *See* Employer
fire,
early strict, 10.02-10.04

Liability—*cont*
source of, 10.01
function of, 1.15-1.19
fundamental principles,
fault, 1.32-1.34
generally, 1.20
intention, 1.21-1.26
negligence, 1.27-1.30
strict liability, 1.31
future of, 1.35-1.37
inducing breach of
contract, 21.31-21.46
injurious falsehood. *See* Injurious
falsehood
malicious prosecution. *See* Malicious
prosecution
nature of,
generally, 1.01
wrong,
idea of, 1.02
legal,
non-legal distinguished
from, 1.03-1.06
other forms, 1.07-1.14
non-legal distinguished from
legal, 1.03-1.06
negligence. *See* Negligence
occupier, of. *See* Occupier
personal, of employers, 3.40-3.41
private nuisance, for,
elements,
continuing state of
affairs, 8.08-8.10
damage, 8.28-8.29
enjoyment of property,
generally, 8.11-8.12
locality, 8.13-8.14
standards, 8.15-8.17
utility, 8.18
malice, 8.19-8.21
negligence, 8.22-8.27
personal comfort,
generally, 8.11-8.12
locality, 8.13-8.14
standards, 8.15-8.17
utility, 8.18
incidence,
creator of nuisance, 8.34
landlord out of
possession, 8.40-8.43
occupier, 8.35-8.39
scope of,
corporation, 2.16-2.19
Crown,
act of state, 2.08-2.12
common law, at, 2.02-2.03
statutory change, 2.04-2.07
foreign sovereign, 2.13-2.15
generally, 2.01
person under disability,
bankrupt, 2.34-2.35
mental incompetent, 2.34-2.35
minor,
action against, 2.28-2.30
action by, 2.24-2.27
personal representative, 2.36-2.39
unincorporated body, 2.20-2.23
statutory duty, breach of,
breach of duty, 16.12-16.14
damage, causation of, 16.15-16.16
injury within scope of
statute, 16.17-16.18
plaintiff, duty owed to, 16.11
strict, 1.31
trespass to land. *See* Land
trespassing livestock, 11.28-11.31
vicarious. *See* Vicarious liability
Libel. *See* Defamation
Liberum tenementum
trespass to land, defence to, 5.37-5.38
Limitation of action
negligence, damages for, 15.19-15.21,
15.47-15.50
Livestock
dogs which attack, 11.25-11.27
meaning, 11.26
trespassing,
detention, 11.32-11.33
liability, 11.28-11.31
Local government
corporation, liability of, 2.17
Locality
private nuisance, liability for, 8.13-8.14
Logic
legal principles, role in formation
of, 1.18
Loss
amenities, of, 15.41-15.43
economic. *See* Economic loss
migration of, 15.10-15.11
non-fatal personal injury. *See* Non-fatal
personal injury
property, of, 15.12-15.14
qualified privilege, of, 18.99-18.102
support, of, 15.58-15.60

Malice
fact, in, 1.22
injurious falsehood, liability
for, 21.61-21.62
intention distinguished from, 1.25
law, in, 1.22
private nuisance, liability for, 8.19-8.21
Malicious prosecution. *See* Abuse of process
Master and servant
negligence, liability for, 1.28
Medieval law
vicarious liability, origin of doctrine
of, 3.01

Mental incompetent
liability, scope of, 2.31-2.33
Mentally incompetent person
trespass to person, characteristics of, 6.06
Minor
action against, 2.28-2.30
action by, 2.24-2.27
occupier's liability, 14.31-14.32
plaintiff, as, 13.30
trespass to person, characteristics of, 6.06
unborn child,
damage to, 1.04
duty to, 2.26-2.27
Misfeasance
non-feasance distinguished from, 3.37
Mis-statement, negligent
duty of care, 12.35-12.39
Mistake
trespass to land, defence to, 5.29
trespass to person, defence to, 6.24-6.25

Nature of liability. *See* Liability
Necessity
land, defence to trespass to, 5.30-5.32
person, defence to trespass to, 6.34-6.35
Rylands v. Fletcher, rule in, 9.50
Negligence
care, duty of,
breach of,
customary practice, 12.79-12.81
general practice, 12.79-12.81
objectivity, 12.76-12.78
proof of, 12.82-12.84
res ipsa loquitur,
application, 12.86
control, 12.87-12.88
generally, 12.85
maxim, effect of, 12.91-12.92
ordinary occurrence, 12.89-12.90
standard of care, 12.72-12.75
contract, and, 12.69-12.71
exclusion of duty, 12.64-12.68
extensions of duty,
developments,
animals, 12.55
defective buildings, 12.56-12.57
omissions, 12.58-12.60
statutory powers, 12.62-12.63
third party, act of, 12.61
limitations, 12.53-12.54
foreseeability,
economic loss, 12.40-12.52
forseeable plaintiff and forseeable harm, 12.21-12.23
generally, 12.11-12.14
negligent mis-statement, 12.35-12.39
nervous shock, 12.24-12.28
rescuers, 12.29-12.34
risk, 12.15-12.20
relevant factors, 12.05-12.10
casual, 3.38
chattels, liability for. *See* Chattels
collateral, 3.38
contributory,
common law doctrine,
damage, negligence causing or contributing to, 13.27-13.28
negligence not considered contributory,
agony of moment, plaintiff acting in, 13.31
child, where plaintiff was, 13.30
defendant obliged to protect plaintiff, 13.29
last clear chance, doctrine of, 13.32-13.36
last opportunity, doctrine of, 13.32-13.36
not dependant of duty, 13.26
employer's liability, defence to, 14.56
historical survey, 13.23-13.25
statute, effect of,
apportionment, 13.39-13.43
generally, 13.37
last opportunity, 13.38
statutory duty, breach of, 16.20
damage,
causation,
generally, 12.93-12.95
proof of,
generally, 12.96
McGhee case and aftermath, 12.102-12.109
several defendants, 12.97
successive accidents, 12.98-12.101
remoteness, and, 12.93-12.95
statutory duty, breach of, 16.15-16.16
contributory negligence, 13.27-13.28
directness versus foreseeability, 12.120-12.122
foreseeability,
directness versus, 12.120-12.122
rise of, 12.115-12.119
remoteness,
causation, and, 12.93-12.95
direct consequences, 12.110-12.114
foreseeability, rise of, 12.115-12.119
generally, 12.93-12.95, 12.109
damages for,
aggravated, 15.03, 15.06
compensation, 15.08-15.09
compensatory, 15.03, 15.07
contemptuous, 15.03, 15.04

Negligence—*cont*
death, dependants' claims,
beneficiaries of action, 15.56
Fatal Accidents Act, 15.52
recoverable damages, 15.57-15.60
right to sue, 15.53-15.55
survival of actions, 15.51
exemplary, 15.03, 15.05
kinds of, 15.03-15.07
mitigation of loss, 15.10-15.11
nominal, 15.03-15.04
non-fatal personal injuries,
limitation of action, 15.47-15.50
non-pecuniary loss,
amenities, loss of, 15.41-15.43
assessment of award, 15.45-15.46
generally, 15.22-15.23
injury, 15.44
pain and suffering, 15.39-15.40
pecuniary loss,
deductions, 15.35-15.37
expenses, 15.30-15.34
future earnings, 15.26-15.29
generally, 15.22-15.23
interest, 15.38
lost earnings, 15.24-15.25
only remedy, 15.01-15.02
property,
damage, 15.15-15.17
date of assessment, 15.18
limitation of action, 15.19-15.21
loss, 15.12-15.14
punitive, 15.03, 15.05
defences to,
consent,
decline of, 13.22
express, 13.10
implied,
consent, 13.18-13.21
generally, 13.11-13.12
knowledge, 13.13-13.17
volenti non fit injuria, 13.05-13.09
contributory negligence,
common law doctrine,
last clear chance, doctrine of, 13.32-13.36
last opportunity, doctrine of, 13.32-13.36
negligence causing or contributing to damage, 13.27-13.28
negligence not considered contributory, 13.29-13.31
not dependant on duty, 13.26
historical survey, 13.23-13.25
statute, effect of,
apportionment, 13.39-13.43
generally, 13.37
last opportunity, 13.38
generally, 13.01
illegality of plaintiff, 13.44-13.47
inevitable accident, 13.02-13.04
employer's liability. *See* Employer
fire, liability for, 10.05-10.06
independent contractor, of, liability for, 3.37
liability,
fire, 10.05-10.06
fundamental principle of, 1.27-1.30
independent contractor, of, 3.37
mental incompetent, of, 2.33
private nuisance, for, 8.22-8.27
mental incompetent, liability of, 2.33
minor, action against, 2.28
occupier's liability. *See* Occupier
private nuisance, liability for, 8.22-8.27
tort of, generally, 12.01-12.04
varieties of,
chattels, liability for. *See* Chattels
employer's liability. *See* Employer
occupier's liability. *See* Occupier
Nervous shock
foreseeability of, 12.24-12.28
legal and non-legal wrong, 1.04
Nominate tort
distinguished from innominate, 1.06
Non-fatal personal injury
limitation of action, 15.47-15.50
non-pecuniary loss,
amenities, loss of, 15.41-15.43
assessment of award, 15.45-15.46
generally, 15.22-15.23
injury, 15.44
pain and suffering, 15.39-15.40
pecuniary loss,
deductions, 15.35-15.37
expenses, 15.30-15.34
future earnings, 15.26-15.29
generally, 15.22-15.23
interest, 15.38
lost earnings, 15.24-15.25
Non-pecuniary loss. *See* Non-fatal personal injury
Nuisance
club, tort committed against, 2.21
coming to, 8.44-8.45
creator of, 8.34
highway, to,
adjoining owners, obstruction causing loss to, 8.76
disrepair, 8.77-8.78
obstruction,
adjoining owners, causing loss to, 8.76
users, to, 8.79-8.80
projections over highway, 8.81-8.82
users, obstruction to, 8.79-8.80
meaning, 8.01-8.02
petition of right in case of, 2.03

Nuisance—*cont*
private, defences,
coming to nuisance, 8.44-8.45
jus tertii, 8.46
prescription, 8.47-8.50
statutory authority, 8.51-8.56
elements of liability,
continuing state of affairs, 8.08-8.10
damage, 8.28-8.29
enjoyment of property,
generally, 8.11-8.12
locality, 8.13-8.14
standards, 8.15-8.17
utility, 8.18
malice, 8.19-8.21
negligence, 8.22-8.27
personal comfort,
generally, 8.11-8.12
locality, 8.13-8.14
standards, 8.15-8.17
utility, 8.18
entitlement to sue, 8.30-8.33
incidence of liability,
creator of nuisance, 8.34
landlord out of possession, 8.40-8.43
occupier, 8.35-8.39
meaning, 8.03, 8.05-8.07
public nuisance distinguished from, 8.03
remedies,
abatement, 8.57-8.61
damages, 8.62-8.65
generally, 8.04
injunction, 8.66-8.68
vicarious liability for, 3.37
public,
civil action, 8.74-8.75
damage, 8.73
meaning, 8.03
persons affected by, 8.72
private nuisance distinguished from, 8.03
remedies, 8.04
special offences, 8.72
servitude, injury to, 8.69-8.71
varieties of,
land, use of, 8.04
private nuisance,
meaning, 8.03
public nuisance distinguished from, 8.03
remedies, 8.04
public nuisance,
meaning, 8.03
private nuisance distinguished from, 8.03
remedies, 8.04
vicarious liability for, 3.37

Obstruction
highway, of, 8.76, 8.79-8.80
Occupier
Crown, liability of, 2.06
independent contractor, liability for act of, 3.36
liability of,
common law, 14.15-14.16
duty of occupier,
common duty of care,
children, 14.31-14.32
contents of duty, 14.28-14.30
knowledgeable visitor, 14.33
defences to liability, 14.39-14.41
discharge of duty,
independent contractors, 14.36
warnings, 14.34-14.35
exclusion of duty, 14.37-14.38
third party, to those entering under contract with, 14.42
trespassers, to, 14.43-14.45
negligence, 1.28
private nuisance, 8.35-8.39
statutory law,
scope of Acts,
damage, 14.24-14.27
occupier, 14.19
premises, 14.17-14.18
visitor, 14.20-14.23
negligence, liability for, 1.28
private nuisance, liability for, 8.35-8.39
Owner
adjoining highway, obstruction causing loss to, 8.76
Ownership
trespass to land as wrong against, 5.02

Pain
non-pecuniary loss, 15.39-15.40
Parent
authority of, as defence to trespass to person, 6.29
Parties
Rylands v. Fletcher, rule in, 9.12-9.15
Passing-off
classical, 21.70-21.72
development of, 21.65-21.69
modern extension, 21.73-21.76
notice of, 21.65-21.69
Paternity
blood test to establish, taking of, as trespass to person, 6.33
Pearson Committee
conclusions of, 1.15, 1.16
Pecuniary loss. *See* Non-fatal personal injury
Perjury
legal and non-legal wrong, 1.05
Person
meaning, 2.01

Person—*cont*
trespass to,
defences,
accident, 6.23-6.25
breathalyser, sample of breath by, 6.33
captain of ship, authority of, 6.32
consent, 6.36-6.42
husband, authority of, 6.31
lawful arrest, 6.43-6.51
necessity, 6.34-6.35
parental authority, 6.29
paternity, taking of blood test to establish, 6.33
pilot of aircraft, authority of, 6.32
schoolmaster, authority of, 6.29-6.30
self-defence, 6.26-6.28
general characteristics,
accident distinguished from trespass, 6.07
anger, 6.03
force, use of, 6.03-6.05
hostility, 6.04
immediate and consequential injury distinguished, 6.02
intention to injure, 6.04
king's peace, trespass entails breach of, 6.01
mentally incompetent person, 6.06
minor, 6.06
proof, onus of, 6.07-6.09
trespass, meaning, 6.02
liability, effect of intention on, 1.24
varieties of trespass,
assault, 6.14-6.17
battery, 6.10-6.13
false imprisonment, 6.18-6.22
Person under disability
insane person. *See* Insane person
mentally incompetent person. *See* Mentally incompetent person
minor. *See* Minor
Personal comfort
private nuisance, liability for,
generally, 8.11-8.12
locality, 8.13-8.14
standards, 8.15-8.17
utility, 8.18
Personal injury
fatal. *See* Death
non-fatal. *See* Non-fatal personal injury
Personal representative
liability, scope of, 2.36-2.39
Pilot of aircraft
trespass to person, defence to, 6.32
Plaintiff
agony of moment, acting in, 13.31
child as, 13.30
deceit, liability for, 17.15
defamation, 18.21-18.25
defendant obliged to protect, 13.29
foreseeable, 12.21-12.23
illegality of, 13.44-13.47
Rylands v. Fletcher, rule in, 9.35-9.45
statutory duty, breach of, 16.11
Plant
employer's liability, 14.51
Policy
legal principles, role in formation of, 1.18
Possession
goods, trespass to, 7.06-7.11
land, trespass to,
basis of action, 5.13-5.15
claim not based on possession,
ejectment, 5.18-5.19
relation, trespass by, 5.16
reversionary interest, injury to, 5.17
right to possess, 5.18-5.19
landlord out of, 8.40-8.43
trespass to land as wrong against, 5.02
Post Office
tort committed by, liability of Crown, 2.07
Pound-breach
goods, wrongful interference with, 7.43
Premises
employer's liability, 14.52
occupier's liability, 14.17-14.18
Prescription
private nuisance, defence to, 8.47-8.50
Privacy
invasion of, legal and non-legal wrong, 1.05
questionable concept, as, 19.01-19.02
scope of,
generally, 19.03-19.06
wrongdoing, different types of, 19.07-19.10
Private nuisance. *See* Nuisance
Privilege
absolute, cases of,
judicial proceedings, 18.76-18.82, 18.86-18.88
official communications, 18.84-18.85
Parliament, statement made to, 18.74
parliamentary papers, 18.75
solicitor and client, communications between, 18.83
nature of, 18.71-18.73
qualified, cases of,
loss, 18.99-18.102
privileged reports, 18.89-18.94
statements, 18.95-18.98
Process, abuse of. *See* Abuse of process
Professional
vicarious liability, application of, 3.04
Prohibition
authority, effect on, 3.09-3.10

Proof
  care, breach of duty of, 12.82-12.84
  trespass to person, of, 6.07-6.09
Property
  damage to, 15.15-15.17
  enjoyment of. *See* Enjoyment of property
  loss, 15.12-15.14
Prosecution
  abuse of process. *See* Abuse of process
Public interest
  defamation, 18.64
Publication
  defamation, of, 18.29-18.36

Reason
  legal principles, role in formation of, 1.18
Reasonable care
  employer's duty of, 3.36
Reciprocity
  liability, fundamental principle of, 1.20
Relation
  trespass by, 5.16
Remedies
  confidence, breach of, 20.13-20.16
  defamation. *See* Defamation
  goods, wrongful interference with,
    damages,
      conversion, 7.49-7.51
      generally, 7.47
      trespass, 7.48
    goods detained, where, 7.46
    improvement of goods, 7.52-7.53
    title, extinction of, 7.54-7.55
  land, trespass to,
    judicial remedies, 5.49-5.51
    self-help, 5.48
  private nuisance,
    abatement, 8.57-8.61
    damages, 8.62-8.65
    generally, 8.04
    injunction, 8.66-8.68
  provision of, 1.07
  public nuisance, 8.04
Remoteness of damage. *See* Damage
Replevin
  goods, wrongful interference with, 7.42
Res ipsa loquitur
  application, 12.86
  control, 12.87-12.88
  generally, 12.85
  maxim, effect of 12.91-12.92
  ordinary occurrence, 12.89-12.90
Rescous
  goods, wrongful interference with, 7.43
Rescuer
  care, duty of, 12.29-12.34
Restitution
  tort and, 1.13
Reversionary interest
  injury to, 5.17
Risk
  foreseeability of, 12.15-12.20
Rylands v. Fletcher, rule in
  analysis of,
    damage, 9.31-9.34
    dangerous things, 9.19-9.22
    escape, 9.16-9.18
    non-natural user, 9.23-9.30
    parties, 9.12-9.15
  character of, 9.07-9.11
  fire, impact on, 10.07-10.11
  qualifications of,
    God, act of, 9.46-9.49
    necessity, 9.50
    plaintiff,
      act of, 9.35-9.37
      consent of, 9.38-9.40
    statutory authority, 9.41-9.42
    stranger, act of, 9.43-9.45
  rule stated, 9.01
  sources of, 9.02-9.06

Schoolmaster
  authority of, as defence to trespass to person, 6.29-6.30
Scope of liability. *See* Liability
Seduction
  legal and non-legal wrong, 1.03
Self-defence
  liability, effect of intention on, 1.24
  trespass to person, defence to, 6.26-6.28
Self-help
  trespass to land, remedy in case of, 5.48
Servant
  agent distinguished from, 3.01, 3.04
  corporation, of, liability of, 2.19
  Crown, of,
    immunity of, 2.08
    liability for act of, 2.04-2.05
    wrong committed by, 2.03
  gratuitous, 3.05
  master and, liability for negligence, 1.28
  transferred, cases relating to, 3.06
Service. *See* Contract of service
Services. *See* Contract for services
Servitudes
  injuries to, 8.69-8.71
Several tortfeasors
  contracts of indemnity, 4.12-4.14
  contribution between tortfeasors, 4.07-4.11
  joint tortfeasors, distinguished from,
    importance of distinction,
      common law, 4.04
      judgment against one of them, effect of, 4.05
      release of tortfeasor, 4.06
    nature of distinction, 4.01-4.03

Several tortfesors—*cont*
  meaning, 4.02
  release of tortfeasor, 4.06
Shock. *See* Nervous shock
Slander. *See* Defamation
Solicitor
  care, duty of, 12.67, 12.68
Sovereign
  foreign, scope of liability, 2.13-2.15
Standards
  care, duty of. *See* Negligence
  private nuisance, liability for, 8.15-8.17
State of affairs
  continuing, liability for private nuisance, 8.08-8.10
Statutes. *See* Construction of statutes
Statutory authority. *See* Authority
Statutory change
  Crown, liability of, 2.04-2.07
Statutory duty, breach of
  construction of statutes,
    court, role of, 16.03-16.05
    rules of construction, 16.06-16.10
  defences,
    contributory negligence, 16.20
    delegation, 16.21
    volenti, 16.19
  generally, 16.01-16.02
  liability, elements of,
    breach of duty, 16.12-16.14
    damage, causation of, 16.15-16.16
    injury within scope of statute, 16.17-16.18
    plaintiff, duty owed to, 16.11
Stranger
  act of, rule in *Rylands v. Fletcher*, 9.43-9.49
Strict liability
  doctrine of, 1.31
Suffering
  non-pecuniary loss, 15.39-15.40
Support
  loss of, 15.58-15.60
Surveyor
  care, duty of, 12.37
Survival of action
  death, following 15.51

Third party
  act of, duty of care, 12.61
  person entering under contract with, occupier's duty of care, 14.42
Title
  extinction of, 7.54-7.55
  plaintiff, of, in action for conversion, 7.31-7.36
Tort
  liability. *See* Liability
  meaning, 1.01
Tortfeasors
  joint. *See* Joint tortfeasors
  several. *See* Several tortfeasors
Trade
  wrongful interference with. *See* Wrongful interference
Trade union
  defamation of, 2.22
  liability, scope of, 2.22-2.23
  quasi-corporation, as, 2.22
Trespass
  ab initio, 5.09
  accident distinguished from, 6.07
  club, tort committed against, 2.21
  continuing, 5.08
  damages, 7.48
  goods, to,
    generally, 7.03
    interference, 7.04-7.05
    possession, 7.06-7.11
    wrongfulness, 7.12-7.15
  land, to. *See* Land
  livestock, by,
    detention, 11.32-11.33
    liability, 11.28-11.31
  meaning, 6.02
  person, to. *See* Person
  quare clausum fregit, 5.01
  vi et armis, 6.01
Trespasser
  occupier's duty with respect to, 14.43-14.45
Trover. *See* Conversion
Trust
  breach of, tort and, 1.14

Unborn child. *See* Minor
Unincorporated body
  liability, scope of, 2.20-2.23
Unjust enrichment. *See* Restitution
User
  non-natural, rule in *Rylands v. Fletcher*, 9.23-9.30
  obstruction to, nuisance to highway, 8.79-8.80
Utility
  private nuisance, liability for, 8.18

Vicarious liability
  agent distinguished from servant, 3.01, 3.04
  application,
    agent distinguished from servant, 3.04
    captain of ship, to, 3.04
    contract for services distinguished from contract of service, 3.05
    control, relevance of, 3.06-3.07
    director, action against, 3.06
    doctor, to, 3.04

Vicarious liability—*cont*
  application—*cont*
    engineer, to, 3.04
    independent contractor,
      meaning, 3.03
    lawyer, to, 3.04
    professional, to, 3.04
    servant distinguished from
      agent, 3.04
  authority,
    actual, 3.11-3.13
    meaning, 3.08
    ostensible, 3.14-3.16
    prohibitions, 3.09-3.10
  corporation, of, 2.18
  doctrine of, 2.01, 3.01-3.02
  employer, personal liability
    of, 3.40-3.41
  employment, course of,
    acts outside, 3.30-3.33
    acts within, 3.19-3.24
    master, acts not in interest
      of, 3.27-3.29
    meaning, 3.17-3.18
    prohibited acts, 3.25-3.26
  independent contractor, of,
    bridge, non-repair of, 3.37
    casual negligence, 3.38-3.39
    collateral negligence, 3.38-3.39
    defective equipment, supply of, 3.36
    extra-hazardous acts, 3.35
    fire, damage by, 3.37
    general principle, 3.34
    highway,
      non-repair of, 3.37
      work done in or on, 3.35
    misfeasance, non-feasance
      distinguished from, 3.37
    negligence, 3.37
    nuisance, 3.37
    occupier, liability of, 3.36
    reasonable care, employer's duty
      of, 3.36
  rationale, 3.01-3.02, 3.39
  servant distinguished from agent, 3.01,
    3.04
Visitor
  knowledgeable, 14.33
  occupier's liability, 14.20-14.23, 14.33
Volenti non fit injuria
  defence of, 1.09
  employer's liability, 14.55
  negligence, consent as defence
    to, 13.05-13.09
  statutory duty, breach of, 16.19

Warning
  occupier's duty of care, 14.34-14.35
Wealth maximisation
  liability, function of, 1.18
Words and phrases, defined
  act of state, 2.09
  authority, 3.08
  cattle, 11.02
  confidence, 20.04-20.06
  conspiracy, 21.03
  conversion, 7.16-7.18
  course of employment, 3.17-3.18
  dangerous animals, 11.10-11.12
  defamation, 18.01-18.02
  defamatory, 18.07-18.12
  household, 11.19
  independent contractor, 3.03
  joint tortfeasors, 4.01
  keeper of animal, 11.20
  livestock, 11.26
  nuisance, 8.01-8.02
  person, 2.01
  private nuisance, 8.03, 8.05-8.07
  public nuisance, 8.03
  several tortfeasors, 4.02
  tort, 1.01
  trespass, 6.02
Wrong
  idea of, 1.02
  legal,
    non-legal distinguished
      from, 1.03-1.06
    other forms,
      breach of contract, tort
        and, 1.10-1.12
      crime, tort and, 1.08-1.09
      generally, 1.07
      restitution, tort and, 1.13
      trust, breach of, 1.14
  non-legal, legal wrong distinguished
    from, 1.03-1.06
  See also Wrongful interference
Wrongful arrest. *See* Person, trespass to
Wrongful dismissal
  damages awarded in, case of, 1.12
Wrongful interference
  conspiracy. *See* Conspiracy
  generally, 21.01-21.02
  goods, with. *See* Goods
  inducing breach of contract. *See* Contract
  injurious falsehood. *See* Injurious
    falsehood
  intimidation. *See* Intimidation
  passing-off. *See* Passing-off